The Complete Guide to PICTURE FRAMING

Techniques ◆ Materials

The Complete Guide to PICTURE FRAMING

Techniques ◆ Materials

JENNY RODWELL & GEORGE SHORT

BLACK CAT

First published in Great Britain in 1986
Published by Macdonald & Co (Publishers) Ltd
Reprinted in 1988 by Macdonald & Co (Publishers) Ltd under the Black Cat imprint

British Library Cataloguing in Publication Data
Rodwell, Jenny
The complete guide to picture framing
1. Picture frames and framing
I. Title II. Short, George
749'.7 N8550

ISBN 0-7481-0199-3

This book was designed and produced by
Quarto Publishing plc
The Old Brewery, 6 Blundell Street
London N7 9BH

Senior editor: Jane Laing
Art editor: Moira Clinch
Editorial: Polly Powell, Michelle Newton
Designer: Rita Wuthrich
Design assistants: Anthony Bussey, Fraser Newman, Ursula Dawson
Illustrators: Ray Brown, Fraser Newman, Mick Hill
Photographers: Mac Campeanu, John Heseltine
Consultants: Peter Worley and staff at the Newgate Gallery, London, Christine Ovel, Aidan Walker
Indexer: Richard Bird

Art Director: Nigel Osborne.
Editorial director: Jim Miles

Typeset by Facsimile Graphics Ltd, Coggeshall
Paste-up by Elly King, Dave Evans
Colour origination by Rainbow Graphic Arts Co Ltd, Hong Kong
Printed by Lee Fung Asco Printers Ltd, Hong Kong

Macdonald & Co (Publishers) Ltd
3rd Floor
Greater London House
Hampstead Road
London NW1 7QX
a member of Maxwell Pergamon Publishing Corporation plc

Contents

Preface

Whether a gilded border of ornate decorations or a simple band of metal, the frame plays a major role in the total visual impact of an artpiece, enhancing or seriously distorting the overall effect of the image. The most suitable choice is not always the most obvious one and this book offers valuable guidelines on selecting frames for a wide variety of artpieces, including the three-dimensional. In many cases you will be unable to find a perfectly suitable ready-made frame and will want to make your own. The *Complete Guide to Picture Framing* tells you how.

The basic principles and techniques of framing and mounting are clearly explained and step-by-step illustrated instructions guide you through all the foundation skills of picture framing, from measuring the artpiece to giving your frames a special finish. A large project section, covering a wide range of framing techniques, will enable you to complete different types of frame for different types of artwork. There is a section on the tools and materials needed – it always pays to buy the best you can afford; cheap tools can let you down badly – and a section on the care and repair of both frames and artworks, which will prove especially useful to all those interested in buying second-hand frames and tailoring them to their own requirements. Many damaged frames can be successfully renovated and even the oldest picture frames can usually be stripped of plaster and gilt and the wooden base used as the foundation for one of your own finishes.

Introduction

Although there have been some spectacular exceptions, such as the ancient cave paintings and some murals, a frame is normally needed to act as a boundary. It therefore plays an important role in the composition of a picture. A church steeple in a landscape painting, for instance, will often be slightly offset, rather than centred, to give a more interesting composition but this is effective only if the limits to the picture are obvious. For, without limits, the whole idea of a composition becomes meaningless and the shapes in the picture merge into the surroundings.

The frame also prevents the 'escape' of colours from an artpiece into the surrounding room. A block of colour in a picture will 'jump out' if there is a similar colour nearby and the picture is not framed. The frame defines the extent of the artpiece and stops this subconscious action of the human eye. It plays exactly the same role in preventing the surface of a picture from becoming merged and confused with the surrounding surface, such as a patterned wallpaper.

On a more practical level, the frame protects the artwork from damage. It guards against general wear and tear and against accident when an artwork is being handled.

THE DEVELOPMENT OF FRAMING

In the ancient classical world, frames were made mainly for mirrors. The Romans and Greeks painted frescos directly onto walls without frames as they are now known. Meanwhile, the Oriental civilizations were developing their own distinct attitude towards paintings. Chinese and Japanese artists painted their works upon folding screens, which divided rooms, and scrolls, which were hung directly on the wall without frames.

In Medieval times, artists began painting onto the slightly hollowed surface of wooden panels and the raised edges, often decorated with separate motifs, gradually developed into a formal picture frame. To begin with frames were frequently part of the solid piece, rather than existing in their own right, and the first separate frames were imitations of their original architectural surroundings – an environment which

The emerging frame
Rich bands of intricate decoration surround these paintings of the early Renaissance. The setting, like the picture itself, was inspired by religion and given up to the glory of God. Intricate patterns (left) *are worked around the* Lamentation over the Body of Christ *by Giotto. The triptych* Madonna and Child *by Duccio* (above) *is an altarpiece painted into hinged, recessed panels which are the forerunners of the modern frame.*

Imitating architecture
Attempts to imitate architectural designs led to the creation of styles which gradually evolved into the modern frame. On each side of the Baptism *by della Francesca* (left) *stand two pilasters, fake 'pillars', such as would be found on a doorway or impressive window recess.*

The simple, sombre frame surrounding Blake's watercolour on wood, The Body of Abel Found by Adam and Eve (above), *highlights the dramatic nature of the painting.*

The contemporary artist, Howard Hodgkin, has incorporated the frame into his oil painting on wood, D H in Hollywood (right) *to vivid and complementary effect.*

was ornate and ecclesiastical. As cathedrals and larger churches were built they demanded even grander architecture. The frame, like the architecture, became more elaborate, as can be seen in the lavish arches, pinnacles and carvings around the Polyptych altarpiece in the Strozzi Chapel, Santa Maria Novella, Florence, by Andrea Orcagna (*c.* 1308–1368). One style which became popular was the Tabernacle frame, a literal imitation of a window recess in which pilasters, make-believe 'pillars' or flattened versions of columns, flanked the painting. The *Madonna and Child with Saints and Donors* in Santo Spirito, Florence, by Filippino Lippi (*c.* 1457–1504), provides an outstanding example of such a Tabernacle frame.

The real breakthrough for the picture frame came in the late fifteenth and early sixteenth centuries when painters began to see themselves as artists in their own right and not simply as servants of architects. They required frames to set their paintings apart from their surroundings. Some of the best frames ever made date from this period. One of the new styles to evolve was the Tondo or circular type exemplified by the intricately carved, wide, gilded frame surrounding the *Holy Family* by Michelangelo, to be found in the Uffizi Gallery in Florence.

Sixteenth-century frame makers began moving towards a more restrained style and the frame gradually became more harmonious with the picture within. Soon, the wealthier classes began seeking paintings for their own homes. Art was no longer merely for public display and it became a product which increasingly needed to be transported after being bought by an individual; and so picture frames became a practical necessity.

As painters became more in demand, they found they had little time to make their own frames. They passed the work on to their apprentices and to outside specialists and so frame making became a skilled craft with its own separate place in the art industry. Increasingly the frame became the property of the cabinet maker and it changed in style as the style of furniture changed. Materials became more sophisticated; in Puritan-influenced northern Europe exotic woods replaced gaudy gilded mouldings.

From time to time conflicts arose between the painter and the frame maker. In the sixteenth century, for instance, frame makers tried to outdo each other and the frames often outshone the paintings, placing them in settings which were extremely elaborate and often inlaid with materials such as jewels, mother of pearl and ivory. The rich rococo style of architecture and interior decoration, popular in early eighteenth-century France, was reflected in frames, and, although a simpler fashion was intro-

duced with the neoclassical revival in Europe in the late part of that century, the rococo designs kept returning. One of these styles, popular for many years, was the Lawrence frame, named after Sir Thomas Lawrence (1769–1830), a fashionable British portrait painter.

With the growth of Modernism in the early twentieth century, frames were widely denounced as over-elaborate and unnecessary visual competition for the picture. Artists increasingly chose simple frames. Some disregarded the traditional restrictions of the frame, such as the American abstract expressionist, Jackson Pollock (1912–1956), who painted huge canvases of dripping and spattered colours, creating an overall image and generating an energy which many argued would have been inappropriate if contained in a fixed wall-piece. Supporters of this idea talked of a 'visual splash' of colour and shape, which, they argued, did not fit into the conventions of pictorial composition and therefore did not require a frame. During the same period, some museums removed more ornate frames from recent paintings and replaced them with simple ones.

In more recent years, however, there has been a definite revival of interest in, and respect for, the frame. There has also been a rise in the popularity of elaborate frames. Critics report that a number of artists have turned to the frame for its ability to enhance and even interact with the painted surface. Several contemporary artists have fitted frames specially designed to interact with their pictures. For example, two modern American painters, the abstract artist Marsden Hartley and the figurative painter Maurice Prendergast, sometimes make their own frames to accord with their images and Georgia O'Keefe, another American artist, has solid metal frames specially made to complement her work.

Altering or abandoning the frame is not a new idea. During the Baroque period, which began in Europe in the early seventeenth century, many paintings were reframed in a more ornate style. The gold leaf of some of the new frames introduced to the Pitti Palace in Florence, for instance, was so bright that some said it distracted seriously from the paintings. In the early nineteenth century, Napoleon had many paintings in the Louvre reframed in the then fashionable Empire style.

The picture frame has endured throughout all these changes in fashion and looks set to continue indefinitely as the necessary boundary for most works of art. It has also increasingly come into its own among browsers of stalls and antique shops who wish to frame collections of old prints, maps, posters and other memorabilia.

The Principles of Framing

Setting off the Artpiece

Displaying Frames

Mounts and Mounting

Types of Moulding

Setting off the artpiece

There is really no such thing as the 'right' frame for an artpiece – one correct frame which must belong to a particular image. A vast choice is open to the collector or framer and in the end the choice of frame is a matter of personal taste, which is why this is such a fascinating subject, appealing to the individualist.

There are some principles, however, which can be followed to advantage. They fall into two basic categories: the general and the specific. Different types of frames should be used for different types of artwork – oils, watercolours, posters, photographs and so on; and a frame should be chosen that enhances the individual characteristics of a particular artwork. In all cases, the artwork should dictate the frame and not vice versa. The style and colour of the frame and mount should not fight the artwork for attention, nor should they detract from the image. Rather they should complement the image, drawing attention to it. The viewer should not notice the frame or mount rather than the artwork.

There is a further interesting demarcation between old and new frames. An old frame is not necessarily the best choice for an old artpiece, nor a new frame for a new one. It is a question of style. You may decide that a new artpiece needs an antique-looking frame and, conversely, many old artworks, especially old photographs, look attractive in modern frames. Within these categories there is much scope for imagination. For instance, if you decide on an old-style frame, you are not confined to a genuinely antique one. There are many modern reproduction frames, and reproduction mouldings can be bought and used to make your own 'antiqued' version.

A host of ready-made new frames can also be purchased. The drawback here is the range of sizes available. Pictures, old prints, maps and any other items you may wish to frame do not fall easily into rigid categories of size and shape. You need specific proportions and this should be dictated by the artpiece rather than by the size of frame that happens to be available in a shop.

For some projects, ready-made equipment – such as clip frames or other simple Perspex framing kits – can be useful. Generally speaking, though, you may find this too limiting as your interest grows. Kits for self-assembly frames are available in plastic, metal or wood but, again, the problem is the severely limited range of sizes and styles.

One alternative to buying new frames is to turn to the bargain or junk market. Here you may find a greater range of sizes and styles, often at reasonable prices, because they are frequently damaged.

No matter what kind of frame you decide on, one factor becomes increasingly important as you gain in expertise. This is the need to match the frame to the subject being framed. This section takes a look at the wide variety of artpieces you might wish to frame and offers general guidelines on the most suitable kinds of frames, mounts and finishes. For a more detailed discussion on mounts and mounting, and mouldings see pages 30–37 and 38–47. Details on specific picture framing techniques are given on pages 56–85.

OILS AND ACRYLICS

Pictures in oils or acrylics are usually painted onto canvas stretchers (the canvas stretched taut over a framework of wooden slats), canvas-covered boards, or hardboard. With the stretcher, a traditional surface for oils, extra care has to be taken when framing because the painting is often slightly asymmetrical, the thickness of the canvas varies round the edge, and the slats can cause problems.

As a general rule, paintings in oils or acrylics are not glazed – that is, they are not covered by glass – although sometimes glass is used to provide protection, especially with smaller paintings, when it may also actively enhance the picture.

Oil and acrylic paintings usually have a vigorous presence. There are exceptions but, broadly speaking, the very nature of oil and acrylic paints gives a texture that makes the painting stand out more boldly than would a watercolour or print, especially when the artist has used them in a thick or impastoed manner. When framing most oil paintings, therefore, you are dealing with something which is in relief, literally 'standing out from the wall'.

It is this that governs your choice of frame; it also helps to broaden the choice. You can sometimes make do with narrow batten frames, such as wooden or metal strips, that do not cover any of the surface of the painting but are merely tacked onto the edge of the stretcher. This is a suitable approach if the painting is strong enough to stand out on its own and a slim boundary will suffice.

On the other hand, a strong painting can also take a strong frame. This is especially useful in the case of a small painting. The presence here of a

Oil and acrylic
The framers' moulding around this picture (above) *gives a strong surround to this rather subdued picture, without overpowering it. The green mount surrounding the rural scene* (above right) *picks out the greens in the picture. The polished wooden frame gives it a solid and permanent look. The garden scene* (right) *is thickly painted with bold colours, using a lot of greens, and the renovated wooden frame complements these textures and colours.*

wider frame will help to focus the eye onto the painting itself, which, although small in size, will still be bold enough not to be dominated by the frame. With larger paintings, the freedom of choice is total. They can stand up to 'rougher' stylistic treatment.

WATERCOLOURS

Unlike oils and acrylics, watercolours can suffer terribly from their frames. Generally, watercolours have delicate, washy surfaces and all too often one sees a thinly painted watercolour languishing inside an intricate or heavy frame that makes the picture look as if it is fading away.

By tradition, watercolour frames have been rather unadventurous. They tend to have a subdued look, reflecting the muted tones of the picture they contain. The rugged moorlands or soft trees mellowly depicted by a typical watercolourist like John Sell Cotman (1782–1842) hang on many walls inside frames which are necessarily low key, with a yellowing, dusty look. This quiet framing style is suited to older watercolours – unfortunately, it has become a tradition for *all* types of watercolours. Some modern pictures, however, deserve a brighter context; the concentrated, luminous colours which many modern watercolourists use can stand up to a more vibrant frame.

Nearly all watercolours stand behind a 'mount', a cardboard 'frame' within the actual frame. This creates a broad expanse of space, providing a sympathetic surround that separates the image from the hard edge of the frame. Since watercolour paints are transparent, they give a fragile, ethereal image and it is generally not a good idea to surround them with an opaque or densely coloured mount. This explains why traditional watercolour

Watercolours
A soft watercolour of Durham Town is given a sympathetic dark brown mount in a gold, antiqued frame (above). *The bevelled edge of the mount is lined with antique gold to match the gold on the frame. A large frame with a simple moulding surrounds a cream mount for this small watercolour* (left).

mounts are white, cream or pastel-coloured. Again, there are exceptions but these are best done consciously – if you use a bright or dark mount, choose it for a specific reason.

Glass is nearly always used to cover watercolour pictures, as they are far less durable than oils or acrylics. Dust is a great enemy of watercolours, making them dull and dark. Moisture wrinkles the paper and, in extreme conditions, causes the spots of brown mildew known as 'foxing', which can be seen on many older prints and watercolours.

Although the mount is often a broad border around the picture – and the smaller the picture, the bigger the mount can be in contrast – the frame itself should be narrow. Visually, it should make as little fuss as possible, so as not to detract from the picture.

A common characteristic of watercolours is that the paint is rarely taken right up to the edge of the paper. This gives the framer the choice of leaving this unpainted area showing or cropping it closely. Usually, watercolours are best left with the 'random edge' uncropped because this enables the viewer to see how the washes of paint are affected by the paper and the picture benefits from the irregular expanse around its composition.

PASTELS

Pastel paintings, like watercolours, are usually framed by a mount and a frame, and the advice given for mounting and framing watercolours *(see page 14)* applies equally well to pastels.

Pastels are fine chalks and smudge easily. Therefore, in addition to fixing the painting with a fixative spray, a double mount is often used to keep the pastel away from the glass.

PHOTOGRAPHS

Old sepia photographs, popular with collectors, can be greatly enhanced by being framed in traditional style, in keeping with their nostaligic appearance. However, you can use a modern mount and frame to good effect with some images.

With modern photographs, you can rarely afford to take such liberties. Most modern photographs belong firmly to their own era and usually demand a modern frame.

Some framers like to trim off the white edges round photographs but this is not advisable when dealing with the older ones, as the edges often contain fascinating signatures, or captions scribbled in faded ink, or fancy edging reflecting bygone fashions. These characteristics deserve to be preserved and they can be included in the visual whole of the frame. Treatment similar to that of a watercolour is best here: use a neutral-coloured mount and leave the captioned edge of the photograph visible inside. Neutral colours for mounts work well with modern photographs, although sometimes a contemporary black-and-white photograph can be set off by a more brightly coloured mount.

With an old portrait photograph, there is plenty of scope. Again, it would probably be unsuitable to crop it and give it a modern setting. A fabric mount, damask or lace perhaps, gives a period touch to a photograph. Alternatively, you could use old-fashioned marbled paper or vellum. In some cases, if the photograph is in good condition, it is possible to frame it directly, without using a mount. This may be especially effective in cases where older photographs have been 'vignetted' – that is, where the image is isolated in the centre of a slightly faded and misty-looking background.

One remarkable way to give a sympathetic setting to most old photographs is to use a fabric-covered frame. Leather can be glued onto a wooden frame, adding textural interest to the picture as a whole. Brown or olive green leather, for instance, works well with the warm tones of old

The collection of photographs (above, far left) *is given cohesion by the formal arrangement and each one is made much more distinctive by the ruled lines that surround each photograph* (see project, page 112). *The sepia photograph* (below, far left) *is given a touch of colour by the fine strips of green and mid-brown inlay set in the wooden frame. The double mount beautifully sets off the modern print* (left). *By inserting strips of black into the light-coloured frame* (above), *the eye is drawn to the simple black-and-white print.*

sepia photographs but any thick material can be used, including velvet and suede.

You can be much more boisterous in the treatment of modern photographs: black-and-white prints can be contrasted with brightly coloured surrounds; coloured photographs can be placed in a black-and-white setting or in a setting or colour which repeats a theme present in the photograph.

Modern photographs usually look their best in an austere setting, although this depends on the subject. A picture in the style of a contemporary photographer such as Ansell Adams, for instance, with its stark quality, sharply defined shapes and contrasting tones would be shown to best advantage in a simple frame – perhaps just a narrow metallic band or a plain black frame. Most modern photographs look best with as little distraction as possible and simple Perspex clipboards are usually sufficient, especially if the picture is to be hung against a plain background.

In modern photo-journalism the image is all-important and the subject is sometimes a serious one, often making a social comment or recording some dramatic event. Again, a fussy frame would be distracting and inappropriate.

PRINTS

There is a brisk market nowadays for prints of all kinds and ages, from faded illustrations torn from old books to bright, graphic lithographs produced by modern artists. As with photographs, contemporary prints can be freely interpreted when it comes to choosing a frame. Simple frames, such as those made of coloured plastic or metal strip, often look effective on strong modern designs.

There is one general rule which applies to both old and new prints: leave the edge of the print showing. In a good print, this edge should be a crisp line but all edges are interesting because they show how the plate is registered – that is, how the colours are laid on top of each other, so that they meet in the exact positions in the composition. With etch-

Posters
Because posters have such a strong graphic content, they nearly always require the simplest of frames. A blue mount and a flat blue frame surround the poster (above). *In some cases, posters can look attractive without any surround at all—as with the poster* (left), *which has been clipped onto a backing board beneath glass. Transparent Perspex clips were used and the backing board was edged with plain wooden battens to give a neater edge* (see project, page 100).

The traditional look
This piece of modern needlework was given a traditional appearance by surrounding it with a velvet-covered slip and a mahogany moulding.

Antique piece
This sampler requires an old-looking surround. It is well worth hunting for the right old-style frame for such an attractive piece.

ings, for instance, an indentation can be seen in the paper where the metal plate was pressed onto the damp paper. By leaving this 'key' intact when you frame the print, you display a facet of the production which many will find interesting.

Old prints can be given a new lease of life by reframing them. The white surround is often discoloured and frequently there will be blotches of mould, or foxing, which is caused by a chemical reaction of moisture in the atmosphere with the iron content in the paper. By reframing the print and giving it a mount, you can often cover up such defects. You will also have had an opportunity to clean up the print before reframing it. Cleaning, care and maintenance is covered in Care and Repair.

When reframing, you do not necessarily have to use an exact replica of the original frame but it is best if you choose one that remains in character with the picture. For example, a modern steel frame would look wrong with an antique print. Experiment with one of the finishes discussed on pages 44–47: the frame could be enhanced perhaps by a gilding or by a patina – a softening tonal wash.

Old prints often have the title underneath the picture. Rather than obliterating this, it is better to cut a small window in the mount.

POSTERS

The inspiration for most posters came from the events for which they were produced to advertise. Thus they began as ephemeral things, pieces of art which were by nature temporary. It is therefore often inappropriate to give them a permanent-looking frame, as if they were classical artefacts. Posters, after all, were designed to stand alone, and they can look striking if this effect is preserved. A simple block mount or clip frame is enough. For details of this style of mounting, see the poster project on pages 100–103.

Recently, posters have been more consciously aimed at being works of art in their own right and, there are many 'art' posters on the market. Yet they still reflect the original bold styles and, like prints, look best when framed in a simple way.

NEEDLEWORK AND OTHER FABRIC IMAGES

The way to prevent a piece of treasured needlework, collage, weaving or silk-screen from becoming tattered or worn is to frame it. The piece of work should be stretched first around a board or similar surface, fixing it at the back with masking tape. Until this is done, it is impossible to know its correct measurements for framing.

Glass is needed to protect the piece but avoid placing glass directly onto the surface. An insert or some other means must be found to separate the fabric from the glass pane where the material could be distorted by pressure from the glass.

In the late nineteenth and early twentieth centuries in America and Europe, embroidered samplers were often placed in tortoiseshelled, woodgrained or otherwise decorated frames and you

Maps and documents *The antique map of Africa (left) has been given a light wooden moulding with green edges. Because there is a lot of space within the actual subject, it does not need a separate mount. A red mount with a traditional tiny black and gilt frame adds a theatrical formality to the small opera souvenir (below left). The simple black script on paper (below) is given a formal appearance by its plain red mount and polished wooden frame.*

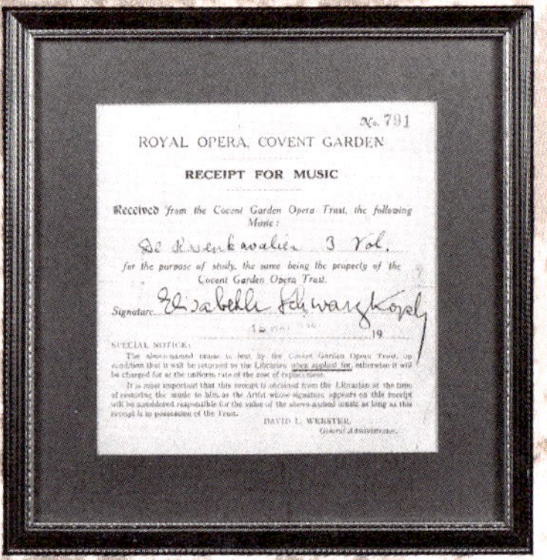

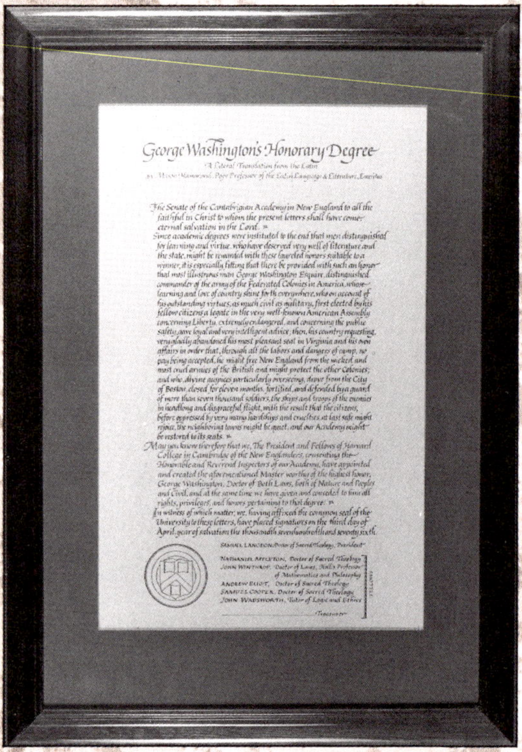

might like to preserve this traditon when framing or reframing such a piece; finishes are discussed on pages 44–47.

MAPS AND DOCUMENTS — OLD AND NEW

It is best to separate quite clearly in your mind the difference between framing a modern map or document and an antique one. The two types are found on the wall for entirely different reasons: the antique one is there mainly for its visual effect, a decorative piece of nostalgia or historic interest; the modern one is there as a colourful reference.

Maps

For the modern map, a simple clip frame or block mount is preferable – a businesslike frame. Some might feel that the style of the frame will make no difference and that a modern map could be set within an old-looking elaborate frame but you will probably find that the result will look incongruous.

Genuinely antique maps, or reproductions of antiques that convey the same atmosphere, are often seen in frames of polished wood such as maple and walnut – woods with warm colours. They can also look good in frames decorated with a special finish, such as imitation tortoiseshell or marble *(see pages 93–97)*. Making a new frame for an old map provides an opportunity to carry out some finishing work to give the frame an antique look.

With an old map, the question immediately arises of whether to trim the edges to remove torn and grubby pieces of the paper edge. This is not advisable, especially if you have been lucky enough to get hold of a map which has not been interfered with too much over the years. Unfortunately, if the map is genuinely old, you are likely to find that it has

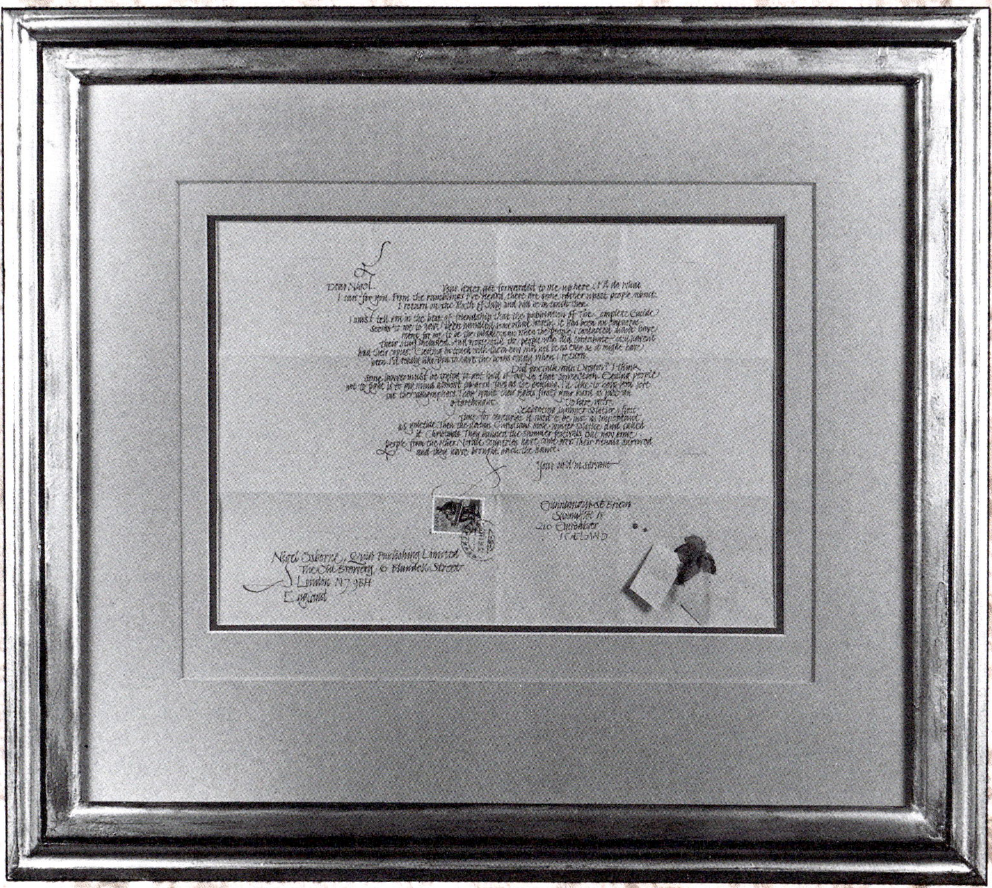

The grey and rather formal appearance of this manuscript (above) *is given just the right amount of uplift by the triple mount and red slip. A blue-black groove contrasts elegantly with the pewter wax finish* (see project, page 116).

already been trimmed too much, as different owners have forced it into available frames. Once removed, an edge cannot be replaced and the map will lose its value as well as the aesthetic effect of the original wide margin. Repair and cleaning of old maps and documents is explained on pages 136–137.

The broad margin which surrounds most old maps makes it generally undesirable to mount them. The margin itself, often with attractively aged and faded paper and interesting keys or titles, is a good enough 'mount' with which to surround the map.

With an old map, or any piece of archive document that you wish to preserve and frame, it is advisable to flatten out the original carefully and place it on a conservation board; the board should be specially purchased. Ordinary mounting board will not do in this case as it absorbs the acid in the air, and this will eventually soak through into the print and discolour or damage it.

Some interesting maps and documents, which you might wish to frame, are printed on both sides. In order that you can see both sides, a double-sided frame, usually a freestanding one, is necessary. Double-sided frames are often used when framing bonds and shares.

Documents

These also fit into two basic categories: the functional, such as a diploma, which is there to inform; and the decorative, such as a piece of calligraphy, an historic manuscript or an illuminated text. With the functional document, a simple frame is better: a plain narrow frame reflects its dignity. With the decorative piece, the choice is broader. A piece of writing is essentially flat, without the illusion of space

Pressed flowers
The attraction of these pressed flowers (above) lies partly in their fragile and faded look. The collector browsed through the junk shops to find this fitting old, plain, narrow frame.

found in most pictures and, for this reason, it is often rewarding to give a spatial feeling to a piece of text by placing it in a frame with moulding that projects outwards to make the whole object three-dimensional. Illuminated lettering is often decorated with gold and bright colours. This can be pleasingly brought out by having gilt on the frame and perhaps adding a narrow strip of one of the colours contained in the text.

THE THREE-DIMENSIONAL

Many people like to display a three-dimensional set piece on the wall. This might be a collection of medals, or a collage made of shells, beads or other materials. Oriental fans, tiny pieces of carvings or sculpture, or arrangements of dried flowers can all look attractive on a wall.

This type of piece calls for a box-like frame, sometimes known as a display frame or 'shadow box', so-called because when lit from an angle it can highlight the three-dimensional aspect of the piece with shadows. The box is basically an ordinary frame but with a deeper insert.

Any subject which is likely to gather dust, such as dried flowers or a delicate fan, should be placed under glass. With the three-dimensional box, you can choose your own background to match the subject. If it is a Chinese fan, for instance, a piece of Chinese paper would make a good background; shells could be placed on a 'beach' effect made by glueing sand evenly across the back board. There is plenty of scope here for creativity.

Extra care is needed for work of a more enduring nature, such as ceramics, jewellery and small pieces of sculpture or antique glass. Such items stand out alone, and often need the simplest of settings. A piece of Roman glass, for instance, is intrinsically interesting and invites close inspection. Such a hard and glossy object would benefit from being placed on a simple, softly textured background which complements the centrepiece, such as coarse silk or linen.

Shadow boxes
For the butterflies (above), *a deep moulding was chosen to create a space between the glass and the fragile subjects. Like the butterflies, the jewels* (right) *were also mounted on black velvet to accentuate them. The glass front of the jewellery frame forms a lid, which gives access to the contents.*

Displaying frames

There is a view – some might call it artistic snobbery – that it is wrong to consider how a painting will fit in with the decor of a room. Painting, they argue, is on a high aesthetic plane far superior to such mundane things as interior decorating. However, this argument ignores the fact that throughout its early history most art was created purely to complement its surroundings.

While the more experimental art forms play an undeniably important cultural role, it would be a pity if the pleasure of choosing pictures and frames to suit the home environment was lost and this section looks at the place of the frame within the larger environment of a room.

PLACING THE ARTPIECE

When deciding where to hang a framed artpiece, several practical points should be borne in mind. Heat can seriously damage the surface of paintings, especially oils, so avoid placing them directly above heaters. Not only will the rising heat damage the picture but dust and grease will also be carried upwards and will gradually concentrate over the picture surface. If for some reason you cannot avoid placing a picture above a heater, then make sure that it is glazed. Artworks should also be kept free of damp and condensation. Direct sunlight can cause watercolours to fade; some pigments are especially vulnerable. A popular material used in modern watercolours is watercolour concentrate, such as Lumar; some of these colours are particularly fugitive. Hang such paintings on walls that are not in the line of direct sunlight.

Aesthetic considerations are also important. If you have only one artpiece on a wall it is usually preferable to hang it so that the centre of the artpiece aligns approximately with the average person's eye-level. This position will vary according to the room in which the artpiece is hung: if you wish to hang a set of pictures in a hallway, for instance, where people rarely sit, then eye-level should be determined when standing; in a sitting-room, however, you should hang the pictures lower as people are likely to view them from a chair or sofa.

A small or narrow space – a hallway or corridor, for instance – is often ideal for small, detailed artpieces, where the interest lies in the content rather than in the general visual impact. A larger picture, however, where the viewer needs to stand back in order to take in the whole image, requires more space. It may look impressive at the end of a long corridor, or you could try placing it opposite the entrance to a room.

GROUPING AND ARRANGING

Often, the striking characteristic of a group of artpieces is their unity: they all seem to belong. This effect does not happen automatically; much thought is needed to achieve it. Attention should be given to the space between each artpiece. If the space is too narrow, the pictures will interfere with each other, whereas if there is too much space, the group will lose its cohesion.

Before hanging a group of pictures, it is a good idea to arrange them on the floor first, matching the shapes and colours. This will give you a reasonable

Vertical arrangement
The arrangement of the frames here (above) have an effect on the appearance of the interior of the hallways as a whole. The irregular rectangles form a pillar of their own and complement the diagonal slope of the banisters and the curved arch of the open doorway.

Colourful abundance
Frames need not be regularly spaced in a formal way. They can often look attractive when thrown together at random, completely covering a wall to present an effect rather like an antique market or junk shop. In the arrangement (right), a colourful mixture of antique and modern frames containing a variety of images creates an exciting impact.

1

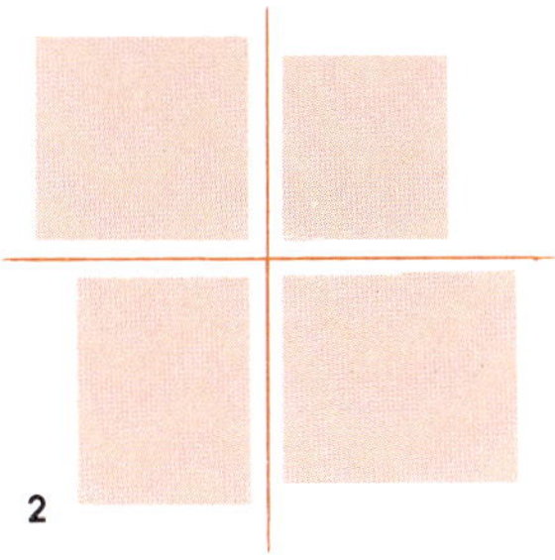
2

3

4

5

The more formal approach
1 *A few smaller frames can be ranged around a very large picture to good effect. Align the tops to give a formal cohesion to the group.*
2 *Four rectangular frames, each of a different size and proportion, can be given form by basing them on vertical and horizontal axes.*
3 *Arrange a variety of rectangular frames sitting on top and hanging underneath a hypothetical line*
4 *This mixture of frames are arranged within what is in effect an overall 'frame'—the rectangle in which they are enclosed.*
5 *When arranging frames on the wall of a stairway, use imaginary verticals to provide form. In this way a 'scattered', unrelated look is avoided.*

DAILY
Mirror

Arranging and displaying
Period frames are arranged symmetrically and aligned with a sideboard to give a neat effect (top left). *Circular objects provide an interesting contrast* (centre top). *A set of framed pictures* (top right) *gives a formal appearance to this elegant bedroom. A set of cards is given form by the fan-shaped frame* (far left). *As the frame is transparent, its shape does not disrupt the wall colour. A bathroom is enlivened with framed documents and charts* (left). *A dense arrangement of pictures makes a feature of a whole wall* (right).

representation of the final effect and the opportunity to experiment before you commit yourself.

One way of making a harmonious group from an array of different shapes and odd proportions is to line up either the tops or the bottoms of the pictures. If you are arranging a group of artpieces for an awkward space, such as the wall next to a staircase, it is not always practical to align them horizontally. In this case, the group spirit can be preserved by lining up the sides of the pictures so that there are regular 'columns' of space between them. Other groupings that can work well include square and circular formations. Experiment with different arrangements to see which suits your artworks best.

MIXING AND MATCHING FRAMES

A set of matching artpieces, or even very different ones, can be given unity by placing each one in an identical frame. This is especially effective if there are other things in the room which are visually 'busy', such as patterned fabrics and wallpapers.

However, one of the most exciting forms of design for a group is to mix the frames, mixing not only the colours, shapes, styles and sizes but also old and new. Although a room that is decorated in a particular period style requires frames that do not jar with the style, most rooms are not designed in such a unified way. Rooms are more often designed according to personal taste and, over a period of years, result in a mixture, which can often benefit from a grouping of pictures and frames that mingles old and new styles and materials. Place a modern plastic frame beside an older-looking wooden moulding, and they may set each other off attractively. Sometimes an oval frame sits nicely in a group of rectangular ones, giving just the right amount of variation. Try to preserve some visual unity, however, or the result will appear random and chaotic.

When it comes to mounts, the scope is unlimited. You can design your mounts to fit into a particular room, or to suit a particular group of images. As mounts can be changed without harming the pictures, there is plenty of room for experiment.

LIGHTING

If you decide to light your artpiece, you are faced with two alternatives. You can either 'spot' it, by placing an ordinary light or spotlight to shine on it from elsewhere in the room, or you can fix lighting on or near the frame itself.

Traditionally, painters have used natural light, often a skylight or northern light, to work by and many painters still follow this tradition. Ideally, therefore, pictures should be lit by daylight from above or from a northerly direction – in other words, 'soft' daylight – but this is rarely practical. Electric bulbs are available which imitate daylight and some galleries use fluorescent lighting under a casing of pearly plastic; long strips of lights are sometimes set in brackets, either above or below the picture. Such lighting techniques could be used in a large room to highlight oil paintings but are not advisable with glazed pictures, as the glass tends to reflect the light detracting from the picture.

Most of us prefer to use normal domestic lighting so that the artpiece blends in with the rest of the room, although, for a special picture, you could make some adjustments. It might be worth buying lighting strips to fit into brackets and attach to the frame itself to look downwards or upwards at the picture, or you may achieve an attractive effect by fixing a spotlight to the ceiling or wall and directing the light at the picture. If you dislike the harshness of spotlights, position ordinary household lighting, such as standard lamps or table lamps, in such a way that they provide good lighting for the pictures. Specially placed lights and spots can be hidden behind a piece of furniture or among plants. Experiment until you achieve exactly the effect that you want.

Variety of style
The use of different shapes, sizes and types of frame bring this bedroom to life (right). *Because the arrangement is interesting, the eye is led to each picture. By mixing bold frames with unstriking frames that blend with the colour scheme of the room, the overall appearance is never overwhelming.*

Lighting and wiring
For more complex arrangements of framed pictures, lighting becomes important. Care must be taken not to beam a light onto a frame in such a way that a deep moulding creates a shadow across part of the picture. Wiring should also be kept as invisible as possible. These pictures and free-standing figures (right) *have been lit in such a way that wiring is not too obtrusive. The movable spotlights in the ceiling can be adjusted to emphasize different artworks or aspects of a collection.*

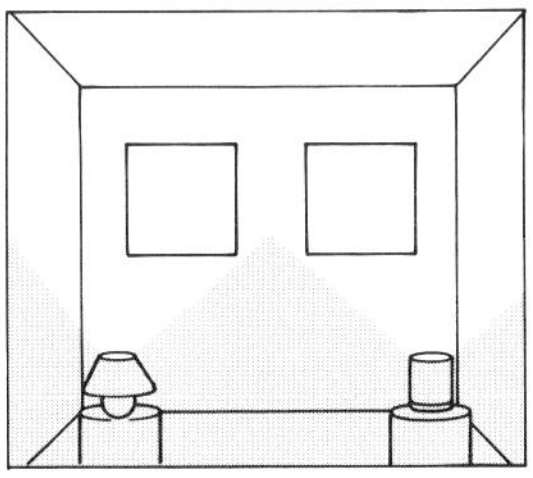

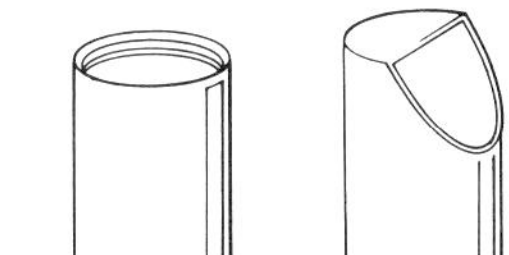

Uplighters
Pictures can be lit by directing lamps from beneath. Special uplighting units create an even, diffused light, spreading upwards and outwards. These are sometimes grouped together to produce an area of even light across the top part of a room or gallery.

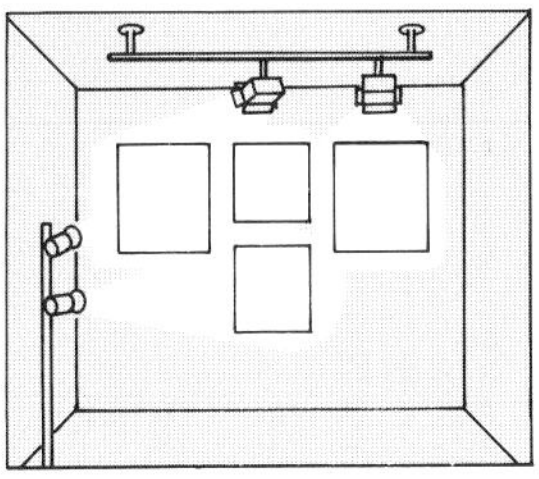

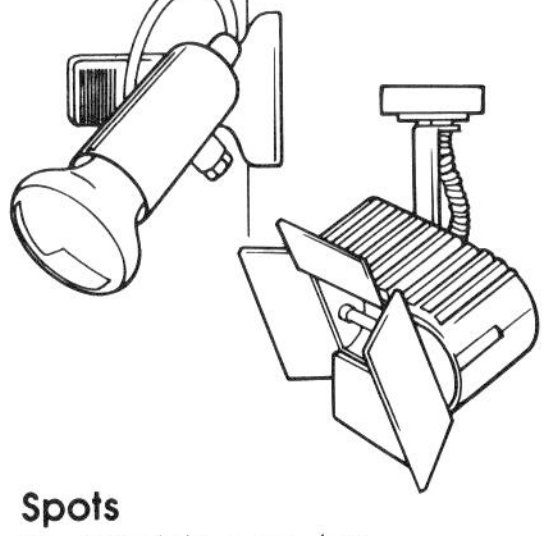

Spots
Spotlights can be adjusted to create direct or reflected light. These can run on a strip track, attached to or hung below the ceiling. Single spots can be fixed to the wall, ceiling or floor, and can also be bought fixed to a stand. Use them singly or in groups.

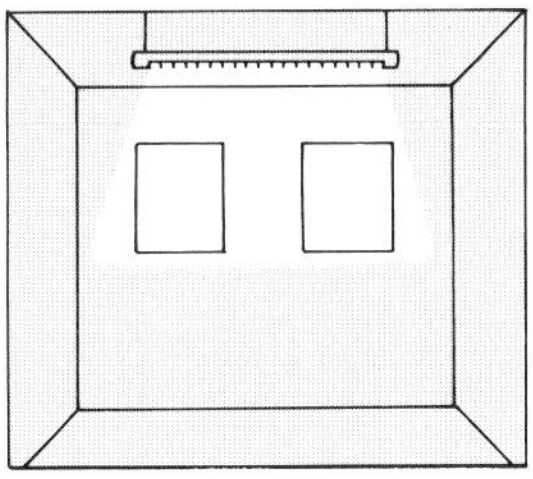

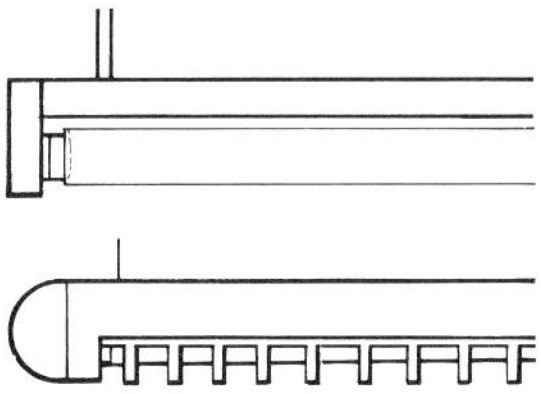

Strips
Sometimes an arrangement of framed pictures looks best when lit by one source. For this, a strip of fluorescent lighting is ideal. Light can be directed onto the pictures by deflectors.

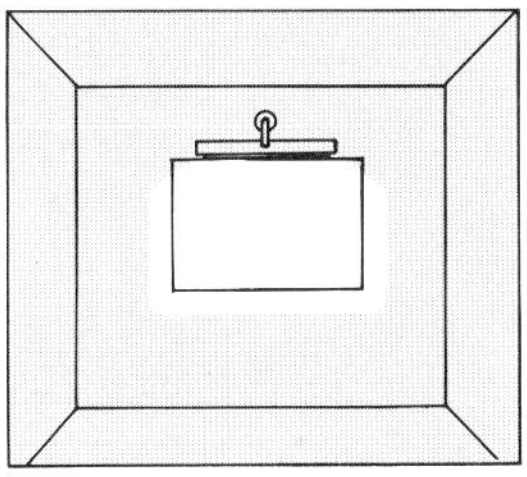

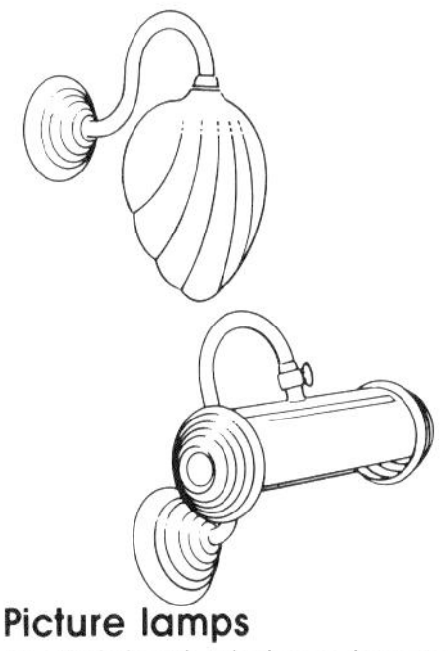

Picture lamps
Individual picture lamps can be bought in a variety of sizes and shapes to suit almost every type of picture. A range of styles is available, from antiqued and old-fashioned to modern designs.

Mounts and mounting

It is important to differentiate clearly between the mount – the 'window' which is placed upon the artwork – and the backing card or board onto which the artwork is stuck before the process begins. Confusion arises because this backing is often referred to as the mount. The means by which the artwork is stuck to this backing is also referred to as 'mounting'. This section discusses the general principles of mounts and mounting. The specific techniques are dealt with in clear, detailed, step-by-step terms in the section entitled the Foundation Skills.

THE BREATHING SPACE

Many artpieces are mounted as well as framed. In other words, the picture does not make direct contact with the frame but is surrounded by a wide margin which separates the picture from the frame. This is the mount. It is the 'breathing space' between the picture content and the frame itself.

There are no rigid rules governing whether you should or should not have a mount within your frame but, as a basic guideline, consider the artpiece itself: does it, for instance, contain large areas of empty space in its composition, as in the case of a line drawing on a plain white background? This sort of picture would look effective with only a small amount of border, or possibly with none at all. On the other hand, a more crowded picture would benefit from a substantial border of space between the image and the frame.

The mount should be chosen before the frame, because it is the mount that comes next to the artpiece. A great deal of mystery has been attached to the 'proportions' of the mount – the amount of space which should be left at the bottom, sides and top of the image. In fact, the choice is personal and there is nothing magical about the measurements. There are some general rules, however.

The proportions of the mount should not compete with the proportions of the artwork; that is, a big picture does not necessarily need a wide mount and a small picture does not always benefit from having a narrow mount. Generally speaking, a small picture is much improved by a wide mount and a grand-looking frame. Do not follow this principle slavishly or you will end up with a postage-stamp-size picture in the middle of a poster-size mount! There are some exceptions. Small photographs can sometimes look good with narrow mounts. A flamboyant modern print can benefit from a wide mount. The result is usually more effective if you avoid giving the visual impression that you have used exactly the same area for the mount as for the artpiece.

There is one important visual illusion which needs

Mount widths
The width of the mount has an immediate effect on the framed picture as a whole. If the mount is too small, it can give the picture a cramped and restricted look. An equal all-round width works well with some images. If the mount is large in comparison with the picture, it is usually better if the picture 'sits' high up in the frame–make sure the mount margin at the bottom of the picture is deeper than that of the other three sides.

Choosing a colour
The landscape (top) is painted in muted, earthy colours. With a picture like this, it is usually advisable to choose a colour that harmonizes with the subject. The light beige mount makes the picture look darker; the dull olive green immediately picks out the green tones in the composition; black emphasizes the linear content. Sometimes a mount of an unrelated colour works: the rich magenta contrasts attractively with the greens and browns in the picture. A picture in bright, expressionistic colours (above) poses a very different problem. The mount generally should be as strong and bright as the colours contained in the painting. The red, blue, yellow, pink and mauve mounts all emphasize these particular colours in the portrait. The lime green provides a contrast; the white mount is effective because it picks out the background of the picture, giving a light, spacious feel.

Assembling block frames
For a neat finish, block frames can be edged with wooden battens and clips screwed into these. The framer (right) *is using Perspex clips, which do not intrude upon the image. These clips are also available in brass and stainless steel.*

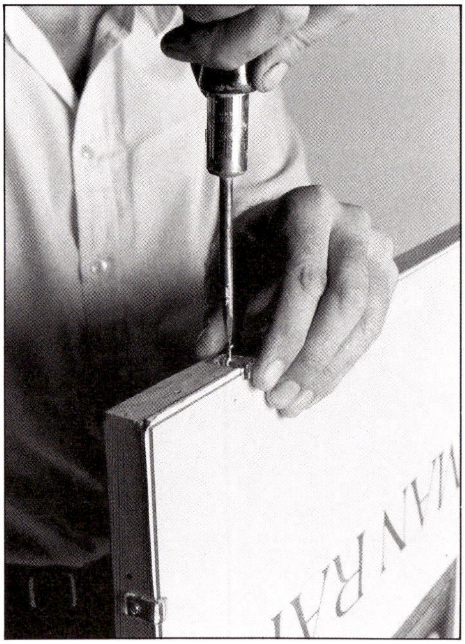

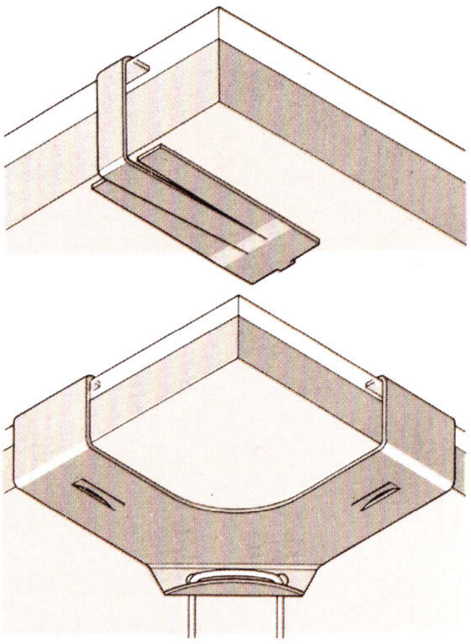

Alternative clips
Spring clips (top) *and metal corner pieces* (above) *are found in most framers' supply shops.*

to be considered. If the width of space around an artpiece is equal, then the bottom will appear smaller than the other margins. Therefore, an impression of symmetry is best produced by having the space at the bottom a little larger than the other margins – between 6mm ($^1/_4$in) and 18mm ($^3/_4$in) is enough in most cases, depending on the size of the artpiece.

THE BASIC MOUNT

Mounting card is available in three different thicknesses: 4-sheet (1000 microns), 6-sheet (1250 microns) and 8-sheet (1900 microns). 6-sheet is the most commonly used and available in the widest variety of colours: maroon, saxe blue, green, grey, pompadour, pale green, holly green, Russian green, mid grey, bottle green, sepia, seal, coffee, ivory and poster black. 8-sheet is the thickest of the three. Thicker card is available but is quite often difficult to obtain and you will probably have to resort to sticking thin pieces of card together if you want to achieve a thick mount. A thick mount is necessary if you wish to create a deeper recess for your picture. For example, if you are working with a very small image and you want to exaggerate its smallness, fragility or preciousness, you might want a deeply recessed effect.

Block Mounts

With modern photographs, a popular method is to use a 'block' mount, in which the image juts out to meet the viewer instead of receding inside a 'window' as is usually the case. Block mounting is inexpensive and simple to do. The photograph can be trimmed first to remove any white edge. Then it is fixed onto a platform, or block, usually of chipboard or wood, which can be hung as it is or stuck onto a flat surface to leave a surround.

CO-ORDINATING THE COLOURS

As with space, the colours of mount and artpiece should not compete with or equal each other. The colour of the mount should not overpower or merge with the colours in the picture. On the whole, the colours of the mount should not be too strong or bright but should be muted and neutral.

Sometimes, contrast can be effective: warm colours in a picture can be offset by a cool colour in the mount, and vice versa. For instance, a sepia drawing can be enhanced by a grey, pale blue or pale green surround. Traditionally, watercolours are given cool-coloured mounts, perhaps because of their mainly delicate washes and subjects, although in recent years dark green and brown have become popular, especially for landscapes. The darker the mount, the more quickly the eye is drawn towards the picture.

With many modern prints, the rules of co-ordination are discarded in favour of dramatic effect and instant impact. Bright colours can often successfully surround a modern print to produce a startling and eye-catching effect.

Mounts are usually made from mounting card. This is available in a variety of colours but, if you are seeking an unusual colour or a different pattern or texture, it is quite possible to buy plain white card and stick coloured or hand-decorated paper onto it.

If you are using acid-free conservation board – for instance, for an old map or document – you may find that this is available in only white or off-white. Again, you can stick a good quality paper – that is, a hand-made paper produced from rags, which is relatively free from impurities – onto an acid-free board. Do not use the usual spray adhesive or commercial glues in this case; you must buy acid-free tape from an art shop or make your own paste from wheatflour and water, otherwise the chemical glue fumes may damage the picture.

WINDOWS

On deciding to use a mount, you are not limited to a single rectangle for the window. You can, if you wish, 'trim' your picture – without actually cutting it – by placing a differently shaped window on top of it. Or you can simply use a window which suits the shape of the original picture.

One extremely effective way in which to set certain artworks, but a more difficult one to cut, is an oval or round mount. Ovals are particularly attractive for mounting vignettes; small pictures which do not have hard edges. Oval and circular-shaped mounts are available from art shops in standard sizes ready-cut.

If you require a specific size which is not available ready-cut, and you do not have access to an oval mount cutter, then it is best to hand-cut ovals and circles, using a scalpel or art knife – and great care. You may need considerable practice with scraps of card before you are ready to cut the final piece but other devices are available, such as compass-cutters and templates.

For the adventurous and the skilled, it is possible to cut an endless variety of window shapes. You do not have to follow any particular traditions, although bizarre shapes can look rather ridiculous unless they are particularly suited to the picture and are well designed. It is advisable to use thin card rather than mounting board, at least until you become more skilled and confident.

An artwork can be made to look richer and more expensive by setting it in a double mount, cutting an inner mount which fits under the main one, so that only a small part of the inner mount shows. This small band can be more adventurous than the main mount, perhaps using a bright colour or even gilt. A third mount can be added, although care is needed in the choice of colour and size – too many confusing edges tend to detract from the artwork.

If you have a collection or series of small artpieces that go well together, they can be set within the same frame. This is called a multiple mount. Two, three, four, six or eight pictures can best be mounted together. This obviously takes a little planning and the layout requires thought. It is advisable to set out the pictures on a piece of paper and then to cut windows from the paper. Use this paper pattern as a guide for the final mount.

THE BEVELLED EDGE

Almost all mounts are cut with a bevelled edge. Instead of cutting a piece of board or card with the knife held vertically, the cutting edge is sloped. Thus, instead of a sheer 'canyon' effect, the picture is placed in a window which has inclining sides. This means that no unwanted trace of shadow will appear, and the eye will be brought directly to the picture without hindrance from a hard edge.

Ready-made mounts
Ready-made mounts (below) *are available in a variety of shapes, sizes and colours. Buy mounts made from rag fibres – those containing wood pulp can cause staining.*

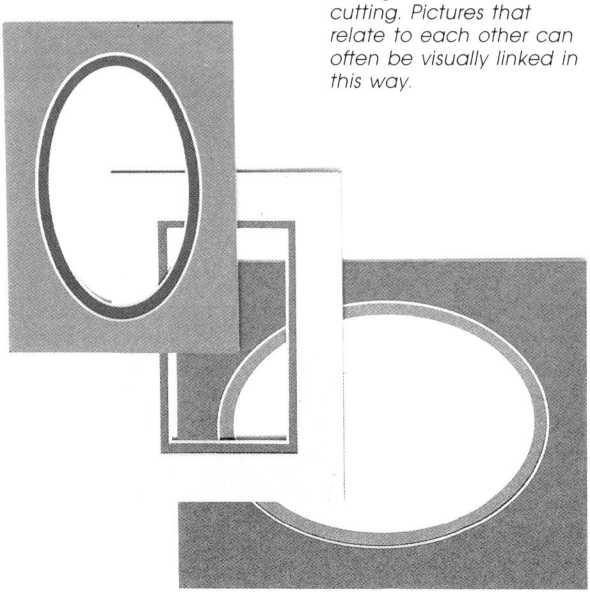

Multi-window mounts
An attractive display can be created by using multi-window mounts (right). *There is no set number of windows that should be cut in a single card, but spacing is crucial and you should try various arrangements before cutting. Pictures that relate to each other can often be visually linked in this way.*

Bevelled edges
Cutting a bevelled edge requires practice, and it is best to experiment first on scraps of card. Keep the knife at a constant angle when cutting. It is essential to have a really sharp scalpel or knife.

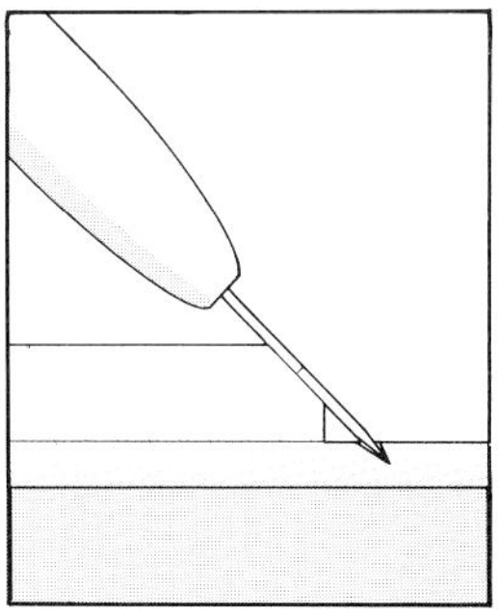

Bought mounts
Mounts can be bought in a rich variety of finishes. In this collection, pale, thin washes contrast with ribboned and marbled borders.
1 *Blue and gold French wash mount.*
2 *Peach and gold English wash-line mount.*
3,5,7 *Line, gold line and wash mounts.*
4,6,8 *Marbled mounts with contrasting overmounts.*
9,10 *Marbled mounts with coloured undermounts.*
11 *Blue-grey marbled mount.*
12 *Taupe marbled mount.*
13 *Cream marbled mount.*
14 *Gold line and wash.*
15 *Green wash.*
16 *Reverse-bevel double mount.*
17 *Marbled mount.*
18 *Yellow wash mount.*
19 *Grey wash mount.*
20 *Pink wash mount.*
21 *Blue wash mount.*
22 *Pink wash mount.*
23 *Line-and-wash mount.*
24 *Marbled mount with contrasting overmount.*
25 *Mulberry paper mount with ribbon inlay.*
26 *Line-and-wash mount.*
27 *Marbled mount with contrasting overmount.*
28 *Line-and-wash, two-tone mount with inlay.*

Bevelling evenly by hand is quite difficult. Again, practice is the answer and an extremely sharp cutting tool is vital. Use a metal ruler fixed in position to guide your hand when cutting such an edge. It is possible to obtain a mount cutter, a tool which holds replaceable blades in position, *(see page 54)* but this tool is difficult to get used to and it can take just as long to learn how to use it as to become proficient in cutting by hand.

A fine finishing touch can be given to a bevelled edge by gilding it or painting it in a contrasting colour.

LINES AND WASHES

There is a refinement which can be added to the process of mounting to give the finished product a genuinely period touch. Lines and washes became popular in Europe during the eighteenth century and the technique is known as French mounting – an arrangement of lines, sometimes filled with a light wash, set around the picture. The point of the arrangement is to guide the eye gently in to the painting or drawing.

Colours are crucial to this process. They must be chosen carefully to complement those in the picture itself. A common mistake is to make them too brash. The secret is to 'understate' rather than 'overstate'. Otherwise, you will find that when you view the finished product, you notice the lines instead of the picture, which defeats the whole purpose.

Lines and washes work best on a neutral-coloured mount, one which does not challenge the arrangement. If you have only a dark-coloured or soiled mount, cover it with watercolour paper before applying lines and washes. The lines themselves are often drawn in gold, producing the luxurious effect which has been traditionally popular. Many people will have frequently looked at watercolours surrounded by lines and washes, without noticing that the technique has been used. This is because it has been done with subtlety.

The use of lines and washes became common in Europe towards the end of the eighteenth century and was still popular in the nineteenth. This was when the classical school of English watercolourists came into its own, reaching great heights with such artists as John Sell Cotman (1782–1842) and Thomas Girtin (1775–1802). The lines and washes employed on the mounts for their pictures have become so familiar, and are so subtly done that we scarely notice them.

Framers still rely on the line-and-wash method when they want to give an extra finish to the product. The method, although traditionally used with neutral colours by the watercolourists, is nowadays sometimes used on vibrant, modern prints. In this case the line and wash is often bolder, using brighter colours for both the wash and the lines.

One of the attractive features of the line-and-wash technique is that you are not limited. You can vary the width of line, the space between the lines

Line-and-wash borders
An English Lady *by Hans Holbein* (above) *has a line-and-wash border, which is painted onto the picture itself. Modern lines and washes include:* **1** *silver, white, gold and red on light grey;* **2** *silver and light grey on Wedgewood blue;* **3** *black, gold and white on cream;* **4** *Ochre edged with gold, with a fine black line.*

Fabric coverings
Mounts and frames can be covered by an enormous variety of materials. Velvet, leather, silk, hessian — there is a host of different textures and patterns to choose from. They can be used to cover the outer frames or mounts, which will add a dash of colour to the artpiece. Spend time experimenting with fabrics, placing them beside pictures to see how they work. Learn how to enhance a picture without overwhelming it. For a less dominant tonal or textural effect, fabrics can also be used for just part of a frame or mount, limited, for instance, to the borders.

and the number of lines. You also have a choice of colour. You can use only one colour, or you can be adventurous and use several.

Do not launch into the technique without careful preparation. You will need to practise first: try using a mount wash kit (available from art shops) to begin with if you are unused to painting with watercolours. Traditionally, an ordinary nibbed pen was used and craftsmen developed great skill in keeping the lines even and in varying their width, by making confident movements with the pen and ensuring that it did not run out of ink at a crucial time, producing an uneven or broken rule.

Today, we are much luckier. Ruling pens are easily available from art and graphic suppliers; these have adjustable nibs, so that the same pen can be used whatever sort of line you are making. The pen is specially made so that the nib effectively acts as a tiny reservoir to ensure a smooth flow of ink.

COVERING A MOUNT

Mounts can be covered with a variety of materials, not only to produce different colours but to give a variety of textural effects. Two of the most popular materials are hessian and linen, easily obtainable from fabric shops. Mounting card can be bought already covered with canvas, hessian or silk but in this case the bevelled edge remains uncovered. Fabric of this kind is also often used to cover the wooden insert of a frame for oil or acrylic paintings to give a suitably textured area between the frame and the painted surface.

A fabric mount can also be used to put a picture in context. For example, an early twentieth-century silhouette or an old portrait photograph could be given a period flavour by using taffeta or shot silk on the mount. Black or deep red velvet could be effective in giving a luxurious feel to a grand picture or to lend distinction and formality to a collection of medals or coins, and a suede or leather mount makes a treasured photograph more enduring and special. Many modern pictures are enhanced by a mount covered in a soft textural weave, such as hessian, canvas or linen. Artists' canvas comes in a range of subtle tones from off-white to a muted dark beige.

Paper, too, has its different textures. Shiny and metallic surfaces can be used as surrounds. In some cases, why not use textured wallpaper? Many people underestimate the amazing variety of patterns available nowadays in paper. Particularly interesting are the unusual, though sometimes expensive, papers used in the bookbinding craft. These include many beautiful marbled patterns and some intricate designs, subtle enough to be useful to the picture framer.

WET AND DRY MOUNTING

As well as deciding on the mount, you must ensure that the artwork itself is stuck firmly onto a backing. Frequently, the works that you wish to frame will not have been executed directly onto paper thick or

Using wallpaper
If you intend covering a frame or mount with wallpaper, make sure that it blends with the furnishings of the room. A wallpaper-covered frame or mount can look extremely attractive on a plain wall. The examples shown here include mounts that offset the moulding, and more exotic cases in which the paper covers both the mount and the moulding.

firm enough to support them without this backing material being added before the artwork is taped to the backing board. Remember that if you are dealing with valuable, old or treasured pictures or documents, acid-free conservation board should be used.

The methods used by craftsmen for sticking the picture to a stiff card or board are known as 'wet mounting' and 'dry mounting'.

Wet mounting simply means glueing a picture onto a board, but this has to be done with great care – it is all too easy to end up with bubbles or ridges, and a treasured picture can be ruined.

First a piece of board or card is cut to exactly the same size as the artwork itself. Then an adhesive, preferably a rubber- or plastic-based glue, is brushed smoothly or sprayed evenly on top and the picture carefully positioned. To smooth out the bubbles and any excess glue, it is flattened with a roller or cloth, moving towards the edges from the centre. It is advisable to clamp the picture and backing between boards while the glue is drying.

A more permanent professional finish is achieved by dry mounting. A sheet of adhesive wax film (available from art and craft shops) is carefully placed between the picture and its backing and the film is then heated to fuse the picture or print to the backing card, giving a perfect product. Professionals use dry-mounting presses but these are expensive. Dry mounting can be done just as effectively by using a regular household iron.

TAPING

If the picture is stiff enough without a backing, or if you do not want to take the irretrievable step of fusing the artpiece to the backing, use tape. Strips of fabric or masking tape should be used, rather than normal transparent tape, as they can be unstuck comparatively easily.

Very narrow tape is usually sufficient for this process. It can be positioned so that it overlaps both the edge of the picture and the backing card, or – if you do not want to stick it onto the top surface of the picture or print – you can fold the tape back onto itself as you would with stamps in an album, creating a double-sided adhesive tape effect. Double-sided tape is not a wise alternative: as with clear tape, it is too firmly adhesive and can cause difficulties should you wish to remove the artwork at a later date. It is also more difficult to position the artwork correctly using double-sided tape.

HINGE MOUNTS

One way of ensuring that you position an artpiece exactly in place on a backing is to construct a hinge mount. Simply hinge the backing onto the window and close them together, placing the artwork in between the two *(see pages 58–61 for details)*. One advantage of this method is that the window mount and backing are fixed permanently in relation to each other, allowing you to move the picture around on the inner backing until you have found exactly the right position for it.

Types of moulding

The mould is the frame itself, the outer edges that most people have in mind when they think of a frame. Moulding is available in the form of strips of wood similar to the carved pieces that surround many doors and windows. This section discusses the types of moulding available for making your own frames, and the variety of finishes you can apply to them. Specific details on the techniques of measuring, cutting, glueing and finishing frames are given in clear, step-by-step format in the section called Foundation Skills.

There are two types of moulding: framers' moulding and builders' moulding. The main difference between the two is that framers' moulding comes with a fitted rebate; that is, it is 'stepped' in order to allow the picture, mount and glass to fit neatly into place without falling right through the frame.

Builders' moulding is primarily intended for trimming doors, windows, skirting boards and for other interior finishes. Its use as picture-framing material is incidental and, consequently, it does not have a fitted rebate. Consequently, if you use builders' moulding, you will either have to cut out the step or create a recess by sticking a narrow strip of wood underneath the moulding.

The other important difference is the price. Framers' moulding is very expensive. It comes pre-finished and is often made of hardwood. However, for the amateur, it is advisable to use framers' moulding initially despite the extra cost because the added complication of having to make rebates is something that can well be left until you have more frame-making experience.

Once you have a little experience, you may want to use builders' moulding. At this stage, when you visit a builders' yard or timber shop, you will probably be surprised at the wide variety of mouldings available Many can be used as picture frames and sometimes two or more types can be put together to make a more elaborate frame.

When browsing through the yards and shops for builders' framing, bear in mind the width of the framing you will need – the picture should not be overshadowed. For a classical or traditional oil painting, a heavy moulding several inches wide is desirable; for a more abstract design, a simpler edging is preferable.

One advantage of using builders' moulding is that it gives a free range to home experts who wish to create their own finishes.

FRAMERS' MOULDING

Ready-made framers' moulding is available in a variety of types and finishes and is to be found in art shops and picture-framing stockists. There is an impressive array of mouldings from reproduction, antique-looking and highly decorated edgings to plain and simple styles.

Framers' mouldings include, at the exotic end of the range, the period mouldings, gilded and ornate, with delicate leaf-like patterns and elegant and formal ribbed designs reminiscent of the flamboyant courts of the *Ancien Régime* in eighteenth-century France. Also to be found are the more mundane, but attractive, spoon or scoop shapes in which the edging appears as if it has been scooped out regularly right along its line. Related to these are the traditional 'window frame' styles which 'step down' in gentle progression towards the picture.

Reproduction frames
From the simple to the extremely ornate, this selection gives an indication of the enormous range of reproduction framers' mouldings available today. They are known as: **1** *'Marlborough';* **2** *Red and gold;* **3** *'Van Huysum';* **4** *Red crackle;* **5** *Reproduction seventeenth-century;* **6** *'Rondo';* **7** *'Ripple';* **8** *Gilt Art Nouveau;* **9** *Black and gold;* **10** *Reproduction sixteenth-century Florentine;* **11** *Gilt;* **12** *'Whistler';* **13** *'Edgar Enigma';* **14** *Faux tortoiseshell;* **15** *'Aschkar';* **16** *'Old Ornate Bourlet';* **17** *'Klanaris';* **18** *Golf leaf on blue, no 11;* **19** *'Rembrandt';* **20** *Dutch veneer, no 6;* **21** *'Marco 1';* **22** *Gilt;* **23** *Red, black and gold;* **24** *Crackled green and bronze;* **25** *Gold leaf;* **26** *'Jap 1';* **27** *'Chinzan';* **28** *Hogarth;* **29** *Gilt;* **30** *Black Flemish-style.*

6
7
8
9
10
11
12
13
14
15
16
17
18
19
20
21
22
23
24
25
26
27
28
29
30

Variety of mouldings
Builders' moulding comes in a surprising amount of different styles. Become more familiar with the range by browsing in timber yards and do-it-yourself shops. Most timber shops have charts giving a 'to scale' range. You will need to make your own rebate.

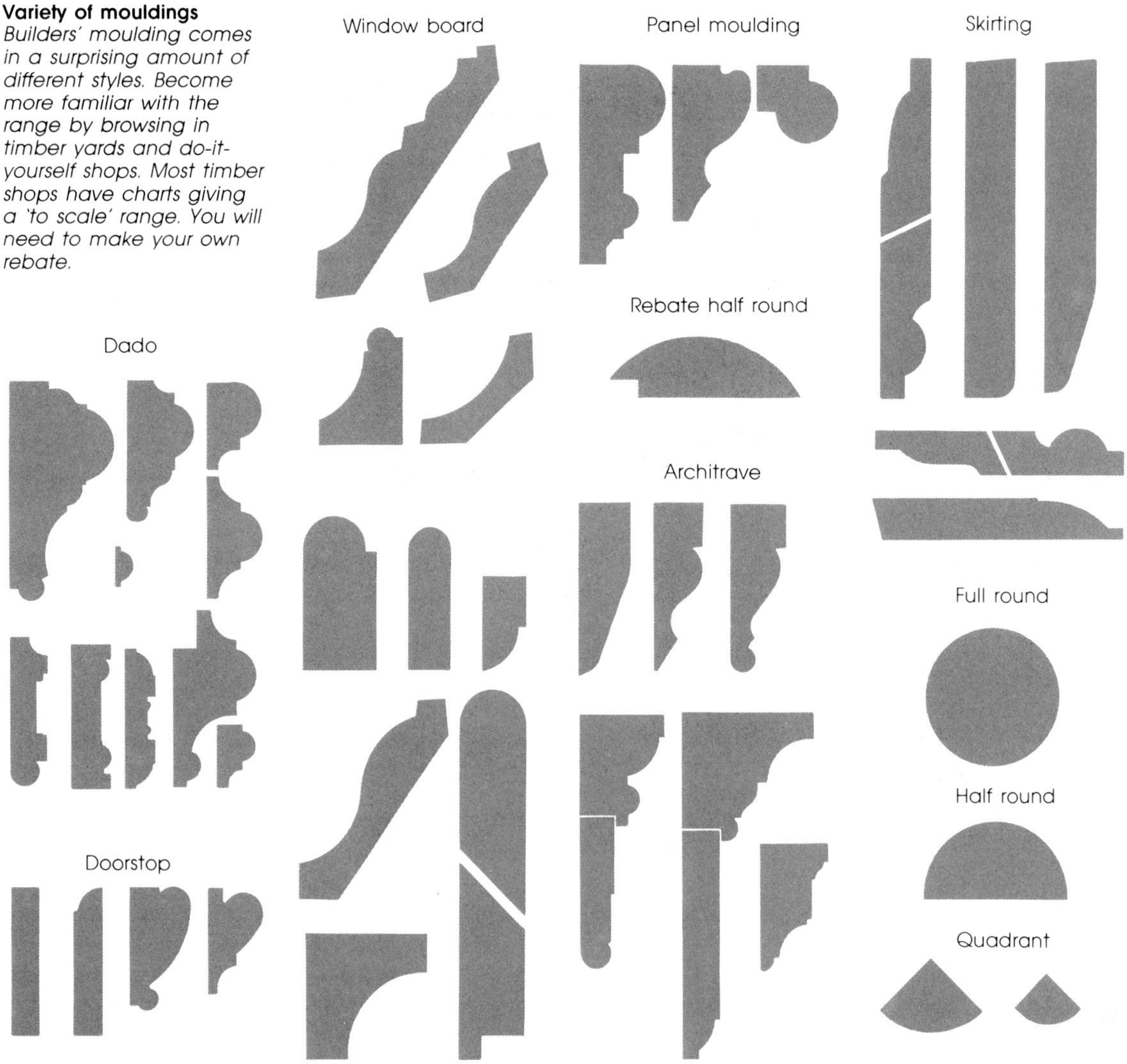

Less expensive are the simple wood slopes and flat edges with aluminium finishes.

If you want a metal frame, it can usually be purchased in the form of straight metal strips. However, metal is more difficult to use than wood and special equipment is needed to drill and saw it *(see page 75)*. It is possible to obtain framers' moulding which is covered in a thin veneer of metal. This looks like solid metal but can be sawn and treated like any other moulding.

One of the more striking characteristics of the range of framers' mouldings available is the large variation in width. Here, keen judgement is necessary. Try to keep in mind the artpiece you are framing when looking over the strip of moulding.

Insert mouldings are also available from picture-frame stockists. They can be fitted inside the outer frame to give endless combinations of colour, shape and texture.

Much variation is provided, too, by different types of wood, each with its own characteristic appearance. One favourite is walnut but you will also find such woods as maple and cherry prominent on the shelves. Further alternatives include mouldings that have been stained, gilded, coloured or waxed.

BUILDERS' MOULDING

At first glance there seems to be less variety of builders' moulding than framers' moulding but great scope is available in the way builders' moulding can be combined and finished.

This is not so unusual as it may appear, for, if you look closely at the framers' mouldings available, you will often find that they themselves comprise subtle combinations of differently shaped strips.

One common type of builders' moulding found in the timber yards and do-it-yourself shops is the heavy, traditional carved strip often found around door frames. This automatically suggests itself for a picture in the grander style, such as a substantial oil painting; but with care and good finishing, some surprising effects are achieved by using this heavy style as a surround for a smaller image, such as a portrait. This can produce the effect of a dramatic

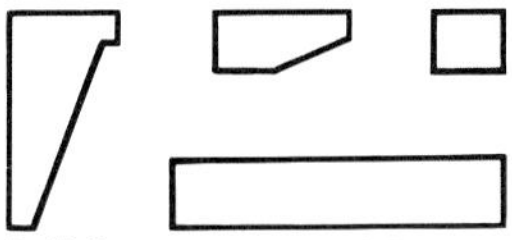

Building up a moulding
You can construct your own more elaborate mouldings by buying separate strips and assembling them to your own design. For instance, the strips illustrated (above) in cross section were used to create all the mouldings at right.

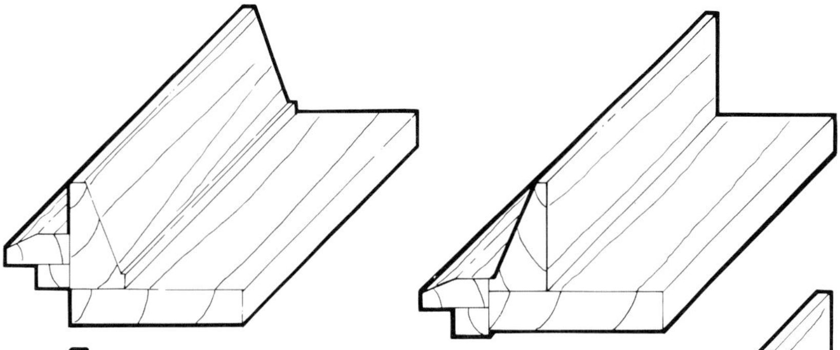

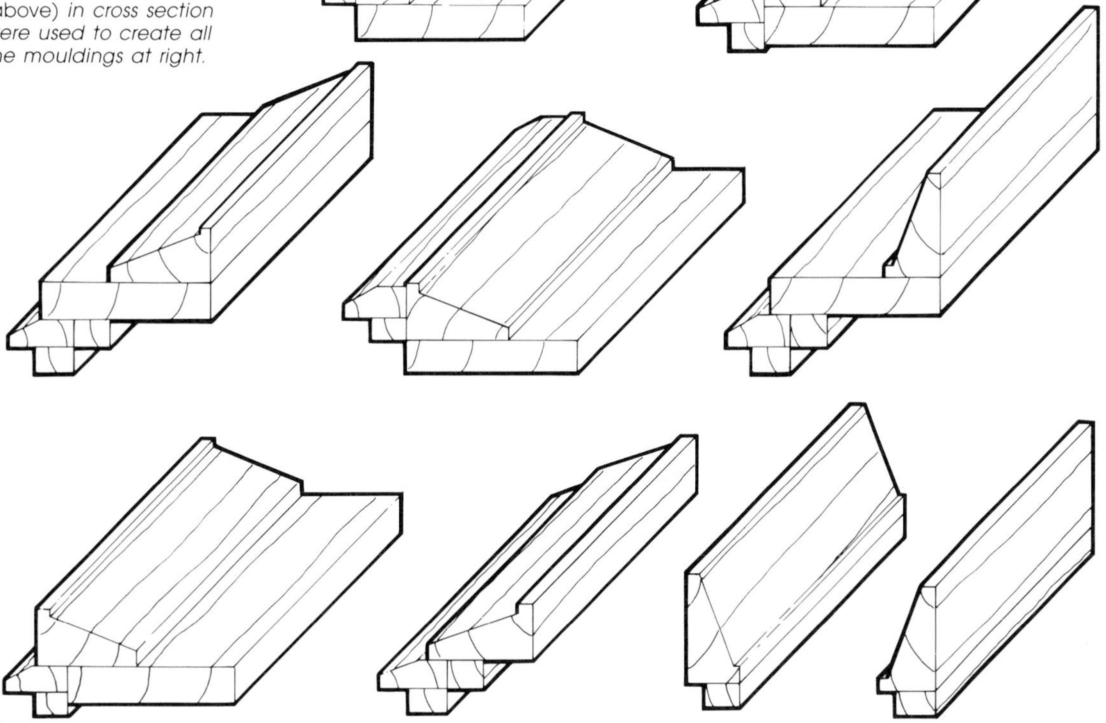

Moulding can often be attractively carved. Use existing frames for inspiration and keep the designs simple and tools very sharp.

recess, almost as if you are looking at the picture down a tunnel.

The door mouldings and the slightly smaller window strips are the obvious choices; they already look like most framers' mouldings. However, there are more unusual styles, such as symmetrical mouldings, where the inside edge is the same as the outside one, and rounded or bevelled beadings.

With builders' mouldings, if the exact profile you had in mind is not manufactured, then you can often come very close to it by combining two or more simpler pieces. If you can persuade your timber merchants' to give you waste pieces or offcuts with which to experiment in different combinations, you will soon become quite expert.

We should stress again the major difference between framers' and builders' mouldings — framers' strips come with a fitted rebate, builders' mouldings do not. Whichever moulding you choose, you must bear in mind the need for a rebate. If the basic moulding is wide enough you could, perhaps, make a rebate by gouging it out of the same piece

but this is complicated and can lead to mistakes. By far the simplest method is to stick a plain strip of wood to the back of the selected moulding*(see page 78)*.

SELECTING THE FRAME

By using an appropriate style of frame you can set off your picture to advantage. When choosing a frame, bear in mind the period and style of the picture. A delicate Japanese print, for example, would not be complemented by a heavy European frame with an eighteenth-century look. Such a mismatch of styles would immediately jolt the senses.

However, selecting a frame is still more a question of personal taste than rules. For instance, many Impressionist and Post-impressionist paintings, their colours brighter and brushwork bolder than that of their predecessors, still look well inside the ornate

Bought frames and mouldings
A fine, grained frame with a raised inner edge stands complete at the top right of this selection. The group of grained woods and veneers illustrates the range of frames and mouldings available. At the bottom left-hand corner are two types of frame for an oval picture, including a gold slip oval that would enhance a particularly treasured period miniature. A more formal style of room cries out for the more formal, polished frames that are typical of those grouped together here. Among the narrower frames is an elegant tortoiseshell and gold, two sides of which are illustrated at the top left. Next to it is a corner piece in antique walnut veneer. Some solid and grand frames lie across the centre of the group, including one with fan-shaped wooden inlays. Take care when choosing frames of this sort—consideration should be given not only to the type of picture to be framed, but also to the suitability of the frame to the environment where the picture will hang.

Colourful paint finishes
Some highly decorative paint finishes are featured in this group of mouldings. All ready-cut frames, they combine a traditional period flavour with modern experimental finishes. The yellow marbled frame across the centre is frankly faked. Yet the result is a tasteful version of a traditional marbling technique, even though the colours are chosen to blend well with a modern interior. It contrasts strongly with the simple green and turquoise ovals that lie next to it in the group. To their bottom right is a series of specimens including a 'faux' or 'made' (imitation) malachite, and two elegant and narrow samples finished in stippled red and sponged blue. At the extreme top left of the whole group is a marbled dark blue frame, followed by frames sporting a variety of decorative finishes, including two rectangles with painted motifs and decoration over white and green stippled backgrounds.

gilded mouldings of the seventeenth and eighteenth centuries.

Most old pictures look best in their original frames but, of course, this is often impossible to achieve, for the original is frequently missing or hopelessly damaged. The search is then on for a moulding that is a modern reproduction of an older look. If possible, the final choice should maintain the original balance: the right proportions between picture and frame, colours that do not clash, and a weight that is not overbearing.

A heavy moulding – a massive look – may be suitable for an image such as a portrait, where the head usually takes up most of the picture surface, but it would be inappropriate for a picture containing many small figures or shapes and a lot of space.

Do not overlook the feelings of the artist. Painters often design and paint the frame as well as the picture. The Pointillist, Georges Seurat (1859–91) extended his 'optical' method of mixing colour used in his pictures to some of his frames, creating a total effect.

It is not easy to decide what sort of mouldings the artist would have wished for a particular painting but some sensitivity and exploration is called for.

Double Frames

Smaller artworks especially can be set off well by double framing, in which a second frame, or 'slip', is inserted within a broader one. The terminology varies but we shall refer to these internal frames throughout the book as 'inserts'.

Why use inserts? They provide a broad ribbon of material between the artwork and the outside world and they do it more gently than would a solid wedge-like frame. The insert provides a gentle transition from the artwork to the outside frame and, in turn, the surrounding environment. More than one insert can be used, giving a multiple frame. They can be made of different materials, can be covered with fabrics such as velvet or canvas, and can be veneered or painted.

The colour and texture of the insert should harmonize with the artpiece, picking up some of its characteristics. A block of dull red in a picture, for instance, can be reflected by a similar colour for the insert. Some purists argue that framers can wrongly emphasize a colour or element in the artpiece by reflecting this in the frame, and certainly with some artworks it may be better to use a more neutral tone,

Velvet slip
Traditional materials have been chosen here for a traditional subject. The needlework has been placed in a mahogany frame with an insert or slip frame which has been covered in rich green velvet.

which does not visually alter the artwork. This is a field in which the framer can have fun learning and experimenting with different effects.

Platform Frames

Another alternative for the smaller artpiece is a platform frame. The artpiece is mounted onto a larger surround, so that it is physically raised up above the surface. The surround can be made of practically any material but wood or cork are favourites, as they allow the picture to 'breathe'.

A VARIETY OF FINISHES

You, too, can paint your own frames, or you can finish them with other materials and techniques. Framers' mouldings are bought ready-finished but builders' mouldings allow you to develop your own artistic talent.

Five basic methods of finishing – waxing, staining, texturing, gilding, and painting – are discussed below with special emphasis on painting, which includes such techniques as marbling and spattering. Details on how to effect these techniques are given on pages 86–97.

Waxing

This finishing technique makes the most of the appearance of the wood itself, whether it is soft or hard. Waxing enriches the natural colour of the wood and also brings out the grain.

Either apply wax straight to the wood surface or use it as a final finish by waxing over another finish, such as staining. Paint the wax on with a brush; several coats can be used and each one should be polished and buffed up with a soft cloth.

For the most effective wax, mix equal parts of melted beeswax, pure turpentine and pure linseed oil. As an alternative to merely enhancing the colour of the wood, you can add your own colouring by mixing wax with artists' oil paint.

Staining

One of the great advantages of staining today is that you are no longer restricted to the traditional, natural colours of wood. Stains are now made in a wide variety of colours and if a shop does not stock exactly the shade you require, mix your own.

Staining preserves the patterns of the wood, simply adding colour. It does leave the wood porous, however, and you will therefore need to seal the finished piece with a wax or varnish.

Some stains are water-based and some spirit-based: be careful not to mix the two types.

Texturing

There are two basic ways of creating a textured surface. You can either cut into the wood, usually with a pointed instrument or 'raking' tool such as a comb, or you can build up a texture by applying certain substances and working on them.

One such substance is a thick coat of paint. Drag

Applying gold leaf
For both these finishes, begin in the same way by giving the basic frame several coats of gesso and bole. The less expensive method of gilding (left) *is transfer gilding, which is bought in the form of gold sheets on a paper backing. Water gilding* (below) *is an old craft, requiring practice and the right equipment.*

a comb or other instrument through the still slightly wet paint to create a pattern. Vinyl paint is particularly well suited to this technique. You can also use gesso, a fine plaster-type finish mixed into a paste from powder and water. Experiment with other materials to achieve interesting or unusual results.

Professional Gilding

Gilding, or 'golding' involves covering the surface with a gold colour or a very fine layer of real gold. For picture frames, the most expensive and difficult method, but also the most professional, is to use real gold leaf. The word 'real' is used here because you can also buy synthentic gold leaf, although this is harder to apply. Real gold leaf is gold beaten into a sheet only 0.0001mm thick. Bought in books or sheets, it is the result of a craft dating back many centuries. Homer's *Odyssey* contains a passage describing how cattle ready for sacrifice had their horns covered with beaten gold. The process of making gold leaf today has changed little since a German monk wrote a basic outline of the technique in the twelfth century.

There are several different types of real gold leaf, all available from art shops. The main ones are named after their countries of origin: English, French and Italian. Although they vary in quality, they all tend to be highly expensive. However, real gold leaf applied well provides a beautiful finish.

Water gilding and oil gilding are the two basic methods of applying gold leaf. With water gilding, the gold is burnished to a very bright finish; with oil gilding, the surface is left matt.

Simple Gilding

There are easier ways of achieving a gilt finish on your picture frame than using real gold leaf. Liquid gold leaf or even gold paint can be used for small areas, such as a narrow band, or for retouching.

Metallic powders are widely available: mix them with a varnish. They are especially good for painting motifs and stencilling patterns but if used for larger areas they tend to look streaky and patchy. Powders can be bought for silver and bronze effects as well as gold.

Another material that can be used for gilding is transfer gold. Similar to gold leaf but easier to apply, transfer gold is a thin layer of gold which is purchased on backing paper. Use it like a traditional transfer, but only for smaller jobs.

Creative finishes
Some wooden frames can be painted so that they resemble different materials, such as the apparent marble (right). *The painted golden and auburn tortoiseshell* (above) *is more obviously stylistic. The effect of wood grain can also be created with paint* (above right).

Paint Effects

A wealth of finishes can be obtained with paint, using various tricks to produce different effects.

Paint can be used to achieve a surface that resembles a more expensive texture, such as marble, tortoiseshell, or a rare and exotic hardwood. Once you have learned the techniques, you will be amazed at how easily you can obtain a finish that has the look of a highly professional product. A brief summary of paint techniques follows; for more details on how to effect them, see pages 92–97.

Marbling is the technique of using broken colour to capture the effect of the irregular streaks of the seams in real marble. It rarely actually deceives but marble is accepted today as a legitimate pattern in its own right.

Wood-graining is one of the older crafts. Victorian decorators became skilled at producing the effect of wood grain on furniture and only a few years ago examples of it could still be found in many homes. Apply a thin layer of paint, so thin that it is transparent, and then carefully drag a dry brush over it to achieve a wavy texture. On top of this, while the paint is still wet, scratch in lines to represent the grains of wood.

Tortoiseshelling makes use of oil-based paint, which is painted into a textured varnish and smoothed out to create the subtly blurred surface of real tortoiseshell.

Rubbing back consists of painting a wet paint onto a dry one of a different colour. Wipe the second colour while it is still wet to leave just a few traces in the grains of the wood. Rubbing back is particularly effective when using gold over a warm colour such as red, or silver over a cool colour or black.

Vinegar painting is sometimes called putty graining. It creates a grain-like pattern but does not attempt to imitate real wood and is most effective when bright colours are used. Any pattern can be pro-

Etched patterns
A combination of gilding, gesso and paint can give spectacular effects (left). *The gesso is etched or scoured with a sharp implement and the gilding and colour applied on top.*

Spattering with a brush
Spattering gives a speckled effect (above): *use bright colours for a modern effect, or neutral or black to create an antique look.*

duced using this technique. Paint one colour onto the frame and allow it to dry. Then paint on a second colour made as a paste from vinegar, sugar, powder colour and a little detergent. While it is still wet, dab it with cork or crumpled paper to make a pattern.

Flicking and spattering require a stiff brush, such as a toothbrush. Run your thumb along the bristles or hit the handle on a strip of wood to spatter the paint onto the moulding. If this is done in a restrained way, using a neutral colour, you can make gilt finishes look old and more subdued. Alternatively, you can let rip and use lots of colours on top of each other to create an exciting effect.

Patinas can be used to create subtle warm and cool tones on the same frame. Begin with a basic pale grey base. Then apply cooler or warmer greys in a thin wash. To make a cooler grey, add blue to the basic grey; for a warmer tone, add burnt sienna or yellow ochre. The best effects are made by mixing warm and cool tones. Apply two or more transparent glazes of warm and cool tones, allowing each layer to dry before applying the next.

Matching the frame to the artpiece can be done with a plain matching colour, matt or gloss, or you can decorate the moulding in a way which is visually sympathetic to the artwork. This is a very old practice: the man generally credited with having discovered oil painting, Jan Van Eyck (1390–1441), is known to have painted his frames to match his pictures. Care is needed, but with flair and imagination frames can be decorated in a way that does not impose an incongruous or overbearing style on the original picture.

Antiquing – making a frame look older and toning down brash colours – can be achieved by using some of the methods mentioned above. Spattering, for instance, if done with black or a dull colour, can tone down a harsh surface. Or rubbing back can be used, again with a dull, neutral top colour.

The Basics of Framing

Materials and Equipment

The Foundation Skills

Finishing Techniques

Materials and equipment

Before you embark on framing a piece, it is essential to become familiar with the parts that make up a framed artpiece and their roles, and to purchase the right tools and equipment. This section takes you through the basic parts of a frame and describes the range of equipment you will need to complete a variety of frames.

PARTS AND FITTINGS

From the outside looking inwards, a framed artpiece is made up of a **rebated moulding**, **glass**, a **mount**, the picture, **inner backing**, and **backing board**. These are all held in position by **veneer pins** and the framed picture is hung with **hanging fittings.**

The names of parts can be confusing as craftsmen have not always been consistent when giving terms to components and techniques. Detailed below are the terms used for a standard glazed frame with a mount and for the fittings that attach it to the wall.

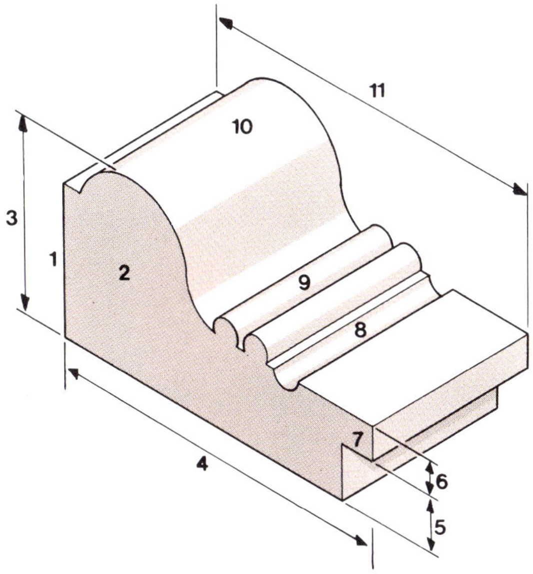

Profile of a moulding
1 *Outside moulding edge*
2 *Moulding profile*
3 *Total moulding height*
4 *Total moulding width*
5 *Rebate*
6 *Moulding inside edge*
7 *Lip of rebate*
8 *Fluting*
9 *Beading*
10 *Ridge*
11 *Moulding face*

Rebated Moulding

You can purchase moulding with rebate already fitted – ie a stepped moulding – otherwise you will need to buy a separate strip to fit along the bottom of your moulding to make the rebate or 'rabbet'.

The back of the rebated moulding, which rests against the wall, is referred to as the 'bottom edge' or sometimes the 'rebated edge'. The side of the moulding, which you would see if you pressed your eye against the wall and looked at the side of the frame, is called the 'back'. The front edge of the moulding, the strip which the viewer sees, is called the 'front' or 'face'. The edge of the moulding, which overlaps the picture slightly is known as the 'sight edge'.

Glass

The pane of glass used for glazing a picture is usually 2mm ($^{1}/_{12}$in) thick. A very common commodity, it is stocked by all main glaziers and it can be bought cut to the correct measure if you do not wish to cut it yourself.

Non-reflective glass can also be purchased but this is more expensive and many people feel that it does not give the picture the bright look usually lent by glass but a duller more matt appearance. It is, however, entirely a matter of personal taste and many pictures are framed in non-reflective glass.

Perspex is sometimes used, as this, too, is non-reflective but it is generally not advisable as it scratches easily, becomes static after wiping, attracting more dust, and yellows with age.

Mount

This is a specially made piece of card, which is white all the way through, except for the surface colour. This means that when you cut the bevel to make the window for the picture, you are left with a uniform clean white edge.

Inner Backing

This is the stiff card against which the picture itself is either stuck or held firm in some other way.

If the picture is rare or antique, the inner backing will need to be acid-free conservation board, which is obtainable from specialist suppliers.

Backing Board and Veneer Pins

This is the final backing, usually made of hardboard or craft board and measured to exactly the same size as the glass. After it has been fitted, the tiny gap between it and the bottom edge of the moulding is sealed with brown gum strip as a guard against dust.

When the backing board is lower than the bottom edge of the moulding, it can be fixed into place with veneer pins.

Sometimes the rebate is too shallow to accommodate the glass, the mount and the inner backing as well as the backing board. In this case, the veneer pins are tapped into the moulding and then bent over so that their heads hold the components in position.

If the hardboard is exactly flush with the back of the frame, it can be either bevelled, to allow the veneer pins to be tapped into the moulding at an angle, or it can be held in place with turn clips.

Hanging Fittings

Many different types of fittings are available. Screw eyes, which sometimes have a second ring, are the most common. Such rings are attached directly to the bottom edge of the moulding. Back hangers are useful when a moulding is narrow. These are fixed into the backing board. For bigger pictures with heavy frames, more substantial fittings are required, such as D-rings or otherwise-shaped back hangers. These rings are fitted into a fold of metal, which is screwed into the bottom edge of the moulding.

Fittings are usually fixed a third of the way down the picture. Take care to use picture wire of the correct thickness for the weight of the framed picture.

Wall Attachments

In most cases, a masonry nail is sufficent for hanging a picture, and is easily banged into the wall: place a small piece of Sellotape on the wall before driving in the nail to avoid cracking the wall or paint. If the wall is unusually hard, it may need to be drilled with a masonry drill bit and plugged with fibre or plastic rawlplugs before inserting screws. A large picture can be made more stable by hanging it on two hooks or nails; this also keeps the picture level. If your picture is particularly heavy, it might be necessary to use a bolt that screws into a special casing with an exact fit.

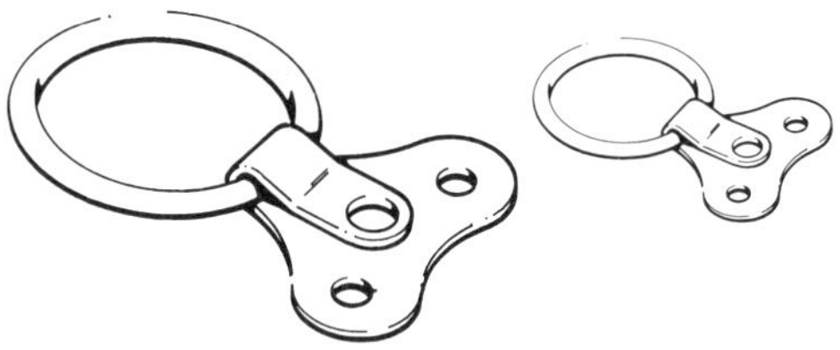
Heavy duty hang rings

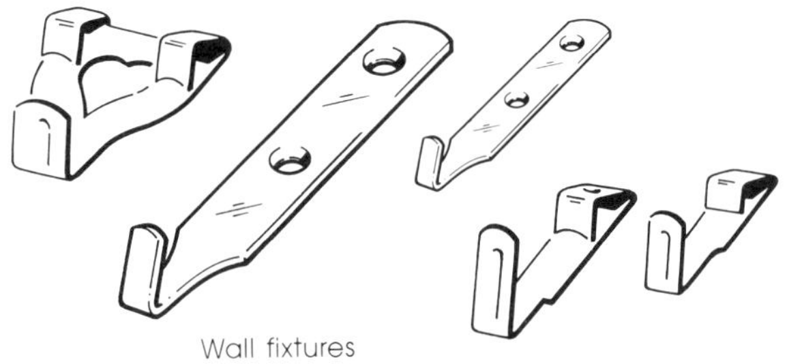
Wall fixtures

Lightweight hang rings

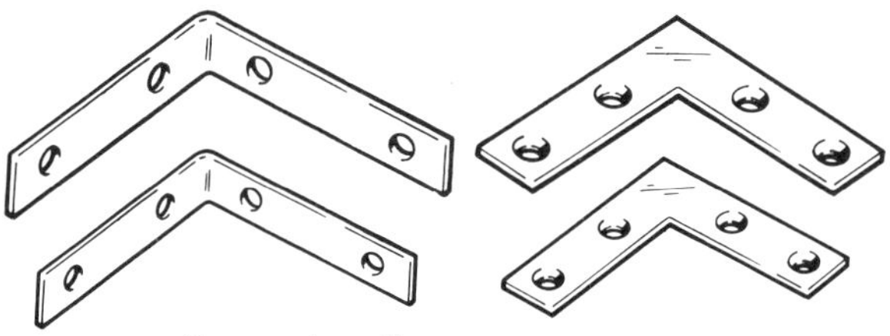
Corner strengtheners

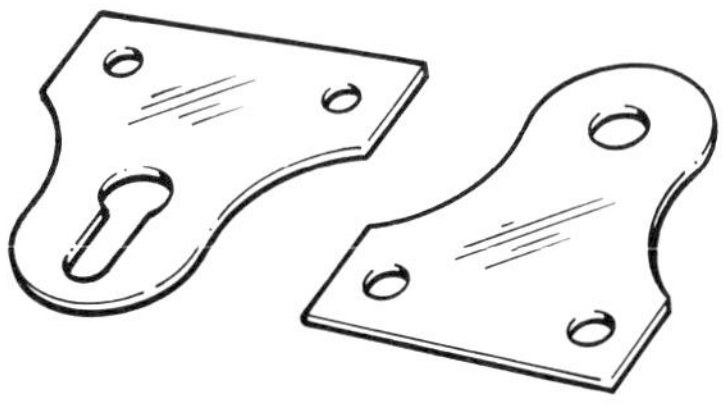
Picture plates

Turn clips

Screw on clips for block mounts

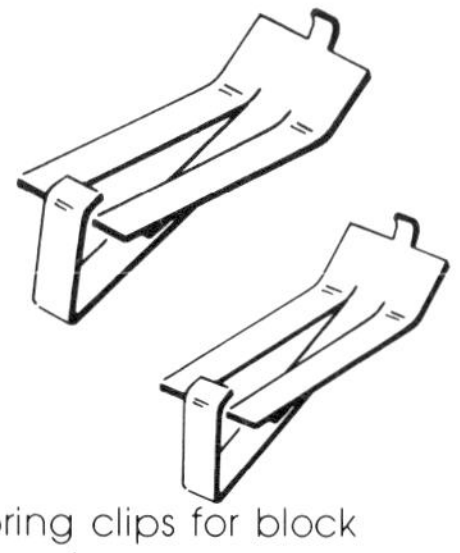
Spring clips for block mounts

Backing board
Artpiece
Mount, can be double or triple; not usually used for oils
Insert
Frame
Glass, not usually used for oils

Directory of Tools and Equipment

Most professional craftsmen regard with horror the old maxim that only a bad workman blames his tools and advise that no work should be undertaken without tools of exactly the right kind and the proper quality. Even if you are not planning anything elaborate, some good basic tools are essential if the job is to be done well. This directory includes all the basic tools and equipment needed for successful picture framing.

Artists' brushes It is useful to have a selection of these for executing oil and acrylic paint finishes.

Backsaw Also known as a tenon saw. Ordinary saws tend to be flexible and bend; the metal reinforcing strip along the top of this saw prevents the saw blade from 'weaving'. It can be fixed to the workbench with screws.

Bole A red clay pigment used especially in water gilding. Bole is painted on the gesso base to provide a soft, satin-like surface for the gold leaf.

Burnisher Needed to make the smooth, shiny finish so characteristic of water gilding. Most burnishers have an ordinary wooden handle and a curved, smooth metal end which is available in different shapes and sizes for different tasks and is used to burnish the leaf onto the frame.

Carpenters' rule The recommended straight-edge to use when glass cutting. An ordinary thin metal rule is too flimsy to hold the cutter.

Coloured paper Useful for covering mount board if the exact colour of mount board that you require is not available.

Conservation board Sometimes known as 'museum board', conservation board has been treated to rvoid the tendency of ordinary mount board to absorb acid from the polluted atmosphere, which leads eventually to discoloration of the picture. It is advisable to use acid-free conservation board if you are mounting old or valuable drawings or prints.

Craft knife A sharp, general-purpose craft knife, able to cut both card and fabric, is essential for mount cutting. Change the craft blade frequently, especially when you are cutting the bevelled edge of a mount, otherwise the finish will be fuzzy and you will have to trim all the edges.

Decorating brushes It is useful to have a selection of these brushes for waxing, staining and some paint finishes. You will probably not need one more than 37mm ($1\frac{1}{2}$in) wide.

Drill Needed to make the pilot holes in the corners of moulding pieces before they are secured together. The most suitable type of drill is a portable household electric drill but a good hand drill is perfectly adequate. Whichever you decide on, you will need a collection of drill bits.

Dry-mounting film Available from graphic suppliers and art shops, this film is placed between the canvas and the backing board and, when heat is applied, fuses the two together.

Dry-mounting press Commercial dry-mounting presses are usually heavy and inappropriate for home framers. Lighter versions are available which are useful if you intend doing a lot of dry mounting; these are basically electric metal presses for use on a table.

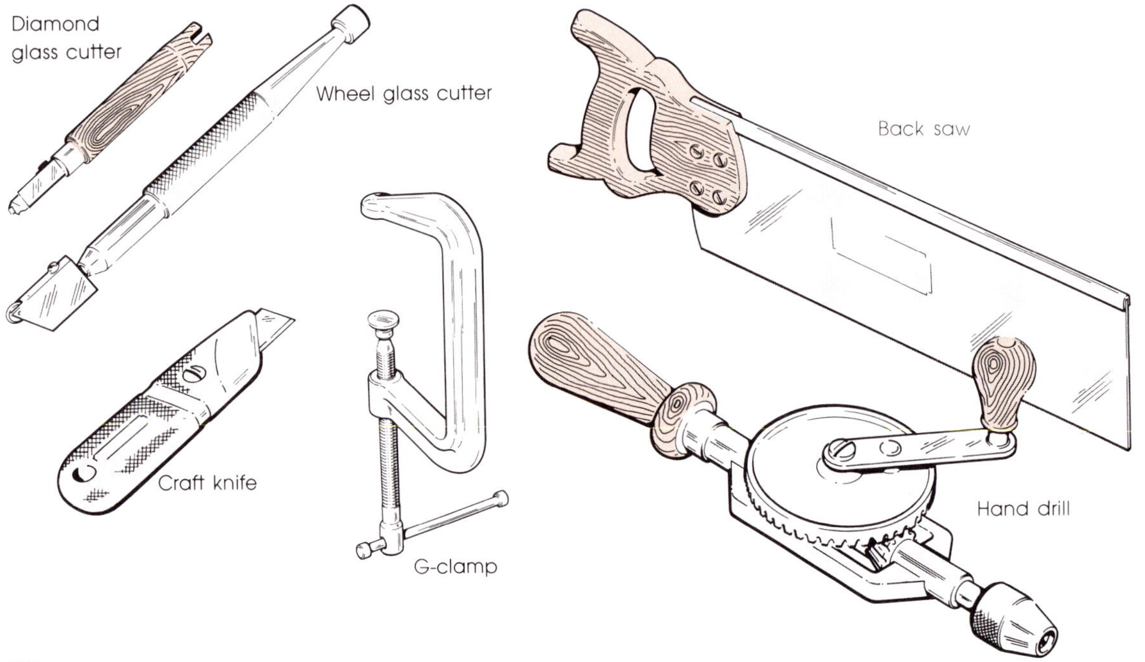

Face-pieces These scraps of wood are inserted in the vice and screwed to the jaws to prevent the moulding from being damaged by the vice as it is being worked on.

Felt-tipped pen (delible) Can be used to mark the size of the piece of glass required directly onto the glass before cutting. Another method is to draw the cutting lines on a piece of paper, place the paper beneath the glass and follow the lines.

Fitch brushes These are inexpensive and useful for stippling and small-scale decoration and for the spattering effect used in antiquing.

G-clamp If you are making your own rebate, G-clamps (also known as C-clamps) can be used to clamp the moulding to the underlying strip of wood. Also useful as an additional grip.

Gesso A gesso base is needed for both water and oil gilding. Mix gesso powder, which is a chalk, with rabbit-skin glue (both available from art shops) to make the gesso or buy it ready-mixed in fluid form.

Gilders' cushion A padded board covered with suede and used for resting gold leaf. A stiff paper screen boxes in one end of the cushion to protect the gold leaf against draughts: the leaf is so fine and fragile that it can be lifted off the cushion surface by the slightest draught and crumpled, making it unfit for further use.

Gilders' knife This knife has a very fine blade and is used for separating sheets of gold leaf.

Gilders' tip A flat brush with thinly spaced camel hairs, a gilders' tip is stroked across the hand or hair so that it gathers just enough natural oil from the human skin to pick up a sheet of gold leaf from the gilders' cushion.

Glass Picture-framing glass is lighter in weight than normal window glass. It is available in a standard thickness of 2mm (1/12in), as opposed to the 3mm (1/8in) thickness of window glass or the very thick plate glass used in shop windows, which is sometimes as much as 4mm (1/6in) thick.

Glass cutter There are two types of glass cutter. The one that is easiest for the beginner to use comprises a handle with a steel revolving wheel. Most experienced framers, however, prefer the glaziers' diamond, a handle which holds a diamond, which is especially suitable for thin picture glass. Both are used manually and rely upon good measurement and judgement.

Glass-paper Fine glass-paper is needed to rub down the layers of gesso as they are applied in both water and oil gilding.

Graining brush This brush has little tufts of bristles for building up layers of grain effect.

Iron If you do not possess a commercial heat press an ordinary domestic iron can be used for small-scale projects to apply heat in the dry-mounting process.

Metal ruler When cutting a straight edge, either with a knife or mount cutter, a metal ruler is essential. If you use a wooden or plastic ruler, you will pare the ruler's edge. An engineers' metal straight-edge is ideal, if a little more expensive than an ordinary metal ruler.

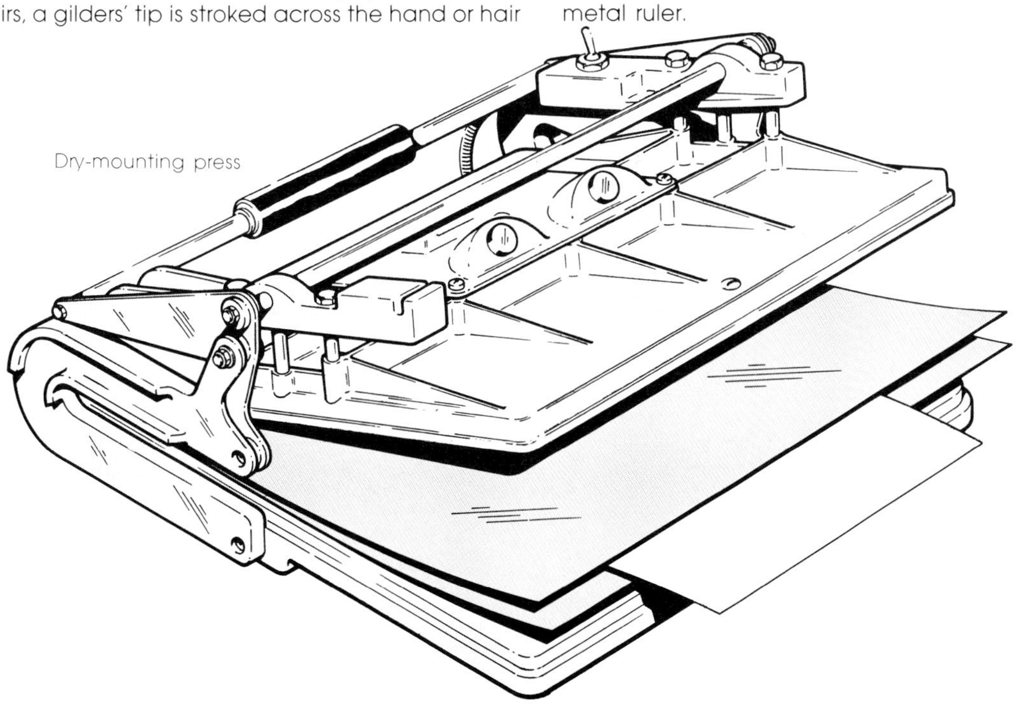
Dry-mounting press

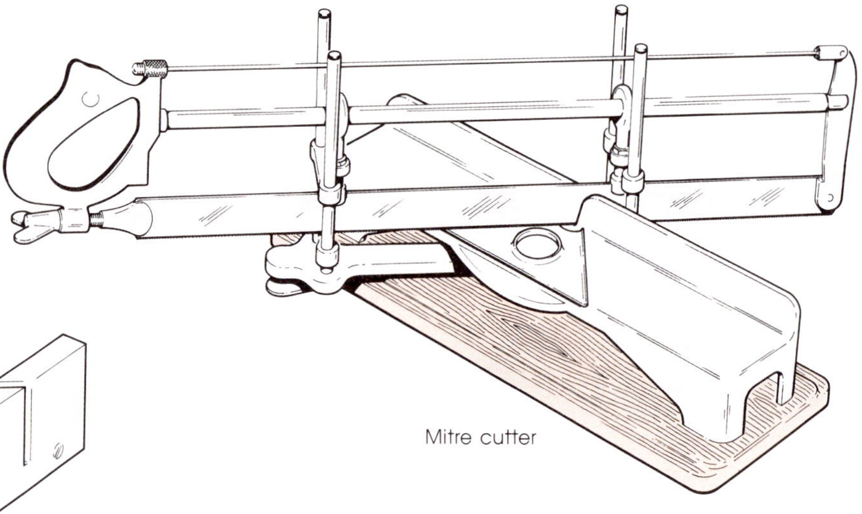

Mitre cutter

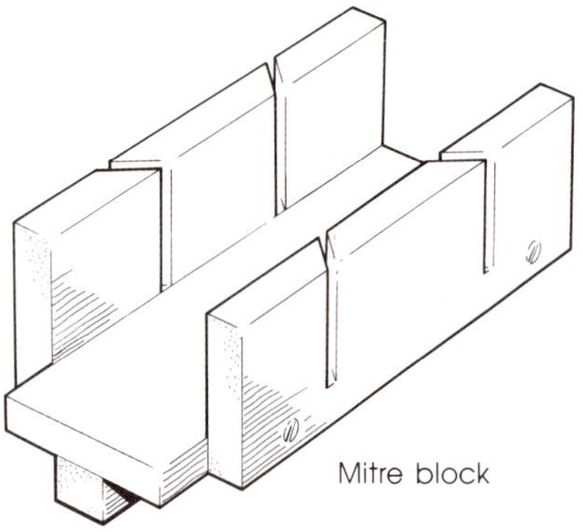

Mitre block

Mitre block Essential for forming the corners of a frame, a mitre block must be absolutely accurate. It cuts at an angle of 45 degrees and if it is out of line by even half a degree, the inaccuracy wil be obvious in the finished frame. It is therefore worthwhile buying a good quality mitre block. Unfortunately, a mitre block may become wobbly with use and therefore lose its accuracy. The simplest sort of mitre block is a wooden frame shaped like an open-ended box with slits in each side to guide the saw at a constant angle of 45 degrees. The block is usually made of hardwood but, even so, continuous sawing can wear away the precise measurements of the slits. A more expensive version can be obtained with metal reinforcements at the top of the slits.

Mitre clamp Once the moulding has been cut at right angles for the corners it needs to be held firmly in place so that the pieces can be glued and nailed, and to be gripped in position until the glue has dried. For this, a mitre clamp, made of metal and sometimes called a corner clamp, is used. If possible, the clamp should be fixed by clamping it onto the corner of the table or work-bench to give added stability. A simpler type of corner clamp is made of four plastic right angles which fit around the pieces of moulding and are tightened by a cord. Both types are suitable for simple framing but, for heavier frames, the metal one is easier to use.

Mitre cutter Some of the more sophisticated mitre blocks are made entirely of metal, and the most advanced of all is the mitre cutter which is a mitre box and saw combined in one piece of equipment. These are designed to give absolute rigidity and to prevent the saw from descending too low and causing damage.

Mottling brush Used for breaking up and highlighting the grain.

Mount boards As picture framing has become more popular, an increasingly large choice of mount boards has come on the market. Almost all of them have the traditional distinction of being white throughout their thickness regardless of outer colouring, so that the bevelled edge shows up white. The edge is usually left white but it provides a good base on which to place a gilt strip, or another colour, if you wish. Choice of thickness is usually limited to 4-sheet, 6-sheet and 8-sheet, although thicker card can be obtained or two boards can be stuck together.

Mount cutter This specialist tool cuts the inside bevelled edge of the mount at an angle of 45 degrees. The most useful type of mount cutter has a replaceable blade which is held firmly at an angle and can be set to different depths, depending on the thickness of the mount board.

Oilstone Useful to rub down sharp, newly cut edges of glass.

Paintbrushes Those cut on the diagonal and normally used for painting awkward angles on windows are useful for painting the crevices in mouldings.

Panel pins Fine, round-wire nails from 12 to 50mm ($^1/_2$ to 2in) long, panel pins can be nailed into the corners of a freshly glued frame to provide a more permanent reinforcement. They have very small heads that can be punched below the surface of the wood.

Mitre clamp

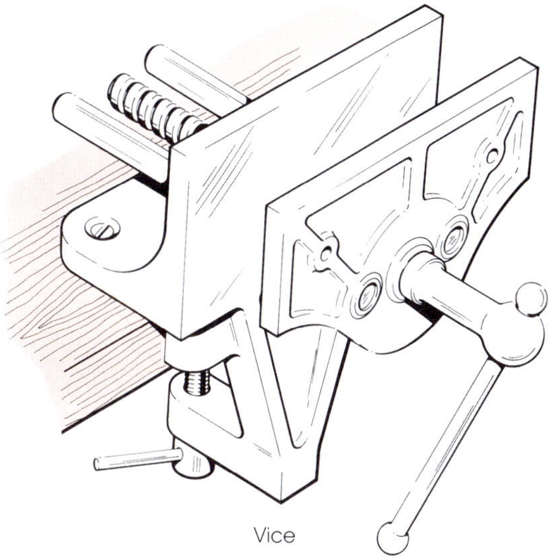

Vice

Rebate plane Also known as a rabbet or fillister plane, it has an adjustable fence, a depth gauge and a cutter that is set in a forward position for planing up to a stopped rebate.

Sable brushes Usually used by watercolourists, sable brushes are useful for fine finishing.

Sandpaper Essential for smoothing a wooden frame before applying a final surface finish.

Shellac varnish Whether you have a gesso or bole final surface, an oil gilding project must be sealed with a coat of shellac varnish.

Set square Essential for drawing accurate right angles when marking out the window in the mount board.

Spray glue Needed in wet mounting to attach the picture to the inner backing as it gives an evenly glued surface.

Table If you do not have a work-bench, a table can be used instead. It must be firm and, if you are setting it up for any length of time, it should be fixed to the floor for extra stability.

Tack hammer A light hammer especially suitable for hammering in the pins and nails used in picture framing. A heavier hammer tends to bend the pins, even if used with care.

Tacking iron For use in conjuction with a dry-mounting press, a tacking iron is like a tiny domestic flat iron but is angled on a handle to enable precision use. It is used to fuse together the picture, dry-mounting sheet and inner backing before final bonding.

T-square Like the set square, a T-square is useful for marking out accurate right angles.

Turpentine When cutting glass, keep the wheel cutter lubricated by frequently dipping it into turpentine or white spirit.

Veneer pins For very lightweight framing, these tiny nails are sufficient to reinforce the corners of the frame.

Vice An ordinary vice can be used to grip pieces of moulding in place while general work is being done on them but its role in picture framing is an all-purpose rather than a specific one. It is also used for drilling and trimming wood, for instance, and should not be confused with the role of the clamp, which is used specifically to hold the corners at rigid right angles.

Wallpaper paste and **water-based glue** Used for wet mounting, although because they are water-soluble they are unsuitable for prints and drawings done in non-waterproof inks.

White spirit Useful for cleaning dirty oil paintings and for lubricating a wheel cutter during glass cutting.

Woodwork glue For glueing the corners of the frame together, a synthetic, PVA-based woodwork glue is most suitable. You do not need to use very much on each corner.

Work-bench Provides a solid and level work surface.

The foundation skills

Before embarking on specific projects, it is necessary to master the foundation skills of picture framing. These fundamental skills are described below in detail, enabling you to tackle with ease any of the projects that follow.

MEASURING THE ARTPIECE

It is important to take precise measurements whether you are measuring the artpiece, the mount or the moulding. In fact, it is often worthwhile taking a measurement twice to double check.

Before you can calculate the length of the moulding you will need to know one of two basic picture measurements: either the 'rebate' measurement or the 'sight' measurement.

For oil and acrylic paintings, canvases, hardboard panels or any type of artpiece which cannot be trimmed, the rebate measurement is usually the most useful as it indicates the total ground area, including that which is hidden beneath the rebate. Measure the length and the width of the artpiece and mount, if there is one, and then add 3mm ($^1/_8$in) all round – this allows for easy insertion of the artpiece into the rebate. Many canvases used for oil paintings, especially home-made ones, are 'off-square'. If this is the case, add the extra 3mm ($^1/_8$in) to the longest measurement.

An oil painting is sometimes fitted very snugly into the rebate, almost as far as it can go, inevitably hiding some of the image. If it is important not to cover any of the composition, and the image reaches virtually to the edge of the canvas, then it will be necessary to frame the picture with the smallest possible fraction of it hidden behind the rebate, using spacers to hold it in place, and you will need to take a sight measurement. A sight measurement gives the distance between the inside edges of the front of the frame, indicating precisely the area of the artpiece which will be finally open to view.

WET, OR COLD, MOUNTING

Some drawings or prints are too flimsy to stand by themselves when being placed between backing board and frame, and need to be stuck fast to a rigid support. Glueing a picture to such a board is called wet mounting. Wet mounting is also the quickest and simplest method of block mounting – fixing an artwork to a platform projecting from the surround.

Paintings executed on canvas, which have been removed from their stretchers, can be wet mounted. The technique is also suitable for photographs, drawings, prints and documents and is a good way

THE PROFESSIONAL METHODS

The professional methods of framing often differ from the basic picture framing techniques. Consequently, throughout this section, in addition to the basic techniques of framing, many of the professional techniques are also illustrated and described in step-by-step format. The professional techniques covered are those for:

- *Wet, or cold, mounting*
- *Dry, or hot, mounting*
- *Attaching the window mount*
- *Cutting a bevelled window*
- *Cutting an aluminium frame*
- *Underpinning*
- *Assembling an aluminium frame*

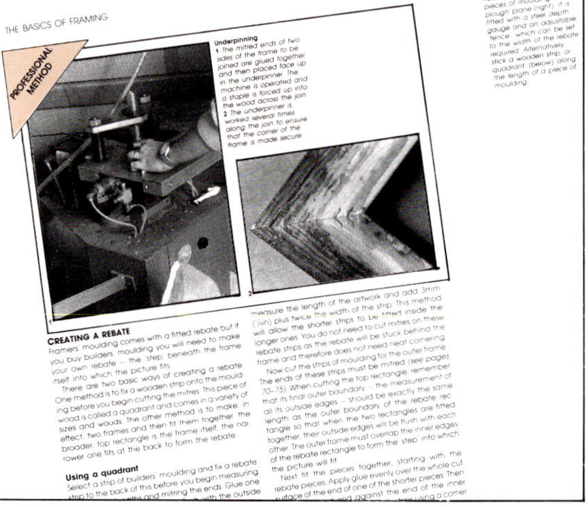

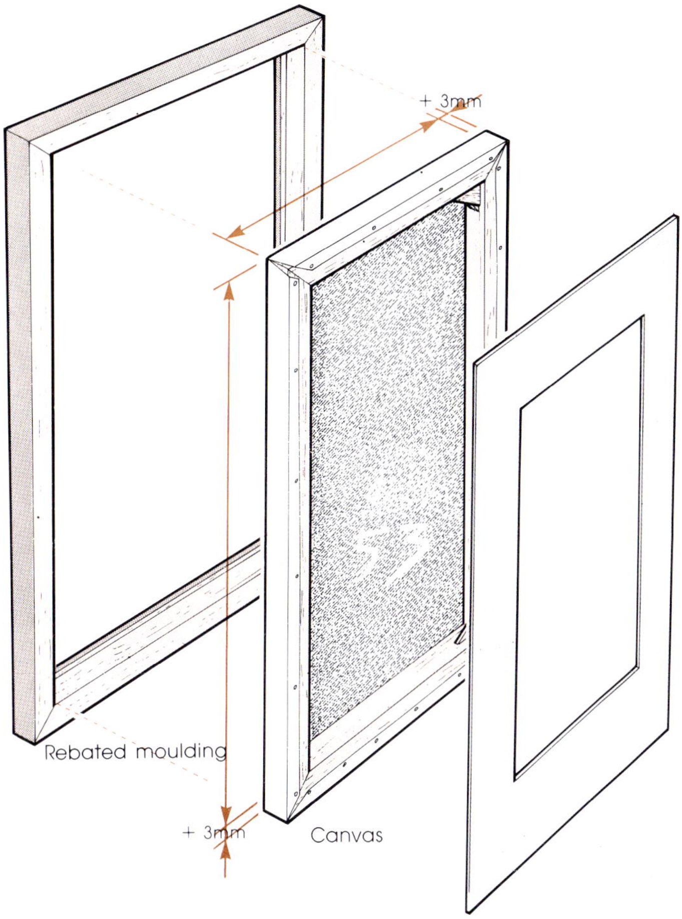

The diagram (left) *illustrates the importance of taking accurate measurements. Whether you have a mounted picture or an oil painting on a stretcher, you must fit the artpiece snugly into the rebate of the frame. The diagram* (below) *clearly shows the difference between the sight and rebate measurements. The sight measurement of a framed artpiece indicates the area of the artpiece open to view. The rebate measurement indicates the total area of the artpiece, including that which is hidden behind the rebate.*

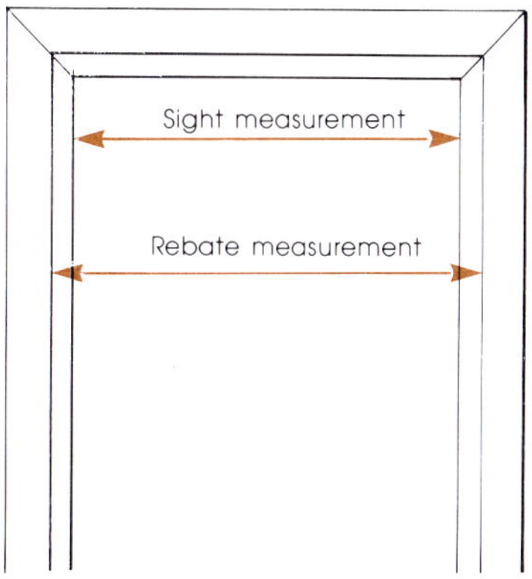

of preserving something of sentimental value, which you would not want creased or torn. However, because it is difficult to reverse, wet mounting should be avoided when dealing with antique or rare pictures.

Various types of glue are suitable for wet mounting. An aerosol spray glue is most suitable for pictures done on thin papers and any synthetic glue is suitable for those carried out on thicker paper.

Wallpaper size is often a less expensive and just as convenient alternative. Mix this according to the instructions on the packet but remember that it is water-soluble, so avoid using it on works of art that are printed or painted using water-soluble materials, as traces of it could soak through. If wallpaper size is applied to plywood, it can cause it to warp. When using wallpaper size, remember to 'pre-size' the board: give it a coat of size and allow it to dry. This will seal the board and prepare the surface for the final sizing, resulting in a better grip.

When using a non-aerosol adhesive, it is common to misjudge the amount needed and place too much glue on the backing, so some practice is advisable. To prevent bubbles appearing when mounting a large print or photograph, wet the picture before positioning it on the glued board. Do not try this, however, with a watercolour or a print effected with water-soluble inks.

When glue and size mounting, flatten the artwork, removing any trapped air, by applying pressure with a roller: roll firmly out from the centre of the picture — a technique also designed to remove any surplus glue. You can ensure that no glue seeps onto the picture by covering it with a sheet of paper before you start rolling. Alternatively, if only a small print is being mounted, or if you do not have a roller, a soft, dry rag can be used: again work outwards from the centre. It is a good idea to weight the picture onto the glued surface while it is drying. This can be done by clamping the picture and mount between two sheets of plywood, or placing them beneath one or two heavy books.

DRY, OR HOT, MOUNTING

Dry mounting is the process of fusing the artpiece to the inner backing by means of heat and a special adhesive sheet. Place the sheet between the picture and the backing and apply the heat. The sheet will melt, fixing the picture firmly on the backing.

If you intend to carry out a lot of dry mounting, it may be worth investing in a press. Place the picture face down on a dry surface while the press is warming up. Position a sheet of mounting tissue – the adhesive sheet – so that it covers the picture's reverse side entirely, and fix the picture and adhesive sheet in position by applying a warm tacking iron along one edge. If more than one adhesive sheet is needed to cover the area, ensure that the edges are butted and do not overlap, otherwise creases and bubbles will mar the result. With each new sheet that is added, apply a tacking iron along one edge to fix it into position.

Trim the edges of the adhesive sheet precisely with a very sharp scalpel or craft blade. Turn the picture and sheet face up and position it on the inner backing. Cover the picture with brown paper and apply the tacking iron again to hold the backing fast along one edge. Place the picture and backing in the press, on top of an extra piece of board for additional stability, and position a sheet of protective paper – usually provided with the adhesive sheet – on top. Close the press and leave for between 30 and 60 seconds to fuse. Remove from the press and place the backing, picture and protective paper under a heavy weight, such as a pile of books.

If you do not have a press, a domestic iron is also suitable both for the tacking and the final bonding. Simply follow the above procedure, substituting an iron for the press. Use a solid, flat working surface and set the iron to 'linen'. Iron out from the centre for the final bonding.

HINGE MOUNTING

In a hinge mount, the inner backing and the mount are hinged together. This keeps the mount board

Spray mounting
The advantage of spray mounting is that it is easy to apply. Place the artwork face down on a clean surface and spray evenly over the back with spray glue (left). *Position the artwork on the mounting board—many spray adhesives have a delayed drying time to allow you to adjust the artwork. Smooth down from the centre outwards* (below).

Glues for mounting

Type	Advantages	Disadvantages	Drying time
Wallpaper size	Cheap and strong	Should not be used for valuable items	A few hours to dry properly
Contact glues	Very strong and quick; multi-purpose; can be used on card, rubber, laminates etc	Should not be used for valuable items—once the glued surfaces touch they cannot be pulled apart again.	Instant
Dry mounts	Strong; extremely professional finish	Requires heat	Instant
Spray mounts	Convenient; allows for adjusting and repositioning	Expensive	Up to a few minutes (some have adjustment times)
PVA (can be diluted with water for sticking paper and card)	Can be used on paper, card and fabric, and is very strong		Half an hour to a few hours (depending on type)
Organic glues (including artists' size)	Good for fabrics, card and paper	It goes off; requires gentle heat—can be 'killed' if overheated	A few hours to dry thoroughly
Latex glues	Good for canvas, card, paper etc	Difficult to remove excess; strong smelling	About one hour

PROFESSIONAL METHODS

Wet, or cold, mounting

1 *The picture is placed carefully on pressure sensitive film, which is then detached from the rest of the roll.*

2 *The backing of the film is then peeled off, leaving a strongly adhesive surface. The picture is now ready to place on the backing. Here, craft board has been used as both inner backing and backing board.*

3 *One end of the print is pressed down on the backing and passed through the rollers of the mounting press. The rest of the picture is held tautly with one hand against the top roller, while the card and picture is gradually wound between the rollers. In this way, no air bubbles are allowed to form. When the entire print has passed through the rollers, the mounted picture is wound back through the press to ensure that the print is stuck firmly to the board.*

1

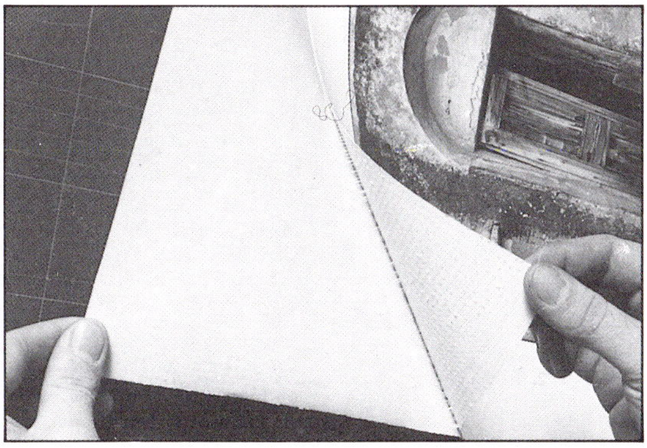

2

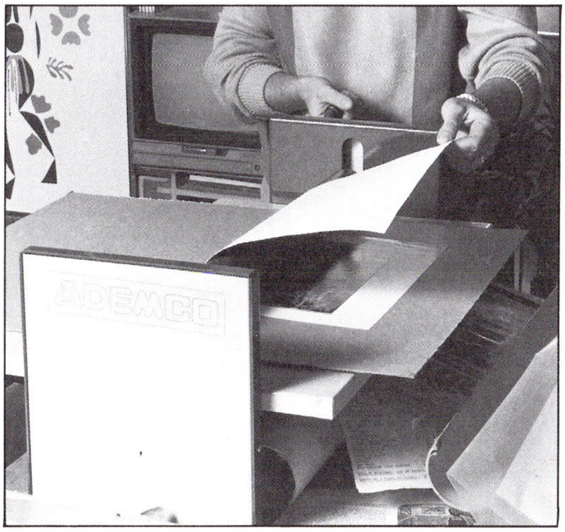

3

Dry, or hot, mounting

Dry mounting provides the strongest and most professional-looking bond. The picture is placed face up on dry-mount tissue, which is coated with wax and placed on top of the backing. It is then covered with a piece of clean board to prevent the wax not covered by the picture from sticking to the lid of the press. It is all inserted in the pre-heated dry-mounting press and left for 1 minute to fuse.

Hinge mounts
1 *The first stage in the making of a hinge mount is to fix the picture onto a backing. Attach the artwork to the backing with tape, so that it can be adjusted when the window is fitted over it and can also be removed later if necessary.*
2 *Cut another mount, exactly the same overall size as the first 'backing' mount and cut out a window.*
3 *Lay the two mounts end to end, and tape them together.*
4 *Finally, carefully fold the window over the mounted picture.*

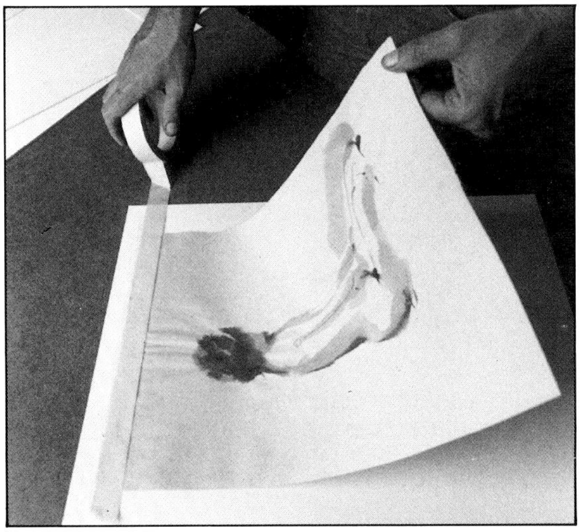

1

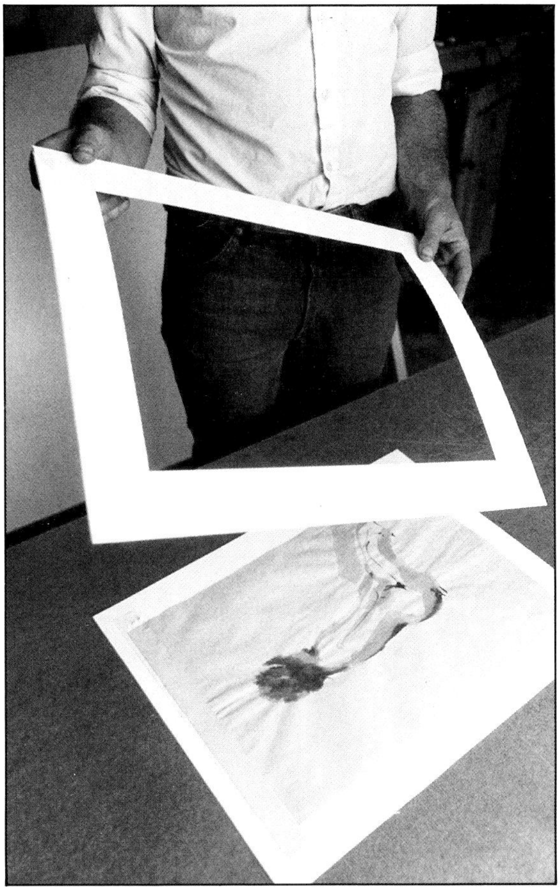

2

3

4

PROFESSIONAL METHOD

1

Attaching the window mount
1 *Double-sided tape is applied to the back of the window along the top and sides, or, if hinge mounting, just to the top edge. The mount is never fixed at both top and bottom as this might result in the picture wrinkling if the picture drops. The mount is then positioned on top of the backing and picture.*
2 *Any additional backing is then cut away with the straight edge of a mount cutter. The window mount is used as a guide to leave a clean edge to the mounted picture.*

2

and inner backing together during framing, preventing them from slipping, and allows you to change the artwork and use the same mount over and over again.

To make a hinge mount, cut the window and lay the mount and the inner backing face down on a clean surface, head-to-head with their top edges flush. Then stick the two together, placing a piece of masking tape, gum strip or fabric tape at the top of the backing. Next, fit the picture: determine the exact postition of the picture by trial and error, moving it by degrees behind the window. Then stick the picture onto the inner backing by one of two methods: either affix small pieces of tape to its edges, or, if you particularly do not want the surface of the artwork to be touched by tape, fold over a piece of tape into a little hinge and place it behind the artwork. Double-sided tape can also be used but is not recommended because of its fiercely adhesive quality, which makes precise positioning and removal of the artwork difficult.

CONSERVATION MOUNTING

Although conservation techniques have always been used to help preserve particularly precious artworks, their use has become more common in recent years as attention has been increasingly drawn to the problems of environmental pollution.

Conservation mounting is not simply a matter of isolating the picture from the atmosphere, which contains acid particles and other harmful chemicals. The picture must also be separated from the actual frame, for much of the material used in frame making contains traces of acids which might be damaging to a picture over a long period of time. Acid traces can be found in almost all materials, including cardboard, paper and wood, when they are not specifically acid-free.

Conservation mounting, therefore, involves selecting acid-free materials and ensuring that these, and no others, are placed next to the artwork. Acid-free mounting board, sometimes known as conservation board or museum board, is widely available from specialist suppliers. Acid-free cloth tape can be used to hinge the mounting board to the inner backing and rice paper can be used to stick the artwork to the inner backing. Tear the rice paper into strips, fold into hinges and stick them to the inner backing and artwork with an acid-free glue. Cardboard, especially corrugated cardboard, which is sometimes used as backing, should be avoided when conservation is important: its acid content tends to be particularly high. When you have completed the framing, turn the picture

Cutting a rectangular mount

1 *First, decide on the size of the mount: the borders on either side of the artwork should be of an identical width and the bottom border should be wider than the top border. Cut the total area of mount card required from the whole sheet, ensuring that all the corners are square. Now, with a pencil, mark the widths of the borders at several points along each side. Join the pencil dots on one side with a ruler and pencil in a line. Do the same for the other three sides of the window, overshooting at the corners so that you make clear right angles.*
2 *Using a protractor or set square, check that the rules of the window form perfect right angles at the corners. Amend the lines if necessary.*
3 *Place a metal straight-edge along one of the marked lines; tap in two nails at either side of the mount board and rest the ruler against them. Using a sharp craft knife, cut along the straight-edge at*

1

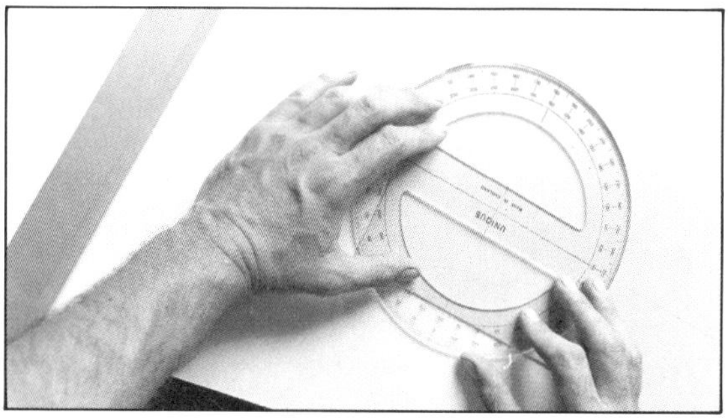

2

3

4

5

6

7

a constant angle of 50 or 60 degrees. Repeat for the other sides of the window.
4 *Tidy the corners of the bevelled window with the point of the craft knife blade.*
5 *The adjoining sides of the window should meet in a clean, precise corner.*
6 *Rub out any pencil marks that are still visible on the mount.*
7 *An interesting variation of the standard rectangular mount can be made by 'clipping' the top two corners. Mark the diagonal rules on the mount with a pencil before you begin cutting the bevelled edges.*

upside down and seal the back securely with a paper dust seal. To achieve a tight seal between the glass and the frame, pack the backing board, mount, artwork and glass tightly and make the seal firm by tacking nails into the rebate.

MEASURING THE MOUNT

As a rule, the mount is cut first, and then the frame around it, enabling you to position the artwork in the mount. Usually, the sides and the top margins around the mount are slightly narrower than the bottom margin, so that the artwork sits up high in the mount.

Remember that you are beginning with two pieces of card – the backing card and the mount itself. Unless you are using conservation board, the inner backing can be of a cheaper material than the mount. The inner backing and the mount should be measured and cut so that they both fit neatly into the rebate.

When measuring the window, place the card face down on a clean surface and mark the measurements on the 'wrong', ie reverse, side. Decide the width of the mount surround and mark the margins in as lines on the reverse side of the card. The final window measurement can now be checked with a set square for corner squareness, after which it is ready for cutting.

CUTTING A BEVELLED WINDOW

A bevelled edge – a sloping, rather than straight, edge – gives a professional finish to the window of a mount.

A simple and easily available tool, such as a craft knife, is usually used to cut a bevelled edge, and a metal straight-edge is necessary to guide your

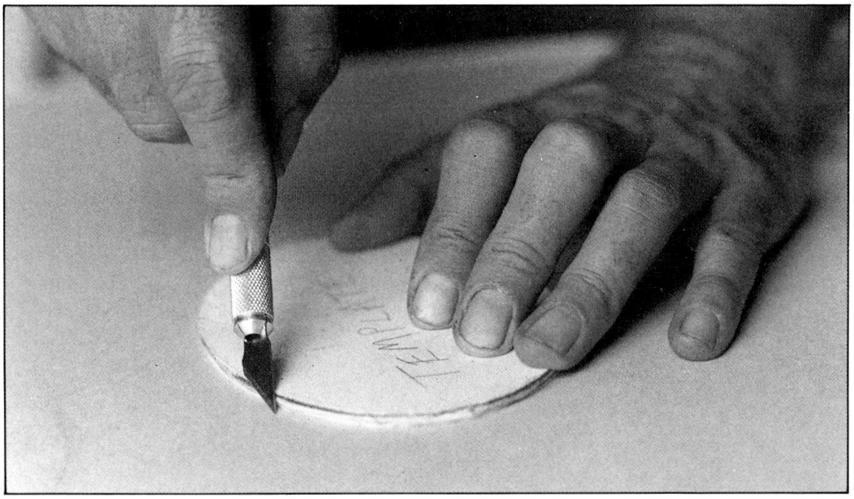

1

Hand cutting an oval with a knife
It is extremely difficult to achieve a neat, clean edge when hand cutting ovals, so restrict hand cut ovals to mounts that will be covered by paper or fabric.
1 *Using a very sharp scalpel, hold the template down firmly and cut round it.*

2 *When you have cut the oval, remove the template and trim any jagged edges. Don't overdo the trimming, however, as this can distort the finished shape.*

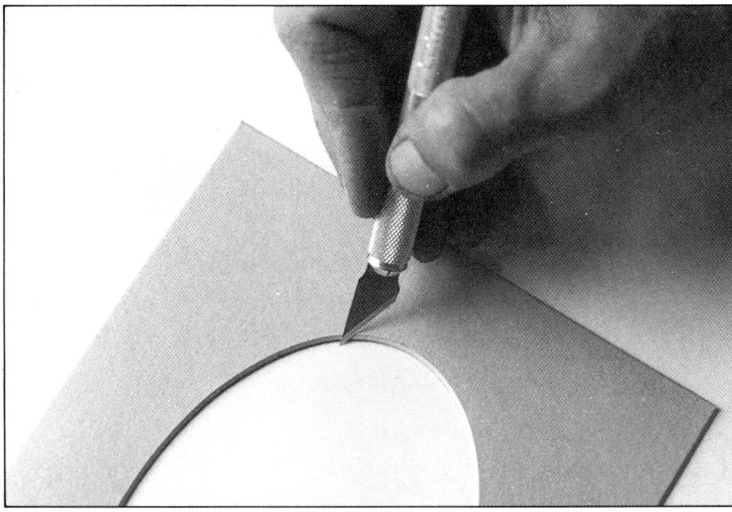

2

hand when you are cutting. The blade used for cutting a bevelled edge must be absolutely razor-sharp. Always keep a supply of spare blades in stock and as soon as cutting becomes slightly difficult, change the blade. Do not use a wooden or plastic ruler, as the knife will shave small flakes from it, not only blunting the blade but quickly ruining the straight-edge and making the ruler unusable.

After measuring and marking out the window, place the card from which it is to be cut face down on a board or table where it won't matter if the surface is cut or damaged. To lengthen the life of your blade, insert newspaper between the card and the board so that you cut into the newspaper rather than the board or table. To prevent the metal straight-edge from slipping while you are cutting, it is a good idea to tap in two nails – one at each side of the mount board – for the ruler to rest against.

With the card still face down, place the ruler along the first marked line to be cut and insert the knife slightly beyond the corner mark outside the window area. This slight overcut – equivalent in distance to the thickness of the card – will not be noticed on the right side of the mount and will ensure that the corners are sharp and precise.

There are two alternative methods for the next part of the procedure, both requiring practice. For the first method, cut along the straight-edge in one smooth stroke, keeping the pressure even, and holding the knife at a constant angle of between 50 and 60 degrees. Cut beyond the corner of the line by the same amount as the overcut at the first corner – the thickness of the card. For the second method, lightly score along the line at the correct angle. Then make another scoring stroke along exactly the same line and at the same angle; repeat until you have cut right through the card. After the first line is lightly scored, you might find it more comfortable to do without the straight-edge.

Repeat the cutting procedure for all four sides of the window. The bevelled edge should be a smooth, clean slope but if you are left with a few jagged

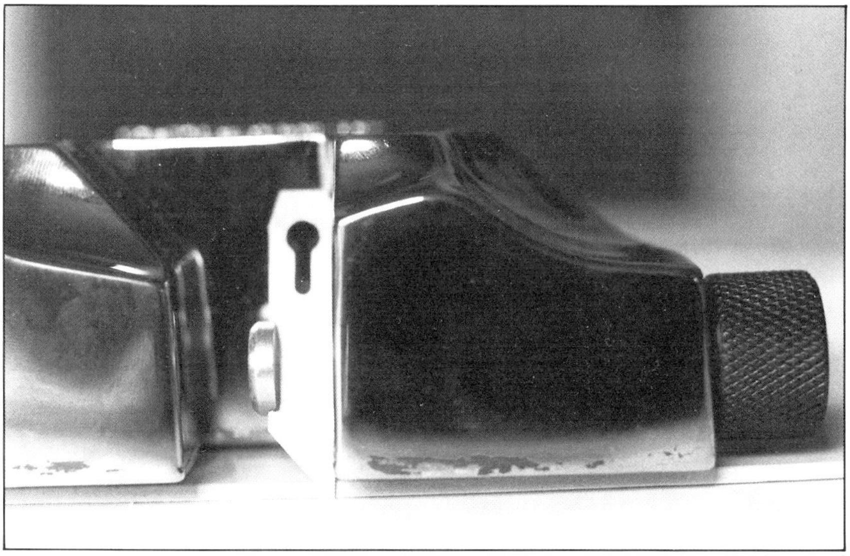

1

Using a hand cutter
1 *There are several types of hand cutters on the market. This is a Dexter cutter.*
2 *Make straight cuts by placing the cutter against a metal straight-edge.*
3 *Hold the straight-edge very firmly and draw the cutter along, applying a firm, even pressure.*
4 *An oval can be cut in a similar manner, using a template.*
5 *Cutting around a template requires practice as it is difficult to manouevre the cutter at the narrow ends of the oval.*

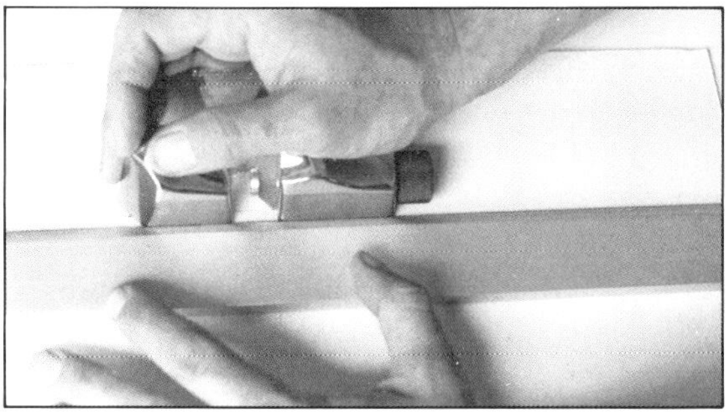

2

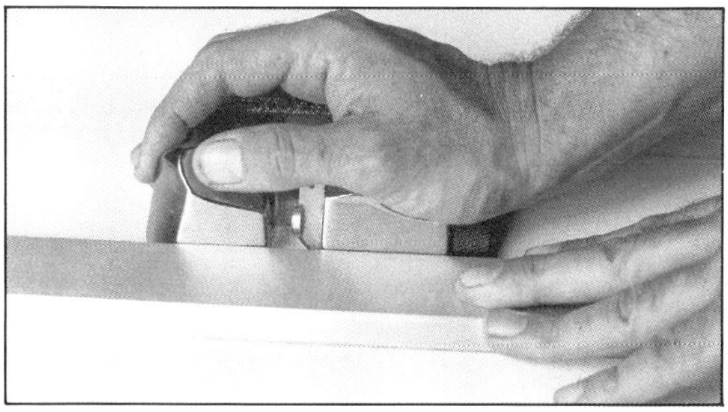

3

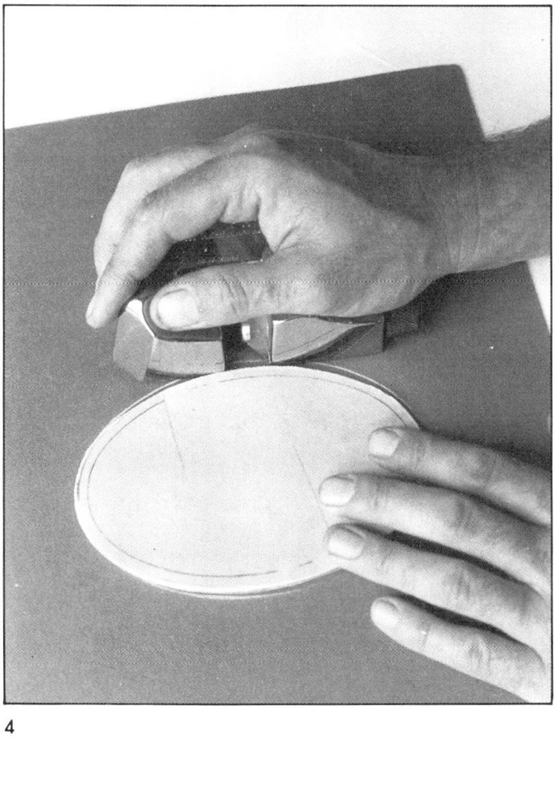

4

5

PROFESSIONAL METHOD

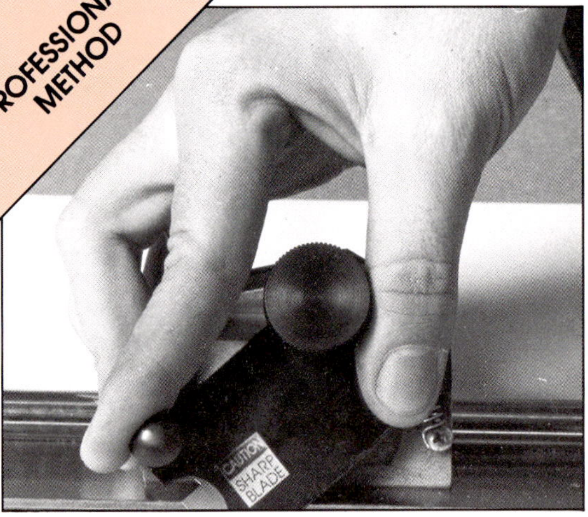

1

Cutting a bevelled window
First the size of the border is determined; the depth of the bottom border is always greater than the depth of the other three, which are usually the same size. Once this is done, the total outside measurement of the window mount is calculated.
1 *Placing the mount card face down and using the straight edge of the mount cutter, the first side of the mount is cut.*
2 *The other three sides are then cut in the same way, altering the stops as appropriate.*
3 *The inner edges are then cut, using the bevelled edge of the mount cutter. A slight overcut is usually made, as this will not show on the right side of the mount and results in the formation of sharp, clean, bevelled corners.*

2

3

pieces, you can often remove them by carefully rubbing them down with very fine sandpaper, glass-paper or emery-cloth.

Some framers recommend using the bevelled edge of the straight-edge to give the hand additional guidance although, since it is the hand itself that maintains the angle, this method still requires practice.

APPLYING LINES AND WASHES

To decorate the mount, lines can be drawn around the window and some of these filled in with washes. For an especially rich look, strips of gold are also applied. The number of lines, their thickness and spacing are important if you wish to avoid an over-fussy appearance and it is advisable to lightly pencil the lines around the window before applying the wash, measuring up in order to keep them strictly parallel.

A typical line-wash mount consists of a ruled line 6mm (¼in) to 12mm (½in) from the bevel, followed by a broader band of wash and enclosed by an outer double line. Ideally, the colour of the wash and lines should echo some of the colours in the picture without swamping the image. Generally, bright colours should be avoided because they detract attention from the picture. If you particularly wish to use a strong colour, such as viridian or magenta, try muting them slightly, without drastically changing them, by mixing a tiny amount of a complementary colour with them. Black may seem an obvious choice for the lines but, on the whole, is better avoided, as the starkness of black dominates a light-coloured mount too much and dark browns, greens or blues are preferable.

Before applying the wash, it is a good idea to wet the area between the lines, lightly wiping it with a soft watercolour brush dipped in water. The colour will then flow onto the paper without leaving unsightly tide marks. Apply the colour in several thin layers, until you achieve the required colour density for your mount.

When the wash is completely dry, define the coloured area with a stronger outline, using a ruling pen; usually the line is drawn in a deeper tone of the wash colour. Wait until this line is completely dry

Lines
Before applying lines and washes, mark off all the measurements from the window outwards (left). *Mark these guidelines in light pencil all the way round the mount, or mark dots at the corners, or make pin holes if the line is to be particularly fine. Lines can be drawn with ruling pens, rapidographs, felt-nibbed pens, pencils or even crayons. A combination of different thicknesses and textures is usually more interesting than a regular arrangement.*

Using a ruling pen
A ruling pen has an adjustable nib, allowing you to alter the thickness of the line. The pen can be filled by dipping it into the ink (below), *but if you do this you must clean the edges afterwards. Alternatively, load a brush with ink and fill the nib from this. Draw a line against a ruler* (right), *making sure that the ruler is upside down so that its bevelled edge* (bottom) *creates a space, preventing the ink from touching the ruler directly.*

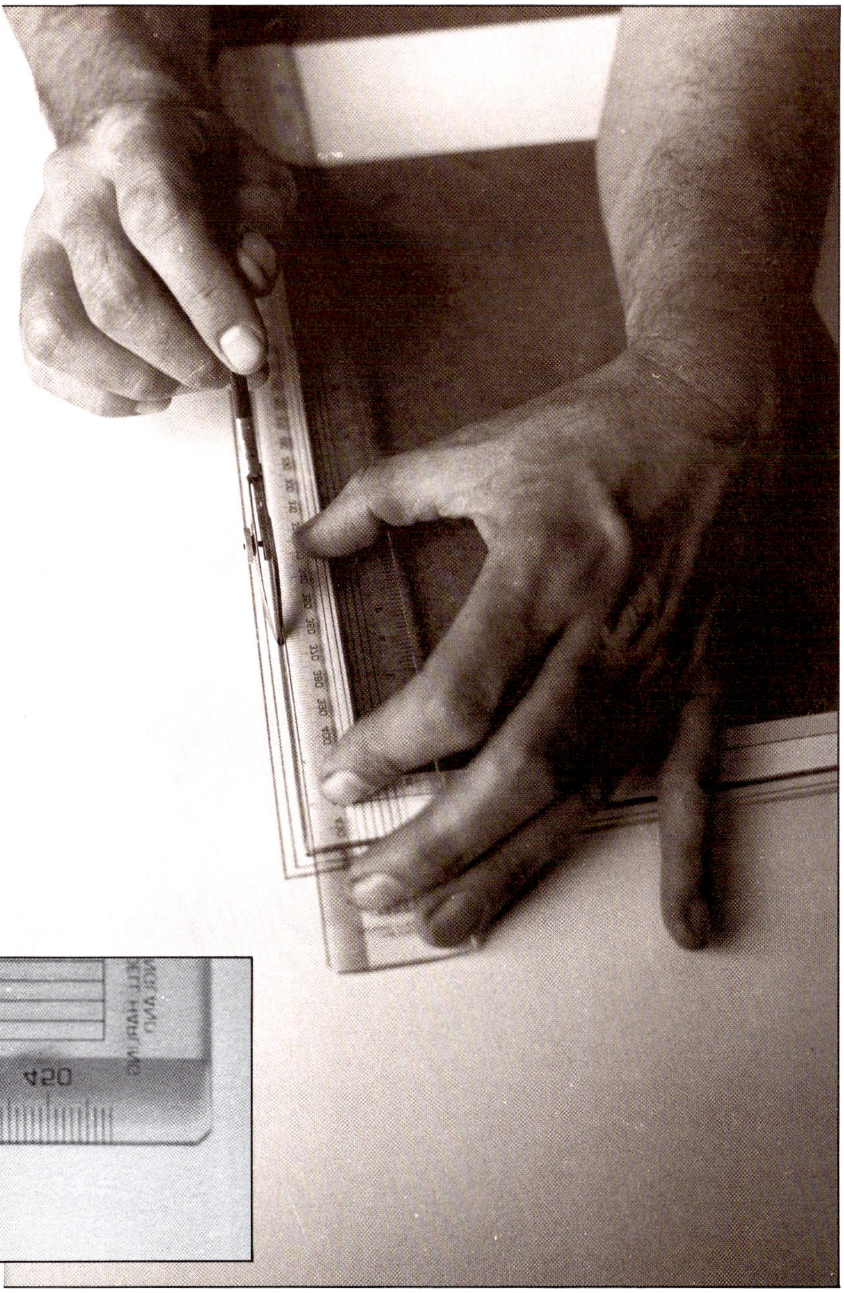

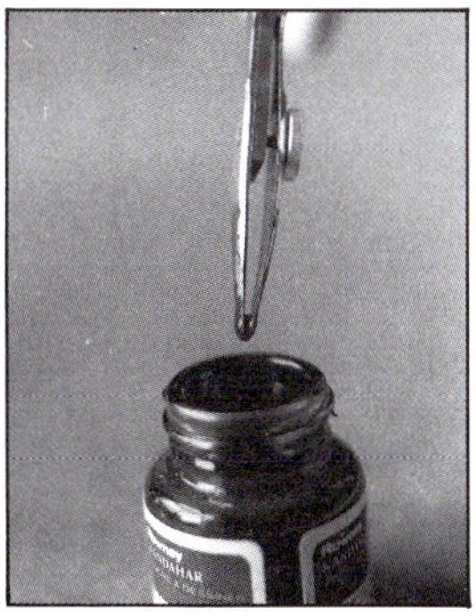

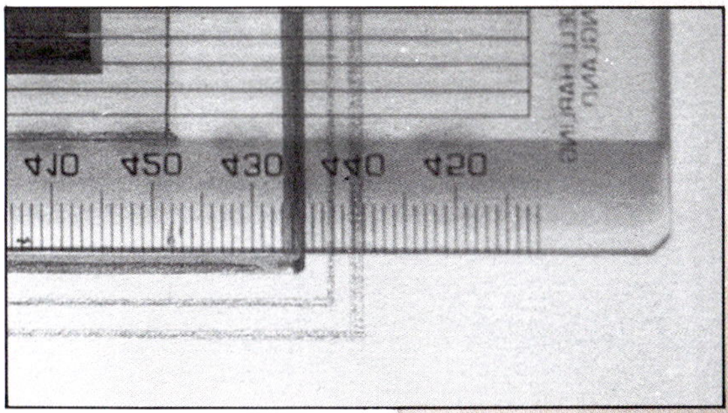

Washes
Use pencil lines to guide you when applying lines and washes to mounts. As a guide for the washes or to the finished lines themselves, draw lightly with a pencil against an ordinary Perspex ruler (right). *You can then apply gouache freehand with a brush* (below). *Make sure the gouache is thin but creamy enough to be opaque.*

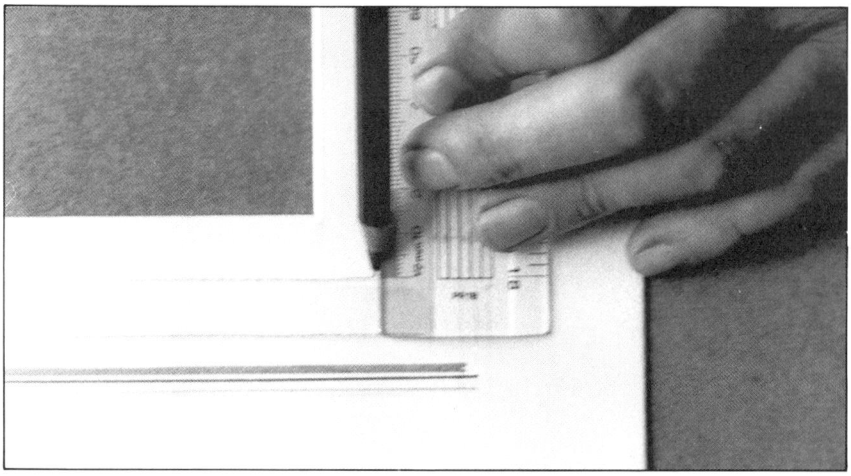

Wash and line
All these washes and lines can be done by the home framer (left to right): *silver and light grey on a dark background; sepia lines and a pale wash on white; black line and wash on medium; black, gold and white on light; compact white and dark on medium.*

Types of line

Apply a line to a mount, using a gold pen (left). *Lines can be drawn along the edges of a strip of wash to tidy it up, or they can be drawn first and a wash applied between them with a brush. They can also stand alone, in varying widths, if desired.*

Wavy lines

Sometimes a wavy or irregular line can look attractive amid all the straight verticals and horizontals of the frame, the picture and the mount (above). *Another attraction of wobbly lines is that they are easier to create than perfectly straight ones!*

before adding any other border lines, otherwise you may cause smudges with your hands, spoiling hours of painstaking work.

Use the bevelled edge of a ruler to draw lines: place the ruler upside down on the mount, leaving a tiny gap between the paper and its raised edge so that the ink or paint will not blot should the colour come into contact with the edge of the ruler.

Ordinary dip pens can be used to draw the lines but they are not very reliable, and by far the best way to achieve a continuous straight line is to use a ruling pen. Turn the knob on the side of the nib to adjust the width of the line but remember that the nib holds a limited amount of ink, so that a very wide line must necessarily be a very short one, as the colour will run out very quickly; it is difficult to continue a broken-off line in a smooth fashion.

Gold and silver inks are more difficult to use than ordinary inks or watercolours: they are not so evenly mixed and can form sediments, making it harder to achieve a smooth flow. It is often a better idea to buy metallic gummed strips, which can be cut to the required width. However, some of these are rather bright and care should be taken not to overdo the banding or the effect will be too brash.

COVERING THE MOUNT

Once the window has been cut, the mount can be covered with fabric. This is generally a better idea for oil paintings and heavier works than for watercolours.

The easiest method of covering a mount is to cut a piece of cloth slightly larger than the whole mount: glue this to the mount and then cut a window from it in such a way that flaps can be folded over to complete the covering. This method can be used with any shaped window, including round and oval ones. Use a spray adhesive for sticking the fabric to the mount.

CALCULATING THE LENGTH OF THE MOULDING

To work out the exact total length of moulding that will be required, first add together the length and width of your picture and mount, if there is one, using the rebate measurements *(see page 56)* and multiply the total by two. Next, to take account of the moulding that will extend beyond the picture at the corners of the frame, measure the width of the moulding you have chosen and multiply this figure by eight. Add this to the first (picture) figure. This gives you the total length of moulding needed.

To discover the total length of moulding you will require, measure the length and width of your artpiece, multiply the total by two and add 12mm (½in) for an easy fitting margin. Next, measure the width of the moulding and multiply this figure by eight to allow for the mitred ends.

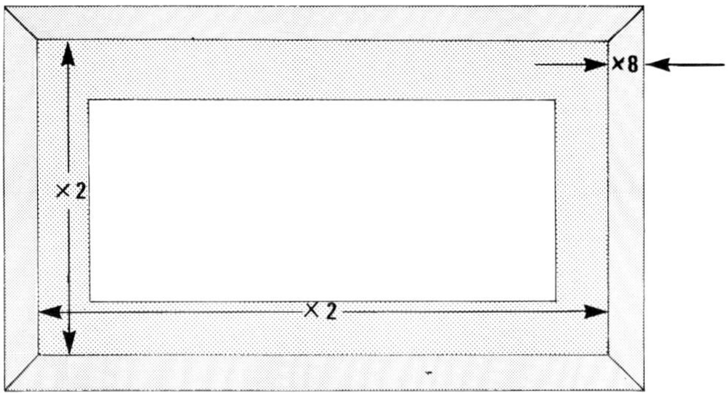

CUTTING THE MOULDING

When cutting framers' moulding into separate pieces it is important to avoid confusion by working always from the back edge, ie from the edge of the strip which contains the rebate and from the same end of the strip. It is also important to make one side of the frame at a time rather than trying to measure up the whole strip for cutting.

Cutting a Mitre

Once you have determined the entire length of the moulding that you require to frame your art-

Fabric-covered mounts
When cutting fabric to cover a rectangular mount, allow enough material to fold over the edges. Cut slots into the inside and outside corners (right), so that they will fold back neatly. Place the fabric face down on a clean surface and spray on adhesive.

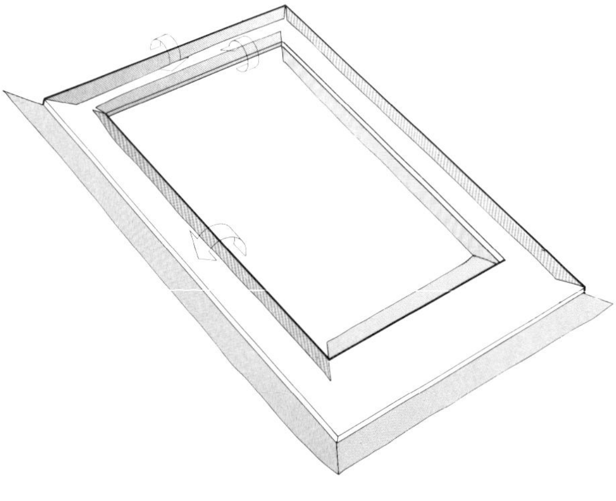

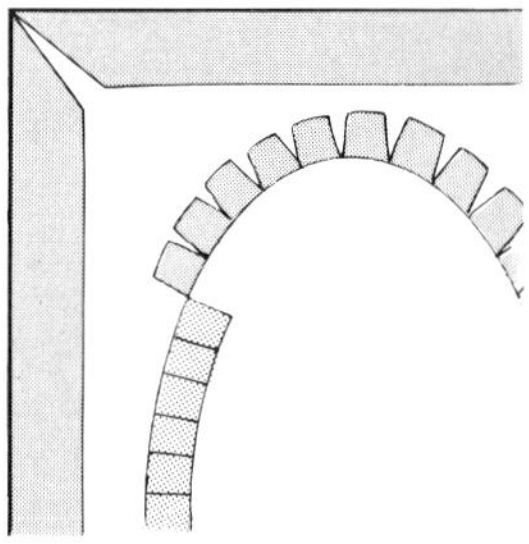

Cut small slots into the inside edge of an oval mount (above), so that they can be folded back in a curve.

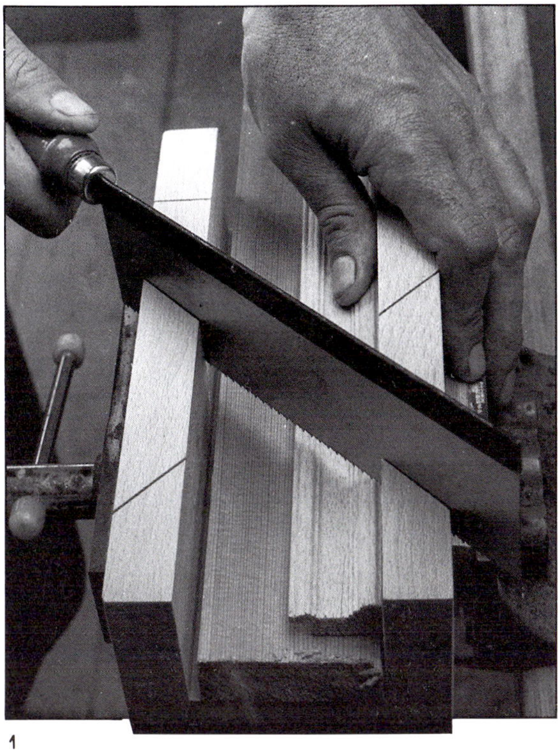

1

Cutting a mitre

1 *Place a piece of moulding face up in a mitre box to make the first cut. The rebate edge of the moulding fits up against the inside edge of the mitre box.*

2 *If you are using a metal mitre box, it can also be used as a corner clamp in the later glueing and nailing stage.*

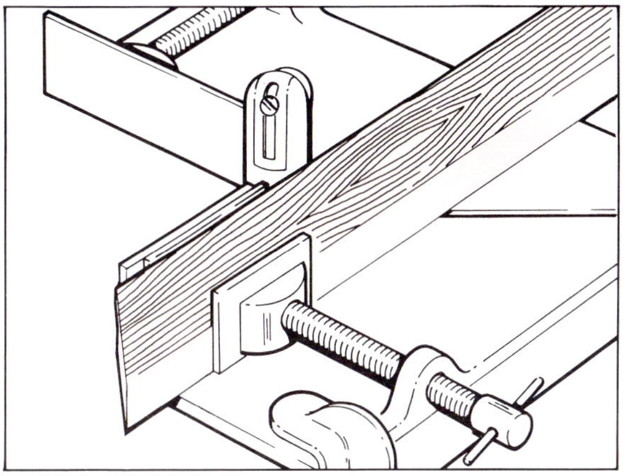

2

3

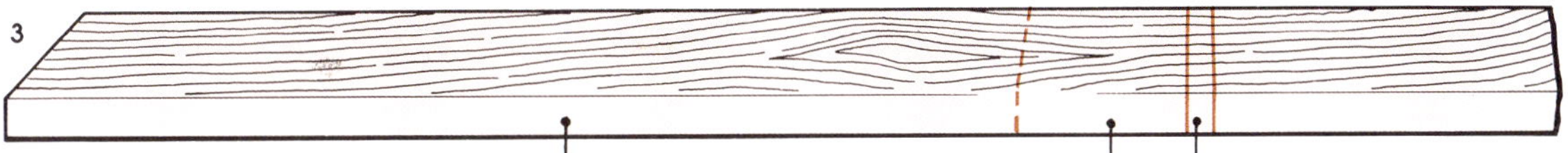

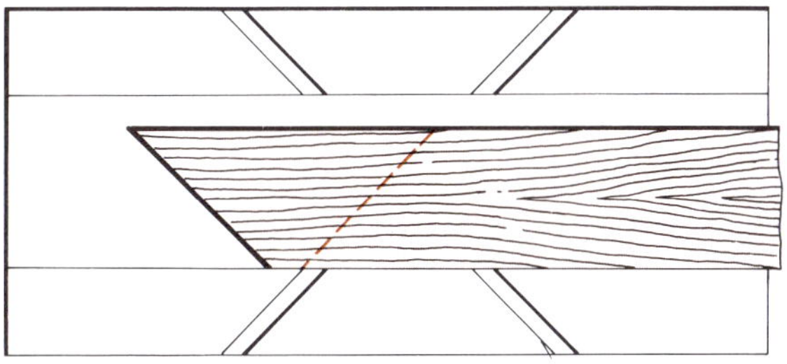

4

3 *Place the moulding face up and measure it from the longest edge of the mitre.*

4 *Mark the outside edge of the frame with a pencil. Line up the pencil mark with the cutting channel of the mitre box and saw, making sure that the saw cut is on the waste side of the moulding.*

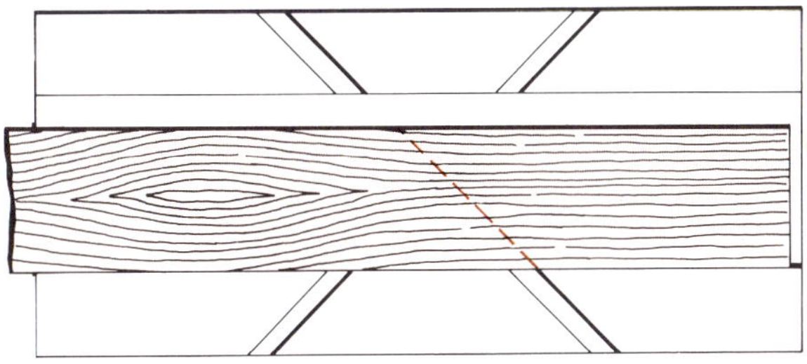

5

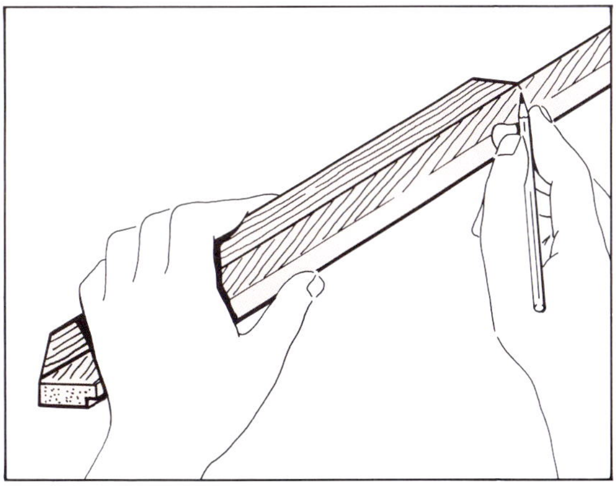

6

5 *Place the remaining piece of moulding in the mitre box and cut the first mitre of the second strip.*

6 *Measure off the length of the second piece. Use the first piece as a guide, placing them back to back.*

piece, your first task is to cut a mitre at the end of the strip. A mitre is the joint of two pieces of wood at an angle of 90 degrees, with the line of the junction exactly bisecting this angle. Precision is vital when cutting a mitre: if the angle on one of the pieces is even slightly off 45 degrees, you will finish with a gap at the corners of the frame where the two pieces of moulding should meet exactly. It is important to rule out the possibility of cutting a mitre by simply measuring the angle and cutting the moulding freehand. You would have to be extremely lucky to succeed in cutting a perfect mitre using this method. A mitre box or a mitre cutter is essential.

Place one end of the moulding in the mitre box, making sure that the back of the moulding is absolutely flat on the bottom, the rebate edge is nearest to you, and the strip is flush with the sides of the box. If you are using a metal mitre box, place a thin batten of wood between the moulding and the edge of the box, so that the metal does not mark the wood. If you are using a metal mitre box and a saw is not built into it, use a backsaw with it: the manufacturers will recommend the most suitable one. A wooden mitre box is less expensive than a metal one and is used with a tenon saw, preferably one with a thin blade. The mitre box will guide the action of your saw precisely. Use a slow, easy cutting motion rather than a fast energetic one, which will cause the saw to turn and twist.

Now mark out the first total measurement – picture height plus twice the width of the moulding plus easy-fitting margin – starting from the mitred end. There is no need to mark any other measurements on the strip at this point as the second strip will be cut based on the first length. Remove the moulding from the mitre cutter and lay it down with the rebate upwards. Mark the measurement on the outside edge of the moulding. Then replace the

1

2

3

Using a metal mitre box
1 *This metal mitre box has holes in its base so that is is not restricted to cutting angles of 45 degrees. Place pieces of dowling in the holes to allow you to change the angles for frames of more complex shapes.*
2 *Whatever type of mitre box you use, always clamp it firmly to the work-table. Here, the framer has chosen to use a G-clamp.*
3 *Hold the moulding firmly in position with one hand. The metal guides keep the sawing at a precise angle to ensure a perfectly fitting corner.*

The Marples mitre box
A popular model, the Marples mitre box is a simple tool, which can be used as a corner clamp as well as a mitre cutter.
1 *Hold the box in position on the work-table with a G-clamp.*
2 *Insert the wood into one of its sections and tighten the screws to hold it in place while the mitre is cut.*
3 *Place the tenon saw into its guides, holding it firmly.*
4 *Use a good quality saw and keep the sawing action steady for a clean cut.*

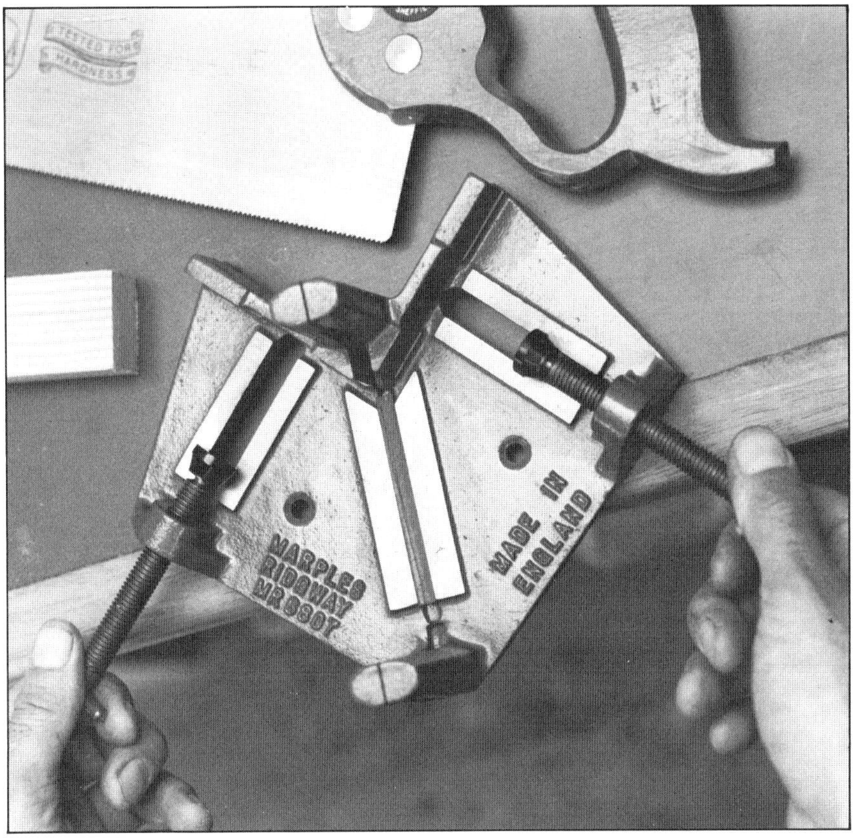

1

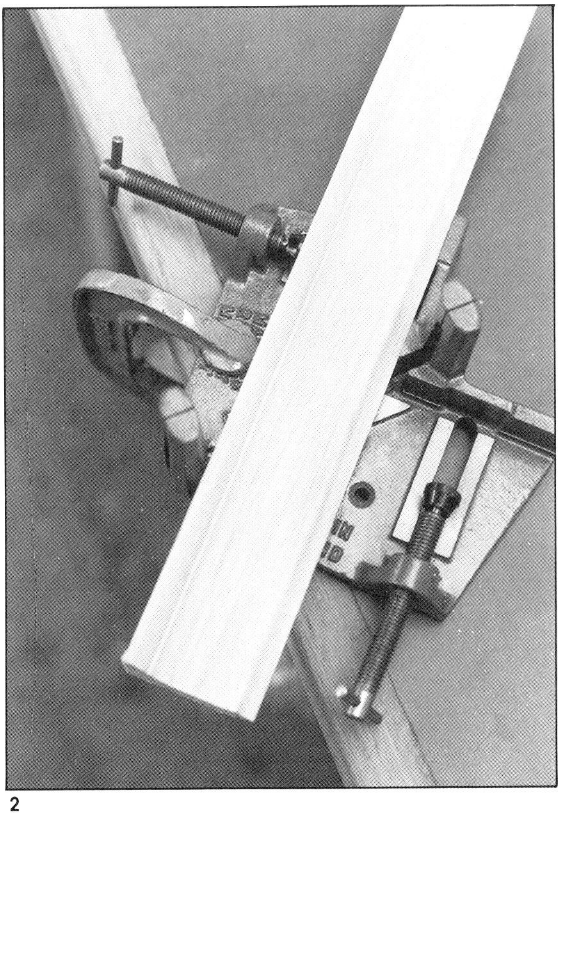

2

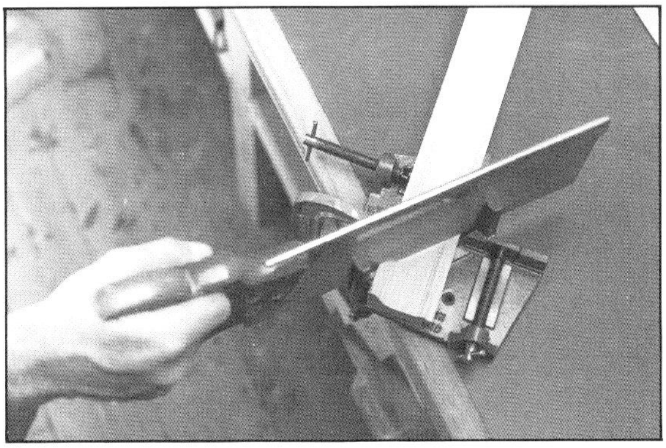

3

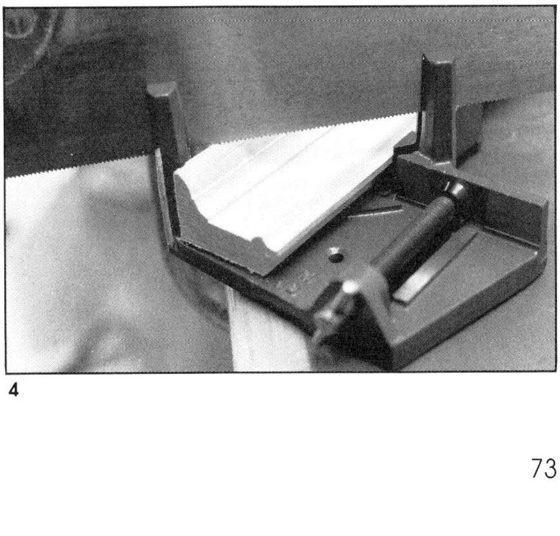

4

Variety of angles
1 *This more complicated mitre box has a protractor fitted to it, which allows the user to cut a wide variety of angles to create triangles or otherwise shaped frames.*
2 *It contains its own saw.*
3 *Set the saw carefully at the appropriate angle.*
4 *Hold the wood firmly in place against the metal support.*
5 *You will then be able to make an accurate cut with the saw.*
This mitre box, like the others, is clamped to the work-bench by G-clamps. Make sure that it is securely held before setting angles and making cuts.

1

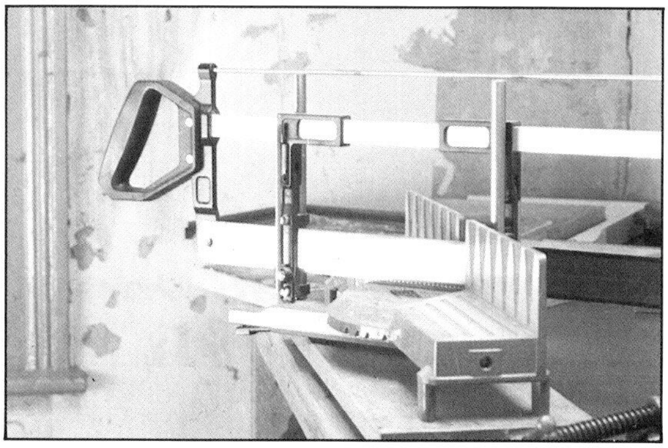

2

3

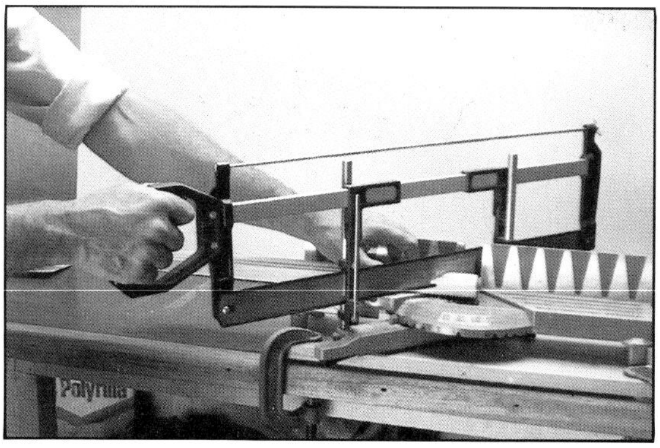

4

5

moulding in the mitre cutter, with the mark in line with the channel of the cutter. This means that the mark is directly beneath the saw blade which will cut diagonally through the point to produce your second mitre. You now have the first complete side of your frame.

You will now find that the remaining piece of moulding already has a diagonal cut at one end, left over from the cut which created your first complete side. However, this is obviously facing the wrong way and, as an initial step to your second complete side, it is once again necessary to cut a first mitre, from this same end. Next, place the complete side back to back with the remainder of the strip, putting the mitre cuts together so that they are completely flush. Now to mark a diagonal line across the uncut strip, using the end of the first side as a guide. Place the uncut strip in the mitre cutter and cut along the marked line to produce a second identical side for your frame.

Repeat this procedure for the other two sides of the frame, substituting the picture width measurement for the picture height measurement.

FORMING THE CORNERS

When joining two pieces of moulding, first place them back to back to ensure that they are exactly the same length.

Using a Vice

Place one piece of moulding in the vice and, if you are right-handed, hold the other piece in your left hand, keeping your right hand free to work with. Apply woodworkers' resin adhesive to the sawn-off mitred end of the length of moulding held in the vice and hold the mitred end of the other piece

PROFESSIONAL METHODS

Cutting a wooden frame
1 *The strip of wooden moulding is placed in the mitre cutter, face up, with the outside edge towards the operator. Supports are wedged under the rebate so that the descending blades do not crush it. The extra amount of moulding required to accommodate the mitred ends is then calculated and allowed for and the machine operated.*
2 *The blades descend on the moulding to cut out a triangle of wood. The cutter is then released. The cutter is worked several more times, each time cutting a little deeper. By cutting through the wood gradually in this way, the moulding is not crushed and two perfect mitres are created. The first length of the frame is then removed from the cutter and the rest of the strip moved along so that the next mitres can be cut and the second length of frame completed.*

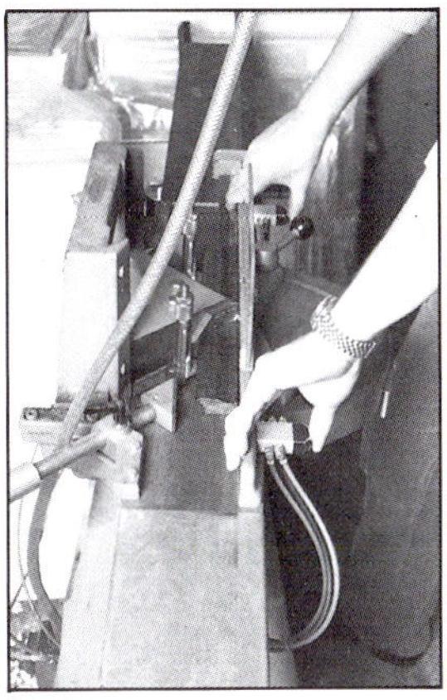

1

2

Cutting an aluminium frame
The strip of metal framing is placed in the metal mitre cutter, with the outside edge facing the operator. The machine allows for the extra length needed to accommodate the mitered ends. The blades slice through the framing, leaving two precise miters.

firmly against it. Using an electric drill with a 1½mm (1/16in) drill bit, make two pilot holes across the join, always ensuring that the drill passes right through into the second piece of wood; it is vital to hold the pieces firmly together so that there is no slipping as you drill. Now drive size 18 panel pins, 18mm (¾in) long, into the pilot holes and release the left-hand piece of wood, which is now fixed to the moulding held in the vice. To achieve a neat finish, countersink the pins, using a nail punch to drive them slightly below the surface, so that the hole can be filled with plastic wood filler.

If you do not have a drill, it is best to leave the glue to harden in the join before making a hole with a bradawl and nailing the pieces together. Modern rapid-dry glues set in half an hour to an hour.

Using a Clamp

If you have a mitre clamp, sometimes called a corner clamp, instead of a vice, the task is made slightly easier, as the clamp holds both pieces together at rigid right angles, leaving both hands free to insert the panel pins after glueing.

Glues for Framing

Type	Advantages	Disadvantages	Drying times
Scotch glue (organic glue available in flakes or sheets	Set glue can be heated to dissolve making it possible to correct mistakes	Time consuming and brittle; not as strong as PVA	Overnight
PVA	Convenient; no heat needed; very strong	Cannot break and re-set	Half an hour to overnight (depending on use and type)
Epoxy resins (there are several of these including Araldite and the 'super glues'	Set quickly; very strong	Cannot break and re-set; spills and drips cannot be removed once set	Few minutes to an hour

1

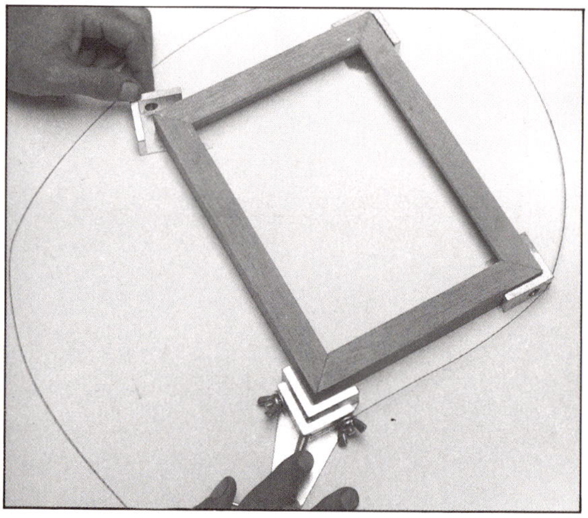

2

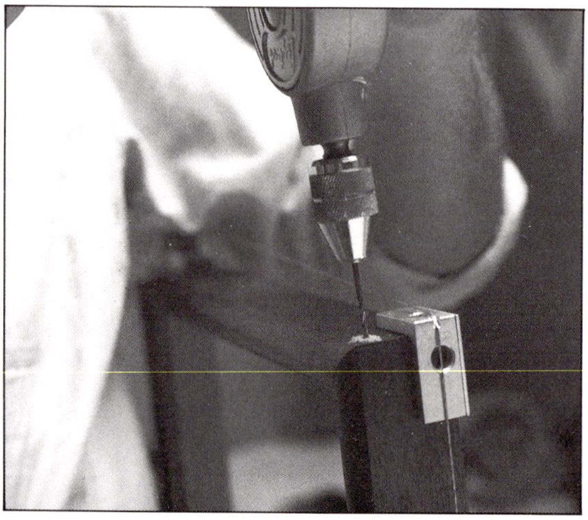

3

Cramping methods
1 *As an alternative to using corner clamps (or cramps), a vice can be used, as long as it can accommodate two pieces of wood. Glue the mitred ends and place the two pieces together. Then make holes for nailing with a bradawl.*
2 *Another method of clamping is to use an Elwood clamp. This consists of four metal corners, one of which has a screw attached. Run wire around the notches in the corners and tighten with the screw.* **3** *With the frame held firmly in place while the glue is drying, drill holes for the nails.*

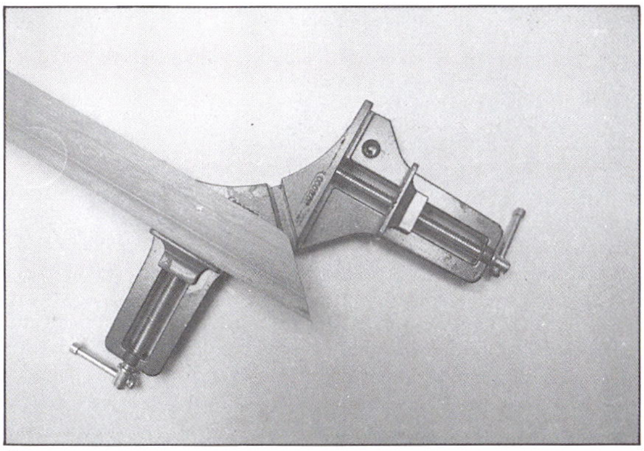

1

Corner clamps

1 *For lighter frames, corner clamps are useful. Fit the first piece of mitred wood into one side of the clamp.*

2 *Glue the second piece and place it into the clamp.*

3 *Ease the pieces together, making sure they are flush. Then tighten the clamp and wipe off any surplus glue.*

4 *If you are making a deep box frame, you may find that the clamps hold the bottom firmly but do not apply sufficient pressure to the top. In this case, position metal spring clips on the corner with pliers that first hold them apart and then release them onto the corner.*

2

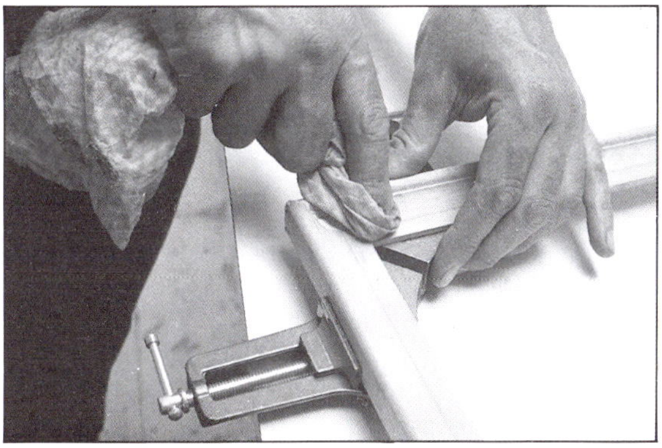

3

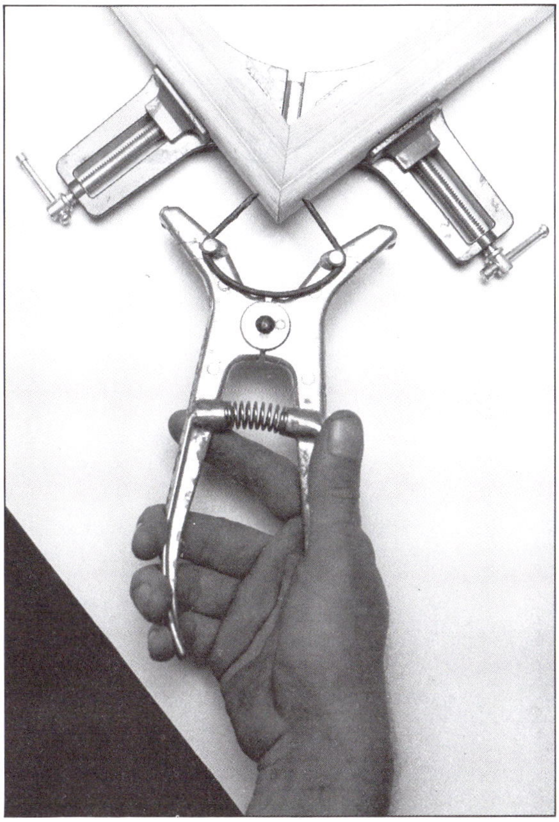

4

Checking corners

Lightweight clamps do not automatically make a precise right angle. Make the two 'L-shapes'. Then check the corner of the first two pieces (above) before fixing them together to form a rectangle.

PROFESSIONAL METHOD

1

Underpinning
1 *The mitred ends of two sides of the frame to be joined are glued together and then placed face up in the underpinner. The machine is operated and a staple is forced up into the wood across the join.*
2 *The underpinner is worked several times along the join to ensure that the corner of the frame is made secure.*

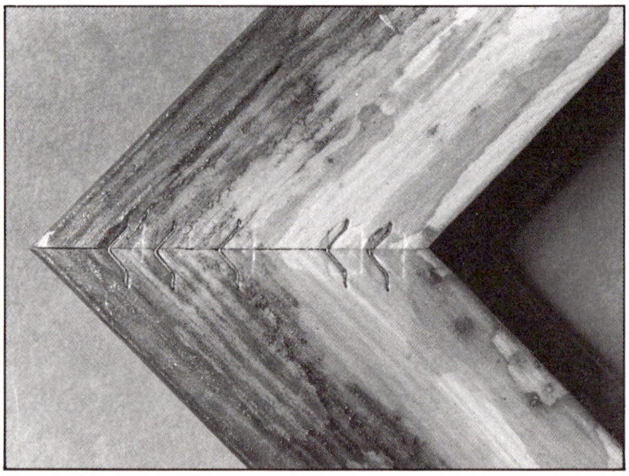

2

CREATING A REBATE

Framers' moulding comes with a fitted rebate but if you buy builders' moulding you will need to make your own rebate – the 'step' beneath the frame itself into which the picture fits.

There are two basic ways of creating a rebate. One method is to fix a wooden strip onto the moulding before you begin cutting the mitres. This piece of wood is called a quadrant and comes in a variety of sizes and woods. The other method is to make, in effect, two frames and then fit them together: the broader, top rectangle is the frame itself; the narrower one fits at the back to form the rebate.

Using a quadrant

Select a strip of builders' moulding and fix a rebate strip to the back of this before you begin measuring the specific lengths and mitring the ends. Glue one side of the rebate strip. Lay it flush with the outside edge of the moulding and fix it from the back of the rebate edge with panel pins. You have now made your own framers' moulding and are ready to measure it and cut the mitres.

Making two frames

Begin by cutting the two shorter rebate strips: measure the width of the artwork and add 3mm ($^1/_8$in) to allow for easy fitting. This margin is particularly important when you frame canvases, as they are often a shade off-square and their corners are frequently bulky. Next cut the two longer strips: measure the length of the artwork and add 3mm ($^1/_8$in) plus twice the width of the strip. This method will allow the shorter strips to be fitted inside the longer ones. You do not need to cut mitres on these rebate strips as the rebate will be stuck behind the frame and therefore does not need neat cornering.

Now cut the strips of moulding for the outer frame. The ends of these strips must be mitred *(see pages 70–75)*. When cutting the top rectangle, remember that its final outer boundary – the measurement of all its outside edges – should be exactly the same length as the outer boundary of the rebate rectangle so that when the two rectangles are fitted together, their outside edges will be flush with each other. The outer frame must overlap the inner edges of the rebate rectangle to form the 'step' into which the picture will fit.

Next fit the pieces together, starting with the rebate pieces. Apply glue evenly over the whole cut surface of the end of one of the shorter pieces. Then hold the glued end against the end of the inner side of one of the longer rebate strips using a corner clamp or a vice to help the adhesive form a strong bond. Tap two panel pins into the end of the join to give extra stability. Repeat this process on all the corners, working in such a way that you produce two L-shapes, and finally join them both together to make the inner rectangle. Follow the same procedure with the mitred strips of wood to form the outer rectangle of the frame.

When the glue is dry, stick the two rectangles

Making a rebate
Rebates can be cut into pieces of moulding with a plough plane (right). *It is fitted with a steel depth gauge and an adjustable 'fence', which can be set to the width of the rebate required. Alternatively, stick a wooden strip, or quadrant,* (below) *along the length of a piece of moulding.*

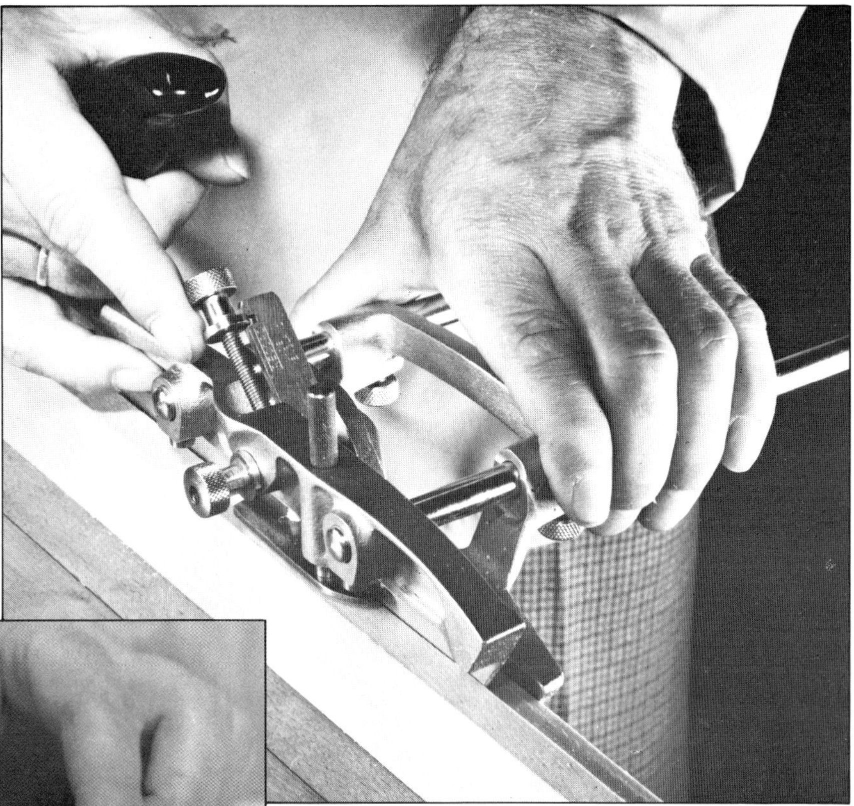

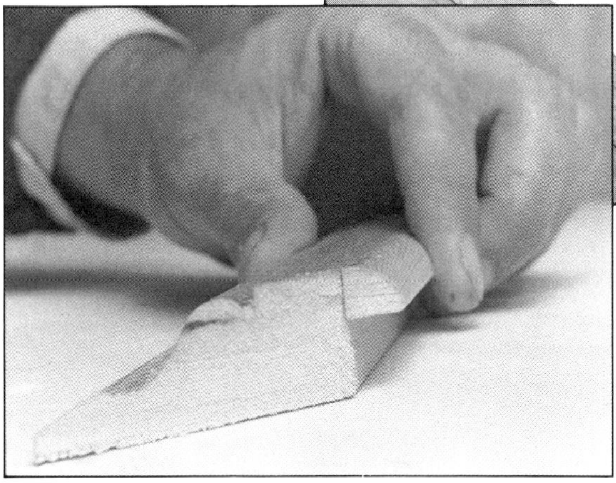

Covering an insert
When making an insert, make sure you completely cover the front and the rebate with fabric, so that no bare wood will show when it is fitted into the main frame (above).

together. Lay the rebate rectangle flat and cover the whole of its top surface with adhesive. Place the outer rectangle face down and place the rebated rectangle adhesive-side down on top of the outer one. Fix it in position with panel pins. Make sure that the surface on which you are working is absolutely clean to avoid marking the front of the frame.

COVERING A FRAME INSERT

Strips of fabric are usually sufficient to cover wooden inserts. As inserts are made from strips of moulding which then fit inside the outer frame, it is possible to cover the separate strips of insert moulding before joining them together. If you do follow this method, the corners of the insert will be neat because the fabric will be glued between the joins.

Alternatively, you can cover the insert after it is assembled. Glue on strips of cloth and then mitre the corners with a very sharp blade. The advantage of covering after assembly is that you avoid the difficulty of keeping the fabric clean while assembling the frame insert.

GLAZING

When your frame is completed, you may well wish to place the artwork beneath glass. For many frames, the procedure for cutting glass can be satisfactorily carried out at home, although any work involving glass must be completed extremely carefully.

Cutting very large pieces of glass, however, is best left to the expert: large pieces are difficult to carry; a

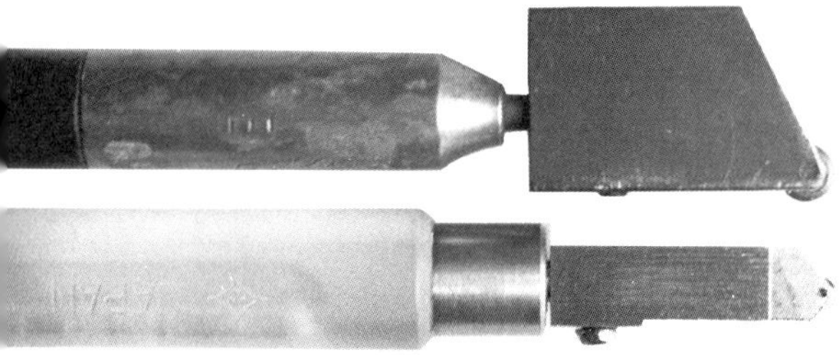

1

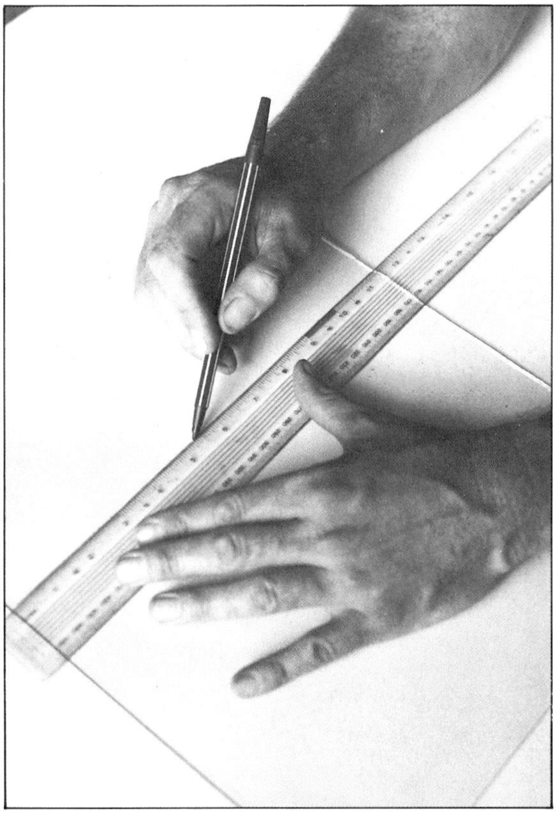

2

3

Cutting glass
1 *There are two basic types of glass cutter. The most common type has a small tungsten carbide wheel. The other, a diamond glass cutter, is used mainly for thicker glass.*
2 *Use a ruler and felt-tipped pen to mark where you are going to cut the glass.*
3 *Keep the glass cutter lubricated by dipping it into special glass-cutting oil, a thin mixture, or methylated spirits.*
4 *To score a line, hold the ruler firmly in place and keep the glass cutter vertical. This requires practice: too little pressure makes no impression at all and too much cracks the glass.*
5 *Tap the glass along the scored line with the knob on the end of the cutter.*
6 *Make the final snap by breaking the glass over the edge of a table.*
7 *If you are cutting a small section you can break it with glass pliers by placing the scored line along a table edge and giving the glass a sharp tweak.*
8 *Alternatively, break the glass by placing the scored line over the edge of a ruler.*

suitable surface may be hard to find for a large operation; and the bigger the frame the greater the chance that your rebate will be inaccurate.

The glass must fit very tightly inside the frame – it should not slip around inside the rebate. Moreover, if the glass is a shade too big when cut, there is little you can do to rectify matters, although, occasionally, it may be possible to sandpaper it down to size. Measuring and cutting must, therefore, be very accurate and the allowance for easier fitting should ideally be no more than 1mm ($^{1}/_{20}$in).

To enable you to avoid accidents with fragile picture glass it is advisable to practice glass cutting. Repeatedly cutting waste pieces of glass will increase your confidence and accuracy and it will also give you a good idea of the correct pressure that should be applied when cutting.

The surface on which you cut the glass should be completely level and non-slip. Use double-sided tape to prevent the glass and your straight-edge from moving.

Measure and mark the glass, preferably with a felt-tipped pen so that any wrong marks can be rubbed out with white spirit if necessary. (Although, if you do leave any measurement marks, they are likely to be covered up in the last instance because the edges of the glass will be fitted under the rebate.)

The next stage is the actual cutting: the object is not to cut through the glass completely but to score it, so that is can be snapped cleanly along the line. Place the straight-edge along the felt-tip mark and pull the cutter towards you with a pressure that is firm but not so firm that it cuts right through the glass. The scored line should pass cleanly over the edges of the sheet. Score the glass once only; twice makes little difference and can damage the cutting wheel even if you are using a tungsten carbide

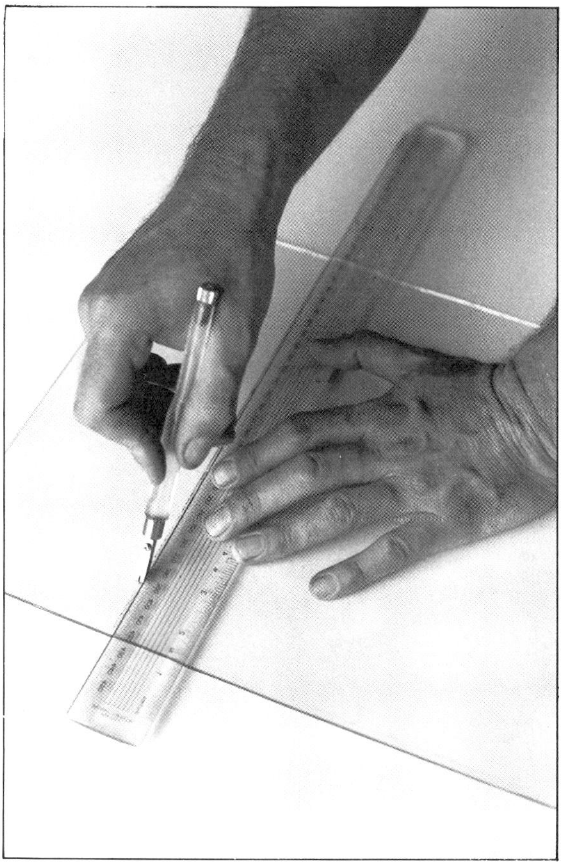

4

5

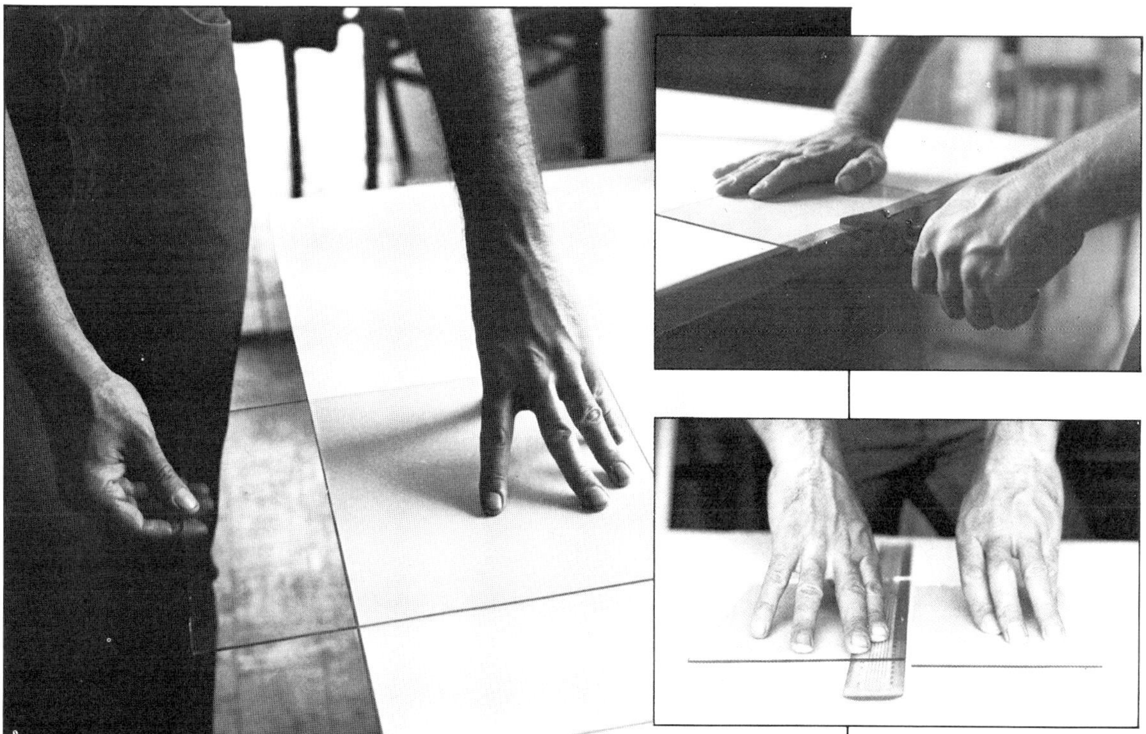

6

wheel, which is superior to and much longer-lasting than an ordinary steel wheel.

There are several ways of snapping the glass. Most glass cutters have knobs on the end, which allow you to tap the glass along the cut: tapping gently but frequently ensures a clean snap. Another method of snapping is to slide the straight-edge beneath the glass, almost up to the score line but just to the immediate left of it. Then, when you press down on the right-hand side, the glass will snap, leaving a clean edge. Another method is to lift the glass slightly with your left hand (if you are right-handed), placing your thumb and first finger, with thumb on top, over the edge of the glass just to the left of the score line. Then take hold of the glass with your right hand just to the right of the score line. With one quick downward movement of your right hand the glass will snap.

Finishing, if required, can now be carried out by rubbing the edge of the glass with wet emery paper.

Remember that throughout the whole operation it is necessary to keep the glass cutter lubricated by frequently dipping it in white spirit.

ASSEMBLING

Always work from the back of the frame and make sure that the surface on which you are working is clean. First insert the glass into the rebate, making sure there is no dirt on it. Then insert the picture and

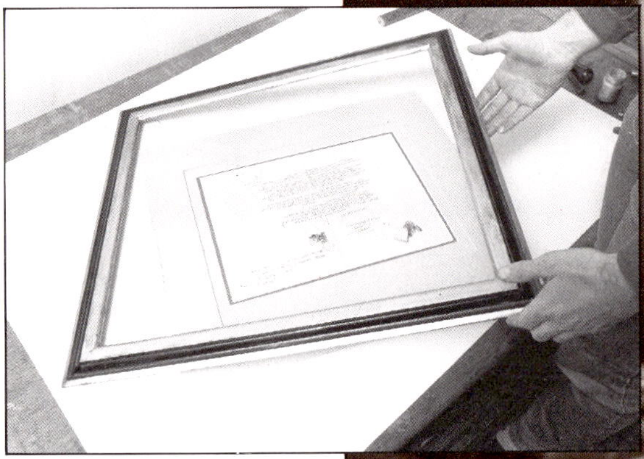

Assembling the frame
When assembling all the components, remember to work from the back. With the frame held face down, fit the glass into the rebate at the rear. Then fit the mounted picture, followed by the backing board, if this is being used. The oil painting and frame (right) *are ready for assembly. Bradawl, steel tacks and hammer are necessary to secure the painting.*

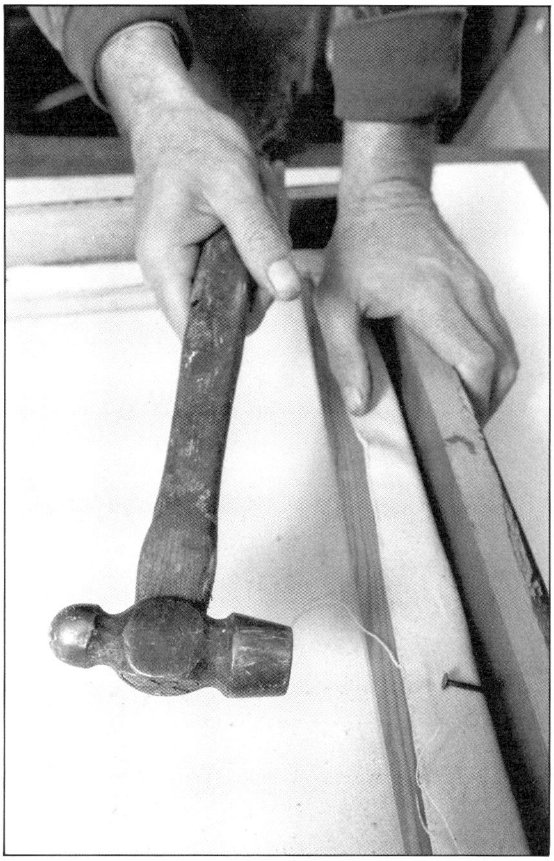

Using tacks
Ordinary steel tacks can be used to hold the components in place. After the frame has been assembled, tap the tacks into the inside edges of the main frame (left). *One on each side should be enough to hold the frame together.*

Using a point-driver
An alternative way of securing the components is to use a point-driver (above). *Holding the machine down firmly onto the back of the assembled parts, pull the trigger to send a diamond tack into the inside edge of the main frame.*

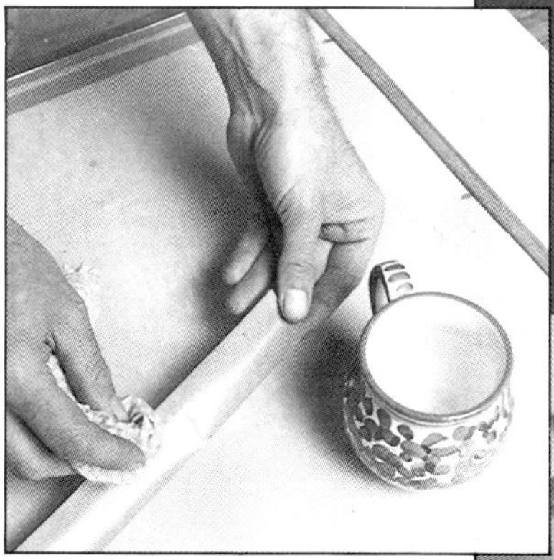

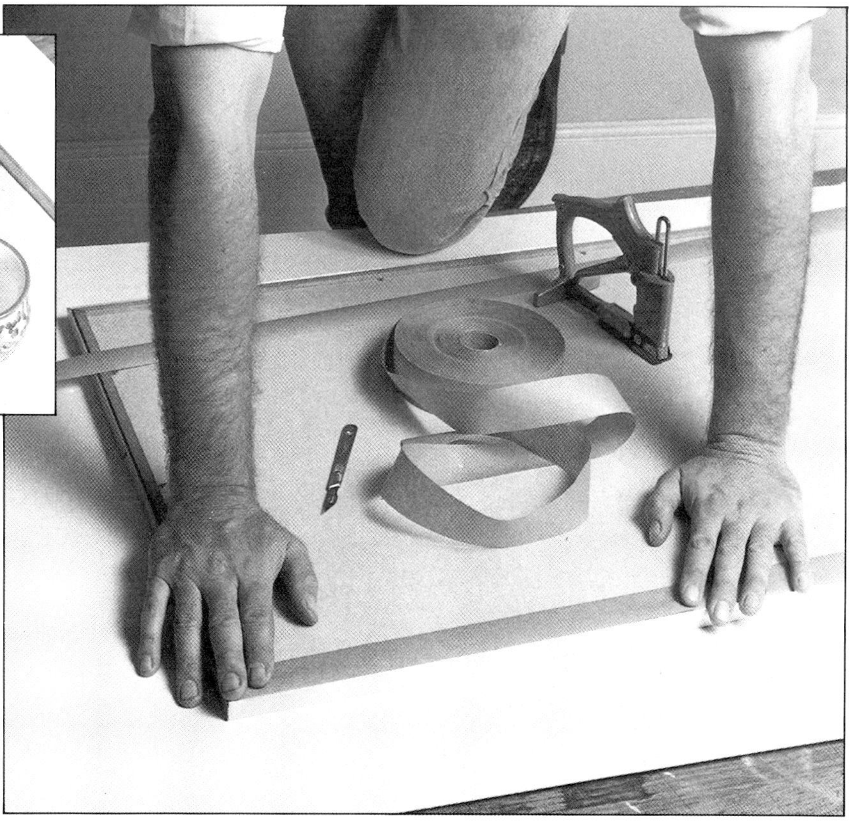

Gummed paper
To prevent dust from entering the framed picture, stick gummed brown paper onto the back of the frame. Wet the paper first (above), *and then stick it firmly along the back edges* (right), *making sure that the picture is completely sealed.*

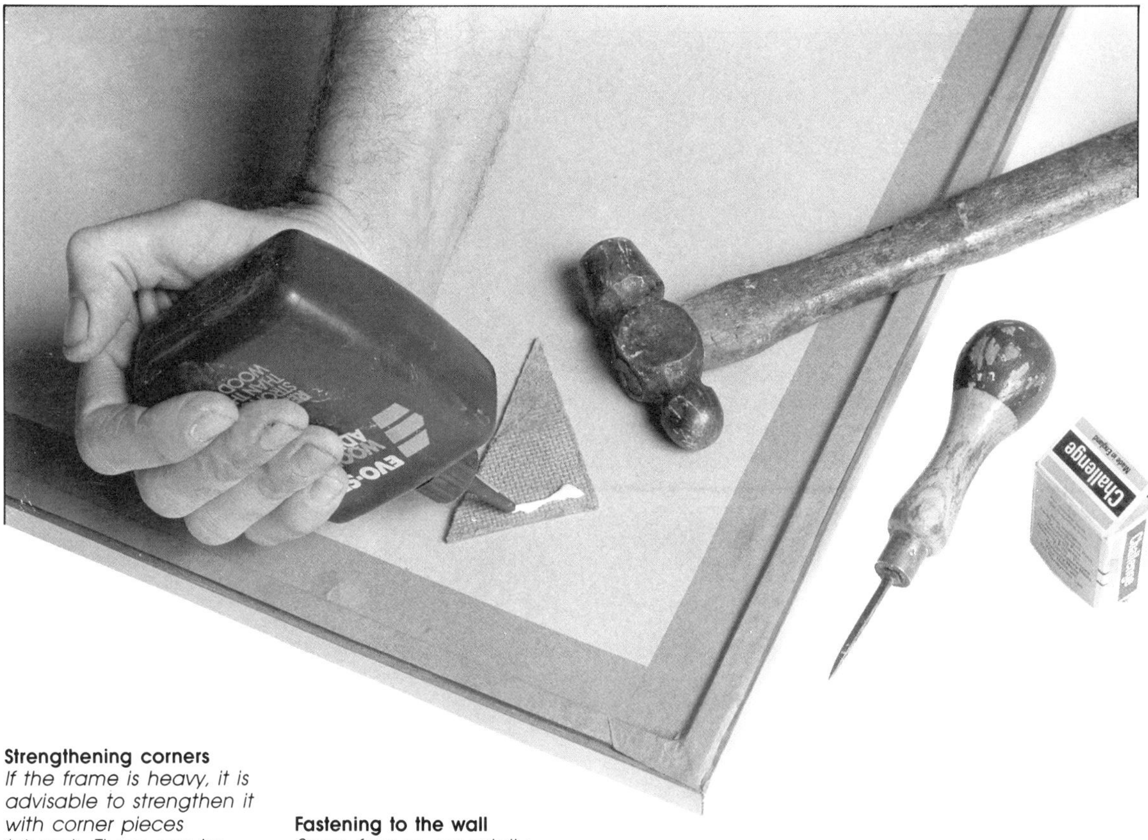

Strengthening corners
If the frame is heavy, it is advisable to strengthen it with corner pieces (above). *These can be home-made triangles of hardboard. Glue and then tack them into place on the back corners of the frame. Make sure that they are placed so that they are not visible from the front.*

Fastening to the wall
Some frames, especially deep ones, look good when screwed up flat against the wall. Fastening plates can be bought for this (right). *For hanging most framed pictures, screw-eyes and wire are ideal* (below right).

mount, if there is one, face down on the glass. Finally, insert the backing board. There are several ways of holding everything in place. If the rebate is deeper than the thickness of all the parts, hammer veneer pins into the rebate, behind the backing board, at intervals of 5cm (2in). If the parts are thicker than the rebate, hammer the veneer pins into the back of the frame and bend the heads over the backing board. If the backing board lies flush with the back of the frame, it is a good idea to hold everything in place with turn clips. Once everything is assembled, seal the edges with strips of brown gummed tape. This prevents any dust from entering.

HANGING

Using a bradawl, punch a hole either side of the frame about a third of the way down. Screw in screw eyes. Then run picture-framing wire through the eyes, knotting it at either end with pliers. Take care not to leave the wire too taut. Finally, wind the spare ends back round the wire.

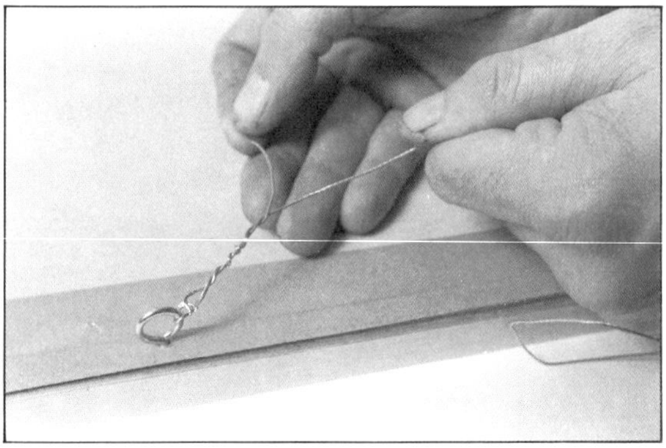

PROFESSIONAL METHOD

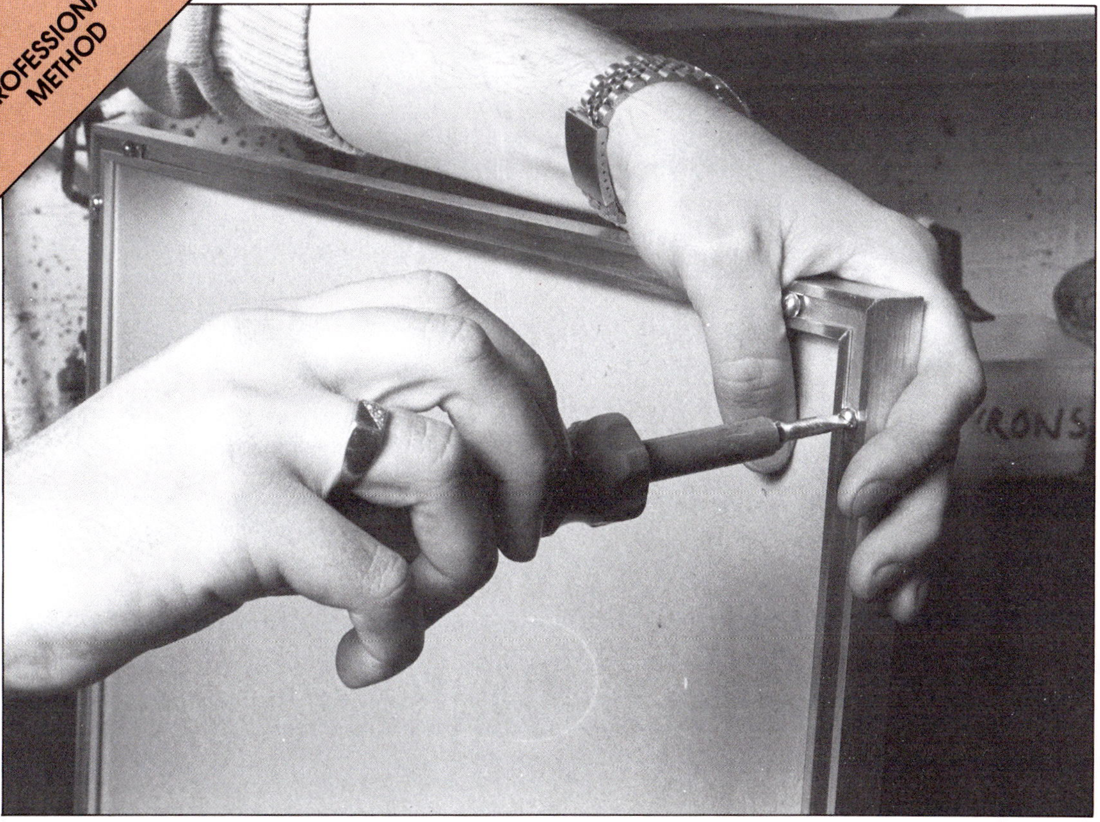

1

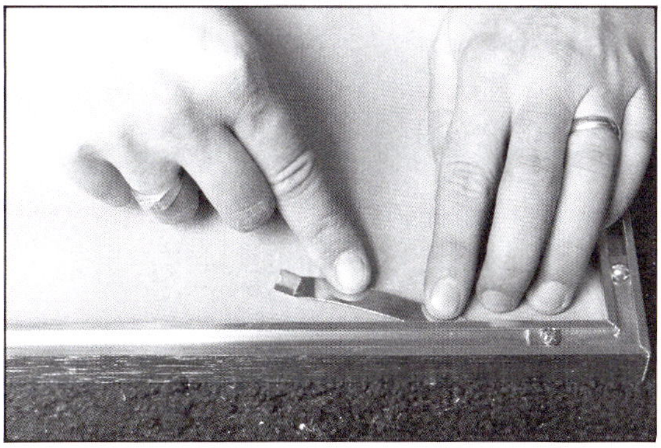

2

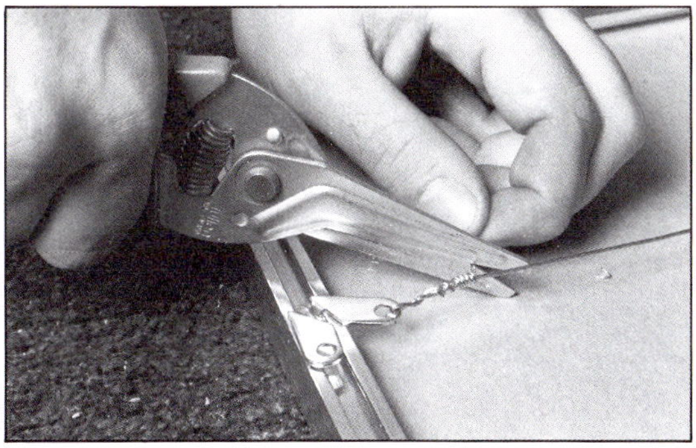

3

Assembling an aluminium frame

1 *Chevrons are placed on either end of the top strip of the frame and screwed into place from the back. The two adjoining strips are then inserted into the chevrons and also screwed into place. The picture, backing and glass are then slid into the frame and the final side of the frame screwed into place.*

2 *Springs are inserted between the backing board and the back of the frame towards the corners to keep the picture pressed against the glass.*

3 *Two butterfly clips are inserted into the frame a third of the way down each side of the picture. These are then turned and knocked firmly into place. Wire is then threaded through one butterfly clip and twisted round on itself. Any extra wire is clipped off with a wire cutter. The wire is threaded through the other clip in the same way and the picture is ready for hanging.*

Finishing techniques

Finishing the frame provides an ideal opportunity for experiment. You can transform the bare appearance of builders' moulding in a wide variety of ways by choosing any of the following basic finishing techniques and adapting them to your own personal taste. Remember to bear in mind the type of artpiece you are framing when deciding on the finish.

APPLYING GESSO

To create a perfect finish, it is advisable to treat the wood surface with gesso before painting or gilding it. This prevents paint or size from sinking into it and also provides a fine, smooth surface on which to apply the final touches.

Gesso is a fine white powder, rather like plaster of Paris, and is available from art shops (full instructions are provided with the product). Work the white gesso powder into rabbit-skin glue to a thin, milk-like consistency; brush onto the surface and allow to dry. Apply a second coat and, when it is dry, lightly rub it down to achieve a completely smooth finish.

GILDING WITH REAL GOLD LEAF

Gilding is the technique of placing a fine film of gold over a surface. Real gold leaf comes in the form of 'leaves' in a booklet and covers a gesso-treated surface best. Gold leaf is so fine that its final colour can be affected by the colour of the surface beneath it. Traditionally, therefore, before applying the gold leaf, the gesso base is given a coat of red bole, a red clay pigment that gives a rich, warm look to the gold finish.

There are two main methods of gilding with real gold leaf: water gilding and oil gilding.

Water Gilding

Used to achieve a high-gloss finish, ideally, you should be taught this method by a professional and even then a great deal of practice is needed to attain perfection. However, it is still a fruitful field for experiment by the more determined home framer.

Gesso and bole are applied to the wooden frame, which is then coated with water, and, finally, gold leaf. The leaf is then burnished to achieve the

Rabbit skin glue
Gesso can be bought ready-made, but if you want to make your own you must first bind the gesso powder by mixing it with rabbit skin glue. The glue is bought in granules or sheets and should be soaked in water overnight. Mix one part soaked glue to nine parts cold water, and gently heat the mixture in a double boiler. Add the gesso powder, usually referred to as gilders' whiting, until it has a creamy white consistency. Sieve out any lumps or strain through muslin.

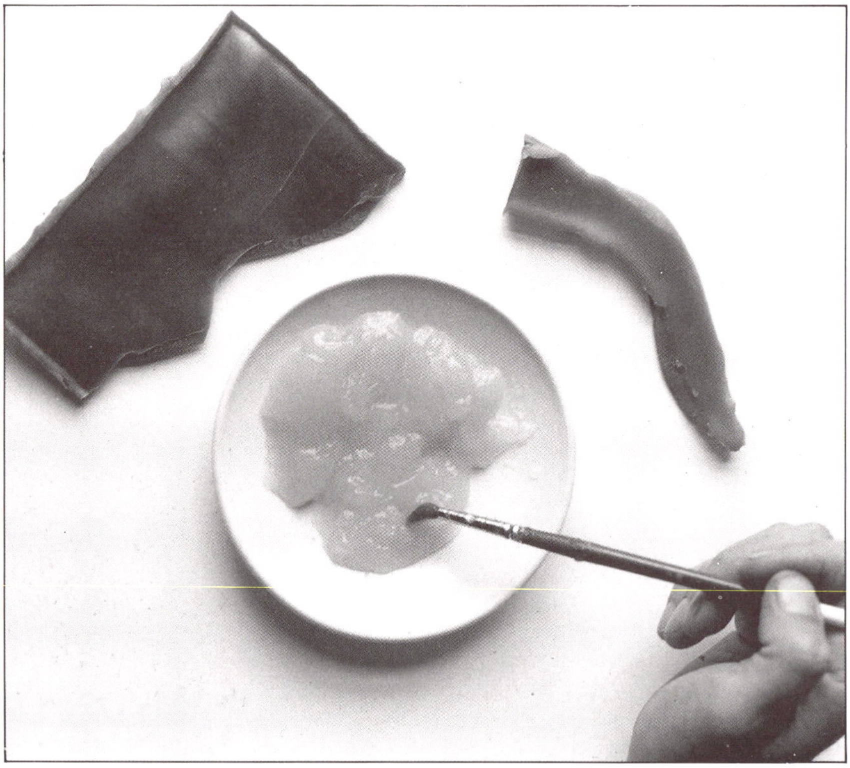

1

2

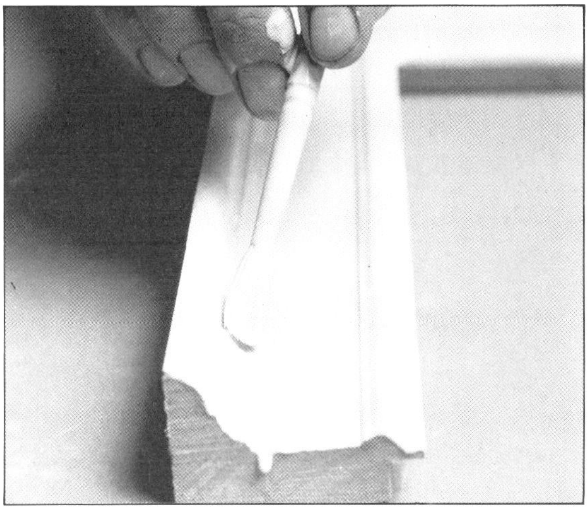

3

Applying gesso
1 *First seal the wooden frame with a weak solution of rabbit skin glue and water.*
2 *Apply the first coat of gesso.*
3 *As soon as this has dried, rub it down with fine sandpaper, or wet and dry. To build up a smooth gesso base, repeat this procedure up to six times.*

Building up gesso
1 *When the final coat of gesso has dried, rub it down to an extremely fine finish with wet and dry. At this stage you can actually wet the wet and dry. (Had you tried this at an earlier stage it would have dissolved the gesso and taken you back to the bare wood.)*
2 *Use a sculpting tool to remove excess build up of gesso in the corners of the frame.*
3 *The gesso coat should be perfectly smooth before adding the final finish.*

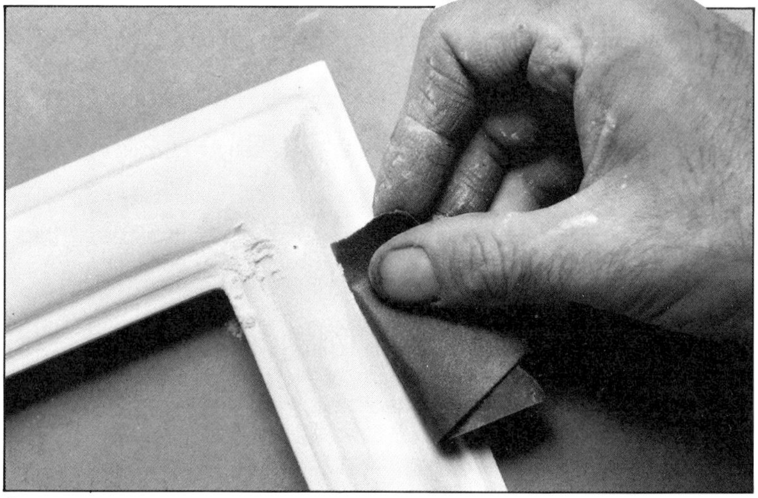
1

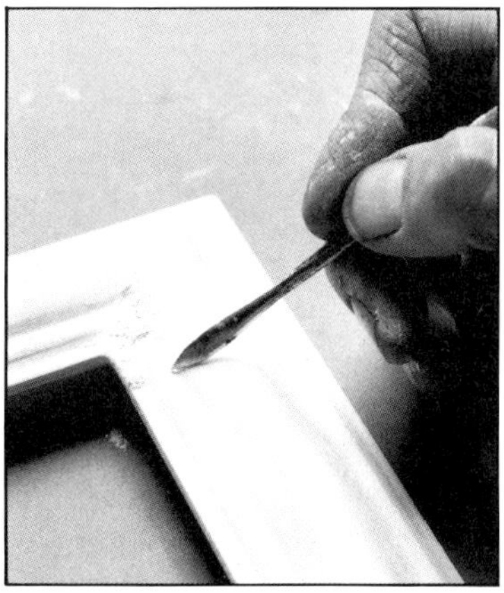
2

3

Applying bole
Before gilding, apply two or three coats of bole (left). *Apply the first coat very thinly* (below). *Allow each coat to dry before rubbing down with fine sandpaper.*

classic shine associated with gilded frames.

First apply the coats of hard gloss, that is, gesso that has been mixed with a large amount of glue to a hard consistency: two coats of hard gesso are usually sufficient. Then apply up to four coats of soft gesso, and sandpaper or glass-paper them finely. Now apply up to four coats of bole and rub down the surface with glass-paper to achieve an absolutely smooth finish. With a soft mop brush apply water containing a small amount of gelatine or methylated spirits and then place the gold leaf in position straight away. Finally, burnish the leaf, using a gilders' burnisher. If the burnisher cannot reach the small indentations in the more intricately moulded or carved frames, leave them matt; this adds to the richness of the finish by producing a variety of tone.

Oil Gilding

For oil gilding there is no need to apply the first coats of hard gesso and you can brush an ordinary coat of paint instead of the bole directly onto the gesso, ignoring the colour aspect altogether.

Oil gilding requires a non-absorbent surface and a coating of shellac glue is required to completely seal the surface. If you do not wish to use bole but do wish to achieve something of the earth-red colour which is such a good base for gold leaf, red colourant can be added to the shellac glue before it is applied. Ordinary red oil paint can also be used in this way. For silver leaf, black or yellow ochre are good colours to use for the base instead of red.

The surface must be slightly sticky before applying the sheets of gold leaf. This is achieved by coating the surface with gold size, a mixture of oil varnish and a drying agent, designed to provide exactly the right degree of 'tackiness', and obtainable from picture framers' supply shops.

SIMPLE GILDING

The alternatives to real gold leaf do not provide such an effective gilded finish but they are less expensive and simpler to apply.

Transfer Gold Leaf

All that is needed prior to positioning the transfer is to give the gessoed frame a coat of thin Venetian red acrylic paint. Then simply lay the transfer gold leaf on the surface and rub over it firmly with your fingers before stripping off the backing.

Metallic Powders

Apply straight onto the tacky surface; again a ground colour is desirable to give a rich sheen. Metallic powders are not suitable for large areas as they tend to look thin and insubstantial. After applying a powder, a coat of varnish is necessary to prevent it from being rubbed off the surface.

Wax Gilding

Again, there is no need for either gesso or bole. Simply apply an undercoat of paint to the wooden frame. Then make your own 'gilt' by mixing wax with metallic powder and rub this over the completely dry painting frame. Polish with a soft rag.

Gold or Silver Paint

Paint cannot usually be used to create the impression of gilding, although it can be useful occasionally for touching up small areas of gilding.

Wax gilding
Mixed wax and metallic powder is applied with a brush over an orange undercoat (left). *It can also be applied with the finger* (below). *The proportion of wax to powder depends on the density of the metal finish required. Pre-mixed metallic wax is also available.*

Transfer gilding

Before applying transfer gilding, make sure that the surface has been coated with gold size. It is important that this has dried to the right degree of tackiness to ensure that the gold adheres properly to the surface. Different types have different setting times, so follow the manufacturers' instructions.

1 *Transfer gold comes in sheets on a paper backing.*

2 *Position a sheet on the frame.*

3,4 *Press it down lightly with the finger. Use a tool if you have to push it into a grooved molding.*

5 *Carefully remove the paper backing. Repeat this procedure until the required area is covered. Traditionally, red-brown bole is used as a base for gold, and black bole for silver. After applying the transfer gold, protect it with a coat of lacquer.*

1

2

4

3

5

Water gilding

You will need a gilders' pad and knife, a badger brush and a thin solution of rabbit skin glue and water.

1 *Cut the gold leaf on the pad with the knife to the required size. This requires practice, as the leaf is very flimsy and tends to waft in the slightest draught.*

2 *Create static on a badger brush by rubbing it gently on the skin or hair, and pick up the leaf with it.*

3 *Place the water solution carefully on the area to be gilded, and brush into place.*

4 *The framer has used red lacquer to complete the design.*

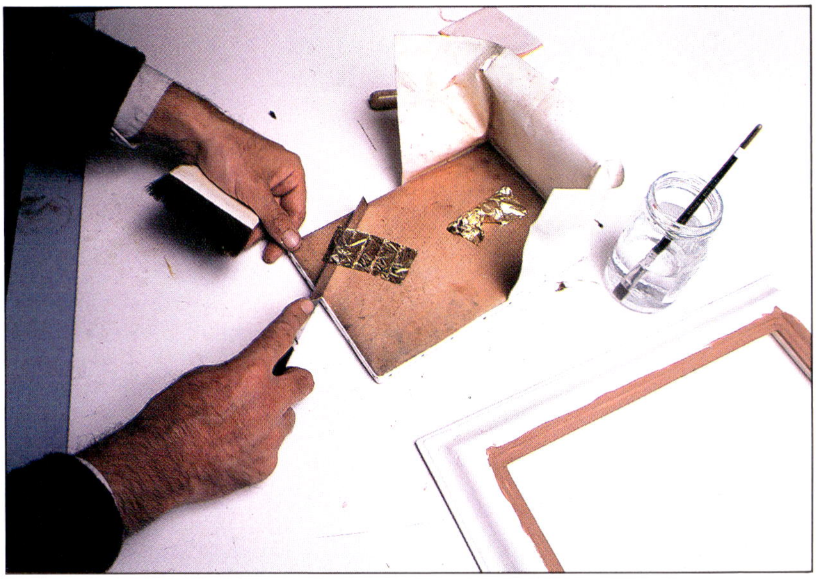

1

2

3

4

STAINING

Staining enhances rather than hides the natural patterns of the wood grain. Hardwoods take the stain particulary well, as their close-grained nature aids the even application of the dye. Softwoods are not so suitable for staining and should be well sanded beforehand.

Many colours of wood dye are available and they can be mixed to give further subtle shades. Stains used to be restricted to the more natural-looking colours but nowadays bright colours, too, are available.

Stains can be oil based or water based and care should be taken not to mix the two. Wood dye can be evenly spread with a soft brush, although it is often best to apply the dye with very fine steel wool, using rubber gloves to protect your hands. It is often easier to dye the separate pieces of moulding before assembling the frame. Rub the wood with turpentine before staining to remove any oil or grease marks.

WAXING

Natural or stained wood should be sealed to preserve its colour. The most natural-looking method of achieving this is to use wax. After the wood has been lightly rubbed down with a fine sandpaper, apply white polish, beeswax or ordinary household wax polish. Then buff the wax to give a sheen.

VARNISHING

A varnish provides a tough, hard-wearing finish but never gives quite the same professional look as wax

Antiquing silver transfer leaf
A silver transfer leaf frame can be antiqued with black staining wax—the type used on furniture. Rub it in with a rag, wait a few minutes, and then buff it up lightly to achieve a polished finish.

The same treatment can be used effectively on other finishes, including watercolour or gouache.

or polish. Varnishes are available in gloss, matt or semi-gloss; the high-gloss varnishes, however, can look shiny and synthetic and are probably best suited to bright and modern subjects.

ANTIQUE GLAZING

One way to give a frame an older look is to coat the frame with a subdued coloured glaze. This can be done over a plain colour or over a decorative painted effect.

Antique glaze can be purchased ready-made but it is simple to make: just add linseed oil, turpentine or white spirit and a drying agent to the oil colour chosen. Artists' oil paints provide a wide choice of colours, and earth pigments, such as raw or burnt umber or raw sienna, are popular because of their natural mature look but if you are antiquing a metal surface, plain black functions well as the basic glaze colour.

When you have mixed the glaze, apply it evenly over the frame: the brush should follow the direction of the wood grain. Then wipe off the glaze with a cloth, taking care not to wipe it away completely but to leave traces in the cracks and corners. This can be made permanent by giving the frame a coat of varnish when it is dry.

Oil-based glazes take a long time to dry, possibly a few days. Water-based tinted washes dry more quickly and can be made easily: tint very thin emulsion with watercolour or acrylic paint.

ANTIQUE SPATTERING

Antique spattering produces a freckled, mature look. The neutral colours that are used with glazes are best suited to this technique, although greys and black can alsolook attractive; use an antique glaze or Indian ink. Spattering can also be effective in toning down a too-bright under-colour.

Dip the stiff bristles of a brush into the glaze, paint or ink and spatter it unevenly over the frame by drawing your thumb over the top of the brush so that tiny spots of paint are flicked onto the surface. If the spatter is applied too evenly it looks like a mechanical paint finish, so make sure to keep the pattern random. If the finished effect looks rather stark, rub it down with a little steel wool when it is dry.

When the spattered frame is dry, add a coat of varnish to protect it. A high-gloss finish is not suitable for a frame that you wish to look old, so use matt or semi-matt varnish.

APPLYING FLAT PAINTS

Acrylic paints give a quick-drying and convenient basic coat, which can be left plain or waxed, or can be varnished or embellished with oil- or water-based paints.

Acrylics allow you to begin with a grey or neutral tone to which you can add subtle shades of a brighter colour to give a slightly warmer or cooler effect. To achieve this, mix a little of the colour to the grey

Scumbling
Apply a flat, oil-based undercoat. Here light grey is being used with brown and blue mottling. You can work with bought scumble glaze or make your own from artists' oil paint, linseed oil and turpentine. Using the lightest glaze and a soft bristle brush, stipple the surface in order to achieve an even but broken colour (left). *Then apply a darker tone of scumble with a smaller brush* (below left), *aiming for a linear, veined effect. The finished frame is shown beside a darker version made with a dark grey undercoat and a light scumble glaze* (below right).

acrylic base and apply it as one coat; or apply a coat of flat grey acrylic paint and, after it has dried, apply a top coat of very diluted paint so that the grey shows through a translucent layer of colour.

Oil-based paints can also be used as finishes but take longer to dry. Modern high-gloss or 'wet-look' paints are more suited to a modern picture or frame. They are most effective as a finish when used with a light undercoat or gesso surface, which is lightly sanded. If gesso is not being used, coat the wood with wood primer before applying an oil-based paint.

Spray paints and enamels give a really professional-looking finish, free of any tell-tale brush marks around the mitred corners. They are particularly effective when applied to a surface that has been primed with gesso. They can be applied directly onto a well-sanded base of acrylic or latex emulsion but should not be used on an oil-based undercoat.

SCUMBLING

Best suited to plain, flat, angular frames, scumbling is a quicker way of achieving a marbling effect, although it does not have the same quality of finish. It consists of a flat undercoat, with more than one tone of scumble glaze on top applied with a circular motion of the brush. Mix scumble glaze from artists' oil paint, linseed oil and turpentine – to give it its 'glaze' or transparent quality. Alternatively, buy it ready-made in a variety of colours.

MARBLING

Like tortoiseshelling, marbling is done not to deceive the eye into thinking that it is seeing real marble but to produce a beautiful pattern based on the subtle markings of marble – it is a visual association rather than an exact replica. Again, it is a technique suited to plain, flat, angular frames rather than ornate mouldings, on which it would be impossible to create this style because of the number of ridges.

Paint an all-over glaze, made from white spirit and artists' oil paint, over the surface. Paint the veins of the marbling pattern onto this in short, jerky strokes, rolling and flicking the brush to give an impression of the actual seams in the stone. Before the veins are dry, blur them very thoroughly with a dry brush. Then go over it again, using the same colours and painting a few better defined veins onto the blurred background. This is surprisingly simple and effective and, providing that you use fairly

1

2

3

Marbling
1 *Starting with a cream ground, apply a loose ochre glaze. Use a smaller brush to rough in veins of dark brown.*
2 *Ruffle and blend the wet surface with crumpled newspaper. Soften the surface with a dry brush.*
3 *With a small artists' brush, add veins in blue and sepia glaze. Soften these with a broad brush or a feather.*
4 *Apply unsoftened, fine white veins with the tip of the feather to cross the existing pattern.*

4

Types of marble
Terra verde or green marble (above left) *is made by applying green and white glazes over a black base. White marble* (centre left) *is created by painting thin black and grey veins over a white base. Golden marble* (below left) *is built up from ochre, sepia, blue and white glazes over cream.*

Pattern and texture

1 *The framer is applying his own mixture of wax and black stain with a cloth to create a pattern.*
2 *A motif has been etched into the gesso base and decorated with a water-based paint and gold wax.*
3 *This frame was made from a piece of flat timber, which was coated with gesso and decorated with gold leaf and blue lacquer.*
4 *In this frame, a dark blue lacquer and gold motifs were used in a similar way.*

1

2

3

4

neutral colours without too much tonal contrast, it will produce a fine marble effect that will not intrude too much upon the picture.

TEXTURING

A textured finish is best suited to simple frames. A texture can be scratched into a paint surface to soften the effects of an austere frame without detracting from its simplicity. The traditional craftsman's method is to scratch or carve out a pattern on a gesso ground. A more practical and quicker way is to use a vinyl paint as the base.

Apply a thick coat of vinyl paint to the frame and texture it when the paint is partially dry so that it will be stiff enough to hold its shape and preserve the patterns you make. A simple, linear texture effected with a metal comb, a stiff brush or any other sharp implement can make an intriguing textured surface, turning a commonplace frame into an unusual one. Once you have created the textured surface, paint it any colour you wish.

WOOD-GRAINING

Wood-graining is a traditional technique, the object of which is not to produce a finish that looks exactly like wood but to produce a frank replica of a wood-grain pattern with paint. A coat of paint is applied, a glaze added and then wood-grain marks made on this. It is not necessary to confine yourself to 'woody' colours — some of the most exciting modern grain has been created in colours which were never seen in any natural habitat.

Start off by applying a coat of flat colour. This should be lighter than the glaze and, ideally, there should not be too much contrast between the two as the effect will be too stark. Use ordinary undercoat, or matt or eggshell emulsion for the first coat; gloss and enamel paints should not be used.

You can either buy the glaze and then tint it with a stainer — a strong, transparent liquid colour — or you can make your own, using the same method as for making antiquing glaze but with any colour. Brush a thin glaze of colour over the dry, undercoated surface, using a small decorator's brush, about the size of one normally used to paint a window-frame.

While the glaze is still wet, drag a brush with slightly spaced bristles across the surface to create hair-like streaks. Now flick a special grainers' brush — a soft brush known as a 'flogger' and available from specialist art shops — evenly over the surface to give a blurred effect.

TORTOISESHELLING

Tortoiseshelling gives a frame a luxurious finish, creating an unusual and special-looking effect. Care should be taken, however, not to overdo it because tortoiseshelling is essentially a paint finish

Wood-graining
There are two methods of wood-graining. In the first (right), *medium oak scumble glaze applied on top of a pale, wood-coloured undercoat. Both are specially available for wood-graining. While the glaze is wet, it is combed with a rubber comb. The combed ridges are then smoothed out diagonally with a soft brush to create a softer line. In the second* (far right, above), *a paint glaze is brushed on freely and combed. Knots are touched in with a fingertip and then strengthened with an artists' brush. In the third method* (far right, below), *a soft dragger is used to create a mahogany pattern in wet, red-brown paint.*

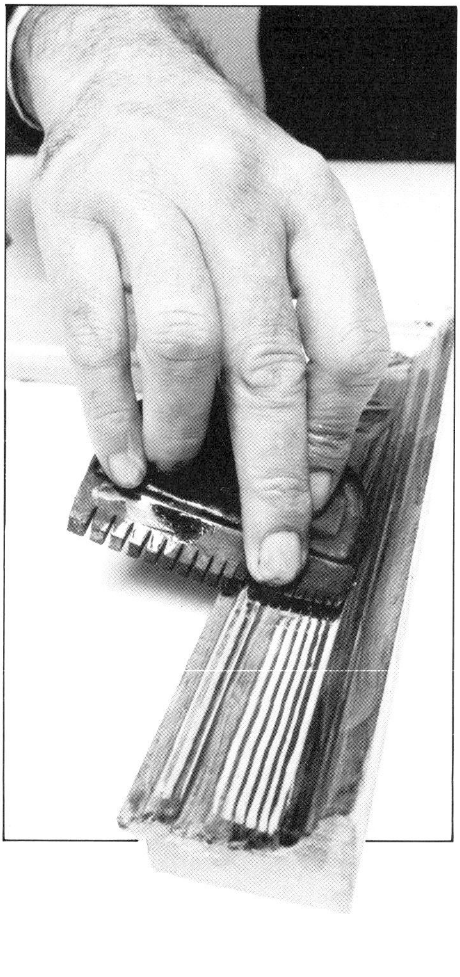

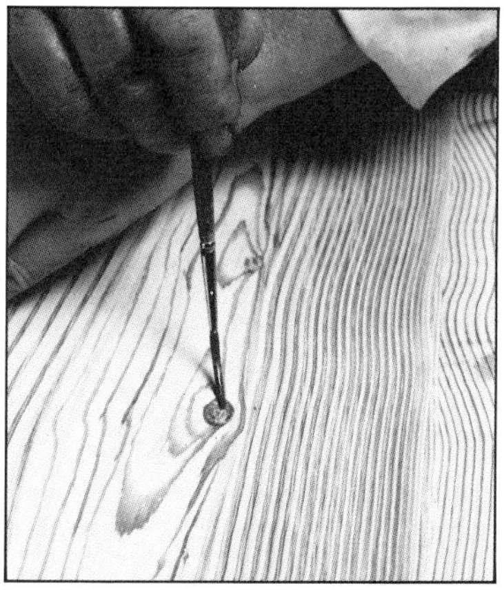

Golden tortoiseshell
1 *On a cream undercoat, apply tinted varnish in short, irregular strokes. Indian red blobs are also put on with a small decorators' brush.*
2 *Blend these in long, smooth strokes.*
3 *Apply blobs of Indian red and burnt sienna and work these in lightly with an artists' brush.*
4 *Blend these with a swift, crossing stroke. Finally, soften the whole surface by criss-crossing lightly with a wide, dry brush.*

1

2

3

4

– a frankly fake, exotic production, which can look overwhelming if it covers a very large area.

The tortoiseshell pattern is based on the polished pieces of tortoiseshell that show the internal seams of organic growth and feature them as a pattern. Originally, tortoiseshelling was applied mainly to small articles, such as combs, hairbrushes and dressing table mirrors, but it is now a popular paint finish for many surfaces, especially the surfaces of small items of furniture and picture frames. Study the style carefully and decide which of the varieties you require. They range from very dark to what is often referred to as blond tortoiseshell and the finished effect can be of blobs of spreading colour or, alternatively, of streaks.

The darkest styles of tortoiseshelling include one which is very distinctive and rich-looking. It was used a great deal on Colonial-style furniture and is usually recognizable by its bold, dark streaks – often black or bronze – running over a mellow red background. Blond tortoiseshelling is effected over a light-coloured background, which may be metallic – using gold or silver. Fawn or light brown is usually used for the streaks.

Use a smooth, oil-based paint for the initial ground on which the pattern is to be based. The ground colour should be of a lighter tone than that of the required finish because the varnish and streaks will darken it. The key to successful tortoiseshelling is to work the design into the varnish while it is still wet, spreading successive layers of paint into patterns by lightly brushing diagonally in opposite directions with a dry brush. Use oil-based paints, such as artists' oil colours, for the streaks.

The Practice of Framing

Project 1: Framing a poster

Project 2: Framing a watercolour

Project 3: Framing an oil painting

Project 4: Framing a collection of photographs

Project 5: Framing a manuscript

Project 6: Framing a piece of needlework

Project 7: Framing the three-dimensional

Project 8: Restoring a gilded frame

Care and repair

THE PROJECTS

PROJECT 1

Framing a poster

This is a simple project—a poster is clipped beneath a sheet of glass, which can be purchased ready-cut, to an ordinary piece of chipboard. However, deterioration will develop unless steps are taken to strengthen this heavy artpiece and to preserve the poster from damage due to contact with the chipboard. To overcome these problems, a backing is provided for the poster and wooden battens are fixed to the edges of the chipboard. Screw clips can then be fixed to the battens rather than the chipboard, which is not really suitable for this, making the artpiece more secure and, at the same time, giving a more professional look to the piece.

Materials and Equipment

- Poster
- Wooden batten, 6mm (¼in) wide
- Chipboard
- Ruler
- Craft knife
- Pencil
- Tenon saw
- Mitre box
- Hammer
- Resin glue
- Regular panel pins
- Small panel pins
- Cardboard
- Clips
- Bradawl
- Short screws, 9mm (⅜in) long
- Cut and smoothed glass, 2mm (½in) or 3mm (⅛in) thick
- Screwdriver
- Screw-eyes or D-rings
- Strong wire or cord

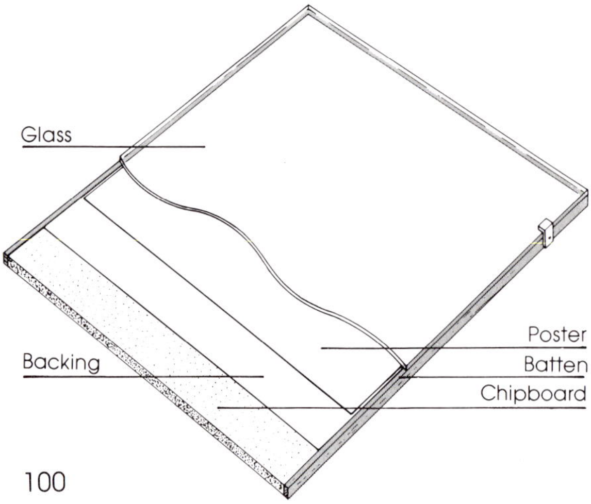

1 Select a length of wooden batten, 6mm (¼in) wide, and a piece of ordinary chipboard. Measure the post to be framed and cut the chipboard to the same size minus 12mm (½in) in both height and width to account for the width of the batten.

2 Cut each piece of batten to a length which is 12mm (½in) longer than the corresponding side of chipboard. Then, using a mitre box, cut the corners of the frame in the battens. Using ordinary resin glue, fix the battens around the edges of the chipboard and nail them together with panel pins.

3 Glue and nail a piece of batten across the back of the chipboard, using small, 12mm (½in) panel pins to avoid penetrating the front of the board. It is from this batten that the artpiece will be hung on the wall, so place it one third of the way down from the top of the chipboard to hide the hanging-wire.

4 From cardboard, cut a piece of backing to the size of the poster. This will be placed between the poster and the chipboard to prevent damage being caused to the poster by the rough texture of the chipboard. The backing also lends a firmness to the final fitting and presents a smooth resting place for the poster.

5 You are now ready to fix glass, poster, backing and chipboard with clips. Sprung-steel emu clips are simple and popular but, for extra strength, a hardware or brass-fitting store can supply clips of the type shown here in brass, stainless steel, or the less noticeable Perspex, which we have chosen.

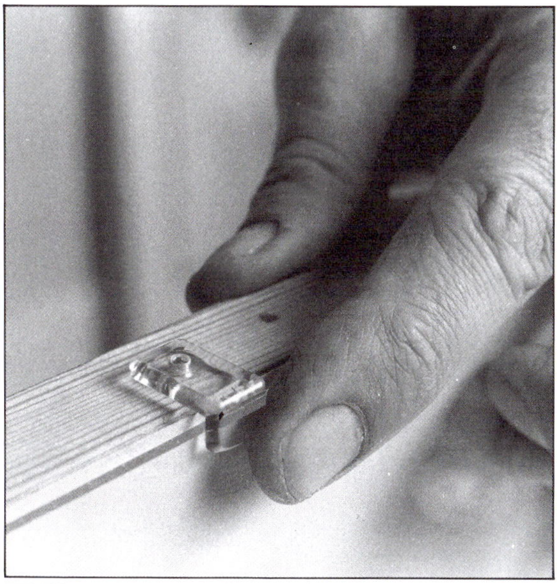

6 Position each clip carefully. Place two clips on the top, two on the bottom, and three on each side to hold the poster and glass securely. Make sure the clips are a few inches away from the corners and are neatly opposite each other. Their positions can now be marked with a bradawl.

7 To make holes for the screws that will fix the clips, hold the bradawl firmly but do not push and twist too hard. Only small holes need be made, as the best type of screw for fixing clips is a short, 9mm (3/8in) one.

8 The component parts are now ready for assembling. Place the chipboard on a flat surface. Lay the backing board on top, then the poster, and finally the glass. Purchase glass either 2mm($^1/_{12}$in) or 3mm ($^1/_8$in) thick but avoid anything thicker. Ask the glazier to smooth off the edges, or smooth them yourself with fine glass-paper.

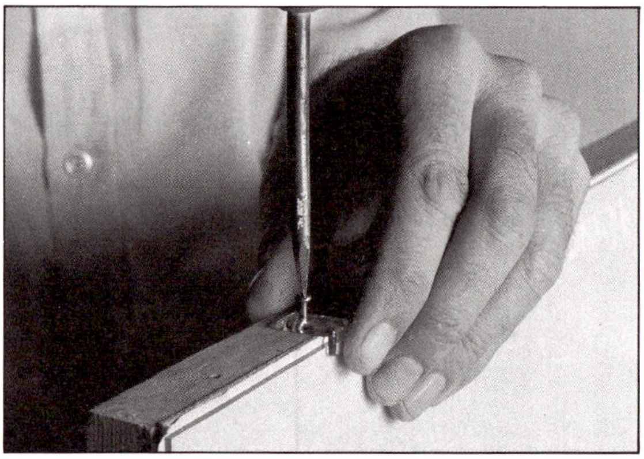

9 Screw the clips into the wooden battens round the edges of the chipboard, using a small screwdriver. You will probably find it easiest to start the screws while the assembled poster and board are lying flat on the work-table. They can then be finished firmly, with the poster upright if necessary.

10 Lay the framed poster face down. Fasten two screw-eyes, or D-rings, to the batten across the back of the chipboard. To make hanging easier, keep these spaced wide apart. Run a strong wire or cord through each eye and fasten it so that it is fairly taut; knot it firmly. You may find it better to use the wire or cord doubled.

MAN RAY

PROJECT 2

Framing a watercolour

1 To frame this large watercolour, it was decided to use a deep, white mount, with two inner slip mounts, in colours matching those in the painting.

The delicate lines and washes of a watercolour usually require a mount to set them off best. Moreover, watercolours are normally framed behind glass, which helps to preserve them, and the mount acts as a fixture to prevent the watercolour being pressed too tightly against the glass.

Materials and Equipment

- Point-driver (optional)
- Nails
- Hammer
- Gummed tape
- Hardboard offcuts for corner pieces
- Bradawl
- Corner clamps
- Screwdriver
- Screw eyes for wall-hanging
- Brass picture-frame wire
- Pliers
- Ruler
- Hard, sharp pencil
- Craft knife or scalpel
- Thick, white mount card
- Thin, coloured mount card
- Aluminium-plated wooden moulding
- Saw
- Mitre box
- Woodwork glue
- Heavy-duty cardboard
- Glass, 2mm ($\frac{1}{12}$in) thick

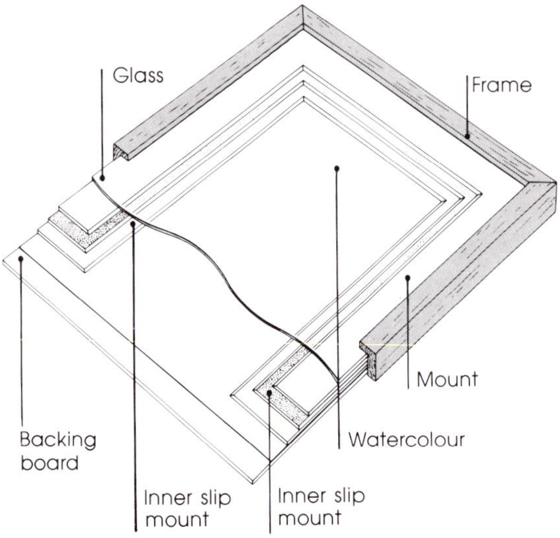

2 Measure with even more care than usual when making slip mounts, as even a slight error is easily noticeable in a multi-mount. Slip mounts are usually the same width all round, while the outside mount is deeper at the bottom than on the other three sides to ensure that the picture sits up well in the frame. Cut the mounts and windows.

3 Measure the perimeter of the outer mount and cut a metal frame, mitring the corners in the usual way. You can obtain solid metal frames, which must be cut with a hacksaw, but the frame we chose was essentially wooden, with a coating of light aluminium, which enabled us to cut it with an ordinary saw. Glue the pieces together; do not nail the pieces in this case – nails would make the metal look untidy. Cut a piece of cardboard, measured to fit inside the frame, for the backing board.

4 Turn the frame over and fit the pre-cut glass into the rebate. Next insert the triple mount, then the watercolour and finally the backing board. To hold this large frame together, a point-driver was used to tack the components together. Position the point-driver right up against the inside wooden part of the frame.

5 Holding the machine down firmly on the backing board, pull the trigger and shoot a diamond-tack into the side of the frame. If you do not have a point-driver, tack the nails sideways into the inside of the frame.

6 It will now be necessary to stick the gummed tape to the edges of the backing board and the back of the frame to reinforce the structure and keep out the dust. Wet strips of ordinary gummed brown paper tape.

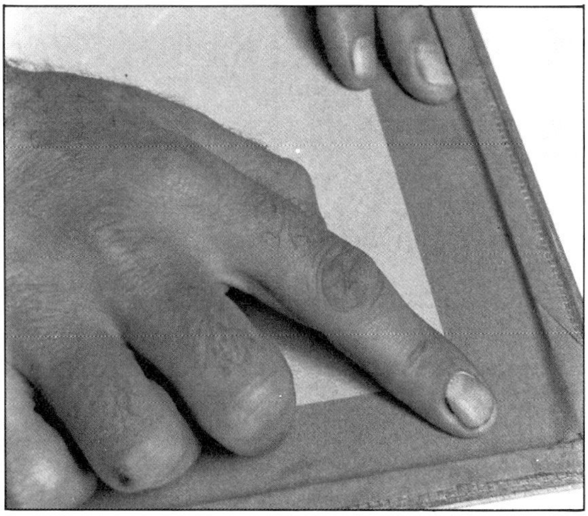

7 Press the tape into place, working slowly and carefully to ensure that no possible space is left for dust to enter. Take extra care when pressing the tape into the corners.

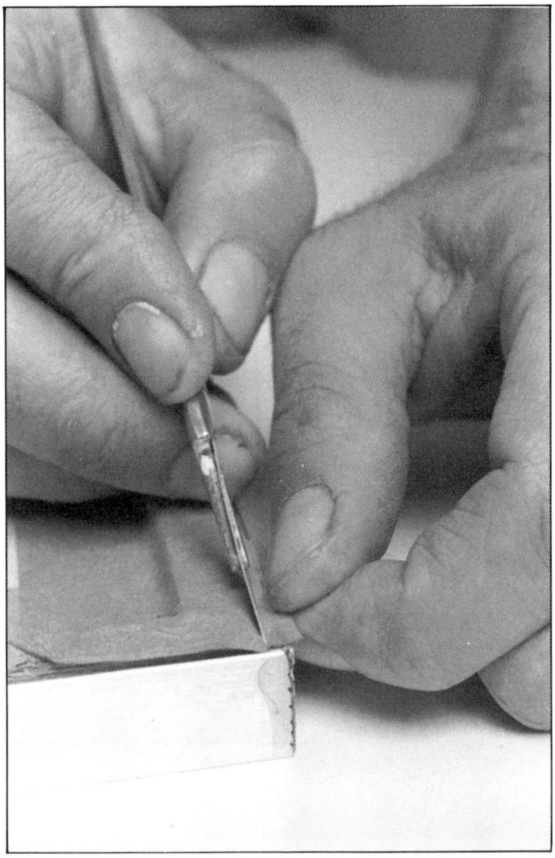

8 Trim off any excess tape with a scalpel. The back of the frame should now be thoroughly sealed. This is very important, as watercolours can be spoiled easily by dust and dirt.

9 To strengthen the corner joins, which were not nailed, as this is a metal frame, we made corner pieces from hardboard. You can also buy ready-made corner pieces in a variety of metals, if you wish.

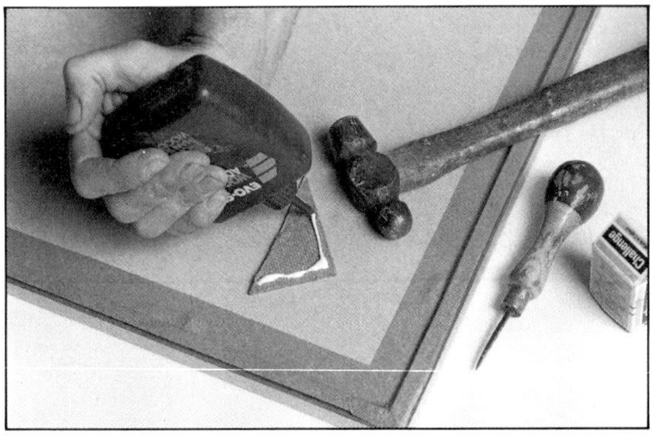

10 The corner pieces are first glued and then nailed into place. Run strips of glue along the edges of the corner pieces. Try not to use too much glue as this might cause slippage.

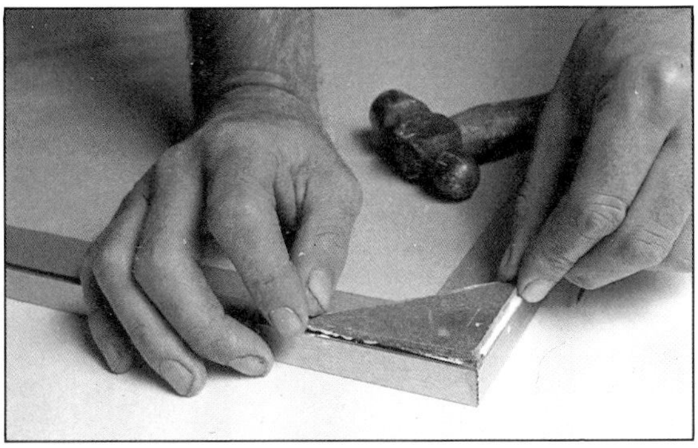

11 Place the corner pieces into position with extreme care; make sure they are not visible from the front of the frame. Glue into place, then wait for the glue to harden.

12 Using a bradawl, make holes in the back of the frame for nailing the corners. A steady hand pressure is essential to ensure that you do not damage the frame. Tap in the nails.

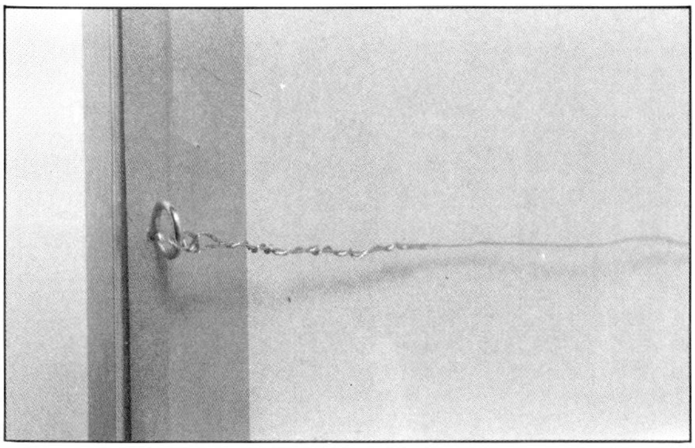

13 We used special brass picture-framing wire, obtainable from art shops, for this project, to bear the weight of the artpiece. Run the wire through one of the eyes and knot it. Tighten the knot with pliers and then wire and knot the other end, taking care not to leave the wire too taut. Wind the spare ends back around the wire.

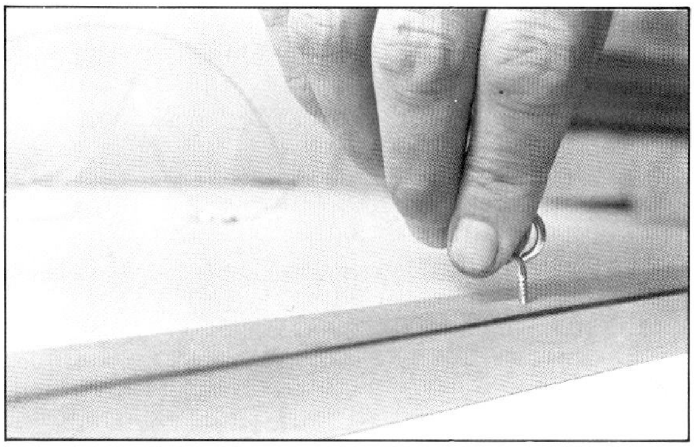

14 A bradawl should be used to make holes in the back of the metal frame for hanging. Position the holes about a third of the way down the picture, one on either side, and screw in screw eyes.

15 The framing is now complete. Without dominating the picture, the slip mounts lead the eye into the watercolour and enhance the pale washes that were used in the painting.

PROJECT 3

Framing an oil painting

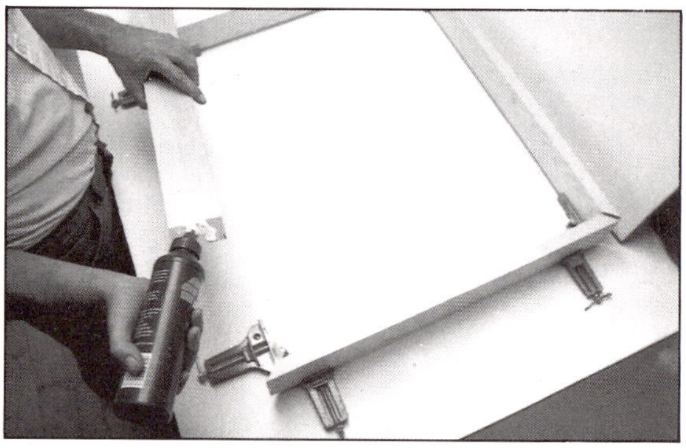

I We chose pinewood, 50mm (2in) by 25mm (1in), generally available from builders' merchants, for the main frame. When measuring for oil painting frames, remember that the canvas on the stretcher is often slightly misshapen, so allow a tiny extra margin. After cutting and mitring, glue the corners and clamp them together.

This modern, dramatic oil painting stares boldly from the canvas. The wintry image is flat and graphic, and we therefore decided to use a deep box frame, painted a stark plain black to highlight the dramatic nature of the picture. We decided not to place the painting under glass; it is generally not necessary to glaze oil paintings.

Materials and equipment

Pine moulding, 50mm (2in) by 25mm (1in)
Hard, sharp pencil
Ruler
Saw
Mitre box
Woodwork glue
Corner clamps
Corner clips (optional)
Pliers
Nails
Hammer
Wooden quadrant
Tape
Bradawl
Punch
Fine surface filler
Sandpaper
Grey undercoat paint
Black enamel spray paint
Paintbrush
Steel tacks
Brass plate wall-fastenings
Brass screws
Screwdriver

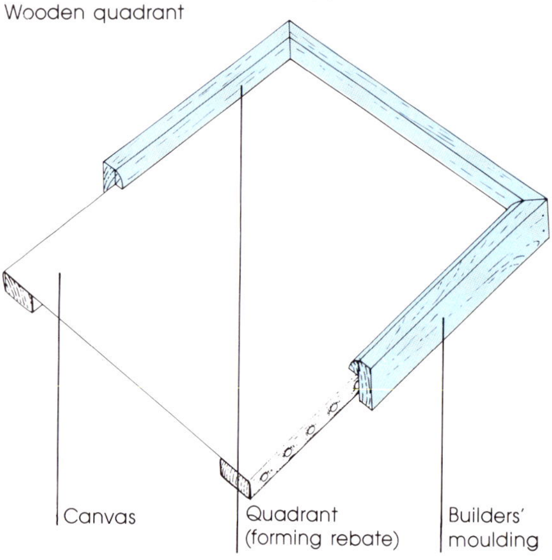

2 This is a deep frame and the clamps are holding it firmly together at the bottom. However, there is no clamping pressure on the top and we used special sprung-steel clips to rectify this.

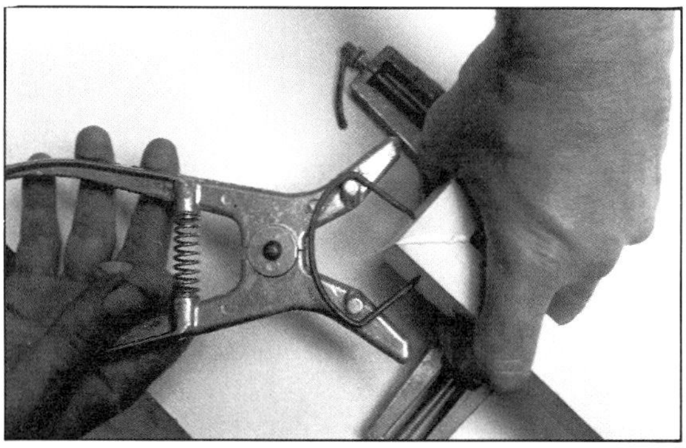

3 To fit the clips, special pliers are required to pull them apart. Position the pliers around the top of one corner, as shown, and release them, allowing the clip to spring into place.

4 Fit clips similarly on each corner, so that the frame is firmly held by clamps and clips. If you do not have special clips, tie string round the frame as a temporary measure. Then tap in nails to secure the corners, using a punch to tap them just below the surface.

5 Allow the time specified by the manufacturer for the glue to dry, before releasing the clamps and clips.

6 The wooden frame should fit snugly around the canvas. A rebate is now fitted to cover the edges of the canvas, giving a neater and more professional look and stopping the canvas from slipping out through the front. A wooden quadrant was chosen to make the rebate. Mitre the quadrant and place the strip onto the front of the frame, so that you can measure the lengths required. Mark off each corner and cut to size.

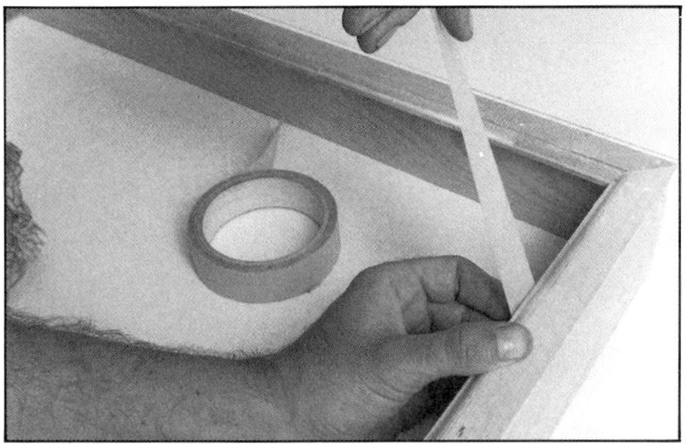

7 Glue the rebate strips into place. Bind strips of tape around the quadrant and frame to hold it in place, and wait for the glue to set.

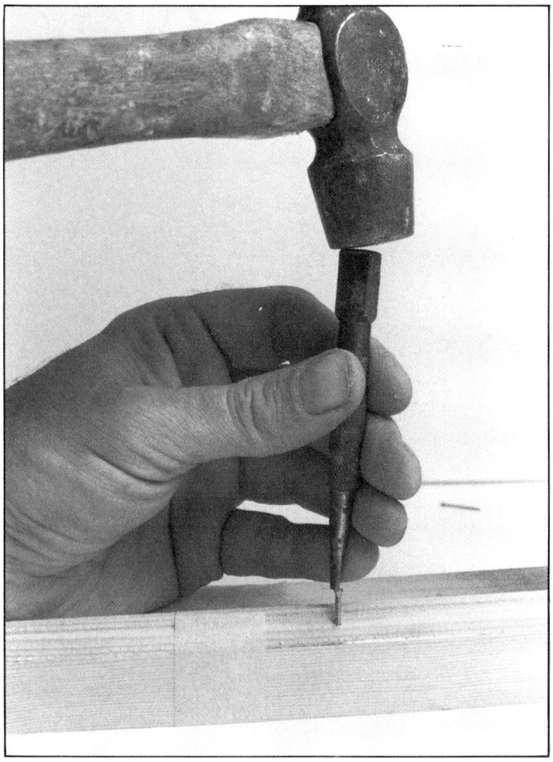

8 This solid, deep frame will stand upright without difficulty, and it is therefore easy to work holes into the quadrant and frame with a hand-held bradawl. Tap in the nails and sink them below the surface with a punch.

9 Fill in the nail holes with fine surface filler, obtainable from most hardware stores. At the same time fill in the holes made in the corners of the main frame. Then rub down the filler with sandpaper.

10 Brush a grey undercoat onto the completed frame, applying two coats. Sand this down. Then spray thinly with black enamel paint. Allow this to dry and then rub down gently with fine steel wool. Spray on several coats in this way, until you have achieved the finish you require.

11 The components are now ready for assembly. You will need a bradawl, hammer and steel tacks. Make sure that you have a flat, uncluttered surface on which to lay the frame for final fitting.

12 Fit the canvas into the main frame, easing it up tight against the rebate. Check that it fits snugly before nailing. Then, using a hand-held bradawl, make the holes in the inside of the frame. Nail steel tacks sideways into the frame to hold the painting in place.

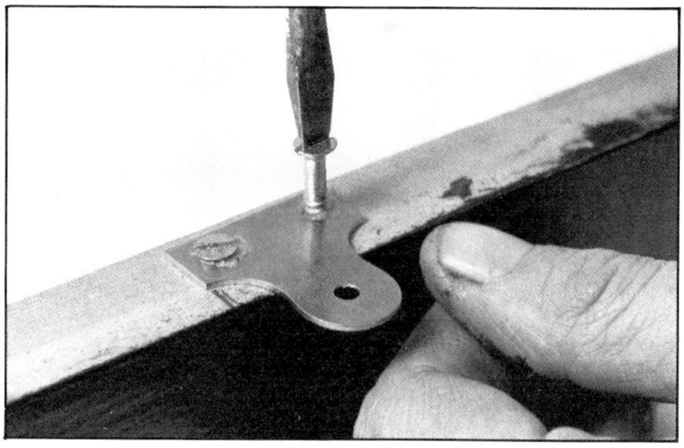

13 It was decided to fit the frame against the wall instead of hanging it and we selected brass plate fastenings for this, to be fitted to the sides of the frame. Position the plates so that they are exactly opposite each other and mark the holes with a bradawl. Screw on the plates with brass screws.

14 Screw the framed painting in place on the wall. It should sit flat against the wall to enhance the depth of the frame and give emphasis to the window effect of this landscape picture.

PROJECT 4

Framing a collection of photographs

All the people in the photographs to be framed are from the same family, and all the photographs have a definite nineteenth-century flavour. They are therefore ideal candidates for a group mounting – all the photographs mounted within one large frame. By using a single mount with several windows cut into it, a backing board and glass – held in the rebate of a polished wooden frame that is enchanced by a gold slip – vitality and unity is given to what could easily be a collection of scattered photographs.

Materials and Equipment

- Stiff card or hardboard
- Mount card
- Sharp, hard pencil
- Ruler with bevelled edge
- Protractor or set square
- Craft knife
- Gummed paper
- Perspex ruler
- Brown sepia ink
- Gold ink
- Lining pen or felt-tipped pen
- Rebated moulding
- Mitre box
- Saw
- Middle oak woodstain
- Rag
- Woodwork glue
- Clear wax
- Gold slip
- Glass, 2mm (1/12in) thick
- Steel tacks, 25mm (1in) long
- Hammer
- Screwdriver
- Brass screw eyes
- Picture-frame wire

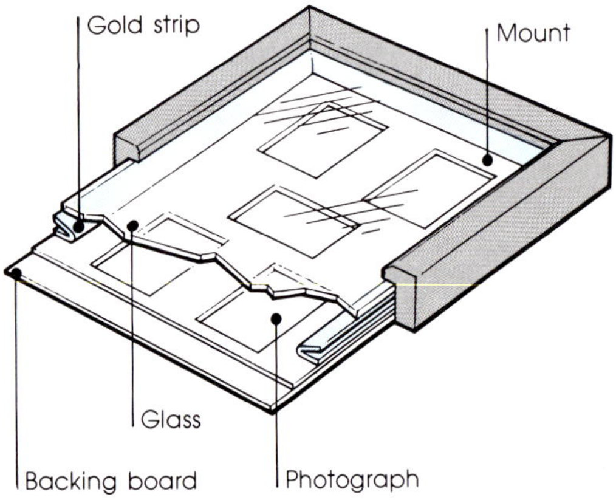

1 Arrange your photographs into a composition: ensure that none looks outwards or away from the group. In our collection, we had four photographs of the same size and one smaller one. It was decided to put the small one in the centre and range the others around it.

2 Use a piece of stiff cardboard – as here – or hardboard to provide a backing. For the mount itself, use mount card. Here, an ivory colour was chosen to give an off-white, subdued paleness, onto which decorative lines could be drawn.

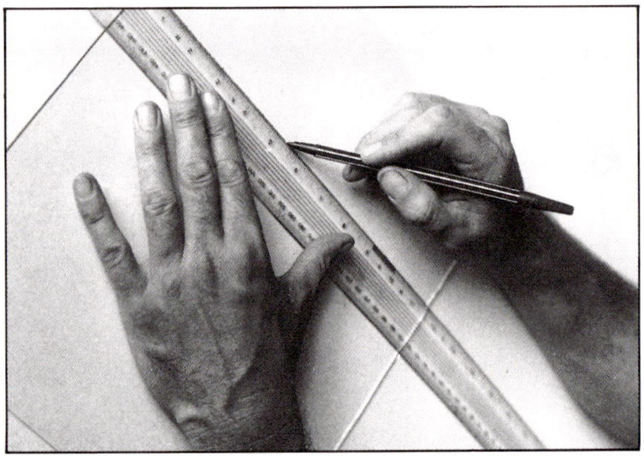

3 Backing board, mount and glass must all be the same size. If you wish to re-use an old frame, measure the height and width of the space within the frame, including the rebate overlap, while the frame is upside down, and cut the board, mount and glass so that they fit snugly into it. Otherwise, determine the size of the mount first, as we have done here, and then cut the frame and mount. Cut the board with a craft knife.

4 Decide where to place the photographs, using your own judgement, but leaving more space at the bottom of the photographs than at the top, so that they sit up high in the mount; we have placed the middle photograph with 150mm (6in) of space above it and 230mm (9in) of space below.

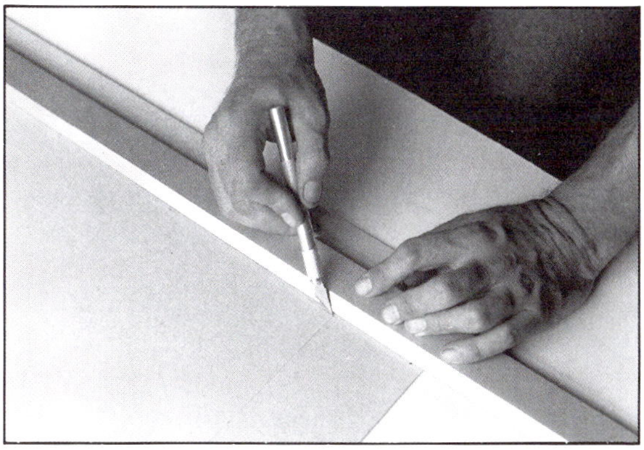

5 Measure each photograph. Subtract about 12mm ($^1/_2$in) from both the height and width measurements to allow for an overlapping margin of mount card – the photo will fit beneath the mount and must be slightly larger than the window, otherwise it will fall out. Lay the mount card flat and measure out the windows. If you are cutting by hand, rule lightly pencilled lines on the front of the mount card before cutting.

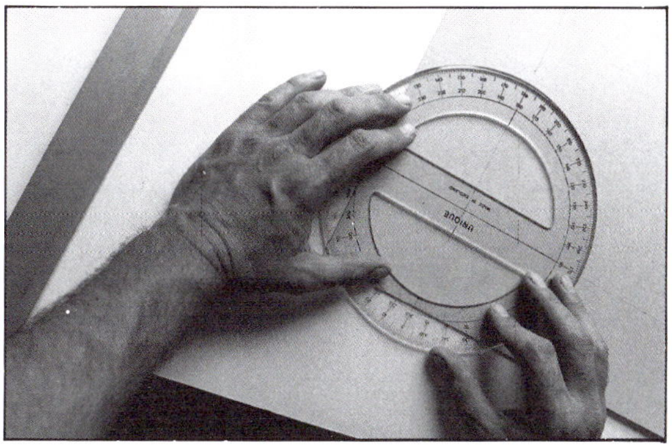

6 Before cutting, check the right angles at the corners of the windows, using a protractor or set square.

7 When cutting the windows, use a straight-edge with a bevelled slope and a rubber tread on the bottom to prevent it from slipping. Lay the straight-edge along the pencilled line on the front of the mount card. Place a craft-knife blade at the top of one line and score a light cut, holding the blade against the bevelled edge to give a sloped window. Run the blade along the line a second or third time until you have cut right through the card. Repeat this process until you have cut out all the windows.

8 Now stick down the photographs. Turn the mount card upside down and lay it flat. Place one photograph face downwards onto its window and stick a piece of tape along one edge of the back of the photograph. Then turn the mount card over to check that the photograph is correctly positioned.

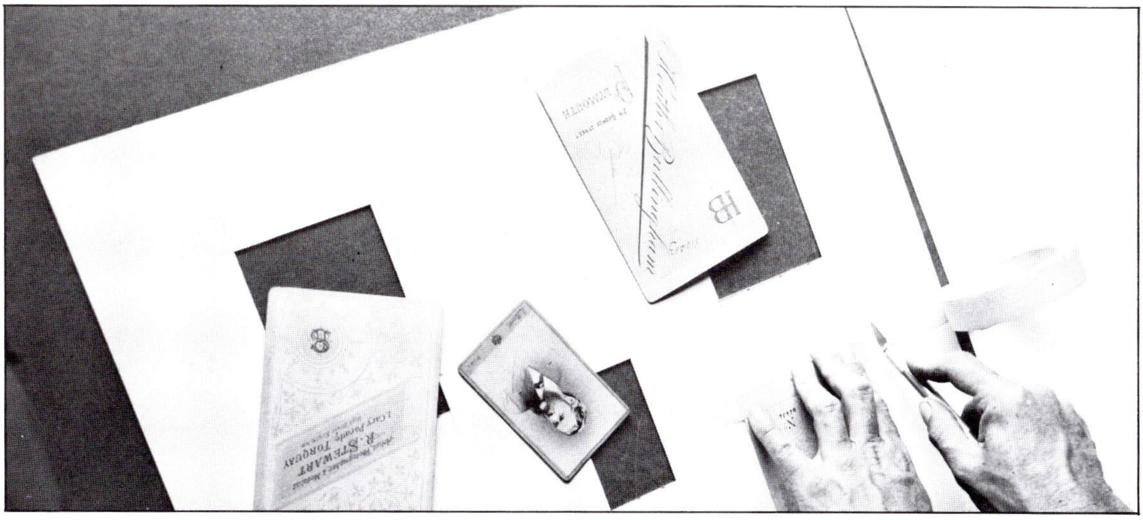

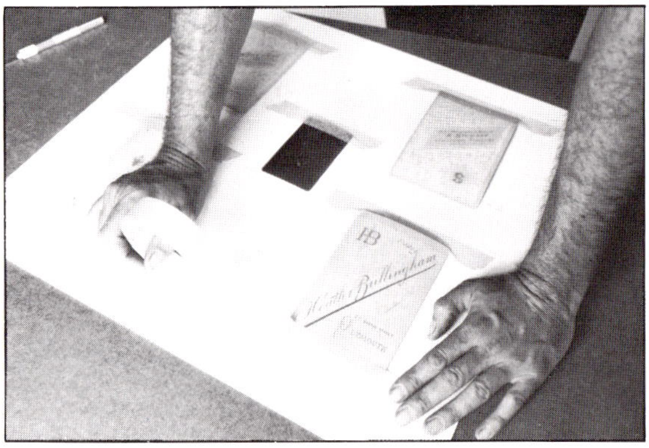

9 Once you are satisfied that the photograph is properly in place, turn the mount card face down again, and apply tape to the other sides of the photograph to secure it. Repeat this procedure with the other photographs.

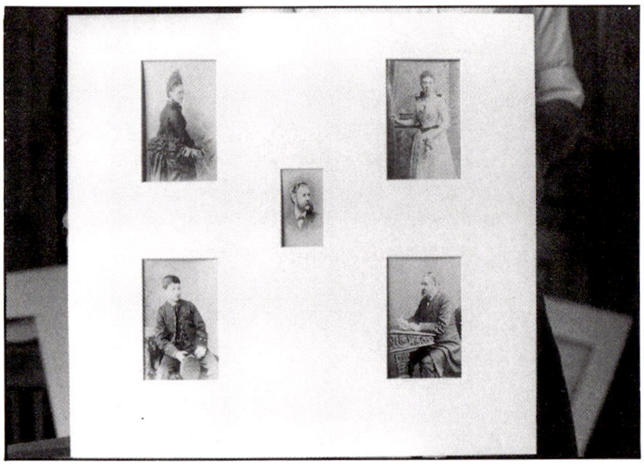

10 Make one final check with all the photographs in place. Notice the final effect, here, of placing the photographs so that they sit high up in the mount-space. The outside photographs have a 50mm (2in) space above them but a 75mm (3in) space below them; and they are arranged symmetrically, with a 12mm (½in) space between each, and a 75mm (3in) space between them and the middle photograph, and a uniform distance from the sides of the mount.

11 Using an ordinary Perspex ruler, draw light lines with a sharp, hard pencil to mark where the decorative lines will fall. Check the right angles with a set square or protractor. It is up to you where you place the lines but avoid spacing them too evenly as this gives a dull effect. We decided to draw three lines around each photograph, one 6mm (¼in) from the edge of the photograph, one 3mm (⅛in) beyond that and a third 15mm (⅝in) beyond that.

12 We used brown sepia ink for the two inner lines and gold ink for the outer one, drawing the lines with a lining pen. Place the rule upside down to avoid smudging the ink. Run the pen along the pencilled line slowly and continuously. Felt-tipped pens can also be used for the lines.

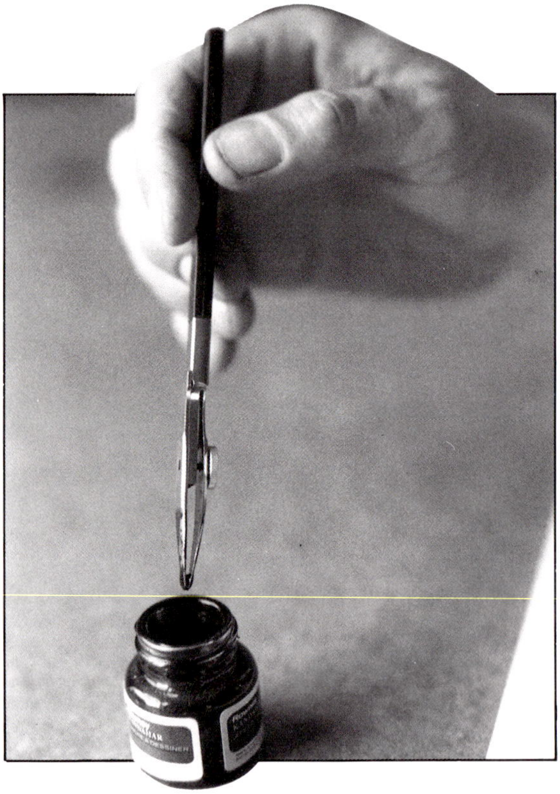

13 For the frame, we used a rebated frame moulding, cut into four pieces and mitred. Before joining, we stained the pieces with middle oak colour, using a rag to spread the stain. After joining, the frame was polished with clear wax.

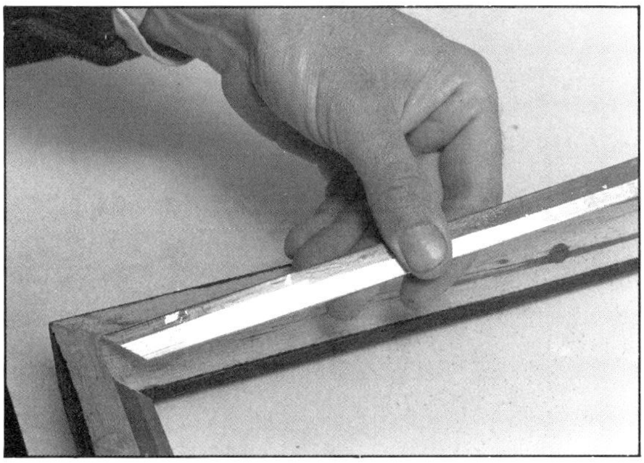

14 Lengths of gold slip add a final touch to the framing. Place a piece along the inside of the back of the frame and measure it by eye, marking it off so that it fits tightly into the rebate. Then mitre the pieces.

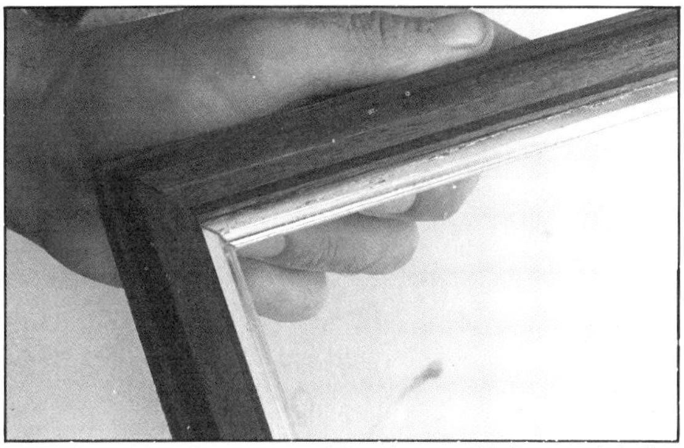

15 Turn the frame upside down. Fit the gold slip snugly into place into the rebate; next fit the glass; then the mount card with the photos; and finally the backing board. Tap 25mm (1in) steel tacks into the frame at an angle so that they hold everything in place against the rebate. There is no need to make holes first with a bradawl as the tacks are extremely sharp.

16 Tape the back along the edges with adhesive paper to keep out the dust. Finally, screw in two brass screw eyes into the back of the moulding, one on each side, a third of the way down the artpiece; run wire through from one side to the other and knot firmly.

PROJECT 5

Framing a manuscript

Manuscripts usually have a serious, grey appearance. They can be brightened up considerably in the framing, without losing their dignity. We decided to use a triple mount for this manuscript, with a red slip included to give a touch of colour. We cut the mounts and windows first in the usual way.

Materials and equipment

- Mount card (red and two tones of grey)
- Hard, sharp pencil
- Ruler
- Scalpel or craft knife
- Pine builders' moulding
- Quadrant
- Woodwork glue
- Nails
- Hammer
- General purpose brush
- Vice or corner clamps
- Mitre box
- Saw
- Panel pins, 25mm (1in) long
- Pigments and shellac
- Pewter wax
- Polishing rag
- Gummed paper
- Bradawl
- Screw eyes
- Wire for wall-hanging
- Pliers

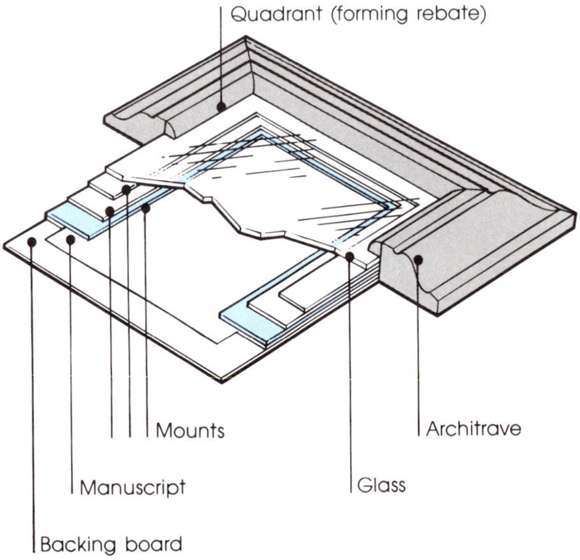

1 Purchase a length of ordinary builders' moulding, or architrave, as it is also known. Professionals may cut a rebate into this with a plough plane but for this project a strip of quadrant was attached to the moulding to make a rebate.

2 Glue the quadrant to the architrave. For extra strength, nail the two pieces together. Cut the finished length into four pieces and mitre in the normal way.

3 As an alternative to corner clamps, a vice can be used for making a main frame. Place one piece of quadrant and architrave firmly in the vice, and apply glue to the end.

4 Adjust the vice to hold another piece against the glued strip. Make a hole ready for a nail, using a bradawl. Hand-held pressure is enough, as this is a piece of soft pine.

5 Check that the glued pieces are held firmly in the vice before nailing the corners. Then hammer in a 25mm (1in) panel pin. One pin in each corner should suffice.

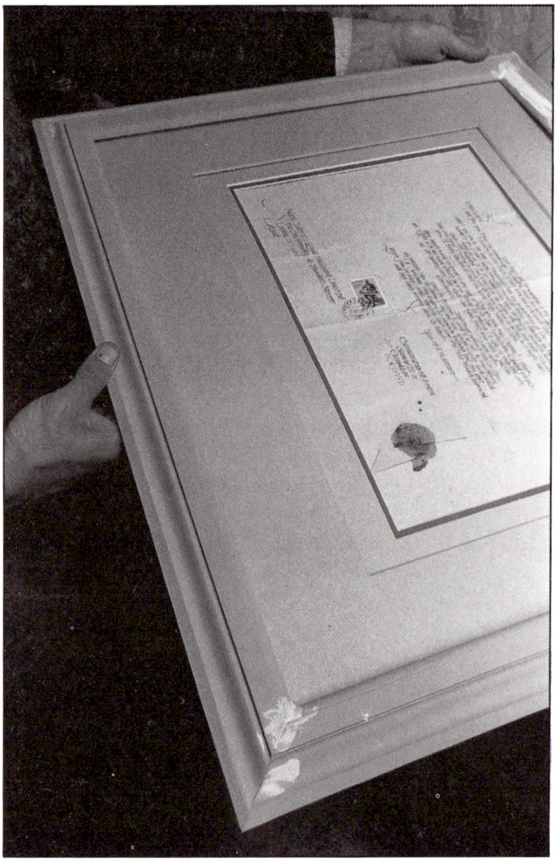

6 When the whole frame has been glued and nailed together, make sure that the mounts fit properly. Assemble the mounts to check, and trim them if necessary. Remove the manuscript and mounts, so that the frame can be decorated.

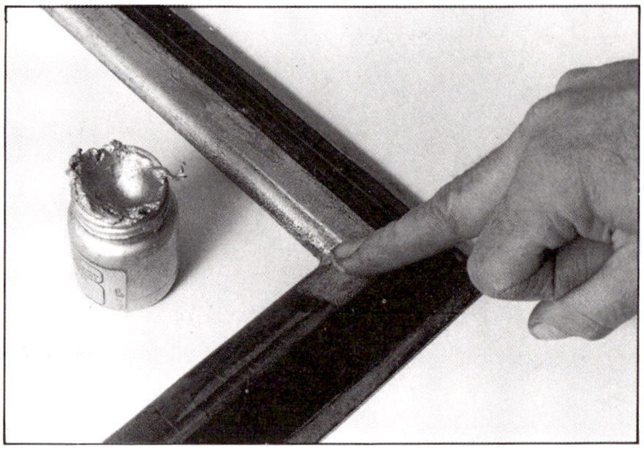

7 We applied a blue-black undercoat, using pigment mixed with shellac. We left a groove in this darker colour to add decorative interest and gave the rest of the frame a pewter wax finish. Ready-made waxes are available in different colours. Apply either with a brush or with the finger. Wait for a few days before polishing, or you will rub off the wax.

8 Assemble the glass, mount, manuscript and backing board and tap nails into the inside edges of the frame to hold the component parts together. Place gummed paper on the back to keep out the dust and attach screw eyes and wire in the usual way for hanging.

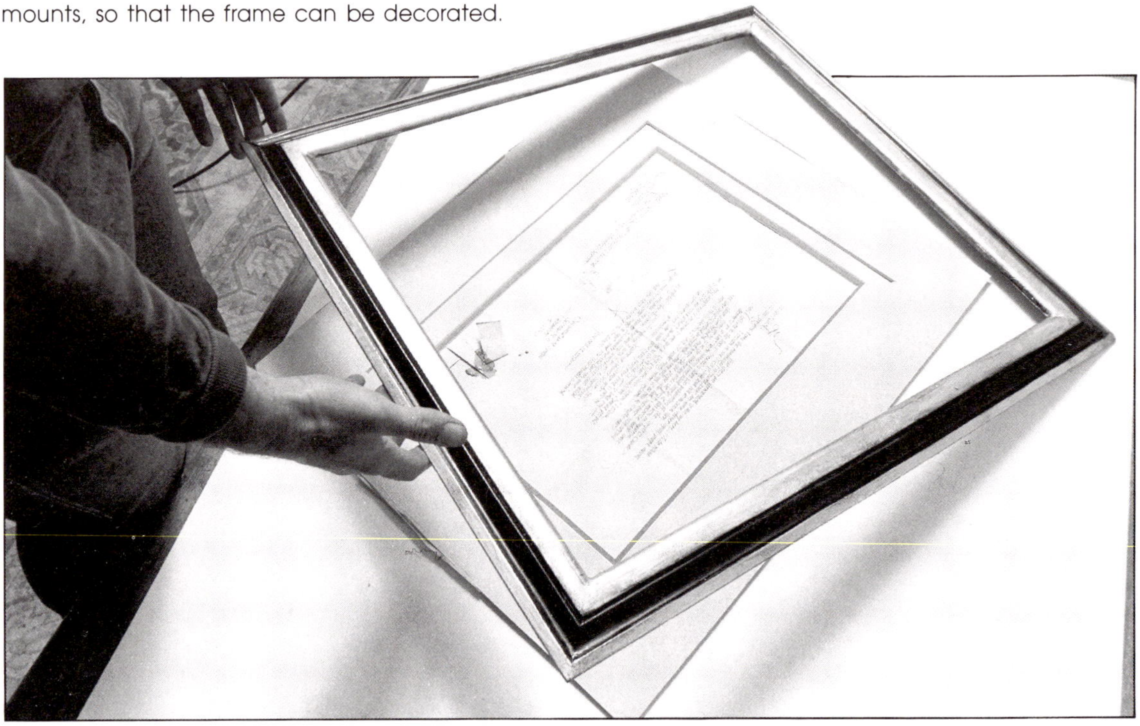

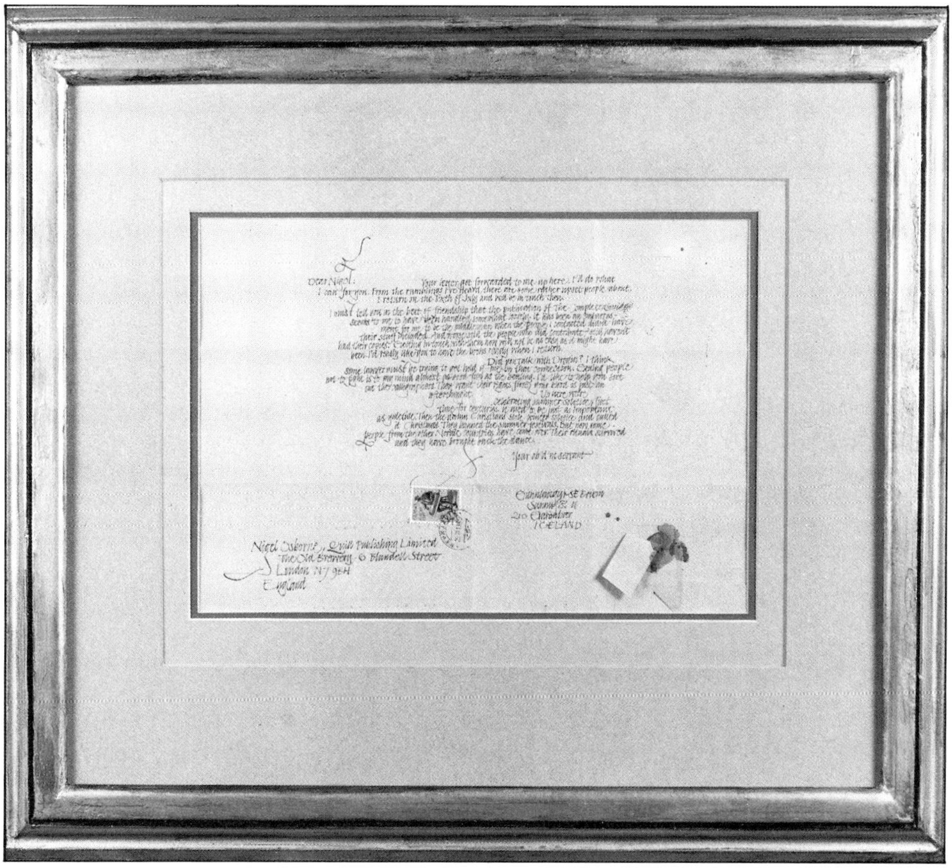
Dear Nigel:
Nigel Osborne, Quill Publishing Limited
The Old Brewery, 6 Blundell Street
London N7 9BH
England
ICELAND

PROJECT 6

Framing a piece of needlework

1 A length of moulding is used for the inner, velvet-covered insert, or slip frame. Make sure that the rebate is deeper than the depth of the stretcher, so that the stretcher will eventually fit right down into the slip frame. Cut and mitre the wood, then spray the pieces with fabric glue.

Needlework is often attached to a stretcher before being framed to give it an extra smartness and tautness. Place the needlework over a stretcher similar to that used for an oil painting, and staple it round the edges.

We framed this piece of embroidery under glass, and it was decided to keep it from contact with the glass in an elegant way by putting a velvet slip frame between the embroidery and the glass.

Materials and equipment

- Battens for stretcher
- Hammer
- Stapler for stretcher
- Moulding with rebate
- Hard, sharp pencil
- Ruler
- Mitre box
- Saw
- Fabric glue
- Velvet
- Scalpel or craft knife
- Mahogany moulding with rebate
- Woodwork glue
- Elwood clamp or corner clamps
- Glass, 2mm ($^{1}/_{12}$in) thick
- Bradawl
- Nails
- Panel pins
- Screw eyes for wall-hanging
- Wire for wall-hanging

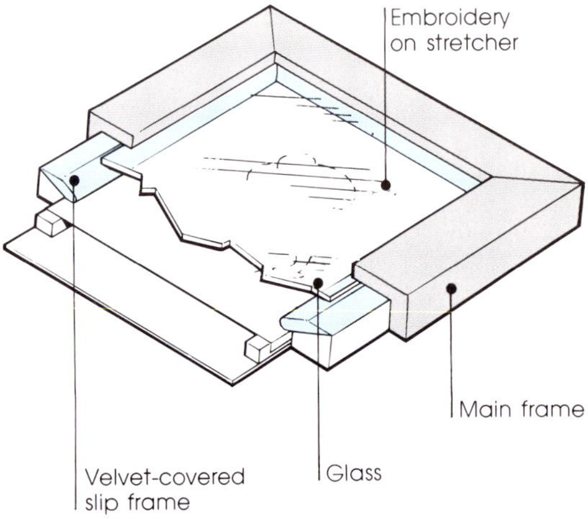

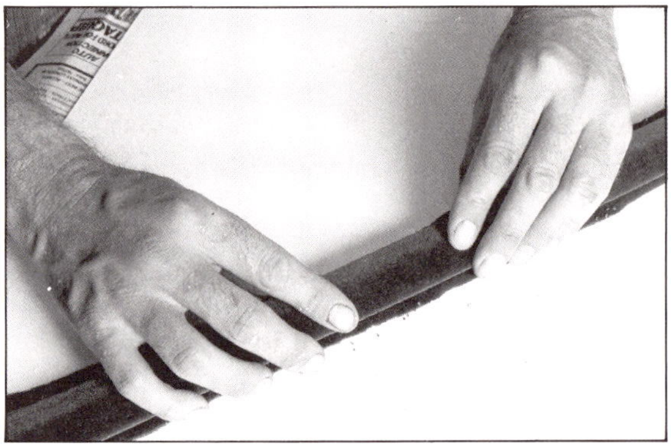

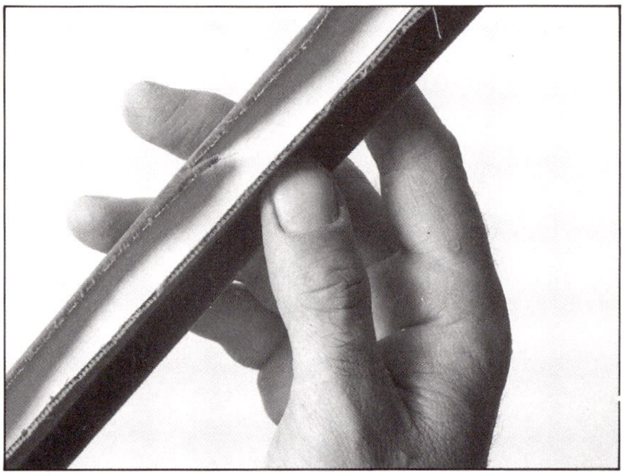

2 With a scalpel cut pieces of velvet large enough to cover the rebate, and front and side of the insert. Wrap each piece of velvet round a glued piece of insert and press home firmly.

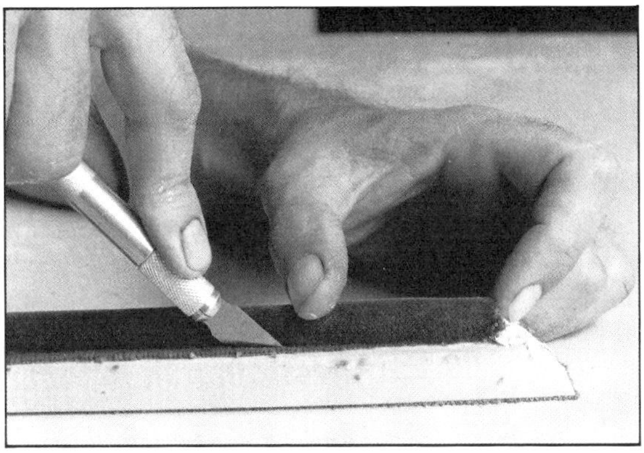

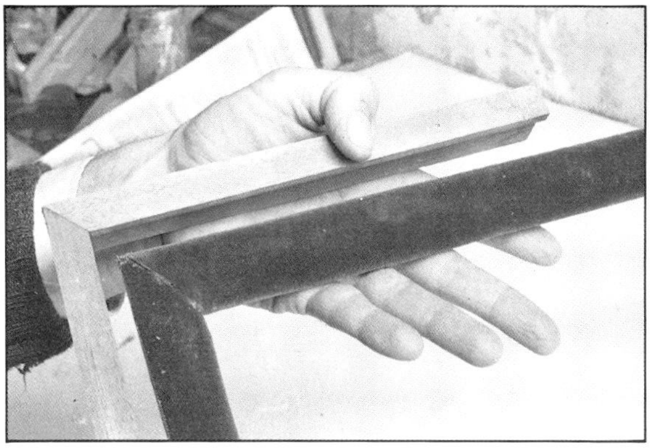

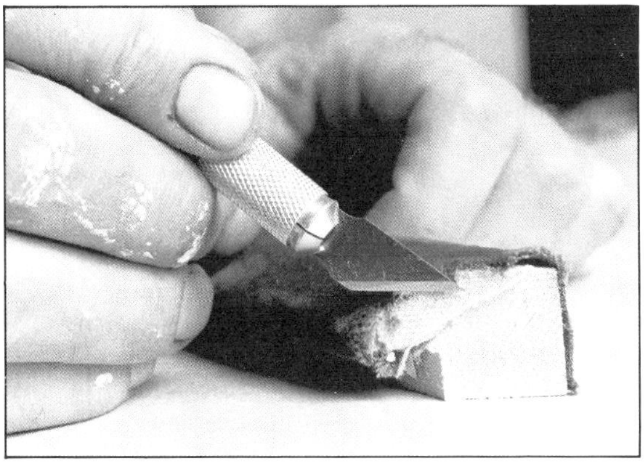

3 Make sure that the velvet covers the insert and rebate except at the back, so that only the velvet will show when the insert is fitted into the main frame. With a scalpel, trim off all the excess velvet from the edges and corners.

4 A length of mahogany moulding was chosen for the main frame. This outer frame, of course, must be deeper than the insert. Cut and mitre the moulding so that the insert will fit snugly into the frame.

5 We used an Elwood clamp for the frame. This clamp consists of four metal corners. The fourth corner has a screw-tightener attached to it and a piece of wire leading from it.

6 Apply glue to the mitred ends of the moulding, and stick together. Fit the corners of the Elwood clamp onto the corners of the frame and run the wire around the whole frame, making sure it sits in the grooves provided for it in the metal corners. Then fasten the wire in the screw-tightener and tighten it up just enough to ensure that the glued corners will be stuck firmly. Wait for the glue to dry and then nail the corners. Make the slip frame in the same way.

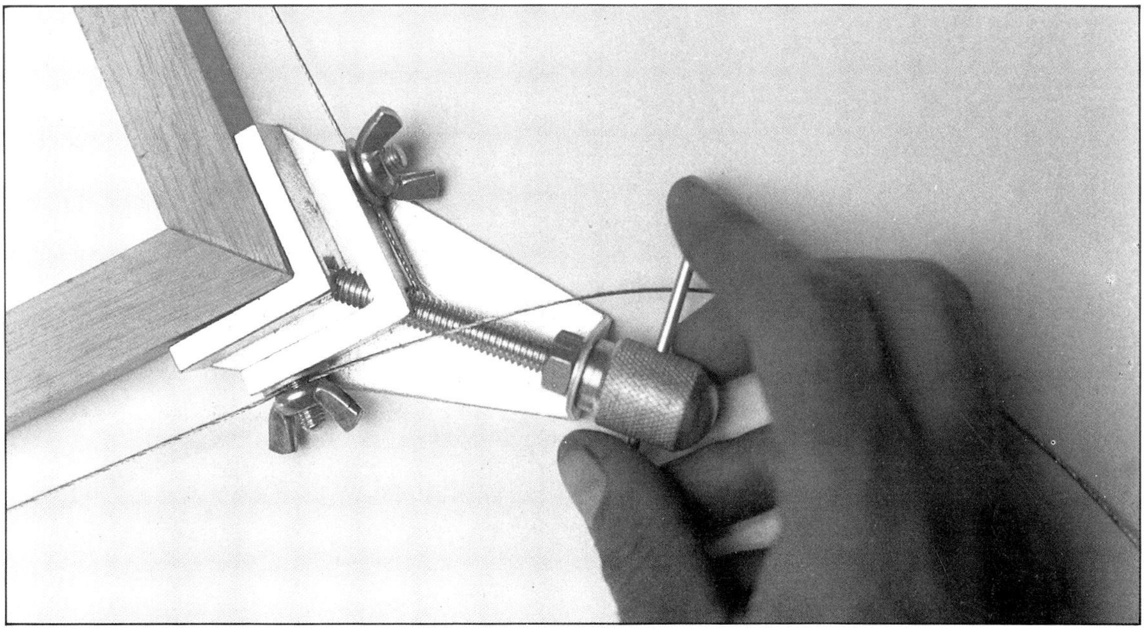

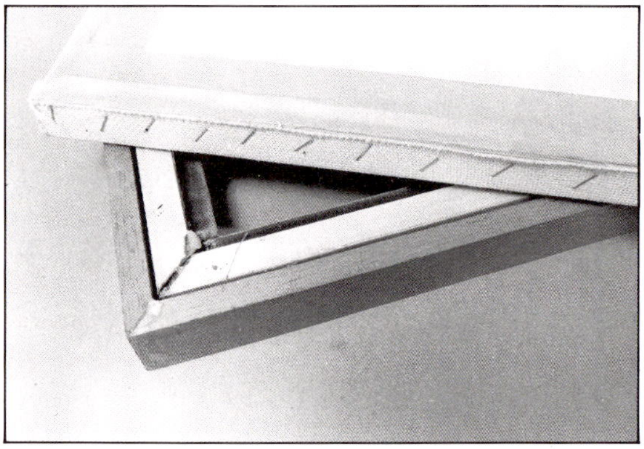

7 The components are now ready for assembly. Lay the main frame face down. Fit a piece of glass into its rebate and then fit the slip frame into the back of the main frame.

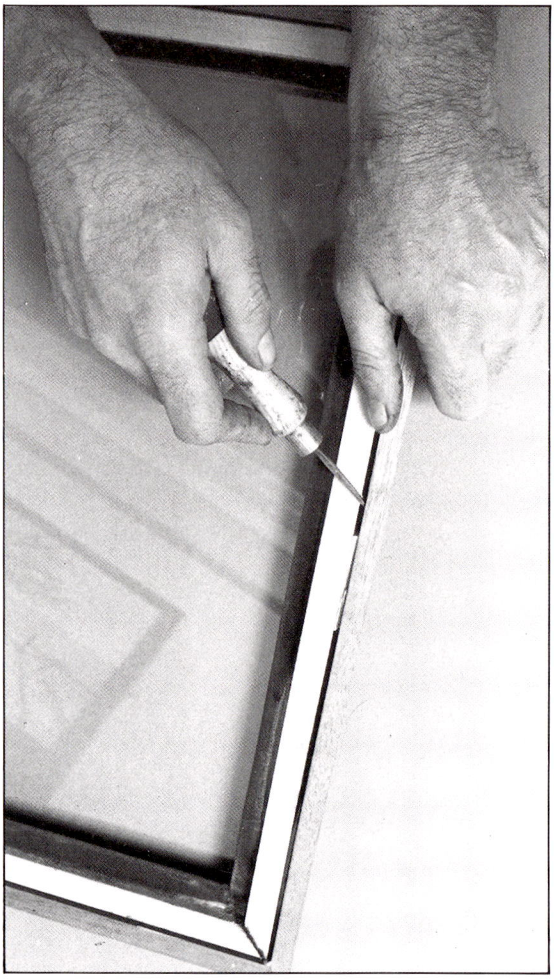

8 Next, secure the slip frame in the outer frame. Make the holes in the outer main frame with a bradawl, one in each side. Remember that you will be doing this with the glass already in place and the slip frame behind it, so work in the bradawl gently.

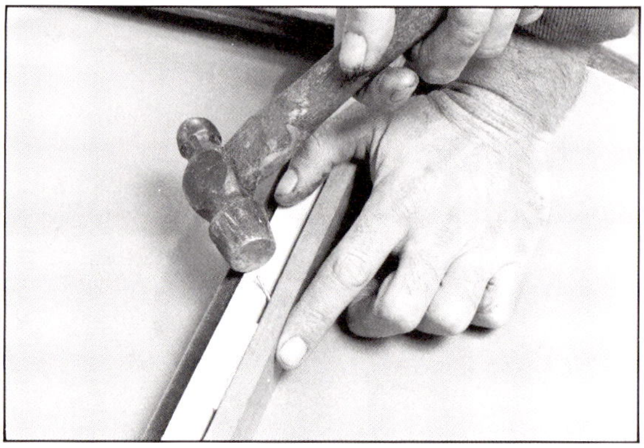

9 Hammer nails into the holes which you have made in the inside edges of the main frame. Use sharp panel pins to ensure that you can tap them into place without using too much force.

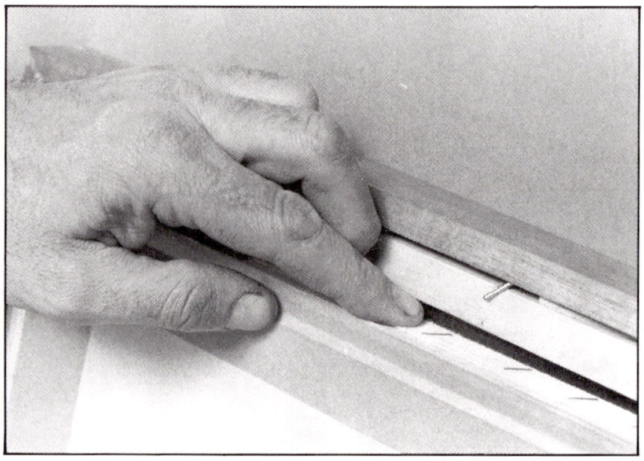

10 Now take the needlework on its stretcher and place it in the rebate of the slip frame. Tap nails into the inside edges of the slip frame to hold the stretcher in place.

11 The frame is now complete. The needlework is protected from dirt and dust by the glass, and protected from direct contact with the glass by the velvet-covered slip frame. A treasured piece of embroidery can be neatly preserved in this way.

ROSE
COTTAGE

PROJECT 7

Framing the three-dimensional

The butterflies to be framed were fixed with pins to cork bases, making framing a tricky, delicate affair. For instance, velvet was chosen for the background: should the cork bases be glued onto velvet? Glue could damage such a delicate material.

Black velvet was chosen to off-set the butterflies, an effect which could easily be ruined by dust. So a dust-free working environment was essential and care had to be taken to make the finished frame tight and secure.

Materials and Equipment

- Box moulding, 50mm (2in) deep, 18mm (3/4in) wide
- Glass, 2mm (1/12in) thick
- Sharp, hard pencil
- Length of wooden quadrant
- Woodwork glue
- Hand drill
- Panel pins, 15mm (5/8in)
- Hammer
- Punch
- Dark woodstain
- Mitre box
- Saw
- Ruler
- Corner clamps
- Counter-sinker (optional)
- Bradawl
- Brass screws
- Screwdriver
- Black matt paint
- Craft knife or scalpel
- Black velvet
- Hardboard
- Fabric glue
- Screws, 15mm (5/8in)
- Gummed paper
- Brass plates and screws

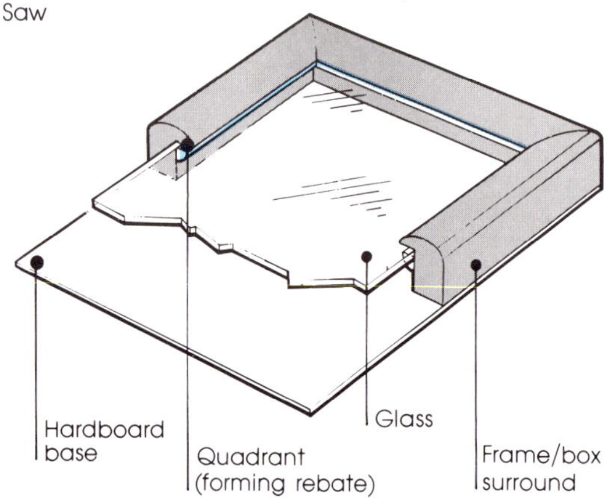

1 Choose a piece of moulding deep enough to ensure that a space large enough to accommodate the items to be framed exists between the glass and the back of the frame. We chose a piece of boxmoulding 50mm (2in) deep and 18mm (3/4in) thick. Hold the glass along the edge of the rebate, and mark its precise thickness along the moulding with a pencil.

2 Select a piece of quadrant. This will be stuck along the inside of the rebate to create a groove in which the glass will be fitted. Make sure the quadrant is not so deep that it will be visible behind the glass.

3 Place the length of quadrant along the moulding, and glue it in place over the pencilled line. Apply tape to give it extra temporary strength. Once the glue has set, drill small holes through the quadrant into the main frame and hammer 15mm ($^5/_8$in) panel pins into it. Punch them beneath the wood surface for a neat effect.

4 Stain the moulding and quadrant with a dark woodstain, and cut it into four pieces, mitring the corners in the usual way. Join two short sides and one long side of the frame to allow the glass to be fitted into the groove.

5 After glueing and nailing the three sides of the frame together, carefully slide the sheet of glass into place in the groove.

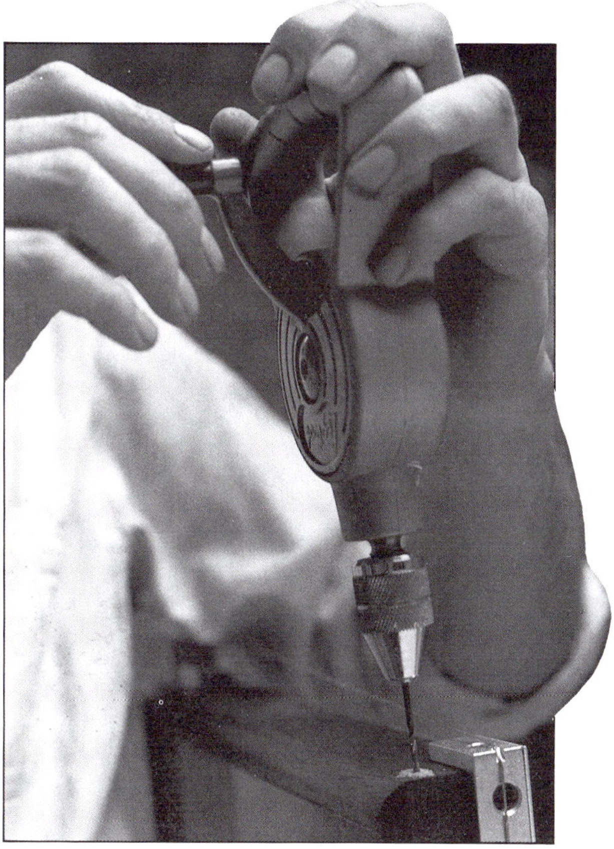

6 The final side of the frame is not glued or nailed, but screwed on, so that it can be removed if the glass ever needs replacing. Holding the frame steady with a clamp, drill into the corners.

7 It is often a good idea to use a counter-sinker for fine-finish work of this type. By making tiny 'craters' at the entrance of the drilled holes, the screws will not jut out above the surface of the wood. Make sure you do not over-do this.

8 Carefully screw brass screws into the holes, resting them snugly in the hollow, to give a professional look.

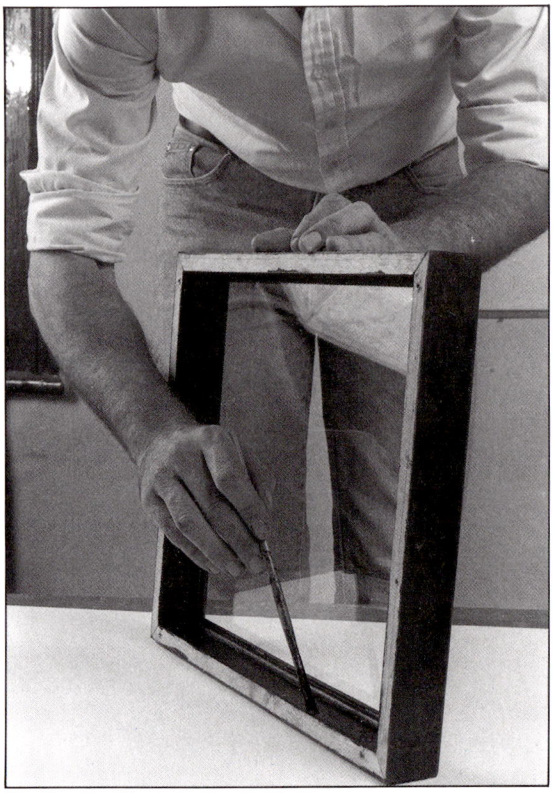

9 Paint the inside of the frame black. The use of a matt black will match, but not overwhelm, the black velvet that will provide a mounting base for the group of butterflies.

10 Measure out a piece of hardboard to the same size as the frame and stick the piece of black velvet onto it with fabric glue. Cut out the piece of hardboard.

11 Decide where you wish to place each specimen and measure out their positions on the back of the hardboard.

12 As the slightest spilling of glue could damage the velvet, we decided to screw the cork bases in place in this project. This is why it was important to plot the positions of the butterflies on the back.

13 Using 15mm ($^5/_8$in) screws, carefully screw through the back of the hardboard, so that the screws protrude through the front. The cork bases of the butterflies are then carefully screwed onto the threads of the screws.

14 Place the hardboard and specimens onto the back of the frame. Make holes with a bradawl, drill and then fix a screw into each corner to provide a firm attachment.

15 Tape over the hardboard with gummed paper to make absolutely sure no dust can get in. Finally, fit brass plates to the sides of the frame so that it can be screwed flat onto a wall.

PROJECT 8

Restoring a gilded frame

This mid-nineteenth century wooden frame, gilded and beautifully embellished with intricate ornamentation, is sadly in need of repair. With skill and patience and some common materials, one of which is widely used by dentists, the frame can be brought back vividly to life.

Materials and equipment

- Soap, water, rag
- Acetone cleaner
- Brush
- Vaseline
- Alginate mould solution
- Knife (for spreading)
- Cooking oil or grease
- Plaster
- Plaster spatula or carving tool
- Woodwork glue
- Sandpaper
- Gesso
- Bole
- Gold leaf
- Ormiline lacquer
- Staining wax
- Container such as a tin lid

1 Some of the ornamentation in this frame has cracked badly and some has been completely lost. There is extensive damage to one corner of the frame, and two sides need general repair.

2 Much can be achieved by cleaning with soap and water. Be careful not to use too much water as this can damage the frame. After cleaning off the surface grease and dust, lightly brush over with acetone, a chemical cleaner used for gold leaf.

3 In many cases, even the lost pieces can be 'recovered' by taking moulds from the good fragments that remain. Search the frame for areas of ornamentation still in good condition.

4 Apply Vaseline with a brush, working thoroughly into all the areas from which you intend to take moulds. This will prevent the moulding material from sticking to the wood.

5 Mix the mould solution. Alginate, similar to the substance dentists use to make moulds for crowns, can be obtained from dental suppliers or from general mould suppliers, such as model shops. It gives a very high definition, and is very useful for moulding intricate embellishments.

6 While the mould is still in a semi-liquid state, apply it to the required spot. Press it into crevices and corners with a knife, working quickly, as it sets in a matter of minutes.

7 Cover all the areas from which you intend to make moulds, and leave for a few minutes to allow it to dry and set. Apply a generous coating so that each mould will be strong and substantial when removed.

8 When they are set, peel the moulds off carefully. They will have a rubbery, flexible texture, but will tear quite easily. Also note that moulds made from alginate do not last very long.

9 Apply cooking oil or grease to the moulds so that the plaster will not stick to them. Select a plaster. Press the plaster paste into the mould and leave it for a few hours to set. Apply glue to the damaged areas and then press the plaster firmly into place, so that it blends with the surrounding ornamentation. Some minor alterations may need to be made; use a plaster spatula or carving tools for these finishing touches. Then rub down lightly with sandpaper.

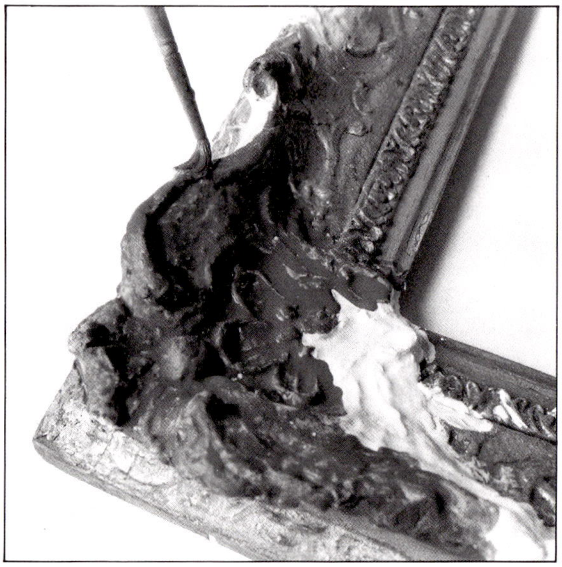

10 Apply two or three coats of gesso to the plaster to provide a base for the gold leaf. Rub down with fine sandpaper. Then apply two coats of bole colouring, a dark, terracotta reddish-brown, allowing time for drying in between applications.

11 Apply gold leaf in the usual way. Lacquer the gold leaf with ormiline lacquer, a hot colourless type, to provide protection. You will notice that the repaired sections of the frame look much newer than the rest of the frame. It is therefore necessary to tone down the new parts so that they blend with the rest. Waxes and pigments can be used for this.

12 Mix the staining wax and pigment in a shallow container; a tin lid is used here. A variety of waxes are available. We chose staining waxes with brown and black colouring.

13 Apply successive layers of wax with a rag, until the right colour is achieved. As an alternative to staining waxes, water and pigments can be used and then waxed afterwards.

14 You may have to work in several layers of wax before you are satisfied that the new areas blend with the original. The result will be a richly decorated frame, with the craftsmanship of an earlier era restored to perfection.

Care and repair

A central part of picture framing is the care and repair of the frames. Apart from looking after your own frames, you may wish to detach an attractive old frame from an unsuitable picture and give it a new lease of life. Or you may have an old print or picture that needs attention before it can be placed in a frame. Consequently, we have also included in this section some tips on simple picture cleaning and restoring.

If you do buy an old frame, first be careful to ensure that you are not spoiling a rare antique by attempting to renovate it. Your local antique shop should be able to advise you on this. If you have bought an old frame without antique value in itself, then you can achieve a great deal by cleaning and renovating it. For instance, if an old moulded plaster frame is damaged in places, it is usually well worthwhile repairing these dents and chips by taking a mould from the good parts of the frame and using this to build up the damaged parts with filler. There are different ways of renovating gilding, from using real gold leaf — if your frame is a particularly fine one — to simpler and quicker retouching. Sometimes it is just the glass which needs replacing and this is an easier task.

Although it is best to leave valuable works to the professional, there are some basic techniques which, once mastered, will enable you to carry out many minor repairs to give a surprisingly new look to pictures and frames.

REPAIRING OLD FRAMES

It is important to be cautious when renovating old frames and if in doubt give the job to a professional.

Most of the frames bought from antique shops are nineteenth- and early twentieth-century reproductions. While these are not particularly valuable, they are well-made frames, more individual and interesting then many modern mouldings, and well worth reviving, as they will probably last for many more years.

Many such frames have some kind of gold finish. Some are basic wooden frames with plaster mouldings and gilded finishes; others are carved wooden frames decorated in gold leaf; and others are gold-painted wooden frames.

When cleaning gold leaf, there is one important 'don't' to remember: never harshly rub or wash it with water, as this action wipes off much of the actual gold surface, a veneer so delicate that it is all too easy to damage. Instead, carefully wipe the gold leaf with a diluted bleach solution or acetone; or brighten the gold with lemon, rubbing a slice of lemon gently over the moulding.

Mending Chipped Gilt

The easiest way to mend small chips in gilt is to touch up the damaged spot with gilt paste, which is available in art and craft shops, or, if very small, with gold paint. However, if a small portion of the moulding is missing, it might be necessary to fill in the missing area with plastic wood, barbola paste, putty or

Replacing decorations
Badly damaged or chipped frames can often be repaired by making plaster replacements for the damaged parts from moulds taken from good portions of the frame. If a frame still has a good corner, for instance, a whole corner piece can be recreated in this way (right).

The gilded frames (left and below) *are both slightly chipped. Such chips can be repaired by casting plaster replacements from moulds. Alternatively, very small areas can sometimes be built up by hand and touched up with gold paint. The gold slip frame* (far left) *is held in place by wooden wedges – a device often used in older frames.*

Secondhand frames

This frame (right) *was bought secondhand, in poor condition. The gesso and gilt were chipped and the corners were worn and loose. The frame was first thoroughly cleaned and then dismantled. The corners were then re-mitred, so that the frame fitted the new painting precisely.*

Damaged frame
The gilded frame around this landscape print (right) *is faded and badly damaged. The chipped, damaged corners* (above) *could be touched up but in this case the framer decided to remove the gesso and gilt completely by soaking and scrubbing. Many such old frames have solid and attractive wooden bases that can be cleaned and polished.*

decorators' filler. Such a filler can be moulded into shape with a paintbrush handle or fine sculpting tool to blend it in with the original. When the area is dry, it can be matched to the original with the gilt paste.

Of course, gold leaf itself can be used to repair original gold leaf surfaces. However, this is rarely advisable as new gold leaf shines brightly and will look out of place on a more mellowed gold leaf frame. All gilt repairs tend to suffer to a certian extent from this problem but there are a few ways of getting round it. One way is to make use of the antiquing technique described on page 92. Another is to age the new gilt instantly: rub tiny amounts of adhesive onto the newly renovated moulding and sprinkle a little dust onto the area. Wipe away the loose dust and you are left with a perfect older-looking frame.

Larger Repairs

If an area of wooden or plaster moulding is missing that is too large or too intricate to build up with filler materials, it is sometimes worth making your own mould for the missing portion. This is usually not too difficult as many of the frames requiring this treatment were themselves originally manufactured from moulds. *(See pages 128–131 for further details.)*

Use a piece of the frame which is intact and undamaged as the base for your mould. Press Plasticine onto this area of the frame to obtain an impression of the pattern. Remove from the frame and build up the edges of the Plasticine mould with more Plasticine. Then pour in plaster of Paris up to the depth required to fit into the missing section. When dry, remove the dried plaster moulding from the Plasticine and glue it into place.

Although Plasticine is easily available from department stores, many modern picture framers use alternative substances, such as silicone rubber and an organic material based on seaweed called Alginate, which can be obtained from specialist stores. The organic material and the silicone rubber give very precise impressions but Alginate lasts only a few days once the mould has been made, so is not suitable for long-term projects.

Stripping Old Frames

Some old plaster frames are beyond repair and may not be to your taste in any case. Do not throw these away, however, as most old plaster mouldings were created on very well made wooden bases, often pine, which make excellent frames in their own right. Remove the plaster by immersing the frames in hot water and scrubbing. When the stripped frame is dry, finely sandpaper it and then wax or stain it to produce a solid, new-look frame.

REPLACING GLASS

Often what seems to be a dingy or yellowed picture is in fact a clean picture languishing behind a dirty, ageing, nicotine-stained piece of old glass. Very old-fashioned glass often distorts a picture. Sometimes the glass can be removed and washed; sometimes it needs replacing.

To dismantle a frame, place the picture face down on a clean, soft surface. Then gently remove the tacks which hold the backing and the picture in place. Lift up the picture and remove the glass.

Renovating oil paintings

Surface Dirt

It is a mistake to assume that your rather gloomy-looking oil painting is necessarily a dirty one. Many such paintings were intended to look dark: portraits and still-lifes, for instance, were traditionally given a dark background in the eighteenth and nineteenth centuries, and many landscape painters used a great deal of brown in their trees and grass. Many paintings look dark because of the mastic varnish covering them. This type of varnish, widely used until twenty years ago, has a dulling effect on paintings that is now familiar – the yellowing skies, brown foliage, and general dinginess often seen on pictures found in attics, junk shops and the more neglected museums.

However, many paintings are simply dirty and there are some basic steps which can be taken to improve them before reframing them. Surface dirt, accumulated through years of exposure to dust, nicotine, oil lamps and open fires is relatively easy to remove without damaging the picture (although it is not advisable to do even this much on a picture of high value). Wipe the surface of the old painting with cotton wool soaked in white spirit. The older the varnish, the safer this method is: if a picture has been varnished recently, the white spirit will tend to dissolve the varnish as well. By removing the surface grime in this way, the colours of the painting can be appreciably brightened.

You may find that a painting has not been varnished at all and that dirt is engrained into the paint. If this is the case you will need to wipe the painting with cotton wool soaked in a weak solution of ammonia to remove the dirt. However, by using ammonia you do run the risk of removing the paint as well as the dirt, so do not attempt it on any paintings that are valuable to you.

Removing Old Varnish

Extreme caution is required when removing a coat of old varnish from a painting. Tackle a small area at a time, using a solvent such as acetone, methyl alcohol or ethyl alcohol; if the varnish is fairly new, white spirit might be sufficient. Starting with the darker areas, apply the solvent cautiously with swabs of cotton wool. It is better to leave fragments of old varnish, which will not necessarily be noticed, than to be so anxious to remove every scrap of old varnish that you also remove a crucial detail of the painting.

Dealing with Flaking Paint

The professional will go to great lengths to recover flakes of paint that are missing from a painting. This is not so ridiculous as it sounds, especially if the painting has been behind glass, since the missing flakes will be stuck somewhere in the frame. Once discovered, the restorer will patiently fit the flakes back into the picture as though completing a jigsaw puzzle. The pieces are stuck into place with beeswax, which has a very low melting point. The beeswax is placed on the appropriate spot in the picture and the flake of paint positioned on top of this. Then a heated spatula – a very fine one – is applied on top of the flake, so that the beeswax beneath melts and the flake can be precisely manoeuvred into position. Although this is a specialist technique, there is no reason why the home renovator cannot become adept at it, using a heated teaspoon handle instead of a spatula if need be.

If the missing flakes of paint are irretrievably lost and you do not wish to hand the painting over to an expert, you might wish to paint over the problem areas.

Sometimes, a fine portion of missing paint will have left an uneven picture surface. An indentation can be built up very carefully, using interior decorators' filler or even putty and, in the case of a very slight indentation, a thicker layer of paint may suffice.

Use either oils or acrylics to paint over the problem spots of the picture. These areas will often be white: where the top paint has flaked off, the white prime – the 'undercoat' which is applied to the canvas before the oil paint – usually remains. The advantage of using acrylic paint, especially if it is to be applied thickly, is that it dries very quickly; the equivalent amount of oil paint can sometimes take weeks to dry.

If you are not used to painting, remember that you must match the tone as well as the colour. For instance, a red jacket may not be red in the simple sense but might actually be a more dingy colour and contain more grey than red. It is advisable to tone down your colours with a neutral pigment, such as raw umber or Payne's grey, and experiment on a separate piece of paper until you obtain exactly the right shade.

Cracks in the Paint

Almost all old paintings have surface cracks, which actually serve to authenticate the picture. By studying the distance between the cracks and identifying the types of cracks that they are, an expert can 'read' a painting, that is, identify when the painting was originally executed. Experts suspect a fake if they can find no cracks, or if the signature contains no cracks, and if one area

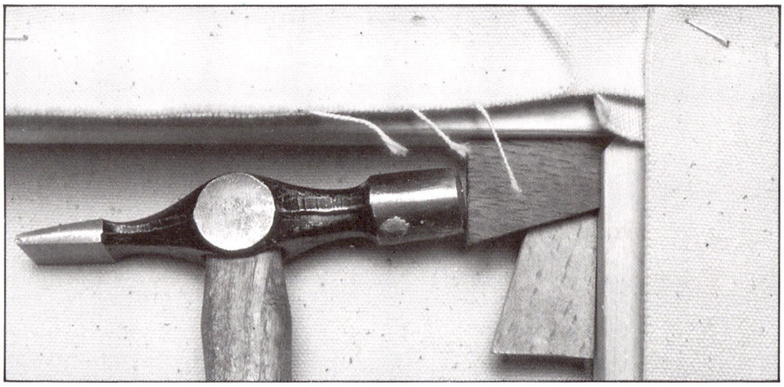

of a painting is without cracks it has probably been repaired.

Therefore, unless the cracks in your old oil painting are really disfiguring, it is best to leave them alone.

Revarnishing

Either matt or gloss varnish can be coated onto an old painting, although a very high-gloss varnish will look unnatural. Dilute the varnish to two parts varnish and one part white spirit and apply it with a brush vertically, then horizontally, using even, parallel strokes to achieve a smooth coat. Avoid applying thick coats of varnish as this will make the picture look as if it has been encapsulated in plastic.

Alternatively, use a spray can of varnish; this is preferable, as an aerosol gives a more even application than a brush. Nevertheless, the varnish must still be sprayed in thin, light coats: hold the picture upright and spray it from about 30cm (1ft) away, avoiding a build-up of varnish in any one area, which would probably drip.

Whichever method you use, it is absolutely essential that you work in clean, dust-free surroundings. If any particles of fluff or dirt become stuck in the varnish, they will look prominent and unsightly.

Making the canvas taut
Purpose-built stretchers have corner wedges which can be tapped in gently (above). *This pushes the sides apart and tightens the canvas.*

Tightening the Canvas

Tightening a canvas that has become loose is a simple task. In many cases, professionally made canvases can be made taut again without having to remove the tacks that join the canvas to the stretcher. If you turn the canvas over, you will usually find that the corners of the stretcher have been slotted together and held slightly apart by tiny wedges of wood to provide the original final tightening of the canvas. A gentle tap will drive these wedges inwards slighly and provide a new tautness for the canvas.

Renovating prints, watercolours, maps and documents

Many prints and watercolours become damp over the years and, like oil paintings, their surface can become dingy with dust. Because prints and watercolours are usually executed on paper, they are also subject to staining, mildew and buckling. They can be ripped and scratched, too.

Removing Surface Dirt

Removing grime from a dingy surface, often the result of the print not having been behind glass, is not simply a case of giving the surface a quick wipe, as it can be sometimes with oil paintings. Because the paper on which the painting was done is porous, the grime will have been absorbed to a certain extent. Removing dirt from the picture surface, therefore, is a job for an expert. However, the white areas

An old print
This print (right) *is typical of many that you will come across. It is badly damaged and in need of flattening as well as cleaning.*

around and within the picture can sometimes be dealt with by the home renovator – and this can often be enough to give the whole picture a facelift. Wipe gently over the white areas with a putty rubber. Alternatively, wipe the whole surface with carbon tetrachloride – a dry-cleaning solution available from the chemist's. This must be wiped evenly all over the picture, including the image area, to avoid a blotchy result.

Dealing with Creases

Creases can sometimes be removed by sandwiching the canvas between two sheets of blotting paper and keeping it under a heavy, even weight for several days. If this does not work, it may be necessary to stretch the paper. Immerse the picture in cold water for just long enough to wet the paper (the water will not make the watercolours run as long as the whole print is immersed). Then place the picture on a flat surface and stick it down with brown paper tape. Allow the picture to dry naturally – artificial drying makes the paper contract too quickly and tear. Remove the tape to leave a completely flat picture.

Removing Damp Stains and Foxing

Damp stains and the little spots of mildew known as foxing can be removed by bleaching. Do not use ordinary commerical bleach; one per cent standardized sodium hypochlorite solution is suitable – the solution used for sterilizing babies' bottles, obtainable from chemists. Mix it in a ratio of one part solution to three parts cold water and put it into a flat photographers' tray or baking dish. Immerse the print or watercolour in the solution for a few minutes until the blemishes start to disappear. As soon as the dark spots begin to fade, remove the print and place it in a bath of water for a few minutes to wash away the bleaching solution. After rinsing, you may well need to stretch the canvas, especially if the watercolour is on light- to medium-weight paper. Partially dry the canvas naturally, then place it between two sheets of clean, dry blotting paper to finish off the drying. The marks should by now have disappeared.

Covering Scratches

Retouching a scratched area is generally a professional job. However, if you do decide to embark on this, begin with a paint that is more diluted than usual and gradually build up the intensity of the colour. When repairing tears, it is important to lay the surfaces together without disturbing the fibres in the paper, which means that you must find their original positions and piece them back together before glueing them into place.

The problem of mould

This print (above) is marred by mould. Most engravings will withstand washing and, sometimes, bleaching. Here, an oxidizing agent will be used to remove the stains and improve overall appearance.

TEARS

Small tears, where there is sufficient overlap, can usually be repaired by applying acid-free, colourless adhesive that does not shrink as it dries. To repair large tears, however, you will probably need to fix thin backing paper to the back of the picture, so that no gap is visible.

Damaged engraving

Varnish, applied to give the appearance of an oil painting, has darkened with age on this hand-coloured print (left). A solvent was needed to remove ingrained varnish deposits.

Glossary

Abstract expressionism
An art form in which expression of the artist's inner experience is more important than realism. Paintings are created from involuntary marks and dribbles of paint.

Acrylic paint
A comparatively new paint in which the pigment is suspended in a synthetic resin.

Ancien Régime
The period in Europe before the French Revolution.

Architrave
The moulded wooden trim used around door and window frames.

Baroque
The richly decorative style of the post-Renaissance, prevalent in the seventeenth and eighteenth centuries.

Batten
Narrow strip of wood, sometimes used to frame an artpiece.

Bevel
The rounded or sloped edge of a ruler or strip of wood, or the sloped inside edge of a window in a mount.

Block mount
A block of wood or chipboard onto which a print or other picture is mounted.

Builders' moulding
Strips of wood used by builders for trimming doors, windows, skirting boards etc, which can be used to make picture frames.

Chipboard
Rigid board made from compressed chips of wood.

Clip frame
A simple frame without an edge or surround, formed by clipping a sheet of glass to a wooden backing.

Cold mounting
See Wet mounting.

Composition
The arrangement of the elements that make up the content of a picture.

Conservation mounting
Mounting carried out with acid-free materials to preserve old or valuable documents and pictures.

Damask
A fabric woven with a pattern which is visible on both sides.

Dry mounting
A method of sticking a picture onto a backing. A sheet of film is placed between the two and heat is applied. The film dissolves, fusing the picture and backing. Also known as hot mounting.

Emery
Cloth or paper covered with emery powder, for sanding a fine finish.

Empire style
The fashion associated with Napoleonic France, in the late eighteenth and early nineteenth centuries.

Foxing
Tiny spots of mildew that can form on old prints and drawings.

Framers' moulding
Strips of rebated wood especially designed for picture frames.

Fresco
Painting carried out on mortar or plaster that is not quite dry.

Gesso
Prepared surface of plaster as a ground for gilding and other finishes.

Gilding
Applying a gold finish.

Glaze
(1) To cover with glass, as with glass in a frame. (2) A thin coat of a transparent colour that is placed over a differently coloured undercoat.

Gold leaf
Thin sheets of beaten gold which can be applied to frames.

Hinge mount
A mount which opens and closes on a hinge, enabling the picture to be positioned and removed easily.

Hot mounting
See Dry mounting.

Insert
A smaller frame within the outer frame. Sometimes referred to as a slip frame.

Mastic
Natural gum from which some paints and varnishes are made.

Memorabilia
Articles and ephemera that have nostalgic associations.

Mitre
The 45-degree angled cut, made in the ends of each side of the frame.

Modernism
Art styles pertaining to and identifying with the twentieth century.

Mount
The card which is used as a backing for a flimsy picture, and the card from which a window is cut, beneath which a picture is placed.

Neoclassical revival
Art movements of the eighteenth and nineteenth centuries that looked back to classical, ie Greek and Roman, times.

Neutral
Without positive or distinctive characteristics.

Patina
A finish often used as a base for glazes or to modify and tone a colour.

Perspex
Tough, inflexible type of plastic available in sheet form and sometimes used in framing instead of glass.

Quadrant
Strip of wood or metal, shaped like a quarter-circle, often used to form a rebate.

Rebate
The L-shaped groove on the reverse side of framers' moulding into which the glass, mount, artpiece and backing board fit.

Sampler
Piece of embroidery worked in a variety of stitches, which was traditionally worked to demonstrate accomplishment in needlework.

Score
To cut, in glass or card, a line that does not pass through the material completely.

Sepia
A rich brown pigment obtained from cuttle fish. Now used to describe the colour only.

Slip frame
An inner frame, usually covered in fabric, inserted between the main frame and picture to provide a decorative border in the same way as a mount. Also known as an insert.

Stretcher
An expandable wooden frame to which a canvas is usually tacked before framing, so that it can be made taut in the frame.

Transfer gold or silver
Thin sheets of beaten gold or silver attached to paper and rubbed onto the surface of a frame.

Veneer
A thin layer or inlay of flat wood applied to a surface.

Vignette
A picture or design, usually done on a small scale, without a boundary.

Wash
Thinly diluted paint used to obtain a transparent or delicate paint finish.

Wet mounting
A method of sticking a picture to a backing, using spray glue or wallpaper size. Also known as cold mounting.

Index

Page numbers in *italic* refer to illustrations and captions

T

U

V

W

Acknowledgements

The pictures on these pages were produced by courtesy of the following:

8 Scrovegni, Padua; **9** National Gallery, London (t,b); **10** National Portrait Gallery, London; **11** Private collection, London; **14** Private collection, London (tr,br); **15** Private collection, London (t,b); **16** Private collection, London (bl,cr); **17** Private collection, London; **18** Private collection, London (t); **19** Private collection, London (r); **20** Private collection, London (tl,bl,br); **23** Private collection, London (t,b); **24** Elizabeth Whiting & Associates; **25** Elizabeth Whiting & Associates; **26** Elizabeth Whiting & Associates (tl,bl,tr,br); **27** Elizabeth Whiting & Associates (t,b); **28** Elizabeth Whiting & Associates; **29** Elizabeth Whiting & Associates (t); **31** Stan Smith (t), Rosie Waites (b); **34** *The World of Interiors*, photograph – John Cook; **35** Trustees of the British Museum, London (t); **39** *The World of Interiors*, photograph – John Cook; **40** Sandell Perkins Ltd, London; **42** *The World of Interiors*, photograph – John Cook; **43** *The World of Interiors*, photograph – John Cook; **136** Victoria and Albert Museum, London (br); **137** Victoria and Albert Museum, London (bl,tr).

With special thanks to Patricia Monahan and John Shrimpton.

All other photographs are the property of Quarto Publishing Ltd.

Key: (t) top; (b) bottom; (l) left; (r) right; (c) centre

While every effort has been made to acknowledge all copyright holders, we apologize if any omissions have been made.

PLANETARY NEBULAE: A UNIVERSAL TOOLBOX
IN THE ERA OF PRECISION ASTROPHYSICS

IAU SYMPOSIUM 384

COVER ILLUSTRATION:

The planetary nebula M57, also known as the Ring Nebula. Image from multiple sources, Hubble Space Telescope (He II, [OIII], [NII]), the James Webb Space Telescope (3.3 micron), the Large Binocular Telescope (2.1 microns), the Subaru Telescope (H alpha)" - Robert Gendler, John Bozeman, NASA, ESA, and C.R. O'Dell (Vanderbilt University).

IAU SYMPOSIUM PROCEEDINGS SERIES

INTERNATIONAL ASTRONOMICAL UNION

UNION ASTRONOMIQUE INTERNATIONALE

International Astronomical Union

IAU

PLANETARY NEBULAE: A UNIVERSAL TOOLBOX IN THE ERA OF PRECISION ASTROPHYSICS

PROCEEDINGS OF THE 384th SYMPOSIUM OF THE INTERNATIONAL ASTRONOMICAL UNION KRAKOW, POLAND 4–8 SEPTEMBER 2023

Edited by

ORSOLA DE MARCO

School of Mathematical and Physical Sciences, Macquarie University, Sydney, 2109 NSW, Australia

ALBERT ZIJLSTRA

School of Physics & Astronomy, University of Manchester, Oxford Road, Manchester M13 9PL, United Kingdom

and

RYSZARD SZCZERBA

AS, CAMK Department of Astrophysics, Ul Rabianska 8, 87-100 Torun, Poland

CAMBRIDGE
UNIVERSITY PRESS

CAMBRIDGE UNIVERSITY PRESS
University Printing House, Cambridge CB2 8BS, United Kingdom
1 Liberty Plaza, Floor 20, New York, NY 10006, USA
10 Stamford Road, Oakleigh, Melbourne 3166, Australia

First published 2025

Printed in Great Britain by Henry Ling Limited, The Dorset Press, Dorchester, DT1 1HD

Typeset in System $\LaTeX$ 2ε

A catalogue record for this book is available from the British Library Library of Congress Cataloguing in Publication data

ISBN 9781009399326 hardback
ISSN 1743-9213

Table of Contents

Preface

In this volume we present the proceedings of IAU Symposium 384: Planetary Nebulae: a Universal Toolbox in the Era of Precision Astrophysics, which was held in city of Krakow, Poland, from the 4th to the 8th September 2023, in the Collegium Novum of the historical Jagiellonian University, where Nicolaus Copernicus studied mathematical astronomy in the 1490's. The symposium was held on the 550th anniversary of Copernicus' birth. The field of astronomy has evolved since his days. Planetary nebulae were only discovered after the invention of the telescope in the 17th century, and were thus not known to Copernicus. We would like to think that had he known them he would have appreciated them for their stunning beauty, and for their significance as the embodiment of our Sun's future.

Planetary nebulae are the ejecta of dying, Sun-like stars, in the mass range 1–8 $M_{\odot}$. Their evanescent beauty seems to celebrate the life of the star that produced it! Lawrence Hugh Aller (1913–2003)† once called them "*The wreaths placed by Nature around dying stars*" ‡. Over 3000 planetary nebulae are now known in the Miky Way galaxy, and many more in other galaxies.

Research on planetary nebulae covers a diverse range of topics, linking to many areas in modern astrophysics. The nebula can be thought of as a star reflecting on its past§: it is a unique tracer of the final stages of stellar evolution. Binary interactions are a major focus of these studies, involving jets, common envelope interactions and transient events. The spectra of the ionised nebulae provide abundances of elements, including light elements and s-process products. This gives insight into the composition of the interstellar medium at the time when the star formed, as well as knowledge of the dredge-up processes that bring to the stellar surface the elements produced deep in the stellar interior. The chemistry occurring in the nebulae is another area of intense research, involving primary production (and destruction) of complex molecules such as fullerenes and PAHs, and solid particles such as those that we find in pre-solar grains in the Solar System. Planetary nebulae are detectable to distances as far as the Coma cluster: they are the brightest phase of the evolution of low- and intermediate-mass star and more than 10% of the luminosity can come out in a single emission line. They are therefore used to study stellar populations in galaxies, including abundance gradients, galaxy dynamics and dark matter. They are also a critical rung of the extragalactic distance scale and a likely excellent tool to help resolve the current Hubble Constant tension. Finally, planetary nebulae are used effectively to engage the public and excite and educate students and teachers, and this topic was also explored during the symposium: a highlight of the meeting was an invited talk by Arianna Cortesi, on astronomical outreach and education in marginalised, indigenous communities in Brazil. The eye-opening talk showed how astronomy can be a tool for social development.

This was the 11th IAU-sponsored planetary nebula symposium, a series that started in 1967. They have been held in 10 different countries and on all continents except South America and Antarctica. The community is as diverse as the topic itself. The current symposium attracted 104 participants from 26 different countries. One third of the participants were female. At the very first of the IAU Symposia in 1967, female participants accounted for only 10% of the group, suggesting we are halfway on the journey to gender parity. Half the invited talks and Invited reviews were by female speakers.

† `https://baas.aas.org/pub/lawrence-hugh-aller-1913-2003/release/1`
‡ Kwitter & Henry, 2022, PASP, 134,02.2001
§ Menzies & Whitelock, 1988, MNRAS, 233, 697

Table 1. IAU Symposia on planetary nebulae, 1967–2023

IAUS 384	09/2023	Planetary Nebulae: a Universal Toolbox in the Era of Precision Astrophysics	Krakow, Poland
IAUS 323	10/2016	Planetary Nebulae: Multi-Wavelength Probes of Stellar and Galactic Evolution	Beijing, China
IAUS 283	07/2011	Planetary Nebulae: an Eye to the Future	Puerto de la Cruz, Tenerife, Spain
IAUS 234	04/2006	Planetary Nebulae in our Galaxy and Beyond	Waikoloa Beach, Hawai'i, USA
IAUS 209	11/2001	Planetary Nebulae: their Evolution and Role in the Universe	Canberra, Australia
IAUS 180	08/1996	Planetary Nebulae	Groningen, the Netherlands
IAUS 155	07/1992	Planetary Nebulae	Innsbruck, Austria
IAUS 131	10/1987	Planetary Nebulae	Mexico City, Mexico
IAUS 103	08/1982	Planetary Nebulae	London, UK
IAUS 76	06/1977	Planetary Nebulae	Ithaca, New York, USA
IAUS 34	09/1967	Planetary Nebulae	Tatranská Lomnica, Tatras Mountains, Slovakia

Because of the 550th anniversary of Copernicus' birth, Polish television interviewed participants at the Symposium. The city of Krakow dates to the 7th century; the Old Town was one of two cities on the very first UNESCO World Heritage list. Many of the old buildings and churches in the city centre still survive. The Jewish quarter retains sacred architecture and a living Jewish culture which is unparalleled in Poland. The Yiddish culture was celebrated with a concert at the conference dinner.

The Jagiellonian University, its staff and students supported the IAU Symposium brilliantly. The organisers gratefully acknowledge financial support from the IAU and from the Polish Ministry of Education and Science under the program Excellent Science II. The meeting was organised by IAU commission H3, Planetary Nebulae. It was coordinated by IAU Division H and endorsed by Divisions C, G and J. IAU funding was used to support students and early-career scientists. 20 people from 15 countries received IAU travel grants.

A prize was awarded for the best poster at the meeting: we are very happy to announce that this was won by Silvia Tosi from Rome Observatory, Italy.

The Organizing Committee

Acknowledgements

The symposium was organised by IAU Commission H3 (Planetary Nebulae). It was sponsored and supported by the IAU Divisions Division C (Education, Outreach and Heritage), G (Stars and Stellar Physics), H (Interstellar Medium and Local Universe; Coordinating Division) and J (Galaxies and Cosmology).

The Local Organizing Committee operated under the auspices of the Nicolaus Copernicus Astronomical Center of the Polish Academy of Sciences (CAMK PAN) and the Jagiellonian University (UJ).

Funding by the International Astronomical Union and the Minister of Education and Science under the program - Excellent Science II, and the Patronage from the Rektor Uniwersytetu Jagielonskiego, Polskie Towarzystwo Astronomiczne, Urania - Postepy Astronomii, Astronarium, TVP NAUKA and TVP3 is gratefully acknowledged.

List of Participants

Muhammad	Akashi	Technion & Kinneret College, Haifa	Israel
Stavros	Akras	National Observatory of Athens	Greece
Javier	Alcolea	Observatorio Astronómico Nacional, Madrid	Spain
Magda	Arnaboldi	ESO, Garching	Germany
Bruce	Balick	University of Washington	United States
Luis Carlos	Bermúdez-Bustamante	Macquarie University, Sydney	Australia
Souradeep	Bhattacharya	Inter-University Center for Astronomy and Astrophysics, Pune	India
John	Black	Chalmers University of Technology, Gothenberg	Sweden
Marissa	Botello	Instituto de Astronomía, Universidad Nacional Autónoma de México	Mexico
Panos	Boumis	National Observatory of Athens	Greece
Konstantinos	Bouvis	National Technical University of Athens	Greece
Martin	Bureau	University of Oxford	UK
Roldan A.	Cala	Instituto de Astrofísica de Andalucía	Spain
Jan	Cami	University of Western Ontario, London	Canada
Nicholas	Chornay	University of Geneva	Switzerland
Emanuele	Contini	Yonsei University, Seoul	South Korea
Arianna	Cortesi	Valongo Observatory, Rio de Janeiro	Brazil
Orsola	De Marco	Macquarie University, Sydney	Australia
Flavia	Dell'Agli	INAF - Observatory of Rome	Italy
Eylul	Demir	Ankara University	Turkey
Sophia	Derlopa	National Observatory of Athens	Greece
Harriet	Dinerstein	University of Texas at Austin	USA
Ana	Ennis	University of Waterloo - Perimeter Institute	Canada
Muhammad	Fajrin	Bandung Institute of Technology; Bosscha Observatory	Indonesia
Xuan	Fang	National Astronomical Observatories of Chinese Academy of Sciences	China
Vasiliki	Fragkou	Federal University of Rio de Janeiro	Brazil
Juris	Freimanis	Ventspils International Radio Astronomy Centre, Ventspils	Latvia
Domingo Aníbal	García Hernández	Instituto de Astrofísica de Canarias, La Laguna	Spain
Krzysztof	Gęsicki	Nicolaus Copernicus University, Torun	Poland
Marco A.	Gómez-Muñoz	Instituto de Astrofísica de Canarias, La Laguna	Spain
Denise R.	Gonçalves	Valongo Observatory, Rio de Janeiro	Brazil
Aija	Grankina	Laser Center, University of Latvia	Latvia
Martin A.	Guerrero	Instituto de Astrofísica de Andalucía, Granada	Spain
Marcin	Hajduk	University of Warmia and Mazury in Olsztyn	Poland
Johanna	Hartke	Finnish Centre for Astronomy with ESO, University of Turku	Finland
Diego	Hernandez-Juarez	Instituto de Astronomía, Universidad Nacional Autónoma de México	Mexico
Todd	Hillwig	Valparaiso University	USA
Bruce	Hrivnak	Valparaiso University	USA

Chih-Hao	Hsia	The Laboratory for Space Research, The University of Hong Kong	China
Teresa	Huertas Roldán	Instituto de Astrofísica de Canarias, La Laguna	Spain
Kim	Hyosun	Korea Astronomy and Space Science Institute, Yuseong	South Korea
Vincent	Icke	Universiteit Leiden	The Netherlands
George	Jacoby	NSF's NOIRLab, Tucson	USA
Palmira	Jimenez	Dublin Institute of Advanced Studies	Ireland
Tomasz	Kamiński	Nicolaus Copernicus Astronomical Center, Torun	Poland
Lydia	Konstantinou	National Technical University of Athens	Greece
Sun	Kwok	University of British Columbia, Vancouver	Canada
Marco	Laversveiler	Valongo Observatory, Rio de Janeiro	Brazil
Yushan	LI	The University of Hong Kong	Hong Kong
Giovanna	Liberato	Valongo Observatory Rio de Janeiro	Brazil
Arturo	Manchado	Instituto de Astrofísica de Canarias, La Laguna	Spain
Minia	Manteiga	Centre for Information and Communications Technology Research, University of A Coruña	Spain
M. Belén	Mari	Valongo Observatory, Rio de Janeiro	Brazil
Mikako	Matsuura	Cardiff University	UK
Roberto	Mendez	Institute for Astronomy, Honolulu	USA
Jose Eduardo	Mendez Delgado	Zentrum für Astronomie der Universität Heidelberg	Germany
Luis F.	Miranda	Instituto de Astrofísica de Andalucía, Granada	Spain
Casper	Moltzer	Radboud University, Nijmegen	Netherlands
Hektor	Monteiro	Universidade Federal de Itajubá	Brazil
Rodolfo	Montez	Center for Astrophysics, Harvard & Smithsonian	USA
Borja	Montoro	Molina Instituto de Astrofísica de Andalucía, Granada	Spain
Paula	Moraga Baez	Rochester Institute of Technology	USA
Christophe	Morisset	Instituto de Astronomia, Universidad Nacional Autónoma de México	Mexico
Roberto	Ortiz	Universidade de São Paulo	Brazil
Masaaki	Otsuka	Okayama Observatory, Kyoto University	Japan
Ishika	Palit	National tsing hua University, Hsinchu,	Taiwan
Quentin	Parker	The University of Hong Kong	Hong Kong
Kerry	Paterson	Max Planck Institute for Astronomy, Heidelberg	Germany
Miriam	Peña	Instituto de Astronomia, Universidad Nacional Autónoma de México	Mexico
Sophie Antonia	Penger	University of Cologne	Germany
Rafael Andres	Pignata	Observatorio Astronómico de Córdoba	Argentina
Lea	Planquart	Université Libre de Bruxelles	Belgium
Karlis	Pukitis	University of Latvia, Riga	Latvia
Guillermo	Quintana-Lacaci	Instituto De Física Fundamental, Madrid	Spain
Gerardo	Ramos-Larios	University of Guadalajara	Mexico
Jackeline Suzett	Rechy-García	Valongo Observatory, Rio de Janeiro	Brazil
Nicole	Reindl	Zentrum für Astronomie der Universität Heidelberg	Germany

Michael	Richer	Instituto de Astronomía, Universidad Nacional Autónoma de México	Mexico
Andreas	Ritter	Hong Kong University	China
Janis Berenice	Rodriguez Gonzalez	Instituto de Radioastronomía y Astrofísica, Morelia	México
Martin	Roth	Leibniz Institute for Astrophysics Potsdam	Germany
Laurence	Sabin	Instituto de Astronomía, Universidad Nacional Autónoma de México	Mexico
Raghvendra	Sahai	Jet Propulsion Laboratory, California Institute of Technology, Pasadena	USA
Carmen	Sánchez Contreras	Center for Astrobiology, Madrid	Spain
Miguel	Santander-García	Observatorio Astronómico Nacional, Madrid	Spain
Saskia	Schlagenhauf	Armagh Observatory and Planetarium	UK
Deborah	Schmidt	Franklin and Marshall College, PA	USA
Mark	Siebert	University of Virginia, Charlottesville	USA
Azlizan Adhyaqsa	Soemitro	Leibniz Institute for Astrophysics Potsdam	Germany
Noam	Soker	Technion, Haifa	Israel
Dimitris	Sourapanis	National Observatory of Athens	Greece
Letizia	Stanghellini	NSF's NOIRLab, Tucson	USA
Grażyna	Stasińska	Paris Observatory	France
Nicholas	Sterling	University of West Georgia, Carrollton	USA
Ryszard	Szczerba	Nicolaus Copernicus Astronomical Center, Torun	Poland
Jesús	Toalá	Instituto de Radioastronomía y Astrofísica, Morelia	Mexico
Silvia	Tosi	Roma Tre University	Italy
Zhijun	Tu	National Astronomical Observatories, Beijing	China
Toshiya	Ueta	University of Denver	USA
Lucero	Uscanga	University of Guanajuato	Mexico
Lucas	Valenzuela	University Observatory Munich	Germany
Griet	Van de Steene	Royal Observatory of Belgium, Brussels	Belgium
Luis	Velilla-Prieto	Institute of Fundamental Physics, Madrid	Spain
Paolo	Ventura	Observatory of Rome	Italia
Jeremy R.	Walsh	ESO, Garching	Germany
Roger	Wesson	Cardiff University	UK
Yong	Zhang	Sun Yat-sen University, Guangzhou	China
Albert	Zijlstra	The University of Manchester	UK
Lucy	Ziurys	University of Arizona, Tucson	USA
Staszek	Zola	Jagiellonian University, Krakow	Poland

Planetary Nebulae: A Universal Toolbox in the Era of Precision Astrophysics
Proceedings IAU Symposium No. 384, 2025
O. De Marco, A. Zijlstra & R. Szczerba, eds.
doi:10.1017/S1743921324000073

Planetary Nebulae as Probes of Kinematics and Abundances to Trace Galaxy Evolution

Letizia Stanghellini

NSF's NOIRLab, Tucson, United States
email: letizia.stanghellini@noirlab.edu

Abstract. We review recent results that utilize planetary nebulae (PNe) to constrain galactic dynamical and chemical evolution in different environments. Planetary nebulae have become essential probes in both these aspects of galaxy evolution, and novel observations illustrate their potential. Dynamical evolutionary models need observational constraints, and PNe uniquely probe the environment far from the galactic centers. In chemical evolution, the PN progenitor population spans a broad range of formation epochs; the oldest progenitors of local PNe are contemporary with H II regions in $z \sim 2$ star-forming galaxies (SFGs). The future will bring even more possibilities in these fields, especially with the advent of extremely large telescopes.

Keywords. extragalactic planetary nebulae, dynamical evolution of galaxies, chemical evolution of galaxies

1. Introduction

Extragalactic planetary nebulae (PNe) have been first observed in the 30s in the Magellanic Clouds (Cannon 1933), but identified as such much later, both in the Magellanic Clouds (Lindsay 1955) and M31 (Baade 1955). In the 70s and 80s the search moves out to other galaxies. A discussion and summary of early extragalactic PN surveys is given in Ford et al. (2002). Planetary nebulae in the intra-cluster (IC) had been first identified much later (Arnaboldi et al. 1996).

Years of studies have consolidate the understanding that extragalactic PNe are excellent kinematic probes of the stellar populations they represent. With the advent of more efficient slitless methods for radial velocity measurement, this potential began to be exploited. We also know of elliptical galaxies where PNe indicate a clear presence of dark matter, in agreement with other techniques, yet probing unique regimes at large galactocentric distances. PNe also provide important kinematic information in spiral galaxies, in particular those which appear edge-on, where the angular separation from the galactic plane yields to the physical distance of the PN from the plane.

Furthermore, the use of PNe as probes of stellar populations in our galaxy and beyond has been essential to advance the knowledge of chemical evolution of star-forming galaxies (SFGs). Planetary nebulae are bright and easily to recognize in galaxies; their chemical abundances are relatively easy to measure; and PNe represent a definite stage of stellar evolution, thus can be associated to a specific progenitor mass range and lookback time by comparing their abundances to the yields from asymptotic giant branch (AGB) evolution. Galactic and Magellanic Cloud PNe, as well as those in nearby galaxies, have been studied in detail by spectroscopic means to determine the metal distribution in our galaxy and beyond.

Both these aspects of extragalactic PNe have flourished, and the usage of PNe as probes for extragalactic astronomy has been conspicuous in the recent years. The last full meeting on extragalactic PNe was within the 2015 IAU General Assembly (Stanghellini et al. 2016), with reviews on the kinematical role of PNe (Coccato 2016; Arnaboldi 2016). Chemical evolution in nearby galaxies has been reviewed by Magrini et al. (2012), and more recently by Stanghellini (2019). The last IAU Symposium on PNe (Liu et al. 2017) also included several topics related to extragalactic PNe. It is refreshing to see that the IAU PN community has kept the field up to task, and in the present Symposium the program includes many extragalactic PN talks and posters. The extragalactic PN community, as other PN communities, is especially suited to establish collaborations with other astrophysical fields, and makes the PN community as a whole known across astronomical expertise.

It is a pleasure to review the research status of PNe as probes of galaxy dynamical and chemical evolution at this Symposium. Similarly to the oral presentation, this paper covers the kinematics of PNe in external galaxies and in the IC (Section 2) and PNe as probes of galactic chemical evolution (Section 3). Each section includes a brief overview of the subject, and a discussion of selected results in the field in the past five years. This paper highlights progress in the field(s) with the attempt to focus on the importance of specific results rather than reference completeness. The intent is to stimulate the audience, especially students and young researchers, to enter in these fascinating scientific realms.

2. Motion and light: Planetary Nebulae Probing the Dynamical Evolution of Galaxies

Extragalactic PNe are kinematic probes of present-day (i. e., low-redshift) galaxies and their dark halos and of the IC and intra-group (IG) environments. The ultimate goal of studying these PNe and their motion is to characterize the evolution of galaxies in the cosmological framework, since present-day galaxies are the result of cosmic evolution.

PNe have a special advantage over other probes in these applications, since they can probe all the way out to 6 R_e and more, where R_e is the effective, or half-light, radius. Most other stellar probes have limitations as of where in space outside the halos are reliable. The distribution of PNe follows the surface brightness distribution, and their kinematics is seamless with the integrated light measurements observed in the central galactic regions, typically with IFU techniques.

In this paper we will go through several different environment. With no pretense of completeness, rather, with the aim of a quick travel across the power of PNe in extragalactic astrophysics, we will discuss Early-type galaxies (ETGs), SFGs, and other environments. Early-type galaxies are elliptical or spheroidal in shape; they tend to be massive, red, having low star formation (SF). These galaxies typically live in clusters and groups; they display random, rather than organized, stellar motions; finally, they can be slow (SR) or fast (FR) rotators. Star-Forming galaxies display a morphology with disks, spiral arms, and bars. They have high SF; they tend to be blue, and their stellar motions are rotational, with $V/\sigma >> 1$. We will also discuss dwarf spheroidal galaxies, streams, and the IC and IG environments.

2.1. *Early-Type Galaxies*

The knowledge of ETG formation is still evolving (Cimatti et al. 2019). The current view of standard cosmology suggests that wet mergers, i.e., mergers of disk galaxies, have an essential role in ETG formation. Wet mergers can destroy disk structures, leading to ETG morphology. It appears most likely that the formation of ETGs is a hybrid process, involving both initial collapse and (or) wet merger events, with in-situ star formation, followed by merger episodes (dry mergers of dwarf galaxies), which populates the ETGs

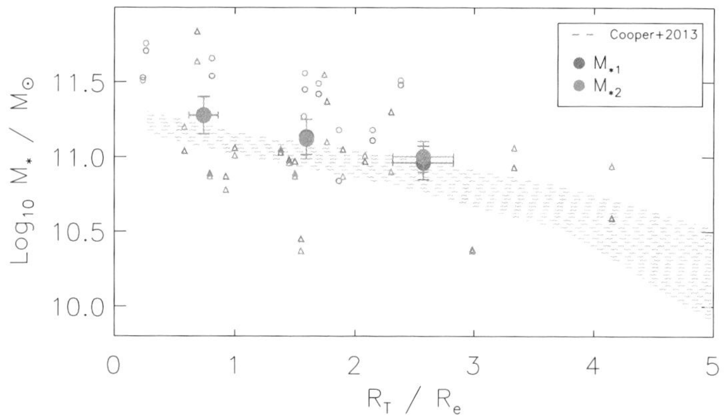

Figure 1. Total stellar mass vs. transition radius R_T in units of R_e (open symbols: circles for SRs, triangles for FRs). The full symbols show the same quantities in bins of $R_\mathrm{T}/R_\mathrm{e}$. Different colors show the results of two different procedures for calculating the total stellar mass. Pulsoni et al. (2018), reproduced with permission, © ESO.

with ex-situ star formation. As a consequence, the central regions and the halos of ETGs are physically diverse, including in the aspects of their kinematics.

PNe are kinematic and light tracers; we can measure their angular momentum (AM), mass distribution, and velocity distributions vs. their dispersion. Early-type galaxies that are FR show a decrease in rotation in their outskirts; the distance at which the decrease in the rotation occurs is consistent with the size of the disk within the galaxy. The spatial transition between the rotation– and dispersion–dominated parts of ETGs is different for galaxies of different masses: More massive galaxies tend to have transition radii, R_T, which are smaller fractions of their R_e, as is seen in Figure 1 (Pulsoni et al. 2018).

Galaxies that are efficient in forming stars are also efficient in retaining their AM. A strong correlation between specific AM (sAM, j) and stellar mass has been known to hold in spiral galaxies (Fall & Efstathiou 1980). Recently, Pulsoni et al. (2023) explored a similar relation in ETGs, where PNe have proven to be of fundamental utility in constraining the models. Pulsoni et al. (2023) pursued a survey of extragalactic PNe in ETG galaxies with the extragalactic PN spectrograph (PN.S), and found that ETGs lose AM during their evolution, while SFGs retain more AM than ETGs of similar mass; lenticular galaxies (S0) retain more ($\sim 25\%$) of their AM from their host halos than ellipticals ($< 10\%$), for masses up to $\log(M/M_\odot) \sim 10.5$.

2.2. *Star-Forming Galaxies*

The characterization of SFGs in the last few years has also taken advantage of the wealth of extragalactic PN data. A systematic study of disk galaxies that include PN analysis (Aniyan et al. 2018, 2021) allowed to resolve the disk-halo of two systems, NGC 628 and NGC 6946.

When the disk dominates the mass in the inner regions, galaxies are labelled *maximal*; when the dark halo is dynamically important in the inner galaxy (e. g. in the Milky Way), the galaxy is *sub-maximal*. Aniyan et al. (2018, 2021) measured the mass-to-light (M/L) ratio in the studied galaxies to assess the degeneracy from the surface mass density – proportional to the $\sigma_\mathrm{z}/h_\mathrm{z}$ ratio – and the surface brightness of the disk. The novel approach here is the usage of the same kinematical component to measure σ_z and h_z, as it should be, resulting in higher estimates of M/L than measured earlier with measurements from different components.

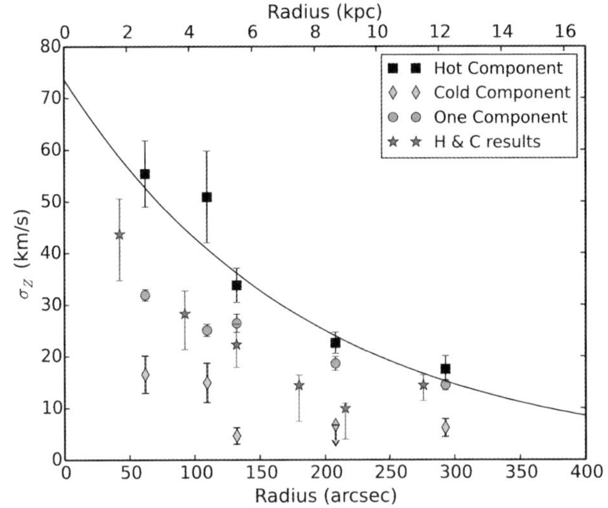

Figure 2. The σ_z per radial bin in NGC 628. The black and grey markers indicate the hot and cold velocity dispersions, respectively, from the two component fits, the cyan markers are the single-component values, and the points in red are the Herrmann & Ciardullo (2009) PNe data (see original text for more details). The data points at R = 62 and 109 arcsec were obtained for integrated light spectra from VIRUS-W and the outer data points are for PNe from PN.S. The solid line denotes an exponential with twice the galaxy's dynamical scale length, fit to the hot component. The errors bars are the 1σ errors obtained from Monte Carlo simulations. From Aniyan et al. (2018).

The result, similar for both studied galaxies, is that the disk is more dominant in the inner regions that we though, making both galaxies likely to be maximal. These studies put strong constraints for future analysis, and demonstrates once more the importance of PNe in dynamical evolution of galaxies.

2.3. *Characterizing the Intra-Cluster Environment*

Planetary nebulae are essential players in the IC and the IG. PNe have been observed in the IC and IG all the way to the Virgo, Hydra, Fornax, and Coma clusters. In local groups, observations are consistent with the scenario where IG stars are formed in the satellite galaxies of the group, setting a strong constrain on the evolution history of galaxies.

The light fraction of stars in the IC/IG environment is less than ten percent that of the whole cluster/group light. These IC/IG stars or stellar probes are not bound to a specific galaxy; they are bounded to the cluster/group cluster potential instead. CMD in clusters revealed that the IC light consists of old (10 Gyr) and metal-poor stars. The review on IC light by Arnaboldi & Gerhard (2022) includes a detailed description of these phenomena and the discoveries leading to the knowledge of IC/IG starlight. In the present review we focus on a recent results that exemplify the power of such IC probes to our understanding of galaxy evolution.

A study of stars and PNe in M87 revealed the galaxy to be strongly triaxial. Red globular clusters have similar dispersion (σ) to that of stars, and appear to belong to the stellar halo (Zhang et al. 2015) while the IC component of PNe have sharply rising σ (Longobardi et al. 2018), separating this population from that of stars (Liepold et al. 2023). In Figure 3 we show the contrast of the two populations, disclosing the nature of the matter distribution in this galaxy.

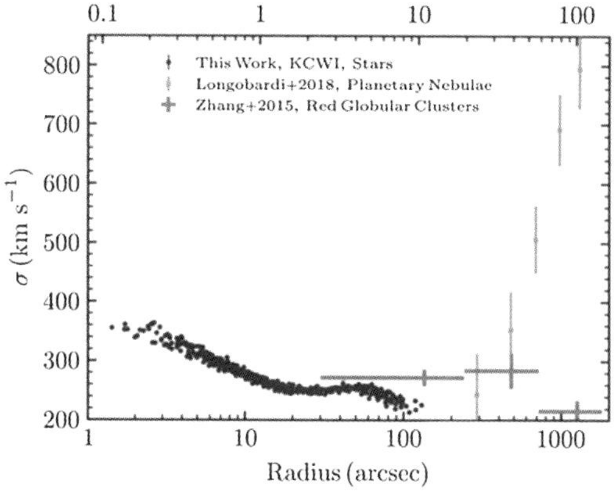

Figure 3. Radial profile of stellar velocity dispersion of M87 out to 100 kpc from Liepold et al. (2023) (in their Fig. 3). Red globular clusters (red symbols) have similar σ as stars (blue symbols) and appear belonging to the M87 stellar halo whereas the IC component of PNe in green, have sharply rising profile. From Liepold et al. (2023).

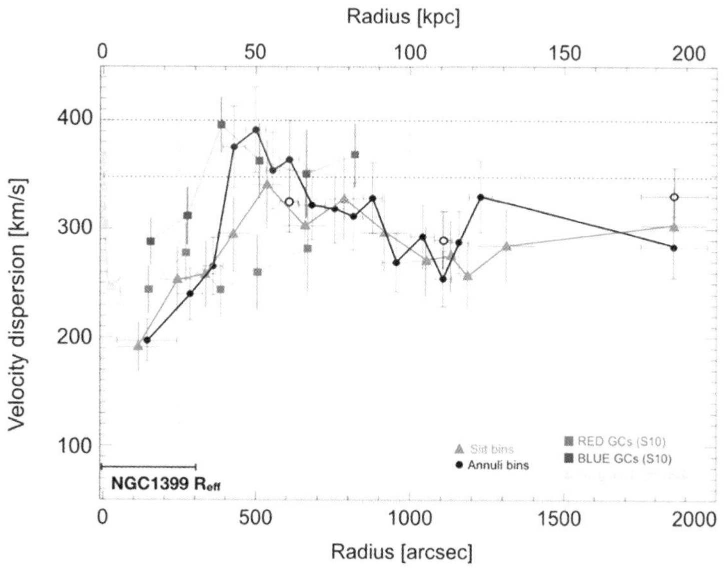

Figure 4. Velocity dispersion vs. radius as observed in PNe (black symbols and lines) and globular clusters (see labels). From Spiniello et al. (2018).

2.4. *Dwarf-Merging, Streams, and Sub-Structures*

Streams carry information about the transformation of the dwarf systems; From stream analysis, is possible to determine the extent to which the baryonic material is distrupted. Sub-structures in halos are hard to detect but essential to constrain the formation of galaxies. In the Fornax cluster, PNe are unbounded at radii larger than 400 arcsec. There may be sub-halos around 1000 arcsec. Further away from the galaxy center the profile flattens out. The Stream-finding algorithm COSTA (COld STream finding Algorithm, Gatto et al. (2020) was applied to PN (and GC) catalogs to characterize streams in the Fornax cluster. The resulting streams (13 identified) at various distances from the core center, the streams' dispersion velocities are compatible with those typical of dwarf galaxies (Spiniello et al. 2018; Napolitano et al. 2022).

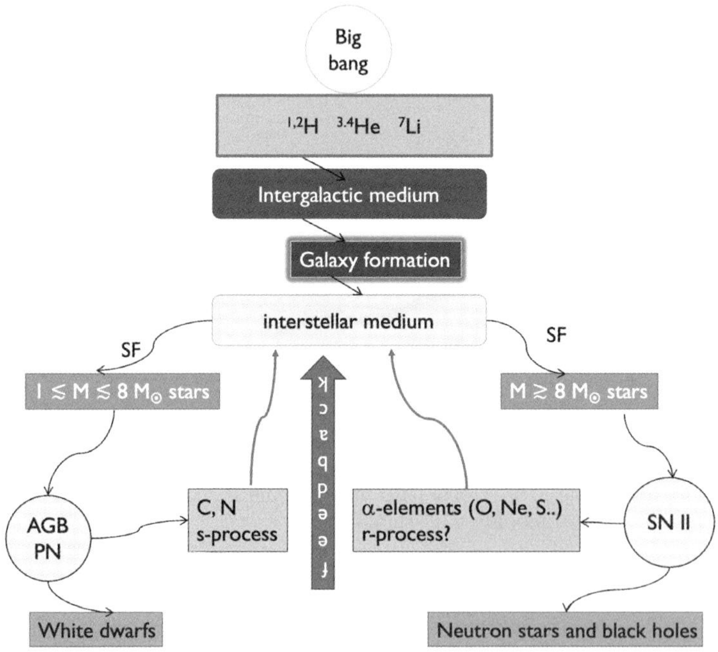

Figure 5. Schematic paths to chemical evolution in galaxies, in the cosmological context.

3. Abundances: Probing the Galactic Chemical Evolution

Figure 5 is a conceptual flow chart illustrating cosmic recycling due to stellar and galactic evolution. The Universe starts off chemically simple and evolves into chemical complexity due to the evolution of galaxies and stars at different times. The metallicity of galaxies carries the signature of their chemical evolution through cosmic time, and it is thus essential to find the best observational probes for it. Star formation occurs upon galaxy evolution. There are two major stellar mass channels: Low- and intermediate-mass stars (LIMS), with masses between ~ 1 and $\sim 8\ M_{\odot}$, follow the evolutionary path of red giants, the AGB, and eventually eject their envelopes in the PN process, are responsible for a sizable fraction of the cosmic carbon and nitrogen; Massive stars, with $M > 8\ M_{\odot}$ produce most of the α-elements in the Universe. Gas accretion, both during early evolutionary stages or subsequent gas inflow and outflow, also determines the final chemical distribution.

Models of galactic chemical evolution have been used to explore the various possible path to galaxy formation and chemical evolution. Nonetheless, they can not tell us how observables should look now, from ab-initio evolution. Just as PNe kinematic is essential to constrain the dynamical evolution of galaxies, abundances of PNe are one of the most powerful tools to constrain chemical evolution. In particular, radial metallicity gradients and especially their cosmic evolution are the ultimate constraints for these models, and different authors have been creative in using a variety of probes marking distinct cosmic times.

The inside-out growth scenario of spiral galaxy formation produces negative metallicity gradients, with higher metallicity at the galactic centers than in their periphery. Intense accretion of external pristine gas may result in inverted (positive) gradients. From the models, there is no consensus on cosmological gradient evolution, i.e., flattening vs. steepening of the gradient with time. Gradient evolution is the best constraints on galaxy growth and assembly history. Gibson et al. (2013) published a set of chemical evolution

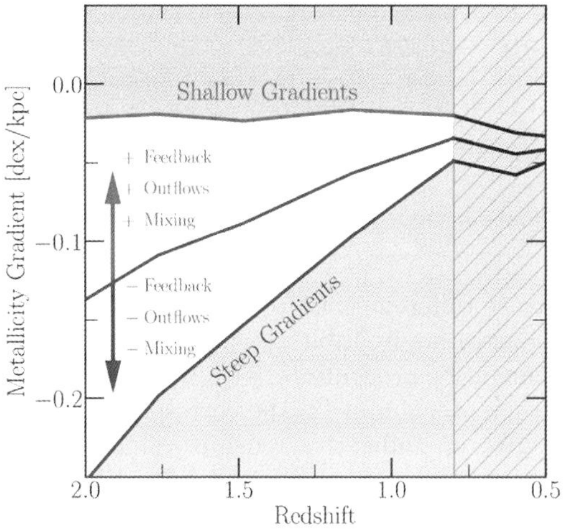

Figure 6. A schematic summarizing the results of Gibson et al. (2013). The gradient evolution of enhanced (i.e. strong) and conventional (i.e. weak) feedback models are shown in red and blue, respectively. The gradient evolution of a hypothetical model with feedback stronger than conventional models but weaker than enhanced models is shown in purple. From Hemler et al. (2021).

models that was seminal for gradient evolution studies. These are numerical models with two branches of gradients, flattening or steepening with time, depending on galaxy feedback. TNG50 models (Hemler et al. 2021) show steep negative gradients at high redshift; FIRE (Ma et al. 2017) gradients are more similar to Gibson et al. (2013)'s models with enhanced feedback.

Figure 6 shows a schematic illustration of the metal gradients in evolution models. We see that adjusting the strength of feedback affects the redshift evolution of metallicity gradients. In this Figure we see the gradient evolution of enhanced (i. e. strong) and conventional (i. e. weak) feedback models in red and blue, respectively. But the models can not tell us a priori wether radial metallicity gradients are flattening or steepening with time if we do not make strong assumptions. In conclusion, the only reasonable way to understand the chemical evolution of SFGs is through observational constraining of the models. In this part of the review we will touch upon the prominent results of the recent past and look at the prospective for the future in this field.

3.1. *Measuring Radial Metallicity Gradients and their Time Evolution*

Radial metallicity gradients in galaxies are measured starting from the galactic center going to the periphery in concentric annuli for diffuse sources, and just by abundance vs. galactocentric distance for discrete sources such as PNe; thus to determine a metallicity gradient, generally identified by the slope of its linear fit in dex kpc^{-1}, we need to measure the abundance and galactocentric distance of the probes. The metallicity depends on the probe; Fe and Mg are both used in stars, while O, Ar, S are the most prominent metals used in nebulae. Fe can not be used for PN gradients since it appears to be depleted compared to the underlying stellar population (Delgado-Inglada & Rodríguez 2014; Stanghellini et al. 2023).

We measure gradients using PNe (and H II regions) in the Milky Way and nearby galaxies with direct abundances; this type of analysis is based, in turn, on weak-line plasma diagnostics. PNe are too faint for weak-line analysis for farther galaxies, where the nebular gradients are measured with strong-line analysis of H II regions. Of course

Table 1. Ages and masses of emission-line progenitors.

$t_\star[Gyr]$	$M_{TO}/M_\odot$	z	Notes
10.5	1	2.2	lower limit of PPN mass
$\gtrsim 7.5$	$\lesssim 1.1$	>0.95	OPPNe
2.35	1.5	0.2	
$\lesssim 1.0$	$\gtrsim 2.0$	0	YPPNe
0.32	3.0	0	
0.22	3.5	0	HBB onset in Galactic AGB stars
0	>8	0	H II region progenitors, upper limit of PPN mass

PNe and H II regions trace different *time zones* of the cosmic evolution, and we define these stellar evolution constraints in Table 1, where we compare typical stellar evolution timescales of emission-line probe progenitors, with their turn-off masses; column (1) gives the stellar age or limit thereof, column (2) the corresponding stellar mass or mass limit, and in column (3) we give an indicative redshift value at progenitor's formation, to compare gradients of nearby galaxies with those of redshifted galaxies. The ages and masses are from Maraston (2005), for solar metallicity, and the redshifts are estimated from standard cosmology. It is worth noting that probes such as PNe with young stellar progenitors probe the same *time zone* than the H II regions, which are equals to constrain the gradient slope at present time.

We use the old progenitor PNe (OPPNe) and young progenitor PNe (YPPNe) as defined in Stanghellini & Haywood (2018), based on the evolving chemistry in the probe, due to AGB evolution, which depends on the progenitor's turn-off mass, see also Ventura et al. (2017). We give the chemical definition of YPPNe and OPPNe in Equations (1) and (2). It is worth noting that other authors have used thin and thick disk populations of PNe to distinguish between young and old, such as in M31 (Bhattacharya et al. 2022).

$$\text{OPPN}\begin{cases}\log(\text{N/H})+12<0.8\times(\log(\text{O/H})+12)+1.40\\ \log(\text{C/H})+12>\log(\text{N/H})+12\end{cases} \tag{1}$$

$$\text{YPPN}\begin{cases}\log(\text{N/H})+12>0.57\times(\log(\text{C/H})+12)+3.67\\ \log(\text{N/H})+12>0.6\times(\log(\text{O/H})+12)+3.30\end{cases} \tag{2}$$

3.2. *Observed Radial Metallicity Gradients and their Evolution in Star-Forming Galaxies*

We can only measure gradients from direct abundances in nearby galaxies. There are 4 galaxies in addition to the Milky Way with metallicity gradients measured this way. Since the last IAU Symposium on PNe (Liu et al. 2017) there was limited progress in this field, with new datasets for the same galaxies as those reviewed by Bresolin (2017). In Table 2, we give the updated references for all and only the oxygen measured gradients in nearby galaxies, where both a young and old population are analyzed together. Column (1) gives the name of the galaxy, column (2) and (3) give the population used in the gradient time evolution, and column (3) indicates the references.

3.3. *Gradients in the Milky Way and Nearby Galaxies*

Figure 7 shows the latest measured oxygen gradients in Galactic PNe (Bucciarelli & Stanghellini 2023), where OPPNe (bottom) and YPPNe (top) are separate, the distances are from Gaia DR3 calibrations, and the abundances are from the general literature. There is mild gradient evolution in the MW when the oxygen gradient is measured with PNe, with slopes from OPPNe and YPPNe respectively -0.0121 ± 0.00465 and -0.022 ± 0.00758 [dex kpc^{-1}], thus disclosing a mild steepening since Galaxy formation,

Table 2. Radial Oxygen Gradients from old and young populations. References for Local Galaxies.

Galaxy	Old Pop.	Young Pop.	References
NGC 300	PNe	H II regions	Peña & Flores-Durán (2019)
M 81	PNe	H II regions	Bresolin (2017)
M 33	non-Type I PNe	Type I PNe	Peña & Flores-Durán (2019)
MW	OPPNe	YPPNe	Bucciarelli & Stanghellini (2023)
M 31	thick disk PNe	thin disk PNe	Bhattacharya et al. (2022)

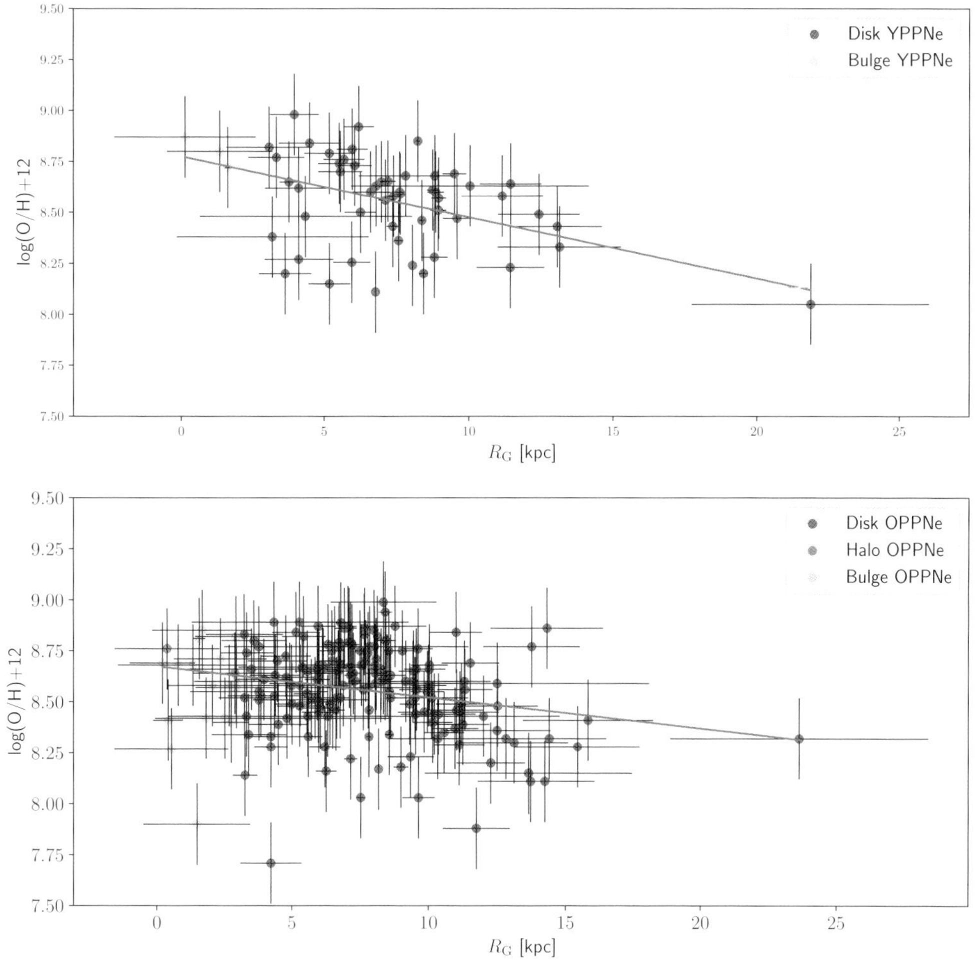

Figure 7. Radial oxygen gradients in Galactic YPPNe (top) and OPPNe (bottom), with distances from the Gaia DR3 calibration (Bucciarelli & Stanghellini 2023). The slopes indicate a steepening of the oxygen gradients with time in the Milky Way.

with a slope change of 0.01 dex. Excluding possible bulge and halo PNe would not change this result sensibly. This paper uses the best distance scale available to date; additionally, Gaia proper motion information allowed to confirm the PN progenitors ages in terms of their kinematics, as shown in Figure 8.

In Figure 9 we plot the gradient slope evolution from the references in Table 2. This figure includes of all local galaxies where this type of analysis is feasible, and it confirms a mild steepening of the gradient slope with time since galaxy evolution for all the galaxies

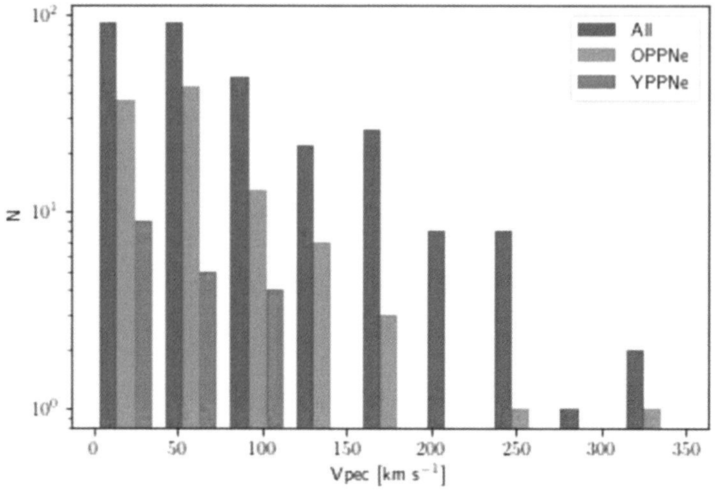

Figure 8. Distribution of peculiar velocity for OPPNe and YPPNe, adapted from Bucciarelli & Stanghellini (2023).

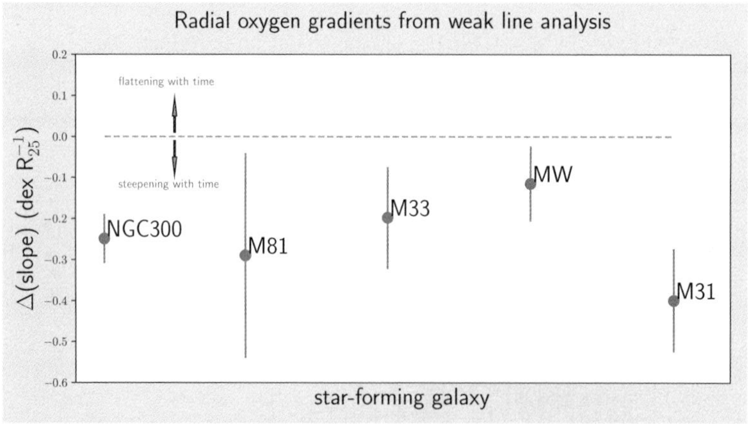

Figure 9. Radial oxygen gradients from emission-line probes in all local galaxies where is possible to measure them based on weak-line abundances of old and young populations. The slopes reflect the gradients given in the references of Tab. 2.

examined. In this figure we plot gradient slopes in [dex R_{25}^{-1}], where R_{25} is the 25% isophot in each galaxy.

3.4. *Cosmology with PNe, and Gradients in High-Redshift Galaxies*

With the analysis of direct abundances of PNe in nearby galaxies we have approximately reached the current capability limit for gradients evolution studies. The next step for PN gradient usage is the cosmological environment. Following the translation of stellar progenitor ages and redshift above and in Table 1, we can plot the metallicity gradients of local and redshifted galaxies in the same regime. Radial migration may affect old stellar populations; migration at the 1-2 kpc level would have no effects on this analysis.

In Figure 10, we show gradient evolution in galaxies in the slope vs. redshift plot, where with PNe are placed at their pseudo-z. In the figure we also plot Gibson et al. (2013) models. We indicate other classes of redshifted gradients in the plot (figure's

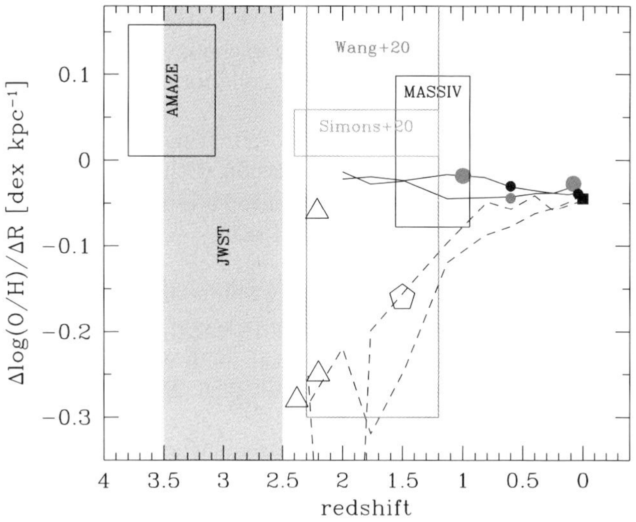

Figure 10. Radial oxygen gradients (slope), in dex kpc^{-1}, using different age populations in nearby galaxies and placing them at their inferred population redshift. Red, blue, and black dots are respectively the emission-line gradients from direct abundances for the MW (red), M33 (blue) and M81 (black), as in Stanghellini (2019). The boxes indicate the loci of external galaxies redshifts and their gradients. The references are: AMAZE (Troncoso et al. 2014), Wang+20 (Wang et al. 2020), Simons+20 (Simons et al. 2021), MASSIV (Queyrel et al. 2012). The JWST rectangle is the locus of expected JWST gradients. The lines represent the models from Gibson et al. (2013), with regular (broken) and enhanced (solid) feedback. Open symbols are lensed galaxies from Jones et al. (2013) (triangles) and Yuan et al. (2011) (pentagons).

legend and caption). We note that mild steepening of the metallicity gradient with time is predominant, with the exception of the lensed galaxies, plotted with open symbols.

Other gradient slopes of redshifted galaxies are available to date from strong-line abundances, see e. g. Figure 8 in Curti et al. (2020) and Figure 2 in Wang et al. (2022), the latter being the only result from the JWST to date. Most of these observations are consistent with steepening since galaxy formation, just as in local galaxies.

The green box in Figure 10 marks the realm of JWST. Data analysis of several programs, some already observed in the first cycles, could yield to metallicity gradients in several high redshift galaxies, where strong-line analysis will determine their gradients; in this case, redshifted emission lines observed in the IR regime for these galaxies.

4. The Future

The fields of constraining dynamical and chemical evolution models of galaxies are healthy and evolving, and PNe play a pivotal role, which we expect to become even more relevant in the future. Surveys with the PN.S and other instrumentation will constrain the motion of many more galaxies, selected by mass and shape, toward a deep understanding of the role of dark matter in galaxy evolution.

Progress can certainly be made in the era of the extremely large telescopes for radial metal gradients. For example, spectra of the brightest PNe in M81 could be acquired in a few minutes down to auroral lines for plasma diagnostics, as opposed to the two nights used in 8m-class telescopes observations. Much fainter PNe and H II regions are also within reach with reasonable exposures. Emission-line probes are within reach in the Virgo cluster, where the variety of galaxy types can be examined in detail for their chemical content, and the field of metallicity gradients is likely to take a leap in the near future.

The subjects reviewed here will especially thrive in the cross-pollination between the fields of PNe and extragalactic astronomy. Such exchange is happening already, and will hopefully continue to provide more grounds for collaborations in the future.

I thank the organizer of this Symposium for inviting me to review these fascinating subjects. I also acknowledge scientific discussion with Drs. Magda Arnaboldi, Paolo Ventura, and Mark Dickinson who provided essential advise respectively on the dynamics of galaxies, stellar evolution, and galaxy evolution.

References

Aniyan, S., Freeman, K. C., Arnaboldi, M., et al. 2018, MNRAS, 476, 1909
Aniyan, S., Ponomareva, A. A., Freeman, K. C., et al. 2021, MNRAS, 500, 3579
Arnaboldi, M., Freeman, K. C., Mendez, R. H., et al. 1996, ApJ, 472, 145
Arnaboldi, M. 2016, IAU Focus Meeting, 29B, 5
Arnaboldi, M. & Gerhard, O. 2022, Frontiers in Astronomy and Space Sciences, 9, 403
Baade, W. 1955, AJ, 60, 151
Bhattacharya, S., Arnaboldi, M., Caldwell, N., et al. 2022, MNRAS 517, 2343
Bresolin F., 2017, IAU S323, by Liu, X., Stanghellini, L., & Karakas, A., 237
Bucciarelli, B. & Stanghellini, L. 2023, arXiv:2309.10096
Cannon, A. J. 1933, Harvard College Observatory Bulletin, 891, 2
Cimatti, A., Fraternali, F., & Nipoti, C. 2019, Introduction to Galaxy Formation and Evolution: From Primordial Gas to Present-Day Galaxies. Cambridge University Press. ISBN: 9781107134768, 2019
Coccato, L. 2016, IAU Focus Meeting, 29B, 20
Cooper, A. P., D'Souza, R., Kauffmann, G., et al. 2013, MNRAS, 434, 3348
Curti, M., Maiolino, R., Cirasuolo, M., et al. 2020, MNRAS, 492, 821
Delgado-Inglada, G. & Rodríguez, M. 2014, ApJ 784, 173
Fall, S. M. & Efstathiou, G. 1980, MNRAS, 193, 189
Ford, H., Peng, E., & Freeman, K. 2002, The Dynamics, Structure & History of Galaxies: A Workshop in Honour of Professor Ken Freeman, 273, 41
Gatto, M., Napolitano, N. R., Spiniello, C., et al. 2020, A&A, 644, A134
Gibson, B. K., Pilkington, K., Brook, C. B., et al. 2013, A&A, 554, A47
Hemler, Z. S., Torrey, P., Qi, J., et al. 2021, MNRAS, 506, 3024
Herrmann, K. A. & Ciardullo, R. 2009, ApJ, 705, 1686
Jones, T., Ellis, R. S., Richard, J., et al. 2013, ApJ, 765, 48
Liepold, E. R., Ma, C.-P., & Walsh, J. L. 2023, ApJL, 945, L35
Lindsay, E. M. 1955, MNRAS, 115, 248
Liu, X., Stanghellini, L., & Karakas, A. 2017, Planetary Nebulae: Multi-Wavelength Probes of Stellar and Galactic Evolution (IAU S323)
Longobardi, A., Arnaboldi, M., Gerhard, O., et al. 2018, A&A, 620, A111
Ma, X., Hopkins, P. F., Feldmann, R., et al. 2017, MNRAS, 466, 4780
Magrini L., Stanghellini L., Gonçalves D. R., 2012, IAU S283, by Manchado, A., Stanghellini, L., & Schönberner, D., 251
Manchado, A., Stanghellini, L., & Schönberner, D. 2012, Planetary Nebulae (IAU S283)
Maraston, C. 2005, MNRAS, 362, 799
Napolitano, N. R., Gatto, M., Spiniello, C., et al. 2022, A&A, 657, A94
Peña, M. & Flores-Durán, S. N. 2019, RMA&A, 55, 255
Pulsoni, C., Gerhard, O., Arnaboldi, M., et al. 2018, A&A, 618, A94
Pulsoni, C., Gerhard, O., Fall, S. M., et al. 2023, A&A, 674, A96
Queyrel, J., Contini, T., Kissler-Patig, M., et al. 2012, A&A, 539, A93
Simons, R. C., Papovich, C., Momcheva, I., et al. 2021, ApJ, 923, 203
Spiniello, C., Napolitano, N. R., Arnaboldi, M., et al. 2018, MNRAS, 477, 1880
Stanghellini, L., Peña, M., & Méndez, R. 2016, IAU Focus Meeting, 29B, 3
Stanghellini, L. & Haywood, M. 2018, ApJ, 862, 45

Stanghellini, L. 2019, IAU Symposium, 343, 174
Stanghellini, L, Smith, Verne V., Cunha, K, and Prantzos, Nikos, 2023, in preparation
Troncoso, P., Maiolino, R., Sommariva, V., et al. 2014, A&A, 563, A58
Ventura, P., Stanghellini, L., Dell'Agli, F., et al. 2017, MNRAS 471, 4648
Wang, X., Jones, T. A., Treu, T., et al. 2020, ApJ, 900, 183. d
Wang, X., Jones, T., Vulcani, B., et al. 2022, ApJL, 938, L16
Yuan, T.-T., Kewley, L. J., Swinbank, A. M., et al. 2011, ApJL, 732, L14
Zhang, H.-X., Peng, E. W., Côté, P., et al. 2015, ApJ, 802, 30

Planetary Nebulae: A Universal Toolbox in the Era of Precision Astrophysics
Proceedings IAU Symposium No. 384, 2025
O. De Marco, A. Zijlstra & R. Szczerba, eds.
doi:10.1017/S1743921323005501

Planetary nebulae as tracers of stellar population properties: unlocking their potential with integral-field spectroscopy

Ana Inés Ennis[1,2], Johanna Hartke[3,4], Magda Arnaboldi[5], Claudia Pulsoni[6], Fuyan Bian[7] and Chiara Spiniello[8,9]

[1]Waterloo Centre for Astrophysics, University of Waterloo, Canada

[2]Perimeter Institute, Canada

[3]Finnish Centre for Astronomy with ESO (FINCA), FI-20014 University of Turku, Finland

[4]Tuorla Observatory, Department of Physics and Astronomy, FI-20014 University of Turku, Finland

[5]European Southern Observatory, Garching bei München, Germany

[6]Max-Planck-Institut für Extraterrestrische Physik (MPE), Garching, Germany

[7]European Southern Observatory, Alonso de Córdova, Vitacura, Santiago, Chile

[8]INAF - Osservatorio Astronomico di Capodimonte, Salita Moiariello 16, 80131 - Napoli, Italy

[9]Department of Physics, University of Oxford, Denys Wilkinson Building, Keble Road, Oxford OX1 3RH, UK

email: ennis.ana@gmail.com

Abstract. Planetary nebulae (PNe) are essential tracers of the kinematics of the diffuse halo and intracluster light where stellar spectroscopy is unfeasible, due to their strong emission lines. However, that is not all they can reveal about the underlying stellar population. In recent years, it has also been found that PNe in the metal-poor halos of galaxies have different properties (specific frequency, luminosity function), than PNe in the more metal-rich galaxy centers. A more quantitative understanding of the role of age and metallicity in these relations would turn PNe into valuable stellar-population tracers. In order to do that, a full characterization of PNe in regions where the stellar light can also be analysed in detail is necessary. In this work, we make use of integral-field spectroscopic data covering the central regions of galaxies, which allow us to measure both stellar ages and metallicities as well as to detect PNe. This analysis is fundamental to calibrate PNe as stellar population tracers and to push our understanding of galaxy properties at unprecedented galactocentric distances.

Keywords. catalogs, surveys, galaxies: elliptical and lenticular, cD, planetary nebulae

1. Introduction

For almost thirty years planetary nebulae (PNe) have been used as kinematic tracers of the extended haloes of galaxies (Arnaboldi et al. 1994; Napolitano et al. 2000; Coccato et al. 2009; Spiniello et al. 2018; Pulsoni et al. 2023). The distinct optical spectral features of PNe, characterized by a flat continuum and prominent emission lines (see Figure 1), render them detectable at large distances from the centre of galaxies, where the emitted light is too faint for absorption line spectroscopy and stellar population analysis. Furthermore, the luminosity-specific PN number ($\alpha = N_{PN}/L_{gal}$ ratio) has been

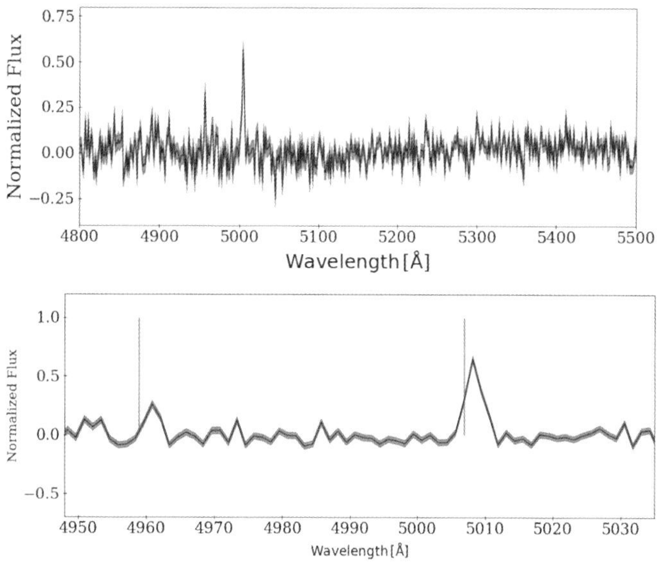

Figure 1. Top: full spectrum for a PN detected in NGC 1387. Bottom: zoom-in of the same spectrum in the [OIII] doublet region.

shown to vary with the age and metallicity of the stellar population of the host galaxy (Buzzoni et al. 2006). A comprehensive understanding of this relationship would unlock the full potential of PNe as tracers of stellar populations, enabling us to characterize age and metallicity in the extended haloes at greater distances than ever before.

Given that stellar population properties vary throughout the full radial span of a galaxy, it is reasonable to expect these differences may also appear in the PN population if they are connected. Currently, there are very few galaxies for which a joint analysis has been performed of the radial variations of α and the age and metallicity of its stellar populations. In Hartke et al. (2017), the α-parameter of M49 was shown to vary with colour, presenting lower values in the inner, red, metal-rich halo. Similarly, for M105 in Hartke et al. (2020) two distinct values of α were estimated for different areas of the galaxy, identifying a diffuse outer component with old halo metal-poor stars. Since these studies rely on photometric data, the relation is estimated in terms of colours, which do not translate directly into age and metallicity.

To resolve this degeneracy, it is necessary to analyse PNe in regions of the galaxy where high SNR spectroscopic data of the stellar population can be obtained in order to estimate their age and metallicity independently. A challenge arises, however, as wherever the stellar population is bright enough to allow this, PNe become much harder to detect using traditional methods. The central regions of galaxies, which are perfect candidates for detailed analysis of stellar populations, are usually blind spots for PNe detection techniques.

In this work, we present a way to overcome these limitations by using IFU data from MUSE and the DELF technique (Differential Emission-Line Filter, Roth et al. 2021). This enables us to detect PNe while simultaneously analysing the underlying stellar population in the same area. By linking α-parameters directly to age and metallicity for a sample of galaxies, we aim to gain a thorough understanding of these relations. This takes us one step closer to PNe becoming reliable tracers of stellar population properties. We aim to perform this analysis on a sample of early-type galaxies which was built using two criteria: that they have MUSE observations publicly available in the ESO Archive, and that they have an available PNe catalogue for their outer halo, for future comparison. We show in these proceedings the results process applied to one of the galaxies in this sample, NGC 1387.

2. Detection and classification of sources

Traditionally, the main detection method for PNe is based on obtaining *on* and *off* images, i.e. a narrowband filter image centered in the [OIII] line, and a broadband filter image which should capture continuum emission (Ford et al. 1973; Ford & Jenner 1975; Jacoby et al. 1992). Because PNe have a negligible continuum, they will not show up in the broadband filter, but they will be very bright in the narrow-band one, making them easy to identify among other sources. The main idea behind DELF is that this is easily emulated using IFU data since we can create images based on any filter, and we can enhance our signal by having access to the entire spectrum with high resolution, thus being able to build customised filters in the most convenient way for our purposes.

As a first step, we subtract the continuum emission from the cubes by fitting a polynomial function to each pixel and creating a "continuum cube", which we then subtract to create an "emission-line cube" (Spriggs et al. 2020). From the emission-line cube, we extract our *on* images. We create our filter considering that PNe have velocity dispersions of about $\pm 500\,\mathrm{km/s}$, so the line can be detected in 5007.8 ± 7.5Å. Rather than creating a narrowband filter with this width, we split this range into 12 slices with a width of 1.25Å, which improves our detection capabilities. We run Source Extractor (Bertin & Arnouts 1996) in each of the slices and require sources to be detected in three consecutive slices in order to be considered positive detections. Once we build our catalogue of detected sources, we filter out spurious detections by fitting a Gaussian profile to the flux across all slices. This ensures that we are not detecting extended emission across the entire wavelength range, or potential artifacts in the spectra. Finally, we extract the full spectrum for each source, and perform a visual check on the lines, as seen in Figure 1.

Since we have access to the full MUSE spectrum for each object, we are able to estimate the flux of multiple emission lines. This makes it possible to construct diagnostic diagrams that separate PNe from other emission-line sources such as supernova remnants and HII regions. We calculate the [OIII] magnitude using the expression from Jacoby (1989):

$$m_{\mathrm{OIII}} = -2.5\, log_{10}(F_{\mathrm{OIII}}) - 13.74 \qquad (1)$$

In Figure 2 we show the diagnostic diagram for NGC 1387, where PNe are identified in the region determined by Ciardullo et al. (2002).

3. Calculation of the luminosity-specific PN number

As a first step, we perform a completeness analysis by injecting artificial stars on the slices using a PSF modeled with a Moffat profile and then repeating the same detection process as before. We compare the fraction of recovered sources to the injected sources in terms of magnitude range and distance to the galactic center.

We also look into the luminosity function of PNe, which is widely known to be a distance indicator due to the universal absolute magnitude value of its bright cut-off (Ciardullo et al. 1989). Due to the small number of PNe given the limited size of our field of view, we do not aim at measuring distances. However, the PNLF also allows us to estimate what proportion of PNe we are detecting within our completeness limit, and to extrapolate towards fainter magnitudes since its shape has been widely studied. In Figure 3 we show the PNLF for NGC 1387.

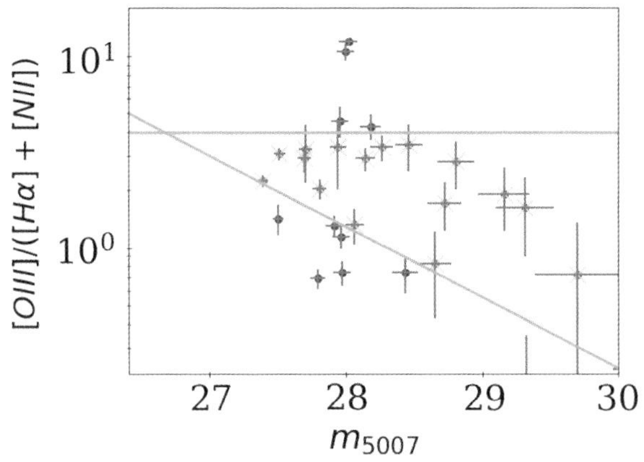

Figure 2. Diagnostic diagram for sources in NGC 1387. Pink triangles indicate PNe, and blue dots, contaminants. The limits shown in light blue solid lines are defined in Ciardullo et al. (2002)

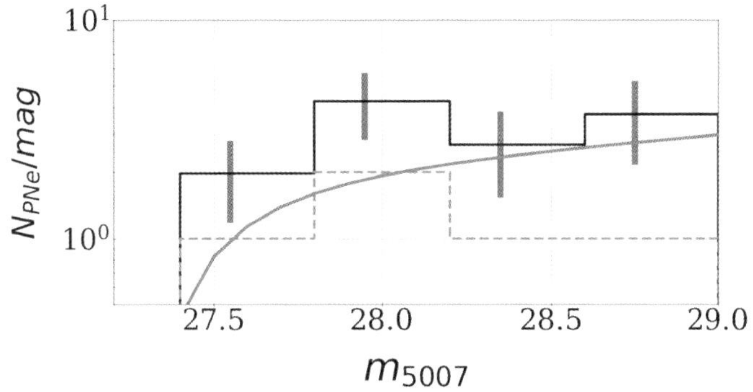

Figure 3. PNLF for NGC 1387. Dashed blue lines show the original histogram, while grey solid lines show the completeness-corrected distribution. The red line shows the function as determined by the distance obtained through the surface brightness fluctuation method for this galaxy.

The luminosity-specific PN number, α, is connected to the total number of PNe, N_{PN}, and the total bolometric luminosity L_{bol} through the following expression:

$$N_{PN} = \alpha L_{bol} \tag{2}$$

We bin PNe into elliptical bins, with their geometry defined by the isophotal properties of the host galaxy, and apply the completeness correction. We then measure the PN logarithmic number density profile as

$$\mu_{PN}(r) = -2.5log_{10}\left(\frac{N_{PN,corr}(r)}{A(r)}\right) + \mu_{off} \tag{3}$$

where $A(r)$ is the area of the respective ellipse. The offset μ_{off} is fit to match the surface brightness profile, as shown in Figure 4, and we refer to Hartke et al. (2020) for a thorough explanation of how to estimate $\alpha_{2.5}$ from it. For NGC 1387, we obtain a value of $\alpha_{2.5} = 4.39 \times 10^{-8}\ N_{PNe} \times L_{bol}^{-1}$.

We use the GIST pipeline to analyse the stellar population in the cubes. GIST utilizes Penalized PiXel-Fitting (Cappellari 2023) in order to obtain kinematics and stellar population properties (i.e. age and metallicity). In Figs. 5 and 6 we show the stellar population properties of NGC 1387 obtained with this method.

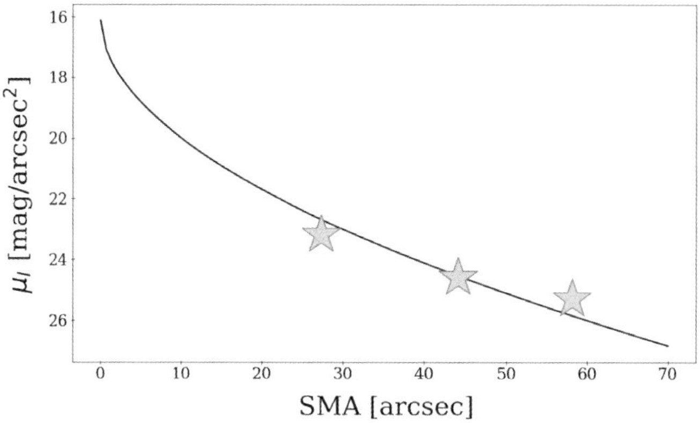

Figure 4. Surface brightness profile of NGC 1387 in a solid black line, with three pink stars indicating the numeric density of PNe at the corresponding radius, offset by the respective amount. The x-axis is the galactocentric distance, measured as the semi-major axis (SMA) of the isophotal ellipses.

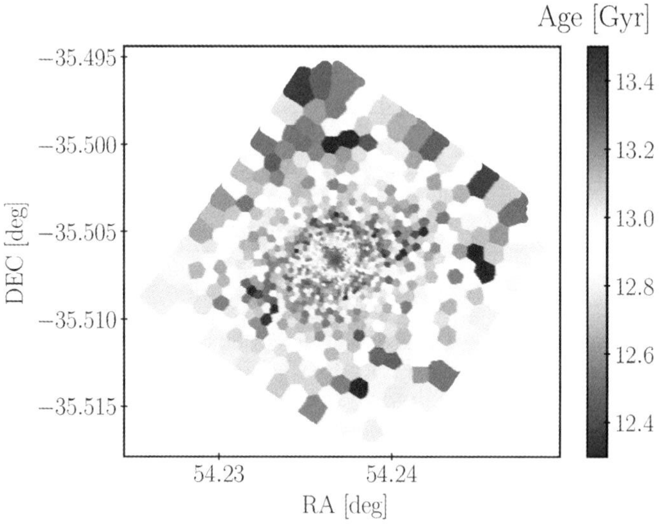

Figure 5. Age estimates for the stellar population of NGC 1387.

In Figure 5 we show the relation between α and the mean metallicity of the host galaxy for the sample studied by Buzzoni et al. (2006), covering a wide range of morphologies, and indicate the position that the inner region of NGC 1387 has in this relation. Adding the remaining nine galaxies in our sample will allow us to populate the relation, examining how it behaves when the measurements of α and stellar properties are performed in the same regions.

4. Conclusions

In this work, we have shown preliminary results for the analysis of PNe in the inner regions of galaxies. We describe the method and show the results for one of the galaxies in our sample. In an upcoming paper, this analysis will be applied to the full sample of ten galaxies, which will enable us to interpret the relation between α and stellar population properties in larger detail.

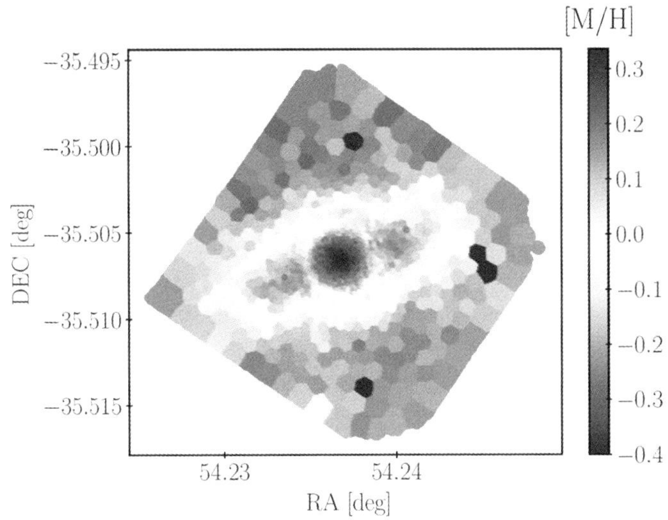

Figure 6. Metallicity estimates for the stellar population of NGC 1387.

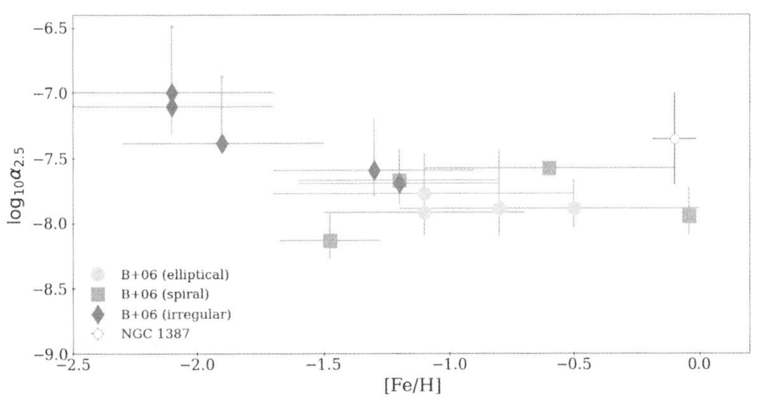

Figure 7. Luminosity-specific PN number of a sample of galaxies from Buzzoni et al. (2006) in relation to their metallicity. The symbols correspond to different morphologies (circles - ellipticals, squares - spirals, diamonds - irregulars). The unfilled circle is our pilot galaxy shown in this work, NGC 1387.

5. Acknowledgements

A.I.E. acknowledges the financial support from the visitor and mobility program of the Finnish Centre for Astronomy with ESO (FINCA), funded by the Academy of Finland grant nr 306531. This research was supported in part by Perimeter Institute for Theoretical Physics. Research at Perimeter Institute is supported by the Government of Canada through the Department of Innovation, Science and Economic Development and by the Province of Ontario through the Ministry of Research and Innovation.

References

Arnaboldi, M., Freeman, K. C., Hui, X., Capaccioli, M., & Ford, H. 1994, The Messenger, 76, 40
Bertin, E. & Arnouts, S. 1996, Astronomy and Astrophysics, Supplement, 117, 393
Buzzoni, A., Arnaboldi, M., & Corradi, R. L. M. 2006, MNRAS, 368, 877
Cappellari, M. 2023, MNRAS, 526, 3273
Ciardullo, R., Feldmeier, J. J., Jacoby, G. H., et al. 2002, ApJ, 577, 31

Ciardullo, R., Jacoby, G. H., Ford, H. C., & Neill, J. D. 1989, ApJ, 339, 53
Coccato, L., Gerhard, O., Arnaboldi, M., et al. 2009, MNRAS, 394, 1249
Ford, H. C. & Jenner, D. C. 1975, ApJ, 202, 365
Ford, H. C., Jenner, D. C., & Epps, H. W. 1973, ApJ, 183, L73
Hartke, J., Arnaboldi, M., Gerhard, O., et al. 2020, A&A, 642, A46
Hartke, J., Arnaboldi, M., Longobardi, A., et al. 2017, A&A, 603, A104
Jacoby, G. H. 1989, ApJ, 339, 39
Jacoby, G. H., Branch, D., Ciardullo, R., et al. 1992, PASP, 104, 599
Napolitano, N. R., Arnaboldi, M., & Capaccioli, M. 2000, Mem. Soc. Astron. Italiana, 71, 1049
Pulsoni, C., Gerhard, O., Fall, S. M., et al. 2023, A&A, 674, A96
Roth, M. M., Jacoby, G. H., Ciardullo, R., et al. 2021, ApJ, 916, 21
Spiniello, C., Napolitano, N. R., Arnaboldi, M., et al. 2018, MNRAS, 477, 1880
Spriggs, T. W., Sarzi, M., Napiwotzki, R., et al. 2020, A&A, 637, A62

Planetary Nebulae: A Universal Toolbox in the Era of Precision Astrophysics
Proceedings IAU Symposium No. 384, 2025
O. De Marco, A. Zijlstra & R. Szczerba, eds.
doi:10.1017/S174392132400022X

Survey of Planetary Nebulae in the Andromeda galaxy (M 31)

Souradeep Bhattacharya[1], Magda Arnaboldi[2], Ortwin Gerhard[3], Nelson Caldwell[4], Chiaki Kobayashi[5], Francois Hammer[6], Yanbin Yang[6], Kenneth C. Freeman[7], Johanna Hartke[8] and Alan McConnachie[9]

[1]Inter University Centre for Astronomy and Astrophysics, Ganeshkhind, Post Bag 4, Pune 411007, India
email: souradeep@iucaa.in

[2]European Southern Observatory, Karl-Schwarzschild-Str. 2, 85748 Garching, Germany

[3]Max-Planck-Institut für Extraterrestrische Physik, Giessenbachstrasse, 85748 Garching, Germany

[4]Harvard-Smithsonian Center for Astrophysics, 60 Garden Street, Cambridge, MA 02138, USA

[5]Centre for Astrophysics Research, Department of Physics, Astronomy and Mathematics, University of Hertfordshire, Hatfield AL10 9AB, UK

[6]GEPI, Observatoire de Paris, Université PSL, CNRS, Place Jules Janssen, F-92195 Meudon, France

[7]Research School of Astronomy and Astrophysics, Mount Stromlo Observatory, Cotter Road, ACT 2611 Weston Creek, Australia

[8]Finnish Centre for Astronomy with ESO (FINCA), University of Turku, FI-20014 Turku, Finland

[9]NRC Herzberg Institute of Astrophysics, 5071 West Saanich Road, Victoria, BC V9E 2E7, Canada

Abstract. We summarize the main results from the survey of Planetary Nebulae (PNe) in M 31 with Megacam@CFHT and subsequent spectroscopy with Hectospec@MMT. We identified ~5000 PNe in M 31 (~1200 with spectroscopy; ~200 with chemical abundances). We find a PN Luminosity Function faint-end rise, linked to a percentage of older stars in the parent population. We utilize PN extinction to distinguish young and old PNe. We find that the [Ar/H] vs [O/Ar] plane for emission-line nebulae is analogous to the [Fe/H] vs [α/Fe] plane for stars, and exploration of the M 31 disc PNe in this plane allowed us to constrain its chemical enrichment history. We find the kinematically and chemically distinct thin and thick discs of M 31, and that the G1-clump substructure is formed from perturbed disc material. We infer that M 31 has had a wet major (mass-ratio~1:5) merger ~2.5-4 Gyr ago, and obtain important constraints on the cannibalized satellite properties.

Keywords. galaxies: abundances, galaxies: individual (M31), galaxies: kinematics and dynamics, galaxies: structure, planetary nebulae: general

1. Introduction

The Andromeda Galaxy (M 31) is the most massive (1.56×10^{12} M$_\odot$; see Bhattacharya 2023a and references therein) member of our local group and the nearest (776 kpc;

Savino et al. 2022) giant galaxy to our Milky Way (MW). Imaging surveys of M 31, covering almost 100 sq. deg. on the sky (e.g. PAndAS; McConnachie et al. 2018), have measured the projected number density of resolved red giant branch (RGB) stars. This has led to the revelation of several faint and diffuse substructures in the M 31 halo, a telltale sign of its turbulent recent formation history. However, chemodynamic measurements of M 31's stellar population is required for shedding light on its recent merger history. Owing to its large angular span on the sky, chemodynamic measurements from absorption line features of individual RGB stars over the entirety of the M 31 disc and inner halo is challenging (e.g. SPLASH – Guhathakurta et al. 2005; DESI – Dey et al. 2023), with substantial contamination from MW halo stars.

Planetary Nebulae (PNe), emission-line nebulae in the late stages of stellar evolution for stars with initial masses $\sim$0.8–8 $M_{\odot}$, are discrete tracers of galaxy stellar population properties such as light (e.g. Hartke et al. 2017), kinematics (e.g. Hartke et al. 2022) and chemistry (see review by Kwitter & Henry 2022, and references therein). At the distance of M 31, PNe can be identified over the entire span of its disc and inner-halo in reasonable time with wide-field narrow- and broad-band imaging and subsequent spectroscopic follow-up. The bright emission line features in PNe efficiently allows for chemodynamic measurements. Additionally the MW halo is transparent to PNe (any MW halo PNe would be much brighter and easily identifiable) and background galaxy contamination is minimal at the distance of M 31.

Studying PNe in M 31 also offers a unique opportunity to connect PN properties with that of their resolved parent stellar populations. The star-formation history and metallicity distribution functions of the M 31 disc have been well-estimated from RGB number counts from the Pan-Hubble Andromeda Treasury (PHAT; Williams et al. 2017) as well as in some of the inner-halo substructures (Bernard et al. 2015). The location and large mass of M 31 within the local group allows the observations (both photometric and spectroscopic) of relatively faint PNe (compared to any other similarly large galaxy) in large numbers in a reasonable time with present-day instrumentation (e.g. Merrett et al. 2006; Sanders et al. 2012). It is thus the prime galaxy wherein to utilise the wealth of observational information to connect PN population properties with that of their parent stellar population.

We can thus utilise PN chemodynamics to understand the recent formation history of M 31, while simultaneously connecting PN properties with that of their parent stellar populations. This is what we endeavored to do through the survey of PNe in M31 whose details and findings have been published in six papers (Bhattacharya et al. 2019a,b, 2021, 2022a, 2023b; Arnaboldi et al. 2022) and one spin-off letter (Kobayashi et al. 2023). We briefly describe the survey characteristics in Section 2. Our main results on the connection of PNe to their parent stellar population properties are described in Section 3 while the main results on the recent formation history of M 31 are described in Section 4. We summarize and conclude in Section 5.

2. The survey of Planetary Nebulae in M 31

As PNe are bright in [OIII] 5007 Å and faint in broad-bands, they can be identified distinctly from continuum emitters. The automatic selection procedure based on this on-off technique was initially developed and validated in Arnaboldi et al. (2002, 2003) and later adapted to larger surveys by Longobardi et al. (2013) and Hartke et al. (2017). PN candidates were photometrically identified in a 54 sq. deg. [OIII] 5007 Å narrow-band and broad g-band imaging survey (Bhattacharya et al. 2019a, 2021) covering the disc and inner halo of M31 with the MegaCam imager at the CFHT. We identified 5265 PN candidates in M 31, the largest PN sample in any galaxy, of which 4085 were

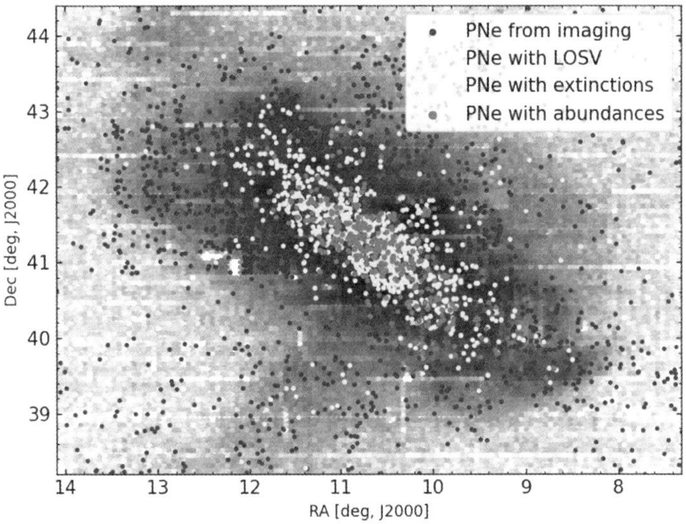

Figure 1. The number density map of RGB stars from PAndAS (McConnachie et al. 2018), binned for visual clarity, is shown in grey. The PN candidates identified in the imaging survey (within this field of view) are marked in blue (see Bhattacharya et al. 2021 for the full sample); those with LOSV measurements are marked in green; those with only extinction measurements are marked in yellow while those with chemical abundance determinations are marked in red (Bhattacharya et al. 2022a).

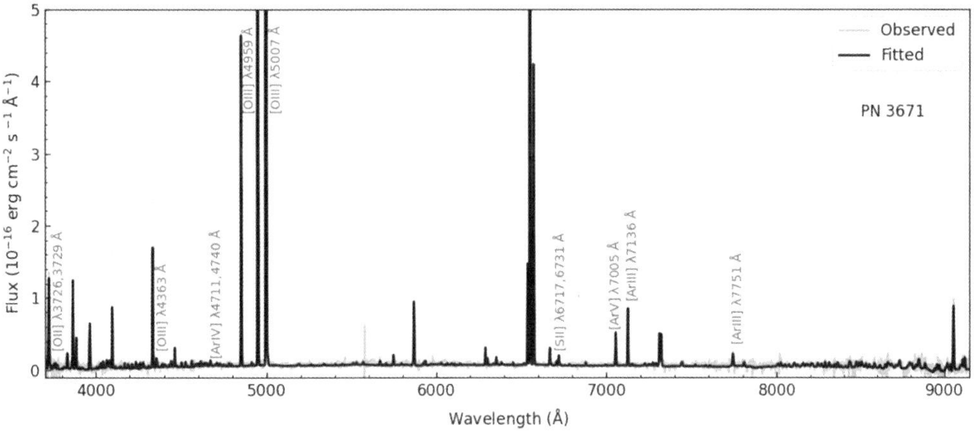

Figure 2. An example of the M 31 PN Hectospec spectrum. The spectrum shown in grey is obtained following heliocentric correction, removal of sky lines and flux calibration. The fitted spectra using ALFA (Wesson 2016) is shown in black. The emission lines with fluxes used for velocity measurement are marked in green while those used for extinction measurement are marked in yellow. Those used for chemical abundance determination are marked in red.

newly discovered (Bhattacharya et al. 2021). Figure 1 shows a part of the sample of the photometrically identified PNe.

Spectroscopic follow-up of a complete sub-sample of these PN candidates were carried out with the Hectospec MOS spectrograph (covering ~3685–9200 Å) on the MMT Telescope (Fabricant et al. 2005). A typical PN spectra with the emission lines of interest is shown in Figure 2. A sample of 413 PN spectra (including those found by Sanders et al. 2012) with confirmed detection of the [OIII] 4959/5007 Å emission lines, allowing us

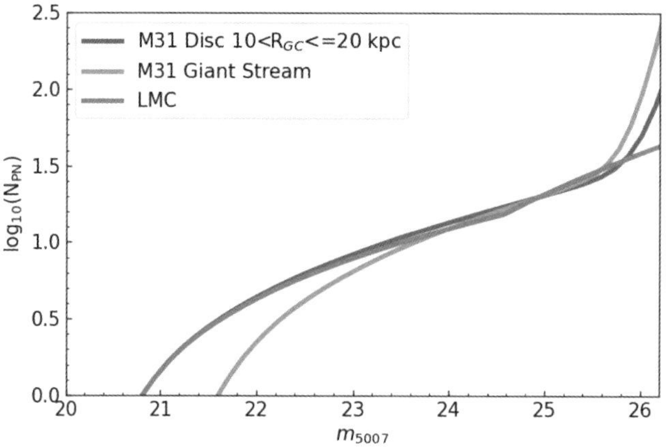

Figure 3. Completeness-corrected PN luminosity function, as described by the generalised analytical formula in Bhattacharya et al. (2021), for the M 31 disc PNe (blue), the PNe co-spatial with the giant stream substructure of M 31 (orange) and those in the Large Magellanic Cloud shifted to the distance of M 31 (green). All three luminosity functions are scaled to the number of PNe in the giant stream.

to obtain their LOSV measurements, were first utilised for the kinematic analysis of the M 31 disc presented in (Bhattacharya et al. 2019b). The survey was extended in Bhattacharya et al. (2022a) to include a total of 1251 PN LOSV measurements in M 31. Their spatial distribution is shown in Figure 1. Of these 1251 PNe, for 745 we have been able to derive extinction values due to detection of the H-β line. They are also shown in Figure 1 Within the M 31 disc, the temperature-sensitive [OIII] 4363 Å line was detected in a magnitude limited sample of 205 PNe (see Figure 1), enabling the computation of oxygen and argon abundances. The details of the chemical abundance analysis are presented in Bhattacharya et al. (2022a).

3. Planetary Nebulae and their parent stellar populations

3.1. *The rise in the faint end of the Planetary Nebula Luminosity Function*

Narrow-band [OIII] 5007 Å surveys have been a staple of extragalactic PN observations, from which the m_{5007} magnitude is measured. For an extragalactic PN population, this allows the construction of the [OIII] 5007 Å luminosity function (hereafter PNLF) that is observed to have an absolute bright cut-off, M*, seemingly invariant with age (although varying slightly with metallicity) of the parent stellar population, and galaxy type (see review by Ciardullo 2022, and references therein).

While M* has been the subject of many studies, inspection of the faint-end of the PNLF has remained elusive, as most extragalactic PN studies are limited to only ~2 magnitudes below M* (e.g. Hartke et al. 2017), even though PNe are theoretically expected to be present down to at least 8 magnitudes below M* (Buzzoni, Arnaboldi, & Corradi 2006). In Bhattacharya et al. (2019a), we obtain the PNLF for M 31 down to ~6 magnitude below M*, identifying a steep rise in the faint-end of the PNLF ~5 magnitude below M*. In Bhattacharya et al. (2021), we were able to construct the PNLFs for different sub-regions of M 31 where the parent stellar population properties were also different, though the PNLFs from all regions showed the faint-end rise (see the PNLF shapes in Figure 3). We found that the PNLF could be characterised in two modes with two slopes, one describing the PNLF just below the brighter end and a second slope, c_{f2}, for the fainter exponential rise (similar to the two-mode PNLF presented by Rodríguez-González et al. 2015). We found that c_{f2} was steeper when the percentage of stellar

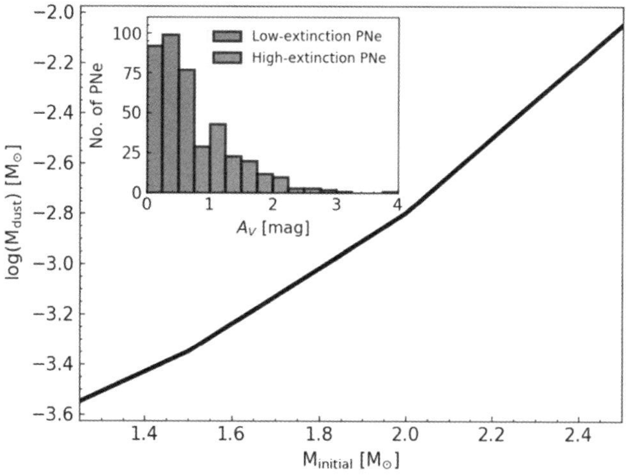

Figure 4. The mass of dust plotted as a function of stellar mass as per the AGB models with $Z = 8 \times 10^{-3}$ by Ventura et al. (2014). Adopted from their Figure 10. [Inset] Histogram showing the distribution of extinction values for the M 31 PNe, with the high- and low-extinction PNe marked in blue and red respectively. Adopted from Figure 1 in Bhattacharya et al. (2019b).

mass older than 5 Gyr was higher (see Figure 7 in Bhattacharya et al. 2021). The stellar masses were obtained from star-formation histories constructed by Bernard et al. (2015) in the different M 31 regions. The relation of c_{f2} and percentage of stellar mass older than 5 Gyr was also consistent with the PNLF of the LMC, the only other galaxy where the PNLF has been characterised to comparable depth by Reid & Parker (2010).

Comparing the PNLF shapes in Figure 3, it becomes apparent that the M 31 disc and LMC have similar shapes except at the faint-end, while the Giant Stream has a faint-end rise more similar to the M 31 disc but a lower M^*. Understanding that parent stellar population properties are leaving noticieable differences in the PNLF shapes, in Bhattacharya et al. 2021 we use an Anderson-Darling test (AD-test†; Scholz & Stephens 1987) to compare the PNLF shapes of different M 31 regions. We find that the Giant Stream and NE-shelf form a set having similar stellar populations, that is distinct from the M 31 disc and G1-clump which are instead self-similar in their PNLFs. The Stream D substructure seems completely distinct in its PNLF that is different from all other M 31 regions.

3.2. *Distinguishing young and old Planetary Nebulae based on their derived extinction*

Stellar models with initial stellar masses lower than ~3 $M_\odot$, show an exponential increase in mass of dust produced during the Asymptotic Giant Branch (AGB) phase as a function of increasing initial stellar mass (Ventura et al. 2014). This trend is plotted in Figure 4 for the models with metallicity most similar to M 31. While AGB stars with higher initial masses would also have stronger winds to disperse the dust in their environment prior to the onset of the PN phase, it is still not unexpected that PNe evolving from larger initial masses (younger) would have higher circumstellar extinction than those evolving from lower initial masses (older).

From this understanding, we developed a novel selection of M 31 PNe based on their measured extinction. Figure 4 [inset] shows the extinction distribution of a complete sub-sample of M 31 disc PNe (from Bhattacharya et al. 2019b) with a notable second peak

† The AD-test usage has been discussed in detail in Bhattacharya et al. (2021, see Section 3.4) along with applications in Bhattacharya et al. (2022a,b, 2023b,c).

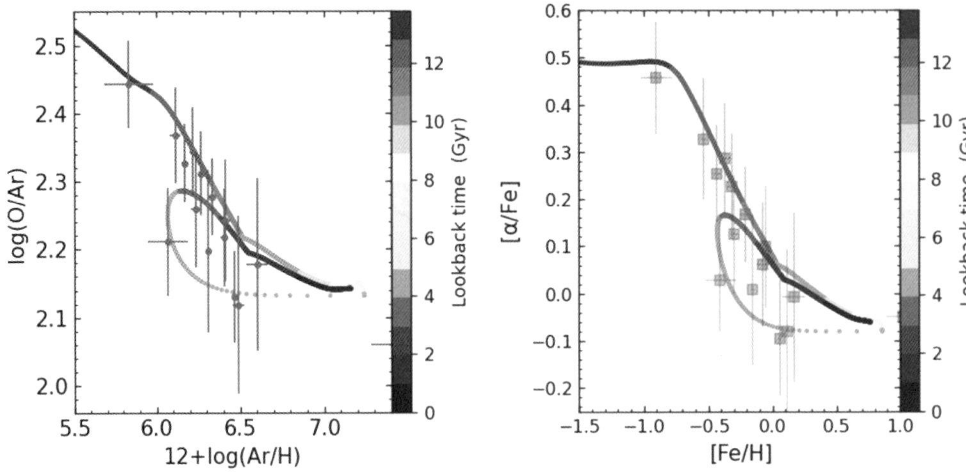

Figure 5. [Left] Mean log(O/Ar) values of the low-extinction M 31 PNe (red) and the high-extinction M 31 PNe (blue) within a galactocentric radius, $R_{GC} < 14$ kpc, and the fiducial two-infall galactic chemical evolution model for the M 31 disc, coloured by lookback time. Adopted from Figure 7 in Arnaboldi et al. (2022). [Right] Same as the left panel but now in the [α/Fe] vs [Fe/H] plane. Adopted from Figure 2 in Kobayashi et al. (2023).

at $A_V \sim 1$. We divided the PNe based on their extinction into high- and low-extinction samples and found that the two samples respectively formed the kinematically distinct thin & thick discs of M 31. Using archival determinations of central star properties of M 31 PNe from Kwitter et al. (2012), compared with the stellar evolution tracks from Miller Bertolami (2016), we found that the high-extinction PNe were ∼2.5 Gyr old while the low-extinction PNe were >4.5 Gyr old. The star-formation history of M 31 (Bernard et al. 2015; Williams et al. 2017) shows a burst of star-formation ∼2 Gyr ago, with the high-extinction PNe temporally consistent with having formed in the burst while the low-extinction PNe would be consistent with having formed earlier.

3.3. *The imprint of chemical enrichment history on oxygen and argon abundance measurements of Planetary Nebulae*

From the detection of relevant emission lines (see Figure 2), we derived oxygen and argon abundances for PNe in the M 31 disc (Bhattacharya et al. 2022a). In Arnaboldi et al. (2022), we identified that the [Ar/H] vs [O/Ar] plane for emission line nebulae is analogous to the [Fe/H] vs [α/Fe] plane for stars (see Figure 5), and exploration of the M 31 PN population in this plane in conjunction with galactic chemical evolution (GCE) models, based on Kobayashi et al. (2020) and constrained by the star-formation history and metallicity distribution function from M 31 RGB stars presented by Williams et al. (2017), allowed us to constrain the chemical enrichment history of the M 31 disc. The older low extinction PNe show a monotonic decrease in log(O/Ar) with increasing 12+log(Ar/H). This is consistent with the old ages in the GCE model. The location of the high-extinction PNe in this plane, however, necessitates the infall of fresh gas and requires the loop in the GCE models seen in Figure 5.

In Kobayashi et al. (2023), we presented the PN abundances in the [Fe/H] vs [α/Fe] plane, using an affine transformation of [Ar/H] vs [O/Ar] plane anchored to the GCE model predictions in both these planes. This enables direct comparison of PN derived chemical enrichment history with that of RGBs, showcasing the potential of using PN chemical abundances as a probe of galaxy chemical enrichment, even for galaxies at

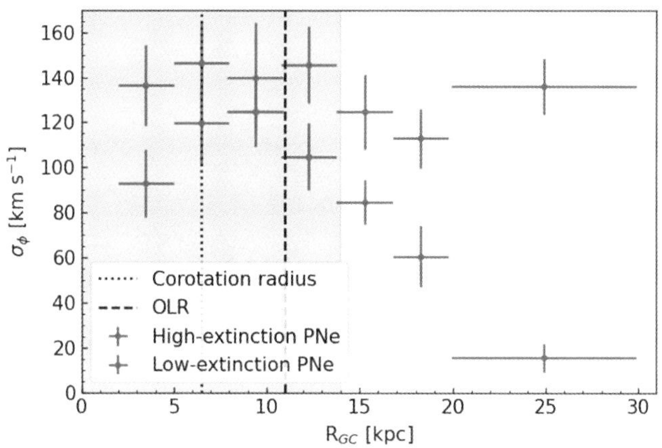

Figure 6. Rotational velocity dispersion for the high- and low-extinction M 31 PNe are shown in blue and red, respectively. The co-rotation radius (black dotted line) and outer Lindblad resonance (OLR; black dashed line) of the M 31 bar are as found in the models by Blaña et al. (2018). The grey shaded region is possibly influenced by different dynamical heating events from the bar.

larger distances where [Fe/H] & [α/Fe] from absorption-line spectroscopy of resolved stellar populations would be observationally prohibitive.

4. Constraints on the recent formation history of M 31

4.1. *The kinematically and chemically distinct thin and thicker discs of M 31*

In Bhattacharya et al. (2019b), through velocity dispersion profiles of high- and low-extinction PNe in the M 31 disc (see Figure 6), we respectively identify the kinematically distinct dynamically colder thin and hotter thicker disc. At the equivalent radius of the solar neighbourhood in M 31, the thin and thicker disc of M 31 are respectively about twice ($\sigma_\phi \sim 61$ km s^{-1}) and thrice ($\sigma_\phi \sim 101$ km s^{-1}) as dynamically hot as the MW thin disc population of the same age (see also Dorman et al. 2015). The age-velocity dispersion relation in the M 31 disc is consistent with a ~1:5 major merger in M 31 ~2.5–4.5 Gyr ago. A minor merger (~ 1:20) would not be able to dynamically heat the M 31 disc to the measured thicker disc velocity dispersion. See Bhattacharya et al. (2019b) for details.

In Bhattacharya et al. (2022a), we found that the kinematically distinct discs are also chemically distinct. The thicker disc has near-flat radial abundance gradients in oxygen (0.006 ± 0.003 dex/kpc) and argon (-0.005 ± 0.003 dex/kpc), typical of discs that have experienced a recent major merger, while the thin disc had steeper gradients for both oxygen (-0.013 ± 0.006 dex/kpc) and argon (-0.018 ± 0.006 dex/kpc) consistent with that of the MW thin disc (accounting for different disc scale lengths). M31 PN abundance gradients are discussed in detail in Bhattacharya et al. (2022a).

From the [Ar/H] vs [O/Ar] distribution of M 31 disc PNe and the use of galactic chemical evolution models, in Arnaboldi et al. (2022), we found that the older M 31 thicker disc PNe show monotonic chemical enrichment in an extended star formation episode up to super-solar values, while the younger M 31 thin disc is formed ~2–4 Gyr ago from accreted metal-poor gas that mixed with the relatively metal-rich M 31 ISM (consistent with that observed from the star-formation history of resolved stars in the M 31 disc; Williams et al. Williams et al. (2017)). This has been presented in detail in Arnaboldi et al. (2022).

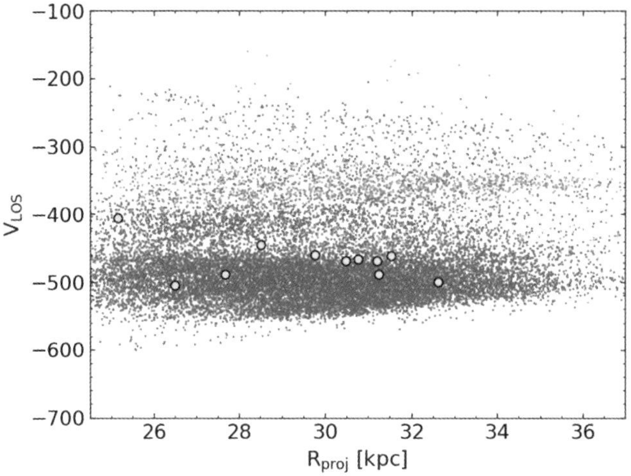

Figure 7. The projected radial distance (R_{proj}), from the center of M 31, of the PNe co-spatial with the G1-Clump substructure is plotted against their line-of-slight velocity (V_{LOS}). The observed PNe are shown in green. Also shown are the host (blue) and satellite (orange) particles in the G1-clump analogue from the major merger simulation by Hammer et al. (2018). The projected distances of the simulated particles has been corrected for an offset, $R_{proj,offset}$ = 3.51 kpc, to account for the slightly different positions of the simulated analogue from the observed substructure on the sky. The figure is adapted from Figure 5 of Bhattacharya (2023a).

In Kobayashi et al. (2023), we showed that there is a α/Fe bimodality in M 31, as inferred from the PN abundances and consistent with *James Webb Space Telescope* measurements of [α/Fe] & [Fe/H] from RGB stars presented provisionally by Nidever et al. (2023). The high-α M 31 thick-disc population formed by an initial starburst that was more intense than that in the MW. The young M 31 low-α thin disc is present within a galactocentric radius of 14 kpc formed during the merger induced secondary star formation. In the outer disc, however, there is only a slightly higher-α thin disc population at a given metallicity, formed from almost pristine gas brought in by the satellite with little to no mixing. Thus, an [α/Fe] bimodality is seen in the inner disc (within 14 kpc), while only a slight [α/Fe] offset of the young population is seen in the outer disk (beyond 18 kpc).

4.2. *The origin of M 31 inner-halo substructures*

From the PNLF comparisons in Bhattacharya et al. (2021), we found that the GS and NE-Shelf are consistent with being composed of stellar debris from an in-falling satellite, while the G1-Clump is linked to the pre-merger M 31 disc (see also Faria et al. 2007). Stream-D would instead have its origin from a distinct metal-poor dwarf galaxy.

In Bhattacharya et al. (2023b), we present the first LOSV measurements of PNe co-spatial with the four M 31 inner-halo substructures (namely Giant Stream, NE-shelf, W-shelf and G1-clump). We compare the measured LOSV distribution and observed projected radial distance vs. LOSV phase space of the PNe (and RGBs where available) to their simulated analogues in the major-merger (mass-ratio $\sim$1:4) simulation by Hammer et al. (2018). The NE- and W-shelves, and Giant Stream are consistent with being satellite debris (with some fraction of host material) while the G1-clump is consistent with being perturbed M 31 disc material (Figure 7). We thus link the formation of the aforementioned substructures in a single unique event, consistent with a major merger. In particular, the G1-clump cannot be formed from perturbed disc material in a minor merger. Details are provided in Bhattacharya et al. (2023b).

5. Summary and conclusions

Through the survey of PNe in M 31, we have identified vital links of observed extragalactic PN population properties with that of their parent stellar populations, while also uncovering vital details about the recent formation history of M 31. The faint-end of the PNLF shows a rise that is linked to the percentage of older (>5 Gyr old) stars in the parent population (Bhattacharya et al. 2019a, 2021). In M 31, young (∼2.5 Gyr old) high-extinction PNe are distinct from older (>4.5 Gyr old) low-extinction PNe, in both their kinematics (Bhattacharya et al. 2019b) and chemistry (Bhattacharya et al. 2022a), forming the thin and thick disc of M 31 respectively. We also find that the [Ar/H] vs [O/Ar] plane for emission line nebulae is analogous to the [Fe/H] vs [α/Fe] plane for stars, allowing us to constrain the chemical enrichment and star formation history of the thin and thick disc in M 31 (Arnaboldi et al. 2022; Kobayashi et al. 2023).

From the aforementioned results, we find that M 31 experienced a 'wet' major merger (mass ratio ∼ 1:5) ∼2.5–4 Gyr ago (Bhattacharya et al. 2023b). This event formed the M 31 thicker disc and the G1-clump from the pre-merger M 31 disc stars, while the thin disc was formed from gas brought in by the satellite mixed with the pre-enriched gas in the pre-merger disc. The satellite debris material formed the other inner-halo substructures.

Acknowledgements

SB thanks the organizers of the IAU Symposium 384 for the opportunity to present an invited talk. Based on observations obtained with MegaPrime/ MegaCam at the CFHT. Based on observations obtained at the MMT Observatory. SB is funded by the INSPIRE Faculty award (DST/INSPIRE/04/2020/002224), Department of Science and Technology (DST), Government of India. SB acknowledges support from the IMPRS on Astrophysics at the LMU Munich during his PhD. A preliminary version of this work appears in his PhD thesis (Bhattacharya 2020).

References

Arnaboldi, M., Aguerri, J. A. L., Napolitano, N. R., *et al.* 2002, *AJ*, 123, 760
Arnaboldi, M., Freeman, K. C., Okamura, S., *et al.* 2003, *AJ*, 125, 514
Arnaboldi, M., Bhattacharya, S., Gerhard, O., *et al.* 2022, *A&A*, 666, A109
Bernard, E. J., Ferguson, A. M. N., Richardson, J. C., *et al.* 2015, *MNRAS*, 446, 2789
Bhattacharya, S., Arnaboldi, M., Hartke, J., *et al.* 2019a, *A&A*, 624, A132
Bhattacharya, S., Arnaboldi, M., Caldwell, N., *et al.* 2019b, *A&A*, 631, A56
Bhattacharya S., 2020, PhD thesis, Ludwig-Maximilians University of Munich, Germany
Bhattacharya, S., Arnaboldi, M., Gerhard, O., *et al.* 2021, *A&A*, 647, A130
Bhattacharya, S., Arnaboldi, M., Caldwell, N., *et al.* 2022a, *MNRAS*, 517, 2343
Bhattacharya S., Rao K. K., Agarwal M., *et al.* 2022b, MNRAS, 517, 3525
Bhattacharya S., 2023a, *arXiv e-prints*, 2305.03293
Bhattacharya S., Arnaboldi M., Hammer F., *et al.* 2023b, *MNRAS*, 522, 6010
Bhattacharya S., Saha K., Mondal C., 2023c, *arXiv e-prints*, 2310.01903
Blaña, M., Gerhard, O., Wegg, C., *et al.* 2018, *MNRAS*, 481, 3210
Buzzoni A., Arnaboldi M., Corradi R. L. M., 2006, MNRAS, 368, 877
Ciardullo R., 2022, FrASS, 9, 896326.
Dey A., Najita, J. R., Koposov, S. E., *et al.* 2023, *ApJ*, 944, 1
Dorman C. E., Guhathakurta, P., Seth, A. C., *et al.* 2015,*ApJ*, 803, 24
Fabricant, D., Fata, R., Roll, J., *et al.* 2005, *PASP*, 117, 1411
Faria D., Johnson R. A., Ferguson A. M. N., *et al.* 2007, *AJ*, 133, 1275

Guhathakurta P., Ostheimer J. C., Gilbert K. M., *et al.* 2005, *arXiv e-prints*, astro-ph/0502366

Hammer F., Yang Y. B., Wang J. L., *et al.* 2018, *MNRAS*, 475, 2754

Hartke J., Arnaboldi M., Longobardi A., *et al.* 2017, *A&A*, 603

Hartke, J., Arnaboldi, M., Gerhard, O., *et al.* 2022, *A&A*, 663, A12

Kobayashi, C., Karakas, A. I., & Lugaro, M., 2020, *ApJ*, 900, 179

Kobayashi C., Bhattacharya S., Arnaboldi M., Gerhard O., 2023, *ApJL*, 956, L14

Kwitter K. B., Lehman E. M. M., Balick B., *et al.* 2012, ApJ, 753, 12

Kwitter K. B., Henry R. B. C. 2022, *PASP*, 134, 022001.

Longobardi, A., Arnaboldi, M., Gerhard, O., *et al.* 2013, *A&A*, 558, A42

McConnachie, A. W., Ibata, R., Martin, N., *et al.* 2018, *ApJ*, 868, 55

Merrett H. R., Merrifield M. R., Douglas N. G., *et al.* 2006, *MNRAS*, 369, 120

Miller Bertolami M. M., 2016, *A&A*, 588, A25.

Nidever D. L., Gilbert K., Tollerud E.,*et al.* 2023, *arXiv e-prints*, 2306.04688

Reid, W. A., & Parker, Q. A. 2010, *MNRAS*, 405, 1349

Rodríguez-González A., Hernández-Martínez L., Esquivel A., *et al.* 2015, A&A, 575, A1.

Sanders, N. E., Caldwell, N., McDowell, J. *et al.* 2012, *ApJ*, 758, 133

Savino A., Weisz D. R., Skillman E. D.,*et al.* 2022, *ApJ*, 938, 101.

Scholz, F. W. & Stephens, M. A. 2010, *Journal of the American Statistical Association*, 399, 918

Ventura P., Dell'Agli F., Schneider R., *et al.* 2014, *MNRAS*, 439, 977

Wesson R., Stock D. J., Scicluna P., 2012, *MNRAS*, 422, 3516

Wesson R., 2016, *MNRAS*, 456, 3774

Williams, B. F., Dolphin, A. E., Dalcanton, J. J., et al. 2017, *ApJ*, 846, 145

Planetary Nebulae: A Universal Toolbox in the Era of Precision Astrophysics
Proceedings IAU Symposium No. 384, 2025
O. De Marco, A. Zijlstra & R. Szczerba, eds.
doi:10.1017/S1743921323005227

Analysis of distances to planetary nebulae

Diego Hernández-Juárez[1], Mónica Rodríguez[2] and Miriam Peña[1]

[1]Instituto de Astronomía, Universidad Nacional Autónoma de México, Apdo. Postal 70264, Ciudad de México, Mexico

[2]Instituto Nacional de Astrofísica, Óptica y Electrónica, Luis Enrique Erro 1, Tonantzintla 72840, Puebla, México.
email: dbhernandez@astro.unam.mx

Abstract. We compare different estimates of distances to planetary nebulae (PNe), namely, *Gaia* parallaxes and statistical values, in order to determine the most reliable distance for each PN. In numerous instances, we find that the distances derived from the Gaia parallaxes are not the most reliable, and that better estimates can be obtained from the median of the available statistical values. Our resulting distances imply that the distributions of distances from the Galactic plane of PNe with [WR] central stars is different from the distributions of both non-[WR] hydrogen-poor central stars and hydrogen-rich central stars.

Keywords. planetary nebulae: general, stars: distances, catalogs

1. Introduction

Distance estimates to planetary nebulae (PNe) can be statistical or individual estimates. Statistical distance estimates are derived using empirical relations among two or more nebular parameters, such as ionized mass and radius (e.g., Shklovsky 1956). On the other hand, individual estimates are direct measures of distance, such as distances derived from parallaxes. Individual distances are generally considered more reliable than statistical estimates, but until recently they were available for just a few PNe. The data provided by *Gaia* has greatly increased the number of PNe with measured parallaxes (see, e.g., Chornay & Walton 2021), but we must be cautious when using these parallaxes.

It can be very difficult to identify the central stars of PNe (CSPNe). Chornay & Walton (2021) and González-Santamaría et al. (2021) look for CSPNe in *Gaia*-EDR3 using the distance to the geometric center of the PN and the color of the objects. They find more than 2000 sources each, but the identifications can be highly uncertain. Besides, some objects have spurious *Gaia* parallaxes, even when the parallax errors are small (Fabricius et al. 2021). There are also objects with negative parallaxes or very large errors. A Bayesian analysis can be used for these objects (Bailer-Jones et al. 2021), but it requires a prior based on the distribution of stars in the Milky Way (Astraatmadja & Bailer-Jones 2016). For negative parallaxes or for parallaxes with large errors ($\delta p/p > 1$), the Bayesian distances converge to the prior (Oudmaijer et al. 2022) and hence, do not provide much information on the individual distances in these cases.

2. Assignment of distances

Fig. 1 shows the ratios of the inverse of the *Gaia* parallaxes, p (top panel) and the Bayesian estimates $D_{\rm B}$ (bottom panel) to the three statistical distance estimates, D_S, considered here plotted as a function of the relative parallax errors, $\delta p/p$. The statistical distances used are from Zhang (1995, $D_{\rm Z95}$), Frew et al. (2016, $D_{\rm FBP16}$), and

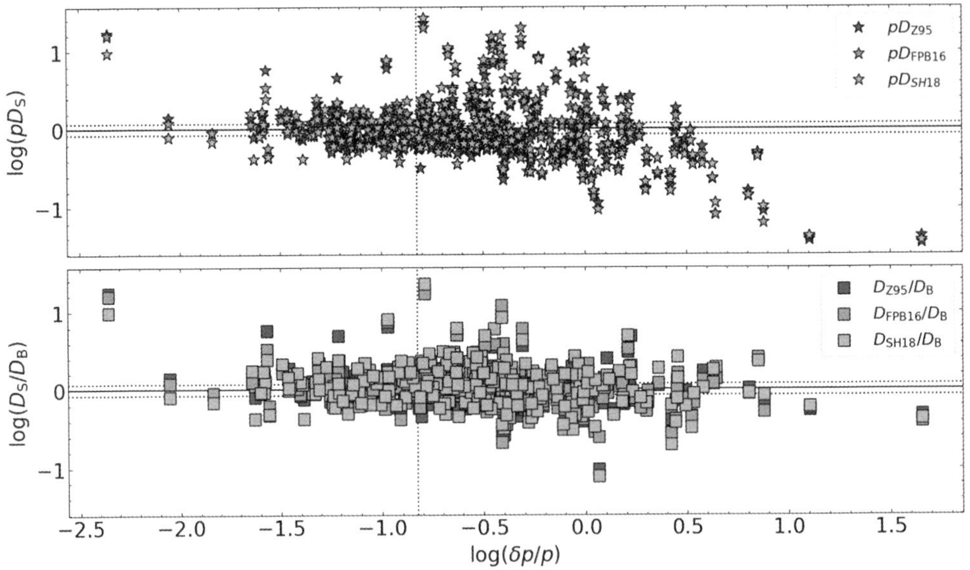

Figure 1. Ratios of *Gaia* distances D_S and statistical distances as a function of the relative parallax errors. Statistical distances are from Frew et al. (2016, blue symbols), Stanghellini & Haywood (2018, orange symbols), and Zhang (1995, brown symbols). *Gaia* distances are derived from the inverse of the parallax (stars, top panel) and from Bayesian estimates (squares, bottom panel). The vertical dotted line indicates an error in the parallax of 15%, and the horizontal dotted lines correspond to differences of ±0.07 dex.

Stanghellini & Haywood (2018, $D_{\rm SH18}$). We can see in the figure that, for small errors, the inverse of the parallax and the Bayesian estimates have similar values. However, for large errors, the inverse of the parallax is biased and can lead to distances which are very different from the statistical estimates. The Bayesian estimates behave better for larger errors. The difference between the two *Gaia* distance estimates is more noticeable for errors larger that 15% (indicated by a dotted vertical line in both panels of Fig. 1). On the other hand, there are some objects in the region of small errors for which the *Gaia* distances are quite different from the statistical distances. An example is Abell 43 (the object with the lowest parallax error). According to Chornay & Walton (2021), this case is probably a misidentification because the identified star is too yellow to be a CSPNe. Other cases could be also misidentifications or result from spurious parallaxes.

So, when should we use each distance estimate? We define four different cases: A, B, C, and D. Case A: if the parallax error is small (less than 15%) and the ratio between at least one statistical distance and the inverse of the parallax is lower than 0.07 dex (indicated by the horizontal dotted lines in Fig. 1), we use the inverse of parallax as the best distance estimate. For errors larger than 15%, we use the median of the statistical distances and the Bayesian distance if the ratio between at least one statistical distance and the Bayesian estimate is lower than 0.07 dex (case B); otherwise, we use the median of the statistical distances (case C). These requirements should allow us to avoid misidentifications and spurious parallaxes. Of course, for those objects with no useful parallax measurement, we also use the median of statistical distances (case C). Finally, there are objects that have only one distance estimate (case D).

We have explored different ways of determining uncertainties for these distances, such as the comparison of different distance estimates, the uncertainties implied by the parallax error, and the uncertainties provided by the Bayesian method. We have decided

Table 1. Available distances and our most reliable distance (all in kpc) for some of our sample PNe.

PN G	D_{Z95}	D_{FBP16}	D_{SH18}	D_B	$1/p$	$\delta p/p$	D_{tw}	Case[(a)]
000.0−01.0	–	–	–	8.20	1.22	0.48	8.20 ± 5.74	D
000.0−06.8	–	6.97	–	8.39	21.28	0.72	6.97 ± 4.88	D
000.1+02.6	–	–	–	4.88	3.82	0.62	4.88 ± 3.42	D
000.1+17.2	8.87	9.46	14.51	7.82	34.56	2.28	9.16 ± 3.66	B
000.1−01.1	6.05	–	8.63	–	–	–	7.23 ± 2.89	C
000.1−01.7	–	6.95	–	–	–	–	6.95 ± 4.87	D
000.1−02.3	–	7.62	5.58	–	–	–	6.52 ± 2.61	C
000.1−05.6	–	6.19	7.92	5.66	2.94	0.79	6.19 ± 2.48	B
000.1−08.0	–	–	–	6.73	4.39	2.70	6.73 ± 4.71	D
000.2+01.7	–	8.50	–	–	–	–	8.50 ± 5.95	D
000.2+06.1	–	9.79	–	–	–	–	9.79 ± 6.85	D
000.2−01.9	6.77	4.89	8.80	9.03	6.10	0.68	6.77 ± 2.71	C
000.3+03.2	–	–	–	6.96	1.54	1.70	6.96 ± 4.87	D
000.3+04.2	–	–	–	6.61	5.57	1.34	6.61 ± 4.63	D
000.3+12.2	3.49	2.35	3.97	2.46	3.07	0.13	3.07 ± 1.23	A

(a): A: Inverse of parallax; B: Median of statistical estimate and Bayesian estimate; C: Median of statistical estimates; D: One useful distance estimate.

to use the conservative uncertainties implied by the comparison among different distance estimates for those objects that have more than one distance estimate (40%). For objects with only one distance estimate, we have decided to assign larger uncertainties (70%) because these distances are less reliable. In Table 1 we show some examples of our results. The table lists the available distances (columns 2-6), the parallax uncertainty (column 7), our selected distance, D_{tw}, with its uncertainty (column 8) and the case (column 9). There are 89 PNe in case A (inverse of the parallax); 177 PNe in case B (median of the statistical estimates and the Bayesian estimate); 635 PNe in case C (median of the statistical estimates); and 1310 PNe in case D (only one useful distance estimate).

3. An application of these distances

We use our derived distances to analyze the galactic distribution of different spectral types of central stars. Several spectral types of central star exist, but most of them can be classified as hydrogen-poor central stars (HP-CSPNe) or hydrogen-rich central stars (HR-CSPNe). Some authors have studied the distributions of the galactic height of these spectral types. For example, Peña et al. (2013) find that [WR] CSPNe (a type of HP-CSPNe) are closer to the galactic plane than HR-CSPNe. Weidmann et al. (2020) use a larger sample and find that HP CSPNe are at lower galactic latitude than HR-CSPNe.

We have studied the distribution of galactic height (z_G) of [WR] and HR CSPNe using the catalog of CSPNe of Weidmann et al. (2020). Fig. 2 shows the distributions of z_G for [WR] CSPNe (upper panel), HP non-[WR] CSPNe (middle panel) and HR CSPNe (bottom panel). We can see in Fig. 2 that [WR] CSPNe are closer to the galactic plane than HR CSPNe, as previously found by Peña et al. (2013). A Kolmogorov-Smirnov test indicates that the distributions of [WR] CSPNe and HR CSPNe have significant differences (with a *p-value* of 0.007). On the other hand, HP non-[WR] CSPNe seem to have a different behavior from the [WR] CSPNe population. A Kolmogorov-Smirnov test indicates that both distributions have significant differences (*p-value* of 0.02). Moreover, the test indicates that the HP non-[WR] and HR CSPNe have similar distributions of z_G (*p-value* of 0.39). This result disagrees with the existence of an evolutionary sequence among HP CSPNe, as proposed by several authors (see Fig. 1 of Weidmann et al. 2020, and references therein). This results can be affected by the different distributions of

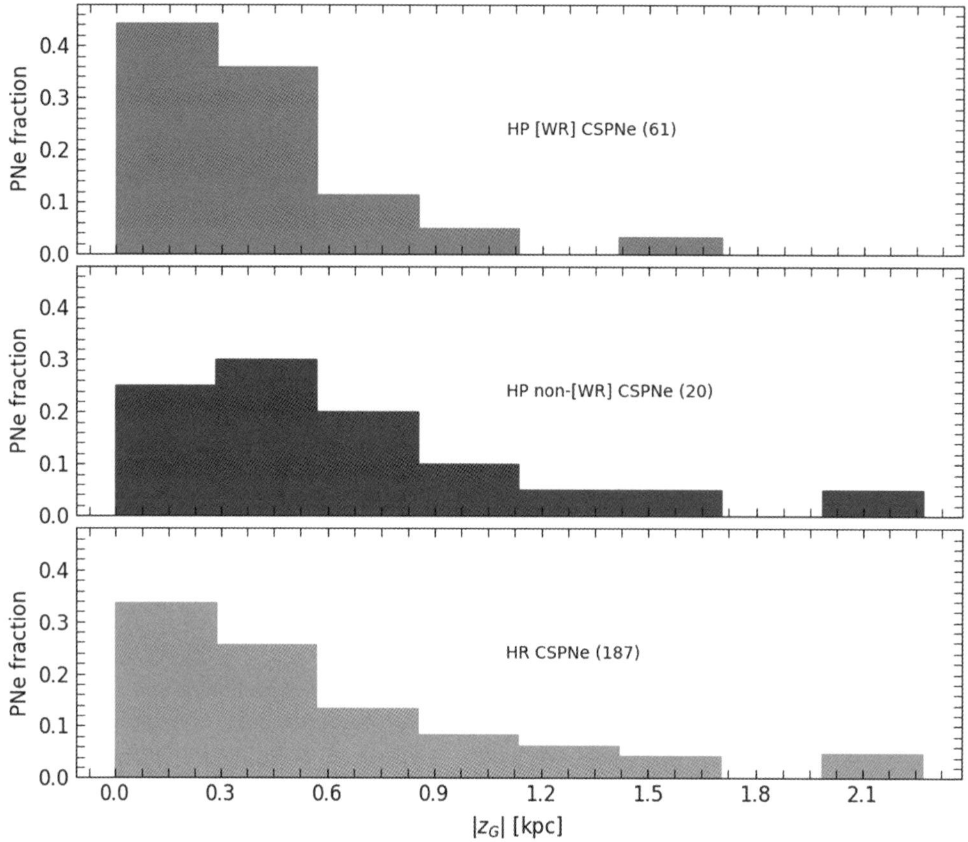

Figure 2. Distributions of distances to the galactic plane (z_G) for [WR] CSPNe (top panel), HP non-[WR] CSPNe (middle panel) and HR CSPNe (bottom panel). The number of objects is indicated in each panel.

heliocentric distances shown by the different CSPNe, something that we explore in our complete work submitted to RevMexAA.

4. Conclusions

We have determined the most reliable distance for a sample of 2211 PNe, using *Gaia*'s parallaxes (Gaia Collaboration et al. 2021, 2016; Bailer-Jones et al. 2021) and statistical distances (Zhang 1995; Frew et al. 2016; Stanghellini & Haywood 2018). Besides, we have confirmed that [WR] CSPNe are closer to the galactic plane than other CSPNe. We have found that the distribution of galactic heights of [WR] CSPNe is different from those of other HP CSPNe. This result disagrees with the existence of an evolutionary sequence among HP CSPNe. A complete version of this work will be submitted to RevMexAA.

DHJ acknowledges financial support from the IAU and UNAM and a scholarship from CONAHCyT, Mexico. This work has made use of data from the European Space Agency (ESA) mission *Gaia* (`https://www.cosmos.esa.int/gaia`), processed by the *Gaia* Data Processing and Analysis Consortium (DPAC, `https://www.cosmos.esa.int/web/gaia/dpac/consortium`). Funding for the DPAC has been provided by national institutions, in particular the institutions participating in the *Gaia* Multilateral Agreement.

References

Astraatmadja, T. L. & Bailer-Jones, C. A. L. 2016, *ApJ*, 833, 119

Bailer-Jones, C. A. L., Rybizki, J., Fouesneau, M., et al. 2021, *AJ*, 161, 147

Chornay, N., & Walton, N. A. 2021, *A&A*, 656, A110

Fabricius, C., Luri, X., Arenou, F., et al. 2021, *A&A*, 649, A5

Frew, D. J., Parker, Q. A., & Bojičić, I. S. 2016, *MNRAS*, 455, 1459

Gaia Collaboration, Brown, A. G. A., Vallenari, A., et al. 2021, *A&A*, 649, A1

Gaia Collaboration, Prusti, T., de Bruijne, J. H. J., et al. 2016, *A&A*, 595, A1

González-Santamaría, I., Manteiga, M., Manchado, A., et al. 2021, *A&A*, 656, A51

Oudmaijer, R. D., Jones, E. R. M., & Vioque, M. 2022, *MNRAS*, 516, L61

Peña, M., Rechy-García, J. S., & García-Rojas, J. 2013, *Rev. Mex. Astron. Astrofis.*, 49, 87

Shklovsky, I. S. 1956, *AZh*, 33, 222

Stanghellini, L., & Haywood, M. 2018, *ApJ*, 862, 45

Zhang, C. Y. 1995, *ApJS*, 98, 659

Weidmann, W. A., Mari, M. B., Schmidt, E. O., et al. 2020, *A&A*, 640, A10

Planetary Nebulae: A Universal Toolbox in the Era of Precision Astrophysics
Proceedings IAU Symposium No. 384, 2025
O. De Marco, A. Zijlstra & R. Szczerba, eds.
doi:10.1017/S1743921324000486

GTC Spectroscopic Surveys of Planetary Nebulae in the Milky Way and M31

Xuan Fang[1,2], Haomiao Huang[1,3], Martín A. Guerrero[4], Letizia Stanghellini[5], Rubén García-Benito[4], Ting-Hui Lee[6] and Yong Zhang[7,2]

[1]National Astronomical Observatories, Chinese Academy of Sciences (NAOC), Beijing 100101, China; fangx@nao.cas.cn

[2]Laboratory for Space Research, Faculty of Science, The University of Hong Kong, Hong Kong, China

[3]School of Astronomy and Space Science, University of Chinese Academy of Sciences, Beijing 100049, China

[4]Instituto de Astrofísica de Andalucía, CSIC, Glorieta de la Astronomía s/n, E-18008 Granada, Spain

[5]NSF's NOIRLab, 950 N. Cherry Ave., Tucson, AZ 85719, USA

[6]Department of Physics and Astronomy, Western Kentucky University, Bowling Green, KY 42101, USA

[7]School of Physics and Astronomy, Sun Yat-Sen University, Zhuhai 519082, China

Abstract. We report spectroscopic surveys of planetary nebulae (PNe) in the Milky Way and Andromeda (M31), using the 10.4-m Gran Telescopio Canarias (GTC). The spectra are of high quality and cover the whole optical range, mostly from 3650 Å to beyond 1 μm, enabling detection of nebular emission lines critical for spectral analysis and photoionization modeling. We obtained GTC spectra of 24 compact (angular diameter <5 arcsec) PNe located in the Galactic disk, ∼3–20 kpc from the Galactic centre, and that can be used to constrain stellar evolution models and derive radial abundance gradients of the Milky Way. We have observed 30 PNe in the outer halo of M31 using the GTC. These halo PNe are uniformly metal-rich and probably all evolved from low-mass stars, consistent with the conjecture that they formed from the metal-rich gas in M31 disk but were displaced to their present locations due to galaxy interactions.

Keywords. (ISM:) planetary nebulae: general, stars: evolution, planetary nebulae

1. Introduction

Planetary nebulae (PNe) evolved from low- to intermediate-mass stars (∼1–8 $M_{\odot}$), which account for an absolute majority of the stellar populations in the universe. PNe are ionized shells of gas ejected episodically by asymptotic giant branch (AGB) stars during the late-stage stellar evolution. Although belonging to the interstellar medium (ISM) and having a very short visible/dynamical age (∼10^4 yr) due to nebular expansion, PNe are a direct link between stellar evolution and the interstellar gas, and can be used to well constrain the theory of AGB nucleosynthesis (e.g. Fang et al. 2018; Henry et al. 2018).

Chemical abundances of PNe, both of α-elements and of N, C and He, can be used to constrain stellar evolutionary models and quantify the contribution of low- to intermediate-mass stars to Galactic chemical enrichment. CNO abundances give a direct indication of whether the AGB stars have gone through hot bottom burning (HBB) and the third dredge-up (Herwig 2005), indicating a more massive progenitor. The α-elements can also be used to constrain Galactic chemical evolution by measuring metallicity gradients in the disk (e.g. Milingo et al. 2010; Stanghellini & Haywood 2010).

Abundances of Galactic PNe have been investigated for decades, but mostly with significant limitations. First, of the current several hundred Galactic PNe with detailed chemical analyses, most are older, extended objects (e.g. Dufour et al. 2015; Henry et al. 2018). Deriving total elemental abundances in extended PNe using small apertures (e.g. narrow slits) involves substantial uncertainties because the ionization is often highly stratified in a PN (Osterbrock & Ferland 2006). It is hard to extrapolate abundances from one part of a PN to the whole nebula. Compact PNe fit into a long slit, so the flux of the entire nebula is measured, and little correction is needed. A second limitation on abundance analyses of Galactic PNe is that results between similar studies by different observations/authors are frequently inconsistent, due to different ionization correction factors (ICFs) adopted. ICFs are used to estimate abundances of ions that are absent in optical spectra (Kingsburgh & Barlow 1994), and work generally well; but since they were never calibrated for extreme metallicity, electron temperature, or ionization levels due to lack of infrared (IR) or UV data at the time, the use of ICFs introduces larger uncertainties in those regimes. Hence, the best way to address this problem is optical spectroscopy in combination with the IR/UV data. That is why we carried out optical spectroscopy of Galactic compact PNe with available *Spitzer* mid-IR and *HST*/STIS UV observations (see Section 2).

The main-sequence progenitors of PNe encompass a wide range of stellar ages, corresponding to a broad range in stellar population. Given their bright, narrow emission lines, PNe are easily detectable in distance galaxies/clusters (e.g. Gerhard et al. 2005, 2007; Longobardi et al. 2018), and are excellent tracers of the chemistry, dynamics and stellar population of host galaxies. The Andromeda Galaxy (M31) is the nearest (785 kpc; McConnachie et al. 2005) large disk system and best candidate for studying galaxy merger and evolution. Numerous large-scale substructures (i.e. stellar streams; e.g. Ibata et al. 2001) as well as inhomogeneity in metallicity have been revealed in M31's extended halo by panoramic surveys such as PAndAS (McConnachie et al. 2009), pointing to a tumultuous merging history of this galaxy.

One long-standing unresolved question is what the origin of M31's stellar substructure is. It has been proposed that the Northern Spur and the Southern Giant Stream, two very prominent substructures, might be connected by a stellar stream (Ibata et al. 2001; Merrett et al. 2003), but this hypothesis needs assessment. Recent hydrodynamical simulations suggests that a single major merger might be responsible for the bulk of the substructures in the M31 halo, including the Southern Giant Stream (Hammer et al. 2018). However, these simulations, including all previous efforts, are still somewhat speculative; accurate observations yet to be used help constrain the modeling. PNe are the only ISM/nebulae that exist in almost every part of a galaxy, from the disk to the bulge as well as the outer halo; the nebular emission lines of a PN can be measured to derive accurate ionic/elemental abundances. PNe thus can be used as a tracer to study the properties of M31 halo substructures. This is the main driving science of our GTC spectroscopy of PNe in M31's halo (see Section 3).

2. Spectroscopic Survey of compact PNe in the Galactic Disk

We carried out deep optical spectroscopy of 24 compact (angular diameter <5 arcsec; Figure 1) PNe in the Galactic disk, using the OSIRIS spectrograph on the 10.4 m Gran Telescopio Canarias (GTC, La Palma). The targets are mostly Northern objects, and

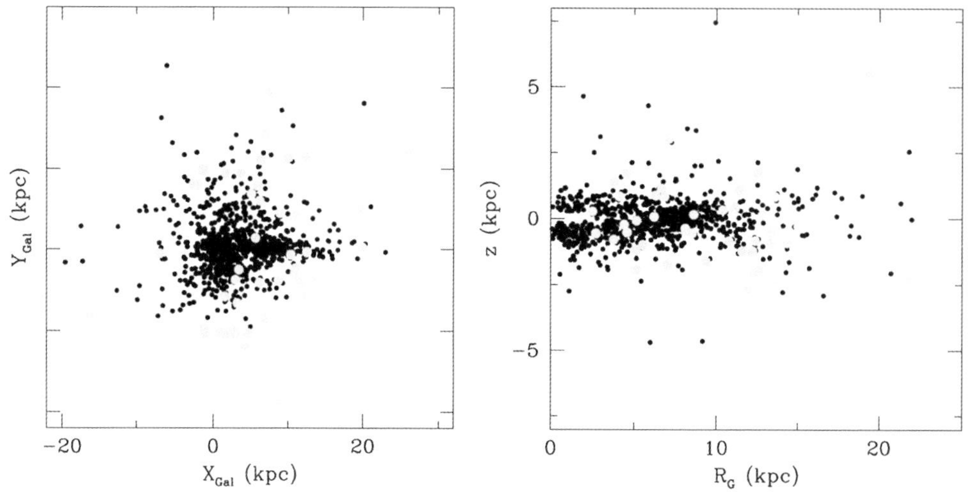

Figure 1. Spatial distribution of compact PNe (large, cyan dots) against the general distribution of Galactic PNe (small, black dots). *Left*: top-view of the Galactic disk. *Right*: galacocentric distance vs. distance from the Galactic plane. Images adopted from Stanghellini, Shaw & Villaver (2016, Figures 8 and 9 therein).

were carefully selected from a well defined sample of 150 compact PNe whose mid-IR spectra were obtained with *Spitzer*/IRS (Stanghellini et al. 2012). They cover an adequate galactocentric range (∼3–20 kpc) so that radial metallicity gradients can be readily available.

The GTC/OSIRIS observations was obtained from June to July in 2016 (GTC program No.: GTC66-16A; PI: X. Fang) in the long-slit spectroscopy mode, with 1 arcsec slit width. The blue and red grisms, R1000B and R1000R, were used, covering spectral ranges ∼3630–7850 Å and ∼5080–10370 Å, respectively. The OSIRIS detector consists of two CCDs with 2048×4096 pixels†. The size of a single pixel is 15 μm, corresponding to angular scale of 0.127 arcsec; the standard observing mode was used where the output images were binned by 2×2. Spectroscopic observations were carried out in the dark moon night with a wonderful seeing of 0.6–0.8 arcsec. During observations, multiplet exposures were made for each PN for purpose of cosmic-ray removal and increasing the signal-to-nose ratio. In total, ∼40 hr observations were completed at GTC for the 24 compact PNe.

Reduction of the GTC OSIRIS spectra generally follows the standard procedure for the long-slit spectra, using IRAF‡. As an example, we present in Figure 2 the final reduced, calibrated and extracted 1D spectrum of one of our targets, PN G068.7+14.8, where C III $\lambda\lambda$4649,5696 and C IV $\lambda\lambda$5801,5811 broad emission lines, probably coming from the PN central star, are well detected. We analyzed the nebular spectra, and carried out photoionization modeling using the CLOUDY code (Ferland et al. 1998, 2017) to derived the PN central star properties (e.g. *bottom-right* panel in Figure 2).

Complete analyses of the GTC spectra of all compact PNe targets, in combination with the archival *HST*/STIS UV–optical and *Spitzer* min-IR data, are underway (Fang et al. 2023a, in preparation). The more reliable ICFs of different elements will be derived for

† In 2023, OSIRIS was updated to OSIRIS+, with a new monolithic 4k×4k CCD installed. `https://www.gtc.iac.es/instruments/osiris+/osiris+.php`

‡ IRAF, the Image Reduction and Analysis Facility, is distributed by the National Optical Astronomy Observatory, which is operated by the Association of Universities for Research in Astronomy under cooperative agreement with the National Science Foundation.

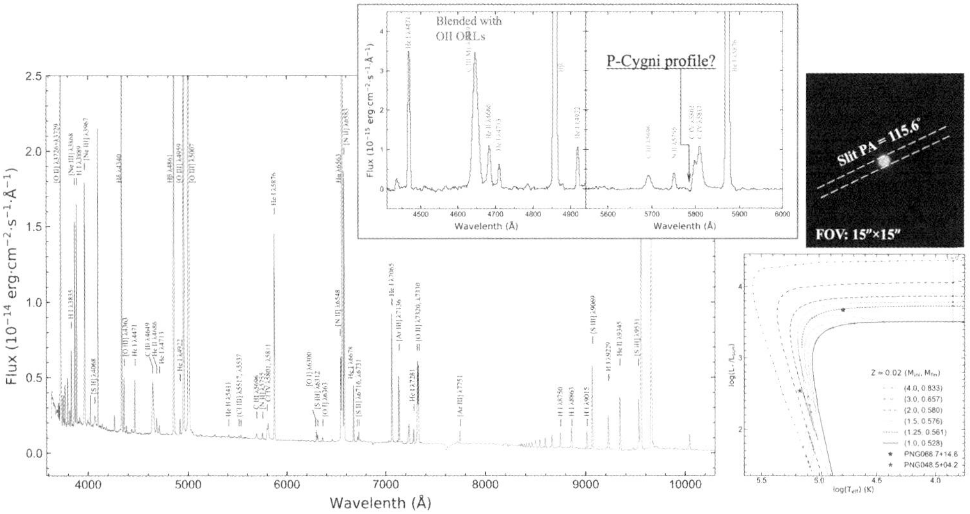

Figure 2. *Left*: GTC OSIRIS long-slit spectrum of Galactic planetary nebula PN G068.7+14.8; blue and red represent the R1000B and R1000R grisms, respectively. *Right-top*: *HST* WFC3 F502N narrowband image of PN G068.7+14.8 in the [O III] λ5007 emission line, adopted from Stanghellini, Shaw & Villaver (2016); the GTC long slit (white-dashed lines) with 1-arcsec width is overlaid. *Right-bottom*: Central star position of PN G068.7+14.8 (blue star) in H-R diagram, where model tracks of the H-burning post-AGB sequences calculated by Miller Bertolami (2016) at $Z = 0.02$ are overplotted, different line types representing different initial and final masses. The red curves are the isochrones for evolutionary ages (τ = 0, 5000, 10,000, 15,000, and 20,000 years) since the beginning of post-AGB defined at $\log T_{\rm eff} = 3.85$. The central star position of another Galactic compact nebula PN G048.5+04.2 (green star) is also presented for purpose of comparison of a different evolutionary status from that of PN G068.7+14.8. *Top-inset*: Zoom-in of the GTC spectrum showing the C III and C IV lines possibly emitted from the central star, with a likely P-Cygni profile marked (Huang & Fang, in preparation).

our PNe using the multi-wavelength spectra. CLOUDY photoionization models, with an aid of the *HST* optical images (Stanghellini, Shaw & Villaver 2016), will be developed based on the UV-optical-IR spectra, to derive the central star masses of our sample PNe and consequently, the main-sequence masses/ages. We will compare the chemical abundances with predictions from the stellar evolution models – in particular the AGB nucleosynthesis models (e.g. Karakas & Lugaro 2016), and correlate them with the dust chemistry, metallicity and central star masses.

Given the distribution (Galactic l and b, distance) of our sample in the Galaxy, it is suitable to explore the nebular and stellar properties across the Galactic disk. Our Northern sample is complemented by the previous observations of the Southern objects (using the 4.1-m SOAR telescope) and other published spectroscopy. With the available *Gaia* distances, we will set strong constraints on the Galactic evolutionary models through the analysis of chemical (oxygen and other α-elements) and population gradients using these compact PNe.

3. Spectroscopic Survey of the PNe in M31 halo

Since 2012, large-aperture (8–10 m class) optical telescopes have been used to obtain the spectra of PNe in M31, mostly in M31's outer disk (Kwitter et al. 2012; Balick et al. 2013; Corradi et al. 2015), and all have oxygen abundances close to the solar level. Spectroscopic analysis of the outer-halo PNe in M31 were extremely scarce. Our first attempt of optical spectroscopy of bright PNe in the outer halo in the Northern Spur

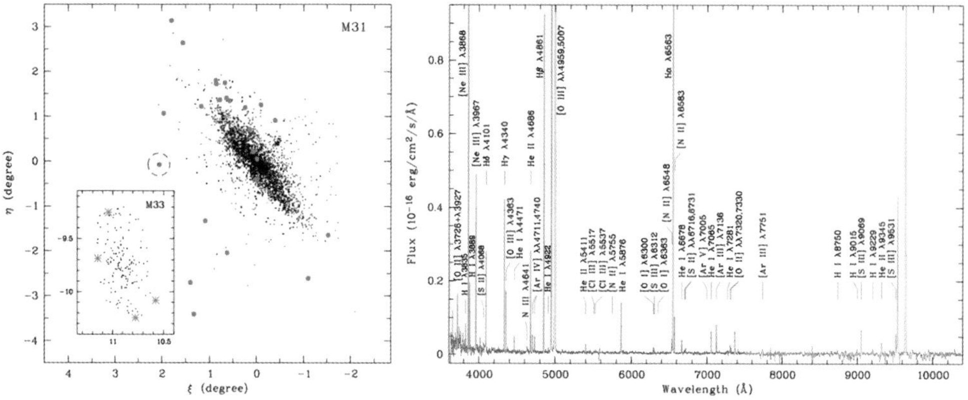

Figure 3. *Left*: Distribution of PNe in M31+M33. The PNe targeted by our GTC observations (Fang et al. 2013, 2015, 2018, and several unpublished objects) are highlighted in red-filled circles and red asterisks. The inset shows the PNe in M33 in M31-centred coordinates. *Right*: GTC OSIRIS long-slit spectrum of a halo PN in M31 (marked by a red-dashed circle in the *left* panel) obtained with the R1000B (blue) and R1000R (red) grisms, with emission lines labeled.

substructure) of M31 was carried out using the 5.1-m Hale telescope, only with limited data quality, although our analysis revealed metal-rich nature of the halo objects (Fang et al. 2013). Since 2014, we continued this effort using the 10.4-m GTC in La Palma. So far, over 100 hr observations have been completed at the GTC for ∼30 PNe in M31's halo (Figure 3), mostly with excellent spectral quality (e.g. Figure 3-*right*). Our halo samples kinematically deviate from the disk population, and were carefully selected so that they are located in different halo substructures, covering a vast spatial extension (Figure 3-*left*). The instrument setup (spectrograph, grisms, slit width and observing mode) and procedure of data reduction are the same as introduced in Section 2.

All the outer-halo PNe of M31 we have published so far also have oxygen abundances close to the Sun, $[O/H]\gtrsim -0.4$ with modest scatter (Fang et al. 2013, 2015, 2018, see also Figure 4), and probably all evolved from low-mass ($<2\,M_{\odot}$) stars mostly with ages of ∼2–5 Gyr. Our halo sample cannot be distinguished from the disk population in metallicity or the main-sequence mass/age (Fang et al. 2018), which is in stark contrast with the underlying, smooth, metal-poor halo of M31 (Figure 4). We conjecture that these halo PNe might have originally formed from metal-rich gas in M31 disk but were displaced to the halo regions and gained their current stream/substructure kinematics as a result of M31's interaction with its satellite(s). This astrophysical picture, although highly speculative, agrees with our present-day knowledge that M31's extended halo evolved from complex galactic mergers and interactions. Further investigation using a combined sample in M31+M33 is underway (Fang et al. 2023b, in preparation).

Photoionization models will be constructed for the halo/substructure PNe in M31 to derive their main-sequence masses ($M_{\rm ini}$). We will then derive the He/H and N/O abundance ratios versus $M_{\rm ini}$ relations for the combined sample of the halo/substructure PNe in M31 together with the Galactic compact PNe observed using GTC (see Section 2). These abundance-mass relations will be used to constrain the AGB models. The surface contents of helium and nitrogen are expected to increase as a consequence of the second dredge up and HBB that occur in intermediate-mass AGB stars with $M_{\rm ini}\gtrsim$3–5 $M_{\odot}$(e.g. Karakas & Lugaro 2016). However, previous spectroscopic analysis of M31 and Galactic PNe indicates that HBB might actually occur at $<3\,M_{\odot}$. Our new observations will be used to carefully assess this (Fang et al. 2023b, in preparation).

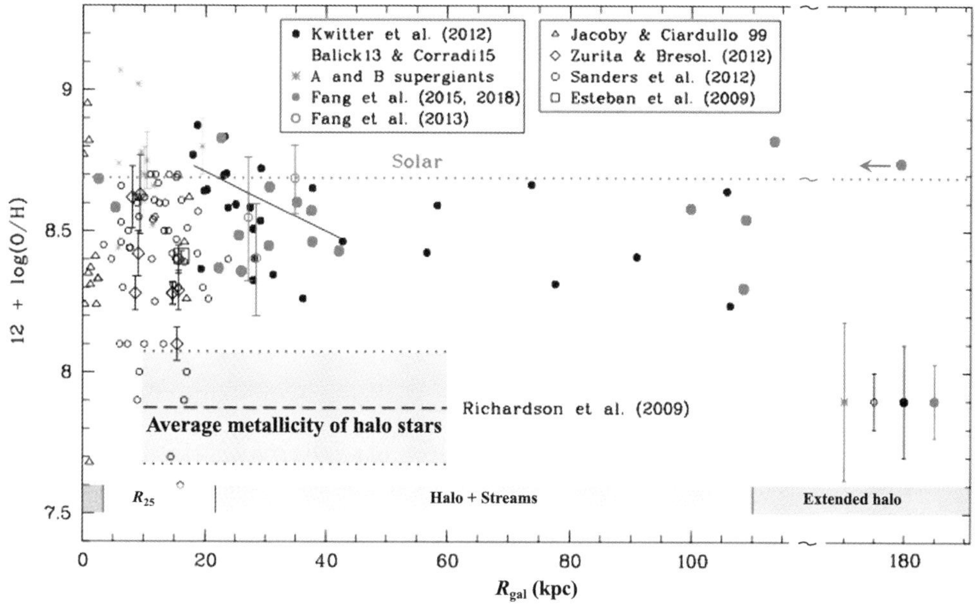

Figure 4. Radial distribution of oxygen abundances in M31 (figure adopted from Fang et al. 2018). The M31 halo PNe previously targeted by our GTC observations are red-filled circles (see Figure 3-*left*). The M31 outer-disk PNe (observed by Kwitter et al. 2012, Balick et al. 2013, and Corradi et al. 2015) are black dots. Other literature samples of PNe, H II regions and supergiants in M31 are over-plotted (see legend). The black-solid straight line is a linear fit to the disk PNe between 20 and 40 kpc (Kwitter et al. 2012). The red-dotted line marks the solar value. The horizontal black-dashed and dotted lines represent the mean metallicity and dispersion (also grey-shaded) of halo stars between 10 and 60 kpc (Richardson et al. 2009).

References

Balick B., Kwitter K. B., Corradi R. L. M., & Henry R. B. C., 2013, *ApJ*, 774, 3, DOI:10.1088/0004-637X/774/1/3

Corradi R. L. M., Kwitter K. B., Balick B., et al., 2015, *ApJ*, 807, 181, DOI:10.1088/0004-637X/807/2/181

Dufour R. J., Kwitter K. B., Shaw R. A., et al., 2015, *ApJ*, 803, 23, DOI:10.1088/0004-637X/803/1/23

Gerhard O., Arnaboldi M., Freeman K. C., et al., 2005, *ApJL*, 621, L93, DOI:10.1086/429221

Gerhard O., Arnaboldi M., Freeman K. C., et al., 2007, *A&A*, 468, 815, DOI: 10.1051/0004-6361:20066484

Fang X., Zhang Y., Garía-Benito R., Liu X.-W., & Yuan H.-B., 2013, *ApJ*, 774, 138, DOI:10.1088/0004-637X/774/2/138

Fang X., García-Benito R., Guerrero M. A., et al., 2015, *ApJ*, 815, 69, DOI:10.1088/0004-637X/815/1/69

Fang X., García-Benito R., Guerrero M. A., et al., 2018, *ApJ*, 853, 50, DOI:10.3847/1538-4357/aaa1e5

Ferland G. J., Chatzikos M., Guzmán F., et al., 2017, *RMxAA*, 53, 385, DOI:10.48550/arXiv.1705.10877

Ferland G. J., Korista K. T., Verner D. A., et al., 1998, *PASP*, 110, 761, DOI:10.1086/316190

Hammer F., Yang Y. B., Wang J. L., et al., 2018, *MNRAS*, 475, 2754, DOI:10.1093/mnras/stx3343

Henry R. B. C., Stephenson B. G., Miller Bertolami M. M., Kwitter K. B., & Balick B., 2018, *MNRAS*, 473, 241, DOI:10.1093/mnras/stx2286

Herwig F., 2005, *ARA&A*, 43, 435, DOI:10.1146/annurev.astro.43.072103.150600

Ibata R. A., Irwin M. J., Lewis G., et al., 2001, *Nature*, 412, 49, DOI:10.1038/35083506
Karakas A. I., & Lugaro M., 2016, *ApJ* 825, 26, DOI:10.3847/0004-637X/825/1/26
Kingsburgh R. L., & Barlow M. J., 1994, *MNRAS*, 271, 257, DOI:10.1093/mnras/271.2.257
Kwitter K. B., Lehman E. M. M., Balick B., & Henry R. B. B., 2012, *ApJ*, 753, 12, DOI:10.1088/0004-637X/753/1/12
Longobardi A., Arnaboldi M., Gerhard O., et al., 2018, *A&A*, 620, A111, DOI:10.1051/0004-6361/201832729
McConnachie A. W., Irwin M. J., Ferguson A. M. N., et al., 2005, *MNRAS*, 356, 979, DOI:10.1111/j.1365-2966.2004.08514.x
McConnachie A. W., Irwin M. J., Ibata R. A., et al., 2009, *Nature*, 461, 66, DOI:10.1038/nature08327
Merrett H. R., Kuijken K., Merrifield M. R., et al., 2003, *MNRAS*, 346, L62, DOI:10.1111/j.1365-2966.2003.07367.x
Milingo J. B., Kwitter K. B., Henry R. B. C., & Souza S. P., 2010, *ApJ*, 711, 619, DOI:10.1088/0004-637X/711/2/619
Miller Bertolami M. M., 2016, *A&A*, 588, A25, DOI:10.1051/0004-6361/201526577
Osterbrock D. E., & Ferland G. J., 2006, Astrophysics of Gaseous Nebulae and Active Galactic Nuclei (Sausalito, CA: Univ. Science Books)
Richardson J. C., Ferguson A. M. N., Mackey A. C., et al., 2009, *MNRAS*, 396, 1842, DOI:10.1111/j.1365-2966.2009.14788.x
Stanghellini L., García-Hernández D. A., García-Lario P., et al., 2012, *ApJ*, 753, 172, DOI:10.1088/0004-637X/753/2/172
Stanghellini L., & Haywood M., 2010, *ApJ*, 714, 1096, DOI:10.1088/0004-637X/714/2/1096
Stanghellini L., Shaw R. A., & Villaver E., 2016, *ApJ*, 830, 33, DOI:10.3847/0004-637X/830/1/33

Planetary Nebulae: A Universal Toolbox in the Era of Precision Astrophysics
Proceedings IAU Symposium No. 384, 2025
O. De Marco, A. Zijlstra & R. Szczerba, eds.
doi:10.1017/S1743921323005513

Probing the Local Planetary Nebula Luminosity Function with *Gaia*

Nicholas Chornay[1,2], **Nicholas Walton**[2], **David Jones**[3,4] **and Henri Boffin**[5]

[1]Department of Astronomy, University of Geneva, Chemin d'Ecogia 16, 1290 Versoix, Switzerland;
email: `Nick.Chornay@unige.ch`

[2]Institute of Astronomy, University of Cambridge, Madingley Road, Cambridge CB3 0HA, UK

[3]Instituto de Astrofísica de Canarias, E-38205 La Laguna, Tenerife, Spain

[4]Departamento de Astrofísica, Universidad de La Laguna, E-38206 La Laguna, Tenerife, Spain

[5]ESO, Karl-Schwarzschild-str. 2, 85748 Garching, Germany

Abstract. The Planetary Nebula Luminosity Function (PNLF) remains an important extragalactic distance indicator despite a still limited understanding of its most important feature - the bright cut-off. External galaxies benefit from consistent distance and extinction, which makes determining the PNLF easier but detailed study of individual objects much more difficult. Now, the advent of parallaxes from the Gaia mission has dramatically improved distance estimates to planetary nebulae (PNe) in the Milky Way. We have acquired ground-based narrowband imagery and measured the [OIII] fluxes for a volume-limited sample of hundreds of PNe whose best distance estimates from Gaia parallaxes and statistical methods place them within 3 kpc of the Sun. We present the first results of our study, comparing the local PNLF to other galaxies with different formation histories, and discussing how the brightness of the PNe relates to the evolutionary state of their central stars and the properties of the nebula.

Keywords. planetary nebulae, surveys, distances

1. Introduction

The [O III] $\lambda5007$ magnitudes of planetary nebulae (PNe) show a remarkably consistent bright-end cutoff largely independent of galactic age and metallicity (Ciardullo et al. 1989; Jacoby 1989), so much so that the [O III] planetary nebula luminosity function (PNLF) continues to serve as an important extragalactic distance indicator (Roth et al. 2021; Scheuermann et al. 2022). The reason for this behaviour is, however, still not fully understood after more than three decades (Ciardullo 2022).

Historically, highly uncertain distances to Galactic PNe (Frew, Parker, & Bojičić 2016) have made the study of the PNLF of the Milky Way difficult, outside of populations at a known (assumed) distance such as the Galactic Bulge (Kovacevic et al. 2011). Milky Way PNLF studies are also challenged by the presence of interstellar dust, whose effects must be disentangled from those of circumnebular dust (Davis et al. 2018; Yao & Quataert 2023) in order to recreate the PNLF's behaviour. These issues mean that studies of the PNLF have largely focused on other galaxies (e.g. M31: Bhattacharya et al. 2019; Galera-Rosillo et al. 2022), where all PNe can be treated as lying at the same distance (not to mention more efficiently imaged). However a unique opportunity of studying the Milky Way PNLF is the direct observability of their CSPNe, which can be probed in detail for indicators of stellar parameters and possible binary evolution. The morphologies of the nebulae are also visible, spectroscopy is easier to obtain, and there is already a wealth of information in the literature.

The advent of precise parallaxes from the *Gaia* mission (Gaia Collaboration et al. 2016) has dramatically improved distance estimates to Galactic PNe (Chornay & Walton 2021), and *Gaia* data has also been used to improve Milky Way extinction maps (see, e.g., Dharmawardena et al. 2022). A missing ingredient is [OIII] λ5007 flux measurements. While it is possible to estimate [OIII] λ5007 fluxes using fluxes in other lines and spectroscopic line ratios, that approach introduces significant systematic uncertainties, particularly for nearby objects with a greater angular extent. The best values come from direct measurement (see e.g. the assessment of Kovacevic et al. 2011).

In this work we introduce our narrowband imaging survey of local PNe within a 3 kpc heliocentric radius. We use those fluxes, combined with extinction and distance estimates, to determine the PNLF of the sample. We compare this PNLF to those of other nearby galaxies, and describe how the properties of the nebulae and the CSPNe relate to the absolute [OIII] magnitudes of the PNe.

2. Observations and Data Reduction

Targets were selected with the aim of obtaining fluxes for a 3 kpc volume-limited sample of PNe. Targets were "true" (spectroscopically confirmed) PNe from the Hong Kong/AAO/Strasbourg Hα (HASH) PN catalogue (Parker, Bojičić, & Frew 2016). The distance estimates used for selection were the median distances from the catalogue of Chornay & Walton (2021) in the cases where there was a sufficiently secure central star identification. PNe were also included if their statistical distance estimate from Frew, Parker, & Bojičić (2016) or the inversion of the (sufficiently high quality) *Gaia* parallax placed them within 3 kpc.

Data for targets visible from the northern hemisphere (northwards of -25° in declination) were obtained with the Wide Field Camera (WFC) on the 2.54m Isaac Newton Telescope (INT) and the Alhambra Faint Object Spectrograph and Camera (ALFOSC) on the 2.56m Nordic Optical Telescope (NOT), both at the Observatorio del Roque de los Muchachos in La Palma, Spain. Southern hemisphere targets were observed at the European Southern Observatory (ESO) New Technology Telescope (NTT) at the La Silla observatory in Chile, using the ESO Faint Object Spectrograph and Camera (EFOSC2). That latter set of observations are not presented here.

Across all instrument setups, targets were observed with a narrowband filter centred around the [OIII] λ5007 emission line as well as a broad filter whose transmission curve enclosed that of the narrow filter (nominally a g filter). Typical exposure times were 300 seconds in the narrowband and 30 seconds in the broadband filter, both repeated twice; these were shortened for very bright targets to avoid saturation.

Images were reduced using standard methods. Sources were extracted from each reduced image using the IMCORE program published by the Cambridge Astronomical Software Unit (CASU).†, and a world coordinate system (WCS) was determined by matching those sources to the *Gaia* EDR3 catalogue, propagated to the epoch of the observations.

PN fluxes were extracted in each [OIII] image using a circular aperture, whose size was adjusted to match that of the PN. The background was estimated using an annulus centred on the PN. Particularly for fainter nebulae, field stars coincident with the nebula can contribute significantly to the aperture flux; this was removed by masking the stars, using the *Gaia* positions and magnitudes as a reference.

† `http://casu.ast.cam.ac.uk/surveys-projects/software-release`

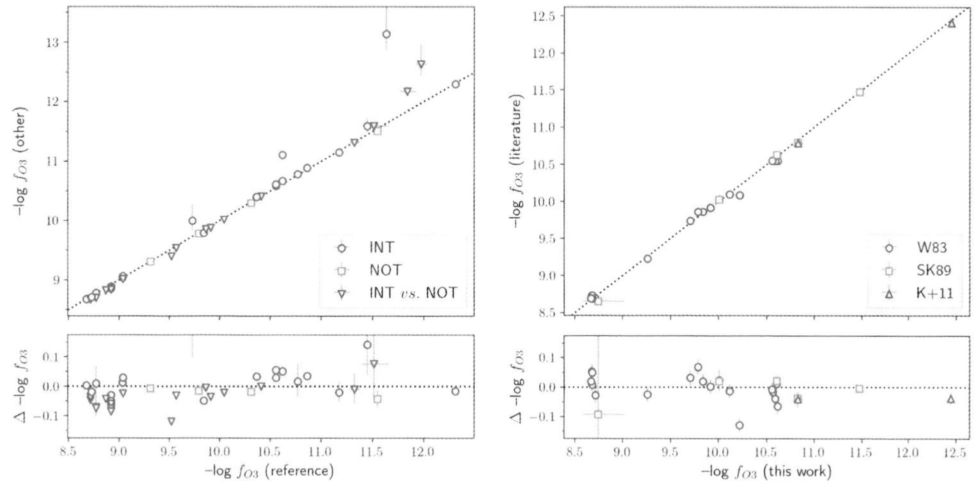

Figure 1. Left: Comparison of log fluxes for targets with repeated measurements, for targets observed by the INT, NOT, and both. The reference value is the observation with the best nominal uncertainties (grey error bars), except for the comparison between the INT and NOT fluxes in which case it is the INT observation with the best nominal uncertainties. Right: Comparisons to previous directly measured fluxes in literature, from Webster (1983) (W83), Shaw & Kaler (1989) (SK89), and Kovacevic et al. (2011) (K+11).

Photometric calibration was bootstrapped from the stellar fluxes of the near contemporaneous g-band image, which were compared to fluxes from the Pan-STARRS survey (for the northern hemisphere data). The nominal central wavelengths of the various g-band filters are all close to that of the [O III] filters, so we expect differences in the atmospheric extinction between these bands to be relatively small and predictable. The relationships between the zero points in the two filters as a function of airmass were determined from standard star observations included in each night of observing.

The uncertainties are dominated by effects other than photon counting: systematic errors due to the image reduction, flux extraction, and the method of determining the zero point, as well as further uncertainties due to potential variations of the zero point of the course of observations. Empirical uncertainties were obtained from repeat exposures. The conversion of narrowband filter to line flux depends on the transmission of the narrowband filters and radial velocity shifts. The former is only be detectable through systematic flux differences between instruments or between our measurements and those from literature; the latter we expect to be small and ignorable for our purposes, with the range of radial velocities of objects in our sample observed by Durand, Acker, & Zijlstra (1998) resulting in a transmission change of at most about 1% in the narrowest [O III] filter, that of the NOT.

3. [O III] Fluxes

We observed 225 different PNe, of which 219 had positive flux measurements, and 216 had positive flux measurements with a signal-to-noise ratio greater than one. The resulting fluxes span five orders of magnitude.

We repeated observations of some of the same targets on different nights and some with different instruments. The purpose of this is both to empirically assess the uncertainty and to look for systematic differences in our calibration between instruments. The results are shown in the left panel of Fig. 1. The INT measurements have a scatter of 0.05 dex,

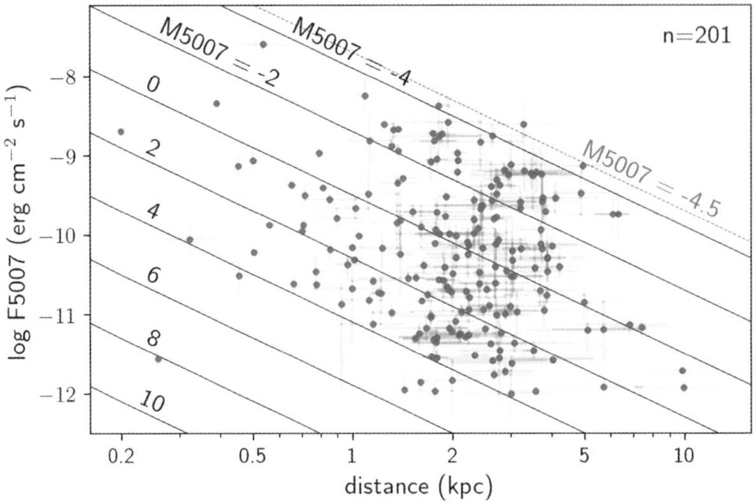

Figure 2. Logarithmic [OIII] fluxes corrected for extinction, for all observed PNe with flux signal-to-noise greater than one and literature extinction estimates. The diagonal lines show different values of M_{5007} with the approximate cutoff magnitude highlighted as the dashed red line.

while the four NOT measurements show about half that. For targets observed with both instruments, the NOT observations tend to be slightly brighter than the INT ones.

A small number of our targets have direct [OIII] flux measurements in literature that can be used for comparison. This was by design, as few nearby northern PNe have such measurements. We included two targets overlapping with Kovacevic et al. (2011), as well as five from Shaw & Kaler (1989) and thirteen from Webster (1983). The results of these comparisons are shown in the right panel of Fig. 1; all of these were measured at the INT, except for the two points closest the the equality line at the bright end which came from the NOT. There is not a significant systematic offset between our flux measurements and those in literature, except that both of the fluxes of Kovacevic et al. (2011) are brighter than ours by 0.04 dex.

While the measurements certainly show repeatability, in general the scatter is larger than expected from the nominal uncertainties, though the obvious outliers do have noticeably larger error bars. More work is needed to disentangle the source of this additional error: whether it is due to the measurement of the nebula flux itself, or uncertainty in the zero point, or some other systematic error introduced in the data reduction process. The comparison to literature fluxes show neither an obvious offset nor a higher scatter than expected from the internal consistency checks, so we consider the internal consistency to be the first priority for improvement.

4. PNLF

The distribution of de-reddened fluxes with distance is shown in Fig. 2, using the median distance estimates from Chornay & Walton (2021) and extinction values from Frew, Parker, & Bojičić (2016). For the purposes of this initial analysis we do not attempt to separate interstellar extinction and self-extinction by the PNe. The sample is nearly complete to 3 kpc (compared to the sample of known, spectroscopically confirmed PNe in the survey area accessible from the Northern hemisphere); we use this as the cutoff distance for most of the subsequent analysis.

The diagonal lines show corresponding values of M_{5007}; its distribution spans 8 magnitudes but is naturally incomplete at the faint end. The uncertainties in M_{5007} are

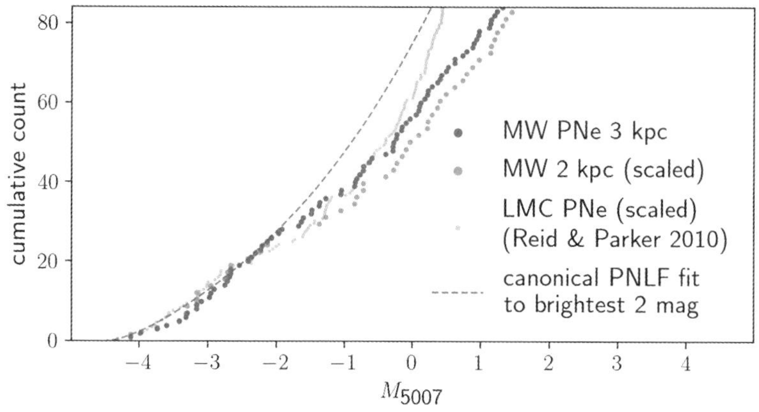

Figure 3. Cumulative distribution of M_{5007} values for our 3 kpc Milky Way sample compared to those of the same sample limited to 2 kpc and of the LMC sample of Reid & Parker (2010). The latter samples have been scaled to match the count in the brightest magnitude bins of the 3 kpc sample. The red dashed line is the canonical PNLF form scaled to match the counts at the bright end.

taken from the uncertainties corresponding to flux, distance, and extinction added in quadrature.

The resulting cumulative distribution of M_{5007} with the 3 kpc sample is shown in Fig. 3. It is compared to the canonical distribution from Ciardullo et al. (1989), $N(M) \propto e^{0.307M}(1 - e^{3(M^* - M)})$, with the cutoff magnitude fixed at $M^* = -4.5$ and the total count scaled to match the total number of PNe in the sample with $M_{5007} < -2.5$. The choice of scale is motivated by the clear departure of the distribution from the canonical one at fainter magnitudes. This corresponds to a dip in the (non-cumulative) PNLF.

Such a feature can be present in other galaxies that have undergone more recent star formation (Ciardullo 2022). For example, the Small Magellanic Cloud (SMC) PNLF of Jacoby & De Marco (2002) also shows a dip starting about 2.5 magnitudes below the bright cutoff, while the dip in the Large Magellanic Cloud (LMC) PNLF of Reid & Parker (2010) occurs even closer to the cutoff magnitude (grey points in Fig. 3). Jacoby & De Marco (2002) speculate that this gap is associated with a phase of fast CSPN evolution, in particular in young populations, noting that, if that is indeed the case, then the position of the dip is related to timing of the most recent period of star formation. We caution that the PNLF presented here is not directly comparable to these PNLFs, because the fluxes are corrected for extinction.

The PN in our sample with the brightest measured [OIII] flux is NGC 6572, with $M_{5007} = -4.1 \pm 0.3$. It has a bipolar morphology and is classified as a Type IIa PN by Quireza, Rocha-Pinto, & Maciel (2007).

The morphologies of the PNe (taken from HASH PN) show a small preference for bipolarity at the bright end, but otherwise bipolar and elliptical PNe are distributed relatively evenly (notably it is more difficult to measure the morphologies of fainter PNe, so the classifications are biased). This is in contrast with the observation of Kovacevic et al. (2011), who noted that bipolar PNe preferentially occupied the faint end of their Bulge PNLF (though without much detail). Round PNe are only present at magnitudes fainter than the dip.

Most known close binary systems occupy the intermediate magnitudes of the PNLF. The brightest known binary is NGC 2392 ($M_{5007} = -2.4 \pm 0.3$), a double-degenerate system detected through radial velocity variations (Miszalski et al. 2019). NGC 6572 has bipolar outflows (Miranda et al. 1999), which are often associated with binary interactions (Boffin & Jones 2019), but the brightness of the object (and indeed of the brightest PNe) makes it difficult to monitor for photometric or radial velocity variations from the ground, so its status has not been conclusively shown.

5. Conclusions

When published our catalogue will represent the largest set of directly measured [O III] fluxes for nearby (non-Bulge) Milky Way PNe, spanning nearly five orders of magnitude in flux and with typical uncertainties of 0.04 dex. The data already shown here will be complemented by recently acquired observations from the Southern hemisphere, and will provide a rich basis for future analysis and studies of Milky Way PNe, more so when combined with more precise parallax measurements from future *Gaia* data releases.

This research is based on observations made with the Isaac Newton Telescope operated on the island of La Palma by the Isaac Newton Group of Telescopes in the Spanish Observatorio del Roque de los Muchachos of the Instituto de Astrofísica de Canarias. This research is based on observations made with the Nordic Optical Telescope, owned in collaboration by the University of Turku and Aarhus University, and operated jointly by Aarhus University, the University of Turku and the University of Oslo, representing Denmark, Finland and Norway, the University of Iceland and Stockholm University at the Observatorio del Roque de los Muchachos, La Palma, Spain, of the Instituto de Astrofisica de Canarias. This research has made use of data from the European Space Agency (ESA) mission *Gaia* (`https://www.cosmos.esa.int/gaia`), processed by the *Gaia* Data Processing and Analysis Consortium (DPAC; `https://www.cosmos.esa.int/web/gaia/dpac/consortium`). Funding for the DPAC has been provided by national institutions, in particular the institutions participating in the *Gaia* Multilateral Agreement. This research has also made use of the HASH PN database (`http://hashpn.space`). This research was supported through the Cancer Research UK grant A24042.

References

Bhattacharya S., Arnaboldi M., Hartke J., Gerhard O., Comte V., McConnachie A., Caldwell N., 2019, *A&A*, 624, A132. doi:10.1051/0004-6361/201834579

Boffin H. M. J., Jones D., 2019, ibfe.book. doi:10.1007/978-3-030-25059-1

Chornay N., Walton N. A., 2021, *A&A*, 656, A110. doi:10.1051/0004-6361/202142008

Ciardullo R., 2022, *FrASS*, 9, 896326. doi:10.3389/fspas.2022.896326

Ciardullo R., Jacoby G. H., Ford H. C., Neill J. D., 1989, ApJ, 339, 53. doi:10.1086/167275

Davis B. D., Ciardullo R., Jacoby G. H., Feldmeier J. J., Indahl B. L., 2018, *ApJ*, 863, 189. doi:10.3847/1538-4357/aad3c4

Dharmawardena T. E., Bailer-Jones C. A. L., Fouesneau M., Foreman-Mackey D., 2022, A&A, 658, A166. doi:10.1051/0004-6361/202141298

Durand S., Acker A., Zijlstra A., 1998, *A&AS*, 132, 13. doi:10.1051/aas:1998356

Frew D. J., Parker Q. A., Bojičić I. S., 2016, MNRAS, 455, 1459. doi:10.1093/mnras/stv1516

Gaia Collaboration, Prusti T., de Bruijne J. H. J., Brown A. G. A., Vallenari A., Babusiaux C., Bailer-Jones C. A. L., et al., 2016, *A&A*, 595, A1. doi:10.1051/0004-6361/201629272

Galera-Rosillo R., Mampaso A., Corradi R. L. M., García-Rojas J., Balick B., Jones D., Kwitter K. B., et al., 2022, A&A, 657, A71. doi:10.1051/0004-6361/202141890

Jacoby G. H., 1989, *ApJ*, 339, 39. doi:10.1086/167274

Jacoby G. H., De Marco O., 2002, *AJ*, 123, 269. doi:10.1086/324737

Kovacevic A. V., Parker Q. A., Jacoby G. H., Miszalski B., 2011, apn5.conf, 44. doi:10.48550/arXiv.1010.1655

Kovacevic A. V., Parker Q. A., Jacoby G. H., Sharp R., Miszalski B., Frew D. J., 2011, *MNRAS*, 414, 860. doi:10.1111/j.1365-2966.2011.18250.x

Miranda L. F., Vázquez R., Corradi R. L. M., Guerrero M. A., López J. A., Torrelles J. M., 1999, *ApJ*, 520, 714. doi:10.1086/307506

Miszalski B., Manick R., Van Winckel H., Escorza A., 2019, *PASA*, 36, e018. doi:10.1017/pasa.2019.11

Parker Q. A., Bojičić I. S., Frew D. J., 2016, *JPhCS*, 728, 032008. doi:10.1088/1742-6596/728/3/032008

Quireza C., Rocha-Pinto H. J., Maciel W. J., 2007, *A&A*, 475, 217. doi:10.1051/0004-6361:20078087

Reid W. A., Parker Q. A., 2010, *MNRAS*, 405, 1349. doi:10.1111/j.1365-2966.2010.16635.x

Roth M. M., Jacoby G. H., Ciardullo R., Davis B. D., Chase O., Weilbacher P. M., 2021, *ApJ*, 916, 21. doi:10.3847/1538-4357/ac02ca

Scheuermann F., Kreckel K., Anand G. S., Blanc G. A., Congiu E., Santoro F., Van Dyk S. D., et al., 2022, *MNRAS*, 511, 6087. doi:10.1093/mnras/stac110

Shaw R. A., Kaler J. B., 1989, *ApJS*, 69, 495. doi:10.1086/191320

Webster B. L., 1983, *PASP*, 95, 610. doi:10.1086/131226

Yao P. Z., Quataert E., 2023, *ApJ*, 957, 30. doi:10.3847/1538-4357/acfed9

Planetary Nebulae: A Universal Toolbox in the Era of Precision Astrophysics
Proceedings IAU Symposium No. 384, 2025
O. De Marco, A. Zijlstra & R. Szczerba, eds.
doi:10.1017/S1743921323005768

Integral Field Spectroscopy: a disruptive innovation for observations of Planetary Nebulae and the PNLF

Martin M. Roth[1], George H. Jacoby[2], Robin Ciardullo[3], Azlizan A. Soemitro[1], Peter M. Weilbacher[1] and Magda Arnaboldi[4]

[1]Leibniz-Institut für Astrophysik Potsdam (AIP), Germany
email: mmroth@aip.de

[2]NSF's NOIRLab, U.S.A.

[3]The Penn State University, U.S.A.

[4]European Southern Observatory

Abstract. A quarter of a century has passed since the observing technique of integral field spectroscopy (IFS) was first applied to planetary nebulae (PNe). Progress after the early experiments was relatively slow, mainly because of the limited field-of-view (FoV) of first generation instruments. With the advent of MUSE at the ESO Very Large Telescope, this situation has changed. MUSE is a wide field-of-view, high angular resolution, one-octave spanning optical integral field spectrograph with high throughput. Its major science mission has enabled an unprecedented sensitive search for Lyα emitting galaxies at redshift up to z=6.5. This unique property can be utilized for faint objects at low redshift as well. It has been demonstrated that MUSE is an ideal instrument to detect and measure extragalactic PNe with high photometric accuracy down to very faint magnitudes out to distances of 30 Mpc, even within high surface brightness regions of their host galaxies. When coupled with a differential emission line filtering (DELF) technique, MUSE becomes far superior to conventional narrow-band imaging, and therefore MUSE is ideal for accurate Planetary Nebula Luminosity Function (PNLF) distance determinations. MUSE enables the PNLF to become a competitive tool for an independent measure of the Hubble constant, and stellar population studies of the host galaxies that present a sufficiently large number of PNe.

Keywords. (ISM:) planetary nebulae: general, galaxies: distances and redshifts, techniques: spectroscopic

1. Introduction

This paper describes the breakthrough for the spectrophotometry of Planetary Nebulae, specifically extragalactic PNe, that has been enabled with the technique of integral field spectroscopy. Most notably, the performance of MUSE, the Multi Unit Spectral Explorer, at the ESO Very Large Telescope (VLT) will be explained, as will how spectral imaging with IFS has essentially superseded narrow-band imaging, the classical technique for the determination of the Planetary Nebula Luminosity Function (PNLF), for distance measurements beyond ~20 Mpc. Not by coincidence, IAU Symposium 384 has yielded several more presentations concerned with the subject, e.g. Jacoby *et al.* (2023b), Soemitro *et al.* (2023b), Bhattacharya *et al.* (2023), Hartke *et al.* (2023). MUSE has also shown to be a powerful tool for spatially resolved plasma diagnostics of Galactic PNe,

Figure 1. A reminiscence of IAU Symposium 131 from 1987 in Mexico City, organized by Silvia Torres-Peimbert and Manuel Peimbert, that publicly marked the birth of the PNLF as a standard candle.

e.g., Montero *et al.* (2023). However this subject deserves a full account on its own merits and is beyond the scope of this review.

We will begin with a somewhat selective, brief history of IFS, an introduction to the MUSE instrument, a description of MUSE data cubes, and a discussion of the data analysis. We will then present a proof of concept and benchmark tests, and conclude with a summary and an outlook to the intended future development of the technique.

Before starting the discussion, it is useful and appropriate to put the problem into historical context and recall some key issues that matter for precision spectrophotometry, which is a prerequisite for accurate distance determinations with the PNLF. It is hoped that the reader will tolerate a slight personal twist when pointing out that a previous IAU Symposium on Planetary Nebulae, No. 131, that was organized on October 5-9, 1987 in Mexico City by Silvia Torres Peimbert, Manuel Peimbert, and Jim Kaler (SOC chair), can be understood as a landmark. It occurred when CCD detectors were beginning to enable precision spectrophotometry, and the less efficient technologies of photomultipliers and image tubes were being retired. In fact, the presentations by Holland Ford (Ford *et al.* 1989) and George Jacoby (Jacoby 1989) signaled the launch of the subsequent success story of the PNLF and the large number of studies that have extended over more than three decades since then – essentially until most of the galaxies within reach of narrow-band imaging on 4-8m class telescopes were completed (Ciardullo 2022). IAU 131 was also the time where CCD cameras revolutionized the study of PN morphology through narrow-band imaging as participants will recall from a memorable talk by Bruce Balick (Balick 1989).

The observational problem can be understood as follows. Until the change of paradigm in the late 1980s, measuring emission line fluxes had conventionally been accomplished either with photoelectric aperture photometers, equipped with narrow-band interference filters, or spectrally dispersed spectrographs/scanners. The former were eventually replaced by narrow-band imaging CCD cameras (Jacoby *et al.* 1987), but the latter are still in use with modern instrumentation. What was probably less rigorously absorbed by the community is the understanding how the accuracy of emission line flux measurements depends on observing conditions and details of the flux calibration. The fact that flux standards are typically hot stars, preferentially with featureless spectral energy distributions, introduces a complication related to the point spread function (PSF) of unresolved point sources: any aperture presented by the apparatus measuring stellar flux, whether it is the diaphragm of a photoelectric photometer, or the slit of a spectrograph, inevitably truncates the extended wings of the PSF, such that only a fraction of the light coming from the star will be registered on the detector. Selecting a very large aperture diameter, or opening the slit jaws may minimize the light loss, but at the expense of the inclusion of background light, or reduced spectral resolution, respectively. Generally, one must ensure that variable atmospheric seeing does not result in the object and flux standard observations having different PSF widths that would result in systematic calibration errors. The paper introducing two-dimensional spectrophotometry with the panoramic CCD detector by Jacoby *et al.* (1987) explains how the effects of a fixed aperture can be circumvented with the calibration techniques of CCD photometry. This pioneering work can be understood as setting the stage for what was exploited fully in subsequent PNLF studies.

An important paper that has pioneered spectrophotometry of extragalactic PNe was presented by Jacoby & Kaler (1993), who investigated in detail the various aperture effects, such as slit losses, seeing effects, differential atmospheric dispersion, etc. It is unfortunate that this presentation of fundamental technical concerns has not received the attention it deserves, but it is highly recommended for study. For illustration, see Soemitro *et al.* (2023a) who discuss an example in the literature where ignoring those principles has likely led to a systematic bias in the PNLF photometry for the nearby galaxy NGC 300.

As will be seen later when we introduce the observing technique of IFS, concerns related to aperture effects vanish as they can be treated by analysis software in the picture of a data cube.

2. A brief history of integral field spectroscopy

As an anecdotal subtlety, it is worthwhile to cite from the conclusion section of Jacoby *et al.* (1987) who proposed an extension of their scheme of narrow-band filters for CCD photometry of PNe, and with foresight contemplated: "*Ideally, one would like a spectrograph having thousands of input apertures which can be configured to a packed array of serveral hundred per side to sample the sky at arc-sec intervals. Some fiber-optic systems now in use are testing this technique (Barden & Scott 1986).*"

The statement was inspired by early experiments with panoramic IFS by French groups (Vanderriest *et al.* 1987; Bacon *et al.* 1988), and at the Kitt Peak National Observatory 4m Telescope (Barden & Wade 1988). Fig. 2 shows an example of a relatively simple fiber bundle integral field unit (IFU), whose purpose was to resample the focal plane (left) onto a fiber pseudo-slit (right), that was fed to a long-slit spectrograph. While the former groups were primarily interested in the study of extragalactic problems, e.g., stellar kinematics in the nuclei of galaxies, or gravitationally lensed QSOs, it was another variant of the DensePak IFU with a total of 91 fibers, attached to the WIYN 3.5 m telescope and the fiber-fed bench spectrograph HYDRA in Echelle configuration, that is arguably the first IFS that was ever used for the study of PNe: Jacoby *et al.* (1998) investigated the spatially resolved expansion velocity field and the expansion age of the born-gain PN V4334 Sgr (Sakurai's object). Other works on Galactic PNe based on IFS include, e.g., Monreal-Ibero *et al.* (2005) and Sandin *et al.* (2008), both of which studied the faint surface brightness haloes of PNe, or Sandin *et al.* (2010) with an investigation of an extremely metal poor galactic halo PN.

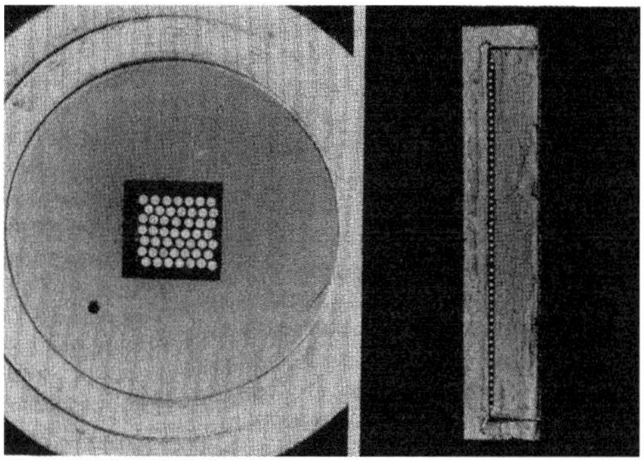

Figure 2. The pioneering fiber bundle integral field unit DensePak II for the KPNO 4m Telescope. The unit featured 49 fibers and subtended 16×19 arcsec^2 on the sky (from Barden & Wade (1988).

Coming back to the importance of aperture effects as discussed in Section 1, it is useful to focus on a first generation effort with IFS that was rigorously designed to enable precision spectrophotometry, as can be appreciated from the acronym PMAS: Potsdam Multi-Aperture Spectrophotometer (Roth *et al.* 1998). Unlike some other spectrographs that were retrofitted with an IFU, PMAS was specifically built and optimized for that purpose. It is a fully self-contained instrument, shown in Fig. 3, at the Cassegrain focus of the Calar Alto Observatory (CAHA) 3.5m telescope (Roth *et al.* 2005). As a unique feature, it offers two IFU modes that are complementary in terms of angular resolution and FoV. The standard lens array IFU covers a FoV between 8×8 arcsec^2 and 16×16 arcsec^2 with a choice of three different magnifications, and Nyquist sampling to accomodate seeing of $1 \ldots 2$ arcsec FWHM; square lenses of projected 0.5 arcsec pitch are used for the highest angular resolution. The PPaK IFU is a bare fiber bundle that was retrofitted to the initial configuration in an off-axis position of the Cassegrain focal plane for the purpose of allowing an approximately 1 arcmin wide FoV with large spatial sampling elements (spaxels). The resulting ≈ 3 arcsec fiber diameter on the sky was built to enable the observation of low surface brightness objects (Kelz *et al.* 2006). Another unique feature of PMAS is its high throughput and sensitivity down to the atmospheric cutoff in the ultraviolet, as demonstrated in a science verification run with observations of the high excitation PN NGC 7027 (Roth *et al.* 2004a).

Analogous to the slicer-based IFS instrument E3D (Weitzel *et al.* 1996), PMAS was initially intended to be a traveling experiment and designed with the goal of being used as a visitor instrument on different telescopes. However, after commissioning at the CAHA 3.5m telescope in 2001, the community interest was found to be so high that it has been there as a shared risk common user instrument ever since. PMAS has been used for a diversity of problems, e.g., Milky Way Herbig-Haro objects (López *et al.* 2008), HII regions in nearby galaxies (López-Hernández *et al.* 2013), supernovae (Christensen *et al.* 2003), ultra-luminous X-ray sources (Lehmann *et al.* 2005), extremely metal-poor starburst galaxies (Kehrig *et al.* 2016), blue compact dwarf galaxies (Cairos *et al.* 2010), luminous infrared galaxies (Alonso-Herrero *et al.* 2009), multiply lensed QSOs (Wisotzki *et al.* 2003), DLA galaxies and their foreground absorbers (Christensen *et al.* 2004), GRB host galaxies (Ferrero *et al.* 2009), and surveys like DiskMass (Bershady *et al.* 2010) and CALIFA (Sánchez *et al.* 2012), and many more.

The seeing-limited spatial sampling of PMAS has been utilized to demonstrate crowded field IFS for stars in globular clusters and the validation of the PampelMuse code, that can be understood as an analogue to DAOPHOT (Stetson 1987) for data cubes (Kamann *et al.* 2013). This latter technique has become an "industry", used on objects

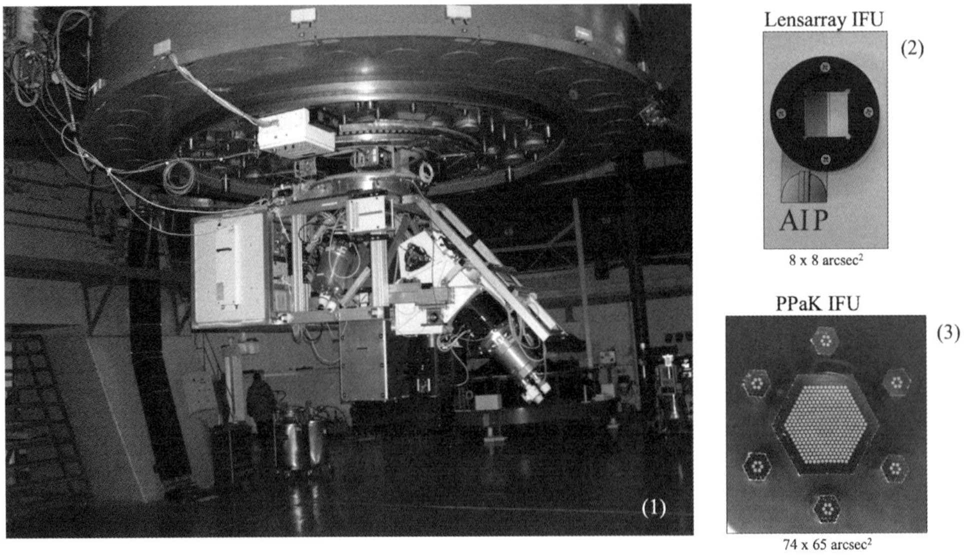

Figure 3. Left: PMAS instrument at the Cassegrain focus of the Calar Alto 3.5m Telescope (1). Right: square lens array IFU (2) with a standard FoV of 8×8 arcsec^2; fiber bundle IFU PPaK with hexagonal footprint and FoV of 74×65 arcsec^2, surrounded by 6 bundles to sample the sky background (3).

ranging from Milky Way globular clusters out to local volume galaxies (Roth *et al.* 2019), and has been applied to data from MUSE at the ESO VLT (see below). This is a satisfying confirmation of the PMAS science case, presented in Roth & Laux (1998). Two other science cases for PMAS included the study of spatially extended Milky Way PNe, and extragalactic PNe, that are, akin to stars, observed as point sources. The idea was driven by the argument that in the absence of aperture effects, IFS was thought to be an ideal tool for spectrophotometry.

Despite the small number of spaxels (256) and the quite limited FoV, a proof of concept was undertaken with PNe in the bulge of the Andromeda galaxy, selected from the sample in Ciardullo et al. (1989), who had obtained narrow-band imaging photometry in [O III] λ5007Å and established the PNLF for M31. The results from observations with three integral field spectrographs were published in Roth *et al.* (2004b): these included early observations with the MPFS instrument in the prime focus of the Selentchuk 6m telescope (Sil'chenko & Afanasiev 2000), from the INTEGRAL IFU (Arribas *et al.* 1998), coupled to the WYFFOS spectrograph at the William Herschel Telescope (WHT), and from the first PMAS science observations that were obtained after commissioning and science verification. Fig. 4 shows example maps and spectra that were extracted from the data cubes that had been obtained from these observations. The validity of the imaging capabilities was independently checked with narrow-band images, obtained with the Fabry Perot camera in the prime focus of the CAHA 3.5m telescope.

Incidentally, it was discovered that one of the objects, PN276, is not a point source as it exhibits a roughly triangular geometry, and displays strong low excitation lines of [O I], [S II], and [N II]. These lines are characteristic for supernova remnants (SNR).

Moreover, Roth *et al.* (2004b) were able to demonstrate that a PSF-fitting technique, which is common-place in crowded field CCD photometry, is useful for distinguishing intrinsic PN emission line strengths from contamination due to diffuse gas emission in the environment of the point source. More observations in Local Group galaxies have

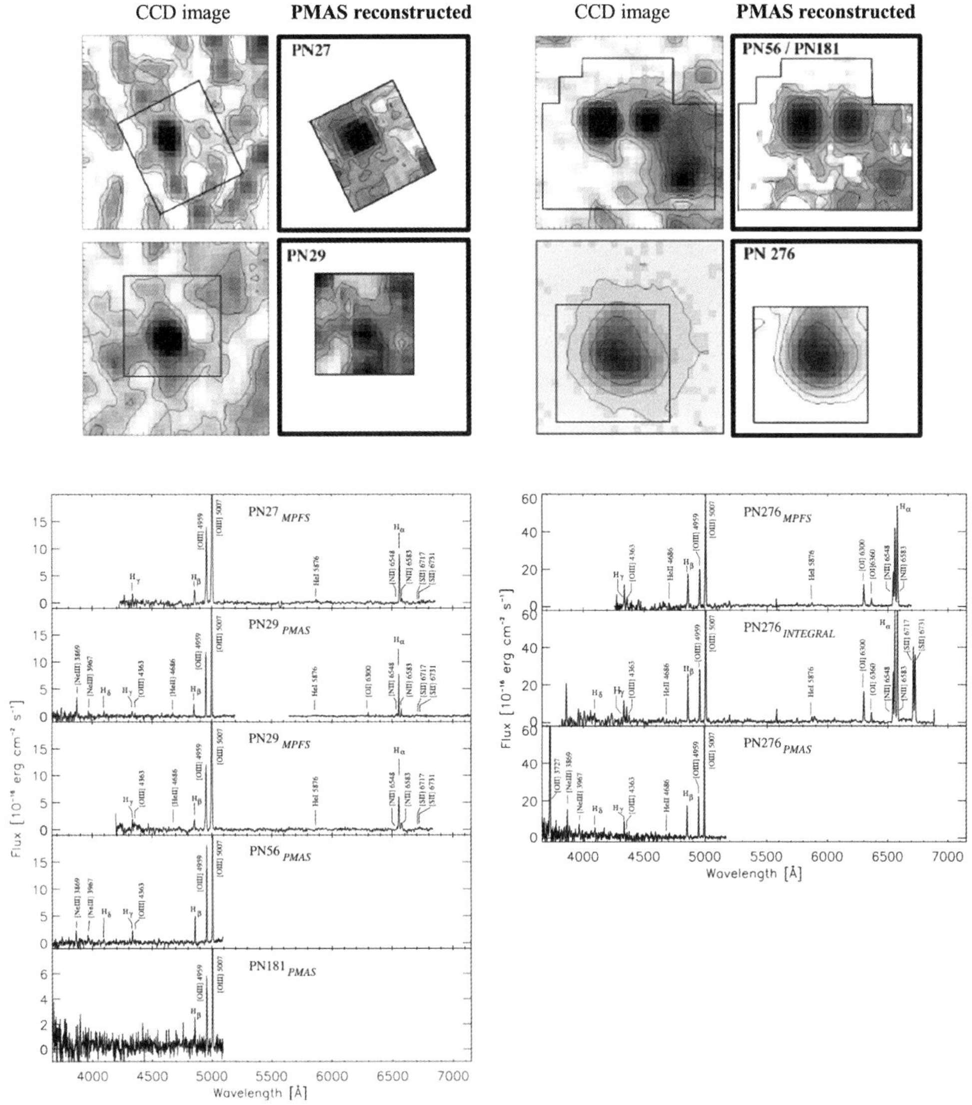

Figure 4. PNe in M31 observed with IFS. Adapted from Roth *et al.* (2004b). Top: the bold outlined frames show reconstructed maps obtained from PMAS data cubes in [O III] λ5007Å for PN27, PN29, PN56, PN181, and PN276 from the sample of Ciardullo et al. (1989); Fabry Perot CCD images are shown on the left for comparison (see explanation in the text). Bottom: corresponding spectra obtained with PMAS, MPFS at the Selentchuk 6m telescope, and with INTEGRAL at the WHT. PN276 is clearly identifiable as a supernova remnant.

shown the usefulness of this approach, albeit with a low efficiency, since the initial PMAS configuration was essentially using only half of the spectrograph's spectral range (the instrument's 2K×4K CCD was later replaced by a 4K×4K chip (Roth *et al.* 2010)). Nonetheless, another misidentification of a PN candidate was reported in (Roth *et al.* 2006). Still, beyond the proof of principle, a more productive use of IFS for the observation of extragalactic PNe had to await the arrival of a large panoramic integral field spectrograph with high angular resolution - such as MUSE.

Figure 5. MUSE at the ESO VLT. The complex arrangement of 24 spectrographs on the Nasmyth platform of UT4 is shown in (1), credit: Ghaouti Hansali (CRAL). The 24 spectrographs are fed by image slicers whose purpose is to map the input sky field into a staggered set of mini-slits. Each image slicer consists of an arrangement of an image dissector array (2) with a focusing mirror array (3), that sends an ordered set of sliced sky area to its associated spectrograph module. Credit: Florence Laurent, CRAL.

3. MUSE, the Multi Unit Spectroscopic Explorer

MUSE is a 2nd generation VLT instrument that was built between 2004 and commissioning in 2014 (Bacon *et al.* 2010), that is mounted on the Nasmyth platform of Unit Telescope 4 (UT4) of the Very Large Telescope (VLT) of the European Southern Observatory (Fig. 5). As a survey instrument built to address faint high redshift galaxies in the optical wavelength domain, MUSE is entirely devoted to single mode IFS. The instrument achieves the best possible stability by avoiding many different observing modes and the usually required moving parts. The primary mirror of UT4 was the last one manufactured for the VLT and exhibits the the smallest wavefront errors due to imperfections of the polishing procedure. It is therefore the telescope of choice for implementation of a ground layer adaptive optics system, called GALACSI (Stuik *et al.* 2006). GALACSI is available for MUSE, both in the standard wide field mode, covering a FoV of 1×1 arcmin^2 with square spaxels of 0.2×0.2 arcsec^2, and the narrow field mode with a FoV of 7.5×7.5 arcsec^2 and 0.025×0.025 arcsec^2 spaxels. The wavelength range is 465 - 930 nm at a spectral resolution of $R = 2000 \ldots 4000$.

As opposed to the fiber-based IFUs shown in Fig. 2 and Fig. 3, MUSE achieves its 90,000 spaxels (and spectra) through a modular design, involving 24 identical spectrographs, each of which is equipped with an image slicer to ensure the densest possible packing of spectra on the detector. The 24 spectrographs are fed from the focal plane of the telescope through a derotator and a field splitter fore optics such that a free space optical system from the telescope pupil to the detector is realized. Each detector pixel is mapped onto a particular spot on the sky and a particular wavelength bin. The data reduction pipeline collects this mapping in a so-called pixel table from which, after appropriate astrometric and wavelength calibration, a final data cube is formed in one single rebinning step (Weilbacher *et al.* 2020).

The slicer concept is depicted in Fig. 5, (2) and (3). It consists of an image dissector array (IDA), made out of 4 identical stacks of 12 slices, which cut the input FoV into thin, narrow strips, thus redirecting the beams in different directions. The telescope pupil is reimaged onto different intermediate pupils that are arranged in a staggered geometry, allowing for straylight removal through pupil stops. The light is further directed to a matching focusing mirror array (FMA), that finally sends the light into the spectrograph collimator for dispersion through a volume phase holographic grating and subsequent imaging onto the CCD detector. A full description of this critical device and its performance is found in Laurent *et al.* (2008).

The complex design of MUSE and its performance, including stringent priorities to optimize throughput, set this instrument aside from other competing large integral field spectrographs on 8-10m class telescopes, like KCWI at Keck (Morrissey *et al.* 2018), or VIRUS at the Hobby Eberly Telescope (Hill *et al.* 2021). The large FoV, high image quality with ground layer adaptive optics support, and high throughput make this instrument unique, to the effect that it has become the most demanded and productive facility of the VLT (e.g., 170 refereed papers in 2022)†.

The science objectives that were identified during MUSE's Phase A study include, first and foremost, the study of the formation of galaxies at high redshift, e.g., Lyα emitters, fluorescent emission and the cosmic web, reionisation, feedback processes and galaxy formation, ultra-deep surveys using strong gravitational lensing, resolved spectroscopy at intermediate redshifts. Also listed are the investigation of nearby galaxies (e.g., kinematics and stellar populations, interacting galaxies, star formation in nearby galaxies, the study of stars and resolved stellar populations, early stages of stellar evolution), and crowded field spectroscopy in the Milky Way, Local Group galaxies, and beyond.

It is beyond the scope or this paper to review the wealth of scientific outcome obtained with MUSE. However for the subject of spectrophotometry of faint extragalactic PNe, it is useful to highlight the sensitivity obtained with a very deep exposure of 140 h, obtained in the Hubble Ultra-Deep Field, aka the MUSE Extremely Deep Field (MXDF; Bacon *et al.* 2021). At a wavelength of 7000 Å, this exposure has enabled an unprecedented 5σ surface brightness detection limit of 1.3×10^{-19} erg cm^{-2}s^{-1} arcsec^{-2} for diffuse extended Lyα emission, while the 5σ point source limiting flux is 2.3×10^{-19} erg cm^{-2}s^{-1} for the same wavelength. Thanks to the adaptive optics system, the image quality of the combined dataset was excellent, with a FWHM of 0.6 arcsec at 4700 Å, and 0.4 arcsec at 9300 Å.

The ability to accumulate long exposures to achieve this level of sensitivity is due to the instrument's stability that was a design goal from the outset. It can of course be utilized for faint objects at low redshift as well, which was indeed envisaged by a proposed study in the nearby galaxy NGC 300 as part of the Phase A science case mentioned above. The MUSE collaboration has therefore conducted observations in selected fields of NGC 300 as part of the guaranteed observing time program with run IDs 094.D-0116(A), 094.D-0116(B), 095.D-0173(A), 097.D-0348(A), 0102.B-0317(A) between September 2014 and October 2018, entitled "*A study of the faint end of the planetary nebulae luminosity function of NGC 300*", PI Roth. The program produced data for a total of 9 fields with total exposure times of 1.5 h each (under photometric conditions), and mostly with excellent image quality (ground layer adaptive optics support during the 2018 run).

A pilot study of the initial 7 pointings was published by Roth *et al.* (2018) and presented results from the technique of crowded field IFS as described in Section 2. This paper presented a catalog of luminous stars, rare objects such as Wolf-Rayet stars, Be stars, carbon stars, symbiotic star candidates, PNe, H II regions, SNR, giant shells, peculiar diffuse and filamentary emission line objects, and background galaxies, along with their spectra.

By mimicking PNe with artificial emission line point sources that were embedded in the observed data cubes, it was demonstrated that 95% completeness could be achieved at a limiting magnitude of m5007 = 28 mag when the image quality was excellent (0.6 arcsec FWHM), and m5007 = 26 mag when the seeing was mediocre (1.2 arcsec FWHM). The definition of monochromatic [OIII] magnitudes m5007 is given in Ciardullo et al. (1989), and is roughly equal to the magnitude of the object through a broadband *V*

† https://www.eso.org/sci/php/libraries/pubstats/

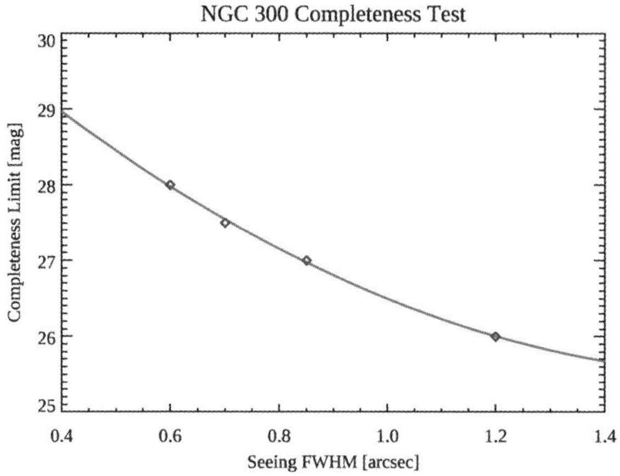

Figure 6. Completeness of PN detections at 95% in MUSE data cubes observed in NGC 300 as a function of seeing FWHM. The total exposure time for each observation was 1.5 h. From Roth *et al.* (2018).

filter. These very encouraging results have prompted the further development of MUSE spectrophotometry of extragalactic PNe as described below.

To date, the rich dataset from NGC 300 has spawned three more papers: González-Torà *et al.* (2022) on the quantitative spectroscopy of BA-type supergiants, Micheva *et al.* (2022) on extremely faint HII regions and diffuse ionized gas, and Soemitro *et al.* (2023a) on the PNLF. The latter work is also discussed in these proceedings (Soemitro *et al.* 2023b). The improved analysis of the partially resolved stellar population is ongoing, and more papers are in preparation.

4. Differential Emission Line Filter (DELF)

As reported by Roth *et al.* (2018), the extremely narrow 1.25 Å bandwidth of a single MUSE data cube layer results in very high contrast for emission line objects, no matter whether the objects are point sources or extended surface brightness distributions. In their analysis, the residual continuum within the chosen 5 . . . 6.25 Å wavelength intervals for the synthetic filters of important emission lines was subtracted with suitably chosen and scaled continuum nearby passbands. Fig. 7 illustrates how this scheme has been further developed to form a Differential Emission Line Filter (DELF) for the [OIII] λ5007 Å line in MUSE data cubes.

The green and orange hues of the sketch are intended to illustrate passbands centered on the [OIII] emission line (on-band), and with a much wider bandwidth on the nearby continuum (off-band). For classical PNLF observations with narrow-band filters, the on-band and off-band exposures would be obtained one after another at different times during an observing night.

The key point here is that a MUSE data cube provides on-band and off-band data obtained *simultaneously*, and under *exactly the same observing conditions*. The spectra shown in Fig. 7 depict an example obtained with deep observations of the lenticular galaxy NGC 1380, featuring various metal absorption lines, and a peak-to-peak variation across the average of roughly 5%. It must be noted that the plot contains the superposition of 10 spectra that were taken from various locations over the face of the galaxy. They are almost indistinguishable, and the variation from spectrum to spectrum is tiny. Also the averaged flux density of the continuum over the entire off-band shows a remarkably small variation on the order of 0.1%.

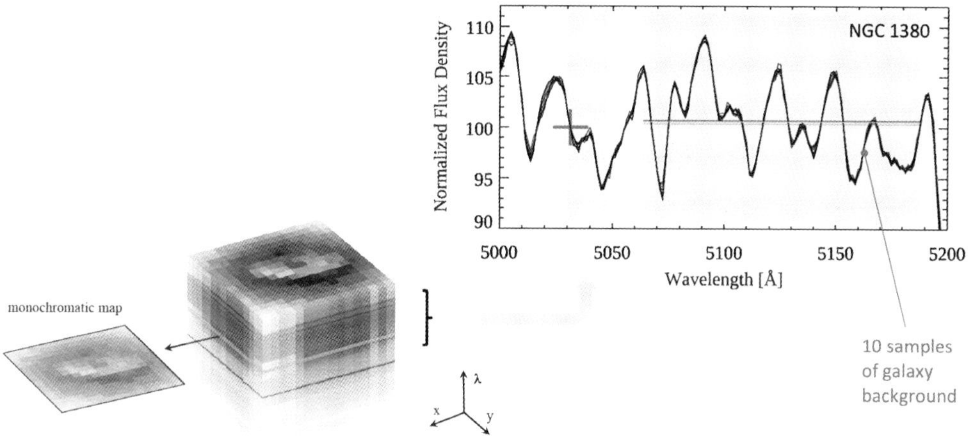

Figure 7. The Differential Emission Line Filter for data cubes (DELF). Figure adapted from Roth *et al.* (2021). For explanation, see text.

We emphasize that the continuum background for emission line objects within the green on-band interval is affected by a blend of absorption lines that happen to show a variation of 5% from the blue end to the red end, corresponding to a radial velocity interval of ± 250 km s^{-1}, which is typical for a large galaxy. The central [OIII] wavelength of the most blue-shifted PN in this picture would correspond to the red cross. However, the *ratio between the intensity at a given wavelength* within the on-band and the *continuum average* of the off-band does not change from spectrum to spectrum. In other words: for each wavelength bin within the green passband, we can apply a calibrated subtraction of the average off-band, which is very well defined because of the large interval, and the small spectral variation. As a result, an accurate, internally calibrated continuum background subtraction is obtained on a spaxel-by-spaxel basis. In essence, this is the reason for the excellent performance of DELF.

A mathematical derivation for the performance of a DELF is presented in Roth *et al.* (2021). In a sense, the DELF technique bears some similarities with the problem of accurate sky background subtraction for the detection of the faintest high redshift galaxies before the advent of the Hubble Space Telescope. The search for background-limited galaxies by Tyson (1990) was only accomplished by achieving an accuracy of 10^{-4} of the sky background through the so-called "shift-and-stare" technique. This methodology overcame pixel-to-pixel sensitivity variations in the flatfield calibration thanks to the linearity and stability of the CCD detector. The advantage of MUSE is that the spaxel-to-spaxel variations cancel out immediately due to the inherent differential principle within a data cube, and no offset pointings are required.

5. MUSE PNLF

Given the favorable performance of the DELF technique, a proof of concept was undertaken using archival data to investigate whether MUSE spectrophotometry can improve the quality and range of PNLF distance determinations significantly beyond the state-of-the art with the classical narrow-band filter technique. The study, published in Roth *et al.* (2021), discusses in detail the test of photometric precision, the calibration of aperture corrections, the additional benefits of discarding interlopers (SNR, HII regions, background galaxies) based on candidate spectra, the utility of avoiding systematic errors due to interference filter passband transmission changes, and the unique opportunity to discover and eliminate systematic errors caused by chance superpositions of PNe, see also

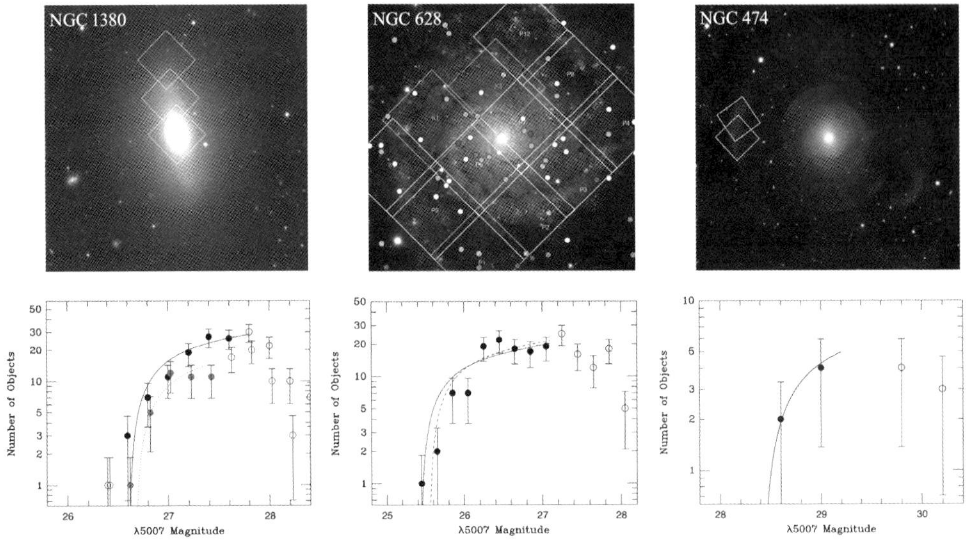

Figure 8. Three benchmark galaxies used to validate the new approach of measuring the PNLF with MUSE and the DELF methodology. Adapted from Roth *et al.* (2021).

Chase *et al.* (2023). The results for three benchmark tests, namely NGC 1380, NGC 628, and NGC 474, are illustrated in Fig. 8.

Comparison with other PNLF studies in the literature based on the same data but using other techniques demonstrates that DELF is superior in terms of signal-to-noise ratio and sensitivity. A more elaborate test with 20 galaxies of various Hubble types and distances has been published in Jacoby *et al.* (2023a) and is discussed in these proceedings as a promising independent technique to measure the Hubble constant (Jacoby *et al.* 2023b).

6. Summary and Conclusions

Integral field spectroscopy has been demonstrated to be the ideal observing technique for precision spectrophotometry: a prerequiste for accurate PNLF distance determinations. However, first generation instruments were offering too small a field-of-view to efficiently use them for that purpose. MUSE, with its wide field-of-view, excellent image quality, and high throughput at an 8m class telescope, has completely changed the situation. Thanks to the superior quality of MUSE spectrophometry, the DELF technique, and the associated flatfield accuracy, we are now able to accurately perform [OIII] λ5007 Å photometry even in high surface brightness regions near the nuclei of galaxies, which contain a high surface density of planetary nebulae. PN surveys in these regions were previously impossible with conventional techniques. After a successful proof of concept study and the exploration of archival data for a sample of 20 galaxy test cases, it is now time for targeted observations and carefully planned calibrations that are optimized for MUSE PNLF determinations. The method holds great promise to provide a new, independent way of measuring the Hubble constant. Looking further into the future, the option of an IFU for WFOS at the TMT (Steidel *et al.* 2022) could potentially increase the reach of PNLF distances out to ∼100 Mpc.

References

Alonso-Herrero A., García-Marín M., Monreal-Ibero A., Colina L., Arribas S., Alfonso-Garzón J., Labiano A., 2009, *A&A*, 506, 1541. doi:10.1051/0004-6361/200911813

Arribas S., del Burgo C., Carter D., Cavaller L., Edwards R., Fuentes J., et al., 1998, *ASPC*, 152, 149

Bacon R., Adam G., Baranne A., Courtès G., Dubet D., Dubois J.-P., et al., 1988, *ESOC*, 30, 1185

Bacon R., Accardo M., Adjali L., Anwand H., Bauer S., et al., 2010, *SPIE*, 7735, 773508.

Bacon R., Mary D., Garel T., Blaizot J., Maseda M., Schaye J., Wisotzki L., et al., 2021, *A&A*, 647, A107. doi:10.1051/0004-6361/202039887

Balick B., 1989, *IAUS*, 131, 83

Bershady M. A., Verheijen M. A. W., Swaters R. A., Andersen D. R., Westfall K. B., Martinsson T., 2010, *ApJ*, 716, 198. doi:10.1088/0004-637X/716/1/198

Bhattacharya, S. et al., 2023, these proceedings

Barden S. C., Scott K., 1986, *BAAS*

Barden S. C., Wade R. A., 1988, *ASPC*, 3, 113

Cairós L. M., Caon N., Zurita C., Kehrig C., Roth M., Weilbacher P., 2010, *A&A*, 520, A90. doi:10.1051/0004-6361/201014004

Chase O., Ciardullo R., Roth M. M., Jacoby G. H., 2023, *ApJ*, 950, 59. doi:10.3847/1538-4357/acc9bd

Ciardullo R., Jacoby G. H., Ford H. C., Neill J. D., 1989, *ApJ*, 339, 53. doi:10.1086/167275

Ciardullo R., 2022, *FrASS*, 9, 896326

Christensen L., Becker T., Jahnke K., Kelz A., Roth M. M., Sánchez S. F., Wisotzki L., 2003, *A&A*, 401, 479. doi:10.1051/0004-6361:20030015

Christensen L., Sánchez S. F., Jahnke K., Becker T., Wisotzki L., Kelz A., Popović L. Č., et al., 2004, *A&A*, 417, 487. doi:10.1051/0004-6361:20034371

Ferrero P., Klose S., Kann D. A., Savaglio S., Schulze S., Palazzi E., Maiorano E., et al., 2009, *A&A*, 497, 729. doi:10.1051/0004-6361/200809980

Ford H. C., Ciardullo R., Jacoby G. H., Hui X., 1989, *IAUS*, 131, 335

Micheva G., Roth M. M., Weilbacher P. M., Morisset C., Castro N., Monreal Ibero A., Soemitro A. A., et al., 2022, *A&A*, 668, A74. doi:10.1051/0004-6361/202244017

González-Torà G., Urbaneja M. A., Przybilla N., Dreizler S., Roth M. M., Kamann S., Castro N., 2022, *A&A*, 658, A117. doi:10.1051/0004-6361/202142372

Hartke J et al., 2023, these proceedings

Hill G. J., Lee H., MacQueen P. J., Kelz A., Drory N., Vattiat B. L., Good J. M., et al., 2021, AJ, 162, 298. doi:10.3847/1538-3881/ac2c02

Jacoby G. H., Quigley R. J., Africano J. L., 1987, *PASP*, 99, 672

Jacoby G. H., Kaler J. B., 1993, *ApJ*, 417, 209

Jacoby G. H., De Marco O., Sawyer D. G., 1998, AJ, 116, 1367

Jacoby G., Ford H. C., Ciardullo R., 1989, *IAUS*, 131, 357

Jacoby G. H., Ciardullo R., Roth M. M., Arnaboldi M., Weilbacher P. M., 2023, arXiv, arXiv:2309.11603. doi:10.48550/arXiv.2309.11603

Jacoby G. H. et al., 2023, these proceedings

Kamann S., Wisotzki L., Roth M. M., 2013, *A&A*, 549, A71. doi:10.1051/0004-6361/201220476

Kehrig C., Vílchez J. M., Pérez-Montero E., Iglesias-Páramo J., Hernández-Fernández J. D., Duarte Puertas S., Brinchmann J., et al., 2016, MNRAS, 459, 2992. doi:10.1093/mnras/stw806

Kelz A., Verheijen M. A. W., Roth M. M., Bauer S. M., Becker T., Paschke J., Popow E., et al., 2006, *PASP*, 118, 129. doi:10.1086/497455

Laurent F., Renault E., Kosmalski J., Adjali L., Boudon D., Bacon R., Caillier P., et al., 2008, *SPIE*, 7018, 70180J. doi:10.1117/12.789285

Lehmann I., Becker T., Fabrika S., Roth M., Miyaji T., Afanasiev V., Sholukhova O., et al., 2005, *A&A*, 431, 847. doi:10.1051/0004-6361:20035827

López-Hernández J., Terlevich E., Terlevich R., Rosa-González D., Díaz Á., García-Benito R., Vílchez J., et al., 2013, MNRAS, 430, 472. doi:10.1093/mnras/sts658

López R., Sánchez S. F., García-Lorenzo B., Gómez G., Estalella R., Riera A., Busquet G., 2008, MNRAS, 384, 464. doi:10.1111/j.1365-2966.2007.12718.x

Monreal-Ibero A., Roth M. M., Schönberner D., Steffen M., Böhm P., 2005, ApJL, 628, L139. doi:10.1086/432664

Montero H. et al., 2023, these proceedings

Morrissey P., Matuszewski M., Martin D. C., et al., 2018, *ApJ*, 864, 93. doi:10.3847/1538-4357/aad597

Roth M. M., Bauer S.-M., Dionies F., Fechner T., et al., 1998, *SPIE*, 3355, 798. doi:10.1117/12.316793

Roth M. M., Laux U., 1998, *ASPC*, 152, 168

Roth M. M., Becker T., Böhm P., Kelz A., 2004, AN, 325, 147. doi:10.1002/asna.200310196

Roth M. M., Becker T., Kelz A., Schmoll J., 2004, *ApJ*, 603, 531. doi:10.1086/381526

Roth M. M., Kelz A., Fechner T., Hahn T., Bauer S.-M., Becker T., Böhm P., et al., 2005, *PASP*, 117, 620. doi:10.1086/429877

Roth M. M., Becker T., Böhm P., Schönberner D., Steffen M., Exter K., 2006, pnbm.conf, 239. doi:10.1007/3-540-34270-2_36

Roth M. M., Fechner T., Wolter D., Sandin C., Kelz A., Bauer S. M., Popow E., et al., 2010, *SPIE*, 7742, 774209. doi:10.1117/12.856936

Roth M. M., Sandin C., Kamann S., Husser T.-O., Weilbacher P. M., Monreal-Ibero A., Bacon R., et al., 2018, *A&A*, 618, A3. doi:10.1051/0004-6361/201833007

Roth M. M., Weilbacher P. M., Castro N., 2019, *AN*, 340, 989. doi:10.1002/asna.201913751

Roth M. M., Jacoby G. H., Ciardullo R., Davis B. D., Chase O., Weilbacher P. M., 2021, *ApJ*, 916, 21

Sánchez S. F., Kennicutt R. C., Gil de Paz A., van de Ven G., Vílchez J. M., Wisotzki L., Walcher C. J., et al., 2012, *A&A*, 538, A8. doi:10.1051/0004-6361/201117353

Sandin C., Schönberner D., Roth M. M., Steffen M., Böhm P., Monreal-Ibero A., 2008, *A&A*, 486, 545. doi:10.1051/0004-6361:200809635

Sandin C., Jacob R., Schönberner D., Steffen M., Roth M. M., 2010, *A&A*, 512, A18. doi:10.1051/0004-6361/200911796

Afanasiev V. L., Sil'chenko O. K., 2000, AJ, 119, 126. doi:10.1086/301162

Soemitro A. A., Roth M. M., Weilbacher P. M., Ciardullo R., Jacoby G. H., et al., 2023a, *A&A*, 671, A142

Soemitro A. et al., 2023b, these proceedings

Steidel C., Peng E., Fucik J., et al., 2022, *SPIE*, 12184, 1218423. doi:10.1117/12.2629464

Stuik R., Bacon R., Conzelmann R., Delabre B., Fedrigo E., Hubin N., Le Louarn M., et al., 2006, *NewAR*, 49, 618. doi:10.1016/j.newar.2005.10.015

Stetson P. B., 1987, *PASP*, 99, 191. doi:10.1086/131977

Tyson J. A., 1990, *ASPC*, 10, 292

Vanderriest C., Haddad B., Lemonnier J. P., 1987, *AnPh*, 12, 207

Weilbacher P. M., Palsa R., Streicher O., et al., 2020, *A&A*, 641, A28. doi:10.1051/0004-6361/202037855

Weitzel L., Krabbe A., Kroker H., et al., 1996, A&AS, 119, 531

Wisotzki L., Becker T., Christensen L., Helms A., Jahnke K., Kelz A., Roth M. M., et al., 2003, *A&A*, 408, 455. doi:10.1051/0004-6361:20031004

Planetary Nebulae: A Universal Toolbox in the Era of Precision Astrophysics
Proceedings IAU Symposium No. 384, 2025
O. De Marco, A. Zijlstra & R. Szczerba, eds.
doi:10.1017/S1743921323005549

Precision spectrophotometry for PNLF distances: the case of NGC 300

Azlizan A. Soemitro[1,2], Martin M. Roth[1,2], Peter M. Weilbacher[1], Robin Ciardullo[3], George H. Jacoby[4], Ana Monreal-Ibero[5], Norberto Castro[1] and Genoveva Micheva[1]

[1]Leibniz-Institut für Astrophysik Potsdam (AIP), Germany
email: asoemitro@aip.de

[2]Universität Potsdam, Germany

[3]Department of Astronomy & Astrophysics, The Pennsylvania State University, USA

[4]NSF's NOIRLab, Tucson, USA

[5]Leiden Observatory, Leiden University, The Netherlands

Abstract. The Multi-Unit Spectroscopic Explorer (MUSE) has enabled a renaissance of the planetary nebula luminosity function (PNLF) as a standard candle. In the case of NGC 300, we learned that the precise spectrophotometry of MUSE was crucial to obtain an accurate PNLF distance. We present the advantage of the integral field spectrograph compared to the slit spectrograph in delivering precise spectrophotometry by simulating a slit observation on integral field spectroscopy data. We also discuss the possible systematic shift in measuring the PNLF distance using the least-square method, especially when the PNLF cutoff is affected by small number statistics.

Keywords. galaxies: luminosity function, stars: planetary nebulae

1. Introduction

The planetary nebula luminosity function (PNLF) is a secondary distance indicator with ~10% accuracy (Ciardullo 2010, 2022). Using narrowband photometry, one can obtain the V-band equivalent [OIII]λ5007 magnitude defined by Jacoby (1989):

$$m_{5007} = -2.5 \log F_{5007} - 13.74 \tag{1}$$

The number distribution of planetary nebulae (PNe) per magnitude bin for a given galaxy can then be modelled using the empirical law described by Ciardullo et al. (1989):

$$N(M) \propto e^{0.307M}\{1 - e^{3(M^{*}-M)}\} \tag{2}$$

Variations of the formula have been introduced to explain the influence of different underlying stellar populations (Longobardi et al. 2013; Rodríguez-González et al. 2015). However, these formulae merely affect the faint end of the PNLF. The definition of the PNLF cutoff, which is crucial for the distance determination, remains unchanged.

The renaissance of the PNLF as standard candles came with the use of the Multi-Unit Spectroscopic Explorer (MUSE; Bacon et al. 2010) on the Very Large Telescope (VLT). As an integral field spectrograph (IFS), it allows simultaneous imaging and spectroscopy to find and classify PNe, even in more crowded regions of galaxies, that previously were not accessible using the classical narrow-band imaging methods (Kreckel et al. 2017; Spriggs et al. 2020; Roth et al. 2021; Scheuermann et al. 2022; Soemitro et al. 2023).

The precision of the m_{5007} defines the precision of the PNLF cutoff of a galaxy, which consequently defines the accuracy of the distance determination. To achieve this, Roth et al. (2021) developed the differential emission line filter (DELF), which suppresses systematic errors and delivers higher signal-to-noise ratios for the photometry, with a typical photometric error of $\sim$ 0.04 mag. They demonstrated that their method was able to reach distances up to $\sim$ 40 Mpc, twice as far as most studies done with the classical narrow-band photometry until the early 2010s.

2. Planetary nebulae in NGC 300

NGC 300 is a nearby spiral galaxy in the foreground of the Sculptor Group, where a few PN surveys have already been conducted, making it a good case to test the DELF technique using MUSE data (Soemitro et al. 2023). Previously, using narrow-band imaging on the New Technology Telescope (NTT), Soffner et al. (1996) found 34 PNe, covering $3 \times 2.2 \times 2.2$ arcmin^2. Another survey with the FORS2 instrument on the VLT found a total of 104 PNe using the narrow-band imaging mode within $2 \times 6.8 \times 6.8$ arcmin^2 (Peña et al. 2012). For the brighter 32 PN candidates, they obtained spectroscopic follow-up data using the multi object spectroscopy mode of the same instrument (MXU-FORS2). Using the MUSE instrument, Roth et al. (2018) observed 7 fields in the wide field mode (WFM, 1×1 arcmin^2 FoV) that cover the nucleus, parts of a spiral arm, and parts of a nearby inter-arm region, as a pilot study for crowded field spectroscopy, which explored a plethora of possible science cases. They identified 45 PNe, which was not ideal to construct a proper PNLF. As a follow up for the PN science case, Soemitro et al. (2023) employed additional archival MUSE data and increased the dataset from 7 fields to a total of 44 fields, and identified 109 PNe. Using the DELF, the study presented a similar number of PNe in comparison to the previous study by Peña et al. (2012), however needing only half of the surveyed area.

3. Precision spectrophotometry: integral field spectrograph vs. slit spectrograph

For the common PNe in the sample, Soemitro et al. (2023) have compared the m_{5007} measurements with the results from Soffner et al. (1996) and Peña et al. (2012). While their m_{5007} values were consistent with the earlier study done with the narrow-band imaging photometry on the NTT, they found that the results from the FORS2 survey study were fainter by an average of 0.71 mag, a discrepancy factor of $\sim$ 2. The m_{5007} comparison can be seen in Figure 1. The speculation was, since Peña et al. (2012) calibrated their photometry using spectroscopic fluxes obtained with the multi object spectrograph, that they might be subject to slit loss effects (Soemitro et al. 2023). Due to atmospheric dispersion, one has to orient the slit along the parallactic angle to obtain precise spectrophotometry (Filippenko 1982; Jacoby & Kaler 1993). This is necessary to minimise the slit loss, because the wavelength dependence of the point spread function full width half maximum (PSF FWHM) might complicate the slit positioning. For instance, if the slit was positioned based on the image in the R-band, the slit position could be off-centre at [OIII]λ5007. Moreover, the PSF FWHM also increases with shorter wavelengths (Fried 1966; Boyd 1978; Kamann et al. 2013), which might causes more loss of flux in blue.

To demonstrate the effect of atmospheric dispersion, we used a standard star observation obtained with another integral field spectrograph, the Potsdam Multi-Aperture Spectrophotometer (PMAS; Roth et al. 2005) whose raw data comes without atmospheric dispersion correction. The star was observed in the lens array mode with 1"/pixel sampling (LARR, 16×16 arcmin^2 FoV) and a wavelength coverage of $\sim 3500 - 6800$ Å(V600

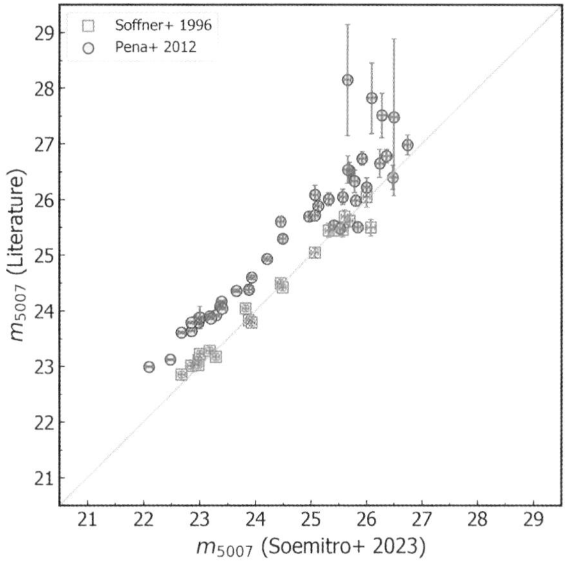

Figure 1. Comparison of the m_{5007} for different PN surveys in NGC 300. The magnitudes from Peña et al. (2012) is 0.71 mag fainter than the other surveys. The plot is adapted from Soemitro et al. (2023).

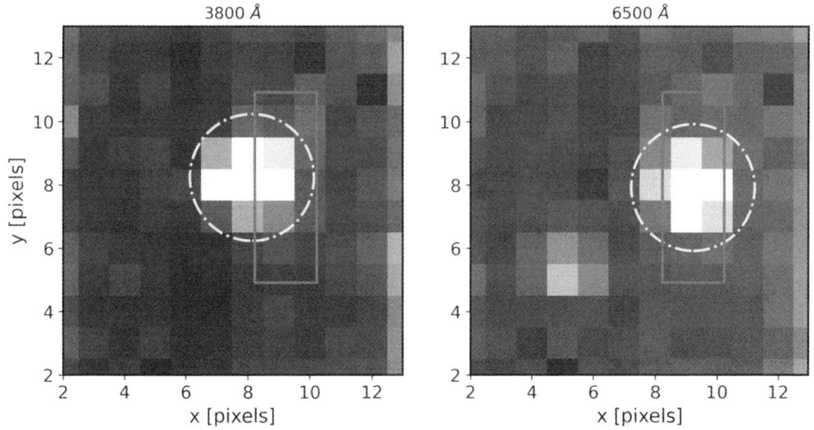

Figure 2. Simulated apertures for testing the light loss effect of atmospheric dispersion for a standard star. The dot-dashed green line represents measurements using IFS. The solid red line represent measurements using a slit spectrograph. This effect can be minimised by aligning the slit with the parallactic angle continuously during observations (Filippenko 1982; Jacoby & Kaler 1993).

Grating, GROT=144.5). We took two wavelength slices: 3800 Åand 6500 Å. We created a rectangular aperture to simulate a slit, using the width of two pixels. The simulated slit position was fixed based on the PSF centroid in 6500 Å, then we performed photometry for both slices. As a comparison, we also did photometry using circular apertures with the radius of two pixels, however, we adjusted their positions based on the PSF centroid in each respective data cube layer. Figure 2 displays the star with the apertures in the two wavelengths. In this configuration, we found that the slit loss in 6500 Åwas $\sim$ 10%. However, with $\sim$ 34%, the light loss in the blue was much more severe.

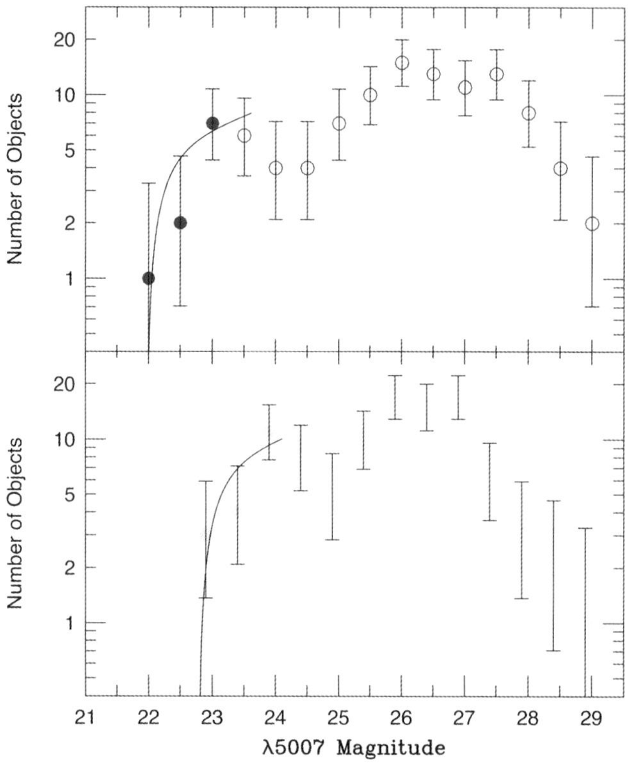

Figure 3. The PNLF for MUSE data (Soemitro et al. 2023) in blue and FORS2 data (Peña et al. 2012) in green. The plot is adapted from Soemitro et al. (2023).

While we cannot prove that the effect was exactly the cause of the discrepancies between Peña et al. (2012) and Soemitro et al. (2023), since it was unclear whether the slit alignment with the parallactic angle was done or not for the FORS2 observations, we can plausibly argue that the effect can have large effects on the flux calibration, in particular knowing that the seeing FWHM can be quite variable over the course of a night. Moreover, we demonstrated that the IFS has an advantage to handle such atmospheric effects, delivering a more precise spectrophotometry and consequently better distances. In the case of MUSE data, the atmospheric dispersion as a function of wavelength is even corrected by lateral shifts that are applied through the data reduction pipeline (Weilbacher et al. 2020).

4. The PNLF of NGC 300

In Soemitro et al. (2023), the PNLF distance to NGC 300 was derived using the maximum likelihood estimation method (Ciardullo et al. 1989). The PNLF maximum likelihood distance estimates for both the MUSE and the FORS2 datasets resulted in $(m-M)_0 = 26.48^{+0.11}_{-0.26}$ and $(m-M)_0 = 27.30^{+0.09}_{-0.20}$, respectively, reflecting the photometric discrepancy explained above. However, in the original study of Peña et al. (2012), they measured a distance of $(m-M)_0 = 26.29^{+0.12}_{-0.22}$, derived on the basis of the least-square fitting method. By using such a method, the distance measurement became very dependent on the binning. Since the PNLF bins of NGC 300 presented only a small number of PNe, the exact definition of the bins has likely caused a systematic shift to the distance measurement (Soemitro et al. 2023). The choice of binning also smeared out the details of the PNLF shape. In their study, Peña et al. (2012) reported that they did not observe

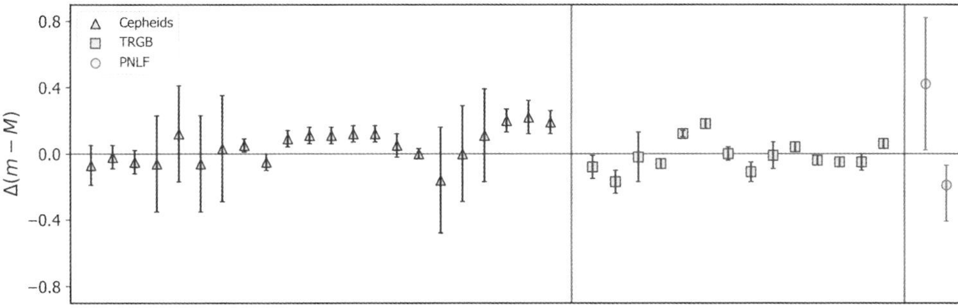

Figure 4. The MUSE-PNLF distance and its uncertainty is presented as a solid green line and the green shaded range, respectively. As a comparison with distances from literature, Cepheids (blue triangles), tip of the red giant branch (red squares), and previous PNLF distance estimates (the two green circles) are shown. A full reference list of literature distances can found in Soemitro et al. (2023).

any PNLF dip, that however is typically being observed in star forming galaxies (Jacoby & De Marco 2002). With a higher resolution of the magnitude bins, Soemitro et al. (2023) showed that the dip can be seen even in the FORS2 data, and also in the MUSE observations, as shown in Figure 3. With the precise spectrophotometry delivered by MUSE, the PNLF distance was brought into good agreement with the Cepheid and the tip of the red giant branch (TRGB) distances. The distance comparison is shown in Figure 4.

5. Summary

The case of NGC 300 has shown that the precision of spectrophotometry can have a significant impact on the distance measurement. We made a test using another integral field spectrograph, PMAS, to show the probable effect of atmospheric dispersion when using a slit spectrograph to do the spectrophotometry. This illustration supports the importance of using an IFS for measuring accurate m_{5007} magnitudes for PNLF distance determinations. Moreover, the methodology of how to fit an analytical PNLF to the observed photometry is crucial. In case of small number statistics at the PNLF cutoff, using the least-square minimisation method that is dependent on the bin size, is likely to bias the distance measurement. Therefore, the maximum likelihood approach is recommended. As the only IFS that to date has the sensitivity and spatial resolution to detect PNe in distant galaxies, the MUSE instrument is crucial for the measurement of PNLF distances in the future. With the currently demonstrated range of up to $\sim$ 40 Mpc, the PNLF can be assumed to be an additional calibration tool for SN Ia distances and a contribution to the ongoing discussion of the Hubble tension (Jacoby et al. 2023).

References

Bacon, R. et al. 2010, *SPIE*, 7735, 773508
Boyd, J. P. 1978, *Journal of Atmospheric Sciences*, 35, 2236
Ciardullo, R. 2010, *PASA*, 27, 149
Ciardullo, R. 2022, *Frontiers in Astronomy and Space Sciences*, 9, 896326
Ciardullo, R. et al. 1989, *ApJ*, 339, 53
Filippenko, A. V. 1982, *PASP*, 94, 715
Fried, D. L. 1966, *Journal of the Optical Society of America* (1917–1983), 56, 1372
Jacoby, G. H. 1989, *ApJ*, 339, 39
Jacoby, G. H., Ciardullo, R., Roth, M. M., Arnaboldi, M., & Weilbacher, P. M. 2023, arXiv e-prints, arXiv:2309.11603

Jacoby, G. H. & De Marco, O. 2002, *AJ*, 123, 269
Jacoby, G. H. & Kaler, J. B. 1993, *ApJ*, 417, 209
Kamann, S., Wisotzki, L., & Roth, M. M. 2013, *A&A*, 549, A71
Kreckel, K. et al. 2017, *ApJ*, 834, 174
Longobardi, A. et al. 2013, *A&A*, 558, A42
Peña, M. et al. 2012, *A&A*, 547, A78
Rodríguez-González, A. et al. 2015, *A&A*, 575, A1
Roth, M. M. et al. 2005, *PASP*, 117, 620
Roth, M. M. et al. 2018, *A&A*, 618, A3
Roth, M. M. et al. 2021, *ApJ*, 916, 21
Scheuermann, F. et al. 2022, *MNRAS*, 511, 6087
Soemitro, A. A. et al. 2023, *A&A*, 671, A142
Soffner, T. et al. 1996, *A&A*, 306, 9
Spriggs, T. W. et al. 2020, *A&A*, 637, A62
Weilbacher, P. M. et al. 2020, *A&A*, 641, A28

Planetary Nebulae: A Universal Toolbox in the Era of Precision Astrophysics
Proceedings IAU Symposium No. 384, 2025
O. De Marco, A. Zijlstra & R. Szczerba, eds.
doi:10.1017/S1743921323005458

PICS: Planetary Nebulae in Cosmological Simulations – Revelations of the Planetary Nebula Luminosity Function from Realistic Stellar Populations

Lucas M. Valenzuela[1], Rhea-Silvia Remus[1], Marcelo M. Miller Bertolami[2,3] and Roberto H. Méndez[4]

[1]Universitäts-Sternwarte, Fakultät für Physik, Ludwig-Maximilians-Universität München, Scheinerstr. 1, 81679 München, Germany
email: lval@usm.lmu.de

[2]Instituto de Astrofísica de La Plata, UNLP-CONICET, La Plata, Paseo del Bosque s/n, B1900FWA, Argentina

[3]Facultad de Ciencias Astronómicas y Geofísicas, UNLP, La Plata, Paseo del Bosque s/n, B1900FWA, Argentina

[4]Institute for Astronomy, University of Hawaii, 2680 Woodlawn Drive, Honolulu, HI 96822, USA

Abstract. Even after decades of usage as an extragalactic standard candle, the universal bright end of the planetary nebula luminosity function (PNLF) still lacks a solid theoretical explanation. Until now, models have modeled planetary nebulae (PNe) from artificial stellar populations, without an underlying cosmological star formation history. We present PICS (PNe In Cosmological Simulations), a novel method of modeling PNe in cosmological simulations, through which PN populations for the first time naturally occur within galaxies of diverse evolutionary pathways. We find that only by using realistic stellar populations and their metallicities is it possible to reproduce the bright end of the PNLF for all galaxy types. In particular, the dependence of stellar lifetimes on metallicity has to be accounted for to produce bright PNe in metal-rich populations. Finally, PICS reproduces the statistically complete part of the PNLF observed around the Sun, down to six orders of magnitude below the bright end.

Keywords. galaxies: distances and redshifts, galaxies: stellar content, planetary nebulae: general, stars: AGB and post-AGB, stars: evolution, stars: luminosity function, mass function

1. Introduction

As bright sources of the nebular emission line [O III] λ5007, planetary nebulae (PNe) have long been used as tracer populations and distance indicators in other galaxies, meanwhile reaching distances as far away as 40Mpc (Jacoby et al. 2023). While the bright end of their luminosity function (planetary nebula luminosity function, PNLF) has observationally been found to be universal among different types of galaxies and thus letting PNe be used as standard candles (e.g., Ciardullo et al. 1989; Jacoby 1989), the theoretical background of the PNLF is still not well understood (e.g., Ciardullo 2022). For that reason, numerous models have attempted to improve our understanding of the bright end of the PNLF (e.g., Dopita et al. 1992; Gesicki et al. 2018; Souropanis et al. 2023; Yao & Quataert 2023) and its overall shape (e.g., Méndez & Soffner 1997;

Valenzuela et al. 2019; Chase et al. 2023). These models have generally been based on artificial stellar populations, oftentimes using the results from studies of Milky Way stars. However, such stellar populations may not be representative of the diverse star formation histories that lead to a wide range of stellar populations in other galaxies, for example in old, metal-rich elliptical galaxies (e.g., Li et al. 2018).

With the advent of hydrodynamical cosmological simulations in the past decade, it has become possible to obtain more realistic stellar populations with a large variety of cosmological star formation histories that are self-consistent with the actual assembly history of the simulated galaxy itself. In this work, we introduce the PNe In Cosmological Simulations (PICS) method, which for the first time can use simulated stellar populations as the underlying systems for PN populations and the PNLF. We present the PICS method and the models used in Section 2. In Section 3, we present first results from applying PICS to a cosmological simulation, focusing on the relevance of metallicity and the reproduction of the Milky Way PNLF. Finally, we summarize and conclude our findings in Section 4.

2. Model

To introduce PNe in cosmological simulations, the Planetary nebulae In Cosmological Simulations (PICS) method provides a modular framework for determining the population of PNe for a given single stellar population (SSP). As each stellar particle in a cosmological simulation represents an SSP, this allows one to apply PICS to all the stellar particles in such a simulation in post-processing. As a result, PNe are obtained with all the inherited properties from their parent stellar particles, such as spatial and kinematic information or their ages, and with the properties of the PNe themselves, such as the [O III] λ5007 (from hereon simply referred to as [O III]) magnitude or the central star mass.

The framework consists of a sequence of models that determine the PNe population for an SSP, which is defined by its age, total mass, initial mass function (IMF), and its element abundances. In its basic form, the sequence is the following:

(1) Lifetime function for the SSP, through which the initial mass of the stars reaching the post-asymptotic giant branch (AGB) phase can be determined from the SSP age.
(2) Initial-to-final mass relation (IFMR), from which the central star mass is obtained.
(3) Post-AGB stellar evolution tracks, which provide the central star properties for a given post-AGB age, that is the time passed since leaving the AGB. In particular, the stellar properties consist of the effective temperature and luminosity of the star.
(4) Planetary nebula model, which determines the nebular properties, most importantly the [O III] magnitude.

For (1), the lifetime function, we consider two different prescriptions: The first is composed of the main sequence lifetime from Padovani & Matteucci (1993), which is the one used in the Magneticum Pathfinder simulations (the implemented stellar evolution models are described by Tornatore et al. 2007), and the post-main sequence lifetime from Renzini & Buzzoni (1986). The second is the group of lifetime functions as obtained from Miller Bertolami (2016), which vary with metallicity. The left panel of Fig. 1 shows the lifetime functions, where it can be seen that the lifetime function from Padovani & Matteucci (1993) and Renzini & Buzzoni (1986) is most similar to the lifetime function at a metallicity of $Z = 0.01$ from Miller Bertolami (2016). It also becomes apparent

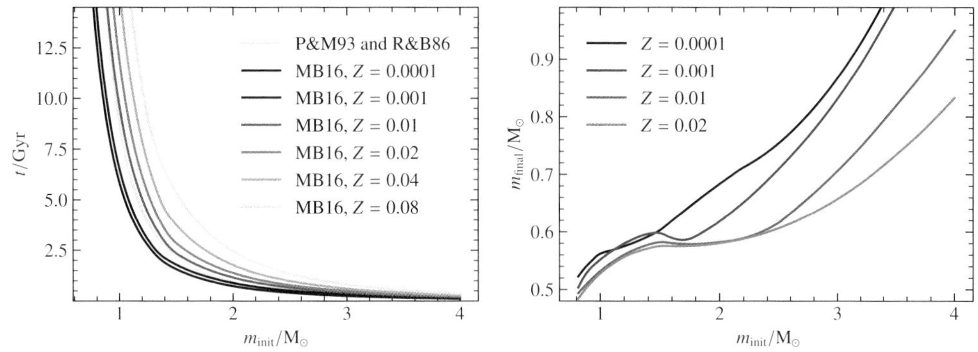

Figure 1. *Left*: Lifetime functions from the main sequence plus post-main sequence lifetime functions by Padovani & Matteucci (1993) and Renzini & Buzzoni (1986), respectively, and from the total lifetimes as computed by Miller Bertolami (2016) for different metallicities, Z, given the initial mass of a star. The lifetime functions for $Z = 0.04$ and 0.08 are extrapolated from the four computed ones. *Right*: Initial-to-final mass relations for the four computed metallicities from Miller Bertolami (2016).

that more metal-rich stars reach the PN phase after significantly longer times than metal-poor stars of the same initial mass. This is due to the impact of metallicity on bound-free opacities, which leads to larger luminosities at lower metallicities.

For (2) and (3), the IFMR and post-AGB stellar evolution tracks, respectively, we use the metallicity-dependent results from Miller Bertolami (2016). The IFMRs for the four metallicities used by Miller Bertolami (2016) are shown in the right panel of Fig. 1. All of the models are interpolated between the metallicities. The lifetime functions are extrapolated beyond the originally computed metallicities, as running new stellar evolutionary simulations for the higher metallicities is beyond the scope of this work. In future studies, we will have such simulated results available to replace the extrapolations. Finally, for (4), the PN model, we use the empirical model presented by Valenzuela et al. (2019), which is also based on the assumption that PNe can be optically thin, thus losing some of their [O III] intensity. The model will be presented in detail in a full paper (Valenzuela et al. in prep.).

3. Application to a Cosmological Simulation

As a first test in applying the model to a cosmological simulation, we use the Magneticum Pathfinder† Box4 (uhr) simulation, which has a side length of 68Mpc and an average stellar particle mass of $1.8 \times 10^6 M_\odot$. We assume a Chabrier IMF (Chabrier 2003) as also used within the simulation. For more details on the simulation and an overview of comparisons with observations, see Teklu et al. (2015) and Valenzuela & Remus (2022), respectively.

3.1. *The Importance of Metallicity*

In recent studies of the PNLF through modeling, it has been customary to only consider PNe of a single fixed solar-like metallicity of $Z = 0.01$ or $Z = 0.02$ (e.g., Gesicki et al. 2018; Valenzuela et al. 2019; Souropanis et al. 2023; Yao & Quataert 2023). To evaluate the importance of taking the actual metallicities of PNe into account, we apply PICS with two different model sequences to the cosmological simulation. For the first, we only use the relations given for a metallicity of $Z = 0.01$ from Miller Bertolami (2016) and the

† `www.magneticum.org`

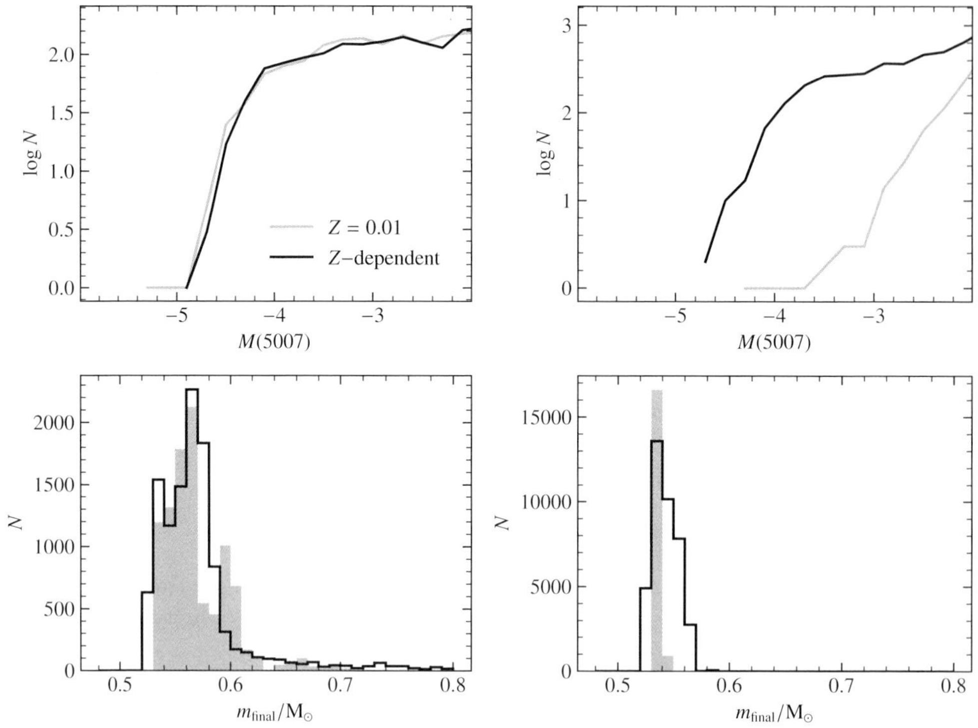

Figure 2. *Top*: Obtained PNLFs for two simulated galaxies (left and right panel each show the results for one galaxy) by running PICS with the models for $Z = 0.01$ (gray) and with the full metallicity-dependent models (black). *Bottom*: Final mass distributions of the PN central stars for the same two galaxies and running the same two varieties of PICS model sequences (in gray and black as for the top row).

lifetime function from Padovani & Matteucci (1993) and Renzini & Buzzoni (1986). For the second, we apply the full metallicity-dependent models to the stellar particles.

We applied the two model sequences of PICS to two different galaxies in the simulation, thus obtaining two PNe populations with [O III] magnitudes for each galaxy, leading to two PNLFs per galaxy. This led to very different results between the two galaxies. The first galaxy, which has a stellar mass of $M_* = 1.8 \times 10^{10} M_\odot$, an average stellar age of $\langle t_{\rm age}\rangle = 6.5$Gyr, and an average metallicity of $\langle Z\rangle = 0.013$, features the well-known PNLF bright end cutoff for both model sequences (top left panel of Fig. 2). In contrast, the second galaxy, which is much more massive, older, and more metal-rich ($M_* = 1.2 \times 10^{11} M_\odot$, $\langle t_{\rm age}\rangle = 9.3$Gyr, $\langle Z\rangle = 0.022$), only features a normal PNLF for the metallicity-dependent model sequence, but completely lacks the brightest PNe when disregarding the metallicity on the stellar lifetimes (top right panel of Fig. 2).

The reason for the large differences between the two PNLFs of the second galaxy can be found in the distribution of the final masses of the PN central stars (bottom row of Fig. 2). While the $Z = 0.01$ model predicts final stellar masses of mostly $M_{\rm final} < 0.54 M_\odot$, the metallicity-dependent model finds final masses of up to $M_{\rm final,max} = 0.57 M_\odot$, which is only slightly lower than the required maximum final mass as obtained by Valenzuela et al. (2019) for old stellar populations. This is a consequence of the lifetimes being longer for any given stellar mass at higher metallicities (left panel of Fig. 1), leading to the metal-rich, more massive stars reaching the PN phase at later times than metal-poor stars of the same mass. As the second galaxy is old and relatively metal-rich, the effect is strongly visible, whereas the first galaxy has metallicities close to the assumed $Z = 0.01$

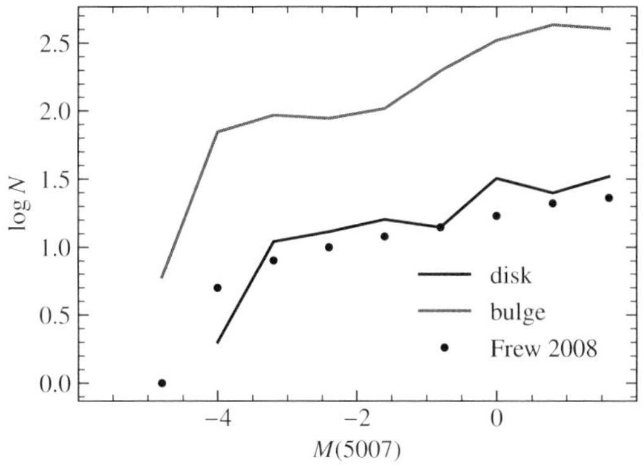

Figure 3. Planetary nebula luminosity functions of PNe in the Milky Way within 2kpc of the Sun from Frew (2008) (black dots), for the modeled PNe within a sphere of 2kpc radius with its center in the disk, 8kpc away from the center of a selected simulated galaxy (black line), and for the modeled PNe within 2kpc of the center of the simulated galaxy (red line). The simulated galaxy is a disk galaxy with a mass similar to that of the Milky Way. The PNe were modeled using the metallicity-dependent lifetime functions. Note that the $M(5007)$-axis reaches much deeper magnitudes than the ones in Fig. 2.

of the metallicity-independent model, thus only leading to minor changes in the PNLF and final mass distribution. As a result, the metallicities clearly cannot be neglected in the general case when modeling the PNLF.

3.2. *Normalization and Shape of the PNLF*

While we have shown that the general shape of the PNLF is qualitatively in agreement with observations, the question remains whether the absolute number of PNe found at a given [O III] magnitude is comparable with observations, that is the normalization of the PNLF. To not only compare this for the brightest PNe, but obtain a result reaching faint PNe as well, we decided to use the PNLF measured for PNe within 2kpc of the Sun by Frew (2008). That PNLF is estimated to be statistically complete up to six orders of magnitude below the bright end cutoff and can be seen in Fig. 3.

From the simulation, we selected a disk galaxy from Magneticum Box4 (uhr) with a Milky Way-like stellar mass ($M_* = 3 \times 10^{10} M_\odot$) to determine an analogous PNLF in the outer regions of the disk. For this, we only considered the stellar particles within a radius of 2kpc from a point in the disk 8kpc away from the galaxy center. The average stellar age in that region is $\langle t_{\rm age} \rangle = 5.6$Gyr and the average metallicity $\langle Z \rangle = 0.027$, which is overall similar to the solar neighborhood. The resulting PNLF from PICS using the metallicity-dependent model sequence is very similar to that from Frew (2008), lying only around 0.2dex higher than the observed PNLF at the dim end and dropping off slightly earlier at the bright end (Fig. 3). As the simulated galaxy is of course not an exact Milky Way-analog, it is expected to also have differences with respect to its PNLF. However, the fact that the overall normalization and absolute number of PNe down to six orders of magnitude below the bright end are in agreement between the observations and simulations shows that the PNLF normalization obtained from the basic metallicity-dependent PICS model sequence is reasonable. In addition, it also shows that the assumption of PNe sometimes being optically thin is necessary to obtain the correct normalization since optically thick PNe lead to more particles being ionized and thus more [O III] emission. It should be noted that a perfect comparison is not only difficult because of the differences between the simulated galaxy and the Milky Way, but also because of the circumstellar extinction not being taken into account for the Milky Way PNe.

Finally, we also determined the PNLF of the inner stellar particles within 2kpc of the galaxy center (red line in Fig. 3). Due to the larger density of stars in the center, there are significantly more PNe in this region. Additionally, the shape of the PNLF is different than that of the disk, which is likely due to the bulge of the simulated galaxy being younger and more metal-rich than the disk (unlike the Milky Way bulge). This difference in stellar population affects the shape of the PNLF, as already observed in previous studies (e.g., Reid & Parker 2010; Valenzuela et al. 2019; Bhattacharya et al. 2021) and will be further investigated in a future study.

4. Summary and Conclusion

In this work, we have introduced a novel method of integrating PNe in cosmological simulations through post-processing, called PICS (PNe In Cosmological Simulations), and have presented first results from it. The method consists of a sequence of models that define the stellar lifetime function, the initial-to-final mass relation, the post-AGB stellar evolutionary tracks, and the nebular model. We employ the models of Miller Bertolami (2016) and Valenzuela et al. (2019) and use the lifetime function from Padovani & Matteucci (1993) and Renzini & Buzzoni (1986), which has been used independently of metallicity in the past, to compare the effect that metallicity-dependent models have: We show that a reasonable bright end of the PNLF of old metal-rich stellar populations can only be obtained when taking into account that metal-poor stars reach the PN phase more quickly than metal-rich stars of the same mass.

We also demonstrate that the metallicity-dependent model sequence of PICS is capable of producing the same shape and normalization (i.e., the same absolute number of PNe) of the PNLF as is observed in the Milky Way disk around the Sun, down to at least six magnitudes below the bright end of the PNLF. As a result, PICS is shown to produce reasonably accurate populations of PNe and PNLFs for different underlying stellar populations. This work therefore lays the foundation for a more detailed analysis of the drivers behind the properties of the PNLF as well as for studies of the PNLF for galaxies across a diverse range of morphologies and formation histories, promising to significantly improve our understanding of the PNLF.

Acknowledgments

LMV acknowledges support by the German Academic Scholarship Foundation (Studienstiftung des deutschen Volkes) and the Marianne-Plehn-Program of the Elite Network of Bavaria.

References

Bhattacharya S., Arnaboldi M., Gerhard O., McConnachie A., Caldwell N., Hartke J., Freeman K. C., 2021, A&A, 647, A130
Chabrier G., 2003, PASP, 115, 763
Chase O., Ciardullo R., Roth M. M., Jacoby G. H., 2023, ApJ, 950, 59
Ciardullo R., 2022, Frontiers in Astronomy and Space Sciences, 9, 896326
Ciardullo R., Jacoby G. H., Ford H. C., Neill J. D., 1989, ApJ, 339, 53
Dopita M. A., Jacoby G. H., Vassiliadis E., 1992, ApJ, 389, 27
Frew D. J., 2008, PhD thesis, Macquarie University, Department of Physics and Astronomy
Gesicki K., Zijlstra A. A., Miller Bertolami M. M., 2018, Nature Astronomy, 2, 580
Jacoby G. H., 1989, ApJ, 339, 39
Jacoby G. H., Ciardullo R., Roth M. M., Arnaboldi M., Weilbacher P. M., 2023, arXiv e-prints, p. arXiv:2309.11603
Li H., et al., 2018, MNRAS, 476, 1765
Miller Bertolami M. M., 2016, A&A, 588, A25

Méndez R. H., Soffner T., 1997, A&A, 321, 898
Padovani P., Matteucci F., 1993, ApJ, 416, 26
Reid W. A., Parker Q. A., 2010, MNRAS, 405, 1349
Renzini A., Buzzoni A., 1986, in Chiosi C., Renzini A., eds, Astrophysics and Space Science Library Vol. 122, Spectral Evolution of Galaxies. pp 195–231, doi:10.1007/978-94-009-4598-2˙19
Souropanis D., Chiotellis A., Boumis P., Jones D., Akras S., 2023, MNRAS, 521, 1808
Teklu A. F., Remus R.-S., Dolag K., Beck A. M., Burkert A., Schmidt A. S., Schulze F., Steinborn L. K., 2015, ApJ, 812, 29
Tornatore L., Borgani S., Dolag K., Matteucci F., 2007, MNRAS, 382, 1050
Valenzuela L. M., Remus R.-S., 2022, arXiv e-prints, p. arXiv:2208.08443
Valenzuela L. M., Méndez R. H., Miller Bertolami M. M., 2019, ApJ, 887, 65
Yao P. Z., Quataert E., 2023, ApJ, 957, 30

Planetary Nebulae: A Universal Toolbox in the Era of Precision Astrophysics
Proceedings IAU Symposium No. 384, 2025
O. De Marco, A. Zijlstra & R. Szczerba, eds.
doi:10.1017/S1743921324000085

Towards Precision Cosmology With Improved PNLF Distances Using VLT-MUSE

George H. Jacoby[1], Robin Ciardullo[2], Martin M. Roth[3] and Magda Arnaboldi[4]

[1]NSF's NOIRLab, U.S.A.

[2]The Penn State University, U.S.A.

[3]Leibniz Institute for Astrophysics Potsdam (AIP), Germany

[4]European Southern Observatory

Abstract. We analyzed VLT/MUSE data for 20 galaxies in the ESO public archive to identify their systems' planetary nebulae (PNe). Using the differential emission line filter (DELF) technique, we performed photometry of the galaxies' PNe and determined their distances via the planetary nebula luminosity function (PNLF). Of the 16 galaxies for which a quality PNLF could be formed, two are isolated and more distant than 30 Mpc and therefore, relatively unaffected by Hubble Flow peculiar velocities. Using these data, we derived a Hubble Constant of 74.2 ± 7.2 (stat) ± 3.7 (sys) km s^{-1} Mpc^{-1}, a value that is similar to that found from other quality indicators (e.g., Cepheids, the tip of the red giant branch, and surface brightness fluctuations), but with a larger uncertainty due to the small number of galaxies. We describe how to improve PNLF measurements so that the precision of the technique is comparable to that of other quality distance indicators. We also describe a path forward in the era of ELTs that supersedes current techniques.

Keywords. Galaxies: distances, galaxies: individual, planetary nebulae

1. Introduction and motivation

The measurement of accurate and precise distances to astronomical objects, particularly external galaxies, has always posed a problem for astronomers. In the 1970s and 1980s, the notable era of the "The Hubble Controversy", the distance debate revolved around whether the Hubble Constant, H_0, was 50 or 100 km s^{-1} Mpc^{-1}, and there was limited discourse about any intermediate values (Jacoby et al. 1992). This factor of two uncertainty permeated all fields of extragalactic astronomy and was considered the most serious problem in cosmology. In fact, since the methodology and instrumentation of the time were not up to the task of resolving the Hubble Constant question, the literature was dominated by a few personalities rather than hard science. The field needed new ideas and techniques, and also new scientists. And, that transition did not occur until the 1990s and beyond.

Over the past two decades, measurement techniques have improved dramatically, so that H_0 values are now generally quoted to 1-2%. But this precision has brought about its own controversy: whether the measured distances to galaxies are consistent with the paradigm of the standard model. Inconsistencies at the $3 - 5\sigma$ level between measurements of H_0 based on the Cepheid calibration of the Type Ia supernova (Riess et al.

2022) and that from the microwave background (Planck Collaboration et al. 2020) have ushered in the era of "The Hubble Tension". If real, the discrepancy means that new physics, beyond ΛCDM cosmology, is needed to explain the universe (Kamionkowski & Riess 2023). Since other distance-ladder (Freedman et al. 2019; Garnavich et al. 2023) and non-distance-ladder (Pesce et al. 2020; Wong et al. 2020) techniques also suggest an H_0 discrepancy, it is once again the case that the distance scale is considered to be one of the most serious problems in cosmology.

Given what is at stake, new, precise (1-2%) techniques are needed to validate the results from Cepheids, and, since Cepheids are Population I objects, those methods must work in galaxies with recent star formation. The planetary nebula luminosity function (PNLF), as implemented by VLT/MUSE, is very promising in this regard (Roth et al. 2021; Jacoby et al. 2023). This paper presents a brief description of our work toward demonstrating that approach.

2. The PNLF method has matured

In the mid-1980s, the concept of using PNe as distance indicators seemed questionable at best, and was poorly received. Distances to Galactic PNe were almost impossible to measure to more than a factor of 2-3, and their morphologies and excitations are so diverse that their consideration as "standard candles" could not be taken seriously. Still, the physics of photoionization is relatively straightforward and common to all PNe, and a single PN was not being proposed as a standard candle: it was the bright-end cutoff of the luminosity function of an ensemble of sources that served as a standard. The lack of a complete theoretical basis for a universal bright-end cutoff did slow acceptance of the technique, but the excellent results obtained in the Local Group, NGC 5128, M81, and the Leo I Group, were hard to dispute (see the review by Ciardullo 2012).

However, beyond ~10 Mpc, evidence emerged that the PNLF distances were too small by ~0.2 mag. Also, unexplained were the "overluminous" PNe appearing in galaxies at larger distances. This fueled speculation that the PNLF distances were being biased, perhaps by contamination from supernova remnants, (Kreckel et al. 2017), H II regions, background Lyα emitting galaxies (Ciardullo et al. 2002b), or even object superpositions (Chase et al. 2023).

Roth et al. (2021) demonstrated that most of these biases could be addressed using MUSE on the VLT. Specifically, the instrument's wide spectral coverage enables PNe to be separated from most other emission line objects via line ratios, in much the same way as the classic BPT diagram (Baldwin et al. 1981). Moreover, MUSE's $R \sim 2000$ spectral resolution allows blended objects to be resolved via their differing radial velocities, leaving any remaining blends to be dealt with using the methodology of Chase et al. (2023).

VLT/MUSE PNLF observations are greatly improved over the original concepts of narrow-band imaging (Ciardullo et al. 1989). The advantages come from utilizing (a) a "dynamically" defined very narrow-band differential emission line filter (DELF) with an effective bandpass of $\sim 3-5$ Å, (b) an 8 m versus a 4 m aperture, and (c) much-improved image quality ($0.''6$-$0.''7$ instead of $0.''9$-$1.''1$). Ultimately, MUSE enables the unbiased application of the PNLF technique to ~40 Mpc in both early and late-type galaxies, where previously the method had been limited to Population II systems within ~15 Mpc.

3. Results

We selected 20 galaxies from the ESO's science archive to help us explore the potential of MUSE for PNLF measurements. With a few exceptions, we chose galaxies having good seeing ($< 1.''0$), exposure times greater than an hour, distances between 20 and 35 Mpc,

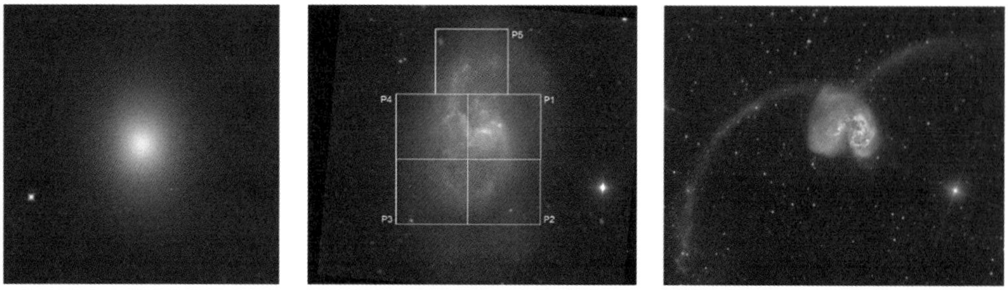

Figure 1. A sample of the galaxies analyzed in this project illustrating the variety of galaxy types. From left to right: the E1 elliptical M 49 (NASA), the Sc spiral NGC 1385 (ESO MUSE), and the interacting Antennae galaxies (Olsen/Subaru). For NGC 1385, the 5 MUSE fields that we used are outlined; the lack of field overlap introduced an additional zero-point error into the photometry.

and luminosities brighter than $M_V < -19$. We also had a preference for galaxies measured by other techniques and selected systems with a diverse range of morphologies and star-forming activity. This allowed us to explore environments where the PNLF works well or not at all. Figure 1 illustrates the diversity of our galaxy selection.

In four galaxies, the PNLF could not be used as a distance estimator: three of the galaxies had too few PNe to form a PNLF, and the fourth had a high inclination with significant and variable internal reddening. A sample of good and typical PNLFs is shown in Figure 2.

A lesson learned from this work is that the brightest magnitude of the PNLF needs to be populated by at least 50 PNe to form a well-defined PNLF (see the curve for NGC 1404). A second lesson learned from NGC 1433 is that each MUSE pointing must be carefully oriented to include a bright point source. Without such a source, photometric aperture corrections can not be measured to the precision necessary for distance scale work. If no bright star is available, the only alternative is to ensure the pointing overlaps a datacube with a bright PSF star, and there must be a number of sources in the regions of field overlap.

4. Distances and H_0

Figure 3 shows a histogram for our 16 galaxies with well-determined PNLF distances. The "cluster" of distances near 18 Mpc is the result of the large collection of MUSE archival data in the Fornax cluster. Two galaxies stand out. NGC 4355 and 6958 are the most distant galaxies yet measured with the PNLF. Both have distances greater than ~ 30 Mpc, both are early-type lenticulars, and both are relatively isolated, meaning their peculiar velocities should be small. The galaxies' radial velocities should therefore be representative of a largely unperturbed Hubble flow.

For these two galaxies, we derive PNLF distances of 32.9 ± 1.3 (for NGC 4355) and 36.2 ± 3.8 Mpc (for NGC 6958), with the large uncertainties driven by the relatively small number of PNe found in each system (24 and 15, respectively). Nevertheless, if we compare these numbers to the galaxies' recessional velocities, we obtain values for H_0 of 75.0 ± 9.6 and 69.2 ± 11.0 km s^{-1} Mpc^{-1} respectively. The weighted average of these two values, 74.2 ± 7.2 km s^{-1} Mpc^{-1} is quite encouraging, especially considering that it is based on archival data that were not optimized for distance scale studies.

Although the $\sim 10\%$ uncertainty is far higher than that derived from the Cepheid, tip of the red giant branch (TRGB) or surface brightness fluctuations (SBF) calibrations of SN Ia, this is mainly due to the targets being relatively small and not optimally

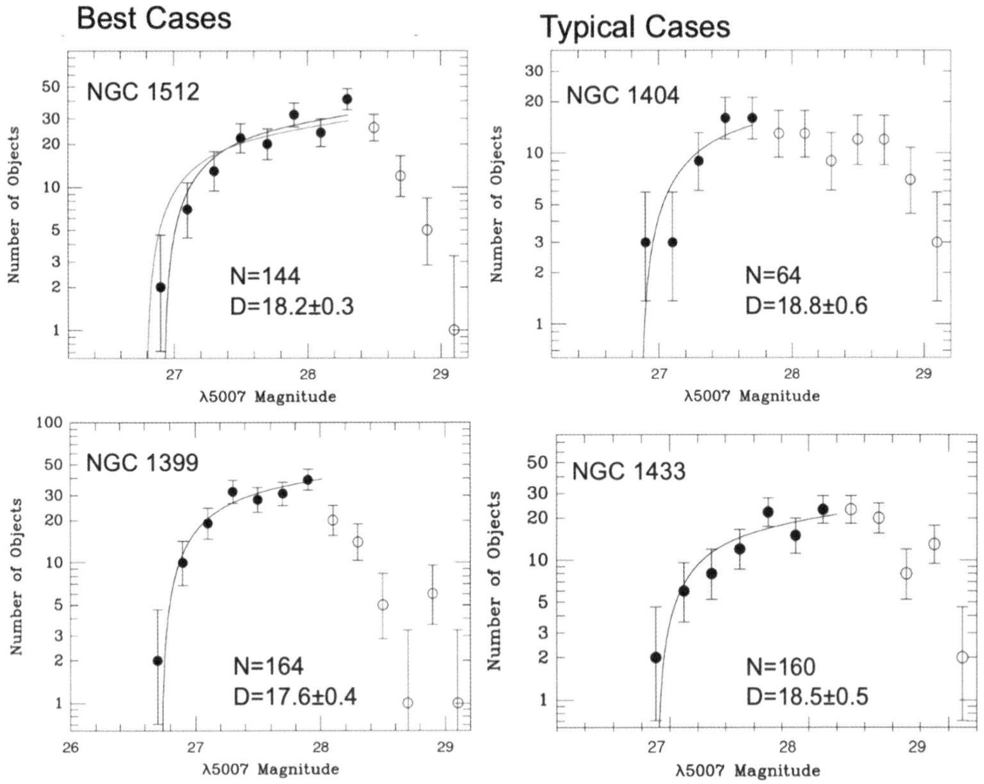

Figure 2. A sample of PNLFs. For NGC 1512, the red curve is the nominal fit to the reference PNLF equation (Ciardullo et al. 1989) and the black curve is the fit to that equation as modified for superpositions (Chase et al. 2023).

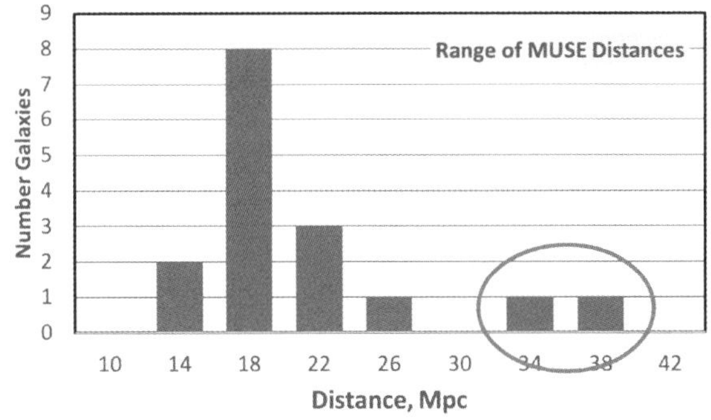

Figure 3. A histogram of the distances derived for the 16 galaxies for which a reasonable PNLF could be formed from the MUSE archive collection. NGC 4355 and 6958 are circled in red.

observed. Moreover, they are just two galaxies. In our new MUSE/PNLF dataset, we see no evidence for distance biases, so, in principle, observations of 25-30 galaxies beyond ~ 30 Mpc can be expected to drive the average error down by a factor of 5, to 2% or better.

Table 1. PNLF compared with Cepheids, TRGB and SBF.

Method	N(galaxies)	Difference
Cepheids	1	+7%
TRGB	3	+4%
SBF	8	−9%

Table 2. PNLF comparison in specific cases.

Galaxy	NGC 1404	NGC 4038/9
PNLF/Cepheid	...	+7.5%
PNLF/TRGB	+0.5%	+4.2%
PNLF/SBF	−7.4%	...

5. Precision

Since there is no collection of test galaxies with *a priori* known distances, the true precision and accuracy of a distance technique is difficult to derive. Can the PNLF really be used to obtain a 2% error on H_0? Note that this goal represents the precision for an ensemble of measurements, not for any one object, and it is a goal that has not been convincingly achieved for any method.

The usual approach to understanding the precision of a method is to compare it against other "gold standard" techniques. Cepheids and TRGB are currently held in the highest regard, with SBF a close third. When we compare our PNLF results to these methods, the results are promising but not yet compelling, as the sample is small. This is summarized in Table 1. Unfortunately, only one galaxy has a Cepheid distance and it is a somewhat peculiar object: NGC 4038/39, otherwise known as the "Antennae Galaxy". Nevertheless, the PNLF distance is within 7% of the Cepheid measurement, well within the combined errors of the two methods.

The TRGB comparison is based on 3 galaxies and the average difference is quite small, with the PNLF generating distances that are, on average 4% further. The 9% difference for the 8 SBF galaxies may seem problematic at first, but it has the opposite sign for that of the Cepheid and TRGB comparisons. Moreover, this difference is considerably smaller than previous checks between these methods (Ciardullo et al. 2002a) where the average difference was 15%. As shown by Ciardullo et al. (1993, 2002a), the fact that PNLF distances are systematically shorter than those of the SBF is consistent with the idea that the calibration galaxies used by the two methods have more internal extinction than the techniques' program galaxies.

For the 16 galaxies in our sample, the internal uncertainties of the PNLF fits are typically 6% and the best targets exhibit errors as small as 4%. The latter galaxies are usually early-type systems containing large numbers of bright PNe that were observed in a manner that was almost optimal for PNLF distance scale studies (see § 6). Table 2 provides a 4-way check for two of these well-observed systems. There is no reason why targeted observations for PNLF distances cannot always achieve this level of precision ($< 4\%$).

6. Achieving H_0 with 2% precision

With a sample of 25–30 well-observed galaxies, the PNLF can deliver a good measurement of H_0 directly from their distances in the relatively unperturbed Hubble flow. Alternatively, the PNLF can calibrate SN Ia luminosities in systems that are not amenable to Cepheid and/or TRGB analyses, thereby linking the technique to measures of the distant universe.

For PNLF measurements to be successful, they must be carefully planned, as (a) the seeing must be better than 0.″75, (b) the galaxies chosen must be isolated E/S0 systems with $M_V < -19.5$, (c) each observation must contain a bright star for PSF determination (or at least overlap a frame that does have a PSF star in order to bootstrap the photometric zero point), and d) the exposure times and enclosed galaxy luminosity must be sufficient to identify 50–100 PNe in the top magnitude of the luminosity function.

Finally, it should be noted that the importance of a single PN to a galaxy's PNLF depends strongly on its luminosity: the brighter the PN, the more weight it carries in defining the system's PNLF cutoff. This fact, coupled with the rarity of bright PNe, means that it is critically important to continually improve our knowledge of the true shape of the function's bright-end cutoff (Jacoby et al. 2023).

7. Future steps

One underlying issue that has slowed the acceptance of PNLF distances is the lack of a complete theoretical understanding of the shape of the luminosity function and its resilience to population variances. Metallicity corrections may be required for some galaxies, and while the response of the PNLF cutoff to oxygen abundance has been modeled (Dopita et al. 1992; Schönberner et al. 2010), the empirical data must be improved (Ciardullo & Jacoby 1992).

Understanding the cutoff's constancy with population age is trickier, though it appears to be related to dust generated within the PN progenitors (Ciardullo & Jacoby 1999; Davis et al. 2018). Briefly put: the PNe from younger populations derive from more massive progenitors which eject more gas and dust on the AGB. The greater amount of ejected dust, and the shorter time it has to disperse before ionization, compensates for the higher luminosities of the central stars that drive the observed [O III] brightness. This correlation between progenitor age and intrinsic extinction has been independently calibrated in M31's disc via their age-velocity-dispersion relation (Bhattacharya et al. 2019).

Looking toward the era of Extremely Large Telescopes with MUSE-like integral-field spectrographs, the PNLF can be extended 2–3 times further. At those distances, cosmic velocity errors will not dominate the error as they do at 35 Mpc. Relatively fewer galaxies will be needed to a achieve high precision measurement of H_0.

8. Acknowledgements

The NSF supported this work through grant AST2206090. Based on data obtained from the ESO Science Archive Facility with DOI(s): `https://doi.org/10.18727/archive/41` and `https://doi.org/10.18727/archive/42`. This work has made use of the SIMBAD database, operated at CDS, Strasbourg, France, and of the NASA/IPAC Extragalactic Database (NED), which is operated by the Jet Propulsion Laboratory, California Institute of Technology, under contract with the National Aeronautics and Space Administration. The Institute for Gravitation and the Cosmos is supported by the Eberly College of Science and the Office of the Senior Vice President for Research at the Pennsylvania State University.

References

Baldwin, J. A., Phillips, M. M., & Terlevich, R. 1981, PASP, 93, 5, doi: 10.1086/130766

Bhattacharya, S., Arnaboldi, M., Caldwell, N., et al. 2019, A&A, 631, A56, doi: 10.1051/0004-6361/201935898

Chase, O., Ciardullo, R., Roth, M. M., & Jacoby, G. H. 2023, ApJ, 950, 59, doi: 10.3847/1538-4357/acc9bd

Ciardullo, R. 2012, Ap&SS, 341, 151, doi: 10.1007/s10509-012-1061-2

Ciardullo, R., Feldmeier, J. J., Jacoby, G. H., et al. 2002a, ApJ, 577, 31, doi: 10.1086/342180

Ciardullo, R., Feldmeier, J. J., Krelove, K., Jacoby, G. H., & Gronwall, C. 2002b, ApJ, 566, 784, doi: 10.1086/338230

Ciardullo, R., & Jacoby, G. H. 1992, ApJ, 388, 268, doi: 10.1086/171150

—. 1999, ApJ, 515, 191, doi: 10.1086/307025

Ciardullo, R., Jacoby, G. H., Ford, H. C., & Neill, J. D. 1989, ApJ, 339, 53, doi: 10.1086/167275

Ciardullo, R., Jacoby, G. H., & Tonry, J. L. 1993, ApJ, 419, 479, doi: 10.1086/173501

Davis, B. D., Ciardullo, R., Jacoby, G. H., Feldmeier, J. J., & Indahl, B. L. 2018, ApJ, 863, 189, doi: 10.3847/1538-4357/aad3c4

Dopita, M. A., Jacoby, G. H., & Vassiliadis, E. 1992, ApJ, 389, 27, doi: 10.1086/171186

Freedman, W. L., Madore, B. F., Hatt, D., et al. 2019, ApJ, 882, 34, doi: 10.3847/1538-4357/ab2f73

Garnavich, P., Wood, C. M., Milne, P., et al. 2023, ApJ, 953, 35, doi: 10.3847/1538-4357/ace04b

Jacoby, G. H., Ciardullo, R., Roth, M. M., Arnaboldi, M., & Weilbacher, P. M. 2023, arXiv e-prints, arXiv:2309.11603, doi: 10.48550/arXiv.2309.11603

Jacoby, G. H., Branch, D., Ciardullo, R., et al. 1992, PASP, 104, 599, doi: 10.1086/133035

Kamionkowski, M., & Riess, A. G. 2023, Annual Review of Nuclear and Particle Science, 73, 153, doi: 10.1146/annurev-nucl-111422-024107

Kreckel, K., Groves, B., Bigiel, F., et al. 2017, ApJ, 834, 174, doi: 10.3847/1538-4357/834/2/174

Pesce, D. W., Braatz, J. A., Reid, M. J., et al. 2020, ApJ, 891, L1, doi: 10.3847/2041-8213/ab75f0

Planck Collaboration, Aghanim, N., Akrami, Y., et al. 2020, A&AP, 641, A6, doi: 10.1051/0004-6361/201833910

Riess, A. G., Yuan, W., Macri, L. M., et al. 2022, ApJ, 934, L7, doi: 10.3847/2041-8213/ac5c5b

Roth, M. M., Jacoby, G. H., Ciardullo, R., et al. 2021, ApJ, 916, 21, doi: 10.3847/1538-4357/ac02ca

Schönberner, D., Jacob, R., Sandin, C., & Steffen, M. 2010, A&A, 523, A86, doi: 10.1051/0004-6361/200913427

Wong, K. C., Suyu, S. H., Chen, G. C. F., et al. 2020, MNRAS, 498, 1420, doi: 10.1093/mnras/stz3094

Planetary Nebulae: A Universal Toolbox in the Era of Precision Astrophysics
Proceedings IAU Symposium No. 384, 2025
O. De Marco, A. Zijlstra & R. Szczerba, eds.
doi:10.1017/S1743921323005586

Using adaptive-optics assisted MUSE observations to measure galaxy distances with the Planetary Nebula luminosity function

Saskia Schlagenhauf[1,2] and Marc Sarzi[1]

[1]Armagh Observatory and Planetarium, UK
email: saskia.schlagenhauf@armagh.ac.uk

[2]Queen's University Belfast, UK

Abstract. Thanks to its characteristic bright cut-off, the planetary nebulae luminosity function (PNLF) has now become a well-established extragalactic distance indicator that is in principle applicable to all types of galaxies. Most recently, several studies have demonstrated how the use of integral-field spectroscopy can lead to even more precise PNLF measurements, in particular as it allows to probe the central regions of galaxies and obtain well-sampled PNLF distributions. In this respect, adaptive optics (AO) is expected to further increase the scope and reach of PNLF measurements, as it should allow for the detection of even more and more distant PNe. This proceeding presents first results of the investigation of the MUSE-AO performance in relation to the detection of PNe in external galaxies, based on all galaxies with wide-field mode AO observations in the ESO archive.

Keywords. instrumentation: adaptive optics, planetary nebulae, galaxies: distances, galaxies: luminosity function

---

1. Introduction

Planetary nebulae have extraordinary bright [OIII] emission, especially the λ5007 line, which makes them detectable even in external galaxies, where they appear as unresolved point sources. So far, PNe have been detected as far as 100 Mpc in the Coma cluster, which makes them the second most distant single-star phenomena whose spectrum can be analysed with 8-m class telescopes, after cosmological supernovae (Arnaboldi and Gerhard 2022). This has allowed to collect samples of PNe in well-studied systems to which we know the distance, e.g. Large and Small Magellanic Cloud, Andromeda and the Leo galaxy group. Ciardullo et al. (1989) analysed PNe in our local group and found that the planetary nebulae luminosity function (PNLF) could be described as:

$$N(M) \propto e^{0.307M} \cdot \left(1 - e^{3(M^* - M)}\right), \tag{1.1}$$

with the number of PNe N, the absolute magnitude of the PN M, and the absolute magnitude cutoff M^*. What is most remarkable about this relation is its sharp brightness cutoff, at $M^* = -4.48$. This makes it possible to determine the distance to a galaxy, in which we can detect enough PNe to determine the apparent magnitude of this cutoff. To do so, it is necessary to convert the λ5007 line flux F_{5007} into and equivalent V-magnitude m_{5007} using

$$m_{5007} = -2.5 \log (F_{5007}) - 13.74 \tag{1.2}$$

from Jacoby (1989).

Table 1. Target galaxies observed with MUSE. For each galaxy, right ascension (RA), declination (Dec), and the Hubble distance D is given. The Hubble distances are taken from the NASA/IPAC Extragalactic Database (NED)[1], where the Hubble distance is determined by assuming a Hubble constant of $67.8\,\mathrm{km\,s^{-1}\,Mpc^{-1}}$.

Target	RA	Dec	D [Mpc]
NGC 0244	$00°45'46''$	$-15°35'47''$	9.26 ± 0.72
NGC 1336	$03°26'32''$	$-35°43'21''$	19.34 ± 1.36
NGC 6958	$20°48'43''$	$-37°59'50''$	36.96 ± 2.60
NGC 1326	$03°23'56''$	$-36°27'52''$	18.47 ± 1.30
NGC 1553	$04°16'10''$	$-55°46'49''$	15.74 ± 1.11
NGC 1440	$03°45'03''$	$-18°15'60''$	21.85 ± 1.59
NGC 3489	$11°00'18''$	$+13°54'03''$	15.09 ± 1.12
NGC 3412	$10°50'53''$	$+13°24'42''$	17.51 ± 1.28
NGC 3593	$11°14'37''$	$+12°49'05''$	14.32 ± 1.07
NGC 1079	$02°43'44''$	$-29°00'12''$	18.87 ± 1.34
NGC 1201	$03°04'08''$	$-26°04'11''$	22.58 ± 1.60
NGC 1320	$03°24'49''$	$-03°02'32''$	38.64 ± 2.71
NGC 3626	$11°20'04''$	$+18°21'24''$	26.98 ± 1.92
NGC 4457	$12°28'59''$	$+03°34'15''$	18.09 ± 1.32
NGC 4379	$12°25'15''$	$+15°36'25''$	20.63 ± 1.48
NGC 4421	$12°27'03''$	$+15°27'39''$	27.66 ± 1.96
NGC 4528	$12°34'06''$	$+11°19'14''$	25.18 ± 1.80
NGC 5121	$13°24'36''$	$-37°40'60''$	25.73 ± 1.83

[1]`https://ned.ipac.caltech.edu`

The greatest advantage of using the PNLF as a distance indicator is, that it can be applied to all Hubble types of galaxies, since PNe appear in all stellar populations. In comparison, the other two main extra-galactic measurement techniques, surface brightness fluctuations and Cepheid variables, can only be applied to early and late type galaxies, respectively. This makes the PNLF a relatively standard method to derive distances, allowing in principle to be an important calibrator of methods further up in the distance ladder, such as the cosmologically all important Supernovae Ia (SNIa) that indeed occur in all sorts of galaxies (see Riess et al. 2022).

In recent years, integral-field spectroscopy has proven particularly useful to deliver abundant samples of PNe in external galaxies and thus ensure robust PNLF distance measurements, in particular as it allows to detect PNe in the central, PNe-rich regions of galaxies (see e.g. Sarzi et al. 2011). With its relatively large field of view ($1' \times 1'$) and broad spectral range ($465\,\mathrm{nm} \times 930\,\mathrm{nm}$)† the MUSE instrument is ideally suited for PNe detection, as it also allows for the identification of PNe impostors such as compact HII regions and supernovae remnants. Furthermore, the MUSE adaptive optics (AO) system promises to deliver even larger PNe sample at a given distance or to detect PNe in galaxies further away by allowing to detect fainter [OIII] point sources.

2. Galaxy Sample

As of June 2023, in total 18 galaxies were available in the ESO archive that were observed with MUSE in Wide-Field Mode (WFM) using AO (Table 1). For each galaxy, right ascension (RA), declination (Dec), and Hubble distance D is given. Hubble distances are taken from the NASA/IPAC Extragalactic Database (NED). In total, the galaxies have Hubble distances between 9 Mpc and 39 Mpc with a median Hubble distance of 20 Mpc. As indicated in the previous section, galaxies in this distance range can act as valuable calibrators for other distance measurements. However, it is important to note, that the present archival sample comes with a some limitations as not all galaxies are ideally suited for applying the PNLF distance method.

† `https://www.eso.org/sci/facilities/paranal/instruments/muse/inst.html`

3. Data Analysis

To detect and measure the flux of PNe in MUSE data and then obtain a distance based on the PNLF we followed the procedures described in Spriggs et al. (2020, 2021), which were used for MUSE WFM observations without AO.

The procedure starts from obtaining a stellar-continuum subtracted cube, following a spaxel-by-spaxel fit to the MUSE spectra using both the pPXF and GandALF codes (Cappellari and Emsellem 2004; Sarzi et al. 2006) to simultaneously model the stellar and nebular components in the MUSE spectra. Whilst this first analysis of the MUSE cubes already deliver an [OIII] map that generally reveals the presence of several PNe, it is not specifically optimised to identify such sources. Indeed PNe have only modest expansion velocities of a few tens of km/s so that their unresolved line profile will generally be narrower than the one coming from diffuse ionised-gas emission. Once the stellar continuum has been subtracted in each spaxel we therefore proceed to run a dedicated spaxel-by-spaxel fit only the the [OIII]$\lambda\lambda 4959, 5007$ doublet imposing a fixed intrinsic line velocity dispersion of 40 km/s (Schönberner et al. 2014) and while also accounting for an instrumental resolution of 75 km/s at 5007 Å (Guérou et al. 2017).

Such a dedicated spaxel-by-spaxel fit gives us a final [OIII] flux emission map and - most important - a map for the ratio between the amplitude (A) of [OIII] emission and the residual-noise level (rN) in each spaxel that we can use to detect PNe candidates, [OIII] point sources using the Python package SEP, which is based on the Sextractor source-finding algorithm by Bertin and Arnouts (1996).

The next step is to validate or reject the identified PNe candidates, whilst also measuring their final flux. To do so a small 9×9 spaxel cube over a restricted wavelength region from 4900 Å to 5100 Å is extracted around each candidate source for a final fit in which all [OIII] lines in the 81 spectra of such a cube are simultaneously fit while imposing the same line profile and a spatially varying overall flux that follows the MUSE point-spread function, as would be expected in the presence of unresolved [OIII] emission from a PN. During this fit, only the overall total flux, velocity and position of such an unresolved [OIII] source is optimised for. Key to this fit, is the prior knowledge of the PSF, which in our case we took to have a Moffat profile (see Moffat 1969), with the shape parameters determined with the pipeline from Fusco et al. (2020).

Such a 1D+2D fit allows to exclude some PNe candidates that are in fact regions with ionised-gas emission or false-positive detections. Spriggs et al. (2020) showed, that sources with a central $A/rN > 3$ and a sufficient fit quality, which means that the χ^2 value was above the 95% confidence level, can be confirmed as [OIII] point sources and used for further analysis.

As brighter PNe are easier to detect than fainter ones, we have to account for the incompleteness of our PNe sample. Therefore, the PNLF (see Equation 1.1) is modified by the completeness ratio for each magnitude, where the completeness ratio is the fraction of the [OIII] image where a PN with that magnitude could be detected. The completeness corrected PNLF has only one free parameter the apparent magnitude cutoff which yields the distance to the galaxy.

4. Sample Limitations

As we did not chose the sample of galaxies because of their properties, but rather because of what is available in the ESO archive, some galaxies are not ideal for PNe detection. This includes galaxies where a large portion of the MUSE field of view presents diffuse and strong ionized-gas emission (e.g, NGC 1320), leaving only a small and insufficient number of PNe detections for an accurate PNLF distance measurement, similarly to the case of objects that are too far away (e.g., NGC 6958) or that are intrinsically not

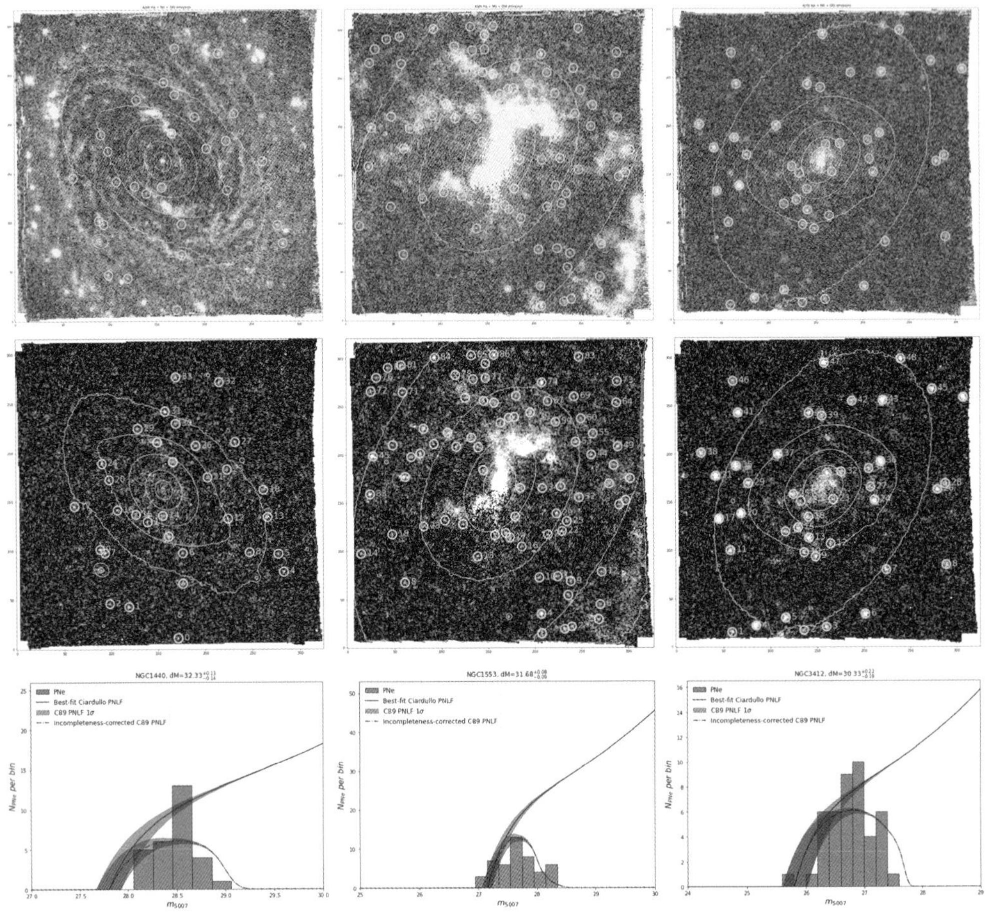

Figure 1. Top: Ar/N map of combined Hα, [NII], and [OIII] emission. The positions of PNe are indicated with green circles, PNe impostors with blue circles. Center: Ar/N map of [OIII] emission. PNe are circled in green, PNe impostors in blue. Bottom: Incompleteness corrected PNLF fit. Galaxies from left to right: NGC 1440, NGC 1553, and NGC 3412.

sufficiently massive to offer abundant PNe populations (e.g., NGC 0244). Work is under way to at least derive robust upper-limits on the distance to such galaxies.

5. First Results

In this Proceeding, we present the distances to the three galaxies NGC 1440, NGC 1553, and NGC 3412. From top to bottom, for each galaxy Figure 1 shows the Ar/N map of the combined Hα, [NII], and [OIII] emission, alerting to the presence of diffuse ionised-gas emission, the Ar/N map of [OIII] emission showing [OIII] point sources and our final PNLF fits. PNe and PNe impostors (HII regions, SNR or PNe too deeply embedded in diffuse gas) are shown by the green and blue circles, respectively. The PNLF show fit with the Ciardullo prescription with and without incompleteness correction. The results of our analysis are summarised in Table 2. For NGC 1440 we found a distance of nearly 30 Mpc at a 6 % accuracy, which effectively pinpoint the location of this object whose previous distance estimates ranged widely between 18 Mpc to 83 Mpc. Furthermore, the accuracy of our distance measurement is comparable to the typical accuracy of the non-AO observations of Spriggs et al. (2021) for Fornax cluster galaxies at 20 Mpc, thus demonstrating the usefulness of AO data in this game. For NGC 3412, the PNLF agrees

Table 2. Results determined from the PNLF fit.

Target	#PNe	dM [mag]	D [Mpc]	D_{ref} [Mpc]	Type	Reference
NGC 1440	29	$32.332^{+0.126}_{-0.138}$	29.26 ± 1.80	18 - 83	TF, FJ	1,2
NGC 1553	47	$31.683^{+0.076}_{-0.086}$	21.71 ± 0.85	18.3	SBF	3
NGC 3412	44	$30.332^{+0.225}_{-0.193}$	11.65 ± 1.28	11.3	SBF	3

TF: Tully-Fisher, FJ: Faber-Jackson, SBF: Surface brightness fluctuations
[1]de Vaucouleurs and Olson (1984), [2]Tully and Fisher (1988), [3]Tully et al. (2013)

with the measurements from surface brightness fluctuations, whereas for NGC 1553 the PNLF gives a slightly larger distance than surface brightness fluctuations.

6. Outlook

Other studies have been carried out with MUSE data using the Differential Emission Line Filter (DELF) technique (Roth et al. 2021) that are generally consistent with our approach (Jacoby et al. 2023). DELF provides excellent results by using less computational resources but our approach may prove more versatile when it will come to disentangling PNe from diffuse ionised-gas emission (see Pastorello et al. 2013) or blended PNe in the crowded central regions of galaxies, thanks to the possibility to account for the separate kinematics of such components. In a coming paper we will complete our analysis of all galaxies available in the ESO archive observed with MUSE in wide field mode using AO to fully assess its usefulness for PNLF distance measurements.

References

Arnaboldi, M. & Gerhard, O. 2022, Kinematics of the diffuse intragroup/intracluster light in groups and clusters of galaxies in the Local Universe (within 100 Mpc distance). Frontiers in Astronomy and Space Sciences, 9, 403.

Bertin, E. & Arnouts, S. 1996, Sextractor: Software for source extraction. Astron. Astrophys. Suppl. Ser., 117(2), 393–404.

Cappellari, M. & Emsellem, E. 2004, Parametric Recovery of Line-of-Sight Velocity Distributions from Absorption-Line Spectra of Galaxies via Penalized Likelihood. PASP, 116(816), 138–147.

Ciardullo, R., Jacoby, G. H., & Ford, H. C. 1989, Planetary Nebulae as Standard Candles. IV. A Test in the Leo I Group. APJ, 344, 715.

de Vaucouleurs, G. & Olson, D. W. 1984, A comparison of distance scales for early-type galaxies. APJS, 56, 91–104.

Fusco, T., Bacon, R., Kamann, S., Conseil, S., Neichel, B., Correia, C., Beltramo-Martin, O., Vernet, J., Kolb, J., & Madec, P. Y. 2020, Reconstruction of the ground-layer adaptive-optics point spread function for MUSE wide field mode observations. AAP, 635, A208.

Guérou, A., Krajnović, D., Epinat, B., Contini, T., Emsellem, E., Bouché, N., Bacon, R., Michel-Dansac, L., Richard, J., Weilbacher, P. M., Schaye, J., Marino, R. A., den Brok, M., & Erroz-Ferrer, S. 2017, The MUSE Hubble Ultra Deep Field Survey. V. Spatially resolved stellar kinematics of galaxies at redshift $0.2 \lesssim z \lesssim 0.8$. AAP, 608, A5.

Jacoby, G. H. 1989, Planetary Nebulae as Standard Candles. I. Evolutionary Models. APJ, 339, 39.

Jacoby, G. H., Ciardullo, R., Roth, M. M., Arnaboldi, M., & Weilbacher, P. M. 2023, Towards Precision Cosmology With Improved PNLF Distances Using VLT-MUSE II. A Test Sample from Archival Data. arXiv e-prints, arXiv:2309.11603.

Moffat, A. F. J. 1969, A Theoretical Investigation of Focal Stellar Images in the Photographic Emulsion and Application to Photographic Photometry. AAP, 3, 455.

Pastorello, N., Sarzi, M., Cappellari, M., Emsellem, E., Mamon, G. A., Bacon, R., Davies, R. L., & de Zeeuw, P. T. 2013, The planetary nebulae population in the nuclear regions of M31: the SAURON view. MNRAS, 430(2), 1219–1229.

Riess, A. G., Yuan, W., Macri, L. M., Scolnic, D., Brout, D., Casertano, S., Jones, D. O., Murakami, Y., Anand, G. S., Breuval, L., Brink, T. G., Filippenko, A. V., Hoffmann, S., Jha, S. W., D'arcy Kenworthy, W., Mackenty, J., Stahl, B. E., & Zheng, W. 2022, A Comprehensive Measurement of the Local Value of the Hubble Constant with 1 km s^{-1} Mpc^{-1} Uncertainty from the Hubble Space Telescope and the SH0ES Team. APJL, 934(1), L7.

Roth, M. M., Jacoby, G. H., Ciardullo, R., Davis, B. D., Chase, O., & Weilbacher, P. M. 2021, Toward Precision Cosmology with Improved PNLF Distances Using VLT-MUSEI. Methodology and Tests. APJ, 916(1), 21.

Sarzi, M., Falcón-Barroso, J., Davies, R. L., Bacon, R., Bureau, M., Cappellari, M., de Zeeuw, P. T., Emsellem, E., Fathi, K., Krajnović, D., Kuntschner, H., McDermid, R. M., & Peletier, R. F. 2006, The SAURON project - V. Integral-field emission-line kinematics of 48 elliptical and lenticular galaxies. MNRAS, 366(4), 1151–1200.

Sarzi, M., Mamon, G. A., Cappellari, M., Emsellem, E., Bacon, R., Davies, R. L., & de Zeeuw, P. T. 2011, The planetary nebulae population in the central regions of M32: the SAURON view. MNRAS, 415(3), 2832–2843.

Schönberner, D., Jacob, R., Lehmann, H., Hildebrandt, G., Steffen, M., Zwanzig, A., Sandin, C., & Corradi, R. L. M. 2014, A hydrodynamical study of multiple-shell planetary nebulae. III. Expansion properties and internal kinematics: Theory versus observation. Astronomische Nachrichten, 335(4), 378–408.

Spriggs, T. W., Sarzi, M., Galán-de Anta, P. M., Napiwotzki, R., Viaene, S., Nedelchev, B., Coccato, L., Corsini, E. M., Fahrion, K., Falcón-Barroso, J., Gadotti, D. A., Iodice, E., Lyubenova, M., Martín-Navarro, I., McDermid, R. M., Morelli, L., Pinna, F., van de Ven, G., de Zeeuw, P. T., & Zhu, L. 2021, The Fornax3D project: Planetary nebulae catalogue and independent distance measurements to Fornax cluster galaxies. AAP, 653, A167.

Spriggs, T. W., Sarzi, M., Napiwotzki, R., Galán-de Anta, P. M., Viaene, S., Nedelchev, B., Coccato, L., Corsini, E. M., de Zeeuw, P. T., Falcón-Barroso, J., Gadotti, D. A., Iodice, E., Lyubenova, M., Martín-Navarro, I., McDermid, R. M., Pinna, F., van de Ven, G., & Zhu, L. 2020, Fornax 3D project: Automated detection of planetary nebulae in the centres of early-type galaxies and first results. AAP, 637, A62.

Tully, R. B., Courtois, H. M., Dolphin, A. E., Fisher, J. R., Héraudeau, P., Jacobs, B. A., Karachentsev, I. D., Makarov, D., Makarova, L., Mitronova, S., Rizzi, L., Shaya, E. J., Sorce, J. G., & Wu, P.-F. 2013, Cosmicflows-2: The Data. AJ, 146(4), 86.

Tully, R. B. & Fisher, J. R. 1988,. Catalog of Nearby Galaxies. Cambridge University Press.

Planetary Nebulae: A Universal Toolbox in the Era of Precision Astrophysics
Proceedings IAU Symposium No. 384, 2025
O. De Marco, A. Zijlstra & R. Szczerba, eds.
doi:10.1017/S1743921324000346

Kinematics of the diffuse intragroup/intracluster light in groups and clusters of galaxies in the Local Universe (within 100 Mpc)

M. Arnaboldi[1] **and O. Gerhard**[2]

[1]European Southern Observatory, Karl-Schwarzschild-Str. 2, 85748 Garching, Germany

[2]Max-Planck-Institut für Extraterrestrische Physik, Giessenbachstr. 1, 85748 Garching, Germany

Abstract. Nearly all intragroup (IGL) and intracluster light (ICL) comes from stars that are not bound to any single galaxy but were formed in galaxies and later unbound from them. Kinematic information on these very low surface brightness structures mostly comes from discrete tracers such as planetary nebulae and globular clusters, showing highly unrelaxed velocity distributions. Cosmological hydrodynamical simulations provide key predictions for the dynamical state of IGL and ICL and find that most IC stars are dissolved from galaxies that subsequently merge with the central galaxy. The increase of the measured velocity dispersion with radius in the outer halos of bright galaxies is a key feature to identify IGL and ICL components. In the local groups and clusters, IGL and ICL are more centrally concentrated than the galaxies, with their typical fractions that are few to ten percent, i.e. significantly lower than the average values in more evolved clusters. The properties of ICPNe, their luminosity functions and specific frequencies were key to further constraint the age (10 Gyr) and the metallicity ($[M/Fe] < -1.0$) of the IC/IGL. The results in the nearby clusters are briefly illustrated.

Keywords. Planetary nebulae: general, galaxies: clusters, galaxies: groups, galaxies: elliptical and lenticular, cD galaxies: halos galaxies: individual: M87

1. Introduction

In our own Milky Way the concept of "stellar populations" characterize their members which differ from each other in various ways, most notably by ages, chemical composition and location. Physical properties, e.g. phase-space, ages and metallicity distributions, of intragroup (IG) and intracluster (IC) light components in groups and clusters within 100 Mpc are key to address the question whether an intragroup/ intracluster light population exists which is distinct in ages/metallicity and kinematics from the stellar population found in the halos of massive galaxies.

The starting point is to be able to constrain the initial dynamic conditions under which these stars were formed (Eggen et al. 1962) from the energies and momenta of the orbits of the IGL/ICL stars.

In dynamically complex and massive structures such as groups and clusters of galaxies, accretion processes and mergers furthermore liberate stars into the so-called intra-group (or intra-cluster) light (IGL/ICL), a diffuse stellar component that is gravitationally bound to the group (or cluster) potential (Zwicky 1937, 1951). As the ICL and IGL formation is intertwined with cluster and group assembly processes, characterising it can provide important constraints on the extended mass assembly in the densest regions of the universe.

As Arnaboldi & Gerhard (2022) present in their recent review, the study of IGL/ICL characterization based on deep photometry defines IGL/ICL through multi-component surface brightness (SB) profiles (e.g. Gonzalez et al. 2005; Rudick et al. 2010; Morishita et al. 2017; Ragusa et al. 2023), or as all the light beyond a fixed SB limit (e.g. Feldmeier et al. 2004a; Mihos et al. 2005; Montes & Trujillo 2018). The ICL surface brightness profile extend from a few to hundreds of kpc (Gonzalez et al. 2005; Morishita et al. 2017), with the typical surface brightness of the IGL/ICL component being one percent of the of the surface brightness of the night sky. The ICL profile gradient or shape varies between clusters (Krick & Bernstein 2007; Kluge et al. 2020; Montes 2022). Ellipticity generally increases with radius, while the position angle sometimes has sharp variations (Gonzalez et al. 2005; Kluge et al. 2021). The transition from the center cluster galaxy (CCG) halo to the ICL/IGL is also characterized by a stronger connection with the clusters, with the latter that can be displaced and more aligned/centered with cluster (Zibetti et al. 2005; Arnaboldi et al. 2012; Kluge et al. 2021).

The ICL fraction in individual clusters varies: 4-21% (in B band, see clusters studied in Krick & Bernstein (2007)), 10-30% (Feldmeier et al. 2004b), 5% in isolated regions of the Virgo cluster (Castro-Rodriguéz et al. 2009) and up to 50% (Bernstein et al. 1995) in a specific field location in the Coma cluster core. The ICL fraction expressed as a number ratio of the light in this component with respect to the light in cluster galaxies is clearly dependent on the radial range investigated and the evolutionary stage of the clusters.

Differently from an imaging/photometry only based definition, an attempt to separate halo and IGL or ICL stars utilizing their different binding energies may provide useful insight. Different binding energies can be translated into differences in the observable line-of-sight velocity distributions (LOSVDs) for ensembles of stars. Those stars bound the gravitational potential of the clusters and thus associated with the ICL or IGL would have broader LOS velocity distributions than any ensemble of halo stars (e.g. Dolag et al. 2010; Cui et al. 2014).

From simulations, the velocity distribution of the star particles in the CCG and ICL is bimodal. Fit by two Maxwellian distributions, with one narrower (colder) for the central galaxy and a broader one (hotter) for the ICL, returns the results that the hotter component drives the "light excess" at large radii. A bonus of the kinematical tagging is that galaxy halo and ICL stars can be separated from their LOSVD at the same spatial location! The spatial and kinematical diversity of halo and ICL/IGL stellar particles corresponds to differences in ages and star formation. ICL/IGL stellar particles in hydro-dynamical cosmological simulations turn out to have different spatial distributions, different star formation history (Kapferer et al. 2010) and to be older (Murante et al. 2004) from those in the CCG halo.

2. PNe as kinematical and population tracers

Measuring the kinematics of faint surface brightness components from integrated-light absorption spectra is very challenging. Therefore, measuring stellar kinematics in the outer haloes and surrounding IGL or ICL of early-type galaxies (ETGs) better relies on discrete tracers, such as planetary nebulae (PNe). PNe are the final stages of intermediate mass stars and their characteristic [OIII] 5007 Å emission-line combined with the absence of a strong stellar continuum make these stars readily identifiable in low surface brightness regions. Once their [OIII] 5007 Å emission is detected in high resolution spectra, it provides the LOS velocity. 2D maps generated from samples of PNe can be used to investigate halos and ICL assembly (Arnaboldi et al. 1996), up to distances of the Coma Cluster ($\sim 100\,$Mpc; Gerhard et al. 2005).

In addition to being excellent tracers of halo and ICL kinematics (Arnaboldi & Gerhard 2010), PN samples may also reveal information about the parent stellar populations. For Local Group galaxies, this can be done with direct abundance measurements (see contribution by by Bhattacharya and Stanghellini, this conference). Still, these measurements are currently not easily accessible for galaxies at larger distances. We return to PN tracers as ensamble of stars and look for correlation among population parameters like the luminosity-specific PN frequency, or α parameter for short, and the PN luminosity function (PNLF) slopes of the ICL/IGL component, selected on the basis of its LOSVD. We refer to the contribution by Hartke, this conference, for the relationship of the ICL/IGL PN populations with the metallicity and ages of the parent resolved stellar population.

In the next section we illustrate the example case of the separation of halo and ICL in the outermost regions of M87 in the Virgo cluster using ICPNe in Sect. 3. We then address the question whether there is an ICL population around M87 which is also distinct from its halo. We then summarise what we learn from this study of IGL/ICL in the nearby cluster and groups in Sect. 4.

3. PNe as tracers of the extended halo in M87 and of the ICL in the core of the Virgo cluster

Since the serendipitous discovery of three ICPNe at $V_{LOS,mean} = 1,400$ kms^{-1} along the LOS of the galaxy M86 (NGC 4406; $v_{sys} = -240$ kms^{-1}) in the Virgo cluster core (Arnaboldi et al. 1996), ICPNe have been used to map both spatial distributions and kinematics of the ICL and IGL component in nearby clusters. Around M87 and in the Virgo cluster core, narrow band imaging (Feldmeier et al. 2004a; Arnaboldi et al. 2002; Aguerri et al. 2005; Longobardi et al. 2013) and spectroscopic follow-up surveys (Arnaboldi et al. 2003, 2004; Doherty et al. 2009) were carried out to constrain the properties of the phase space of the stars at these locations. Information from ICPNe was key to separate the distincts components that contribute to the entwined network of structures visible in the deep images by Mihos et al. (2005).

The ICPN survey carried out with Subaru SuprimeCam (imaging) and Flames at UT2 on the VLT (spectroscopy) delivered 287 spectra for individual PNe (Longobardi et al. 2015a). The sample was analysed including additional 11 v_{LOS} from independent PN spectra measured by Doherty et al. (2009) in the same area, giving a combined total sample of 298 PN v_{LOS}. Interestingly, the entire PN LOSVD displays broad asymmetric wings that cannot be matched by a single Gaussian, see Figure 1. Instead it can be approximated by two Gaussians, one as a narrow component centred at the systemic velocity of M87 ($v_{sys,M87} \simeq 1,300$ kms^{-1}), with $\sigma_{narrow} \sim 300$ kms^{-1}, and a second additional one, much broader, Gaussian with an average velocity at $v_{broad} \simeq 1,000$ kms^{-1} and $\sigma_{broad} \simeq 900$ kms^{-1}. Each PN in the projected phase-space, V_{LOS} vs. R_{major}, around M87 can be assigned a probability to belong either to the narrow Gaussian, i.e. the M87 halo component, or to the broad component, i.e. the ICL. The ICPNe in the Virgo cluster core were thus identified by Longobardi et al. (2015a) via a multi- Gaussian decomposition of their LOSVD. The ICPN sample was later expanded by Longobardi et al. (2018), who added the un-relaxed component that overlaps with the M87 smooth halo in the 40-150 kpc radial range. Using the combined ICPN sample, i.e., ICL from the broad Gaussian ($\sigma_{broad} \simeq 900$ kms^{-1}) in the Virgo core plus the unrelaxed components at the location of the M87 halo (including the crown, Longobardi et al. (2015b)), the resulting ICPN LOSVD is statistically undistinguishable from the LOSVD for satellite galaxies (Longobardi et al. 2018) in the Virgo core region (Binggeli et al. 1993). This approach is

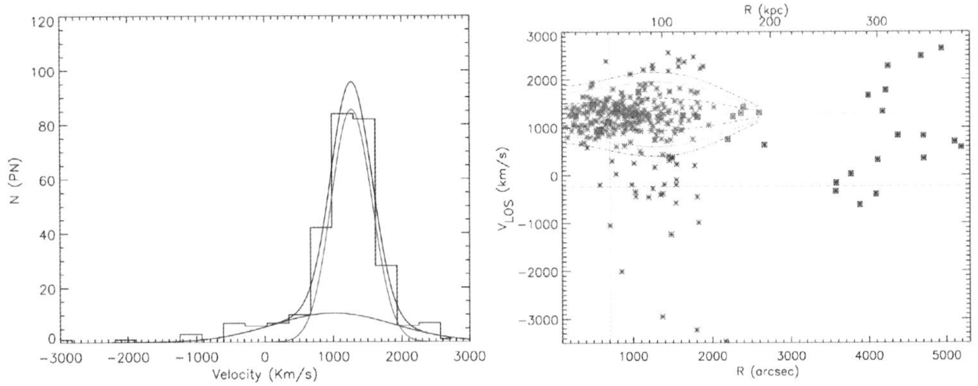

Figure 1. PN velocities tracing the diffuse light around M87 in the Virgo cluster. Left: histogram of the V_{LOS} of the spectroscopically confirmed PNe (black histogram) fitted with a double Gaussian (black curve). Red and blue lines represent the two Gaussians associated with the M 87 halo and the IC components. Right: projected phase-space diagram, V_{LOS} vs. major axis distance from the centre of M 87, for all spectroscopically confirmed PNe in Longobardi et al. (2015a). The major axis distance is given both in arcsec (bottom axis), and in kpc (top axis), where 73 pc = 1". The PNe are classified as M 87 halo PNe (red asterisks) and ICPNe (blue asterisks), respectively; see text. Black squares identify spectroscopically confirmed PNe from Doherty et al. (2009). The smoothed 1, 2, and 2.5σ thresholds are represented by the dashed, dotted, and dot-dashed lines, respectively. The dashed horizontal line shows the M 87 systemic velocity $V_{sys} = 1,275$ kms^{-1}, while the continuous green vertical line shows the effective radius $R_e = 704$" determined by Kormendy et al. (2009). At $V_{LOS} = -220$ kms^{-1}, we plot the M 86 systemic velocity (long dashed line). Image reproduced from Longobardi et al. (2015a) with permission.

the implementation in the observable parameter space of the CCG halo/ICL decomposition of the diffuse stellar component in simulated clusters, as illustrated by Dolag et al. (2010).

3.1. *Distinct spatial distribution for kinematically selected halo and IC PNe in the core of the Virgo cluster*

In M87, the CCG of Virgo sub-cluster A, the V band profile (Kormendy et al. 2009) follows a Sersic profile with high index (n = 10.0), out to 150 kpc major axis distance, with the two furthest photometric points reflecting the additional contribution from the ICL (Mihos et al. 2005). Longobardi et al. (2013) showed that PN distribution can be decomposed into an inner halo component following the Sersic profile and an outer ICL component with 3 times larger PN luminosity specific yield. From the kinematic decomposition described previously, Longobardi et al. (2018) showed that the number density distribution of the PNe identified as the "smooth" M87 halo follow the same Sersic profile as the light, and the ICPN component, which includes the unrelaxed component of the M87 halo and the $\sigma_{broad} = 900$ km^{-1} component, follows a power law distribution $\mu_{ICPNs} \propto R^{\gamma}$ with $\gamma = [-0.79 \pm 0.15]$.

Longobardi et al. (2018) showed that their kinematically separated halo PN and IC PN populations had different PNLFs. The IC PNLF differs from the M 87 halo PNLF by having a small value of the c2 parameter in the generalised PNLF formula (Longobardi et al. 2013) and by the presence of a morphological signature denoted as a "dip" located about $1 - 1.5$ magnitudes below the bright cut-off of the PNLF, see Figure 2. PN population studies relate the presence of this dip to recent star formation (Ciardullo 2010).

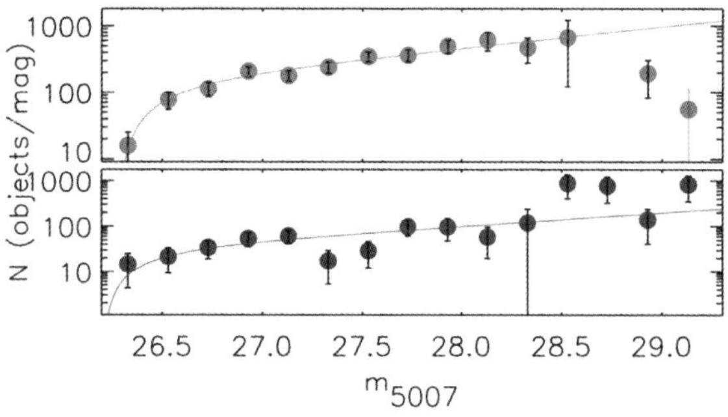

Figure 2. Top: luminosity function of the M 87 halo PNs (red circles) together with the fit of the generalised analytic formula to the halo PNLF, with $c2 = 20.72$ and bright cut-off at magnitude 26.3. After the statistical subtraction of the reassessed ICL component no residual of a dip is seen. Bottom: PNLF for the ICPNs (blue circles). The blue line shows the fit of the generalised analytic formula to the ICPNLF, with $c2 = 0.66$ and bright cut-off magnitude at 26.3. Image reproduced from Longobardi et al. (2018) with permission.

4. What have we learnt on ICL and IGL from studies in the local groups and clusters?

The study of the ICL and IGL in the local groups and clusters in the nearby Universe allows us a privileged view on these components and their phase space properties, which is complementary to the photometric studies carried out for clusters at higher redshifts. In the nearby Universe it is possible to measure the projected phase space-radius and velocity-for a sparse but still significant sample of individual IGL and ICL tracers. Nearby clusters are also within reach of HST, and pointed observations provide specific information on the age and metallicity distribution function of the resolved stellar populations in these clusters and groups. The IGL and ICL surface brightness distributions in the nearby clusters are more centrally concentrated than the azimuthally averaged light of group and cluster galaxies excluding the CCG: by itself it is an indication that stars are gravitationally unbound and added to the group or cluster volume from those galaxies that plunge deeper into the group or cluster potential. The ICL and IGL fractions are a few to ten percent of the light in cluster and group galaxies. These fractions are lower than those measured in more concentrated, dynamically evolved clusters at larger distances. The ICL stars are not bound to a single galaxy, but by the cluster or group potential (Murante et al. 2007). The binding energy of the ICL may, in fact, be a continuum depending on the whether the cluster is relaxed/compact or affected by sub-cluster mergers. From the measured color-magnitude diagrams of resolved stellar populations in deep HST images, the theoretical stellar evolution models suggest that the IC population is dominated by stars with old ages (≥ 10 Gyr) with a significant number of very metal-poor stars ($[Fe/H] < -1.5$) (Williams et al. 2007). See also the very recent results on the color gradients in the ICL towards bluer color in intermediate redshift ($0.2 - 0.8$) clusters (Golden-Marx et al. 2023). To conclude, the selection based on the kinematics returns distinct stellar population properties supporting the presence of an IGL/ICL population which is different from those of the CCG halos.

Both the observations and the simulations show that the ICL *in-situ* star formation from gas in clusters (Peng et al. 2010) is not an important channel, see discussion in Contini (2021). But it does happen: see the tidally stripped gas in the Virgo core (Oosterloo & van Gorkom 2005) and the isolated HII around NGC 4388 (Gerhard et al. 2002). Hence the majority of IC stars in the nearby groups and clusters were formed in galaxies and then unbound in the cluster space.

Acknowledgements

MAR would like to thank the organisers of IAU Symposium 384 for the invitation to present this work and for the stimulating conference.

References

Aguerri, J. A. L., Gerhard, O. E., Arnaboldi, M., et al. 2005, AJ, 129, 2585
Arnaboldi, M., Aguerri, J. A. L., Napolitano, N. R., et al. 2002, AJ, 123, 760
Arnaboldi, M., Freeman, K. C., Mendez, R. H., et al. 1996, ApJ, 472, 145
Arnaboldi, M., Freeman, K. C., Okamura, S., et al. 2003, AJ, 125, 514
Arnaboldi, M. & Gerhard, O. 2010, Highlights of Astronomy, 15, 97
Arnaboldi, M. & Gerhard, O. 2022, Frontiers in Astronomy and Space Sciences, 9, 403
Arnaboldi, M., Gerhard, O., Aguerri, J. A. L., et al. 2004, ApJ, 614, L33
Arnaboldi, M., Ventimiglia, G., Iodice, E., Gerhard, O., & Coccato, L. 2012, A&A, 545, A37
Bernstein, G. M., Nichol, R. C., Tyson, J. A., Ulmer, M. P., & Wittman, D. 1995, AJ, 110, 1507
Binggeli, B., Popescu, C. C., & Tammann, G. A. 1993, A&AS, 98, 275
Castro-Rodriguéz, N., Arnaboldi, M., Aguerri, J. A. L., et al. 2009, A&A, 507, 621
Ciardullo, R. 2010, PASA, 27, 149
Contini, E. 2021, Galaxies, 9, 60
Cui, W., Murante, G., Monaco, P., et al. 2014, MNRAS, 437, 816
Doherty, M., Arnaboldi, M., Das, P., et al. 2009, A&A, 502, 771
Dolag, K., Murante, G., & Borgani, S. 2010, MNRAS, 405, 1544
Eggen, O. J., Lynden-Bell, D., & Sandage, A. R. 1962, ApJ, 136, 748
Feldmeier, J. J., Ciardullo, R., Jacoby, G. H., & Durrell, P. R. 2004a, ApJ, 615, 196
Feldmeier, J. J., Mihos, J. C., Morrison, H. L., et al. 2004b, ApJ, 609, 617
Gerhard, O., Arnaboldi, M., Freeman, K. C., et al. 2005, ApJ, 621, L93
Gerhard, O., Arnaboldi, M., Freeman, K. C., & Okamura, S. 2002, ApJ, 580, L121
Golden-Marx, J. B., Zhang, Y., Ogando, R. L. C., et al. 2023, MNRAS, 521, 478
Gonzalez, A. H., Zabludoff, A. I., & Zaritsky, D. 2005, ApJ, 618, 195
Kapferer, W., Schindler, S., Knollmann, S. R., & van Kampen, E. 2010, A&A, 516, A41
Kluge, M., Bender, R., Riffeser, A., et al. 2021, ApJS, 252, 27
Kluge, M., Neureiter, B., Riffeser, A., et al. 2020, ApJS, 247, 43
Kormendy, J., Fisher, D. B., Cornell, M. E., & Bender, R. 2009, ApJS, 182, 216
Krick, J. E. & Bernstein, R. A. 2007, AJ, 134, 466
Longobardi, A., Arnaboldi, M., Gerhard, O., et al. 2013, A&A, 558, A42
Longobardi, A., Arnaboldi, M., Gerhard, O., & Hanuschik, R. 2015a, A&A, 579, A135
Longobardi, A., Arnaboldi, M., Gerhard, O., & Mihos, J. C. 2015b, A&A, 579, L3
Longobardi, A., Arnaboldi, M., Gerhard, O., Pulsoni, C., & Söldner-Rembold, I. 2018, A&A, 620, A111
Mihos, J. C., Harding, P., Feldmeier, J., & Morrison, H. 2005, ApJ, 631, L41
Montes, M. 2022, Nature Astronomy, 6, 308
Montes, M. & Trujillo, I. 2018, MNRAS, 474, 917
Morishita, T., Abramson, L. E., Treu, T., et al. 2017, ApJ, 846, 139
Murante, G., Arnaboldi, M., Gerhard, O., et al. 2004, ApJ, 607, L83
Murante, G., Giovalli, M., Gerhard, O., et al. 2007, MNRAS, 377, 2
Oosterloo, T. & van Gorkom, J. 2005, A&A, 437, L19
Peng, C. Y., Ho, L. C., Impey, C. D., & Rix, H.-W. 2010, AJ, 139, 2097
Ragusa, R., Iodice, E., Spavone, M., et al. 2023, A&A, 670, L20
Rudick, C. S., Mihos, J. C., Harding, P., et al. 2010, ApJ, 720, 569
Williams, B. F., Ciardullo, R., Durrell, P. R., et al. 2007, ApJ, 656, 756
Zibetti, S., White, S. D. M., Schneider, D. P., & Brinkmann, J. 2005, MNRAS, 358, 949
Zwicky, F. 1937, ApJ, 86, 217
Zwicky, F. 1951, PASP, 63, 61

Planetary Nebulae: A Universal Toolbox in the Era of Precision Astrophysics
Proceedings IAU Symposium No. 384, 2025
O. De Marco, A. Zijlstra & R. Szczerba, eds.
doi:10.1017/S1743921325000961

A new population of stars between the LMC and the MW revealed by post-AGB stars

Iker González Santamaría[1], Óscar Jiménez-Arranz[2], Minia Manteiga[3], Arturo Manchado[3], Eva Villaver[3], Merce Romero[2] and Xavi Luri[3]

[1]University of A Coruña, Spain

[2]University of Barcelona, Spain

[3]Instituto de Astrofísica de Canarias, Spain
email: `minia.manteiga@udc.es`

Abstract. Gaia astrometry was used to explore the properties of Galactic Post-AGB stars in the literature. DR3 precise parallaxes allowed us to isolate a small group of stars in the direction of the Large Magellanic Cloud (LMC) previously reported as post-AGB stars in the LMC, but that, according to their distances, seem to be located in an intermediate region between the LMC and the Galaxy. In order to verify this, we have used a classifier that allows us to evaluate the probability of a star belonging to the Milky Way (MW) or the LMC. This classifier is based on an Artificial Neural Network (ANN) algorithm and is fed with the astrometry and photometry published in DR3. In this presentation, we study the membership probabilities of several samples of stars in the direction of the LMC. As a result, we have obtained that around 25-30% of stars in our samples, suspected to belong to the LMC, have indeed low probabilities of belonging to either one galaxy or the other. On the contrary, they seem to be located in an intermediate region between the two galaxies. We also analysed the radial velocity distributions of the different samples and the location of the stars in a colour-magnitude diagram. APOGEE data was also used to study the chemical abundances of stars in the different regions (LMC, MW, and intermediate population).

Keywords. LMC – stellar populations – post-AGB stars – machine learning

1. Introduction

The gravitational interaction between the Milky Way (MW) and the Large Magellanic Cloud (LMC) seems to be responsible for the existence of stellar populations and streams of gas and dust in intermediate locations between both galaxies (Chandra et al. 2023, Vasiliev 2023). Such stars could have been released from the LMC in the past due to the MW gravitational influence. Gaia accurate astrometric and photometric data and machine learning techniques, make it possible to search for them and confirm their origin.

2. Catalogue of post-AGB stars

In previous work, González-Santamaría et al. (2023), we studied galactic post-AGB stars' properties by using Gaia DR3. Gaia astrometry allowed us to derive distances and luminosities which were used to disclose post-AGB stars from stars in other evolutive stages and build a comprehensive and accurate catalogue of objects in this quite elusive late evolutionary phase. To do so, we started gathering all post-AGB candidates from the literature: the online† Torun catalogue of galactic post-AGB stars

† `https://fox.ncac.torun.pl/camkweb/postagb2.php`

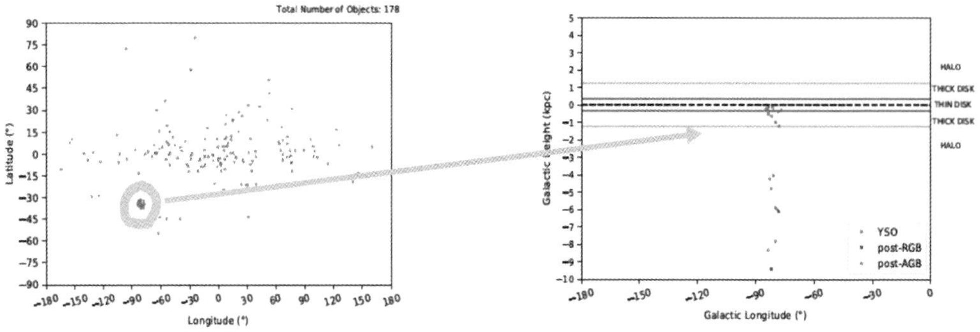

Figure 1. Galactic distribution of the 178 stars (left) and galactic height of the 21 stars in LMC direction (right).

(Szczerba et al. 2012), the spectroscopic atlas of post-AGB and planetary nebulae by Suárez et al. (2006) and Simbad astronomical database.

By applying an astrometric quality filtering (parallax and distance relative uncertainties below 30% and Renormalised Unit Weight Error, RUWE, below 1.4), we ended up with a sample of 178 post-AGB candidates with accurate parameters in Gaia DR3. Next, we calculated the luminosity of these objects in order to be able to discern between post-AGB stars and other similar objects such as supergiants, post-Red Giant Branch (post-RGB) stars, or Young Stellar Objects (YSO).

The galactic distribution of these stars showed a small group of 21 objects in the direction of the LMC (as shown in Fig. 1) that remain in our astrometric filtered sample. We then calculated their galactic height obtaining two separated populations: one of them composed of 11 galactic objects, possibly YSOs, all with galactic heights below 2 kpc, and the other formed by 10 post-AGB, or possibly some post-RGB stars according to their luminosities, with galactic heights beyond 4 kpc.

In conclusion, we found a small population of post-AGB candidates that, according to Gaia DR3 distances (estimated by a statistical method developed by Bailer-Jones et al. 2021), are all located in an intermediate region between the MW and the LMC. These stars share proper motions, which are very similar to those of LMC stars.

3. ANN classifier for MW and LMC stars

With the aim of clarifying the location of these objects in the LMC direction, we used the algorithm developed by Jiménez-Arranz et al. (2023) that allows us to classify objects as members of either the MW or the LMC on the basis of their Gaia astrometry and photometry. This algorithm is based on an Artificial Neural Network (ANN) with an architecture of three hidden as shown in Figure 2. The input layer contains the following parameters: RA (α), Dec (δ), parallax (ω), parallax error (σ_ω), proper motion in R.A. and its error ($\mu\alpha*$ and $\sigma_{\mu\alpha*}$), proper motion in Dec. and its error ($\mu\delta$ and $\sigma_{\mu\delta}$), and the three Gaia photometric magnitudes (G, G_{BP}, G_{RP}).

A probability value of 0 indicates that the object belongs to the MW with a probability of 100% and a value of 1 means that the object belongs to the LMC with a probability of 100%. In practice, we will consider that a source is in the LMC if it has a probability higher than 0.9, and in the MW if it is lower than 0.1. For the remaining probabilities, we will assume that the object is located in an intermediate region between both galaxies.

When we ran this algorithm over the 10 post-AGB stars mentioned before, we obtained that while six of them are indeed located in the LMC, the remaining four objects are located in the intermediate region. In order to shed more light on this possible intermediate population (IP), we ran the algorithm over the following two samples of stars

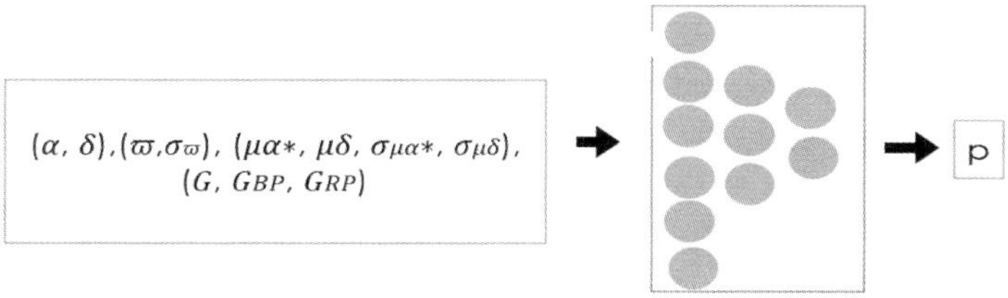

Figure 2. Classifier based on an ANN algorithm which, based on Gaia astrometric and photometric measurements, gives the probability of a source belonging to the LMC or to the MW.

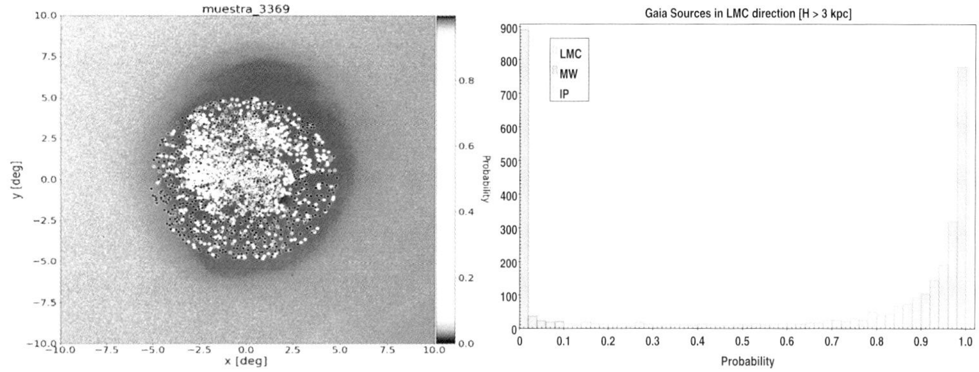

Figure 3. Spatial distribution of the 3369 objects in the Gaia sample (left) and their corresponding probabilities distribution (right).

located within the LMC region in the sky: a sample of sources with high-quality astrometry in Gaia DR3 and a sample of stars within the LMC direction with measurements and derived abundances from the APOGEE survey.

3.1. *Gaia DR3 sample*

To build this sample we started by selecting all Gaia DR3 sources located in a radius of 5 degrees around the coordinates of the LMC (RA:80.8958, Dec:-69.7561), obtaining a total of more than 21 million sources. We discarded those sources without known parallaxes in Gaia and kept only objects with high astrometric quality (parallax and distances errors below 30% and RUWE value below 1.4) obtaining a sample of 266,440 sources. Finally, we also discarded those objects with a galactic height below 3 kpc, as they should be located within the MW. So, we ended up with a sample of 3369 objects (which includes the 10 post-AGB candidates). If we run the classifier over this sample, we obtain the following results:

- 1533 objects in the LMC [46%]
- 988 objects in the MW [29%]
- 845 objects in the intermediate region [25%]

In the left panel of Fig. 3 we show the spatial distribution of the sample over the LMC region as well as the membership probabilities color-coded according to the probability distribution shown on the right.

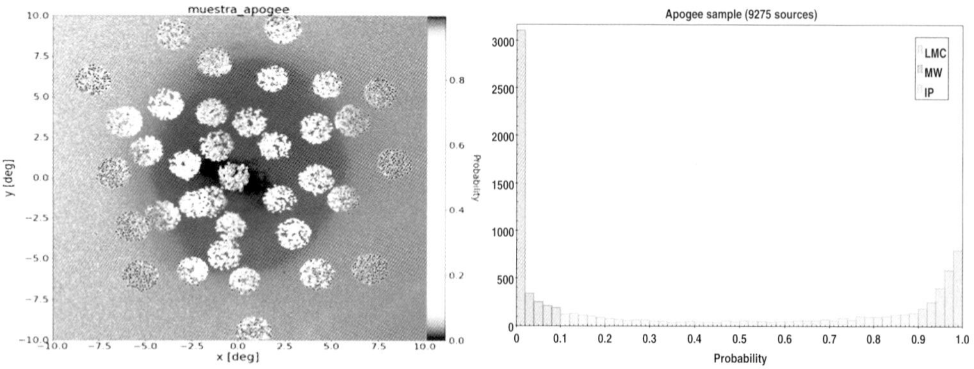

Figure 4. Spatial distribution of the 9273 objects in the APOGEE sample (left) and their corresponding probabilities distribution (right).

3.2. *APOGEE sample*

APOGEE DR17 survey includes observations of 9273 sources in the LMC direction with elementary chemical abundances and radial velocities derived by the survey pipeline. Concretely, the chemical abundances provided are: [M/H], [α/Fe], [C/Fe], [Cl/Fe], [O/Fe], [Mg/Fe], [Si/Fe], [Ca/Fe], [Fe/H] and [Ni/Fe]. Applying the classifier over this sample we obtained (Figure 4):

- 2234 objects in the LMC [24%]
- 4104 objects in the MW [44%]
- 2910 objects in the intermediate region [31%]

The proportion of objects located in the IP is quite similar to that obtained previously with the Gaia DR3 sources. The left panel of Fig. 3 shows the spatial distribution of the sample as well as the probabilities of memberships following the color code shown in the probability distribution on the right.

3.3. *Other post-AGB samples*

In view of the results obtained, it could be also interesting to run this classifier over other literature samples of post-AGB stars in the LMC direction. One of these samples is the one by Van Aarle et al. (2011), where they presented a sample of 144 bright LMC post-AGB stars. If we apply the classifier, we obtain that while 61% of the objects are located in the LMC, 11% of objects would belong to the MW, and the remaining 28% are located in the IP. In the left panel of Fig. 5 we show the probability distribution of such a sample.

Another LMC post-AGB sample is the one presented by Kamath et al. (2015). In this work, they analyse a sample of 33 objects. We can confirm that 76% of those stars are indeed located in the LMC, while the remaining 24% would be in an IP. The probability distribution given by the algorithm in this case is shown in the right panel of Fig. 5.

4. Analysis of radial velocities, HR diagram, and chemical abundances

In order to complement the results of the classifier, we analysed other available properties such as their radial velocities, and compared them with the radial velocities distributions in the LMC and in the MW.

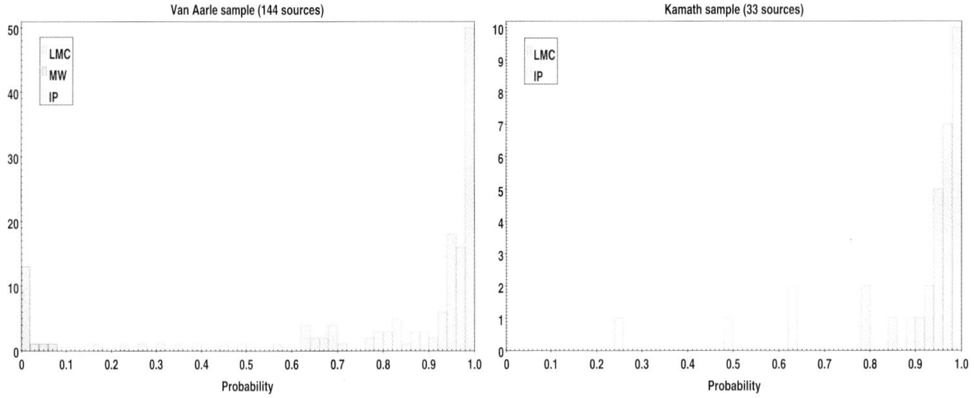

Figure 5. Probability distribution of the objects in Van Aarle et al. (2011) (left) and in Kamath et al. (2015) (right).

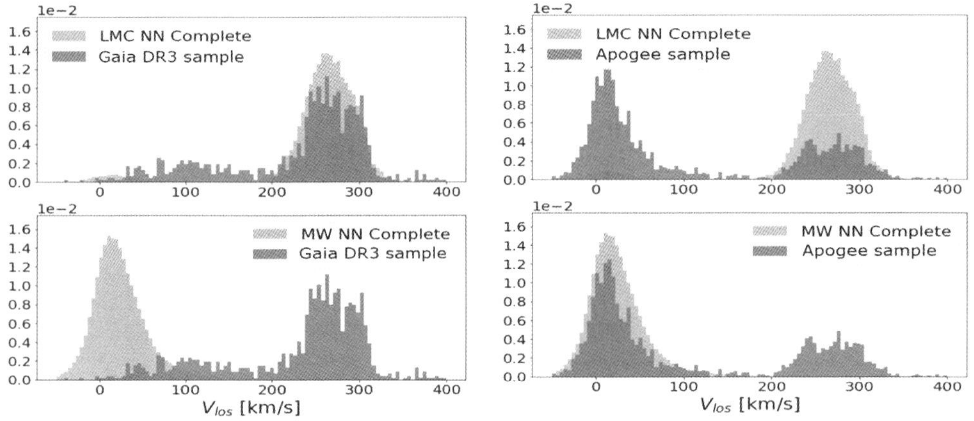

Figure 6. Radial velocities distribution of stars in Gaia sample (left) and in APOGEE sample (right), compared with radial velocities in the LMC (up) and MW (bottom) samples of stars.

The left panels of Fig. 6 show Gaia DR3 sample velocities as compared with that of the LMC stars (upper panel) as well as those of the MW (lower panel). The right panels show the same for the APOGEE sample. While stars in the Gaia sample display a similar distribution as those stars located in the LMC, stars in the APOGEE sample display a distribution closer to that of the MW stars. The distribution of radial velocities of the Gaia sample shows an overdensity of stars around radial velocities of about 100 Km/s, which seems rather peculiar.

It is also interesting to compare the location of the stars in a colour ($G_{BP} - G_{RP}$) vs magnitude (G) diagram (CMD). In the first and third columns of Fig. 7, we have plotted the CMD diagrams obtained for both the LMC (upper figure) as well as for the MW (lower figure) stars in the classifiers training sample as a reference. The second column shows the same CMDs together with sample 1 stars (Gaia sample) and the fourth together with sample 2 stars (APOGEE sample). The stars are color-coded according to their probabilities of membership, being the stars in the IP in white color, those in the MW brown coloured, and those in the LMC in green. While some IP stars are located in regions scarcely populated with MW or LMC stars, there are also stars located in regions with overdensities of LMC stars.

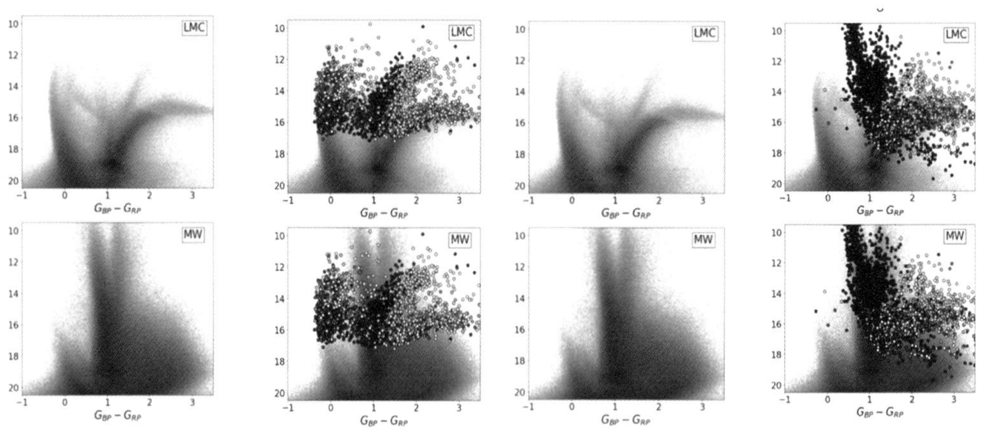

Figure 7. $G_{BP} - G_{RP}$ vs G magnitude diagrams of the Gaia sample (left) and APOGEE sample (right). In the background are plotted the diagrams of the LMC (upper) and the MW (lower).

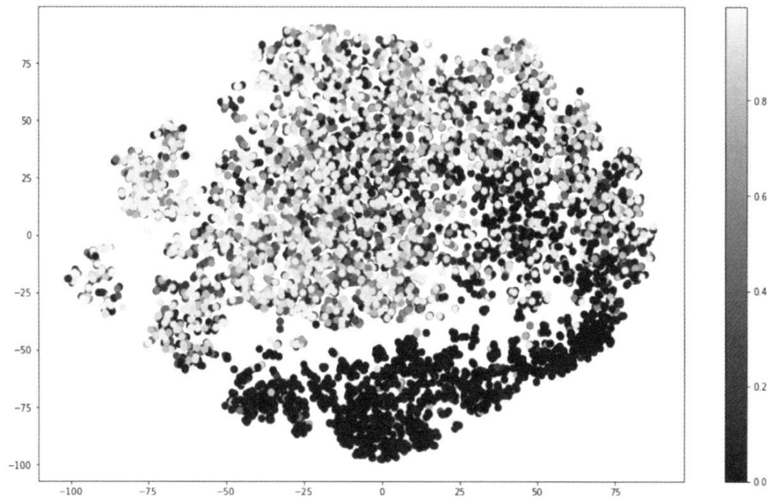

Figure 8. t-SNE clustering of chemical abundances in sample 2 stars (APOGEE sample).

We also carried out an analysis of the chemical abundances using APOGEE measurements. To do so, we ran a t-distributed stochastic neighbour embedding (t-SNE) test on the individual elementary abundances data of sample 2, and colored the obtained distribution according to the classification probability label. t-SNE is a statistical method for visualising high-dimensional data by giving each data point a location in a two-dimensional map. The result of the clustering is shown in Fig. 8.

It can be appreciated that while a subsample of MW objects ($P<0.1$) are clearly clustered apart, stars from LMC ($P>0.9$) and from the IP ($0.1<P<0.9$) are clustered approximately together.

5. Conclusions

(1) Gaia astrometry + photometry allows building a classifier that separates LMC stars from background MW stars.
(2) About 25-30% of Post-AGB stars in the LMC direction have low probabilities of membership to the LMC and seem to form an Intermediate Population.

(3) This result is supported by additional samples of non-superluminous stars
(4) A fraction of the line of sight velocities seems also peculiar.
(5) Chemical abundances are indistinguishable from those in the LMC.

6. Acknowledgements

This work has made use of data from the European Space Agency (ESA) Gaia mission. The authors thank financial support from Spanish Ministry grants PID2021-122842OB-C22 and PID2021-122842OB-C21.

References

Chandra, V., Naidu, R. P., Conroy C., 2023, arXiv e-prints. doi:10.48550/arXiv.2306.15719

González-Santamaría I., Manteiga M., Manchado A., Ulla A., Dafonte C., 2023, *A&A*, (*under revision*)

Jiménez-Arranz Ó., Romero-Gómez M., Luri X., et al., 2023, *A&A*, 669, A91

Kamath D., Wood P. R., Van Winckel H, 2015, *MNRAS* 454, Issue 2, pp. 1468-1502

Suárez, O. and García-Lario P., Manchado A., et al., 2006, *A&A*, 458, Issue 1, pp. 173-180

Szczerba, R., Siódmiak, N., Stasińska, G., et al., 2012, Planetary Nebulae: An Eye to the Future, Proceedings of the International Astronomical Union, IAU Symposium, Volume 283, pp. 506-507

Van Aarle E., van Winckel H., Lloyd Evans T., 2011, *A&A*, 530, A90

Bailer-Jones C. A. L., Rybizki J., Fouesneau M., Demleitner, M., Andrae, R., 2021, *AJ* 161, 147

Vasiliev E., 2023, Galaxies, Vol. 2, p. 59

Planetary Nebulae: A Universal Toolbox in the Era of Precision Astrophysics
Proceedings IAU Symposium No. 384, 2025
O. De Marco, A. Zijlstra & R. Szczerba, eds.
doi:10.1017/S1743921323005203

Diverse Science from VLT imagery and spectroscopy of PNe in the Galactic Bulge

Quentin A. Parker[1], **Shuyu Tan**[1], **Andreas Ritter**[1] **and Albert Zijlstra**[2]

[1]Laboratory for space research, University of Hong Kong, HK SAR PRC

[2]Manchester University, U.K.
email: quentinp@hku.hk

Abstract. We have undertaken a deep investigation of a well defined sample of 136 PNe located in a 10×10 degree central region of the Galactic Bulge observed with the ESO VLT and supplemented by archival HST images. These studies have provided precise morphologies, major axes position angles and the most robust sample of consistently derived chemical abundances available to date. Using these data we have statistically confirmed, at 5σ, the precise PNe population that provides the PNe alignment of major axes previously suggested in the Galactic Bulge, revealed a partial solution to the sulfur anomaly and uncovered interesting morphological, abundance and kinematic features. We summarise the most significant findings here with detailed results appearing in a series of related publications.

Keywords. planetary nebulae, wide-field surveys, statistical analysis

1. Introduction

There are currently ~ 3800 Galactic planetary nebulae (PNe) known as recorded in the HASH database, e.g. Parker et al. (2016) with half arising from discoveries over the last 25 years by our group, e.g. Parker et al. (2006), Miszalski et al. (2008), Sabin et al. (2014). These PNe have been found in crowded, wide-field, narrow-band Hα surveys in the Galactic plane including the Galactic Bulge. Here we present summary results from our ESO VLT narrow-band imagery for PNe located in the inner 10×10 degree region of the Galactic bulge selected to be highly likely physical bulge members. This is based on the criteria detailed in Rees & Zijlstra (2013). The 136 original targets were spectroscopically obtained using FORS2 on the ESO 8.2m VLT between 2015 and 2019 for PIs Rees, Zijlstra and Parker using the same instrumental configurations and observing strategies. We believe this represents the most self-consistent and well characterised sample of PNe available with high S/N spectra, from which well-determined spectroscopic properties and deep analysis can be performed. FORS2 narrow-band pre-imaging was also obtained and supplemented by 40 objects previously observed with *HST*. These data have provided the basis for several detailed investigations either recently published, in press or about to be submitted. Selected scientific results that emerged are summarised conveniently below.

2. The bulge PNe morphology, central stars and kinematic ages project

Our high quality VLT pre-imaging and, when available, HST imagery, shows that a large fraction (68%) of our compact bulge sample are bipolars Tan et al. (2023a). The increase in the fraction of bipolar PNe comprising our bulge sample is very significant for

Figure 1. Example of a PN (PHR1150-6704, HASH # 2722) where the correct CSPN is clear in the HASH imagery but has been incorrectly identified from Gaia data.

a population ostensibly dominated by older stars. If bipolars generally derive from higher mass progenitors, as inferred by their preponderance at lower Galactic scale heights in the Galactic disk, as well as being in binaries, then that would suggest a significant, young stellar population in the bulge feeding the observed population today. They dominate all PNe emerging from the general, several Giga year old bulge stellar population.

Four new planetary nebula central stars are also identified which are not in *Gaia*. Some 11 putative central stars previously reported, based on *Gaia* positions, are now shown not to be the true central star, refer Figure 1 for an example. Furthermore, *Gaia* central stars reported in the literature are often based on the overall centroid position of a very compact planetary nebula rather than the actual central star within it that is often below Gaia limits. We find that 15% of *Gaia* CSPN identified by (Chornay & Walton 2021) are not confirmed. Great care is needed when using *Gaia* CSPN compilations and we strongly recommend using the HASH database† Parker et al. (2016) for such studies where every CSPN listed has been holistically vetted. HASH consolidates and federates available multi-wavelength imaging, spectroscopic and other data for Galactic PNe.

We also provided in Tan et al. (2023a) the most complete and accurate kinematic age estimates for our compact bulge PNe ever compiled. This included *Gaia* distances for 33, accurate expansion velocities for 77, improved angular size determinations for all (from the HST, VLT and Pan-STARRS imagery) and average distance and expansion velocities for the rest. The expected young age of the PNe sample is confirmed with an average kinematic age of $6{,}400 \pm 3{,}800$ years. Kinematically older PNe are dominated by bipolars with 14/16 PNe with estimated ages >10,000 years being bipolars (refer Figure 2). The best current work also puts the short-period binary fraction of bulge PNe at 15-20% - maximum 60% in bipolars (Miszalski et al. 2009), giving 9-12% of PNe in binaries are bipolars. This is a factor of up to 7 lower than the bipolar fraction we find. A younger stellar population in the bulge, wider period binaries and the relationship between PN formation and the CSPN binarity may play a role but the issue of the progenitor masses of bipolars remains.

† HASH: available online `http://www.hashpn.space`

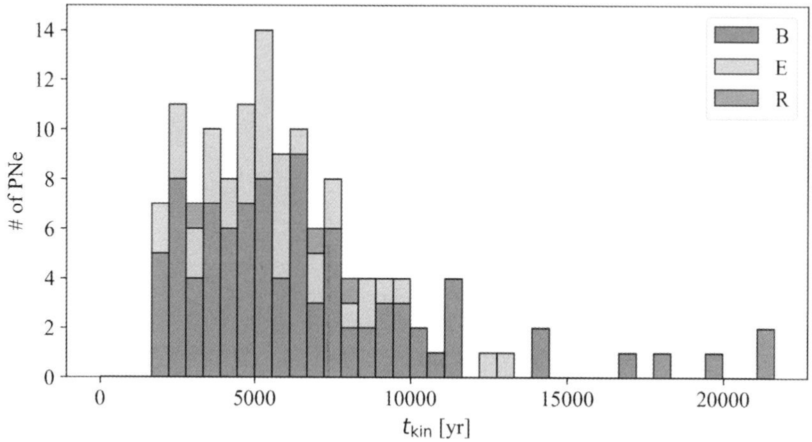

Figure 2. Distribution of kinematic ages determined for our bulge PNe. Histograms are color-coded according to the main morphological classes.

3. The bulge PN major axes alignment project

We have recently reported a 5σ PNe major axes alignment, almost parallel to the Galactic plane, for a subset of bulge PNe that host, or are inferred to host, short period binaries (Tan et al. 2023b). Almost all are bipolar. It is only this very particular PNe sub-population that gives this result compared to the much weaker statistical alignments reported previously for PNe in the bulge where this signal is diluted (refer Figure 3). We now have clear, irrefutable evidence of a organised and long lived process at play at the centre of our Galaxy for this particular PNe subgroup. Not only that but it has to have endured over cosmologically significant time periods given the age differences estimated for several PNe in the sample (Tan et al. 2023b) that emerge from stars of different progenitor mass. The only plausible mechanism that could affect multiple close binary star orbits across large volumes of the Galaxy, as revealed by the observed major axes orientations of their eventual PNe, is thought to be magnetic fields. We speculate that PNe forming from wider binaries could have their symmetry axes change over time more randomly due to the ambient field where directions may evolve due to Galactic wind or bulk ISM motions. This provides a possible explanation for the observed alignment only being seen in post-CE binary PNe. If this is the process then it must remain ordered, potent and have endured for billions of years. The only alternative is a pervasive force (magnetic?) acting currently only on the PNe bipolar lobe ejection mechanism that host short-period binaries. This must be sufficiently strong to align Galactic Position Angles (GPAs, see (Tan et al. 2023b) for definition) over entire Galactic bulge in only a few thousand years which seems unlikely as current Galactic magnetic field strengths are too weak.

4. The bulge PN abundance project

We have obtained well determined chemical abundances for 124 PNe in the Galactic bulge from our VLT data together with logarithmic extinctions and plasma diagnostics of n_e and T_e. Prior to our work there were about ~ 240 bulge PNe with chemical abundances determined over the last 50 years and of very variable quality. For 34 we have now determined abundances for the first time which alone adds $\sim$14% to the available sample of bulge PNe abundances. We have significantly improved the accuracy and reliability of the rest. Interstellar reddening, physical conditions (e.g. electron densities, n_e, temperatures, T_e), and chemical compositions are derived for each PN using a variety

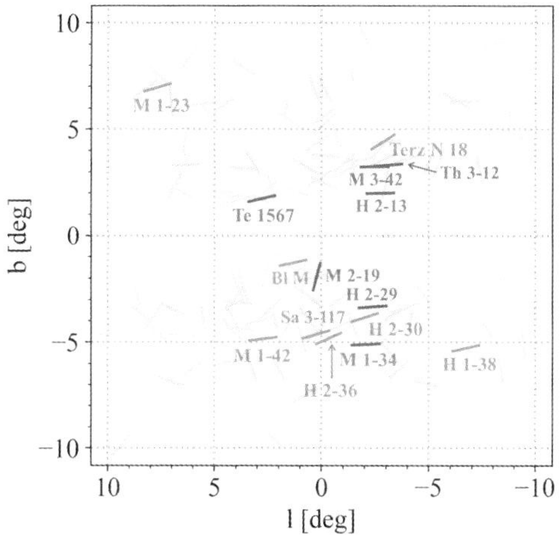

Figure 3. Distribution of measured GPAs for our bulge PNe. Grey vectors are the general sample, those with confirmed binary central stars are blue vectors and those with high abundance discrepancy factors, *adfs* (that are taken as a reliable proxy for PNe hosting short-period binaries) are pink vectors. M 1-34, suspected of hosting a short period binary, is plotted with a green vector.

of line diagnostics. Comparisons with the best available literature values for 75 PNe in common shows that our significant new data are reliable, robust and internally self-consistent. They represent the largest well understood and high quality compilation of PNe abundances currently available. Our VLT low-to-medium resolution spectroscopic observations exhibit excellent consistency with previous high-resolution spectra with 2-m class telescope, demonstrating the reliability of weak line detection, the line deblending methods and our line flux measurement, particularly for weak recombination lines. Our abundance compilation, which adopted updated atomic data and ionisation correction factor (ICF) schemes introduced in (Delgado et al. 2014), results in overall higher abundances of alpha elements than solar compared to the general abundance pattern in the literature. The lockstep behavior of alpha elements, which was less evident in previous studies, is clearly observed in our results. In Figure 4 we plot [O III] line ratios for 100 PNe from our sample. It is clear our data consistency provides solid confidence in the reliability and quality of our data and its reduction and hence for our abundances.

5. The PN sulfur anomaly project

We have undertaken a detailed investigation of the so-called "sulfur anomaly" (Tan & Parker, submitted). This is a long-standing puzzle that has perplexed astronomers for decades. The anomaly for PNe was first identified by (Henry et al. 2004). Sulfur is expected to be in lockstep with other α elements like oxygen, neon, argon, and chlorine in more massive stars, so its cosmic abundance should also be proportional. Strong correlations of [S/H] and [O/H] are seen in H II regions and blue compact galaxies. However, PNe sulfur abundances, which arise from low-to-intermediate mass progenitors, have consistently been lower, giving rise to the sulfur anomaly. ICFs have suggested to be a potential suspect (Reichel et al. 2022).

Our analysis uses our robust VLT based bulge PNe chemical abundances. With our significantly improved accuracy and reduced abundance uncertainties and by using argon as a superior PNe metallicity indicator, we show that the sulfur anomaly is reduced and better constrained. Furthermore, for the first time, we demonstrate sulfur α-element lockstep behaviour in PNe with both oxygen and argon. Our work dispels earlier hypotheses

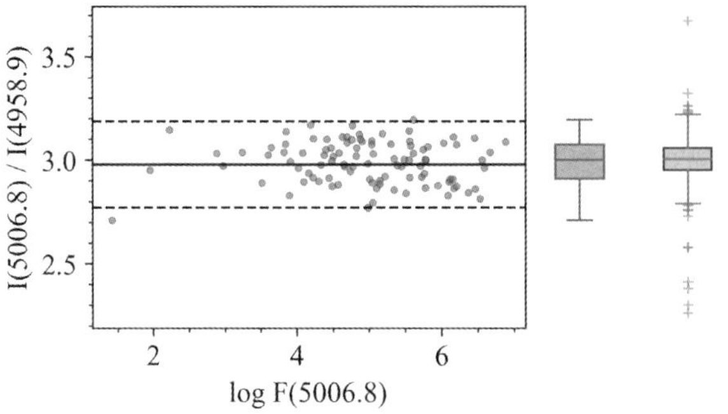

Figure 4. Comparison of flux ratios of our measured de-reddened [O III] lines with theoretical values with their line ratios plotted against the [O III] $\lambda5007$ flux in 10^{-16}erg cm^{-2}s^{-1} on a log scale. The black line is the theoretical line ratio value of 2.98 while the dashed lines indicate 7% deviation for typical uncertainties. The right shows box plots that compare our results (blue) with those for 124 Galactic PNe from Rodriguez (2020) (grey). The boxes depict the 25th to 75th percentiles, with the median indicated by a horizontal line. The whiskers extend to the 10th and 90th percentile, while outliers are represented by individual crosses. The results show excellent agreement to within 7% errors and no bias as a function of flux.

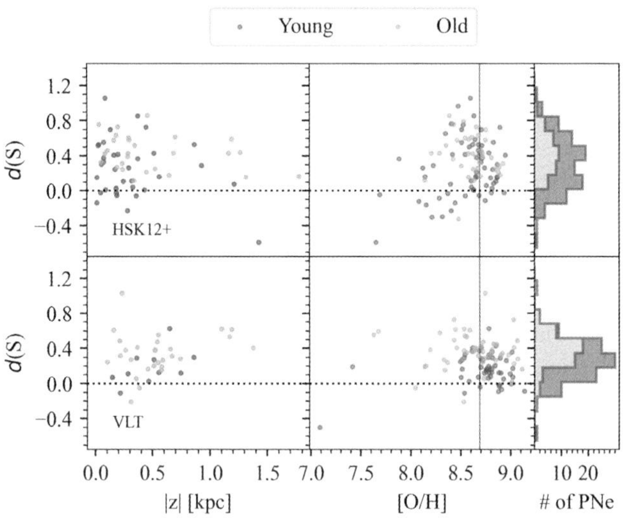

Figure 5. A combined figure for sulfur deficit $d(\mathrm{S})$ on the vertical axis for the HSK12+ sample (top row) and VLT sample (bottom row) against i) absolute height above the Galactic plane '$|z|$' in kpc, ii) [O/H] and iii) stacked histograms of $d(\mathrm{S})$ values with bin size 0.15 dex. The Galactic disk and bulge PNe samples are color-coded to their basic age group from criteria outlined in Paper V with green indicating young and orange old progenitor stars. The middle panel red vertical line indicates solar oxygen abundance.

that the anomaly originates from underestimation of higher sulfur ionization stages. Using a machine learning approach, we reveal that earlier ICF schemes contributed to the anomaly. We also identify a correlation between the sulfur anomaly and the age/mass of PNe progenitors, with the anomaly being either absent or significantly reduced in PNe with young progenitors (refer Figure 5). Despite inherent challenges and uncertainties, we link this relationship to PNe dust chemistry, noting those with carbon-dust chemistry exhibit a more pronounced anomaly. By integrating these findings, we provide a plausible explanation for the residual sulfur anomaly and propose its potential as an indicator of relative age compositions in galaxies based on their PNe observations.

6. Summary

We have used a well defined sample of 136 PNe carefully selected to be members of the Galactic Bulge and consistently observed with the same instrumentation and set-up on the 8m ESO VLT. The resulting high-quality data has been used to undertake a series of investigations covering morphological distribution, central star identification and kinematic ages (Tan et al. 2023a), major axes orientation (Tan et al. 2023b), abundance determinations, Tan et al. (in press) and the sulfur anomaly (Tan & Parker, 2023, submitted). These studies have resulted in some important findings:

• 68% of our bulge sample are bipolars. This is significant for a population ostensibly dominated by old stars. If bipolars emerge from higher mass progenitors, and are in binaries there has to be a young stellar bulge population feeding the observed population we see today.

• 15% of *Gaia* CSPN identified by (Chornay & Walton 2021) are incorrect.

• We provide the most complete and accurate kinematic age estimates for our compact bulge PNe ever compiled.

• The expected young age of the compact bulge PNe sample is confirmed with an average kinematic age of 6,400 $\pm$ 3,800 years.

• Kinematically older PNe are dominated by bipolars with 14/16 PNe with estimated ages greater than 10,000 years being bipolars.

• We have found a 5σ major axes alignment for bulge PNe that host short period binaries. Almost all are bipolar. The bulge PNe alignment signal reported previously was diluted.

• As a result there has to have been an organised, long lived process at play at the centre of our Galaxy that has to have endured over cosmologically significant time periods given several PNe in our sample emerge from stars of different progenitor mass.

• We have obtained well determined chemical abundances for 124 PNe in the Galactic bulge to produce the largest self-consistent well understood and high quality compilation of PNe abundances currently available.

• We show sulfur α-element lock-step in PNe for oxygen and argon for the first time.

• We dispel the hypotheses that the sulfur anomaly originates from underestimation of higher sulfur ionization stages.

• Using a machine learning approach, we reveal that earlier ICF schemes contributed to the anomaly. The sulfur anomaly correlates with the age/mass of PNe progenitors, being absent or significantly reduced in PNe with young progenitors.

References

Chornay, N., Walton, N. A., 2021, *A&A*, 656, 110. doi: 10.1051/0004-6361/202142008

Delgado-Inglada G., Morisset C., Stasińska G., 2014, *MNRAS*, 440, 536. doi: 10.1093/mnras/stu341

Drew, J. E., Greimel, R., Irwin, M. J. et al. 2005, *MNRAS*, 362, 753. doi: 10.1111/j.1365-2966.2005.09330.x

Drew, J. E., Gonzalez-Solares, E., Greimel, R. et al. 2014, *MNRAS*, 440, 2036. doi: 10.1093/mnras/stu394

Henry, R. B., Kwitter, K., Balick, B., 2004, *AJ*, 127, 2284. doi: 10.1086/382242

Miszalski, B., Parker, Q. A., Acker, A., Birkby, J. L., Frew, D.J. and Kovacevic, A., 2008, *MNRAS*, 384, 525. doi: 10.1111/j.1365-2966.2007.12727.x

Miszalski, B., Acker, A., Moffat, A. F. Parker, Q. A., Udalski, A., 2009, *A&A*, 496, 813. doi: 10.1051/0004-6361/200811380

Parker, Q.A., Bojičić, I. S. and Frew, D. J., 2016, *JPhCS*, 728, 32008. doi:10.1088/1742-6596/728/3/032008

Parker, Q. A., Acker, A., Frew, D. J. et al. 2005, *MNRAS*, 373, 79. doi:10.1111/j.1365-2966.2006.10950.x,

Rees, B., Zijlstra, A. A., 2013, *MNRAS*, 435, 975. doi:10.1093/mnras/stt1300

Reichel, M., Kimeswenger, S., van Hoof, P. A. M., et al. 2022, *ApJ*, 939, 103. doi:10.3847/1538-4357/ac90c4

Rodríguez, M, 2020, *MNRAS*, 495, 1016. doi: 10.1093/mnras/staa1286

Sabin, L., Parker, Q. A., Corradi, R. L. M. et al. 2014, *MNRAS*, 443, 3388. doi: 10.1093/mnras/stu1404

Tan, S., Parker, Q. A., Zijlstra, A. A., Ritter, A., 2023, *MNRAS*, 519, 1049. doi: 10.1093/mnras/stac3490

Tan, S., Parker, Q. A. Zijlstra, A. A., Ritter, A., Rees, B., 2023, *ApJ Letters*, 951, 44. doi: 10.3847/2041-8213/acdbcd

Planetary Nebulae: A Universal Toolbox in the Era of Precision Astrophysics
Proceedings IAU Symposium No. 384, 2025
O. De Marco, A. Zijlstra & R. Szczerba, eds.
doi:10.1017/S174392132300577X

Planetary nebulae populations in the haloes of nearby massive early-type galaxies

J. Hartke[1,2], M. Arnaboldi[3], O. Gerhard[4], A. I. Ennis[5,6], C. Pulsoni[4], L. Coccato[3], A. Cortesi[7], K.C. Freeman[8], K. Kuijken[9], M. Merrifield[10] and N. Napolitano[11]

[1]Finnish Centre for Astronomy with ESO, (FINCA), University of Turku, 20014 Turku, Finland
email: johanna.hartke@utu.fi

[2]Tuorla Observatory, Department of Physics and Astronomy, University of Turku, 20014 Turku, Finland

[3]European Southern Observatory, Karl-Schwarzschild-Str. 2, 85748 Garching, Germany

[4]Max-Planck-Institut für Extraterrestrische Physik, Giessenbachstr. 1, 85748 Garching, Germany

[5]Perimeter Institute for Theoretical Physics, Waterloo, Ontario N2L 2Y5, Canada

[6]Waterloo Centre for Astrophysics, University of Waterloo, Waterloo, Ontario, N2L 3G1, Canada

[7] Instituto de Fisica, Universidade Federal do Rio de Janeiro, 21941-972, Rio de Janeiro, RJ, Brazil

[8]Research School of Astronomy & Astrophysics Mount Stromlo Observatory, Cotter Road, 2611 Canberra, Australia

[9]Leiden Observatory, Leiden University, PO Box 9513, 2300 RA Leiden, The Netherlands

[10]School of Physics and Astronomy, University of Nottingham, NG7 2RD, United Kingdom

[11]School of Physics and Astronomy, Sun Yat-sen University, DaXue Road 2, 519082 Zhuhai, China

Abstract. Planetary nebulae (PNe) are excellent tracers of the metal-poor haloes of nearby early-type galaxies. They are commonly used to trace spatial distribution and kinematics of the halo and intracluster light at distances of up to 100 Mpcs. The results on the early-type galaxy M105 in the Leo I group represent a benchmark for the quantitative analysis of halo and intragroup light. Since the Leo I group lies at just a 10 Mpc distance, it is at the ideal location to compare results from resolved stellar populations with the homogeneous constraints over a much larger field of view from the PN populations. In M105, we have – for the first time – established a direct link between the presence of a metal-poor halo as traced by resolved red-giant branch stars and a PN population with a high specific frequency (α-parameter). This confirms our inferences that the high α-parameter PN population in the outer halo of M49 in the Virgo Cluster traces the metal-poor halo and intra-group light.

Keywords. planetary nebulae: general, galaxies: clusters, galaxies: groups, galaxies: elliptical and lenticular, cD galaxies: halos galaxies: individual: NGC 4479, galaxies: individual: NGC 3379

1. Introduction

In the current paradigm, the evolution of early-type galaxies (ETGs) is a two-phase process (e.g. Naab et al. 2009; Oser et al. 2010; Rodriguez-Gomez et al. 2016), where the second phase is responsible for the substantial size growth from redshift $z \approx 2$ until today (e.g. Daddi et al. 2005; De Lucia et al. 2006). This phase is governed by numerous mergers and accretion events that are imprinted in the galaxies' haloes, where dynamical time scales are long (e.g. Bullock & Johnston 2005). Observationally, the transition from the *in-situ*-dominated galaxy centres to the *ex-situ*-dominated stellar haloes is signalled by radially varying light profiles (morphology, colours; e.g. D'Souza et al. 2014; Capaccioli et al. 2015; Iodice et al. 2016; Spavone et al. 2017) and kinematics (e.g. Coccato et al. 2009; Forbes et al. 2016; Foster et al. 2016; Pulsoni et al. 2018; Dolfi et al. 2021; Spavone et al. 2022). However, despite the considerable efforts to observationally distinguish in-situ from ex-situ stellar populations, these observational methods do not reliably separate those populations when applied to data from cosmological simulations where the accretion histories are known (Pulsoni et al. 2021; Remus & Forbes 2022).

In dynamically complex and massive structures such as groups and clusters of galaxies, accretion processes and mergers furthermore liberate stars into the so-called intra-group (or intra-cluster) light (IGL/ICL), a diffuse stellar component that is gravitationally bound to the group (or cluster) potential (Zwicky 1937, 1951). As the ICL and IGL formation is intertwined with cluster and group assembly processes, characterising it can provide important constraints on the second phase of the two-phase formation scenario in dense environments.

As Arnaboldi & Gerhard (2022) discuss in their recent review, there is no uniform definition facilitating IGL- and ICL-halo separation based on deep photometry, where the ICL can either be defined through multi-component surface brightness (SB) profiles (e.g. Gonzalez et al. 2005; Rudick et al. 2010; Morishita et al. 2017; Ragusa et al. 2023), or as all the light beyond a fixed SB limit (e.g. Feldmeier et al. 2004; Mihos et al. 2005; Montes & Trujillo 2018). A kinematic approach to separate halo and IGL or ICL stars based on their different binding energies can be translated to observable line-of-sight velocity distributions (LOSVDs), i.e. the ensemble of stars bound to the ICL or IGL should have larger LOS velocity dispersions than the ensemble of halo stars (e.g. Dolag et al. 2010; Cui et al. 2014).

However, measuring kinematics from integrated-light absorption spectra in the low-SB regime is notoriously challenging. Therefore, measuring stellar kinematics in the outer haloes and surrounding IGL or ICL of ETGs relies on discrete tracers, such as planetary nebulae (PNe). Their characteristic emission-line features combined with the absence of a strong stellar continuum make PNe viable tracers of halo and ICL assembly (Arnaboldi et al. 1996) up to distances of the Coma Cluster ($\sim 100\,\mathrm{Mpc}$; Gerhard et al. 2005).

While being excellent discrete tracers of halo and ICL kinematics, PN populations may also reveal information about the underlying stellar populations. For Local Group galaxies, this can be done with direct abundance measurements (see contributions by Bhattacharya and Stanghellini in these proceedings). Still, these measurements are currently not easily accessible for galaxies at larger distances. Instead, in this proceeding, we summarise our findings on the relation of PN population properties such as the α parameter and PN luminosity function (PNLF) slope with the colours, ages, and metallicities of their host stellar populations. Figure 1 summarises the different methods and tools used to study extragalactic PN populations, especially in the halo-IGL transition context discussed here.

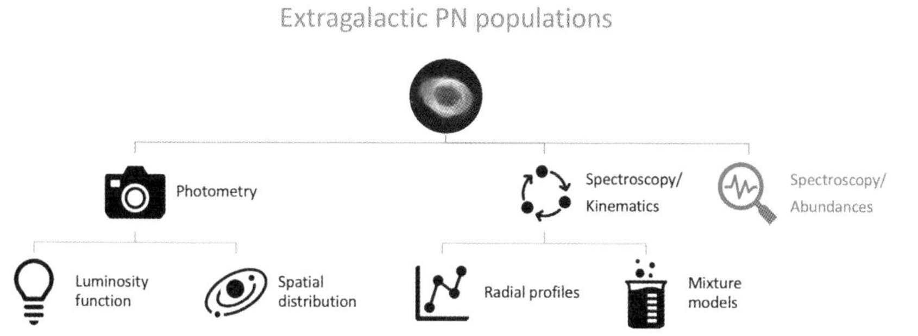

Figure 1. Overview of methods and tools used to study extragalactic PN populations. In this proceeding, we focused on photometry, i.e. deep [OIII] narrow-band surveys and spectroscopy, with the goal of obtaining the PN velocities.

The α-parameter, also known as luminosity-specific PN number, relates the number of PNe $N_{\rm PN}$ with the total bolometric luminosity $L_{\rm bol}$ of the parent stellar population (Jacoby 1980):

$$\alpha = \frac{N_{\rm PN}}{L_{\rm bol}}. \tag{1}$$

In the context of evolving stellar populations, one can also relate the α-parameter with the visibility lifetime $\tau_{\rm PN}$ of a PN population with specific evolutionary flux $\mathcal{B}$ (e.g., Buzzoni et al. 2006)

$$\alpha = \mathcal{B}\tau_{\rm PN}. \tag{2}$$

The PNLF describes the m_{5007} magnitude distribution of a PN population and can be analytically described by a combination of two exponential functions:

$$N_{\rm PN}(m_{5007}) \propto {\rm e}^{c_2(m_{5007}-\mu)}{\rm e}^{3(M^\star - m_{5007}+\mu)}. \tag{3}$$

The first term describes the fading brightness of a spherical gas cloud around the PN central star (Henize & Westerlund 1963), where c_2 is the faint-end slope that was fixed to $c_2 = 0.307$ when this form of the PNLF was first introduced based on observations of M31 (and other Local Group galaxies; Ciardullo et al. 1989). This parameter was later left to vary to reconcile observations of the PNLF in the halo of the massive ETG M87 (Longobardi et al. 2013). The second term describes the bright cut-off at the absolute magnitude $M^\star$ for a galaxy with distance modulus μ. Considering that, empirically, the absolute magnitude of the bright cut-off is near invariant with galaxy type at $M^\star = -4.5$ (Ciardullo 2022), by measuring a galaxy's apparent bright cut-off $m^\star$ it is thus possible to infer its distance. The use of the PNLF as a secondary distance indicator is extensively discussed in the contributions by M. Roth and G. Jacoby in these proceedings.

This proceeding is organised as follows: in Sect. 2 we discuss the ePN.S survey of ETGs, and, building up on this, in Sect. 3 and Sect. 4, we discuss extensions of these surveys mapping the halo-to-IGL transitions in M49 and M105 respectively. We conclude with an outlook on PN studies with current and upcoming novel instrumentation in Sect. 5.

2. Mapping the transition from in-situ to ex-situ stellar halo with the ePN.S survey

The extended Planetary Nebulae Spectrograph (ePN.S) ETG survey (Arnaboldi et al. 2017; Pulsoni et al. 2018) targetted 33 ETGs, of which 25 were observed with the PN.S (including literature data from Coccato et al. 2009; Cortesi et al. 2013; McNeil et al. 2010), and the remaining eight ones either with other slitless spectroscopic facilities or multi-object spectrographs (Teodorescu et al. 2005, 2011; Méndez et al. 2009; Walsh et al. 2015). The survey covers a median of 5.6 effective radii ($R_{\rm eff}$) with a range from $3-13\,R_{\rm eff}$. Containing a total 8354 PNe, it is the largest kinematic survey of extragalactic PNe to date. For each of the 33 galaxies, Pulsoni et al. (2018) published adaptively kernel-smoothed velocity and velocity dispersion fields, complemented with absorption-line kinematics from the literature in the galaxies' centres.

The ePN.S sample contains both galaxies classified as "fast" and as "slow rotators" according to the kinematics in their central regions (Emsellem et al. 2007; Cappellari et al. 2011). As discussed in Pulsoni et al. (2018), this classification mainly pertains to processes governing the assembly of the in-situ dominated centres of ETGs. It may thus not be representative beyond the central $R_{\rm eff}$. In fact, Pulsoni et al. (2018) found that ETGs may have very different kinematics in the halos than the slow-/fast rotator classification suggests based on the kinematics in the central regions, e.g. the onset of rotation in the halos of galaxies that were classified as slow rotators. In fact, one of the main findings of the ePN.S survey is the existence of a kinematic transition radius demarcating the inner regions and the halo. This transition is signalled by a change in the rotation velocity or the kinematic position angle. Pulsoni et al. (2018) found that the transition radii anticorrelate with the stellar mass of the galaxies, similar to the in-situ/ex-situ transition radius found in simulations (Cooper et al. 2013; Rodriguez-Gomez et al. 2016; Remus & Forbes 2022). However, later Pulsoni et al. (2021) argue that kinematic transition radii defined by a drop in rotation or peak in the λ_R-profile† (see also Schulze et al. 2020) do not necessarily trace the in-situ/ex-situ transition in the IllustrisTNG ETGs.

In the following two sections, we discuss findings from two projects that build on the ePN.S survey but have even more extended radial coverages due to additional PN.S observations and wide-field narrow-band imaging with Subaru's SuprimeCam, allowing us to uncover the kinematic transitions from the ex-situ stellar halo to the intra-group light with PNe as discrete kinematic and stellar population tracers.

3. M49: the brightest group galaxy in the Virgo Subcluster B

The Virgo Cluster is the closest cluster of galaxies ($D = 16.5 \pm 0.1$, Mei et al. 2007). Its proximity has facilitated many observational campaigns that revealed a complex dynamical history. In fact, the Virgo Cluster is not virialised yet, and three subclusters/groups (A, B, and C), whose centres coincide with the massive ETGs M87, M49, and M60, were identified by Binggeli et al. (1987). First detections of intracluster PNe tracing the ICL were focused on the centre of the cluster, i.e. Virgo A, (Feldmeier et al. 2004; Aguerri et al. 2005; Castro-Rodriguéz et al. 2009). Later, Longobardi et al. (2013, 2015, 2018) found that the Virgo A ICL has a significantly higher α-parameter than the halo of M87 and that the change from halo to ICL is signalled not only by a tell-tale change in stellar kinematics but also by a variation in the PNLF slope (see also contribution by Arnaboldi in these proceedings).

An extended bow shock north of M49 indicates that we are currently witnessing the infall of the Virgo Subcluster B into the centre of Virgo (Irwin & Sarazin 1996). Stars that will eventually be deposited in the ICL of Virgo A are pre-processed in the Virgo Subcluster B and its IGL. Investigating the IGL in this subcluster environment may, therefore, shed light on the different processes contributing to IGL *and* ICL assembly. Interestingly, the environment around M49 is characterised by a very extended halo,

† The λ_R parameter, introduced by Emsellem et al. (2007), can be used to quantify whether a galaxy is rotation- or dispersion-supported. The λ_R- and specific angular momentum profiles of 32 ePN.S galaxies derived from PN.S and integral-field spectroscopic data are presented in Pulsoni et al. (2023).

with a significant colour gradient, reaching blue colours of $B-V=0.65$ at 100 kpc ($\sim 6.25\,R_{\rm eff}$, Mihos et al. 2013).

Due to the age-metallicity degeneracy, one cannot directly infer the stellar population properties from the observed colours; therefore, the outer halo of M49 may be blue due to a relatively young (and metal-rich), or a metal-poor (and old) stellar population (or a combination of the two). A young stellar population (~ 2 Gyr, Mihos et al. 2013) would have to be due to a recent merger with a relatively massive star-forming galaxy, but a recent merger is not visible in the deep photometry (Mihos et al. 2013; Capaccioli et al. 2015; Mihos et al. 2017). If the observed colour gradient would instead correspond to a metallicity gradient of an old stellar population (5 Gyr or older), the outermost stars would have to have metallicities below $[\mathrm{Fe/H}] \leq -1$ (Mihos et al. 2013). If their progenitor host galaxies lie on the mass-metallicity relation (Zahid et al. 2017), their masses would be of the order of 10^{-3} times smaller than that of M49. This is in tension with the dominant accretion channel predicted by numerical simulations, that is, mergers with mass ratios of about 1:5 (Oser et al. 2012; Rodriguez-Gomez et al. 2016). To address this tension, we use PNe as discrete kinematic tracers that can help us to constrain the orbital precession time in the outer halo and IGL and thus also the dynamical ages of stars therein.

3.1. *A PN-rich IGL revealed from deep narrow-band photometry*

Before addressing this interesting dynamical issue, by studying the distribution of PN candidates from deep Subaru SuprimeCam (Miyazaki et al. 2002) narrow-band imaging in magnitude and position space, we could already identify indicators for a change in the PN population parameters from M49's inner to outer halo. In Hartke et al. (2017), we reported an excess of PNe at large radii compared to what would be expected from the V-band stellar light distribution, even when considering that the stellar light distribution itself deviates from a single-slope Sérsic profile at large radii (Capaccioli et al. 2015).

We could reconcile these observations with a two-component photometric model, where the inner halo is dominated by a Sérsic profile, and the light distribution at large radii is approximated by a constant surface brightness value of $\mu_{V,\rm outer} = 28.0\,\mathrm{mag\,arcsec^{-2}}$. The two model components are weighted by their respective α-parameters. We found a 3.2 times higher α-parameter for the constant-surface-brightness component compared to that describing the main galaxy halo. In light of the findings of Longobardi et al. (2013) for Virgo A, we interpreted this as a change of the parent stellar population from galaxy to IGL. In Fig. 2, we show the light-weighted α-parameter versus colour profiles from our two-component models. As expected for massive ETGs, the α-parameter is lowest in the inner red and metal-rich halo and then increases with decreasing colour, reaching values similar to that of star-forming local group (LG) galaxies with similarly blue colours.

While in M87 the ICL and halo PNLFs have similar faint-end slopes ($c_{2,\rm Halo}=0.72$ and $c_{2,\rm ICL}=0.66$, Longobardi et al. 2015, 2018), but the ICL PNLF exhibits a dip 1-1.5 magnitudes fainter than the bright cut-off, in M49 the PNLFs have significantly different faint-end slopes of $c_2=0.69\pm0.07$ in the inner and $c_2=1.08\pm0.36$ in the outer halo, also indicating a stellar population change from halo to IGL (Hartke et al. 2017). However, these results alone are not enough to confirm the presence of IGL PNe. For that, it is necessary to measure the PN kinematics.

3.2. *Three distinct PN populations in the halo of M49*

Combining the data from the deep SuprimeCam narrow-band survey discussed above with that from the ePN.S survey allowed us to identify three distinct PN populations

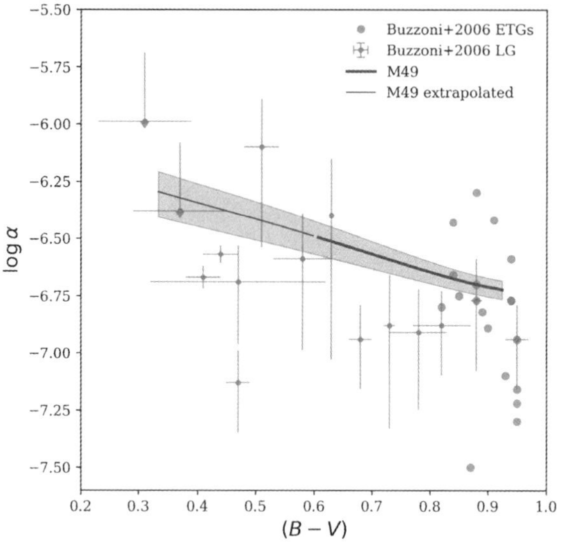

Figure 2. Variation of the M49 α-parameter with galaxy colour (solid line, colour data from Mihos et al. 2013) in comparison with data from other galaxies collated in Buzzoni et al. (2006, circles and errorbars). The colour-α-parameter profile for M49 is based on the two-component model discussed in Sect. 3.1 and extrapolated beyond the radial range of the colours measured by Mihos et al. (2013) assuming a linear colour gradient in the inner halo and a constant colour for the IGL. Adapted from Hartke et al. (2017).

in the halo of M49 (Hartke et al. 2018). Two of them were already discussed previously, namely the main halo of M49 and the IGL of the Virgo Subcluster B. However, the decomposition of the line-of-sight velocity distribution (LOSVD) into halo and PN components was not straightforward due to the presence of a third component, namely the dwarf irregular galaxy VCC 1249. It is interacting with M49 and dominates the blue wing of the LOSVD due to a velocity difference of $\sim 500\,\mathrm{km\,s^{-1}}$ between the two galaxies. By assessing the reduced velocity as function of magnitude (Sambhus et al. 2006) along the major and minor axes of M49, we identified a sample of bright ($m_{5007} < 27.5$ mag) PNe (258) with large reduced velocities, of which ten can be firmly associated with the interaction of M49 and VCC 1249 (see also poster by Penger in these proceedings). Their imprint on the line-of-sight velocity dispersion profile as a function of radius can be clearly seen in Fig. 3, where the profile of the bright PNe (blue) peaks at the major-axis radius at which VCC 1249 is located.

In the faint sample ($m_{5007} < 27.5$ mag, 178 PNe), the excess of PNe with large reduced velocities is absent and the influence of the VCC 1249 interaction negligible, facilitating the decomposition of its strongly-winged LOSVD into halo and IGL components. The transition from halo to IGL is indicated by a tell-tale rise of the line-of-sight velocity dispersion profile as a function of major-axis radius, reaching dispersion values of the Subcluster B, as illustrated in Fig. 3. This indicates that the outermost halo of M49 is controlled by the subcluster's gravity. By using Gaussian mixture models, we find that the IGL component has a significantly larger velocity dispersion $\sigma_{\mathrm{IGL}} = 400\,\mathrm{km\,s^{-1}}$ than the halo ($\sigma_{\mathrm{halo}} = 170\,\mathrm{km\,s^{-1}}$). This agrees well with the expectations from simulated galaxy clusters (e.g. Dolag et al. 2010; Cui et al. 2014). In the faint sample, the IGL-PN fraction is about 40% on average and reaches values of 57% at the largest radii covered by the survey. M49 is one of the first galaxies where the transition from galaxy to cluster velocity dispersion was measured based on individual stars.

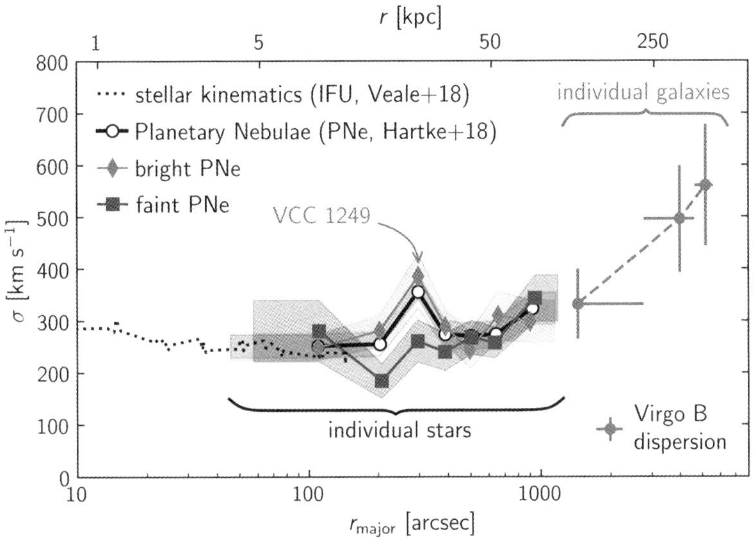

Figure 3. Line-of-sight velocity dispersion profile as a function of major-axis radius for all PNe (black), and the bright (blue) and faint (red) subsamples. Stellar kinematics derived from Veale et al. (2018) are denoted by the dashed line and those of dwarf galaxies in the Virgo Subcluster B (from Kim et al. 2014) by grey error bars. Adapted from Hartke et al. (2018).

3.3. *Constraints on blue IGL formation channels in the Virgo Subcluster B from PNe*

Combining the information from deep broad- and narrow-band surveys in the Virgo Subcluster B with the dynamical information from PNe described in the previous section, it became possible to constrain the formation channels for the extended blue diffuse light first identified by Mihos et al. (2013). In Hartke et al. (2018), we argued that its smooth appearance and regular, point-symmetric velocity field with large dispersion put a lower limit of 5 Gyr on the orbital precession time, therefore ruling out a recent moderately massive merger. Instead, a viable formational channel is the early accretion of metal-poor ($[Fe/H] < -1$ and low-mass ($\sim 10^8\,M_\odot$) dwarf galaxies. These accretion events have much lower merger-mass ratios (about $1:10^{-4}$) than the mergers predominantly responsible for halo growth in cosmological simulations (e.g. Rodriguez-Gomez et al. 2016). This may be due to a combination of resultion and/or feedback effects.

Finally, having dynamically confirmed the presence of IGL PNe in the outer halo of M49, we can now also link back the high α-parameter and steep faint-end PNLF slope, to the blue and metal-poor IGL stellar population.

4. M105 and the IGL of the Leo I group

Compared to the Virgo Cluster, the Leo I group in which M105 resides is a dynamically tame environment. The group's mass is two orders of magnitudes smaller (e.g. Kourkchi & Tully 2017) and at $D = 10.3$ (Tonry et al. 2001) it is the closest galaxy group to contain both early-and late-type massive galaxies (de Vaucouleurs 1975). Its proximity makes it a viable target for resolved stellar population studies of red giant branch (RGB) stars with the *Hubble Space Telescope (HST)*, which revealed the emergence of a metal-poor stellar population in the outskirts of M105 based on two ACS/WFC fields at $4\,R_{\rm eff}$ and $12\,R_{\rm eff}$ respectively (Harris et al. 2007b; Lee & Jang 2016).

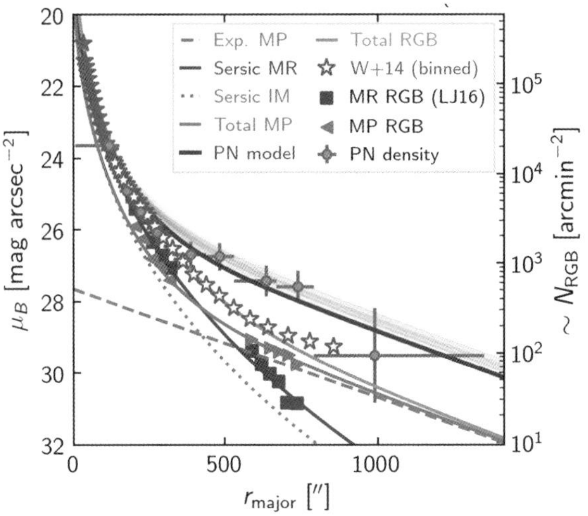

Figure 4. Observed tracer profiles and models in the halo of M105. Green dots with errorbars denote the PN number density scaled to observed B-band surface brightness via the α-parameter measured in the inner halo. The best fit two-component model (including a high α-parameter halo component, see text) and its uncertainty are indicated by the solid green line. Stars show the integrated surface brightness profile from Watkins et al. (2014), red squares [blue triangles] the number density of metal-rich [metal-poor] RGB stars from Lee & Jang (2016). The RGB number density profile (solid grey line) is decomposed into an exponential profile (dashed blue line) for the metal-poor ([M/H] < -1), and two Sérsic profiles for the intermediate-metallicity ($1 \leq$[M/H]< -0.5, dotted blue line) and metal-rich ([M/H]≥ -0.5, solid red line) populations. Adapted from Hartke et al. (2020).

4.1. *A direct link of a high α-parameter with a metal-poor stellar population in the Leo I Group*

Similar to the reasoning described in Sec. 3 for M49, we used deep SuprimeCam [OIII] narrow-band imaging covering M105 and its neighbouring galaxy NGC 3384 to study the distribution of PN candidates in magnitude and position space (Hartke et al. 2020). As shown in Fig. 4, the PN number density (green symbols and error bars) in the outer halo of the galaxy is higher than what would be expected considering a constant α-parameter and the observed B-band surface brightness profile (grey stars, Watkins et al. 2014). The number density distribution of metal-poor (blue triangles) and metal-rich RGB stars (red squares, Lee & Jang 2016) can be modelled with an exponential profile for the most metal-poor stars ([M/H] < -1, dashed blue line) and two Sérsic profiles with the same slope for the intermediate-metallicity ($1 \leq$[M/H]< -0.5, dotted blue line) and metal-rich ([M/H]≥ -0.5, solid red line) populations. This decomposition can be used to inform a two-component photometric model, where the inner halo is dominated by the combined Sérsic profile for the intermediate metallicity and metal-rich stellar populations and the outer halo by the exponential profile.

The α-parameter of the extended, metal-poor halo is more than seven times higher than that of the metal-rich inner halo. In addition to that, we also measure a steeper PNLF slope in the outer halo ($c_2 = 1.42 \pm 0.18$) compared to the inner halo ($c_2 = 0.51 \pm 0.13$). Previously, the link of an increased α-parameter with metal-poor IGL/ICL stellar populations could only be indirectly inferred (Hartke et al. 2017; Longobardi et al. 2013). The origin of this stellar population, i.e. whether it was built up from pristine gas whose star-formation was truncated early as proposed by Harris et al. (2007a) or formed by accretion of metal-poor galaxies (Lee & Jang 2016), is addressed in the following.

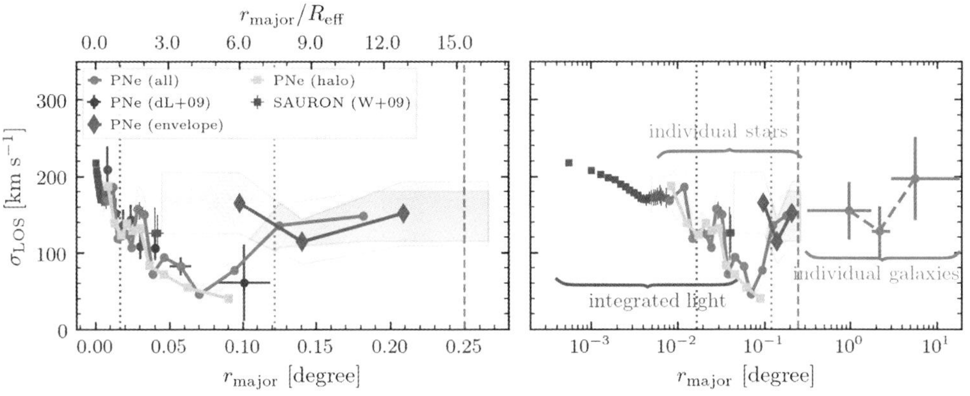

Figure 5. Line-of-sight velocity dispersion profiles in the halo of M105. Black squares denote absorption-line kinematics from Weijmans et al. (2009), black circles the PN velocity dispersion based on the central PN.S pointing (de Lorenzi et al. 2009), grey circles the more extended data from Hartke et al. (2022), and purple and yellow symbols the decomposition into envelope and halo kinematics. Blue symbols on the right panel denote the dwarf galaxy kinematics derived from data compiled by Müller et al. (2018, see also references therein). The vertical lines denote the kinematic transition from rotating core to inner halo already identified in Pulsoni et al. (2018, red dotted line), and from the inner halo to the exponential envelope (grey dotted). The latter transition radius agrees with the inner photometric transition radius identified independently by Ragusa et al. (2022). We also show the outer photometric transition radius that Ragusa et al. (2022) interpret as the photometric transition to the IGL (dashed grey line).

4.2. *Evidence for a kinematic transition to the metal-poor IGL*

Early PN.S observations of the central 6 $R_{\rm eff}$ of M105 (Romanowsky et al. 2003) triggered a series of papers on the dark matter (DM) content and spatial distribution of massive ETGs, as the decreasing line-of-sight velocity dispersion profile was consistent with both low-mass and low-concentration DM haloes, if any (Romanowsky et al. 2003; Douglas et al. 2007), as well as with DM halos in the expected mass range for massive ETGs when considering the mass-anisotropy degeneracy and viewing angle effects (Dekel et al. 2005; Douglas et al. 2007; de Lorenzi et al. 2009; Weijmans et al. 2009). Using new, extended kinematics of PNe allowed us to investigate whether the line-of-sight velocity dispersion profile consistent with a small DM content continued in the outer halo, as well as to constrain the formation channel of the high-α metal-poor stellar population discussed in the previous subsection.

The extended kinematic survey spans 15 $R_{\rm eff}$ and also covers the neighbouring galaxy NGC 3384, which is also a member of the Leo I group, that was targetted as part of the PN.S survey of S0 galaxy kinematics (Cortesi et al. 2013). In Hartke et al. (2022), we build on the photo-kinematic decomposition techniques of Cortesi et al. (2011) to determine membership probabilities for each PNe to belong to NGC 3384 or M105 and its surrounding exponential envelope.

By studying the PN smoothed velocity fields, LOS velocity dispersion (as shown in Fig. 5), rotation, and λ_R profiles, we separate the PNe associated to M105 into three kinematically distinct components: (1) the rotating core covering the central 1 $R_{\rm eff}$ of M105, with a metal-rich stellar population (see, e.g. Weijmans et al. 2009) and an in-situ origin, (2) the inner halo, whose light distribution is described by a Sérsic profile, and composed of intermediate-metallicity stars that may either have formed in-situ or were brought in through few major mergers, and (3) the exponential envelope beyond 7.5 $R_{\rm eff}$, with a metal-poor and PN-rich stellar population and high velocity dispersion, reaching that of dwarf galaxies in the Leo I group.

The increase of the velocity dispersion profile at large radii, driven by PNe associated with the exponential envelope, may indicate that those stars are bound to the gravitational potential of the Leo I group at large and thus part of its IGL. This is corroborated by the observation of the exponential envelope having similar kinematics (line-of-sight velocity dispersion, rotation amplitude, and kinematic major axis) to dwarf galaxies orbiting the Leo I group (see right panel of Fig 5). The transition from halo to IGL is also signalled by a break in the surface brightness profile and isophotal twists as measured by Ragusa et al. (2022).

Our PN kinematics support the two-mode formation scenario for the metal-rich and metal-poor stellar populations in M105 and its envelope proposed by Lee & Jang (2016): the inner, metal-rich halo was likely formed in situ, while the metal-poor exponential envelope that is part of the IGL of the Leo I group was formed via accretion. The high α-parameter of the IGL PNe discussed in the previous subsection, similar to that of Local Group dwarf irregular galaxies (see also Buzzoni et al. 2006), independently supports this formation channel.

5. Outlook and perspectives for extragalactic PN studies with current and upcoming instrumentation

Our work presented above shows conclusive evidence for empirical correlations between the α-parameter, PNLF faint-end slope c_2, and the underlying stellar population properties such as metallicity and colour. It builds on the seminal work of Buzzoni et al. (2006) on PNe of galaxy stellar populations, however, their sample of PNe and stellar population properties was derived from a heterogeneous set of observations. What is now needed is a systematic survey where PN and stellar population properties are measured simultaneously for galaxies along the entire mass-metallicity relation. However, traditional PN detection techniques, such as the on-off band technique with follow-up spectroscopic surveys or counter-dispersed imaging, are unsuited to detect PNe in the bright centres of galaxies where stellar population parameters are most easily accessible from absorption-line measurements. Integral-field spectrographs (IFSs) allow for a pixel-by-pixel decomposition of the spectra into their respective nebular and stellar (i.e. galaxy light) contributions. The SAURON IFS provided a first view of the PN population in the central regions of M31 (Sarzi et al. 2011).

With its 1×1 arcmin^2 field-of-view (FoV) and large wavelength range, the Multi-Unit Spectroscopic Explorer (MUSE, Bacon et al. 2010) at ESO's *Very Large Telescope (VLT)* has opened a new window for PN discoveries in the very centres of galaxies and allows for a simultaneous measurement of stellar kinematics, ages, and metallicities. The combination of MUSE with the adaptive optics system GALACSI (Arsenault et al. 2008; Ströbele et al. 2012) can significantly boost the detection of PNe due to their point-like nature. Different strategies have been established for optimising the detection of PNe in MUSE cubes, such as (1) the Diffuse Emission Line Filter technique (DELF, Roth et al. 2021, see also contribution by Soemitro in these proceedings), (2) using "pure" emission-line datacubes after subtracting the stellar continuum (Spriggs et al. 2020, see also contribution by Schlagenhauf in these proceedings), or (3) the detection based on line maps (Scheuermann et al. 2022). The methods can also be combined, as demonstrated by Ennis et al. (2022, 2023, these proceedings), who used the DELF technique on continuum-subtracted MUSE cubes.

The imaging Fourier transform spectrometer Spectrograph SITELLE (Spectromètre Imageur à Transformée de Fourier pour l'Etude en Long et en Large de raies d'Emission, Drissen et al. 2019) at the *Canada-France-Hawaii Telescope* with its large FoV (11×11 arcmin^2) and IFU capabilities in spectral filters covering some of the most important emission lines of PNe ([OIII], Hα, Hβ, [SII]) has the capabilities of mapping PN populations in nearby galaxies in a single pointing. First results in the scope of the SIGNALS survey (Rousseau-Nepton et al. 2019) were recently published by Vicens-Mouret et al. (2023). In light of current and upcoming large surveys with IFSs, machine learning has become increasingly important to classify a large number of ionised nebulae, including, but not limited to PNe (Congiu et al. 2023; Rhea et al. 2020).

Combining IFS data with that obtained with "traditional" techniques in the halos of nearby galaxies may provide constraints on the variation of the α-parameter and PNLF within a galaxy, representing the different stellar populations of in-situ and ex-situ origins, as we illustrated with the example of M105, where a combination of MUSE, *HST*, and PN.S data showed a trend of a decreasing α-parameter with metallicity. To interpret these observations and advance our understanding of PNe as stellar population tracers, it is important that extragalactic PN populations can also be adequately modelled and compared with other stellar population properties in numerical simulations of galaxy evolution. The extension of the formalism described in (Valenzuela et al. 2019) to cosmological simulations, as presented at this meeting, is an important milestone.

In the coming decade(s), several upcoming instruments and facilities may open new and exciting discovery spaces for extragalactic PN science. One of them is BlueMUSE (Richard et al. 2019) at the *VLT*, with an instrumental design similar to MUSE, but with a larger FoV and providing access to bluer emission lines such as [OII] at 3727 Å, Hγ at 4340 Å, and [OIII] at 4346 Å, with the latter being an important ingredient in direct abundance determinations. Spectroscopic facilities with high multiplexing and IFS capabilities and unprecedentedly large FoVs, such as the Maunakea Spectroscopic Explorer (The MSE Science Team et al. 2019) in the northern and the Wide-field Spectroscopic Telescope (Pasquini et al. 2018) in the southern hemisphere at 10-m class telescopes have the potential to be transformational for extragalactic studies of PNe.

Acknowledgements

J.H. would like to thank the organisers of IAU Symposium 384 for the invitation to present this work and for the stimulating conference. J.H. and A.I.E. acknowledge the financial support from the visitor and mobility program of the Finnish Centre for Astronomy with ESO (FINCA), funded by the Academy of Finland grant nr 306531. The authors would like to acknowledge the contribution from Dr Nigel Douglas, first P.I. of the PN.S. We also would like to thank the staff at the WHT for their support during the many PN.S observing runs.

References

Aguerri, J. A. L., Gerhard, O. E., Arnaboldi, M., et al. 2005, *AJ*, 129, 2585

Arnaboldi, M., Freeman, K. C., Mendez, R. H., et al. 1996, *ApJ*, 472, 145

Arnaboldi, M. & Gerhard, O. 2022, Frontiers in Astronomy and Space Sciences, 9, 403

Arnaboldi, M., Pulsoni, C., Gerhard, O., & PN.S Consortium. 2017, in IAU Symposium, Vol. 323, Planetary Nebulae: Multi-Wavelength Probes of Stellar and Galactic Evolution, ed. X. Liu, L. Stanghellini, & A. Karakas, 279–283

Arsenault, R., Madec, P. Y., Hubin, N., et al. 2008, in Society of Photo-Optical Instrumentation Engineers (SPIE) Conference Series, Vol. 7015, Adaptive Optics Systems, ed. N. Hubin, C. E. Max, & P. L. Wizinowich, 701524

Bacon, R., Accardo, M., Adjali, L., et al. 2010, in Society of Photo-Optical Instrumentation Engineers (SPIE) Conference Series, Vol. 7735, Ground-based and Airborne Instrumentation for Astronomy III, ed. I. S. McLean, S. K. Ramsay, & H. Takami, 773508

Binggeli, B., Tammann, G. A., & Sandage, A. 1987, *AJ*, 94, 251

Bullock, J. S. & Johnston, K. V. 2005, *ApJ*, 635, 931
Buzzoni, A., Arnaboldi, M., & Corradi, R. L. M. 2006, *MNRAS*, 368, 877
Capaccioli, M., Spavone, M., Grado, A., et al. 2015, *A&A*, 581, A10
Cappellari, M., Emsellem, E., Krajnović, D., et al. 2011, *MNRAS*, 413, 813
Castro-Rodriguéz, N., Arnaboldi, M., Aguerri, J. A. L., et al. 2009, *A&A*, 507, 621
Ciardullo, R. 2022, Frontiers in Astronomy and Space Sciences, 9
Ciardullo, R., Jacoby, G. H., Ford, H. C., & Neill, J. D. 1989, *ApJ*, 339, 53
Coccato, L., Gerhard, O., Arnaboldi, M., et al. 2009, *MNRAS*, 394, 1249
Congiu, E., Blanc, G. A., Belfiore, F., et al. 2023, *A&A*, 672, A148
Cooper, A. P., D'Souza, R., Kauffmann, G., et al. 2013, *MNRAS*, 434, 3348
Cortesi, A., Arnaboldi, M., Coccato, L., et al. 2013, *A&A*, 549, A115
Cortesi, A., Merrifield, M. R., Arnaboldi, M., et al. 2011, *MNRAS*, 414, 642
Cui, W., Murante, G., Monaco, P., et al. 2014, *MNRAS*, 437, 816
Daddi, E., Renzini, A., Pirzkal, N., et al. 2005, *ApJ*, 626, 680
de Lorenzi, F., Gerhard, O., Coccato, L., et al. 2009, *MNRAS*, 395, 76
De Lucia, G., Springel, V., White, S. D. M., Croton, D., & Kauffmann, G. 2006, *MNRAS*, 366, 499
de Vaucouleurs, G. 1975, *ApJ*, 202, 610
Dekel, A., Stoehr, F., Mamon, G. A., et al. 2005, *Nature*, 437, 707
Dolag, K., Murante, G., & Borgani, S. 2010, *MNRAS*, 405, 1544
Dolfi, A., Forbes, D. A., Couch, W. J., et al. 2021, *MNRAS*, 504, 4923
Douglas, N. G., Napolitano, N. R., Romanowsky, A. J., et al. 2007, *ApJ*, 664, 257
Drissen, L., Martin, T., Rousseau-Nepton, L., et al. 2019, *MNRAS*, 485, 3930
D'Souza, R., Kauffman, G., Wang, J., & Vegetti, S. 2014, *MNRAS*, 443, 1433
Emsellem, E., Cappellari, M., Krajnović, D., et al. 2007, *MNRAS*, 379, 401
Ennis, A., Hartke, J., Arnaboldi, M., et al. 2023, arXiv e-prints, arXiv:2311.09176
Ennis, A. I., Hartke, J., & Bian, F. 2022, Boletin de la Asociacion Argentina de Astronomia La Plata Argentina, 63, 175
Feldmeier, J. J., Ciardullo, R., Jacoby, G. H., & Durrell, P. R. 2004, *ApJ*, 615, 196
Forbes, D. A., Romanowsky, A. J., Pastorello, N., et al. 2016, *MNRAS*, 457, 1242
Foster, C., Pastorello, N., Roediger, J., et al. 2016, *MNRAS*, 457, 147
Gerhard, O., Arnaboldi, M., Freeman, K. C., et al. 2005, ApJ, 621, L93
Gonzalez, A. H., Zabludoff, A. I., & Zaritsky, D. 2005, *ApJ*, 618, 195
Harris, W. E., Harris, G. L. H., Layden, A. C., & Stetson, P. B. 2007a, *AJ*, 134, 43
Harris, W. E., Harris, G. L. H., Layden, A. C., & Wehner, E. M. H. 2007b, *ApJ*, 666, 903
Hartke, J., Arnaboldi, M., Gerhard, O., et al. 2018, *A&A*, 616, A123
Hartke, J., Arnaboldi, M., Gerhard, O., et al. 2022, *A&A*, 663, A12
Hartke, J., Arnaboldi, M., Gerhard, O., et al. 2020, *A&A*, 642, A46
Hartke, J., Arnaboldi, M., Longobardi, A., et al. 2017, *A&A*, 603, A104
Henize, K. G. & Westerlund, B. E. 1963, *ApJ*, 137, 747
Iodice, E., Capaccioli, M., Grado, A., et al. 2016, *ApJ*, 820, 42
Irwin, J. A. & Sarazin, C. L. 1996, *ApJ*, 471, 683
Jacoby, G. H. 1980, The Astrophysical Journal Supplement Series, 42, 1
Kim, S., Rey, S.-C., Jerjen, H., et al. 2014, *ApJS*, 215, 22
Kourkchi, E. & Tully, R. B. 2017, *ApJ*, 843, 16
Lee, M. G. & Jang, I. S. 2016, *ApJ*, 822, 70
Longobardi, A., Arnaboldi, M., Gerhard, O., et al. 2013, *A&A*, 558, A42
Longobardi, A., Arnaboldi, M., Gerhard, O., & Hanuschik, R. 2015, *A&A*, 579, A135
Longobardi, A., Arnaboldi, M., Gerhard, O., Pulsoni, C., & Söldner-Rembold, I. 2018, *A&A*, 620, A111
McNeil, E. K., Arnaboldi, M., Freeman, K. C., et al. 2010, *A&A*, 518, A44
Mei, S., Blakeslee, J. P., Côté, P., et al. 2007, *ApJ*, 655, 144
Méndez, R. H., Teodorescu, A. M., Kudritzki, R. P., & Burkert, A. 2009, *ApJ*, 691, 228
Mihos, J. C., Harding, P., Feldmeier, J., & Morrison, H. 2005, *ApJ*, 631, L41

Mihos, J. C., Harding, P., Feldmeier, J. J., et al. 2017, *ApJ*, 834, 16
Mihos, J. C., Harding, P., Rudick, C. S., & Feldmeier, J. J. 2013, *ApJ*, 764, L20
Miyazaki, S., Komiyama, Y., Sekiguchi, M., et al. 2002, PASJ, 54, 833
Montes, M. & Trujillo, I. 2018, *MNRAS*, 474, 917
Morishita, T., Abramson, L. E., Treu, T., et al. 2017, *ApJ*, 846, 139
Müller, O., Jerjen, H., & Binggeli, B. 2018, *A&A*, 615, A105
Naab, T., Johansson, P. H., & Ostriker, J. P. 2009, *ApJ*, 699, L178
Oser, L., Naab, T., Ostriker, J. P., & Johansson, P. H. 2012, *ApJ*, 744, 63
Oser, L., Ostriker, J. P., Naab, T., Johansson, P. H., & Burkert, A. 2010, *ApJ*, 725, 2312
Pasquini, L., Delabre, B., Ellis, R. S., et al. 2018, in Society of Photo-Optical Instrumentation Engineers (SPIE) Conference Series, Vol. 10700, Ground-based and Airborne Telescopes VII, ed. H. K. Marshall & J. Spyromilio, 107004E
Pulsoni, C., Gerhard, O., Arnaboldi, M., et al. 2018, *A&A*, 618, A94
Pulsoni, C., Gerhard, O., Arnaboldi, M., et al. 2021, *A&A*, 647, A95
Pulsoni, C., Gerhard, O., Fall, S. M., et al. 2023, *A&A*, 674, A96
Ragusa, R., Iodice, E., Spavone, M., et al. 2023, *A&A*, 670, L20
Ragusa, R., Mirabile, M., Spavone, M., et al. 2022, Frontiers in Astronomy and Space Sciences, 9, 852810
Remus, R.-S. & Forbes, D. A. 2022, *ApJ*, 935, 37
Rhea, C., Rousseau-Nepton, L., Prunet, S., Hlavacek-Larrondo, J., & Fabbro, S. 2020, *ApJ*, 901, 152
Richard, J., Bacon, R., Blaizot, J., et al. 2019, arXiv e-prints, arXiv:1906.01657
Rodriguez-Gomez, V., Pillepich, A., Sales, L. V., et al. 2016, *MNRAS*, 458, 2371
Romanowsky, A. J., Douglas, N. G., Arnaboldi, M., et al. 2003, Science, 301, 1696
Roth, M. M., Jacoby, G. H., Ciardullo, R., et al. 2021, *ApJ*, 916, 21
Rousseau-Nepton, L., Martin, R. P., Robert, C., et al. 2019, *MNRAS*, 489, 5530
Rudick, C. S., Mihos, J. C., Harding, P., et al. 2010, *ApJ*, 720, 569
Sambhus, N., Gerhard, O., & Méndez, R. H. 2006, *AJ*, 131, 837
Sarzi, M., Mamon, G. A., Cappellari, M., et al. 2011, *MNRAS*, 415, 2832
Scheuermann, F., Kreckel, K., Anand, G. S., et al. 2022, *MNRAS*, 511, 6087
Schulze, F., Remus, R.-S., Dolag, K., et al. 2020, *MNRAS*, 493, 3778
Spavone, M., Capaccioli, M., Napolitano, N. R., et al. 2017, *A&A*, 603, A38
Spavone, M., Iodice, E., D'Ago, G., et al. 2022, *A&A*, 663, A135
Spriggs, T. W., Sarzi, M., Napiwotzki, R., et al. 2020, *A&A*, 637, A62
Ströbele, S., La Penna, P., Arsenault, R., et al. 2012, in Society of Photo-Optical Instrumentation Engineers (SPIE) Conference Series, Vol. 8447, Adaptive Optics Systems III, ed. B. L. Ellerbroek, E. Marchetti, & J.-P. Véran, 844737
Teodorescu, A. M., Méndez, R. H., Bernardi, F., et al. 2011, *ApJ*, 736, 65
Teodorescu, A. M., Méndez, R. H., Saglia, R. P., et al. 2005, *ApJ*, 635, 290
The MSE Science Team, Babusiaux, C., Bergemann, M., et al. 2019, arXiv e-prints, arXiv:1904.04907
Tonry, J. L., Dressler, A., Blakeslee, J. P., et al. 2001, *ApJ*, 546, 681
Valenzuela, L. M., Méndez, R. H., & Miller Bertolami, M. M. 2019, *ApJ*, 887, 65
Veale, M., Ma, C.-P., Greene, J. E., et al. 2018, *MNRAS*, 473, 5446
Vicens-Mouret, S., Drissen, L., Robert, C., et al. 2023, *MNRAS*, 524, 3623
Walsh, J. R., Rejkuba, M., & Walton, N. A. 2015, *A&A*, 574, A109
Watkins, A. E., Mihos, J. C., Harding, P., & Feldmeier, J. J. 2014, *ApJ*, 791
Weijmans, A.-M., Cappellari, M., Bacon, R., et al. 2009, *MNRAS*, 398, 561
Zahid, H. J., Kudritzki, R.-P., Conroy, C., Andrews, B., & Ho, I. T. 2017, *ApJ*, 847, 18
Zwicky, F. 1937, *ApJ*, 86, 217
Zwicky, F. 1951, *PASP*, 63, 61

Planetary Nebulae: A Universal Toolbox in the Era of Precision Astrophysics
Proceedings IAU Symposium No. 384, 2025
O. De Marco, A. Zijlstra & R. Szczerba, eds.
doi:10.1017/S1743921323005781

On determining the chemical composition of planetary nebulae

Grażyna Stasińska

LUTH, Observatoire de Paris, CNRS, Université Paris Diderot; Place Jules Janssen, F-92190 Meudon, France
e-mail: grazyna.stasinska@obspm.fr

Abstract. We present literature on abundance determinations in planetary nebulae (PN) as well as public tools that can be used to derive them. Concerning direct methods to derive abundances we discuss in some depth such issues as reddening correction, use of proper densities and temperatures to compute the abundances, correction for unseen ionic stages, effect of stellar absorption on nebular spectra, and error analysis. Concerning photoionization model-fitting, we discuss the necessary ingredients of model stellar atmospheres, the problem of incomplete slit covering and the determination of the goodness of fit. A note on the use of IFU observations is given. The still unsolved problem of temperature fluctuations is briefly presented, with references to more detailed papers. The problem of abundance discrepancies is touched upon with reference to more extensive discussions in the present volume. Finally carbon footprint issues are mentioned in the context of extensive PN modeling and large databases.

Keywords. atomic data, dust, extinction, ISM: abundances, planetary nebulae: general

1. Introduction

The first elemental abundance determinations in planetary nebulae (PN) date back to the study of Bowen & Wyse (1939), who elaborated a way to derive the abundances from the observed emission lines and showed that, in spite of PN spectra being very different from those of stars, their chemical composition is very similar.

Since then, abundances studies in PNe have flourished, with the aim both to determine the chemical composition of the gas out of which they were formed and to estimate the amount of element production by the PN progenitors.

For any PN, the derived chemical composition depends on the available observations, on the adopted methods and on the atomic data that have been used. Table 1 shows the abundances of He, C, N, O, Ne and S determined by various authors for the brightest PN: NGC 7027, using various methods. The bottom line shows the standard deviation of all these determinations, and gives a *rough* idea of the expected uncertainties in PN abundances including all possible sources of errors.

A recent study by Rodríguez (2020) compared abundances derived with the same methods and same atomic data for about 20 Galactic PNe that have more than one spectrum of good quality. The derived one-sigma observational uncertainties from these objects are: 0.11 dex for O/H, 0.14 dex for N/H, 0.14 dex for Ne/H, 0.16 dex for S/H, 0.11 dex for Ar/H, and 0.14 dex for Cl/H an less than 0.05 dex for He/H.

Several reviews have been published recently on abundance determinations in ionized nebulae with special attention to PNe, (eg, Stasińska 2004, 2009, Peimbert et al. 2017). The present text is not a tutorial on abundance determination, but a complement to the

Table 1. Comparison of abundances for NGC 7027 in units of log X/H + 12.

	He	C	N	O	Ne	S
Stanghellini et al. 2006	11.21		8.43	8.43	7.67	
Zhang et al. 2005	11.00	9.10	8.14	8.66	8.07	6.92
Kwitter et al. 2003	11.00		8.62	8.37	7.85	6.64
Bernard-Salas et al. 2001	11.03	8.78	8.20	8.61	8.00	6.97
Kwitter & Henry 1996	11.00	8.98	8.21	8.71	8.14	7.85
Keyes et al. 1990	11.05	8.84	8.10	8.49	8.00	6.86
Middlemass 1990	11.02	9.11	8.28	8.75	8.04	6.90
Perinotto et al. 1980		9.11	8.52	8.62		
Péquignot et al. 1978	11.00	9.48	8.30	8.86	8.34	7.23
Aller 1954	10.96		8.52	8.96	8.44	8.17
Standard deviation	0.06	0.21	0.17	0.18	0.22	0.50

afore mentioned papers incorporating recent studies and emphasizing issues that need a careful treatment.

There are basically two ways to determine element abundances in PNe from their emission lines. One is the 'direct method' which obtains ionic abundances from ratios of the observed emission-line fluxes and next derives total elemental abundances by using ionization-correction factors (ICFs). The other is to fit the observed line intensities using photoionization models. Both approaches will be discussed here, but first we will examine the issue of correcting for extinction due to interstellar dust.

2. Reddening correction

2.1. *Generalities*

The nebular flux after attenuation by a purely absorbing intervening dust slab is given by:

$$F(\lambda)_{\rm obs} = F(\lambda)_{\rm em} \times \exp(-\tau(\lambda)), \tag{1}$$

where $F(\lambda)_{\rm em}$ is the emitted flux at wavelength λ and $F(\lambda)_{\rm obs}$ is the observed flux at this wavelength.

In nebular astrophysics, one often uses the following expression to relate $F(\lambda)_{obs}$ and $F(\lambda)_{em}$:

$$F(\lambda)_{\rm obs} = F(\lambda)_{\rm em} \times 10^{Cf(\lambda)} \tag{2}$$

where C is the logarithmic extinction at H$\beta$and $f(\lambda)$ is called the 'extinction law' considered as universal, equal to 1 at 4861Å.

Knowing the form of $f(\lambda)$, C can be derived from the observed Hα/Hβratio by comparing it to the theoretical one for case B recombination:

$$C = [\log(\mathrm{F(H}\alpha)/\mathrm{F(H}\beta)_{\rm B} - \log(\mathrm{F(H}\alpha)/\mathrm{F(H}\beta)_{\rm obs}]/(\mathrm{f(H}\alpha) - \mathrm{f(H}\beta)) \tag{3}$$

Emission line ratios are then dereddened using the formula:

$$\log(\mathrm{F}(\lambda_1)/\mathrm{F}(\lambda_2))_{\rm corr} = \log(\mathrm{F}(\lambda_1)/\mathrm{F}(\lambda_2))_{\rm obs} + \mathrm{C} \times (\mathrm{f}(\lambda_1) - \mathrm{f}(\lambda_2)) \tag{4}$$

2.2. *Complications*

- The intrinsic Hα/Hβratio depends slightly on the electron temperature $T_{\rm e}$ and electron density $n_{\rm e}$. This can easily be dealt with a iterative scheme, i.e.,first dereddening the line ratios using canonical values for $T_{\rm e}$ and $n_{\rm e}$ (for example 10,000 K and 100 cm^{-3}), then computing $T_{\rm e}$ and $n_{\rm e}$ from dereddened line ratios and iterate, as advocated e.g.,by Ueta & Otsuka (2021). Such a procedure has been adopted in many studies. However, unless the temperature or densities are very different from the ones that were chosen a priori, the error on abundances is not very large (only of a few percent for 8,000 K $< T_e <$ 12,000K, Morisset et al. 2023) so the results obtained by authors who, for some reason, do not apply an iterative approach, remain acceptable.

• The intrinsic Hα/Hβratio may be different from that of the theoretical case B due to collisional excitation of H^0. The effect is larger in objects where the proportion of neutral hydrogen is larger and the electron temperature is high. For example for $T_e$equal for 17,000 K and $H^0/H = 10^{-2}$, Hα/H$\beta$is equal to 3, while it would be of 2.75 in absence of collisional excitation (see Fig. 1 of Luridiana 2009).

• The extinction law is actually not universal. It has been shown by Cardelli et al. (1989) that its form can be parametrized by the parameter: $R_V = A(V)/E(B-V)$, i.e.,the ratio of total to selective extinction at V. While 3.1 is the standard value adopted for R_V in the vast majority of studies, the actual values vary from 2.3 to 5.5 (Cardelli et al. 1989, Fitzpatrick 1999). This is almost never considered in spectroscopic studies of PNe. The value of R_V is related to the environment. Large values of R_V, which correspond to a flatter extinction law, are found for lines-of-sight crossing dense interstellar clouds, where grain growth occurs, while lower values of R_V are found in the diffuse interstellar medium. In absence of any information on the value of R_V, the uncertainties on reddening correction due to the form of the 'extinction law' can be taken into account using Table 1 of Fitzpatrick (1999).

• If some dust is mixed with the ionized gas and strongly contributes to the extinction, no 'extinction law' applies. Such a situation, however, is unlikely to occur in planetary nebulae, except in very young and compact objects.

• Instead of using only H$\alpha$and Hβone can force the observed Balmer decrement to its theoretical value. Such a procedure avoids the problem of the extinction law as well as of the flux calibration in the blue (which is difficult to achieve) but it requires a correct treatment of the observational uncertainties. This procedure returns correct line ratios even in the case where internal dust plays a role. However, is feasible only if the signal-to-noise ratio of all the lines that are used is sufficiently high.

• In many cases only H$\alpha$and Hβintensities are of sufficient accuracy so that the use of an extinction law cannot be avoided. In case of calibration problems, the resulting intensities of Hγ, Hδ etc. may be far from the theoretical values. This has to be artificially corrected, otherwise the intensities of nearby lines will be wrong. An important case is that of the [O III]λ4363line, which lies near the Hγ line, and has a strong impact of the derived chemical composition of the PNe.

• The observed Balmer lines can be affected by stellar absorption. This happens when the slit covers the central star. The effect of absorption on Balmer lines can be tackled with an adjusted model of the stellar atmosphere or by observations with good spectral resolution (stellar lines are generally broader than emission lines). An example of such a procedure is described in Sect 2.2.3 of Stasińska et al. (2010). Another case is that of extragalactic PNe, when the slit encompasses a lot of light from the stars located in the galaxy. The best practice to deal with such a case would be to fit the observed stellar continuum using a stellar population synthesis code and subtract it from the observed spectrum. Such a procedure is routinely applied in studies of emission-line galaxies (see e.g.,Asari et al. 2007, Thomas et al. 2013, Belfiore et al. 2022), and should also be implemented in studies of extragalactic PNe.

3. Abundance determinations using direct methods

Direct methods are very simple in their principle. The abundance ratio of two ions is obtained from the observed intensity ratio of lines emitted by these ions. For example,

O^{++}/H^{+} can be derived from

$$O^{++}/H^{+} = \frac{[\text{O III}]\ \lambda5007/\text{H}\beta}{j_{[\text{O III}](T_e,n_e)}/j_{\text{H}\beta(T_e,n_e)}}. \quad (5)$$

$j_{[\text{O III}]}(T_e, n_e)$ and $j_{\text{H}}\beta(T_e, n_e)$ are the emission coefficients of the [O III]λ5007 and Hβlines respectively, which depends on T_e and n_e(assumed uniform in the nebula). Both $T_e$and $n_e$can be derived from specific line ratios.

However, as will be seen, the devil is in the details.

3.1. *Softwares for direct abundance determinations*

Over the years, many softwares have been developed for public use: ABELION (Stasińska 1978), FIVEL (de Robertis et al. 1987), NEBULAR (Shaw & Dufour 1995), ELSA (Johnson et al. 2006), NEAT (Wesson et al. 2012), PyNeb (Luridiana et al. 2015). Of all these softwares, PyNeb (https://pypi.org/project/PyNeb/) is the most complete and versatile, regularly updated by C. Morisset and deserves a more detailed description here.

PyNeb is easy to install. It is written in Python and uses standard Python libraries such as numpy, matplotlib, pyfits, scipy and other. While PyNeb was originally designed to compute nebular abundances, it can perform many tasks which help understand the processes giving rise to the intensities of emission lines in ionized nebulae and thus have a better control on the results. Examples of things PyNeb can do:

- compute physical conditions from suitable diagnostic line ratios.
- compute level populations, critical densities and line emissivities.
- compute and display emissivity grids as a function of $T_e$and n_e.
- correct line intensities for reddening using various extinction laws.
- read and manage observational data.
- plot and compare atomic data from different publications.
- compute ionic abundances from line intensities and physical conditions.
- compute elemental abundances from ionic abundances and ICFs.

Note however that, when using PyNeb *it is the user's responsibility* to make all the choices concerning reddening correction, electron temperatures and densities, etc. These choices must be clearly described in the publications. Also, it is important to always mention the version of PyNeb and list the references for the atomic data that are being used. Before publishing, it is recommended to analyze the reliability of the results and perform some checks by computing a few abundances 'by hand' using the emission-line tables that can be produced by PyNeb.

3.2. *Choosing a set of atomic data*

As shown by Juan de Dios & Rodríguez (2017), atomic data variations introduce differences in the derived abundance ratios as low as $0.1 - 0.2$ dex at low density, but that reach $0.6 - 0.8$ dex at densities above 10^4 cm^{-3} in several abundance ratios, such as O/H and N/O.

Note that the most recent atomic data are not always the best. Even if the methods are more refined, computations may still involve approximations or even errors. For example, Palay et al. (2012) were the first to calculate collision strengths for the O III forbidden transitions using a relativistic Breit-Pauli R-matrix method with resolved resonance structures. Their results were significantly different from those of previous authors. However, Storey et al. (2014) noted that Palay et al. (2012) had omitted the three 2p^4 terms from their scattering target, leading to a downshift of the temperature derived from [O III]λ4363/5007by up to 600 K.

A default data set is now provided by PyNeb thanks to the collaboration with C. Mendoza, and will be regularly updated (Morisset et al. 2020, Mendoza et al. 2023). In any case, it is always necessary to publish the exact source of atomic data that are used in a given computation.

3.3. *What about the general density stucture of PNe?*

The density derived from [Ar IV]λ4740/4711is generally larger than that derived from [S II]λ6731/6717(e.g. Wang & Liu 2007, Méndez-Delgado et al. 2023). This can be due either to the different sensitivity of the line ratios or to density stratification in PNe. If [S II]λ6731/6717is not available, or very uncertain, this has an important consequence on the derived N/O abundance ratio, which could be overestimated by up to 50%.

However, comparing the densities derived from [S II]λ6731/6717, [O II]λ3726/3729, [Cl III]λ5537/5517and [Ar IV]λ4740/4711in a large sample of PNe Juan de Dios & Rodríguez 2021 concluded that 'the density structures derived for the objects depend strongly on the atomic data used in the calculations: atomic data are shaping the derived density pattern.'

Another and completely independent way to derive the density structure of PNe is to use Hαsurface brightness maps (see e.g.,Stasińska et al. 2010). However, no systematic study comparing this approach to that of line ratios has been made yet.

All the above concerns large scales. But what happens when looking on smaller scales? The James Webb Space Telescope has shown that the bright shell of the ring nebula, NGC 6720, is fragmented in thousands of dense globules of molecular gas, with a characteristic diameter of 0.2 arcsec and density of $10^5 - 10^6$ cm^{-3}, embedded in ionized gas (Wesson et al. 2023). This implies that the ionized gas at the frontier of these globules cannot be of uniform density. Chemical abundances derived under the hypothesis of constant density are therefore likely to be biased.

3.4. *Choosing $T_e$and n_e*

In direct abundance determinations in PNe, the common practice is to build a T_e, $n_e$diagram for the various observed line ratios that are sensitive to $T_e$and/or n_e. From such a diagram one reads out the values of $T_e$and $n_e$representative of the different zones in the nebula.

This empirical procedure needs some clarifications. First of all, it is important to visualize the effect of the error bars on the line ratios. This is easily achieved with the PyNeb software. Even so, the various temperature or density indicators do not always seem to give reasonable values of $T_e$and n_e(see e.g.,García-Rojas et al. 2012). However, one must recall that these diagrams are built under the hypothesis of uniform $T_e$and $n_e$for each diagnostic line ratio, which obviously cannot be the case in real objects. So any choice of $T_e$and $n_e$from such diagrams is just an educated guess which gives an incomplete (and biased) idea of temperature and density stratifications. Abundances derived from different lines of the same ion may differ. For example, in NGC 7027, adopting T_e= 12,600 K for all the lines emitted by O^{++}Zhang et al. (2005) find O^{++}/H^{+}= 2.5610^{-4} from the O III]λ1661 line but O^{++}/H^{+}= 3.0810^{-4} from the [O III]λ5007and [O III]λ4363lines. This difference is due to the fact that ultra-violet lines are more sensitive to high temperatures.

3.5. *More on temperature diagnostics*

As known from some time, collisionally excited lines (CELs) can be affected by recombination of the upper ion. This is the case, for example, of [N II]λ5755, [O II]λ7720 + 7730 and [O III]λ4363, which are all used for temperature diagnostics. Liu et al. (2000)

proposed formulae to estimate the recombination contribution. These formulae depend on the abundance of the upper ion and on T_e. They are generally used assuming that $T_e$is equal to the temperature derived from [O III]λ4363/5007. But this is wrong in the presence of cold zones, and the actual recombination contribution is larger than computed! Gómez-Llanos et al. (2020) proposed a formula to correct [O III]λ4363for recombination for the case if high excitation PNe, but they do warn against its blind use in cases where the gas has two phases of different chemical composition, with the recombination contribution coming mainly from the cold regions.

García-Rojas et al. (2022) have proposed a more direct empirical method using the strongest observed recombination lines N IIλ5679 and O IIλ 4649+50, whose emissivity ratio is almost independent of T_e. To correct the [N II]λ5755 for the contribution of recombination they write:

$$I(\lambda 5755)_{\rm corr} = I(\lambda 5755) - j(\lambda 5755)/j(\lambda 5679) \times I(\lambda 5679) \qquad (6)$$

It must be added that recently Nemer at al (2019) reported the first observational evidence of Rydberg Enhanced Recombination (RER), an important recombination process that has so far been unexplored. First estimates on carbon ions shows that RER has a significant impact on the ionization structure of ionized nebulae containing cold zones and on the derived abundances.

3.6. *Correction for unseen ionic stages*

The ICFs computed by Kingsburgh and Barlow (1994) on the basis of a few tailored PN models have been used for decades.

In 2014, Delgado Inglada et al. have published ICFs for He, O, N, Ne, S, Ar, Cl, and C, based on a grid of ionization- and density-bounded photoionization models of different values of stellar luminosities and effective temperatures, nebular masses and internal radii. The models were computed with the photoionization code CLOUDY c10.01 (Ferland et al. 1998). The initial grid was trimmed so as to keep only those models that could represent PNe in terms of nebular masses, surface brightness and exciting star masses. This resulted in 2820 models which were used to compute analytical expressions of ICFs for different ions as a function of $O^{++}/(O^{+}+ O^{++})$ or $He^{++}/(He^{+}+ He^{++})$, which are quantities that can be obtained from the observations. With this procedure, the authors were able to estimate for the first time the values of the uncertainties linked to ICFs. However, it turns out that the grid of models was slightly too large and that the uncertainties were not well evaluated. More recently, Amayo et al. (2021) produced ICFs for giant H IIregions, based on a much more refined grid of models taking into account the probability that each model can represent a giant H IIregion in the real world and using a more correct procedure to estimate the uncertainties. Such an enterprise should also be undertaken for PNe.

Another option is now offered by machine learning techniques, which can easily provide ICFs that are tailored to a given object. For example, Sabin et al. (2022) and García-Rojas et al. (2022) have used an enhanced grid of PN photoionization models (3MdB, Morisset et al. 2015, https://sites.google.com/site/mexicanmillionmodels/) and selected the models that have *all* of the He^{++}/He^{+}, O^{++}/O^{+}, Ne^{4+}/Ne^{3+}, Ne^{3+}/ Ne^{++}, and $Ar^{4+}/Ar^{3+}/$ ratios close to the observed ones. With such a technique, it should also be easy to estimate error bars.

3.7. *Error analysis*

The best way to perform reliable error analyses is through Monte-Carlo techniques. A proper analysis should start right from data acquisition and go through all the processes involved in abundance determination, that is:

- Photometric calibration.
- Line intensity measurement.
- Extinction 'law'.
- Reddening computation
- Determination of plasma parameters $T_e$and n_e
- Ionization correction factors

Some difficulties are however involved in the process, which are not always recognized.
• The form of the distribution in errors in line intensities is not always known, and depends on the detection and measurement process: gaussian, log gaussian, something else? (See Wesson et al. 2016).
• If only one temperature diagnostic is available, e.g.,T_e[O III], one has to adopt a relation between its value and the values of the other characteristic temperatures,e.g.,T_e[N II]. What distribution to use for this relation?
• What distribution to consider for uncertainties in the ICFs?

It is not sufficient to state that uncertainties have been obtained with Monte-Carlo technique. A proper description is necessary. For example in the case of gaussian distributions, the intensities may become negative. How is this taken into account? When using several hydrogen lines to determine the reddening and simultaneously determine the plasma parameters $T_e$and n_e, it is important to first determine which hydrogen lines are to be included in the process, and to check the final results for reliability (for example the final abundance results of Ueta & Otsuka 2022 on the N/O abundances are obviously wrong since in some of the PNe they studied, the found a 'corrected' Hα/Hβratio that is impossible to achieve in any nebula (see Morisset et al. 2023 for a detailed discussion of this case).

Finally let us point out that resulting abundance distributions may be strongly asymmetric so it is recommended to use medians and quartiles rather than means and dispersions to describe them.

4. Abundance determination with photoionization models

Many studies have considered that, especially in absence of direct information on the electron temperature, e.g.,T_e[O III], the chemical composition of PNe can be derived through photoionization model fitting. This is only partly true. First of all, in absence of adequate constraints, the solution may not be unique, while generally the search is stopped after one solution is found. A proper photoionization modeling may give incorrect abundances if the nebula is density bounded while the model is ionization bounded, or if helium lines are not fitted.

The most recent review dealing with photoionization models is the one by Morisset (2017). Here we mainly comment on the question of abundance determination using photoionization models.

Many photoionization codes have being written, but only a few are of public use. They are listed below.

4.1. *Open-source photoionization codes*

4.1.1. Spherical Geometry

Cloudy. This photoionisation code has been in continuous development since 1978, led by Gary Ferland, and in collaboration with many scientists. The latest full description in a journal is by Ferland et al. (2017) and the website https://gitlab.nublado.org/cloudy/cloudy. The current version is C23. This code is the most widely used to model dusty H IIregions, PNe and active galactic nuclei. It comes along with a thorough documentation and contains a very complete and regularly updated collection of atomic processes including molecules.

Mappings V. The original MAPPINGS code (Binette et al. 1985) was developed to model the emission line and continuum spectra of H IIregions, PNe and active galactic nuclei and do the same for plasmas that are out of collisional or photoionization equilibrium, such as the radiative shocks in supernova remnants and their precursor zones. The interaction with dust was introduced in 2000. Mappings V has an expanded database for cooling and recombination lines and is described in Sutherland & Dopita (2017). It can be found on https://bitbucket.org/RalphSutherland/mappings/src/public/

4.1.2. Pseudo-3D

pyCloudy. This is a Python library developed by Morisset (2013) to generate 3D nebula models from various runs of the 1D Cloudy code. It can also be used more generally to handle Cloudy input and output files and easily build grids of Cloudy models. It has been employed to build the models of the 3MdB database. It is found at https://pythonhosted.org/pyCloudy/. Note that, although the treatment of the diffuse ionizing radiation is largely simplified, pseudo-3D models are a convenient substitute to full 3D models in the case where the PN geometries are not too complicated and have the advantage of being much faster, which is appreciable when carrying-out model-fitting of PNe observations (e.g.,Gesicki et al. 2016)

4.1.3. 3D

Mocassin. This is a fully 3D or 2D photoionization and dust radiative transfer code which uses a Monte Carlo approach to the transfer of radiation through media of arbitrary geometry and density distribution (Ercolano et al. 2003, 2005, 2008) https://mocassin.nebulousresearch.org/. It allows modeling PNe with such extreme morphologies as NGC 6302 (Wright et al. 2011).

Messenger Monte Carlo MAPPINGS V (M^3) M^3 (Jin et al. 2022) is a 3D photoionization code, combining the Monte Carlo radiative transfer technique with the MAPPINGS V photoionization code. Its purpose is to produce reliable diagnostic emission lines in ionized nebulae with arbitrary geometry. This code is not yet publicly available.

4.2. *Why and how use photoionization models for abundances?*

Photoionization model-fitting is much more time-consuming than direct abundance determination. So, is it worthwhile undertaking such a task? When no direct determination of $T_e$are available, this is the only way to put some limits on the abundances. Even if $T_e$measurements exist, it may be useful to consider photoionization modeling, because there is no ICF issue: the chemical composition of the object under study is that of the model which fits all the lines.

The model is supposed to take into account all the relevant physical processes occurring in the nebula. The chemical composition of the nebula is that of the model that fits *all* the observed line ratios.

The model should use properly all the available constraints

- density structure from an Hαimage,
- line ratios (in the appropriate apertures),
- properties of the exciting star, if known,
- luminosity, if known.

While often published models of PNe assume that they are ionization-bounded, this is not necessarily the case. They can be matter-bounded, especially in some directions.

If the observational slits do not cover the entire nebula, the comparisons with the models must account for it, by extracting from the model a portion of the nebula which corresponds to the slit, like e.g.,in Morisset & Georgiev (2009), or Stasińska et al. (2010).

One important ingredient of photoionization modeling is the description of the ionizing radiation. While blackbodies can be useful for exploratory studies, proper model atmospheres of the central stars are required for a detailed model-fitting. Such models are discussed by Kudritzki et al. (2006). Grids of plane-parallel NLTE model atmospheres of hot white dwarfs using TMAP have been computed by Rauch (2003), Rauch & Reindl (2014). NLTE models for central stars with winds are computed by using CMFGEN (Hillier 2006) and using METUJE by Krtička et al. (2020).

A model should fit *all* the observed line ratios within the uncertainties (observational and model). If it does not (which is often the case), it is not easy to determine what are the real abundances. Perhaps some important physical parameter is not correctly treated or missing (erroneous assumed geometry, distribution of dust grains, missing of cooling or heating mechanisms etc.)

To estimate the goodness of a model, it is not recommended to use a khi-square approach as is sometimes done (e.g.,Henry et al. 2015) because *each* of the mismatched line intensity has a significance that is worth investigating. One can instead (Morisset & Georgiev 2009, Stasińska et al. 2010, Bandyopadhyay et al. 2021, Miranda-Marques et al. 2023) use a quality factor for each observable

$$\kappa(\mathrm{O}) = (\log \mathrm{O}_{\mathrm{mod}} - \log \mathrm{O}_{\mathrm{obs}})/\tau(\mathrm{O}) \tag{7}$$

where $\tau(\mathrm{O})$ is the accepted tolerance in dex, which takes into account the observational uncertainty in flux ratio and reddening as well the expected ability of the model to reproduce the observable. $\tau(\mathrm{O})$ is defined as follows:

$$\tau(\mathrm{O}) = \log(1 + \Delta(\mathrm{O})/\mathrm{O}), \tag{8}$$

where $\Delta(\mathrm{O})$ is the absolute value of the maximum 'acceptable' error on the observable, A good model should have all the values of $\kappa(\mathrm{O})$ between -1 and $+1$. Of course, a preliminary condition is that the model returns the correct value of the Hαflux.

How to estimate error bars on elemental abundances? They cannot be easily deduced from errors in the observed line intensities. One must find *all* the models that are compatible with the observational error bars. This would be a huge task, almost never undertaken. Stasińska et al. (2010) have done such an exercise for the most oxygen-poor PN, PN G 135.9+55.9, but this was a relatively easy case, because the abundances of metals being small, they did not impact on the thermal balance.

There is a remaining problem with abundances derived from models. It often occurs that, while the intensities of the strongest lines are fitted, those of the weak lines are not, in particular those which indicate the value electron temperature (see e.g.,Kwitter & Henry 1996, 1998). Such a mismatch indicates that the temperature of the model is incorrect and therefore the chemical composition of the model cannot be considered as the correct one. Such cases require a discussion to understand why the predicted thermal balance is off.

4.3. *Do integral field unit (IFU) observations help for abundance determinations?*

Spectra provided by IFUs are extremely valuable in PNe studies since they allow one to determine the distributions of

- extinction,
- densities,
- local inhomogeneities (clumps, filaments, low ionization structures),
- electron temperatures,

- zones possibly affected by shocks,
- ionic ratios,
- ionic abundance discrepancy factors (see next section).

But they do not allow a direct determination of the distribution of elemental abundances, because the ICFs on different lines of sight are not known. The available ICFs have been obtained using PN photoionization models that represent entire objects and cannot be applied on a spaxel-by-spaxel basis. However, adding up all the spaxels in a given object provides an integrated spectrum which, indeed, can be treated by the direct method.

The integrated spectrum, together with the observed surface brightness distribution, is also ideal to confront with self-consistent photoionization models, which are, at the same time, required to reproduce the observed distribution of electron temperatures and densities (see Basurah et al. 2016). Undertaking this with all the accuracy allowed by the observations is a phenomenal task successfully achieved by H.Monteiro (these proceedings).

5. Temperature fluctuations and abundance discrepancies

Before leaving, we must evoke a very important problem which has been with us for decades and is still harshly debated. It is the so-called problem of 'temperature fluctuations' and the associated one of 'abundance discrepancies'. Temperature fluctuations were suggested by Peimbert (1967) to explain the discrepancy between electron temperatures derived from collisionally excited lines and those derived from the hydrogen Balmer jump. A technique was then proposed to correct the derived abundances for this effect. These temperature fluctuations are often ignored in direct abundance derivations. The question of the discrepancy between abundances derived from collisionally excited lines and from recombination lines is thoroughly discussed by Méndez-Delgado & Garcia-Rojas and by Morisset et al. (these proceedings). Previous reviews on these topics are by Esteban (2002), Liu (2002), Ferland (2003), Peimbert & Peimbert (2003), Stasińska (2004, 2009), García-Rojas et al. (2019), where many references can be found.

Some recent studies have provided an important progress in the observational evidence of the existence of temperature fluctuations (Peimbert & Peimbert 2013, Méndez-Delgado et al., 2023b) since now the evidence is based on lines from O^{++}only and does not require additional information from hydrogen lines which introduced some approximation in the derivation. However, it has not been proven that the formulation of Peimbert (1967) to derive the temperature fluctuation parameter t^2 gives correct results in the case of extreme temperature jumps such as may occur even in the case of a canonical $t^2 = 0.04$ (see Stasińska 2004). Indeed the formulation is based on Taylor series which may not be appropriate in this case. The other remaining problem is to find mechanisms that can *quantitatively* reproduce the inferred 'fluctuations'. Perhaps the more promising one is photoelectric heating of small grains in nebulae with density condensations which, as showed by Stasińska & Szczerba (2001) spectacularly boosts the temperature of the diluted component. However, there is presently no direct evidence of the presence of small grains in such nebulae.

Regarding abundance discrepancies, the presence of oxygen-rich inclusions in some PNe has also been clearly demonstrated (see Espiritu & Peimbert 2021 and references in Méndez-Delgado & Garcia-Rojas, these proceedings) as well as their concentration in the central zones. It has also been shown that the most extreme abundance discrepancies are found in PNe with binary central stars (Wesson et al. 2018) suggesting than they may be caused by a nova-like eruption occurring soon after the common-envelope phase.

6. Carbon footprint issues

While the complexity of computations in the field of PNe is far from comparing with that of cosmological or weather forecast simulations in terms of both CPU and memory, it is still worth asking the question of the carbon footprint of computational tasks (Lannelongue et al. (2001).

With modern computers, calculating an abundance or producing a photoionization model is almost instantaneous. To the point that not much effort is spent nowadays on reducing computing times (in contrast to the situation in the 70-80'ties when computations were much slower and optimization was vital).

However, with IFUs now producing spectra in many spaxels (e.g.,40,000 spaxels for MUSE observations of PNe), with Monte-Carlo simulations requiring random sampling for each process and each spaxel, computation times may become huge.

For example, for the 724,386 PN entries in the 3Mdb_17 database which required 145,150 runs of Cloudy 17.01, the total computation time would be of nearly 500 days if using one processor on an Intel(R) Xeon(R) CPU E5-2640-v3@2.60GHz. With 50 processors, the time is reduced by a factor 50. Note that if the code had been paralleled (which is not the case here), the carbon footprint would at the same time have increased by a factor of 2 (see Fig. 3 in Lannelongue et al 2021).

Therefore, reducing computing times again becomes a concern nowadays. The first thing is to improve computer programs with efficient coding, and, perhaps, to use more suitable programming languages. For the building of large grids of PNe models, an alternative to Cloudy would be needed since Cloudy, because it treats so many physical processes in detail, is very slow compared to other photoionization codes that are no so complete but still useful for most studies on PNe (e.g.,PHOTO, last described in Stasińska 2005 is at least 10 times faster).

Another road is to use databases of precomputed models (e.g.,3MdB) as much as possible. Finally it is a good idea to ask oneself whether the gain in scientific result is worth the computational cost. Artificial intelligence (AI) techniques are now very useful to reduce the number of simulations in a given project. Some examples can be found in Sabin et al. (2021) or García-Rojas et al. (2022).

7. Summary

Over the 80 years of abundance determinations in PNe, the basic methods have remained the same. Abundances are believed more reliable today mainly due to progress in atomic data computations. PNe in external galaxies are now within reach for abundance analyses thanks to large telescopes and appropriate instrumentation. Public tools are now available for direct abundance derivation as well as for photoionization modeling (but should not be used without caution).

Here we have revised some problems which still need attention such as reddening correction, use of proper densities and temperatures to compute the abundances, correction for unseen ionic stages and error analysis.

As in many fields in astrophysics, machine learning techniques are starting to be used to perform specific tasks such as deriving ionization correction factors based a grids of photoionization models or speeding up computational process in Monte-Carlo estimation of plasma parameters in the case of IFU observations of PNe.

Contrary to what one might believe, elemental abundances derived from photoionization modeling are not necessarily better than abundances derived from a direct analysis of the spectra and the related uncertainties are very difficult to assess.

Important progress in the long standing problem of temperature fluctuations and abundance discrepancies (see Sect. 5) has been made, but the topic remains the most challenging one in nebular astrophysics.

References

Aller, L. H., 1954, *ApJ*, 120, 401. doi:10.1086/145931

Amayo, A., Delgado-Inglada, G., Stasińska G., 2021, *MNRAS*, 505, 2361. doi:10.1093/mnras/stab1467

Asari N. V., Cid Fernandes R., Stasińska G., Torres-Papaqui J. P., Mateus A., Sodré L., Schoenell W., et al., 2007, *MNRAS*, 381, 263. doi:10.1111/j.1365-2966.2007.12255.x

Bandyopadhyay R., Das R., Mondal S., 2021, *MNRAS*, 504, 816. doi:10.1093/mnras/stab860

Basurah H. M., Ali A., Dopita M. A., Alsulami R., Amer M. A., Alruhaili A., 2016, *MNRAS*, 458, 2694. doi:10.1093/mnras/stw468

Belfiore F., Santoro F., Groves B., Schinnerer E., Kreckel K., Glover S. C. O., Klessen R. S., et al., 2022, *A&A*, 659, A26. doi:10.1051/0004-6361/202141859

Bernard Salas J., Pottasch S. R., Beintema D. A., Wesselius P. R., 2001, *A&A*, 367, 949. doi:10.1051/0004-6361:20000435

Binette L., Dopita M. A., Tuohy I. R., 1985, *ApJ*, 297, 476. doi:10.1086/163544

Bowen I. S., Wyse A. B., 1939, *LicOB*, 495, 1. doi:10.5479/ADS/bib/1939LicOB.19.1B

Cardelli J. A., Clayton G. C., Mathis J. S., 1989, *ApJ*, 345, 245. doi:10.1086/167900

Delgado-Inglada G., Morisset C., Stasińska G., 2014, *MNRAS*, 440, 536. doi:10.1093/mnras/stu341

De Robertis M. M., Dufour R. J., Hunt R. W., 1987, JRASC, 81, 195

Ercolano B., Barlow M. J., Storey P. J., Liu X.-W., 2003, *MNRAS*, 340, 1136. doi:10.1046/j.1365-8711.2003.06371.x

Ercolano B., Barlow M. J., Storey P. J., 2005, *MNRAS*, 362, 1038. doi:10.1111/j.1365-2966.2005.09381.x

Ercolano B., Young P. R., Drake J. J., Raymond J. C., 2008, ApJS, 175, 534. doi:10.1086/524378

Espíritu J. N., Peimbert A., 2021, *MNRAS*, 508, 2668. doi:10.1093/mnras/stab2746

Esteban C., 2002, *RMxAC*, 12, 56

Ferland G. J., 2003, *ARA&A*, 41, 517. doi:10.1146/annurev.astro.41.011802.094836

Ferland G. J., Korista K. T., Verner D. A., Ferguson J. W., Kingdon J. B., Verner E. M., 1998, *PASP*, 110, 761. doi:10.1086/316190

Ferland G. J., Chatzikos M., Guzmán F., Lykins M. L., van Hoof P. A. M., Williams R. J. R., Abel N. P., et al., 2017, RMxAA, 53, 385. doi:10.48550/arXiv.1705.10877

Fitzpatrick E. L., 1999, *PASP*, 111, 63. doi:10.1086/316293

García-Rojas J., Peña M., Morisset C., Mesa-Delgado A., Ruiz M. T., 2012, *A&A*, 538, A54. doi:10.1051/0004-6361/201118217

García-Rojas J., Wesson R., Boffin H. M. J., Jones D., Corradi R. L. M., Esteban C., Rodríguez-Gil P., 2019, arXiv, arXiv:1904.06763. doi:10.48550/arXiv.1904.06763

García-Rojas J., Morisset C., Jones D., Wesson R., Boffin H. M. J., Monteiro H., Corradi R. L. M., et al., 2022, *MNRAS*, 510, 5444. doi:10.1093/mnras/stab3523

Gesicki K., Zijlstra A. A., Morisset C., 2016, *A&A*, 585, A69. doi:10.1051/0004-6361/201526653

Gómez-Llanos V., Morisset C., García-Rojas J., Jones D., Wesson R., Corradi R. L. M., Boffin H. M. J., 2020, *MNRAS*, 498, L82. doi:10.1093/mnrasl/slaa131

Henry R. B. C., Balick B., Dufour R. J., Kwitter K. B., Shaw R. A., Miller T. R., Buell J. F., et al., 2015, *ApJ*, 813, 121. doi:10.1088/0004-637X/813/2/121

Hillier D. J., 2012, *IAUS*, 282, 229. doi:10.1017/S1743921311027426

Jin Y., Kewley L. J., Sutherland R., 2022, *ApJ*, 927, 37. doi:10.3847/1538-4357/ac48f3

Juan de Dios L., Rodríguez M., 2021, *MNRAS*, 507, 5331. doi:10.1093/mnras/stab2488

Keyes C. D., Aller L. H., Feibelman W. A., 1990, *PASP*, 102, 59. doi:10.1086/132607

Kingsburgh R. L., Barlow M. J., 1994, *MNRAS*, 271, 257. doi:10.1093/mnras/271.2.257

Krtička J., Kubát J., Krtičková I., 2020, *A&A*, 635, A173. doi:10.1051/0004-6361/201937150

Kudritzki R. P., Urbaneja M. A., Puls J., 2006, IAUS, 234, 119. doi:10.1017/S1743921306002857

Kwitter K. B., Henry R. B. C., 1996, *ApJ*, 473, 304. doi:10.1086/178145
Kwitter K. B., Henry R. B. C., 1998, *ApJ*, 493, 247. doi:10.1086/305094
Kwitter K. B., Henry R. B. C., Milingo J. B., 2003, *PASP*, 115, 80. doi:10.1086/345108
Jin Y., Kewley L. J., Sutherland R., 2022, *ApJ*, 927, 37. doi:10.3847/1538-4357/ac48f3
Johnson M. D., Levitt J. S., Henry R. B. C., Kwitter K. B., 2006, *IAUS*, 234, 439. doi:10.1017/S1743921306003632
Lannelongue L., Grealey J., Inouye M, 2021, *Adv. Sci.* 8, 2100707
Liu X.-W., 2002, *RMxAC*, 12, 70
Liu X.-W., Storey P. J., Barlow M. J., Danziger I. J., Cohen M., Bryce M., 2000, *MNRAS*, 312, 585. doi:10.1046/j.1365-8711.2000.03167.x
Luridiana V., Morisset C., Shaw R. A., 2015, *A&A*, 573, A42. doi:10.1051/0004-6361/201323152
Luridiana V., 2009, *Ap&SS*, 324, 361. doi:10.1007/s10509-009-0095-6
Méndez-Delgado J. E., Esteban C., García-Rojas J., Arellano-Córdova K. Z., Kreckel K., Gómez-Llanos V., Egorov O. V., et al., 2023, *MNRAS*, 523, 2952. doi:10.1093/mnras/stad1569
Méndez-Delgado J. E., Esteban C., García-Rojas J., Kreckel K., Peimbert M., 2023, b, *Nature*, 618, 249. doi:10.1038/s41586-023-05956-2
Méndez-Delgado J. E., García-Rojas J., 2023, arXiv, arXiv:2311.10280. doi:10.48550/arXiv.2311.10280
Middlemass D., 1990, *MNRAS*, 244, 294
Miranda Marques B. L., Monteiro H., Aleman I., Akras S., Todt H., Corradi R. L. M., 2023, *MNRAS*, 522, 1049. doi:10.1093/mnras/stad1055
Morisset C., 2013, ascl.soft. ascl:1304.020
Morisset C., Delgado-Inglada G., Flores-Fajardo N., 2015, *RMxAA*, 51, 103. doi:10.48550/arXiv.1412.5349
Morisset C., Georgiev L., 2009, *A&A*, 507, 1517. doi:10.1051/0004-6361/200912413
Morisset C., Luridiana V., García-Rojas J., Gómez-Llanos V., Bautista M., Mendoza, Claudio, 2020, *Atoms*, 8, 66. doi:10.3390/atoms8040066
Morisset C., Corradi R. L. M., García-Rojas J., Mampaso A., Jones D., Kwitter K. B., Magrini L., et al., 2023, *A&A*, 674, L6. doi:10.1051/0004-6361/202346296
Nemer A., Sterling N. C., Raymond J., Dupree A. K., García-Rojas J., Wang Q., Pindzola M. S., et al., 2019, *ApJL*, 887, L9. doi:10.3847/2041-8213/ab5954
Peimbert M., 1967, *ApJ*, 150, 825. doi:10.1086/149385
Peimbert M., Peimbert A., 2003, *RMxAC*, 16, 113. doi:10.48550/arXiv.astro-ph/0207186
Peimbert A., Peimbert M., 2013, *ApJ*, 778, 89. doi:10.1088/0004-637X/778/2/89
Peimbert M., Peimbert A., Delgado-Inglada G., 2017, *PASP*, 129, 082001. doi:10.1088/1538-3873/aa72c3
Péquignot D., Aldrovandi S. M. V., Stasińska G., 1978, *A&A*, 63, 313
Perinotto M., Panagia N., Benvenuti P., 1980, *A&A*, 85, 332
Rauch T., 2003, *A&A*, 403, 709. doi:10.1051/0004-6361:20030412
Rauch T., Nickelt I., Stampa U., Demleitner M., Koesterke L., 2009, ASPC, 411, 388. doi:10.48550/arXiv.0901.4204
Rauch T., Reindl N., 2014, apn6.conf, 77
Rodríguez M., 2020, *MNRAS*, 495, 1016. doi:10.1093/mnras/staa1286
Sabin L., Gómez-Llanos V., Morisset C., Gómez-González V. M. A., Guerrero M. A., Todt H., Fang X., 2022, *MNRAS*, 511, 1. doi:10.1093/mnras/stab3649
Shaw R. A., Dufour R. J., 1995, *PASP*, 107, 896. doi:10.1086/133637
Stanghellini L., Guerrero M. A., Cunha K., Manchado A., Villaver E., 2006, *ApJ*, 651, 898. doi:10.1086/507840
Stasińska G., 2004, cmpe.conf, 115
Stasińska G., 2005, *A&A*, 434, 507. doi:10.1051/0004-6361:20042216
Stasińska G., 2009, elu..book, 1. doi:10.1017/CBO9780511552038.003
Stasińska G., Morisset C., Tovmassian G., Rauch T., Richer M. G., Peña M., Szczerba R., et al., 2010, *A&A*, 511, A44. doi:10.1051/0004-6361/200912405
Stasińska G., Szczerba R., 2001, *A&A*, 379, 1024. doi:10.1051/0004-6361:20011403

Sutherland R. S., Dopita M. A., 2017, ApJS, 229, 34. doi:10.3847/1538-4365/aa6541

Thomas D., Steele O., Maraston C., Johansson J., Beifiori A., Pforr J., Strömbäck G., et al., 2013, *MNRAS*, 431, 1383. doi:10.1093/mnras/stt261

Ueta T., Otsuka M., 2021, *PASP*, 133, 093002. doi:10.1088/1538-3873/ac20ab

Ueta T., Otsuka M., 2022, *A&A*, 667, L8. doi:10.1051/0004-6361/202244744

Wang W., Liu X.-W., 2007, *MNRAS*, 381, 669. doi:10.1111/j.1365-2966.2007.12198.x

Wesson R., Stock D. J., Scicluna P., 2012, *MNRAS*, 422, 3516. doi:10.1111/j.1365-2966.2012.20863.x

Wesson R., Stock D. J., Scicluna P., 2016, *MNRAS*, 459, 3475. doi:10.1093/mnras/stw826

Wesson R., Matsuura M., Zijlstra A. A., Volk K., Kavanagh P. J., García-Segura G., McDonald I., et al., 2023, arXiv, arXiv:2308.09027. doi:10.48550/arXiv.2308.09027

Wright N. J., Barlow M. J., Ercolano B., Rauch T., 2011, *MNRAS*, 418, 370. doi:10.1111/j.1365-2966.2011.19490.x

Zhang Y., Liu X.-W., Luo S.-G., Péquignot D., Barlow M. J., 2005, *A&A*, 442, 249. doi:10.1051/0004-6361:20052869

Planetary Nebulae: A Universal Toolbox in the Era of Precision Astrophysics
Proceedings IAU Symposium No. 384, 2025
O. De Marco, A. Zijlstra & R. Szczerba, eds.
doi:10.1017/S1743921324000462

The structure of emission lines in planetary nebulae at very high spectral resolution†

Michael G. Richer[1], José Alberto López[1], Anabel Arrieta[2], Lorena Arias[2] and Silvia Torres-Peimbert[3]

[1]Instituto de Astronomía, Universidad Nacional Autónomo de México, Apartado Postal 106, CP 22800 Ensenada, Baja California, México

[2]Departamento de Física y Matemáticas, Universidad Iberoamericana, Prolongación Paseo de la Reforma 880, Lomas de Santa Fe, CP 01210, Ciudad de México, México

[3]Instituto de Astronomía, Universidad Nacional Autónomo de México, Apartado Postal 70-264, CP 04510 Ciudad de México, México

Abstract. We present spectroscopy of NGC 3242, NGC 6153, and NGC 7009 at very high spectral resolution ($\lambda/\delta\lambda = 75,000 - 100,000$) obtained with the Manchester Echelle Spectrograph at the 2.1m telescope of the Observatorio Astronómico Nacional on the Sierra San Pedro Mártir. We study the kinematics of the plasma within the nebular shells, decomposing the observed line profiles considering the microscopic, macroscopic, and observational processes that broaden them. The residual kinematic structure, defined as the sum of velocity gradients, kinematic structure, and seeing dominates the broadening of the lines of heavy elements. We estimate the effect of velocity gradients, finding that it can account only for a minority of this residual kinematic structure. Whatever the origin of this residual kinematic structure, it is an important component of the kinematics of the ionized plasma within the nebular shell and implies an important energy source that is not contemplated in photoionization models of planetary nebulae.

Keywords. planetary nebulae, spectroscopy, kinematics, turbulence

1. Introduction

We present preliminary results of observations of the planetary nebulae NGC 3242, NGC 6153, and NGC 7009 at very high spectral resolution. Our objective is to study the structure of the plasma within the nebular shell, as illustrated in Figure 1. In contrast to traditional studies of the internal kinematics of planetary nebulae, where the focus is usually on studying the expansion of the nebular shell as a function of the ions observed, here we study the motions within the nebular shell itself. To do so, we must separate the effects of microscopic physical processes from the physical processes that operate on macroscopic scales. We mostly follow the precepts laid out in Sabbadin et al. (2008).

A variety of processes contribute to broaden the emission line profile arising from a plasma. We may quantify several of these effects. First, each line has a natural line width due to the lifetime of the line's upper level. For the permitted lines we consider, the width is of order m/s in velocity space (Gaussian σ; e.g., Pradhan & Nahar 2011). For the much longer lifetimes of the forbidden lines, the width is orders of magnitud smaller than this. We ignore this natural line width because it is much less than the effects that follow. Second, the H and He lines have components whose spacing is less than the thermal broadening, and so are not resolved even when the instrumental resolution would allow

† MGR and JAL acknowledge funding from DGAPA-UNAM grants IG101233 and IN111124.

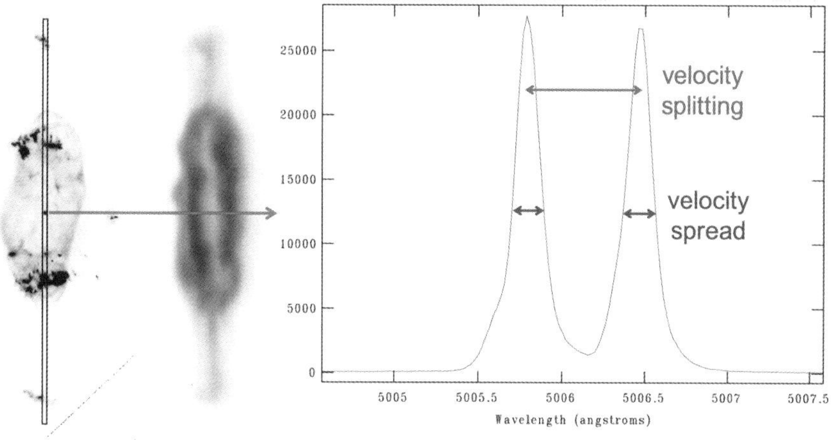

Figure 1. This figure illustrates our experiment. The left panel sketches our slit over the HST image of NGC 7009 ([N II] λ6584; Prop. ID 11122, PI Balick). The middle panel presents the resulting two dimensional spectrum, the position-velocity (PV) diagram. The approaching (left) and receding (right) sides of the nebular shell are clearly distinguished due to their differing Doppler shifts. The ellipse in the PV diagram, due to the main shell, closes at the top and bottom because the velocity is perpendicular to the line of sight at those positions. The right panel presents a spatial cut of the PV diagram at the position of the central star (the position of the arrow) from the [O III] λ5007 spectrum. The two peaks represent the emission from the approaching and receding sides of the shell, separated by their velocity splitting. What interests us here is the widths of these emission peaks (FWHM), the velocity spread, and the physical processes responsible for these widths.

it. This broadening has a typical width of 5 km/s, but will depend upon the particular lines (e.g., Clegg et al. 1999). Third, the thermal motions of the ions in the plasma imply a broadening, $\sigma_{th} = \sqrt{83.1(T_e/10^4/A)}$ km/s (e.g., Lang 1980), where T_e is the electron temperature (in K) and A the atomic mass of the ion involved (in atomic mass units), i.e., $\sigma_{th} = 9.1$ km/s for H and 2.3 km/s for O at 10^4 K. Fourth, the instrumental point spread function will broaden the line profile by $1.3 - 5.4$ km/s for spectral resolutions between 10^5 and 20,000 respectively.

There are other broadening mechanisms, whose effect upon the observed line width are much less clearly defined. There may be both organized and disorganized motions within the nebular shell. Apart from the expansion of the nebular shell, it is well-known that the velocity splitting observed between the approaching and receding sides varies as a function of the ionization potential of the ions involved (Wilson 1950), i.e., there is often a velocity gradient from the inner to the outer edge of the nebular shell. Both the expansion of the nebular shell and the velocity gradient are ordered motions, but there may also be macroscopic turbulence, due to large-scale, disordered motions within the plasma. In what follows, we will refer to the sum of these macroscopic effects as the nebular shell's "kinematic structure".

Finally, the spatial resolution of the observations is finite. So, if nearby lines of sight have different kinematics and if these lines of sight cannot be spatially resolved, they will contaminate and broaden the emission profile along any given line of sight. Our experiments indicate that this effect is probably not important for scales of $1'' - 2''$ in our objects, whose sizes are of order $30''$.

2. Observations

The observations were undertaken at the Observatorio Astronómico Nacional on the Sierra San Pedro Mártir (OAN-SPM), Baja California, México using the Manchester Echelle Spectrograph (MES; Meaburn et al. 2003) installed on the Cassegrain focus of the 2.1m telescope. The MES is a long-slit, echelle spectrograph that uses narrow-band filters to isolate the spectral order of interest. The spectral resolution is set by the width of the entrance slit. For the observations used here, a $39\,\mu$m slit was used, yielding a maximum spectral resolution ($\lambda/\delta\lambda$) of order 10^5 at the C II λ6578 line. The observations were obtained in various observing runs beginning with the first trial observations in 2018 and continuing to June 2023. We obtained spectra with filters that allowed observing the following emission lines: O II $\lambda\lambda$4639,4649,4662, N III $\lambda\lambda$4634,4641, He II $\lambda\lambda$4686,6560, [O III] λ5007, He I λ5016, [N II] $\lambda\lambda$6548,6563, Hα, and C II λ6578. Here, we present observations of NGC 3242, NGC 6153, and NGC 7009, but we also have similar spectra for IC 418, NGC 6543, NGC 6572, NGC 6826, and NGC 7027.

The reduction of these spectra followed the standard practice for long-slit spectroscopy (e.g., Massey et al. 1992) and is described in Richer et al. (2017). When necessary, cosmic rays were edited out of the object spectra. The overscan area of the images was then averaged and subtracted for all images. Mean, overscan-subtracted bias images were used to create two-dimensional bias patterns and subtracted from all other images. In some cases, flat field images were obtained of the internal tungsten lamp and used to create flat field images that were then applied to the object spectra. We did not calibrate in flux.

We also consider observations of NGC 6153 obtained on 2002 June 8 at the European Southern Observatory (ESO) using the Ultraviolet and Visual Echelle Spectrograph (UVES; Dekker et al. 2000) mounted on the Very Large Telescope (VLT) Kuyen (UT2) and retrieved from the ESO archives (program 69.D-0174A, PI Danziger). These spectra include the entire optical range at a spectral resolution of approximately 30,000 and have been described in detail elsewhere (Richer et al. 2022).

3. Analysis and Results

For the MES spectra, we measure the velocity spread (Figure 1) of two sides of the nebular shell along the line of sight to the central star (NGC 3242, NGC 6153, and NGC 7009), what Sabbadin et al. (2008) refer to as the "central star pixel line". We consider a spatial extent of $1''$ for the analysis. We measure the FWHM of the emission peaks, fitting a Gaussian function, or several if the line can be reliably decomposed into several components. In all cases, one component strongly dominates the emission profile and we present results only for that component. As the spectrum in Figure 1 illustrates, the profiles may be complex within the main shell, but usually one emission component dominates along any given line of sight.

We decompose the width of this dominant component assuming that the line fine structure, the thermal broadening, and the instrumental point spread function are all Gaussian in form. Hence, we compute the residual kinematic structure, ΔW_{ks} as

$$\Delta W_{ks}^2 = FWHM_{obs}^2 - FWHM_{fs}^2 - FWHM_{th}^2 - FWHM_{psf}^2$$

where $FWHM_{obs}$, $FWHM_{fs}$, $FWHM_{th}$, and $FWHM_{psf}$ are the observed width, the fine structure broadening, the thermal width, and the instrumental broadening, all as $FWHM = 2.355\sigma$. The only lines affected by fine structure are Hα and He II $\lambda\lambda$4686,6560. For Hα, we adopt $FWHM_{fs} = 7.5\,\mathrm{km/s}$ based upon García-Díaz et al. (2008). We are working on estimates for the He II lines (see also Sabbadin et al. 2008). For the thermal broadening, we currently assume $T_e = 9,000\,\mathrm{K}$, though this may be an over-estimate for the C II and O II lines in these objects. For the instrumental broadening,

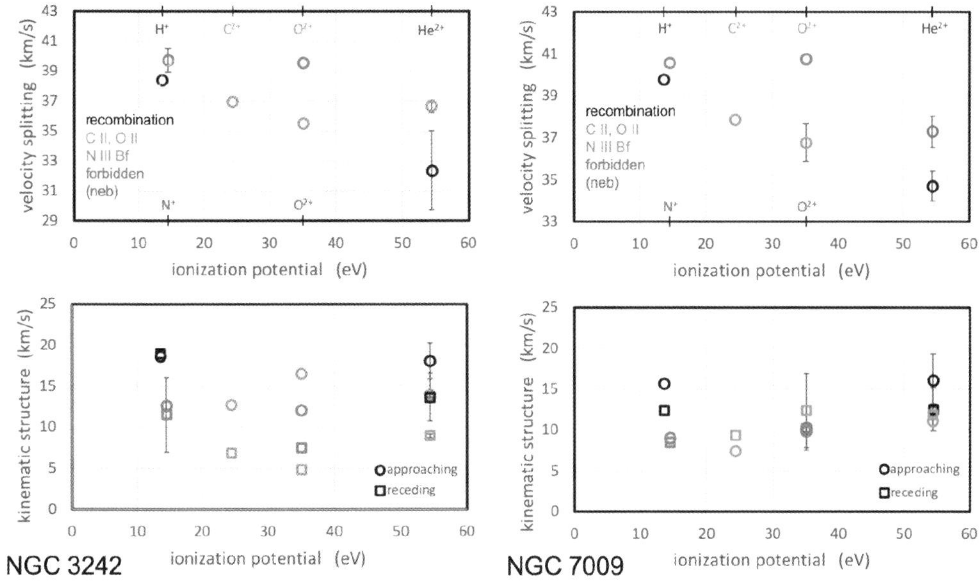

Figure 2. We present our results for NGC 3242 (left) and NGC 7009 (right) using the MES spectra. In the top panels, we present the usual "Wilson diagram" of velocity splitting plotted as a function of the ionization potential of the parent ion. The different colours indicate lines formed from different physical mechanisms. The bottom panels present the residual kinematic structure as a function of the ionization potential of the parent ion (shown, top/bottom axes). The circles and squares present the results for the approaching and receding sides, respectively. For NGC 3242, the velocity splitting varies from about 32 km/s for He II to 40 km/s for [N II], which means that the velocity gradient from the innermost part of the shell to the outermost part is of order 4 km/s. On the other hand, the residual kinematic structure is of order $10-15$ km/s, which is several times higher. The same situation occurs in NGC 7009: The velocity gradient is again of order 4 km/s while the residual kinematic structure is again aproximately three times larger, $10-15$ km/s.

we measure the FWHM of the arc lines closest to the wavelength of the line of interest since the spectral resolution of the MES spectra varies across the spectral intervals (at this very high resolution; $FWHM_{psf} = 3 - 5\,\mathrm{km/s}$).

For the UVES spectra of NGC 6153, the foregoing applies generally. However, the spectral resolution varies rather little, so we adopted a constant value of the instrumental broadening of $FWHM_{psf} = 11\,\mathrm{km/s}$.

Figures 2 and 3 present our results. The top panel for each object presents the "Wilson diagram" of velocity splitting as a function of the ionization potential of the parent ion of the line (Wilson 1950). For permitted lines, the parent ion is the ion that captures the electron whose emission cascade is observed, e.g., H^+ ions capture electrons, but we observe H I lines, so the relevant ionization potential is that to produce H^+. On the other hand, forbidden lines arise from the excitation of electrons already attached to the ions, e.g., [O III] λ5007 arises from the excitation of electrons attached to O^{2+} ions, so the relevant ionization potential is that to produce O^{2+}. The other case we observe are the Bowen fluorescence lines of N III whose ultimate origin is due to emission of He II Lyα photons, so the relevant ionization potential is that to produce He^{2+}.

From the Wilson diagrams, we can easily estimate the velocity gradient from the innermost to the outermost parts of nebular shell based upon the He II and [N II] lines. We estimate the velocity gradient as half the difference between the velocity splitting observed for the He II and [N II] lines. For example, in NGC 3242, the velocity splitting

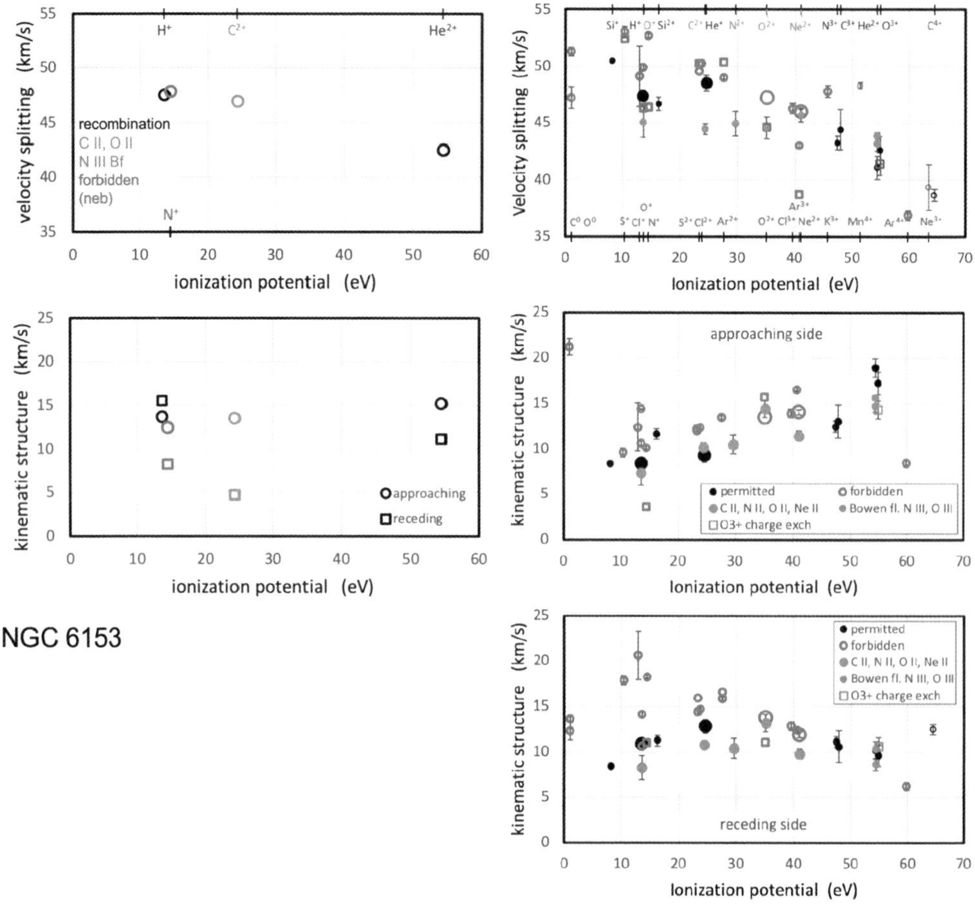

Figure 3. This figure presents our results for NGC 6153 using the MES spectra (left) and UVES spectra (right). Given the large number of lines measured in the UVES spectra, we present the kinematic structure for the approaching (middle panel) and receding (bottom) sides separately. The measurements are made along the line of sight to the central star for the MES spectra, but along a line of sight slightly offset from the central star (towards the ESE; Richer et al. 2022) for the UVES spectrum. Both datasets reveal results similar to NGC 3242 and NGC 7009: The velocity gradient through the nebular shell is $3-4\,\mathrm{km/s}$ while the residual kinematic structure is aproximately three times larger, about $12\,\mathrm{km/s}$.

is approximately $32\,\mathrm{km/s}$ for He II and $40\,\mathrm{km/s}$ for [N II], so the difference is $8\,\mathrm{km/s}$. However, this velocity difference is measured over a line of sight that crosses both the approaching and receding sides of the nebular shell. Hence, the velocity gradient from the inner to outer edge of the nebular shell should be only about half of this value, or $4\,\mathrm{km/s}$.

The bottom (or subsequent) panels in each column in Figures 2 and 3 present the residual kinematic structure, ΔW_{ks}, as a function of the ionization potential of the parent ion. Contrary to the velocity splitting, the kinematic structure does not vary in a systematic way with the ionization potential in these three objects. In some cases in Figures 2 and 3 there is a trend of ΔW_{ks} with ionization potential, but the sense of this trend is not systematic from one object to another. The most fundamental result from Figures 2 and 3 is that the residual kinematic structure is always substantially larger than the velocity gradient through the nebular shell, typically by a factor of 3 or more.

4. Discussion

If we compare the residual kinematic structure we find in these three objects with the broadening mechanisms listed earlier, the residual kinematic structure is more important than any of them, except for thermal broadening of H and He lines. For the heavy elements C, N, and O, the residual kinematic structure is the dominant line broadening mechanism.

The fine structure of the H and He lines varies as a function of the electron temperature and density, but they are not a source of concern. The calculations of Clegg et al. (1999) indicate that temperature variations over the $300 - 30,000\,\mathrm{K}$ range produce a change in the central wavelength of the blend by only 0.3 km/s for the H I lines. For He II $\lambda4686$, the effect is of 0.5 km/s for a temperature variation of $1,000 - 30,000\,\mathrm{K}$. Variations in the electron density have even less effect. So, this is not an important concern, as it is at least an order of magnitude smaller than the residual kinematic structure that we observe.

As we have defined it here, the residual kinematic structure includes all non-microscopic broadening mechanisms. One of these broadening mechanisms is the velocity gradient that is often observed through the nebular shell (Wilson 1950). This velocity gradient is well-understood from hydrodynamical models and arises because the innermost plasma cannot overrun the plasma that surrounds it (e.g., Villaver et al. 2002; Perinotto et al. 2004). The velocity gradient is a largely ordered velocity structure, so it's effect on broadening lines should be modest, except perhaps for lines like those of H that are emitted thoughout the entire nebular volume. However, we measure the velocity gradient directly here and find that it is always much less than the observed residual kinematic structure, with the two differing typically by a factor of 3 or more. Here, we consider only lines of sight toward or near the central star. These lines of sight are maximally sensitive to the effect of the velocity gradient, which only serves to emphasize that it is only a fraction of the residual kinematic structure. Hence, there is considerably more kinematic structure in nebular shells than the velocity gradient.

By considering the line of sight towards the central star (or very near it), we minimize the effects of projection along the line of sight (Sabbadin et al. 2008). This line of sight is radial through the nebular shell with respect to the central star. Other lines of sight will potentially intercept more structure, since they will traverse longer paths through nebular shell, if it is of constant thickness. However, as both the image and spectrum in Figure 1 clearly illustrate, the local structure is very variable and may well dominate over simple geometrical expectations.

Turbulence is likely the most obvious explanation for the residual kinematic structure we observe, as has been noted before (Sabbadin et al. 2008). Turbulence is also likely to have ample opportunity to be generated, since the small-scale structure (molecular) of planetary nebulae is notoriously non-uniform, even in highly evolved objects such as NGC 6720 or NGC 7293 where time might have been expected to allow the matter distribution to smooth itself out (Wesson et al. 2023; Su et al. 2007, respectively). This small-scale structure persists and must be continuously evaporated over the lifetime of the ionized shell and so provides many local sources of random velocity anomalies.

Whatever the origin of the residual kinematic structure, it is an energy source that contributes to the total energy budget. It would appear that it is also an important energy source, since the associated velocity, typically $10 - 15\,\mathrm{km/s}$ here, is a large fraction of the thermal velocity of H atoms ($21\,\mathrm{km/s}$ at $10^4\,\mathrm{K}$). At face value, the energy associated with the residual kinematic structure may amount to of order 25% of the thermal energy, so this energy will affect the microphysics of the plasma. To our knowledge, this energy source has not been included thus far when modelling planetary nebulae.

References

Clegg, R. E. S., Miller, S., Storey, P. J., & Kisielius, R. 1999, A&AS, 135, 359
Dekker, H., D'Odorico, S., Kaufer, A., Delabre, B., & Kotzlowski, H. 2000, Proc. SPIE, 4008, 534
García-Díaz, Ma. T., Henney, W. J., López, J. A., & Doi, T. 2008, RMxAA, 44, 181
Lang, K. R. 1980, Astrophysical Formulae (Berlin: Springer)
Massey, P., Valdes, F., & Barnes, J. 1992, IRAF User Guide 2B, A User's Guide to Reducing Slit Spectra with IRAF (Tucson, AZ: National Optical Astronomy Observatory)
Meaburn, J., López, J. A., Gutiérrez, L., et al. 2003, RMxAA, 39, 185
Perinotto, M., Schönberner, D., Steffen, M., & Calonaci, C. 2004, A&A, 414, 993
Pradhan, A. K., & Nahar, S. N. 2011, Atomic Astrophysics and Spectroscopy (Cambridge University Press)
Richer, M. G., Arrieta, A., Arias, L., et al. 2022, AJ, 164, 243
Richer, M. G., Suárez, G., López, J. A., & García-Díaz, Ma. T 2017, AJ, 153, 140
Sabbadin, F., Turatto, M., Benedetti, S., Ragazzoni, R., & Cappellaro, E. 2008, A&A, 488, 225
Su, K. Y., Chu, Y.-H., Rieke, G. H., et al. 2007, ApJL, 657, 41
Villaver, E., García-Segura, G., & Manchado, A. 2002, ApJ, 581, 1204
Wesson, R., Matsuura, M., Zijlstra, A. A., et al. 2023, arXiv:2308.09027
Wilson, O. C. 1950, ApJ, 111, 279

Planetary Nebulae: A Universal Toolbox in the Era of Precision Astrophysics
Proceedings IAU Symposium No. 384, 2025
O. De Marco, A. Zijlstra & R. Szczerba, eds.
doi:10.1017/S1743921323005215

Precise Determination of Extinction Corrections and Plasma Diagnostics

Toshiya Ueta[1] **and Masaaki Otsuka**[2]

[1]Department of Physics and Astronomy, University of Denver, USA
email: Toshiya.Ueta@du.edu

[2]Okayama Observatory, Kyoto University, Japan

Abstract. Extinction correction is the quintessence of astronomy. To achieve precision astrophysics in plasma diagnostics as in the theme of the present Proceedings, one must perform extinction correction properly before executing any line diagnostics of line-emitting objects including planetary nebulae. By making use of the inseparable relationship between extinction correction and plasma diagnostics, we establish a novel method to determine the physical conditions of a line-emitting target and the extinction characteristics along the line of sight toward the target simultaneously and self-consistently. This approach is made possible by the exact analytical expressions for the extinction parameters in terms of the emission properties of the target and by statistical optimization of the extinction parameters to find the robust physical conditions of the target.

Keywords. plasmas, methods: analytical, methods: statistical, techniques: spectroscopic, dust, extinction

1. Introduction

Plasma diagnostics are the gold standard to understand the physical conditions of line-emitting gaseous systems (e.g., Osterbrock & Ferland 2006; Pradhan & Nahar 2011). Given the observed relative strengths of diagnostic emission lines from various astrophysical targets, it is possible to determine the excitation states of specific gaseous species in terms of the electron density (n_{e}) and temperature (T_{e}), from which ionic and elemental abundances can also be derived (e.g., Peimbert, Peimbert, & Delgado-Inglada 2017; Kewley, Nicholls, & Sutherland 2019). Thus, measuring line strengths at high accuracy and precision is of the utmost importance to succeed.

Meanwhile, it must also be recognized that one's success in plasma diagnostics hinges on the quality of extinction correction, because observed strengths of diagnostic emission lines are all subject to the circumsource and interstellar extinction (e.g., Savage & Mathis 1979; Salim & Narayanan 2020; Gordon et al. 2023). No matter how precise and accurate line measurements are, inadequate extinction correction could potentially ruin the rest of the data analysis and compromise all the subsequent derivatives and implications. In the era of precision astrophysics in the 21st century as in the theme of the present Proceedings, one should really refrain from making a naive assumption such as extinction being benign or negligible. It is imperative that extinction is rigorously accounted for and that observed line strengths are properly corrected for extinction *before any subsequent analysis is performed.*

Hence, it is not too hard to see that extinction correction and plasma diagnostics are to be performed simultaneously and self-consistently for the best results. This is simply because the degree of extinction is usually determined by comparing observed line strength ratios with their unattenuated theoretical counterparts, provided that the physical conditions of the target are known *a priori*. In this contribution, we outline a robust update on the "Direct Method" to streamline both extinction correction and plasma diagnostics so that the physical conditions of the line emitting target and the extinction toward the target are determined *all at once* based exclusively on spectroscopic data of the most abundant and prevalent gas species, hydrogen.

2. Extinction Correction of Line-Emitting Gaseous Nebulae

According to the theory of radiative transfer, the amount of radiation from a target source $I_0(\lambda)$ is reduced to the observed value $I(\lambda)$ as

$$I(\lambda) = I_0(\lambda)\exp(-\tau_\lambda) \tag{1}$$

upon passing through the circumsource and interstellar media, which as a whole amount to the optical depth τ_λ along the line of sight. Observationally, this reduction of the intrinsic signal is often expressed by means of the wavelength-dependent base-10 power index $c(\lambda)$ as

$$I(\lambda) = I_0(\lambda) \cdot 10^{-c(\lambda)} = I_0(\lambda) \cdot 10^{-\tau_\lambda / \ln 10}. \tag{2}$$

This base-10 power index c is usually referred to as "the extinction c" where $c(\lambda) \approx 0.434\tau_\lambda$.

Meanwhile, the magnitude-based total extinction A_λ is defined to be

$$A_\lambda = -2.5\log_{10}\frac{I(\lambda)}{I_0(\lambda)}, \tag{3}$$

for which we immediately see the relationship between A_λ and $c(\lambda)$ as $A_\lambda = 2.5c(\lambda)$. The total extinction A_λ is often normalized by A_V, the total extinction at the V band, to define an extinction law of the form

$$\left\langle \frac{A_\lambda}{A_V} \right\rangle = a_\lambda + b_\lambda \cdot R_V^{-1}. \tag{4}$$

Here, R_V is the total-to-selective extinction, $A_V/E(B-V) = A_V/(A_B - A_V)$, which is meant to capture the wavelength-dependent nature of extinction along a line of sight (e.g., Cardelli, Clayton, & Mathis 1989). It can alternatively be understood as the color excess at the V band with respect to an infinitely red band (i.e., $A_\infty \equiv 0$) normalized by the $B-V$ color excess. More broadly, R_V is often considered to represent the average dust size along a particular line of sight: the larger the dust size is, the greater R_V value becomes. Mathematicaly, the a_λ and b_λ parameters in Eq. 4 are the y-intercept and slope, respectively, of the fit of the extinction curve A_λ/A_V to R_V^{-1} averaged over many lines of sight in the Milky Way or toward a specific galaxy (hence the angle brackets $\langle\rangle$ are used to mean it is the "average"). These parameters are usually expressed as a combination of polynomials representing the continuum and Drude profiles describing significant spectral features (e.g., Gordon et al. 2023).

When a gaseous nebula of the electron density n_e and electron temperature T_e radiates emission lines, the ratio of intrinsic line strengths of a particular ionic species X^{i+} can be expressed as a ratio of volume emissivities or emission coefficients $\epsilon_{X^{i+}}$ between two lines as

$$\frac{I_0(\lambda_2)}{I_0(\lambda_1)} = \frac{n_\mathrm{e} n_{i+} \epsilon_{X^{i+}}(\lambda_2; n_\mathrm{e}, T_\mathrm{e})/4\pi}{n_\mathrm{e} n_{i+} \epsilon_{X^{i+}}(\lambda_1; n_\mathrm{e}, T_\mathrm{e})/4\pi} = \frac{\epsilon_{X^{i+}}(\lambda_2; n_\mathrm{e}, T_\mathrm{e})}{\epsilon_{X^{i+}}(\lambda_1; n_\mathrm{e}, T_\mathrm{e})} \tag{5}$$

where n_{i+} is the number density of the ionic species X^{i+} given that emission lines arise from the same part of the target nebula. This means that the intrinsic line ratios are practically functions of n_e and T_e of the line emitting region of the target (e.g., Pradhan & Nahar 2011).

Then, based on the base-10 power-law formalism (Eq. 2), the modification of the intrinsic line ratio $I_0(\lambda_2)/I_0(\lambda_1)$ into the observed line strength ratio $I(\lambda_2)/I(\lambda_1)$ is expressed as

$$\frac{I(\lambda_2)}{I(\lambda_1)} = \frac{I_0(\lambda_2) \cdot 10^{-c(\lambda_2)}}{I_0(\lambda_1) \cdot 10^{-c(\lambda_1)}} = \frac{I_0(\lambda_2)}{I_0(\lambda_1)} \cdot 10^{-c(\lambda_1)\left(\frac{c(\lambda_2)}{c(\lambda_1)}-1\right)} = \frac{I_0(\lambda_2)}{I_0(\lambda_1)} \cdot 10^{-c(\lambda_1)\left(\frac{A_{\lambda_2}}{A_{\lambda_1}}-1\right)} \tag{6}$$

where the relationship between $c(\lambda)$ and A_λ introduced above is used at the last step. This equation gives us the basis for the determination of the absolute amount of extinction c at some reference wavelength λ_1 as

$$c(\lambda_1) = \left(1 - \frac{A_{\lambda_2}}{A_{\lambda_1}}\right)^{-1} \log_{10}\left(\frac{\frac{I(\lambda_2)}{I(\lambda_1)}}{\frac{I_0(\lambda_2)}{I_0(\lambda_1)}}\right) \tag{7}$$

in which the coefficient involving the ratio of total extinction A at λ_1 and λ_2 can be replaced by adopting an R_V-dependent extinction law (e.g. Eq. 4) as

$$\left(1 - \frac{A_{\lambda_2}}{A_{\lambda_1}}\right) \approx \left(1 - \frac{\left\langle \frac{A_{\lambda_2}}{A_V} \right\rangle}{\left\langle \frac{A_{\lambda_1}}{A_V} \right\rangle}\right) = \left(1 - \frac{a_{\lambda_2} + b_{\lambda_2} \cdot R_V^{-1}}{a_{\lambda_1} + b_{\lambda_1} \cdot R_V^{-1}}\right). \tag{8}$$

Here, we emphasize that the inseparable relationship between extinction correction and plasma diagnostics arises from the dependence of the intrinsic line ratio $I_0(\lambda_2)/I_0(\lambda_1)$ on n_e and T_e (Eq. 7) via the line emissivities (Eq. 5). In other words, the extinction c at a reference wavelength λ_1 cannot be determined unless the physical conditions of the line emitting gas, n_e and T_e, are known *a priori*. Thus, extinction correction and plasma diagnostics must be performed together – iteratively or otherwise – for the maximum consistency. To restate it further, *extinction can be, and hence, should be, determined as part of plasma diagnostics.*

3. Analytical Solutions for the Relative Visibility and Extinction Index

In the literature, there is a long history of plasma diagnostics (e.g., Aller 1999). Naturally, diagnostics have long been performed most often in the optical using the H I Balmer lines with the Hβ line as a reference. The initial choice of the Hβ line as a reference was most likely motivated because this line happens to be relatively isolated from other major lines in the optical. However, there is no particular theoretical reason why the Hβ line must be used as a reference. For that matter, there is no particular theoretical reason why the Hα-to-Hβ ratio must be treated as a canon. As long as measurements are accurate and precise enough, one can adopt other H I recombination lines or even lines of other species.

Theoretically, line strength ratios are adopted as proxies for the ratio of emissivities of the corresponding lines (Eq. 5 above; see Hummer & Storey 1987; Storey & Hummer 1995; Storey & Sochi 2014 for cases of hydrogenic ions). In fact, Osterbrock (1989) originally suggested the use of a Paschen line and a Balmer line from the same upper set of levels, because then line intensity ratios would depend mostly on the ratio of their transition probabilities. However, they hesitated to go with the Paschen-to-Balmer ratio method stating that "the relative insensitivity of photomultipliers and of CCDs at wavelengths longward of 1 μm." This statement reflected the state of IR detectors when the first edition of the book was published (Osterbrock 1989) and was somehow kept in the second edition even when sensitive IR spectroscopic measurements were enabled routinely (Osterbrock & Ferland 2006). Of course, such is no longer a source of concern now in the 21st century.

At any event, we continue our discussion below using λ_1 as the wavelength of a reference line to keep the generality of the discussion. Provided that a specific R_V-dependent extinction law is adopted, by combining Eqns. 7 and 8, we can determine the extinction $c(\lambda_1)$ as

$$c(\lambda_1) = \frac{a_{\lambda_1} \cdot R_V + b_{\lambda_1}}{(a_{\lambda_1} - a_{\lambda_2}) \cdot R_V + (b_{\lambda_1} - b_{\lambda_2})} \log_{10} \left(\frac{\frac{I(\lambda_2)}{I(\lambda_1)}}{\frac{I_0(\lambda_2)}{I_0(\lambda_1)}} \right), \tag{9}$$

and similarly the relative visibility R_V as

$$R_V = \frac{b_{\lambda_1} \cdot \log_{10} \left(\frac{\frac{I(\lambda_2)}{I(\lambda_1)}}{\frac{I_0(\lambda_2)}{I_0(\lambda_1)}} \right) - (b_{\lambda_1} - b_{\lambda_2}) \cdot c(\lambda_1)}{(a_{\lambda_1} - a_{\lambda_2}) \cdot c(\lambda_1) - a_{\lambda_1} \cdot \log_{10} \left(\frac{\frac{I(\lambda_2)}{I(\lambda_1)}}{\frac{I_0(\lambda_2)}{I_0(\lambda_1)}} \right)} \tag{10}$$

for a particular line at λ_2 with respect to a reference line at λ_1. The above two equations form a system of equations for unknowns, R_V and $c(\lambda_1)$, given the observed line ratio $I(\lambda_2)/I(\lambda_1)$ and its unattenuated theoretical counterpart $I_0(\lambda_2)/I_0(\lambda_1)$, which is a function of n_e and T_e via Eq. 5. Because both $c(\lambda_1)$ and R_V characterize extinction along the line of sight to a specific target source, we should find the same $c(\lambda_1)$ and R_V irrespective of the choice of the line at λ_2. Therefore, we can analytically solve this system of equations for $c(\lambda_1)$ and R_V, if we have at least another set of equations with yet another line at λ_3, i.e., Eqns. 9 and 10 in terms of another line ratio, $I(\lambda_3)/I(\lambda_1)$. Then, with the $c(\lambda_1)$ and R_V values determined, we can also fix the n_e and T_e values as those that yield $I_0(\lambda_2)/I_0(\lambda_1)$ and $I_0(\lambda_3)/I_0(\lambda_1)$ consistently. Thus, we have established *a new method to determine the extinction parameters toward the source from line measurements alone simultaneously in a self-consistent and self-contained manner.*

4. The Optimum Solutions for the Electron Density and Temperature

In practice, however, this is not the end of the analysis. We must now find the optimum solutions for the physical conditions of the target, (n_e, T_e). Based on the above system of equations, when we secure measurements of two line ratios, e.g., $I(\lambda_2)/I(\lambda_1)$ and $I(\lambda_3)/I(\lambda_1)$, or measurements of three lines at λ_1, λ_2, and λ_3, the R_V and $c(\lambda_1)$ surfaces can be defined over a certain range of the (n_e, T_e) space. Then, we can make use of the same expectation that R_V and $c(\lambda_1)$ represent extinction along the same line of sight to the target and conclude that the same R_V and $c(\lambda_1)$ values must always result irrespective of the choice of diagnostic line pairs. That is, we can determine the optimum (n_e, T_e) values as the location in the (n_e, T_e) space at which the same R_V and $c(\lambda_1)$ always result for any diagnostic line ratio pairs $I(\lambda_i)/I(\lambda_1)$ and $I(\lambda_j)/I(\lambda_1)$ where $i \neq j > 1$.

In reality, however, because of observational uncertainties, these R_V and $c(\lambda_1)$ surfaces would vary for each pair of diagnostic line ratios or each trio of diagnostic line measurements. In fact, when we have more than three line strengths measured so that more than two line ratios can be defined (as is fairly routinely done nowadays), we can establish multiple R_V and $c(\lambda_1)$ surfaces to compare against each other. To be more precise, there are ${}_nP_2$ distinct surfaces (where n is the number of line ratios) for each of R_V and $c(\lambda_1)$. Then, it is expected that the R_V and $c(\lambda_1)$ values among all the R_V and $c(\lambda_1)$ surfaces formed with distinct line ratio pairs would vary the least amount at the optimum (n_e, T_e) location. Such a point in the (n_e, T_e) space can easily be determined via some statistical method.

For example, if we obtain four line strength measurements ($I(\lambda_i)$ for $i = 1$ to 4 and λ_1 is used as a reference), we can form three line ratios, $I(\lambda_2)/I(\lambda_1)$, $I(\lambda_3)/I(\lambda_1)$, and $I(\lambda_4)/I(\lambda_1)$, to establish the R_V and $c(\lambda_1)$ surfaces for each pair of line ratios among the ${}_3P_2 = 3$ permutations over a certain (n_e, T_e) range. Thus, we can find the optimum (n_e, T_e) solutions as the location where both of the R_V and $c(\lambda_1)$ values remain the most consistent (i.e., the least amount of variation). Then, the R_V and $c(\lambda_1)$ values at the convergence point in the (n_e, T_e) space would of course be the corresponding optimum solutions for R_V and $c(\lambda_1)$. When a greater number of line measurements, and hence, a greater number of line ratio pairs are available, we can form more R_V and $c(\lambda_2)$ surfaces with every single permutation of line ratio pairs. Then, the optimum values of n_e, T_e, $c(\lambda_1)$, and R_V are determined by the location in the (n_e, T_e) space where $c(\lambda_1)$ and R_V vary the least amount.

In this way, we can seek out the optimum solution for $(R_V, c(\lambda_1))$ and (n_e, T_e) simultaneously and self-consistently if we have the line strength measured at more than three H I recombination lines. Now, we have implemented *an updated method to determine the physical conditions of a line emitting source and the extinction parameters toward the source simultaneously and self-consistently based exclusively on one's own line measurements.*

5. Conclusion and Implications

Following the procedure outlined above, one can simultaneously determine the physical conditions of line emitting plasma (n_e, T_e) together with the base-10 power-law extinction index c at some reference wavelength and the relative visibility R_V along the line of sight to the line emitting plasma, provided that (i) we have measurements of at the very least four H I recombination lines, and (ii) a certain extinction law $\langle A_\lambda/A_V \rangle$ of the R_V-dependent form covering the wavelength range of the measured lines is adopted (e.g., Cardelli, Clayton, & Mathis 1989; Gordon et al. 2023). This is a remarkable improvement on the presently widely-exercised Direct Method of plasma diagnostics, because the proposed method yields (i) all the pertinent quantities simultaneously and self-consistently and (ii) based solely on one's own spectroscopic measurements of H I recombination lines. In other words, the proposed method is *completely data-driven and self-contained*, and *no need to make unnecessary assumptions and rely on separate extinction studies*. In addition, the method can be used effectively for *fainter line emission objects in which only H I recombination lines are readily available*, significantly lowering the requirement threshold for the applicability of the analysis.

Lines to be used in the proposed procedure do not have to be exclusively H I recombination lines. As originally suggested by (Osterbrock 1989), comparing the [S II] lines at $\lambda\lambda$ 4069 and 4076 (^{4}S–^{2}P) with those at $\lambda\lambda$ 10287, 10320, 10336, and 10370 (^{2}D–^{2}P) is a viable option. The He II lines are also possible alternatives, while these lines probe higher excitation regions of the target. At any rate, it would make the most sense to adopt H I recombination lines because hydrogen is obviously the most abundant and prevalent species and these lines are readily available in various wavelength ranges, especially in the optical and infrared that are routinely observed nowadays. For that matter, higher order H I recombination lines within the JWST/MIRI range alone will suffice for the proposed method to yield results.

However, some caution needs to be exercised when practicing the proposed analysis. Obviously, the precision and accuracy of line measurements must be sufficiently high. Among all the sources of uncertainty in the analysis, the measurement uncertainties of the input line measurements impose the largest influence on the precision and accuracy of the derived values. The H I recombination line emissivities show relatively weak n_e dependence over a relevant n_e range. Therefore, it is comparatively more difficult to pinpoint the optimum n_e value than the optimum T_e value. Moreover, line ratio measurements that are offset too much by measurement uncertainties may not yield valid solutions for R_V and $c(\lambda_1)$ (i.e., unphysical negative values may result).

In our preliminary assessment of the validity and effectiveness of the proposed method with a large number of randomly generated models with simulated measurement uncertainties, we have found that (i) T_e, R_V, and $c(\mathrm{H}\beta)$ can be recovered with precision and accuracy within 1 % and n_e can be recovered with precision and accuracy within around 10 % as long as the (n_e, T_e) space is searched at the 0.001 dex resolution in the absence of measurement uncertainties, while (ii) assumed 1 % uncertainties in typical line measurements would translate to 0.1 ± 2.0, 20 ± 50, 5 ± 12, and 6 ± 8 % deviations in the resulting $\log T_e$, $\log n_e$, R_V, and $c(\mathrm{H}\beta)$, respectively. The resulting T_e is always fairly precise and accurate thanks to the relatively large gradient in the line emissivity along the T_e dimension. Therefore, we can in practice fix T_e, R_V and $c(\mathrm{H}\beta)$ first, and further optimize n_e (and R_V and $c(\mathrm{H}\beta)$ again) using other n_e-diagnostic lines already recognized in the traditional Direct Method or any line ratio pairs that would yield a large gradient in the n_e dimension.

If we were to rely on the single fixed line ratio of $I_0(\mathrm{H}\alpha)/I_0(\mathrm{H}\beta) = 2.85$ (corresponding exclusively to gas at $T_e = 10^4$ K and $n_e = 10^3\,\mathrm{cm}^{-3}$) as has been traditionally practiced, the extinction correction would immediately be inconsistent unless the target object is of exactly $T_e = 10^4$ K and $n_e = 10^3\,\mathrm{cm}^{-3}$ (via Eqns. 9 and 10), which of course is never guaranteed. Hence, we must be wary of unnecessary assumptions that can lead to imprecise and inaccurate results by way of inconsistent extinction correction, which in turn can invite unwarranted discussions to mend the incidental inconsistencies (e.g. Ueta & Otsuka 2021, 2022).

Similarly, assuming the "standard" MW value of $R_V = 3.1$ for *any* Galactic object may introduce some unwanted consequence. For example, Moraga Baez et al. (2023) have reported a discrepancy in the resulting $c(\mathrm{H}\beta)$ value for NGC 7027 based on the $\mathrm{H}\alpha/\mathrm{H}\beta$ and $\mathrm{Pa}\beta/\mathrm{H}\beta$ ratios according to the "canonical" Direct Method (i.e., assuming $T_e = 10^4$ K and $n_e = 10^3\,\mathrm{cm}^{-3}$ as well as $R_V = 3.1$). By a quick search for the optimum $c(\mathrm{H}\beta)$ and R_V values by minimizing the discrepancy among the $c(\mathrm{H}\beta)$ values based on seven Balmer and Paschen line ratios for the target observed by us (using the KOOLS-IFU instrument on the Seimei 4 m telescope; e.g. Otsuka 2022), we obtain the optimum value of $R_V = 3.39$, which is consistent with the previous result toward the direction of the target (Seaton 1979). This is potentially a significant issue because the R_V value greatly influences extinction in the UV and can affect the resulting elemental abundances based on UV lines (such as C III 1909 Å). For this particular case, $R_V = 3.1$ yields the C/O abundance ratio of 1.37, while $R_V = 3.4$ gives 1.04, suggesting that the stellar chemistry for NGC 7027 is not as C-rich as previously thought.

In the 21st century, we can *start performing precision astrophysics* in plasma diagnostics with all associated uncertainties quantified. There is no reason not to invest in a method that is clear and straightforward as well as self-consistent and self-contained, leaving no room for any simplifying assumptions that are totally unnecessary. Those who are interested in the present method are encouraged to refer to our forthcoming set of publications, in which more detailed formulation of this solution method will be presented (Ueta & Otsuka *in preparation*) and various case studies in which the method is applied to various types of astrophysical targets are introduced (Otsuka & Ueta *in preparation*).

References

Aller, L. H. 1999, *ApJ*, 525C, 265.
Moraga Baez P., Kastner J. H., Balick B., Montez R., Bublitz J. 2023, *ApJ*, 942, 15.
Cardelli, J. A., Clayton, G. C., Mathis, J. S. 1989, *ApJ*, 345, 245.

Gordon K. D., Clayton G. C., Decleir M., Fitzpatrick E. L., Massa D., Misselt K. A., Tollerud E. J. 2023, *ApJ*, 950, 86.

Hummer D. G., Storey P. J. 1987, *MNRAS*, 224, 801.

Kewley L. J., Nicholls D. C., Sutherland R. S. 2019, *ARA&A*, 57, 511.

Osterbrock, D. E. 1989, *Astrophysics of Gaseous Nebulae and Active Galactic Nuclei.* (Sausalito, CA: University Science Books).

Osterbrock D. E., Ferland G. J. 2006, *Astrophysics of gaseous nebulae and active galactic nuclei, 2nd. ed.* (Sausalito, CA: University Science Books).

Otsuka M. 2022, *MNRAS*, 511, 4774.

Peimbert M., Peimbert A., Delgado-Inglada G. 2017, *PASP*, 129, 082001.

Pradhan A. K., Nahar S. N. 2011, *Atomic Astrophysics and Spectroscopy* (Cambridge, UK: Cambridge University Press).

Salim S., Narayanan D. 2020, *ARA&A*, 58, 529.

Savage, B. D., Mathis, J. S. 1979, *ARA&A*, 17, 73.

Seaton, M. J. 1979, *MNRAS*, 187, 785.

Storey P. J., Hummer D. G. 1995, *MNRAS*, 272, 41.

Storey P. J., Sochi, T. 2014, *MNRAS*, 446, 1864.

Ueta T., Otsuka M. 2021, *PASP*, 133, 093002.

Ueta T., Otsuka M. 2022, *A&A*, 667, L8.

Planetary Nebulae: A Universal Toolbox in the Era of Precision Astrophysics
Proceedings IAU Symposium No. 384, 2025
O. De Marco, A. Zijlstra & R. Szczerba, eds.
doi:10.1017/S1743921323005537

Abundance determination in PNe: How to deal with large chemical inhomogeneities

C. Morisset[1,2], J. García-Rojas[3,4], V. Gomez-Llanos[3,4] and H. Monteiro[5]

[1]Instituto de Astronomía (IA), Universidad Nacional Autónoma de México, Apdo. postal 106, C.P. 22800 Ensenada, Baja California, México
email: chris.morisset@gmail.com

[2]Instituto de Ciencias Físicas, Universidad Nacional Autónoma de México, Av. Universidad s/n, 62210 Cuernavaca, Mor., México

[3]Instituto de Astrofísica de Canarias, E-38205 La Laguna, Tenerife, Spain

[4]Departamento de Astrofísica, Universidad de La Laguna, E-38206 La Laguna, Tenerife, Spain

[5]Instituto de Física e Química, Universidade Federal de Itajubá, Av. BPS 1303-Pinheirinho, 37500-903, Itajubá, Brazil

Abstract. Abundance determinations in planetary nebulae (PNe) are crucial for understanding stellar evolution and the chemical evolution of the host galaxy.

We discuss the complications involved when the presence of a metal-rich phase is suspected in the nebula. We demonstrate that the presence of a cold region emitting mainly metal recombination lines necessitates a detailed treatment to obtain an accurate assessment of the enrichment of this cold gas phase.

Keywords. (stars:) binaries: general, ISM: abundances, (ISM:) planetary nebulae: general

1. Introduction

For more than 80 years, the abundance discrepancy (AD) has been a challenge in the field of abundance determination in ionized nebulae. This discrepancy is the fact that the ionic abundances relative to hydrogen (X^{+i}/H^{+}) obtained from observations of weak recombination lines (RLs) of ions heavier than helium are systematically higher than those obtained from much brighter collisionally excited lines (CELs) corresponding to the same ion (Wyse 1942). This discrepancy is generally parameterized through the abundance discrepancy factor (ADF, Tsamis et al. 2003), which is the ratio between RLs and CELs abundances determined for a given ion (i. e. ADF $= [X^{+i}/H^{+}]_{RLs}/[X^{+i}/H^{+}]_{CELs}$). Recently, it has been found that a scenario in which the presence of temperature fluctuations (Peimbert 1967) in the zones where the gas is most ionized, possibly produced due to the stellar feedback effect, may be responsible for the AD in H II regions (Méndez-Delgado et al. 2023). However, this scenario does not appear to work in the case of planetary nebulae (PNe; Méndez-Delgado & García-Rojas 2023, these proceedings).

The problem is further complicated when considering that in some PNe, the AD is much greater (ADF ≥ 10) than that measured in the vast majority of ionized nebulae (ADF $\sim$ 2–4). In these cases, a binary star that has gone through a common-envelope phase is usually present. It has been shown that a large part of the AD is caused by two plasma components with very different physical conditions. The first component has temperatures similar to those of typical photoionized nebulae with a spectrum mainly composed of RLs of H and He and CELs of heavy elements. The second component is much colder and emits almost no CELs, but its spectrum of RLs of heavy elements is very strong (Corradi et al. 2015; Wesson et al. 2018). The presence of this cold component significantly affects the determination of the physical conditions of the gas and the determination of the chemical abundances in both components (Gómez-Llanos et al. 2020; García-Rojas et al. 2022).

Gómez-Llanos & Morisset (2020) developed a grid of photoionization models that combine cold metal-rich clumps embedded in a normal metallicity region and found that the real contrast between chemical abundances relative to H in both components (the Abundance Contrast Factor, ACF) could be different from the observationally computed ADF. These results call for a review of the methodology for computing ion abundances in this type of objects.

2. Using a correct temperature for Hβ

In the following, we use the same formalism and equations as in Gómez-Llanos et al. (2024, in prep.).

The classical way of determining ionic abundances from emission line is using the following relations:

$$I_\lambda = \int_V n_\mathrm{e}.n_{X^i}.\epsilon_\lambda(T_\mathrm{e}, n_\mathrm{e})dv \simeq \frac{X^i}{H^+}.n_\mathrm{e}^2.\epsilon_\lambda(T_\mathrm{e}, n_\mathrm{e}).V, \tag{1}$$

where n_e and n_{X^i} are, respectively, the densities of electrons and of the ions under consideration, $\epsilon_\lambda(T_\mathrm{e}, n_\mathrm{e})$ is the line emissivity in erg/s.cm^3, X^i/H^+ is the ionic abundance to be determined, T_e is the electron temperature (but see below). The integral is carried out over the volume V of the nebula. In the case of Hβ line this relation is:

$$I_\beta = \int_V n_\mathrm{e}.n_{H^+}.\epsilon_\beta(T_\mathrm{e}, n_\mathrm{e})dv \simeq n_\mathrm{e}^2.\epsilon_\beta(T_\mathrm{e}, n_\mathrm{e}).V, \tag{2}$$

neglecting the contribution of elements other than H to free electrons. Combining both relations leads to:

$$\frac{X^i}{H^+} = \frac{I_\lambda}{I_\beta}.\frac{\epsilon_\beta(T_\mathrm{e}, n_\mathrm{e})}{\epsilon_\lambda(T_\mathrm{e}, n_\mathrm{e})}, \tag{3}$$

where I_λ/I_β is the line ratio involving the X^i ion. Here, we find the first potential problem: the temperature and density used in both emissivities are not necessarily the same. It is very common in detailed analysis to consider two or even tree zones in the considered nebula, the difference between the zones being described by the main ions it contains. For example, a two-zone description could have a low ionization zone where the temperature is determined from [N II] $\lambda5755/\lambda6584$, while the high ionization zone is described by the [O III] $\lambda4363/\lambda5007$ temperature diagnostic. The important issue here is the temperature (and density in a less important way) used in the Hβ emissivity: as the Hβ line is the same in both zones, its emissivity should not depend on where the metal line is coming from. The emissivity of the Hβ line must be obtained from a pair of T_e, N_e representative of the whole H^+ region, which encloses both zones.

As an illustration, we consider a nebula where the low ionization zone has a temperature of 12,000 K, while the high ionization zone is at 9,000 K. The H I line can be considered at 10,000 K. The classical way to determine abundances, using the same electron temperature for the metal line and for Hβ would underestimate the N^+/H^+ ionic abundance in the low ionization zone (using [N II] $\lambda6584$) by 15%, while it would overpredict the O^{++}/H^+ ionic abundance in the high ionization zone (using [O III] $\lambda5007$) by 9%.

The PyNeb `getIonabunce` method gives the user the opportunity to specify the electron temperature for the line under consideration, as well as the temperature for the Hβ line used to normalize the observation:

```
O3.getIonAbundance(int_ratio=350, tem=9000, den=100., wave=5007,
                   Hbeta=100, tem_HI=10000)
```

3. Cold regions disguised as hot ones

In the case of a metal-rich cold phase, the dominant channel to produce emission lines such as [N II] λ5755 or [O III] λ4363 is not longer the radiative decay following a collisional excitation of N^+ or O^{++} ions, but rather the recombination of N^{++} to N^+ or O^{3+} to O^{++}, respectively.

This phenomenon has already been reported in observations (e.g. Jones et al. 2016; García-Rojas et al. 2016, 2022) and in theoretical studies (e.g. Gómez-Llanos & Morisset 2020). Failing to consider the contribution of the recombination to the auroral lines leads to significantly inaccurate estimations of the electron temperature and subsequently the chemical abundances.

4. Detailed abundance determinations for two-components plasma

In the case of two different phases of gas mixed in the line of sight, the previous relations lead to the following.

$$
\begin{aligned}
I_\lambda &= I_\lambda^w + I_\lambda^c \\
&= \left[\frac{X^i}{H^+}\right]^w \cdot (n_e^w)^2 \cdot \epsilon_\lambda(T_e^w, n_e^w) \cdot V^w \\
&\quad + \left[\frac{X^i}{H^+}\right]^c \cdot (n_e^c)^2 \cdot \epsilon_\lambda(T_e^c, n_e^c) \cdot V^c \\
&= \left[\frac{X^i}{H^+}\right]^w \cdot [N_e.n_e]^w \cdot \epsilon_\lambda(T_e^w, n_e^w) \\
&\quad + \left[\frac{X^i}{H^+}\right]^c \cdot [N_e.n_e]^c \cdot \epsilon_\lambda(T_e^c, n_e^c),
\end{aligned}
\tag{4}
$$

the case of Hβ being:

$$
\begin{aligned}
I_\beta &= I_\beta^w + I_\beta^c \\
&= (n_e^w)^2 \cdot \epsilon_\beta(T_e^w, n_e^w).V^w + (n_e^c)^2 \cdot \epsilon_\beta(T_e^c, n_e^c).V^c \\
&= [N_e.n_e]^w \cdot \epsilon_\beta(T_e^w, n_e^w) + [N_e.n_e]^c \cdot \epsilon_\beta(T_e^c, n_e^c) \\
&= (1-\omega) \cdot I_\beta + \omega \cdot I_\beta,
\end{aligned}
\tag{5}
$$

where the w and c superscripts are used for the warm and cold regions, respectively, and ω is defined as the weight of the cold region in the I_β emission: $\omega = I_\beta^c / I_\beta$. The total number of electrons in each region is $N_e = n_e.V$.

Combining the 2 previous equations, we obtain:

$$
\begin{aligned}
\frac{I_\lambda}{I_\beta} &= \left[\frac{X^i}{H^+}\right]^w \cdot (1-\omega) \cdot \frac{\epsilon_\lambda(T_e^w, n_e^w)}{\epsilon_\beta(T_e^w, n_e^w)} \\
&\quad + \left[\frac{X^i}{H^+}\right]^c \cdot \omega \cdot \frac{\epsilon_\lambda(T_e^c, n_e^c)}{\epsilon_\beta(T_e^c, n_e^c)}.
\end{aligned}
\tag{6}
$$

When a line is mainly emitted through collisional excitation followed by radiative transitions, the ratio of its emissivities $\epsilon_\lambda / \epsilon_\beta$ vanishes at low electron temperature, and the line is produced exclusively by the warm region. On the other hand, when a line originates from recombination followed by radiative transitions, the ratio of emissivities $\epsilon_\lambda/\epsilon_\beta$ remains almost independent of the electron temperature. The contribution of the warm (cold) region to the observed line intensity depends primarily on $1-\omega$ (ω respectively), as well as on the ionic abundance of the emitting ion.

Using the findings of bi-abundance models built by Gómez-Llanos & Morisset (2020) and depicted in their Fig. 18, in the following we explore the hypothesis that [O III] and O II come from exclusive regions (warm and cold, respectively). The ionic abundances for each region are determined from different lines using the following equations:

$$\left[\frac{X^i}{H^+}\right]^w = \frac{I_\lambda}{(1-\omega)\cdot I_\beta}\cdot\frac{\epsilon_\beta(T_e^w, n_e^w)}{\epsilon_\lambda(T_e^w, n_e^w)}, \tag{7}$$

when $I_\lambda^c = 0$, and:

$$\left[\frac{X^i}{H^+}\right]^c = \frac{I_\lambda}{\omega\cdot I_\beta}\cdot\frac{\epsilon_\beta(T_e^c, n_e^c)}{\epsilon_\lambda(T_e^c, n_e^c)}, \tag{8}$$

when $I_\lambda^w = 0$.

It is important to note here that the T_e and n_e values used to compute the Hβ emissivity should correspond to the specific region under consideration (warm or cold). Refer to Sec. 2 for the case of the warm region.

The ionic abundances derived from both collisionally excited lines and recombination lines using the generic eq. 3 are both underestimated by a factor close to $1/(1-\omega)$ and $1/\omega$ respectively. If the effect of ω is not taken into account, the ratio between the two determinations is the classical ADF. Thus, ACF is linked to ADF by a factor of $(1-\omega)/\omega$, which can be notable. Hence, there is a clear necessity to determine ω for each spaxel in the images to attain reliable abundances.

The determination of the weight of the cold region ω is a challenging task. It can be computed by considering that the hydrogen emission arises from both regions, and that the Balmer or Paschen jump normalized to an H I line is indicative of the emission contribution from each region. This ratio is commonly employed to determine the so-called Balmer or Paschen temperature. In the case of two regions with very different temperatures, the derived temperature from the Balmer or Paschen jump may not accurately reflect the actual temperature of any plasma component within the observed object.

The theoretical Paschen jump and H-lines are computed as the sum of contributions from both the cold and the warm regions:

$$\begin{aligned} PJ\,(\omega, T_e^w, T_e^c, n_e^w, n_e^c) &= [N_e.n_e]^w\cdot C_{8100}(T_e^w, n_e^w) + [N_e.n_e]^c\cdot C_{8100}(T_e^c, n_e^c)\\ &\quad - [N_e.n_e]^w\cdot C_{8400}(T_e^w, n_e^w) - [N_e.n_e]^c\cdot C_{8400}(T_e^c, n_e^c)\\ &= \left[(1-\omega)\cdot\frac{I_\beta}{\epsilon_\beta(T_e^w, n_e^w)}\cdot(C_{8100}(T_e^w, n_e^w) - C_{8400}(T_e^w, n_e^w))\right]\\ &\quad + \left[\omega\cdot\frac{I_\beta}{\epsilon_\beta(T_e^c, n_e^c)}\cdot(C_{8100}(T_e^c, n_e^c) - C_{8400}(T_e^c, n_e^c))\right] \end{aligned} \tag{9}$$

$$\begin{aligned} I_{9229}\,(\omega, T_e^w, T_e^c, n_e^w, n_e^c) &= (1-\omega)\cdot\frac{I_\beta}{\epsilon_\beta(T_e^w, n_e^w)}\cdot\epsilon_{9229}(T_e^w, n_e^w)\\ &\quad + \omega\cdot\frac{I_\beta}{\epsilon_\beta(T_e^c, n_e^c)}\cdot\epsilon_{9229}(T_e^c, n_e^c) \end{aligned} \tag{10}$$

In the first equation, we omit explicitly stating the dependencies of the continuum on He^+/H^+ and He^{2+}/H^+, but they are considered.

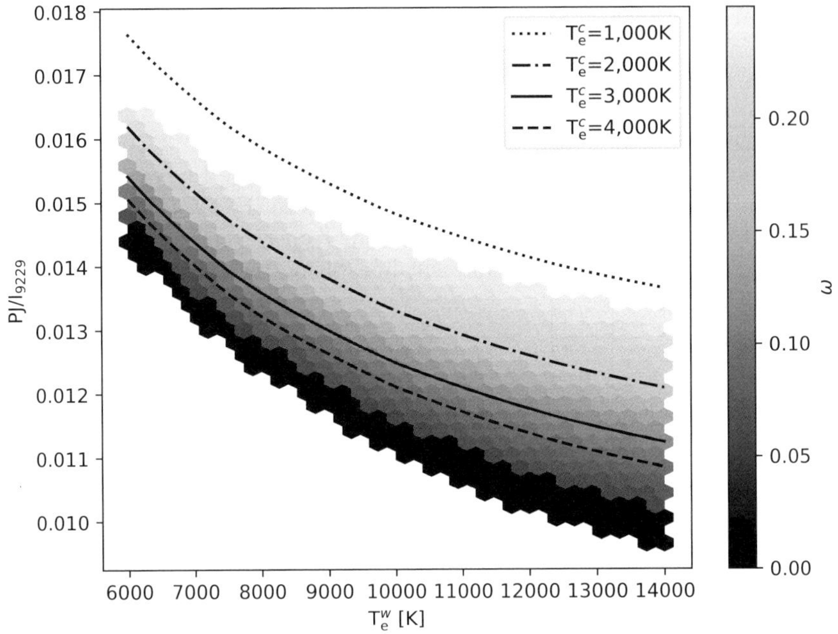

Figure 1. Colored hexagons show the variation of ω when T_e^w varies from 6,000 to 14,000 K and the normalized Paschen jump PJ/I_{9229} varies from 0.010 to 0.017. Fixed values are set to: T_e^c = 3,000 K, $n_e^w = n_e^c$ = 1,000 cm^{-3}, He^+/H^+ = 0.1, and He^{2+}/H^+ = 0.005. Lines of different styles show the values of PJ/I_{9229} for different values of T_e^c and a fixed value of $\omega = 0.1$.

The normalized Paschen jump PJ/I_{9229} is computed using PyNeb (Luridiana et al. 2015) across a grid of T_e^w, T_e^c, and ω, and constant values for n_e^w, n_e^c, He^+/H^+, and He^{2+}/H^+. These numerical values must be adapted for each object. As an illustration, the values of PJ/I_{9229} obtained for T_e^w between 6,000 and 14,000 K, and ω between 0 and 0.25, and fixed values of T_e^c = 3,000 K, $n_e^w = n_e^c$ = 1,000 cm^{-3}, He^+/H^+ = 0.1, and He^{2+}/H^+ = 0.005 are used in Fig. 1 to draw as colored hexagons the variations of ω relative to PJ/I_{9229} and T_e^w. Lines are also showing the effect of changing T_e^c to 1,000, 2,000, 3,000 (the same value used for the colored hexagons), and 4,000 K for the case $\omega = 0.1$.

A numerical algorithm (which can be an Artificial Neuron Network) is then used to interpolate the inverse problem to predict ω from T_e^w, T_e^c, and PJ/I_{9229}.

In the case of NGC 6153, Gómez-Llanos et al. (2024, in prep.) generate a spatially resolved map of ω and use it to compute the ACF of O^{2+}.

5. Conclusions

As highlighted by Richer et al. (2022) regarding the PN NGC 6153, "reality is complicated" when determining the chemical abundances in PNe, particularly in those with high ADFs. It is essential to pay close attention to details when attempting to obtain accurate chemical abundances in these objects, as has been shown in this proceeding.

CM acknowledges funding from PAPIIT/UNAM grants IN101220 and IG101223. JG-R and VG-LL acknowledge funding from the Canarian Agency for Research, Innovation and Information Society (ACIISI), of the Canary Islands Government, and the European

Regional Development Fund (ERDF), under grant with reference ProID2021010074. JG-R also acknowledges the support of the Spanish Ministry of Science and Innovation (MICINN) through the Spanish State Research Agency, under the Severo Ochoa Centers of Excellence Program 2020-2023 (CEX2019-000920-S).

References

Corradi R. L. M., García-Rojas J., Jones D., Rodríguez-Gil P., 2015, ApJ, 803, 99

García-Rojas J., Corradi R. L. M., Monteiro H., Jones D., Rodríguez-Gil P., Cabrera-Lavers A., 2016, ApJ, 824, L27

García-Rojas J., Morisset C., Jones D., Wesson R., Boffin H. M. J., Monteiro H., Corradi R. L. M., Rodríguez-Gil P., 2022, MNRAS, 510, 5444

Gómez-Llanos V., Morisset C., 2020, MNRAS, 497, 3363

Gómez-Llanos V., Morisset C., García-Rojas J., Jones D., Wesson R., Corradi R. L. M., Boffin H. M. J., 2020, MNRAS, 498, L82

Jones D., Wesson R., García-Rojas J., Corradi R. L. M., Boffin H. M. J., 2016, MNRAS, 455, 3263

Luridiana V., Morisset C., Shaw R. A., 2015, A&A, 573, A42

Méndez-Delgado J. E., García-Rojas J., 2023, arXiv e-prints, p. arXiv:2311.10280

Méndez-Delgado J. E., Esteban C., García-Rojas J., Kreckel K., Peimbert M., 2023, Nature, 618, 249

Peimbert M., 1967, ApJ, 150, 825

Richer M. G., Arrieta A., Arias L., Castañeda-Carlos L., Torres-Peimbert S., López J. A., Galindo A., 2022, AJ, 164, 243

Tsamis Y. G., Barlow M. J., Liu X. W., Danziger I. J., Storey P. J., 2003, MNRAS, 345, 186

Wesson R., Jones D., García-Rojas J., Boffin H. M. J., Corradi R. L. M., 2018, MNRAS, 480, 4589

Wyse A. B., 1942, ApJ, 95, 356

Planetary Nebulae: A Universal Toolbox in the Era of Precision Astrophysics
Proceedings IAU Symposium No. 384, 2025
O. De Marco, A. Zijlstra & R. Szczerba, eds.
doi:10.1017/S1743921323005446

A statistical view of low-ionization structures in planetary nebulae

M. Belén Mari[1], Stavros Akras[2] and Denise R. Gonçalves[1]

[1]Valongo Observatory, Federal University of Rio de Janeiro, Rio de Janeiro, Brazil
email: mbmari@unc.edu.ar

[2]Institute for Astronomy, Astrophysics, Space Applications and Remote Sensing, National Observatory of Athens, Greece

Abstract. More than three decades after the pioneering imaging catalog by Balick (1987), where the small-scale and low-ionization structures (LISs) in planetary nebulae (PNe) became evident, the present study conducts a comprehensive statistical analysis of LISs' physical-chemical and excitation properties. Gathering the largest dataset to date, we compare LISs with high-ionization components (rims/shells) across a diverse sample of PNe. Key findings include lower electron densities (N_e[S II]) in LISs than in adjacent rims/shells and comparable electron temperatures (T_e [N II] and [O III]) between these two nebular componets. Various optical diagnostic diagrams, while revealing a clear excitation stratification between these groups of components, are not good enough to clearly pinpoint the main excitation mechanism behind the LISs line-emission. Photoionization and shock models highlight a notable overlap between mechanisms, emphasizing the coexistence of both excitation processes. Contrary to expectations, shocks are unlikely to be the primary excitation source for most of LISs in PNe.

Keywords. ISM: jets and outflows; ISM; kinematics and dynamics; planetary nebulae: general

1. Introduction

Planetary nebulae (PNe) exhibit a variety of morphologies, which are based on the shape of the large-scale, high-ionization) structures such as rims, shells or haloes. In addition, PNe possess small-scale structures prominent in low-ionization species, such as [N II], [S II], [O II] and also [O I]. Gonçalves et al. (2001) classified these low-ionization structures (LISs) considering not only the morphology but also the kinematics, into four main groups: knots, which can appear isolated or in pairs, displaying an aspect ratio close to 1; filaments, when this aspect ratio mentioned before is larger than 1; jets, which appear in opposite pairs, oriented in radial direction from the central star (CS) and have velocities notably higher than the surrounding gas; and jet-like structures, when the velocity of these jets is similar to that of the large-scale structures on which the LISs are embedded. Note that this term, *LISs*, encompasses a broader category that includes various structures falling under this classification, which, in the literature, may also be referred to by more specific nomenclatures: fast low-ionization emission regions (FLIERs) by Balick et al. (1993), bipolar rotating episodic jets (BRETs) by Lopez et al. (1995) or slow moving low-ionization emission regions (SLOWERs) by Perinotto (2000).

Many authors have tried to understand the LISs' properties through, in particular, optical spectra (e.g. Balick et al. 1993, 1994; Gonçalves et al. 2003, 2009; Akras & Gonçalves 2016; Mari et al. 2023a). The conclusions arrived so far are: (i) LISs appear in all morphological type of PNe; (ii) the electron temperature (T_e) between LISs and the larger structures is almost the same; (iii) the electron density (N_e), in general, is lower in LISs than in the surrounding medium; and (iv) there is no significant difference in the chemical abundance between LISs and their surrounding medium. Regarding the excitation mechanisms, there is no consensus yet, LISs could be excited by photoionization from the CS (e.g. Hajian et al. 1997; Ali & Dopita 2017), by shocks interactions (Gonçalves et al. 2004) or by both mechanisms (Fang et al. 2015; Akras & Gonçalves 2016).

In an effort to gain deeper insights into the characteristics of LISs, we initiated a comprehensive study by compiling optical properties obtained from published research over the years. Similar to Guerrero et al. (2020), where efforts were made to enhance the understanding of kinematic properties of LISs within PNe, our objective here is to attain robust and reliable results concerning physico-chemical properties. Section 2 provides an overview of the data we have gathered and our approach to visualizing it. In Section 3, we present the key findings, while Section 4 highlights the discuss and main conclusions arrived.

2. Collected data and visualization

Considering optical spectroscopic studies aimed at understanding LISs within PNe published over the years (e.g. Balick et al. 1994; Hajian et al. 1997; Gonçalves et al. 2003; Fang et al. 2015; Akras & Gonçalves 2016; Ali & Dopita 2017; Miranda et al. 2021; Mari et al. 2023a) we have compiled a dataset of 33 PNe, encompassing 88 rims/shells and 104 LISs. Our choice was to conduct a statistical analysis, employing violinplots – a hybrid visualization method that combines elements of both boxplots and kernel density distributions. One of the most important quantities, in addition to the quartiles and the median, which represents the most expected value, pertains to the *notches*. They serve as boundaries for the 95% confidence interval (CI) of the median value within the analyzed data group (Hintze & Nelson 1998). With the objective of contrasting the features of rims/shells and LISs to discern potential similarities or differences, notches emerge as a valuable analytical tool. Non-overlapping confidence intervals (CIs) imply statistical dissimilarity between groups, while overlapping CIs suggest similarity in the specified property (Chambers & et al. 2017).

3. Results

This section compiles the primary results obtained through the utilization of violin plots.

3.1. *Electron density*

Upon the examination of electron density based on sulfur diagnostic lines (N_e[S II]), in Fig. 1 it can be observed two distinct distributions: one represented in green denoting the LISs distribution, and the other in cyan, signifying the rims/shells distribution. A split violinplot analysis revealed non-overlapping CIs for both distributions, corroborated by the statistical values in Table 1. Consequently, it can be deduced that the two groups exhibit statistically significant differences with respect to N_e[S II]. Further accentuating the contrasting N_e[S II] between the two distinct nebular components is illustrated in the right panel of Fig. 1. This panel directly compares the median N_e[S II] per PN for rims/shells and LISs. This analysis leads to the same unequivocal inference that the electron densities of LISs are notably lower than those of rims/shells.

3.2. *Electron temperature*

In terms of electron temperature (T_e) derived from the [N II] diagnostic lines, the analysis indicates an overlap in the CIs, as presented in Table 1. This result is further

Table 1. N_e (in particles per cm^{-3}) and T_e (in K) for the samples of rims/shells and LISs. The CI correspond to the approximated 95 per cent of confidence intervals for the median value. The last two rows show the number of outliers and sample size, respectively.

	log(N_e[S II])		log(T_e[N II])		log(T_e[O III])	
	Rims/Shells	LISs	Rims/Shells	LISs	Rims/Shells	LISs
Median	3.42	3.23	4.03	4.04	4.01	4.06
CI	[3.35;3.50]	[3.15;3.31]	[4.01;4.05]	[4.02;4.06]	[3.98;4.03]	[4.05;4.08]
#Outliers	4	3	2	2	0	3
#Sample	79	98	64	81	79	83

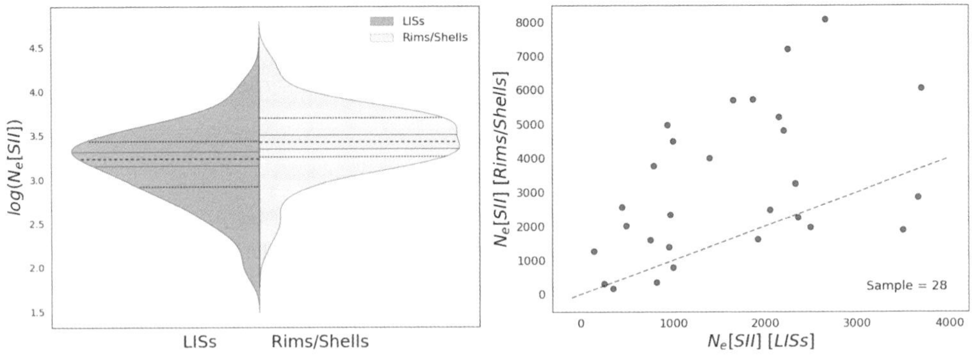

Figure 1. Comparison of N_e[S II] between LISs and rims/shells groups. *Left panel*: split violinplot of both groups with the median, 25th and 75th quartiles shown by dashed and dotted lines, respectively, and the CIs represented by solid lines. *Right panel*: median N_e[S II] values per PN for each group. The dashed line represents the identity function.

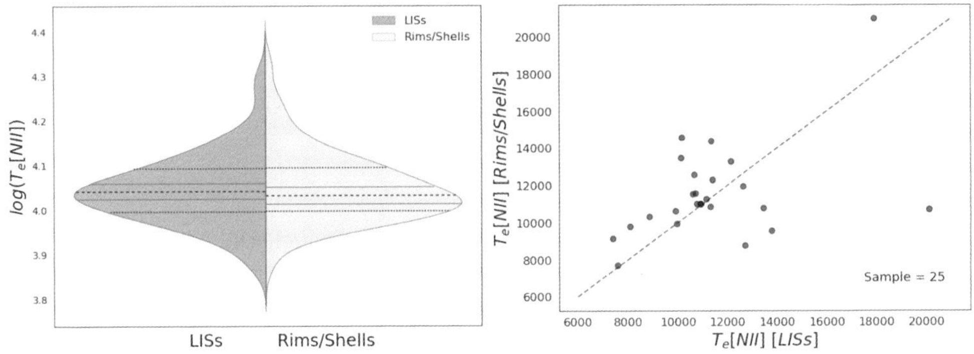

Figure 2. Same as Fig. 1, for T_e[N II].

supported by the similarity observed in the distributions, illustrated in Fig. 2. Therefore, a reasonable conclusion can be drawn that the two groups exhibit a considerable degree of similarity in terms of this electron temperature (T_e[NII]).

When examining the T_e via the [O III] lines, an unexpected bimodality is revealed in the rims/shells group (see Fig. 3), accompanied by non-overlapping CIs (see Table 1). This unanticipated result yields a T_e for LISs that is approximately 1400 K higher than that of rims/shells. Nevertheless, scrutinizing the median values within each group per nebula exposes a dispersion of roughly ± 2000 K for both T_e measurements, whether derived from [N II] or [O III] diagnostic lines. Moreover, the right panel of Fig. 3 illustrates minimal discrepancies in median values among the groups within each nebula. In light of this, it can be concluded that the 1400 K difference between the groups falls well within the scatter and does not carry statistical significance. Hence, the datasets indicate comparability in T_e measurements, even when using the [O III] lines.

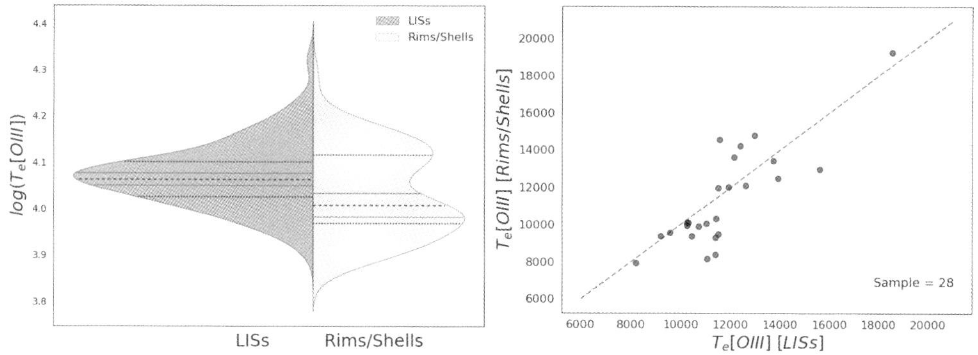

Figure 3. Same as Fig. 1, for T$_e$[O III].

3.3. *Excitation mechanisms*

In our exploration of excitation mechanisms, we have employed various diagnostic diagrams (DDs), such as those of Sabbadin, Minello & Bianchini (1977) (SMB) and Baldwin, Phillips & Terlevich (1981) (BPT), to distinguish between different objects like H II regions, supernova remnants (SNR) or PNe. SMB relies on Hα/[S II] and Hα/[N II] line ratios to separate these objects. On the other hand, BPT diagrams utilize the [O III]/Hβ line ratio in addition to low-ionization lines over Hα. In our analysis, we employed these DDs to discern excitation mechanisms among the distinct components within the analyzed PNe. As illustrated in Fig. 4, the line ratios involving low-ionization lines do not show overlap in terms of CIs between the groups, which can be interpreted as distinct states of excitation among the analyzed components. In the case of the ratios involving [O III], there are overlapping CIs.

To mitigate potential effects from differences in elemental abundances, we have introduced a new DD centered on a single chemical element, specifically oxygen (Fig. 5). Our analysis of split violinplots for [O I]/Hα and [O II]/[O III] reveals distinct separation, with non-overlapping CIs indicating a clear differentiation between the groups – although with a transition region with both groups mixed, evident on the scatter plot. Nevertheless, it is worth noting that the detection of [O I] is not always feasible, resulting in a smaller sample size that requires cautious interpretation of the results.

3.4. *Photoionization and shocks models*

Examining Figs. 4 and 5, it becomes evident that even though LISs and rims/shells fall into statistically distinct groups concerning excitation state, both appear to be associated with regions excited purely by photoionization except for a few structures that fall near the SNR region – i.e., shocks may be the responsible for the excitation of these structures. A grid of photoionization and shock models from the 3MdB (Morisset et al. 2015; Alarie & Morisset 2019) were used in order to look for the range of various emission lines produced by these two mechanisms. Using these models, we applied the same DDs mentioned in the previous section, delineating regions for data corresponding to pure photoionization, as well as low- and high-velocity shock regions.

A substantial overlap between both excitation mechanisms, encompassing not only low-velocity shock models but also those associated with higher velocities, was found. Nonetheless, by employing DDs that take into account the low-ionization line ratios [N II]/[S II] (see left panel of Fig. 6), we managed to differentiate high-velocity shock regions from the region defined by low-velocity shocks, both of which still overlap with the region primarily dominated by photoionization. Furthermore, when

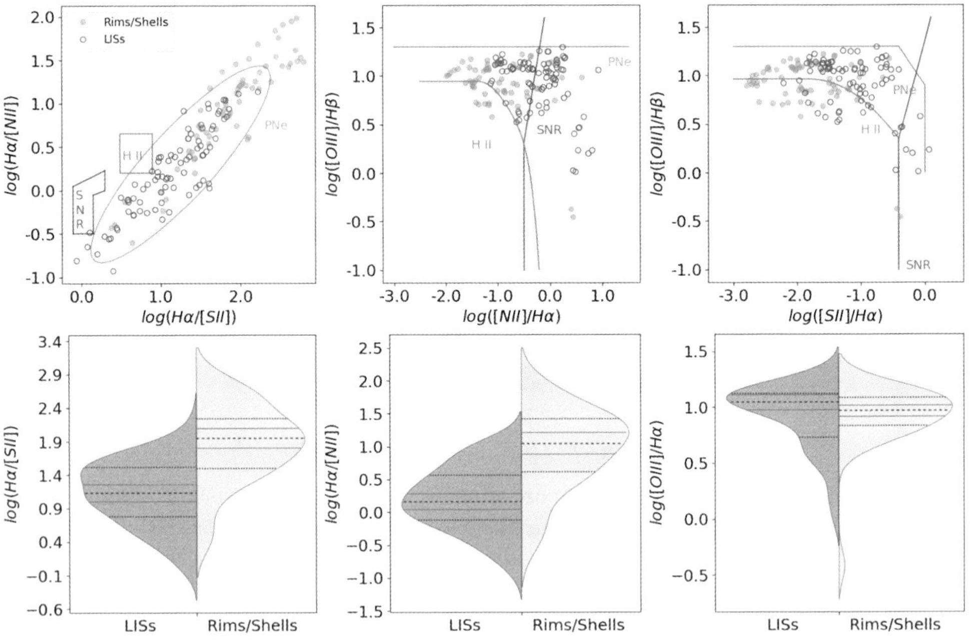

Figure 4. Diagnostic diagrams employed in this work (upper panels) and the split violinplots of their ratio lines (lower panels).

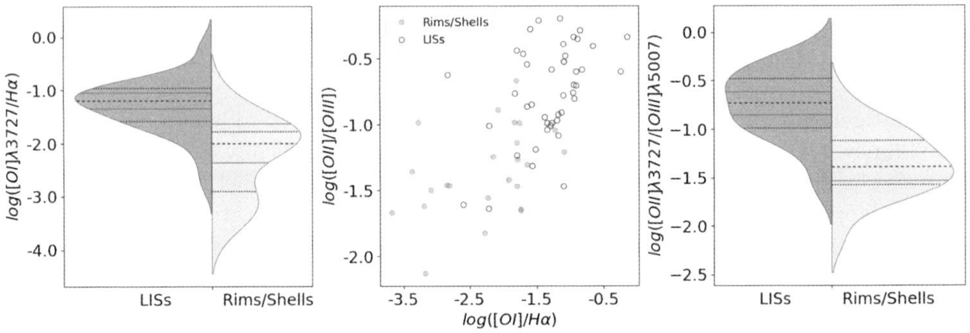

Figure 5. Diagnostic diagram depending on oxygen (middle panel), together with its split violinplots.

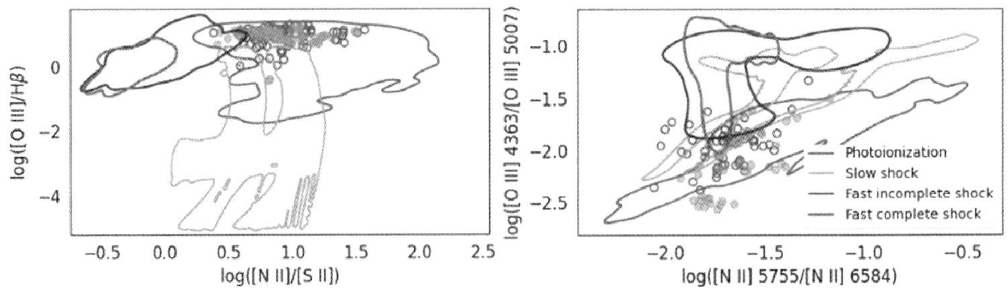

Figure 6. Diagnostic diagrams generated from grids of photoionization and shocks models available in the 3MdB. The photoionization models are in blue contour, the low- and high-velocity shock models are in orange and purple contours, respectively. Our sample of LISs and rims/shells are shown with unfilled green circles and filled cyan circles as before.

utilizing temperature-sensitive line ratios, specifically [N II]λ5755/[N II]λ6584 versus [O III]λ4363/[O III]λ5007 (right panel of Fig. 6), we can distinguish high- and low-velocity shock regions from the location of the objects predominantly excited by photoionization (Mari et al. 2023b).

4. Discussion and conclusions

Returning to the contrast observed in electron density (N_e) between the two groups, a follow-up investigation involving the median values of each group per nebula confirmed that the N_e for rims/shells is indeed higher than that for LISs, with measured median value around 1700 cm^{-3}. Notably, this result appear contradictory to models predicting higher total densities for observed knots (Raga et al. 2008) in comparison with their surrounding gas, or more recently for knots at the tip of the jets having total density in the range of 10^6 to 10^7 cm^{-3}, coupled with low temperatures in the range of 1 to 300 K (Balick et al. 2020). In an effort to address this discrepancy, Gonçalves et al. (2009) proposed the possibility that a substantial fraction of the gas may exist in a neutral or molecular state, which is supported by the limited number of LISs in PNe with the detection of H_2 in the near-IR (Fang et al. 2015, 2018; Akras et al. 2017, 2020). Nonetheless, additional investigations are required to explore new results in the near-IR by examining H_2 and, similarly, in the millimeter range to search for CO, the two most abundant molecules in the universe.

Therefore, considering that this study utilized the most extensive sample of LISs to date and employed statistical analysis, the overall conclusions are more robust. The key findings are as follows: (i) There is no significant difference between the two groups in terms of T_e when using either [N II] or [O III] diagnostic lines. (ii) LISs do indeed exhibit lower electron density compared to the surrounding gas, reinforcing the hypothesis of the presence of neutral and/or molecular matter in their interiors. (iii) Using classical diagnostic diagrams, it is evident that the separation between the groups demonstrates an excitation stratification within PNe, meaning two distinct groups in terms of excitation. However, the majority of LISs are primarily excited by photoionization, with only a few potentially influenced by shocks. (iv) The utilization of multiple DDs may provide a more reliable method of distinguishing between different excitation mechanisms.

Acknowledgements. We acknowledge the partial support: MBM (Capes; IAU and FAPERJ/ 200.527/2023); DRG (CNPq313016/2020-8 and FAPERJ/200.527/2023); SA (H.F.R.I. Project Number: 15665).

References

Akras S., Gonçalves D. R., 2016, MNRAS, 455, 930
Akras S., Gonçalves D. R., Ramos-Larios G., 2017, MNRAS, 465, 1289
Akras S., Gonçalves D. R., Ramos-Larios G., Aleman I., 2020, MNRAS, 493, 3800
Alarie A., Morisset C., 2019, RMxAA, 55, 377
Ali A., Dopita M. A., 2017, PASA, 34, e036
Baldwin J. A., Phillips M. M., Terlevich R., 1981, PASP, 93, 5
Balick B., Rugers M., Terzian Y., Chengalur J. N., 1993, ApJ, 411, 778
Balick B., Perinotto M., Maccioni A., Terzian Y., Hajian A., 1994, ApJ, 424, 800
Balick B., Frank A., Liu B., 2020, ApJ, 889, 13
Chambers J. M., et al. 2017, Graphical Methods for Data Analysis. 1st Ed., doi:10.1201/9781351072304
Fang X., Guerrero M. A., Miranda L. F., Riera A., Velázquez P. F., Raga A. C., 2015, MNRAS, 452, 2445
Fang X., Zhang Y., Kwok S., Hsia C.-H., Chau W., Ramos-Larios G., Guerrero M. A., 2018, ApJ, 859, 92

Gonçalves D. R., Corradi R. L. M., Mampaso A., 2001, ApJ, 547, 302
Gonçalves D. R., Corradi R. L. M., Mampaso A., Perinotto M., 2003, ApJ, 597, 975
Gonçalves D. R., Mampaso A., Corradi R. L. M., Perinotto M., et al. 2004, MNRAS, 355, 37
Gonçalves D. R., Mampaso A., Corradi R. L. M., Quireza C., 2009, MNRAS, 398, 2166
Guerrero M. A., Suzett Rechy-García J., Ortiz R., 2020, ApJ, 890, 50
Hajian A. R., Balick B., Terzian Y., Perinotto M., 1997, ApJ, 487, 304
Hintze J. L., Nelson R. D., 1998, The American Statistician, 52, 181
Lopez J. A., Vazquez R., Rodriguez L. F., 1995, Astrophys. J. Let., 455, L63
Mari M. B., Gonçalves D. R., Akras S., 2023a, MNRAS, 518, 3908
Mari M. B., Akras S., Gonçalves D. R., 2023b, MNRAS, 525, 1998
Miranda L. F., et al., 2021, arXiv e-prints, p. arXiv:2105.05186
Morisset C., Delgado-Inglada G., Flores-Fajardo N., 2015, RMxAA, 51, 103
Perinotto M., 2000, Astrophys. Space Sci., 274, 205
Raga A. C., Riera A., Mellema G., Esquivel A., Velázquez P. F., 2008, A&A, 489, 1141
Sabbadin F., Minello S., Bianchini A., 1977, A&A, 60, 147

Planetary Nebulae: A Universal Toolbox in the Era of Precision Astrophysics
Proceedings IAU Symposium No. 384, 2025
O. De Marco, A. Zijlstra & R. Szczerba, eds.
doi:10.1017/S1743921323005434

What do we really know about the low-ionization structures in planetary nebulae?

Stavros Akras

Institute for Astronomy, Astrophysics, Space Applications and Remote Sensing, National Observatory of Athens, GR 15236 Penteli, Greece
email: stavrosakras@gmail.com

Abstract. We do know that planetary nebulae (PNe) are ionized gaseous clouds of material ejected by evolved dying stars. The intense ultraviolet radiation field of these stars leads to the dissociation of the cold molecular gas and then to the ionization/excitation of the resultant atomic gas. The chemical composition, ionization structure, physical conditions and formation process of nebular shells, rims, and halos are well comprehended. On the contrary, the origin of low-ionization structures (LISs) frequently found in PNe break the overall picture, and it still remains poorly understood. The latest discoveries of molecular hydrogen (H_2) in LISs have changed how we think about their origin. Besides the detection of H_2 emission, the [Fe II] 1.644μm and [C I] 8727Å lines have also been detected in LISs. These results add new pieces to the puzzling problem of LISs opening a new window to enrich our knowledge and understanding on these microstructures.

Keywords. (ISM:) planetary nebulae: general, ISM: atoms, ISM: molecules, planetary nebulae, (ISM:) dust, extinction

1. Introduction

Planetary nebulae (PNe) are complex batches of expanding and interacting shells of gas and dust expelled from low-to-intermediate mass stars (1-8 $M_\odot$), during the active red-giant (RG) and asymptotic giant branch (AGB) evolutionary stages via stellar winds and pulsations. The gas (ionic, atomic and molecular) forming a PN is the debris of these progenitors stars. The intense UV radiation field of the exposed hot and luminous central star (CS) is the dominant source of highly energetic photons that lead, first, to the dissociation of the cold molecular circumstellar envelope (mainly H_2, CO) and, then, to the ionization/excitation of the resulting atomic gas causing the nebula to glow (Kwitter & Henry 2022).

From a morphological point of view, PNe display a number of nebular structures such as rims, shells and halos surrounding the CS, as well as structures in smaller-scales prominent in low-ionization species e.g. [N II], [S II], [O II], [O I] (hereafter LISs; Gonçalves et al. 2001), and easily discerned from the host nebulae. Moreover, based on their kinematic properties, LISs are also divided into the fast, low-ionization emission regions (FLIERs, Balick et al. 1993, 1998), the bipolar, rotation episodic jets (BRETs, López et al. 1995), and the slow moving low ionization emitting regions (SLOWERs, Perinotto 2000).

Considering the intense UV radiation from the CSs, photo-ionization/excitation processes are innately considered as the predominant mechanism for the observed emission-line spectra of PNe. However, this fails to explain simultaneous the enhanced emission in LISs and the surrounding shell, indicating significantly different physical conditions. The origin of LISs continues intriguing the scientists. Their formation cannot be explained by the Generalized Interacting Stellar Wind model (GISW, Balick 1987) and additional mechanisms such as (i) collimated jets/outflows (e.g., Balick et al. 2020) and/or (ii) hydrodynamical instabilities (Kelvin-Helmholtz and/or Rayleigh-Taylor) at the ionization and shock fronts (e.g. Steffen & López 2004; Segura et al. 2006) are required to elucidate their origins.

2. Low-ionization structures: the atomic/ionic component

Based on observations in the visible wavelengths (e.g. Akras & Gonçalves 2016; Mari et al. 2023a,b), it has been found that LISs are characterized by (I) systematically lower electron density (N_e) which contradicts the predictions of dense clumps formation models, (II) comparable electron temperatures (T_e) and (III) similar chemical composition relative to the host nebula. LISs also display significantly lower ionization state than the host nebulae, as it has been shown by the [O I]/Hα vs [O II]/[O III] diagnostic diagram (Mari et al. 2023b). Regarding their excitation mechanisms, the comparison of the observations with the predictions from photoionization and shock models indicates that the vast majority of LISs are more likely photo-dominated structures, but shocks cannot fully rule out yet (Mari et al. 2023b). Overall, LISs akin to photodissociated regions (PDRs).

MUSE data of PNe have offered the opportunity to carry out a spectroscopic analysis in both spatial dimensions covering the host nebulae and LISs (e.g. Walsh et al. 2018; Monreal-Ibero & Walsh 2020). An increase in interstellar extinction c(Hβ) and electron temperature derived from the [S III] diagnostic lines (T_e) have been found in the LISs of NGC 7009 relative to the host nebula (Walsh et al. 2018; Akras et al. 2022). These findings likely indicates the presence of more dust and the contribution of photoelectric dust heating. Based on emission line diagnostic diagrams, LISs occupy the regime of low-ionization nebulae, and they are well distinguished from the host nebula (Akras et al. 2022).

The spectral range of MUSE (4560Å to 9300Å) may not allow the detection of the [O III] λ4363 line flux and consequently, the estimation of T_e, but we can look for the detection of the far-red [C I] λ8727 line. [C I] lines are important coolants of gas in PDRs (Burton et al. 1992) and they imply the presence of free carbon and an oxygen/carbon (O/C) zone. Surprisingly, the [C I] λ8727 line is present in LISs of NGC 6778 (García-Rojas et al. 2022), NGC 7009 (Akras et al. in prep.) and NGC 3242 (Konstantinou et al. in prep.).

Moreover, a pilot [Fe II] 1.644 μm narrowband image survey has been conducted in PNe with LISs [Program ID: GN-2017A-Q-58, PI: S. Akras]. [Fe II] lines are common tracers of shocks, and they have been detected in different astronomical environments. The preliminary analysis has shown that LISs also emit in the [Fe II] 1.644 μm line. Figure 1 displays the PN NGC 7009 in the optical (HST, left panel and MUSE, right panel) and near-infrared (Gemini, middle and inner panels). The LISs in this nebula are characterized by the detection of the [N II], [C I], H_2 and [Fe II] emission lines. All these lines are typical for low-ionization environments such as PDRs.

3. Low-ionization structures: the molecular component

Molecular gas concentrated in small clumps/knots or filamentary structures has already been found in the Helix nebula (Speck et al. 2002; Matsuura et al. 2009), NGC 2346 (Manchado et al. 2015) and very recently in NGC 3132 (De Marco et al. 2022) and the Ring nebula (Wesson et al. 2023) with the remarkable data from the James Webb Space Telescope (JWST).

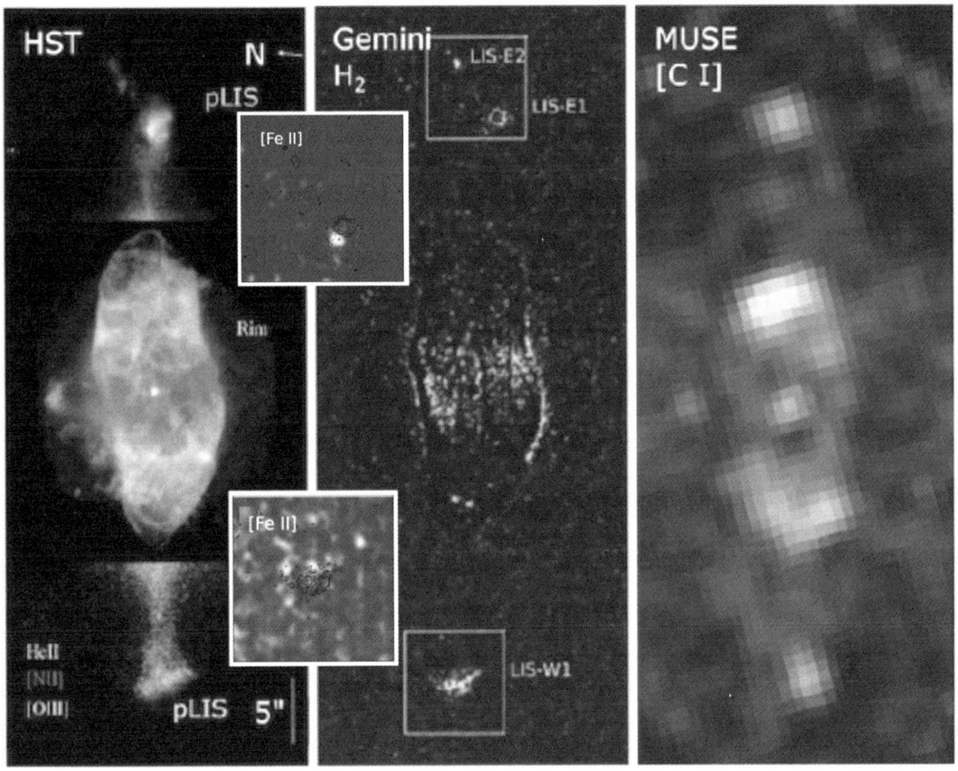

Figure 1. Multi-wavelength picture of the archetypal NGC 7009. Left panel: The optical RGB HST image ([O III] λ5007 in green, [N II] λ6584 in red and He II λ4686 in cyan from Balick et al. (1998). Middle panel: The near-IR continuum-subtracted H_2 v=1-0 2.12 μm Gemini image (Akras et al. 2020). The white squares indicate the two LISs of the nebula. Right panel: The optical MUSE [C I] λ8727 emission line map (Akras et al., in prep.). Inner panels: The near-IR continuum-subtracted [Fe II] 1.644 μm Gemini image of the LISs (Akras et al. in prep.). The solid black and dashed red contours indicate the H_2 1-0 and Brγ emission lines. Both LISs in NGC 7009 are composed of ionic, atomic and molecular gas components.

Gonçalves et al. (2009) suggested that the mass of LISs must be mostly neutral, and, therefore, unobserved in the visible light. The enhanced [O I] λ6300 line in LISs was a strong indicator for the presence of an H_2 component (Reay et al. 1988). Recent near-IR observations have unveiled that LISs are also made of molecular gas (Akras et al. 2017; Akras et al. 2020; Fang et al. 2018). Figure 1 shows the continuum-subtracted H_2 2.12 μm line images of NNG 7009 and Figure 2 presents the optical and continuum-subtracted H_2 images of three new PNe: NGC 6818, NGC 2392, and NGC 7354. [N II] λ6584 is found to be co-spatial with H_2 emission line. This reinforces the idea that some LISs, if not all, are made of molecular gas.

Therefore, LISs and H_2 clumps are apparently the two sides of the same coin of ("Dense Molecular Low-Ionization structures" (hereafter DMLISs; see Figure 3). Yet, the origin of H_2 gas still remain an open question. **Are DMLISs fossils of AGB winds surviving for thousands of years, or formed in situ during the PN stage due to shocks and UV radiation?**

The flux ratio of the two brightest molecular hydrogen lines, $R(H_2)=H_2$ 2.12 μm/H_2 2.24 μm, is commonly used to disentangle the photo-heated ($R(H_2)\sim3$) and shock-heated regions ($R(H_2)>10$) (e.g. Marquez-Lugo et al. 2015). However, it is well-known that the UV pumping H_2 emission can also be thermalized in high densities (10^{4-7} cm^{-3})

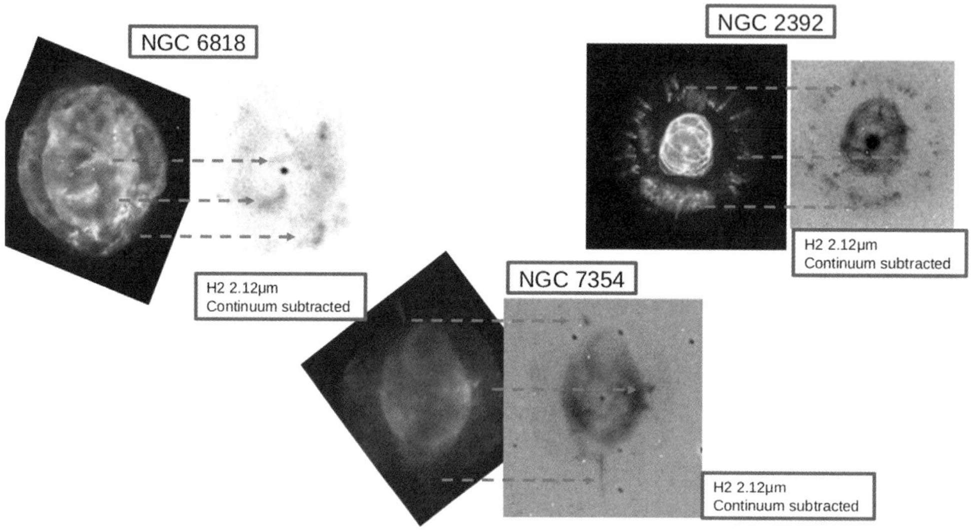

Figure 2. Optical (left panels) and Gemini near-IR (right panels) images of three PNe: NGC 6818, NGC 2392, and NGC 7354. The red arrows indicate the ([N II]) and H_2 emission from the same low-ionization structures.

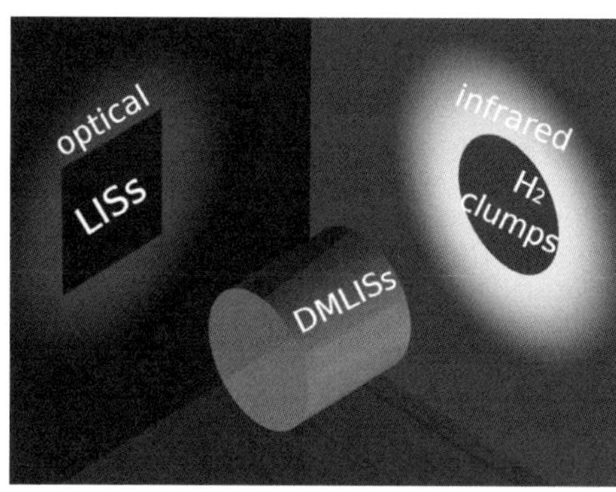

Figure 3. The two sides of the same coin. Low-ionization structures are the DMLISs in the optical wavelengths and H_2 clumps in the near-Infrared wavelengths.

environments (Sternberg & Dalgarno 1989; Burton et al. 1990), yielding to ratios as high as those of shocks. As a consequence, the $R(H_2)$ ratio is not an adequate parameter for the determination of the excitation mechanisms in DMLISs. The observed $R(H_2)$ values of LISs have not yet led to a firm conclusion about their excitation mechanism (Akras et al. 2020).

The bombardment of H_2 clumps by highly energetic FUV photons results in the dissociation and photoevaporation of the gas (e.g. Mellema et al. 1998) and consequently in the formation of a photodissociation region (PDR) around the dense H_2 core (see Figure 4 and Speck et al. 2002). An equivalent stratification has also been observed in the LISs of NGC 7009 (Akras et al. 2022). High-to-moderate ionization lines (He II, [O III]) have their peak intensity closer to the CS than the low-ionization ([N II], [S II]) ones. The latter lie closer to the CS than the atomic ones ([O I]), which also lie closer to the CS than the H_2 lines. This overall picture of DMLISs resembles the structure of PDRs (Black & van Dishoeck 1987) and the photoevaporation process can provide a reasonable explanation for the lower N_e measured in the LISs relative to the surrounding gas and line stratification.

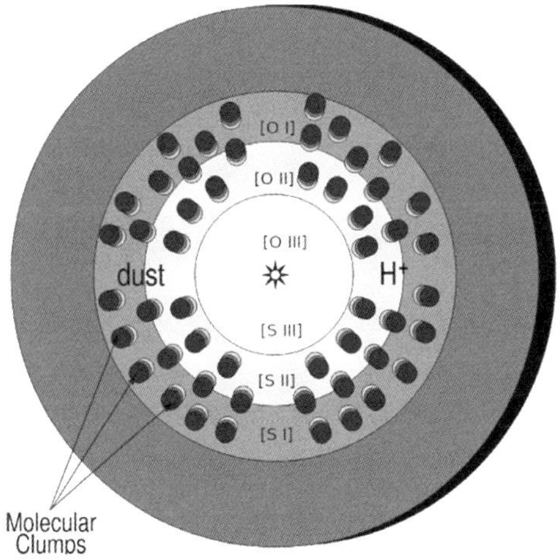

Figure 4. A cartoon of the clumpy envelope in PNe taken from Speck et al. (2002). The ionization stratification is indicated with the O and S emission lines.

PDRs are neutral gaseous regions formed by the penetration of FUV radiation into molecular clouds. A characteristic feature of PDRs is the presence of polycyclic aromatic hydrocarbon (PAH) molecules. PAHs play a crucial role as catalysts in the formation of H_2 via the absorption of H atoms. Despite the detection of PAHs in PNe with Spitzer (e.g. Perea-Calderón et al. 2020), the low spatial resolution of the data have not allowed the direct association of PAHs with DMLISs yet. A very narrow region at the outer parts of NGC 6720 is found to exhibit an excess in the JWST bands that contain the 3.3 and 11.3 μm PAH features (Wesson et al. 2023).

4. Dense molecular low-ionization structures: their origin

Despite the intense UV radiation from CS, H_2 molecules can survive, given that the timescale to dissociate them is still larger than the lifetime of PNe (thousands of years). Observations of cool evolved stars have shown that their highly in-homogeneous winds are composed of large amount of dust and molecules, while dense clumps are constantly formed and destroyed (Weigelt et al. 2002; Ziurys 2006; Ramstedt et al. 2020; Decin 2021) and indicated by 2D hydrodynamic models (e.g. Woitke 2006). While the photodissociation front is propagated into the circumstellar envelope, it destroys some of these molecular clumps, but not the extremely dense ones, which may survive for thousands of years, and they eventually turn out to be engulfed by the resultant ionized nebular gas (Graham et al. 1993). As a consequence, DMLISs plausibly represent fossil condensations of the AGB winds which have not been fully dissociated yet, and they are currently being photo-evaporated (see Redman et al. 2003). On the other hand, dynamic instabilities (e.g. Rayleigh-Taylor, Vishniac or thin-shell instabilities) due to the interaction of the stellar winds or at the ionization-shock front may also lead to the in situ formation of molecular clumps (e.g. Dyson et al. 2000; Steffen & López 2004; Segura et al. 2006).

Both mechanisms have been proposed to explain the formation of the cometary globules in the Helix nebula. Matsuura et al. (2009) argued that some portion of H_2 gas in the globules is primordial from the AGB phase, whereas Segura et al. (2006) claimed based on hydrodynamical simulations that a portion of the globules may have formed by the dynamic instabilities.

5. Discussion and Conclusions

Low-ionization structures have being studied mainly in the visible wavelength, and only a portion of their true structure has been unveiled. The recent observational attempts in the near-IR have complemented the optical studies and unveiled their true structure as "Dense Molecular Low-Ionization structures". NGC 7009 serves as the archetypal planetary nebulae for the study of LISs. Besides the typical low-ionization lines [N II], [S II] and [O I], both LISs in NGC 7009 have been detected in the [C I], [Fe II] and H_2 1-0 lines.

A new window of multi-wavelength study of LISs is now open to get new pieces to the puzzling problem of LISs and valuable insights in their origin and formation mechanisms, as well as explore their possible link with clumps from previous evolutionary stages.

Acknowledgments. The research project is implemented in the framework of H.F.R.I call "Basic research financing (Horizontal support of all Sciences)" under the National Recovery and Resilience Plan "Greece 2.0" funded by the European Union - NextGenerationEU (H.F.R.I. Project Number: 15665).

References

Akras S., Gonçalves D. R., 2016, *MNRAS*, 455, 930A
Akras S., Gonçalves D. R., Ramos-Larios G., 2017, *MNRAS*, 465, 1289A
Akras S., Gonçalves D. R., Ramos-Larios G., Aleman I., 2020, *MNRAS*, 493, 3800A
Akras S., et al., 2022, *MNRAS*, 512, 2202A
Balick B., 1987, *AJ*, 94, 671B
Balick B., Rugers M., Terzian Y., et al., 1993, *ApJ*, 411, 778
Balick B., Alexander J., Hajian A. R., et al., 1998, *AJ*, 116, 360B
Balick B., et al., 2020, *ApJ*, 889, 13
Black J. H., van Dishoeck E. F., 1987, *ApJ*, 322, 412
Burton M. G., Hollenbach D. J., Tielens A. G. G. M., 1990, *ApJ*, 365, 620B
Burton M. G., Bulmer M., Moorhouse A., et al., 1992, *MNRAS*, 257, 1P
Decin L., 2021, *ARA&A*, 59, 337D
De Marco O., Akashi M., Akras S., et al., 2022, *NatA*, 6, 1421D
Dyson J. E., Hartquist T. W., Redman M. P., et al., 2000, *Ap&SS*, 272, 197D
Fang X., et al., *2018*, *ApJ*, 859, 92
García-Rojas J. et al., 2022, *MNRAS*, 510, 5444G
Garcia-Segura et al. 2006, *ApJ*, 646L, 61G
Gonçalves D. R., Corradi R. L. M., Mampaso A., 2001, *ApJ*, 547, 302G
Gonçalves D. R. et al., 2009, *MNRAS*, 398, 2166G
Graham J. R., et al., 1993, *ApJ*, 408L, 105G
Kwitter K. B., Henry R. B. C., 2022, *PASP*, 134, 2001
López J. A., V ázquez R., Rodríguez L. F., 1995, *ApJ*, 455, L63
Manchado A., et al., 2015, *ApJ*, 808, 115M
Mari M. B., Gonçalves D. R., Akras S., 2023a, *MNRAS*, 518, 3908M
Mari M. B., Akras S., Gonçalves D. R., 2023b, *MNRAS*, 525, 1998M
Marquez-Lugo R. A., Guerrero M. A., Ramos-Larios G., et al., 2015, *MNRAS*, 453, 1888M
Matsuura, M., et al., 2009, *ApJ*, 700, 1067M
Mellema G., et al., 1998, *A&A*, 331, 335M
Monreal-Ibero A., Walsh J. R., 2020, *A&A*. 634A, 47M
Perea-Calderón J. V., García-Hernández D. A., García-Lario P., et al., 2009, *A&A*, 495L, 5P
Perinotto M., 2000, *Ap&SS*, 274, 205
Ramstedt S., et al., 2020,*A&A*, 640A, 133R
Reay et at. 1988, *MNRAS*, 232, 615R
Redman M. P., Viti S., Cau P., Williams D. A., 2003, *MNRAS*, 345, 1291R
Speck K. A., et al., 2002, *AJ*, 123, 346S

Steffen W., López J. A. 2004, *ApJ*, 612, 319S
Sternberg A., Dalgarno A., 1989, *ApJ*, 338, 197S
Walsh J. R, et al., 2018, *A&A*, 620A, 169W
Weigelt G., et al. 2002, *A&A*, 392, 131W
Wesson R., Matsuura M., Zijlstra A. A., et al., 2023, arXiv230809027W
Woitke P., 2006, *A&A*, 452, 537W
Ziurys L. M., 2006, *PNAS*, 10312274Z

Planetary Nebulae: A Universal Toolbox in the Era of Precision Astrophysics
Proceedings IAU Symposium No. 384, 2025
O. De Marco, A. Zijlstra & R. Szczerba, eds.
doi:10.1017/S1743921323005811

Probing the physical and chemical properties of planetary nebulae using precision photoionization modeling

H. Monteiro[1], C. Mendes de Oliveira[2], P. Amram[3], Bruno C. Quint[4], L. Stanghellini[5] and R. Wesson[6]

[1]Universidade Federal de Itajubá - UNIFEI
email: hmonteiro@unifei.edu.br

[2]Departamento de Astronomia, Instituto de Astronomia, Geofísica e Ciências Atmosféricas da USP, Cidade
Universitária, 05508-900, São Paulo, SP, Brazil

[3]Aix Marseille Université, CNRS, LAM (Laboratoire d'Astrophysique de Marseille), Marseille, France

[4]Rubin Observatory Project Office, 950 N. Cherry Ave., Tucson, AZ 85719, USA

[5]NSF's National Optical-Infrared Astronomy Research Laboratory, Tucson, AZ 85719

[6]Department of Physics and Astronomy, University College London, Gower Street, London WC1E 6BT, United Kingdom

Abstract. Planetary nebulae (PNe) are remnants of evolved stars, fundamental for understanding stellar life cycles and galactic enrichment. In this work, we present a summary of our recent work using three-dimensional models and spatially resolved constraints to examine the physical and chemical properties of PNe, with a particular focus on preliminary results for the PN NGC 3132. Our results indicate that a star of about $3M_\odot$, surrounded by a shell, wind, or disk with approximately $5.0 \times 10^{-6} M_\odot$ and extending to about 300AU is necessary to adequately reproduce the observations, consistent with recent JWST findings. We also discuss the importance of this methodology in studying the properties of the progenitor stars and making abundance determinations.

Keywords. Catalogs, Surveys, stars: binaries, planetary nebulae

1. Introduction

Planetary nebulae (PNe) are remnants of evolved stars, fundamental for understanding stellar life cycles and galactic enrichment. It is well documented that PNe exhibits a large range in size, from a few hundred astronomical units to several parsecs and a multitude of morphological features, with intricate and often asymmetric or point symmetric structures (Balick and Frank 2002). In general the transition from the thermally pulsing asymptotic giant branch (TP-AGB) phase to the PN stage is governed by the interaction between the stellar wind and the circumstellar material. The canonical understanding of this transition is based on the interacting wind model (Kwok 2000; Kwok et al. 1978), which describes how the fast wind from the central star interacts with the previously ejected AGB material, shaping the PN structure. Although the general framework of the interacting wind model is well established, other factors influence the diverse and complex morphologies observed in PNe.

The complexity in PN morphologies can be attributed to a confluence of factors, primarily involving the interplay between interacting winds (IW), binary systems, inhomogeneities in circumstellar material, and magnetic fields. The role of binaries in the shaping of PNe has garnered increasing attention, as binary central stars can lead to complex mass ejection and shaping mechanisms (De Marco 2009). Additionally, inhomogeneities in the circumstellar environment, such as density variations and turbulence, play a crucial role in the formation of morphological features (Blackman et al. 2001). Magnetic fields also have a significant impact on the shaping of PN structures (García-Segura 2002), and observations have indicated the presence of magnetic fields in the envelope of certain proto-PNe (Sabin et al. 2007, 2014). Although progress has been made in understanding the general transition from TP-AGB to PN via the interacting wind model, the intricate details of how these elements collectively influence the emergence of the diverse and complex morphologies in PNe remain an active area of research.

Overall, the study of PNe involves a blend of observational and theoretical approaches, with photoionization models having an important role. As elegantly said by Dr. Christophe Morisset in Morisset (2017) "One can see a photoionization code as a detailed quantitative summary of our knowledge of gas-photon interactions in the interstellar medium". One-dimensional (1D) photoionization models have been widely employed to study PNe because of their simplicity and computational tractability. They provide estimates for fundamental parameters such as electron temperatures, ionization states, and element abundances. In general, 1D models have been quite successful in explaining many observed properties of PNe. In Morisset (2017) a very comprehensive review of the characteristics, properties, uses, and limitations of photoionization models is given and we refer the reader to that work and references therein for further details.

Related to the modeling efforts are the observational data used to constrain them. Imaging and spectroscopy data have been widely used for empirical and theoretical studies and a good sample of the myriad of applications can be seen in Liu et al. (2017). In recent years, integral field spectroscopy (IFS) has become a crucial observational technique, particularly in the study of extended objects such as PNe (Mediavilla et al. 2011). Compared to traditional long-slit strategies, IFS offers the advantage of complete spatial sampling, allowing for the study of spatially resolved physical, chemical and kinematic properties, from the central star to the very outer edge of the nebulae. After the initial use of IFS in the study of galactic PNe by Tsamis et al. (2008), an increasing number of publications have used this technique to investigate various aspects of PNe. Recent studies of PNe using IFS include the work of Ali and Dopita (2019), Akras et al. (2020a), Akras et al. (2022), Walsh et al. (2016), Walsh et al. (2018), and Monreal-Ibero and Walsh (2020). In addition to studying the PN gas, the central star of these objects can also be analyzed using 3D spectroscopy data, as demonstrated in the works of Ali et al. (2016), Basurah et al. (2016), and Danehkar (2014).

The advances in observational capabilities lead to the increased use of three dimensional photoionization models to study PNe. Since the work of Kirkpatrick (1970) 3D photoionization models have been used to replicate PN observed morphologies, accounting for the spectroscopic data taken with distinct aperture sizes and placements, and constraining velocity fields measured with high resolution spectroscopy. Three-dimensional photoionization modelling combined with the spatially resolved constraints has provided significant insight into the properties of PNe and their the central stars (Danehkar 2018; Morisset 2017; Jones et al. 2020; Ercolano et al. 2003b,a, 2004; Gonçalves et al. 2006; Yuan et al. 2011; Wright et al. 2011). Although it has helped explain the observed diversity in PN morphologies and shed light on the factors influencing their chemical abundances and kinematics, its prevalence is still limited. This

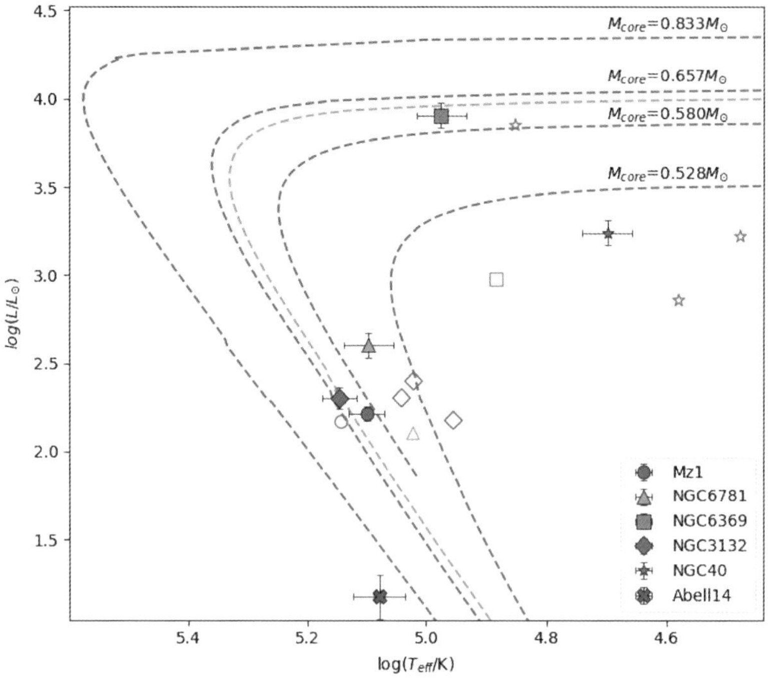

Figure 1. HR diagram of all PNe modeled by our group using 3D photoionization codes. For each nebula a symbol is used where model results are presented in filled symbols and literature values in open symbols. The blue dashed lines are evolutionary tracks from Miller Bertolami (2016). The orange dashed line is the interpolated track for the model of NGC 3132 discussed in Sec. 3.

is primarily due to the complexity of determining a detailed three-dimensional density structure as well as the actual model fitting procedure.

2. Improved 3D structures for specific objects

Over the past few decades, our group has dedicated its efforts to advancing the development of highly detailed three-dimensional photoionization models for specific objects, leveraging high-quality spatially resolved constraints where available. Some examples of these works are Monteiro and Falceta-Gonçalves (2011), Akras et al. (2016) and references therein.

2.1. *3D structure for NGC 40 from hydrodynamical models*

In Monteiro and Falceta-Gonçalves (2011) we obtained a 3D density structure from hydrodynamical models and combined it with the photoionization model to obtain consistent physical, chemical and velocity distributions for the nebula NGC 40. By combining the velocity field with emission-line data, we generated synthetic position-velocity plots for comparison with observations. From theoretical evolutionary tracks for intermediate- and low-mass stars, we deduced the mass and age of NGC 40's central star as (0.567 $\pm$ 0.06) $M_\odot$ and (5810 $\pm$ 600) years, respectively, as well as $T_{eff} = 50$kK for the effective temperature, $log(L/L_\odot) = 3.2$ for the luminosity and (1150 $\pm$ 120) pc for the distance. The good agreement of the distance determination, which was the original focus, contrasts with the lack of agreement of T_{eff} and $log(L/L_\odot)$ found in the literature. This can be seen in Fig. 1 where we show results of our 3D model compared to other determinations from the literature. For NGC 40 the reported values are from Stanghellini et al. (2002), Pottasch and Bernard-Salas (2010) and Toalá et al. (2019), showing that important discrepancies remain. The abundances obtained from the model fit are different from previous empirical determinations found in the literature, which were determined from different portions of the nebula, using ionization correction factors (Monteiro and Falceta-Gonçalves 2011, details in Table 3).

As a by-product of the work on NGC 40, in Monteiro et al. (2014) we examined the effectiveness of empirical abundance determination methods in accurately retrieving predefined parameters and abundance variations within a realistically modeled planetary nebula. To conduct this assessment, we processed the density structure used for the nebula, obtained from a hydrodynamical simulation, through a 3D photoionization code. The input parameters, including ionizing source, density, and chemical abundances adopted were typical values for Type I PNe. Emissivities from the model were projected along the line of sight to generate synthetic emission line maps, which, in turn, yielded temperature and density diagnostic maps. These diagnostics and line emission maps were subsequently used to derive spatially resolved abundance maps. The study explored abundance variations for two distinct orientations of the density structure and input He abundances. The findings reveal that given typical signal-to-noise ratios obtained from long-slit spectroscopy or IFU data, the usual empirical method was unable to detect abundance variations and introduced artificial fluctuations. Significant artificial variations were detected in both the abundances derived from total line fluxes and those obtained from emission line maps. The most substantial disparities were evident in the nitrogen (N) abundances, exhibiting a notable increase of 50%. Furthermore, variations were observed in the abundances of oxygen (O), showing a decrease in 23% and in the abundances of sulfur (S), indicating an increase in 18%.

2.2. *3D structure for Abell 14 from velocity fields*

Taking it one step further, with the recognition that the detailed definition of the spatial distribution of gas and dust was a crucial component to infer precise physical and chemical properties for the PN and its central star, we tackled the modeling of the poorly studied PN Abell 14, classified as a born-again planetary nebula. In Akras et al. (2016) we used the SHAPE code to derive a detailed 3D gas structure based on high resolution echelle spectroscopy and MOCASSIN codes to analyze its ionization structure. This procedure reduces the number of assumptions that had to be made when compared to the method using the MHD modeling. The model reproduced with good precision the available spatially resolved constraints. Our findings revealed that Abell 14 is a highly evolved bipolar nebula with a kinematical age of approximately 19,400 years, at a distance of 4 kpc. The elevated helium abundance and N/O ratio suggested a progenitor star with a mass of $5M_{\odot}$, undergoing the third dredge-up and hot bottom-burning phases. However, the evolved stage of the central star, near the white dwarf cooling track, does not support the born-again scenario. Surprisingly, the nebula exhibits strong [NI]λ5200 and [OI]λ6300 emission lines, which could not be reproduced by a pure photoionization model, implying potential shock interactions. The combination of low central star luminosity and expansive nebular size results in a minimal photoionization rate, making any contribution from shock interaction quite noticeable, even at relatively low velocities.

Better observations for the PN were obtained with the VIMOS-IFU spectrograph and presented in Akras et al. (2020b) with results confirming the previous findings. The data also allowed for the classification of the star located at the center of Abell 14 indicating it is of A5 spectral type with effective temperature of $T_{eff} = 7909 \pm 135$ K and surface gravity log(g) $= 1.4 \pm 0.1$ cm s^{-2}. This star is not capable of ionizing the nebula. Recent Gaia parallaxes of this star give distances between 3.6 and 4.5 kpc, which is consistent with the distance determined from the 3D photoionization model of Abell 14, suggesting the presence of a binary system at the center of the PN. Interestingly, even with the better IFU data, again we find no agreement between the empirical abundance determination and the one from the photoionization model based on a precise density structure.

The model results, when compared to the more up-to-date evolutionary tracks of Miller Bertolami and Althaus (2007), show agreement in the estimated dynamical age, which was not the case when using the previous models from Bloecker (1995), which underscores the importance of using a detailed photoionization model constrained by comprehensive, high-quality, and spatially resolved data.

3. Minimizing Assumptions in 3D Gas structure determination

The determination of the detailed 3D structure of PNe encounters certain limitations in the methods described previously. On the one hand, hydrodynamical models, while producing self-consistent results, require numerous assumptions regarding the physical processes involved for which there are no direct observational constraints other than the observed morphologies. The assumptions can lead to degeneracy and uncertainties into the reconstructed 3D structure. On the other hand, kinematical modeling approaches, which make use of a limited number of high-resolution slit observations, often necessitate the use of idealized assumptions about the 3D structures which will be combined, such as cylinders, toruses, cones, and other geometric shapes. These idealizations may not fully capture the complex and diverse details of the morphologies of real PNe. Consequently, these inherent limitations should be carefully considered when interpreting the results of 3D structural studies of PNe.

For the case of PNe, there is ample evidence that, in general, the velocity vector at any given point is proportional to the position vector of that point in the nebula (Wilson 1950; Weedman 1968; Corradi 2004; Meaburn et al. 2008; Uscanga et al. 2014, among many others). According to Zijlstra et al. (2001), this type of velocity distribution can be expected if the nebula has evolved from a relatively short mass-loss event and is now moving ballistically. Also, Steffen and López (2004) argue that a continuous interaction of a wind with small-scale structures can also develop a positive velocity gradient with distance. The result of this type of expansion is that the nebula conserves its shape over time.

The assumption described above has been used in numerous studies aimed at reconstructing the spatial structure of planetary nebulae. In particular, Sabbadin et al. (2006) focused extensively on this technique, successfully obtaining three-dimensional structures for a sample of objects. Another important effort is the work of Steffen and López (2006), in which they developed a computational tool to analyze and untangle the three-dimensional geometry and kinematic structure of gaseous nebulae. Subsequent studies, widely cited and still in use today, have applied this methodology to a diverse range of complex objects, recovering detailed information about their kinematics and structure.

Here we present preliminary results obtained by applying the same strategy to analyze data from high resolution scanning Fabry-Perot interferometer, SAM-FP, mounted on the SOAR telescope adaptive module for the PN NGC 3132. Observations were obtained in the [NII] filter (SAMI 6584-20) and Hα filter (BTFI 6569-20) with a spectral resolution of about 11200 at Hα. The observations employed an e2v CCD detector with dimensions of 4096 $\times$ 4112 pixels, covering a total field of view of 180 arcseconds $\times$ 180 arcseconds and a pixel size of 0.18 arcseconds.

To obtain the final 3D density structure from these data we started from an initial guess of the proportionality constant used to translate the velocity field information to distance.

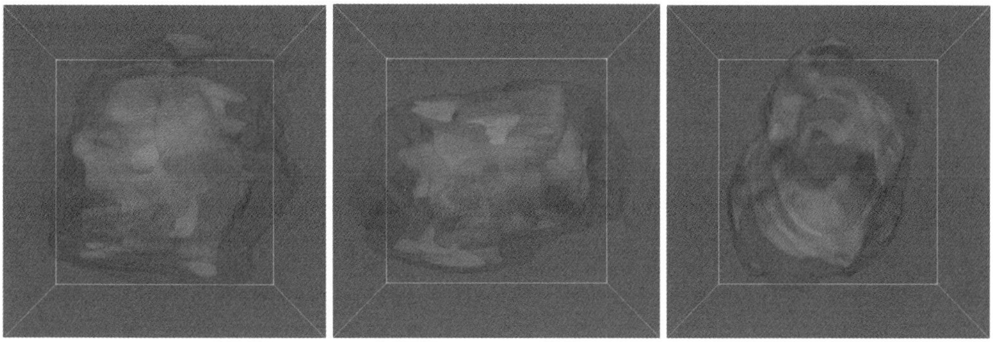

Figure 2. Visualization of the 3D density structure derived from the SAM-FP velocity data for NGC 3132. The left panel shows a side view in the direction the z axis, the middle panel in the direction of the y axis and the left panel in the direction of the x axis which is also the same as the line of sight from Earth.

With the inferred structure we start the iterative procedure to fit the photoionization model to the available observational data constraints. In this sense, the proportionality constant is taken as a free parameter of the modeling process. A visualization of the obtained 3D density structure is shown in Fig. 2. The photoionization code Mocassin, version 2.02.73.2 using the Chianti 7 atomic data base was used.

We start by adopting that, to first order, the $H\alpha$ emission intensity can be approximated by $I_{H\alpha} \propto n^2$, where n is the gas density. Using the velocity and position proportionality, we convert $H\alpha$ velocity data cubes into a three-dimensional density structure. With this density structure, we start the iterative process of fitting the photoionization model to the observational constraints. Once a preliminary agreement is achieved, we further extend our analysis by establishing a relation between the [NII]λ6584 line intensity and density finding that, for this particular case, $I_{[NII]} \propto n^{2.5}$ which enabled us to convert [NII]λ6584 velocity data cubes into a corresponding 3D density structure. These two density structures are then combined as the iterative process continues until a reasonable fit to the observational constraints is found. The combination of velocity data and precise density structure dimensions also yields a dynamical age of 2061 years.

The ionizing source with its T_{eff} and luminosity is one of the critical free parameters that is fit using the model. We started with the usual blackbody sources and quickly found that they were not able to reproduce the observations completely, specially when considering the gas temperature as measure through the diagnostic diagrams, always giving significantly hotter plasmas. Reproducing the gas temperature is critical to guarantee that the abundances found with the model fitting are indeed accurate. We then explored more detailed NLTE stellar model atmospheres provided by T. Rauch † which gave better results but still lead to gas temperatures that were few hundred degrees too hot when compared to observational diagnostics.

At this point, the observations obtained by the JWST telescope became available and were analyzed by a group of researchers in De Marco et al. (2022). One of the striking results presented was the detection of a dusty envelope around the central star of the nebula. The JWST data provided critical observational constraints including precise photometry for the central source. In De Marco et al. (2022) they found that the observations were consistent with a dust disk with an inner radius of 55 au, an outer radius of 140AU, and a dust mass of $2 \times 10^{-7} M_\odot$. In Sahai et al. (2023), using the same observations, the authors find that a $3.9 \times 10^{-8} M_\odot$, a radius of 1785 au, with a composition of 70%

† `http://astro.uni-tuebingen.de/~rauch/`

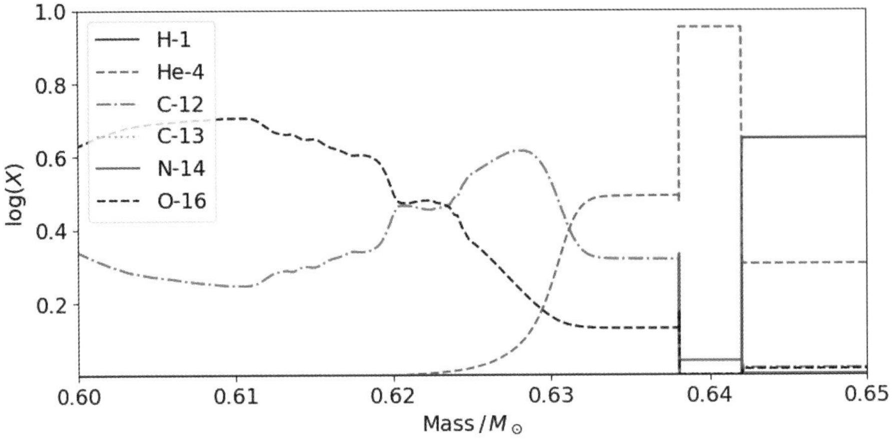

Figure 3. Mass fraction profiles for a $3M_\odot$ model star at the end of the last thermal pulse. Model details are presented in Pignatari et al. (2016)

silicate and 30% amorphous carbon could explain the available photometry. However, it was already clear from the work in De Marco et al. (2022) that a dust only shell or disk was not capable of improving the photoionization models results, reducing the gas temperature obtained. These results motivated us to explore the influence of a dust and gas shell in our models.

We included a dust and gas spherical shell with uniform density surrounding our model ionizing source. To accomplish this with the available resolution of the model density grid, we first calculated a photoionization model for the central region, and then used the calculated spectral energy distribution (SED) as input ionization source for the PN photoionization model.

After iterating with the free parameters of the introduced shell, we found that it allowed the model to reproduce the line diagnostic ratios, in particular for the temperature. A shell with a radius of 334 AU, $4.3 \times 10^{-5}M_\odot$ gas and $1.5 \times 10^{-10}M_\odot$ dust was found to produce the best fit to the observational constraints. We note that the fit was also sensitive to the mass fractions used in the shell abundances. The best fit corresponds to a He-poor, C and O-rich shell with mass fractions of $X_{He} = 5.0 \times 10^{-7}$, $X_C = 0.5$, $X_N = 1.0 \times 10^{-7}$, $X_O = 0.49$. Interestingly, these mass fractions are consistent with what some models of stellar evolution obtain for the inner layers of a $3M_\odot$ progenitor star remnant (Pignatari et al. 2016, for example), as shown in Fig. 3. However, since these are preliminary results, the actual value ranges are yet to be determined by improved model fitting and constraints and should also be checked by independent determinations if possible.

The constraints used in the model fitting were spatially resolved VLT-MUSE observations obtained by Monreal-Ibero and Walsh (2020), long-slit scans from Tsamis et al. (2004), and long-slit observations from (Krabbe and Copetti 2005, 2006) and remeasured International Ultraviolet Explorer (IUE) large aperture (10.3 by 23 arcseconds) observations. Model integrated line intensities are presented and compared to observations in Table 1. To scale the UV to optical line data, we used the theoretical intensity ratio for HeII $\lambda1640/\lambda5411$, measuring the HeII $\lambda5411$ flux using the MUSE data on the same aperture configuration to ensure accurate scaling factors without introducing errors due to the ionization structure or aperture position. The IUE observations were crucial in constraining the C abundance. In Fig. 4 we show the comparison of the emission line

Table 1. Preliminary results for the photoionization model fit of integrated line intensities for some of the most important emission lines.

Line	M00	Tsamis04	MUSE	Krabbe05	Model
Hbeta ($erg\ cm^{-2}\ s^{-1}$)			9.18×10^{-11}		9.6×10^{-11}
Halpha	2.900	2.860	2.880	2.860	2.847
[OII] 3729+3727	–	5.510	–	5.330	5.997
CII 4267	–	0.007	–	–	0.004
[OIII] 4364	0.050	0.040	–	0.050	0.063
HeII 4686	0.106	0.040	–	0.070	0.120
[OIII] 5008	8.300	7.890	8.360	8.860	8.185
[NI] 5200	0.120	0.010	0.080	0.100	0.014
HeII 5411	–	0.004	0.007	–	0.009
[NII] 5756	0.093	0.080	0.080	0.080	0.092
HeI 5877	0.184	0.160	0.160	0.170	0.159
[OI] 6302	0.329	0.370	0.330	0.330	0.338
[SIII] 6312	–	0.024	0.024	0.026	0.033
[NII] 6585	5.591	6.420	5.560	–	5.455
HeI 6678	–	0.045	0.050	0.040	0.045
[SII] 6732	0.533	0.540	0.510	0.510	0.434
[SIII] 9072	–	–	0.384	–	0.518

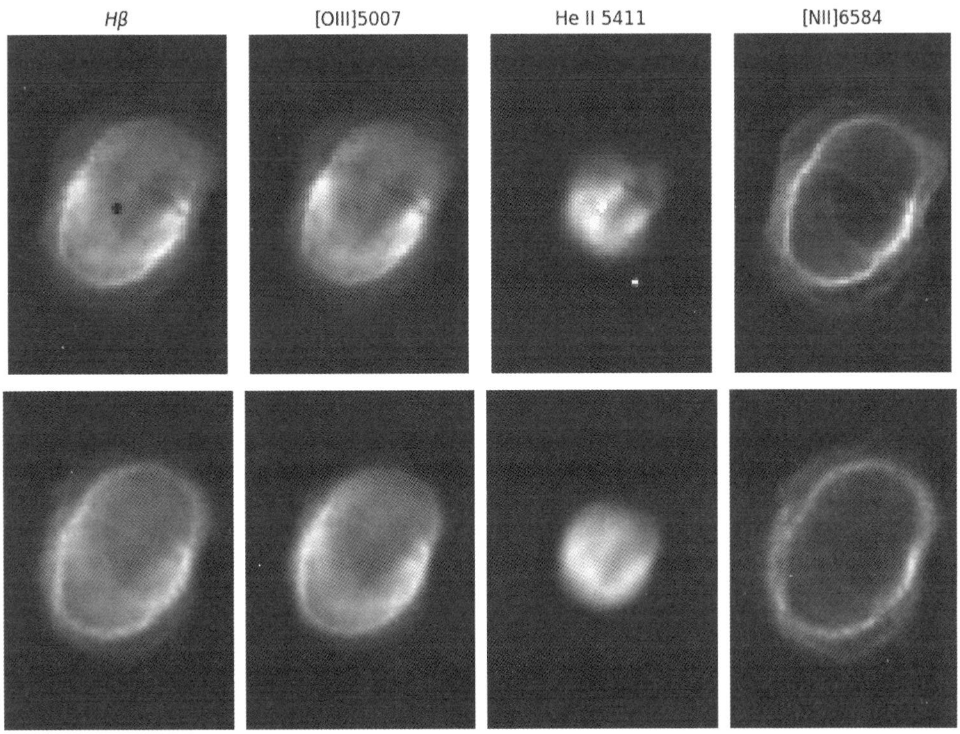

Figure 4. Comparison between MUSE data (top row) and photoionization model (bottom row) for some important emission line maps for NGC 3132.

map of H_β obtained from the model and from MUSE data. A detailed description of the constraints and model results will be presented in a forthcoming paper.

The final abundances obtained by the model fit for the most important elements are presented in Table 2. It is important to clarify here that model abundances are free parameters in the fitting process and are not adopted from the empirical method determinations. The results show that the He abundances in general agree, but significant

Table 2. Abundances from the 3D model compared with values from the literature. Abundances are ratio of elements to hydrogen by number.

	3D Model fit	**Tsamis (2003)**	**Krabbe (2003)**	**Monreal-Ibero (2020)**
He	0.113	0.12	0.126	0.124
C	6.00×10^{-4}	3.20×10^{-4} [a]	–	7.10×10^{-4}
N	1.70×10^{-4}	2.40×10^{-4}	2.91×10^{-4}	3.60×10^{-4}
O	4.20×10^{-4}	6.60×10^{-4}	5.72×10^{-4}	8.60×10^{-4}
C/O	1.4	0.48	–	0.8
N/O	0.40	0.36	0.51	0.42

differences in the C,N and O abundances are present, just as in the PNe described in previous sections. The largest discrepancy is found for the C abundance; however, inspecting the ratios of C/O and N/O obtained from the model, we see that again, the values are consistent with what is expected for a $3M_{\odot}$ star.

4. Conclusions

The combination of observational and theoretical approaches, with photoionization models serving as a tool, has been key in obtaining a comprehensive understanding of the complexities of PNe properties. The transition from widely-used one-dimensional models and simple long slit observational data to integral field spectroscopy (IFS) combined with three-dimensional photoionization models have contributed valuable insights into both complex PN and their central stars properties.

Here we discussed the improvement in determining the three-dimensional structures for specific objects, exemplified by the detailed models for NGC 40 and Abell 14, showing the importance in reconstructing spatial structures accurately and performing model fits constrained by high-quality spatially resolved data. We pointed to the still existing discrepancies in abundance determinations when the results are compared to the ones obtained with the usual empirical method.

Preliminary findings for PN NGC 3132 were presented, based on a 3D photoionization model using a detailed density structure reconstructed from high-resolution Hα and [NII] velocity data from the SAM-FP instrument at the SOAR telescope. The iterative model fitting process taking as free parameters the ionizing source properties and chemical composition of the gas, uses a diverse set of spatially resolved observational constraints from UV to the IR regions of the spectrum. Incorporating detailed NLTE stellar models and accounting for a gas and dust envelope around the central star, a good fit was obtained. The results of the best-fit model indicate that the derived central source and chemical properties of the nebular gas are consistent with a $3M_{\odot}$ progenitor star, in agreement with recent JWST results presented in De Marco et al. (2022).

In all PNe presented in this work, the abundances derived by the 3D photoionization model fitting differed significantly from the empirical determinations. However, for these PNe the models reproduced well the diverse observational constraints available. Notably the properties derived by the model fits for the ionizing source are in better agreement with what is expected from evolutionary models when considering their T_{eff}, luminosity and dynamical ages (Fig. 1). In particular for NGC 3132, the precision to which the observational constraints (ionization structure, emission line maps, integrated line intensities across the spectrum, central source and nebular photometry in the IR) are reproduced together with the agreement of dynamical age with the values from the evolutionary tracks of Miller Bertolami and Althaus (2007), is remarkable.

Although we cannot establish how accurate the results really are, the level of agreement of the models presented to the observational constraints suggest that the abundances obtained from the usual empirical method can give inaccurate values for complex PNe.

This has been shown to be the case in at least one controlled modeling experiment using a specific 3D density structure as described in Monteiro et al. (2014). Further studies to quantify these effects could lead to relevant improvements to the empirical abundance determination method.

Overall, the results presented indicate that, to precisely constrain the physical and chemical properties of complex PNe and their central sources, detailed 3D density structures coupled with 3D photoionzation models should be used.

Acknowledgements

This work has made use of the computing facilities available at the Laboratory of Computational Astrophysics of the Universidade Federal de Itajubá (LAC-UNIFEI). The LAC-UNIFEI is maintained with grants from CAPES, CNPq and FAPEMIG. This research has made use of the VizieR catalogue access tool, CDS, Strasbourg, France (DOI: 10.26093/cds/vizier). The original description of the VizieR service was published in A&AS 143, 23. This research has made use of NASA's Astrophysics Data System.We acknowledge funding from the EU Horizon2020 program through grant 101004214.

References

Akras, S., Clyne, N., Boumis, P., Monteiro, H., Gonçalves, D. R., Redman, M. P., & Williams, S. 2016, Deciphering the bipolar planetary nebula Abell 14 with 3D ionization and morphological studies. MNRAS, 457(4), 3409–3419.

Akras, S., Monteiro, H., Aleman, I., Farias, M. A. F., May, D., & Pereira, C. B. 2020,a Exploring the differences of integrated and spatially resolved analysis using integral field unit data: the case of Abell 14. MNRAS, 493a(2), 2238–2252.

Akras, S., Monteiro, H., Aleman, I., Farias, M. A. F., May, D., & Pereira, C. B. 2020,b Exploring the differences of integrated and spatially resolved analysis using integral field unit data: the case of Abell 14. MNRAS, 493b(2), 2238–2252.

Akras, S., Monteiro, H., Walsh, J. R., García-Rojas, J., Aleman, I., Boffin, H., Boumis, P., Chiotellis, A., Corradi, R. M. L., Gonçalves, D. R., Gutiérrez-Soto, L. A., Jones, D., Morisset, C., & Papanikolaou, X. 2022, Spectroscopic analysis tool for intEgraL fieLd unIt daTacubEs (SATELLITE): case studies of NGC 7009 and NGC 6778 with MUSE. MNRAS, 512(2), 2202–2221.

Ali, A. & Dopita, M. A. 2019, IFU spectroscopy of southern PNe - VII. Photoionization modelling of intermediate excitation class objects. MNRAS, 484(3), 3251–3266.

Ali, A., Dopita, M. A., Basurah, H. M., Amer, M. A., Alsulami, R., & Alruhaili, A. 2016, IFU spectroscopy of southern planetary nebulae - III. MNRAS, 462(2), 1393–1404.

Balick, B. & Frank, A. 2002, Shapes and Shaping of Planetary Nebulae. ARA&A, 40, 439–486.

Basurah, H. M., Ali, A., Dopita, M. A., Alsulami, R., Amer, M. A., & Alruhaili, A. 2016, Problems for the WELS classification of planetary nebula central stars: self-consistent nebular modelling of four candidates. MNRAS, 458(3), 2694–2709.

Blackman, E. G., Frank, A., & Welch, C. 2001, Magnetohydrodynamic Stellar and Disk Winds: Application to Planetary Nebulae. ApJ, 546(1), 288–298.

Bloecker, T. 1995, Stellar evolution of low- and intermediate-mass stars. II. Post-AGB evolution. A&A, 299, 755.

Corradi, R. L. M. Multiple, Coeval and Hubble-Like Bipolar Outflows. In Meixner, M., Kastner, J. H., Balick, B., & Soker, N., editors, Asymmetrical Planetary Nebulae III: Winds, Structure and the Thunderbird 2004, volume 313 of Astronomical Society of the Pacific Conference Series, 148.

Danehkar, A. 2014, Evolution of Planetary Nebulae with WR-type Central Stars.

Danehkar, A. 2018, Bi-Abundance Ionisation Structure of the Wolf-Rayet Planetary Nebula PB 8. PASA, 35, e005.

De Marco, O. 2009, The Origin and Shaping of Planetary Nebulae: Putting the Binary Hypothesis to the Test. PASP, 121(878), 316.

De Marco, O., Akashi, M., Akras, S., Alcolea, J., Aleman, I., Amram, P., Balick, B., De Beck, E., Blackman, E. G., Boffin, H. M. J., Boumis, P., Bublitz, J., Bucciarelli, B., Bujarrabal, V., Cami, J., Chornay, N., Chu, Y.-H., Corradi, R. L. M., Frank, A., García-Hernández, D. A., García-Rojas, J., García-Segura, G., Gómez-Llanos, V., Gonçalves, D. R., Guerrero, M. A., Jones, D., Karakas, A. I., Kastner, J. H., Kwok, S., Lykou, F., Manchado, A., Matsuura, M., McDonald, I., Miszalski, B., Mohamed, S. S., Monreal-Ibero, A., Monteiro, H., Montez, R., Baez, P. M., Morisset, C., Nordhaus, J., Mendes de Oliveira, C., Osborn, Z., Otsuka, M., Parker, Q. A., Peeters, E., Quint, B. C., Quintana-Lacaci, G., Redman, M., Ruiter, A. J., Sabin, L., Sahai, R., Contreras, C. S., Santander-García, M., Seitenzahl, I., Soker, N., Speck, A. K., Stanghellini, L., Steffen, W., Toalá, J. A., Ueta, T., Van de Steene, G., Van Winckel, H., Ventura, P., Villaver, E., Vlemmings, W., Walsh, J. R., Wesson, R., & Zijlstra, A. A. 2022, The messy death of a multiple star system and the resulting planetary nebula as observed by JWST. Nature Astronomy, 6, 1421–1432.

Ercolano, B., Barlow, M. J., Storey, P. J., Liu, X. W., Rauch, T., & Werner, K. 2003,a Three-dimensional photoionization modelling of the hydrogen-deficient knots in the planetary nebula Abell 30. MNRAS, 344a(4), 1145–1154.

Ercolano, B., Morisset, C., Barlow, M. J., Storey, P. J., & Liu, X. W. 2003,b Three-dimensional photoionization modelling of the planetary nebula NGC 3918. MNRAS, 340b(4), 1153–1172.

Ercolano, B., Wesson, R., Zhang, Y., Barlow, M. J., De Marco, O., Rauch, T., & Liu, X. W. 2004, Observations and three-dimensional photoionization modelling of the Wolf-Rayet planetary nebula NGC 1501. MNRAS, 354(2), 558–574.

García-Segura, G. 2002, MHD Models of Planetary Nebulae: Review. arXiv e-prints, astro–ph/0202041.

Gonçalves, D. R., Ercolano, B., Carnero, A., Mampaso, A., & Corradi, R. L. M. 2006, On the nitrogen abundance of fast, low-ionization emission regions: the outer knots of the planetary nebula NGC 7009. MNRAS, 365(3), 1039–1049.

Jones, D., Boffin, H. M. J., Hibbert, J., Steinmetz, T., Wesson, R., Hillwig, T. C., Sowicka, P., Corradi, R. L. M., García-Rojas, J., Rodríguez-Gil, P., & Munday, J. 2020, The post-common-envelope binary central star of the planetary nebula PN G283.7-05.1. A possible post-red-giant-branch planetary nebula central star. A&A, 642, A108.

Kirkpatrick, R. C. 1970, Axially Symmetric Model Planetary Nebulae. ApJ, 162, 33.

Krabbe, A. C. & Copetti, M. V. F. 2005, Electron temperature fluctuations in planetary nebulae. A&A, 443(3), 981–994.

Krabbe, A. C. & Copetti, M. V. F. 2006, Chemical abundances in seven galactic planetary nebulae. A&A, 450(1), 159–166.

Kwok, S. 2000,. The Origin and Evolution of Planetary Nebulae. Cambridge Astrophysics. Cambridge University Press.

Kwok, S., Purton, C. R., & Fitzgerald, P. M. 1978, On the origin of planetary nebulae. ApJ, 219, L125–L127.

Liu, X., Stanghellini, L., & Karakas, A. 2017, Planetary Nebulae: Multi-Wavelength Probes of Stellar and Galactic Evolution. Proceedings of the International Astronomical Union,(S323).

Meaburn, J., Lloyd, M., Vaytet, N. M. H., & López, J. A. 2008, Hubble-type outflows of the high-excitation poly-polar planetary nebula NGC 6302 - from expansion proper motions. MNRAS, 385(1), 269–273.

Mediavilla, E., Arribas, S., Roth, M., Cepa-Nogué, J., & Sánchez, F. 2011,. 3D Spectroscopy in Astronomy. Cambridge University Press.

Miller Bertolami, M. M. 2016, New models for the evolution of post-asymptotic giant branch stars and central stars of planetary nebulae. A&A, 588, A25.

Miller Bertolami, M. M. & Althaus, L. G. 2007, The born-again (very late thermal pulse) scenario revisited: the mass of the remnants and implications for V4334 Sgr. MNRAS, 380, 763–770.

Monreal-Ibero, A. & Walsh, J. R. 2020, The MUSE view of the planetary nebula NGC 3132. A&A, 634, A47.

Monteiro, H. & Falceta-Gonçalves, D. 2011, Three-dimensional Photoionization Structure and Distances of Planetary Nebulae. IV. NGC 40. ApJ, 738(2), 174.

Monteiro, H., Santos, P. M., & Falceta-Gonçalves, D. Detecting Abundance Variations in Planetary Nebulae. In Morisset, C., Delgado-Inglada, G., & Torres-Peimbert, S., editors, Asymmetrical Planetary Nebulae VI Conference 2014, 61.

Morisset, C. Photoionization models of Planetary Nebulae. In Liu, X., Stanghellini, L., & Karakas, A., editors, Planetary Nebulae: Multi-Wavelength Probes of Stellar and Galactic Evolution 2017, volume 323 of IAUS, pp. 43–50.

Pignatari, M., Herwig, F., Hirschi, R., Bennett, M., Rockefeller, G., Fryer, C., Timmes, F. X., Ritter, C., Heger, A., Jones, S., Battino, U., Dotter, A., Trappitsch, R., Diehl, S., Frischknecht, U., Hungerford, A., Magkotsios, G., Travaglio, C., & Young, P. 2016, NuGrid Stellar Data Set. I.Stellar Yields from H to Bi for Stars with Metallicities Z = 0.02 and Z = 0.01. ApJS, 225(2), 24.

Pottasch, S. R. & Bernard-Salas, J. 2010, Planetary nebulae abundances and stellar evolution II. A&A, 517, A95.

Sabbadin, F., Turatto, M., Ragazzoni, R., Cappellaro, E., & Benetti, S. 2006, The structure of planetary nebulae: theory vs. practice. A&A, 451(3), 937–949.

Sabin, L., Zhang, Q., Zijlstra, A. A., Patel, N. A., Vázquez, R., Zauderer, B. A., Contreras, M. E., & Guillén, P. F. 2014, Submillimetre polarization and magnetic field properties in the envelopes of protoplanetary nebulae CRL 618 and OH 231.8+4.2, 438(2), 1794–1804.

Sabin, L., Zijlstra, A. A., & Greaves, J. S. 2007, Magnetic fields in planetary nebulae and post-AGB nebulae. MNRAS, 376(1), 378–386.

Sahai, R., Bujarrabal, V., Quintana-Lacaci, G., Reindl, N., Van de Steene, G., Sánchez Contreras, C., & Ressler, M. E. 2023, The Binary and the Disk: The Beauty is Found within NGC3132 with JWST. ApJ, 943(2), 110.

Stanghellini, L., Villaver, E., Manchado, A., & Guerrero, M. A. 2002, The Correlations between Planetary Nebula Morphology and Central Star Evolution: Analysis of the Northern Galactic Sample. ApJ, 576(1), 285–293.

Steffen, W. & López, J. A. 2004, On the Velocity Structure in Clumpy Planetary Nebulae. ApJ, 612(1), 319–331.

Steffen, W. & López, J. A. 2006, Morpho-Kinematic Modeling of Gaseous Nebulae with SHAPE. Rev. Mexicana Astron. Astrofis., 42, 99–105.

Toalá, J. A., Ramos-Larios, G., Guerrero, M. A., & Todt, H. 2019, Hidden IR structures in NGC 40: signpost of an ancient born-again event. MNRAS, 485(3), 3360–3369.

Tsamis, Y. G., Barlow, M. J., Liu, X. W., Storey, P. J., & Danziger, I. J. 2004, A deep survey of heavy element lines in planetary nebulae - II. Recombination-line abundances and evidence for cold plasma. MNRAS, 353(3), 953–979.

Tsamis, Y. G., Walsh, J. R., Péquignot, D., Barlow, M. J., Danziger, I. J., & Liu, X. W. 2008, Integral field spectroscopy of planetary nebulae: mapping the line diagnostics and hydrogen-poor zones with VLT FLAMES. MNRAS, 386(1), 22–46.

Uscanga, L., Velázquez, P. F., Esquivel, A., Raga, A. C., Boumis, P., & Cantó, J. 2014, Modelling the 3D morphology and proper motions of the planetary nebula NGC 6302. MNRAS, 442(4), 3162–3165.

Walsh, J. R., Monreal-Ibero, A., Barlow, M. J., Ueta, T., Wesson, R., & Zijlstra, A. A. 2016, The extinction and dust-to-gas structure of the planetary nebula NGC 7009 observed with MUSE. A&A, 588, A106.

Walsh, J. R., Monreal-Ibero, A., Barlow, M. J., Ueta, T., Wesson, R., Zijlstra, A. A., Kimeswenger, S., Leal-Ferreira, M. L., & Otsuka, M. 2018, An imaging spectroscopic survey of the planetary nebula NGC 7009 with MUSE. A&A, 620, A169.

Weedman, D. W. 1968, Observational Spatial and Kinematic Models of Planetary Nebulae. ApJ, 153, 49.

Wilson, O. C. 1950, A Survey of Internal Motions in the Planetary Nebulae. ApJ, 111, 279.

Wright, N. J., Barlow, M. J., Ercolano, B., & Rauch, T. 2011, A 3D photoionization model of the extreme planetary nebula NGC 6302. MNRAS, 418(1), 370–389.

Yuan, H. B., Liu, X. W., Péquignot, D., Rubin, R. H., Ercolano, B., & Zhang, Y. 2011, Three-dimensional chemically homogeneous and bi-abundance photoionization models of the 'super-metal-rich' planetary nebula NGC 6153. MNRAS, 411(2), 1035–1052.
Zijlstra, A. A., Chapman, J. M., te Lintel Hekkert, P., Likkel, L., Comeron, F., Norris, R. P., Molster, F. J., & Cohen, R. J. 2001, Bipolar outflows in OH/IR stars. MNRAS, 322(2), 280–308.

Planetary Nebulae: A Universal Toolbox in the Era of Precision Astrophysics
Proceedings IAU Symposium No. 384, 2025
O. De Marco, A. Zijlstra & R. Szczerba, eds.
doi:10.1017/S1743921325001413

JWST imaging observations of the Ring Nebula

R. Wesson[1,2], Mikako Matsuura[1], Albert Zijlstra[3], Kevin Volk[4], Patrick J. Kavanagh[5,6], Guillermo García-Segura[7], I. McDonald[3,8], Raghvendra Sahai[9], M. J. Barlow[2], Nick L. J. Cox[10], Jeronimo Bernard-Salas[10,11], Isabel Aleman[12,13], Jan Cami[14,15,16], Nicholas Clark[14,15], Harriet L. Dinerstein[17], K. Justtanont[18], Kyle F. Kaplan[17], A. Manchado[19,20,21], Els Peeters[14,15,16], Griet C. Van de Steene[22] and Peter A. M. van Hoof[22]

[1]Cardiff Hub for Astrophysics Research and Technology (CHART), School of Physics and Astronomy, Cardiff University, The Parade, Cardiff CF24 3AA, UK

[2]Department of Physics and Astronomy, University College London, Gower Street, London WC1E 6BT, United Kingdom

[3]Jodrell Bank Centre for Astrophysics, Department of Physics & Astronomy, The University of Manchester, Oxford Road, Manchester M13 9PL, UK

[4]Space Telescope Science Institute, 3700 San Martin Drive, Baltimore, MD 21218, USA

[5]Department of Experimental Physics, Maynooth University, Maynooth, Co Kildare, Ireland

[6]School of Cosmic Physics, Dublin Institute for Advanced Studies, 31 Fitzwilliam Place, Dublin 2, Ireland

[7]Instituto de Astronomía, Universidad Nacional Autónoma de México, Ensenada, Mexico

[8]Department of Physical Sciences, The Open University, Walton Hall, Milton Keynes, MK7 6AA, UK

[9]Jet Propulsion Laboratory, California Institute of Technology, Pasadena, CA, USA

[10]ACRI-ST, Centred'Etudes et de Recherche de Grasse (CERGA), 10 Av. Nicolas Copernic, 06130 Grasse, France

[11]INCLASS Common Laboratory., 10 Av. Nicolas Copernic, 06130 Grasse, France

[12]Department of Computer Science, Institute of Mathematics and Statistics, University of São Paulo, Rua do Matão 1226, Cidade Universitária, 05508-090, São Paulo, SP, Brazil

[13]Instituto de Física e Química, Universidade Federal de Itajubá, Av. BPS 1303, Pinheirinho, 37500-903, Itajubá, MG, Brazil

[14]Department of Physics and Astronomy, University of Western Ontario, London, Ontario, Canada

[15]Institute for Earth and Space Exploration, University of Western Ontario, London, Ontario, Canada

[16]SETI Institute, Mountain View, CA, USA

[17]University of Texas at Austin, Austin, TX 78712, USA

[18]Chalmers University of Technology, Onsala Space Observatory, S-439 92 Onsala, Sweden

[19]Instituto de Astrofísica de Canarias, E-38205 La Laguna, Tenerife, Spain

[20]Departamento de Astrofísica, Universidad de La Laguna, E-38206 La Laguna, Tenerife, Spain

[21]Consejo Superior de Investigaciones Científicas (CSIC), Spain

[22]Royal Observatory of Belgium, Ringlaan 3, B-1180 Brussels, Belgium
email: `rw@nebulousresearch.org`

Abstract. We present *JWST* images of NGC 6720 (the Ring Nebula), covering wavelengths from 1.6 μm to 25 μm. The bright shell is strongly fragmented with some 20 000 dense globules, bright in H_2, with a characteristic diameter of 0.2 arcsec and density $n_H \sim 10^5$–10^6 cm^{-3}. The shell contains a narrow ring of polycyclic aromatic hydrocarbon (PAH) emission. H_2 is found throughout the shell and also in the halo. The central cavity is filled with high ionization gas and shows two linear structures seen in projection against the cavity. The central star is located 2 arcsec from the emission centroid of the cavity and shell. Linear features ('spikes') extend outward from the ring, pointing away from the central star. Around ten low-contrast, regularly spaced concentric arc-like features are present; they suggest orbital modulation by a low-mass companion with a period of about 280 yr. A previously known much wider companion is located at a projected separation of about 15 000 au; we show that it is an M2–M4 dwarf. NGC 6720 is therefore a triple star system. These features, including the multiplicity, are similar to those seen in the Southern Ring Nebula (NGC 3132) and may be a common aspect of such nebulae.

Keywords. stars: planetary nebulae; abundances dust; molecular abundances

---

1. Introduction

The Ring Nebula (NGC 6720 or M 57) is located at a distance of 790±30 pc, as derived from the *Gaia* parallax of the central star of 1.2696 ± 0.0438 mas (Lindegren et al. 2021). It has a visual diameter of about 4 arcmin (equivalent to $\sim 2 \times 10^5$ au or ~1 pc) and shows a complex morphology (O'Dell et al. 2013). The distance puts the central star 190 pc above the Galactic plane, consistent with membership of the thin disk.

The central star currently has a temperature of $T_{\rm eff} = 1.35 \times 10^5$ K and a luminosity of $L \approx 310$ $L_\odot$ (Sahai et al, in prep.) which places it on the white dwarf cooling track. The current mass and progenitor mass of the central star are difficult to determine for objects on the cooling track, as the tracks tend to converge in that region of the HR diagram. González-Santamaría et al. (2021) quote 0.58 $M_\odot$ and 1.5 $M_\odot$, respectively, while the models of Miller Bertolami (2016) for the current temperature and luminosity are also consistent with a progenitor mass close to 2 $M_\odot$.

A post-AGB star of these masses reaches peak temperature at a luminosity $L \sim 3000\,L_\odot$. Fom this point, the luminosity declines to $\sim 200\,L_\odot$ within a few hundred years, before the decline slows down (Miller Bertolami 2016). The stellar luminosity of NGC 6720 ($L \approx 310\ L_\odot$) indicates that the star is currently in this phase of rapid fading. Part of the ionized nebula is likely recombining.

2. JWST Observations

The Ring Nebula was observed with *JWST* (Gardner et al. 2023) in Cycle 1 General Observers (GO) program 1558 (Figure 1). The observations were carried out in July and August 2022, using both NIRCam (Rieke et al. 2023) and MIRI (Wright et al. 2023).

The NIRCam observations were obtained on 2022 August 4th. Four filters were used, with two filters for each of the Short Wavelength Camera (F162M and F212N) and the Long Wavelength Camera (F300M and F335M). The nebula was covered by a single field of view (FOV) with a 4-point dither pattern yielding a FOV of 2.45 arcmin with some gaps near the edges of the fields which depend on the camera. The observing log is summarized in Table 1.

Imaging observations with MIRI were carried out on 2022 August 20th, using nine filters. The exposure time was 444 sec in each filter. The nebula was covered by a 1×2 mosaic with a 4-point dither pattern. The field size was 2.35×1.9 arcmin.

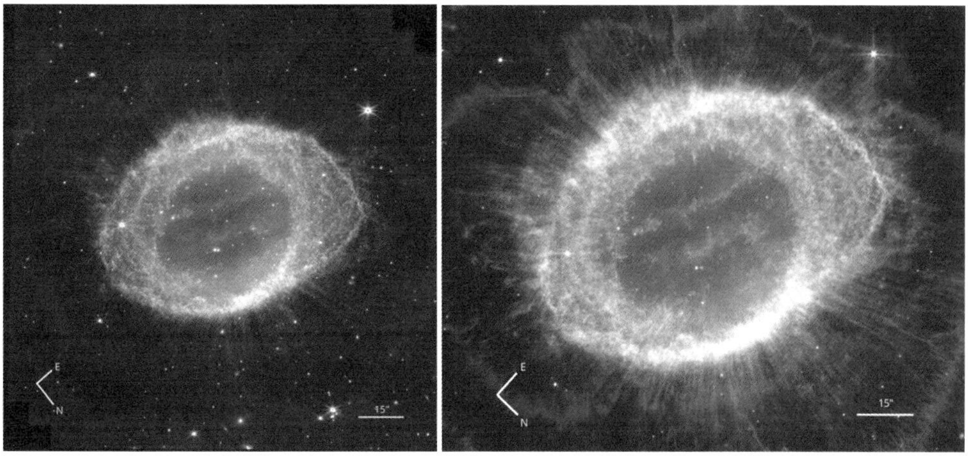

Figure 1. (l) NIRCam three colour image: F212N (blue), F300M (green) and F335M (red). (r) MIRI three-colour image: F2550W (blue), F560W (green) and F1130W (red). Directions of north and east are indicated.

Table 1. Observing log.

Instrument	**Filter**	λ_p (μm)	**BW** (μm)	**PSF** (″)	$t_{\rm exp}$ (sec)	$F_{\rm tot}$ (Jy)	**North Spec contributions** Cont	H I	H_2	Others	**Notes**
NIRCam	F162M	1.626	0.168	0.053	1933	0.113±0.017	81%	10%	4%	He I (1%)	
	F212N	2.121	0.027	0.069	1933	0.9±0.08	13%		85%		
	F300M	2.996	0.318	0.097	483	0.1511±0.0002	58%	10%	27%	He II (1%)	
	F335M	3.365	0.347	0.109	483	0.2124±0.0003	53%	6%	37%		PAHs
MIRI	F560W	5.6	1.2	0.207	444	0.44±0.02	62%	2%	32%		
	F770W	7.7	2.2	0.269	444	0.816±0.01	68%	5%	14%	[Ar II] (9%)	PAHs
	F1000W	10.0	2.0	0.328	444	1.86±0.02	46%		11%	[S IV] (26%); [Ar III] (14%)	
	F1130W	11.3	0.7	0.375	444	0.7253±0.003	94%			[Ni I] (3%)	PAHs
	F1280W	12.8	2.4	0.420	444	1.20±0.02	45%	2%	1%	[Ne II] (49%)	
	F1500W	15.0	3.0	0.488	444	7.43±0.02	4%			[Ne III] (94%)	
	F1800W	18.0	3.0	0.591	444	4.01±0.02	42%			[S III] (54%)	
	F2100W	21.0	5.0	0.674	444	5.57±0.03	71%			[S III] (25%); [Ar III] (1%)	
	F2550W	25.5	4.0	0.803	444	20±2	88%			[O IV] (8%)	
MIRI Simul	F770W				951						
	F1130W				951						
	F1000W				951						

λ_p: pivot wavelength in μm (NIRCam: Rieke et al. 2023; MIRI: Bouchet et al. 2015). BW: band width in μm. PSF: FWHMs of PSFs in arcsec. For NIRCam simulated values are taken. $t_{\rm exp}$: exposure time on source in sec. $F_{\rm tot}$: photon-weighted mean flux density of the nebula in Jy. North Spec contributions: Estimated contributions to the images in each filter, calculated using NIRSpec-IFU and MIRI-MRS observations of a region in the northern part of the bright ring (van Hoof et al. in prep).

The pixel scales of the reduced data are 0.031 arcsec per pixel for the NIRCam short wavelength camera images, 0.063 arcsec for the NIRCam long wavelength camera images, and 0.111 arcsec for the MIRI images.

Table 1 lists the photon-weighted mean flux densities ($F_{\rm tot}$ in Jy) of the main body (the bright shell) of the Ring Nebula.

3. Nebular structure and stratification

The nebular images show three distinct regions: the central cavity, bright shell, and halo (Figure 2). The latter can be further divided into inner and outer halos. Multi-colour images reveal these components with different colours, indicating stratification

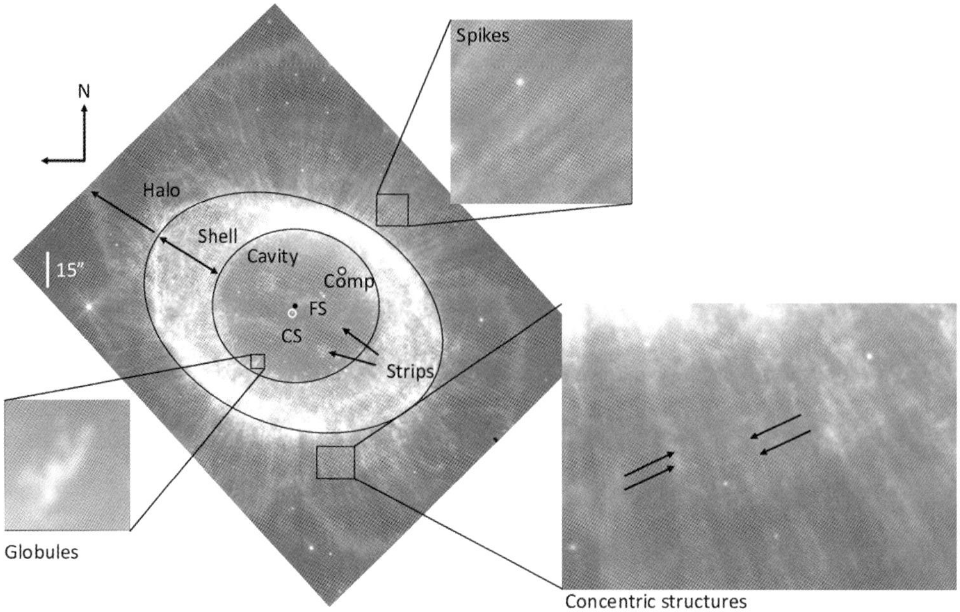

Figure 2. The names of the nebula components superposed on the NIRCam and MIRI three-colour image: F300M (blue), F560W (green) and F770W (red). CS (the white circle) is the central star, FS (black spot) is the first-moment centroid of the flux in the F300M image, and Comp is the companion star candidate. North is at the top in this image. The locations of some low-contrast concentric features are indicated, but they are much more easily seen in Fig. 3.

based on line emission. The low-density central cavity, emitting mainly in high-excitation [S IV] and [O IV] lines, has a circular outer edge. It contains a linear structure along its major axis, visible in various filters. The shell, surrounding the cavity, is an elliptical, clumpy region with a well-defined inner and outer edge. Its outer edge shows distortion, possibly related to the central star's proper motion. The inner halo, seen in various images, displays intricate structures including concentric arcs and radial spikes. The central star is detected in NIRCam and the two shortest-wavelength MIRI images.

Although the outer edge of the inner cavity is close to circular, its centre does not exactly correspond to the position of the central star, but instead appears to be offset to the north-west (roughly in the direction of the *Gaia* companion; see Sect. 3.5) by about 2 arcsec. The flux-weighted centres of the F300M and F335M images (calculated as the first moment of the images) are also offset from the central star, and nearly coincide with the centre of the inner cavity.

3.1. *Globules*

Even the angular resolution of the *JWST* images does not allow the system of globules to be cleanly resolved. To estimate their total number, we applied a peak-finding algorithm from the Python package PHOTUTILS (Bradley 2023) to the F212N image. The algorithm identifies about 17 500 peaks, which, given the density of clumps and resulting overlap, is likely to be an underestimate of the total number. A manual count was done in small regions, which, extrapolated to the full area, gives an estimated population of $\sim$25 000 globules.

The H_2 images reveal few cometary tails emanating from the globules. This is in contrast to the Helix Nebula where the majority of the globules (at least in the inner region)

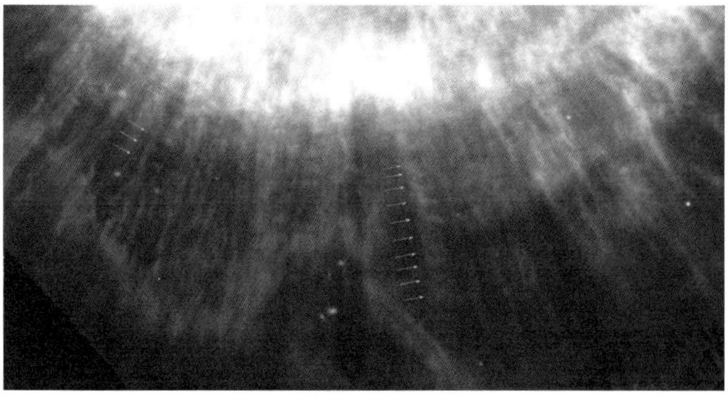

Figure 3. Regular concentric features in the outer regions of the F770W image of the Ring Nebula. Green arrows indicate the locations where these regularly-spaced features are most easily seen.

have well-developed tails seen in H_2 (Matsuura et al. 2009). Some short extensions of around 1 arcsec in length can be seen in absorption in the *HST* F502N and F658N images but these mostly do not have clear counterparts in the *JWST* images. The extensions seen in the *HST* images tend not to be straight. They may trace an early stage of tail formation.

3.2. *Radial spikes*

The halo shows multiple narrow, radial features pointing away from the central star, which following De Marco et al. (2022) we call 'spikes' (Fig. 3). They are seen only outside the bright shell, and mainly in H_2. The spikes are mainly a feature of the inner halo (O'Dell et al. 2013).

In a section of the F770W image covering 20 degrees of azimuth, we count 15–20 spikes. From this, we estimate that there are about 300–400 spikes in total. The exact number is imprecise due to the low contrast, small separation, and partial overlap of many spikes. The typical width appears to be around 0.4 arcsec. The typical length of the visible spikes is around 20 arcsec, but they may in a few cases extend twice as far, to the outer edge of the nebula.

The spikes are expected to arise from illumination effects where stellar light escapes through holes in the shell (De Marco et al. 2022). They line up better with the central star than with the offset centre of emission, which indicates that the dominant cause lies in the current or recent radiation from the star. There are some cases of misalignment with the star, possibly where there is partial overlap between spikes.

The number of spikes is of order 2 per cent of the number of globules. This suggests that there is no direct relation between the globules and spikes. O'Dell et al. (2013) argue that some of the spikes can be the shadows of large globules but this is not evident from the data here.

3.3. *Concentric arcs*

A series of faint, broken concentric arcs is apparent outside the bright ring in the H_2 halo. In places, up to 10 arcs can be identified (Figure 3). In some directions, the arcs appear to have been disrupted, possibly due to density variations in the nebula, but in general the curvature is regular.

The concentric structures are most apparent in the F770W image, which contains emission lines of H_2, H I and [Ar II]. They are also clearly visible in the F1000W and

F1130W images and can be distinguished at longer wavelengths in the F1800W and F2100W filters, but at lower contrast due to the poorer spatial resolution. At shorter wavelengths with better spatial resolution, the much clumpier appearance of the nebula in the lines isolated by these filters makes the features harder to trace. The arcs are seen in most directions but are obscured by the shell along the major axis.

A common scenario invoked to explain arc systems like these is one in which a close binary companion modulates the outflow from the AGB star. The time interval of 280 years then corresponds to the orbital period of the companion. If the combined mass of the original AGB star and its companion is $1.5 \pm 0.5 M_\odot$, the orbital separation would be about 50 ± 15 au.

3.4. *PAHs*

The polycyclic aromatic hydrocarbon (PAH) feature at 11.3 μm has been detected in *Spitzer* spectra of the Ring Nebula (Cox et al. 2016) based on Program 40536 (P.I. H. Dinerstein). *Spitzer*'s Infrared Spectrograph (IRS) covered a 99×18 arcsec area along the major axis of the elliptically-shaped Ring Nebula, with a pixel scale of 1.8 arcsec. This spectral map showed that the PAH feature is emitted from the outer half of the shell, a more or less similar emitting region to the H_2 S(1) and S(2) lines at 17.04 and 12.28 μm.

The higher angular resolution *JWST* images allow the PAH-emitting regions to be studied in much more detail. The F335M filter encompasses the 3.3 μm PAH feature, while the F300M filter lacks this band but otherwise contains similar nebular emission (Table 1). The F1130W filter has the lowest contribution from emission lines (Table 1), and best reflects the contributions of the continuum and PAH bands. Both the F335M/F300M ratio image and the F1130W/F1000W ratio image show indications of a narrow ring of excess emission located at the outer edge of the shell.

This narrow ring shows up only in the two filters containing PAH bands and is not seen in other filter combinations. From Table 1, the PAH contribution to F335M and F1000W is < 14 per cent and < 7 per cent respectively, but this is estimated from MIRI IFU spectra which are not centred on the narrow ring. We interpret these narrow ring excesses as possible PAH emission.

3.5. *Multiplicity*

A distant companion to the central star was identified by González-Santamaría et al. (2021). This star, *Gaia* DR3 2090486687506009472, lies 18.5 arcsec from the central star, corresponding to a projected distance of 0.07 pc. González-Santamaría et al. (2021) proposed that this companion is a white dwarf, based on the *Gaia* DR3 photometry. However, the B_P and R_P photometry is discrepant from the G-band photometry by 2.74 mag, and appears to be significantly affected by nebular emission lines. We combined photometry from our NIRCam and MIRI observations as well as archival Hubble Space Telescope images to establish the properties of the companion star, using the Python Stellar Spectral Energy Distribution toolset (PySSED), an SED-fitting code based on the software presented in McDonald et al. (2009, 2012, 2017). We assume a distance to the star of 790 pc, and that the star has a composition of between $[Fe/H] = -0.4$ and $+0.0$ dex and a corresponding $[\alpha/Fe] = +0.1$ to $+0.0$ dex, based on its height of 190 pc from the Galactic plane. The Ring Nebula has a metallicity which is approximately solar (Liu et al. 2004; Guerrero et al. 1997). For a plausible range of values of extinction, the luminosity and temperature that we obtain correspond to a main sequence star of approximate spectral type M2–M4 with a mass of 0.3–0.5 $M_\odot$ (Cifuentes et al. 2020).

4. Conclusion

JWST images have revealed a wealth of structural detail in NGC 6720. The nebula has a highly ionized inner cavity, a shell containing some 20 000 dense clumps, a thin ring of possible PAH emission, and a halo that contains around 10 concentric arcs and 400 spikes. Much of this detail is shown by the H_2 emission. The globules in the Ring Nebula have little or no tails, unlike those in the Helix Nebula. The globules in the Helix are also larger. These differences could be due to the Helix Nebula being more evolved and the Ring Nebula being in an earlier phase of evolution.

The central exciting star is inferred to be a member of a triple system. This consists of: the central star itself, with a progenitor mass of $\sim$1.5–2 $M_\odot$; a binary companion at some 50 au, responsible for the evenly spaced concentric arc structures in the nebula; and a distant, common proper motion companion at 0.07 pc which is a low-mass M2–M4 main sequence star.

Many features we see in the *JWST* images of the Ring Nebula, including the spikes, are shared by several other well-studied PNe of similar morphology. The time when planetary nebulae could be modelled as uniform density spheres is long gone. They contain a wide variety of structures and phases, with very different conditions and size scales, ranging from highly ionized hot gas to dense molecular clumps.

References

Bouchet P., et al., 2015, PASP, 127, 612
Bradley L., 2023, astropy/photutils: 1.8.0, doi:10.5281/zenodo.7946442
Cifuentes C., et al., 2020, A&A, 642, A115
Cox N. L. J., Pilleri P., Berné O., Cernicharo J., Joblin C., 2016, MNRAS, 456, L89
De Marco O., et al., 2022, Nature Astronomy, 6, 1421
Gardner J. P., Mather J. C., Abbott R., et al. 2023, arXiv e-prints, p. arXiv:2304.04869
González-Santamaría I., Manteiga M., Manchado A., Ulla A., Dafonte C., López Varela P., 2021, A&A, 656, A51
Guerrero M. A., Manchado A., Chu Y. H., 1997, ApJ, 487, 328
Lindegren L., et al., 2021, A&A, 649, A4
Liu Y., Liu X. W., Barlow M. J., Luo S. G., 2004, MNRAS, 353, 1251
Matsuura M., et al., 2009, ApJ, 700, 1067
McDonald I., van Loon J. T., Decin L., Boyer M. L., Dupree A. K., Evans A., Gehrz R. D., Woodward C. E., 2009, MNRAS, 394, 831
McDonald I., Zijlstra A. A., Boyer M. L., 2012, MNRAS, 427, 343
McDonald I., Zijlstra A. A., Watson R. A., 2017, MNRAS, 471, 770
Miller Bertolami M. M., 2016, A&A, 588, A25
O'Dell C. R., Ferland G. J., Henney W. J., Peimbert M., 2013, AJ, 145, 92
Rieke M. J., Kelly D. M., Misselt K., et al. 2023, PASP, 135, 028001
Wright G. S., Rieke G. H., Glasse A., et al. 2023, PASP, 135, 048003

Planetary Nebulae: A Universal Toolbox in the Era of Precision Astrophysics
Proceedings IAU Symposium No. 384, 2025
O. De Marco, A. Zijlstra & R. Szczerba, eds.
doi:10.1017/S1743921324000358

Remarkable Chemical Complexity in Planetary Nebulae: A Molecule and Dust Perspective

L. M. Ziurys[1] and D. R. Schmidt[2]

[1]Departments of Chemistry and Astronomy, The University of Arizona, USA

[2]Department of Physics and Astronomy, Franklin & Marshall College, USA

Abstract. Despite model predictions, many planetary nebulae appear to have a relatively rich molecular content. Observational studies of over 30 such objects show the presence of a variety of gas-phase molecules, from simple species such as CN and CS, to more complex organics including H_2CO, HC_3N, c-C_3H_2, and CH_3CN. Other PNe contain fullerenes; carbonaceous and silicate dust features are also found. Molecular abundances also do not appear to vary with nebular age. Remnant material from the asymptotic giant branch appears to undergo chemical processing in the protoplanetary nebula phase and then is frozen out in planetary nebulae. PN ejecta are thus in part molecular in content and may account for the observation of complex molecules in diffuse clouds.

Keywords. stars: planetary nebulae, molecular abundances, dust

---

1. Planetary Nebulae: A Problem for the "Organic Continuum"

Planetary nebulae (PNe) are the final stage in stellar evolution for most stars (1–8 $M_\odot$) following the Asymptotic Giant Branch (AGB). Significant mass loss on the AGB creates a roughly spherical circumstellar envelope, which, by uncertain processes, evolves into the wide variety of morphologies observed in PNe, from elliptical to bipolar to multipolar (Balick & Frank 2002). The ejected envelope also becomes highly ionized by the strong ultraviolet (UV) radiation field generated by the star as it evolves into a white dwarf. The presence of strong UV emission has led to the belief that only atomic and diatomic species would survive from the molecule-rich AGB envelope because of widespread photodissociation. Models of the chemical evolution of PNe predict orders of magnitude decrease in gas-phase molecular abundances over the nebular lifetime (Redman et al. 2003); for example, the HCN abundance falls by ~ 7 orders of magnitude by 10,000 yrs into the PN lifespan.

About $\sim 85\%$ of the material that forms the interstellar medium (ISM) has its origins in ejecta from low and intermediate mass stars through the PN phase (Dorschner & Henning 1995). The predicted widespread destruction of gas-phase molecules in PNe therefore implies that there is a sharp discontinuity in molecular chemistry between the AGB and diffuse clouds. The copious production of carbon-carbon bonds that occurs in C-rich AGB stars associated with the so-called "organic continuum" is disrupted such that molecule formation in diffuse clouds must begin from the atomic level. Yet, observations have shown that diffuse clouds contain far more polyatomic molecules than can be produced in situ in the low density environment present (Snow & McCall 2006). Therefore, an outside source must be supplying diffuse clouds with molecular material, suggesting that the molecular content of PNe is more complex than models had predicted. PNe could be seeding diffuse clouds and preserving the organic continuum.

CO has long been known to be present in PNe, as demonstrated by the early surveys of Huggins et al. (2005) and Huggins et al. (1996). More recent observations also showed widespread H_2 in objects such as the Helix and Ring Nebulae and other PNe (Speck et al. 2003; Davis et al. 2003). The presence of other molecules in PNe, in particular polyatomic species, was not well-known. A few objects were observed in CN, HCN and HCO^+ in the millimeter range (Bachiller et al. 1997; Cox et al. 1992), and the very young PN NGC 7027 was investigated in some detail (Zhang et al. 2008). This nebula was found to contain molecules as complex as HC_3N and c-C_3H_2; such findings could be attributed to its age of $\sim$700 yrs in the PN phase, which agreed with chemical models at some level.

2. Molecular Clues from the Aging Helix Nebula

The mystery of polyatomic molecules in diffuse clouds and the problem of the organic continuum led to further investigations into the molecular content of PNe at millimeter wavelengths. Following on the study of Bachiller et al. (1997), Tenenbaum et al. (2009) found H_2CO, c-C_3H_2 and CCH at the same position in the Helix Nebula where HCN and HCO^+ were detected. In contrast to NGC 7027, the Helix is quite old ($\sim$12,000 years) and the presence of 4-5 atom molecules completely contradicted the models. Subsequent observations of the Helix by Zack & Ziurys (2013) and Zeigler et al. (2013) showed widespread HCO^+ and H_2CO across the $\sim 1000''$ source. A complete map of the Helix of the J = 1$\rightarrow$0 transition of HCO^+ at 89 GHz using the 12 m telescope of the Arizona Radio Observatory (ARO) demonstrated that the molecule was present throughout the nebula (see Figure 1), except in the inner highly-ionized region traced by He^+ emission. Given the radio beam size of $\sim$ 1 arcmin, over 270 individual positions were measured to produce this image. These high spectral resolution data helped to show that the Helix Nebula was not a helix, but rather bipolar in structure and shaped like a "barrel" oriented almost along the line-of-sight (Zeigler et al. 2013). Subsequent observations revealed that HCN, HNC, CCH, and c-C_3H_2 also had extended distributions in the Helix (Schmidt & Ziurys 2017a; Schmidt et al. 2018a). Even at its advanced stage of evolution, the Helix is chemically-rich, suggesting that indeed its ejecta may contain significant molecular material.

3. The "Level 1" and "Level 2" Planetary Nebula Surveys of HCN and HCO^+

The molecular detections in the Helix Nebula prompted a mini-survey of HCO^+ and CS in five nebulae that spanned the age range 900–10,000 years: K4-47, NGC 6537 (Red Spider), M2-48, NGC 6720 (Ring), and NGC 6853 (Dumbbell). The J = 1$\rightarrow$0 and 3$\rightarrow$2 transitions of HCO^+ at 89 and 267 GHz and the J = 2$\rightarrow$1, 3$\rightarrow$2, and J = 5$\rightarrow$4 lines of CS (98, 147, and 245 GHz) were observed using the ARO Submillimeter Telescope (SMT) and 12 m antenna (Edwards et al. 2014).The thrust of this work was to examine the change in molecular abundances of these two species with nebular age. Surprisingly, the abundances did not appear to vary significantly, with $f(CS/H_2) \sim 1$–4×10^{-8} and $f(HCO^+/H_2) \sim 10^{-8}$ - 10^{-7}. This very suggestive result led to the more extensive surveys of Schmidt & Ziurys (2016), Schmidt & Ziurys (2017a), Schmidt & Ziurys (2017b), and Schmidt et al. (2022), which initially focused on HCO^+ and HCN identifications in over a dozen PNe, using their J = 1$\rightarrow$0 and 3$\rightarrow$2 transitions at 3 and 1.2 mm, respectively. These objects were chosen on the basis of their strong CO emission as determined previously in the Huggins et al. surveys, and covered a range of morphologies (bipolar, multipolar,

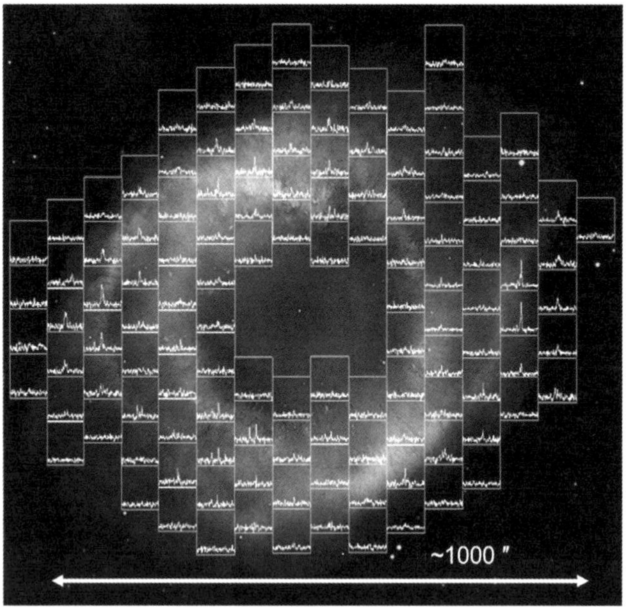

Figure 1. Spectra of the J = 1→0 transition of HCO^+ at 89 GHz observed throughout the Helix Nebula with $\sim 70''$ spacings, showing the widespread distribution of this molecule (Zeigler et al. 2013).

elliptical) and ages (900 to 13,000 yrs.) Most of the sample nebulae are displayed in Figure 2.

Measurements were carried out again at ARO, but this time with the new ARO 12 m for the 3 mm work. Of the 17 target PNe in this "Level 1" survey, detections were made of at least one molecule in 13 objects, with sensitivities of a few mK. Fractional abundances found were in the ranges $f(HCO^+/H_2) \sim 0.04$–7×10^{-7} and $f(HCN/H_2) \sim 0.1$–9×10^{-7}. Radiative transfer modeling, also done in multiple CO transitions, indicated that the molecules were present in warm but quite dense gas, with a typical gas kinetic temperature of $T_K \sim 20$–30 K and 1–5 $\times 10^6$ cm^{-3} (Schmidt & Ziurys 2016; Edwards & Ziurys 2013, 2014). The non-detections in certain nebulae may require longer integration times and/or a smaller telescope beam size. Representative Level 1 spectra of the J = 3→2 transition of HCN are presented in Figure 3.

The HCN and HCO^+ detections were subsequently followed by searches for both HNC and CCH in many of the Level 1 objects, as well as the Helix Nebula, as mentioned (Schmidt & Ziurys 2017a,b). These observations were also carried out with the ARO telescopes and focused on the J (or N) = 1→0 and 3→2 transitions at 3 and 1.2 mm. HNC was found in 12 PNe with abundance relative to H_2 of $f \sim 0.02$–2×10^{-7}, resulting in an [HCN]/[HNC] ratio of 1–8. Such low ratios, favoring HNC, are quite different from those found in AGB stars and are important clues to the chemical transformations into the PN phase. CCH was found in the 10 nebulae searched with $f \sim 0.2$–47×10^{-7}, making it one of the more abundant molecules in PNe (Schmidt & Ziurys 2017b; Schmidt et al. 2018a).

The success of the Level 1 studies prompted observations of additional planetary nebulae in HCN and HCO^+, in this case with lower CO intensities, also conducted at ARO at 1 and 3 mm. These so-called "Level 2" sources are shown in Figure 2, and again

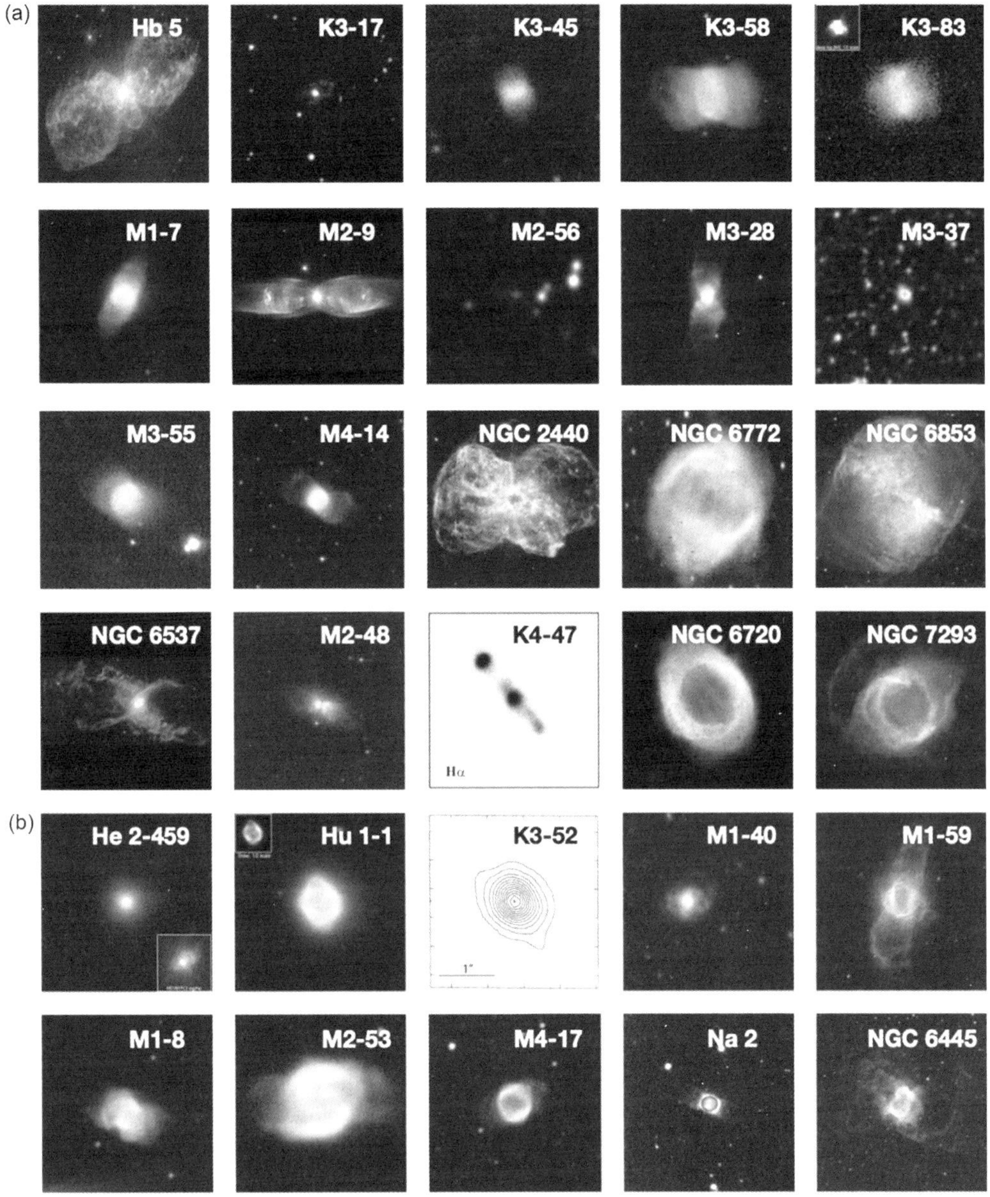

Figure 2. a) PNe from the Level 1 survey and associated studies. b) PNe from the Level 2 survey. All images were acquired from the Planetary Nebula Image Catalog (PNIC) and sources therein, save for M2-9 (source: ESA/Hubble), M2-56 and M3-37 (source: Aladin), NGC 6853 (source: ESO), K4-47 (source: Corradi et al. 2000), and K3-52 (source: Aaquist & Kwok 1990).

represent varied morphologies and ages (Schmidt et al. 2022). Out of the 13 original nebulae, 10 were found to foster at least one of these two polyatomic molecules. A surprising result was the identification of HCO^+ in Na 2, a very old PN estimated to have a kinematic age of ~28,000 years. The abundances derived were very similar to those of the Level 1 sources, with $f(\mathrm{HCN}) \sim 0.2$–1.5×10^{-7} and $f(\mathrm{HCO^+}) \sim 0.3$–$5.1 \times 10^{-8}$. The abundances also did not significantly vary with nebular age.

Combined with previous observations, at least 30 PNe contain HCN and/or HCO^+, indicating that polyatomic molecules are common constituents of these objects. The data

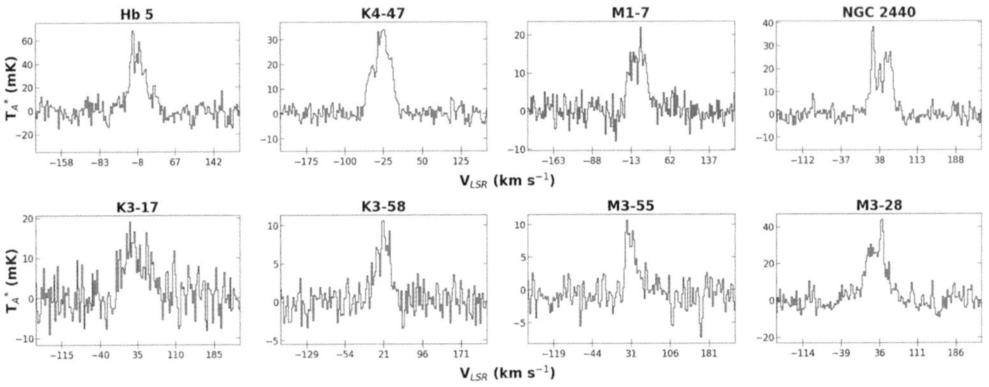

Figure 3. Representative spectra of the J = 3 → 2 line of HCN near 265 GHz observed with the ARO SMT toward several of the "Level 1" PNe (Schmidt & Ziurys 2016).

strongly support a scenario where dense ejecta from PNe seed the interstellar medium with molecular matter.

4. Remarkable Chemical Complexity in Select Planetary Nebulae: K4-47 and M2-48

Some of the Level 1 sources were studied in other molecules. The most chemically-rich PN found to date is the young nebula K4-47 (Schmidt & Ziurys 2019). Measurements at 1, 2, and 3 mm of multiple transitions were carried out at the ARO and Institut de Radioastronomie Millimètrique (IRAM) 30 m telescopes to ensure the accuracy of all molecular identifications. K4-47 is thought to be a young (400–900 yrs), highly collimated, bipolar nebula observed in vibrationally-excited H_2 (Akras et al. 2017). K4-47 was found to contain some unusual species seen in a few other PNe, including HC_3N, N_2H^+, H_2CO, c-C_3H_2, and SiO. However, the more complex molecules CH_3CN, H_2CNH, and CH_3CCH were additionally detected in multiple transitions; see Schmidt & Ziurys (2019) and Figure 4. These species have never before been observed in PNe. In addition, a wide variety of ^{13}C-substituted isotopologues were observed, such as c-$^{13}CCCH_2$, c-$CC^{13}CH_2$, $CH_3{}^{13}CN$, $^{13}CH_3CN$, $CH_3{}^{13}CCH$, and $^{13}CH_3CCH$, adding additional evidence for the presence of these complex molecules. Moreover, all three doubly ^{13}C-substituted varieties of HC_3N were identified - the first known object in which all three species have been detected. After CO and H_2, the most abundant molecules in K4-47 were found to be CCH and CN, which have abundances of $f \sim 8 \times 10^{-7}$, relative to molecular hydrogen. Surprisingly, the next most abundant molecule is CH_3CCH, which has $f \sim 6 \times 10^{-7}$. The abundances of CH_3CN and H_2CNH were estimated to be $f \sim 5 \times 10^{-8}$ and $f \sim 10^{-7}$, respectively.

Another PN that was found to have striking properties is M2-48 (Edwards & Ziurys 2014). This object is estimated to be middle-aged at ∼ 4,800 years and has a bipolar morphology and an intricate structure in [N II]. There is a bright, bipolar core, roughly $30'' \times 20''$ in extent, from which the highly collimated bipolar outflow extends, terminating in two symmetric bow-shocked knots, extending $\pm\ 2'$ from the center (López-Martín et al. 2002). H_2 emission has also been detected toward M2-48 by Marquez-Lugo et al. (2013). M2-48 was one of the original sources in the Edwards et al. (2014) survey.

M2-48 was the first PN where SiO and SO_2 were detected; also found were CN, HCN, HNC, CS, SO, HCO^+, N_2H^+, and the isotopologues ^{13}CN, $H^{13}CN$, $HN^{13}C$, and $H^{13}CO^+$. A radiative transfer analysis of multiple SiO transitions showed a slightly higher gas kinetic temperature than found in other nebulae, with $T_K \sim 55$ K. SO and SO_2 were

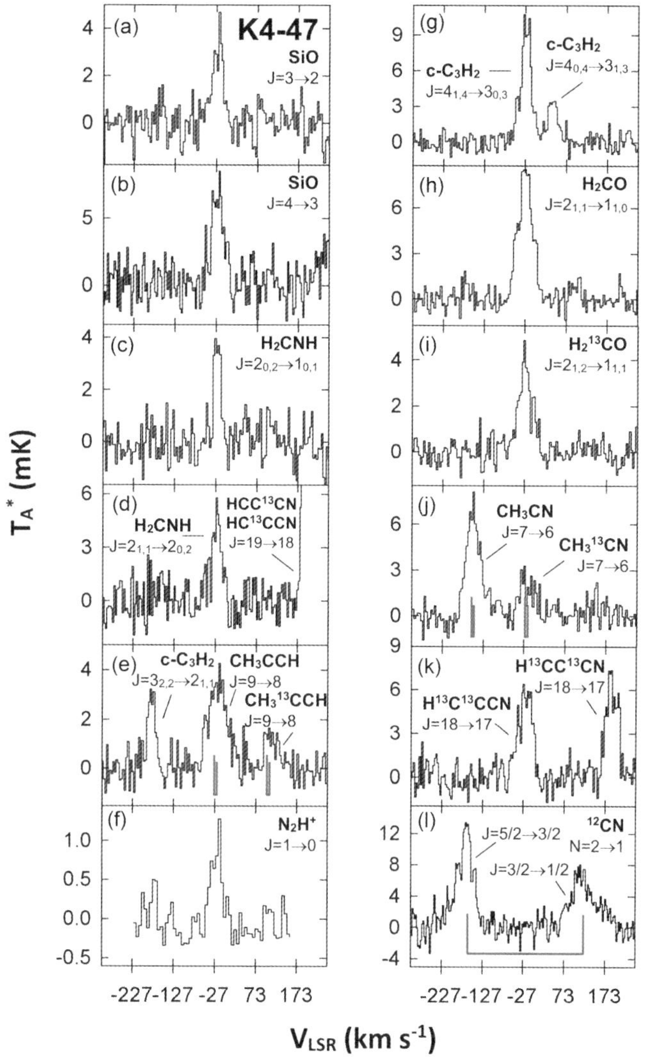

Figure 4. Spectra of unusual and complex molecules found in K4-47, including the organics CH_3CN, H_2CNH, and CH_3CCH (Schmidt & Ziurys 2019).

found to be some of the most prevalent molecules in this nebula, with fractional abundances, relative to H_2, of $f \sim 2.4 \times 10^{-7}$ and 1.2×10^{-7}, indicating an $[SO]/[SO_2]$ ratio of ~ 2. Relatively high ion abundances were measured in M2-48 as well, with $f \sim 10^{-7}$ for both HCO^+ and N_2H^+. An [HCN]/[HNC] ratio of ~ 2 was determined, as typically observed in other PNe. The high abundances of SO and SO_2, along with the presence of SiO with $f \sim 2.9 \times 10^{-8}$, suggest $O/C > 1$ in this source. Furthermore, the prevalence N_2H^+ indicates possible nitrogen enrichment. Unlike many other PNe, CCH was absent in this nebula, despite extensive searches.

More recent observations by Schmidt et al. have led to the detection of H_2S in M2-48 and a few other PNe. This molecule was identified on the basis of its fundamental transition $J_{Ka,Kc} = 1_{1,0} \rightarrow 1_{0,1}$ which lies at 169 GHz, as shown in Figure 5. A new very

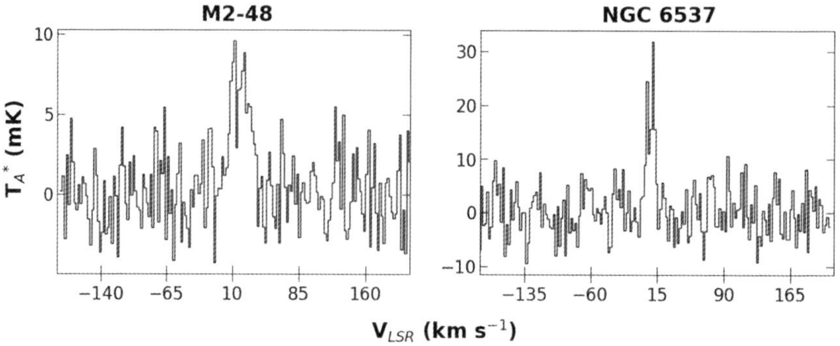

Figure 5. Spectra of the $J_{Ka,Kc} = 1_{1,0} \rightarrow 1_{0,1}$ transition of H_2S near 169 GHz, detected towards the nebulae NGC 6537 and M2-48 (Schmidt et al., in prep.).

sensitive 2 mm receiver built at ARO for the 12 m telescope was used for the measurements. Although the data analysis is preliminary, the presence of H_2S may provide some insight into the so-called "sulfur anomaly" in PNe. A study of O, Ne, S, Cl, and Ar abundances in 85 PNe by Henry et al. (2004), systematically found lower sulfur abundances, relative to H II regions of the same metallicity. This discrepancy has been verified by other observations. Henry et al. suggested that sulfur may be sequestered into grains. However, molecules such as H_2S, SO, and SO_2 may provide an alternative sink.

M2-48 appears to be an O-rich nebula while K4-47 is clearly carbon-rich. The molecular content thus can be used as an indicator of the C/O ratio in PNe. These ratios are likely those from the original AGB stars.

5. Other Nebulae of Interest

The studies of K4-47 and M2-48 are only sampling a small subset of all PNe that have a noteworthy chemistry. Bublitz et al. (2019), for example, has identified interesting molecules such as HCN, CN and HNC in NGC 6853 and NGC 6445. They found a correlation between the [HCN]/[HNC] ratio and UV flux. Further observations of NGC 7027 by the same group has revealed a very complex morphology consisting of multipolar structures actively driven by collimated winds (Moraga Baez et al. 2023). This nebula also contains CH^+ and the rare ion HeH^+ (Neufeld et al. 2020; Güsten et al. 2019).

Several of the Level 2 sources from Schmidt et al. (2022) have also been further investigated for their molecular content. One object of note is NGC 6445, the "Little Gem" Nebula. This PN was initially studied in molecular lines by Bublitz et al. (2019), who identified HCO^+, CN, HCN, and HNC in the nebula in the 3 mm window. Schmidt et al. expanded this data set by measuring the $J = 3 \rightarrow 2$ transitions of HCN and HCO^+, followed by Gold et al. (in prep.) who added CCH, HC_3N, H_2CO, CS, H_2S and c-C_3H_2 to the molecular list. High sensitivity spectra in CO and other molecules suggest that this nebula has four distinct velocity components (Schmidt et al. 2022). The complexity of this structure is currently being unraveled by both ALMA observations (Moraga Baez et al. this volume) and single-dish mapping (Gold et al).

Hu 1-1 is another "Level 2" nebula with some striking properties. Most of the molecule-rich nebulae are bipolar or multipolar in shape, but Hu 1-1 is thought to be elliptical with a binary companion (Weidmann & Gamen 2011). The previous detections of HCN and HCO^+ have been complemented recently by H_2CO, CCH, CN, CS, and c-C_3H_2 (Figure 6; Gold et al. in prep.) These results suggest that morphology may not play a decisive role in the chemistry, but further exploration is clearly needed. Further observations of this

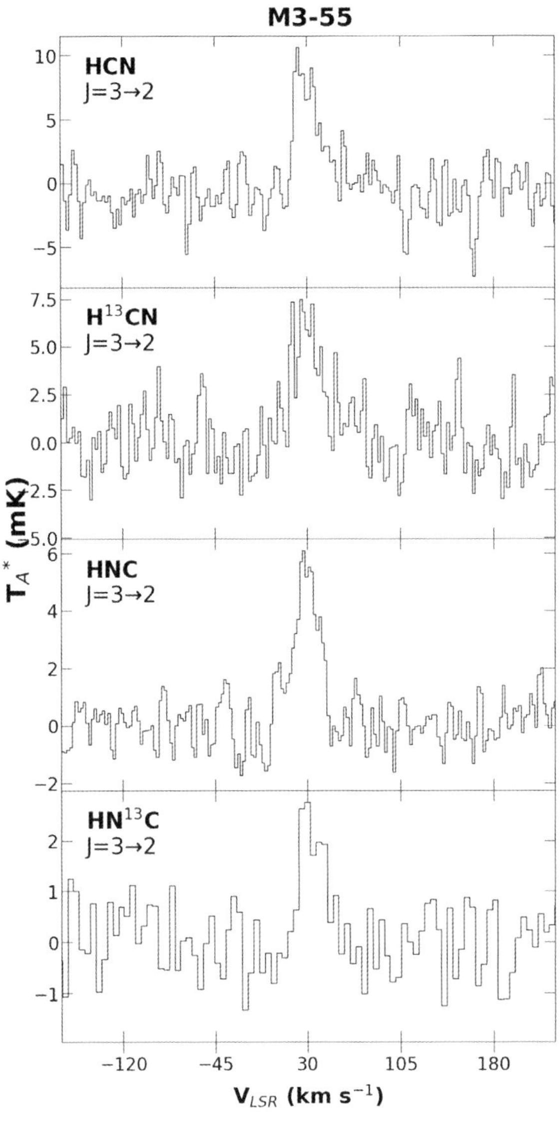

Figure 6. Spectra of molecules observed towards Hu 1-1, an elliptical PN with a binary companion, including H_2CO and c-C_3H_2 (Gold et al. in prep).

rare source are in progress. It is also noteworthy that the spectra from Hu 1-1 have an unusual line profile with a strong central peak combined with a broad, redshifted wing, most visible in CO (Schmidt et al. 2022). This line shape may be related to the binary structure, but high-resolution imaging would give a more complete picture.

6. An Overview of Molecular Abundances in Planetary Nebulae: Beyond CO

The current work has led to the identification of many molecules in PNe, often with multiple transitions (see Table 1 for a complete list). Accurate radiative transfer modeling can then be carried out, establishing not only abundances but densities and temperatures,

Table 1. Molecules Observed in Planetary Nebulae.

H_2	CH^+	HNC	SO_2	CH_2NH
CO	OH	CCH	H_2S	CH_3CN
CO^+	SiO	N_2H^+	H_2CO	CH_3CCH
CN	SO	HCO^+	c-C_3H_2	C_{60}
CS	HCN	HeH^+	HC_3N	C_{70}

as mentioned. Over 30 PNe have now been observed in a variety of species. Although this number is a small subset of the PNe in the Galaxy, it does provide a snapshot of the chemical complexity in these objects. Note that most molecular lines detected in planetary nebulae are quite weak - about 1–20 mK, as shown in Figures 4–6. Many of the PNe observed have a small angular size, such that mm-wave observations are typically "beam-diluted." Systemic studies with long integration times, sensitive receivers, and multiple frequency bands are needed for these detections. Such obstacles have made the study of the molecular content of PNe sporadic until recently. The establishment of a consistent set of molecular abundances in PNe has been a decade-long effort and finally a statistical sample, albeit small, is available.

A summary of molecular abundances measured in PNe for almost all species thus far identified is given in Table 2. The criterion for inclusion in the table is the appearance of a given molecule in at least three nebulae. Therefore, the more complex organics currently unique to K4-47 are not included, but their abundances have been reported in an earlier section. For nebulae with small angular sizes, relative to the mm-wave antenna beam, abundances have been corrected for the source size, based on the optical image. For extended sources, a "clumping" factor is also applied, which compensates for the presence of molecules in knots as opposed to a uniform distribution (see Schmidt & Ziurys 2016). Such clumps are known to exist in the Helix from H_2 observations, for example Meixner et al. (2005). All corrections have been applied to the data in a consistent manner such that meaningful comparisons can be made. Note that when three or more transitions of a given molecule are detected, an estimate of the density and temperature of the gas can be calculated. This situation is common for CO, CS, and larger molecules such as HC_3N. The typical density and temperature range found for the gas in the >30 sample of PNe is $T_k \sim$ 15–70 K and n(H_2) $\sim 10^5$-10^7 cm^{-3}. As mentioned, the molecular material is dense but not very hot. These physical properties support the concept that the molecules exist in dense, self-shielding clumps, mixed with dust, embedded in an ionized medium, as theorized decades ago by Howe et al. (1994). Evidence for the "knots" model is apparent in the H_2 observations of sources such as the Helix (e.g. Meixner et al. 2005; Speck et al. 2003). However, contrary to some theoretical predictions (Redman et al. 2003), the clumps apparently do not dissipate on a $t^{-3/2}$ timescale and are more robust than assumed.

As shown in Table 2, CO is the most abundant molecule after (presumably) H_2. The abundance of this molecule is fairly constant across all PNe at $f \sim 10^{-4}$. The next most prevalent species is a polyatomic, CCH, with $f \sim 0.02$–4.7×10^{-6}, with the emphasis on the upper end of the given range. CCH, however, has not been observed in any O-rich PNe. HCN and CN closely follow with $f \sim 0.1$–9×10^{-7} and $f \sim 0.7$–9.9×10^{-7}. These species are abundant in oxygen-rich M2-48 (Edwards & Ziurys 2014) and are also common in O-rich stellar envelopes (Ziurys et al. 2009). HCO^+ is also relatively common, having $f \sim 0.02$–7.4×10^{-7}, with HNC, H_2CO, SO, and c-C_3H_2 equally abundant with $f \sim 0.2$–2×10^{-7}, although HNC has a somewhat lower range. It is also noteworthy that the abundance of HC_3N is as high as $f \sim 10^{-7}$. N_2H^+, SiO, and H_2S (in prep.) are about a factor of 10 lower than the other molecules.

Table 2. Representative Abundances in Planetary Nebulae.

Molecule	$f(X/H_2)^a$	References
CO	$\sim 10^{-4}$	-
HCN	$0.1–9.1 \times 10^{-7}$	b, c, d, e, f, g
HCO^+	$0.02–7.4 \times 10^{-7}$	b, c, d, e, g, h, i
CCH	$0.02–4.7 \times 10^{-6}$	b, c, j, k
HNC	$0.02–2.2 \times 10^{-7}$	c, d, f
H_2CO	$0.22–2.50 \times 10^{-7}$	c, i, l
CS	$0.05–1.1 \times 10^{-7}$	c, d, h
CN	$0.7–9.9 \times 10^{-7}$	b, c, d, k, l
SO	$0.21–2.40 \times 10^{-7}$	c, d
SO_2	1.2×10^{-7}	d
c-C_3H_2	$0.1–1.5 \times 10^{-7}$	b, k, l
N_2H^+	$0.38–9.80 \times 10^{-8}$	b, c, d, l
SiO	$1.4–2.9 \times 10^{-8}$	d, l
HC_3N	$0.09–2.2 \times 10^{-7}$	b, l

[a] Abundance relative to H_2, [b] Zhang et al. (2008), [c] Edwards & Ziurys (2013), [d] Edwards & Ziurys (2014), [e] Schmidt & Ziurys (2016), [f] Schmidt & Ziurys (2017a), [g] Schmidt et al. (2022), [h] Edwards et al. (2014), [i] Zack & Ziurys (2013), [j] Schmidt & Ziurys (2017b), [k] Schmidt et al. (2018a), [l] Schmidt & Ziurys (2019)

Another important characteristic of the molecular abundances is that they do not appear to vary with the age of the PNe, as mentioned in Section 3 for HCN and HCO^+. This finding is illustrated in Figure 7. Here abundances for HCN, HCO^+, CCH, CS, H_2CO, c-C_3H_2 and N_2H^+ are plotted vs. the age of the nebula host, in circles of varying colors. For a given species, the abundances do not typically vary more than a factor of 10 across 12,000 yrs. For example, the abundance of CCH remains at 10^{-7}-10^{-6}, while the values for H_2CO fluctuate slightly around 10^{-7}. Even more striking is that of HCN, which never drops below 10^{-8} for over 30 PNe. In contrast, the model of Redman et al. (2003) predicts that the abundances of HCN and HCO^+ decrease by factors of 10^6 and 100, respectively. No such decrease is observed. This result strongly supports the idea that PNe seed the diffuse ISM with molecular material, as discussed.

7. The Isotope Mystery

The $^{12}C/^{13}C$ ratio is a sensitive indicator of nucleosynthesis and mixing in the interior of stars (e.g. Abia et al. 2017). ^{13}C is an intermediate product of hydrogen-shell burning in the CNO cycle (e.g. Wiescher et al. 2010), produced on the red giant branch (RGB) and brought to the stellar surface in the First, and for more massive stars, Second Dredge-Up. ^{12}C, in contrast, is created by the triple alpha process during helium-burning, which occurs on the AGB and also in supernovae (Herwig 2005). Thermal pulsing on the AGB creates a convective envelope, which, through Third Dredge-Up, brings the ^{12}C to the stellar surface. As a consequence, low $^{12}C/^{13}C$ ratios are expected on the RGB, typically 5–25. The ratios increase on the AGB to > 30, in the process creating carbon stars where $C > O$ (Lebzelter et al. 2019). Overall, observations of $^{12}C/^{13}C$ ratios in evolved stars have supported this picture with lower ratios for oxygen-rich stars, and higher values for carbon-rich objects. For example, in Ramstedt & Olofsson (2014), typical ratios determined for the shells with $C < O$ were $^{12}C/^{13}C \sim 5$–15, while values of $^{12}C/^{13}C \sim$ 8–46 were found for those with $C > O$. Milam et al. (2009) found $^{12}C/^{13}C \sim$ 25-90 in C-rich AGB envelopes and substantially lower values of $^{12}C/^{13}C \sim$ 3–35 in oxygen-rich shells.

As molecular observations of PNe were conducted, spectra of ^{13}C-substituted molecules were often observed, enabling a determination of $^{12}C/^{13}C$ ratios. These species include

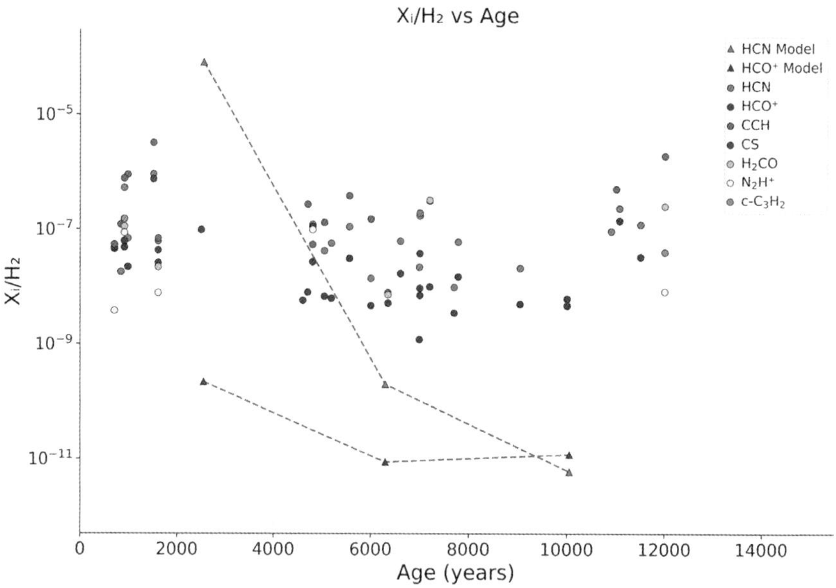

Figure 7. A plot of molecular abundances (circles) for series of PNe vs. their age. Data are shown for HCN, HCO^+, CCH, CS, H_2CO, c-C_3H_2 and N_2H^+. For a given species, the abundances typically do not vary more than a factor of 10 across 12,000 yrs. Theoretical predictions are shown by triangles and dashed lines for HCN and HCO^+, which show orders of magnitude decrease with age, in contrast to the observations.

Table 3. $^{12}C/^{13}C$ Isotope Ratios in PNe [a].

Source	Morphology	Molecular Tracers	$^{12}C/^{13}C$	Previous $^{12}C/^{13}C$[b]	C/O
NGC 6537	Multipolar	HCN, HNC	2.4–3.5 ± 0.5	-	0.95[c] $\geq$1[d]
M2-48	Bipolar	HCN, HNC HCO^+, CN	2–4 ±0.6	-	<1[d]
K4-47	Bipolar	CO, CN, HCN, HNC, HCO^+, H_2CO	1.3–3.4 ± 0.6	-	>1[e]
NGC 7293[f]	Bipolar	HCO^+	12.4 ± 5.4	9, 10, 9.4 ± 0.6	0.9–1[g,h] >1[i]
M3-55	Bipolar	HCN, HNC	1.0–1.8 ± 0.8	-	$\geq$1[i]
M3-28	Quadrupolar	HCN	7.2 ± 4.4	-	$\geq$1[i]
M2-9	Bipolar	CO, HCO^+	3.3 ± 1.9 (CO) 13.2 ± 4.9 (HCO^+)	>2	<0.5[j]
NGC 2440	Quadrupolar?	CO, HCN	1.2–1.6 ± 0.7	-	0.5–1.9[h,k]
NGC 6720	Bipolar	HCN, CN	10.8–12.2 ± 4.5	22, 9.5 ± 1.6	1.1[h]
K3-52	Irregular	HCN	1.5 ± 0.5	-	-
K3-70	Elliptical	CO	1.75	-	-
M3-3	Bipolar	HCN	~ 2.5	~ 3	-

[a] From Ziurys et al. (2020) except where indicated, [b] From Palla et al. (2000), Balser et al. (2002), Andriantsaralaza et al. (2020); from CO, [c] Pottasch et al. (2000), [d] Edwards et al. (2014), [e] Schmidt et al. (2018b), [f] (+390″, -30″) position, [g] Henry et al. (1999), Henry et al. (2018), [h] Ventura et al. (2017), [i] Based on molecular content, [j] Liu et al. (2001), [k] Bernard-Salas et al. (2002)

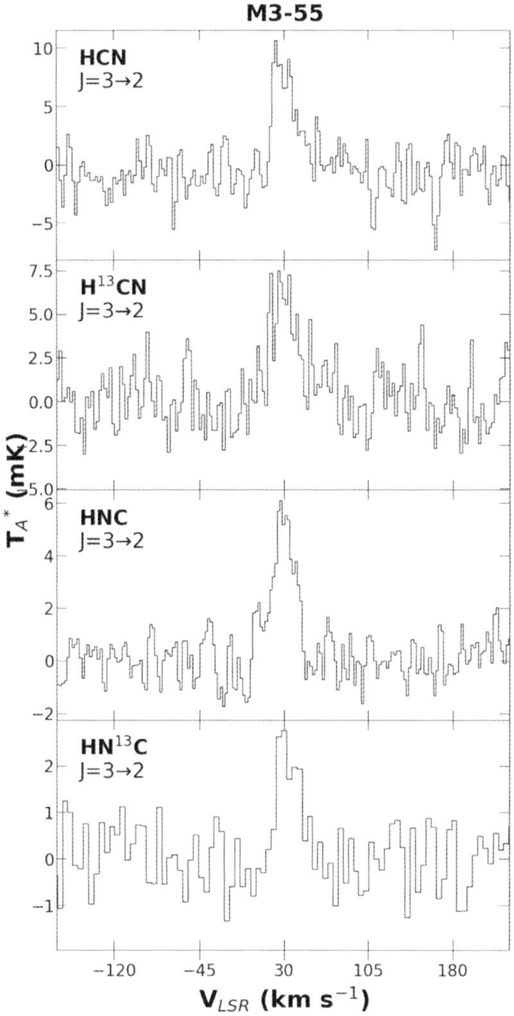

Figure 8. Spectra of the J = 3→2 transition of HCN, $H^{13}CN$, HNC, and $HN^{13}C$ measured toward the PN M3-55. Note the relative strengths of the lines.

CO, HCN, HNC, CN, and others, as previously mentioned for K4-47. Sample spectra are shown in Figure 8, specifically lines of HCN, $H^{13}CN$, HNC, and $HN^{13}C$ in M3-55.

Currently, the ratio has been measured in a sample of 12 PNe, 9 from Ziurys et al. (2020) and new data. These values are summarized in Table 3. The ratios fall in the range 1.0 ± 0.8 to 13.2 ± 4.9. In 7 out of 12 sources, more than one molecule was used in the determination, and often with multiple transitions. Values are very consistent between molecules. It is therefore clear in this sample, many of which are C-rich PNe, that the $^{12}C/^{13}C$ ratios are unexpectedly low - significantly less than in normal carbon stars. Furthermore, in several nebulae, the ratio is < 3.5, the minimum achieved in equilibrium CNO burning (Herwig 2005).

The objects chosen here have ages $\sim$ 900 to 12,000 years and thus sample the entire PN lifespan. However, because nucleosynthesis ceases at the beginning of the PN stage,

age should not play a role in the ratio values. Fractionation is not likely, as Schmidt & Ziurys (2016), Schmidt & Ziurys (2017a), Schmidt & Ziurys (2017b), Zack & Ziurys (2013), Schmidt et al. (2018a), and Edwards et al. (2014) have shown that the molecular gas in PNe is warm, typically 20–50 K. Therefore, the low ratios reflect the end of the AGB.

The lowest isotope ratio that can possibly be produced by equilibrium CNO cycle H-burning is 3.5; yet, for ten nebulae with measured $^{12}C/^{13}C$, the ratio is < 3.5. Non-equilibrium models of abruptly initiated and terminated high temperature proton capture reactions can produce carbon isotope ratios as low as 0.5 (Audouze et al. 1973), commonly accompanied by conversion of C to N. The consistently low $^{12}C/^{13}C$ ratios observed in a dozen PNe, combined with often a high N/O ratio, suggest that a rapid hot process involving proton-capture occurred on the AGB.

8. More Detailed Structure and Chemistry in Planetary Nebulae: ALMA Imaging

Single-dish observations at millimeter wavelengths have clearly demonstrated that molecules are widespread in PNe and can achieve significant complexity. That being said, there is limited information available regarding the spatial distribution of these molecules in the nebulae in which they are found. With few exceptions, the angular sizes of PNe tend to be smaller than the beam size of the single-dish telescopes at the frequencies observed; as a result, it can be determined what molecules are present in these nebulae but not where they reside. Even in cases in which multiple pointings across the PN are possible, there is generally incomplete coverage of the source.

In order to attain the higher spatial resolutions needed to trace the kinematic structure of the molecular outflows, interferometers are needed. Arrays such as SMA and NOEMA have provided such insight. For instance, images of CO^+ and HCO^+ in NGC 7027 made using NOEMA exhibit notably different emission morphologies, with HCO^+ displaced radially outward compared to CO^+ (Bublitz et al. 2023). On the basis of these observations, the authors suggest that the two ions trace different environments, with CO^+ delineating the inner boundaries of the photon-dominated region (PDR) and HCO^+ the signpost of an X-ray dominated region (XDR) surrounding the PDR.

Currently, the most powerful tool to study the distribution of the molecular outflow in PNe is the Atacama Large Millimeter Array (ALMA). One of the earliest objects to be studied with ALMA was the Boomerang Nebula, which was imaged in the CO $J = 1 \rightarrow 0$ and $J = 2 \rightarrow 1$ lines (Sahai et al. 2013). Low angular resolution single dish images suggested a spherical molecular outflow, in contrast to its visible-light morphology. The high resolution ALMA data revealed dense walls of molecular gas surrounding hollow cavities (the bipolar outflow observed in the optical), as well as a compact mass of millimeter-sized grains in the nebula's waist observed through continuum emission. The waist was determined to shape the nebula's illumination, resulting in its hourglass morphology. Subsequent observations of both $J = 1 \rightarrow 0$ and $J = 3 \rightarrow 2$ CO emission provided further insight into the nebula's central waist and bipolar outflow and suggested that it arose from a common-envelope binary interaction (Sahai et al. 2017).

The well-studied Helix Nebula (NGC 7293) has been imaged with ALMA as well. In particular, the C1 globule was observed at the $J = 2 \rightarrow 1$ transitions of ^{12}CO, ^{13}CO, and $C^{18}O$ (Andriantsaralaza et al. 2020). The measurements were used to derive a molecular mass of $\sim 2 \times 10^{-4}$ for the globule, indicating that it may have been previously highly underestimated, along with $^{12}C/^{13}C$ and $^{16}O/^{18}O$ ratios of $\sim$10 and $\sim$115, respectively. Two other globules were observed at 1 mm and 3 mm with ALMA, yielding images of

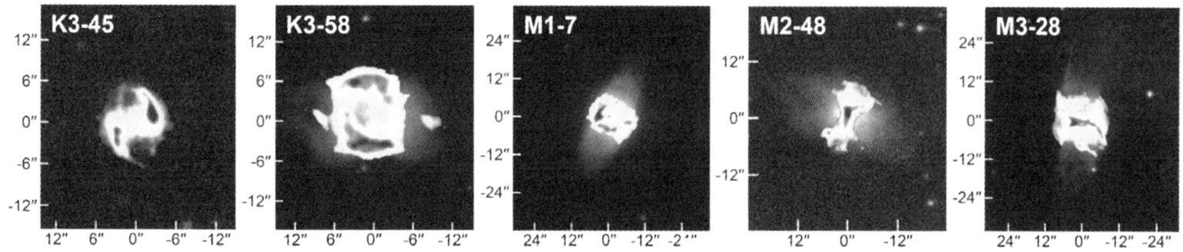

Figure 9. Moment 0 maps of CO J = 2→1 emission in K3-45, K3-58, M1-7, M2-48, and M3-28 overlaid on optical images of the nebula from the PNIC.

^{12}CO, HCN, HCO$^+$, and HNC which revealed their filamentary nature (Bublitz et al. 2020).

Interferometric observations have also been performed on some lesser-known PNe. In particular, five PNe whose molecular composition had been studied to varying degrees using the ARO facilities were recently imaged using ALMA, specifically K3-45, K3-58, M1-7, M2-48, and M3-28 (see Figure 2 for optical images). The nebulae are diverse, covering a range of kinematic ages, from the young (K3-45 at ~ 800 years) to the middle-aged (M1-7 at ~ 6000 years, M2-48 at ~ 5000 years, and M3-28 at ~ 8000 years) to the old (K3-58 at ~ 11,000 years). Further, these PNe exhibit varying morphologies; for instance, K3-45, based on its U-shaped line profiles, is expected to be bipolar, while M3-28 is thought to be quadrupolar.

The ALMA Band 6 receiver in combination with the 12 m array antennas were used to observe the CO J = 2 → 1 line in each source, which had been previously identified using the ARO SMT. M1-7, M2-48, and M3-28 were also imaged at the J = 3 → 2 lines of HCN and HCO$^+$, which had also been originally measured using the SMT. Given an angular resolution of ~1″, the regions of molecular emission were readily resolved in each source. The ALMA datacubes were combined with their single-dish SMT data in order to recover all flux. The resulting CO images are shown in Figure 9.

When overlaid on optical images of the corresponding nebulae, these images demonstrate that the molecular material is generally confined to the central regions of the nebula. This indicates that the molecular material is funneling the bipolar outflows seen in the optical, and suggests that the remnant AGB shell may be transformed into a disk or other structures. Thus, remnant molecular material may play a role in the shaping of PNe.

9. Molecule Survival and the Chemical Transition from the Asymptotic Giant Branch to Planetary Nebulae

The envelopes of AGB stars are resplendent in molecules and set the stage for the formation of PNe. Abundances of molecules in AGB envelopes and PNe do differ substantially. The typical abundance of HCN is $f \sim 10^{-5}$ in C-rich AGB shells, as opposed to $f \sim 10^{-8}$-10^{-7} in observed PNe, most of which also appear to be carbon-rich - a factor of 100–1000 decrease. On the other hand, HCO$^+$ is almost non-existent in C-rich AGB envelopes but has $f \sim 10^{-8}$-10^{-7} in O-rich shells (Pulliam et al. 2011). In PNe, the abundance is $f \sim 0.02$–7.4×10^{-7} and thus far is universally present, despite the C/O ratio of a given nebula. HCO$^+$ therefore is more prevalent in PNe. The abundance of HNC increases dramatically from the AGB to PNe, altering the [HCN]/[HNC] ratios from > 100 to 1–8, as discussed (Schmidt & Ziurys 2017a). In contrast, the CCH abundance drops by no more than a factor of 5, staying relatively constant throughout the AGB-PN transitions (Schmidt & Ziurys 2017b).

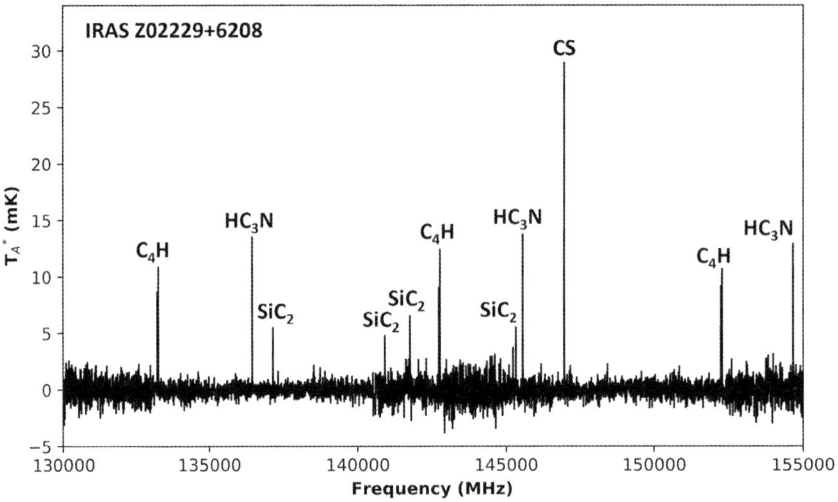

Figure 10. Spectrum of the C-rich PPNe IRAS Z02229+6208 near 145 GHz, showing its diverse chemical composition (Gold et al., in prep.).

Because abundances remain fairly constant across time with PNe, the chemical changes must come in the protoplanetary nebulae (PPN) phase. This stage is a fleeting episode in stellar evolution that lasts just a few thousand years (Hrivnak et al. 2020), nestled in between the AGB and planetary nebulae. It is characterized by very fast ($\sim$ 100 km s^{-1}) collimated outflows that interact with the slower AGB wind, likely causing shocks and elevated temperatures (e.g. Lorenzo et al. 2021). In addition, the central star is beginning to evolve towards a white dwarf and emit UV radiation, causing photoionization. These conditions alter the AGB molecular content. There have been several in-depth studies of the molecular content of PPNe, most notably the C-rich objects CRL 2688 and CRL 618 (e.g. Qiu et al. 2022; Zhang et al. 2013; Pardo *et al.* 2007). Abundances of certain molecules do change from the AGB stage. For example, Zhang et al. found that both CS and HCN had lower abundances in CRL 2688 than IRC+10216 by a factor of 15. HNC becomes more prevalent with [HCN]/[HNC] $\sim$ 1 in CRL 2688 and CRL 618 (Zhang et al. 2013; Herpin & Cernicharo 2000). Molecular inventories are also being assembled for O-rich PPNe such as M1-92 and the Cotton Candy Nebula (e.g. Gold et al., in prep). Other, less well-studied objects such as IRAS Z02229+6208 also appear to have interesting chemistries (Figure 10). As a larger statistical sample is obtained for PPNe, a clearer picture of the chemical transformation will emerge for comparison with PNe.

10. A Few Comments on Dust

Both silicates and carbonaceous dust grains have been found in PNe. They are thought to reflect the grain composition formed in the AGB phase. A summary of observed dust features is given in Table 4. Common grain composition includes aromatic and aliphatic carbon dust, and amorphous and crystalline silicates (e.g. Kwok 2022). Also, in certain cases, PNe show a mixed dust grain composition, or no dust features at all (e.g. García-Hernández & Górny 2014). Surprisingly, the SiC dust feature that is almost ubiquitous in C-rich circumstellar shells is absent in PNe (Chen et al. 2022). Thus far there has been no systematic comparison of dust types and molecular composition. Perhaps of even more interest is the presence of the fullerenes C_{60} and C_{70} in certain PNe and PPNe (e.g. Zhang et al. 2016; Cami et al. 2010). The formation of these large molecules composed

Table 4. Common Dust Features in PNe.

Feature	Wavelength (μm)
Aromatic carbon	3.3, 6.2, 7.7, 8.6, 11.3
Aliphatic carbon	3.4
Amorphous silicates	9.7, 17
Crystalline silicates	19, 24, 28, 34

of pure carbon is difficult to explain. Their origin has been attributed to PAHs and HACs (Berné & Tielens 2012). More recently, experimental work has suggested that the fullerenes arise from the destruction of SiC grains, commonly produced in circumstellar shells (Bernal et al. 2022, 2019). Shock heating of the grains leaches the silicon from the surface, creating graphitic layers that can deform into spherical structures. Nanotubes are also formed, suggesting that they may be present in the ISM.

11. Perspectives

The past decade of molecular observations of planetary nebulae have demonstrated that many of these objects are rich in gas-phase molecules, despite the presence of strong UV radiation. The molecules are present in warm, dense gas, and appear to survive in self-shielding clumps. These molecules likely represent remnant AGB material, but with abundances becoming modified in the PPN stage. Once the PN stage is attained, abundances appear to be "frozen" throughout the nebular lifetime. Therefore, the PN ejecta that populate the diffuse ISM may be in part molecular in nature, and can account for the chemistry in diffuse clouds. This molecular material also appears to play an important role in the shaping of PNe. The extreme ^{13}C enrichment observed in some PNe may additionally hold clues to unknown processes in AGB nucleosynthesis that may help shape these fascinating objects as well.

12. Acknowledgements

This work was supported by NSF Grants AST-1907910 and AST-2307305. We also thank Katherine Gold for her help and contributions of data in preparation.

References

Aaquist, O.B., & Kwok, S. 1990, *A&AS*, 84, 229

Abia, C., Hedrosa, R.P., Domínguez, I., & Straniero, O. 2017, *A&A*, 599, A39. doi:10.1051/0004-6361/201629969

Akras, S., Gonçalves, D.R., & Ramos-Larios, G. 2017, MNRAS, 465, 1289. doi:10.1093/mnras/stw2736

Andriantsaralaza, M., Zijlstra, A., & Avison, A. 2020, MNRAS, 491, 758. doi:10.1093/mnras/stz3026

Audouze, J., Truran, J.W., & Zimmerman, B.A. 1973, *ApJ*, 184, 493. doi:10.1086/152346

Bachiller, R., Forveille, T., Huggins, P.J., & Cox, P. 1997, *A&A*, 324, 1123

Balick, B., & Frank, A. 2002, *ARA&A*, 40, 439. doi:10.1146/annurev.astro.40.060401.093849

Balser, D.S., McMullin, J.P., & Wilson, T.L. 2002, *ApJ*, 572, 326. doi:10.1086/340309

Bernal, J.J., Haenecour, P., Howe, J., et al. 2019, *ApJL*, 883, L43. doi:10.3847/2041-8213/ab4206

Bernal, J.J., Zega, T.J., & Ziurys, L.M. 2022, *J. Phys. Chem.*, 126, 5761. doi:10.1021/acs.jpca.2c01441

Bernard-Salas, J., Pottasch, S. R., Feibellman, W. A., & Wesselius, P. R. 2002, A&A, 387, 301. doi:10.1051/0004-6361:2002035

Berné, O., & Tielens, A.G.G.M. 2012, *PNAS*, 109, 401, doi:10.1073/pnas.1114207108

Bublitz, J., Kastner, J.H., Hily-Blant, P., et al. 2020, *Galaxies*, 8, 32. doi:10.3390/galaxies8020032

Bublitz, J., Kastner, J.H., Hily-Blant, P., et al. 2023, *ApJ*, 942, 14. doi:10.3847/1538-4357/aca405

Bublitz, J., Kastner, J.H., Santander-García, M., et al. 2019, *A&A*, 625, A101. doi:10.1051/0004-6361/201834408

Cami, J., Bernard-Salas, J., Peeters, E., & Malek, S.E. 2010, *Sci*, 329, 1180. doi:10.1126/science.1192035

Chen, T., Xiao, C.Y., Li, A., & Zhou, C.T. 2022, *MNRAS*, 509, 5231. doi:10.1093/mnras/stab3175

Corradi, R.L.M., Gonçalves, D.R., Villaver, E., et al. 2000, *ApJ*, 535, 823. doi:10.1086/308877

Cox, P., Omont, A., Huggins, P.J., Bachiller, R., & Forveille, T. 1992, *A&A*, 266, 420

Davis, C.J., Smith, M.D., Stern, L., Kerr, T.H., & Chiar, J.E. 2003, *MNRAS*, 344, 262. doi:10.1046/j.1365-8711.2003.06820.x

Dorschner, J., & Henning, T. 1995, *A&ARv*, 6, 271. doi: 10.1007/BF00873686

Edwards, J.L., Cox, E.G., & Ziurys, L.M. 2014, *ApJ*, 791, 79. doi:10.1088/0004-637X/791/2/79

Edwards, J.L., & Ziurys, L.M. 2013, *ApJL*, 770, L5. doi:10.1088/2041-8205/770/1/L5

Edwards, J.L., & Ziurys, L.M. 2014, *ApJL*, 794, L27. doi:10.1088/2041-8205/794/2/L27

García-Hernández, D.A., & Górny, S.K. 2014, *A&A*, 567, A12. doi:10.1051/0004-6361/201423620

Güsten, R., Wiesemeyer, H., Neufeld, D., et al. 2019, *Natur*, 568, 357. doi:10.1038/s41586-019-1090-x

Henry, R.B.C., Kwitter, K.B., & Balick, B. 2004, *AJ*, 127, 2284. doi:10.1086/382242

Henry, R.B.C., Kwitter, K.B., & Dufour, R.J. 1999, *ApJ*, 517, 782. doi:10.1086/307215

Henry, R.B.C., Stephenson, B.G., Miller Bertolami, M.M., Kwitter, K.B., & Balick, B. 2018, MNRAS, 473, 241. doi:10.1093/mnras/stx2286

Herpin, F., & Cernicharo, J. 2000, *ApJ*, 530, L129. doi:10.1086/312507

Herwig, F. 2005, *ARA&A*, 43, 435. doi:10.1146/annurev.astro.43.072103.150600

Howe, D.A., Hartquist, T.W., & Williams, D.A. 1994, *MNRAS*, 271, 811.

Hrivnak, B.J., Henson, G., Hillwig, T.C., et al. 2020, *ApJ*, 901, 9. doi:10.3847/1538-4357/abad8c

Huggins, P.J., Bachiller, R., Cox, P., & Forveille, T. 1996, *A&A*, 315, 284.

Huggins, P.J., Bachiller, R., Planesas, P., Forveille, T., & Cox, P., 2005, *ApJSS*, 160, 272

Huggins, P.J., & Healy, A.P., 1989, *ApJ*, 346, 201.

Kwok, S. 2022, *FrASS*, 9, 893061. doi:10.3389/fspas.2022.893061

Lebzelter, T., Hinkle, K.H., Straniero, O., et al. 2019, *ApJ*, 886, 117. doi:10.3847/1538-4357/ab4e9b

Liu, X.-W., Barlow, M.J., & Cohen, M. 2001, MNRAS, 323, 343. doi:10.1046/j.1365-8711.2001.04180.x

López-Martín, L., López, J.A., Esteban, C., et al. 2002, *A&A*, 388, 652. doi:10.1051/0004-6361:20020502

Lorenzo, M., Teyssier, D., Bujarrabal, V., et al. 2021, *A&A*, 649, A164. doi:10.1051/0004-6361/202039592

Marquez-Lugo, R.A., Ramos-Larios, G., Guerrero, M.A., & Vázquez, R. 2013, 429, 973. doi:10.1093/mnras/sts381

Meixner, M., McCullough, P., Hartman, J., Son, M., & Speck, A. 2005, *AJ*, 130, 1784. doi:10.1086/444539

Milam, S.N., Woolf, N.J., & Ziurys, L.M. 2009, *ApJ*, 690, 837. doi:10.1088/0004-637X/690/1/837

Moraga Baez, P., Kastner, J.H., Balick, B., Montez, Jr., R., & Bublitz, J. 2023, ApJ, 942, 15. doi:10.3847/1538-4357/aca401

Neufeld, D.A., Goto, Miwa, Geballe, T.R., et al. 2020, 894, 37. doi:10.3847/1538-4357/ab7191

Palla, F., Bachiller, R., Stanghellini, L., Tosi, M., & Galli, D. 2000, *A&A*, 355, 69.

Pardo, J.R., Cernicharo, J., Goicoechea, J.R., Guélin, M., Asensio Ramos, A. 2007, *ApJ*, 661, 250. doi:10.1086/513734

Pottasch, S.R., Beintema, D.A., & Feibelman, W.A. 2000, *A&A*, 363, 767

Pulliam, R.L., Edwards, J.L., & Ziurys, L.M. 2011, *ApJ*, 743, 36. doi:10.1088/0004-637X/743/1/36

Qiu, J.-J., Zhang, Y., Zhang, J.-S., & Nakashima, J. 2022, *ApJS*, 259, 56. doi:10.3847/1538-4365/ac5180

Ramstedt, S., & Olofsson, H. 2014, *A&A*, 566, A145. doi:10.1051/0004-6361/201423721

Redman, M.P., Viti, S., Cau, P., & Williams, D.A., 2003, *MNRAS*, 345, 1291. doi:10.1046/j.1365-2966.2003.07047.x

Sahai, R., Vlemmings, W.H.T., Huggins, P.J., & Nyman, L.-Å. 2017, *ApJ*, 841, 110. doi:10.3847/1538-4357/aa6d86

Sahai, R., Vlemmings, W.H.T., Huggins, P.J., Nyman, L.-Å, & Gonidakis, I. 2013, *ApJ*, 777, 92. doi:10.1088/0004-637X/777/2/92

Schmidt, D.R., Gold, K.R., Sinclair, A., Bergstrom, S., & Ziurys, L.M. 2022, *ApJ*, 927, 46. doi:10.3847/1538-4357/ac4474

Schmidt, D.R., Woolf, N.J., Zega, T.J., & Ziurys, L.M. 2018b, *Natur*, 564, 378. doi:10.1038/s41586-018-0763-1

Schmidt, D.R., Zack, L.N., & Ziurys, L.M. 2018a, *ApJL*, 864, L31. doi:10.3847/2041-8213/aadc09

Schmidt, D.R., & Ziurys, L.M. 2016, *ApJ*, 817, 175. doi:10.3847/0004-637X/817/2/175

Schmidt, D.R., & Ziurys, L.M. 2017a, *ApJ*, 835, 79. doi:10.3847/1538-4357/835/1/79

Schmidt, D.R., & Ziurys, L.M. 2017b, *ApJ*, 850, 123. doi:10.3847/1538-4357/aa8a6a

Schmidt, D.R., & Ziurys, L.M. 2019, *ApJL*, 881, L38. doi:10.3847/2041-8213/ab3663

Snow, T.P., & McCall, B.J. 2006, *ARA&A*, 44, 367. doi:10.1146/annurev.astro.43.072103.150624

Speck, A.K., Meixner, M., Jacoby, G.H., & Knezek, P.M. 2003, *PASP*, 115, 170. doi:10.1086/345911

Tenenbaum, E.D., Milam, S.N., Woolf, N.J., & Ziurys, L.M. 2009, *ApJ*, 704, L108. doi:10.1088/0004-637X/704/2/L108

Ventura, P., Stanghellini, L., Dell'Agli, F., & García-Hernández, D.A., 2017, MNRAS, 471, 4648. doi:10.1093/mnras/stx1907

Weidmann, W.A., & Gamen, R. 2011, *A&A*, 526, A6. doi:10.1051/0004-6361/200913984

Wiescher, M., Görres, J., Uberseder, E., Imbriani, G., & Pignatari, M. 2010, *Ann. Rev. Nucl. Part. Sci.*, 60, 381. doi:10.1146/annurev.nucl.012809.104505

Zack, L.N., & Ziurys, L.M. 2013, *ApJ*, 765, 112. doi:10.1088/0004-637X/765/2/112

Zeigler, N.R., Zack, L.N., Woolf, N.J., & Ziurys, L.M., 2013, *ApJ*, 778, 16. doi:10.1008/0004-637X/778/1/

Zhang, Y., Kwok, S., & Dinh-V-Trung 2008, *ApJ*, 678, 328. doi:10.1086/529428

Zhang, Y., Kwok, S., Nakashima, J., Chau, W., & Trung, D.-V. 2013, *ApJ*, 773, 71. doi:10.1088/0004-637X/773/1/71

Zhang, Y., Kwok, S., & Sadjadi, S. 2016, *JPhCS*, 728, e052004. doi:10.1088/1742-6596/728/5/052004

Ziurys, L.M., Schmidt, D.R., & Woolf, N.J. 2020, *ApJL*, 900, L31. doi:10.3847/2041-8213/abb082

Ziurys, L.M., Tenenbaum, E.D., Pulliam, R.L., Woolf, N.J., & Milam, S.N. 2009, *ApJ*, 695, 1604. doi:10.1088/0004-637X/695/2/1604

Planetary Nebulae: A Universal Toolbox in the Era of Precision Astrophysics
Proceedings IAU Symposium No. 384, 2025
O. De Marco, A. Zijlstra & R. Szczerba, eds.
doi:10.1017/S1743921324000243

ALMA Observations of Molecular Line Emission from High-excitation Bipolar Planetary Nebulae

Paula Moraga Baez[1], Joel H. Kastner[1,2], Jesse Bublitz[3], Javier Alcolea[4], Miguel Santander-García[4], Thierry Forveille[5], Pierre Hily-Blant[5], Bruce Balick[6], Rodolfo Montez, Jr.[7] and Caroline Gieser[8]

[1]School of Physics and Astronomy and Laboratory for Multiwavelength Astrophysics, Rochester Institute of Technology, Rochester, NY, USA

[2]Chester F. Carlson Center for Imaging Science, Rochester Institute of Technology

[3]Green Bank Observatory, Green Bank, WV, USA

[4]Observatorio Astronómico Nacional, Madrid, Spain

[5]Institut de Planetologie et d'Astrophysique de Grenoble, France

[6]Department of Astronomy, University of Washington, Seattle, WA USA

[7]Center for Astrophysics, Harvard & Smithsonian, Cambridge, MA, USA

[8]Max Planck Institute for Extraterrestrial Physics, Munich, Germany

Abstract. We present early results from our program of ALMA Band 6 (1.3mm) molecular line mapping of a sample of nearby, well-studied examples of high-excitation, bipolar/pinched-waist and molecule-rich planetary nebulae (Hubble 5 and NGC 2440, 2818, 2899, 6302, and 6445). We have mapped these planetary nebulae (PNe) in isotopologues of CO as well as various molecular line tracers of high-energy irradiation, such as HCN, CN, HNC, and HCO^+, with the complementary goals of establishing nebular kinematics as well as the zones of UV-heated and X-ray-ionized molecular gas within each nebula. The resulting high-resolution ALMA molecular emission-line maps reveal the regions of high-excitation bipolar PNe in which molecular gas, presumably ejected during asymptotic giant branch stages of the PN progenitor stars, survives and evolves chemically. We present a summary of molecular species detected to date in the sample nebulae, and we use example results for one PN (NGC 6455) to demonstrate the power of the ALMA data in revealing the structures, kinematics, and compositions of the equatorial molecular tori that are a common feature of the sample objects.

Keywords. stars: binaries, planetary nebulae, stars: evolution, molecular data

1. Introduction

For several decades, mm-wave CO emission lines have been used as probes of the molecular gas components of planetary nebulae (PNe; e.g., Huggins & Healy 1989). Numerous single-dish mm-wave radio telescope surveys targeting CO, HCO^+, HNC, HCN, CN, CS, and other species have been carried out so as to advance our understanding of the molecular masses and chemistries of PNe (e.g., Huggins et al. 2000; Edwards & Ziurys 2013; Edwards et al. 2014; Bublitz et al. 2019; Schmidt et al. 2022). Interferometric mm-wave molecular line mapping observations of PNe are somewhat fewer and farther between, and have usually involved mapping of individual PNe (e.g., Bublitz et al. 2023).

Table 1. Properties of Survey Targets

Object	Central Star[a]			Molecular Torus[b]		
	D^a (kpc)	$\log L_\star$ ($L_\odot$)	$T_{\rm eff}$ (kK)	R (pc)	$V_{\rm exp}$ (km s^{-1})	Age (yr)
Hubble 5	1.7	3.64	170	0.033	50	1300
NGC 2440	1.9	3.32	210	0.05	35	2800
NGC 6302	1.0	3.62	220	0.05	20	5000
NGC 6445	1.14[c]	2.80	170	0.11	55	5000
NGC 6537	2.0	3.30	180	0.08	20	8000
NGC 2818	2.1	2.80	145	0.14	20	15000
NGC 2899	1.9[c]	4.25[d]	270[d]	0.16	20	17000

Notes: a) Distances (D) and central star properties ($\log L_\star$, $T_{\rm eff}$) as listed in Frew et al. (2013) except where noted. b) Radius (R), deprojected expansion velocity ($V_{\rm exp}$), and dynamical age of molecular torus as estimated from ALMA ^{12}CO (2–1) data. c) D from Gaia DR3. d) $\log L_\star$ and $T_{\rm eff}$ from González-Santamaría et al. (2019).

Here, we present initial results from Atacama Large Millimeter Array (ALMA) Band 6 (1.3 mm) observations of a sample of relatively nearby, molecule-rich, high-excitation bipolar PNe. This program constitutes among the first molecular line surveys of PNe to exploit ALMA's unique high spatial and spectral resolution mapping capabilities. The main goals of our ALMA bipolar PN survey are twofold: *(1)* to use velocity-resolved mm-wave molecular line mapping to pinpoint the locations and study the structures and kinematics of the regions of cold, dense molecular gas within high-excitation bipolar PNe; and *(2)* to ascertain the effects of UV vs. X-ray irradiation from PN central stars on the composition and heating of PN molecular gas.

Ultimately, these observations of an evolutionary sequence of bipolar PNe ranging from young and rapidly evolving nebulae to more "mature" bi-lobed nebulae will help us constrain PN shaping models that involve binary-influenced AGB and post-AGB mass loss.

2. Observations

2.1. *Sample*

Our target nebulae (Table 1) have been selected from comprehensive catalogs of solar neighborhood PNe (Cahn et al. 1992; Frew et al. 2013; Stanghellini et al. 2002) on the basis of (*i*) distances $D \lesssim 2$ kpc; (*ii*) pinched-waist bipolar morphologies; (*iii*) large molecular gas masses, as evidenced by bright near-IR H_2 and/or mm-wave CO emission (Fang et al. 2018; Guerrero et al. 2000; Huggins et al. 1996, 2005; Kastner et al. 1996; Phillips et al. 1992); and (*iv*) hot, luminous central stars (i.e., central star effective temperatures $T_{\rm eff} \gtrsim 150$ kK and luminosities $L_\star \gtrsim 10^3 L_\odot$). All of the Table 1 objects are hence likely the descendants of relatively massive progenitor stars, with initial masses in the range ~3–8 $M_\odot$ (Corradi & Schwarz 1995; Kastner et al. 1996; Karakas & Lugaro 2016; Miller Bertolami 2016).

2.2. *ALMA data*

Our ALMA Band 6 survey, conducted under ALMA programs 2021.1.00456.S, 2021.2.00004.S, and 2022.1.00401.S, used a half-dozen spectral setups in the 220–270 GHz frequency range to target emission lines of CO, CN, HCN, HNC, HCO^+, CO^+, CS, SO, and isotopologues of CO, HCN, and HCO^+ in the sample PNe. By observing molecular emission from these molecular species, we seek to determine the dynamical ages (ejection timescales) of their molecular emitting regions and (hence) AGB-terminating mass loss, and we can place constraints on the molecular gas optical depths, PN progenitor masses, and zones of UV-irradiated and X-ray-ionized molecular gas (see, e.g., Bublitz et al. 2019,

Table 2. Band 6 Targeted Molecular Lines.

Molecule (Trans.)	ν (GHz)	Hb 5	NGC 6302	NGC 2440	NGC 6445	NGC 2818	NGC 2899
^{12}CO (2–1)	230.538	✓	✓	✓	✓	✓	✓
^{13}CO (2–1)	220.398	O	✓	✓	O	✓	✓
C^{18}O (2–1)	219.560	O	✓	×	O	×	×
CS (5–4)	244.936	×	✓	×	✓	✓	×
C^{34}S (5–4)	241.016	O	✓	×	O	×	×
CN (2–1)	226.697^b,226.874^b	✓	✓	✓	✓	✓	✓
HCN (3–2)	265.886	✓	✓	✓	O	✓	✓
H^{13}CN (3–2)	259.011	O	✓	✓	×	×	×
HNC (3–2)	271.981	O	✓	✓	✓	✓	✓
HCO$^+$ (2–1)	267.557	✓	✓	✓	O	✓	✓
H^{13}CO$^+$ (3–2)	260.255	✓	✓	✓	×	×	×
CO$^+$ (2–1)	235.789^b, 236.063^b	O	×	×	O	×	×
SO (5_6–4_5)	251.857	O	✓	×	O	×	×
SO (6_5–5_4)	219.949	O	✓	✓	O	×	×

Notes: a) ✓ = detected; × = not detected; O = data not obtained. b) Hyperfine complex; representative transition frequency listed.

2023, and references therein). Table 2 lists the molecular lines targeted in the survey. We used both ALMA's 12-m array and Atacama Compact Array (ACA) in configurations that yielded ∼0.5″ and ∼5″ resolution imaging, respectively. Details of the ALMA array and spectrometer configurations and data processing, as well as results from archival ALMA Band 3 mapping of NGC 6537 (obtained via ALMA program 2018.1.00424.S; Gieser et al. 2023), will be presented in forthcoming papers (Moraga Baez et al. 2024a,b, in prep.). Here, we present selected initial results from ALMA Band 6 observations of six Table 1 PNe, as obtained from the ALMA ADMIT pipeline†: Hb 5 and NGC 2440, 2818, 2899, 6302, and 6445.

3. Initial Survey Results: Overview

Fig. 1 presents velocity-integrated ACA and 12-m array ^{12}CO (2–1) maps for the six PNe. Archival Hα images are displayed above the velocity-integrated ^{12}CO (2–1) maps for comparison. It is immediately evident that the brightest ^{12}CO (2–1) in each nebula is confined to its central, pinched-waist equatorial region. In the case of Hb 5, NGC 6302, NGC 2440, and NGC 6445, the ^{12}CO emission appears to take the form of a molecular torus. In NGC 2818 and NGC 2899, however, the ^{12}CO emission lies in more isolated structures (clumps) that appear to surround, or perhaps lie embedded within, the central, equatorial, UV-ionized zones of these nebulae.

The ^{12}CO (2-1) maps and spatially integrated spectral line profiles were used to estimate molecular torus dynamical ages for the sample PNe (Table 1, last column). It is noteworthy that the nebulae with the brightest and most spatially coherent molecular tori (Hb 5, NGC 6302, NGC 2440, and NGC 6445) have the youngest dynamical ages (<5000 yr); while NGC 2818 and NGC 2899, the oldest PNe in our sample (dynamical ages of ∼15000 yr and ∼17000 yr, respectively), display faint, clumpy ^{12}CO (2–1) emission. In the youngest nebulae (Hb 5, NGC 2440, NGC 6302), some ^{12}CO (2–1) emission structures are observed to sit within the large ionized lobes, suggesting that in young bipolar PNe, some molecular gas survives in these more heavily irradiated, fast-expanding regions.

Table 2 summarizes the molecular emission lines that have been detected and not detected to date for each of the six PNe that were the subjects of ALMA Band 6 observations. The PNe are listed (from left to right) in order of increasing estimated dynamical age, and there appears to be a general trend wherein the detection of rare isotopologues

† https://admit.astro.umd.edu

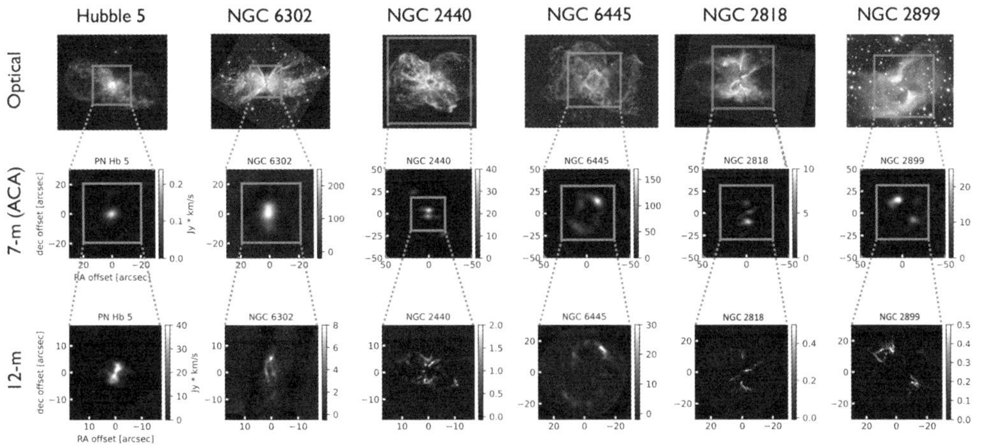

Figure 1. Comparison of optical and ALMA ^{12}CO images of (from L to R) PNe Hb 5, NGC 6302, NGC 2440, NGC 6445, NGC 2818, and NGC 2899. *Top row*: color composites of optical images of the six PNe. Archival HST images are presented for Hb 5, NGC 6302, NGC 2440, and NGC 6445; archival ESO and NOT images are presented for NGC 2899 and NGC 6445, respectively. *Middle* and *bottom rows*: Band 6 ^{12}CO (2–1) velocity-integrated images obtained with ALMA's ACA and 12-m arrays, respectively.

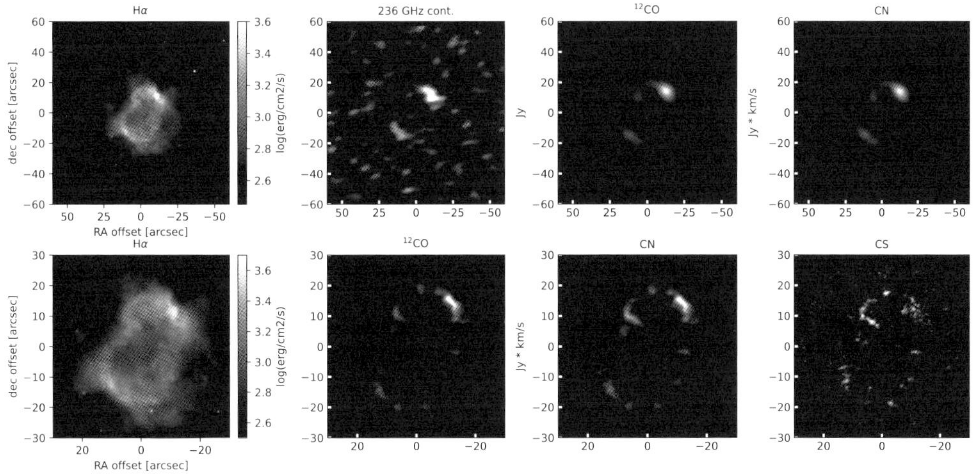

Figure 2. Below: Montages of ALMA continuum and velocity-integrated ^{12}CO, CN and CS images of NGC 6445 as obtained with ACA (*top panels*) and the 12-m array (*bottom panels*). Each ALMA montage is presented alongside the NOT Hα image (Fang et al. 2018), for reference.

(e.g., $H^{13}CN$, $H^{13}CO^+$) as well as S-bearing species (SO, CS) falls off from the youngest (NGC 6302) to oldest (NGC 2818, NGC 2899) objects. The lack of detections of rare isotopologues and S-bearing molecules in the older PNe likely reflects their relatively small residual molecular gas masses, although it remains to establish whether this potential trend might also be indicative of PN progenitor mass.

4. A Closer Look at NGC 6445

To illustrate how the ALMA line survey data are revealing the detailed molecular emission structures within these bipolar PNe, we present selected line (and continuum) emission maps for the PN NGC 6445 (Figs. 2–4). Fig. 2 provides a comparison between

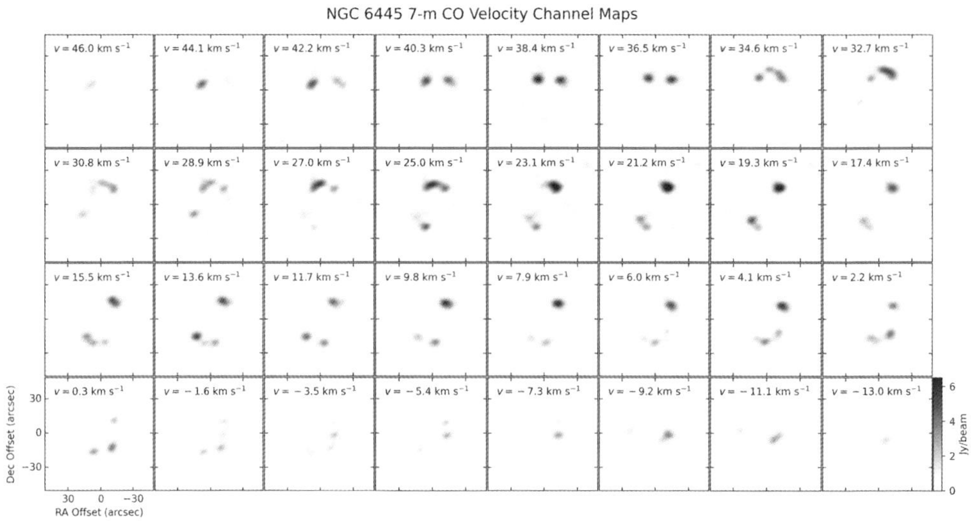

Figure 3. Velocity channel maps extracted from the NGC 6445 ^{12}CO (2–1) ACA data cube. From left to right and top to bottom, the maps are displayed from $\sim$46 km s^{-1} to ~ -13 km s^{-1} in increments of 1.9 km s^{-1}.

optical (Hα) and ALMA ACA and 12-meter array images of the central region of NGC 6445. In the wider-field ACA maps, the molecular emission is seen to be confined to the central region of the nebula, precisely outlining the PN's bright, central Hα ring. The ACA maps hence establish that the molecules previously (spectroscopically) detected in NGC 6445 with single-dish mm-wave facilities (Schmidt et al. 2022) are in fact confined to an equatorial torus within the PN. The higher-resolution 12-m array maps reveal the detailed, clumpy morphology of this equatorial molecular torus. The positions and structures of individual molecular clumps within the torus seen in the 12-m maps closely correspond to features within the central ionized ring traced by Hα. The detection of CN and CS molecules within the clumpy central region of NGC 6445 furthermore suggests the PN is rich in carbon, sulfur, and nitrogen.

Fig. 3 displays velocity channel maps extracted from the ACA ^{12}CO (2–1) data cube. The same data are presented in the form of contour plots of emission integrated over specific velocity ranges, overlaid on the Nordic Optical Telescope (NOT) Hα image, in Fig. 4. The knotty structure of NGC 6445's molecular torus is even more apparent in these velocity-resolved representations. Overall, as one moves from redshifted ($V_{\rm LSR} \sim +25$ to $+45$ km s^{-1}) to blueshifted ($V_{\rm LSR} \sim +5$ to -15 km s^{-1}) emission, the knot system is observed to shift position around the torus from the northwest to the southeast of the central star, with knots at intermediate velocities (i.e., near the PN's systemic velocity, $V_{\rm LSR} \sim +15$ km s^{-1}) found at the limbs of the torus closest to its major axis.

The radial velocity pattern in the ACA ^{12}CO data thus demonstrates that NGC 6445's complex system of molecular knots, taken together, trace an expanding equatorial torus within the nebula. Furthermore, given the structures of the molecular knots as revealed in the 12-m array maps, it appears this torus is in the midst of being torn apart by the central star's high-energy radiation and/or fast winds. It seems reasonable to speculate that, as the nebula continues to evolve and the torus expands, it will further disintegrate, perhaps eventually resembling the highly fragmented systems of molecular clumps observed in the oldest Table 1 PNe, NGC 2818 and NGC 2899.

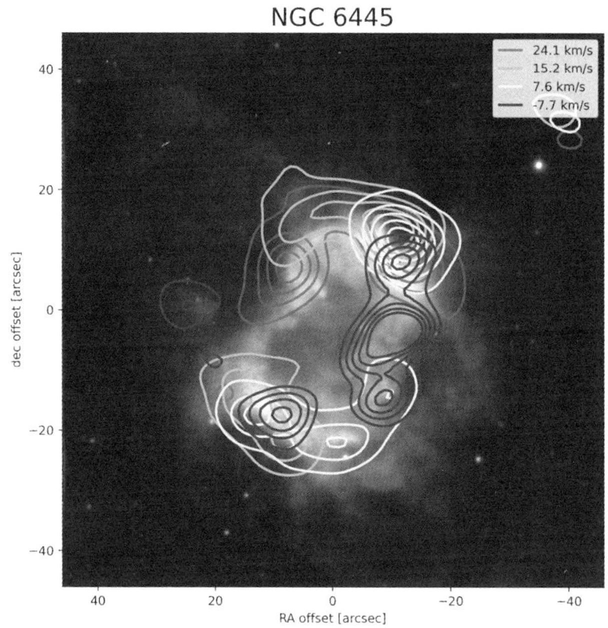

Figure 4. Contours of velocity-resolved ^{12}CO (2–1) emission extracted from the NGC 6445 ACA data cube, overlaid on a color composite of NOT archival optical images (Hα, green; [N II], red; [O III], blue). The contours are color-coded as indicated in the legend (LSR velocities), with red, orange, cyan, and blue indicating a range from more highly redshifted to more highly blueshifted emission with respect to the systemic velocity of NGC 6445 ($V_{LSR} \sim +15$ km s^{-1}).

5. Preliminary Conclusions and Future Prospects

The same basic spatio-kinematic signature of an expanding molecular torus observed within NGC 6445 (Figs. 3, 4) is also seen, to greater or lesser extents, in the ALMA data we have obtained for each of the Table 1 nebulae. Our initial ALMA results hence provide new evidence supporting the notion that the molecular gas reservoirs within bipolar PNe — which presumably can be ascribed to high rates of mass loss near the end of the asymptotic giant branch evolutionary stages of the progenitor stars — are largely confined to the equatorial regions of the nebulae. Furthermore, in the context of the dynamical ages estimated thus far from our ALMA mapping of the molecular emitting regions within the Table 1 objects, the implication is that these high-excitation bipolar PNe display a temporal sequence of increasingly fragmented equatorial molecular gas structures — from the apparently nearly complete, massive tori in Hb 5 and NGC 6302, to the clumpy central molecular rings in NGC 2440 and NGC 6445, and (finally) to the ragged systems of molecular clumps within the pinched-waist regions of NGC 2818 and NGC 2899 (Fig. 1). Evidently, as molecule-rich bipolar PN age and expand, the combination of intense UV and winds from their very hot and luminous stars disrupts and disperses their AGB-ejecta-derived molecular tori, over $\sim 10^4$ yr timescales. Our ongoing analysis of the molecular gas structures, kinematics, and chemical compositions revealed by the ALMA data summarized here will be aimed, in part, at confirming and elaborating on this proposed sequence describing the physical and chemical evolution of the equatorial tori within bipolar PNe descended from massive progenitor stars.

6. Acknowledgment

This research is supported by U.S. National Science Foundation (NSF) grant AST-2206033 to RIT as well as by the NSF through award SOSPADA-009 from National Radio Astronomy Observatories.

References

Bublitz, J., Kastner, J. H., Santander-García, M., et al. 2019, A&A, 625, A101.
Bublitz, J., Kastner, J. H., Hily-Blant, P., et al. 2023, ApJ, 942, 14.
Cahn, J. H., Kaler, J. B., & Stanghellini, L. 1992, A&AS, 94, 399
Corradi, R. L. M. & Schwarz, H. E. 1995, A&A, 293, 871
Edwards, J. L. & Ziurys, L. M. 2013, ApJL, 770, L5
Edwards, J. L., Cox, E. G., & Ziurys, L. M. 2014, ApJ, 791, 79
Fang, X., Zhang, Y., Kwok, S., et al. 2018, ApJ, 859, 92
Frew, D. J., Bojičić, I. S., & Parker, Q. A. 2013, MNRAS, 431, 2
Gieser, C., Beuther, H., Semenov, D., et al. 2023, A&A, 674, A160.
González-Santamaría, I., Manteiga, M., Manchado, A., et al. 2019, A&A, 630, A150.
Guerrero, M. A., Villaver, E., Manchado, A., et al. 2000, ApJs, 127, 125.
Huggins, P. J. & Healy, A. P. 1989, ApJ, 346, 201
Huggins, P. J., Bachiller, R., Cox, P., et al. 1996, A&A, 315, 284
Huggins, P. J., Forveille, T., Bachiller, R., *et al.* 2000, *ApJ*, 544, 889
Huggins, P. J., Bachiller, R., Planesas, P., Forveille, T., & Cox, P. 2005, ApJs, 160, 272
Karakas, A. I. & Lugaro, M. 2016, ApJ, 825, 26.
Kastner, J. H., Weintraub, D. A., Gatley, I., Merrill, K. M., & Probst, R. G. 1996, ApJ, 462, 777
Miller Bertolami, M. M. 2016, A&A, 588, A25.
Phillips, J. P., Williams, P. G., Mampaso, A., et al. 1992, ApSS, 188, 171.
Schmidt, D. R., Gold, K. R., Sinclair, A., et al. 2022, ApJ, 927, 46
Stanghellini, L., Villaver, E., Manchado, A., et al. 2002, ApJ, 576, 285.

Planetary Nebulae: A Universal Toolbox in the Era of Precision Astrophysics
Proceedings IAU Symposium No. 384, 2025
O. De Marco, A. Zijlstra & R. Szczerba, eds.
doi:10.1017/S1743921323005483

Morpho-kinematical modelling in the molecular zoo beyond CO: the case of M 1-92

Miguel Santander-García, Elisa Masa, Javier Alcolea and Valentín Bujarrabal

Observatorio Astronómico Nacional (OAN-IGN), Spain
email: m.santander@oan.es

Abstract. Ongoing improvements of sub-mm- and mm-range interferometers and single-dish radiotelescopes are progressively allowing the detailed study of planetary nebulae (PNe) in molecular species other than ^{12}CO and ^{13}CO. We are implementing a new set of tables for extending the capabilities of the morpho-kinematical modelling tool `SHAPE+shapemol`, so radiative transfer in molecular species beyond ^{12}CO and ^{13}CO, namely C^{17}O, C^{18}O, HCN, HNC, CS, SiO, HCO$^+$, and N$_2$H$^+$, are enabled under the Large Velocity Gradient approximation with the ease of use of `SHAPE`. We present preliminary results on the simultaneous analysis of a plethora of IRAM-30m and HERSCHEL/HIFI spectra, and NOEMA maps of different species in the pre-PN nebula M 1-92, which show interesting features such as a previously undetected pair of polar, turbulent, high-temperature blobs, or a ^{17}O/^{18}O isotopic ratio of 1.7, which indicates the AGB should have turned C-rich, as opposed to the apparent nature of its O-rich nebula.

Keywords. radiative transfer, molecular data, stars: AGB and post-AGB, binaries: close, ISM: kinematics and dynamics, planetary nebulae: general, planetary nebulae: individual (M 1-92)

1. Introduction

Over the last few decades, morpho-kinematical modelling of planetary nebulae (PNe) has provided a wealth of information useful for gaining insight into PN formation (e.g., Solf & Ulrich 1985; Santander-García et al. 2004; Akashi & Soker 2013, 2018). Parameters derived from these models include the current 3D geometry and 3D velocity field of the ejecta, as well as its spatial orientation and kinematical (distance-dependent) age. These allow for instance to establish the evolutionary sequence of formation in the case of a ejecta composed of multiple structures, or investigating whether the equator of the PNe is aligned with the orbital plane of a close-binary central star (as models predict, see e.g. Jones 2020), provided the latter is known.

Despite its proved usefulness, this kind of modelling has its limitations: it only provides a snapshot of the current state of the nebula, and it lacks information on other physical parameters necessary for hydrodynamic or magnetohydrodynamic modelling, such densities, temperatures and pressures at each location throughout the PN.

This shortcoming can be overcome, in the case of the molecular regime, by the inclusion of radiative transfer calculations of molecular species in these models. In this regard, the inclusion of `shapemol` (Santander-García et al. 2015) in the user-friendly, successful morphokinematical modelling code `SHAPE` (Steffen et al. 2011) enabled accurate non-LTE calculations of excitation and radiative transfer in ^{12}CO and ^{13}CO rotational lines under the Large Velocity Gradient (LVG) approximation (e.g. Castor 1970), producing both synthetic single-dish profiles and spectral maps to match observations. Simultaneous fitting of lines of low- and high-excitation in this manner allows to derive

Table 1. Molecules included and parameter coverage of the version of `shapemol` presented in this work.

Species	n (cm^{-3})	T (K)	$X \times \frac{r}{V}$ (cm km^{-1} s)
^{12}CO	$10^2 - 10^{12}$	5 – 1000	$1.2 \times 10^9 - 6.1 \times 10^{13}$
^{13}CO	$10^2 - 10^{12}$	5 – 1000	$3.8 \times 10^7 - 2.0 \times 10^{12}$
C^{17}O	$10^2 - 10^{12}$	5 – 1000	$2.3 \times 10^7 - 1.2 \times 10^{12}$
C^{18}O	$10^2 - 10^{12}$	5 – 1000	$1.2 \times 10^7 - 6.1 \times 10^{11}$
HCN	$10^2 - 10^{12}$	5 – 1000	$5.0 \times 10^3 - 5.0 \times 10^{10}$
HNC	$10^2 - 10^{12}$	5 – 1000	$1.7 \times 10^3 - 1.7 \times 10^{10}$
CS	$10^2 - 10^{12}$	5 – 1000	$2.0 \times 10^4 - 1.1 \times 10^9$
SiO	$10^2 - 10^{12}$	5 – 1000	$5.0 \times 10^3 - 2.7 \times 10^8$
HCO^+	$2.7\times10^2 - 10^{12\star}$	5 – 1000	$5.0 \times 10^5 - 2.7 \times 10^{10}$
N_2H^+	$2.7\times10^2 - 10^{12\star}$	5 – 1000	$5.0 \times 10^2 - 5.0 \times 10^9$

Note: The lower limit of the coverage marked by $\star$ is planned to expand in the final version provided in Masa et al. (in preparation).

the excitation conditions of the gas, namely its density and temperature, as well as the abundance of each species relative to that of molecular hydrogen. These in turn lead to estimates of the mass of the molecule-rich region of the PNe, provides some insight about the conditions for molecular chemistry, and further informs models of formation of PNe.

We introduce the addition of several new molecular species in `shapemol`, as well as a code to better allow for direct matching of interferometric observations. We use these tools to show preliminary results on the simultaneous analysis of a plethora of IRAM-30m and HERSCHEL/HIFI spectra, and NOEMA interferometric maps of different species in the pre-PN M 1-92.

The work presented here will be further discussed in much deeper detail by Masa et al. (in preparation).

2. Expanding `shapemol`

The emission j_ν and absorption k_ν coefficients calculated by `shapemol` for each molecular species and individual transition rely on pre-generated tables according to the density n of each model grid cell, its temperature T, and the product $X \times \frac{r}{V}$, where X is the abundance of the species with respect to H_2, and r and V are the distance to the central star and the expansion velocity, respectively. Tables provided for the previous version of `shapemol` (Santander-García et al. 2015) spanned a range of physical parameters expected to be found in the circumstellar environment of evolved low- and intermediate-mass stars, allowing to model ejecta with n in the range $10^2 - 10^7$ cm^{-3}, T from 10 to 1000 K, and $X \times \frac{r}{V}$ in the range $2.5 \times 10^{10} - 1.3 \times 10^{13}$ cm km^{-1} s, and $8.3 \times 10^8 - 4.2 \times 10^{11}$ cm km^{-1} s for ^{12}CO and ^{13}CO respectively. These coverage was more focused on modelling of PNe, and were therefore insufficient for some projects. Modelling Asymptotic Giant Branch (AGB) stars, for instance, represented quite a struggle. Consequently, the new version of `shapemol` considerably expands the table coverage for ^{12}CO and ^{13}CO by several orders of magnitude in n, and a broader range in $X \times \frac{r}{V}$.

In addition, we have expanded the capabilities of `shapemol` by including a whole new set of molecular species, namely C^{17}O, C^{18}O, HCN, HNC, CS, SiO, HCO^+, and N_2H^+. The preliminary parameter coverage in these molecules, as well as the new coverage for ^{12}CO and ^{13}CO, can be found in Table 1. Note that the parameter coverage is susceptible to expand in the final version presented in Masa et al. (in preparation). An illustrative example of the emission coefficient j_ν of HCN and HNC for a broad range of physical conditions is shown in Figure 1.

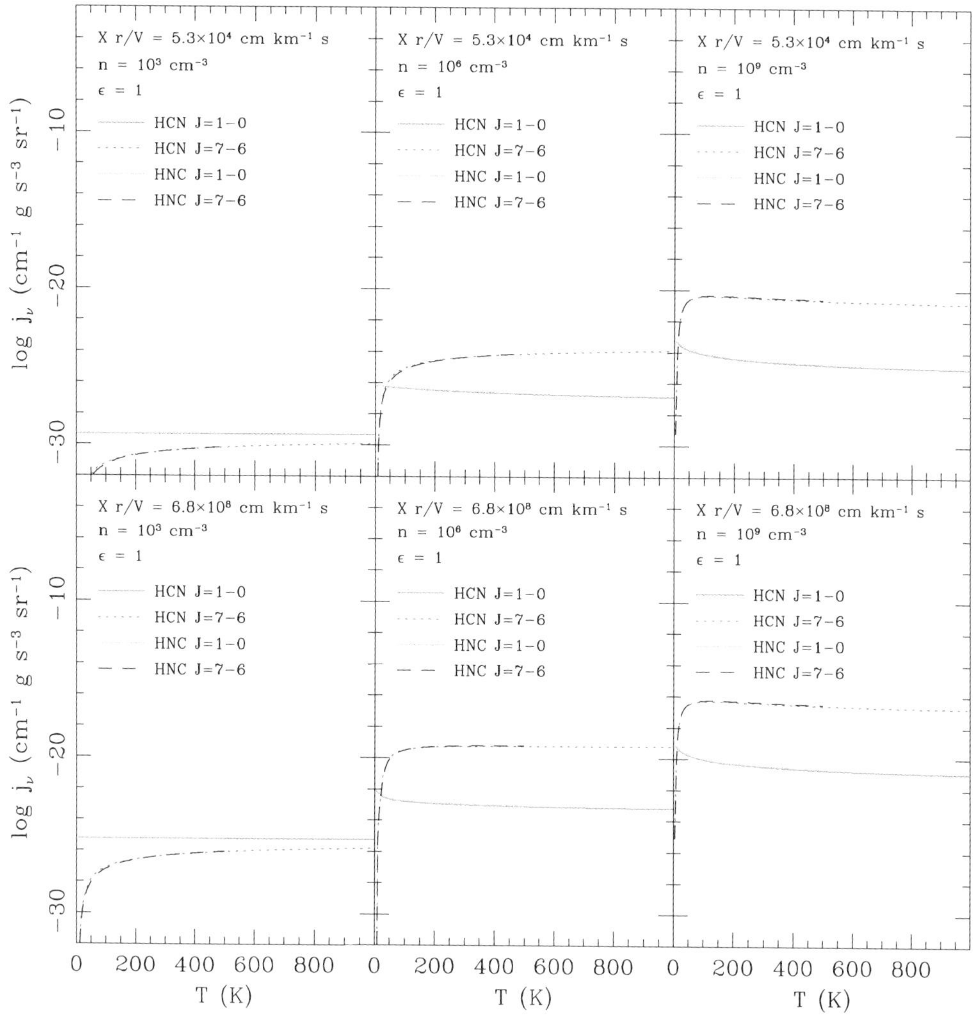

Figure 1. Example of the emission coefficient j_ν of HCN and HNC under a range of conditions of abundance, density and temperature (and a unique value of the logarithmic velocity gradient, $\epsilon = dV/dr\ r/V$, corresponding to ballistic expansion.

The computed j_ν and k_ν were tested in two different manners. We first compared a simple, spherical model computed with `SHAPE+shapemol` with theoretical calculations of the optical depth τ under LVG conditions, finding typical errors of a few ‰ in the optically thin case, increasing to a few % as the nebula becomes optically thick. We also performed a battery of emission and absorption coefficients checks against the results provided by `RADEX` (Van Der Tak et al. 2007). Although RADEX is not a LVG code, the small offsets we found (with typical values of ~5%) ensure our calculations are accurate enough.

3. Proper comparison of synthetic models and interferometric observations

Interferometry involves emission filtering depending on the baselines and UV coverage. As a result, interferometric maps are not akin to Integral Field Spectroscopic data in the sense that they should not be compared with models in a direct fashion. Otherwise,

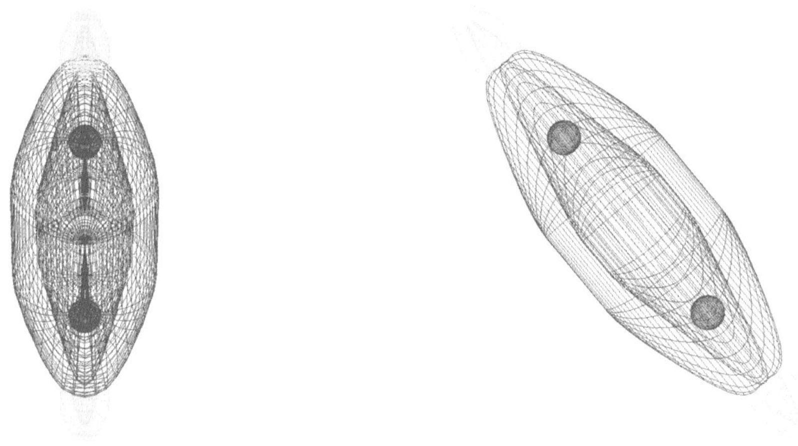

Figure 2. Sketch of the preliminary morpho-kinematical model of M 1-92 presented in this work.

flux lost in the observations (usually from extended, smooth structures) prevents a fair reconstruction by morpho-kinematical modelling.

Models simple enough (e.g. a flaring disk observed through an optical interferometer) can circumvent this limitation by direct comparison of model and observations in the UV plane. However, complex models with many parameters are a different story. In practice, comparisons are only possible in the image plane. Therefore, the model needs to undergo the same filtering and cleaning process suffered by the actual observations. This requires having accurate information of the interferometer configuration, baselines, etc., as well as of the source position in the sky at the moment(s) of observation. Essentially, we need the UV tables of the observation in order to apply the same filtering and cleaning process to the morpho-kinematical model. A proper comparison would also include the application of random noise similar to that of the observations to ensure an even better direct comparison.

We have devised a code for the radioastronomy `GILDAS` suite† that allows to quickly apply this process to models exported from `SHAPE`, provided the UV table of the observation is available.

4. Preliminary model of M 1-92

In order to illustrate the new capabilities of `SHAPE+shapemol` as well as the aforementioned `GILDAS` code, we present a preliminary morpho-kinematical model of the pre-PN M 1-92. We use it to simultaneously fit NOEMA interferometric maps of the J=2−1 transition of ^{13}CO, C^{17}O, C^{18}O, HCN, and HCO^{+}, as well as a large number of single-dish observations from different species made with the IRAM 30 radiotelescope and HERSCHEL/HIFI, namely ^{12}CO (J=1−0, J=2−1, J=5−4, J=7−6, J=9−8); ^{13}CO, C^{17}O and C^{18}O (J=1−0, J=2−1); HNC and N$_2$H^{+} (J=1−0, J=3−2); HCN and HCO^{+} (J=1−0, J=2−1, J=3−2); CS (J=2−1, J=3−2); and SiO (J=2−1, J=3−2, J=4−3, J=5−4, J=6−5). We have kept the number of parameters down to a reasonable value in order to provide a comprehensive description of the geometry, motion, and physical conditions of the real ejecta.

A model sketch of this bipolar pre-PN is shown in Figure 2. A preliminary fit to different single-dish spectral profiles and interferometric maps can be seen in Figures 3, 4, and 5.

† `https://www.iram.fr/IRAMFR/GILDAS`

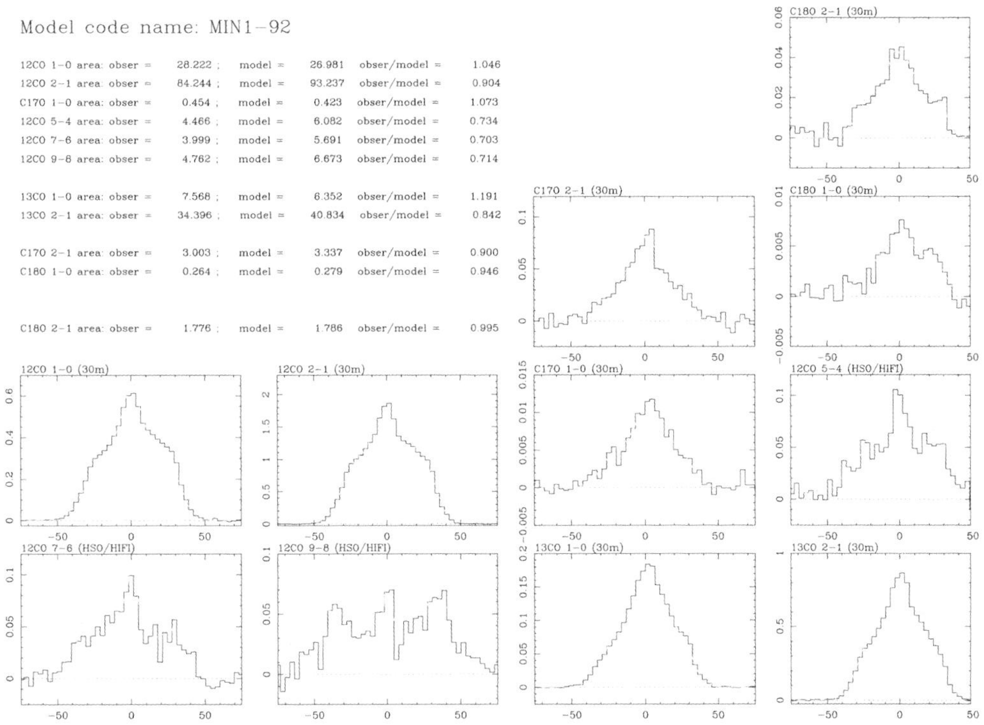

Figure 3. Preliminary model fit to different single-dish spectral profiles from ^{12}CO, ^{13}CO, C^{17}O, and C^{18}O in M 1-92. Numbers in the top left section refer to integrated intensities of both the observation and model in each line, as well as their ratio in order to better assess the fairness of the fit.

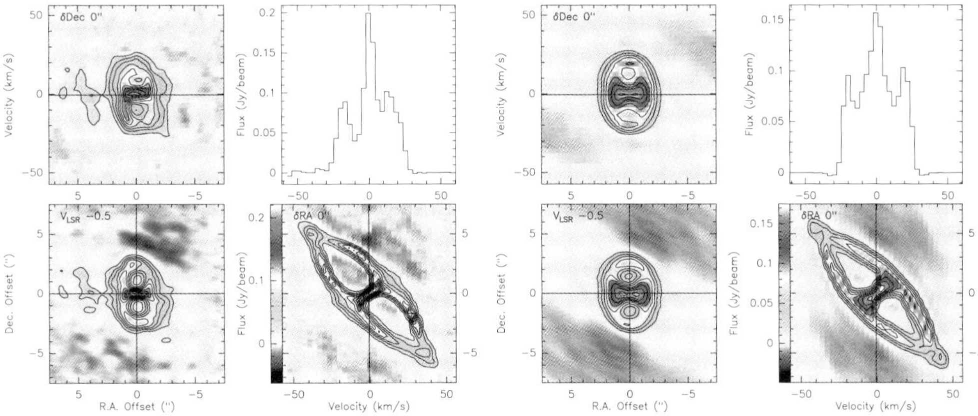

Figure 4. *Left:* A four-panel sample of the ^{13}CO J=2−1 NOEMA interferometric observations of the pre-PN M 1-92. The central (systemic velocity) channel of the spectral map is shown in the bottom left panel. The top left and bottom right panels show position velocity maps along the horizontal and vertical directions, respectively. The top right panel shows the spectral profile at the central position. *Right:* Same for the preliminary model of M 1-92, after application of the GILDAS code to allow direct comparison with the observations.

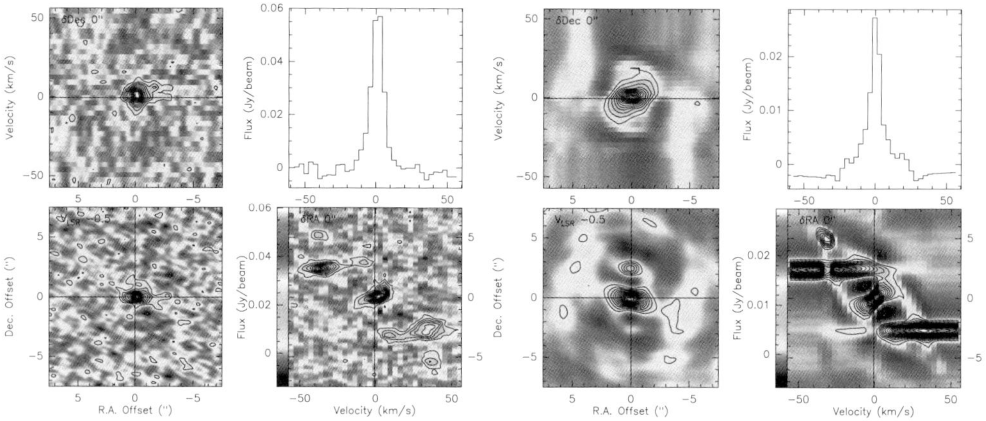

Figure 5. *Left:* A four-panel sample of the HCN J=2−1 NOEMA interferometric observations of the pre-PN M 1-92. The central (systemic velocity) channel of the spectral map is shown in the bottom left panel. The top left and bottom right panels show position velocity maps along the horizontal and vertical directions, respectively. The top right panel shows the spectral profile at the central position. *Right:* Same for the preliminary model of M 1-92, after application of the GILDAS code to allow direct comparison with the observations.

The modelling so far suggests that the tapered shape of the nebula is topped by two polar tips carved out by a hot polar outflow. The inner and outer regions of these tips have very different physical conditions. The density of the model ranges from 1.8×10^5 cm^{-3} in the equatorial inner region to a mere 10^4 cm^{-3} in the inner region of the polar tips, which also are the hotter ones of the model, at ∼450 K, as opposed to the much colder walls of the nebula at 17 K. The nebula expands homologously, except for a couple of small, dense and hot blobs half way along the main axis which dash through the nebula at a much higher velocity (55 km s^{-1}) than the surrounding regions. These blobs, as well as the polar tips, are significantly bright in $HCO^+$and HCN, but difficult to tell apart in low-J ^{12}CO and ^{13}CO transitions.

In summary, the data suggests an active chemistry is taking place in shocked, hot regions within M 1-92. Additionally, an ^{17}O/^{18}O isotopic ratio of 1.7 indicates the progenitor AGB should have turned carbon-rich during its evolution towards the tip of the AGB, whereas the resulting nebula is oxygen-rich. This discrepancy can be removed if the evolution of the AGB was suddenly interrupted by the event that gave rise to the current nebula in a sudden ejection, either by a close binary in common envelope or some other similar phenomenon.

A full description of the final version of this model will be given in Masa et al. (in preparation).

We acknowledge funding from the Spanish Ministry of Science and Innovation (MICINN) through project EVENTs/Nebulae-Web (grant PID2019-105203GB-C21).

References

Akashi, M., Soker, N., 2013, *MNRAS*, 436, 1961. doi: 10.1093/mnras/stt1704

Akashi, M., Soker, N., 2013, *MNRAS*, 481, 2754. doi:10.1093/mnras/sty2479

Castor, J. I., 1970, *MNRAS*, 149, 111

Jones, D., 2020, Observational Constraints on the Common Envelope Phase, in *Reviews in Frontiers of Modern Astrophysics: From Space Debris to Cosmology* (eds. Kabath, Jones and Skarka; publisher Springer Nature), 123–153. doi:10.1007/978-3-030-38509-5_5

Santander-García, M., Corradi, R. L. M., A. Mampaso, B. Balick, 2004, *A&A*, 426, 185. doi:10.1051/0004-6361:20041147
Santander-García, M., Bujarrabal, V., Koning, N., Steffen, W., 2015, *A&A*, 573, 56. doi:10.1051/0004-6361/201322348
Solf, J., Ulrich, H., 2022, *A&A*, 148, 274
Steffen, W., Koning, N., Wenger, S., Morisset, C., Magnor, M., 2011, *IEEE Transactions on Visualization and Computer Graphics*, 17, 454. doi:10.1109/TVCG.2010.62
Van Der Tak, F. F. S., Black, J. H., Schöier, F. L., Jansen, D. J., van Dishoeck, E. F., 2007, *A&A*, 468, 627. doi:10.1051/0004-6361:20066820

Planetary Nebulae: A Universal Toolbox in the Era of Precision Astrophysics
Proceedings IAU Symposium No. 384, 2025
O. De Marco, A. Zijlstra & R. Szczerba, eds.
doi:10.1017/S1743921324000474

Dust production from low- and intermediate-mass stars: new insights from post-AGB stars and PNe

F. Dell'Agli

INAF, Osservatorio Astronomico di Roma, Via Frascati 33, 00077, Monte Porzio Catone, Italy

Abstract. Low- and intermediate-mass (LIM) stars play a pivotal role in the life cycle of their host environment. During the asymptotic giant branch (AGB) phase, they eject gas reprocessed by the internal nucleosynthesis and dust formed in their cool and dense circumstellar envelopes. The production of dust is strongly linked to the evolution of the central object during the AGB phase. Even after the AGB evolution, the effects of the stars' previous evolutionary history, including nucleosynthesis, mass loss, and dust production processes, are still evident. Recently, we introduced a novel approach to address clues connected to the dust production and mass loss history of LIM stars looking at the post-AGB and planetary nebula (PN) evolutionary stage. By utilizing stellar evolution and dust formation models, we analyze the spectral energy distribution (SED) of sources currently undergoing various evolutionary phases, which are believed to have originated from progenitors with similar mass and chemical composition. Comparing the results from different stages along the AGB to PNe transition can provide valuable insights into the amount of dust and gas released during the very late AGB phases. While the post-AGB phase allows us to trace the history of dust production back to the AGB phase's tip, investigating the PNe is crucial for reconstructing the mass-loss process that occurred after the last thermal pulse.

Keywords. stars: abundances - stars: AGB and post-AGB - stars: evolution.

---

1. Introduction

Stars with masses ranging between 1 and 8 times the mass of the Sun significantly contribute to the chemical enrichment of the environment where they form (e.g. D'Antona et al. 2023; Kobayashi et al. 2020; Romano et al. 2019; Vincenzo et al. 2016; Maraston 2005). During this phase, stars can reach luminosities of 10^4-$10^5 L_\odot$, expanding to several hundred times their initial radius and cooling their surface temperatures to as low as 2000 K. A substantial loss of mass occurs during the AGB evolution: the extremely low surface gravity facilitates the ejection of the envelopes into the interstellar medium via stellar winds. This gas bears the imprint of nucleosynthesis and mixing processes experienced by the stars during their evolution (Karakas & Lattanzio 2014; Ventura et al. 2022). The rate at which this material can be expelled can be as high as $10^{-4} M_\odot$/yr. These cool and dense winds create ideal conditions for dust particle condensation in the star's vicinity (Ferrarotti & Gail 2006; Höfner & Olofsson 2018).

Understanding the contribution of LIM stars to the overall dust content in galaxies holds significant relevance across various aspects of astrophysics studies (Schneider & Maiolino 2023). Remarkable progresses have been made in advancing our comprehension of dust formation mechanisms and in aligning theoretical models with observational data (e.g. Nanni et al. 2013, 2019; Ventura et al. 2014, 2020). Both observational and theoretical findings indicate an increase in the dust production rate during the latter phases of the AGB evolution (Dell'Agli et al. 2015a; Marini et al. 2021, 2023). However, accurately describing mass-loss remains one of the most challenging aspects to model (Höfner & Olofsson 2018). This uncertainty not only impacts our understanding of the material ejected by these stars, but also influences the quantity and types of dust released into the interstellar medium (ISM).

Recent studies have explored the feasibility of constraining the description of mass-loss and dust production during the AGB phase by analyzing subsequent stages (Tosi et al. 2022; Dell'Agli et al. 2023a,b). Post-AGB stars and PNe are invaluable to achieve this objective. By comparing their physical properties and chemical compositions with predictions from stellar evolution models, it becomes possible to reconstruct their preceding evolutionary history, thereby connecting it to expectations for the AGB phase. This contribution presents the results obtained thus far through the application of this methodology. The manuscript is organized as follows: Section 1.1 describes the primary properties of the adopted stellar evolution models and the schematic representation used to describe dust production from evolved stars. Section 1.2 outlines the principal characteristics of dust production depending on initial mass, metallicity, and evolutionary stage during the AGB phase. Sections 1.3 and 1.4 present the outcomes derived from the analysis of post-AGB stars and planetary nebulae.

1.1. *Modelling the evolved phases of LIMs*

Over the past few decades, extensive research has focused on studying the AGB and subsequent phases in the lifespan of LIM stars. Various research groups have dedicated their efforts to describing the physical and nuclear processes that characterize these stars. The interested reader can find the current knowledge and theoretical findings in this area in the review by Karakas & Lattanzio (2014). In this contribution, we present the results obtained using the ATON code for stellar evolution (Ventura et al. 1998). This code computes the evolution of stars from the pre-main sequence to the end of the AGB phase, incorporating nuclear burning and chemical mixing self-consistently via a diffusive scheme. A comprehensive grid of models has been generated, yielding gas production by stars within the mass range of 1 to 8 $M_{\odot}$ and metallicities spanning from $Z=10^{-7}$ to $Z=0.04$. These models have been extensively applied in different contexts: from the the analysis of the chemical evolution of the Milky Way (Romano et al. 2019), to the study of globular clusters to explore the role of AGB stars in the formation of multiple populations within these systems (D'Antona 2020, and references therein). For an in-depth discussion of these findings, interested readers can refer to Ventura et al. (2022).

During the last ten years, significant efforts have been made to incorporate the description of the dust formation process into the modeling framework (Ventura et al. 2012, 2014). The code has been integrated with a model previously developed by the Heidelberg group (Ferrarotti & Gail 2006), which involves a stationary, spherically symmetric wind where dust grains grow on preexisting seeds. The thermodynamic structure of the wind relies on the physical parameters of the stars during the AGB phase, specifically the star's mass, luminosity, and effective temperature. The density profile of the wind is determined by the continuity equation, which is based on the computed mass-loss rate during the AGB evolution. The optical depth of the wind is influenced by the growth of the dust particles and their chemical composition. Radiation pressure acting on dust grains plays a crucial role in the wind dynamic. If the grain sizes are sufficiently large and they are highly opaque, they drive the wind, facilitating the ejection of material into the interstellar medium. The formation of different dust species with varying chemistry

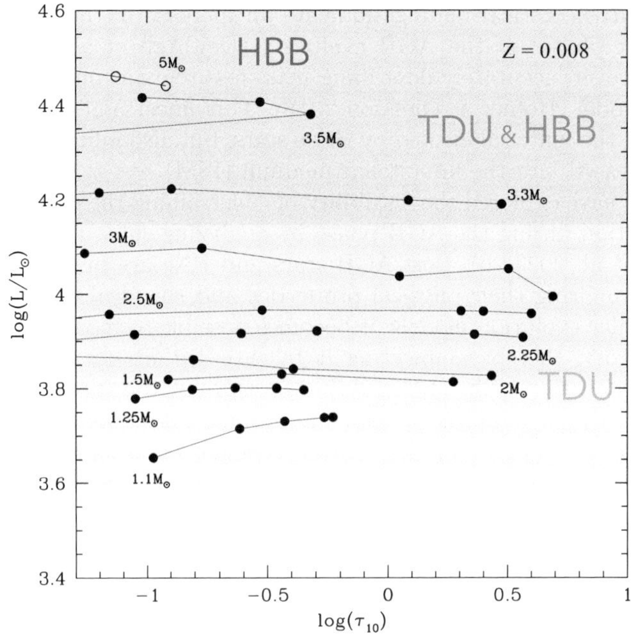

Figure 1. Evolutionary tracks in the optical depth at 10 microns versus luminosity plane. Full dots refer to the carbon star evolutionary phase while open points indicate the oxygen-rich stage of the AGB evolution.

is regulated by the surface chemical composition of the stars. Despite its simplicity, this model has proven to be the most efficient method thus far to couple dust production with a comprehensive description of the AGB phase, thereby aiding in the production of dust yields. These yields have been extensively utilized to evaluate the contribution of LIM stars to the dust production rate and dust budget in galaxies (Dell'Agli et al. 2015a, 2016, 2018, 2019a; Palla et al. 2020, 2023), especially when compared with predictions for supernovae, another major stellar dust producer (Schneider et al. 2014).

Recently, the self-consistent description of stellar evolution has been expanded to encompass the phase that succeeds the AGB phase, namely the post-AGB and planetary nebula phases. A few adjustments to the numerical structure of the stellar evolution code were necessary to achieve this goal. These adjustments involve adopting shorter timescales and freezing the rezoning of mesh points for a limited number of models following the onset of contraction into the post-AGB phase. It has been demonstrated that the results obtained in terms of post-AGB luminosity and surface chemistry are not influenced by the choice of time step adopted. Published models are currently available for masses ranging from 0.8 to 4 $M_\odot$ and some metallicities in studies such as Kamath et al. (2023) and Marini et al. (2020), which provide further details on the methodology used to model the post-AGB phase. Additionally, valuable discussions regarding the evolution from the AGB to the PN phase can be found in the contribution by Ventura in these conference proceedings.

1.2. *Dust production during the AGB evolution*

During the AGB phase, LIM stars undergo various physical processes that significantly impact their surface chemical composition. Of these processes, the third dredge-up (TDU) and hot bottom burning (HBB) have direct effects on the composition of produced dust

(Ventura et al. 2012). TDU occurs after each thermal pulse, wherein the star's envelope penetrates into its inner regions, dredging up the products of 3-α nucleosynthesis, predominantly ^{12}C, to the surface (Iben 1974). After several TDU episodes, the star progresses to the carbon star stage, characterized by a surface C/O number ratio exceeding unity. HBB involves the activation of proton-capture nucleosynthesis at the convective envelope's base (Scalo, Despain, & Ulrich 1975). This phenomenon occurs in stars more massive than 3−4 $M_{\odot}$†. It occurs when the temperature at the convective envelope's base surpasses 30−40 million Kelvin. Several chemical elements participate in this nucleosynthesis, altering their abundances on the star's surface. For the purposes of this discussion, it is notable that carbon and, eventually, oxygen are depleted, while nitrogen is produced. Therefore, massive AGB stars do not reach the carbon star stage, evolving with a C/O ratio lower than unity. This distinction between oxygen-rich (O-rich) and carbon-rich (C-rich) AGB stars influences the dust generated during the AGB phase (Ventura et al. 2014). The presence of the CO molecule in these stars' winds binds all available carbon and oxygen, allowing only the excess of one element to condense. In C-rich environments, solid carbon and silicon carbide are the primary species formed, while in O-rich circumstellar envelopes, silicates and alumina dust are the more prevalent species produced (Ferrarotti & Gail 2006).

Based on the modeling detailed in the preceding section, we can track dust production throughout the AGB evolution and observe how it varies as a function of the star's initial mass, TDU efficiency and HBB intensity. AGB stars can broadly be categorized into three main groups (Ventura et al. 2022). Stars with very low masses ($0.7\,M_{\odot} < M < 1\,M_{\odot}$‡) undergo few thermal pulses and TDU episodes, insufficient to transition them to the carbon star stage. Consequently, they produce silicate dust in limited quantities due to their reduced envelopes and low mass-loss rates. Stars within the mass range of 1−3 $M_{\odot}$ generate approximately up to $10^{-2}\,M_{\odot}$ of carbon dust during their carbon star stage, accompanied by smaller amounts of silicon carbide. The production of carbon dust hinges on the carbon availability in the wind. Being a primary element, the surface fraction of carbon is more affected by the number of TDU episodes rather than the metallicity of the star. Carbon dust production gradually increases after each TDU, peaking toward the end of the AGB phase. During the O-rich phase preceding the carbon star stage, radiation pressure and wind density are unfavorable for substantial silicate dust production. More massive AGB stars (4−8$M_{\odot}$) primarily produce silicate dust, with a notable dependency on metallicity (Dell'Agli et al. 2019b).

In recent years, the ATON models of AGB evolution and dust production have been extensively utilized to study observations of evolved stars across various galaxies. Photometric data from populations of AGB stars in the Magellanic Clouds (Dell'Agli et al. 2015a,b) and in some dwarf galaxies (Dell'Agli et al. 2016, 2018, 2019a) have been considered to assess the contribution of these sources to the dust production rate within these systems. Detailed analyses of the Large and Small Magellanic Clouds have been conducted and compared, revealing that the primary sources of dust from AGB stars in these galaxies are those within the mass range of 1.5−3.0 $M_{\odot}$ upon reaching the carbon star stage. While more massive AGB stars theoretically have the potential to produce significant amounts of silicate dust (up to $10^{-2}\,M_{\odot}$ during the entire AGB phase), they are fewer in number, thus their contribution depends significantly on the star formation history and metallicity of the environment.

† This mass limit varies depending on the star's metallicity and the adopted convective prescription (Ventura et al. 2015).

‡ The masses given here refer to the beginning of the AGB phase. The masses of the progenitors are generally higher and are sensitive to the mass lost during the red giant branch phase.

In Figure 1, black ATON tracks are depicted for various masses at Z=0.008. This plot illustrates the evolution of LIM stars' luminosity during the final stages of the AGB as a function of the optical depth at 10 micron, τ_{10}†. Toward the end of the AGB evolution, the availability of carbon for dust condensation increases, favoring a higher dust production rate. A greater quantity of dust in the circumstellar envelope corresponds to an increase in the optical depth. Consequently, both gas and dust mass-loss rates rise with τ_{10}, eventually reaching 1.5×10^{-4} $M_\odot$/yr and dust production rate $\sim 10^{-6}$ $M_\odot$/yr.

The substantial contribution of carbon stars to the dust production rate renders the low-mass regime particularly intriguing. Since their dust production increase toward the conclusion of the AGB phase, the timescales, number of TDU episodes, and consequently, dust production are intricately linked to the mass-loss rate experienced during this phase. Hence, it becomes imperative to map the AGB phase comprehensively until its conclusion and then compare the modeling outcomes with observational data. In pursuit of this objective, Marini et al. (2021) recently scrutinized carbon stars and their dust production in the LMC. They analyzed the IRS/Spitzer spectra of carbon stars observed in the galaxy (Kemper et al. 2010), which are well-suited for mapping the infrared (IR) emission from these sources. Employing the radiative transfer code DUSTY (Nenkova et al. 1999), they reproduced the spectra, determining the luminosity, optical depth, and chemical composition of these stars for comparison with model predictions.

Marini et al. (2021) present the results for the stars' parameters (luminosity and τ_{10}) obtained from the SED fitting (see their Fig. 5). Stars with luminosities below ~7500 $L_\odot$ constitute the oldest objects in the sample originating from stars with an initial mass below 2 $M_\odot$, formed during epochs earlier than 1 billion years ago. Brigther sources, with luminosities in the range 7500 $L_\odot$ <L<16000 $L_\odot$, are objects younger than 1 billion years, descending from stars with an initial mass above 2 $M_\odot$. In particular, objects exhibiting luminosities surpassing 10^4 $L_\odot$ are interpreted as progenies originating from stars with initial masses ranging from 2.5 to 3.3 $M_\odot$, formed during the peak of the LMC's star formation history, approximately 300 to 600 million years ago. The interpretation of stars with $\tau_{10} > 3$ present challenges within this framework. Dell'Agli et al. (2021) emphasized that the substantial IR excess should be associated to mass-loss rates higher than the ones achievable within a single star model, particularly for a 1−1.5 $M_\odot$ star. They showed that these objects could plausibly be explained as closely interacting binaries, which underwent exceptionally high mass-loss and dust production rates when they interact during the carbon star stage.

1.3. *Studying mass loss and dust production from the post-AGB stars perspective*

After the tip of the AGB, stars progress towards the PN phase via the post-AGB phase. Stars undergo a true metamorphosis, transitioning from a cool and extended configuration to a compact and extremely hot object. The residual envelope contracts, increasing the effective temperature of the central object, while the residual gas and dust move away from the star, laying the groundwork for the future nebula. During this transition, stars traverse the HR diagram, evolving at a constant luminosity until the effective temperature reaches approximately ~ 50000 K. The luminosity value is primarily determined by the core mass, serving as a proxy for the initial mass of the stars. The surface chemical composition mirrors the final surface chemistry at the conclusion of the AGB phase.

† The optical depth is given by $\tau_{10} = \int n_d \sigma_{10} dr$, where n_d is the number density of the seeds over which the dust grains grow, σ_{10} is the cross section of the dust grains at 10 micron and the integral is computed from the photosphere to 200 stellar radii from the stellar surface.

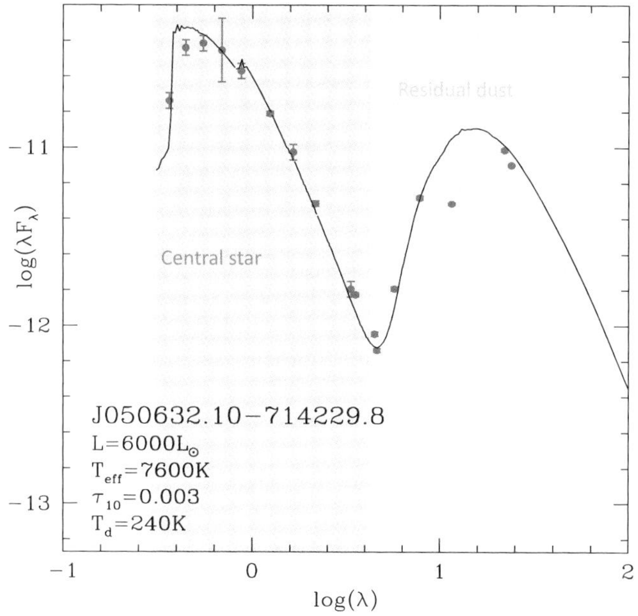

Figure 2. Photometric data (blue points) of the source J050632.10-714229.8 (Kamath, Wood, & Van Winckel 2015) showing the typical double-peaked SED shape of single post-AGB stars. Overlapped to the best fit obtained by Tosi et al. (2022) (black line, see Section 1.3).

Observationally, post-AGB stars are rarer than AGB stars due to the shorter evolutionary timescales of the contraction. However, owing to their higher effective temperatures, determining the surface chemical composition is more straightforward, while AGB spectra typically exhibit several molecular bands, and dust significantly obscures the emission in the optical and, eventually, in the near-IR wavelengths (e.g. Gonneau et al. 2016). Furthermore, during the post-AGB phase, the peculiar shape of the SED of post-AGB stars, displaying a typical double-peaked behavior, allows for the separation of the dust shell's contribution from the emission of the central object (Kamath et al. 2023; Tosi et al. 2022), as shown in Figure 2.

Hence, the determination of the luminosity of post-AGB stars, combined with knowledge about their surface chemical composition, not only facilitates the study of the post-AGB phase but also provides significant insight into the preceding AGB evolution. In particular, it helps in finding consistency between model predictions for the efficiency of TDU and HBB, which significantly alter surface chemistry during the AGB phase, and the observation in post-AGB stars (Kamath et al. 2023). Moreover, the examination of the IR excess serves to illuminate the dust formation process during the very late AGB phases and potentially post the onset of contraction into the post-AGB phase (Tosi et al. 2022). This kind of investigation provides information about the timescale of the AGB to post-AGB transition and allows for an exploration of the dynamics of the wind moving away from the star after the cessation of dust production.

Recently, several studies have presented results derived from this methodology, applied to a sample of single post-AGB stars within our Galaxy (Tosi et al. 2023; Dell'Agli et al. 2023a) as well as in the Magellanic Clouds (MCs; Tosi et al. 2022). These studies involved modeling the SED of a selection of C- and O-rich, single post-AGB stars. They determined the effective temperature and luminosity by analyzing the peak emission of the central object centered around 1μm. Combining these data with surface chemical abundances gathered from the literature and employing [Fe/H] as a tracer for metallicity, a comprehensive comparison of all physical and chemical parameters was conducted. These comparisons were made against results obtained from evolutionary tracks generated using the ATON code (see Section 4), enabling the determination of the progenitor mass of the stars. Additionally, radiative transfer modeling was utilized to investigate the dust mineralogy around individual sources, the optical depth, and the distance of the dusty region from the central star.

The main conclusion drawn in this context is that the observed dust around post-AGB stars was released after the commencement of contraction into the post-AGB phase, where effective temperatures increased to approximately ~4000 K. The detected IR excess predominantly depends on the timescale of post-AGB evolution, which crucially determines the current location of the dusty region and the dust-production rate experienced during the transition from the tip of the AGB to the early post-AGB phase. The majority of investigated sources evolved from low-mass ($M<1.5M_{\odot}$) carbon stars, primarily producing solid carbon. Notably, in the case of carbon stars, the IR excess correlates with the luminosity of the stars. This correlation can be explained by the anticipation that $2-3M_{\odot}$ stars undergo more efficient dust formation, and their faster evolution towards the post-AGB phase results in the dusty region being closer to the central star in more massive carbon stars.

In contrast, the oxygen-rich stars in the sample are interpreted as the progeny of low-mass stars that failed to reach the C-star stage. The dust surrounding these stars predominantly comprises crystalline silicates. Additionally, the dusty shells around M-type stars tend to be, on average, closer to the central star compared to carbon stars. This result is interpreted as a consequence of lower radiation pressure acting on silicates compared to carbon dust, resulting in slower winds.

Both in the Galaxy and the Magellanic Clouds, there is an observed anti-correlation between optical depth and the metallicity of these sources. Lower metallicities are associated with higher carbon-to-oxygen excesses achieved during AGB evolution for stars evolving at similar luminosities. This phenomenon arises due to the lower initial abundance of oxygen locked in stars with lower metallicities.

These studies provide crucial insight into the mass-loss experienced by carbon-rich stars during the transition from the tip of the AGB phase and the beginning of the post-AGB. To replicate the presently observed IR excesses, the required mass-loss rates after the tip of the AGB need to be on the order of $4-5\times10^{-5}\,M_{\odot}/yr$, approximately three times higher than standard evolution modeling suggests. However, the expected mass-loss rates for low-mass stars with solar chemistry evolving through the final AGB phases (around $1-1.5\times10^{-5}\,M_{\odot}/yr$) align with the observed scenario.

1.4. *Insight from the PN phase*

The concept of exploring the final stages of AGB dust production and mass-loss, extending into subsequent evolutionary phases, is also applicable in the study of planetary nebulae (PNe). As central stars transition towards the white dwarf cooling sequence, they heat up to one-to-two hundred thousand Kelvin, leading to the ionization of the gas lingering in their vicinity. The ionized nebula displays a forest of lines in its spectrum, enabling the determination of the gas's chemical composition. In the near-IR spectrum, the presence of dust in the nebula remains visible, typically at lower temperatures and more dispersed spatially compared to the characteristics observed during the post-AGB phase. Recognizing the powerful tool that aided in studying post-AGB sources, recent studies are underway to establish the final linkage between the later stages of low to

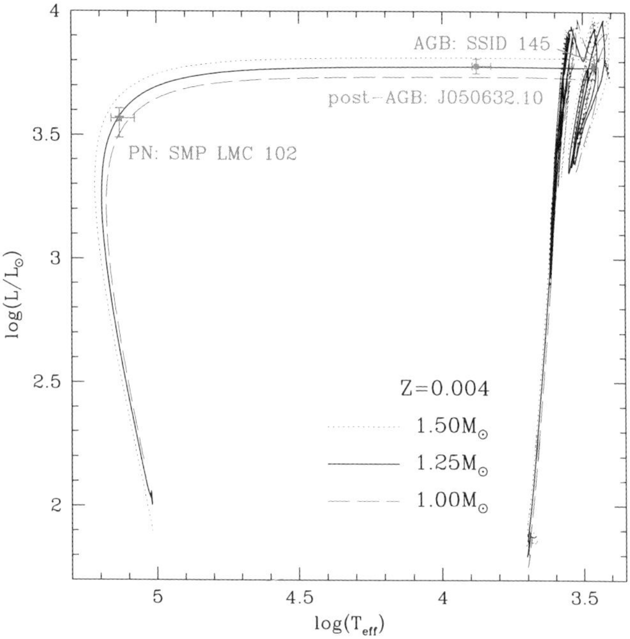

Figure 3. Evolutionary tracks on the HR diagram of the 1.0, 1.25, and 1.5 $M_\odot$ model stars of metallicity Z = 0.004; the location of the AGB (orange full dot), post-AGB (green full square), and PN (magenta open star) sources are reported.

intermediate star evolution. This aims to bridge what is currently observed in the PN phase with the preceding history of mass-loss and dust production.

With this objective, Tosi et al. (in prep) have examined 10 PNe in the LMC, specifically selecting those PNe identified as spherical or elliptical and well-documented in the existing literature (Shaw et al. 2001). These sources' SEDs are comprehensively covered by multiple programs, including Hubble Space Telescope (HST) spectra in the UV region (Stanghellini, Shaw, & Gilmore 2005), Spitzer spectra in the IR (Stanghellini et al. 2007), and diverse photometric data from the optical to the mid-IR ranges (Cutri & et al. 2012; Reid 2014). An extensive SED coverage was crucial to maximize constraints on the photoionization model constructed using the code CLOUDY (Ferland et al. 2017). Previous analysis by Stanghellini et al. (2007) focused on the intensity of lines emitted in the UV. Achieving agreement between the intensities derived from the photoionization model and those available in the existing literature contributes to determining the nebula's ionization level, its chemical composition and metallicity.

The key physical parameters derived from the photoionization models are luminosity, effective temperature, nebular gas mass, type, and quantity of dust, allowing the calculation of the dust-to-gas ratio. Literature-based measurements of C, N, O abundances (Leisy et al. 2006; Stanghellini, Shaw, & Gilmore 2005) are fundamental for reconstructing the nucleosynthesis experienced by the star in preceding phases (Ventura et al. 2015, 2016, 2017). In the low- and intermediate-mass regime of AGB stars (below 4$M_\odot$, depending on the star's metallicity), the carbon abundance at the AGB phase's culmination increases in tandem with the star's initial mass. Essentially, as previously explained (see Section 1.2), a higher envelope mass translates to more episodes of TDU experienced by the star. The increase in nitrogen and the carbon depletion indicates the activation of HBB. As detailed in Section 1.2, this process necessitates temperatures exceeding 30–40 MK at the convective envelope's base, which stars with masses above

$3\,M_\odot$ can attain, depending on the metallicity. Although oxygen could serve as a metallicity indicator, caution is advised as it might also experience slight enhancement due to multiple TDU events. Utilizing oxygen abundance alongside other elements (e.g. argon if available) fortifies the accuracy of the metallicity estimation. By integrating information gleaned from photoionization modeling (primarily luminosity and effective temperature), abundance measurements, and their comparison with evolutionary tracks of different metallicities, it becomes feasible to characterize the progenitor mass of the central star, along with its evolutionary stage during the PN phase. This characterization is pivotal to establish links between current observations and the preceding evolutionary history, encompassing internal processes (like nucleosynthesis and mixing) as well as mechanisms of mass-loss and dust formation.

The recent pilot study by Dell'Agli et al. (2023b) aimed to illustrate how the examination of the AGB to PNe transition can offer new insight into this field. Among those investigated in the LMC (Marini et al. 2021; Tosi et al. 2022, and Tosi in prep.), the authors identified three sources representing distinct evolutionary steps of a $\sim 1.25\,M_\odot$ star, aligning with the same evolutionary tracks. They are shown in Figure 3 with their location in the H-R diagram.

Through the study of post-AGB sources, comprehensive details about the late AGB phases and the beginning of the contraction phase can be derived. In the specific case highlighted by Dell'Agli et al. (2023b), the dust observed during the post-AGB phase originated shortly after the commencement of the contraction phase, at an effective temperature of approximately 3000 K. Their estimation suggests that a mass-loss rate of $1.4 \times 10^{-5}\,M_\odot/yr$ would be required to generate the observed optical depth of the dust observed nowadays (for a detailed explanation, refer to Dell'Agli et al. (2023b) and Tosi et al. (2022)).

Investigating PNe contributes to a more comprehensive understanding of the mass-loss and dust formation processes that occurred during the final two thermal pulses of AGB evolution. Analysis of PN SEDs provided estimates of the quantity of gas and dust retained within the surrounding nebula. These findings were compared with results obtained from stellar evolution models, aiming to comprehend the extent to which gas released by the star during the late AGB phases remains trapped in the nebula. In the specific case studied by Dell'Agli et al. (2023b), $0.5\,M_\odot$ of gas is found to makes up the nebula, which is the amount of gas released during the final interpulse phase of the $1.25\,M_\odot$ AGB phase. Comparisons between the amount of extant dust in the nebula and dust formation models led to an estimation that only about ~ 40 per cent of the dust produced during those phases survived ejection and potential sublimation processes. Further investigations are necessary to ascertain if this behavior is consistent across different scenarios or if other factors might influence this outcome.

Acknowledgements

F.D.A. is in debt to the SOC and LOC of the "IAU Symposium 384: Planetary Nebulae: a Universal Toolbox in the Era of Precision Astrophysics" for the support received to attend the conference. She also acknowledges the support received from the INAF-Mini-GRANTS 2022 ("Disclosing the stellar dust production in the Milky Way", PI. E. Marini).

References

Cutri, R. M. & et al. 2012, VizieR Online Data Catalog, II/311

D'Antona F., 2020, IAUS, 351, 289.

D'Antona F., Vesperini E., Calura F., Ventura P., D'Ercole A., Caloi V., Marino A. F., et al., 2023, arXiv, arXiv:2311.14558

Dell'Agli F., Ventura P., Schneider R., Di Criscienzo M., García-Hernández D. A., Rossi C., Brocato E., 2015, MNRAS, 447, 2992.

Dell'Agli F., García-Hernández D. A., Ventura P., Schneider R., Di Criscienzo M., Rossi C., 2015, MNRAS, 454, 4235.

Dell'Agli F., Di Criscienzo M., Boyer M. L., García-Hernández, D. A. 2016, MNRAS, 460, 4230

Dell'Agli F., Di Criscienzo M., Ventura P., Limongi M., García-Hernández D. A., Marini E., Rossi C., 2018, MNRAS, 479, 5035

Dell'Agli F., Di Criscienzo M., García-Hernández D. A., et al. 2019, MNRAS, 482, 4733

Dell'Agli F., Valiante R., Kamath D., Ventura P., García-Hernández D. A., 2019a, MNRAS, 486, 4738

Dell'Agli F., Marini E., D'Antona F., Ventura P., Groenewegen M. A. T., Mattsson L., Kamath D., et al., 2021, MNRAS, 502, L35.

Dell'Agli F., Tosi S., Kamath D., Ventura P., Van Winckel H., Marini E., Marchetti T., 2023a, A&A, 671, A86

Dell'Agli F., Tosi S., Kamath D., Stanghellini L., Bianchi S., Ventura P., Marini E., et al., 2023b, MNRAS, 526, 5386

Ferland G. J., Chatzikos M., Guzmán F., Lykins M. L., van Hoof P. A. M., Williams R. J. R., Abel N. P., et al., 2017, RMxAA, 53, 385

Ferrarotti A. S., Gail, H.-P. 2006, A&A, 447, 553

Gonneau A., Lançon A., Trager S. C., Aringer B., Lyubenova M., Nowotny W., Peletier R. F., et al., 2016, A&A, 589, A36.

Höfner S., Olofsson H., 2018, A&ARv, 26, 1.

Iben I., 1974, ARA&A, 12, 215

Karakas A. I., Lattanzio J. C. 2014, PASA, 31, e030

Kamath D., Wood P. R., Van Winckel H., 2015, MNRAS, 454, 1468

Kamath D., Dell'Agli F., Ventura P., Van Winckel H., Tosi S., Karakas A. I., 2023, MNRAS, 519, 2169

Kemper F., Woods P. M., Antoniou V., et al. 2010, PASP, 122, 683

Kobayashi, C., Karakas, A. I., & Lugaro, M. 2020, ApJ, 900, 179

Leisy P., Dennefeld M., 2006, A&A, 456, 451

Maraston C., 2005, MNRAS, 362, 799

Marini E., Dell'Agli F., Di Criscienzo M., García-Hernández D. A., Ventura P., Groenewegen M. A. T., Mattsson L., et al., 2020, MNRAS, 493, 2996

Marini E., Dell'Agli F., Groenewegen M. A. T., García-Hernández D. A., Mattsson L., Kamath D., Ventura P., et al., 2021, A&A, 647, A69

Marini E., Dell'Agli F., Kamath D., Ventura P., Mattsson L., Marchetti T., García-Hernández D. A., et al., 2023, A&A, 670, A97

Nanni A., Bressan A., Marigo P., Girardi L., 2013, MNRAS, 434, 2390

Nanni A., Groenewegen M. A. T., Aringer B., et al. 2019, MNRAS, 487, 502

Nenkova M., Ivezic Z., Elitzur M., 1999, LPICo, 20, LPICo.969

Palla M., Calura F., Matteucci F., Fan X. L., Vincenzo F., Lacchin E., 2020, MNRAS, 494, 2355

Palla M., De Looze I., Relaño M., van der Giessen S., Dayal P., Ferrara A., Schneider R., et al., 2023, arXiv, arXiv:2311.16071.

Reid W. A., 2014, MNRAS, 438, 2642 Riebel D., Srinivasan S., Sargent B., Meixner M., 2012, ApJ, 753, 71

Romano D., Matteucci F., Zhang Z.-Y., Ivison R. J., Ventura P., 2019, MNRAS, 490, 2838

Scalo J. M., Despain K. H., Ulrich R. K., 1975, ApJ, 196, 805

Schneider R., Valiante R., Ventura P., et al. 2014, MNRAS, 442, 1440

Schneider R., Maiolino R., 2023, arXiv, arXiv:2310.00053

Shaw R. A., Stanghellini L., Mutchler M., Balick B., Blades J. C., 2001, ApJ, 548, 727.

Stanghellini L., Shaw R. A., Gilmore D., 2005, ApJ, 622, 294

Stanghellini L., García-Lario P., García-Hernández D. A., Perea-Calderón J. V., Davies J. E., Manchado A., Villaver E., et al., 2007, ApJ, 671, 1669

Tosi S., Dell'Agli F., Kamath D., Ventura P., Van Winckel H., Marini E., 2022, A&A, 668, A22

Tosi S., Kamath D., Dell'Agli F., Van Winckel H., Ventura P., Marchetti T., Marini E., et al., 2023, A&A, 673, A41
Ventura P., Zeppieri A., Mazzitelli I., D'Antona F. 1998, A&A, 334, 953
Ventura P., Di Criscienzo M., Schneider R., et al. 2012, MNRAS, 420, 1442
Ventura P., Dell'Agli F., Schneider R., et al. 2014, MNRAS, 439, 977
Ventura P., Stanghellini L., Dell'Agli F., García-Hernández D. A., Di Criscienzo M., 2015, MNRAS, 452, 3679
Ventura P., Stanghellini L., Di Criscienzo M., García-Hernández D. A., Dell'Agli F., 2016, MNRAS, 460, 3940
Ventura P., Stanghellini L., Dell'Agli F., García-Hernández D. A., 2017, MNRAS, 471, 4648.
Ventura P., Marini E., Tosi S., Dell'Agli F., 2020, Univ, 6, 223
Ventura P., Dell'Agli F., Tailo M., Castellani M., Marini E., Tosi S., Di Criscienzo M., 2022, Univ, 8, 45
Vincenzo F., Belfiore F., Maiolino R., Matteucci F., Ventura P., 2016, MNRAS, 458, 3466

Planetary Nebulae: A Universal Toolbox in the Era of Precision Astrophysics
Proceedings IAU Symposium No. 384, 2025
O. De Marco, A. Zijlstra & R. Szczerba, eds.
doi:10.1017/S1743921324000048

Deep radio observations of (proto-) planetary nebulae

Teresa Huertas-Roldán[1,2], **D. Aníbal García-Hernández**[1,2], **José Jairo Díaz-Luis**[3], **Javier Alcolea**[3], **Daniel Tafoya**[4], **Ransel Barzaga**[1,2], **Arturo Manchado**[5], **Marco A. Gómez-Muñoz**[1,2] **and Valentín Bujarrabal**[3]

[1]Instituto de Astrofísica de Canarias (IAC), C/ Vía Láctea s/n, E-38205 La Laguna, Spain
email: thuertas@iac.es

[2]Departamento de Astrofísica, Universidad de La Laguna (ULL), E-38206 La Laguna, Spain

[3]Observatorio Astronómico Nacional (OAN), C/ Alfonso XII 3, E-28014 Madrid, Spain

[4]Department of Space, Earth and Environment, Chalmers University of Technology, Onsala Space Observatory, 439 92 Onsala, Sweden

[5]Consejo Superior de Investigaciones Científicas (CSIC), Spain

Abstract. Planetary nebulae (PNe) are known to be extreme radiation environments. However, these extreme conditions do not preclude the presence of different types of molecules. PNe appear as unique laboratories where atoms and simple and complex molecules, including radicals and ions, coexist. Our recent high-resolution radio observations of the C-rich PNe IC 418 and NGC 7027 and proto-PN (pPN) IRAS 22272+5435 have provided us with a precise database of the molecular content of these three objects. In our aim to study the organic molecules in the radio domain, we have found very deep radio recombination lines (RRLs) of neutral and ionized atoms never observed before. These new detected RRLs, along with the molecular content, will give information on the evolutionary state of the sources, as well as the chemical reactions taking place in such complex astrophysical environments.

Keywords. planetary nebulae, astrochemistry, ISM: molecules, radio astronomy

1. Introduction

The observation of astronomical sources, such as evolved stars or molecular clouds, in the radio range allows the unambiguous detection of very different molecules (both organic and inorganic) with significant dipolar moment. In particular, radio observations of circumstellar envelopes (CSEs) around asymptotic giant branch (AGB) stars and (proto-) planetary nebulae (pPNe and PNe) are crucial to analyse these circumstellar environments and to understand the key chemical processes that take place during the evolution of the central star from the AGB to the PN phase. A lot of work has been already done since the first molecule, CH, was detected in 1937 (Dunham 1937; Swings and Rosenfeld 1937; McKellar 1940). Up to date, the number of molecular detections in different astrophysical environments rise to ∼240 (see e.g. McGuire 2022, for a recent review). However, even though the current list of molecules detected in space is quite large, sometimes the exact chemical pathways necessary to produce each species remain unclear: this is the case of fullerenes. In order to drive the field forward, more molecular species (e.g. key molecular by-products or precursors) need to be detected. Such key possible molecular species may have remained undetected because of their weak rotational transitions, caused by their low abundances or low dipolar moment values.

In this context, deep radio observations, whose main characteristic is the use of very large dishes and long exposure times, are essential to detect weak rotational transitions of the possible key molecular species. The great noise reduction in deep radio spectra may reveal new weak features that have remained undetected by previous radio observations, allowing the astronomers to detect new key chemical species in space. Here we present a preliminary analysis of deep radio observations of three C-rich evolved stars: the PNe IC 418 and NGC 7027 and the pPN IRAS 22272+5435. In our search for new weak molecular features, we have found very deep radio recombination lines (RRLs) of neutral and ionized atoms never observed before.

2. Observations

We have observed three C-rich (p)PNe: IRAS 22272+5435, NGC 7027 and IC 418. Even though all the sources have a similar chemical composition, the different progenitor masses, morphologies and the time passed since they left the AGB phase have led them to a different evolutionary and chemical state. By comparing them we will be able to analyse the chemical evolution of C-rich CSEs throughout the post-AGB phase and beyond.

The extensively studied post-AGB or pPN IRAS 22272+5435 is an elliptical envelope around an evolved star with a relatively cold G-type central star. It is known for its rich content in small C-based molecules, so it has been chosen in our study to help us to identify spectral emission lines in the other two more evolved sources. NGC 7027 is a bipolar/multipolar PN, possibly hosting a central binary system (e.g. Moraga Baez et al. 2023) with a central star effective temperature, $T_{\rm eff}$, of $\sim$200 000 K. The PN IC 418 displays an elliptical morphology and has a central star much cooler ($T_{\rm eff} \sim$ 30 000 K) than NGC 7027 (e.g. González-Santamaría et al. 2021).

These deep radio data were obtained using the Yebes-40m and the IRAM-30m antennas. In both radio telescopes the observations were carried out during the winter semester and under really good weather conditions. The radio spectra were collected at 2 mm, 3 mm and 7 mm with a sensitivity measured in antenna temperature of $\sim$1 mK [T_a^*] for a spectral resolution of 2.5 km/s. For data reduction, the GILDAS-CLASS software package† was used. The final spectra are obtained in corrected main beam temperature ($T_{\rm mb}$).

3. Results

The three (p)PNe observed had been previously analysed in the infrared (IR) domain. IRAS 22272+5435 and NGC 7027 are known to contain both aliphatic and aromatic molecular species as well as broad and discrete unidentified infrared bands (UIRs) (e.g. Beintema et al. 1996). Indeed, the still unidentified 21 μm feature, usually observed in post-AGB stars, is clearly visible in the pPN IRAS 22272+5435 (see e.g. Zhang 2020, and references therein). Furthermore, the IR spectrum of the PN IC 418 displays aliphatic and aromatic molecular bands (and other UIRs) in conjunction with the IR bands of fullerenes (more precisely, C_{60}) (Otsuka et al. 2014).

Previous studies at radio frequencies show a rich molecular content in IRAS 22272+5435 (sensitivity of $\sim$5 mK; Zhang 2020) and NGC 7027 (sensitivity $<$ 8 mK; Zhang et al. 2008), with small organic species such as C_2H, $H^{13}CN$ or HCO^+ (see some examples in Fig. 1a, 1b), among others. To our best knowledge, the PN IC 418

† GILDAS is a radio astronomy software developed by IRAM. See `https://www.iram.fr/IRAMFR/GILDAS/`

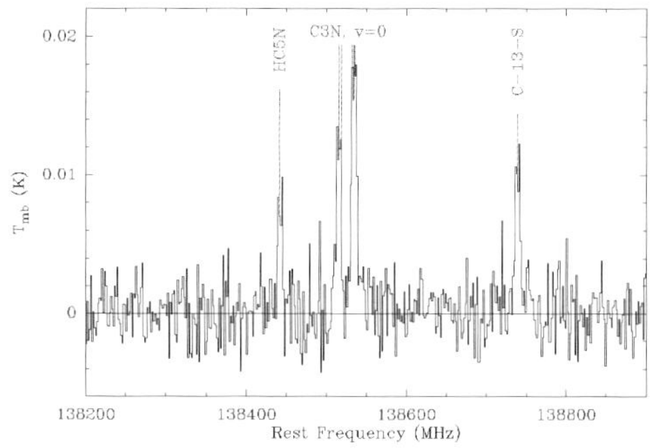

(a) IRAS 22272+5435

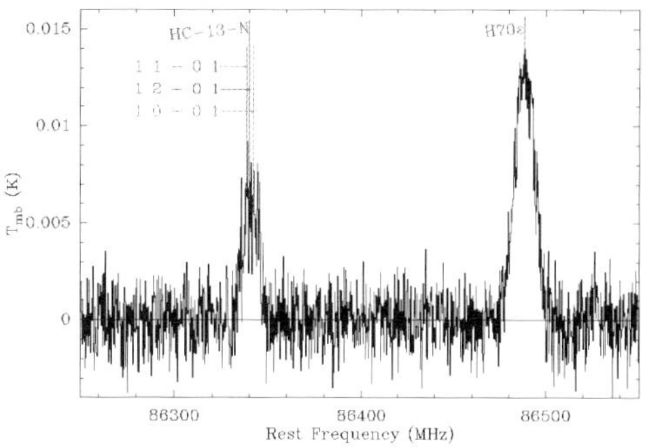

(b) NGC 7027

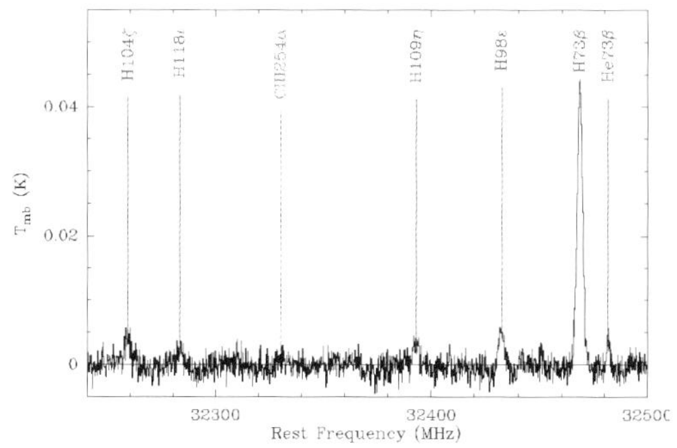

(c) IC 418

Figure 1. Examples of the several radio emission features detected towards our sample of (p)PNe. Panel 1a: rotational transitions of small organic molecules (e.g. HC_5N, C_3N, ^{13}CS) in the pPN IRAS 22272+5435. Panel 1b: hyperfine structure transitions of $H^{13}CN$ and an intense deep RRL ($\Delta n = 5$) in the PN NGC 7027. Panel 1c: deep RRLs of neutral/ionised species of H, He and C.

has not been so well studied in comparison with the other two sources. Narrow-band Very Large Array (VLA) radio observations centered at ~ 14.7 GHz and ~ 4.8 GHz with a resolution of 8 and 12 km/s, respectively, showed the detection of the RRLs H76α and H110α (Garay et al. 1989). A subsequent study with the NRAO 10 m radio telescope on Kitt Peak found that the spectrum of IC 418 is dominated by hydrogen RRLs and reported non detection of both J=1–0 and 2–1 of ^{12}CO (Dayal and Bieging 1996). The most recent study was carried out in the small $\sim 8.2 - 9.0$ GHz range with a rms noise of $\sim 0.3 - 2.3$ mK using the Deep Space Station 63 (DSS-63) single dish, showing the detection of a weak $^3He^+$ emission line and some RRLs in conjunction with the lack of rotational transitions from small organic molecules like those mentioned above (Guzman-Ramirez et al. 2016). These are just three examples manifesting the peculiar fact that IC 418, at radio frequencies, only seems to display strong RRLs and no molecular content in spite of the large abundance of much complex C-compounds as explained before.

Our deep radio observations confirm the presence of the already detected small organic molecules in IRAS 22272+5435 and NGC 7027, which are listed in previous radio line surveys (see e.g. Zhang et al. 2008; Zhang 2020) but allow us, e.g. the observation of some transitions corresponding to the hyperfine structure of those molecules. Moreover, we confirm the complete absence of well known (i.e. already detected in space) small organic molecules in IC 418. Our very deep radio observations reveal also another surprising result in both PNe. The significant reduction of the rms allows us to observe, for the first

Table 1. List of RRLs observed in PNe IC 418 and NGC 7027 with each antenna.

	NGC 7027		IC 418	
Status	Yebes-40m	IRAM-30m	Yebes-40m	IRAM-30m
Detections	Hα - Hδ	Hα - Hθ	Hα - Hθ	Hα - Hλ
	Heα - Heβ	Heα - Heβ	Heα - Heβ	Heα - Heγ
	3HeIIα	3HeIIα	-	-
	HeIIα	HeIIα - HeIIβ	-	
Tentatives	Heϵ	Hι - Hκ	Hι	Hμ
	Heγ	Heγ	Heγ	Heδ
	Cα	Cα	-	-
	-	3HeIIβ	-	-
	HeIIβ	HeIIγ - HeIIδ	-	-
Doubtfulls	Hζ - Hθ	Hλ	Hκ	Hν
	-	Heδ - Heϵ	-	-
	-	3HeIIγ - 3HeIIδ	-	-
	-	HeIIϵ	-	-
	CIIIα/OIIIα - CIIIβ/OIIIβ	CIIIα/OIIIα - CIIIβ/OIIIβ	CIIIα/OIIIα - CIIIβ/OIIIβ	-

time, very deep (i.e. the difference between the upper and the lower electronic level is $\Delta n > 4$) RRLs of neutral and ionised H, He, C-O† in NGC 7027 and IC 418. Table 1 lists the RRLs detected in both PNe with the Yebes-40m and IRAM-30m antennas (~ 120 and ~ 160 RRLs in NGC 7027 and IC 418, respectively); RRLs tentatively detected as well as doutbfull RRLs are also listed (see also Fig. 1 panels 1b and 1c).

Finally, we detect a small number of unidentified features (UFs) in both PNe but the number of UFs in IC 418, curiously a C_{60}-rich PN, is higher than in NGC 7027 (a non C_{60}-rich PN). The UFs appear in the spectra as single and well-defined weak lines (whose frequencies do not match with any well known molecular frequency) or as weak contributions to some RRLs.

4. Conclusions and work in progress

Our deep radio observations show that, even if the sources are all C-rich, their organic chemistry inventory is quite different. The pPN IRAS 22272+5435 is the only source with small organic molecules and no RRLs neither UFs, as expected. However, we found that PN IC 418 does not contain any well known organic molecule but many RRLs and various UFs. The spectrum of PN NGC 7027 is the richest one, showing many RRLs, molecular emission lines of well known small organic species and just a few UFs.

The different results found in PN IC 418 and PN NGC 7027 could be related with their different morphologies and central star temperatures (e.g. their radiative environments). The failed search for well known C-based molecules in PN IC 418 along with the detection of tens of RRLs may be a consequence of its elliptical shape. Due to the absence of shielding structures (such as a dusty torus) around the central star, the UV radiation coming from the expanding ionised front could easily have destroyed the molecules formed during the previous AGB and post-AGB phases. In addition, the PN NGC 7027, even hosting a much hotter central star ($T_{\rm eff} \sim 200\,000$ K), has a richer molecular content combined with a complex bipolar/multipolar morphology. Similar bipolar/multipolar sources, like the pPN IRAS 16594-4656, show a dusty equatorial torus (e.g. García-Hernández et al. 2006) that could protect the molecules from being destroyed by the UV radiation. Several studies (e.g. Nakashima et al. 2010; Moraga Baez et al. 2023) confirm the presence of a dusty equatorial belt and a X-ray dominated region (XDR) where the synthesis of molecules such as HCO^+ is favoured (Bublitz et al. 2023). Therefore, such shielding

† Our high resolution is not enough to resolve the C and O radio spectral lines, so we observe a wide emission line formed by both C and O atoms.

structures and radiative processes could protect and/or enhance the production of some organic molecules.

Other options to have in mind could be the evolution velocity of the PN or the density of the medium. We could be comparing two PNe of a similar age, but one of then could have reached a more evolved phase more rapidly than the other. The more evolved one, in this case IC 418, would be completely ionised. Hence, it would be imposible to detect molecules there because all of them would have been destroyed by the extreme radiation. Differences in the density of the medium could act also as shielding areas in which molecules could be protected. A denser medium or area could block (totally or partially) the central star's radiation and hinder its journey accross the nebula.

Remarkably, most of the UFs detected in PN IC 418 are not present in PN NGC 7027. This fact suggests that these unidentified radio emission lines could be produced by molecules not present in PN NGC 7027. It is well known that the IR spectrum of PN IC 418 displays the C_{60} emission features. Therefore, it is tempting to think that most of these UFs could be originated by C_{60} derivatives or other complex species with a strong dipolar moment, which could be present in IC 418 and absent in NGC 7027.

The next steps are focused on the confirmation of the detection of all the weak RRLs observed in the spectra. For this, specific radiative transfer models, considering the spontaneous emission for each RRL and the main physical characteristics of each source are needed. After this analysis, more UFs are expected to appear, providing us with a larger UF database. We expect that after a comparison of the database of confirmed UFs with experimental rotational spectra and theoretical predictions of complex C-based molecules, we will be able to unambiguously identify such emission lines with specific, likely bigger, organic molecules. Our deep radio observations and potential results may be crucial to find the key molecular species that would help to understand the chemical pathways taking place in circumstellar environments as well as to answer the question of why similar sources have drastically different molecular inventories. However, more laboratory and theoretical efforts are clearly needed to have a better database of both experimental and theoretical rotational spectra of large and complex organic species.

Acknowledgements

THR, DAGH, RB, AM and MAGM acknowledge the support from the State Research Agency (AEI) of the Spanish Ministry of Science and Innovation (MCIN) under grant PID2020-115758GB-I00. THR acknowledges support from grant PID2020-115758GB-I00/PRE2021-100042 financed by MCIN/AEI/10.13039/501100011033 and the European Social Fund Plus (ESF+). JA, VB and, JJDL acknowledge the support from the State Research Agency (AEI) of the Spanish Ministry of Science and Innovation (MCIN) grant 10.13039/501100011033, under project PID2019-105203GB-C21. This publication is based upon work from COST Action CA21126 - Carbon molecular nanostructures in space (NanoSpace), supported by COST (European Cooperation in Science and Technology).

References

Beintema, D. A., van den Ancker, M. E., Molster, F. J., Waters, L. B. F. M., Tielens, A. G. G. M., Waelkens, C., de Jong, T., de Graauw, T., Justtanont, K., Yamamura, I., Heras, A., Lahuis, F., & Salama, A. 1996, The rich spectrum of circumstellar pahs. *A&A*, 315, L369–L372.

Bublitz, J., Kastner, J. H., Hily-Blant, P., Forveille, T., Santander-García, M., Alcolea, J., Bujarrabal, V., Wilner, D. J., Montez, R., & Aleman, I. 2023, Mapping NGC 7027 in new light: CO^+ and HCO^+ emission reveal its photon- and X-ray-dominated regions. *ApJ*, 942(1), 14.

Dayal, A. & Bieging, J. H. 1996, Millimeter-wave observations of CO in planetary nebulae. *ApJ*, 472, 703.

Dunham, T., J. 1937, Interstellar neutral potassium and neutral calcium. *PASP*, 49(287), 26–28.

Garay, G., Gathier, R., & Rodriguez, L. F. 1989, Radio recombination line observations of compact planetary nebulae. *A&A*, 215(1), 101–112.

García-Hernández, D. A., Manchado, A., García-Lario, P., Cañete, A. B., Acosta-Pulido, J. A., & García, A. M. 2006, Revealing the mid-infrared emission structure of IRAS 16594-4656 and IRAS 07027-7934. *ApJ*, 640(2), 829–841.

González-Santamaría, I., Manteiga, M., Manchado, A., Ulla, A., Dafonte, C., & López Varela, P. 2021, Planetary nebulae in Gaia EDR3: Central star identification, properties, and binarity. *A&A*, 656, A51.

Guzman-Ramirez, L., Rizzo, J. R., Zijlstra, A. A., García-Miró, C., Morisset, C., & Gray, M. D. 2016, First detection of $^3He^+$ in the planetary nebula IC 418. *MNRAS*, 460(1), L35–L39.

McGuire, B. A. 2022, 2021 census of insterstellar, circumstellar, extragalactic, protoplanetary disk, and exoplanetary moleculess. *ApJS*, 259(2), 30.

McKellar, A. 1940, Evidence for the molecular origin of some hitherto unidentified interstellar lines. *PASP*, 52(307), 187.

Moraga Baez, P., Kastner, J. H., Balick, B., Montez, R., & Bublitz, J. 2023, Panchromatic HST/WFC3 imaging studies of young, rapidly evolving planetary nebulae. II. NGC 7027. *ApJ*, 942(1), 15.

Nakashima, J.-i., Kwok, S., Zhang, Y., & Koning, N. 2010, Three-dimensional structure of the central region of NGC 7027: A quest for trails of high-velocity jets. *AJ*, 140(2), 490–499.

Otsuka, M., Kemper, F., Cami, J., Peeters, E., & Bernard-Salas, J. 2014, Physical properties of fullerene-containing galactic planetary nebulae. *MNRAS*, 437(3), 2577–2593.

Swings, P. & Rosenfeld, L. 1937, Considerations regarding interstellar molecules. *ApJ*, 86, 483–486.

Zhang, Y. 2020, Molecular gas in 21 and 30 μm sources: The 2 mm and 1.3 mm spectra of IRAS 21318+5631 and 22272+5435. *ApJ*, 898(2), 151.

Zhang, Y., Kwok, S., & Dinh-V-Trung 2008, A spectral line survey of NGC 7027 at millimeter wavelengths. *ApJ*, 678(1), 328–346.

Planetary Nebulae: A Universal Toolbox in the Era of Precision Astrophysics
Proceedings IAU Symposium No. 384, 2025
O. De Marco, A. Zijlstra & R. Szczerba, eds.
doi:10.1017/S1743921325000912

Synthesis of Complex Organics in Planetary Nebulae

Sun Kwok[1,2], SeyedAbdolreza Sadjadi[2] and Yong Zhang[2,3]

[1]Department of Earth, Ocean and Atmospheric Sciences, University of British Columbia, Vancouver, Canada

[2]Laboratory for Space Research, The University of Hong Kong, Hong Kong, China

[3]School of Physics & Astronomy, Sun Yat Sen University, Zhuhai, China
email: `sunkwok@hku.hk`

Abstract. A family of unidentified infrared emission (UIE) bands is widely observed in planetary nebulae. We suggest that the carriers of the UIE bands are mixed aromatic/aliphatic organic nanoparticles (MAONs) synthesized over thousand-year time scales in the nebulae. The possible chemical pathways of synthesis is discussed. These organics are ejected into the interstellar medium and could have enriched the primordial Solar System, leading to the reservoir of complex organics in comets, asteroids, planetary satellites, and interplanetary dust particles.

Keywords. stars: AGB and post-AGB, ISM: molecules, planetary nebulae: general

1. Introduction

Planetary nebulae (PNe) have long been recognized as sources of heavy element enrichment of the Galaxy. Advances in infrared and millimeter-wave astronomical spectroscopy have led to the realization that PNe are also major distributors of molecules and solids in the interstellar medium. Gas-phase molecules and various inorganic solids such as silicates, silicon carbide, and refractory oxides have been detected in the circumstellar envelopes of asymptotic giant branch (AGB) stars, the immediate progenitors of planetary nebulae. In spite of the very low density conditions, molecules and solids are formed in the circumstellar environment over very short ($\sim 10^3$ yr) time scales (Kwok 2004).

The discovery of complex organics in PNe was totally unexpected. A family of unidentified infrared emission (UIE) bands at 3.3, 6.2, 7.7, 8.6, and 11.3 μm, superimposed on an underlying continuum, was first detected in the young planetary nebula NGC 7027 (Russell, Soifer, & Willner 1977). Soon after the discovery, the 3.3 μm feature was identified by Roger Knacke as due to C–H stretching mode of aromatic compounds (Knacke 1977). This would be the first identification of organic compounds in an astronomical source, but the interpretation was not accepted at the time.

The UIE bands have since been detected in many PNe, as well as in reflection nebulae, diffuse interstellar medium, and external galaxies. In some active galaxies, the amount of energy emitted in the UIE bands can be as high as 20% of the total energy output of the galaxy (Smith et al. 2007). Since the carrier is synthesized in situ, PNe are the best objects to study their origins. While the UIE bands are strong in young PNe, they are not seen in AGB stars. The best way to determine when the carriers of the UIE bands are synthesized is to study proto-planetary nebulae (PPNe), the missing link between AGB and PNe. After the discovery of about 30 PPNe (Hrivnak, Kwok, & Volk 1989; Kwok 1993), we proceeded to take infrared spectroscopy of these objects. In addition to the UIE bands, the 3.4 μm feature (identified as C–H stretching mode of aliphatic compounds) were found in the spectra of PPNe (Geballe et al. 1992; Hrivnak et al. 2007). Also found were broad plateau emission features around 8 and 12 μm (Kwok, Volk, & Hrivnak 1999), which we proposed as the result of superpositions of in-plane and out-of-plane bending modes of aliphatic compounds (Kwok, Volk, & Bernath 2001).

Subsequent observations, especially by the *Infrared Space Observatory (ISO)* and *Spitzer* telescopes show that the UIE phenomenon consists of major emission features at 3.3, 6.2, 7.7, 8.6, and 11.3 μm, minor emission features at 3.4, 6.9, 12.1, 12.4, 12.7, 13.3, 15.8, 16.4, 17.4, 17.8, and 18.9 μm and strong, broad emission plateaus features at $6-9$, $10-15$, and $15-20$ μm. The 3.3 and 11.3 μm features are generally attributed to C–H stretching and C–H out-of-plane bending modes of aromatic compounds, and the 3.4 and 6.9 μm attributed to C–H stretching and bending modes of aliphatic compounds (Duley & Williams 1981). The origin of the strong features at 6.2, 7.7, 8.6 μm features is less clear, and are possibly due to coupled vibrational modes of complex organics. A successful model must be able to explain all these properties. The key question is: what is the chemical structure of the carrier?

2. The PAH hypothesis

After the development of millimeter-wave astronomy and the wide detection of molecules through their rotational transitions, the polycyclic aromatic hydrocarbon (PAH) molecules became the most popular hypothesis for the UIE phenomenon. In the PAH hypothesis, the UIE features are the result of infrared fluorescence from small (~ 50 C atoms) gas-phase PAH molecules being pumped by far-ultraviolet photons, However, the PAH hypothesis has a number of problems. PAH molecules are primarily excited by UV with little absorption in the visible, but UIE features are seen in PPNe and reflection nebulae with no UV background radiation. The predicted strong and narrow electronic transitions of PAH molecules in the UV are not seen in interstellar extinction curves. The upper limits of PAH/H of $10^{-10} - 10^{-8}$ derived from UV absorption spectroscopy are orders of magnitude lower than the abundance needed to account for the infrared bands (Clayton et al. 2003; Salama et al. 2011; Gredel et al. 2011). PAH molecules are well studied in the laboratory by chemists (Schlemmer et al. 1994; Cook et al. 1996; Cook & Saykally 1998), who found "No PAH emission spectrum has been able to reproduce the UIE spectrum w.r.t. either band positions or relative intensities" (Wagner, Kim, & Saykally 2000). The PAH model predicts that the UIE band ratios are strongly dependent on the UV background as individual UIE bands are assumed to arise from different neutral or ionized PAHs (Hudgins and Allamandola 2004; Draine et al. 2011), but the profiles and peak wavelengths of UIE bands are found to be independent of temperature of exciting star (Uchida et al. 2000).

The initial identification of the PAH model was based on the 3.3 and 11.3 μm features but there are no obvious counterparts in PAH molecules for the 6.2, 7.7, and 8.6 μm features. To quote Cook & Saykally (1998): "In order to reproduce the narrow 6.2 and 11.2 μm UIR bands, the carriers must consistently exhibit bands at these positions with a consistency similar to that which is observed with the 3.3 μm emission. In addition, the carriers of the UIRs must, in general, exhibit an absence of strong bands in the gap between the 6.2 and 7.7 μm UIR features. The PAHs used in these model spectra simply do not meet these criteria; hence they do not reproduce the details of the UIR spectra". Based on a comparison between the astronomical UIE spectra with the laboratory spectrum of coronene, Léger and Puget (1984) assign the 6.2 μm band to C–C stretch and the 8.6 μm to C–H in-plane bending mode of PAH molecules. Peeters (2011) assigns the infrared bands between 6.1 and 6.5 μm to pure aromatic C–C stretching modes, bands from 6.5 to 8.5 μm to coupled C–C stretching and C–H in-plane bending modes, and bands between 8.3 to 8.9 μm to C–H in-plane bending modes. However, all C–C stretching modes are very weak in comparison to the C–H modes in neutral PAH molecules. In order to explain the prominence of the features, PAH ions are suggested to be responsible for the UIE features in the 6−9 μm region Hudgins and Allamandola (2004).

In part to address the above list of problems, the PAH hypothesis has been revised to incorporate different ionization states and large sizes to increase the absorption cross sections in the visible. The molecular size range has been extended to >1,000 atoms (Peeters et al. 2021). The PAH molecules are also modified to include dehydrogenation, superhydrogenation, and minor aliphatic side groups (Li & Draine 2012). Heteroatoms (defined as those atoms other than C or H) such as N are also introduced to explain the 6.2 μm band (Hudgins & Allamandola 1999).

By using the NASA Ames PAH database and fitting routines (Boersma et al. 2014), the PAH model can fit astronomical observations by including a mixture of PAH of different sizes, structures (compact, linear, branched) and ionization states, as well as artificial broad intrinsic line profiles. However, the number of free parameters in these fits is so large that this procedure has been shown to be able to fit any artificial spectra (Zhang & Kwok 2015).

3. Mixed aromatic/aliphatic organic nanoparticles as carriers of the UIE bands

Amorphous organic solids are often the natural results of combustion. When a mixture of hydrocarbon gases is subjected to energy injection (laser ablation/pyrolysis, electric discharge, photolysis, radio waves), the evaporated condensates collected in cooled substrates are often amorphous carbonaceous compounds. The infrared spectra of these laboratory-synthesized organics show general similarities to the astronomical UIE spectra (Dischler et al. 1983; Herlin et al. 1998) (Figure 1). A recent experiment designed to simulate molecular and solid synthesis in circumstellar low-temperature and low-density conditions yielded the production of simple molecules such as acetylene and ethylene, as well as carbonaceous solids such as amorphous carbon nanograins and aliphatic carbon clusters (Martinez et al. 2020).

As an alternative to the PAH hypothesis, a mixed aromatic-aliphatic model (MAON) has been proposed (Kwok & Zhang 2011, 2013). MAONs consist of small units of aromatic rings linked by aliphatic chains, as well as heteroatoms such as O, N, and S. A typical nanoparticle may contain multiple of structures shown in Figure 2.

As the vibrational spectra of complex organics are not known, we have made initial studies to identify the vibrational mode of all major bands using quantum chemistry techniques. We start with PAH molecules with aliphatic side groups (Sadjadi, Zhang, & Kwok 2015) and proceed to study the nature of the 3.3/3.4, 6.2, and 11.3 μm UIE bands (Sadjadi, Zhang, & Kwok 2015; Hsia et al. 2016; Sadjadi, Zhang, & Kwok 2017). From the study of a small number of MAON-like molecules, we find that many spectral bands are due to coupled vibrational modes and their origin is not straight forward to interpret (Sadjadi, Kwok, & Zhang 2016). Further work is needed to explore the spectral properties of MAON-like molecules.

4. PAH vs MAON

There are fundamental differences between the chemical structures of PAHs and MAONs and these distinctions are not just semantics. For example, is the carrier of UIE free-flying molecules or solids? Is the carrier purely aromatic or has a mixed sp^2/sp^3 structure? Is the geometry two or three dimensional? Is the carrier small (< 50 C) or large ($\sim 10^3$ C)? Does it consist of pure C and H or does it also contain impurities? Is

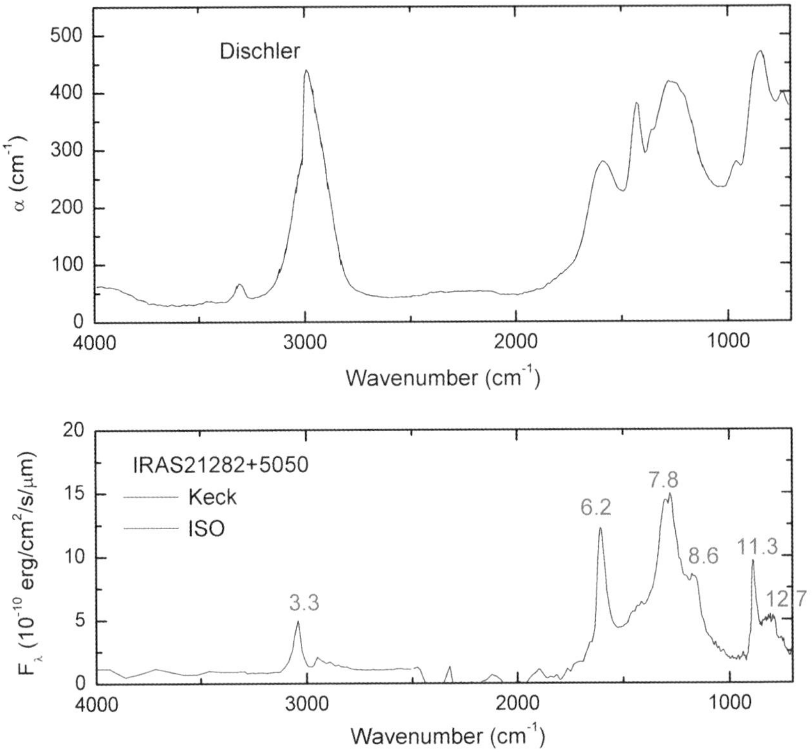

Figure 1. Laboratory infrared spectra of hydrogenated amorphous carbon (top, Dischler et al. 1983) compared to the astronomical spectrum of the planetary nebula IRAS 21282+5050 (bottom panel). The UIE bands are labeled by their wavelengths in μm.

the structure made of pure rings or with a variety of functional side groups? Is the chemical structure regular with repeatable patterns or amorphous with aromatic islands with variable sizes and aliphatic chains with random length and orientations? We hope with time that these distinctions will be clarified and the carrier of the UIE bands identified.

5. Circumstellar synthesis of complex organics

Acetylene (C_2H_2) is commonly detected in evolved carbon stars through its ν_5 fundamental band at 13.7 μm (Volk, Xiong, & Kwok 2000). Polymerization of C_2H_2 leads to the formation of diacetylene (C_4H_2) and triacetylene (C_6H_2) in PPNe, culminating in the formation of benzene (C_6H_6). During the PPNe phase, benzene molecules are clustered together to form islands of aromatic rings. Various aliphatic side groups (CH_2, CH_3, $(CH_3)_2$, $C(CH_3)_3$....) are attached to the peripheral of the rings, linking the aromatic islands together with aliphatic bridges. With the onset of photoionization during the PNe phase, there could be a loss of peripheral H and progressive formation of larger clusters into MAONs.

6. Implications

PPNe, PNe, and novae are the only astronomical objects that we have direct observations of organic synthesis. As chemical synthesis takes place in an expanding circumstellar envelope, the time scale of synthesis is limited by the dynamical timescale of expansion. In PPNe and PNe, chemical evolution leading to complex organic compounds is observed to take place over only a few thousand years. If complex organics are routinely made by

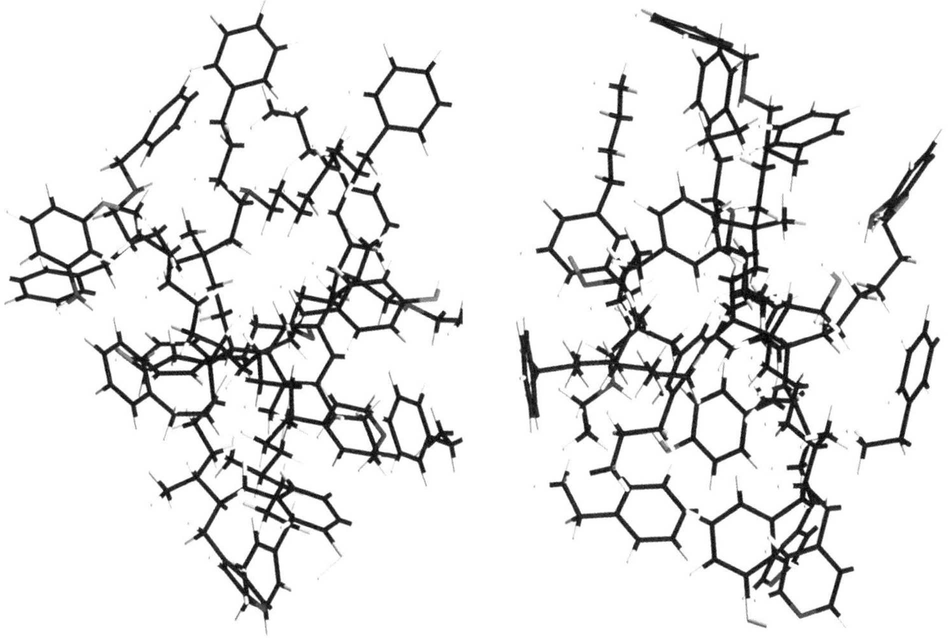

Figure 2. Two views of the molecule $C_{169}H_{225}N_7O_4S_3$. The MAON structure is characterized by a highly disorganized arrangement of small units of aromatic rings linked by aliphatic chains. The C atoms are shown in black, H atoms in white, O in red, N in blue, and S in yellow. A typical MAON particle may consist of multiple structures similar to this one.

old ordinary Sun-like stars and distributed throughout the Galaxy by PNe, these stellar organics may have spread throughout the Galaxy and have even possibly enriched the primordial Solar System. The fact that macro-organics with MAON-like structures have been identified in meteorites, comets, interplantary dust particles, and planetary satellites suggests that there may be a stellar-Solar System connection (Kwok 2016). It is also plausible that the early Earth may have inherited some of these stellar organics (Kwok 2017). The possible role of stellar organics on the origin of life on Earth represents a fascinating topic for future investigations.

Acknowledgment

We thank Ryszard Szczerba and the Local Organizing Committee for organizing a wonderful conference. This work is supported by a grant from the Natural Sciences and Engineering Research Council of Canada.

References

Boersma, C., Bauschlicher, C. W., Jr., Ricca, A., et al. 2014, *ApJS*, 211, 8
Clayton, G. C., Gordon, K. D., Salama, F., et al. 2003, *ApJ*, 592, 947
Cook, D. J., & Saykally, R. J. 1998, *ApJ*, 493, 793
Cook, D. J., Schlemmer, S., Balucani, N., et al. 1996, *Nature*, 380, 227
Dischler, B., Bubenzer, A., & Koidl, P. 1983, *Solid State Commun*, 48, 105
Draine, B. T., Li, A., Hensley, B. S., et al. 2021, *ApJ*, 917, 3
Duley, W. W., Williams, D. A. 1981, *Mon. Not. R. Astron. Soc.* 196, 269
Geballe, T. R., Tielens, A. G. G. M., Kwok, S., Hrivnak, B. J. 1992, *ApJ*, 387, L89
Gredel, R., Carpentier, Y., Rouillé, G., et al. 2011, *A&A*, 530, 26
Herlin, N., Bohn, I., Reynaud, C., et al. 1998, *A&A*, 330, 1127

Hrivnak, B. J., Kwok, S., & Volk, K. M. 1989, *ApJ*, 346, 265
Hrivnak, B. J., Geballe, T. R., Kwok, S. 2007, *ApJ*, 662, 1059
Hsia, C. H., Sadjadi, S., Zhang, Y., Kwok, S. 2016, *ApJ*, 832, 213
Hudgins, D. M., & Allamandola, L. J. 1999, *ApJ*, 513, L69
Hudgins, D. and Allamandola, L. J. 2004, in Astrophysics of Dust, Witt, A. N., Clayton, G. C., and Draine, B. T. (eds.), ASP Conf. Ser. vol. 309, p. 665
Knacke, R. F. 1977, *Nature*, 269, 132
Kwok, S. 1993, *Ann. Rev. Astr. Ap.*, 31, 63
Kwok, S. 2004, *Nature*, 430, 985
Kwok, S. 2016, *Astr. Ap. Rev.*, 24, 8
Kwok, S. 2017, *Nature Astronomy*, 1, 642
Kwok, S., Volk, K., & Bernath, P. 2001, *ApJ*, 554, L87
Kwok, S., Volk, K., & Hrivnak, B. J. 1999, *A&A*, 350, L35
Kwok, S., & Zhang, Y. 2011, *Nature*, 479, 80
Kwok, S., & Zhang, Y. 2013, *ApJ*, 771, 5
Léger, A., Puget, J. L. 1984, *A&A*, 137, L5
Li, A., and Draine, B. T. 2012, *ApJ*, 760, L35
Martínez, L., Santoro, G., Merino, P., et al. 2020, *Nature Astronomy*, 4, 97
Peeters, E. 2011, in *IAU Symposium 280 The Molecular Universe*, Cernicharo, J. & Bachiller, R. (eds), CUP, p. 149
Peeters, E., Mackie, C., Candian, A., Tielens, A. G. G. M. 2021, *Acc. Chem. Res.*, 54, 1921
Russell, R. W., Soifer, B. T., & Willner, S. P. 1977, *ApJ*, 217, L149
Sadjadi, S., Kwok, S., Zhang, Y. 2016, *IOP J. Phys. Conf. Ser. 728*, 062003
Sadjadi, S., Zhang, Y., & Kwok, S. 2015 *ApJ*, 801, 34
Sadjadi, S., Zhang, Y., & Kwok, S. 2017 *ApJ*, 845, 123
Salama, F., Galazutdinov, G.A., Krelowski, J., et al. 2011, *ApJ*, 728, 154
Schlemmer, S., Cook, D., Harrison, J., et al. 1994, *Science*, 265, 1686
Smith, J. D. T., Draine, B. T., Dale, D. A., et al. 2007, *ApJ*, 656, 770
Uchida, K. I., Sellgren, K., Werner, M. W., & Houdashelt, M. L. 2000, *ApJ*, 530, 817
Volk, K., Xiong, G.-Z., & Kwok, S. 2000, *ApJ*, 530, 408
Wagner, D. R., Kim, H., & Saykally, R. J. 2000, *ApJ*, 545, 854
Zhang, Y., & Kwok, S. 2015, *ApJ*, 798, 37

Planetary Nebulae: A Universal Toolbox in the Era of Precision Astrophysics
Proceedings IAU Symposium No. 384, 2025
O. De Marco, A. Zijlstra & R. Szczerba, eds.
doi:10.1017/S1743921323005094

NanoSpace: Networking as a tool to understand carbon molecular nanostructures in planetary nebulae

D. A. García-Hernández

Instituto de Astrofísica de Canarias (IAC), E-38205 La Laguna, Tenerife, Spain
Departamento de Astrofísica, Universidad de La Laguna (ULL), E-38206
La Laguna, Tenerife, Spain
email: agarcia@iac.es

Abstract. I present a short overview of the COST Action NanoSpace ("Carbon molecular nanostructures in space"; CA21126) together with the most recent updates. This includes the main motivation and scientific challenges, Action structure and organization (e.g., working groups, tasks, etc.) as well as the main objectives and deliverables. A special emphasis is given to the interdisciplinary approach proposed to attack the Action challenge and the main needs to drive the field forward. Planetary nebulae (PNe) are wonderful astrochemistry laboratories and a dominant source of complex carbon molecular nanostructures (i.e., nanocarbons) in space, being key astronomical objects for NanoSpace. The main goal is to show the power of networking as a tool to understand nanocarbons in PNe as well as to encourage the participation and collaborations between the PNe community and the multiple interdisciplinary research fields represented in NanoSpace.

Keywords. astrochemistry, molecular processes, ISM: molecules, methods: laboratory, planetary nebulae

---

1. Key Scientific challenges and the fullerene revolution

NanoSpace (`https://research.iac.es/proyecto/nanospace/`) is an EU-funded COST (European Cooperation in Science and Technology) Action; CA21126 "Carbon Molecular nanostructures in space" (`https://www.cost.eu/actions/CA21126/`) running from 1st November 2022 to 31st October 2026.

The main motivation of the Action is to solve one of the hot topics in present day Astrochemistry. This is the understanding of carbon molecular nanostructures, what we call nanocarbons (nC), in space. The main scientific challenges are the following:

- What nanocarbon species are present in space and how can we identify them?
- What are the chemical pathways that lead to their formation and destruction?
- What is the role of nC species in non-terrestrial environments? This is in cosmic and in prebiotic chemistry and in astrophysics. In addition, nanocarbon species form in planetary atmospheres and moons such as Titan and Enceladus (Sittler et al. 2020) and are highly relevant to astrobiology.

Once injected into the interstellar medium (ISM), the most stable nanocarbon species survive and may contribute to interstellar extinction, heating processes, and complex chemical reactions. Recent progress on cosmic fullerenes (e.g., Cami et al. 2010; García-Hernández et al. 2010, 2011a,b) has strongly motivated this Action and these special molecules are central to NanoSpace. For example, nowadays we know that fullerene species may explain several astrophysical phenomena like the unidentified infrared bands (UIRs), the diffuse interstellar bands (DIBs) (Omont 2016) or the so-called UV bump, among other astrophysical mysteries (see e.g., Kwok 2016, for a review).

All these astrophysical phenomena are widespread in the universe, from evolved stars like planetary nebulae (PNe), proto-planetary disks and solar system bodies to galactic nuclei and very distant galaxies. Their carriers are believed to be nanocarbon species but we have not identified them yet.

However, in order to attack the scientific challenge we clearly need an interdisciplinary approach, combining the expertise from a wide range of disciplines like observational astronomy, laboratory astrophysics, astrobiology, theoretical chemistry, synthetic chemistry, molecular reaction dynamics, material science, spectroscopy, graph theory, and data science (e.g., artificial intelligence, machine learning, big data). NanoSpace is also very timely, given the recent successful operation of the James Webb Space Telescope (JWST) with a nominal lifetime of 5 years, the new facilities that can better simulate the circumstellar and interstellar media on the ground as well as the recent developments in the computational facilities and in laboratory techniques.

In order to drive the field-forward we need: first, to build a common scientific language; and second, to understand and accept the challenge and the limitations of the laboratory, theoretical and astronomical approaches. Thus, the main aim and objective of the Action is to advance, by promoting the interdisciplinary combination of state-of-the-art astronomical, laboratory, and theoretical studies, among others above, the fundamental understanding of the physics and chemistry of cosmic carbon nanomaterials and their relevance in non-terrestrial environments. This will be achieved through the specific objectives detailed in the Memorandum of Understanding (MoU) of the Action (`https://www.cost.eu/actions/CA21126/`).

2. Research coordination and capacity building objectives, and deliverables

The Action has several research coordination and capacity building objectives as well as a list of deliverables (see below). Most of these objectives provide great opportunities for students and young researchers (i.e., researchers under the age of 40). In particular to those from inclusiveness target countries (ITC) (most eastern European countries) and near-neighbour countries (NNC). All this information is available in the MoU of the Action at the COST website (`https://www.cost.eu/actions/CA21126/`).

In short, the main research coordination objectives are the following:

- To develop a common understanding
- To develop and implement new theoretical approaches
- To coordinate the access to observational data
- To promote the creation of interdisciplinary research teams
- To enhance the collaboration with Enterprises for future research
- To disseminate the research broadly
- To develop an Action roadmap for a post-NanoSpace era

On the other hand, the main capacity building objectives are the following:

- To promote knowledge exchange
- To provide young researchers with translational skills as well as with opportunities to those from ITC to attend international conferences
- To increase the collaboration opportunities for young and ITC researchers

- To increase the success rate of access to user infrastructures (e.g., astronomical, laboratory, and supercomputing facilities)
- To build the next generation of scientists

Finally, the main deliverables of the Action are the following:

- Preliminary Roadmap reports for each Working Group
- The collection of training inputs for each Working Group
- Priority inputs needed for astrochemical modelling
- A reference chart linking molecular physics processes to large scale nanocarbons (including bio-molecules)
- An art collaboration in 2- and 3-D linked to the NanoSpace outputs
- The release of the new open source standards developed
- A special thematic issue with review articles and Roadmap

3. General Action structure and international participation

The general action structure with the several leadership positions (e.g., coordinators, working group leaders and co-leaders, etc.) can be found in the Action website (`https://research.iac.es/proyecto/nanospace/`). The management committee (MC) is composed by 56 members from 35 European countries (54% are ITC). Some of the several leadership positions of the Action are taken by researchers well known in the PNe field. The core group is formed by 7 persons, those with the mandatory positions. The Action actually have 317 working group (WG) members but continuously growing; the number of members to each WG varies between 80 and 220. There is 52% of young researchers and 35% of females.

Apart from the 35 COST European countries, the action has a broad international participation with participants worldwide from up to 20 additional international countries.

The action is formed by four working groups (WG) with several tasks as summarized in Fig. 1. The WG1 is about "The Cosmic Inventory of nanocarbons" and the WG2 is about the "Processing, reactivity and relaxation pathways of nC", while the WG3 is about the "Role and Importance of nC in Non-Terrestrial Environments". Finally, the WG4 is about the "Impact, Inclusiveness and Outreach".

4. Action updates

The most recent Action updates are the following. A NanoSpace mailing list (`nanospace@iac.es`) is already created and being used as an Action communication channel. This mailing list is moderated by the Action Chair and contains already more than 380 persons interested in the NanoSpace activities and events. So, everybody can use it to announce any conference, school, etc. relevant to the NanoSpace participants. Also, NanoSpace Twitter (`https://twitter.com/CostNanospace`) and Linkedin (`https://www.linkedin.com/groups/9310268/`) accounts, a Slack Channel (`https://costnanospace.slack.com/`), and a YouTube Channel (`https://www.youtube.com/@NanoSpace-gd5qn`) have been created and starting to be used. We are considering the NanoSpace presence in other social media like Facebook and Instagram, among others.

The Action website at the IAC (`https://research.iac.es/proyecto/nanospace/`) is already running and it has been used for the planning of the several activities. In the left menu of the NanoSpace website, we can find all relevant information. The Participants and Working Groups, the Mobility Grants like the Short-Term Scientific Missions

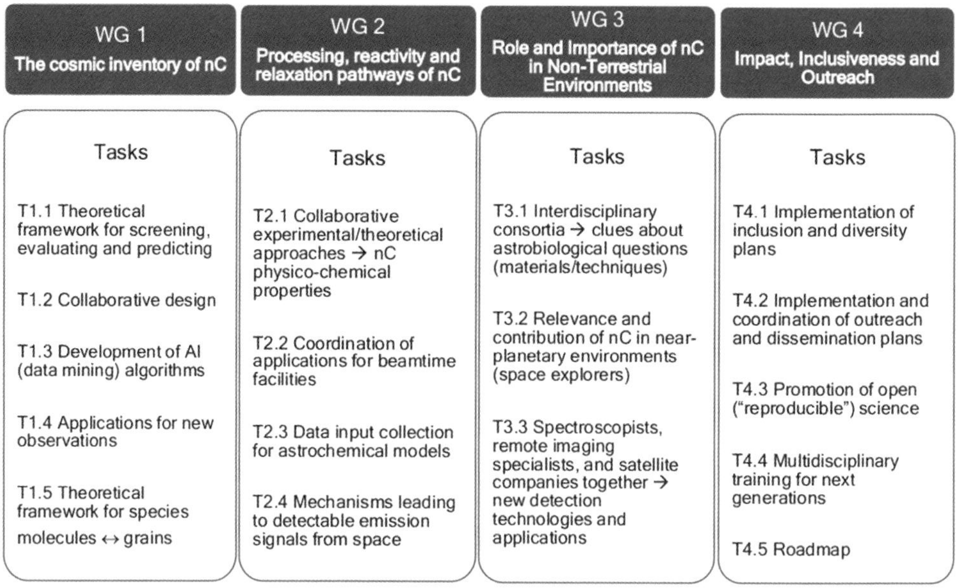

Figure 1. NanoSpace WGs and corresponding tasks in a nutshell.

(STSMs) and ITC Conference Grants, the several Action Events like Joint Scientific and Working Group Meetings, Training Schools, and Online Webinars/Lectures, the grants for Open Source/Access, the Action Publications, the Database of the Network Experimental and Theoretical Resources, the Deliverables as well as the promotional Action Videos.

Finally, considering the great interest of the PNe community on the data from the James Webb Space Telescope (JWST), we want to highlight that NanoSpace recently organized a JWST Training School, where the participants learnt the tools on data analysis and proposals preparations, with a special emphasis on the spectroscopy and on the mid-infrared spectral range. All the relevant information and the programme is at the COST NanoSpace JWST Training School website (`https://meetings.iac.es/jwstworkshop2023/pages/en/motivation.php`). In particular, the several presentations and hands-on exercises are public at the IAC Cloud (`https://cloud.iac.es/index.php/s/eqErrD5MY2AL428`); the IAC (Instituto de Astrofísica de Canarias, Spain) is the NanoSpace Grant Holder institution.

5. Networking to understand nanocarbons in PNe

For the PNe field, perhaps the most important activities are within the WG1 ("The Cosmic Inventory of nanocarbons"; see Fig. 1). The Action needs to expand the cosmic inventory of nanocarbons. For this, we need the spectroscopic match between the astronomical, experimental and theoretical data. We can achieve this via the collaboration of researchers from very diverse disciplines and creating an active networking environment for making a common ground and language. We are continuously updating the database containing the expertise, facilities, and availabilities of each NanoSpace member.

A clear example of this is the kind of interdisciplinary research that we need to carry out in the PNe field in order to understand the organic chemistry diversity that we observe in PNe and their precursors, the post-AGB and AGB stars (see Fig. 2). The PNe are wonderful astrochemistry laboratories and a dominant source of complex nanocarbons in space. Their organic diversity, their simplicity like geometry and well known

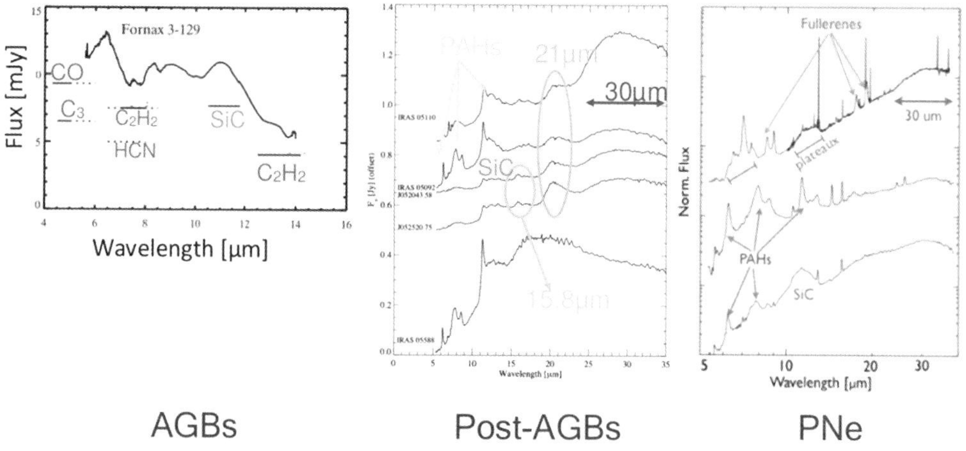

Figure 2. Infrared space-based spectra of key NanoSpace astronomical sources like AGB and post-AGB stars and planetary nebulae (PNe). Several well identified species like small hydrocarbons (CO, C_2H_2, C_3 and HCN), unidentified infrared features (UIRs) (e.g., those at 15.8, 21, and 30 μm) as well as IR features under dispute (e.g., PAHs, SiC, and broad plateaus) are indicated. The figures are updated from Matsuura et al. (2007, 2014); Sloan et al. (2014); Bernard-Salas et al. (2012).

physical conditions together with their short chemical timescales makes PNe to be key astronomical objects for NanoSpace.

In the PNe field, a main goal is to identify the carriers of the unidentified IR features (see Fig. 2) and to understand the formation pathways of these nanocarbon species. For this, NanoSpace offers the opportunity to cross the boundaries between Astronomy, Chemistry and Physics in order to understand the formation of carbon nanostructures in circumstellar envelopes. For example, to combine the astronomical observations at different spectral regions, from the UV to the radio domain, with synthetic chemistry, with theoretical calculations of quantum chemistry, and sophisticated laboratory experiments simulating the circumstellar conditions. Thus, NanoSpace gives PNe researchers the experimental and theoretical contacts as well as all relevant information to establish new national/international collaborations and/or consortia.

With the unprecendented JWST, PNe researchers can do, for example, much more sensitive observations that would allow the confirmation of previous tentative detections (e.g., with the previous *Spitzer Space Telescope*) and later identify the responsible species; e.g., by comparing the astronomical spectra with laboratory spectra and theoretical simulations. In fact, many complex nanocarbons (e.g., fullerene derivatives, nanotubes, etc.) studied in the laboratory and/or theoretically show strong IR emission bands in the JWST spectral ranges.

6. Concluding remarks

In short, we strongly encourage all PNe researchers to enjoy NanoSpace and participate. PNe researchers can collaborate to develop the several Action databases, participate and lead Action events, and benefit from the different multidisciplinary networking activities.

Acknowledgements

DAGH acknowledges support from the State Research Agency (AEI) of the Spanish Ministry of Science and Innovation (MICINN) under grant PID2020-115758GB-I00.

This article is based upon work from European Cooperation in Science and Technology (COST) Action NanoSpace, CA21126, supported by COST.

References

Bernard-Salas, J., Cami, J., Peeters, E., Jones, A. P., Micelotta, E. R. & Groenewegen, M. A. T. 2012, *ApJ*, 757, 41. doi:10.1088/0004-637X/757/1/41

Cami, J., Bernard-Salas, J., Peeters, E., & Malek, S. E 2010, *Science*, 329, 1180. doi:10.1126/science.1192035

García-Hernández, D. A., Manchado, A. García-Lario, P., Stanghellini, L., Villaver, E., Shaw, R. A., Szczerba, R., Perea-Calderón, J. V. 2010, *ApJ*, 724, L39. doi:10.1088/2041-8205/724/1/L39

García-Hernández, D. A., Iglesias-Groth, S., Acosta-Pulido, J. A., Manchado, A., García-Lario, P., Stanghellini, L., Villaver, E., Shaw, R. A., Cataldo, F. 2011a, *ApJ*, 737, L30. doi:10.1088/2041-8205/737/2/L30

García-Hernández, D. A., Kameswara Rao, N. K., & Lambert, D. L. 2011b, *ApJ*, 729, 126. doi:10.1088/0004-637X/729/2/126

Kwok, S. 2016, *A&ARv*, 24, 8. doi:10.1007/s00159-016-0093-y

Matsuura, M., Zijlstra, A. A., Bernard-Salas, J., Menzies, J. W., Sloan, G. C., Whitelock, P. A., Wood, P. R., Cioni, M. -R. L. et al. 2007, *MNRAS*, 382, 1889. doi:10.1111/j.1365-2966.2007.12501.x

Matsuura, M., Bernard-Salas, J., Lloyd Evans, T., Volk, K. M., Hrivnak, B. J., Sloan, G. C., Chu, Y.-H., Gruendl, R. et al. 2014, *MNRAS*, 439, 1472. doi:10.1093/mnras/stt2495

Omont, A. 2016, *A&A*, 590, A520

Sittler, E. C., Cooper, J. F., Sturner, S. J.; Ali, A. 2020, *Icarus*, 344, 113246. doi:10.1016/j.icarus.2019.03.023

Sloan, G. C., Lagadec, E., Zijlstra, A. A., Kraemer, K. E., Weis, A. P., Matsuura, M., Volk, K., Peeters, E. 2014, *ApJ*, 791, 28. doi:10.1088/0004-637X/791/1/28

Planetary Nebulae: A Universal Toolbox in the Era of Precision Astrophysics
Proceedings IAU Symposium No. 384, 2025
O. De Marco, A. Zijlstra & R. Szczerba, eds.
doi:10.1017/S1743921324000103

Dust formation in AGB stars and planetary nebulae

Mikako Matsuura

Cardiff Hub for Astrophysical Research and Technology (CHART), School of Physics and Astronomy, Cardiff University, The Parade, Cardiff CF24 3AA, UK

Abstract. A high sensitivity and high-angular resolutions infrared space telescope, the *James Webb Space Telescope (JWST)*, allowed us to study dust and molecules in unprecedented details. This contribution highlights the first year of *JWST*'s scientific operation, and reports prospects of dust and molecular studies in the coming future.

Keywords. (ISM:) dust, extinction; infrared: stars; (ISM:) planetary nebulae: general; stars: AGB and post-AGB

1. Introduction

The circumstellar envelopes of asymptotic giant branch (AGB) stars are considered to be important dust formation sites. They have a reasonably high density ($> 10^{10}\,\mathrm{cm}^{-3}$) and warm ($\sim$1000 K) gas at the inner region of the circumstellar envelope, which enables reasonably fast chemical reactions (e.g. Cherchneff 2012). Once the stars leave the AGB phase, their circumstellar envelopes are irradiated by strong UV from the central star of the planetary nebula (PN). UV radiation can cause post-formation processing of dust, changing the properties of the grains. In general, a diverse range of dust species have been detected in AGB stars, post-AGB stars and PNe. The detected species of dust grains include amorphous and crystalline silicates, SiC, and polycyclic aromatic hydrocarbons (PAHs), though PAHs might be considered to be large molecules rather than dust grains.

As the near- and mid-infrared spectral range covers a wide range of dust features, the near- and mid-infrared *James Webb Space Telescope* (*JWST*) (Gardner et al. 2023) is an excellent telescope to study dust grains in AGB stars and PNe. At the time of this IAU symposium, *JWST* has completed just over one year of scientific operations, and some highlights from its first year of operation are reported.

2. Highlights of *JWST* observations of PNe

2.1. *NGC 3132: H_2 clumps and dusty disk*

On 12th July 2022, the Space Telescope Science Insitute (STScI) released the first scientific images and spectra, taken by *JWST* (Gardner et al. 2023). One of the four targets of the first scientific data release was PN NGC 3132, showing the stunning detailed structures of this PN (Fig 1). The left-side image of Fig 1 is taken by NIRCam (Rieke et al. 2023) in six filter bands: F090W, F187N, F212N, F356W, F405N and F470N. The ionised gas, traced by [S III] in the F090W band and Paα in the F187N band, is enclosed within the blue elliptical nebula, and is surrounded by clumps and filaments of H_2 in orange-red colour (De Marco et al. 2022). The right-side image of Fig 1 shows a MIRI (Wright et al. 2023) image of the nebula, taken in four filter bands (F770W, F1130W, F1280W and F1800W). Similar to the NIRCam image, H_2 filaments and clumps, which are in blue

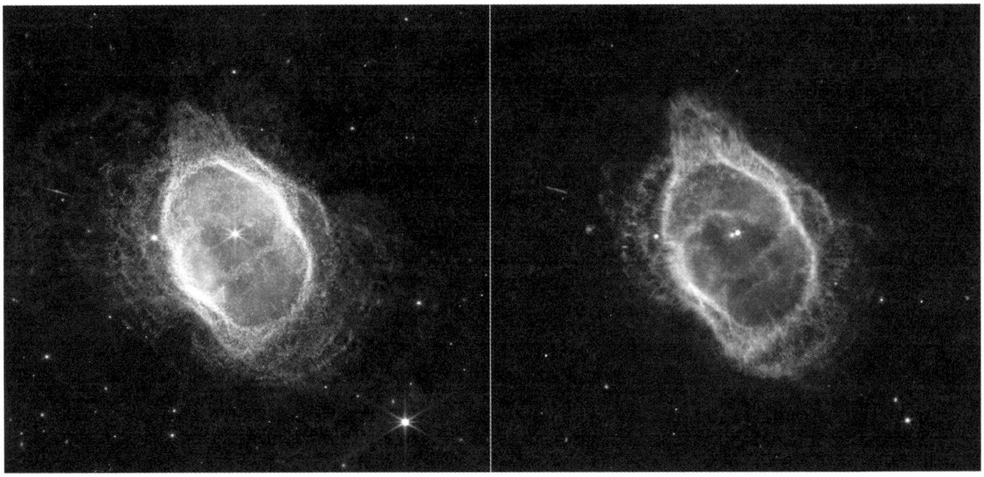

Figure 1. *JWST* images of NGC 3132, taken by the NIRCam (left) and the MIRI (right). The image is from the JWST Early Release Observations (Pontoppidan et al. 2022). Image credit: NASA, ESA, CSA, STScI.

and are traced by the F770W band, are found outside of the elliptically-shaped ionisation front in red. Although not too obvious in this press release image, there are layers of H_2 concentric arcs, surrounding the ionised gas, and H_2 spikes extending in a radial direction.

One of the surprising results is the detection of the mid-infrared excess from the central star of NGC 3132. Fig. 2 shows the image of the central star and its A-type star companion (De Marco et al. 2022). In the optical, the A-type companion is far brighter, but at wavelengths longer than 10 μm, the central star is brighter. Moreover, the central star is not a point source, and is marginally resolved at these wavelengths, with an approximate size of 300 au in the full-width at half-maximum (FWHM). The fit to this mid-infrared excess (Fig. 3) shows that it is explained by a dust mass of $2 \times 10^{-7}\, M_{\odot}$, with an inner radius of 55 au. In order to retain such a quantity of AGB dust near the central star after the central star left the AGB phase approximately 10,000 years ago, the most likely explanation is that dust grains are trapped in a binary disk (Mastrodemos and Morris 1999).

In NGC 3132, H_2 emission is found in clumps (Fig. 4). That is similar to H_2 clumps found in the Helix Nebula (Meixner et al. 2005; Matsuura et al. 2007, 2009) and the Ring Nebula (this contribution). Fig. 4 shows the images of clumps found in NGC 3132 in three different regions (from top to bottom rows) at six different wavelengths (from right to left columns). Some clumps and filaments are seen in obscuration due to dust extinction in optical images taken by the *Hubble Space Telescope (HST)* in Fig. 4. Some clumps are even seen in absorption in the infrared NIRCam F187N and F405N images.

Using the dust extinction of clumps against the bright background nebular emission, clump masses can be estimated. We measured the extinction at 1.87 μm for two clumps seen in extinction against the Paα nebula background: the largest knot on the west side of the nebula (coordinates RA=10:07:00.4, Dec=−40:26:08.8), and one of the darkest on the east side of the nebula (RA=10:07:02.5, Dec=−40:26:00.3). The diameters of these clumps are ~0.36 arcsec and ~0.15 arcsec, and their extinction is ~0.57 mag and ~0.25 mag at 1.87 μm, respectively. Using the dust extinction law $A(\lambda)/A(V)$, where $A(\lambda)$ is the extinction at a given wavelength, λ, and $A(V)$ is the extinction in the V-band (Cardelli et al. 1989), the corresponding values of $A(V)$ are 3.9 mag and 1.7 mag assuming $R_V = 3.1$. Using the conversion between $A(V)$ and the total hydrogen density

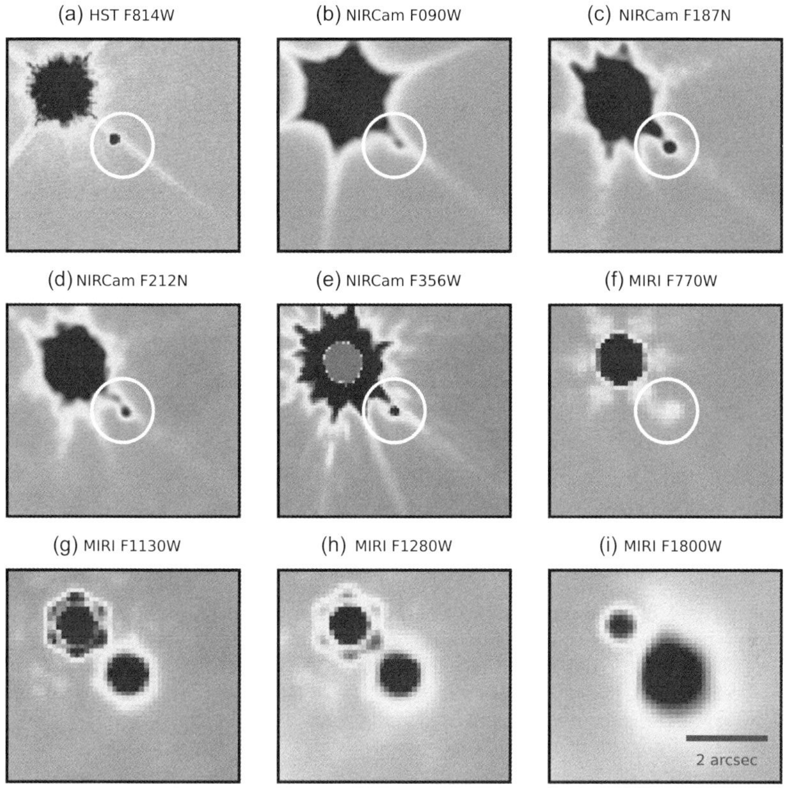

Figure 2. The multiple-wavelength images of the central star (white circle) and A-type companion star of NGC 3132. The companion star is far brighter in the optical, while in the mid-infrared wavelength range longer than F1130W, the central star is brighter, showing dust excess around the central star. The comparison with an A-type star shows that at F1130W, F1280W and F1800W, the central star is not a point source but extended. The figure is from De Marco et al. (2022).

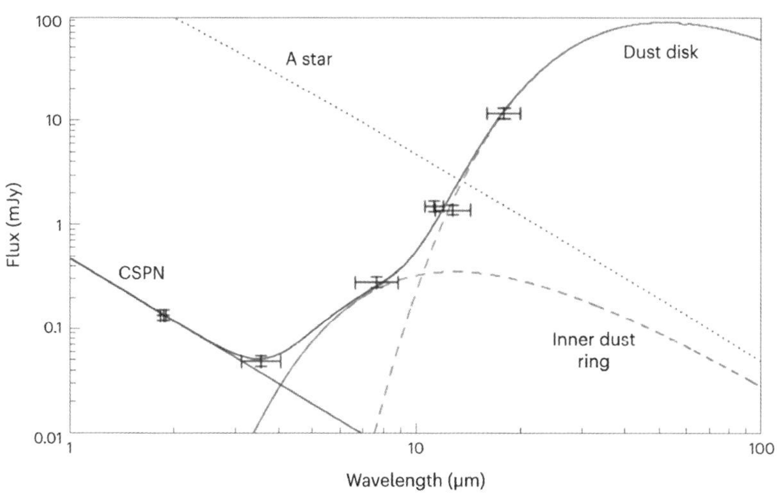

Figure 3. The spectral energy distribution of the central star of NGC 3132 and its dust disk, showing the dust excess, starting at about 3 μm. The figure is from De Marco et al. (2022).

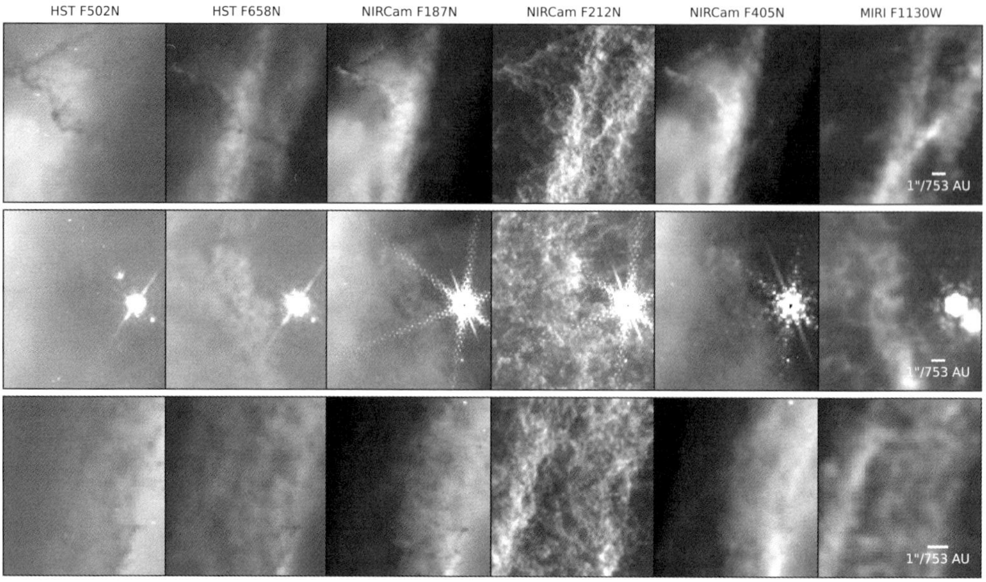

Figure 4. Enlarged images of clumps in three representative regions in NGC 3132: the west side of the ring (top row), near the centre of the ring (middle row) and the east side of the ring (bottom row). Filament structures stand out in the NIRCam F212N images. A few filaments are extinguished by dust, as clearly seen in the HST optical images (first two columns of *HST* F502N and F658N), but also even in infrared images at NIRCam F187N and F405N (third and fifth columns). The figure is from De Marco et al. (2022).

along the line of sight, $N(H)$ (Bohlin et al. 1978), the estimated column densities of these two clumps are $N(H) = 7.3 \times 10^{21}$ cm^{-2} and $N(H) = 3.2 \times 10^{21}$ cm^{-2}, respectively. For the adopted distance of 754 pc, the estimated densities are $n(H) \sim 2 \times 10^{6}$ cm^{-3} for both clumps. These densities suggest clump masses of $10^{-5}\,M_{\odot}$, similar to the typical clump ('globule') masses found in the Helix Nebula (Meixner et al. 2005; Matsuura et al. 2009). Considering the total number of clumps, there is about $0.1\,M_{\odot}$ in the H_2 clumps (De Marco et al. 2022). A substantial fraction of the nebula mass is therefore in H_2.

2.2. *The Ring Nebula: H_2 globules, radial spikes, and the PAH shell*

JWST (Gardner et al. 2023) observed the Ring Nebula (M 57, NGC 6720) during Cycle 1 as part of the General Observers (GO) program 1558 (PI M.J. Barlow). Fig. 5 shows the NIRCam (left) and MIRI (right) false-colour images of the Ring Nebula. The main part of the nebula is filled with numerous clumps of H_2, shown in cyan (F212N), green (F300M) and red (F335M) colours in the NIRCam image. These clumps are also seen in the MIRI image in purple (F560W), blue (F770W) and cyan (F1000W) colours. The clumpy nebula is filled with ionised gas, traced in blue (F162M) in the NIRCam image and orange (F1800W, dominated by [S III]) in the MIRI image. A summary table of the main contributing emissions to each filter band is found in Wesson et al. (this contribution) and Wesson et al. (2023). On top of the clumpy structure of the main body of the nebula, the Ring Nebula shows up to 10 concentric arcs in H_2 and about 300–400 radial spikes (Wesson et al. 2023).

Compared with H_2 clumps detected in the Helix Nebula (Meixner et al. 2005; Matsuura et al. 2007, 2009) and NGC 3132 (De Marco et al. 2022), those detected in the Ring Nebula tend to have less defined heads or tails (Wesson et al. 2023). This is not due to the fact that the Ring Nebula (790±30 pc; Lindegren et al. 2021) is farther than

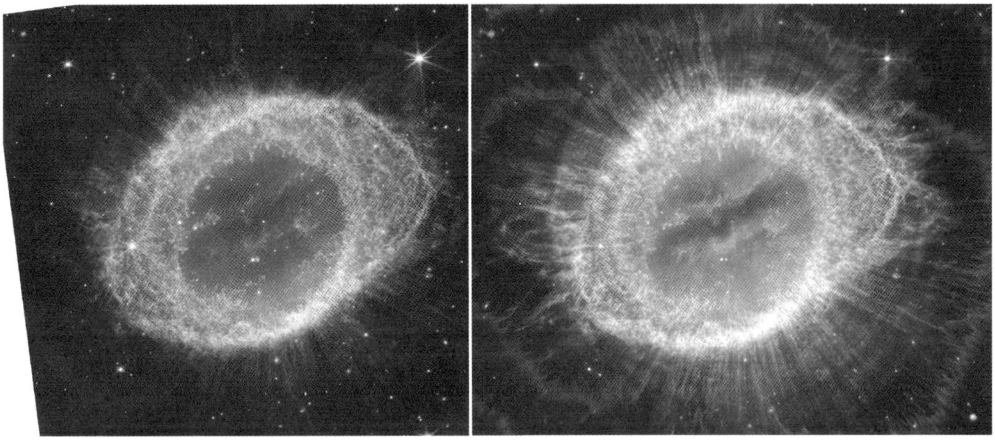

Figure 5. *JWST* images of the Ring Nebula, taken by the NIRCam (left) and the MIRI (right). The images use the data from the General Observers (GO) program 1558 (Wesson et al. 2023). Credit: ESA/Webb, NASA, CSA, M. Barlow, N. Cox, R. Wesson

the Helix Nebula (200±30 pc; Lindegren et al. 2021); NGC 3132 has a similar distance (750 pc; De Marco et al. 2022). Instead, it is probably because the Ring Nebula has had a shorter time since its central star left the peak of its luminosity, and is less evolved.

Hydrodynamic models (García-Segura and Mac Low 1995; Garcia-Segura and Franco 1996) demonstrated that instabilities in existing gas layers being swept up can form clumpy structures. Initially, the range of clump sizes is quite uniform as found in the Ring Nebula, but as the nebula evolves, instabilities build up and tails gradually develop, so that the range of clump sizes grows, as found in NGC 3132 and the Helix Nebula.

JWST's high sensitivity and high angular resolution images of the Ring Nebula show a distinct thin shell, associated with PAHs, in the Ring Nebula. Fig. 6 includes intensity ratios of (a) F335M/F300M and (b) F1130W/F1000W. The F335M and F1130W filters contain PAH bands, while the F300M and F1000W filters include nearby continuum, though there are some weak line contributions, too (Wesson et al. 2023). Nevertheless, the similar thin shell morphology found in both F335M/F300M and F1130W/F1000W images shows that the thin shell represents the location of PAHs. Compared with the overall shell of the Ring, seen in the F212N H_2 image (Fig. 6 (d)), the PAH shell is located approximately at the edge of the main body of the Ring, which contains H_2 clumps.

Spitzer spectral mapping at 11.3 μm is shown at Fig. 6 (c). This map is a single wavelength bin with a spectral resolution of $R \sim 100$ (Houck et al. 2004). The data were taken by Program 40536 (P.I. H. Dinerstein) and published by Cox et al. (2016). This spectral map covers the 11.3 μm PAH band. The black circle, which traces the PAH emission in Fig. 6 (a) and (b) is also plotted in panel (c), and indeed, the PAH emission is strongest in region 3, where the black circle crosses.

Fig. 7 shows *Spitzer* spectra, extracted in the three regions, indicated in Fig. 6 (c). As expected, region 3 has a clear indication of the PAH band at 11.3 μm, with region 2 having weak PAH emission. Regions 2 and 3 both show an excess of the F1130W over the F1000W flux, relative to a simply rising continuum, suggesting the presence of PAH emission in F1130W/F1000W. There is no trace of PAHs in the central ionised region 1. Region 1, the innermost region of the ring, lacks PAH emission at 11.3 μm but has strong [S IV] emission in the *JWST* F1000W filter. This confirms that the thin emission shell, found in F335M/F300M (Fig. 6 (a)) and F1130W/F1000W (Fig. 6 (b)), is indeed due to PAHs.

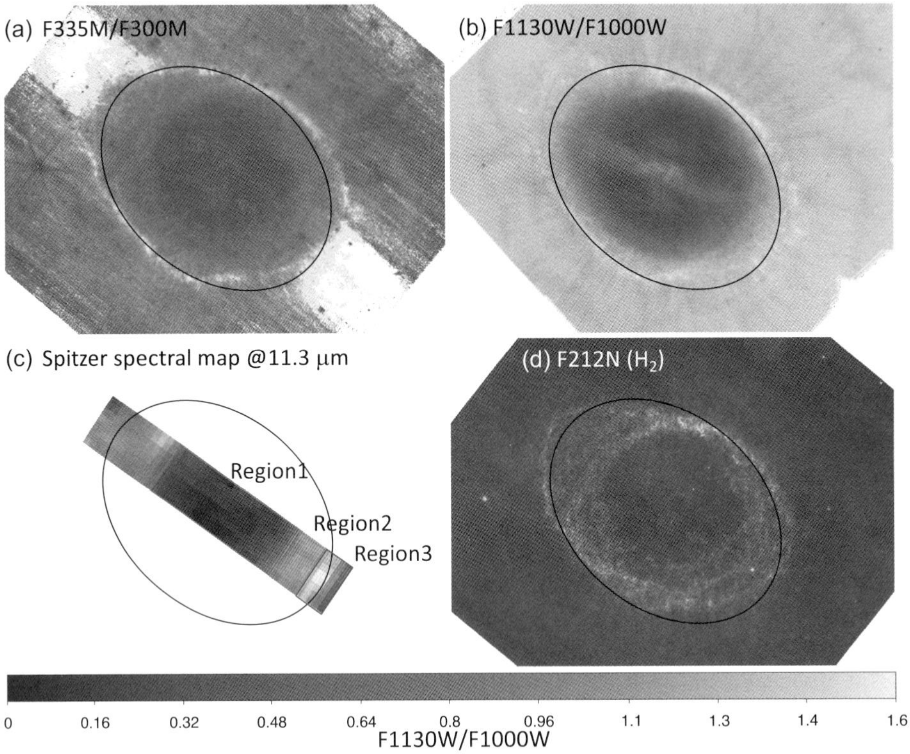

Figure 6. The PAH shell found in the Ring Nebula. The four panels show (a) F335M/F300M ratio, (b) F1130W/F1000W ratio and (c) *Spitzer* spectral map at 11.3 μm (10.95–11.65 μm, corresponding to *JWST* F1130W filter) (Cox et al. 2016) on the same scale. For reference, the black ellipse approximately traces the narrow ring at the edge of the shell, which is interpreted as the peak PAH emission. For comparison, the F212N H_2 image is plotted at the panel (d). The *Spitzer* spectra were extracted at three different regions as indicated in the bottom left panel, and plotted at Fig. 7. North is at the top. The figure is from Wesson et al. (2023)

The location of the PAH-emitting peak at the edge of the H_2 clumps is most likely due to favourable UV excitation of PAHs at this particular distance from the central star. As traced by a black ellipse in Fig. 6, the PAH shell is centred on the current location of the central star, rather than the offset centre found for other emission features, and follows the outer contour of the H_2 distribution (Wesson et al. 2023). As expected from Fig. 6 (d), the peak of H_2 is offset from the central star by about 2 arcsec (Wesson et al. 2023). This offset seems to be associated with the proper motion of the central star, since the nebula material was expelled from the central star about 4000 yrs ago (O'Dell et al. 2004). Although PAHs and H_2 are both associated with clumps, there is a difference in their brightness distributions; PAH brightness peaks are outside of H_2 brightness peaks, and PAH brightness is centred on the current position of the star, while the H_2 brightness is not. This strongly suggests that the PAH excitation, rather than PAH abundance or density distribution within the nebula, contributes to the presence of the PAH peaks.

2.3. *Spectroscopic signature of dust in PN SMP LMC 058*

Another early *JWST* result of dust in PNe came from the commissioning data of the MIRI spectrometer (Wright et al. 2023). SMP LMC 058 is a PN located in the Large Magellanic Cloud (LMC) which was initially identified by an emission source survey

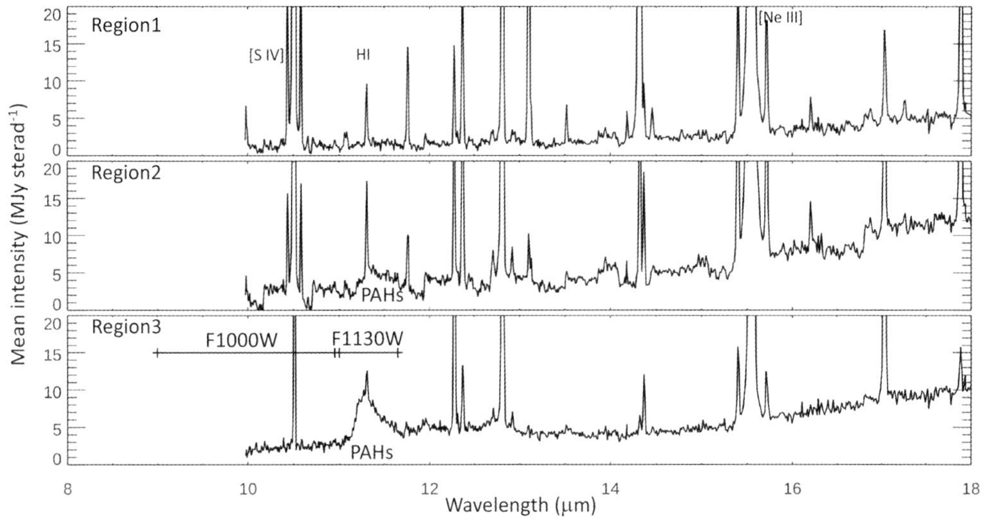

Figure 7. The extracted *Spitzer* spectra of the Ring Nebula (Cox et al. 2016), from the top towards the inner ring from regions 1 to 3. (bottom left panel of Fig. 6). Region 3 has an excess of PAHs at 11.3 μm in Figure 6, and *Spitzer* spectra confirm the presence of 11.3 μm PAHs. In contrast, region 1, the innermost region of the ring, lacks observed PAHs. The figure is from Wesson et al. (2023)

(Sanduleak et al. 1978). *Spitzer* IRS spectra ($R = 60$–127) have identified the SiC feature at 11.3 μm. The PAH features at 6–9 μm were identified, but the PAH feature at $\sim$11.3 μm was unclear (Bernard-Salas et al. 2009).

Higher spectral resolution ($R = 1500$–4000) MIRI spectra clearly identified over 50 emission lines from the 4.9–27.9 μm spectra of SMP LMC 058 (Fig.8; Jones et al. 2023). More relevant to this contribution is the detection of PAHs and SiC dust emissions at 11 μm in this PN. With *Spitzer*'s spectral resolution, it was difficult to disentangle contributions from the 11.3 μm SiC, the 11.2 μm PAHs, and the 11.3 μm H I 9–7. On the other hand, the higher spectral resolution of MIRI was capable of disentangling these three components. Fig. 8 shows the identification of the broad $\sim$11.3 μm SiC. The SiC band is rarely to be found in Galactic high mass-loss rate AGB stars, post-AGB stars and PNe (Speck et al. 2005), while it is rather common in their LMC counterparts (Gruendl et al. 2008; Bernard-Salas et al. 2009; Matsuura et al. 2014; Sloan et al. 2014). On top of the broad SiC band, a narrower and fainter PAH 11.2 μm is clearly detected in MIRI spectra (Fig. 8). That is the power of the higher spectral resolution of the MIRI spectrometer, compared with the *Spitzer* IRS in the low-spectral resolution mode.

2.4. *End of the era of discrete C-rich and O-rich chemistry?*

Finally, *JWST* discovered chemical processes related to dust formation in general, not specific to PNe, but very relevant to dust formation in PNe. The Solar abundance pattern indicates that the gas contains more oxygen than carbon atoms, and the majority of stars were formed from gas with more oxygen than carbon atoms. During the AGB phase, carbon atoms are synthesised and dredged up to the surface, and hence, surface abundances might show a carbon-to-oxygen ratio larger than unity.

In AGB stars, post-AGB stars and PNe, distinct C-rich or O-rich chemistry is operating, depending on which elemental abundance of oxygen or carbon is higher. In a chemical process, carbon monoxide (CO) has the highest binding energy among molecules, hence

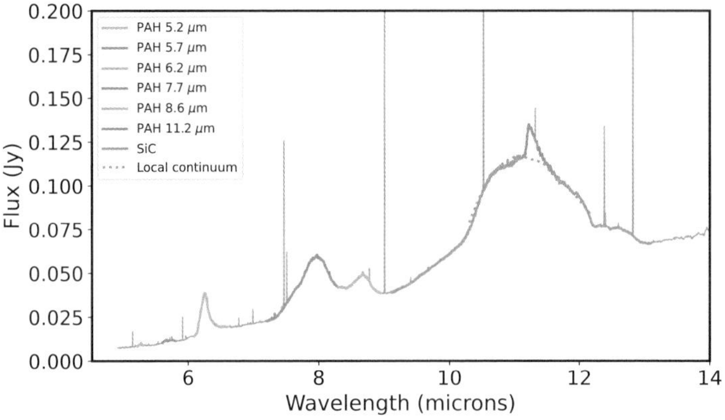

Figure 8. *JWST*/MIRI spectra of the PN, SMP LMC 058. The broad SiC band at 11.3 μ is identified, and on top of that PAH 11.2 μm is found. Other PAH features, such as 5.2, 5.7, 6.2,.7.7 and 8.6 μm are also found. The figure is from Jones et al. (2023)

CO molecules are formed first in AGB stars, when the gas is sufficiently cool. In an oxygen-rich environment (C/O<1), the remaining oxygen atoms react with other atoms, forming H_2O, SiO, CO_2 and silicate dust (e.g. Mg_2SiO_4, $MgSiO_3$). In a carbon-rich environment (C/O>1), the excess carbon atoms react with other atoms, producing molecules such as C_2H_2, HCN, CS, CH, as well as carbonaceous dust (amorphous carbon, SiC and PAHs). Occasionally, molecules and dust which have been formed both in oxygen-rich and carbon-rich environments are found within a single object, and these objects are called dual chemistry objects. Often dual-chemistry objects show silicate dust with PAHs (e.g. Waters et al. 1998; Molster et al. 2002). Some PNe show oxygen-rich abundances from atomic line analysis, and yet also show PAHs. The prime example is the Ring Nebula. As discussed in Sect. 2.2, the Ring Nebula does present PAHs, which are carbon-rich molecules/dust, but its gas abundances were measured to be oxygen-rich from atomic lines (Liu et al. 2004).

There are several hypotheses on how to form dual chemistry objects. One possible explanation is that binary discs have been formed in AGB stars/post-AGB stars and PNe, and past oxygen-rich material has been stored in these discs (Waters et al. 1998; Winckel et al. 2006). The central star eventually became carbon-rich, and carbon-rich molecules and dust were formed in this later phase.

The hypothesis of storing oxygen-rich gas in binary-formed discs might work in AGB stars/post-AGB stars and PNe. However, PAHs are widely found in the diffuse interstellar medium (ISM), and their origin there is not clear, as the ISM gas is oxygen-rich. Another issue is that the mass of PAHs formed in AGB stars is expected to be far too small, compared with the mass found in the ISM in galaxies. In carbon-rich AGB stars, PAHs may be formed via combining C_2H_2 (Allamandola et al. 1989). However, the abundance of C_2H_2 is quite low, and even across the entire AGB population in the Small Magellanic Cloud (SMC), only $10^{-8}\,M_\odot\,\mathrm{yr}^{-1}$ of PAHs may be injected to the ISM (Matsuura et al. 2013). That would make only about 100 $M_\odot$ of PAHs during the lifetime of PAHs in the ISM (1.4–1.6×10^8 yr; Micelotta et al. 2010). On the other hand, Sandstrom et al. (2010) estimated the fractional abundance of PAHs in the SMC ISM to be 0.6 per cent with respect to the total dust mass. Considering the SMC dust mass of 8×10^4–$5 \times 10^5\,M_\odot$ (Gordon et al. 2014), the resultant PAH mass in the SMC ISM would be 500–3000 $M_\odot$. Though there are a lot of uncertainties involved in these estimates, AGB-injected PAHs seem to be insufficient to explain the whole PAH mass in the ISM.

In order to explain the large mass of PAHs found in the ISM, there is a long-term debate on whether PAHs may be formed within the ISM in situ, instead of being injected from AGB stars to the ISM. *JWST* opened clues to this hypothesis. Berné et al. (2023) reported the detection of CH^{+3}, which has been predicted to trigger organic chemistry (Black and Dalgarno 1977), potentially leading to the formation of PAHs. That was detected in the proto-planetary disc d203−506 in the Orion Nebula. The proto-planetary disc is exposed to UV radiation from the Trapezium stars, and this strong UV ($G_0 > 10^4$) irradiation triggered the formation of CH^{+3}, and subsequent organic molecule formation in this high density ($n > 10^5\,\mathrm{cm}^{-3}$) region. Although the first detection of CH^{+3} was in a proto-planetary disc, the implication of this chemistry might be relevant to organic chemistry in the oxygen-rich environment in PNe (Berné et al. 2023).

Another finding from *JWST* was dual chemistry being detected in young stellar objects,. Tabone et al. (2023) reported the detection of C_2H_2, C_6H_6, CO_2, C_4H_2 from a young (2.6±1.6 Myr old) low-mass star 2MASS J16053215−1933159. CO_2 forms in the oxygen-rich environment, while C_2H_2, C_6H_6 and C_4H_2 are carbon-rich in origin. This star is a member of a star-forming region and has an accreting disc around it. One possible explanation is that oxygen atoms are frozen in H_2O ice, so the abundance of carbon-bearing molecules is higher. This has implications for AGB stars and PNe. Some high-mass loss rate AGB stars can have ice (Justtanont et al. 2006), so ice-induced carbon-chemistry might be applicable to evolved stars, too. Future investigations in AGB stars, post-AGB stars and PNe will be important.

Acknowledgements

This work is based on observations made with the NASA/ESA/CSA James Webb Space Telescope. The data were obtained from the Mikulski Archive for Space Telescopes at the Space Telescope Science Institute, which is operated by the Association of Universities for Research in Astronomy, Inc., under NASA contract NAS 5-03127 for *JWST*. These observations are associated with program #1558.

M.M. acknowledges support from STFC Consolidated grant (ST/W000830/1).

References

Allamandola, L. J., Tielens, A. G. G. M., & Barker, J. R. 1989, Interstellar polycyclic aromatic hydrocarbons - The infrared emission bands, the excitation/emission mechanism, and the astrophysical implications. *Astrophysical Journal Supplement Series (ISSN 0067-0049)*, 71, 733–775.

Bernard-Salas, J., Peeters, E., Sloan, G. C., Gutenkunst, S., Matsuura, M., Tielens, A. G. G. M., Zijlstra, A. A., & Houck, J. R. 2009, UNUSUAL DUST EMISSION FROM PLANETARY NEBULAE IN THE MAGELLANIC CLOUDS. *The Astrophysical Journal*, 699(2), 1541–1552.

Berné, O., Martin-Drumel, M.-A., Schroetter, I., Goicoechea, J. R., Jacovella, U., Gans, B., Dartois, E., Coudert, L. H., Bergin, E., Alarcon, F., Cami, J., Roueff, E., Black, J. H., Asvany, O., Habart, E., Peeters, E., Canin, A., Trahin, B., Joblin, C., Schlemmer, S., Thorwirth, S., Cernicharo, J., Gerin, M., Tielens, A., Zannese, M., Abergel, A., Bernard-Salas, J., Boersma, C., Bron, E., Chown, R., Cuadrado, S., Dicken, D., Elyajouri, M., Fuente, A., Gordon, K. D., Issa, L., Kannavou, O., Khan, B., Lacinbala, O., Languignon, D., Gal, R. L., Maragkoudakis, A., Meshaka, R., Okada, Y., Onaka, T., Pasquini, S., Pound, M. W., Robberto, M., Röllig, M., Schefter, B., Schirmer, T., Sidhu, A., Tabone, B., Putte, D. V. D., Vicente, S., & Wolfire, M. G. 2023, Formation of the methyl cation by photochemistry in a protoplanetary disk. *Nature*, 1–4.

Black, J. H. & Dalgarno, A. 1977, Models of interstellar clouds. I - The Zeta Ophiuchi cloud. *The Astrophysical Journal Supplement Series*, 34, 405.

Bohlin, R. C., Savage, B. D., & Drake, J. F. 1978, A survey of interstellar H I from L-alpha absorption measurements. II. *Astrophysical Journal*, 224, 132. A&AA ID. AAA022.131.015.

Cardelli, J. A., Clayton, G. C., & Mathis, J. S. 1989, The relationship between infrared, optical, and ultraviolet extinction. *Astrophysical Journal*, 345, 245.

Cherchneff, I. 2012, The inner wind of IRC+ 10216 revisited: new exotic chemistry and diagnostic for dust condensation in carbon stars. *A&A*, 545, A12.

Cox, N. L. J., Pilleri, P., Berne, O., Cernicharo, J., & Joblin, C. 2016, Polycyclic aromatic hydrocarbons and molecular hydrogen in oxygen-rich planetary nebulae: the case of NGC 6720. *MNRAS*, 456(1), L89–L93.

De Marco, O., Akashi, M., Akras, S., & et al. 2022, The messy death of a multiple star system and the resulting planetary nebula as observed by JWST. *Nature Astronomy*, 6(12), 1421–1432.

Garcia-Segura, G. & Franco, J. 1996, From Ultracompact to Extended H II Regions. *ApJ*, 469, 171.

García-Segura, G. & Mac Low, M.-M. 1995, Wolf-Rayet Bubbles. II. Gasdynamical Simulations. *ApJ*, 455, 160.

Gardner, J. P., Mather, J. C., Abbott, R., & et al. 2023, The James Webb Space Telescope Mission. *PASP*, 135(1048), 068001.

Gordon, K. D., Roman-Duval, J., Bot, C., Meixner, M., Babler, B., Bernard, J.-P., Bolatto, A. D., Boyer, M. L., Clayton, G. C., Engelbracht, C., Fukui, Y., Galametz, M., Galliano, F., Hony, S., Hughes, A., Indebetouw, R., Israel, F. P., Jameson, K., Kawamura, A., Lebouteiller, V., Li, A., Madden, S. C., Matsuura, M., Misselt, K., Montiel, E., Okumura, K., Onishi, T., Panuzzo, P., Paradis, D., Rubio, M., Sandstrom, K. M., Sauvage, M., Seale, J., Sewiło, M., Tchernyshyov, K., & Skibba, R. 2014, Dust and gas in the Magellanic Clouds from the Heritage Herschelkey Project. I. Dust properties and insights into the origin of the submillimeter excess emission. *The Astrophysical Journal*, 797(2), 85.

Gruendl, R. A., Chu, Y.-H., Seale, J. P., Matsuura, M., Speck, A. K., Sloan, G. C., & Looney, L. W. 2008, Discovery of Extreme Carbon Stars in the Large Magellanic Cloud. *The Astrophysical Journal*, 688(1), L9–L12. (c) 2008: The American Astronomical Society.

Houck, J. R., Roellig, T. L., van Cleve, J., & et al. 2004, The Infrared Spectrograph (IRS) on the Spitzer Space Telescope. *ApJS*, 154(1), 18–24.

Jones, O. C., Álvarez-Márquez, J., Sloan, G. C., Kavanagh, P. J., Argyriou, I., Law, D. R., Labiano, A., Patapis, P., Mueller, M., Larson, K. L., Bright, S. N., Klaassen, P. D., Fox, O. D., Gasman, D., Geers, V. C., Glauser, A. M., Guillard, P., Nayak, O., Noriega-Crespo, A., Ressler, M. E., Sargent, B., Temim, T., Vandenbussche, B., & García Marín, M. 2023, Observations of the planetary nebula SMP LMC 058 with the JWST MIRI medium resolution spectrometer. *MNRAS*, 523(2), 2519–2529.

Justtanont, K., Olofsson, G., Dijkstra, C., & Meyer, A. W. 2006, Near-infrared observations of water-ice in OH/IR stars. *A&A*, 450(3), 1051–1059.

Lindegren, L., Bastian, U., Biermann, M., Bombrun, A., de Torres, A., Gerlach, E., Geyer, R., Hernández, J., Hilger, T., Hobbs, D., Klioner, S. A., Lammers, U., McMillan, P. J., Ramos-Lerate, M., Steidelmüller, H., Stephenson, C. A., & van Leeuwen, F. 2021, Gaia Early Data Release 3. Parallax bias versus magnitude, colour, and position. *A&A*, 649, A4.

Liu, Y., Liu, X., Luo, S., & Barlow, M. J. 2004, Chemical abundances of planetary nebulae from optical recombination lines – I. Observations and plasma diagnostics. *Monthly Notices of the Royal Astronomical Society*, 353(4), 1231–1250.

Mastrodemos, N. & Morris, M. 1999, Bipolar Pre–Planetary Nebulae: Hydrodynamics of Dusty Winds in Binary Systems. II. Morphology of the Circumstellar Envelopes. *Astrophysical Journal*, 523(1), 357–380.

Matsuura, M., Bernard-Salas, J., Evans, T. L., Volk, K. M., Hrivnak, B. J., Sloan, G. C., Chu, Y.-H., Gruendl, R., Kraemer, K. E., Peeters, E., Szczerba, R., Wood, P. R., Zijlstra, A. A., Hony, S., Ita, Y., Kamath, D., Lagadec, E., Parker, Q. A., Reid, W. A., Shimonishi, T., Winckel, H. V., Woods, P. M., Kemper, F., Meixner, M., Otsuka, M., Sahai, R., Sargent, B. A., Hora, J. L., & McDonald, I. 2014, Spitzer Space Telescope spectra of post-AGB stars in the Large Magellanic Cloud - polycyclic aromatic hydrocarbons at low metallicities.

Monthly Notices of the Royal Astronomical Society, 439(2), 1472–1493.
Matsuura, M., Speck, A. K., McHunu, B. M., Tanaka, I., Wright, N. J., Smith, M. D., Zijlstra, A. A., Viti, S., & Wesson, R. 2009, A "Firework" of H_2 Knots in the Planetary Nebula NGC 7293 (The Helix Nebula). *ApJ*, 700(2), 1067–1077.
Matsuura, M., Speck, A. K., Smith, M. D., Zijlstra, A. A., Viti, S., Lowe, K. T. E., Redman, M., Wareing, C. J., & Lagadec, E. 2007, VLT/near-infrared integral field spectrometer observations of molecular hydrogen lines in the knots of the planetary nebula NGC 7293 (the Helix Nebula). *MNRAS*, 382(4), 1447–1459.
Matsuura, M., Woods, P. M., & Owen, P. J. 2013, The global gas and dust budget of the Small Magellanic Cloud. *Monthly Notices of the Royal Astronomical Society*, 429(3), 2527–2536.
Meixner, M., McCullough, P., Hartman, J., Son, M., & Speck, A. 2005, The Multitude of Molecular Hydrogen Knots in the Helix Nebula. *AJ*, 130(4), 1784–1794.
Micelotta, E. R., Jones, A. P., & Tielens, A. G. G. M. 2010, Polycyclic aromatic hydrocarbon processing in interstellar shocks. *Astronomy and Astrophysics*, 510, A36.
Molster, F. J., Waters, L. B. F. M., Tielens, A. G. G. M., & Barlow, M. J. 2002, Crystalline silicate dust around evolved stars. I. The sample stars. *Astronomy and Astrophysics*, 382, 184.
O'Dell, C. R., McCullough, P. R., & Meixner, M. 2004, Unraveling the Helix Nebula: Its Structure and Knots. *AJ*, 128(5), 2339–2356.
Pontoppidan, K. M., Barrientes, J., Blome, C., & et al. 2022, The JWST Early Release Observations. *ApJ*, 936(1), L14.
Rieke, M. J., Kelly, D. M., Misselt, K., & et al. 2023, Performance of NIRCam on JWST in Flight. *PASP*, 135(1044), 028001.
Sandstrom, K. M., Bolatto, A. D., Draine, B. T., Bot, C., & Stanimirović, S. 2010, The Spitzer Survey of the Small Magellanic Cloud (S3MC): Insights into the Life Cycle of Polycyclic Aromatic Hydrocarbons. *The Astrophysical Journal*, 715, 701.
Sanduleak, N., MacConnell, D. J., & Philip, A. G. D. 1978, The planetary nebula systems of the Magellanic Clouds. *PASP*, 90, 621–635.
Sloan, G. C., Lagadec, E., Zijlstra, A. A., Kraemer, K. E., Weis, A. P., Matsuura, M., Volk, K. M., Peeters, E., Duley, W. W., Cami, J., Bernard-Salas, J., Kemper, F., & Sahai, R. 2014, Carbon-rich Dust Past the Asymptotic Giant Branch: Aliphatics, Aromatics, and Fullerenes in the Magellanic Clouds. *Astrophysical Journal*, 791(1), 28.
Speck, A. K., Thompson, G. D., & Hofmeister, A. M. 2005, The Effect of Stellar Evolution on SiC Dust Grain Sizes. *The Astrophysical Journal*, 634, 426. (c) 2005: The American Astronomical Society.
Tabone, B., Bettoni, G., Dishoeck, E. F. v., Arabhavi, A. M., Grant, S., Gasman, D., Henning, T., Kamp, I., Güdel, M., Lagage, P. O., Ray, T., Vandenbussche, B., Abergel, A., Absil, O., Argyriou, I., Barrado, D., Boccaletti, A., Bouwman, J., Garatti, A. C. o., Geers, V., Glauser, A. M., Justannont, K., Lahuis, F., Mueller, M., Nehmé, C., Olofsson, G., Pantin, E., Scheithauer, S., Waelkens, C., Waters, L. B. F. M., Black, J. H., Christiaens, V., Guadarrama, R., Morales-Calderón, M., Jang, H., Kanwar, J., Pawellek, N., Perotti, G., Perrin, A., Rodgers-Lee, D., Samland, M., Schreiber, J., Schwarz, K., Colina, L., Östlin, G., & Wright, G. 2023, A rich hydrocarbon chemistry and high C to O ratio in the inner disk around a very low-mass star. *Nature Astronomy*, 7(7), 805–814.
Waters, L. B. F. M., Jong, T. d., Molster, F. J., Loon, J. T. v., Bouwman, J., Koter, A. D., Waelkens, C., Winckel, H. V., Morris, P. W., Cami, J., & Graauw, T. d. 1998, An oxygen-rich dust disk surrounding an evolved star in the Red Rectangle. *Nature*, 391, 868.
Wesson, R., Matsuura, M., Zijlstra, A. A., & et al. 2023, JWST observations of the Ring Nebula (NGC 6720): I. Imaging of the rings, globules, and arcs. *arXiv e-prints*, arXiv:2308.09027.
Winckel, H. V., Evans, T. L., Reyniers, M., Deroo, P., & Gielen, C. 2006, Binary post-AGB stars and their Keplerian discs. *Memorie della Societa Astronomica Italiana*, 77, 943. (c) 2006: SAIt.
Wright, G. S., Rieke, G. H., Glasse, A., & et al. 2023, The Mid-infrared Instrument for JWST and Its In-flight Performance. *PASP*, 135(1046), 048003.

Planetary Nebulae: A Universal Toolbox in the Era of Precision Astrophysics
Proceedings IAU Symposium No. 384, 2025
O. De Marco, A. Zijlstra & R. Szczerba, eds.
doi:10.1017/S1743921323005562

The Red Rectangle: a thin disk with big grains

Javier Alcolea[1], Valentín Bujarrabal[1], Arancha Castro-Carrizo[2], Jacques Kluska[3], Carmen Sánchez Contreras[4] and Hans van Winckel[3]

[1]Observatorio Astronómico Nacional (IGN/CNIG), MITMA, Spain
email: j.alcolea@oan.es

[2]Institut de Radioastronomie Millimétrique, France

[3]Instituut voor Sterrenkunde, KU Leuven, Belgium

[4]Centro de Astrobiología (CAB), CSIC-INTA, Spain

Abstract. The Red Rectangle is a nebula surrounding the post-AGB star HD 44179. It is the prototype of a particular class of nebulae associated with post-AGB binaries characterised by the presence of stable circumbinary disks in (quasi-)Keplerian rotation. Here we present the results of new high-resolution ($0\farcs02$–$0\farcs05$) ALMA observations of continuum and line emissions at 0.9 mm. The continuum maps are analysed through a simple model of dust emission, which can reproduce the observational data. We find that most dust emission in the Red Rectangle is concentrated in the central regions of the rotating disk and that the settlement of dust grains onto the equatorial plane is very significant, particularly in comparison with the much larger scale height displayed by the gas distribution. The diameter of the dust-emitting region is about 250 au, with a total width of about 50 au. This region coincides with the warm PDR where certain molecules (like HCN), CI, and CII are presumably formed, as well as probably PAHs. From the spectral index, we confirm the presence in the disk of large grains, with a typical radius of about 150 μm, which supports the long-lived hypothesis for this structure. We also confirm the existence of a compact ionised wind at the centre of the nebula, probably emerging from the accretion disk around the companion, for which we derive an extent of about 10 au and a total flux of 8 mJy. We also briefly present the results on molecular lines of ^{12}CO, ^{13}CO, and other less abundant species.

Keywords. stars: AGB and post-AGB — circumstellar matter — radio continuum: stars — radio lines: stars — binary — planetary nebulae: individual: Red Rectangle

1. Introduction

There is a class of binary stars consisting of a post-AGB primary and a main-sequence secondary, with about 85 members in our galaxy (Van Winckel 2003; Kluska *et al.* 2022). These sources are systematically surrounded by circumbinary disks in (sub-)Keplerian rotation (Deroo *et al.* 2006; Bujarrabal *et al.* 2013a,b, 2015, 2016; Kluska *et al.* 2019). Very often, they also present a disk-wind bipolar outflow (Gallardo Cava *et al.* 2022, 2023). It is also believed that these disks are responsible for the observed orbital periods of $\sim 150-2000$ d: these values lie in between the bimodal distribution of periods predicted for post-AGB binaries (Nie *et al.* 2012; Oomen *et al.* 2018; Van Winckel 2018), suggesting a strong angular momentum exchange between the stellar system and the circumbinary rotating disk.

Table 1. Observed continuum ranges and detected spectral lines.

Observed frequency range and native spectral resolution	Detected lines	Adopted rest frequency	Upper level energy	Spectral resolution used in the maps
330.350 – 330.827 GHz (0.21 $\mathrm{km\,s^{-1}}$)	^{13}CO J=3–2	330 587.965 MHz	31.7 K	(0.5 $\mathrm{km\,s^{-1}}$)
330.744 – 332.658 GHz (0.85 $\mathrm{km\,s^{-1}}$)	H_2O ν_2=2 J_{K_a,K_c}=$3_{2,1}$–$4_{1,4}$	331 123.730 MHz	4881.4 K	(1.0 $\mathrm{km\,s^{-1}}$)
343.563 – 345.448 GHz (0.85 $\mathrm{km\,s^{-1}}$)	SiO ν=1 J=8–7	344 916.247 MHz	1843.6 K	(1.0 $\mathrm{km\,s^{-1}}$)
	H^{13}CN ν_2=1 J=4–3 l=1e	345 238.771 MHz	1057.2 K	(1.0 $\mathrm{km\,s^{-1}}$)
	H^{13}CN J=4–3	345 339.769 MHz	41.4 K	(1.0 $\mathrm{km\,s^{-1}}$)
345.558 – 346.032 GHz (0.21 $\mathrm{km\,s^{-1}}$)	^{12}CO J=3–2	345 795.990 MHz	33.2 K	(0.5 $\mathrm{km\,s^{-1}}$)

One of the best-studied members of this class is the post-AGB star HD 44179 in Monoceros, which lies at the centre of an X-shaped nebula known as the Red Rectangle (Cohen *et al.* 2004; Bujarrabal *et al.* 2013b, 2016). At a distance of 710 pc, this source has been modelled in detail by Menshchikov *et al.* (2002) from IR imaging. The axis of the nebula is slightly off the plane of the sky, and the equatorial plane is oriented at a parallactic angle (PA) of 103°. The binary has a period of 317 d, and the total stellar mass is 1.8 $M_\odot$ (Thomas *et al.* 2011). The source has a peculiar chemistry with an O-rich component and strong C-rich extended red emission (ERE) and PAH IR features in the nebula (see *e.g.* Cohen *et al.* 2004), which in addition to the detection of CI, CII, and some molecular lines, points to the existence of a photon-dominated region (PDR) at the centre of this object (Bujarrabal *et al.* 2016).

The nebula was previously mapped with ALMA at a resolution of 0.″5 by Bujarrabal *et al.* (2013b, 2016), revealing the structure and velocity field of the molecular gas in both the disk and the biconical outflow. Here we present new band 7 ALMA observations of the Red Rectangle but at a much higher spatial resolution, down to 0.″020 (20 mas).

2. The new ALMA observations

The observations presented here have been obtained at the ALMA project 2019.1.00177.S (Bujarrabal *et al.* 2023). These are band 7 observations in two array configurations with baseline lengths from 14 m to 14.9 km. The observed frequency ranges and native spectral resolutions, as well as the main properties of the spectral lines detected in addition to the continuum, are given in Table 1.

The attained spatial resolution is about 20 mas (14 au) for the continuum data (using robust weighting) and about 55 mas (40 au) for the spectral line data (using natural weighting). All data has been calibrated with the standard ALMA pipeline plus self-calibration using the pure continuum emission. We have verified that the present data are consistent with the previous 0.″5 resolution ALMA observations, and that no flux is filtered out in the new dataset within the 20% calibration uncertainty. Additional information on the observations and data analysis procedure can be found in Bujarrabal *et al.* (2023).

3. Continuum emission results

The image of the continuum emission, shown in Fig. 1, left panel, consists of a central compact component (CCC) plus the contribution of a thin disk seen almost edge-on (dust disk component, DDC hereafter). The orientation of the equatorial plane is at PA=103°, with the symmetry axis close to the plane of the sky. For the central peak, we derive J2000 coordinates of R.A.=$06^h19^m58\overset{s}{.}1988$ and Dec.=$-10°38'15\overset{''}{.}216$, which have been adopted as the centre of our maps. Comparing these coordinates with those from

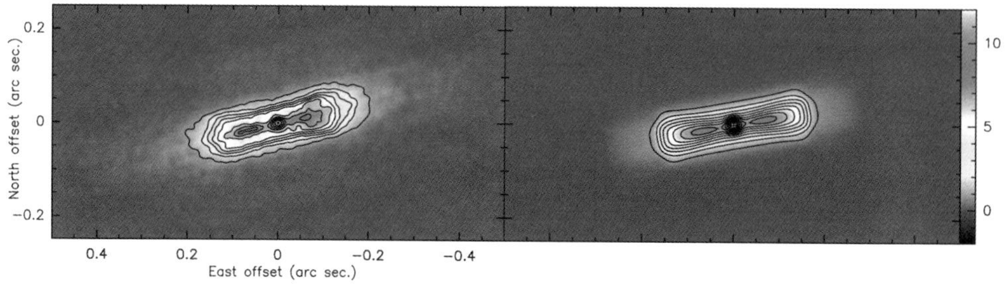

Figure 1. To the left, the new ALMA 0.9 mm continuum map of the Red Rectangle. The size of the circular restoring beam is 20 mas (14 au at 710 pc). To the right, results from our best-fit model of the continuum emission of the Red Rectangle at 0.9 mm as observed by ALMA (see Sect. 4). The model includes the contribution of the dust grain emission (DDC) and of the free-free of the central ionised wind (CCC). Intensity units are mJybeam^{-1}. Colour-coded scale is on the right side. Plotted contours are 1 to 12 by 1 mJybeam^{-1} (36 to 432 by 36 K in Rayleigh-Jeans equivalent brightness temperature). Colour-code scale and contours are the same in both real observed data and the results of the radiative transfer code.

previous VLA and ALMA observations (Jura *et al.* 1997; Bujarrabal *et al.* 2013b, 2016), we derive proper motion values of μ_x=–13.4±0.1 masa^{-1} and μ_y=–26.3±1.4 masa^{-1}.

The total detected fluxes are 664 and 722 mJy at 331.7 and 344.5 GHz respectively, from which we estimate a spectral index (SI) of about 2, compatible with the emission from dust grains of relatively large size (see Jura *et al.* 1997). To isolate the contribution of the CCC we have performed a compact source model fitting in the uv-plane just considering baselines longer than 5 km, eliminating the contribution from the more extended structures of the DDC. We have obtained a total flux of 8.3 mJy and a size of 15 mas (10 au) for the CCC, which we attribute to the free-free emission of an ionised gas wind (see Jura *et al.* 1997). After removing this contribution of the CCC, we find that the strongest continuum emission comes from a region 200 mas wide in diameter (140 au) and 25 mas in height (18 au).

We can get a better estimate of the SI for both CCC and DDC by comparing these new fluxes with those from the literature at cm- and sub-mm-wavelengths (Jura *et al.* 1997; Bujarrabal *et al.* 2013b, 2016). The results of the SIs fittings are shown in Fig. 2, left panel. The derived SI for the CCC is 0.8, very close to the expected value of 0.6 for an isothermal ionised wind of constant mass loss (Panagia & Felli 1975). This confirms the free-free nature of this emission but suggests deviations from the simple case of a homogeneous wind with a $1/r^2$ density. Using the CCC flux value at 0.9 mm, and assuming that the size measured for this component is several times the "so-called" characteristic radius, we derive a temperature of 3 600 – 10 000 K and a mass loss rate of $8\,10^{-8}$ – $1.7\,10^{-7}$ M$_\odot$a^{-1} for this ionised wind, very probably released by an accretion disk around the companion (Witt *et al.* 2009). The derived SI for the DDC, 2.13, is much closer to the value expected for an optically thick emission or the emission by very big grains regardless of the opacity (SI = 2.0), than to the value expected for an optically thin emission of small grains (SI = 3). In addition, the brightness measured in the disk reaches values larger than 200 K, implying that the opacity can not be very small (because the temperature of the grains cannot exceed ∼1000 – 1500 K). This suggests the presence of effective grain growth (see Jura *et al.* 1995, 1997) and moderate opacities in the strongest emitting regions of our disk.

4. Continuum modelling

To derive the physical parameters of the dusty disk that reproduces the continuum emission of the Red Rectangle at 0.9 mm, we have developed a simple model of radiative

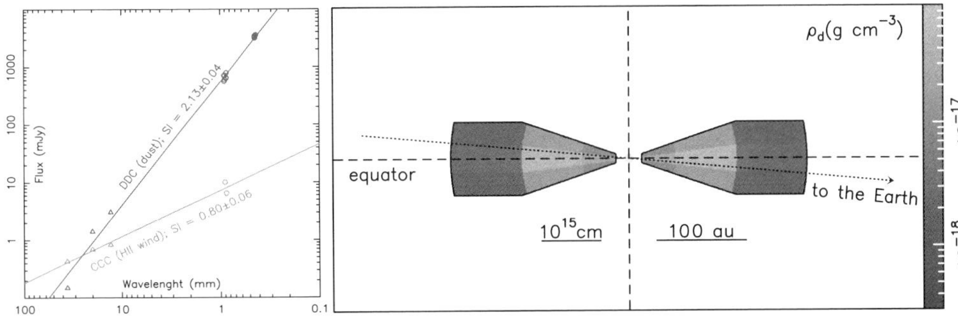

Figure 2. To the left, total integrated continuum fluxes in the Red Rectangle for the CCC in cyan, and the more extended DDC in red: we are assuming that the DDC flux is the total flux minus that from the CCC. cm-wave data (triangles) are from Jura *et al.* (1997), while sub-mm measurements (circles) are from Bujarrabal *et al.* (2013b, 2016), and this work (see Bujarrabal *et al.* 2023). The spectral indexes (and the corresponding formal errors), computed from regression lines, are also indicated. To the right, a sketch of the geometry, sizes, density distribution (grey scale), and viewing angle used for the model of the best fit of the data. The cyan dot at the centre represents the CCC, the compact ionised wind discussed in Sect. 3. See Sect. 4 and Bujarrabal *et al.* (2023) for additional details.

transfer for a dusty disk. Following Tielens (2005), we have adopted very simple laws for grain absorption/emissivity (scattering is not important at these wavelengths). We have assumed constant emissivity for wavelengths smaller than a characteristic one, about 10 times the grain radius, r_g, and an emissivity that decreases inversely proportional to the wavelength elsewhere. We have also adopted a grain density of 3.0 grcm^{-3}, typical of O-rich dust material. The best fitting of the data has been obtained for a r_g value of 150 μm, comparable to the value of 200 μm previously inferred by Jura *et al.* (1997). The density structure of the disk is described in Fig. 2, right panel. The temperature of the dust varies inversely to the square root of the distance to the centre, with a value of 400 K at 1.8 10^{15} cm (120 au), and an upper limit of 1200 K. The predicted emission from the model, directly comparable to the observations, is shown in Fig. 1, right panel, where we have also included the contribution from a small central component to account for the free-free emission of the CCC. Our best model geometry and density distribution are compatible with those of Menshchikov *et al.* (2002). For the assumed grain density, we derive a total dust mass in the disk of 5 10^{-5} – 10^{-4} M$_\odot$. This is 150 times smaller than the total molecular mass of the disk (Gallardo Cava *et al.* 2023). This gas/dust mass ratio value may look a bit low for O-rich environments but note that these circumbinary disks around binary post-AGB sources, including the Red Rectangle, are molecule deficient compared to standard AGB circumstellar envelopes (see Gallardo Cava *et al.* 2022).

Apart from effective grain growth, our model also finds a strong settlement of solid material onto the equatorial plane of the disk: 80% of the disk's solid mass lies at distances from the equatorial plane smaller than 5 10^{14} cm ($\sim$35 au). The extent of this dense disk is also relatively small, with a width-to-height ratio of about 5: disk radius of 2.5 10^{15} cm ($\sim$175 au). These sizes are significantly smaller than the distribution shown by the molecular gas detected in quasi-Keplerian rotation (see Bujarrabal *et al.* 2016, and Sect. 5). The temperature of this dense dust disk varies between 350 and 1200 K at its outer and inner layers, respectively.

5. Molecular line results

Although the flux filtered out in these new high-resolution observations is low or negligible, even for the most sensitive molecular gas probes like ^{12}CO, the new observations

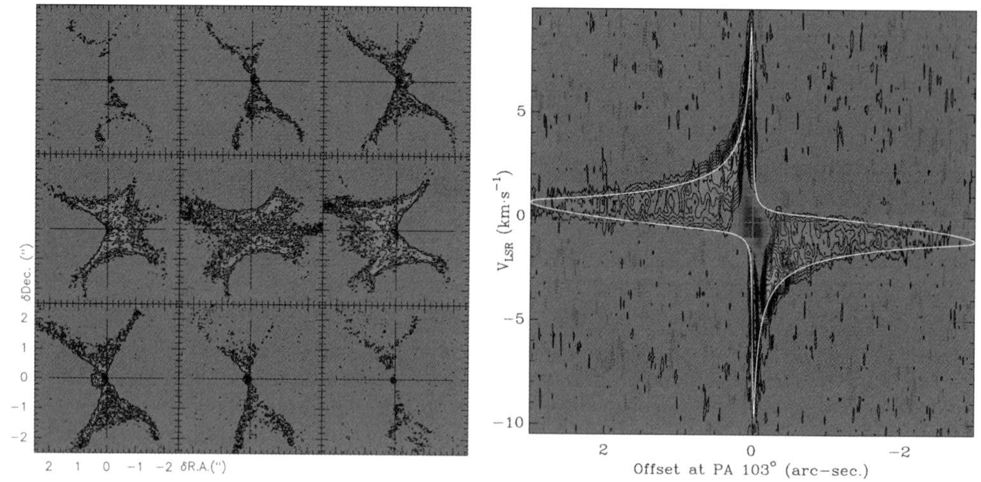

Figure 3. Results from the new ALMA band 7 observations of the Red Rectangle for the J=3–2 line of ^{12}CO. Here the restoring beam is $\sim$55 mas and the velocity resolution is 0.5 kms^{-1}. On the left panel, maps of the ^{12}CO emission for selected velocities (indicated in red figures at the top right corner). To the right, the velocity-position (PV) diagram along the equatorial direction (at PA=103°, i.e., positive offsets are in the east by south-east direction). The red cross marks the assumed central position and systemic velocity of the source (–0.25 kms^{-1}). The yellow line comprises the locations of the gas in the PV diagram according to the velocity law described in Sect. 5. In both panels, the contours are drawn every 0.005 mJybeam^{-1} ($\sim$20 K); negative levels are drawn in dashed blue.

mostly trace the rotating disk; the X-shaped wind is detected very noisily due to sensitivity limitations (see Fig. 3, left panel). On the contrary, the disk and its characteristic Keplerian-like rotation are traced with superb detail in both CO lines (see Figs. 3, right panel, and 4 respectively for ^{12}CO and ^{13}CO). The size of the molecular disk is much larger than that traced by the dust, 6″×1″ ($\sim$4000×700 UA) in ^{12}CO (2.″0×0.″5 in the case of ^{13}CO), i.e. up to $\sim$10 times bigger. We do not see signs of gas concentration or depletion at the equatorial plane: the negative flux seen at low velocities at the nebula's centre is due to the removal of the continuum emission from the line maps and the presence of opaque cold gas in between the continuum source and the observer. In the disk, ^{12}CO is mostly opaque: thus, the observed intensities provide direct information on the excitation of the gas. We derive $T_{\rm exc}$ ($\approx T_{\rm kin}$ for CO) up to 300 K, similar to the dust temperatures. ^{13}CO is partially opaque in the disk: therefore the estimation of parameters such as the ^{12}C/^{13}C ratio and the molecular disk mass requires detailed modelling. In the disk, we detect an inner radius of the molecular gas emission, $R_{\rm int}$, of $\sim$0.″04 (28 au): we are not claiming that there is a central region devoid of molecular gas, just that these central parts do not emit in any of the detected lines above our detection threshold (of about 10 K). Reconciling the observed velocities with central stellar mass requires the presence of rotation and radial expansion that decrease with the square root of the distance to the center: $V_{\rm rot} = 8\sqrt{(R_{\rm int}/r)}$ kms^{-1} and $V_{\rm exp} = 5\sqrt{(R_{\rm int}/r)}$ kms^{-1} (see Fig. 3, right panel).

In addition to the previously mapped lines of ^{12}CO and ^{13}CO J=3–2, and of H^{13}CN J=4–3 (Bujarrabal *et al.* 2013b, 2016), we have also detected vibrationally excited lines of H^{13}CN, H_2O and SiO, with upper-level excitation energies over 1000 K (see Table 1). The emission of these three vibrationally excited lines is very similar (see Fig. 4): they show a very compact central emission, just tracing the inner regions of the rotating disk, from a very narrow range of distances from the centre, $\sim$150 mas (100 au). This is probably related to the presence of the central PDR (Bujarrabal *et al.* 2016), and/or

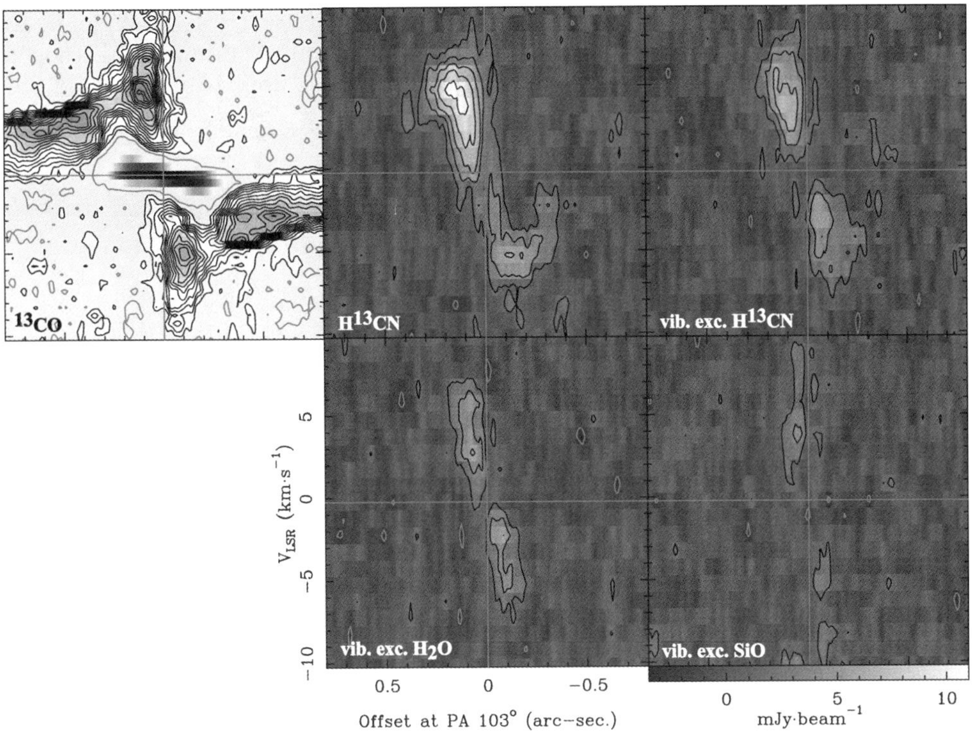

Figure 4. Results from the new ALMA band 7 observations of the Red Rectangle for species other than ^{12}CO. Velocity-position (PV) diagrams along the equatorial direction (PA=103°) for ^{13}CO (top left), ground and vibrationally excited H^{13}CN (top middle and top right respectively), and for vibrationally excited H_2O and SiO (bottom middle and bottom right respectively). The restoring beam is ~ 55 mas and the velocity resolution is 0.5 kms^{-1} for ^{13}CO and 1.0 kms^{-1} in the rest of the cases. The red cross marks the assumed central position and systemic velocity of the source (−0.25 kms^{-1}). The plot zooms into the central region of the disk where species other than CO are detected. On the top left panel, ^{13}CO clearly shows the signature of the quasi-Keplerian rotation. Here positive/negative contours are drawn in black/red. The negative values at the centre of the ^{13}CO panel (cyan and dark blue pixels) are due to the subtraction of the continuum emission and the presence of cold molecular gas in front of the dust disk. The rotation signature is barely hinted at in the H^{13}CN emission, which extends about $\pm 0\farcs35$. For the vibrationally excited emissions, just the inner rim of the molecule-rich rotating disk, extending just $\pm 0\farcs15$, is detected. Except for ^{13}CO, contours are drawn every 0.0025 mJybeam^{-1} (equivalent to ~ 10 K) and negative levels are drawn in dashed blue: the colour-code scale is shown below the SiO emission panel.

strong IR-pumping due to the dense warm dust at these locations. In the case of H^{13}CN J=4–3 from the ground vibrationally state, we observe a slightly more extended emission, up to 250 au from the centre. The detection of both C-rich (H^{13}CN) and O-rich species (H_2O), together with the detection of CI, CII, and PAHs strongly support the existence of a PDR at the centre of the nebula (Bujarrabal *et al.* 2016). ALMA mapping of CI is mandatory to confirm the presence of this PDR and derive its main properties.

Acknowledgements

This work is supported by the I+D+i coordinated project Nebulae Web, PID2019-105203GB-C21 EVENTs (JA, VB, ACC) and PID2019-105203GB-C22 Genesis (CSC), funded by the Spanish MCIN/AEI grant 10.13039/501100011033. The results presented in this contribution were obtained at the ALMA project 2019.1.00177.S (PI V. Bujarrbal).

ALMA is a partnership of ESO (representing its member states), NSF (USA) and NINS (Japan), together with NRC (Canada) and NSC and ASIAA (Taiwan), in cooperation with the Republic of Chile. The Joint ALMA Observatory is operated by ESO, AUI/NRAO and NAOJ.

References

Bujarrabal, V., Alcolea, J., Van Winckel, H., *et al.*, 2013a, *A&A*, 557, A104
Bujarrabal, V., Castro-Carrizo, A., Alcolea, J., *et al.*, 2013b, *A&A*, 557, L11
Bujarrabal, V., Castro-Carrizo, A., Alcolea, J., & Van Winckel, H., 2015, *A&A*, 575, L7
Bujarrabal, V., Alcolea, J., Van Winckel, H., *et al.*, 2016, *A&A*, 557, L11
Bujarrabal, V., Alcolea, J., Castro-Carrizo, A., *et al.*, 2023, *A&A*, 677, L18
Cohen, M., Van Winckel, H., Bond, H. E., & Gull, T. R., 2004, AJ, 127, 2362
Deroo, P., Van Winckel, H., Min, M., *et al.*, 2006, *A&A*, 450, 181
Gallardo, Cava, I., Bujarrabal, V., Alcolea, J., *et al.*, 2022, *A&A*, 659, A134
Gallardo Cava, I., Alcolea, J., Bujarrabal, V., *et al.*, 2023, *A&A*, 671, A80
Jura, M., Balm, S. P., & Kahane, C., 1995, *ApJ*, 453, 721
Jura, M., Turner, J., & Balm, S. P., 1997, *ApJ*, 474, 741
Kluska, J., Van Winckel, H., Hillen, M., *et al.*, 2019, *A&A*, 631, A108
Kluska, J., Van Winckel, H., Coppée, Q., *et al.*, 2022, *A&A*, 658, A36
Menshchikov, A. B., Schertl, D., Tuthill, P. G., *et al.*, 2002, *A&A*, 393, 867
Nie, D. J., Wood, P. R., & Nicholls, C. P., 2012, *MNRAS*, 423, 2764
Oomen, G.-M., Van Winckel, H., Pols O., *et al.*, 2018, *A&A*, 620, A85
Panagia, N. & Felli, M., 1975, *A&A*, 39, 1
Thomas, J. D., Witt, A. N., Aufdenberg, J. P., *et al.*, 2011, MNRAS, 417, 2860
Tielens, A. G. G. M., 2005, The Physics and Chemistry of the Interstellar Medium. Cambridge Univ. Press
Van Winckel, H., 2003, *ARAA*, 41, 391
Van Winckel, H., 2018, arXiv:1809.00871
Witt, A. N., Vijh, U. P., Hobbs, L. M., *et al.*, 2009, *ApJ*, 693, 1946

Planetary Nebulae: A Universal Toolbox in the Era of Precision Astrophysics
Proceedings IAU Symposium No. 384, 2025
O. De Marco, A. Zijlstra & R. Szczerba, eds.
doi:10.1017/S1743921324001224

Dust formation during the interaction of binary stars by common envelope

Luis C. Bermúdez-Bustamante[1,2], Orsola De Marco[1,2], Lionel Siess[3], Daniel J. Price[4], Miguel González-Bolívar[1,2], Mike Y. M. Lau[4,5,6], Chunliang Mu[1,2], Ryosuke Hirai[4,5], Taïssa Danilovich[4,7] and Mansi Kasliwal[8]

[1]School of Mathematical and Physical Sciences, Macquarie University, Balaclava Road, North Ryde, Sydney, NSW 2109, Australia

[2]Astrophysics and Space Technologies Research Centre, Macquarie University, Balaclava Road, North Ryde, Sydney, NSW 2109, Australia

[3]Institut d'Astronomie et d'Astrophysique, Université Libre de Bruxelles (ULB), CP 226, 1050 Brussels, Belgium

[4]School of Physics and Astronomy, Monash University, Clayton, Victoria 3800, Australia

[5]OzGrav: The ARC Centre of Excellence for Gravitational Wave Discovery, Australia

[6]Heidelberger Institut für Theoretische Studien, Schloss-Wolfsbrunnenweg 35, 69118 Heidelberg, Germany

[7]ARC Centre of Excellence for All Sky Astrophysics in 3 Dimensions (ASTRO 3D), Clayton 3800, Australia

[8]Division of Physics, Mathematics, and Astronomy, California Institute of Technology, Pasadena, CA 91125, USA

Abstract. We performed numerical simulations of the common envelope (CE) interaction between two intermediate-mass asymptotic giant branch (AGB) stars and their low-mass companions. For the first time, formation and growth of dust in the envelope is calculated explicitly. We find that the first dust grains appear as early as ~1–3 yrs after the onset of the CE, and are smaller than grains formed later. As the simulations progress, a high-opacity dusty shell forms, resulting in the CE photosphere being up to an order of magnitude larger than it would be without the inclusion of dust. At the end of the simulations, the total dust yield is $\sim 8.2 \times 10^{-3}$ $M_\odot$ ($\sim 2.2 \times 10^{-2}$ $M_\odot$) for a CE with a 1.7 $M_\odot$ (3.7 $M_\odot$) AGB star. Dust formation does not substantially lead to more mass unbinding or substantially alter the orbital evolution.

Keywords. stars: AGB and post-AGB, stars: winds, outflows, (stars:) binaries (including multiple): close

1. Introduction

Unstable mass transfer from an expanding, more massive star to a compact star leads to a CE interaction (Ivanova et al. 2013). The envelope of the giant eventually surrounds both the donor star's core and the companion. At the end of this phase, the envelope may be ejected and a binary system with a much smaller orbital separation or a merger is left behind.

The exact source(s) of energy driving the expansion and ejection of the envelope is not fully identified, and there are problems when considering only orbital energy and angular momentum transfer from the stars to the envelope (but see Valsan et al. 2023), although the work done by recombination energy released in inner layers of the donor likely plays a major role (e.g., Ivanova et al. 2015; Reichardt et al. 2020; Lau et al. 2022).

The CE interaction leads to the formation of systems such as cataclysmic variables, X-ray binaries or progenitors of type Ia supernovae (Paczynski 1971; Ivanova et al. 2013; De Marco & Izzard 2017). It is also likely responsible for at least a fraction of intermediate luminosity transients (Kasliwal et al. 2011), such as luminous red novae (e.g., Blagorodnova et al. 2017), some of which produce dust (Tylenda et al. 2011; Nicholls et al. 2013). From the above, dust might act as an additional driving mechanism, altering the appearance of transient objects by increasing their opacity.

Previous studies on dust in interacting binary stars were conducted in 1D (Lü et al. 2013), analyzed envelope thermodynamic properties without explicitly calculating dust formation (Glanz & Perets 2018; Reichardt et al. 2019), calculated dust formation but in post-processing (Iaconi & De Marco 2019; Iaconi et al. 2020), or focused on the phase before the common envelope (Bermudez et al. 2020).

In González-Bolívar et al. (2023, hereafter paper I) we performed CE simulations with intermediate-mass AGB stars, using a simplified formulation by Bowen (1988) to calculate the dust opacity. We find that dust does not significantly increase the mass loss, but it does increase the envelope opacity. Unfortunately, the Bowen formulation does not provide us with information about the properties of the dust, such as its mass or grains size. For this reason, we perform CE simulations with an explicit calculation of the dust formation process.

2. Numerical Setup

We use the same stellar models as in Paper I, calculated with the 1D stellar evolution code of MESA (e.g., Paxton et al. 2011). The first model is an AGB star, evolved from the main sequence, with a total mass of 1.7 $M_\odot$ (0.56 $M_\odot$ in the core), a radius of 260 $R_\odot$, undergoing its seventh thermal pulse. The second model is an AGB star with a total mass of 3.7 $M_\odot$ (0.72 $M_\odot$ in the core), a radius of 343 $R_\odot$, experiencing its fourth thermal pulse. Both models feature a 0.6 $M_\odot$ companion star initially positioned at the critical distance for triggering Roche lobe overflow, i.e., at a distance of 550 $R_\odot$ (637 $R_\odot$) from the 1.7 $M_\odot$ (3.7 $M_\odot$) AGB star.

We use the smoothed particle hydrodynamics (SPH) code PHANTOM (Price et al. 2018) with 1.37×10^6 SPH particles as was done by González-Bolívar et al. (2022). We also use PHANTOM's implementation of MESA's OPAL/SCVH equation of state tables (as done by Reichardt et al. 2020) to account for recombination energy. We assume the formation of carbon-rich dust with a C/O ratio of 2.5, despite both AGB stars having a C/O ratio of 0.32 when our MESA models ceased. The C/O ratio is not anticipated to impact the AGB convective structure.

We use the treatment described in Siess et al. (2022) for carbon dust nucleation and growth, which takes place in two steps: i) the formation of seed particles from the gas phase in the so-called nucleation stage, followed by ii) a growth phase where monomers (dust building blocks) accumulate on the seed particles to reach macroscopic dimensions. The treatment is based on the theory of moments presented by Gail et al. (1984, and subsequent papers).

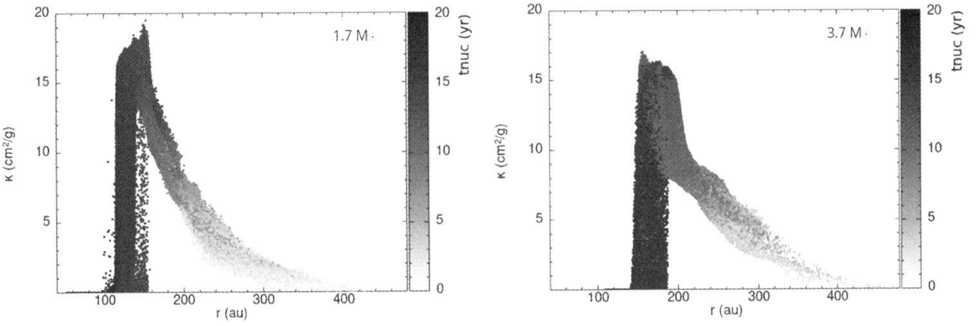

Figure 1. Dust opacity versus distance from the centre of mass for the 1.7 M$_\odot$ (left) and 3.7 M$_\odot$ (right) models after 20 years of simulation. The color bar indicates $t_{\rm nuc}$, the time in years after the start of the simulations, when dust nucleation occurred for each SPH particle.

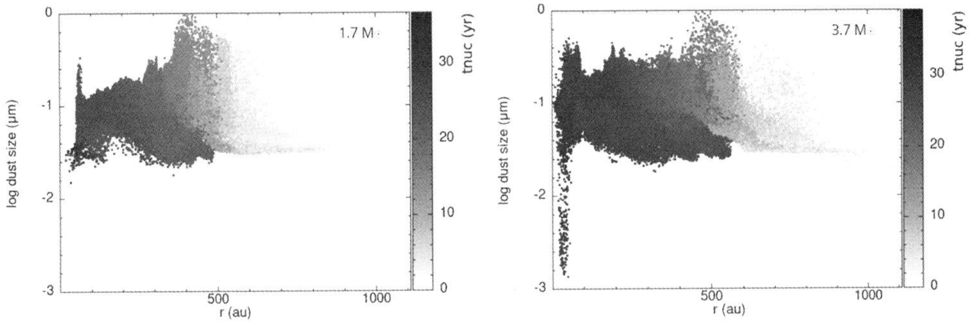

Figure 2. Average dust grains size versus distance for the 1.7 M$_\odot$ (top) and 3.7 M$_\odot$ (bottom) model, after 44 years of simulations. Same color bar as in Figure 1.

3. Dust properties and its impact on orbital and thermodynamics properties

3.1. *Opacity of dust grains*

Figure 1 shows a snapshot† of the dust opacity as a function of distance from the center of mass (the color bar depicts nucleation time $t_{\rm nuc}$ as explained in the caption) at 20 years from the start of the simulation. In the inner regions where there is no dust, the opacity is constant, at a user-defined value of 2×10^{-4} cm^2 g^{-1}. This value is appropriate for recombined gas, but too low for the ionised regions where electron scattering opacities are of the order of 0.5 cm^2 g^{-1}. However, this is not important for now as these inner hot regions do not experience dust formation, which happens ∼1–3 yrs from the start of the simulation, in a shell with radii of ∼10–20 au. When dust forms, the opacity rapidly increases to values of ∼17–20 cm^2 g^{-1} and decreases to almost zero again at larger radii. The dust forming shell radius expands over time and at 20 years it is ∼130 au (160 au) from the 1.7 M$_\odot$ (3.7 M$_\odot$) model. The dust forming shell thickness is also variable.

3.2. *Dust size*

Figure 2 shows a snapshot of dust grains size as a function of distance (same color bar as in Figure 1). Early dust grains (yellow colour in Figure 2) have a narrow range in size around ∼0.02–0.04 μm, and late dust grains (darker colours) have a lager size between ∼0.03 and 1 μm. In the 1.7 M$_\odot$ (3.7 M$_\odot$) model, the largest dust grains are formed at

† Movies corresponding to the figures are available at: `https://tinyurl.com/y455avdj`.

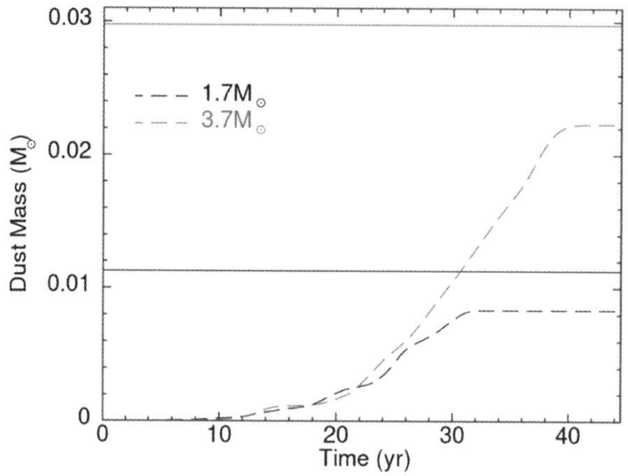

Figure 3. Dashed lines show the total dust mass over time in CE simulations. Horizontal lines represent the maximum carbon available in the envelope for 1.7 M$_\odot$ (black solid) and 3.7 M$_\odot$ (red solid) AGB stars.

~12 yrs (~15 yrs). Interestingly, at the very end of the 3.7 M$_\odot$ simulation (~44 years), dust formation resumes in a thin shell near the centre, but at a low rate.

Depending on t_{nuc}, dust grains grew to different maximum sizes. Our formalism does not include dust destruction, so once a grain stops growing, its size remains constant. However, what is plotted in Figure 2 is the average grain size in a given SPH particle, which can contain many dust grains because it has a set total mass, e.g., 1.7×10^{27} g or 8.3×10^{-7} M$_\odot$ in the 1.7 M$_\odot$ simulation. As such, the average dust grain size in an SPH particle can decrease if new small grains are formed, even after previously-formed grains have become large.

3.3. *Dust mass*

Figure 3 shows that for the 1.7 M$_\odot$ (3.7 M$_\odot$) model, the total dust mass increases steadily until it plateaus at ~32 yrs (~38 yrs) with a value of ~8.2×10^{-3} M$_\odot$ (~2.2×10^{-2} M$_\odot$). Although it is difficult to establish a pattern with only two stars, we see that the more massive the donor star, the longer it takes for the total amount of dust to plateau.

After ~40 yrs, the 1.7 M$_\odot$ (3.7 M$_\odot$) model has produced roughly four (ten) times more dust than during the first ~20 yrs. The drastic increase and subsequent plateauing of dust mass is a consequence of a large fraction of the expanding envelope reaching temperatures below the condensation threshold. Because of that, nucleation is efficient (i.e., there is a large number of dust seeds) and the addition of monomers contribute to dust growth, producing the increase in the dust mass. However, with further gas expansion the nucleation rate decreases, fewer monomers are available and dust production is consequently reduced.

Compared to simulations by Iaconi et al. (2020) for carbon grains, the amount of dust formed in our 1.7 M$_\odot$ (3.7 M$_\odot$) model is four (ten) times larger for a star twice (four times) as massive. In Iaconi et al. (2020), the total dust mass plateaus at $\sim 2.2 \times 10^{-3}$ M$_\odot$ after ~14 yrs for a 0.88 M$_\odot$ RGB star, which started off with a radius of 83 R$_\odot$. It is difficult to comment on whether these differences are due to the different type of stars, to the fact that Iaconi et al. (2020) post-processed the dust formation in their star, or to the nucleation formalism used.

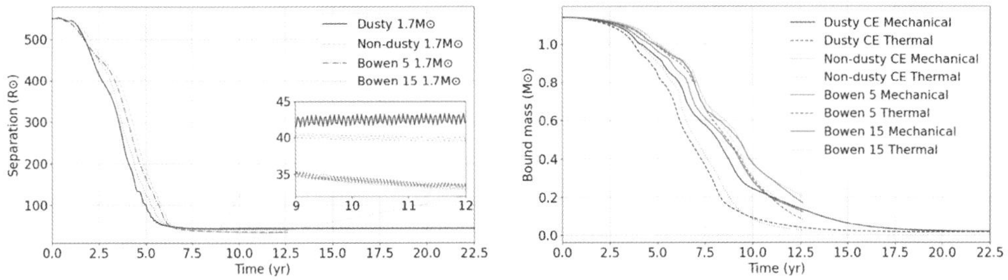

Figure 4. Left panel: orbital separation over time in CE simulations with a 1.7 $M_\odot$ AGB star. Dust formation is explicitly calculated (blue lines), or assumed with a maximum dust opacity of 5 $cm^2\,g^{-1}$ (red lines) or 15 $cm^2\,g^{-1}$ (green lines) as in Paper I. Also shown is a CE simulation without dust (yellow lines). The inset displays the orbital separation at the end of the in-spiral phase. Right panel: Mechanical bound mass (solid lines) and thermal bound mass (dashed lines) over time.

3.4. *Orbital evolution, unbound mass and comparison with non-dusty simulations*

For all simulations, the dynamic in-spiral phase ends after ~7.5 yr (Figure 4, left panel). The orbital separation decreases faster in models where dust opacity is calculated either explicitly (blue line), or using the Bowen opacity approximation (green and red lines), than in the model with no dust (yellow line). Radiative forces have a significant impact on accelerating the envelope, which interact through gravitational friction with the stars. On the other hand, the final (plateau) separation is similar, being ~42 $R_\odot$ (blue line) and ~33 $R_\odot$ (yellow line), although the latter is still decreasing somewhat.

In the right panel of Figure 4, "mechanical" bound mass (solid lines) is the mass of SPH particles whose sum of kinetic and gravitational potential energy is negative, while "thermal" bound mass (dashed lines) is the mass of SPH particles whose sum of kinetic, gravitational and thermal energy (not including recombination energy) is less than zero. The bound mass decreases faster in models with explicit dust formation (blue lines) than in models (i) without dust (yellow lines) or (ii) with a maximum Bowen opacity of 5 $cm^2 g^{-1}$ (red lines); however, when the latter increases to 15 $cm^2 g^{-1}$ (green lines), the evolution of the bound mass is similar. High-opacity dust is located too far in the wind† to generate effective driving on a dynamical timescale required to aid with envelope ejection, because at those distances, the radiative flux is greatly diluted and the material is mostly unbound already. We conclude that dust formation does not lead to substantially more mass unbinding, although $\sim 10^{-2}$ $M_\odot$ of dust is produced.

4. The photospheric size

Figure 5 shows the average radius, in the polar and orbital directions, of the stellar surface where the optical depth, calculated using the Planck-mean opacity, becomes 1 (i.e. the photosphere). We note that after ~5 yrs the size of the photosphere is an order of magnitude larger when dust is included. This is expected, since dust opacity will be high enough for the expanding envelope to become optically thick. We also note that in the dusty model, the equatorial photosphere grows approximately one year before the polar photosphere, effectively indicating that there is a "hole" at the poles where an observer would see deeper into the object. However, this hole is filled rapidly and the size of the photosphere in the two orthogonal directions becomes very comparable, indicating an approximately spherical object.

† See movies of dust opacity versus distance at `https://tinyurl.com/y455avdj`.

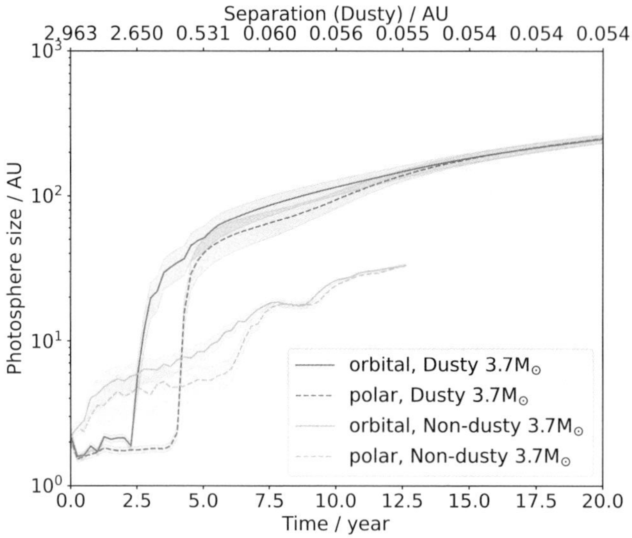

Figure 5. Photosphere size over time in the orbital (solid lines) and the "polar" plane (dashed lines) for the 3.7 $M_\odot$ model with and without dust (blue and orange, respectively). Shaded areas depict uncertainty.

5. Summary

We have carried out simulations of CE interactions of two intermediate-mass AGB stars (1.7 and 3.7 $M_\odot$) with a 0.6 $M_\odot$ companion. To test the dust grains properties, simulations include a self-consistent treatment of dust formation with a C/O ratio of 2.5 (by number). Our main conclusions are:

(1) Dust formation starts ~1–3 yrs after the onset of the CE and leads to the formation of a dusty shell that moves outward. At ~20 yrs the shell has a thickness of ~ 40 au and it is located at ~ 130 au (~ 160 au) in the 1.7 $M_\odot$ (3.7 $M_\odot$) model.
(2) Dust begins as tiny seeds and grows via monomer addition. The growth halts once the dust moves away along with the expanding envelope. Dust grains formed at ~1–3 yrs are smaller (~0.02–0.04 μm) than dust grains formed after ~10 yrs (~0.03–1 μm).
(3) The amount of dust rises and plateaus just below the theoretical maximum, yielding $\sim 8.2 \times 10^{-3}$ $M_\odot$ ($\sim 2.2 \times 10^{-2}$ $M_\odot$) for the 1.7 $M_\odot$ (3.7 $M_\odot$) model.
(4) High-opacity dust is located too far in the wind to generate effective driving on a dynamical timescale required to aid with envelope ejection. Because of that, although $\sim 10^{-2}$ $M_\odot$ of dust is produced, it does not lead to substantially more mass unbinding.
(5) Dust greatly impacts the optical appearance of the CE. At ~12 yrs, the photosphere is an order of magnitude larger if dust is included.

Movies corresponding to the figures are available at: `https://tinyurl.com/y455avdj`.

OD, LS, MK and LB acknowledge support through the Australian Research Council Discovery Program grant DP210101094. LS is senior research associates from F.R.S.-FNRS (Belgium). TD is supported in part by the Australian Research Council through a Discovery Early Career Researcher Award (DE230100183). This work was supported in part by Oracle Cloud credits and related resources provided by Oracle for Research. This work was performed in part on the OzSTAR national facility at Swinburne University of Technology. The OzSTAR program receives funding in part from the Astronomy National Collaborative Research Infrastructure Strategy (NCRIS) allocation provided by the Australian Government, and from the Victorian Higher Education State Investment Fund (VHESIF) provided by the Victorian Government. Some of the simulations were undertaken with the assistance of resources and services from the National Computational Infrastructure (NCI), which is supported by the Australian Government. This research was supported in part by the Australian Research Council Centre of Excellence for All Sky Astrophysics in 3 Dimensions (ASTRO 3D), through project number CE170100013.

References

Bermúdez-Bustamante L. C., García-Segura G., Steffen W., Sabin L., 2020, MNRAS, 493, 2606.
Blagorodnova N., Kotak R., Polshaw J., Kasliwal M. M., Cao Y., Cody A. M., Doran G. B., et al., 2017, yCat, J/ApJ/834/107.
Bowen G. H., 1988, ApJ, 329, 299.
De Marco O., Izzard R. G., 2017, PASA, 34, e001.
Gail H.-P., Keller R., Sedlmayr E., 1984, A&A, 133, 320
Glanz H., Perets H. B., 2018, MNRAS, 478, L12.
González-Bolívar M., Bermúdez-Bustamante L. C., De Marco O., Siess L., Price D. J., Kasliwal M., 2023, arXiv, arXiv:2306.16609.
González-Bolívar M., De Marco O., Lau M. Y. M., Hirai R., Price D. J., 2022, MNRAS, 517, 3181.
Iaconi R., De Marco O., 2019, MNRAS, 490, 2550.
Iaconi R., Maeda K., Nozawa T., De Marco O., Reichardt T., 2020, MNRAS, 497, 3166.
Ivanova N., Justham S., Chen X., De Marco O., Fryer C. L., Gaburov E., Ge H., et al., 2013, A&ARv, 21, 59.
Ivanova N., Justham S., Podsiadlowski P., 2015, MNRAS, 447, 2181.
Kasliwal M. M., Cenko S. B., Kulkarni S. R., Ofek E. O., Quimby R., Rau A., 2011, ApJ, 735, 94.
Lau M. Y. M., Hirai R., González-Bolívar M., Price D. J., De Marco O., Mandel I., 2022, MNRAS, 512, 5462.
Lü G., Zhu C., Podsiadlowski P., 2013, ApJ, 768, 193.
Nicholls C. P., Melis C., Soszynski I., Udalski A., Szymanski M. K., Kubiak M., Pietrzynski G., et al., 2013, MNRAS, 431, L33.
Paczyński B., 1971, ARA&A, 9, 183.
Paxton B., Bildsten L., Dotter A., Herwig F., Lesaffre P., Timmes F., 2011, ApJS, 192, 3.
Price D. J., Wurster J., Tricco T. S., Nixon C., Toupin S., Pettitt A., Chan C., et al., 2018, PASA, 35, e031.
Reichardt T. A., De Marco O., Iaconi R., Tout C. A., Price D. J., 2019, MNRAS, 484, 631.
Reichardt T. A., De Marco O., Iaconi R., Chamandy L., Price D. J., 2020, MNRAS, 494, 5333.
Siess L., Homan W., Toupin S., Price D. J., 2022, A&A, 667, A75.
Tylenda R., Hajduk M., Kamiński T., Udalski A., Soszyński I., Szymański M. K., Kubiak M., et al., 2011, A&A, 528, A114.
Valsan V., Borges S. V., Prust L., Chang P., 2023, MNRAS, 526, 5365.

Planetary Nebulae: A Universal Toolbox in the Era of Precision Astrophysics
Proceedings IAU Symposium No. 384, 2025
O. De Marco, A. Zijlstra & R. Szczerba, eds.
doi:10.1017/S1743921324002011

The evolutionary path from the AGB to the PN phases: certainties and open issues

Paolo Ventura

INAF - Observatory of Rome
email: paolo.ventura@inaf.it

Abstract. The modelling of the evolutionary phases beyond the asymptotic giant branch attracts the interest of the astrophysical community because it allows the determination of the properties of progenitor stars and to deduce the efficiency of the mechanisms able to alter the surface chemistry of the stars evolving through the asymptotic giant branch. This has been possible since improvements in the modelling of these phases, which allow a reliable determination of the luminosity with which stars evolve after the termination the asymptotic giant branch evolution.

The surface chemistry of post-asymptotic giant branch stars and planetary nebulae is shown to be tightly correlated to the various processes taking place during the asymptotic giant branch evolution. The possibility of using the observed infrared excess of these evolved stars to derive information on the dust formation process during the previous evolutionary phases is also discussed.

Keywords. stars: AGB and post-AGB, stars: planetary nebulae

1. Introduction

About half century has passed since the early, pioneering attempts (Paczyński 1970a,b) to model the evolution of stars during the phases following the asymptotic giant branch (AGB), when a general contraction process begins as a reaction to the gradual ejection of the external envelope, wich precedes the white dwarf phase, not before evolving through the post-AGB and the PNe phases (Iben & Renzini 1983).

The modelling of these evolutionary phases is exceptionally difficult, owing to the combination of numerical complexities, which naturally arise along the transition from the AGB to the post-AGB, and long computational times. After the aforementioned studies, driven by Paczynski (Paczyński 1971), in which only the post-AGB phases were modelled, significant steps forward were made thanks to the studies by the Potzdam team (Bloecker & Schoenberner 1990; Bloecker 1995; Schönberner & Blöcker 1996), until the most recent investigations by Miller Bertolami (2016) and Kamath et al. (2023).

The interest towards the evolutionary phases that follow the AGB stems from the relatively easy analysis of their spectra, which allows a solid determination of the surface chemical composition (van Winckel 2003); this is at odds with AGB stars, whose spectral energy distribution is characterized by the presence of large molecular bands, which prevents a reliable estimate of the abundances of the individual chemical species (García-Hernández et al. 2006, 2009). In this regard, post-AGB and PNe sources offer notable information on the AGB phase, because their surface chemistry reflects the efficiency of the various processes able to alter the surface chemistry, primarily hot bottom burning (Renzini & Voli 1981; Bloecker & Schoenberner 1991) and third dredge-up (Iben 1974). The knowledge of the surface chemistry of the stars evolving beyond the AGB offers a notable opportunity for their characterization: this approach was recently followed by Kamath et al. (2023), to identify a sample of Galactic post-AGB stars, and by Ventura et al. (2015, 2016, 2017); and by Stanghellini et al. (2022), to study samples of PNe in the Magellanic Clouds and in the Milky Way.

The study of post-AGB stars and PNe is also important to study dust formation in the winds of evolved stars. While significant dust formation takes place during the AGB phase (Zhukovska, Gail, & Trieloff 2008; Sloan et al. 2009), no condensation of gas molecules into solid grains is expected to occur during the very late evolutionary phases of stars. However, the dust produced during the previous AGB phases leaves a clear signature in the spectral energy distribution (SED) of post-AGB stars and PNe, in the form of a significant infrared excess. Moreover, this can be easily analysed, since the peak of the emission in the mid-IR spectral interval is clearly separated from the black-body like emission from the central stars, which peaks in the visible. In this regard, the analysis of the SED of the stars evolving through evolutionary phases beyond the AGB allows one to draw important conclusions on the dust formation rate taking place during the very late AGB phases (Tosi et al. 2022; Dell'Agli et al. 2023). Because it is during these phases that most of the dust is released, this approach opens the way towards a better comprehension of the role that AGB stars play as dust manufacturers.

In this review we will first present, in Section 2, a brief overview of the evolution of the stars through the AGB, with particular emphasis given to the role of the initial mass; in Section 3 we describe the most relevant aspects of the evolution of the stars during the phases following the AGB, along with the thermal and chemical structure; Section 4 is devoted to a historical account of the attempts to model the post-AGB phases; the importance of the study of post-AGB stars and PNe to draw information on the physical mechanisms able to alter the surface chemistry of AGB stars and as important tracers of the dust formation process during the final AGB phases are addressed, respectively, in Sections 5 and 6; the conclusions are given in the final section.

2. The evolution through the AGB: stellar structure and evolution

The evolution of the stars through the AGB is characterized by the gradual growth of the core mass, favoured by the continuous flux of H-exhausted matter into the core, connected to the CNO burning activity in a shell laying between the core and the external convective mantle (Busso, Gallino, & Wasserburg 1999; Karakas & Lattanzio 2014). The increase in core mass leads to the increase in the luminosity (Paczyński 1971), while the mass of the envelope decreases, owing to the intense mass loss experienced by these stars. The AGB evolution is also characterized by the expansion of the stellar structure. This is primarily due to the fact that the gradients of the thermodynamic variables become steeper and steeper as the AGB evolution proceeds; for carbon stars the cooling and expansion of the outer regions is further enhanced by the gradual increase in the surface carbon, which leads to the increase in the surface molecular opacities (Marigo 2002).

As far as the behaviour of the surface chemical composition is concerned, we can broadly distinguish three behaviours, related to the (initial) mass and also to the metallicity of the stars, which we describe briefly below. We note that the role of mass and metallicity are tightly connected in this context: both the minimum mass required to reach the C-star stage and the lower threshold in mass required to ignite HBB increase with metallcity (Karakas & Lattanzio 2014; Ventura et al. 2022). In what follows, we will refer to the mass of the star at the beginning of the AGB phase. These are approximately consistent with main sequence masses for $M > 1.5 M_{\odot}$; on the other hand, for lower mass stars the mass loss taking place during the red giant branch evolution must be considered, thus the masses given below must be considered as lower limit of the initial masses.

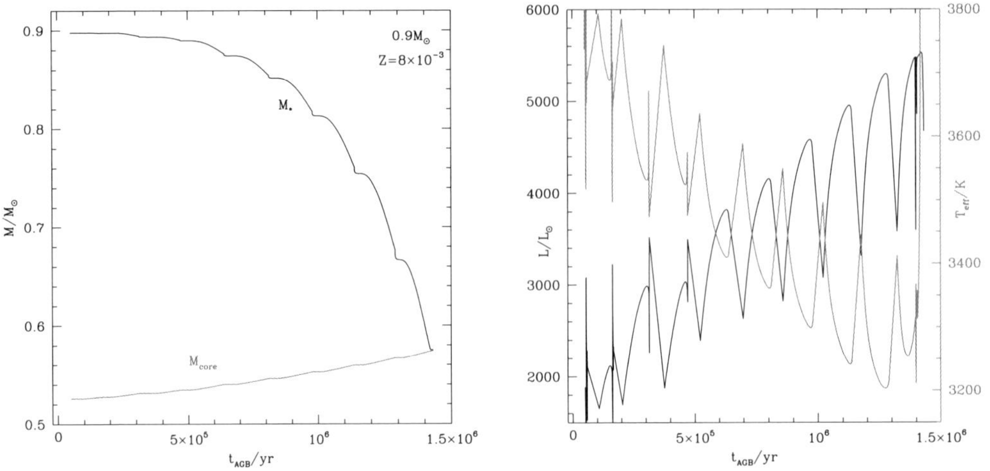

Figure 1. Left: time variation of the total mass (black line) and of the core mass (red) of a 0.9 M$_\odot$ (this mass refers to the beginning of the AGB phase, and corresponds to 1 M$_\odot$ at ZAMS) model star of metallicity $Z = 4 \times 10^{-3}$. Right: time variation of the luminosity (black line, scale on the left y-axis) and effective temperature (red, scale on the right) of the same model star.

2.1. *Low-mass stars*

The stars of mass below ~ 1 M$_\odot$ undergo a gradual loss of the external mantle, which proceeds on time scales of the order of ~ 1 Myr. An example of this kind of evolution is shown in Fig. 1, which reports the time evolution of the core and total mass of the star (left panel), and of the luminosity and effective temperature (right panel). We note the gradual rise in the luminosity, which increases from ~ 2000 L$_\odot$ to ~ 6000 L$_\odot$ during the AGB lifetime. This is accompanied by the cooling of the external regions, witnessed by the decrease in the effective temperature.

The surface chemistry of these stars is not expected to undergo significant changes during the AGB, because of the small number of thermal pulses experienced, of the order of 4-5, which prevents third dredge-up (TDU) from favouring the surface carbon enrichment. Therefore, the final chemical composition of these stars reflects the effect of the first dredge-up only (Karakas & Lattanzio 2014).

2.2. *Carbon stars*

The AGB evolution of stars of initial mass in the $1 - 3$ M$_\odot$ range is characterized by the occurrence of several TDU events, which leads to the formation of carbon stars, after the surface carbon abundance by number exceeds that of oxygen (Iben 1974).

As shown in the left panel of Fig. 2, the luminosity increases with the core mass, similarly to the low-mass counterparts discussed earlier in this section. On the other hand, we see in the right panel of the figure that repeated TDU events eventually result in the surface carbon abundance to exceed that of oxygen, which stars the carbon star phase (grey-shaded region in Fig. 2).

The achievement of the carbon star stage favours a rapid expansion of the external regions, the consequent decrease in the surface gravity, and a fast increase in the rate of mass loss (Marigo 2002; Ventura & Marigo 2009, 2010). This can be intuitively understood by looking at the behaviour of the total mass of the star in the left panel of Fig. 2, where it is clear that the rate at which the envelope is lost suddenly increases after the carbon star stage is reached. A straight consequence of this is that while the star evolves as M-type for the majority of the AGB lifetime, most of the gas ejected is carbon rich:

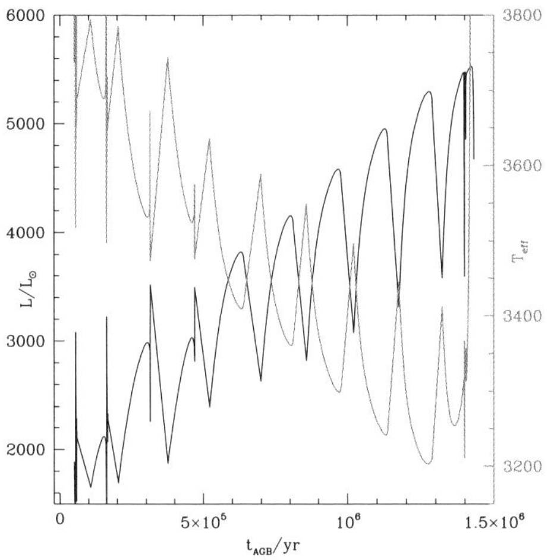

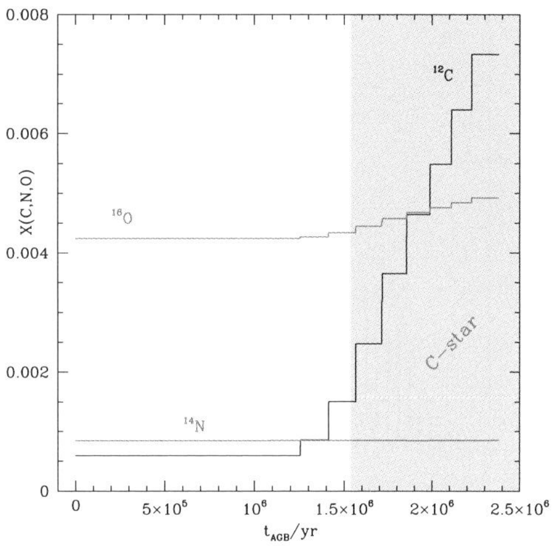

Figure 2. Left: time variation of the total and core mass (black and red lines, respectively, scale on the left y-axis) and of the luminosity (blue line, scale on the right) of a 2 $M_\odot$ model star (this is approximately the ZAMS mass, given the small mass lost by stars in this mass range during the evolutionary phases preceding the core helium burning) of metallicity $Z = 4 \times 10^{-3}$. Right: time variation of the CNO surface mass fractions of the same model star. The grey shaded area indicates the phases during which the star is a carbon star.

this is extremely important when the role of these stars as pollutants of the interstellar medium is considered.

2.3. *Massive AGB stars*

The AGB evolution of stars descending from $M > 3\ M_\odot$ progenitors is characterized by the activation of hot bottom burning (HBB), the physical mechanism consisting in the activation of an advanced proton capture nucleosynthesis at the base of the surface envelope (Renzini & Voli 1981).

On the physical side, the activation of HBB leads to significant deviations from the core mass - luminosity relationship found by Paczyński (1971), and the luminosity of the stars, particularly of those of mass above 6 $M_\odot$, can reach $10^5\ L_\odot$ (Ventura et al. 2013). A typical example of the evolution of massive AGB stars is shown in Fig. 3, which shows the time variation of the luminosity and the temperature at the bottom of the convective envelope (top panels), and of the surface mass fractions of some chemical species (bottom panels).

We note the initial rise in the luminosity, related to the increase in the core mass, and the decline during the final AGB phases, after a significant fraction of the envelope mass was lost, which causes a general cooling of the regions of the star above the core, which gradually turn HBB off. This is confirmed by the behaviour of the temperature at the bottom of the external envelope (see top, right panel of Fig. 3), which also exhibits a decreasing trend in the second part of the AGB phase, after reaching a peak value, at an intermediate stage.

In the bottom-left panel of Fig. 3 we recognize the effects of CNO cycling, with the depletion of the surface carbon, the synthesis of nitrogen, and the reduction of the surface oxygen. We also show the behaviour of lithium, which is produced during the initial part of the AGB evolution, shortly after the ignition of HBB, owing to the activation of the Cameron & Fowler (1971) mechanism.

The bottom-right panel of Fig. 3 shows the time variation of other chemical species, from which we deduce the activation of the Ne-Na nucleosynthesis (the surface sodium

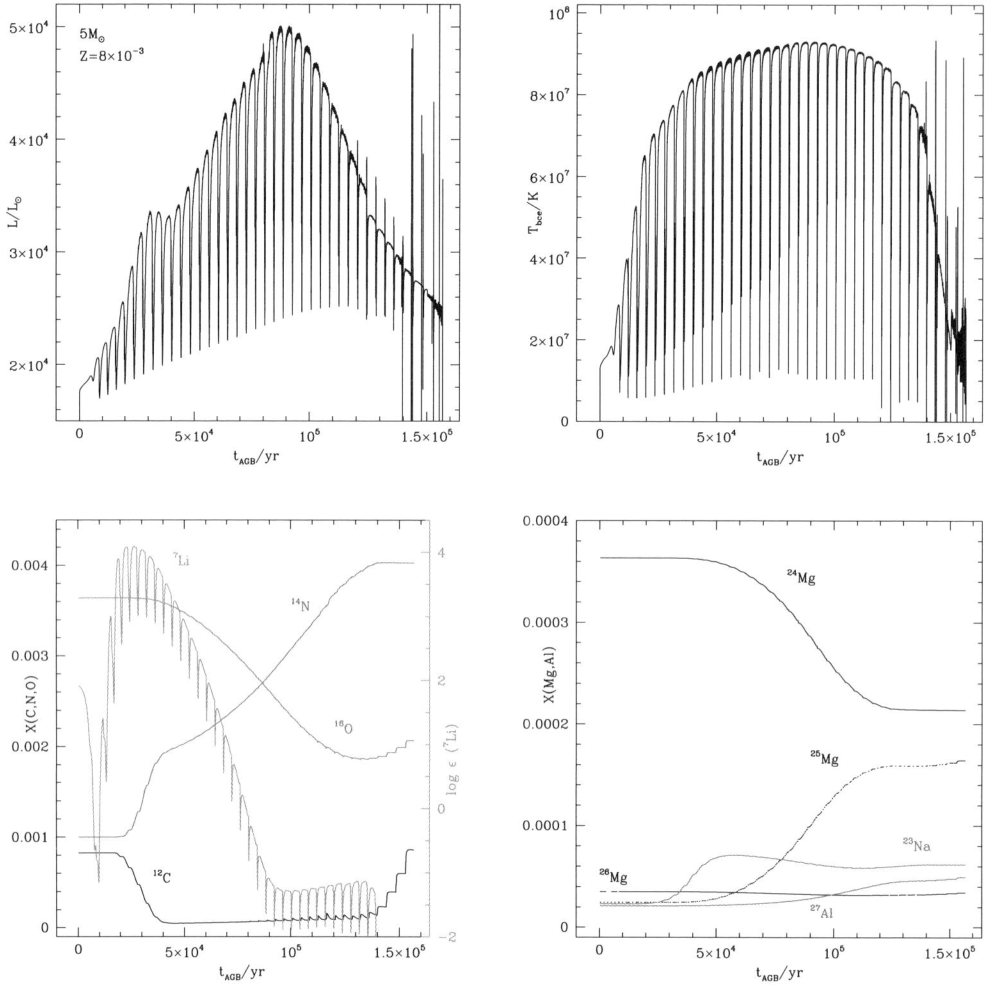

Figure 3. Top row: time variation of the luminosity (left) and temperature at the base of the convective envelope (right) of a 5 $M_\odot$ model star of metallicity $Z = 4 \times 10^{-3}$. Bottom: time variation of the surface mass fractions of lithium and of the CNO species (left), and of those involved in the Ne-Na and Mg-Al nucleosynthesis.

rises by a factor ~ 4 during the AGB phase), and of the Mg-Al chain, witnessed by the decrease in the surface ^{24}Mg and the ^{27}Al increase. The strength of the advanced p-capture nucleosynthesis associated to the ignition of HBB is extremely sensitively to the metallicity of the star (Dell'Agli et al. 2018a).

3. Post-AGB phases: stellar structure and evolution

Once the mass of the envelope of AGB stars drops below a few percents of the core mass, a contraction process begins, so that the evolutionary track moves initially to the blue, at constant luminosity (Iben & Renzini 1983). An example of such a track is shown in Fig. 4, which refers to the descendant of a 2 $M_\odot$ star of metallicity $Z = 0.004$, typical of the stars in the Small Magellanic Cloud (SMC) (Harris & Zaritsky 2004).

The structure of these stars, once they begin the contraction to the blue, is shown in Fig. 5, where the thermodynamic stratification in the pressure vs temperature plane is shown. In the left panel of the figure we can easily recognize: a) the core, composed by

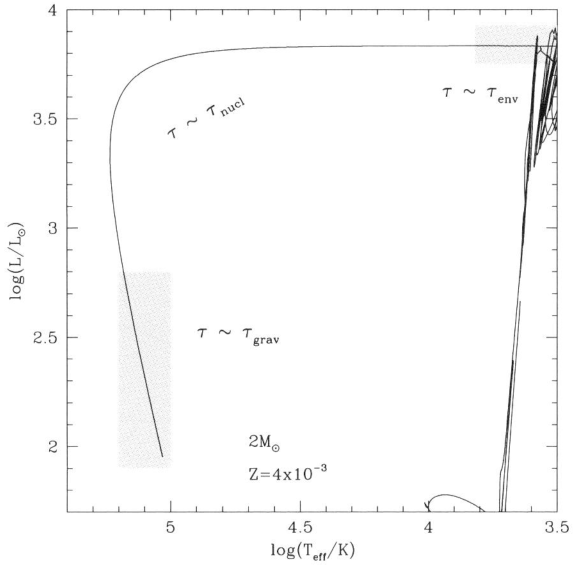

Figure 4. Evolutionary track on the HR diagram of a 2 $M_\odot$ model star of metallicity $Z = 4 \times 10^{-3}$, evolved from the start of core helium burning to the white dwarf cooling sequence. The evolutionary time scales characterizing the different parts of the track are indicated. The grey boxes in the upper and lower part of the plane indicate the parts of the evolution during which the time scale is mainly determined by the rate of mass loss and by the release of gravo-thermal energy, respectively.

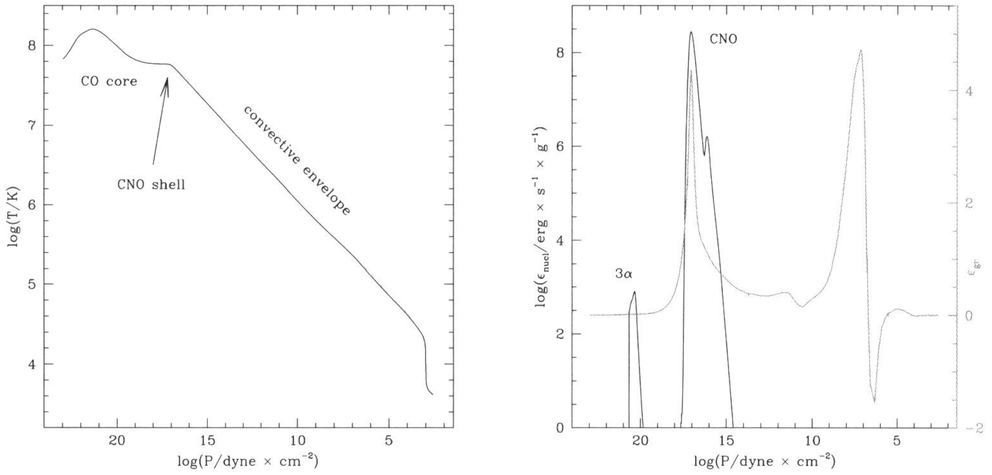

Figure 5. Left: thermodynamic structure of a 2 $M_\odot$ model star of metallicity $Z = 4 \times 10^{-3}$ during the post-AGB phase, in the pressure vs temperature plane. Right: the nuclear (black line) and gravothermal (red) coefficients for the energy release for the same structure reported in the left panel.

carbon and oxygen, supported by the pressure of degenerate electrons, which is almost isothermal; b) the CNO burning shell, located in the region where the decline of the temperature towards the outer regions of the star begins; c) the tenuous and expanded envelope, of mass ~ 0.003 $M_\odot$, which extends across more that 10 orders of magnitude in pressure. The right panel of Fig. 5 shows the gravitational and nuclear contributions to the overall energy release: we deduce that during these evolutionary phases most of the energy is related to CNO activity, with smaller contribution from gravitational

when the bluewards excursion of the track begins is senstitive to the core mass: the higher the core mass, the lower the fractional mass of the envelope below which the contraction process begins (Paczyński 1971).

The path traced by the evolutionary tracks on the HR diagram occurs at constant luminosity, until the CNO nuclear channel is able to provide the required energy supply, then continues towards lower luminosities, along constant radius lines, when the release of gravitational energy takes over.

A significant step forward in the modelling of the evolutionary phases following the AGB was taken by Schoenberner (1979), who calculated for the first time evolutionary sequences extended to the post-AGB and the PN phases, based on the full, self-consistent integration of the stellar structure equations, including the modelling of mass loss from the surface regions of the star. The analysis by Schoenberner (1979) was focused on two model stars descending from 1 $M_\odot$ and 1.45 $M_\odot$ progenitors.

The studies by the Potzdam group were of paramount importance to outline the role played by mass loss modelling on the results obtained, particularly for what pertains the transition time from the AGB to the post-AGB phase. A further important result regarding the evolutionary properties of these phases is the fact that the fading time scale characterizing the transition from the horizontal part of the track to the cooling sequence is given by the rate with which the gravitational energy stored into the star is dissipated (Bloecker & Schoenberner 1990): this highlights the need for a self-consistent calculation of the whole evolution through the AGB phase, in order to determine the gravitational energy reservoir of the star when contraction begins.

A more recent study on the evolutionary phases beyond the AGB was published by Miller Bertolami (2016), who presented tracks and isochrones of $0.8 - 4$ $M_\odot$ stars with metallicity in the $10^{-4} \leq Z \leq 2 \times 10^{-2}$ range. The times required for the star to move from the tip of the AGB to the post-AGB and the PN phase in the Miller Bertolami (2016) compilation are significantly shorter than in the models by Bloecker & Schoenberner (1990) and Vassiliadis & Wood (1994): this can be explained by the difference in the final mass versus luminosity relationship, due to the difference in the input physics and the more detailed treatment of the convective boundaries and the TDU phenomenon used. Regarding the latter point, the results reported in the recent work focused on the description of the AGB and post-AGB phases by Kamath et al. (2023) are in good agreement with those by Miller Bertolami (2016).

5. Post-AGB stars and PNe as tracers of AGB evolution

As discussed earlier in this contribution, the AGB evolution is characterized by the action of different mechanisms able to alter the surface chemical composition, primarily TDU and HBB, whose comprehension is of paramount importance to assess the role played by low and intermediate mass stars as pollutants of the interstellar medium.

On this side the analysis of the chemical composition of post-AGB stars and PNe may offer notable information on the efficiency of these processes, as it reflects the chemistry with which the stars leave the AGB, thus the results of the cumulated action of HBB and TDU over the whole AGB lifetime.

This is the approach used by Ventura et al. (2015, 2016, 2017) to investigate the PN populations of the Magellanic Clouds and of the Milky Way. These works characterized the individual sources observed in terms of mass, formation epoch and metallicity of the progenitors, based on the derived surface chemistry, which, in turn, reflects the efficiency of the aforementioned physical mechanisms.

An example of the approach followed is seen in Fig. 8, which shows the position of individual Galactic PNe studied by Ventura et al. (2017) in the (surface) C vs N plane, compared with the model predictions, found via AGB modelling. This plane was shown

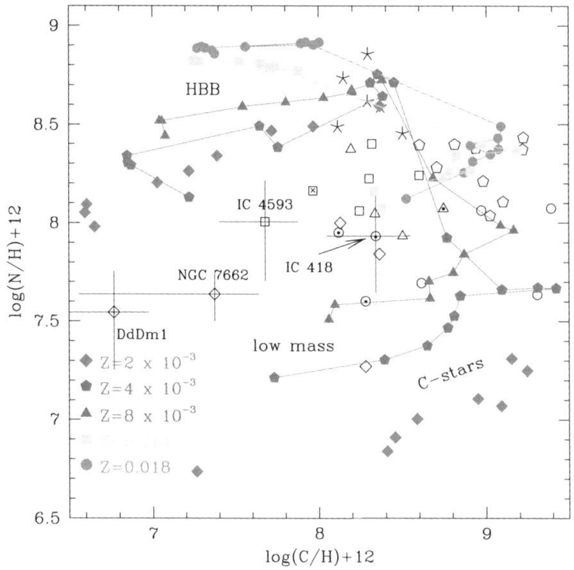

Figure 8. The final surface abundances of carbon and nitrogen of AGB models of different mass, indicated with different symbols, according to the metallicity, in the $2 \times 10^{-3} - 0.018$ range. Black symbols refer to the sample of Galactic PNe discussed in Ventura et al. (2017), for which the surface carbon is available. The different symbols correspond to the characterization of the individual sources and in particular their progenitors: open squares - descend from low-mass, solar metallicity star, which failed to reach the C-star stage; open diamonds - low-mass stars of sub-solar metallicity; open pentagons and circles: carbon stars of solar and sub-solar metallicity, respectively; open traingles and asteriscks: the progeny of stars that experienced HBB of solar and sub-solar metallicity, respectively. Dots inside symbols indicate PNe with evidence of carbon dust, whereas crosses refer to PNe with evidence of silicates. The regions of the plane where low-mass stars, C-stars and the progeny of massive AGBs that experienced HBB are indicated.

to allow the most exhaustive analysis, as stars descending from progenitors of different mass populate specific regions of the plane, according to the efficiency of the two main mechanisms responsible for the alteration of the surface chemistry. In particular, as indicated in Fig. 8, this method allows the identification of the three groups of stars discusses in Section 2: low-mass stars, carbon stars, and the progeny of massive AGBs, which experienced the HBB, easily recognized in the significant increase in the surface N.

This analysis outlined the importance of the knowledge of surface carbon, as indeed carbon is, among the different chemicals, the most sensitive to the efficiency of HBB and TDU, which cause opposite effects on the surface carbon content. The availability of the surface carbon allowed Stanghellini et al. (2022) to characterize a wide sample of Galactic PNe.

A similar approach was used by Kamath et al. (2023) to study a sample of Galactic post-AGB stars, for which the intrinsic luminosities were derived by the measured bolometric flux, benefiting from knowledge of the distances measured by Gaia. In agreement with the investigations on the PN samples of the Magellanic Clouds and the Milky Way presented by L. Stanghellini and collaborators, discussed earlier, Kamath et al. (2023) highlighted the crucial role played by the knowledge of the surface carbon as indicator of the efficiency of TDU and HBB experienced by the stars during the AGB phase. The analysis by Kamath et al. (2023) was mostly developed by studying the position of the sources considered in the surface carbon vs luminosity plane, which was shown to allow the most complete and reliable characterization of the individual stars considered in terms of mass, metallicity and formation epoch of the progenitors.

6. Dust around evolved stars: the new frontier

It is generally recognized that the circumstellar envelope of cool stars prove extremely favourable environment for the formation of dust, via condensation of gaseous molecules into solid particles. Among others, the dust species forming in largest quantities, thus providing the largest contribution to the overall reddening of the SED and to the acceleration of the wind via radiation pressure, are silicates, solid carbon, silicon carbide (SiC), alumina dust and solid iron (Ferrarotti & Gail 2006).

The mineralogy of the dust formed is sensitive to the surface chemistry, owing to the stability of the CO molecule, which absorbs the least abundant between carbon and oxygen in its entirety. Therefore, in C-rich environment the dust is composed of solid carbon, SiC and solid iron, whereas the winds of M-type stars, which have O-rich environments, are characterized by the formation of silicates, alumina dust and solid iron (Ferrarotti & Gail 2001, 2002, 2006).

6.1. *Dust formation modelling*

To adress the topic of dust formation in the surroundings of evolved stars some stellar evolution codes have been implemented with the schematization to model dust formation set up by the Heidelberg team (Ferrarotti & Gail 2006). In particular, Ventura et al. (2012, 2014) applied the Heidelberg method to the ATON code (Mazzitelli 1979; Ventura et al. 1998), whereas Nanni et al. (2013, 2014) coupled the same formalism to the evolutionary models calculated by means of the Colibri code (Marigo et al. 2013).

An interesting application of the combination of stellar evolution and dust formation modelling was proposed by Dell'Agli et al. (2014, 2015), to characterize the whole AGB population of the Magellanic Clouds. Later applications to this approach regarded IC 1613 (Dell'Agli et al. 2016), IC 10 (Dell'Agli et al. 2018b) and Sextans A (Dell'Agli et al. 2019). These studies will be of paramount importance now that we have entered the JWST era, which opened the way to test and extend this approach to many more galaxies in the Local Group.

6.2. *Understanding the infrared excess in the SED of post-AGB stars and PNe*

Once the AGB evolution is finished, dust formation stops, because the stars contract, the external temperature increase, thus the environmental conditions become less and less favourable to allow the condensation of gas molecules into dust. This is not the end of the story though, as the dust released until the end of the AGB leaves a distinct feature in the SED of the stars, identified as a clear IR excess. Indeed the dust moves away from the surface of the star after dust formation stops, but the dust layer is still sufficiently close to the star to leave some observational signatures, while the stars evolve through the post-AGB and the PN phases.

In this regard, Tosi et al. (2022) have recently proposed a novel approach, which allows one to use the SED of dusty post-AGB stars, to reconstruct the modality of the transition from the late AGB to the post-AGB phases, to deduce the rate of dust production during the very late AGB phases and to draw information on the dynamics of the wind, as it moves away from the star after dust formation stops. The method proposed by Tosi et al. (2022) will be of paramount importance to understanding the dust budget expected from low and intermediate mass stars during their life, as it was demonstrated that most of the dust released by these stars is produced during the final AGB phases, when the mass-loss rate is highest (Dell'Agli et al. 2014, 2015).

The analysis by Tosi et al. (2022) benefits from the spectral properties of post-AGB stars, particularly from the fact that the IR excess due to dust is well separated from the emission from the central star, thus the two contributions can be easily disentangled. Following Tosi et al. (2022), we find that the detailed inspection of the SED of post-AGB stars allows one to deduce the following quantities: a) the infrared optical depth, based on the relative height of the peak in the mid-IR, related to dust, compared to the main peak, related to the photospheric emission; b) the dust temperature, by the depth of the minimum in the SED separating the two peaks; c) the bolometric flux from the star, by fitting the near-IR part of the SED; d) the dust mineralogy, by examining the shape of the SED in the mid-IR wavelength region.

Point (c) proves crucial for the characterization of the individual sources considered, given the tight correlation between core mass and luminosity of these objects, discussed in Section 3. Points (a) and (b) above provide important information on the dust production rate during the very late AGB phases, as Tosi et al. (2022) demonstrated the relationship between the optical depth characterizing the star today, and that of the epoch when dust formation stopped.

This method was successfully applied by Tosi et al. (2022), to study the sample of SMC and LMC stars investigated by Kamath et al. (2014) and Kamath et al. (2015), which were classified as single stars, based on their radial velocities. Further application of this scheme was used by Dell'Agli et al. (2023) and Tosi et al. (2023) to investigate and characterize the post-AGB stars in the Milky Way presented in Kamath et al. (2022).

7. Conclusions

Progresses in stellar structure modelling allows robust modelling of the stars evolving past the AGB phase towards the white dwarf cooling sequence. This is now possible thanks to the pioneering investigations on this subject, presented over half century ago. It is now well established that these sources are mainly supported by proton-capture nucleosynthesis taking place in a H-rich shell, and that when the mass of the envelope drops below a few 10^{-3} $M_{\odot}$ the nuclear activity gradually ceases, and the release of gravothermal energy becomes the dominant energy source.

The evolutionary time scale of the post-AGB phases are first given by the speed with which the envelope is consumed, then by growth rate of the H-free core. The first is made uncertain by the poor knowledge of the mass-loss mechanism, whereas the second time scale is more robust, as it is related to the efficiency of the nuclear activity.

The synergy between the modelling of the post-AGB phases and the results from high-resolution spectroscopy of post-AGB stars and PNe allows a reliable classification of the sources investigated, in terms of mass and formation epoch of the progenitors. Furthermore, these investigations offer notable information on the previous AGB phase, as the chemical composition of post-AGB stars and PNe is the outcome of the balance between the action of TDU and HBB in modifying the surface chemical composition of the stars.

The latest research in this field have also outlined the possibility of using the SED of post-AGB stars and PN sources to infer the properties of the dust currently surrounding these stars, and to deduce the efficiency of the dust formation process during the very late AGB phases. This method proves highly effective to evaluate the role of AGB stars as dust manufactures, considering that most of the dust is produced during the late AGB phases.

Acknowledgements

The author acknowledges support from the National Institute for Astrophysics (INAF) within the theory grant *Understanding mass loss and dust production from evolved stars* (Ob. 1.05.12.06.07, PI. P. Ventura) and the PRIN 2019 grant *Building up the halo: chemodynamical tagging in the age of large surveys* (Ob. 1.05.01.85.14, PI. S. Lucatello)

References

Blöecker, T., Schöenberner, D. 1990, *A&A*, 240, L11
Blöecker, T., Schöenberner, D. 1991, *A&A*, 244, L43
Blöecker, T. 1995, *A&A*, 299, 755
Busso, M., Gallino, R., Wasserburg, G. J. 1999, *ARA&A*, 37, 239
Cameron, A. G. W., Fowler, W. A. 1971, *ApJ*, 164, 111
Dell'Agli, F., Ventura, P., García-Hernández, D. A., Schneider, R., Di Criscienzo, M., Brocato, E., D'Antona, F., et al. 2014, *MNRAS*, 442, L38
Dell'Agli, F., Ventura, P., Schneider, R., Di Criscienzo, M., García-Hernández, D. A., Rossi, C., Brocato, E. 2015, *MNRAS*, 447, 2992
Dell'Agli, F., Di Criscienzo, M., Boyer, M. L., García-Hernández, D. A. 2016, *MNRAS*, 460, 4230
Dell'Agli, F., García-Hernández, D. A., Ventura, P., Mészáros, S., Masseron, T., Fernández-Trincado, J. G., Tang, B., et al. 2018a, *MNRAS*, 475, 3098
Dell'Agli, F., Di Criscienzo, M., Ventura, P., Limongi, M., García-Hernández, D. A., Marini, E., Rossi, C. 2018b, *MNRAS*, 479, 5035
Dell'Agli, F., Di Criscienzo, M., García-Hernández, D. A., Ventura, P., Limongi, M., Marini, E., Jones, O. C. 2019, *MNRAS*, 482, 4733
Dell'Agli, F., Tosi, S., Kamath, D., Stanghellini, L., Bianchi, S., Ventura, P., Marini, E., et al. 2023, *MNRAS*, 526, 5386
Ferrarotti, A. S., Gail, H.-P. 2001, *A&A*, 371, 133
Ferrarotti, A. S., Gail, H.-P. 2002, *A&A*, 382, 256
Ferrarotti, A. S., Gail, H.-P. 2006, *A&A*, 447, 553
García-Hernández, D. A., García-Lario, P., Plez, B., D'Antona, F., Manchado, A., Trigo-Rodríguez, J. M., 2006, *Sci*, 314, 1751
García-Hernández, D. A., Manchado, A., Lambert, D. L., Plez, B., García-Lario, P., D'Antona, F., Lugaro, M., et al. 2009, *ApJL*, 705, L31
Harris, J., Zaritsky, D. 2004, *AJ*, 127, 1531
Iben, I. 1974, *ARA&A*, 12, 215
Iben, I., Renzini, A. 1983, *ARA&A*, 21, 271
Kamath, D., Wood, P. R., Van Winckel, H. 2014, *MNRAS*, 439, 2211
Kamath, D., Wood, P. R., Van Winckel, H. 2015, *MNRAS*, 454, 1468
Kamath, D., Van Winckel, H., Ventura, P., Mohorian, M., Hrivnak, B. J., Dell'Agli, F., Karakas, A. 2022, *ApJL*, 927, L13
Kamath, D., Dell'Agli, F., Ventura, P., Van Winckel, H., Tosi, S., Karakas, A. I. 2023, *MNRAS*, 519, 2169
Karakas, A. I., Lattanzio, J. C. 2014, *PASA*, 31, e030
Marigo, P. 2002, *A&A*, 387, 507
Marigo, P., Bressan, A., Nanni, A., Girardi, L., Pumo, M. L. 2013, *MNRAS*, 434, 488
Mazzitelli, I. 1979, *A&A*, 79, 251
Miller Bertolami, M. M. 2016, *A&A*, 588, A25
Nanni, A., Bressan, A., Marigo, P., Girardi, L. 2013, *MNRAS*, 434, 2390
Nanni, A., Bressan, A., Marigo, P., Girardi, L. 2013, *MNRAS*, 438, 2328
Paczyński, B. 1970a, *AcA*, 20, 47
Paczyński, B. 1970, *AcA*, 20, 287
Paczyński, B. 1971, *AcA*, 21, 417
Renzini, A., Voli, M. 1981, *A&A*, 94, 175

Schöenberner, D. 1979, *A&A*, 79, 108

Schönberner, D., Blöcker, T. 1996, *Ap&SS*, 245, 201

Sloan, G. C., Matsuur,a M., Zijlstra, A. A., Lagadec, E., Groenewegen, M. A. T., Wood, P. R., Szyszka, C., et al. 2009, *Sci*, 323, 353

Stanghellini, L., Bushra, R., Shaw, R. A., Dell'Agli, F., García-Hernández, D. A., Ventura, P. 2022, *ApJ*, 929, 148

Tosi, S., Dell'Agli, F., Kamath, D., Ventura, P., Van Winckel, H., Marini, E. 2022, *A&A*, 668, A22

Tosi, S., Kamath, D., Dell'Agli, F., Van Winckel, H., Ventura, P., Marchetti, T., Marini, E., et al. 2023, *A&A*, 673, A41

van Winckel, H. 2003, *ARA&A*, 41, 391

Vassiliadis, E., Wood, P. R. 1994, ApJS, 92, 125

Ventura, P., Zeppieri, A., Mazzitelli, I., D'Antona, F. 1998, *A&A*, 334, 953

Ventura, P., Marigo, P. 2009, *MNRAS*, 399, L54

Ventura, P., Marigo, P. 2010, *MNRAS*, 408, 2476

Ventura, P., Di Criscienzo, M., Schneider, R., Carini, R., Valiante, R., D'Antona, F., Gallerani, S., et al. 2012, *MNRAS*, 424, 2345

Ventura, P., Di Criscienzo, M., Carini, R., D'Antona, F. 2013, *MNRAS*, 431, 3642

Ventura, P., Dell'Agli, F., Schneider, R., Di Criscienzo, M., Rossi, C., La Franca, F., Gallerani, S., et al. 2014, *MNRAS*, 439, 977

Ventura, P., Stanghellini, L., Dell'Agli, F., García-Hernández, D. A., Di Criscienzo, M. 2015, *MNRAS*, 452, 3679

Ventura, P., Stanghellini, L., Di Criscienzo, M., García-Hernández, D. A., Dell'Agli, F. 2016, *MNRAS*, 460, 3940

Ventura, P., Stanghellini, L., Dell'Agli, F., García-Hernández, D. A. 2017, *MNRAS*, 471, 464

Ventura, P., Dell'Agli, F., Tailo, M., Castellani, M., Marini, E., Tosi, S., Di Criscienzo, M., 2022, *Univ*, 8, 45

Zhukovska, S., Gail, H.-P., Trieloff, M. 2008, *A&A*, 479, 453

Planetary Nebulae: A Universal Toolbox in the Era of Precision Astrophysics
Proceedings IAU Symposium No. 384, 2025
O. De Marco, A. Zijlstra & R. Szczerba, eds.
doi:10.1017/S1743921324000954

Nova remnants ... the fast siblings of planetary nebulae

Martín A. Guerrero[1] **and Edgar I. Santamaría**[2]

[1]Instituto de Astrofísica de Andalucía, IAA-CSIC, Glorieta de la Astronomía s/n, E-18008 Granada, Spain

[2]Instituto de Radioastronomía y Astrofísica (IRyA), UNAM Campus Morelia, Apartado postal 3-72, 58090 Morelia, Michoacán, Mexico

Abstract. Classical and recurrent novae are luminous eruptions taking place in binary star systems in which a white dwarf accretes material from a non-degenerate stellar companion. After the nova event, a shell of gas is expelled and expands into the surrounding environment at hundreds to thousands of km s^{-1}. This shell, the so-called nova remnant, experiences interactions with the binary system, the accretion disk, the surrounding environment, and very notably with continuous winds from the white dwarf powered by radiation from nuclear burning on its surface. The similarities with the formation of planetary nebulae are obvious, yet the shaping of nova remnants occurs on much shorter time-scales. This results in the prevalent round to mild elliptical 3D shape of nova remnants. Here we describe the morphology, kinematics and dynamics of nova remnants based on our multi-epoch imaging and long-slit and integral field spectroscopic studies and compare them with those of planetary nebulae.

Keywords. Catalogs, Surveys, stars: binaries, planetary nebulae

1. Introduction

The term nova (plural novae) comes from the latin phrase *"stella nova"*†, meaning the presence of a new star in the sky. Novae are actually luminous eruptions taking place in binary systems composed of a white dwarf (WD) and a non-degenerate stellar companion (e.g., Gallagher & Starrfield 1978). The WD accretes material from the companion until its envelope reaches a critical mass and a thermo-nuclear (TNR) event takes place (Starrfield et al. 1972).

There are a great variety of nova types, depending on the nature of the host binary system, the accretion rate, and the accretion history and mode. In a classical nova (CN), the host binary is a cataclysmic variable (CV) with the secondary, typically a main sequence star, in a short-period orbit, P $\approx$ 1.4-10 hours, thus overflowing its Roche lobe (Warner 2003). Meanwhile, in an embedded nova, proposed to be 20-40% of all nova events, most likely including symbiotic novae and luminous red variable, the WD companion is an evolved red giant star in a long-period orbit, P $\gtrsim$ 100 days (Mikolajewska 2010; Tylenda et al. 2011). These two different types of novae differ notably on the accretion modes and circumstellar media (CSM). In classical novae, the accretion onto the WD is channeled through an accretion disk (Bode & Evans 2008) and the CSM has low (or even negligible) density resulting from the high efficiency of the accretion process. On the other hand, in embedded novae, the accretion onto the WD is mainly through

† First time used by the Danish astronomer Tycho Brahe referring (actually) to a supernova, the so-called Tycho's Supernova or Supernova 1572.

direct wind accretion, resulting in a low accretion efficiency that produces a high-density CSM, i.e., the WD (and the nova as well) is embedded within the red giant wind.

1.1. *The Thermo-Nuclear Runaway (TNR) Event*

In pre-outburst, during most of the life-time of the binary system, the WD accretes H-rich material†. Hydrogen burns at the base of the WD envelope stably either through the p-p chain or the ^{3}He-burning reaction at a rate equal to the accretion rate, $\dot{M}_{\rm acc}$. The energy produced at the bottom of the envelope is transported away by radiation and e^- conduction. As time goes by, the envelope mass increases and it also does the density and temperature at its base. This results in a subsequent increase of the energy release rate.

When a critical mass $M_{\rm crit}$ is accreted, the energy release rate becomes too high for radiative and conductive transport of the energy outwards, and the envelope becomes convective. This, in fact, further increases the nuclear burning rate, as fresh, H-rich material is injected into the burning layer. The result is the onset of the so-called Thermo-Nuclear Runaway (TNR).

The TNR is a complex physical process, involving convection, mixing, instabilities, and nuclear processes. It is important to remark that there is no detonation or deflagration, as convection redistributes very efficiently the energy released throughout the envelope. As a result, the thermal energy of the envelope grows until it reaches the gravitational binding energy and expands. This quenches the nuclear burning rate, so that the TNR then enters a prolonged phase of enhanced, steady burning. The energy release and radioactive heating resulting from the release of energy from β-unstable nuclei eject a fraction of the envelope within minutes to hours.

"All novae are recurrent, but some are more recurrent than others." After a classical nova eruption, accretion may undergo a "hibernation period" due to the disruption of the accretion disk, to disk instabilities, to the inhibition of accretion by the WD wind, ... but the system will finally return to the previous accretion conditions (Shara et al. 1986). With time, another TNR will be triggered with a recurrence time

$$\tau_{\rm rec} \approx \frac{M_{\rm crit}}{\dot{M}_{\rm acc}} \qquad (1)$$

The critical mass for the TNR trigger $M_{\rm crit}$ ranges from 10^{-7} to $10^{-3} M_\odot$. It is a decreasing function of the WD mass and accretion rate, as higher values of $M_{\rm WD}$ and $\dot{M}acc$ imply higher temperatures at the base of the envelope and thus smaller envelope mass for the ignition. There is thus a bias towards the detection of CNe (and recurrent novae) events towards more massive WDs with higher accretion mass rates.

For the particular field of research of planetary nebulae (PNe), it is interesting comparing the case of nova events with born-again PNe. During the post-Asymptotic Giant Branch (post-AGB) phase of their evolution, the central stars of a PN (CSPN) may build a shell of helium with the critical mass to ignite a thermal pulse (Schoenberner 1979; Iben et al. 1983). This so-called very late thermal pulse (VLTP) expands the envelope, which cools dramatically and pushes the CSPN back to the low $T_{\rm eff}$ locus of the Hertzprung-Russell diagram of AGB stars. In a sense, the CSPN is born-again. Meanwhile the incomplete ashes of the He-burning are ejected at high-speeds inside the old PN. This ejecta has high C/O ratio (Miller Bertolami et al. 2006), unlike the products of nova events (Starrfield et al. 1998).

† It is also possible to accrete He-rich material from a degenerate evolved companion, but this seems to have a very low frequency rate, with V445 Pup the most notorious candidate for a helium nova (Ashok & Banerjee 2003).

1.2. *Mass Ejection Modes and Nova Shaping*

The expansion velocity of the ejecta $V_{\rm ej}$ in nova events ranges from 200 to 7000 km s^{-1}. Since the expansion velocity of the ejecta should equal at least the escape velocity from the launching radius, R, this implies

$$V_{\rm ej} \geq V_{\rm esc} = \sqrt{\frac{2GM}{R}}. \qquad (2)$$

Assuming the mass of the system is basically that of the WD, which is actually the most massive component, the launching radius has values between the typical WD radii, $R_{\rm WD} \leq 10^9$ cm, and the binary separation

$$a_{\rm bin} = 3.5 \times 10^{10} M^{1/3} P^{2/3} \ ({\rm cm}), \qquad (3)$$

where the system mass M is in units of $M_\odot$ and the orbital period P in hours. This suggests that the launching radius is above the surface of the WD, but below the orbital radius of the companion.

Another critical piece of evidence to understand the nova event comes from the early detection of X-rays, which arises from shocks within the ejecta itself. This implies the presence of a slow outflow that is shocked and pushed forward by a fast outflow. Nowadays the most accepted scenario for the nova ejection considers the interaction of a series of stellar winds formed at different times after the TNR.

There is an initial impulsive ejection of mass caused by the TNR. This prompt ejection occurs within a few hours after the TNR is triggered. The mass and velocity of the ejecta depend on the mixing between the envelope and underlying WD core, which can vary largely from case to case, although only a fraction of envelope is expected to be ejected.

This impulsive ejection is followed by a short-lived stellar wind driven by radiation pressure. Its mass-loss rate is known to decline by a factor $\approx$10 over just a few hours, because otherwise the supersoft X-ray phase of novae would last longer.

Finally this short-lived wind is superseded by a prolonged optically thick wind with terminal velocity $V_{\rm ej} \geq 1000$ km s^{-1}. This speed implies that the launching radius is smaller than the binary separation, close to the WD surface. The wind is indeed driven by radiation pressure, with acceleration taken place deep below the photosphere. The wind driver is actually the Fe opacity bump at $T \approx 1.6 \times 10^5$ K in the nova envelope. As the mass the WD H-rich envelope decreases, owing to nuclear burning and wind loss, the wind mass loss rate $\dot{M}_{\rm w}$ itself decreases. At the same time the photosphere recedes to smaller radii to reach regions of higher temperature, producing the increase of the wind velocity as the wind launching radius moves inward. Once the temperature drops below 1.6×10^5 K, there are no additional sources of opacity and the wind ceases after a time period from a few days to a few months.

The duration of this phase is expected to be longer for WD with lower mass and higher values of critical mass for the TNR ignition. These novae are classified as "slow novae", in opposition to "fast novae", given their slower decay from brightness peak, as measured by t_3, the time it takes to decline 3 mag from the peak brightness. These "slow novae" do not only last longer, but also their ejecta have slower velocity. Nova remnants are thus shped by wind-wind interactions, as much as PNe (Kwok, Purton, & Fitzgerald 1978; Balick 1987).

2. Nova remnants morphology

2.1. *Early Observations*

It is necessary to remark that the early phases of the TNR are very complex. The TNR may not be triggered simultaneously over the full WD envelope layer, resulting in asymmetric ejecta on small spatial scales. On coherent larger scales, the fast rotation of a WD would produce latitude-dependent variations of the pressure and temperature at the base of the envelope and thus of the TNR. The envelope corotation with the spinning WD surface can be enhanced by magnetic coupling.

At the nova brightness peak, the photosphere of the WD would have expanded largely, up to $10^{12} - 10^{13}$ cm, engulfing the binary system if their orbital period is shorter than 12 hours. This is a scenario similar to a common-envelope phase, well known to occur in PNe (De Marco 2009) and stellar mergers (Ivanova et al. 2013). Therefore processes of frictional drag, binary orbital motion (centrifugal forces), companion's gravity, ... will be active, focusing the mass loss towards the orbital plane, preferentially through the outer L2 Lagrange point, on the far side of the secondary. The binary influence would be greater for slow novae, with $V_{\rm ej} \leq 1000$ km s^{-1} and launching radius of the wind beyond the orbital separation $a_{\rm bin}$.

Early spectral observations of novae in their nebular stage detect double- or triple-peaked line profiles that imply the asphericity in the ejecta. These can be interpreted as a bipolar ejecta and an equatorial torus or disk (Chochol et al. 1997). Early images of nova ejecta are consistent with an elliptical shell whose ellipticity changes with time, becoming either rounder or more prolate. One of the most remarkable cases is that of V959 Mon (a.k.a. nova Mon 2012), whose binary system edge-on inclination favors observing these changes. Indeed, multi-epoch radio images of V959 Mon captured an orthogonal flip in the major axis of the ejecta from a bi-lobed ejecta on day 126 interpreted as a fast bipolar flow to a slower, equatorially concentrated flow on day 615 (Chomiuk et al. 2014). All these are observational evidence of the interaction of two winds or outflows with different symmetry.

Moreover, there are features in spectral lines that persist at a particular velocity. These are believed to originate in discrete clumps, revealing the ejecta clumpy nature. The presence of spectral features around the brightness peak of both low- and high-ionization species also supports a broad range of densities and temperatures within the ejecta, which can result from self-shielding by these clumps.

2.2. *Nova Remnant Morphological Catalog*

Nova ejecta have expansion velocities of a few hundreds up to 1000 km s^{-1}, thus their apparent angular diameter grows so fast

$$\theta = 0.115 \left(\frac{d}{1\ \rm kpc}\right)^{-1} \left(\frac{V_{\rm ej}}{1000\ \rm km\ s^{-1}}\right) \left(\frac{t}{100\ \rm day}\right) \ \rm arcsec \qquad (4)$$

that high-resolution facilities like the *Hubble Space Telescope* (*HST*), near-IR adaptive-optics, and radio/millimeter interferometers can resolve nova ejecta starting a few months to a few years after their eruption. Otherwise ground-based optical imaging would resolve novae from a few years to a few decades after the eruption.

We have undertaken (Santamaría et al. 2024, in prep.) a compilation of archival and proprietary ground-based and *HST* optical narrow-band Hα, Hα+[N II], [N II], and [O III] images of resolved nova remnants. So far this compilation includes images for ≈50 nova remnants with ages from 15 up to 600 years.

Among the nova remnants in this catalog, the most typical morphology is an elliptical shell (see also Slavin, O'Brien, & Dunlop 1995; Gill & O'Brien 1998; Downes & Duerbeck 2000). In a few cases, such RR Pic and HR Del (Figure 1), it is noted an equatorial enhancement (ring), with bipolar over-densities, sometimes observed at different emission lines. Overall the frequency rate of bipolar morphology is very low, with V959 Mon (a NeO

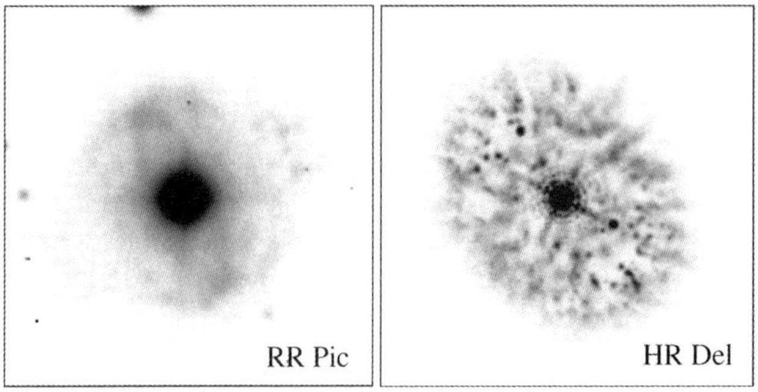

Figure 1. Hα images of the nova remnants RR Pic (left) and HR Del (right). RR Pic shows a clear equatorial enhancement, which is only present in forbidden emission line images of HR Del. Images adopted from the morphological catalog of nova remnants (Santamaría et al. 2024, in preparation).

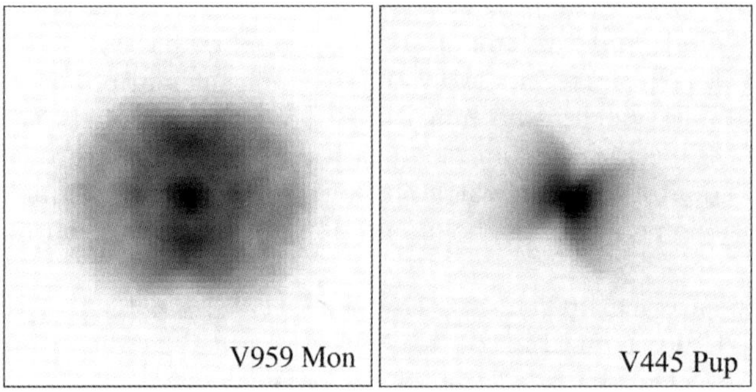

Figure 2. Hα and broad-band images of the bipolar nova remnants V959 Mon (left) and V445 Pup (right), respectively. Images adopted from the morphological catalog of nova remnants (Santamaría et al. 2024, in preparation).

nova detected in GeV γ rays) and V445 Pup (the best candidate for a degenerate, He-donor companion) the only clear cases for this asymmetric morphology (Fig. 2).

In a few other cases the nova remnants exhibit an one-sided clumpy ring, with cometary tail morphology for the individual clumps. The nova remnants IPHASX J210204.7+471015 and AT Cnc (Figure 3) can be thus attributed to an ejection through the L2 point after a common envelope phase (Guerrero et al. 2018; Shara et al. 2012).

There is no clear evidence for fast collimated outflows (jets) in nova remnants, with only a confirmed jet detected in X-rays in DQ Her, probably resulting from the collimation of the current stellar wind (Toalá et al. 2020). Otherwise the jet claimed in GK Per (Shara et al. 2012b) might actually be a section of a larger nebular structure, probably a PN (Harvey et al. 2016).

The detailed morphology of the elliptical shells of nova remnants can be considered smooth, but there is also the presence at different degrees of clumps embedded within those diffuse shells. These clumps shed light into the possible novae yields trapped into clumps, with head and cometary tail morphology that inform on the presence of ablated flows as in GK Per and DQ Her (Liimets et al. 2012; Santamaría et al. 2020; Santamaria et al. 2022a). The comparison of the ALMA interferometric observations of V5668 Sgr ($d = 1450$ pc) with *HST* observations seems actually to imply that novae

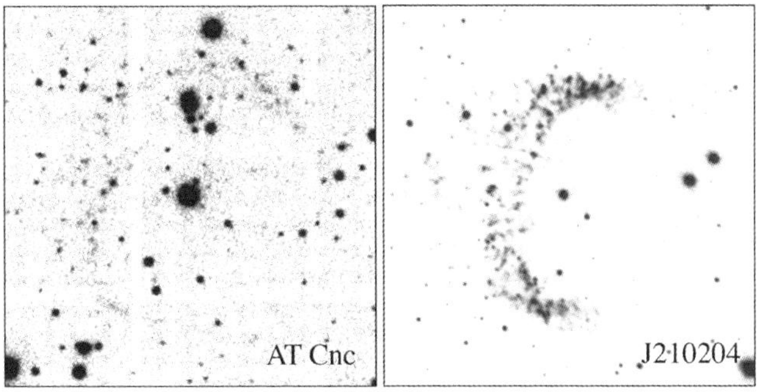

Figure 3. Hα images of the one-sided ring nova remnants AT Cnc (left) and IPHASX J210204.7+471015 (right). Images adopted from the morphological catalog of nova remnants (Santamaría et al. 2024, in preparation).

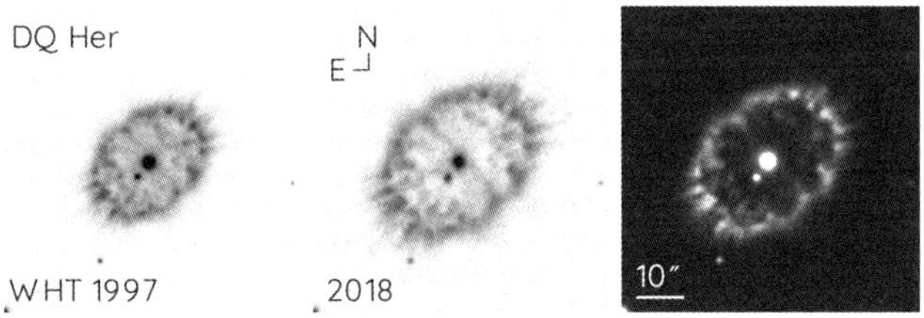

Figure 4. Hα images of DQ Her obtained on 1997 and 2018 at the William Herschel Telescope and Nordic Optical Telescope, respectively. Adopted from Santamaría et al. (2020).

remnants are mostly clumpy, but the limited spatial resolution hinders resolving those clumps, resulting in an apparent smooth morphology (Diaz et al. 2018).

The upcoming morphological catalog of nova remnants will allow us investigating in detail their morphology statistics, and the effects of time-evolution and distance in the observed morphology. There will be soon a dedicated webpage with FITS and JPG files available to the astronomical community. Contributions of images are most welcomed.

3. Angular expansion of nova remnants

The fast angular expansion of nova shells noted in Eq. 4 allows using multi-epoch images of nova remnants to assess their distance, compare the radial and tangential expansion velocity, and their 3D physical structure. It also allows to witness morphological changes.

Notorious examples of multi-epoch imaging of nova remnants that have revealed their expansion are those of DQ Her (a.k.a. Nova Her 1934) based on images from 1977 to 2019, i.e., for a nova age from 43 to 85 years old (see Fig. 4, Santamaría et al. 2020), and GK Per (a.k.a., Nova Per 1901) based on images from 1953 to 2011, i.e., for a nova age from 52 to 110 years old (Liimets et al. 2012). Another well studied cases are those of IPHASX J210204.7+471015 and T Pyx (Santamaría et al. 2019; Schaefer, Pagnotta, & Shara 2010).

We have also undertaken a comprehensive investigation of the expansion of nova shells (Santamaría et al. 2020). A first study has included a sample of five nova remnants with ages in the range from 50 to 130 years. All these have resulted to be in a free expansion phase, with the ejecta mass being 7-45 times larger than the swept-up CSM/ISM medium around the novae (Fig. 5). Combined with the surface brightness decline, it implies that

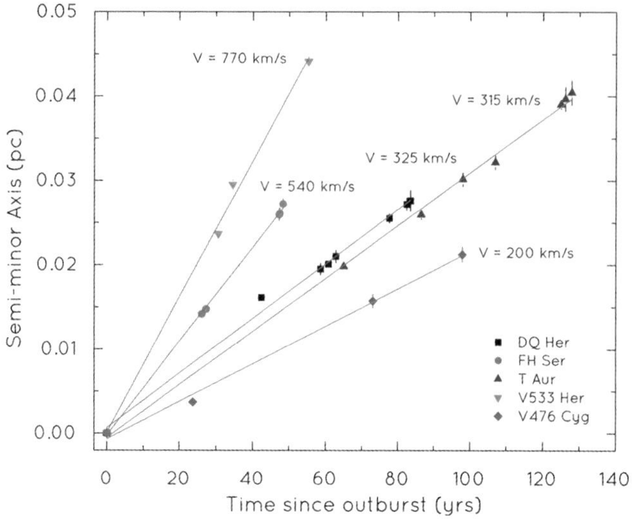

Figure 5. Semi-minor axis expansion of a sample of five nova remnants. The slope determines the tangential velocity on the sky. Adopted from Santamaría et al. (2020).

the life-time of nova remnants is smaller than a few hundred years, with implications for nova remnants dispersal time into ISM and the occurrence of nova events.

It is notorious the case of IPHASX J210204.7+471015 (Santamaría et al. 2019). The [N II]-bright one-sided ring-like feature expands freely, but the [O III] bow-shock-like features seems to have experienced a notable slow down in its interaction with the ISM.

A study based on a larger sample drawn from the morphological catalog of nova remnants is coming soon (Santamaría et al. 2024, in preparation). A preliminary inspection confirms the free expansion of most nova remnants.

4. Physical structure of nova remnants

Angular expansion studies of nova remnants have shown that the radial expansion velocity along the line of sight is not always coincident with the tangential velocity on the plane of the sky (e.g., Slavin, O'Brien, & Dunlop 1995). These differences reveal projection effects, as a shell with elliptical morphology can actually be a tilted oblate or prolate ellipsoid, but also that spectroscopy and multi-epoch imaging probe different structural components, including ring-like structures, outflows, or clumps among others. Otherwise it also unveils errors in distance estimate based on *Gaia* data, as the stellar emission might be contaminated by the "red" nebular emission of the nova remnant, or very notably unreliable radial expansion velocity measurements based in the misleading interpretation of early spectroscopic data.

4.1. *Long-slit Spectroscopic Studies*

Long-slit spectroscopic data along the two main minor and major symmetry axes of nova remnants have proven very efficient to assess their true 3D physical structure (Slavin, O'Brien, & Dunlop 1995). No extreme high-dispersion is required given the fast expansion velocity of nova remnants, with a spectral resolution $R \approx 5000$ being the best trade off between resolution and sensitivity.

A recent long-slit spatio-kinematic investigation of four nova remnants, namely T Aur, DQ Her, QU Vul, and HR Del, and the nova-like source CK Vul (Santamaria et al. 2022a) has clarified their 3D physical structure. Besides CK Vul, with an hour-glass bipolar morphology, the bona-fide nova remnants in this sample can be described as mild prolate ellipsoidal shells with equatorial density enhancements, that in a few cases (e.g., T Aur) is better described by a peanut-shape with open caps.

The comparison of the unprojected (true) axial ratio of these novae with their expansion velocity and decline time t_3 reveals notorious trends. Slow novae, with longer decline time t_3, have slower expansion velocities and are more aspherical than fast novae. Apparently the slower ejecta of these novae have longer interaction times with the companion star, producing more pronounced effects on their shape (Livio et al. 1990; Lloyd, O'Brien, & Bode 1997) as discussed in Section 1.1.

4.2. *Integral Field Spectroscopic Studies*

Long-slit spectroscopic studies of nova remnants are largely superseded by integral field spectroscopic (IFS) observations. These provide a complete spatial coverage, which is essential to identify the symmetry axes and to resolve small-scale (filaments, clumps) structures embedded in the nebular shell (or may be even being its main structural component).

The IFS instrument MEGARA (Gil de Paz et al. 2016) at the GTC 10.4m telescope is well suited for this task. With a spectral resolution up to 18700 in the Hα line, for a velocity resolution $\approx$16 km s^{-1}, it can provide a truly tomographic view of nova remnants. This has been tested with QU Vul, which shows nebular Hα emission in the range from -616 to $+664$ km s^{-1}. Its 3D physical structure is shown to consists of a prolate ellipsoid with axial ratio 1.4$\pm$0.2, inclination with the line of sight $12^\circ \pm 6^\circ$, and polar and equatorial velocities of 560 km s^{-1} and 400$\pm$60 km s^{-1}, respectively (Santamaría et al. 2022b). This greatly improves the morpho-kinematic model obtained by Santamaria et al. (2022a) using a long-slit spectrum.

The tomographic view of QU Vul helps greatly to interpret many different aspects (Fig. 6). For instance, the ionized mass can be derived from the Hα flux at each spatio-kinematic element of the IFS data cube, thus reducing the uncertainty associated to the macroscopic filling factor. The determination of the kinetic energy benefits both from the more accurate value of the ionized mass and from the assessment of the space velocity on each data cube element as well.

Moreover the integrated nebular Hα line profile shows a "castellated" shape (Fig. 7), which is typically seen in early spectroscopic observations of novae. The peaks in the profiles, i.e., the "battlements in the wall of the castle" of this profile, can be unambiguously associated with individual knots moving along radial directions with different inclinations with the line of sight. The association of profile peaks with clumps allows an accurate determination of the expansion velocity, which is typically overestimated on early spectroscopic observations of nova ejecta that assumes either

$$V_{\rm exp} = FWHM \tag{5}$$

or more geometrically exact

$$V_{\rm exp} = \frac{FWHM}{2\sqrt{\ln 2}} = 0.72 \times FWHM \tag{6}$$

but can be defined more precisely by the semi-difference between the velocities of the bluest and reddest profile peaks

$$V_{\rm exp} = \frac{V_{\rm red} - V_{\rm blue}}{2}. \tag{7}$$

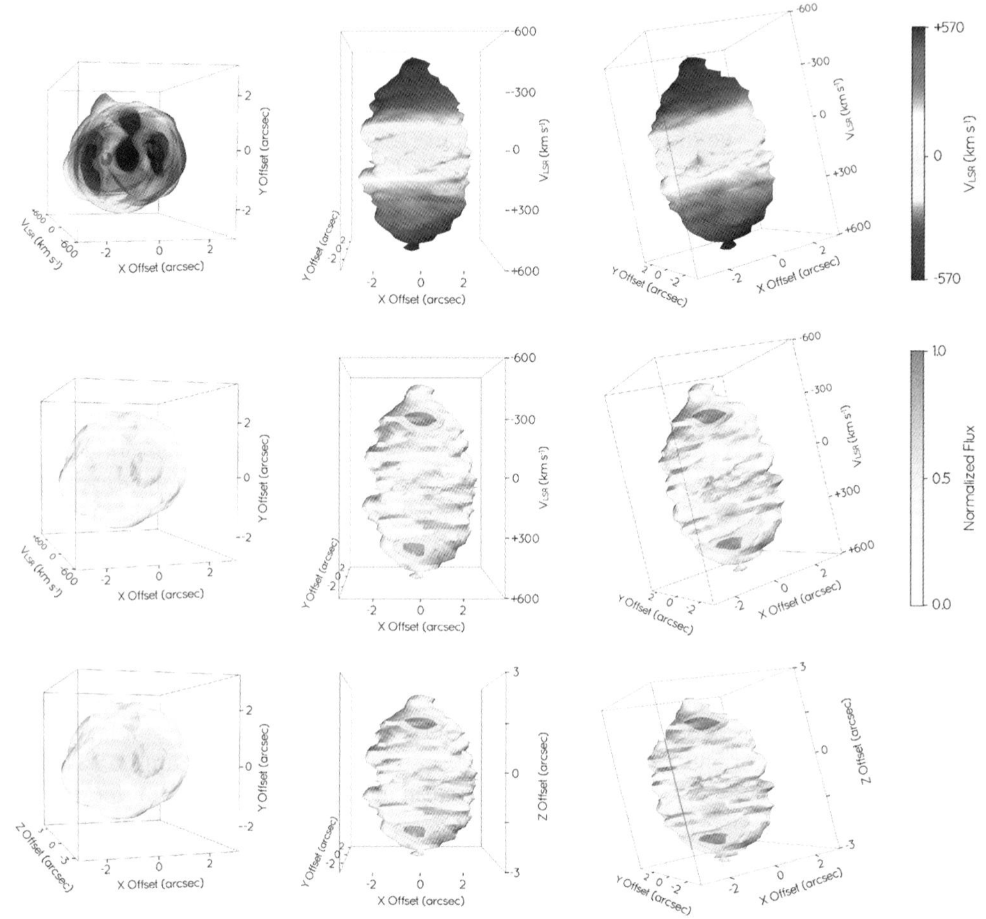

Figure 6. Hα emission velocity-coloured (top) and intensity (middle) position-position-velocity (PPV) diagrams of QU Vul, and true 3D intensity distribution (bottom) along the observer's point of view (i.e. the direct image, left), and the projection from the plane of the sky along directions orthogonal (middle) and parallel (right) to the main axis. Adopted from Santamaría et al. (2022b).

Finally note that the Hα decline of QU Vul implies that the nova remnant will be not detectable in a short time period of 40-60 years from now.

5. Concluding Remarks

The expansion and morphological evolution of nova remnants can be followed from a few years up to a few hundred years after the nova eruption. The expansion of nova remnants is not slowed down by their interaction with the tenuous CSM around them or the surrounding ISM. The importance of binary shaping effects in the nova remnants differs among nova types, being larger in those with slow expansion velocities. On the other hand it is noted that clumping may dominate nova remnants, with nova yields trapped into clumps.

Nova remnants and PNe are both shaped by wind-wind interactions, but it takes much shorter time-scales, from hours to months, in the former. As many PNe, nova remnants are shaped by binary interactions, but most nova remnants have mild ellipsoidal 3D

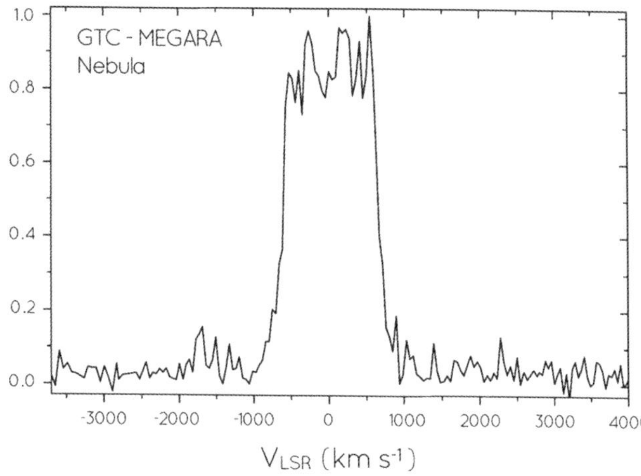

Figure 7. Hα emission line profile of the nebular emission of QU Vul detected by GTC MEGARA. The spectral line profile has a flat, 'castellated' top. Adopted from Santamaría et al. (2022b).

shapes with very few bipolar and even less show jets. This results from the binary shaping effects diluting in short time-scales in nova remnants. The time dilution of nova remnants, ≈ 200 years, is much shorter than in PNe. In a sense, nova remnants are fast-forward PNe, but the longer different time-scale of the wind-wind interactions in PNe makes their morphology more inclined to depart from spherical symmetry.

We deeply appreciate the collaboration of Drs. Sara Cazzoli, Gerardo Ramos-Larios, Laurence Sabin and Jesús A. Toalá to the results based on multi-epoch imaging and spectroscopic observations of nova remnants described here. MAG acknowledges financial support from grants CEX2021-001131-S funded by MCIN/AEI/10.13039/501100011033 and PGC 2018-102184-B-100 and PID 2022-142925NB-I00 from the Spanish Ministerio de Ciencia, Innovación y Universidades (MCIU) cofunded with FEDER funds. MAG also warmly acknowledges funding support provided by the Local Organizing Committee of the International Astronomical Union Symposium 384.

References

Ashok N. M., Banerjee D. P. K., 2003, A&A, 409, 1007. doi:10.1051/0004-6361:20031160
Balick B., 1987, AJ, 94, 671. doi:10.1086/114504
Bode M. F., Evans A., 2008, clno.book
Chochol D., Grygar J., Pribulla T., Komzik R., Hric L., Elkin V., 1997, A&A, 318, 908
Chomiuk L., Linford J. D., Yang J., O'Brien T. J., Paragi Z., Mioduszewski A. J., Beswick R. J., et al., 2014, Natur, 514, 339. doi:10.1038/nature13773
De Marco O., 2009, PASP, 121, 316. doi:10.1086/597765
Diaz M. P., Abraham Z., Ribeiro V. A. R. M., Beaklini P. P. B., Takeda L., 2018, MNRAS, 480, L54. doi:10.1093/mnrasl/sly121
Downes R. A., Duerbeck H. W., 2000, AJ, 120, 2007. doi:10.1086/301551
Gallagher J. S., Starrfield S., 1978, ARA&A, 16, 171. doi:10.1146/annurev.aa.16.090178.001131
Gil de Paz A., Carrasco E., Gallego J., Iglesias-Páramo J., Cedazo R., García Vargas M. L., Arrillaga X., et al., 2016, SPIE, 9908, 99081K. doi:10.1117/12.2231988
Gill C. D., O'Brien T. J., 1998, MNRAS, 300, 221. doi:10.1046/j.1365-8711.1998.01899.x
Guerrero M. A., Sabin L., Tovmassian G., Santamaría E., Michel R., Ramos-Larios G., Alarie A., et al., 2018, ApJ, 857, 80. doi:10.3847/1538-4357/aab669

Harvey E., Redman M. P., Boumis P., Akras S., 2016, A&A, 595, A64. doi:10.1051/0004-6361/201628132
Iben I., Kaler J. B., Truran J. W., Renzini A., 1983, ApJ, 264, 605. doi:10.1086/160631
Ivanova N., Justham S., Chen X., De Marco O., Fryer C. L., Gaburov E., Ge H., et al., 2013, A&ARv, 21, 59. doi:10.1007/s00159-013-0059-2
Kwok S., Purton C. R., Fitzgerald P. M., 1978, ApJL, 219, L125. doi:10.1086/182621
Liimets T., Corradi R. L. M., Santander-García M., Villaver E., Rodríguez-Gil P., Verro K., Kolka I., 2012, ApJ, 761, 34. doi:10.1088/0004-637X/761/1/34
Livio M., Shankar A., Burkert A., Truran J. W., 1990, ApJ, 356, 250. doi:10.1086/168836
Lloyd H. M., O'Brien T. J., Bode M. F., 1997, MNRAS, 284, 137. doi:10.1093/mnras/284.1.137
Mikolajewska J., 2010, arXiv, arXiv:1011.5657. doi:10.48550/arXiv.1011.5657
Miller Bertolami M. M., Althaus L. G., Serenelli A. M., Panei J. A., 2006, A&A, 449, 313. doi:10.1051/0004-6361:20053804
Santamaría E., Guerrero M. A., Ramos-Larios G., Sabin L., Vázquez R., Gómez-Muñoz M. A., Toalá J. A., 2019, MNRAS, 483, 3773. doi:10.1093/mnras/sty3364
Santamaría E., Guerrero M. A., Ramos-Larios G., Toalá J. A., Sabin L., Rubio G., Quino-Mendoza J. A., 2020, ApJ, 892, 60. doi:10.3847/1538-4357/ab76c5
Santamaría E., Guerrero M. A., Zavala S., Ramos-Larios G., Toalá J. A., Sabin L., 2022a, MNRAS, 512, 2003. doi:10.1093/mnras/stac563
Santamaría E., Guerrero M. A., Toalá J. A., Ramos-Larios G., Sabin L., 2022b, MNRAS, 517, 2567. doi:10.1093/mnras/stac2789
Schaefer B. E., Pagnotta A., Shara M. M., 2010, ApJ, 708, 381. doi:10.1088/0004-637X/708/1/381
Schoenberner D., 1979, A&A, 79, 108
Shara M. M., Livio M., Moffat A. F. J., Orio M., 1986, ApJ, 311, 163. doi:10.1086/164762
Shara M. M., Mizusawa T., Wehinger P., Zurek D., Martin C. D., Neill J. D., Forster K., et al., 2012, ApJ, 758, 121. doi:10.1088/0004-637X/758/2/121
Shara M. M., Zurek D., De Marco O., Mizusawa T., Williams R., Livio M., 2012, AJ, 143, 143. doi:10.1088/0004-6256/143/6/143
Slavin A. J., O'Brien T. J., Dunlop J. S., 1995, MNRAS, 276, 353. doi:10.1093/mnras/276.2.353
Starrfield S., Truran J. W., Sparks W. M., Kutter G. S., 1972, ApJ, 176, 169. doi:10.1086/151619
Starrfield S., Truran J. W., Wiescher M. C., Sparks W. M., 1998, MNRAS, 296, 502. doi:10.1046/j.1365-8711.1998.01312.x
Toalá J. A., Guerrero M. A., Santamaría E., Ramos-Larios G., Sabin L., 2020, MNRAS, 495, 4372. doi:10.1093/mnras/staa1502
Tylenda R., Kamiński T., Schmidt M., Kurtev R., Tomov T., 2011, A&A, 532, A138. doi:10.1051/0004-6361/201116858
Warner B., 2003, cvs..book, 592. doi:10.1017/CBO9780511586491

Planetary Nebulae: A Universal Toolbox in the Era of Precision Astrophysics
Proceedings IAU Symposium No. 384, 2025
O. De Marco, A. Zijlstra & R. Szczerba, eds.
doi:10.1017/S1743921324000516

Evolution From Asymptotic Giant Branch to Pre-planetary Nebula: Whorled Patterns and Stellar Companions

Hyosun Kim

Korea Astronomy and Space Science Institute, 776, Daedeokdae-ro, Yuseong-gu, Daejeon 34055, Republic of Korea

Abstract. Bipolar or multipolar lobes in pre-planetary nebulae (pPNe) often exhibit intertwined outer whorled patterns, resulting from stellar wind matter accumulation during the asymptotic giant branch (AGB) phase. These structures are likely triggered by stellar or substellar companions. We regard that CW Leonis currently stands at a critical transition moment, providing a vivid illustration of the progression from an AGB star in a binary system to a pPN. We have found that CW Leonis has shown significant enhancements in its optical and near-infrared light curves over the past two decades, with the recent Hubble Space Telescope image finally revealing the long-awaited central star. Utilizing an eccentric-orbit binary model, we can reproduce the position-angle dependence of the expansion velocity in the whorled pattern around CW Leonis, suggesting a nearly face-on orbital inclination. Its contradiction to the features in the innermost circumstellar envelope, corresponding to a nearly edge-on inclination, may imply the presence of an additional companion. Our updated theoretical framework explores the complexity of the whorled pattern. Further identifying and monitoring phase-transition candidates at the tip of the AGB will provide valuable insights into the AGB-pPN transition and the role of companions in shaping the morphological evolution of these stellar objects.

Keywords. circumstellar matter, stars: AGB and post-AGB, stars: binaries, stars: evolution, stars: mass loss, stars: winds, outflows

---

1. Introduction

The motivation of this work is to better understand the morphological transition between the asymptotic giant branch (AGB) and pre-planetary nebula (pPN) phases. Most circumstellar envelopes of AGB stars are spherical, or near-spherical, but the majority of (p)PNe are not spherical (e.g., Zuckerman & Aller 1986; Sahai et al. 2007, 2011). In particular, a bipolar (p)PN is believed to be formed in the condition that the matter ejection is confined by a surrounding flat disk, which is believed to be produced in a close binary star system.

As an example, V Hydrae observed with the Hubble Space Telescope indicates the high-speed bullet-type ejections every 8.5 yr, and it is proposed that the pericenter passages of an unseen companion having a very elongated orbit with such an orbital period may provoke that phenomenon (Sahai et al. 2016). However, whether such an eccentric orbit can survive against the tendency toward circularization can be an issue (Salas et al. 2019).

Another example can be the PN IRAS 17150-3224. A successful modeling by Huang et al. (2020) showed that at least 3 different directional bipolar structures ejected at different times are overlaid in this source, in addition to the whorled pattern in the outer circumstellar envelope. The adopted geometry was attributed to the precession of

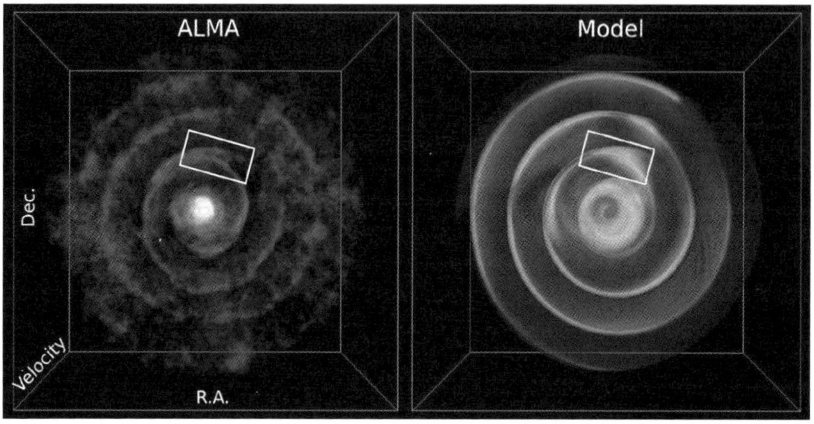

Figure 1. Comparison between the Atacama Large Millimeter/submillimeter Array (ALMA) map of AFGL 3068 (LL Pegasi) for the ^{12}CO molecular line emission and a hydrodynamic model; a snapshot of the supplementary animation of Kim et al. (2017). Bifurcation is identified as evidence for an eccentric orbit of the central binary (white box).

a hypothesized disk, and then the disk precession was concluded to be quite severe in the angle change.

To understand the AGB-(p)PN shape transition, the important thing we need to understand is the binary system, in particular the accretion disk, at the phase *immediately before* the phase transition. We consider the closest carbon star, CW Leonis (a.k.a. IRC+10216), having experiencing extraordinary brightening for nearly two decades until now, as an appropriate target so that a continuous monitoring is desired.

A simultaneously important task is to build up a theoretical framework to comprehend the stellar orbital properties and accretion processes by analyzing density and velocity distributions of the pattern whorled around the central stars. Following the archetypal works on the spiral-shell pattern driven by reflex motion of the mass-losing star in a circular orbit (Soker 1994; Mastrodemos & Morris 1999; Kim & Taam 2012b), eccentric-orbit binary cases are also intensively studied (e.g., He 2007; Kim et al. 2019). Many interferometric observations indeed have shown the whorled patterns in the circumstellar media of AGB stars, which are well reproduced by theoretical models based on the reflex motions (e.g., Maercker et al. 2012; Kim & Taam 2012c; Kim et al. 2013; Cernicharo et al. 2015; Kim et al. 2017; Decin et al. 2020; Bujarrabal et al. 2021, see also Figure 1).

This paper reports recent progress in both theoretical and observational aspects of such investigations on the whorled patterns and stellar companions, and in particular for an example carbon star CW Leonis, which is possibly currently evolving off the AGB.

2. Propagation of Whorled Pattern Hinting at Geometry

The propagation speed (differential proper motion) of a circumstellar whorled pattern is frequently adopted as the (often-assumed isotropic) expansion velocity of the wind. For example, Balick et al. (2012) measured the angular translation of the ensemble of all observed arcs of the pPN CRL 2688 between the Hubble Space Telescope images in 2002 and 2009 epochs, from which their attempt to match this transverse velocity to the line-of-sight velocity (Doppler shift velocity measured from molecular line observations) yielded a distance of 340 pc, differing from a distance of 420 pc measured by a different method (Ueta et al. 2006). Here, we can naturally question whether the isotropic wind assumption is valid or not. For the same source, Ueta et al. (2013) found that the derived

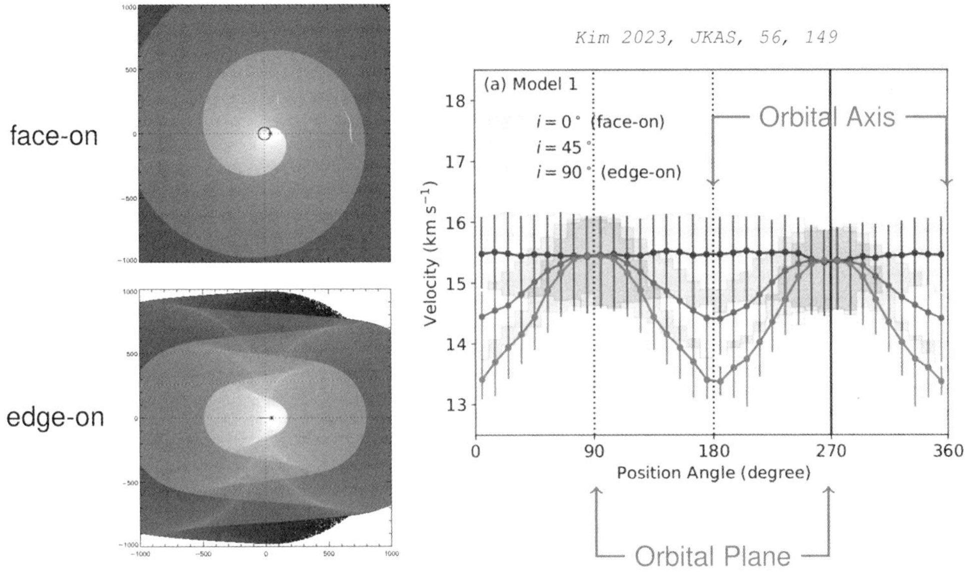

Figure 2. (Left) Face-on and edge-on views of the circumstellar spiral-shell pattern driven by the orbital motions of the central binary system, calculated by a particle simulation using the first version of the pinwheel code (Kim et al. 2024). A perfectly circular orbit is assumed. In the bottom panel (for the edge-on image), the orbital axis lies along the vertical axis. (Right) Figure 2(a) of Kim (2023). The expansion velocity profiles as a function of position angle at three different inclination angles.

transverse wind velocity varies across the Hubble Space Telescope image, but the reason for the position-angle dependence was not provided. The transverse velocities of two AGB stars (AFGL 3068 and CW Leonis) and two PNe (NGC 6543 and NGC 7027) also show a very large dependence of the transverse velocities on the position angle (Guerrero et al. 2020; Kim et al. 2021).

Recently, Kim (2023) reported the theoretical study on the velocity variation of the spiral-shell pattern whorled around the mass-losing star with an intrinsically isotropic and continuous wind ejection, which becomes anisotropic due to the orbital motion in a binary system. If the orbital shape is perfectly circular and the orbital axis is aligned with the line of sight (i.e., the orbital plane is face-on), the transverse velocity derived from the differential proper motion of the whorled pattern is independent on the position angle of the image (see Figure 2, blue). In the cases that the orbital axis is misaligned, the transverse velocity is minimized at the position angles corresponding to the projection of the orbital axis (see Figure 2, red and green). Although the eccentric orbit cases are more complicated, one indubitable finding from Figure 3 is that the transverse wind velocity is minimized at the position angle to the pericenter of the mass-losing star, regardless the current orbital phase.

Based on these simulational results and the position angle dependence on the expansion velocity of circumstellar pattern surrounding CW Leonis (Figure 4), it is proposed that CW Leonis may be an eccentric binary with the pericenter of the AGB star projected toward the northern direction on the nearly face-on orbit (Kim et al. 2021; Kim 2023). Note that a nearly face-on eccentric-orbit binary was also suggested by Guélin et al. (2018) to reproduce the offsets of centers of pattern shells in CW Leonis, although the pericenter located at a different position angle in this consideration.

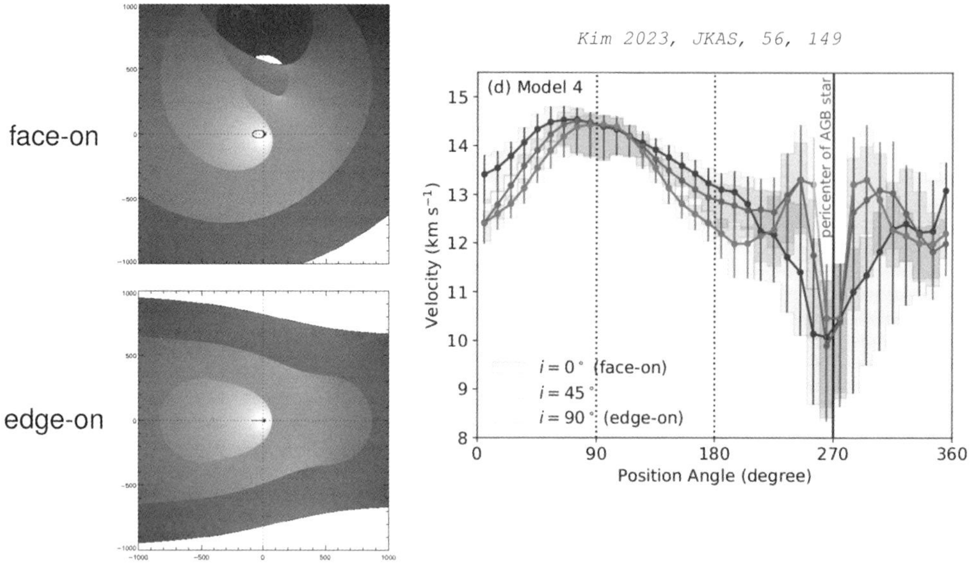

Figure 3. Same as in Figure 2, but for an eccentric orbit binary. Right panel is a copy of Figure 2(d) of Kim (2023), which shows the minimum transverse wind velocity at the pericenter of the mass-losing star.

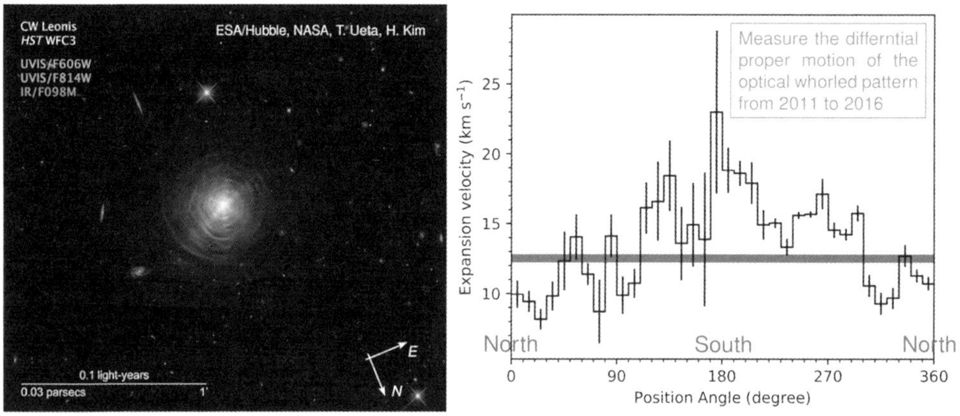

Figure 4. (Left) Pseudo-color image of CW Leonis in the Hubble Space Telescope's gallery https://hubblesite.org/contents/news-releases/2021/news-2021-059. Image dimension is 2.4 arcmin across (about 0.2 light-years). Image credit: ESA/Hubble, NASA, Toshiya Ueta (Univ. of Denver), Hyosun Kim (KASI). (Right) Expansion velocity measured by Kim et al. (2021) using differential proper motion of the whorled pattern from the year of 2011 to 2016, as a function of the position angle (from north to the east).

There is, however, a problem in that the inclination (nearly face-on orbital plane) is contradictory to the previous interpretation for its geometry as nearly edge-on (e.g., Decin et al. 2015) mainly based on the bipolar-like structure observed in the optical, being remained for at least a decade or longer until its disappearance in the 2011 Hubble Space Telescope image (Kim et al. 2015), and the elongation of radio continuum emission that is supposed to indicate the flattened disk-like structure, viewed edge-on, possibly paving the bipolar-like optical light path. Here, a new suggestion can be made to engage the seemingly contradictory geometries: does CW Leonis contains a triple star system

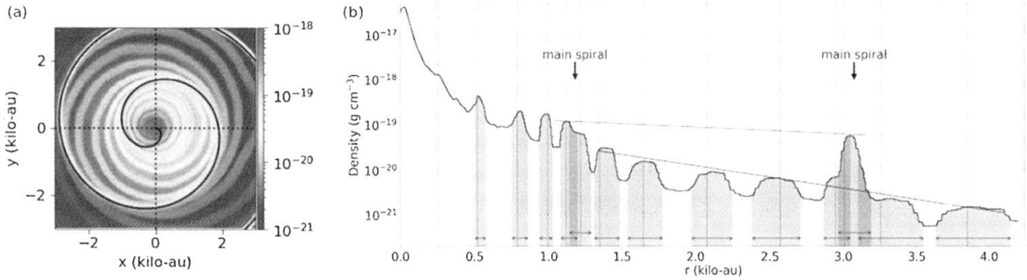

Figure 5. (a) Circumstellar density pattern formed in the orbital plane of a triple star system using a hydrodynamic simulation, overlaid by a black line (main spiral, hereafter) presenting the location of the Archimedean spiral that would be produced by the outer binary alone. (b) Density profile along an angle of 45 degrees with respect to the y axis. Individual shaded regions (and horizontal two-headed arrows) indicate the radial extensions of the individual fine spiral ridges, which converge upon each other at the main spiral. Red and blue lines show the difference in the radial rates of the density decrease in the main and fine patterns. Refer to Kim et al. (2024) for details.

at the center having the inner companion orbit nearly edge-on and the outer companion orbit nearly face-on?

3. Whorled Pattern in a Triple System

A stable, hierarchical triple system is investigated through hydrodynamic and particle simulations to provide a physical framework for interpreting the complex circumstellar patterns whorled around AGB stars (Kim et al. 2024). As shown in Figure 5, the introduction of a third star as a close companion to the mass-losing star causes a periodic variation in the orbital motion of the AGB star, creating an additional finer pattern in the otherwise inter-spiral region of the Archimedean spiral pattern that would be formed by the outer binary alone. The peak density of the finer pattern is comparable to that of the main spiral pattern in the innermost region but the density contrast of the finer pattern more quickly decreases (and plausibly becomes nondetectable) with increasing radius (blue in Figure 5(b)), while that of the main pattern (i.e., the Archimedean spiral) declines slowly (red in Figure 5(b)) by a factor that is related to the ratio between the outer and inner orbital periods. This situation may lead observers to perceive an apparent, but unreal jump in the pattern interval, as has been reported for CW Leonis (e.g., Mauron & Huggins 2000; Guélin et al. 2018). In addition, the fine spiral pattern can be very well approximated by circular rings with centers that are systemically offset from each other, which is also a known characteristic of the structure observed in the circumstellar medium of CW Leonis (e.g., Mauron & Huggins 2000; Guélin et al. 2018). The abrupt radial change in the interval of the pattern, the off-centering of the pattern, and some intertwining with other ridges that are the characteristic features found in observations of CW Leonis, all direct to this source as possibly being a triple system.

4. Extraordinary Brightening of the Carbon Star, CW Leonis: AGB–pPN phase transition?

The extreme carbon star CW Leonis located at the tip of AGB had been completely obscured and thus invisible for at least a few decades due to the dense circumstellar matter it had ejected (Haniff & Buscher 1998; Skinner et al. 1998; Mauron & Huggins 2000; Leão et al. 2006; Kim et al. 2015). Therefore, it was surprising and unbelievable when a local brightness peak appeared exactly at the expected (proper-motion-corrected) stellar position in the Hubble Space Telescope's 0.8 μm image taken in 2016 (Kim et al.

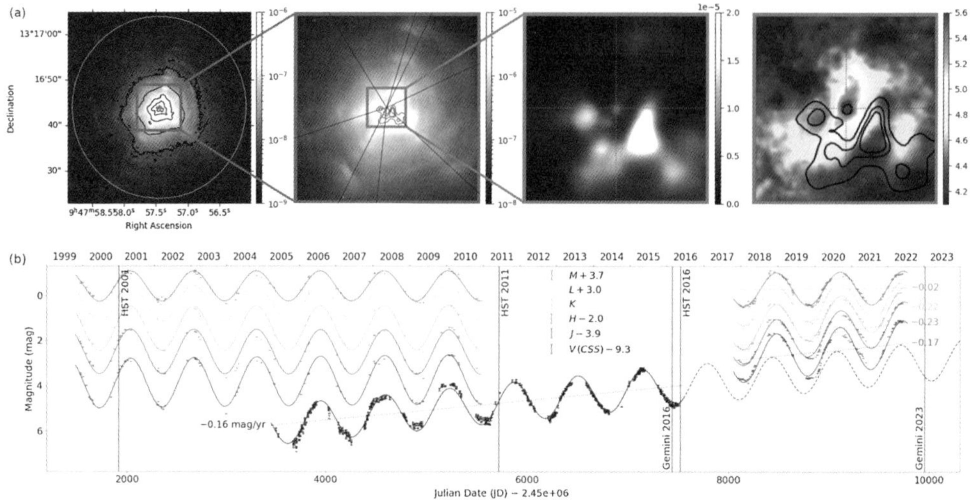

Figure 6. (a) Hubble Space Telescope image at the optical 0.8 μm band with the size of 20 arcsec (first panel), 10 arcsec (second panel), and 2 arcsec (third panel) in Jansky units; the last panel displays the color map (in units of magnitudes) generated by the third panel and the corresponding 0.6 μm image. The reddest spot coincides with the proper-motion-corrected stellar position (at the junction of red dotted lines), where a point-like optical source is detected for the first time (marked by black contours of brightness). The radial beams and nearly circular rings appearing prominent in the central 5 arcsec region are the intriguing features (second panel). See Kim et al. (2021) for details. (b) CW Leonis' photometric data on the Catalina Sky Survey (V) and the light curve fit (black), overlaid with the J (blue), H (green), K (yellow), L (pink), and M (red) light curves. The $JHKLM$ data in 1999–2008 are from Shenavrin et al. (2011), and the latest $JHKLM$ data (2017–current) are obtained through private communication. Vertical lines indicate the previous Hubble Space Telescope epochs (in 2001, 2011, and 2016) and the Gemini epochs (in 2016 and 2023). The near- to mid-infrared light curves show gradual brightening.

2021) (see Figure 6(a), third panel). The local optical peak was compact and the reddest spot in the color map (fourth panel of Figure 6(a)), revealing the red nature of the evolved giant star.

Currently the star's brightness grows very fast (Figure 6(b)), possibly indicating that this star may be unveiling the essential clues for conditions required for the phase transition from AGB to pPN. At the same time, its recent brightening makes the adjacent clumpy structures overwhelmed (relatively dimmer). In the near-infrared, high-resolution observations using adaptive optics and speckle interferometry performed in 1995–2005 showed several near-infrared clumps (Osterbart et al. 2000; Tuthill et al. 2000; Weigelt et al. 2002; Stewart et al. 2016), but these clumps have disappeared around 2005 (Stewart et al. 2016). Because these previous observations were obtained with very small fields of view, therefore registering sky coordinates for these images was impossible, perhaps new monitoring observations on this source with a larger field of view, including field stars, and without central saturation may be critical to understand the late stellar evolution.

5. Porous Envelope Scenario: Period for Redistribution of Halo Illumination linked to Binary Orbital Motion or Stellar Pulsation?

Outer parts of the Hubble Space Telescope images of CW Leonis exhibit 8 radial beams (Figure 6(a), second panel). These radial beams reveal the pathways of starlight escaping from inner holes in the circumstellar envelopes, along which dust particles are illuminated. This porous envelope scenario also explains the redistribution of relative brightness in the extended halo of CW Leonis from the elongated shape to the northwest in 2011 to the fairly symmetric shape about the central star in 2016, which cannot be attributed to dynamical motion of the halo material (Kim et al. 2021). It is speculated that one of the radial beams is nearly aligned with the line of sight but with a slight angular precession directing toward the northwest in 2011 and to the line of sight (but slightly southwest) in 2016. Based on these two epochs, the precession period seems to be about two decades. This time scale is close to the time interval of innermost shells surrounding the central star of CW Leonis, measured on an Hubble Space Telescope's optical image (Mauron & Huggins 2000), which is attributed to the orbital motion of a binary. On the other hand, these two epochs are in different stellar pulsation phases (Figure 6(b)), therefore the possibility of a fast rotation cannot be ruled out without more frequent monitoring observations on this source.

6. Accretion Disk: the Key to the AGB–pPN Shape Transition

Our main motivation is to understand the physical conditions yielding the morphological transition from the AGB to the pPN, for which the accretion disk surrounding either the binary stars or the companion of the mass-losing star is one of the unavoidable part for investigation.

Lee et al. (2022) particularly focused on the inner structure of accretion disk surrounding the companion of a red giant star in a hydrodynamic simulation for a circular-orbit binary system. The disk surface, defined by a steep decline in density and temperature, indicates a vertically flared shape of the disk and two inflowing spirals in the disk are identified through close examination (Figure 7). By carefully tracing the matter inflowing the accretion disk, it is found that not all positions at the disk surface are passed by the streamlines; instead, the half of inflows go through one single point in the opposite side of the bow shock (red in Figure 8) and the other half pass over a wide portion of the disk surface (blue in Figure 8). It leads to different nature of the two spirals in the disk (See Lee et al. 2022, for details). Further investigation for the variations of the disk along the orbital phase in its size, morphology, and accretion rate would be the next step toward the comprehension on the link between the companion's disk and the late stellar evolutionary phase transition.

7. Summary

Whorled patterns reserve the information on the central stars, because the overall morphology of the circumstellar envelope of an AGB star is governed by the velocity fields that are influenced by the reflex motion of the mass-losing star. In addition to the orbital period and eccentricity, the inclination and the number of companions may be hinted from a careful inspection of the whorled pattern.

CW Leonis is chosen as a timely example, because its central star is getting brighter gradually and continuously for already two decades, possibly revealing the AGB-pPN phase transition. The evidences for its porous envelope are reported; the redistribution of its extended halo is interpreted as a slight angular precession of one of the radial beams, which may be also linked to the innermost pattern interval. In particular, the abrupt radial change in the interval of the pattern and the off-centering of the pattern with intertwining with other ridges suggest that CW Leonis may consist of a triple system.

Further systematic monitoring of this high mass-loss carbon star possibly at the critical transition moment by multi-scale multi-wavelength observations and multi-scale computations for theoretical investigation on the whorled patterns in multi-body systems are highly required, in order to properly approach the triggering conditions responsible

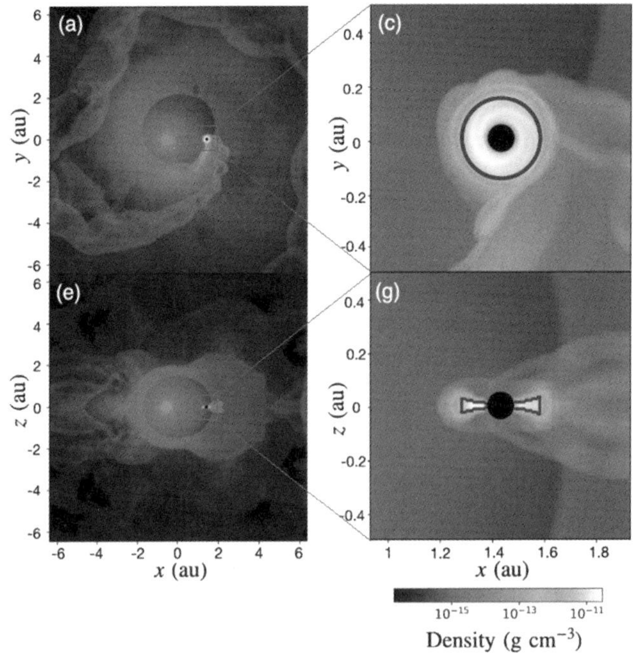

Figure 7. Density distribution in a hydrodynamic simulation for the wind material ejected from a red giant star at $(x, y, z) = (-0.57\,\text{au}, 0, 0)$ circularly orbiting with its white dwarf companion separated by 2 au. The right panels show the accretion disk surrounding the companion star, having a vertically flared shape. Blue lines indicate the surface of the accretion disk, as defined in Lee et al. (2022).

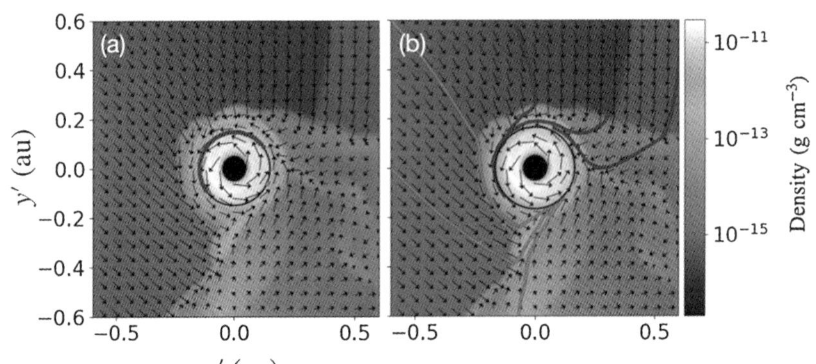

Figure 8. Figure 7 of Lee et al. (2022), showing the density distribution near the accretion disk of companion of the mass-losing red giant star, overlaid by the velocity vectors of matter and some representative streamlines (in red and blue).

for the AGB–pPN shape transition from nearly spherical to highly bipolar/multipolar morphology.

This research was supported by the National Research Foundation of Korea (NRF) grant (No. NRF-2021R1A2C1008928) and Korea Astronomy and Space Science Institute (KASI) grant (Project No. 2023-1-840-00), both funded by the Korea Government (MSIT).

References

Balick B., Gomez T., Vinković D., *et al.* 2012, *ApJ*, 745, 188. doi:10.1088/0004-637X/745/2/188

Bujarrabal V., Agúndez M., Gómez-Garrido M., *et al.* 2021, *A&A*, 651, A4. doi:10.1051/0004-6361/202141002

Cernicharo J., Marcelino N., Agúndez M., Guélin M. 2015, *A&A*, 575, A91. doi:10.1051/0004-6361/201424565

Decin L., Montargès M., Richards A. M. S., *et al.* 2020, *Science*, 369, 1497. doi:10.1126/science.abb1229

Decin L., Richards A. M. S., Neufeld D., *et al.* 2015, *A&A*, 574, A5. doi:10.1051/0004-6361/201424593

Guélin M., Patel N. A., Bremer M., *et al.* 2018, *A&A*, 610, A4. doi:10.1051/0004-6361/201731619

Guerrero M. A., Ramos-Larios G., Toalá J. A., *et al.* 2020, *MNRAS*, 495, 2234. doi:10.1093/mnras/staa1225

Haniff C. A., Buscher D. F. 1998, *A&A*, 334, L5.

He J. H. 2007, *A&A*, 467, 1081. doi:10.1051/0004-6361:20066435

Huang P.-S., Lee C.-F., Sahai R. 2020, *ApJ*, 889, 85. doi:10.3847/1538-4357/ab5f09

Kim H. 2023, *Journal of Korean Astronomical Society*, 56, 149. doi:10.5303/JKAS.2023.56.2.149

Kim H., Hsieh I.-T., Liu S.-Y., Taam R. E. 2013, *ApJ*, 776, 86. doi:10.1088/0004-637X/776/2/86

Kim H., Lee H.-G., Mauron N., Chu Y.-H. 2015, *ApJL*, 804, L10. doi:10.1088/2041-8205/804/1/L10

Kim H., Lee H.-G., Ohyama Y., *et al.* 2021, *ApJ*, 914, 35. doi:10.3847/1538-4357/abf6cc

Kim H., Liu S.-Y., Taam R. E. 2019, *ApJS*, 243, 35. doi:10.3847/1538-4365/ab297e

Kim H., Morris M. R., Kim J., He J. H. 2024, *ApJ*, subm.

Kim H., Taam R. E. 2012b, *ApJ*, 759, 59. doi:10.1088/0004-637X/759/1/59

Kim H., Taam R. E. 2012c, *ApJL*, 759, L22. doi:10.1088/2041-8205/759/1/L22

Kim H., Trejo A., Liu S.-Y., *et al.* 2017, *Nature Astr.*, 1, 0060. doi:10.1038/s41550-017-0060

Leão I. C., de Laverny P., Mékarnia D., de Medeiros J. R., Vandame B. 2006, *A&A*, 455, 187. doi:10.1051/0004-6361:20054577

Lee Y.-M., Kim H., Lee H.-W. 2022, *ApJ*, 931, 142. doi:10.3847/1538-4357/ac67d6

Maercker M., Mohamed S., Vlemmings W. H. T., *et al.* 2012, *Nature*, 490, 232. doi:10.1038/nature11511

Mastrodemos N., Morris M. 1999, *ApJ*, 523, 357. doi:10.1086/307717

Mauron N., Huggins P. J. 2000, *A&A*, 359, 707.

Osterbart R., Balega Y. Y., Blöcker T., *et al.* 2000, *A&A*, 357, 169. doi:10.48550/arXiv.astro-ph/0003328

Sahai R., Morris M., Sánchez Contreras C., *et al.* 2007, *AJ*, 134, 2200. doi:10.1086/522944

Sahai R., Morris M. R., Villar G. G. 2011, *AJ*, 141, 134. doi:10.1088/0004-6256/141/4/134

Sahai R., Scibelli S., Morris M. R. 2016, *ApJ*, 827, 92. doi:10.3847/0004-637X/827/2/92

Salas J. M., Naoz S., Morris M. R., *et al.* 2019, *MNRAS*, 487, 3029. doi:10.1093/mnras/stz1515

Shenavrin V. I., Taranova O. G., Nadzhip A. E. 2011, *Astron. Rep.*, 55, 31. doi:10.1134/S1063772911010070

Skinner C. J., Meixner M., Bobrowsky M. 1998, *MNRAS*, 300, L29. doi:10.1046/j.1365-8711.1998.300004l29.x

Soker N. 1994, *MNRAS*, 270, 774. doi:10.1093/mnras/270.4.774

Stewart P. N., Tuthill P. G., Monnier J. D., *et al.* 2016, *MNRAS*, 455, 3102. doi:10.1093/mnras/stv2454

Tuthill P. G., Monnier J. D., Danchi W. C., *et al.* 2000, *ApJ*, 543, 284. doi:10.1086/317082

Ueta T., Murakawa K., Meixner M. 2006, *ApJ*, 641, 1113. doi:10.1086/500642

Ueta T., Tomasino R. L., Ferguson B. A. 2013, *ApJ*, 772, 133. doi:10.1088/0004-637X/772/2/133

Weigelt G., Balega Y. Y., Blöcker T., *et al.* 2002, *A&A*, 392, 131. doi:10.1051/0004-6361:20020915

Zuckerman B., Aller L. H. 1986, *ApJ*, 301, 772. doi:10.1086/163943

Planetary Nebulae: A Universal Toolbox in the Era of Precision Astrophysics
Proceedings IAU Symposium No. 384, 2025
O. De Marco, A. Zijlstra & R. Szczerba, eds.
doi:10.1017/S1743921323005495

NGC 1514 and the post-AGB mass-luminosity relation

Roberto H. Méndez[1], **Rolf-Peter Kudritzki**[1,2] and **Miguel A. Urbaneja**[3]

[1]Institute for Astronomy, University of Hawaii, 2680 Woodlawn Drive, Honolulu, HI 96822, USA
email: mendez@ifa.hawaii.edu

[2]University Observatory Munich, Scheinerstr. 1, D-81679 Munich, Germany

[3]Universität Innsbruck, Institut für Astro- und Teilchenphysik, Technikerstr. 25/8, 6020 Innsbruck, Austria

Abstract. We present a radial velocity and model atmosphere analysis of both components of the spectroscopic binary central star of NGC 1514, based on high-resolution, high-signal-to-noise-ratio spectrograms taken with the CFH and Subaru telescopes at Maunakea, Hawaii. Together with the Gaia parallax and other data from the literature, all this information permits to determine the basic stellar parameters (Teff, L, log g, masses) of both binary components. This allows us to empirically test the theoretical post-AGB mass-luminosity relation.

Keywords. planetary nebulae: individual (NGC 1514), stars: AGB and post-AGB

1. Introduction

The central star of NGC 1514 is among the brightest in the sky, with $V = 9.5$. Eventually it became clear that it shows a composite spectrum: A-type absorption features (Balmer lines, Fe II, Mg II, Si II, etc.) plus He II $\lambda4686$ in absorption, which can only occur in a much hotter star. This hotter star must be responsible for the ionization of the nebula. The two stars have been confirmed to be members of a spectroscopic binary system (Jones et al. 2017).

In some ways NGC 1514 is a unique system: (1) Spectral features of both stars are visible in the spectrum, so we can obtain accurate radial velocities and, from them, the mass ratio. (2) Given the long orbital period (about 9 years) and the large orbital eccentricity, PN ejection by a common envelope phase can be rejected. (3) We have a good Gaia parallax; the distance to NGC 1514 is 453 pc (Chornay and Walton 2021; see the SIMBAD database). (4) We have good visual and UV spectrophotometry, allowing us to tell, at each wavelength, how much light is contributed by each star (Aller et al. 2015). (5) Model atmosphere analysis allows us to determine $T_{\rm eff}$ and log g. With this information we can get the masses and luminosities of both stars.

This offers a chance to empirically test the new theoretical post-AGB mass-luminosity relation (Miller Bertolami 2016), which differs from the classical one (e.g. Vassiliadis and Wood 1994). Here we summarize the result of this test. A more detailed report is being submitted to the european journal Astronomy and Astrophysics.

2. High-resolution spectrograms

This study is based on high-resolution, high signal to noise spectrograms of the central star of NGC 1514. A total of 22 spectra were taken with the Espadonsspectrograph and

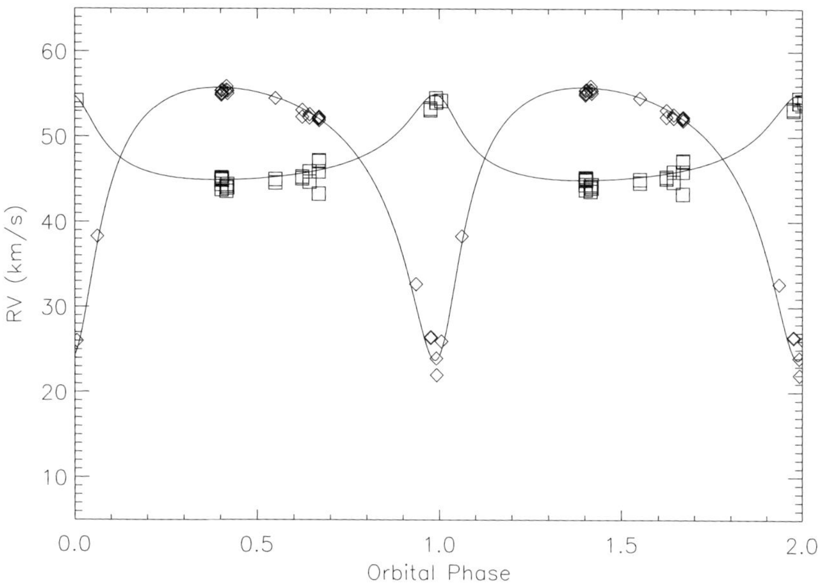

Figure 1. The Espadons and HDS radial velocities of NGC 1514. The squares indicate the cooler component and the diamonds indicate the hotter component.

the Canada France Hawaii Telescope (CFHT) on Maunakea from 2014 to 2019. Five more spectra were taken with the High Dispersion Spectrograph (HDS) and the Subaru Telescope on Maunakea in January and February 2020. The first 12 CFHT spectrograms (2014-2016) were described and analyzed earlier (Mendez et al. 2016).

3. The nature of the cool component

Several authors from Greenstein (1972) to Aller et al. (2015) have hypothesized that the cool component could be a horizontal-branch star. However, such a low-mass star, to be hot enough (Teff = 9850 K from Aller et al. 2015) must have a very low metallicity; otherwise it would appear close to the red giant branch. We have tested this using our Espadons spectra. In order to isolate the light coming from the cool component we subtracted the contaminating light from the hot component and renormalized. The result of the abundance analysis was a metallicity $[Z]$ approximately -0.3 (Mendez et al. 2016). The conclusion was that the cooler star cannot be evolving from the horizontal branch; it must be a more massive and luminous star. This was confirmed by the radial velocities of Jones et al. (2017) and by the Gaia parallax.

4. Radial velocities

The radial velocities of Jones et al. (2017) had a large dispersion, particularly for the cool component, so that the mass ratio could not be estimated with enough precision. We have produced an improved orbital solution using our CFHT and Subaru spectrograms. The new radial velocity curves are shown in Figure 1.

The new orbital parameters are the following:
Orbital period: 3200 days.
System radial velocity: 47.5 km/s.
Orbital eccentricity: 0.5.
Longitude of periastron (hot, cool): 195 degrees, 15 degrees.
Semiamplitude (hot, cool): 16 km/s, 5 km/s.

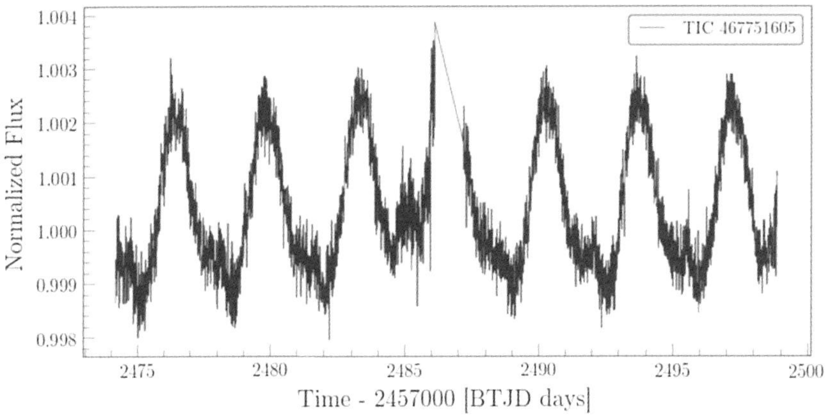

Figure 2. TESS photometry of NGC 1514.

5. Stellar parameters of the A-type component

As a preliminary step we need to isolate the Balmer profiles of the hot star.

We start from the combined spectrum and subtract the contribution from the cool star, using a model Balmer profile (Gonzalez Delgado and Leitherer 1999) corresponding to some log g, and see what remains. If we use a too high log g for the cool star, we will not subtract enough flux, and the resulting continuum of the hot star will be too high at the center of the Balmer line. So we can adjust log g of the cool star until we obtain a satisfactory, straight continuum for the hot star. The result of this exercise is the following: H gamma, beta and alpha can be best decomposed using log g (cool) of 3.65, 3.5 and 3.6 respectively. Thus we obtain for the cool star an average log $g = 3.58$.

Next we adopt $T_{\rm eff} = 9850$ K, a corrected visual magnitude $V = 9.66$, and a visual extinction $A_V = 1.4$ mag, from Aller et al. (2015). Then $V_0 = 8.26$. We also adopt a bolometric correction $BC = -0.25$ mag from Flower (1996).

Then, from elementary definitions,

$$\log L = 2 \log d - 0.10 - 0.4(V_0 + BC) = 2.01$$

where d is in pc and L is in solar luminosities. Finally, from $g = GM/R^2$ we get:

$$\log M = \log g + \log L - 4 \log T_{\rm eff} + 10.61 = 0.2254$$

So the mass M of the A-type star is 1.68 $M_\odot$.

Our calculations imply a specific value for the radius of the cool star. Can this be tested? Fortunately it turns out that NGC 1514 has been observed by the Transiting Exoplanet Survey Satellite (TESS, Ricker et al. 2015), and its photometry shows a clear variability, presumably due to the A-type star rotation. Figure 2 shows the light curve, and Figure 3 shows the power spectrum.

Since the spectra of the two stars are visible, we can find the reduced masses. The formulas are taken from Chapter IX of Underhill (1966). Knowing $K_2 = 16$ km/s, $K_1 + K_2 = 21$ km/s, P=3200 days and e=0.5, we can calculate $M_1 \sin^3(i) = 1.518$. Since $M_1 = 1.68\ M_\odot$, we obtain sin i = 0.967 and i = 75 deg. From our Espadons spectra, working on the Mg II λ4481 profile, we also know that the v sin i for the A-type star is 50 km/s; then the rotational velocity is 52 km/s. Knowing the radius of the cool star, we can calculate the rotation period, which turns out to be 3.38 days. The inverse of that is 0.296, in agreement with the peak in the power spectrum.

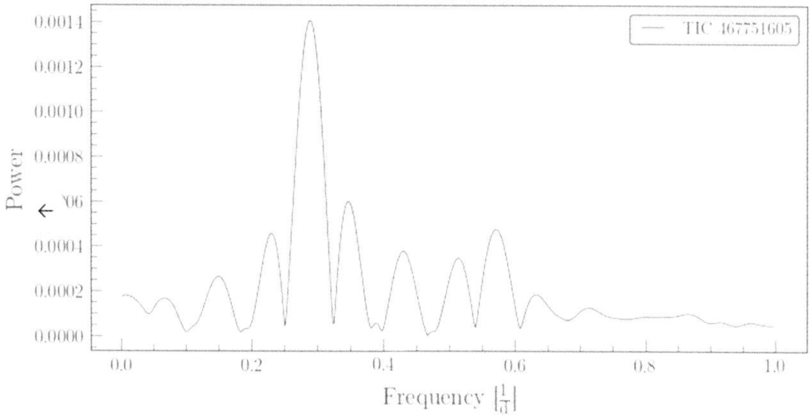

Figure 3. Power spectrum corresponding to Figure 2. There is a clear peak at 0.29.

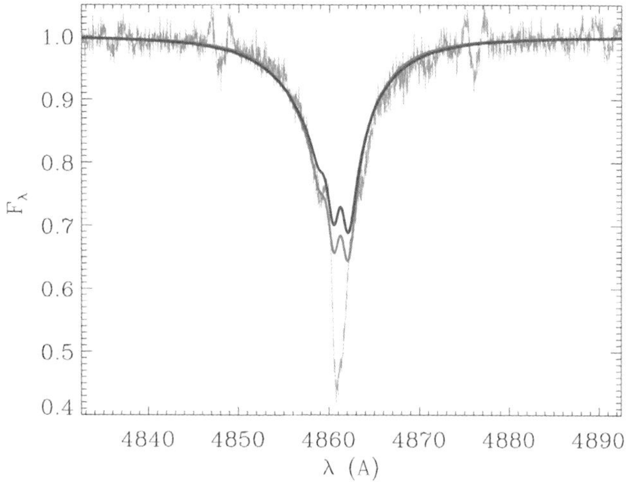

Figure 4. Hot star Hβ profile, compared to FASTWIND profiles calculated for Teff = 90,000 K, N(He)/N(H)=0.4, and log g = 5.0 and 5.2 (blue and red profiles, respectively).

6. Stellar parameters of the hot component

By isolating the visual flux contribution from the hot star we obtain $V = 10.97$, and knowing $A_V = 1.4$ mag, we get $V_0 = 9.57$. We adopt $T_{\rm eff}$=90,000 K (Aller et al. 2015). To calculate the bolometric correction we need the monochromatic flux F_V at the visual wavelength of 5480 Angstroms; from FASTWIND model atmospheres (Puls et al. 2005) we get $F_V = 20.44 \times 10^{-8}$ erg cm^{-2} s^{-1} Å^{-1}. Then

$$BC = 40.23 - 10 \log T_{\rm eff} + 2.5 \log F_V = -6.03 \text{ mag}$$

Therefore,

$$\log L = 2 \log d - 0.10 - 0.4(V_0 + BC) = 3.8$$

Knowing the mass of the A-type star (1.68 $M_\odot$) and the mass ratio from the ratio of semiamplitudes, we get the mass of the hot star: 0.525 $\pm$ 0.06 $M_\odot$, where the error bar comes mostly from uncertainties in the radial velocities and in the hot star temperature. For example, changing the mass ratio to 5/15 would increase the hot star mass to 0.56 $M_\odot$.

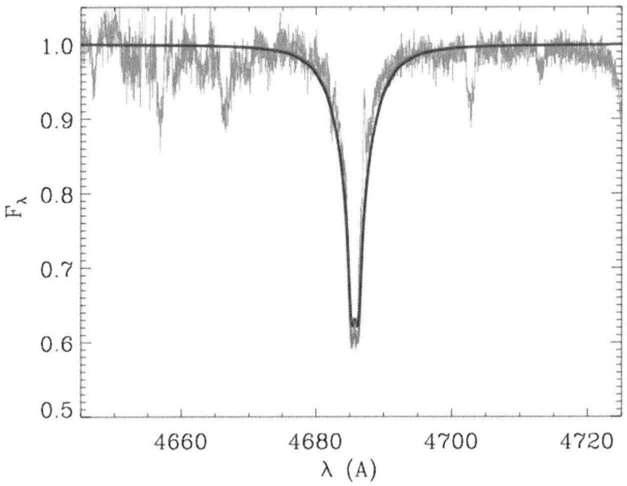

Figure 5. Hot star He II λ4686 profile, compared to FASTWIND profiles calculated for the same parameters as in the previous figure.

Having obtained these stellar parameters, we can predict the value of log g for the hot star:

$$\log g = \log M - \log L + 4 \log T_{\rm eff} - 10.61 = 5.1$$

Figure 4 and Figure 5 show that indeed this value of log g leads to FASTWIND profiles that provide a good fit to the hot star profiles.

7. Comparison with post-AGB tracks

For a log L = 3.8, log $T_{\rm eff}$ = 4.95 and a metallicity slightly below solar, we would expect a mass of 0.59 $M_\odot$ according to Miller Bertolami (2016) and 0.63 $M_\odot$ according to Vassiliadis and Wood (1994). The comparison favors the new tracks by Miller Bertolami.

Acknowledgements

This work is based on observations obtained at the CFHT and at the Subaru Telescope. We are grateful to Ari Heinze for taking a few of the Subaru spectrograms of NGC 1514 in January 2020, and to Dan Huber and Dan Hey for alerting us that NGC 1514 had been observed by TESS.

References

Aller, A., Montesinos, B., Miranda, L. F., Solano, E., and Ulla, A. 2015, *MNRAS*, 448, 2822
Chornay, N., and Walton, N. A. 2021, *A&A*, 656, A110
Flower, P. J. 1996, *ApJ*, 469, 355
Gonzalez Delgado, R. M., and Leitherer, C. 1999, *ApJS*, 125, 479
Greenstein, J. L. 1972, *ApJ*, 173, 367
Jones, D., Van Winckel, H., Aller, A., Exter, K., and De Marco, O. 2017, *A&A*, 600, L9
Mendez, R. H., Kudritzki, R.-P., and Urbaneja, M. A. 2016, *ApJ*, 829, 73
Miller Bertolami, M. M. 2016, *A&A*, 588, A25
Puls, J., Urbaneja, M. A., Venero, R., et al. 2005, *A&A*, 435, 669
Ricker, G. R., Winn, J. N., Vanderspek, R. et al. 2015, *JATIS*, 1, 014003
Underhill, A. B. 1966, Astrophysics and Space Science Library, Vol. 6 (Dordrecht: Reidel)
Vassiliadis, E., and Wood, P. R. 1994, *ApJS*, 92, 125

Planetary Nebulae: A Universal Toolbox in the Era of Precision Astrophysics
Proceedings IAU Symposium No. 384, 2025
O. De Marco, A. Zijlstra & R. Szczerba, eds.
doi:10.1017/S174392132300488X

Monitoring of dynamical processes in outer atmospheres of cool protoplanetary nebulae

Kārlis Puķītis[1], **Laimons Začs**[1], **Julius Sperauskas**[2] **and Aija Grankina**[1]

[1]Laser Center, Faculty of Physics, Mathematics, and Optometry, University of Latvia, Raiņa bulvāris 19, LV-1586 Rīga, Latvia
email: karlis.pukitis@lu.lv

[2]Vilnius University Observatory, Saulėtekio al. 3, 10257 Vilnius, Lithuania

Abstract. Dynamics in the atmospheres of central stars of cool protoplanetary nebulae can contribute to shaping of the subsequent planetary nebulae by giving rise to stellar wind. We have investigated variation in high-resolution spectra of three relatively cool post-asymptotic giant branch stars that are surrounded by non-spherical nebulae. Spectra of HD 161796 show variability in blue wings of weak and medium strength absorption lines while red wings remain unchanged. This could be caused by warm variable outflow. An episode of infall of matter is revealed in spectra of IRAS 22272+5435. Also, episodes of molecular lines in emission are detected for this star. The emissions appear to be related to the star's brightness changes. Qualitatively the same molecular line variability is observed in the spectrum of IRAS Z02229+6208. Possibly, the observed spectral variations are a consequence of similar dynamics as in the atmospheres of asymptotic giant branch stars.

Keywords. stars: AGB and post-AGB, stars: atmospheres, stars: winds, outflows, stars: individual (HD 161796, IRAS 22272+5435, IRAS Z02229+6208)

1. Introduction

Outflows that originate in the atmospheres of post-asymptotic giant branch (post-AGB) stars, including central stars of protoplanetary nebulae (PPNe), are poorly understood, especially in the case of the coolest objects. While the progenitors – AGB stars – have dust-driven winds (Höfner & Olofsson 2018), and hot post-AGB stars develop line-driven winds (Krtička et al. 2020), the nature of the outflow immediately after the termination of AGB is unclear. As the star reaches post-AGB phase the mass-loss rate decreases by orders of magnitude, but in early stage of this phase it could still be significant (Schönberner & Steffen 2007). Additionally, mass loss exactly on this early stage has a considerable impact on evolution of the star (Miller Bertolami 2016). Although binary interactions are generally thought to be responsible for shaping the nebula surrounding the star, also the wind from the central star itself can have an impact.

We present results of investigation of spectral variability of three relatively cool central stars of PPNe: HD 161796 (Puķītis et al. 2022), IRAS 22272+5435 (Začs & Puķītis 2021; Puķītis et al. 2023), and IRAS Z02229+6208 (Začs & Puķītis 2023). All of the stars have shell type spectral energy distribution (Gezer et al. 2015) and for none of the stars there is conclusive evidence for binarity (Hrivnak et al. 2017; Parthasarathy 2022; Hrivnak et al. 2022). All three PPNe are of non-spherical form (Ueta et al. 2000).

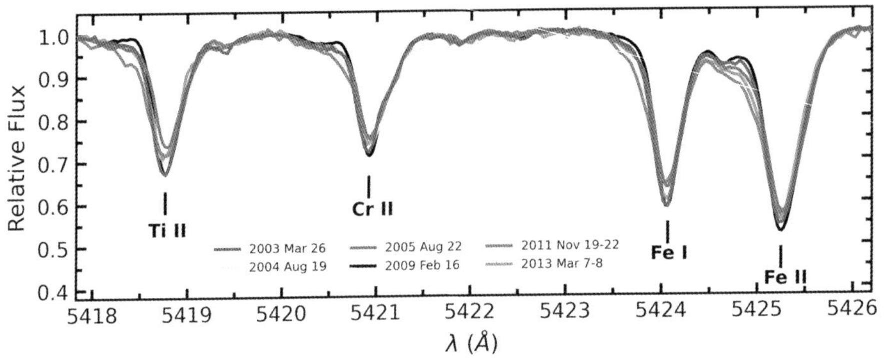

Figure 1. Typical variation of medium-strength absorption lines in spectrum of HD 161796.

2. HD 161796

HD 161796 is an oxygen-rich post-AGB star with surface temperature of around 7200 K (Takeda et al. 2007). This PPNe object pulsates with a primary period of around 45 days (Hrivnak et al. 2015). We compared multiple spectra of the star, that have been acquired during the time span from 2003 to 2021, and detected variability in red wings as well as in central parts of weak and medium strength absorption lines while blue wings remain unchanged (Figure 1). Such behaviour is seen for virtually every line irrespective of the chemical element, ionization stage, and excitation potential. We interpret this variability to be caused by warm variable outflow from the stellar surface. This idea is corroborated by variations in the strong lines. The shape of Hα line in HD 161796, as interpreted by Sánchez Contreras et al. (2008), is a combination of atmospheric absorption and emission that forms in close stellar surroundings and is caused by shocks. Spectra of the star show the central emission-related part of the Hα profile to be highly variable. Profiles of some other strong absorptions also indicate presence of shocks, for example, Fe II 5169.03 Å line clearly shows splitting in some epochs (Figure 2).

3. IRAS 22272+5435

The carbon-rich post-AGB star IRAS 22272+5435 has a surface temperature of around 5500 K (Začs et al. 2016), and it pulsates with a primary period of approximately 132 days (Hrivnak et al. 2022). Two sets of spectra were investigated to search for interday variability. No short-term variability was seen in six spectra acquired within 7 days in 2011 November, when the star was at pulsation phase light minimum. On the other hand, seven spectra observed within 11 days during light maximum phase in 2010 September show significant variability in CN Red (1,0) absorption lines as they increase in radial velocity and decrease in intensity (Figure 3). For example, CN 9203 Å line changes velocity with respect to the photosphere from approximately +16 to +23 km s^{-1} while its equivalent width decreases from 80 to about 20 mÅ. The variation suggests an infall of matter from a height of no less than 25 $R_{\odot}$ above the photosphere. The decrease in intensity is probably related to increase in temperature due to inward motion. Also strong metal absorption lines bear evidence of infall. These lines have photopsheric and additional redshifted absorption component. This excess absorption increases its radial velocity; however, the radial velocity range is different than for CN Red (1,0) lines, presumably due to formation in different heights.

By comparing 2015-2017 spectra of IRAS 22272+5435, we notice numerous emission lines at some epochs and identify them with the CN Red and C_2 Swan system transitions (Figure 4), that belong to multiple vibrational bands. For example, 2015 September 22 spectrum is one of the spectra with the most intense observed emissions reaching up to

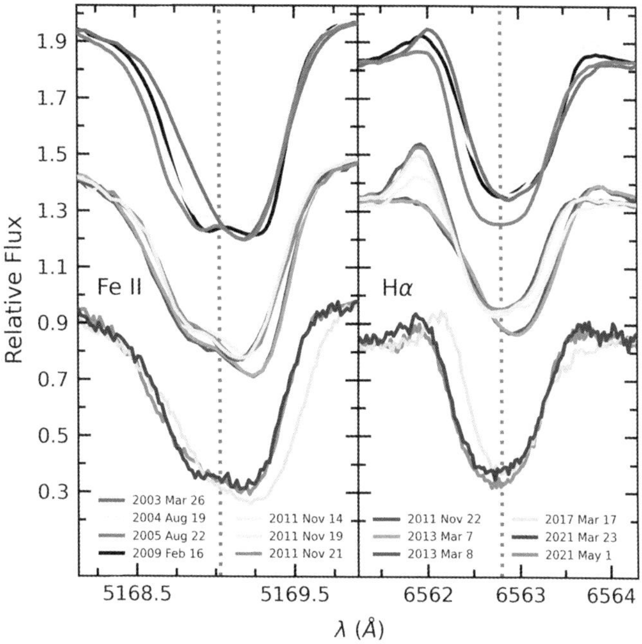

Figure 2. Variability of Fe II 5169.03 Å line and the central part of the Hα profile in the spectrum of HD 161796.

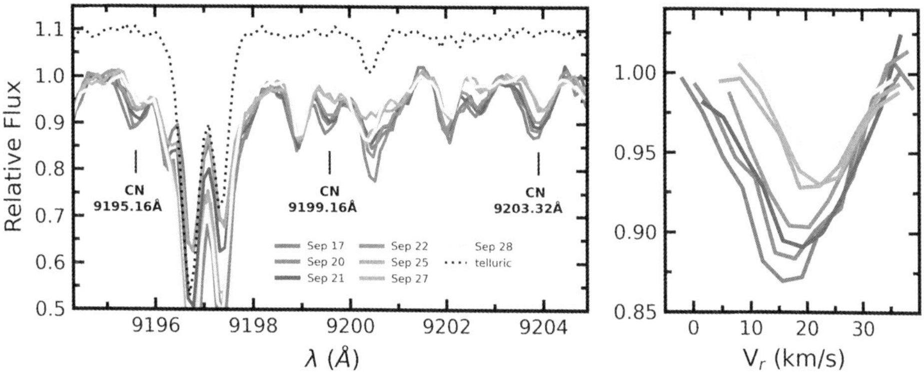

Figure 3. Left: some CN Red system (1,0) lines in 2010 September spectra of IRAS 22272+5435. Right: variability of CN 9203.32 Å line in radial velocity scale with respect to the photosphere.

10 % and even more above the continuum level. Emissions from high rotational quantum number (J) transitions are detected. For example, in the case of CN Red (1,0) and (2,1) bands the emissions are seen in lines arising from transitions with J up to around 70. The spectra suggest that it takes around 2-3 weeks for emissions to reach maximum observed intensity or to decrease to absorption. It appears that molecular emissions are related to pulsation of the star as they are seen only in those phases that are closer to light maximum than minimum. Also Začs et al. (2016) suspected weak CN Red (5,1) emission lines in spectra that were observed during light maxima. However, for example, in 2017 October 31, that corresponds to pulsation phase light maximum, molecular spectrum is described by absorptions. The emissions have radial velocities that are shifted by up to few km s^{-1} with respect to the centre of mass velocity of the star and do not

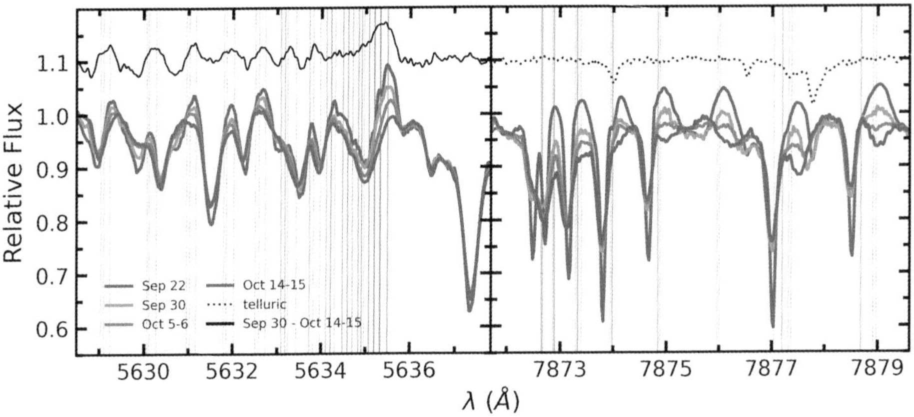

Figure 4. Molecular emissions in the 2015 September-October spectra of IRAS 22272+5435. Left: changes in the C_2 Swan system (0,1) bandhead. Positions of the strongest (highest oscillator strength) molecular lines are marked by vertical gray lines. Subtraction of October 14-15 from September 30 spectrum illustrates the variability that is partially masked by absorptions. Right: variation in the CN Red system (2,0) lines. Along with the slightly redshifted variable emissions also narrow blueshifted CSE absorptions are visible.

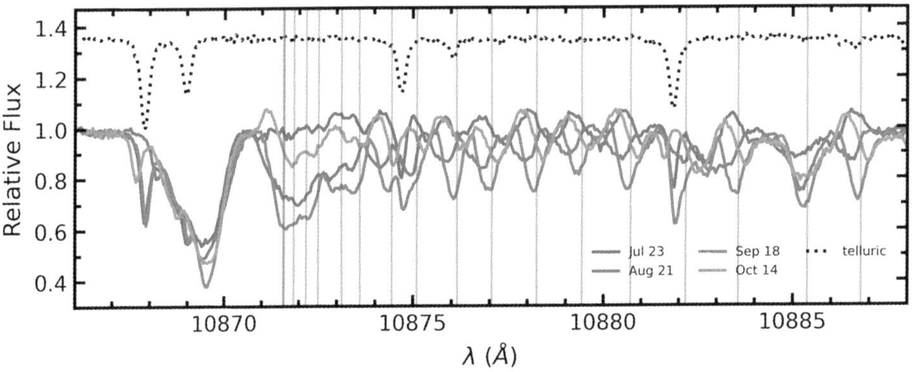

Figure 5. CN Red system (0,0) lines in the 2022 spectra of IRAS Z02229+6208. Vertical gray lines mark the wavelengths of the strongest CN Red system (0,0) lines.

appear to follow pulsation of the star. Some weaker components can have larger shifts, for example, in the September 22 spectrum the emissions are accompanied by weak absorption located at around -12 km s^{-1}. On this epoch the emission lines have a full width at half maximum that corresponds to 13 km s^{-1}. The absorptions, that emissions appear to precede or succeed, are broader than the absorption lines that are formed in the circumstellar envelope (CSE). The relatively fast changes and the widths of the molecular lines suggest that the emissions are formed close to the star. The observed velocities of the molecular features are similar to typical velocities found in modelling of AGB star atmosphere dynamics. Perhaps, similar processes, such as shocks and large scale convection, are responsible for the molecular line behaviour in IRAS 22272+5435.

4. IRAS Z02229+6208

The carbon-rich post-AGB star IRAS Z02229+6208 has a 5500 K surface temperature (Reddy et al. 1999) and primary pulsation period of around 155 days (Hrivnak et al. 2022). We observed it four times in 2022 over a single pulsation cycle. Most notability, we detect variability in CN Red lines (Figure 5) belonging to multiple vibrational bands.

Overall, the molecular lines behave in a qualitatively similar fashion as in the case of IRAS 22272+5435 – shapes, intensities and radial velocities are alike. Also the apparent correlation of emissions with the pulsation of the star is present. The observed molecular line behaviour could be common for the coolest carbon rich post-AGB stars.

We acknowledge support from the Latvian Science Council under the FLPP grant lzp-2020/1-0088" Advanced spectroscopic methods and tools for the study of evolved stars".

References

Hrivnak, B. J., Van de Steene, G., Van Winckel, H., et al. 2017, *ApJ*, 846, 96. doi:10.3847/1538-4357/aa84ae

Parthasarathy, M. 2022, RNAAS, 6, 33. doi:10.3847/2515-5172/ac54bb

Sánchez Contreras, C., Sahai, R., Gil de Paz, A., et al. 2008, *ApJS*, 179, 166. doi:10.1086/591273

Začs, L., Musaev, F., Kaminsky, B., et al. 2016, *ApJ*, 816, 3. doi:10.3847/0004-637X/816/1/3

Hrivnak, B. J., Lu, W., Bakke, W. C., et al. 2022, *ApJ*, 939, 32. doi:10.3847/1538-4357/ac938a

Höfner, S. & Olofsson, H. 2018, *A&ARv*, 26, 1. doi:10.1007/s00159-017-0106-5

Krtička, J., Kubát, J., & Krtičková, I. 2020, *A&A*, 635, A173. doi:10.1051/0004-6361/201937150

Gezer, I., Van Winckel, H., Bozkurt, Z., et al. 2015, *MNRAS*, 453, 133. doi:10.1093/mnras/stv1627

Schönberner, D. & Steffen, M. 2007, Why Galaxies Care About AGB Stars: Their Importance as Actors and Probes, 378, 343

Miller Bertolami, M. M. 2016, *A&A*, 588, A25. doi:10.1051/0004-6361/201526577

Začs, L. & Puķītis, K. 2021, *ApJ*, 920, 17. doi:10.3847/1538-4357/ac1671

Puķītis, K., Začs, L., & Grankina, A. 2022, *ApJ*, 928, 29. doi:10.3847/1538-4357/ac4bc8

Puķītis, K., Začs, L., & Sperauskas, J. 2023, *ApJ*, 948, 70. doi:10.3847/1538-4357/acc52b

Začs, L. & Puķītis, K. 2023, *ApJ*, 952, 49. doi:10.3847/1538-4357/acdcfe

Ueta, T., Meixner, M., & Bobrowsky, M. 2000, *ApJ*, 528, 861. doi:10.1086/308208

Takeda, Y., Taguchi, H., Yoshioka, K., et al. 2007, *PASJ*, 59, 1127. doi:10.1093/pasj/59.6.1127

Hrivnak, B. J., Lu, W., & Nault, K. A. 2015, *AJ*, 149, 184. doi:10.1088/0004-6256/149/6/184

Reddy, B. E., Bakker, E. J., & Hrivnak, B. J. 1999, *ApJ*, 524, 831. doi:10.1086/307858

Planetary Nebulae: A Universal Toolbox in the Era of Precision Astrophysics
Proceedings IAU Symposium No. 384, 2025
O. De Marco, A. Zijlstra & R. Szczerba, eds.
doi:10.1017/S1743921323005756

The discovery of hidden jets in planetary nebulae

J. S. Rechy-García[1], M. A. Guerrero[2], J. A. Toalá[3], D. R. Gonçalves[1], S. Cazzoli[2], G. Ramos-Larios[4], L. Sabin[5], E. I. Santamaría[3], V. M. A. Gómez-González[6] and S. Akras[7]

[1]Valongo Observatory, Federal University of Rio de Janeiro, Brazil;
email: jrechygarcia@gmail.com

[2]Instituto de Astrofísica de Andalucía, España

[3]Instituto de Radioastronomía y Astrofísica, Mexico

[4]Universidad de Guadalajara, Mexico

[5]Instituto de Astronomía, Mexico

[6]Institute for Physics and Astronomy, Universität Potsdam, Germany

[7]Institute for Astronomy, Astrophysics, Space Applications and Remote Sensing, National Observatory of Athens, Greece

Abstract. Almost 80% of mature planetary nebulae (PNe) have non spherical symmetry. Small-scale torii, knots, filaments and jets, frequently of low-ionization, were found embedded in PNe large-scale structures. In particular, the presence of stellar jets has been investigated through morpho-kinematic studies of PNe, from narrow-band imagery and high-dispersion long-slit spectroscopic observations. However, the latter technique is limiting the understanding of the global 3D structure of the PNe. MEGARA – the optical IFU attached to the 10.4-m Gran Telescopio Canarias – provides the ideal data to study the 3D morpho-kinematic structure of PN, allowing to discover, young jets hidden in the nebula. The access to the early evolution and interaction of these jets with the nebular envelope give us the opportunity of elucidating the formation of the non-spherical morphologies observed in most nebulae. We will present the results obtained from the MEGARA, unveiling for the first time hidden jets embedded in the ionized nebular envelope of NGC 2392, HuBi 1, M 2-31, M 3-38.

Keywords. ISM: kinematics and dynamics, ISM: jets and outflows, planetary nebulae

1. Introduction

Planetary nebulae (PNe) are formed by mass lost from low-intermediate mass stars (between 0.8 - 8 $M_\odot$) during the final stages of the asymptotic giant branch (AGB) phase. Based on optical imaging, the main morphological classification for PNe are round, elliptical, bipolar, multipolar or point-symmetric (Stanghellini, Corradi, & Schwarz 1993; Manchado et al. 2000) considering lobes, waist, and halos (Sahai, Morris, & Villar 2011). In additions to the large-scale components, small-scale as filaments, knots, jets and jet-like structures, prominent in low-ionization species are also present in PNe, and they are called low-ionization structures (LIS, Gonçalves, Corradi, & Mampaso 2001; Gonçalves et al. 2009). High-dispersion spectra in the Hα and [N II] emission lines have been used to find evidence of fast collimated outflows still embedded in the nebular envelope. There is a group of PNe called spectroscopic bipolar nebulae - generally round and compact with showing collimated outflows based in spectroscopy 2D (resolved spatiallly and high spectroscopy resolution). These PNe are called spectroscopic bipolar nebulae, some examples: M 1-32, M 3-15 and H 1-67 (Rechy-García et al. 2017; Rechy-García, Peña, & Velázquez 2019). A more detail study of PNe can be done through the simultaneous acquisition of spatial and kinematics data by means of the Integral Field Unit (IFU) technique, which allows the acquisition of a tomography, in the spatial plane and velocity direction. In this proceeding, we present a summary of our findings obtained with MEGARA, revealing for the first time the hidden jets within the ionized nebular shell of HuBi 1, NGC 2392, M 2-31, and M 3-38.

2. Observations

We used the IFU MEGARA (High Resolution GTC Multi-Spectrograph for Astronomy, (Gil de Paz et al. 2018)) mounted on the Gran Telescopio Canarias (GTC) in its LCB (Large Compact Bundle) mode with Field of View (FoV) of 12".5×11."3 with a spaxel size of 0."62. HuBi 1, NGC 2392, M 2-31 and M 3-38 were observed on 2020 August 6, 2020 January 6 and 25, 2020 August 19 and 2021 August 21 respectively. We used the high-resolution (HR) Volume-Phased Holographic (VPH) grism VPH665-HR covering the 6405.6-6797.1 Å wavelength range at a spectral dispersion of 0.098 Å /pix with a resolution of R=18,700 ($\simeq$ 16 km s^{-1}). We apply the regularization grid task *megararss2cube*† to obtain square spaxels with sizes of 0."215.

3. Hidden jets in planetary nebulae

We observed four PNe aiming to discover hidden jets and that can only be detected from their high-resolution spectral observations in the [N II] emission line. For the first case, we studied HuBi 1, a PN with a [WC 10]-type star, which has experienced a very late thermal pulse (VLTP, Iben et al. (1983)), which would make it an member within the born-again class. Moreover, it presents an unusual ionization structure, where the outer shell has higher ionization than the innermost regions (Guerrero et al. 2018). The tomography in velocity of the innermost shell-like structure shows an expansion of $\simeq$ 300 km s^{-1} (Rechy-García et al. 2020).

The second case is the PN NGC 2392, which displays a very complex morphology with multiple components and its orientation is near the pole along the line of sight. It presents an inner shell with expansion velocity of $\simeq$ 120 km s^{-1} (García-Díaz et al. 2012). Although its high-velocity bipolar outflow has been known for more than 30 years, it was not until MEGARA observations that its jets were imaged for the first time, providing detailed information on the PN morphology and kinematics. The velocity range of the approaching componet jet is between −190 km s^{-1} to −150 km s^{-1}, and receding from +150 km s^{-1} to +190 km s^{-1} (Guerrero et al. 2021).

The third PN studied was M 2-31, which is a compact PN with an angular size of 4".0×3".7 (Frew, Parker, & Bojičić 2016), and hosts a Wolf-Rayet C-rich [WC4-6] type central star (Tylenda, Acker, & Stenholm 1993; Acker & Neiner 2003). M 2-31 belongs to the group of spectroscopic bipolar nebulae (Rechy-García et al. 2017), and it has collimated bipolar outflows with expansion velocities up to ±90 km s^{-1} (Akras & López 2012). With the new data with MEGARA, we found five kinematic components with different spatial extents: (i) a pair of fast spectroscopic outflows (ii and iii) with receding and approaching components, (iv) a low velocity component, almost orthogonal to the

† Task developed by J. Zaragoza-Cardiel available at `https://github.com/javierzaragoza/megararss2cube`

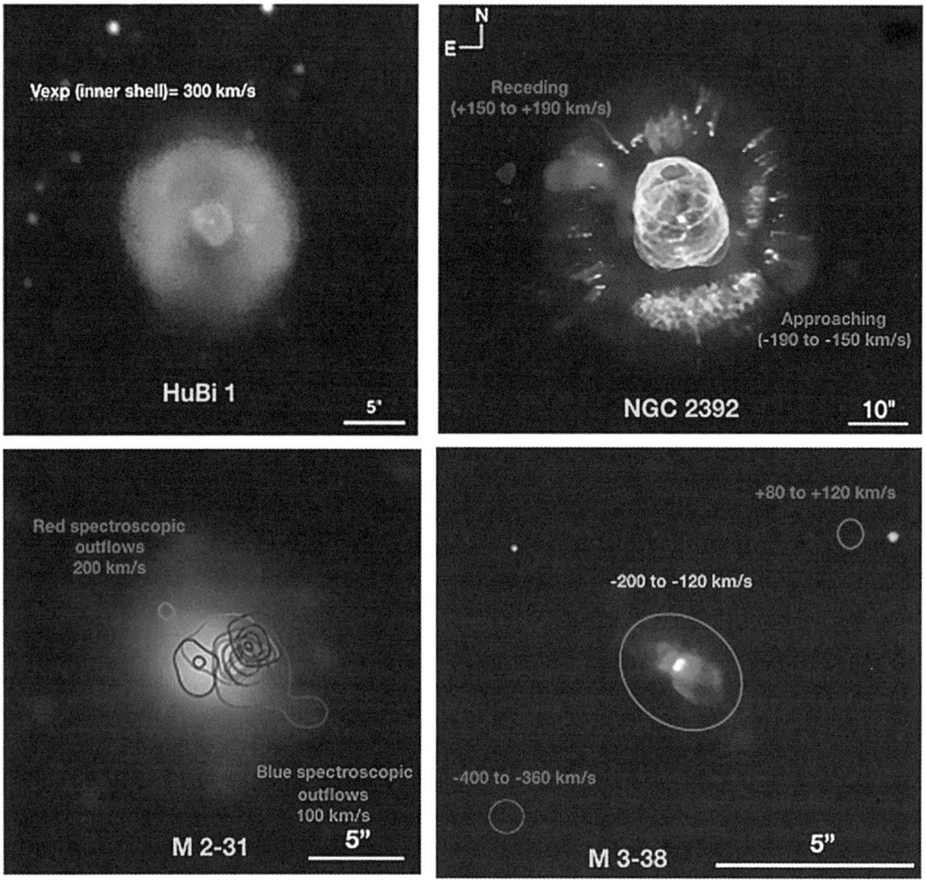

Figure 1. Hidden jets in four PNe. The original images are in the papers: HuBi 1 (Rechy-García et al. 2020), NGC 2392 (Guerrero et al. 2021), M 2-31 (Rechy-García et al. 2021) and M 3-38 (Rechy-García et al. 2022).

spectroscopic outflows and, (v) two knots in the northern and southern parts (Rechy-García et al. 2021).

Finally, we also studied the PN M 3-38, which presents a binary star and a fast collimated outflow with an expansion velocity of ± 225 km s^{-1}. The MEGARA observations also detect another pair of high-velocity clumps which is almost orthogonal to the bipolar axis of M 3-38 (Rechy-García et al. 2022). Figure 1 shows the four PNe studied, displaying their radial velocities in the Local System of Rest.

4. Conclusions

Thanks to the high-resolution spectroscopic observations of four PNe with the optical IFU MEGARA, we, for the first time, revealed collimated and highly-collimated (jet) outflows which had been uncovered in analyses based on the traditional narrow-band images and long-slit spectra. Identifying this type of sources is not easy, since the other nebular components are brighter than these jets and outflows, often making their detection almost impossible. The discovery of hidden components in PNe helps us to better interpret the three-dimensional structure of these objects, both spatially and spectroscopically. Hidden jets can be found in both, compact and large PNe. However, so far, compact PNe with high-velocity jets have received less attention. Now, as we have shown, through high resolution IFU spectroscopy these collimated outflows can be "easily" identified. What is the impact of such discoveries on our understanding of PNe?

5. Future work

As the very first step to answer the above question, or, to understand the action of these collimated outflows on the previously known nebular components, we are attempting to carry out the first spatially resolved spectroscopic analysis of the LIS (tips of the jets) in the near-IR regime. The detection of H_2 lines from different ro-vibrational and excitation states, H I lines (Brγ, Paβ) and the brightest [Fe II] lines at 1.257 and 1.644 μm, in the PNe known to have hidden jets, will thus enable us to check for the existence of shocks, so far unseen in optical studies.

JSRG is supported by the Brazilian research funding FAPERJ through the fellowship and grant E-26/205.846/2022 and E-26/205.847/2022 and IAU grant. DRG acknowledges the grants 200.527/2023 (FAPERJ) and 313016/2020-8 (CNPq).

References

Akras, S., López, J. A., 2012, *MNRAS*, 425, 2197. doi:10.1111/j.1365-2966.2012.21578.x

Acker, A., Neiner, C., 2003, *A&A*, 403, 659. doi:10.1051/0004-6361:20030391

Frew, D. J., Parker, Q. A., Bojičić, I. S., 2016, *MNRAS*, 455, 1459. doi:10.1093/mnras/stv1516

García-Díaz, M. T., López, J. A., Steffen, W., Richer, M. G., 2012, *ApJ*, 761, 172. doi:10.1088/0004-637X/761/2/172

Gil de Paz, A., Carrasco, E., Gallego, J., Iglesias-Páramo, J., Cedazo, R., García-Vargas, M. L., Arrillaga, X., et al., 2018, *SPIE*, 10702, 1070217. doi:10.1117/12.2313299

Gonçalves, D. R., Corradi, R. L. M., Mampaso, A., 2001, *ApJ*, 547, 302. doi:10.1086/318364

Gonçalves, D. R., Mampaso, A., Corradi, R. L. M., Quireza, C., 2009, *MNRAS*, 398, 2166. doi:10.1111/j.1365-2966.2009.15266.x

Guerrero, M. A., Cazzoli, S., Rechy-García, J. S., Ramos-Larios, G., Montoro-Molina, B., Gómez-González, V. M. A., Toalá, J. A., et al., 2021, *ApJ*, 909, 44. doi:10.3847/1538-4357/abe2aa

Guerrero, M. A., Fang, X., Miller Bertolami, M. M., Ramos-Larios, G., Todt, H., Alarie, A., Sabin, L., et al., 2018, NatAs, 2, 784. doi:10.1038/s41550-018-0551-8

Iben, I., Kaler, J. B., Truran, J. W., Renzini, A., 1983, *ApJ*, 264, 605. doi:10.1086/160631

Manchado, A., Villaver, E., Stanghellini, L., Guerrero, M. A., 2000, *ASPC*, 199, 17. doi:10.48550/arXiv.astro-ph/0002073

Rechy-García, J. S., Guerrero, M. A., Santamaría, E., Gómez-González, V. M. A., Ramos-Larios, G., Toalá, J. A., Cazzoli, S., et al., 2020, *ApJL*, 903, L4. doi:10.3847/2041-8213/abbe22

Rechy-García, J. S., Toalá, J. A., Cazzoli, S., Guerrero, M. A., Sabin, L., Gómez-González, V. M. A., Ramos-Larios, G., 2021, *MNRAS*, 508, 2254. doi:10.1093/mnras/stab2531

Rechy-García, J. S., Toalá, J. A., Guerrero, M. A., Rodríguez-López, C., Sabin, L., Ramos-Larios, G., 2022, *ApJL*, 933, L24. doi:10.3847/2041-8213/ac78dc

Rechy-García, J. S., Peña, M., Velázquez, P. F., 2019, *MNRAS*, 482, 1163. doi:10.1093/mnras/sty2758

Rechy-García, J. S., Velázquez, P. F., Peña, M., Raga, A. C., 2017, *MNRAS*, 464, 2318. doi:10.1093/mnras/stw2524

Sahai, R., Morris, M. R., Villar, G. G., 2011, *AJ*, 141, 134. doi:10.1088/0004-6256/141/4/134

Stanghellini, L., Corradi, R. L. M., Schwarz, H. E., 1993, *A&A*, 279, 521

Tylenda, R., Acker, A., Stenholm, B., 1993, *A&AS*, 102, 595

Planetary Nebulae: A Universal Toolbox in the Era of Precision Astrophysics
Proceedings IAU Symposium No. 384, 2025
O. De Marco, A. Zijlstra & R. Szczerba, eds.
doi:10.1017/S1743921323005422

History of two mass loss processes in VY CMa.

G. Quintana-Lacaci, L. Velilla, J. P. Fonfría, J. Cernicharo, A. Castro-Carrizo, M. Agúndez and L. Decin

Dept. of Molecular Astrophysics. IFF-CSIC; Centro de Astrobiología (CAB), CSIC-INTA; Instituut voor Sterrenkunde, KU Leuven; Institut de Radio Astronomie Millimétrique
email: `guillermo.q@csic.es`

Abstract. Red Supergiant stars (RSGs) are known to eject large amounts of material during this evolutionary phase. However, the processes powering the mass ejection in low- and intermediate-mass stars do not work for RSGs and the mechanism that drives the ejection remains unknown. Different mechanisms have been proposed as responsible for this mass ejection including Alfvén waves, large convective cells, and magnetohydrodynamical (MHD) disturbances at the photosphere, but so far little is known about the actual processes taking place in these objects. Here we present high angular resolution interferometric ALMA maps of VY CMa continuum and molecular emission, which resolve the structure of the ejecta with unprecedented detail. We reconstructed the 3D structure of the gas traced by the different species. It allowed us to study the morphology and kinematics of the gas traced by the different species surrounding VY CMa. Two types of ejecta are clearly observed: extended, irregular, and vast ejecta surrounding the star that are carved by localized fast outflows. The structure of the outflows is found to be particularly flat. We present a 3D reconstruction of these outflows and proof of the carving. This indicates that two different mass loss processes take place in this massive star. We tentatively propose the physical cause for the formation of both types of structures. These results provide essential information on the mass loss processes of RSGs and thus of their further evolution.

Keywords. supergiants, radio lines: stars, stars: mass-loss, stars: individual: VY CMa, circumstellar matter

1. Introduction

The processes driving the mass loss ejections in Asymptotic Giant Branch stars (AGBs) is more or less well established due to the effect of the radiation pressure pushing the dust grains formed in the stars' outer photosphere, and the dust's drift on the gas, generating an effective mass ejection (Höfner and Olofsson 2018). However, while we know Red Supergiant stars (RSGs) lose mass, regarding the detection of extended circumstellar material, the mechanism driving such ejections remains mostly unknown.

The amplitude and the irregular period of the pulsation observed in RSGs rule out the mechanism observed in AGB stars (Josselin and Plez 2007). Certain mechanisms have been proposed to be those responsible for the mass ejections in RSGs as the presence of giant convective cells that generate an extended photosphere where dust can be massively formed, as reported to be present in Betelgeuse (Lim et al. 1998). This type of mechanism would generate an inhomogeneous circumstellar envelope, with no preferential directions for the ejection events. However, certain objects as VY CMa or NML Cyg, present well-localized outflows. Due to this, some works have suggested that such ejections are compatible with events of magnetic origin such as the presence of cold spots on the stellar photosphere (O'Gorman et al. 2015). Such cold spots would trigger a

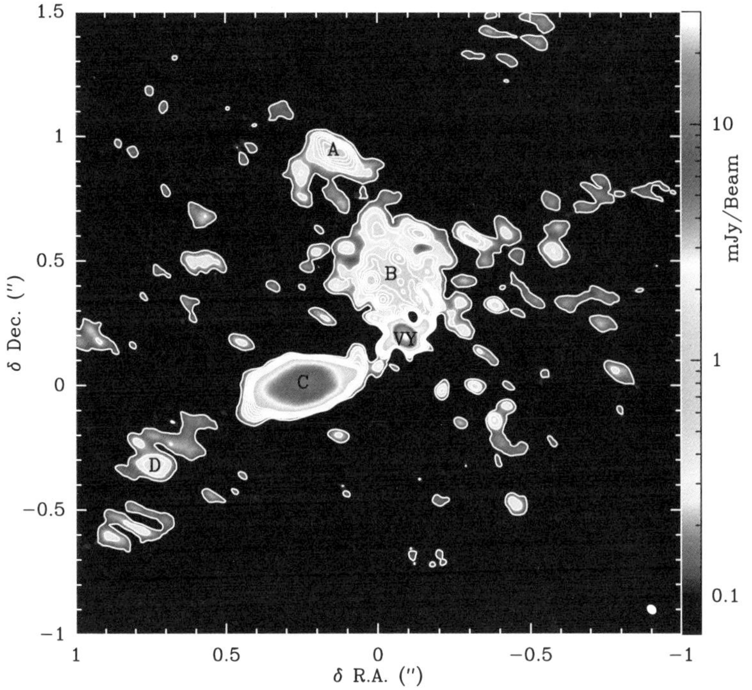

Figure 1. Continuum emission obtained from the ALMA data at $\lambda = 1\,mm$. The Half power beam-width (HPBW) is $0.''04 \times 0.''03$ with a position angle (P.A.) of 29° (see bottom-right corner). The contours correspond to steps of 5σ ($\sigma = 0.023$ mJy/beam). The labels of the different regions follow Kamiński (2019).

localized dust formation and thus a localized gas drifting and mass ejection. In any case, the source powering both types of mass ejections would be radiation pressure on dust, as in AGB objects.

In this work, we focused on VY CMa. The structure of the ejecta observed towards this object is complex, showing clumps, arcs, and other asymmetries (see e.g. Humphreys et al. 2007). Here we present ALMA high-angular resolution maps of a series of molecular species towards VY CMa, and explore the implications to the structures observed.

2. Results

The continuum emission observed toward VY CMa in our maps at 1 mm (Fig. 1) shows three main structures: VY, which is the central compact sources corresponding to the star, a northern elongation and a clump to the East of VY, which is called Clump C in literature.

When comparing these structures with the emission traced by different species (see Fig. 2) we observed that some of these transitions follow relatively well the structure observed in the continuum (e.g. H_2S, or NaCl) while the structures inferred in other molecular lines is very different (e.g. SiO, SO_2,..).

In order to understand the characteristics of the ejecta, we first focused on the H_2S emission, which very accurately traces the emission from the continuum. We obtained a position-velocity diagram along the line connecting VY with clump C, and found that the velocity field is compatible with a Hubble-like velocity field ($v \propto r$).

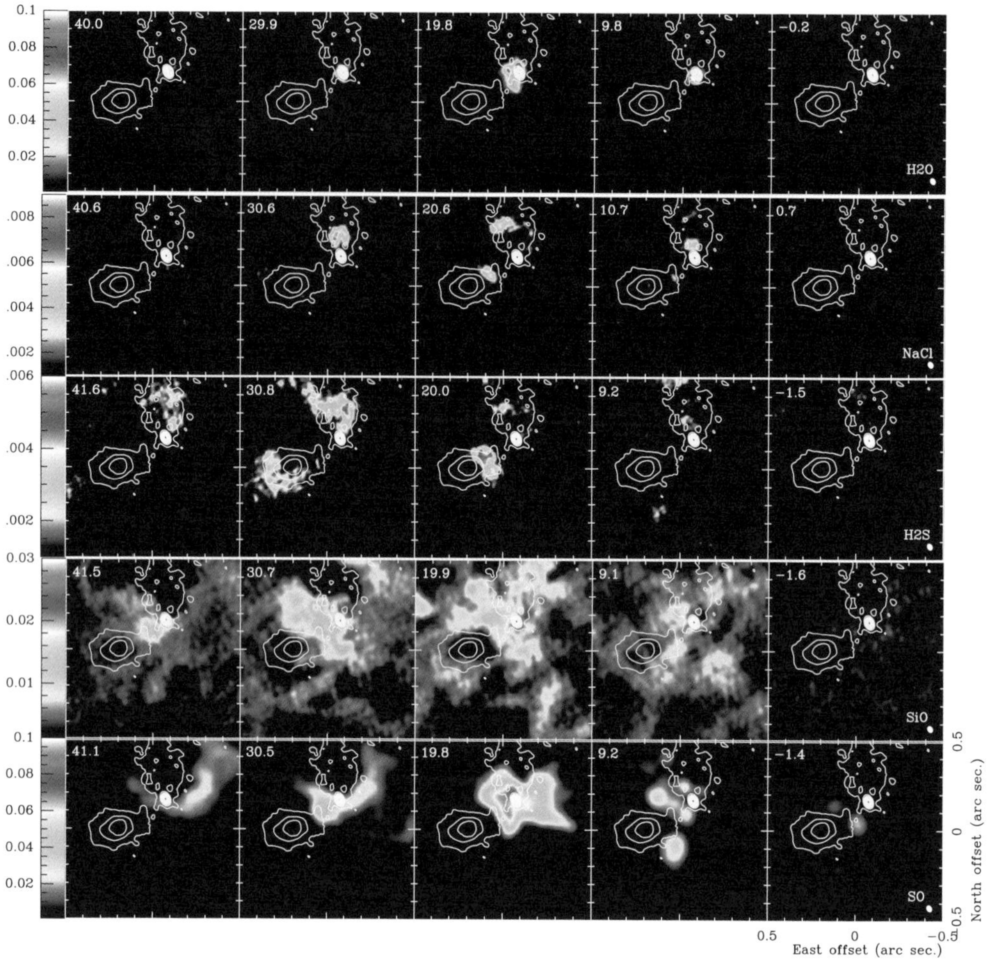

Figure 2. Channel maps of some lines showing the complexity of VY CMa ejecta (continuum shown in contours). From top to bottom in color: H_2O $v = 2$ $5_{5,0} - 6_{4,3}$; NaCl 18–17; H_2S $2_{2,0}$–$2_{1,1}$ SiO 5–4; SO $5_6 - 4_5$. The value of V_{LSR} of each panel is shown in their upper-left corner. The HPBW is 0.″04 × 0.″03 with a P.A. of 29° (see the bottom-right corner of the last panel). The continuum emission is shown in white contours.

Using this velocity field we were able to reconstruct the 3D structure of the H_2S emission. For this purpose, we made use of the `Astructures` program†. This 3D structure revealed that the elongation observed towards the North in the continuum and in H_2S emission is actually composed of a series of outflows. It is worth noting that the velocity these outflows reach in their outermost regions reaches values above ∼100km s^{-1}.

The velocity field and the structure of the SO $5_6 - 4_5$ is relatively complex for an accurate 3D reconstruction. However, we observed a series of shell-like structures coincident with those regions where the fast outflows traced by H_2S are located (see Fig. 3).

This suggests that the VY CMa ejecta consists of two different types of ejections. First, a slow and inhomogeneous, yet not-localized, mass ejection. Second, fast high-collimated outflows carving the formerly ejected slow gas.

Another particular feature observed in the outflows of H_2S is the relative flatness of these structures.

† `https://github.com/GQuintanaL/Astructures`

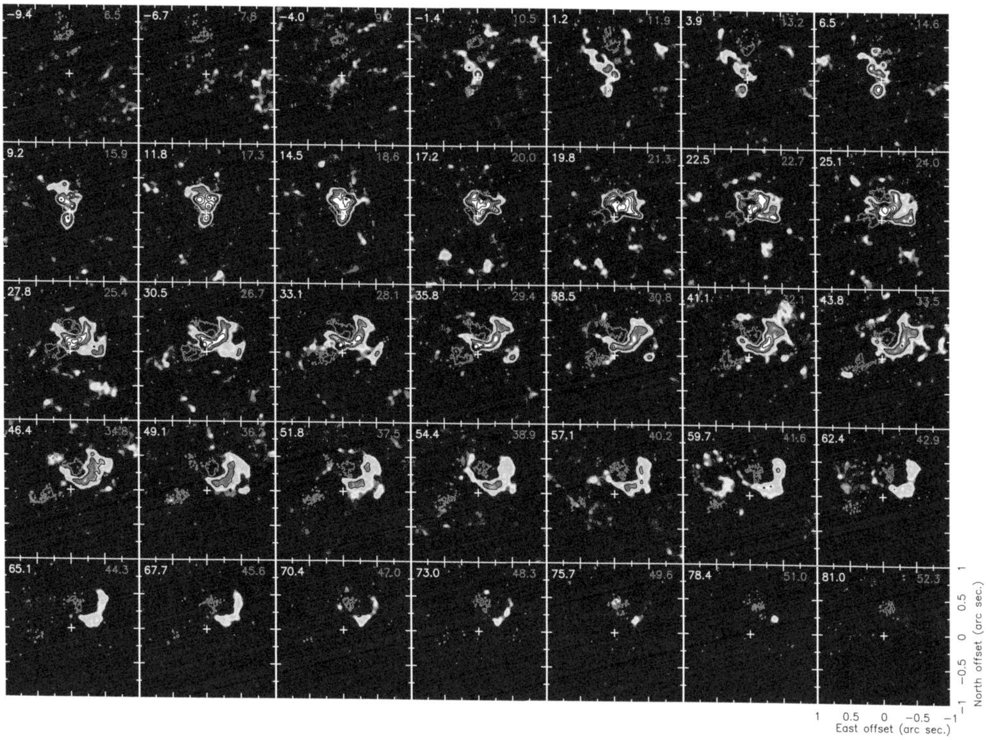

Figure 3. Comparison of the SO $5_6 - 4_5$ emission (colors & black contours) and H_2S $2_{2,0}$–$2_{1,1}$(red contours). $V_{\rm LSR}$ for SO is shown in the upper-left corner, while that of H_2S if shown in red in the upper-right corner. Video available as supplementary material.

In order to explain this flatness we explore if it would be due to the effect of the stellar rotation on the ejection arising from a single point of the photosphere, i.e. a mass ejection arising from a single point in the photosphere would create an emission contained to the angle given by a given angle w.r.t the rotation axis. In the first place, we inspected the 3D structure to see if all the ejections and their flatness could be constrained to different "latitudes". We found that assuming that the rotation axis is in an angle of $\sim 95°$ w.r.t the plane of the sky, all the ejections would lay within a single latitude.

Furthermore, we created a simple expansion model to recreate those ejections. This model had as inputs the latitude of the emitting spot, the duration of the ejection, the velocity field provided by the H_2S maps, and the rotation velocity. We were able to reconstruct the 5 fast outflows observed (Fig. 4).

It is worth noting that, while for RSGs 1 km s^{-1} is a standard value for the rotation velocity, velocities as high as 15 km s^{-1} have been observed and related to processes such as planet engulfment and strong dynamos (Wheeler et al. 2017). The ejection time derived, t_e, in general would be $t_e = 120/V_{rot}[\mathrm{months\,s\,km^{-1}}]$ (for a $V_{rot} = 15$km s^{-1} the value of t_e would be 8 months.)

Finally, we estimated the total linear momentum associated with clump C, in order to explore if an event of magnetic origin could power such an ejection. We found a value for the momentum of 9.3×10^{38} $\mathrm{gr\,cm\,s^{-1}}$. If we estimate the strength needed for a magnetic field to power such momentum, scaling what we know from the Solar coronal mass ejections (Welsch 2018), we found that this value should be of at least 5 kG.

Such high values for the magnetic field have indeed been derived for VY CMa. In particular Shinnaga et al. (2017) found values up to 20 kG. As mentioned above, these

Table 1. Parameters of the Sprinkler model outflows. The rotation velocity of the star is 1 km s^{-1}. V_{16} is the value for a Hubble-like expansion velocity at 10^{16} cm.

Outflow	θ_i (°)	ϕ_i (°)	V_{16} (km s^{-1})	t_e (yr)
1	100	190	94.44	10
2	85	287	94.44	10
3	140	320	85.86	10
4	100	260	85.86	10
5	120	300	85.86	10

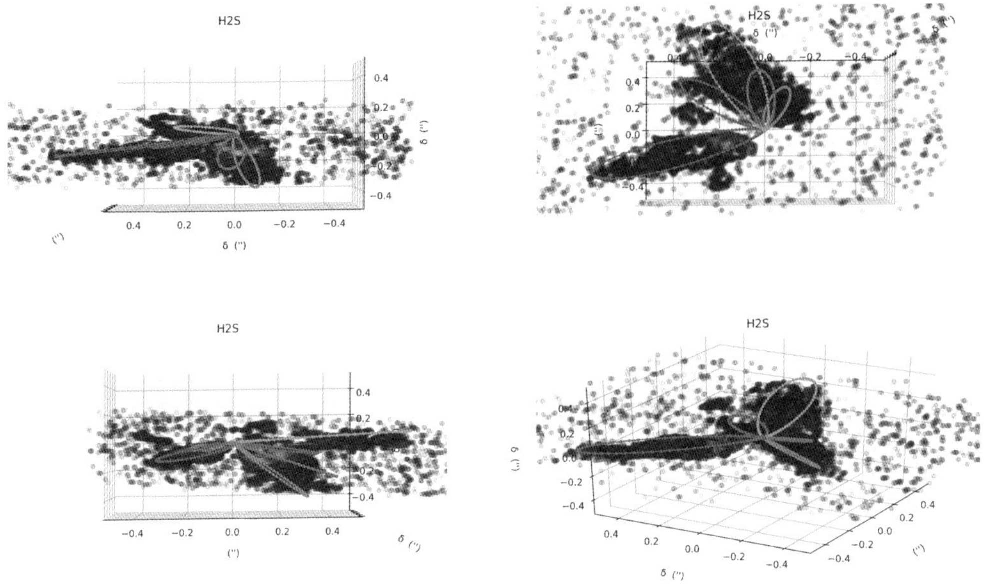

Figure 4. H_2S emission rotated so that the rotation axis corresponds to the Z axis, overplotted to the result of the sprinkler model applied to 5 ejections.

high values can be related to a strong dynamo and a fast rotation. This latter phenomenon can be associated with events such as planets' engulfment (Wheeler et al. 2017).

3. Conclusions

Our analysis reveals that, in the case of the RSG VY CMa, the formation of its circumstellar envelope is formed by two different and independent processes:

• A slow wind. A mass ejection that forms somehow ubiquitous and inhomogeneous ejecta, expanding at relatively low velocities (30 – 40km s^{-1}). These values are compatible with a mass ejection driven by radiation pressures on dust. The mechanism driving this ejection might be the formation of giant convective cells, as those proposed by Lim et al. (1998).

• A fast wind. A fast, collimated and well-localized mass ejection. Its velocity field is similar to the fast collimated outflows observed in proto-planetary nebulae (e.g. Alcolea et al. 2007), i.e. $V_{exp} \propto r$. These fast outflows are compatible with a magnetic-driven event. The magnetic field needed for these outflows is compatible with the momentum derived from the observations. In addition, the structure of these outflows suggests that rotation might leave an imprint in these ejections. A fast rotation velocity would explain these structures as well as the high dynamo needed to power the magnetic field observed.

The results presented here are essential in the context of massive star evolution and in particular in the evolutionary path of these objects shall follow during their final evolution. For the first time, we have shown that mass loss can take place in two completely different ways within this phase.

Future detailed studies of RSGs ejecta will help us to determine the characteristics favoring each type of mass event and the mechanism powering them.

Two of the questions to be addressed in the future regarding the paradigm suggested in by these findings are whether the slow expanding wind is the standard mass ejection process within this evolutionary phase, and if the jets are restricted only to those RSGs presenting higher rotation velocities and strong dynamos.

The research leading to these results has received funding from the European Research Council under the European Union's Seventh Framework Programme (FP/2007-2013) / ERC Grant Agreement n. 610256 (NANOCOSMOS). We would also like to thank the Spanish MINECO for funding support from grants CSD2009-00038, AYA2012-32032. M.A. also thanks for funding support from the Ramón y Cajal programme of Spanish MINECO (RyC-2014-16277). This publication is part of the "I+D+i" (research, development, and innovation) projects PID2019-107115GB-C21, and PID2019-106110GB-I00, and PID2020-117034RJ-I00, supported by the Spanish "Ministerio de Ciencia e Innovación" MCIN/AEI/10.13039/501100011033.

References

Alcolea, J., Neri, R., & Bujarrabal, V. 2007, Minkowski's footprint revisited. Planetary nebula formation from a single sudden event? *A&A*, 468(3), L41–L44

Höfner, S. & Olofsson, H. 2018, Mass loss of stars on the asymptotic giant branch. *The Astronomy and Astrophysics Review*, 26(1), 1

Humphreys, R. M., Helton, L. A., & Jones, T. J. 2007, The Three-Dimensional Morphology of VY Canis Majoris. I. The Kinematics of the Ejecta. *AJ*, 133(6), 2716–2729

Josselin, E. & Plez, B. 2007, Atmospheric dynamics and the mass loss process in red supergiant stars. *A&A*, 469, 671–680

Kamiński, T. 2019, Massive dust clumps in the envelope of the red supergiant VY Canis Majoris. *A&A*, 627, A114

Lim, J., Carilli, C. L., White, S. M., Beasley, A. J., & Marson, R. G. 1998, Large convection cells as the source of Betelgeuse's extended atmosphere. *Nature*, 392(6676), 575–577

O'Gorman, E., Vlemmings, W., Richards, A. M. S., Baudry, A., De Beck, E., Decin, L., Harper, G. M., Humphreys, E. M., Kervella, P., Khouri, T., & Muller, S. 2015, ALMA observations of anisotropic dust mass loss in the inner circumstellar environment of the red supergiant VY Canis Majoris. *A&A*, 573, L1

Shinnaga, H., Claussen, M. J., Yamamoto, S., & Shimojo, M. 2017, Strong magnetic field generated by the extreme oxygen-rich red supergiant VY Canis Majoris. *Publications of the Astronomical Society of Japan*, 69(6). L10

Welsch, B. T. Flux Accretion and Coronal Mass Ejection Dynamics. In *AGU Fall Meeting Abstracts* 2018,, volume 2018, pp. SH13B–2934

Wheeler, J. C., Nance, S., Diaz, M., Smith, S. G., Hickey, J., Zhou, L., Koutoulaki, M., Sullivan, J. M., & Fowler, J. M. 2017, The Betelgeuse Project: constraints from rotation. *MNRAS*, 465(3), 2654–2661

Planetary Nebulae: A Universal Toolbox in the Era of Precision Astrophysics
Proceedings IAU Symposium No. 384, 2025
O. De Marco, A. Zijlstra & R. Szczerba, eds.
doi:10.1017/S1743921324000036

Zooming on the emerging ionized regions of pPNe with ALMA

C. Sánchez Contreras[1], D. Tafoya[2], J. P. Fonfría[1], J. Alcolea[3], A. Castro-Carrizo[4] and V. Bujarrabal[3]

[1]Centro de Astrobiología (CAB), CSIC-INTA. Postal address: ESAC, Camino Bajo del Castillo s/n, E-28692, Villanueva de la Cañada, Madrid, Spain.
email: csanchez@cab.inta-csic.es

[2]Department of Space, Earth and Environment, Chalmers University of Technology, Onsala Space Observatory, 439 92 Onsala, Sweden.

[3]Observatorio Astronómico Nacional (IGN), Alfonso XII No 3, 28014 Madrid, Spain.

[4]Institut de Radioastronomie Millimetrique, 300 rue de la Piscine, 38406 Saint Martin d'Heres, France.

Abstract. We report on recent results from our successful and pioneering observational program with ALMA to study emerging ultracompact HII regions of pre-planetary nebulae (pPNe) using mm-wavelength recombination lines (mRRLs) as new optimal tracers. We focus on our study of two poster-child pPNe, namely, M 2-9 and CRL 618. We reveal the structure and kinematics of the enigmatic inner nebular regions of these objects with an unprecedented angular resolution down to 20-30 mas (~15-30 AU linear scales). For both targets, the ionized central regions are elongated along the main symmetry axis of the large-scale nebulae, consistent with bipolar winds, and show notable axial velocity gradients with expansion velocities of up to ~100 kms. The intensity and width of the H30α profiles are found to be time variable, denoting changes on scales of a few years of the physical properties and kinematics of the present-day post-AGB ejections. Our ongoing analysis involves 3D, non-LTE radiative transfer modeling of the mRRLs and free-free continuum emission. This approach allows us to provide an exceptionally detailed description of the physical conditions in the innermost layers of these well known pPNe.

Keywords. stars: AGB and post-AGB, circumstellar matter, stars: mass-loss, stars: winds, outflows, planetary nebulae: individual (M 2-9, CRL 618).

1. Introduction

Previous studies of pPNe and young PNe (yPNe) suggest that multiple lobes and high velocities may result from collimated fast winds (CFWs or "jets") interacting with slowly expanding circumstellar envelopes formed during the previous AGB phase (see e.g. Balick & Frank 2002, for a comprehensive review). However, directly characterizing post-AGB jets and their launch regions within a few hundred astronomical units is challenging due to their small angular sizes and significant obscuration caused by optically thick circumstellar dust shells or disks. A recent pilot study using millimeter radio recombination lines (mRRLs) in a sample of pPNe/yPNe observed with the IRAM-30 m radiotelescope shows that mRRLs are optimal tracers to probe very deep ionized nebular regions ($\lesssim$150 au), taking us closer to the sites where CFWs are launched and facilitating the measurement of the mass-loss rate of ongoing post-AGB ejections (Sánchez Contreras et al. 2017, hereafter CSC+17). CSC+17 reported the detection of mRRLs in three (out of eight) objects within their sample: MWC 922, M 2-9, and CRL 618, resulting in the first characterization of the spatio-kinematic structure and physical conditions of their central ionized regions.

For M2-9 and CRL 618, the data revealed the existence of young ($\lesssim$15-20 yr) bipolar outflows characterized by moderate average velocities (of a few tens of km s^{-1}) and relatively high mass-loss rates ($\approx 10^{-7}$–10^{-6} $M_{\odot}$ yr^{-1}). In the case of MWC 922, an IR excess B[e]-type star surrounded by a large-scale reflection nebulosity displaying a remarkable X-shape morphology, the line profiles suggested the presence of both a rotating disk and a wind. Through a subsequent ALMA study, Sánchez Contreras et al. (2019) provided evidence for a spatially resolved, nearly edge-on rotating disk and also uncovered a fast ($\sim$100 km s^{-1}) bipolar wind perpendicular to the disk, which was found to rotate in tandem with the disk itself.

This contribution outlines our ongoing ALMA-based study of the emerging compact ionized region at the cores of M 2-9 and CRL 618.

2. Observations

The observations of M 2-9 and CRL 618 were conducted using the ALMA 12-m array as part of projects 2016.1.00161.S and 2017.1.00376.S. The observations were carried out in Band 3 (3 mm) and Band 6 (1 mm), with a total of twelve different spectral windows (SPWs) dedicated to mapping the emission of various mRRLs (and CO lines) as well as the continuum. Observations were conducted in October and November 2017 using 45–50 antennas, with baselines ranging from 41.4 m to 16.2 km for Band 3, and from 41.4 m to 14.9 km for Band 6. The maximum recoverable scale (MRS) of the observations is $\sim$0$''$.8 and $\sim$0$''$.7 at 3 and 1 mm, respectively. Full details on the observations and imaging techniques for M 2-9 and CRL 618 can be found in Sánchez Contreras et al. and Fonfría et al., in preparation, respectively. The final mRRLs cubes and continuum maps presented here have angular resolution of $\sim$40-60 mas at 1 mm and $\sim$70-90 mas at 3 mm.

3. M 2-9 or "The Butterfly Nebula"

M 2-9 is a very well-documented yPNe candidate that has gathered significant attention in the existing literature (e.g. Kwok et al. 1985; Corradi et al. 2011; Castro-Carrizo et al. 2012, 2017; Sánchez Contreras et al. 2017; Balick et al. 2018, and references therein). It has prominent large-scale lobes (oriented along the NS direction) with a dominant expansive kinematics. Indirect, yet compelling evidence suggests that M 2-9 hosts a binary system with an orbital period of $\sim$90 yr, although the nature of this binary remains unknown. The extended lobes display observable radio-continuum free-free emission, contributing to a nearly flat spectral energy distribution at centimeter wavelengths. Additionally, a compact ($\lesssim$0$''$.2) region at the core emits radio-continuum, inferred to be an ionized wind based on the spectral index ($S_{\nu} \propto \nu^{(0.6-0.8)}$), which has been mapped using ALMA as part of this project.

The distance to M 2-9 is highly uncertain, with values spanning from 50 pc to 3 kpc in the literature. The two most accepted values are d=1.3 kpc (Corradi et al. 2011) and d=650 pc (Castro-Carrizo et al. 2012) from the analysis of proper motions and other nebular properties at optical and mm wavelengths, respectively. We adopt a value of d=650 pc, which allows direct comparison with the study by CSC+17.

3.1. *An ionized bent jet surrounded by a circumbinary disk*

The ALMA continuum maps at 1 and 3 mm (Fig. 1), show an elongated structure that resembles what is seen at longer wavelengths. At 3 mm, we discern a C-shaped curvature similar to that observed in 2015 in the VLA 7 mm maps (de la Fuente et al. 2022) consistent with a bent collimated wind or jet emerging from the core. This wind has

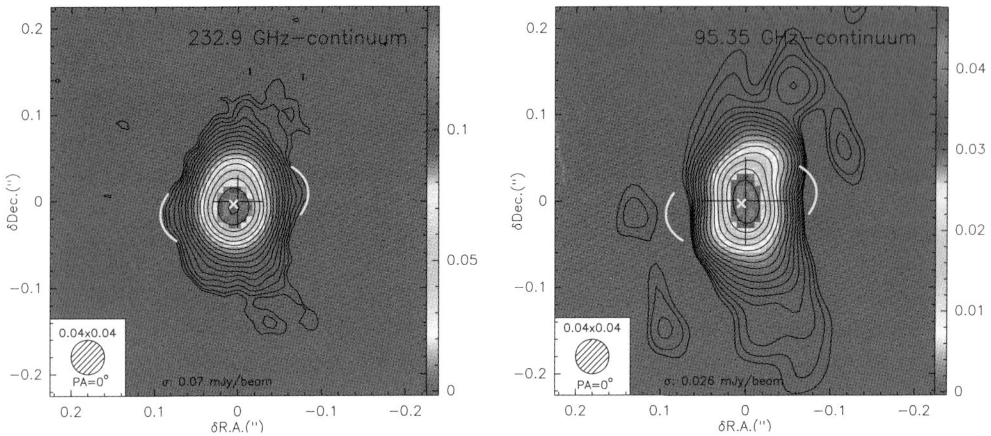

Figure 1. ALMA continuum emission maps of M 2-9 at 232.9 GHz (left) and 95.4 GHz (right) using a circular restoring beam with half power beam width of HPBW=0.″04. The level contours are $(3\sigma)\times1.5^{(i-1)}$ Jy beam^{-1}, i=1,2,3... The central cross marks the 3 mm continuum surface brightness peak at coordinates J2000 R.A.=17^{h}05^{m}37^{s}.96679 and Dec.=−10°08′32.″65 (J2000). The yellow arcs, centered at the small yellow cross, represent the broad-waist structure, plausibly a dust disc.

dimensions of 0.″4×0.″13 (260×85 au at d=650 pc) at 3 mm. We measure a spectral index of the continuum of $S_\nu \propto \nu^{0.92\pm0.10}$, which suggests predominantly free-free emission from the ionized jet, with a minor contribution from dust.

There are some differences between the 1 mm and 3 mm maps that partly arise from the frequency-dependence of the free-free continuum optical depth and from the increased contribution of thermal emission from dust to the continuum at shorter wavelengths. In particular, the 1 mm maps show a broad-waist of emission, absent at 3 mm and in the mRRLs maps, which very likely represents a dusty equatorial disk (with a radius of ∼50 au) surrounding the ionized jet. This mm-continum disk is probably the counterpart of the compact, dust disk known to exist at the core of M 2-9 based on mid-infrarred observations (Lykou et al. 2011).

Further support for the existence of an equatorial disk around the ionized jet comes from our observation of CO compact absorption at the center (not shown). Notably, this absorption is slightly offset to the north (by ∼0.″012). Considering the system's inclination, with the north lobe oriented at an angle of i∼17° away from the plane of the sky, this offset is in line with the absorption of the background free-free continuum (from the ionized core) occurring by the front part of an equatorial disk. The CO absorption feature is redshifted by ∼6 km s^{-1} from the centroid of the mRRLs, which is most likely due to infall motions from the inner regions of the circumbinary disk.

3.2. *Kinematics of the ionized jet*

As shown in Fig. 2, the H30α and H39α line emission span a wide velocity range of ∼140 km s^{-1}, sharing a similar extent and morphology with the mm continuum emission (with the exception of the broad waist at 1 mm). The comparison between the ALMA line profiles (integrated over the emitting area) with those obtained 2 years earlier with the IRAM-30 m antenna (CSC+17) shows that the lines are now more intense and broader, implying changes of in the wind properties over yearly time scales.

The ionized jet's kinematics can be examined using the moment-1 maps and position-velocity diagrams. We observe a global expansion indicated by an overall velocity gradient along the nebula's symmetry axis (PA=0°). The velocity gradient suggests very short

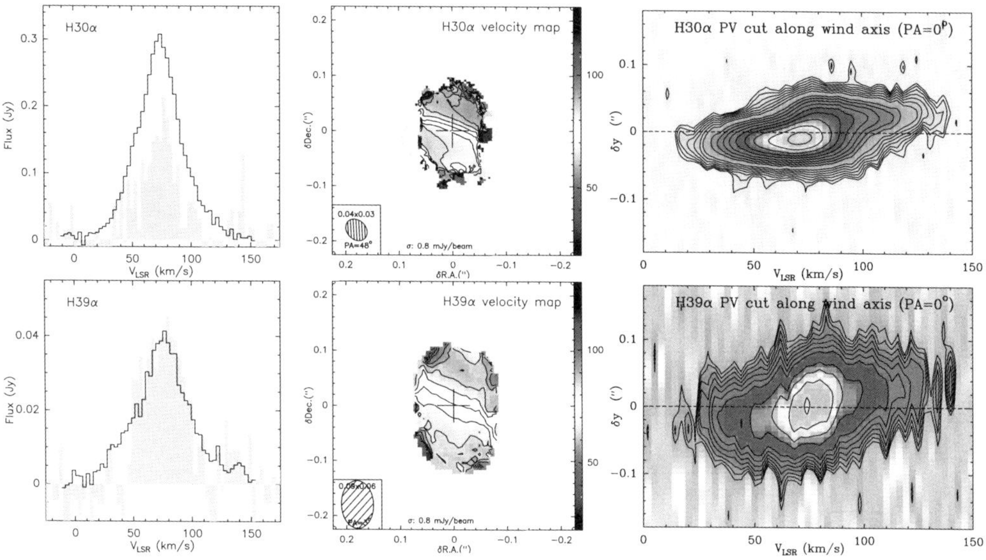

Figure 2. Summary of ALMA data of the H30α (top) and H39α (bottom) recombination lines. Left: Integrated line spectrum obtained with ALMA (black lines) and with the IRAM-30 m antenna (grey histogram, CSC+17). Middle: First moment map. Contours going from $V_{\rm LSR}$=45 to 115 km s^{-1} by 5 km s^{-1}. The wedge indicates the $V_{\rm LSR}$-color relationship. Right: Position velocity cuts through the center along the wind axis (PA=0°). Levels are $2.5\times(1.3)^{(i-1)}$ for H30α and $1.5\times(1.3)^{(i-1)}$ for H39α with i=1,2,3...

kinematical ages of less than approximately one year, consistent with the observed changes in the line profiles over the course of a year. Additionally, we note a slight velocity gradient perpendicular to the lobes, which is evident in the sloping (non-horizontal) isovelocity contours in the momentum-1 map, tentatively suggesting jet rotation. The axial position-velocity diagrams display a distinctive S-shape, showing maximum line widths at two compact regions located diametrically opposed along the axis (at offsets of ~20–30 mas), indicating either rapid/abrupt wind acceleration or shocks at these compact regions (referred to as *HV spots*).

3.3. *Non-LTE radiative transfer modeling*

For a comprehensive analysis of the spatio-kinematics and physical conditions of the ionized jet, we are currently conducting radiative transfer modeling using the co3Ral code developed by co-I D. Tafoya (Sánchez Contreras et al. in prep.). Although the modeling is ongoing, it appears that a wind with a non-uniform density structure is necessary to account for the observations. Notably, the HVspots are well depicted by two regions of high-density and high-velocity, resembling the shock-compressed bipolar structure proposed by Livio & Soker (2001) in their model for M 2-9, which is based on the interaction of a tenuous companion-launched jet and the dense primary star's wind. We find an average electron temperature of ~15000 K and electron densities ranging from $n_e \approx 10^6$ to 10^9 cm^{-3}. The average mass-loss rate of the ionized wind is deduced to be of $\dot{M} \approx 10^{-7}\,M_\odot$ yr^{-1}.

4. CRL 618 or "The Westbrook Nebula"

CRL 618 is a well-studied pPN exhibiting a complex and intricate multipolar structure, including fast outflows reaching expansion velocities of up to ~200 km s^{-1} and

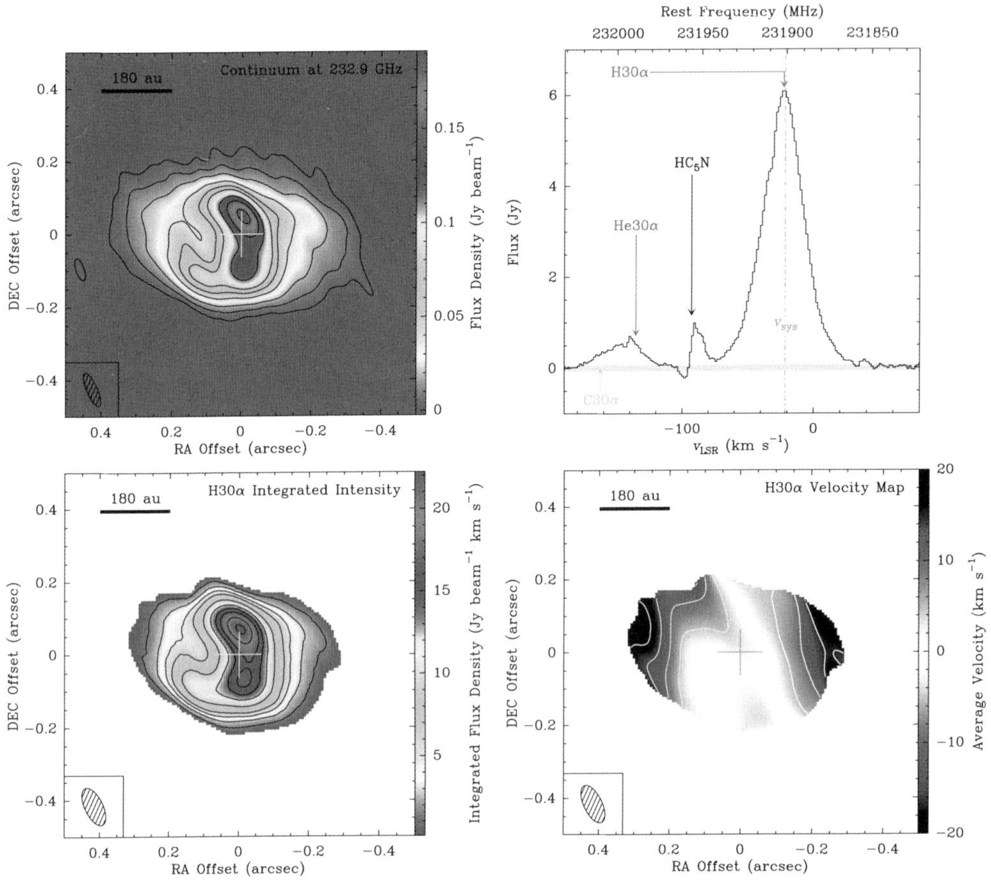

Figure 3. Summary of ALMA data for CRL 618. Top-left: Continuum emission map at 232.9 GHz. Top-right: Spectrum of H30α integrated within the emitting area (other lines are also labeled). Bottom: Zeroth and first moment maps (left and right, respectively) of H30α. The ellipse at the bottom-left corner of the maps represents the HPBW. The central cross marks the coordinates of the tracking center at R.A.= $04^{h}42^{m}53^{s}.583$ and Dec.= $36^{\circ}06'53''.34$ (J2000).

predominantely oriented in the east-west direction (e.g. Cernicharo et al. 1989; Sánchez Contreras et al. 2002, 2004; Riera et al. 2014). Compared with M2-9, CRL 618 has a younger and denser envelope, with the majority of its mass existing in the form of molecular gas (Sánchez Contreras & Sahai 2004; Pardo et al. 2007). A small fraction of material at its core gets ionized by a central B-type star, resulting in the emission of free-free continuum radiation and mRRLs (Kwok & Feldman 1981; Martin-Pintado et al. 1988; Tafoya et al. 2013). These mRRLs were initially observed by Martin-Pintado et al. (1988) and revisited by us in 2015 using the IRAM-30 m antenna (CSC+17), uncovering significant changes in their profiles and confirming ongoing fluctuations in free-free continuum emission over the past few decades.

We observed with ALMA the central ionized region of CRL 618 in 2017 within projects 2016.1.00161.S and 2017.1.00376.S. Regrettably, in this case, the 3 mm data failed the quality assessment, leaving us only with the band 6 data (Fig. 3). Similarly to M 2-9, the 1 mm continuum emission exhibits an elongation aligned with the main nebula axis, mirroring patterns observed at cm wavelengths, albeit on a smaller scale due to the lower opacity of the free-free continuum at mm-wavelengths. The brightness distribution is non-uniform and suggests a hollow cylindrical geometry, with inner and outer radius of ~70 and 110 au, respectively, with a dense equatorial zone.

The H30α line profile exhibits broad wings, implying gas movements at speeds of ~70-100 km/s within the cylindrical shell emitting the free-free continuum. The velocity map reveals a gradient along the east-west direction, i.e., the nebula main symmetry axis, indicating expansion and resulting in kinematical ages of just a few years. Despite the seemingly smooth appearance of the velocity map, a closer examination of the position-velocity diagrams indicates underlying complexity that we are currently investigating. For instance, the velocity field might encompass radial and axial expansions in varying proportions for the equator and the lobes. Additionally, we have noticed potential asymmetries in the geometry, such as the west lobe appearing shorter, and the cylindrical shell possibly being incomplete. We are currently exploring these and other intricacies using a 3D non-LTE radiative transfer model. This effort aims to provide the most comprehensive characterization to date of the central regions, within ~300 au, of this iconic object.

5. Concluding remarks

In this presentation, we underscore the significance of mRRLs in probing the enigmatic central ionized regions of pPNe/yPNe. These lines offer a unique opportunity to closely investigate the jet engine and estimate the mass-loss rate of the ongoing ejections.

In conjunction with the previously published results from our ALMA project on MWC 922 (Sánchez Contreras et al. 2019), the current analysis of our ALMA mRRL emission maps of M 2-9 and CRL 618 is delivering a comprehensive and detailed account of the structure, kinematics, and physical conditions in the central regions of pPNe. We are observing diverse properties of the ionized central regions in the three targets observed within our project, emphasizing the need for additional similar observations to gain meaningful statistical insights and advance our understanding of the developement of nebular asymmetries and rapid outflows in these late evolutionary stages of low-to-intermediate mass stars.

We acknowledge funding from the Spanish MCIN/AEI/10.13039/501100011033 (projects PID2019-105203GB-C22 and PID2019-105203GB-C21). This paper makes use of the following ALMA data: ADS/JAO.ALMA#2016.1.00161.S and ADS/JAO.ALMA #2017.1.00376.S. ALMA is a partnership of ESO (representing its member states), NSF (USA) and NINS (Japan), together with NRC (Canada), MOST and ASIAA (Taiwan), and KASI (Republic of Korea), in cooperation with the Republic of Chile. The Joint ALMA Observatory is operated by ESO, AUI/NRAO and NAOJ.

References

Balick, B., & Frank, A. 2002, *ARA&A*, 40, 439

Balick, B., Frank, A., Liu, B., et al. 2018, *ApJ*, 853, 168

Castro-Carrizo, A., Neri, R., Bujarrabal, V., et al. 2012, *A&A*, 545, A1

Castro-Carrizo, A., Bujarrabal, V., Neri, R., et al. 2017, *A&A*, 600, A4

Cernicharo, J., Guelin, M., Martin-Pintado, J., et al. 1989, *A&A*, 222, L1

Corradi, R. L. M., Balick, B., & Santander-Garc´ ia, M. 2011, *A&A*, 529, A43

de la Fuente, E., Trinidad, M. A., Tafoya, D., et al. 2022, *PASJ*, 74, 594

Kwok, S. & Feldman, P. A. 1981, *ApJL*, 247, L67

Kwok, S., Purton, C. R., Matthews, H. E., & Spoelstra , T. A. T. 1985, *A&A*, 144, 321

Lim, J., & Kwok, S. 2000, Asymmetrical Planetary Nebulae II: From Origins to Microstructures, 1 99, 259

Lim, J., & Kwok, S. 2003, Symbiotic Stars Probing Ste llar Evolution, 303, 437

Livio, M. & Soker, N. 2001, *ApJ*, 552, 685

Lykou, F., Chesneau, O., Zijlstra, A. A., et al. 2011, *A&A*, 527, A105
Martin-Pintado, J., Bujarrabal, V., Bachiller, R., et al. 1988, *A&A*, 197, L15
Pardo, J. R., Cernicharo, J., Goicoechea, J. R., et al. 2007, *ApJ*, 661, 250
Riera, A., Velázquez, P. F., Raga, A. C., et al. 2014, *A&A*, 561, A145
Sánchez Contreras, C., Bujarrabal, V., Castro-Carrizo, A., et al. 2004, *ApJ*, 617, 1142
Sánchez Contreras, C. & Sahai, R. 2004, *ApJ*, 602, 960
Sánchez Contreras, C., Sahai, R., & Gil de Paz, A. 2002, *ApJ*, 578, 269
Sánchez Contreras, C., Báez-Rubio, A., Alcolea, J., et al. 2017, *A&A*, 603, A67
Sánchez Contreras, C., Báez-Rubio, A., Alcolea, J., et al. 2019, *A&A*, 629, A136
Smith, N. & Gehrz, R. D. 2005, *AJ*, 129, 969
Schwarz, H. E., Aspin, C., Corradi, R. L. M., et al. 1997, *A&A*, 319, 267
Tafoya, D., Loinard, L., Fonfría, J. P., et al. 2013, *A&A*, 556, A35

Planetary Nebulae: A Universal Toolbox in the Era of Precision Astrophysics
Proceedings IAU Symposium No. 384, 2025
O. De Marco, A. Zijlstra & R. Szczerba, eds.
doi:10.1017/S1743921324000498

High-Speed Outflows and Dusty Disks during the AGB to PN Transition: The PANORAMA survey

Raghvendra Sahai[1], Javier Alcolea[2], Bruce Balick[3], Eric G. Blackman[4], Valentin Bujarrabal[2], Arancha Castro-Carrizo[5], Orsola De Marco[6], Joel H. Kastner[7], Hyosun Kim[8], Eric Lagadec[9], Chin-Fei Lee[10], Laurence Sabin[11], M. Santander-García[2], Carmen Sánchez Contreras[12], Daniel Tafoya[13], Toshiya Ueta[14], Wouter Vlemmings[13] and Albert Zijlstra[15]

[1]Jet Propulsion Laboratory, Pasadena, CA, USA

[2]Observatorio Astronómico Nacional (IGN/CNIG), MITMA, Spain

[3]Dept. of Astronomy, University of Washington, Seattle, WA 98195-1580, USA

[4]Dept. of Physics & Astronomy, U. Rochester Rochester, NY, 14621, USA

[5]Institut de Radioastronomie Millimétrique, 300 rue de la Piscine, 38406 Saint-Martin-d'Heres, France

[6]School of Mathematical and Physical Sciences, Macquarie University, Sydney, New South Wales, Australia

[7]Rochester Institute of Technology, Rochester, NY 14623 USA

[8]Korea Astronomy and Space Science Institute, 776, Daedeokdae-ro, Yuseong-gu, Daejeon 34055, Republic of Korea

[9]Université Côte d'Azur, CNRS, Boulevard de l'observatoire, CEDEX 4, 06304 Nice, France

[10]Academia Sinica Institute of Astronomy and Astrophysics, No. 1, Sec. 4, Roosevelt Road, Taipei 106, Taiwan

[11]Instituto de Astronomía, Universidad Nacional Autónoma de México, Apdo. Postal 877, C.P. 22860, Ensenada, B.C., México

[12]Centro de Astrobiología (CAB), CSIC-INTA. Postal address: ESAC, Camino Bajo del Castillo s/n, E-28692, Villanueva de la Cañada, Madrid, Spain

[13]Chalmers University of Technology, Onsala Space Observatory, Onsala, Sweden

[14]University of Denver, USA

[15]Jodrell Bank Centre for Astrophysics, Dept. of Physics and Astronomy, University of Manchester, Manchester, UK

Abstract. As AGB stars evolve to planetary nebulae (PNe), the geometry of the ejected mass transforms from nearly spherical to extremely aspherical. The mechanisms governing this transformation are plausibly linked to binarity and the associated production of disks and jets during the transitional (post-AGB) evolutionary stage. We are carrying out an ALMA survey of a representative sample of bipolar/multipolar post-AGB objects to obtain high angular-resolution ($0\farcs1$) observations of the CO(3–2) and 6–5 emission and study the collimated outflows and central disks. We present highlights from our ongoing survey – e.g., the presence of bipolar or multipolar high-velocity outflows, dense toroidal waists, and in one case, a circular ring around the central bipolar nebula. We will use radiative transfer modeling to derive accurate outflow momenta, masses, and mass-loss rates for our sample, thereby constraining different classes of binary PN-shaping models.

Keywords. stars: AGB and post-AGB, stars: mass loss, binaries, planetary nebulae, ISM: jets and outflows, surveys

1. Introduction

Understanding the impact of binary interactions on stellar evolution is a major challenge – these interactions dominate a substantial fraction of stellar phenomenology (Ivanova et al. 2013; Bond et al. 2003; Tylenda et al. 2011), and likely play a major role in the formation of most Planetary Nebulae (PNe), objects that represent the bright end-stages of most stars in the Universe. Such interactions can help explain why, even though the progenitors of PNe – AGB stars and their circumstellar envelopes – are generally slowly-expanding ($V_{exp} \sim$ 5-15 km s^{-1}) round structures, the vast majority of PNe deviate strongly from spherical symmetry, showing a dazzling variety of bipolar, multipolar, and elliptical morphologies (Sahai & Trauger 1998; Ueta et al. 2000; Sahai et al. 2011; Stanghellini et al. 2016). A morphological survey of objects in the evolutionary transition stage between AGB stars and PNe, i.e., pre-planetary nebulae (PPNe), shows a complete lack of round objects (Sahai et al. (2007), hereafter *Setal*07; Siódmiak et al. (2008); Lagadec et al. (2011)). In addition, PPNe also show the presence of fast outflows ($V_{exp} \gtrsim$ 50-100 km s^{-1}), which, when resolved (using interferometric observations), are generally highly-collimated. Dense, dusty, equatorial waists are also frequently found in PPNe and PNe, and recognized as an important morphological feature of this class of objects (*Setal*07, Sahai et al. (2011)). About half of post-AGB objects that are known (or likely) binaries show prominent disks (van Winckel 2003) (dubbed "dpAGB" objects: Sahai et al. 2011), and have very weak (or no) outflows.

The current consensus is that the primary PN formation/shaping process is hydrodynamic sculpting of the progenitor AGB mass-loss envelopes, from the inside-out by wandering and/or episodic jets during the short-lived ($\sim$ 1000 yr) PPN phase (Sahai & Trauger 1998; Soker 2002; Balick & Frank 2002). Support for this conclusion is provided by the fact that the momenta associated with PPN outflows, as inferred from analysis of CO observations of PPNe, either single-dish (e.g., Bujarrabal et al. (2001)) or interferometric (mostly with angular resolution poorer than $\sim 1'' - 2''$ (e.g., Cox et al. (2000); Alcolea et al. (2007); Castro-Carrizo et al. (2010); Sahai & Patel (2015); Olofsson et al. (2019)) show that these cannot be radiatively-driven. The jets are believed to result from the binary interaction; magnetic fields may play a role in PN-shaping as well, but are also most likely induced by close binaries (e.g., García-Segura et al. (2016)).

Hydrodynamic simulations of close binary interaction (e.g., leading to common-envelope evolution) have long struggled to describe even the simplest cases (e.g., Reichardt et al. (2019)), hence quantitative models that can explain the resulting jet and waist formation are lacking. An analytical approach by Blackman & Lucchini (2014) (hereafter *BL*14) predicts specific observational signatures corresponding to various possible modes of binary interaction. *BL*14 used the (limited) outflow data known for a sample of PPNe at "face-value", to derive the minimum required mass-accretion rates ($\dot{M}_a \propto M_j V_j / t_{acc}$), where $M_j V_j$ is the total jet momentum and t_{acc} is the accretion time-scale, and inferred that accretion modes such as Bondi-Hoyle-Lyttleton (BHL) wind-accretion and wind Roche lobe overflow (wRLOF) were too weak to power these

Table 1. Target Sample: Physical Properties.

Name (IRAS)	Spec. Typ.	[a]HST Prim. Morph.	[b]Point Symm. *PS*	[c]Size (″) × (″)	Dist. (kpc)	[d]CO Morph., Kinematics; (FWZI[km s^{-1}])	[e]Continuum (TM1)
06530−0213	F 5Ia	M	s	0.6 × 1.1	1.3	Mp Ofl,W,oR; (30)	NoCen
08005−2356	F 5Ie	B	s	0.6 × 1.4	3	Mp Ofl; (270)	Cen
09371+1212	K 7III	M	m, an, s	?	3	?; (55)	Cen
10197−5750	A 2Iab	B	s	2.1 × 3.6	2	Bp Ofl,W; (100)	Cen
17047−5650	WC 10	M	m	2.6 × 6.2	1.35	Mp, W; (142)	Cen
17106−3046	F 5I	B	s	0.7 × 1.1	4	Bp Ofl; (55)	Cen(1″ × 0.″45)
19024+0044	G 0-5	M	m, an	1.5 × 2.1	3.5	Mp Ofl; (100)	NoCen
19374+2359	B 3-6	B	s	1.8 × 2.4	5	Mp Ofl; (375)	NoCen

Notes to Table: (a) Optical (HST) Prim. Morph.: B=Bipolar, M=Multipolar; (b) Point Symmetry: multiple pairs of lobes=$PS(m)$, ansae=$PS(an)$, shape=$PS(s)$ (details in Sahai et al. (2011)); (c) Semi-minor and semi-minor axes of smallest ellipse that includes observed CO emission (for IRAS 06530, the size refers to the inner aspherical nebula, and excludes the outer ring); (d) CO (ALMA) Prim. Morph. (from TM1 & TM2 data): Bp Ofl=bipolar outflow, Mp Ofl=Multipolar Outflows, W=waist/torus, oR=outer ring, ps=point-symmetry present, ?=unclear (most flux apparently resolved out), FWZI=full-width at zero-intensity; (e) Continuum (ALMA): NoCen=no centrally-peaked continuum source in TM1 observations, Cen=centrally-peaked continuum source [FWHM (major×minor) if resolved].

outflows. However, successful application of BL14's method needs an accurate determination of the fast outflows' physical properties in a representative morphological sample of PPNe, especially $M_j\, V_j$, and t_{acc}.

To this end, we are carrying out a systematic program of high-fidelity, 0.″1 ALMA imaging of PPNe (*P*re-planet*A*ry *N*ebulae high-angular-res*O*lution su*R*vey with *ALMA* or PANORAMA). From our observations, we will estimate the minimum mass-accretion rate using (a) $\dot{M}_a = Q\sum_{k=1}^{n} M_{j,obs}\, V_{j,obs}/t_{accr(k)} = \sum_{k=1}^{n}\int dm(V_{off}) \times |V_{off}|\,/(sin(i_k)\, t_{accr(k)})$ (using eqns. 2 from $BL14$ and Bujarrabal et al. (2001)), where $dm(V_{off})$ is the emitting mass in a small velocity interval at an offset velocity $V_{off} = V_{lsr} - V_{sys}$, n is the number of multiple outflow-pairs, i_k is the inclination angle relative to the sky-plane and $t_{accr(k)} \lesssim t_{exp(k)}$ is the acretion time-scale for the k'th outflow-pair, and Q is a numerical factor typically satisfying $1 < Q < 5$ in jet models. For a bipolar outflow, n=1. The value of $dm(V_{off})$ is sensitive to the excitation temperature, $T_{ex}(V_{off})$, which we will estimate using the CO(6–5)/CO(3–2) ratio as a function of V_{off}.

2. The PANORAMA Survey

The PANORAMA survey covers a small (8), but representative sample of bipolar and multipolar Pre-Planetary Nebulae (PPNe), with the ultimate goal of providing quantitative constraints on the shaping mechanism(s). All objects have been previously imaged in the optical with HST, allowing a detailed classification of their morphology ($Setal07$). The survey sample includes objects that are (i) at the high end of the range of observed fast-outflow momenta ($M_j \sim 10^{39}$ g cm s^{-1}: extreme outflow object IRAS 19374) or at the low end ($M_j \sim 10^{36}$ g cm s^{-1}: IRAS 19024, Sahai et al. (2005)); (ii) with different kinds of point-symmetry, indicative of different kinds of jet activity – e.g., $PS(s)$: continuous jet with time-variable axis as in IRAS 10197; $PS(an)$: episodic jet with time-variable axis, or simultaneous multiple jets as in IRAS 19024; and (iii) with and without halos (e.g., IRAS 19374 & IRAS 17106), i.e., with high and low progenitor AGB mass-loss rates, respectively.

Survey Highlights: Although the survey, requiring observations with the 12-m array in the TM1, TM2 configurations and the 7-m array (with angular resolutions of ∼0.″1, ∼0.″5, ∼5″, respectively) is still in progress, the existing data includes TM1 imaging of all 8 objects in one or both of Bands 7 and 9, which include the CO(3–2) and CO(6–5) lines, respectively. The results are remarkable, generally showing the presence of extended, collimated lobe-structures in CO that presumably result from bipolar or

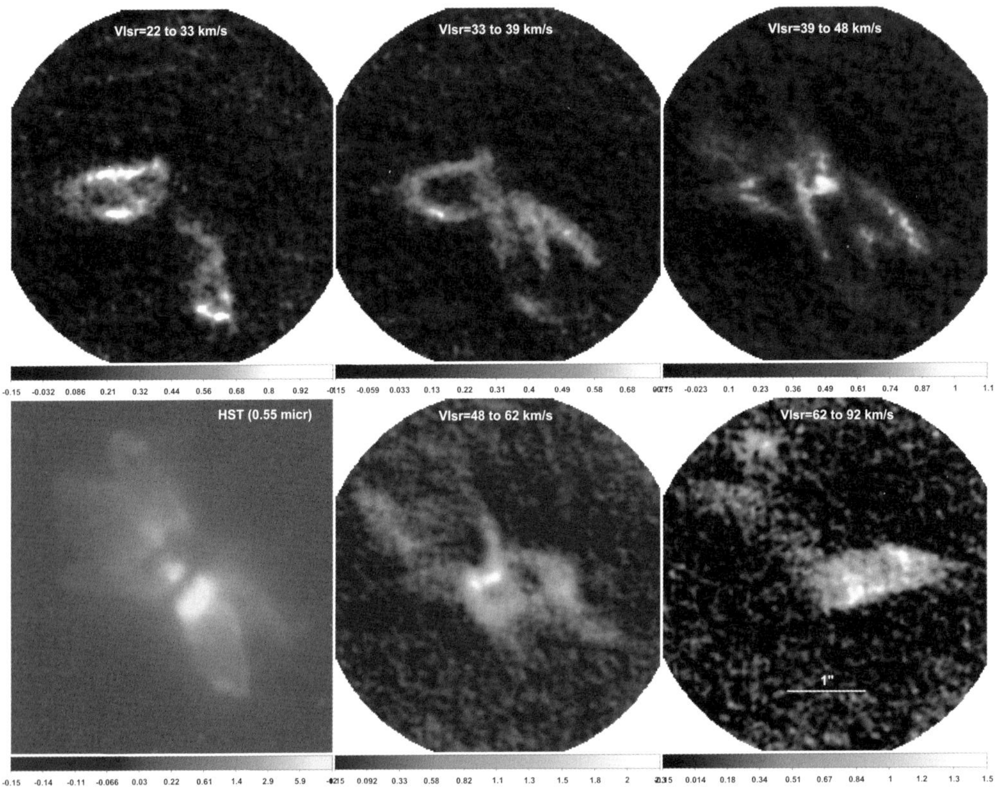

Figure 1. CO(6–5) TM1 images of IRAS 19024 in different velocity ranges within its spectrum chosen to show the shapes of its multipolar lobes for comparison with those seen in scattered light with HST in the optical. The systemic velocity is $V_{lsr} \sim 50\,\mathrm{km\ s^{-1}}$.

multipolar ($V_{exp} \sim 30\,\mathrm{km\ s^{-1}}$) outflows (Figs. 1,2). For IRAS 09371, the imaging suffers from strong artifacts that obscure its structure (Castro-Carrizo et al. 2005). The maximum (projected) outflow velocities, estimated from the spectra, can be broadly classified into 3 classes: extreme (i.e., $V_{exp} \gtrsim 70\,\mathrm{km\ s^{-1}}$: IRAS 17047 and IRAS 19374), medium ($70 > V_{exp} > 30\,\mathrm{km\ s^{-1}}$: IRAS 09371, IRAS 10197, IRAS 17106, and IRAS 19024) and low (IRAS 06530: we discuss this object in detail below). Three optically-classified bipolar objects show the possible presence of an additional (fainter) outflow with a different orientation than the optical symmetry axis, indicating that these objects may also be intrinsically multipolar.

The high angular-resolution maps enable us to isolate the dense waists from the low-latitude region of the outflows in the target sample and resolve their true structure. One of the surprising results is the conspicuous absence of gas close to the central star in the majority of objects, suggesting that the waist structures have a toroidal structure, resulting from an episode of equatorially-enhanced mass-loss from the progenitor AGB, as for e.g., in a CE system (e.g., Sandquist et al. (1998); Passy et al. (2012)). This result is in marked contrast to dpAGB objects, such as the Red Rectangle, AC Her, and IW Car (Bujarrabal et al. 2013, 2015, 2017), that show compact rotating disks of gas+dust, with masses of $\sim 0.0012 - 0.006\,M_{\odot}$; these may have formed due to enhanced RLOF (*BL*14).

Continuum emission was detected towards all sources in the existing data, which can be divided into 3 broad classes, using the TM1 images (i) extended emission + unresolved central source, (ii) extended central source, (iii) extended emission and no central source

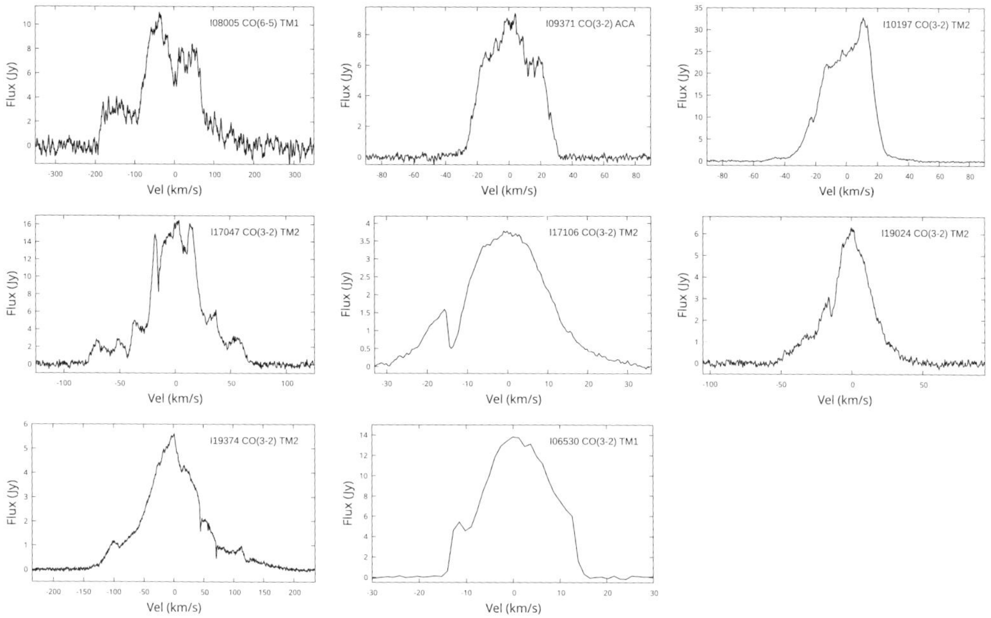

Figure 2. Representative (spatially-integrated) CO J=6-5 or 3-2 spectra, for the PANORAMA sample of PPNe. The systemic velocity has been set to zero for each object.

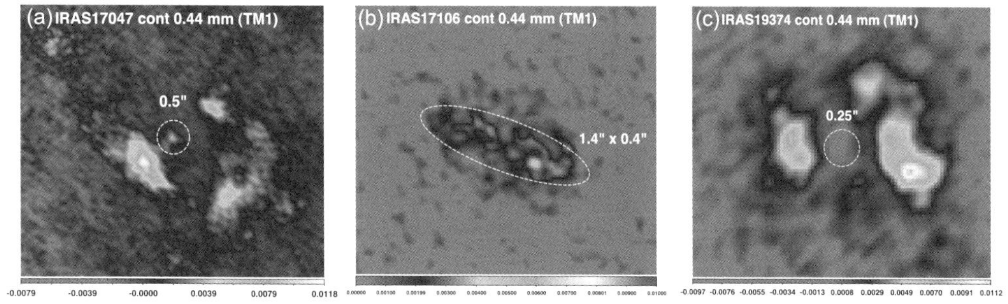

Figure 3. Three classes of continuum emission (0.44 mm TM1 data) (a) extended emission + compact central source, (b) extended central source, (c) extended emission, no central source. The dashed circles or ellipse (with sizes) show the location of the central star.

(e.g., Fig. 3). These data emphasize the importance of high-resolution observations to characterize the origin and nature of the (sub)mm emission, since lower-reolution studies, with angular resolution $\gtrsim 0\farcs5$ would tend to merge the compact and extened emission into one structure, which could then be mis-interptreted as being a dpAGB-type disk, for example.

IRAS 06530: IRAS 06530 shows a large geometrically-thin ring, surrounding a compact central nebula that has a high degree of point-symmetry (Table 1). Unlike the other PPNe in our sample, no high-velocity emission is seen – the value of V_{exp} ($\lesssim 12.5$ km s^{-1}) is similar to what is typically found for outflows during the AGB phase. Such rings have been seen in several carbon stars and attributed to an episodic increase in the mass-loss rate due to a thermal pulse. Thus, the ring in IRAS 06530 is due to the last thermal pulse while its central star was still on the AGB. Following the thermal pulse, there was a steep decrease in the mass-loss rate (by a factor $\gtrsim 10$) for ~ 600 yr. During this latter period, the mass loss was not spherically symmetric (Fig. 4a). It was then followed by a new episode

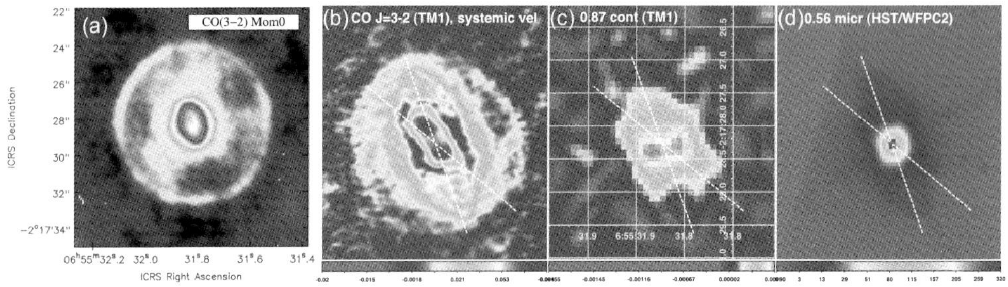

Figure 4. The multipolar PPN IRAS 06530: (a) Moment 0 map of the CO(3–2) (TM2), (b) Map of CO(3–2) at the systemic velocity showing the structure of the central bipolar nebula (TM1), (c) 0.89 mm TM1 continuum image, (d) HST/WFPC2 0.56 μm image of scattered light. The dashed lines show the axes of two pairs of lobes seen in the optical. Panels $b-d$ have the same field-of-view.

of enhanced mass loss immediately preceding the start of the CS's post-AGB evolution; the resulting shell shows extended arc-like structures that are likely part of a 3-D spiral structure resulting from interaction with a companion (such spiral structures are being found in a growing list of AGB stars, see e.g. Decin et al. (2020)). From the expansion ages of the ring (5500 yr) and waist (750 yr), we infer that IRAS 06530 transitioned from an AGB star to a post-AGB star 4750 yr ago. A full description and analysis of these data will be presented in a forthcoming paper (Sahai et al. (2024)).

In summary, the PANORAMA survey has produced several exciting results and some unexpected ones as well. The morphology of the molecular gas, in almost all cases shows the presence of collimated outflows that correspond to the lobes seen in optical scattered light, confirming that the latter result from sculpting of the ambient circumstellar envelope (ejected by the prognenitor AGB star). But there is one notable exception, the C-rich PPN IRAS 06530, which shows an extended ring due to the last thermal pulse. In a few optically-bipolar objects, additional faint outflows misaligned with the symmetry axis are found, indicating that these objects may be multipolar. Compact continuum emission around the central star is seen in some sources, but not in others – in contrast to dpAGB objects, where such emission is one of their defining characteristics.

Acknowledgements

RS's contribution to the research described here was carried out at the Jet Propulsion Laboratory, California Institute of Technology, under a contract with NASA, and funded in part by NASA via ADAP awards, and multiple HST GO awards from the Space Telescope Science Institute.

References

Alcolea et al. 2007, *A & A*, 468, L41
Balick, B. & Frank, A. 2002, *ARA & A*, 40, 439
Balick et al. 2020, ApJ, 889, 13
Blackman & Lucchini 2014, MNRAS, 440, L16 (*BL*14)
Bond, H. E., Henden, A., Levay, Z. G., et al. 2003, *Nature*, 422, 405
Bujarrabal, V., Castro-Carrizo, A., Alcolea, J., et al. 2001, *A & A*, 377, 868
Bujarrabal, V., Castro-Carrizo, A., Alcolea, J., et al. 2013, *A & A*, 557, L11
Bujarrabal, V., Castro-Carrizo, A., Alcolea, J., et al. 2015, *A & A*, 575, L7
Bujarrabal, V., Castro-Carrizo, A., Alcolea, J., et al. 2017, *A & A*, 597, L5
Castro-Carrizo, A., Bujarrabal, V., Sánchez Contreras, C., et al. 2005, *A & A*, 431, 979
Castro-Carrizo, A., Quintana-Lacaci, G., Neri, R., et al. 2010, *A & A*, 523, A59
Cox, P., Lucas, R., Huggins, P. J., et al. 2000, *A & A*, 353, L25

Decin, L., Montargès, M., Richards, A. M. S., et al. 2020, Science, 369, 1497
De Marco, O. & Izzard, R. G. 2017, *Publ. Astr.. Soc. of Australia*, 34, e001
García-Segura, G., Villaver, E., Manchado, A., et al. 2016, *ApJ*, 823, 142
Ivanova, N., Justham, S., Chen, X., et al. 2013, A&ARv, 21, 59
Lagadec, E., Verhoelst, T., Mékarnia, D., et al. 2011, *MNRAS*, 417, 32
Olofsson, H., Khouri, T., Maercker, M., et al. 2019, *A & A*, 623, A153
Passy, J.-C., De Marco, O., Fryer, C. L., et al. 2012, *ApJ*, 744, 52
Reichardt, T. A., De Marco, O., Iaconi, R., et al. 2019, *MNRAS*, 484, 631
Sahai, R. & Patel, N. A. 2015, *ApJ Let*, 810, L8
Sahai, R. & Trauger, J. T. 1998, *AJ*, 116, 1357
Sahai, R. and the PANORAMA consortium, 2024, ApJ (in prep.)
Sahai, R., Sánchez Contreras, C., & Morris, M. 2005, *ApJ*, 620, 948
Sahai, R., Morris, M., Sánchez Contreras, C., et al. 2007, *AJ*, 134, 2200
Sahai, R., Morris, M. R., & Villar, G. G. 2011, *AJ*, 141, 134
Sahai, R., Claussen, M. J., Schnee, S., et al. 2011, *ApJ Let*, 739, L3
Sandquist, E. L., Taam, R. E., Chen, X., et al. 1998, *ApJ*, 500, 909
Siódmiak, N., Meixner, M., Ueta, T., et al. 2008, *ApJ*, 677, 382
Soker, N. 2002, *ApJ*, 568, 726. doi:10.1086/339065
Stanghellini, L., Shaw, R. A., & Villaver, E. 2016, *ApJ*, 830, 33
Tocknell et al. 2014, *MNRAS*, 439, 2014
Tylenda, R., Hajduk, M., Kamiński, T., et al. 2011, *A & A*, 528, A114
Ueta et al. 2000, ApJ, 528, 861
van Winckel, H. 2003, *ARA & A*, 41, 391
Zou, Y. et al. 2020, MNRAS, 497, 2855

Planetary Nebulae: A Universal Toolbox in the Era of Precision Astrophysics
Proceedings IAU Symposium No. 384, 2025
O. De Marco, A. Zijlstra & R. Szczerba, eds.
doi:10.1017/S1743921325000924

Red novae, stellar mergers in binary and triple systems, and bipolar nebulae

Tomek Kamiński

Nicolaus Copernicus Astronomical Center, Polish Academy of Sciences,
Rabiańska 8, 87-100 Toruń, Poland
email: tomkam@ncac.torun.pl

Abstract. Red novae are transients powered by collisions of non-compact stars. Among their progenitors are systems of evolved subgiants and giants stars. Remnants of such red novae display bipolar structures which have remarkably close characteristics to many post-AGB or pre-PN systems. It is important to ask (and eventually verify) whether some of the less known post-main-sequence objects (mis-)classified as pre-PNe can be merger remnants similar to the red nova remnants.

Keywords. stars: imaging, stars: binaries, stars: winds, outflows, circumstellar matter

1. Red novae as stellar mergers

Red novae, also known as luminous red novae, represent a subset of eruptive stars resulting from stellar mergers, particularly non-compact stars. This group includes five Galactic objects: CK Vul, V4332 Sgr, V838 Mon, V1309 Sco, and EWS 2002-OGLE-BLG-360. Unlike supernovae and classical novae, red novae primarily derive their energy from accretion (Tylenda & Soker 2006), not nuclear processes, leading to lower temperatures of their immediate remnants. The stellar products of red novae are cool giants or supergiants with temperatures of 2000–3000 K, surrounded by complex circumstellar environments rich in cool gas and dust (Kamiński et al. 2020, 2018).

Despite being a relatively small sample, Galactic red novae offer insights into a diverse range of variables. The timescales for studying these remnants typically span decades, with CK Vul's outburst observed as early as 1670. Extragalactic red nova analogs in the Local Group, while numerous, lack sufficient spectral observations; observations of the merger products and of their progenitors are also sparse (Pastorello et al. 2019).

Red novae are believed to be mergers involving non-compact stars, including solar-mass giants/subgiants (e.g., Stępień 2011) and main-sequence stars (e.g., Tylenda et al. 2005), but the collision in CK Vul involved a red-giant-branch (RGB) star with a He white dwarf (WD; Tylenda et al. 2023). These events might also encompass planetary engulfment (De et al. 2023; Soker 2023; O'Connor et al. 2023). The luminous extragalactic objects tend to involve higher mass stars (say 3–10 $M_\odot$ or higher), often in the Hertzsprung gap (e.g. Blagorodnova et al. 2017, 2021). The diversity of binary configurations is large in the context of stellar evolution and stellar masses involved, but collectively, red novae have introduced a unique new opportunity to investigate the intricate physical mechanisms destabilizing binaries and resulting in extreme stellar interactions. There is hope that these transients and their remnants will aid our understanding of the common envelope phase (Ivanova et al. 2013).

Distinguishing characteristics of red novae include their eruptive durations lasting from a few months to a year, intermediate luminosities ($\lesssim 10^6$ $L_\odot$) between classical novae and

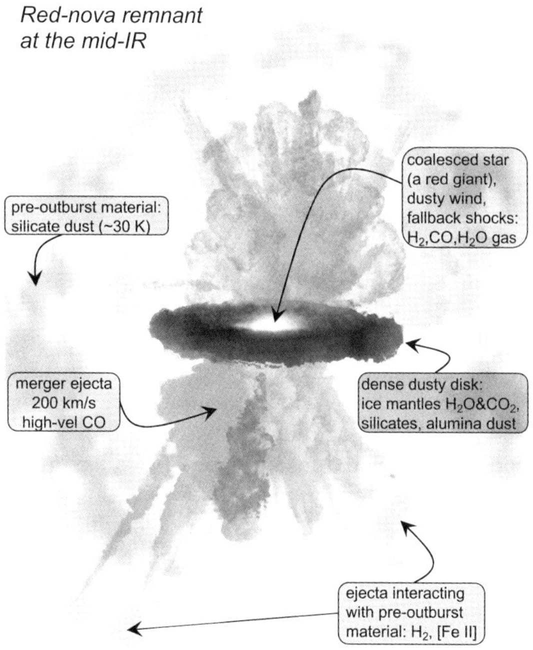

Figure 1. A schematic representation of the complex architecture of a red nova remnant. Observable features are labeled. They are not in scale. The scheme matches well observation of V1309 Sco and V4332 Sgr discussed in the text.

supernovae, multipeaked light curves, and rapid cooling to low photospheric temperatures (1800–2000 K) after the eruption. This abrupt cooling sets red novae apart from classical novae, which progress to the coronal phase at 10^5 K. The cooling process facilitates efficient formation of molecules and dust, processes which are relatively easy to observe but not easy to model (e.g., Iaconi et al. 2020; MacLeod et al. 2022). There are other Galactic objects thought to be of a similar nature as red novae (mergers), including for example objects like the Blue Ring Nebula (Hoadley et al. 2020) or Phoenix giants (Melis 2020), but because there is no record of their outburst ("mergeburst"), they are not part of the red nova classification. It is hard to obtain realistic statistics of these transients but the best efforts predict two bright red novae per decade per galaxy (Kochanek et al. 2014; Howitt et al. 2020; Karambelkar et al. 2023). Red novae are considered to be easily discoverable by the Vera C. Rubin Legacy Survey of Space and Time (LSST; Hambleton et al. 2023). As no new Galactic red nova has been observed since 2008, an overdue event is in the offing. A search for red nova progenitors is ongoing as well (Addison et al. 2022).

A fuller review of Galactic red nova properties was given in Kamiński et al. (2018).

2. Bipolar structures in red nova remnants

2.1. *Coalesced binaries*

Recent studies of the Galactic objects emphasize the complexity of circumstellar envelopes, suggesting the formation of disks, jets, wide-angle outflows, and inhomogeneous winds in the aftermath of mergers (see Mobeen et al. 2021; Steinmetz et al. 2023, for the most recent discussions). This complex architecture is illustrated in Fig. 1. The bipolar structures discovered in red nova remnants are most relevant to the connection to planetary and pre-planetary nebulae.

One important example of such a bipolar circumstellar remnant is V1309 Sco which erupted as a red nova in 2008. V1309 Sco stands out as a key case supporting the merger scenario for red novae due to its well-documented variability before the 2008 eruption. Photometric data revealed V1309 Sco as an eclipsing contact binary with an exponentially decreasing orbital period, showcasing the spiraling-in of two non-compact stars (Tylenda et al. 2011). The subsequent release of gravitational energy and shocks directly triggered the red nova flash (Metzger & Pejcha 2017). Optical, infrared, and submillimeter observations a few years to decade after the outburst display characteristics which can only be explained by a highly bipolar structure (Steinmetz et al. 2023). Spatially unresolved spectral observations of the V1309 Sco's remnant display two fast outflows which produce shocks of different excitation and chemical properties — one giving rise to H_2 IR emission, the other hinted by emission of HCO^+ through pure rotational transitions. Additionally, emission of molecular gas at lower gas temperatures was mapped directly in rotational lines of CO and SiO by the Atacama Large Millimeter Array (ALMA) interferometer (Kamiński et al. 2018; Steinmetz et al. 2023). These maps show that the merger ejecta has a bipolar structure, but whether it is caused by wide-angle outflows or a pair of well collimated jets is currently unclear, as the ALMA observations only barely resolve the source. Observations with ALMA at higher angular resolutions will certainly be feasible in the future and should be more reveling, especially since the source is rapidly expanding.

V4332 Sgr is the older twin of V1309 Sco. It erupted in 1994 and so far has shown spectral and photometric behavior remarkably similar to V1309 Sco (Kamiński et al. 2015). It is thus believed that V4332 Sgr originated from a merger of evolved (post-MS) solar-mass stars, but, unlike in V1309 Sco, no direct observations of the progenitor system are available. Nevertheless, the remnant of V4332 Sgr has been much better resolved by ALMA and a three-dimensional model of its cool component was constructed (Kamiński et al. 2018) with the Shape-X software (Steffen et al. 2014). The study reconstructs the remnant as a fully bipolar structure of $\sim$600 AU expanding according to the Hubble law (i.e., expansion velocity is proportional to the distance from the expansion center). The model architecture is very similar to bipolar planetary nebulae and, even more, to young pre-planetary nebulae, but the amount of detail in V4332 Sgr is very limited by the angular resolution which loses the fight against the large distance to the source of 4–6 kpc. Kamiński et al. (2018) interpret the structure of V4332 Sgr's circumstellar medium as a result of outflow which was deflected into bipolar lobes by a pre-existing dense disk or torus formed in the orbital plane of the evolving binary. This scenario gains a lot of support in merger simulations of Pejcha et al. (2017), which reproduce well the general shape of the circumstellar remnant and its kinematical structure. The observations of V1309 Sco and V4332 Sgr seem to suggest that the bipolar structure arises as an intrinsic feature of the merger event and is directly linked to the parameters (e.g., orientation) of the decaying binary.

2.2. *Mergers in triple systems?*

Mergers are likely to take place in triple and higher systems (e.g., Glanz & Perets 2021; Hamers et al. 2022), for instance, as a consequence of Kozai-Lidov cycles. The most famous example of a red-nova progenitor which was triple is V838 Mon (Tylenda et al. 2005; Kamiński et al. 2021), and *source I* in the Orion Molecular Cloud 1 may be an example of a merger in a multiple system (Bally et al. 2017). Both objects are very young, while we are interested here in evolved objects which may shed light on our understanding of planetary and pre-planetary nebulae. It happens that the oldest known red nova, CK Vul, was likely a triple system.

Figure 2. Reconstructed distribution of molecular ions in the remnant of CK Vul. Adopted from Kamiński et al. (2021). The remnant has a very complex structure when viewed in three dimensions.

CK Vul, initially thought to be the earliest documented nova (Shara & Moffat 1982), is a unique object with a complex history. Discovered in 1670, CK Vul has defied classification as a typical nova due to its peculiar light curve, displaying multiple peaks, and a reddish color, both features – as understood now – characteristic of red novae (Kamiński et al. 2015). The object's nature became clearer with modern observations, lending a large body of evidence for coalescence of a He white dwarf (WD) and a red giant branch (RGB) star (Tylenda et al. 2023). The evidence is most compelling in the elemental and isotopic composition of the circumstellar gas (Kamiński et al. 2017), especially due to the presence of AlF molecules containing the radioactive isotope of ^{26}Al (Kamiński et al. 2018).

This hypothesized stellar collision led to the ejection of material, forming a large hourglass nebula with multiple bullets and a dust-rich waist (Hajduk et al. 2007, 2013; Banerjee et al. 2020). The large nebula is mostly traced in emission of recombining plasma and can easily be taken for a planetary or pre-planetary nebula (if not the bizarre central object). Studied through millimeter and submillimeter observations, in particular with the Submillimeter Array and ALMA, CK Vul also revealed a smaller and cooler molecular component (Kamiński et al. 2015, 2020, 2021). While the large hourglass and the bullets very likely originate in the 1670–1672 events, the age of the molecular component remains practically unconstrained. With detailed spatio-kinematic maps (i.e., spectral cubes) of emission from neutral and ionic molecular species, Kamiński et al. (2021) constructed thorough three-dimensional models of the remnant. The observations and models of the CK Vul remnant are of a much better quality than those for V1309 Sco and V4332 Sgr discussed above, in part because CK Vul is much older and the expansion velocities are twice higher there. A sample view of the reconstructed structure of CK Vul is presented in Fig. 2 and a full movie can be seen at `https://www.aanda.org/articles/aa/olm/2021/02/aa39634-20/aa39634-20.html`. Based on these models, the molecular gas exhibits an overall bipolar structure and intricate three-dimensional architecture which exhibits strong point symmetry. Shocks play an important role in excitation of the molecular gas and determine its chemical composition (including the formation of complex organic molecules like methanol or methylamine). The analysis strongly suggests multiple ejections with varying inclinations and position angles. It is unlikely that these were created during the 1670–1672 outburst. One possible interpretation is that some material originally ejected during the mergeburst falls back on the coalesced star causing episodic accretion and (feedback) mass loss through collimated streams. However, it is unclear whether such a mechanism could ensemble a cool molecular nebula of significant mass (see below). Another interpretation is that CK Vul was a triple system before the merger, and the surviving companion interacts with the merger ejecta. This is a highly speculative scenario but explains more naturally an observed misalignment of the main axis of the large hourglass-shaped recombining nebula with respect to the axis of the molecular lobes.

With submillimeter observations of CO and under some assumptions on CO abundance, one can calculate the mass of the lobes. Kamiński et al. (2021) found a mass of at least $0.8\,M_{\odot}$. This is a very high mass when compared to simulations of stellar mergers where only a few percent of the mass of the entire stellar system is dispersed. This mass is, however, not much larger than masses of envelopes of some pre-planetary nebulae. Moreover, the linear momentum of 10^{40} g cm s^{-1} and the kinetic energy of 10^{47} erg stored in the molecular outflows of CK Vul are comparable to those of many pre-planetary nebulae (cf. Bujarrabal et al. 2001).

3. Curious relation of red nova remnants to pre-PNe

I have highlighted the many correspondences between the merger remnants and (some) pre-planetary nebulae (PPNe). There is a possibility that mechanisms responsible for creating the red nova remnants are similar, if not the same, as in PPNe. Binary interactions and common-envelope ejections certainly play a crucial role in the formation of both classes of objects, and it is worth studying how far the parallels go. Some authors go as far as to suggest that merger and related events could have created some of the well known bipolar planetary nebulae (Soker & Kashi 2012). Since some bipolar flows in PPNe must be created in a short time (often shorter than a timespan of years) and with an extra source of energy other than the radiative energy of the central star, a merger event is a scenario worth considering for each of these cases. The remarkable commonalities in the *appearance* of the circumstellar media of these objects might also mean that some of the sources classified today as evolved stars with the PPN status can in fact be merger products. Whether some particular PPNe could be interpreted as stellar collision products have been discussed in the past, e.g., for Frosty Leo (Bourke et al. 2000), the Rotten Egg Nebula, or PN K4-47 (Schmidt et al. 2018). One important difference between the discussed red novae remnants discussed here and PPNe is a low luminosity of the central object, which is the case of CK Vul is 12–60 $L_{\odot}$. These are much lower than 10^4 $L_{\odot}$ expected for any post-AGB star. This distinguishing feature is, however, of limited use for objects of unknown distance and total extinction, which unfortunately is a frequent case. Nevertheless, I remain hopeful that the next merger remnant will be recognized among PNe or PPNe.

I acknowledge funding from the Polish National Science Center grant SONATA-BIS no. 2018/30/E/ST9/00398.

References

Addison, H., Blagorodnova, N., Groot, P. J., et al. 2022, *MNRAS*, 517, 1884. doi:10.1093/mnras/stac2685

Bally, J., Ginsburg, A., Arce, H., et al. 2017, *ApJ*, 837, 60. doi:10.3847/1538-4357/aa5c8b

Banerjee, D. P. K., Geballe, T. R., Evans, A., et al. 2020, *ApJL*, 904, L23. doi:10.3847/2041-8213/abc885

Blagorodnova, N., Kotak, R., Polshaw, J., et al. 2017, *ApJ*, 834, 107. doi:10.3847/1538-4357/834/2/107

Blagorodnova, N., Klencki, J., Pejcha, O., et al. 2021, *A&A*, 653, A134. doi:10.1051/0004-6361/202140525

Bourke, T., Hyland, A. R., Robinson, G., et al. 2000, Asymmetrical Planetary Nebulae II: From Origins to Microstructures, 199, 171. doi:10.48550/arXiv.astro-ph/9909500

Bujarrabal, V., Castro-Carrizo, A., Alcolea, J., et al. 2001, *A&A*, 377, 868. doi:10.1051/0004-6361:20011090

De, K., MacLeod, M., Karambelkar, V., et al. 2023, *Nature*, 617, 55. doi:10.1038/s41586-023-05842-x

Glanz, H. & Perets, H. B. 2021, *MNRAS*, 500, 1921. doi:10.1093/mnras/staa3242

Hajduk, M., Zijlstra, A. A., van Hoof, P. A. M., et al. 2007, *MNRAS*, 378, 1298. doi:10.1111/j.1365-2966.2007.11825.x

Hajduk, M., van Hoof, P. A. M., & Zijlstra, A. A. 2013, *MNRAS*, 432, 167. doi:10.1093/mnras/stt426

Hambleton, K. M., Bianco, F. B., Street, R., et al. 2023, *PASP*, 135, 105002. doi:10.1088/1538-3873/acdb9a

Hamers, A. S., Glanz, H., & Neunteufel, P. 2022, *ApJSS*, 259, 25. doi:10.3847/1538-4365/ac49e7

Hoadley, K., Martin, D. C., Metzger, B. D., et al. 2020, *Nature*, 587, 387. doi:10.1038/s41586-020-2893-5

Howitt, G., Stevenson, S., Vigna-Gómez, A., et al. 2020, *MNRAS*, 492, 3229. doi:10.1093/mnras/stz3542

Iaconi, R., Maeda, K., Nozawa, T., et al. 2020, *MNRAS*, 497, 3166. doi:10.1093/mnras/staa2169

Ivanova, N., Justham, S., Chen, X., et al. 2013, *AnRevA&A*, 21, 59. doi:10.1007/s00159-013-0059-2

Kamiński, T., Menten, K. M., Tylenda, R., et al. 2015, *Nature*, 520, 322. doi:10.1038/nature14257

Kamiński, T., Mason, E., Tylenda, R., et al. 2015, *A&A*, 580, A34. doi:10.1051/0004-6361/201526212

Kamiński, T., Menten, K. M., Tylenda, R., et al. 2017, *A&A*, 607, A78. doi:10.1051/0004-6361/201731287

Kamiński, T., Steffen, W., Tylenda, R., et al. 2018, *A&A*, 617, A129. doi:10.1051/0004-6361/201833165

Kamiński, T., Tylenda, R., Menten, K. M., et al. 2018, *Nature Astronomy*, 2, 778. doi:10.1038/s41550-018-0541-x

Kamiński, T., Menten, K. M., Tylenda, R., et al. 2020, *A&A*, 644, A59. doi:10.1051/0004-6361/202038648

Kamiński, T., Menten, K. M., Tylenda, R., et al. 2020, *A&A*, 644, A59. doi:10.1051/0004-6361/202038648

Kamiński, T., Tylenda, R., Kiljan, A., et al. 2021, *A&A*, 655, A32. doi:10.1051/0004-6361/202141526

Kamiński, T., Steffen, W., Bujarrabal, V., et al. 2021, *A&A*, 646, A1. doi:10.1051/0004-6361/202039634

Karambelkar, V. R., Kasliwal, M. M., Blagorodnova, N., et al. 2023, *ApJ*, 948, 137. doi:10.3847/1538-4357/acc2b9

Kochanek, C. S., Adams, S. M., & Belczynski, K. 2014, *MNRAS*, 443, 1319. doi:10.1093/mnras/stu1226

MacLeod, M., De, K., & Loeb, A. 2022, *ApJ*, 937, 96. doi:10.3847/1538-4357/ac8c31

Melis, C. 2020, Research Notes of the American Astronomical Society, 4, 238. doi:10.3847/2515-5172/abd32a

Metzger, B. D. & Pejcha, O. 2017, *MNRAS*, 471, 3200. doi:10.1093/mnras/stx1768

Mobeen, M. Z., Kamiński, T., Matter, A., et al. 2021, *A&A*, 655, A100. doi:10.1051/0004-6361/202142297

O'Connor, C. E., Bildsten, L., Cantiello, M., et al. 2023, *ApJ*, 950, 128. doi:10.3847/1538-4357/acd2d4

Pastorello, A., Mason, E., Taubenberger, S., et al. 2019, *A&A*, 630, A75. doi:10.1051/0004-6361/201935999

Pejcha, O., Metzger, B. D., Tyles, J. G., et al. 2017, *ApJ*, 850, 59. doi:10.3847/1538-4357/aa95b9

Shara, M. M. & Moffat, A. F. J. 1982, *ApJL*, 258, L41. doi:10.1086/183826

Schmidt, D. R., Woolf, N. J., Zega, T. J., et al. 2018, *Nature*, 564, 378. doi:10.1038/s41586-018-0763-1

Soker, N. 2023, *MNRAS*, 524, L94. doi:10.1093/mnrasl/slad086

Soker, N. & Kashi, A. 2012, *ApJ*, 746, 100. doi:10.1088/0004-637X/746/1/100

Stępień, K. 2011, *A&A*, 531, A18. doi:10.1051/0004-6361/201116689
Steffen, W., Koning, N., & Santander-García, M. 2014, Asymmetrical Planetary Nebulae VI Conference, 96
Steinmetz, T., Kamiński, T., Schmidt, M., et al. 2023, *A&A* in press, arXiv:2308.14588. doi:10.48550/arXiv.2308.14588
Tylenda, R., Soker, N., & Szczerba, R. 2005, *A&A*, 441, 1099. doi:10.1051/0004-6361:20042485
Tylenda, R., Hajduk, M., Kamiński, T., et al. 2011, *A&A*, 528, A114. doi:10.1051/0004-6361/201016221
Tylenda, R., Kamiński, T., & Smolec, R. 2023, *A&A in press*, arXiv:2312.07433. doi:10.48550/arXiv.2312.07433
Tylenda, R., Kamiński, T., & Smolec, R. 2023, arXiv:2312.07433. doi:10.48550/arXiv.2312.07433
Tylenda, R. & Soker, N. 2006, *A&A*, 451, 223. doi:10.1051/0004-6361:20054201

Planetary Nebulae: A Universal Toolbox in the Era of Precision Astrophysics
Proceedings IAU Symposium No. 384, 2025
O. De Marco, A. Zijlstra & R. Szczerba, eds.
doi:10.1017/S1743921323005112

From an amateur PN candidate to the Rosetta Stone of SN Iax research

A. Ritter[1], Q. A. Parker[1], F. Lykou[2], A. Zijlstra[3,1], M. A. Guerrero[4] and P. Le Dû[5]

[1]Laboratory for Space Research, FoS, The University of Hong Kong, Hong Kong (S.A.R.)
email: azuri.ritter@gmail.com

[2]Konkoly Observatory, Research Centre for Astronomy and Earth Sciences, Budapest, Hungary

[3]The University of Manchester, Manchester, U.K.

[4]Instituto de Astrofísica de Andalucía (IAA-CSIC), Granada, Spain

[5]Kermerrien Observatory, Porspoder, France

Abstract. On August 25th 2013 Dana Patchick from the "Deep Sky Hunters" (DSH) amateur astronomer group discovered a diffuse nebulosity in the Wide-field Infrared Survey Explorer (WISE) mid-IR image archive that had no optical counterpart but appeared similar to many Planetary Nebulae (PNe) in WISE. As his 30th discovery he named it Pa 30 and it was added to the HASH PN database as a new PN candidate. Little did he know how important his discovery would become. 10 years later this object is the only known bound remnant of a violent double WD merger accompanied by a rare Type Iax SN, observed and recorded by the ancient Chinese and Japanese in 1181 AD. This makes Pa 30 and its central star IRAS 00500+6713 (WD J005311) the only SN Iax remnant in our Galaxy, the only known bound remnant of any SN, and based on the central star's spectrum the only Wolf-Rayet star known that neither has a massive progenitor nor is the central star of a Planetary Nebula. We cover this story and our key role in it.

Keywords. emission nebulae, supernova remnants, type Ia supernovae, Wolf-Rayet stars

1. Introduction

While the number of known Supernovae (SNe) of the type Iax is relatively small, they constitute a significant fraction of the total number of SNe Ia, $\sim 5\% - 30\%$ (Foley et al. 2013; White et al. 2015). Yet they are probably the least understood subclass of type Ia SNe. The distribution of host-galaxy morphologies for SNe Iax is strongly skewed toward star-forming, late-type host galaxies (e.g. White et al. 2015, and references therein), which may indicate massive star progenitors for this class (e.g. Valenti et al. 2009). However, the maximum-light spectra of SNe Iax show clear evidence for C/O burning, providing a strong link between SNe Iax and White Dwarf (WD) progenitors (Foley et al. 2010).While the exact mechanisms leading to a Type Iax SN are still not fully understood, they are believed to arise from either the failed detonation of a CO WD accreting material from a Helium donor star (single degenerate scenario, e.g. Kromer et al. 2015) or from a CO WD merging with a heavier Oxygen-Neon (ONe) WD (double degenerate scenario, Kashyap et al. 2018) where the accretion disk itself deflagrates. All SNe Iax observed so far are in distant galaxies and they quickly fade below detectability, even with the biggest telescopes. Using X-ray spectroscopy, Zhou et al. (2021) found high Mn/Fe and

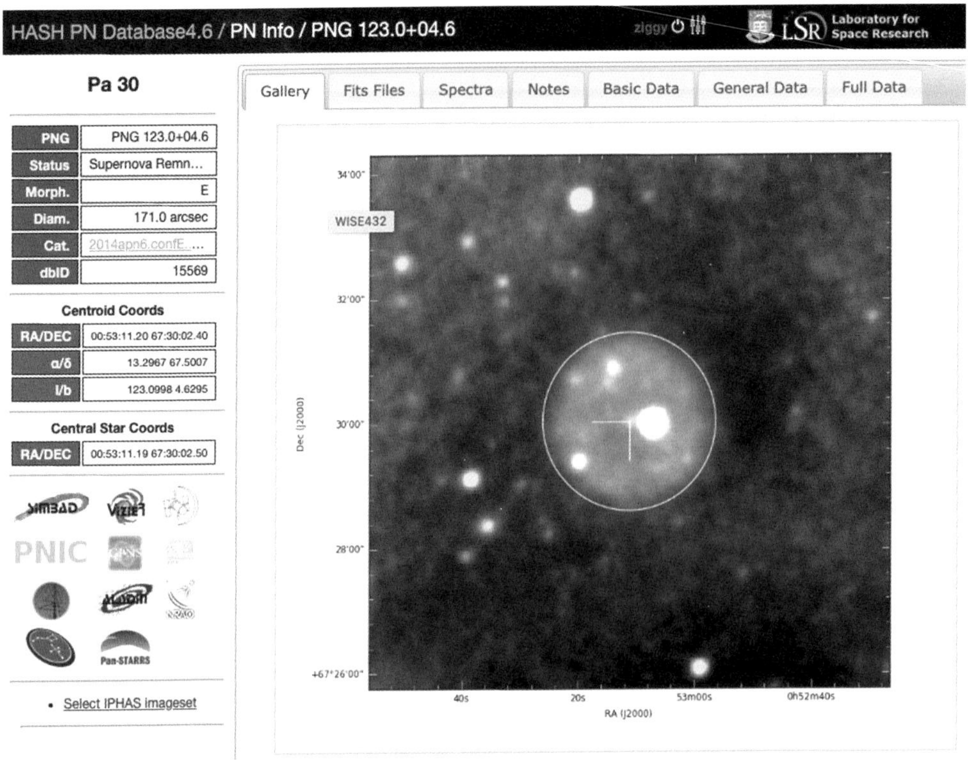

Figure 1. False colour image of Pa 30 and Parker's star in the HASH database. *Blue* stands for *WISE/W2*, *green* for *WISE/W3*, and *red* for *WISE/W4*.

Ni/Fe ratios in the Galactic SNR Sgr A East, interpreting it as the remnant from an Iax event involving a CO WD. However, Zhang et al. (2023) have casted doubt on that interpretation given its low X-ray luminosity. Identifying a Galactic SNR of the type Iax is of utmost importance for understanding this type of SN. Here we will chronologically line out the path from an amateur PN candidate (2) to a WD merger remnant (3) to a SNR (4) to the historical SN 1181 AD (5) to a bound remnant of a SN Iax in our Galactic neighborhood (6). Our latest results are presented in (7), and the conclusions in (8).

2. Pa 30 as an amateur PN candidate

When Dana Patchick (Kronberger et al. 2016) from our affiliated "Deep Sky Hunters" (DSH) amateur group discovered a diffuse nebulosity (Fig. 1) in the Wide-field Infrared Survey Explorer (*WISE*) mid-IR image archive on August 25th 2013, little did he realise what he had found. As Patchick's 30th PN candidate it was originally included into the HASH database † (Parker et al. 2016) as Pa 30 as it possessed certain PN-like characteristics (but see Parker 2022). The *WISE* W3 (11μm) band shows a disk-like nebula, whereas the dominant shape in the W4 (22μm) band is donut-like inside a much fainter halo. Narrow-band [O III] imaging observations obtained by the DSH group on the 2.1 m KPNO telescope in September 2013 (see Fig. 2) indicate very faint circular emission with hints of radial structure confirmed in the [S II] images in (Fesen et al. 2023).

† HASH the consolidated 'gold-standard' PN data repository and catalogue: `http://www.hashpn.space`

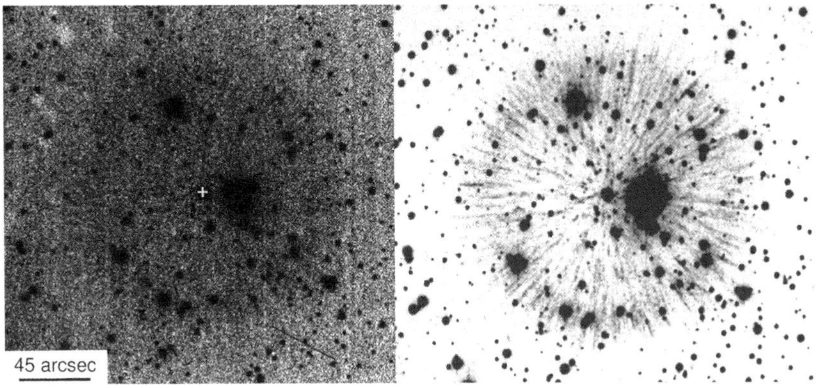

Figure 2. Left: The 2.1-m KPNO [O III] image, which we have stacked and rebinned from individual frames to enhance the low surface brightness, diffuse shell though with hints of radial structure that are seen clearly in the [S II] image of (Fesen et al. 2023, Right). The green cross in the center of the left image marks the location of the CS.

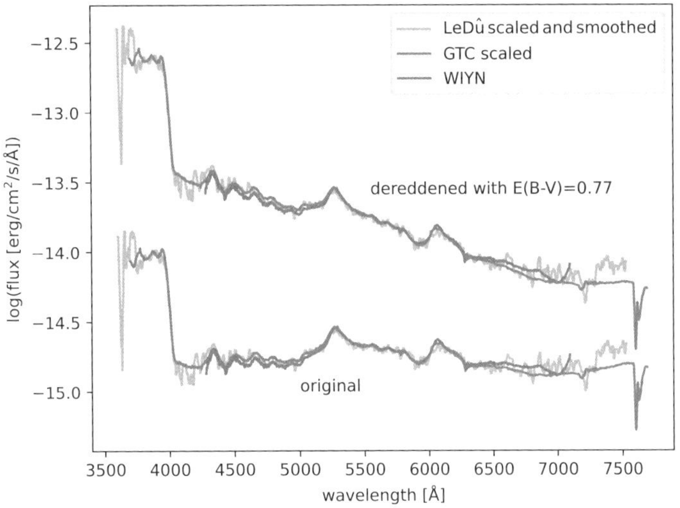

Figure 3. Stellar spectra from SparsePak/WIYN, OSIRIS/GTC, and a small amateur telescope (P. Le Dû) smoothed and scaled to the same flux level. The dereddened spectra are also shown for comparison (using interstellar extinction from Ritter et al. 2021). The major discontinuity bluewards of 4,000 Å is seen in the OSIRIS and amateur spectra but the SparsePak spectrum did not go below 4,200 Å. The OSIRIS spectrum had the slit slightly off-center to avoid a nearby bright star. To correct for the resulting slight flux underestimation after flux calibration the spectrum was scaled to match the reliable SparsePak/WIYN flux level. From Lykou et al. (2023)

On October 15th 2014, the DSH team used the SparsePak integral field unit (IFU) on the 3.5-m WIYN telescope at KPNO to observe Pa 30 as a PN candidate. They did not see the expected PN emission lines and did not extract the central star's spectrum.

We obtained deep optical spectroscopy of both the star and the nebula on July 8th 2016 using long slit observations with the OSIRIS instrument of the 10-m GranTeCan (GTC) telescope. The spectra of the central star are shown in Fig. 3.

The spectrum of the CS is dominated by broad emission lines of highly ionised Oxygen (O VI to O VIII) and Carbon (C IV to C VI) lines. The measured wind velocities of 16,000 km s^{-1} (0.05 c) are unprecedented. On careful scrutiny both sets of our

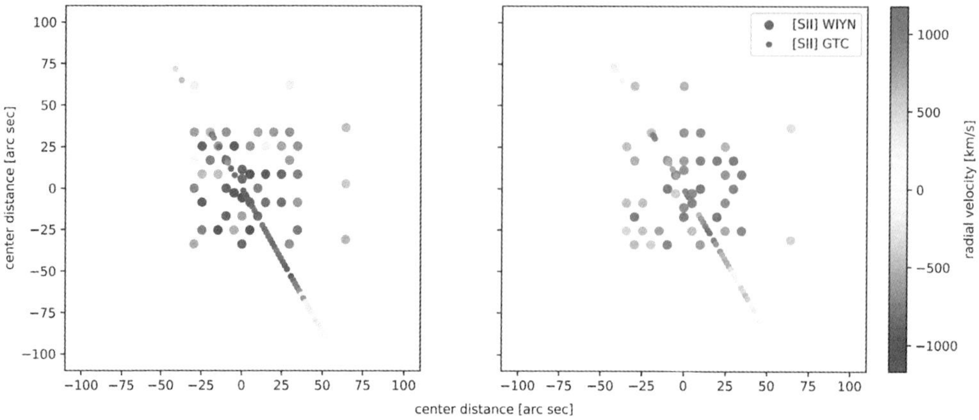

Figure 4. Position-velocity diagram of the [S II] doublet lines (6,716/6,731 Å) from WIYN/SparsePak, overplotted with GTC/OSIRIS along the slit, color-coded to the radial velocity for each measured fibre/CCD column. North is up, East is left. The left/right plots show the near/far side of the nebula. The images show sharp velocity variations where the two sets of [S II] doublet lines are also much brighter than for the rest of the nebula, indicating strong shock excitation both for the near as well as the far side.

spectroscopic observations revealed two sets of faint optical emission lines species in the nebula: the [S II] 6716 and 6731Å doublet, and the [Ar III] 7136Å line. The well resolved [S II] doublet in particular shows two sets of lines due to extreme velocity expansion of the nebula gas, with radial velocities of up to $v_{\rm rad} \approx$1,100±100 km s^{-1} (Fig. 4). The observed velocity structure shows sharp variations across the field of view and declines to systemic velocity at $\approx 100''$. We also extracted the star's GTC spectrum after its remarkable features were first brought to our attention from a spectrum taken by Pascal Le Dû, an amateur collaborator of the corresponding author. We recognised its extreme and unique nature (e.g. see Gvaramadze et al. 2019; Lykou et al. 2023), believing we were the first group to do so. We thereafter referred to IRAS 00500+6713 as "Parker's star".

3. Pa 30's Central Star as a WD merger remnant

While our Nature Astronomy paper on Pa 30 and its CS was in second review, Gvaramadze et al. (2019) published their own Nature paper on the same source. They proposed that the CS was from a double-degenerate CO + ONe WD merger. They identified the CS as an oxygen-rich Wolf Rayet (WO-type) star. The star's spectrum was modelled with the Potsdam Wolf Rayet (PoWR) code and they derived a stellar temperature at the base of the 16,000 km s^{-1} wind of $211,000^{+40,000}_{-23,000}$ K. They determined that the chemical composition is dominated by oxygen and carbon with mass fractions of 0.8 ± 0.1 and 0.2 ± 0.1, respectively. No Hydrogen or Helium lines were detected as expected for WD merger remnants (e.g. Schwab et al. 2016). As driver for the fierce stellar wind they proposed a strong magnetic field of the order of 10^8 G.

4. Pa 30 as a SNR

The same group then published X-ray observations of Pa 30 and its CS (Oskinova et al. 2020). In their X-ray nebula spectra they detected carbon-burning ashes, indicating that Pa 30 is a supernova remnant (SNR), possibly a type Iax, and that the double WD merger was accompanied by an episode of carbon burning. From SNR scaling relations

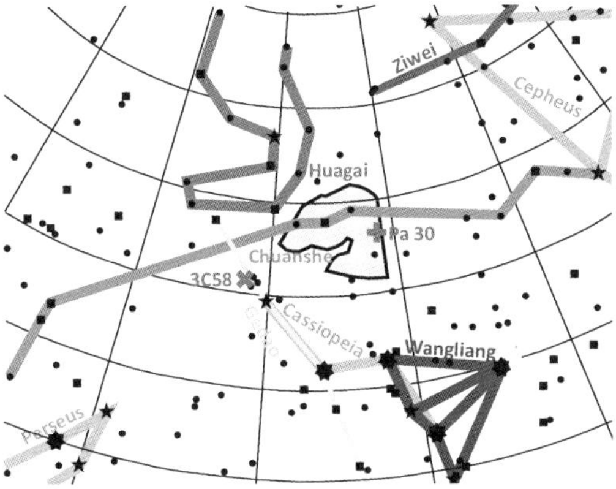

Figure 5. The final map of the most likely position of SN 1181 AD (cyan area) from the detailed interpretation of historical records by Schaefer (2023). Pa 30 is inside this region, 3C58 is not.

they estimated an age of ~1,000 years. Given the *GAIA* DR2 distance of 3.1 kpc they estimated that the SN would have been visible for 2 weeks and so could have been missed by the ancient astronomers. They did not check the historical records.

5. Pa 30 and the historical SN 1181 AD

The only SN of the last millennium that did not have a firmly identified counterpart on the sky was the historical SN 1181 AD. It was described in 3 ancient Chinese and 1 Japanese record that it looked like Saturn and lasted for 185 days. Averaging the best positional estimates from all 4 records places SN 1181 AD in the vicinity of Pa 30. The only other SNR possibly linked to SN 1181 is the pulsar wind nebula G130.7+3.1 (3C58 hereafter, e.g. Stephenson & Green 1999; Kothes 2013). However, a precise estimate of the expansion age of this nebula of 7,000 years, based on radio observations over 20 years Bietenholz (2006), and the spin-down age of the pulsar (5,400 years, Chevalier 2004) have put the association in serious doubt, although not completely excluding it (Kothes 2013). Ritter et al. (2021) showed that Pa 30 and its CS are almost certainly the true remnants of the 1181 AD event. This was later supported by Schaefer (2023), who analysed the historical records in more detail (Fig. 5), and Fesen et al. (2023), who calculated an age estimate of 844±55 years, in excellent agreement with the current 842 years age of SN 1181.

6. Pa 30 as type Iax SNR

With the new *GAIA* eDR3 distance of 2.3 kpc (Bailer-Jones et al. 2021), the maximum absolute brightness ($M_V \sim -14$ to -12.5, Ritter et al. 2021) and duration of naked-eye visibility (185 days, Hsi 1957), together with the expansion velocity (1,100±100 km s^{-1}, Ritter et al. 2021) and inferred kinematical age (990^{+280}_{-220} years, Ritter et al. 2021) of the surrounding nebula, are all consistent with a type Iax SN in 1181 AD.

7. Ruling out a strong magnetic field and kicked remnant star

In Lykou et al. (2023) we analysed our high signal-to-noise spectroscopic data of both star and nebula which were obtained with the OSIRIS instrument on the 10-m Gran Telescopio Canarias (GTC) telescope in 2016, as well as archival ultraviolet spectra from the Space Telescope Imaging Spectrograph (STIS) on the Hubble Space Telescope (HST) under program GO15864 (P.I. G. Graefener; epoch: 4 November 2020). We modeled the stellar wind with the NLTE code CMFGEN adapted to WC and WO stars

Table 1. Range of stellar parameters for CMFGEN models. The last two columns show the values from Gvaramadze et al. (2019) and from the hot gas model. From Lykou et al. (2023)

Parameter	Explored range	Best fit range	Gvaramadze et al. (2019)	Hot gas model
L_* ($L_\odot$)	10,000 – 200,000	30,000 – 60,000	$39,810^{+20,144}_{-10,970}$	
T_* (K)	145,000 – 580,000	200,000 – 280,000	$211,000^{+40,000}_{-23,000}$	
$\dot{M}$ ($M_\odot$/yr)	7.5×10^{-7} – 2.5×10^{-6}	$\leq 4\times 10^{-6}$	$3.5(\pm0.6)\times 10^{-6}$	
R_* ($R_\odot$)	0.04 – 0.22	≤ 0.2	0.15 ± 0.04	
v_∞ (kms)	–	~15,000	$16,000\pm1,000$	
Mass fractions				
X_H	–	–	–	–
X_{He}	0.017 – 0.135	< 0.4	< 0.1	≤ 0.44
X_C	0.0 – 0.261	≤ 0.26	0.2 ± 0.1	0.13
X_O	0.414 – 0.697	≤ 0.7	0.8 ± 0.1	0.39
X_{Ne}	0.011 – 0.501	≤ 0.5	0.01	0.04

(Hillier & Dessart 2012) and an additional high temperature (~4MK) gas component using the CLOUDY code (ver. 17.03 Ferland et al. 2017). The best fit ranges of the individual parameters are shown in Table 1, together with a comparison to the parameters stated by Gvaramadze et al. (2019). We provided an upper limit for a magnetic field of $B < 2.5$ MG, far below the suggestions by Gvaramadze et al. (2019). We also rule out the possibility that the CS received a substantial kick, and suggest that the stellar remnant has dimmed by ~0.5 magnitudes over the last 100 years.

8. Conclusions

WD J005311 (Parker's star) and Pa 30 are the result of a violent double-degenerate merger (ONe/CO or CO/CO WDs) accompanied by a Type Iax SN. It remains the only Iax SNR known in our Galaxy and the only one that can be studied in detail. The CS is also the only bound SNR and the only known WR star which has neither a massive progenitor star nor is the CS of a PN. It has an unprecedented wind speed of 16,000 km s^{-1} (0.05 c) and is the hottest star known (>220,000 K). The CS was not kicked as predicted by most WD merger models. The lack of a companion star (see Schaefer 2023) strongly supports the double degenerate merger scenario for SN Iax.

References

Bailer-Jones, C. A. L., Rybizki, J., Fouesneau, M., Demleitner, M., & Andrae, R. 2021, *Astron. J.* , 161, 147, doi: 10.3847/1538-3881/abd806

Bietenholz, M. F. 2006, *Astrophys. J.* , 645, 1180, doi: 10.1086/504584

Chevalier, R. A. 2004, Advances in Space Research, 33, 456, doi: 10.1016/j.asr.2003.04.018

Ferland, G. J., Chatzikos, M., Guzmán, F., et al. 2017, Revista Mexicana de Astronomía y Astrofísica, 53, 385. https://arxiv.org/abs/1705.10877

Fesen, R. A., Schaefer, B. E., & Patchick, D. 2023, *Astrophys. J. Lett.* , 945, L4, doi: 10.3847/2041-8213/acbb67

Foley, R. J., Brown, P. J., Rest, A., et al. 2010, *Astrophys. J. Lett.* , 708, L61, doi: 10.1088/2041-8205/708/1/L61

Foley, R. J., Challis, P. J., Chornock, R., et al. 2013, *Astrophys. J.* , 767, 57, doi: 10.1088/0004-637X/767/1/57

Gvaramadze, V. V., Gräfener, G., Langer, N., et al. 2019, Nature, 569, 684, doi: 10.1038/s41586-019-1216-1

Hillier, D. J., & Dessart, L. 2012, MNRAS, 424, 252, doi: 10.1111/j.1365-2966.2012.21192.x

Hsi, T.-T. 1957, Smithsonian Contributions to Astrophysics, 2, 109

Kashyap, R., Haque, T., Lorén-Aguilar, P., García-Berro, E., & Fisher, R. 2018, *Astrophys. J.* , 869, 140, doi: 10.3847/1538-4357/aaedb7

Kothes, R. 2013, *Astron. Astrophys.* , 560, A18, doi: 10.1051/0004-6361/201219839

Kromer, M., Ohlmann, S. T., Pakmor, R., et al. 2015, *Monthly Notices Roy. Astron. Soc.* , 450, 3045, doi: 10.1093/mnras/stv886

Kronberger, M., Parker, Q. A., Jacoby, G. H., et al. 2016, in Journal of Physics Conference Series, Vol. 728, Journal of Physics Conference Series, 072012, doi: 10.1088/1742-6596/728/7/072012

Lykou, F., Parker, Q. A., Ritter, A., et al. 2023, *Astrophys. J.* , 944, 120, doi: 10.3847/1538-4357/acb138

Oskinova, L. M., Gvaramadze, V. V., Gräfener, G., Langer, N., & Todt, H. 2020, *A&A*, 644, L8, doi: 10.1051/0004-6361/202039232

Parker, Q. A. 2022, Frontiers in Astronomy and Space Sciences, 9, 895287, doi: 10.3389/fspas.2022.895287

Parker, Q. A., Bojičić, I. S., & Frew, D. J. 2016, in Journal of Physics Conference Series, Vol. 728, Journal of Physics Conference Series, 032008, doi: 10.1088/1742-6596/728/3/032008

Ritter, A., Parker, Q. A., Lykou, F., et al. 2021, *Astrophys. J. Lett.* , 918, L33, doi: 10.3847/2041-8213/ac2253

Schaefer, B. E. 2023, *Monthly Notices Roy. Astron. Soc.* , 523, 3885, doi: 10.1093/mnras/stad717

Schwab, J., Quataert, E., & Kasen, D. 2016, *Monthly Notices Roy. Astron. Soc.* , 463, 3461, doi: 10.1093/mnras/stw2249

Stephenson, F. R., & Green, D. A. 1999, *Astronomy and Geophysics*, 40, 27

Valenti, S., Pastorello, A., Cappellaro, E., et al. 2009, *Nature*, 459, 674, doi: 10.1038/nature08023

White, C. J., Kasliwal, M. M., Nugent, P. E., et al. 2015, *Astrophys. J.* , 799, 52, doi: 10.1088/0004-637X/799/1/52

Zhang, M., Li, Z., Hua, Z., & Morris, M. R. 2023, *Monthly Notices Roy. Astron. Soc.* , 522, 3568, doi: 10.1093/mnras/stad1215

Zhou, P., Leung, S.-C., Li, Z., et al. 2021, *Astrophys. J.* , 908, 31, doi: 10.3847/1538-4357/abbd45

Planetary Nebulae: A Universal Toolbox in the Era of Precision Astrophysics
Proceedings IAU Symposium No. 384, 2025
O. De Marco, A. Zijlstra & R. Szczerba, eds.
doi:10.1017/S1743921323005367

Violent mass ejection by the progenitors of the brightest planetary nebulae: supernova progenitors

Noam Soker

Department of Physics, Technion, Haifa, 3200003, Israel
email: soker@physics.technion.ac.il

Abstract. I examine the morphologies of the brightest planetary nebulae (PNe) in the Milky Way Galaxy and conclude that violent binary interaction processes eject the main nebulae of the brightest PNe. The typical morphologies of the brightest PNe are multipolar, namely have been shaped by two or more major jet-launching episodes at varying directions, and possess small to medium departures from pure point symmetry. I discuss some scenarios, including a rapid onset of a common envelope interaction and the merger of the companion, mainly a white dwarf, with the asymptotic giant branch core at the termination of the common envelope. Some of these might be progenitors of type Ia supernovae (SNe Ia), as I suggest for SNR G1.9+0.3, the youngest SN Ia in the Galaxy.

Keywords. stars: binaries, planetary nebulae, supernovae: general, jets

1. Introduction

The planetary nebula (PN) luminosity function (PNLF) has a more or less universal cutoff at the bright end (e.g., Ciardullo et al. 1989; Jacoby 1989; van de Steene et al. 2006; Ciardullo 2022; Chornay 2023a; Jacoby et al. 2023), although variations exist (e.g., Bhattacharya et al. 2021). In this study, I do not attempt to explain this cutoff as it requires the calculations of the evolution of the central star of the PN and radiative transfer (e.g., Méndez 2017; Gesicki, Zijlstra, & Miller Bertolami 2018; Sabach & Soker 2018; Valenzuela, Méndez, & Miller Bertolami 2019). I limit myself to examining the morphologies of the brightest PNe in the Milky Way Galaxy.

I examine some morphological features that are much more common in the brightest Milky Way PNe (Section 2) than in the hundreds of well resolved PNe that different surveys and catalogs present (e.g., Balick 1987; Chu, Jacoby, & Arendt 1987; Schwarz, Corradi, & Melnick 1992; Corradi & Schwarz 1995; Manchado et al. 1996; Sahai & Trauger 1998; Sahai, Morris, & Villar 2011; Parker, Bojičić, & Frew 2016; Parker 2022). Many PNe and proto-PNe with points-symmetric morphologies and/or with pairs of opposite lobes were likely shaped by jets (e.g., Morris 1987; Soker 1990; Sahai & Trauger 1998; Sahai 2000; Sahai et al. 2000, 2007; Sahai, Morris, & Villar 2011; Boffin et al. 2012).

Based on the shaping of point-symmetric morphologies by jets, I argue in Section 3 that the newly identified point-symmetry in the youngest supernova in the Galaxy implies that this type Ia supernova (SN Ia) exploded inside a PN (Soker 2023).

In Section 4, I summarize this short study by speculating that many of the brightest PNe are the results of interaction with a WD companion. A small fraction of these PNe eventually explodes as SNe Ia.

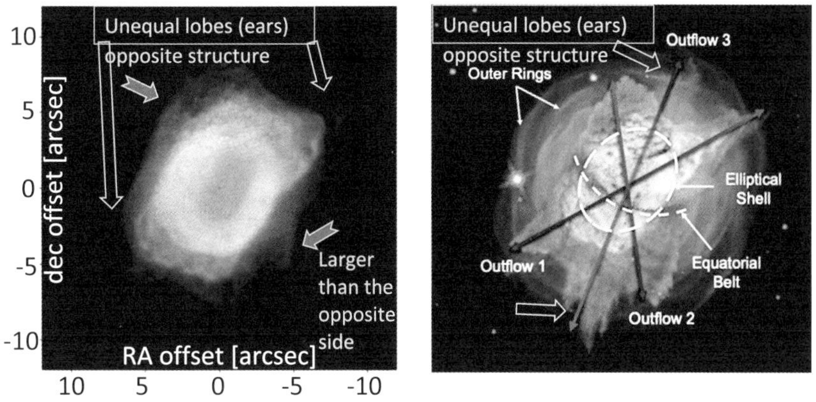

Figure 1. Two panels from Moraga Baez et al. (2023) (their figure 10) of NGC 7027. On the left the red color depicts the Paβ/Hβ line ratio, the green is extinction-corrected Hα emission, and the blue is 1.3 mm radio continuum from Bublitz et al. (2023). On the right panel, Moraga Baez et al. (2023) schematically mark some structural components. They mark the three pairs of jets as Outflow 1, 2, and 3, where red/blue colors indicate the redshift/blueshift. Also marked are the nebulas outer ring system, central elliptical shell, and equatorial belt. I added double-lined yellow arrows that point to morphological features that depart from pure point symmetry, as the insets indicate.

2. Morphological features of the brightest Galactic PNe

Chornay (2023b) lists extinction corrected bright PNe in [O III] (M(5007); for an earlier list see Mendez et al. (1993). The 13 brightest PNe in his list are as follows (from brightest to dimmest). NGC 6572; IC 4670 (Hb 6); K 3-17; M 1-40; NGC 7027; NGC 6369; NGC 7354; NGC 7662; NGC 6537; NGC 7026; NGC 6567; NGC 2440; NGC 6210. I take the 13 brightest PNe and not more because of limited space in this Proceedings paper.

I start with NGC 7027, one of the brightest PNe in the Galaxy, and refer to the recent analysis of this PN by Moraga Baez et al. (2023). In this thorough analysis Moraga Baez et al. (2023) present images in different lines and line ratios. In Figure 1 I present two of their images. Several clear morphological features deviate from pure point symmetry. For example, the two opposite lobes (ears) in all outflows are not equal to each other (I mark two pairs). I mark a pair of opposite bright edges (yellow-red arrows). These are not equal in size, nor do they have the same distance from the center.

The image of NGC 7027 presents the following properties, which are also seen in many earlier studies of NGC 7027 (e.g., Bublitz et al. 2023).

(1) *Multipolar.* It is a multipolar PN, with three outflow directions (e.g., Cox et al. 2002).

(2) *Departure from symmetry.* There is a departure from pure point symmetry in the sense that opposite clumps/lobes/arcs/filaments are not equal in one or more of their properties, including differences in brightness, size, structure, distance from the center, and/or bending such that the two clumps are not exactly opposite to each other through the center.

(3) *Not messy.* Despite these departures from pure point-symmetry, the structure is not 'messy'. Namely, all morphological features present some symmetry and there are no strong and large morphological features that lack any symmetry. Messy PNe are most likely to result from triple-star interaction (e.g., Bear & Soker 2017). NGC 7027 does not require a tertiary star to explain its basic morphology.

The brightest PN is NGC 6572 (Figure 2). A recent study by Bandyopadhyay et al. (2023) reveals its 3D structure with morphokinematic and photoionization modeling. It

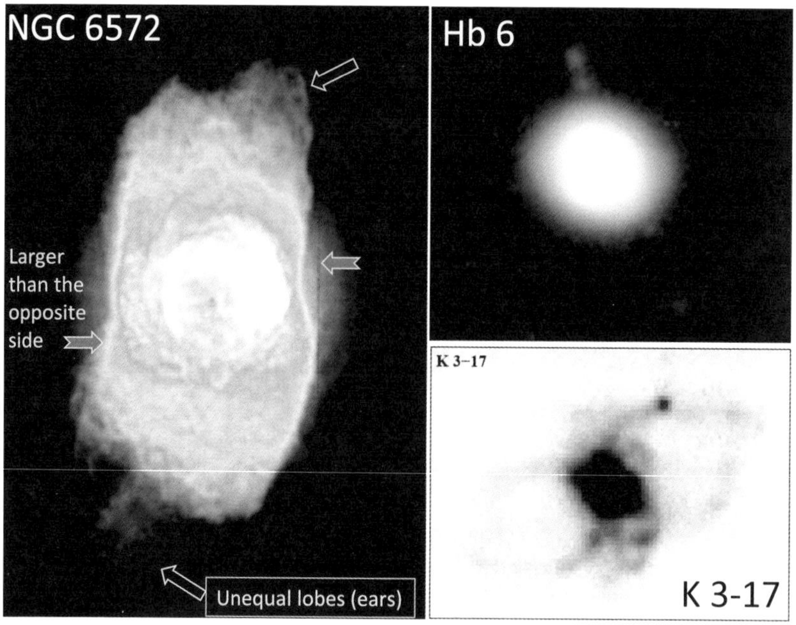

Figure 2. Left: An HST image of NGC 6572 in Hα (red), Hβ (dark blue), oxygen (blue), and a yellow broadband filter (green) (credit: ESA/Hubble & NASA). I indicated departures from point symmetry. For more details on the multipolar structure see, e.g., Bandyopadhyay et al. (2023). The marks emphasize the three properties of (1) multipolar morphology, (2) departure from symmetry, and (3) non-messy morphology (only a small to moderate departure from pure point symmetry). Upper right: an HST image of IC 4670 (Hb 6; Chambers et al. 2016). Lower right: K3-17 (from Steffen et al. 2013).

is also multipolar (2 pairs of lobes) with a clear departure from pure point symmetry, but it is not a messy PN. Namely, it shares the same three properties that I listed above for NGC 7027. The image of IC 4670 (Hb 6) that I take from Chambers et al. (2016) is of too low a resolution to examine the three properties in detail. However, the jet-like structures above and below the main ring in the image suggest that it might share these three properties. In the same figure I also present K3-17 taken from Steffen et al. (2013) who studied this PN as a multipolar PN. It also shares the three properties that I listed for NGC 7027.

In Figure 3 I present the images of six bright PNe. The PN NGC 7026 has two pairs of lobes and has a departure from pure point symmetry as the structural analysis by Clark et al. (2013) shows (lower-right panel of Figure 3). As with some other PNe above, it does not have a strong messy morphology. The image of the PN NGC 7354 in the upper-right panel of Figure 3 presents only one symmetry axis (from upper left to lower right) and clumps near the equatorial plane (in red; perpendicular to the main symmetry axis). However, deeper analysis by Contreras et al. (2010) reveals two axisymmetrical axes inclined to each other. It seems that NGC 7354 also shares the properties I listed for NGC 7027, although only with a weak departure from axisymmetry. NGC 6369 shows two lobes on one side (left in the upper-middle panel). Clearly, its morphology departs from pure point symmetry and it seems to be multipolar, sharing the three properties with the other PNe mentioned above. The PN M1-40 might also share the three properties, although a better-resolution image is required. The case with NGC 6567 is unclear, while NGC 7662 does not reveal a multipolar structure.

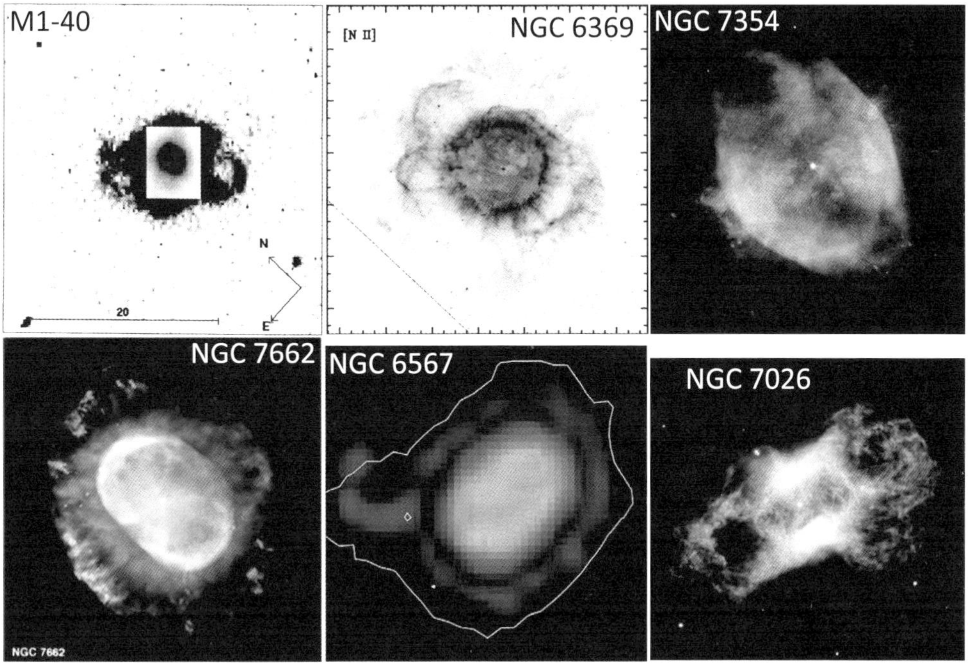

Figure 3. Six bright PNe, from upper left to lower right. An [O III] image of M1-40 (Schwarz, Corradi, & Melnick 1992), an HST [N II] image of NGC 6369 (Ramos-Larios et al. 2012), an image of NGC 7354 from HST site (where more details can be found; credit ESA/Hubble & NASA), NGC 7662 (from the Chandra site based on Kastner et al. 2012), an HST [N II] (log flux scale) image of NGC 6567 from Danehkar (2022), and an HST image of NGC 7026 from the HST site (credit ESA/Hubble & NASA).

The PN NGC 2440 has two pairs of bipolar lobes as the morpho-kinematical modeling by Lago & Costa (2016) shows, and as can also be seen in the upper left panel of Figure 4. A departure from pure point symmetry is seen. NGC 2440 also shares the three properties that I listed for NGC 7027. Bear & Soker (2017) mark NGC 2440 as likely (moderate probability) shaped by a triple stellar system. The PN NGC 6210 is a multipolar PN (e.g., Rechy-García et al. 2020; Henney et al. 2021). It is different than most PNe in this study in that Bear & Soker (2017) classified it as high-probability messy PN. In that case, it requires a triple star system interaction to explain its morphology (Bear & Soker 2017). However, its outer structure might be viewed as composed of two S-shaped pairs of lobes (as I marked in the figure), which would then make NGC 6210 morphology less dominated by the messy parts. The morphology of NGC 6537 is different than those of the other PNe in this study but shares the basic properties. On a large scale, it is a bipolar PN with two opposite large lobes. The boundaries of the lobes are not smooth, and the two lobes are not exactly equal to each other in shape. In the inner region (white) there is a hint of a multipolar PN, although on a smaller scale than the large lobes. The inner regions depart from pure-point symmetry. Although it is different than the other PNe, it is a multipolar PN with a departure from pure point symmetry, but not a messy PN.

Overall, I find that most, but not all, bright PNe tend to be multipolar with small to medium degree departures from pure point-symmetry. These properties suggest that they were shaped by a strong (violent) binary interaction, but not necessarily by a triple-star interaction that most likely leads to messy PNe. On the opposite extreme, there are faint PNe that tend to be round (e.g., Jacoby et al. 2010), most likely because they did not

Figure 4. Upper left: NGC 2440 (The HST site where more details can be found; credit: NASA, ESA, and K. Noll, STScI). Upper right: An [O III] image in log scale of the PN NGC 6210 (Henney et al. 2021). I added two S-shaped double-headed arrows to mark the S-shaped pairs of lobes. Bottom: an HST image of NGC 6537 (credit: SA & Garrelt Mellema). It has a large-scale bipolar morphology, but with clear departures from pure point symmetry and a multipolar morphology in the inner (white) region.

have a binary interaction at all or had an interaction with a sub-stellar object (e.g., Soker & Subag 2005). Out of the 13 PNe I study here, Bear & Soker (2017) attributed a high probability for shaping by triple stellar interaction only to NGC 6210 (but see the marks for more ordered S-shaped pairs of lobes in Figure 4), and a medium probability for NGC 2440. But there are no indications of a large influence by a tertiary star in the other bright PNe. The binary interaction, though, seems to require the change of the symmetry axis of the jets within a relatively short time, during which the system launches two or more energetic pairs of jets (this is what I refer to as 'violent interaction').

3. The case of SN Ia SNR G1.9+0.3 that destroyed its planetary nebula progenitor

Enokiya et al. (2023) published a new X-ray image of the youngest supernova remnant (SNR) in the Galaxy, the type Ia SNR G1.9+0.3. In a recent paper (Soker 2023) I presented my identification of a point-symmetrical structure in this SNR Ia. Explosion models of SNe Ia do not form point-symmetrical ejecta. Therefore, I concluded that the point-symmetrical morphology is an imprint of the circumstellar material (CSM) into which the ejecta expanded since the explosion in about 1890-1900. Furthermore, the known substantial deceleration of the ejecta of SNR G1.9+0.3 (e.g., Borkowski et al. 2017) suggests a relatively massive CSM of $\gtrsim 1 M_{\odot}$. I therefore suggested that SNR G1.9+0.3

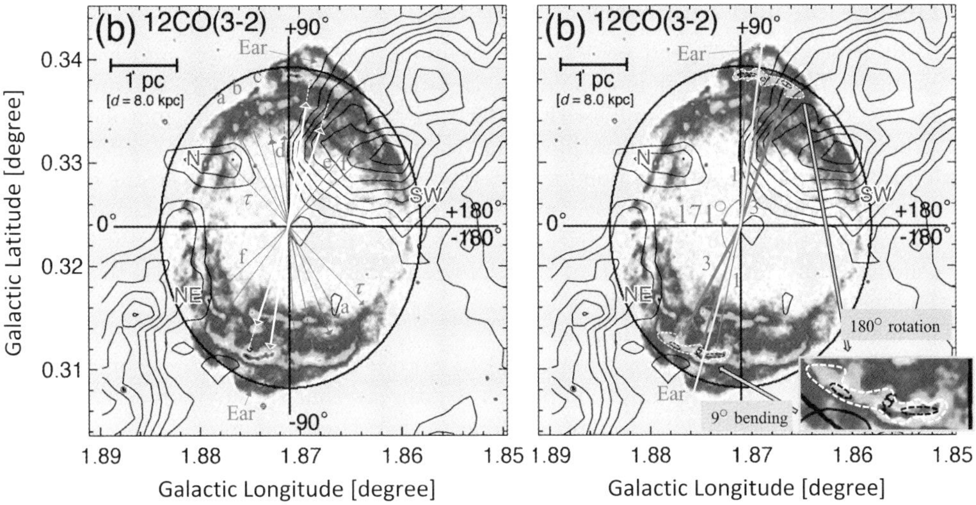

Figure 5. An X-ray image image of SNR G1.9+0.3 with CO contours from Enokiya et al. (2023). The ellipse and the coordinate lines are in the original image. Left panel: an image with annotations from Soker (2023) to present the point symmetric morphology: a mark of the two ears and the double-headed arrows (DHA), including dashed line continuations. DHA-a to DHA-f point at twin clumps of a point symmetric structure, while DHA-τ is a tentative pair because the clumps are small and faint. The two white double-headed arrows point at pairs of clumps that require a different analysis as presented on the right panel (from Soker 2023). The right panel includes the identification of the arc at the base of the upper (western) ear by a white dashed line, and its three peaks with dashed black lines. This is rotated around itself by 180° and matched to the arc at the base of the bottom (eastern) ear, as the inset indicates. This procedure reveals a 9° bend point symmetry of the two ears (DHA-0) and of the two base arcs (DHA-1 to DHA-3).

was an SN Ia inside a PN (SNIP). I present the identification of the point-symmetry in the two panels of Figure 5 (see caption for more details).

The most likely scenario to account for such a SNIP is the core degenerate scenario, where a WD companion spiralling inside the AGB progenitor merges with the core at the end of the common envelope. In this case, there is a PN with a massive central star that is a merger product. The explosion of SNR G1.9+0.3 took place within $\lesssim 10^5$ yr after the common envelope and the formation of the PN. Another possible, but less likely, scenario for such a SNIP is the double degenerate scenario in which the WD companion ended the common envelope at a very close orbit to the core. Gravitational wave radiation brought the WD-core system to interact and explode within $\lesssim 10^5$ yr. The PN in this case was ionized by the core and the WD companion.

The point symmetry extends over a large angle from the double-headed arrow (DHA) line DHA-τ to line DHA-f (left panel). The two double ear structure (lines DHA-0 to DHA-3 on the right panel) has a bend of 9°. The pairs of clumps to the two sides of the ears do not share this bend. I, therefore, speculate that the PN progenitor of SNR G1.9+0.3 was a multipolar PN with some small departures from pure point symmetry. Due to the required massive nebula (as inferred from the decelerated SNR ejecta) and the ionizing source, which was a massive WD or a binary system of two WDs (as discussed above), I further speculate that this might have been a PN at or near the bright cutoff of the PNLF. I note that Yao & Quataert (2023) discuss the WD-WD merger as a scenario to form a bright hydrogen-poor PN (although no such bright PN is known). However, they do not consider the core degenerate scenario evolution through a regular (hydrogen-rich) PN.

4. Discussion and Summary

In this Proceedings paper I presented a preliminary attempt to try and learn about the brightest PNe from their morphologies. Because morphology analysis requires good resolution, this study deals only with Galactic PNe. Examining the morphologies of the brightest Galactic PNe, I identified that they tend to be multipolar with small to moderate departures from pure point symmetry (Section 2). These lead to the first three conclusions below. Adding to these conclusions my very recent claim (Soker 2023) that the youngest Galactic supernova, SNR G1.9+0.3, was an SN Ia inside a PN (SNIP) and my conclusion in Section 3 above that this PN was multipolar, bring me also to speculate on the fourth and fifth conclusions below.

The main conclusions are as follows.

- (1) The brightest PNe progenitors tend to experience strong (violent) binary interaction. This rules out a low-mass companion. I estimate that the companion has a mass of $M_2 \gtrsim 0.5 M_\odot$, which implies a main sequence or a WD companion.
- (2) They are generally not the result of a triple stellar interaction. Namely, a tertiary star does not play a role in explaining the bright cutoff of the PNLF.
- (3) Theoretical studies of the universal bright cutoff of the PNLF cannot ignore binary interaction.
- (4) Consider the claim that SNR G1.9+0.3 was an SN Ia inside a multipolar PN, as I discussed in Section 3. The likely scenario is one where a WD companion merged with the core of the AGB star at the end of the common envelope (the core degenerate scenario), or that they came very close to each other (the double degenerate scenario). The ionizing source of the pre-explosion PN progenitor of SNR G1.9+0.3 was either a massive WD that is a merger remnant, or a system of two close WDs. Theoretical studies should take into account the possibilities of such ionizing sources of the brightest PNe.
- (5) I further speculate that some (but not all) of the central star of the brightest PNe are the merger product of a WD companion with the core. Some, but not all, of these, might explode as SNe Ia, possibly while the nebula still exists, i.e., SNIPs.

Acknowledgement

I thank Nick Chornay for the list of the brightest PNe. In this research, I used the *PNIC: Planetary Nebula Image Catalogue* composed by Bruce Balick (http://faculty.washington.edu/balick/PNIC/). I acknowledge funding from the Pazy Research Foundation in Israel.

References

Balick B., 1987, *AJ*, 94, 671.

Bandyopadhyay R., Das R., Parthasarathy M., Kar S., 2023, *MNRAS*, 524, 1547.

Bear E., Soker N., 2017, *ApJL*, 837, L10.

Bhattacharya S., Arnaboldi M., Gerhard O., McConnachie A., Caldwell N., Hartke J., Freeman K. C., 2021, *A&A*, 647, A130.

Boffin, H. M. J., Miszalski, B., Rauch, T., Jones, D., Corradi, R. L. M., Napiwotzki, R., Day-Jones, A. C., & Köppen, J. 2012, Science, 338, 773

Borkowski K. J., Gwynne P., Reynolds S. P., Green D. A., Hwang U., Petre R., Willett R., 2017, *ApJL*, 837, L7.

Bublitz J., Kastner J. H., Hily-Blant P., Forveille T., Santander-García M., Alcolea J., Bujarrabal V., et al., 2023, ApJ, 942, 14.

Chambers K. C., Magnier E. A., Metcalfe N., Flewelling H. A., Huber M. E., Waters C. Z., Denneau L., et al., 2016, arXiv:1612.05560.

Chornay N., 2023a, PhDT.

Chornay N., 2023b, Proceedings of IAU Symposium 384: Planetary Nebulae: a Universal Toolbox in the Era of Precision Astrophysics. Eds: O. De Marco, A. Zijlstra, R. Szczerba
Chu Y.-H., Jacoby G. H., Arendt R., 1987, ApJS, 64, 529.
Ciardullo R., 2022, FrASS, 9, 896326.
Ciardullo R., Jacoby G. H., Ford H. C., Neill J. D., 1989, ApJ, 339, 53.
Clark D. M., López J. A., Steffen W., Richer M. G., 2013, *AJ*, 145, 57.
Contreras M. E., Vázquez R., Miranda L. F., Olguín L., Zavala S., Ayala S., 2010, *AJ*, 139, 1426
Corradi R. L. M., Schwarz H. E., 1995, *A&A*, 293, 871
Cox P., Huggins P. J., Maillard J.-P., Habart E., Morisset C., Bachiller R., Forveille T., 2002, *A&A*, 384, 603.
Danehkar A., 2022, *ApJS*, 260, 14. doi:10.3847/1538-4365/ac5cca
Enokiya R., Sano H., Filipović M. D., Alsaberi R. Z. E., Inoue T., Oka T., 2023, PASJ..tmp.
Gesicki K., Zijlstra A. A., Miller Bertolami M. M., 2018, *NatAs*, 2, 580.
Henney W. J., López J. A., García-Díaz M. T., Richer M. G., 2021, *MNRAS*, 502, 1070
Jacoby G. H., 1989, ApJ, 339, 39.
Jacoby G. H., Ciardullo R., Roth M. M., Arnaboldi M., Weilbacher P. M., 2023, arXiv:2309.11603.
Jacoby G. H., Kronberger M., Patchick D., Teutsch P., Saloranta J., Howell M., Crisp R., et al., 2010, *PASA*, 27, 156
Kastner J. H., Montez R., Balick B., Frew D. J., Miszalski B., Sahai R., Blackman E., et al., 2012, *AJ*, 144, 58
Lago P. J. A., Costa R. D. D., 2016, RMxAA, 52, 329.
Manchado A., Guerrero M. A., Stanghellini L., Serra-Ricart M., 1996, iacm.book
Méndez R. H., 2017, *IAUS*, 323, 298.
Mendez R. H., Kudritzki R. P., Ciardullo R., Jacoby G. H., 1993, *A&A*, 275, 534
Moraga Baez P., Kastner J. H., Balick B., Montez R., Bublitz J., 2023, *ApJ*, 942, 15.
Morris, M. 1987, *PASP*, 99, 1115
Parker Q. A., 2022, *FrASS*, 9, 895287.
Parker Q. A., Bojičić I. S., Frew D. J., 2016, *JPhCS*, 728, 032008.
Ramos-Larios G., Guerrero M. A., Vázquez R., Phillips J. P., 2012, *MNRAS*, 420, 1977
Rechy-García J. S., Guerrero M. A., Duarte Puertas S., Chu Y.-H., Toalá J. A., Miranda L. F., 2020, *MNRAS*, 492, 1957
Sabach E., Soker N., 2018, *MNRAS*, 479, 2249.
Sahai R., 2000, *ApJL*, 537, L43.
Sahai R., Bujarrabal V., Castro-Carrizo A., Zijlstra A., 2000, *A&A*, 360, L9
Sahai R., Morris M., Sánchez Contreras C., Claussen M., 2007, *AJ*, 134, 2200.
Sahai R., Morris M. R., Villar G. G., 2011, *AJ*, 141, 134.
Sahai R., Trauger J. T., 1998, *AJ*, 116, 1357.
Schwarz H. E., Corradi R. L. M., Melnick J., 1992, *A&AS*, 96, 23
Soker, N. 1990, *AJ*, 99, 1869
Soker N., 2023, *RAA*, in press, arXiv:2309.15093
Soker N., Subag E., 2005, *AJ*, 130, 2717
Steffen W., Koning N., Esquivel A., García-Segura G., García-Díaz M. T., López J. A., Magnor M., 2013, *MNRAS*, 436, 470
Valenzuela L. M., Méndez R. H., Miller Bertolami M. M., 2019, *ApJ*, 887, 65.
van de Steene G. C., Jacoby G. H., Praet C., Ciardullo R., Dejonghe H., 2006, *A&A*, 455, 891.
Yao P. Z., Quataert E., 2023, *ApJ*, 957, 30.

Planetary Nebulae: A Universal Toolbox in the Era of Precision Astrophysics
Proceedings IAU Symposium No. 384, 2025
O. De Marco, A. Zijlstra & R. Szczerba, eds.
doi:10.1017/S1743921324000255

Spectroscopic monitoring of V Hydrae: a binary eclipsed by a jet?

Léa Planquart and Alain Jorissen

Institut d'Astronomie et d'Astrophysique, Université Libre de Bruxelles, CP 226,
Boulevard du Triomphe, 1050 Brussels, Belgium.
email: lea.planquart@ulb.be

Abstract. The carbon-rich star V Hydrae is known to be in its transition from the asymptotic giant branch phase to a bipolar planetary nebula. However, the origin of its bipolar shape, as well as its long-term periodic obscuration, are not well understood. Using high-resolution spectra from the HERMES/Mercator spectrograph spanning over 10-yr monitoring, we disentangled the orbital signal from the intrinsic Mira-like variations of V Hya. The orbital solution obtained is compatible with the light-curve modulation, which we interpret as an obscuration caused by an extended dusty environment surrounding the unseen companion. Additionally, we report high-velocity phase-dependent absorption features in the sodium doublet and explain them by the presence of a conical jet ejected from the (accretion disc of the) companion. We confront our binary scenario with previous radio observations and discuss how this jet could shape the large-scale bipolar outflow of the system.

Keywords. stars: AGB and post-AGB, stars: binaries, AGB star, ISM: jets and outflows

1. Introduction and target

Most planetary nebulae (PN) show aspherical morphology with the emergence of bi- or multi-polar structures. These structures are believed to be shaped by the presence of a companion in a binary system (De Marco 2009). However, there is a lack of observational evidence for binaries among their direct progenitors, the asymptotic giant branch (AGB) stars. AGB stars being bright and pulsating (with periods ranging from 10 d to 600 d), detecting the orbital signature is not an easy endeavour as it requires to correctly disentangle the intrinsic variations from the Keplerian ones.

Here we report on the temporal analysis of the radial-velocity and light curves of the AGB star V Hydrae (V Hya). V Hya is a well-studied carbon-rich star at the late stage of the AGB phase. It exhibits two periodic modulations in its light curve, with periods of 530 d and 17 yr (Campbell 1926, Knapp *et al.* 1999). The shorter period is commonly associated with the Mira-type pulsation while the origin of the longer period was not clearly understood. Large-scale ALMA images reveal a complex structure made of a dense equatorial torus and a bipolar high-velocity outflow (Sahai *et al.* 2022). Those peculiarities, together with the presence of a UV excess (Sahai *et al.* 2008), led to the suspicion that V Hya could be a binary system.

In this paper, we show that an unprecedented long-term spectral monitoring provides an orbital solution for the system and reveals spectral similarities with post-AGB binaries, making V Hya the missing link between AGB stars and bipolar pre-planetary nebula.

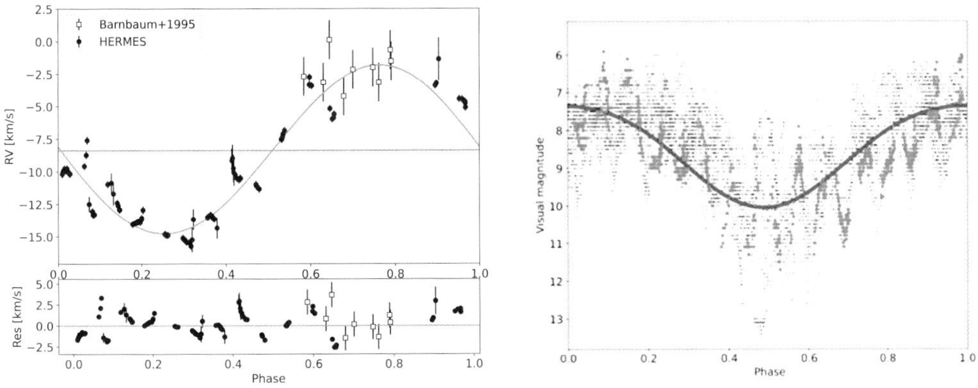

Figure 1. Left: Orbital-phase-folded RV data and Keplerian solution (solid curve; adapted from Planquart *et al.* 2023). **Right**: Visual light curve from AAVSO, phase-folded with the 17-yr orbital period. Photometric data along the most recent orbital cycle are shown as thick blue dots, and the red solid line represents the best-fit Gaussian curve.

2. Observations and methods

V Hya was observed from 2011 to 2023 with the high-resolution HERMES spectrograph mounted on the Mercator telescope (Raskin *et al.* 2011). In the first step of the analysis, the orbital elements are retrieved by fitting the radial-velocity (RV) curve, obtained through cross-correlation of the spectra with a mask constructed from a R-star template. Additional archive RV measurements from Barnbaum *et al.* (1995) are added to the curve to ensure a complete orbital-phase coverage (Fig. 1). The RV-curve is cleaned from the pulsation signal by removing a sinusoidal contribution with a period equal to the 530 d pulsation period. Once cleaned from the Mira pulsation, the RV data set is combined with the astrometric proper motions (Hipparcos, Gaia, and long-term motion obtained by combining Hipparos and Gaia positions). All these data are fitted together using the ORVARA routine (Brandt *et al.* 2021) to obtain the best-fitting set of orbital parameters, which may be found in Planquart *et al.* (2023).

In a second step, a temporal analysis of selected spectral lines is performed, to correlate the varying spectral profiles with the orbital and pulsation phases. The Na I D-line profiles are found to be correlated with the orbital period. They were fitted using a spatio-kinematic model of an absorbing gaseous jet originating from the companion, following the method used to fit Hα profiles in post-AGB binaries (see Bollen *et al.* 2019 and Planquart *et al.* 2023 for details).

3. Results and discussion

The orbital solution has a 17-yr period, equal to the photometric variation, and a low eccentricity. Figure 1 (left panel) displays the phase-folded RV curve, where phase 0.5 refers to the superior conjunction (SC) where the AGB star is behind its companion as seen by the observer. Phase 0 (or 1) corresponds to the opposite situation (inferior conjunction, IC). The SC epoch coincides with the epochs of the light-curve dimming events, implying that the obscuration is linked with the companion motion around the primary. With a dip of ~ 3.5 mag lasting for about a third of the orbital cycle (right panel of Fig. 1), such a broad-band extinction requires the presence of an extended and dense dusty environment surrounding the companion. This is consistent with the infrared interferometric VLTI/MATISSE images of V Hya, which reveal the presence of a dust clump at the position of the companion predicted by the orbital ephemeris (see Fig. 2 and Planquart *et al.* 2024).

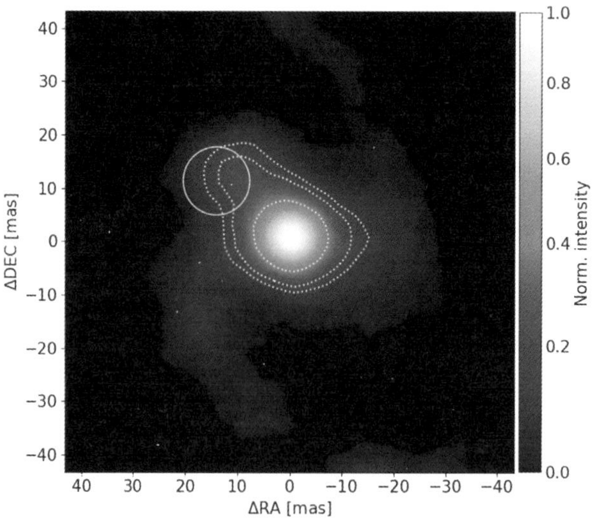

Figure 2. Reconstructed image of the circumstellar environment of V Hya, obtained in the thermal infrared (10.5-11.5 μm). The white circle is the expected companion position from the best-fitting orbit. The 15%, 20%, and 40% intensity levels are drawn in dotted lines. North is up, East is left.

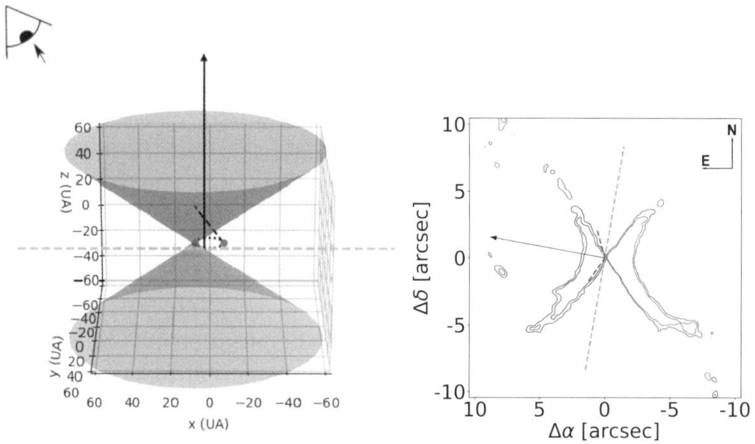

Figure 3. Left: To-scale sketch of the jet geometry. The blue (red) cone is blue-(red-)shifted as seen by the observer (the blueshifted half of the cone is oriented upward). The system is represented at phase 0.5 (SC), with V Hya displayed as a red dot and the companion as a blue one at the central point of the cone. The dashed oblique line represents the line of sight, the green horizontal dashed line the trace of the orbital plane, and the vertical arrow the jet axis direction. **Right**: Stereogram image at $\pm$100 km/s of the CO emission, highlighting the high-velocity bipolar outflow. The system geometry (jet axis and line of nodes) is projected on the plane of the sky according to the orbital solution with clockwise rotation of the companion.

The spectral profile of the sodium doublet exhibits a varying blueshifted absorption with a projected velocity ranging from -150 km/s at phase 0.5 (SC) to -50 km/s at phase 0 (IC). The best-fitting jet model has an opening angle of about 60 degrees, larger than the orbital inclination, implying that the absorption by the jet is present at all phases, with the most blueshifted value occurring when the line of sight crosses the jet axis. The cone geometry, parameterized with the highest velocity along its axis (low-density region) and lowest velocity (denser region) along its edge, is represented in Fig. 3 (left panel).

Details on the observed and modelled spectral profiles can be found in Planquart *et al.* (2023). The right panel of Fig. 3 compares the jet orientation (arrow) and the line of nodes of the orbital plane (dashed line; as derived from the orbital parameters) with the bipolar outflow mapped in the ^{12}CO $J = 2 - 1$ line (using ALMA archive data from project ID 2018.1.01113.S with PI R. Sahai).

4. Summary

The radial-velocity monitoring of V Hya allowed us to confirm the binary nature of the system and to obtain its orbital elements. Furthermore, combining our spectroscopic data with archive astrometric and photometric data, the dust and gas distribution around the system could be constrained. While the temporal variation of the line profile of the Na I resonance doublet could be modelled consistently, a further in-depth investigation should be performed to quantify the density and temperature of the gas and dust around the system.

For the gas distribution, the proposed conical jet model matches the large-scale morphology of the bipolar jet imaged in the radio range as well as the orientation of the collimated ejection seen in the forbidden lines of sulfur (right panel of Fig. 3 and Sahai 2003). This consistency hints at a common shaping mechanism induced by the binary interaction at the orbital scale (about 10 au) that shapes the large-scale (about 1000 au) bipolar outflow. The exact launching site and mechanism(s) of the jet should be investigated through 3D magneto-hydrodynamic models.

For the dust distribution, the particular shape of the dimming events puts strong constraints on the dust location and density around the companion, which require a dense vertical extension. Further modelling is needed to constrain the gas-dust interaction within the jet and to reproduce the light-curve modulation.

Acknowledgements

L.P. is FNRS research fellow.

References

Barnbaum, C., Morris, M., & Kahane, C. 1995, ApJ, 450, 862
Bollen, D., Kamath, D., Van Winckel, H., & De Marco, O. 2019, *A&A*, 631, A53
Brandt, T. D., Dupuy, T. J., Li, Y., *et al.* 2021, AJ, 162, 186
Campbell, L., 1926, Popular Astronomy, 34, 551
De Marco, O., 2009, PASP, 121, 878
Knapp, G. R., Dobrovolsky, S. I., Ivezić, Z., *et al.* 1999, *A&A*, 351, 97
Planquart, L., Jorissen, A., Escorza, A., *et al.* 2023, *A&A*, in press
Planquart, L., Paladini, C., Jorissen, A., *et al.* 2024, *A&A*, submitted
Raskin, G., van Winckel, H., Hensberge, H., *et al.* 2011, *A&A*, 526, A69
Sahai, R., Morris, M., Knapp, G. R., *et al.* 2003, Nature, 426, 6964
Sahai, R., Findeisen, K., Gil de Paz, A. *et al.* 2008, ApJ, 689, 2
Sahai, R., Huang, P. S., Scibelli, S., *et al.* 2022, ApJ, 929, 59

Planetary Nebulae: A Universal Toolbox in the Era of Precision Astrophysics
Proceedings IAU Symposium No. 384, 2025
O. De Marco, A. Zijlstra & R. Szczerba, eds.
doi:10.1017/S174392132400005X

The abundance discrepancy in ionized nebulae: which are the correct abundances?

J. E. Méndez-Delgado[1] and J. García-Rojas[2,3]

[1]Astronomisches Rechen-Institut, Zentrum für Astronomieder Universität Heidelberg, Mönchhofstraße 12-14, D-69120 Heidelberg, Germany
email: jemd@uni-heidelberg.de

[2]Instituto de Astrofísica de Canarias, E-38205 La Laguna, Tenerife, Spain

[3]Departamento de Astrofísica, Universidad de La Laguna, E-38206 La Laguna, Tenerife, Spain

Abstract. Ionized nebulae are key to understanding the chemical composition and evolution of the Universe. Among these nebulae, H II regions and planetary nebulae are particularly important as they provide insight into the present and past chemical composition of the interstellar medium, along with the nucleosynthetic processes involved in the chemical evolution of the gas. However, the heavy-element abundances derived from collisionally excited lines (CELs) and recombination lines (RLs) do not align. This longstanding abundance discrepancy problem calls into question our absolute abundance determinations. Which of the lines (if any) provides the correct heavy element abundances? Recently, it has been shown that there are temperature inhomogeneities concentrated within the highly ionized gas of the H II regions, causing the reported discrepancy. However, planetary nebulae do not exhibit the same trends as the H II regions, suggesting a different origin for the abundance discrepancy. In this proceedings, we briefly discuss the state-of-the-art of the abundance discrepancy problem in both H II regions and planetary nebulae.

Keywords. ISM: abundances, (ISM:) HII regions, (ISM:) planetary nebulae: general

---

1. Introduction

At the beggining of the universe, baryonic matter was composed exclusively of hydrogen, helium and small amounts of lithium (Peebles 1966a,b; Wagoner 1973). The rest of the heavier elements were formed later through nucleosynthetic processes related to the life and death of stars (Bethe 1939; Caughlan 1965; Truran & Cameron 1971). Due to this interconnection between star formation, nucleosynthesis, and chemical composition, the study of the chemical abundances of ionized nebulae in the interstellar medium (ISM) has been crucial in understanding galaxies formation and evolution (Peimbert et al. 2017; Maiolino & Mannucci 2019). For this purpose, star-forming regions, known as H II regions, and planetary nebulae (PNe) are particularly important. The former are clouds of gas ionized by the ultraviolet radiation emitted by newly formed massive O type or early B type stars (Osterbrock & Ferland 2006). The latter are clouds of gas formed by the ejections of matter from low mass stars between $0.8M_{\odot}$ to $8M_{\odot}$ in their final stage of evolution, being ionized by the hot stellar remnant (Osterbrock & Ferland 2006).

H II regions reflect the current chemical composition of the interstellar medium (ISM) (Shaver et al. 1983; Arellano-Córdova et al. 2020; Méndez-Delgado et al. 2022; Groves et al. 2023), while PNe show the composition of the ISM at the time of the formation of the original star, along with nucleosynthetic changes that occurred during its lifetime

(Péquignot et al. 2000; Leisy & Dennefeld 2006; Karakas & Lattanzio 2014; Delgado-Inglada et al. 2015). These characteristics make them very useful for complementary analysis of the distribution of their chemical composition in galaxies. (Magrini et al. 2016; Esteban & García-Rojas 2018; Stanghellini & Haywood 2018; Espinosa-Ponce et al. 2022).

However, there is a problem, and it is a big one: we are not certain about the correct abundance of heavy elements like O, C, N, Ne, collectively known as "metals". Since the pioneering works of Bowen & Wyse (1939) and Wyse (1942), it has been known that the abundances of these elements determined from the bright collisionally excited lines (CELs) (e.g., [O III] $\lambda\lambda$5007, 4959) are systematically lower than those inferred from the faint recombination lines (RLs) (e.g., O II $\lambda\lambda$4649, 4650). The ratio between both estimates is known as the "abundance discrepancy factor" (ADF), and it has been found to be around a factor of 2-4 in H II regions (García-Rojas & Esteban 2007), but can reach values of more than 500 in some PNe (Wesson et al. 2003). The adoption of one metallicity or another can imply significant changes in the interpretation we would make about the chemical evolution of galaxies. Therefore, it is important to consider: which (if any) are the correct abundances?

2. The favourite scenarios

Since the emergence of this long-standing problem, several ideas have been proposed to explain the observed ADF. For instance, fluorescent excitations contaminating heavy element RLs (Seaton 1968); errors in the atomic parameters that model the emissivity of spectral lines (Rodríguez & García-Rojas 2010); the presence of a κ velocity distribution in free electrons instead of a Maxwellian one (Nicholls et al. 2012); temperature inhomogeneities (Peimbert 1967) and chemical inhomogeneities in the gas (Torres-Peimbert et al. 1990; Liu et al. 2000).

The last two scenarios have gained particular relevance in the overall study of chemical abundances in H II regions (Peimbert 1967, 2003; O'Dell et al. 2003; Esteban et al. 2004; García-Rojas & Esteban 2007; Stasińska et al. 2013; Méndez-Delgado et al. 2023b,a) and PNe (Torres-Peimbert et al. 1990; Liu et al. 2000, 2006; Fang & Liu 2011; García-Rojas et al. 2022). Both scenarios are supported by solid theoretical foundations, but the observational evidence to accept or discard either of these scenarios (or both) remains a matter of debate.

2.1. *Temperature inhomogeneities*

To explain differences between the values obtained from several temperature diagnostics in ionized nebulae, Peimbert (1967) proposed the existence of temperature inhomogeneities within the ionized gas. Since the CEL-emissivities have an exponential dependency on temperature (Osterbrock & Ferland 2006), in the case of internal variations, their emissions will be substantially enhanced in the hotter volumes. On the other hand, RLs have emissivities depending on $\sim T_e^{-1}$, so their emission is favored in cooler regions, although with substantially smaller bias. Mathematically, this implies that the temperature inferred from the CEL intensity ratios (such as [O III] $\lambda4363/\lambda5007$) will be systematically higher than the average gas temperature within the volume where the CEL-emitter ion coexists (in the case of [O III] $\lambda4363/\lambda5007$, the ion would be O^{2+}). In such case, the temperature structure of each ionization volume will be characterized by two parameters: T_0, which is the average gas temperature, and t^2, which quantifies how inhomogeneous the temperature is. The mathematical formalism is presented in equations (1) and (2):

$$T_0(X^{i+}) = \frac{\int T_e n_e n(X^{i+}) dV}{\int n_e n(X^{i+}) dV}, \tag{1}$$

$$t^2(X^{i+}) = \frac{\int [T_e - T_0(X^{i+})]^2 n_e n(X^{i+}) dV}{T_0(X^{i+})^2 \int n_e n(X^{i+}) dV}. \quad (2)$$

In these equations, in a specific volume of the nebula, dV, T_e, n_e are the electron temperature and density and $n(X^{i+})$ is the ion's particle density.

Under this paradigm, when the estimated temperature from CEL intensity ratios (e.g., T_e([O III] λ4363/λ5007)) is adopted to calculate chemical abundances relative to H using CEL/RL intensity ratios (e.g., [O III] λ5007/Hβ), the overestimation of temperature will result in an underestimation of ionic abundances. Conversely, if chemical abundances relative to hydrogen are calculated using RL/RL intensity ratios (e.g., O II V1 4649/Hβ), both lines will cancel their linear dependence on temperature, and the derived ionic abundances will be correct.

Despite the simplicity and elegance of this proposal, its adoption as a generalized explanation for the observed ADF has not been universal, and various arguments against the existence of temperature variations have been put forward. Although classical photoionization models predict the existence of temperature inhomogeneities, these are too small ($t^2 \sim 0.004$) (Kingdon & Ferland 1995; Stasińska & Szczerba 2001; Ercolano et al. 2007; Ferland et al. 2017) to account for the observed ADF in H II regions ($t^2 \sim 0.04$) or PNe ($t^2 \sim 0.06$) (Peimbert et al. 2017). An exception might be nebula models with very high metallicity, where temperature gradients are more pronounced (Stasińska 2005). Temperature inhomogeneities in the gas tend to balance out over relatively short timescales (Ferland et al. 2016), so their existence requires an additional physical mechanism to create and maintain them. Additionally, some PNe (Liu et al. 2000; Corradi et al. 2015; García-Rojas et al. 2022) exhibit ADF values that are too large and appear irreconcilable with the t^2 formalism.

However, observational evidence seems to favour temperature variations as the cause of the ADF in H II regions with precise measurements of O II RLs. For instance, García-Rojas & Esteban (2007) found that the ADF of various ions in several Galactic H II regions depends on the excitation energy of the atomic levels giving rise to CELs, which is one of the predictions of the formalism by Peimbert (1967). Recently, Méndez-Delgado et al. (2023b) analyzed 32 spectra from extragalactic H II regions, 20 from Galactic H II regions, and 8 from Galactic ring nebulae with simultaneous detections of O II RLs, T_e([O III] λ4363/λ5007) and T_e([N II] λ5755/λ6584). As shown in Fig. 1, these authors demonstrated that $t^2(O^{2+})$, measured by comparing O II RLs and [O III] CELs (Peimbert & Peimbert 2013), is linearly correlated with the temperature difference T_e([O III] λ4363/λ5007) − T_e([N II] λ5755/λ6584). This shows that $t^2(O^{2+})$ is indeed related to the gas temperature structure. Moreover, it shows that temperature variations are concentrated in regions of higher ionization degree.

The fact that temperature variations are concentrated in the zones of higher ionization, closer to the ionizing stars of the gas, points to stellar feedback as a possible cause of temperature variations. Phenomena such as shocks, winds, or even variations in the ionizing spectrum of stars can cause significant inhomogeneities in the temperature of the surrounding gas (Peimbert et al. 1991; Perez 1997; Ercolano et al. 2007). These are not entirely understood physical phenomena, and their incorporation into photoionization models is not widespread. Méndez-Delgado et al. (2023b) then analyzed 8 spectra of ring nebulae, bubbles of ionized gas created by the ejection of material from young massive stars. Five of these analyzed spectra are from NGC 6888, a nebula associated with a Wolf-Rayet WN6 star, and three others from NGC 7635 associated with an O6.5(n)fp star (Esteban et al. 2016). The authors found that the observed trend between $t^2(O^{2+})$ and T_e([O III] λ4363/λ5007) − T_e([N II] λ5755/λ6584) in the ring nebulae is very similar to what is observed in H II regions. Interestingly, the spectra of NGC 6888 exhibit the

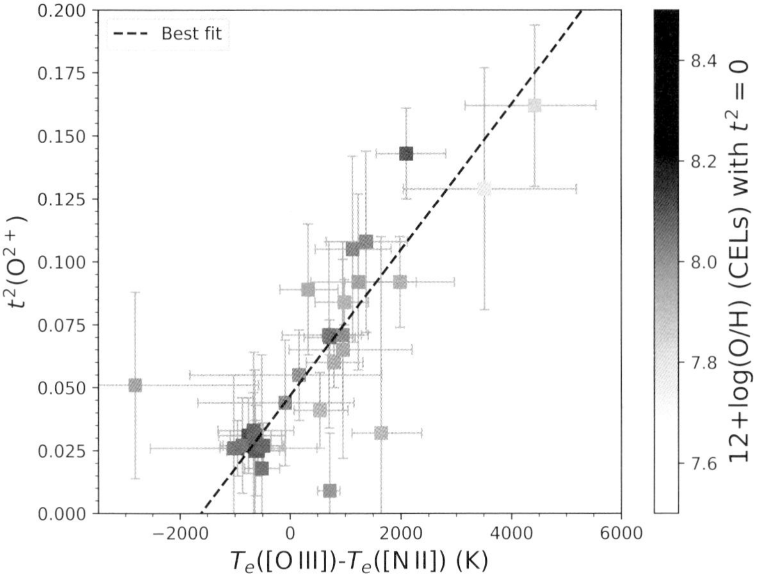

Figure 1. Relationship between $t^2(O^{2+})$, measured from O II RLs and [O III] CELs, with T_e([O III] $\lambda4363/\lambda5007$) and T_e([N II] $\lambda5755/\lambda6584$) in a sample of 32 extragalactic H II regions, all the existing ones in the literature with reliable measurements of all the mentioned indicators. Reproduced from Fig. 1 and extended data Fig. 2 of Méndez-Delgado et al. (2023b).

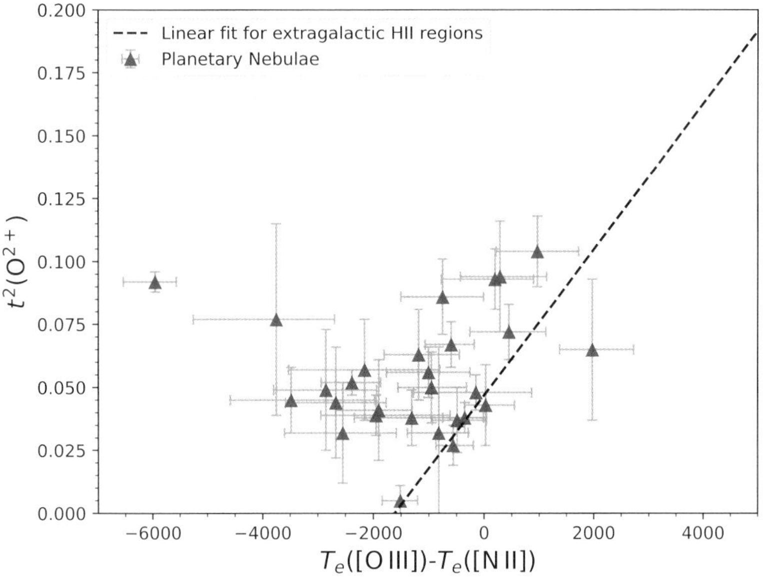

Figure 2. Figure analogous to Figure 1 but considering Galactic PNe. Reproduced from Fig. 10 (ArXiv version) of Méndez-Delgado et al. (2023b).

most extreme temperature variations ($t^2(O^{2+}) > 0.08$), while the values for NGC 7635 are lower ($t^2(O^{2+}) < 0.06$).

However, Méndez-Delgado et al. (2023b) tested this same hypothesis in Galactic PNe, and these do not exhibit a similar correlation as in H II regions, as shown in Fig. 2. This indicates that the cause of the ADF in H II regions and PNe is different. Although obvious, it is important to note that even if temperature variations alone are not able to explain the observed ADF in PNe, this does not rule out their presence and impact on the determination of chemical abundances in these objects. The ADF in PNe may be caused by various linked physical phenomena. For example, the observational evidence presented by Richer et al. (2022) for NGC 6153 shows that while most of the ADF in this region may be due to chemical inhomogeneities, temperature variations are not negligible, finding values of $t^2(O^{2+}) \approx 0.03$, which is typically found in H II regions.

2.2. *Chemical inhomogeneities*

An alternative explanation to the ADF is the existence of chemical inhomogeneities. If in a gas with a typical nebular temperature of $\sim 10\,000$ K there are gas components of different metallicity, they will induce temperature variations (Zhang et al. 2007). However, if the metallicity of these inclusions is extremely high compared to their hydrogen abundance, their temperature can drop to a few thousand kelvin or even lower. Under such circumstances, the flux of O II RLs may surpass the flux of the optical [O III] CELs (Liu 2003), and a different mathematical formalism than that proposed by Peimbert (1967) must be applied (note the dV dependence on Eq. (2)), as the emission from RLs and CELs will essentially come from different volumes (Stasińska 2002).

The existence of these high-metallicity clumps has been particularly important to explain cases of extreme ADF (Liu et al. 2000; Yuan et al. 2011; Corradi et al. 2015; Gómez-Llanos & Morisset 2020; García-Rojas et al. 2022) that have been associated with the existence of central binary stellar systems (Corradi et al. 2015; Jones et al. 2016; Wesson et al. 2018). Narrow-band imaging and Integral Field Unit (IFU) observations of Galactic PNe have been particularly crucial (García-Rojas et al. 2016; Ali & Dopita 2019; García-Rojas et al. 2022) as they have revealed morphological differences in the distribution of heavy-element RLs and their optical CEL counterparts. In addition, there are indications of kinematical differences between [O III] optical CELs and O II RLs (Richer et al. 2013, 2022; Peña et al. 2017), which strengthens this scenario.

However, although this scenario provides a plausible explanation for the extreme ADF in some PNe, it does not entirely answer the initial question of which of the abundances, based on CELs or RLs, is correct. One of the most interesting proposals to assess how important the error in chemical abundance determinations is under this scenario is the "Abundance Contrast Factor (ACF)" formalism (see Gómez-Llanos & Morisset 2020, and the proceeding by Morisset et al. in this series). The ACF measures the proportion of flux emitted by the cold component relative to the total emission. If the cold component is extremely hydrogen-poor, heavy-element RLs will have the most significant errors. However, H I RLs can also have a significant bias by increasing their emission in the cold component, affecting the inferred abundances from heavy-element CEL to H I RL intensity ratios.

Even in cases where the high-metallicity clumps are so hydrogen-poor that the impact on H I RLs is negligible, abundances observationally determined with CELs may not be reliable. Besides potential existence of real temperature inhomogeneities in the "hot" gas component emitting CELs, the existence of extremely cold clumps emitting a large amount of heavy element RLs could bias the T_e values inferred from auroral to nebular CEL ratios by contaminating the emission of auroral lines (e.g., [O III] λ4363, [N II] λ5755) (Rubin 1986; Gómez-Llanos et al. 2020). In order to "decontaminate" the temperatures determined with CEL ratios, it is necessary to know precisely the temperature and ionic abundances of the high metallicity clump that is emitting the "RL contamination". This requires determining the physical conditions using heavy element RLs such as O II $\lambda4089/\lambda4649$ to determine T_e or O II $\lambda4661/\lambda4649$ to determine n_e (Wesson et al. 2005; Peimbert & Peimbert 2013; Storey et al. 2017). This involves measuring heavy

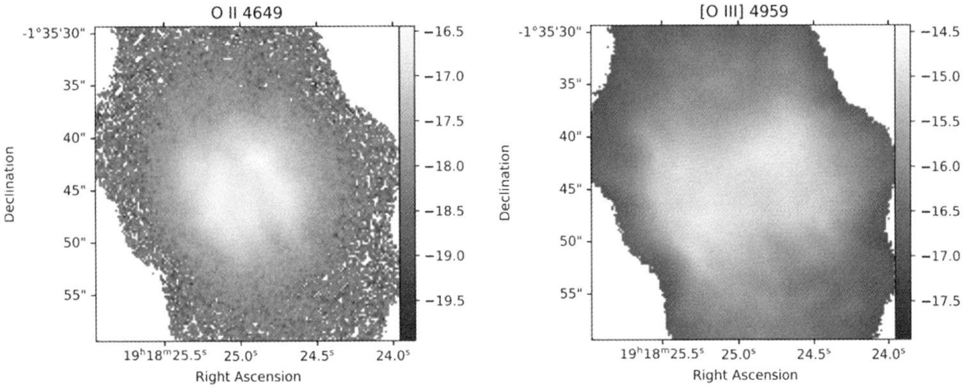

Figure 3. MUSE distribution of the emission of O II $\lambda\lambda$4649+4650 and [O III] λ4959 in the high-ADF Galactic planetary nebula NGC 6778 taken from García-Rojas et al. (2022). The morphological differences are evident and have been interpreted as evidence of the existence of components with different metallicity in the nebula.

element RLs that are comparatively fainter than those traditionally used to determine chemical abundances. A correction like the one proposed by Liu et al. (2000) in their equations (1) and (2) using physical conditions and ionic abundances determined in the "hot" gas component is conceptually incorrect, and it has not been demonstrated to be "less incorrect" than not making any correction.

In addition to the difficulty of explaining the creation and survival of high metallicity clumps (Henney & Stasińska 2010), extrapolating the existence of chemical inhomogeneities to explain the ADF in all PNe, not just extreme cases, could imply the existence of a wide variety of ACF values. If the high-metallicity component is not so hydrogen-poor, the emission of both CELs and RLs can come from both volumes. Such a scenario would imply that both estimates of CELs and RLs using the standard "direct method" are essentially incorrect. On the other hand, there are still some interesting questions about the observational evidence of the high metallicity components. For example, García-Rojas et al. (2022) has shown that the emission of O II RLs has a different morphology than its collisionally excited counterparts, as shown in Fig. 3. This has been argued as evidence of the presence of a cold gas component with a temperature of ~ 800 K. However, excellent MUSE maps show that highly ionized CELs such as [Cl IV] or [Ar IV] have a similar distribution to O II RLs (Figure 4). This does not seem to be a contrast problem since weaker lines than O II λ4649, such as [Cl III] λ5518, have a distribution similar to that of [O III] CELs. Since both Cl and Ar are third-row elements in the periodic table, this also does not seem to be a recombination contribution to these CELs (Barlow et al. 2003). How could a clump with a temperature of ~ 800 K emit these highly ionized CELs?

3. Conclusions

The systematic difference between heavy element abundances determined with RLs and CELs, the so-called abundance discrepancy problem, is one of the most interesting and important enigmas in the study of the chemical composition of ionized nebulae. This long-standing problem has significant implications for models of galaxy formation and evolution, and until its complete clarification, these models may be called into question. However, over the years, significant progress has been made thanks to deep observations of ionized nebulae collected over several decades by numerous researchers worldwide.

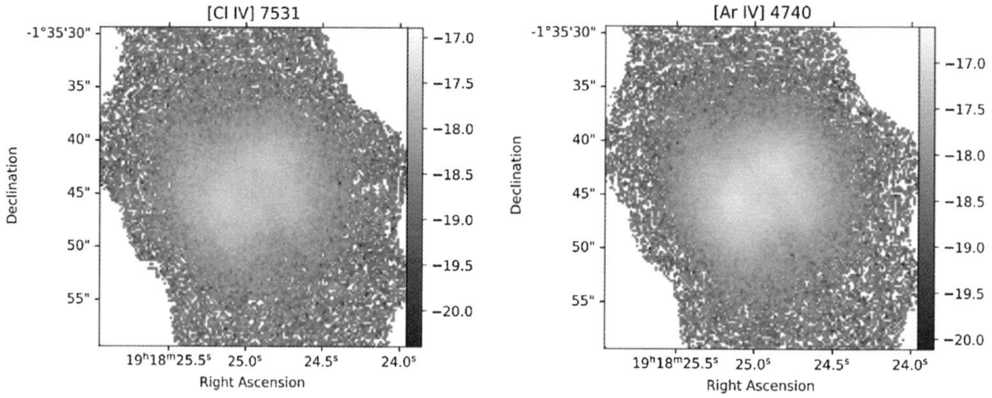

Figure 4. MUSE distribution of the emission of [Cl IV] λ7531 and [Ar IV] λ4740 in the high-ADF Galactic planetary nebula NGC 6778 taken from García-Rojas et al. (2022). The morphology of these highly ionized CELs are more similar to those of heavy element RLs (see Fig. 3).

The evidence suggests that the ADF may have different origins in H II regions and PNe. Recent observational studies seem to favor the presence of temperature inhomogeneities in highly ionized gas as the cause of the ADF in H II regions, in consistency with the formalism of Peimbert (1967). In this case, heavy element RLs appear to provide the correct chemical abundances, being 2−4 times higher than those obtained using CELs with the "direct method" (which assumes homogeneous electron temperature, see Méndez-Delgado et al. 2023b).

The case of PNe appears more intriguing. The evidence suggests that the presence of temperature variations alone is not able to quantitatively explain the observed ADFs in many PNe. In these regions, especially in those with the highest ADF values, there are indications that components of gas with different metallicity could exist. In fact, narrow-band imaging and IFU observations reveal that heavy element RLs have morphological distributions different from their collisionally excited counterparts, which is qualitatively consistent with this scenario. However, the quantitative impact of the presence of high metallicity clumps in the gas remains an open question which is now being addressed by several research groups (Gómez-Llanos & Morisset 2020; García-Rojas et al. 2022). Finally, although the differentiated morphological distribution between heavy element RLs and CELs is evident in PNe with high ADFs, it is important to understand exactly why this is also observed in highly ionized CELs such as [Cl IV] or [Ar IV]. More detailed IFU observations of PNe considering the morphological distribution of RLs and CELs of more ions will shed light on this interesting problem.

JEMD thanks the organizers for their invitation to this excellent symposium as an invited speaker. JEMD gratefully acknowledge funding from the Deutsche Forschungsgemeinschaft (DFG, German Research Foundation) in the form of an Emmy Noether Research Group (grant number - KR4598/2-1, PI Kreckel). JG-R acknowledges financial support from the Canarian Agency for Research, Innovation and Information Society (ACIISI), of the Canary Islands Government, and the European Regional Development Fund (ERDF), under grant with reference ProID2021010074, and from grant P/308614 financed by funds transferred from the Spanish Ministry of Science, Innovation and Universities, charged to the General State Budgets and with funds transferred from the General Budgets of the Autonomous Community of the Canary Islands by the MCIU. JG-R also acknowledges funds from the Spanish Ministry of Science and

Innovation (MICINN) through the Spanish State Research Agency, under Severo Ochoa Centres of Excellence Programme 2020-2023 (CEX2019-000920-S).

References

Ali A., Dopita M. A., 2019, MNRAS, 484, 3251

Arellano-Córdova K. Z., Esteban C., García-Rojas J., Méndez-Delgado J. E., 2020, MNRAS, 496, 1051

Barlow M. J., Liu X. W., . Péquignot D., Storey P. J., Tsamis Y. G., Morisset C., 2003, in Kwok S., Dopita M., Sutherland R., eds, Vol. 209, Planetary Nebulae: Their Evolution and Role in the Universe. p. 373

Bethe H. A., 1939, Physical Review, 55, 434

Bowen I. S., Wyse A. B., 1939, Lick Observatory Bulletin, 495, 1

Caughlan G. R., 1965, ApJ, 141, 688

Corradi R. L. M., García-Rojas J., Jones D., Rodríguez-Gil P., 2015, ApJ, 803, 99

Delgado-Inglada G., Rodríguez M., Peimbert M., Stasińska G., Morisset C., 2015, MNRAS, 449, 1797

Ercolano B., Bastian N., Stasińska G., 2007, MNRAS, 379, 945

Espinosa-Ponce C., Sánchez S. F., Morisset C., Barrera-Ballesteros J. K., Galbany L., García-Benito R., Lacerda E. A. D., Mast D., 2022, MNRAS, 512, 3436

Esteban C., García-Rojas J., 2018, MNRAS, 478, 2315

Esteban C., Peimbert M., García-Rojas J., Ruiz M. T., Peimbert A., Rodríguez M., 2004, MNRAS, 355, 229

Esteban C., Mesa-Delgado A., Morisset C., García-Rojas J., 2016, MNRAS, 460, 4038

Fang X., Liu X. W., 2011, MNRAS, 415, 181

Ferland G. J., Henney W. J., O'Dell C. R., Peimbert M., 2016, Rev. Mex. Astron. Astrofis., 52, 261

Ferland G. J., et al., 2017, Rev. Mex. Astron. Astrofis., 53, 385

García-Rojas J., Esteban C., 2007, ApJ, 670, 457

García-Rojas J., Corradi R. L. M., Monteiro H., Jones D., Rodríguez-Gil P., Cabrera-Lavers A., 2016, ApJ, 824, L27

García-Rojas J., Morisset C., Jones D., Wesson R., Boffin H. M. J., Monteiro H., Corradi R. L. M., Rodríguez-Gil P., 2022, MNRAS, 510, 5444

Gómez-Llanos V., Morisset C., 2020, MNRAS, 497, 3363

Gómez-Llanos V., Morisset C., García-Rojas J., Jones D., Wesson R., Corradi R. L. M., Boffin H. M. J., 2020, MNRAS, 498, L82

Groves B., et al., 2023, MNRAS, 520, 4902

Henney W. J., Stasińska G., 2010, ApJ, 711, 881

Jones D., Wesson R., García-Rojas J., Corradi R. L. M., Boffin H. M. J., 2016, MNRAS, 455, 3263

Karakas A. I., Lattanzio J. C., 2014, Publ. Astron. Soc. Australia, 31, e030

Kingdon J. B., Ferland G. J., 1995, ApJ, 450, 691

Leisy P., Dennefeld M., 2006, A&A, 456, 451

Liu X. W., 2003, in Kwok S., Dopita M., Sutherland R., eds, Vol. 209, Planetary Nebulae: Their Evolution and Role in the Universe. p. 339

Liu X. W., Storey P. J., Barlow M. J., Danziger I. J., Cohen M., Bryce M., 2000, MNRAS, 312, 585

Liu X. W., Barlow M. J., Zhang Y., Bastin R. J., Storey P. J., 2006, MNRAS, 368, 1959

Magrini L., Coccato L., Stanghellini L., Casasola V., Galli D., 2016, A&A, 588, A91

Maiolino R., Mannucci F., 2019, A&ARv, 27, 3

Méndez-Delgado J. E., Amayo A., Arellano-Córdova K. Z., Esteban C., García-Rojas J., Carigi L., Delgado-Inglada G., 2022, MNRAS, 510, 4436

Méndez-Delgado J. E., et al., 2023a, MNRAS, 523, 2952

Méndez-Delgado J. E., Esteban C., García-Rojas J., Kreckel K., Peimbert M., 2023b, Nature, 618, 249

Nicholls D. C., Dopita M. A., Sutherland R. S., 2012, ApJ, 752, 148
O'Dell C. R., Peimbert M., Peimbert A., 2003, AJ, 125, 2590
Osterbrock D. E., Ferland G. J., 2006, Astrophysics of gaseous nebulae and active galactic nuclei
Peña M., Ruiz-Escobedo F., Rechy-García J. S., García-Rojas J., 2017, MNRAS, 472, 1182
Peebles P. J., 1966a, Phys. Rev. Lett., 16, 410
Peebles P. J. E., 1966b, ApJ, 146, 542
Peimbert M., 1967, ApJ, 150, 825
Peimbert A., 2003, ApJ, 584, 735
Peimbert A., Peimbert M., 2013, ApJ, 778, 89
Peimbert M., Sarmiento A., Fierro J., 1991, PASP, 103, 815
Peimbert M., Peimbert A., Delgado-Inglada G., 2017, PASP, 129, 082001
Péquignot D., Walsh J. R., Zijlstra A. A., Dudziak G., 2000, A&A, 361, L1
Perez E., 1997, MNRAS, 290, 465
Richer M. G., Georgiev L., Arrieta A., Torres-Peimbert S., 2013, ApJ, 773, 133
Richer M. G., Arrieta A., Arias L., Castañeda-Carlos L., Torres-Peimbert S., López J. A., Galindo A., 2022, AJ, 164, 243
Rodríguez M., García-Rojas J., 2010, ApJ, 708, 1551
Rubin R. H., 1986, ApJ, 309, 334
Seaton M. J., 1968, MNRAS, 139, 129
Shaver P. A., McGee R. X., Newton L. M., Danks A. C., Pottasch S. R., 1983, MNRAS, 204, 53
Stanghellini L., Haywood M., 2018, ApJ, 862, 45
Stasińska G., 2002, in Henney W. J., Franco J., Martos M., eds, Revista Mexicana de Astronomia y Astrofisica Conference Series Vol. 12, Revista Mexicana de Astronomia y Astrofisica Conference Series. pp 62–69 (arXiv:astro-ph/0102403), doi:10.48550/arXiv.astro-ph/0102403
Stasińska G., 2005, A&A, 434, 507
Stasińska G., Szczerba R., 2001, A&A, 379, 1024
Stasińska G., Morisset C., Simón-Díaz S., Bresolin F., Schaerer D., Brandl B., 2013, A&A, 551, A82
Storey P. J., Sochi T., Bastin R., 2017, MNRAS, 470, 379
Torres-Peimbert S., Peimbert M., Pena M., 1990, A&A, 233, 540
Truran J. W., Cameron A. G. W., 1971, Ap&SS, 14, 179
Wagoner R. V., 1973, ApJ, 179, 343
Wesson R., Liu X. W., Barlow M. J., 2003, MNRAS, 340, 253
Wesson R., Liu X. W., Barlow M. J., 2005, MNRAS, 362, 424
Wesson R., Jones D., García-Rojas J., Boffin H. M. J., Corradi R. L. M., 2018, MNRAS, 480, 4589
Wyse A. B., 1942, ApJ, 95, 356
Yuan H. B., Liu X. W., Péquignot D., Rubin R. H., Ercolano B., Zhang Y., 2011, MNRAS, 411, 1035
Zhang Y., Ercolano B., Liu X. W., 2007, A&A, 464, 631

Planetary Nebulae: A Universal Toolbox in the Era of Precision Astrophysics
Proceedings IAU Symposium No. 384, 2025
O. De Marco, A. Zijlstra & R. Szczerba, eds.
doi:10.1017/S1743921324000371

Astronomical outreach and education in marginalised and indigenous communities: astronomy as a tool for social development

Arianna Cortesi[1,2], Claudia Mignone[3], Alan Alves-Brito[4], Gracy Moreira[5], Claudia Magnani[6], Nilson Moreira[5], Guilherme Moreira[5], Roberto Romeiro[7], André Victor[8], Maria Clara Herdinger Lourenço[2], Gabriela Rufino Travasso[2], Ana Gomes[7] and Lorena Anastácio[7]

[1]Instituto de Física, Universidade Federal do Rio de Janeiro, Brazil

[2]Observatório do Valongo, Universidade Federal do Rio de Janeiro, Rio de Janeiro, Brazil

[3]Istituto Nazionale di Astrofisica, Rome, Italy

[4]Institute of Physics, Federal University of Rio Grande do Sul, Porto Alegre, Brazil

[5]Organização Cultural Remanescentes de Tia Ciata, Rio de Janeiro, Brazil

[6]Independent Researcher

[7]Federal University of Minas Gerais, Belo Horizonte, Brazil

[8]Universidade do Estado do Rio de Janeiro Centro de Tecnologia e Ciências Escola Superior de Desenho Industrial, Rio de Janeiro, Brazil

Abstract. The way we look at the sky is connected to the cosmological paradigm embraced by the society we live in. On the other hand, several astronomical concepts reinforce the idea of a common humanity. Yet, scientific outreach is frequenty reaching out only to a specific part of the world population, often excluding people living in extreme social vulnerability, victims of violence and prejudice, fighting for their lives and for the right of living according to their traditions. We present two outreach projects, developed in Brazil, funded by the Office of Astronomy for Development (OAD) of the International Astronomical Union (IAU), i.e. "Under Other Skies" & "OruMbya", which tackle the importance of ethno-astronomy, and the collaboration with leaders and cultural agents of marginalised communities. We also describe an educational project born in the favela of Cantagalo Pavão Pavãozinho (PPG), in Rio de Janeiro, during the COVID19 pandemic, which started a collaboration with local educators and artists to offer classes of astronomy and English language to children in the favela.

Keywords. Astronomical outreach; astronomy for development; Social Development Goals

1. Introduction

The sky offers humanity a window to study the origin and evolution of the universe, from the Big Bang till the formation of the solar system and planet Earth. Beneath this sky, the contemporary socio-economical structure developed during centuries and millennia, leading to the highly unequal distribution of resources, and life quality and expectancy we observe nowadays, see Figure 1 for a global comparison between light pollution levels, population size, and indexes of violence. In this context, astronomy can be used as a unifying tool for the development and promotion of peace among peoples, fighting inequality and supporting cultural integration, as well

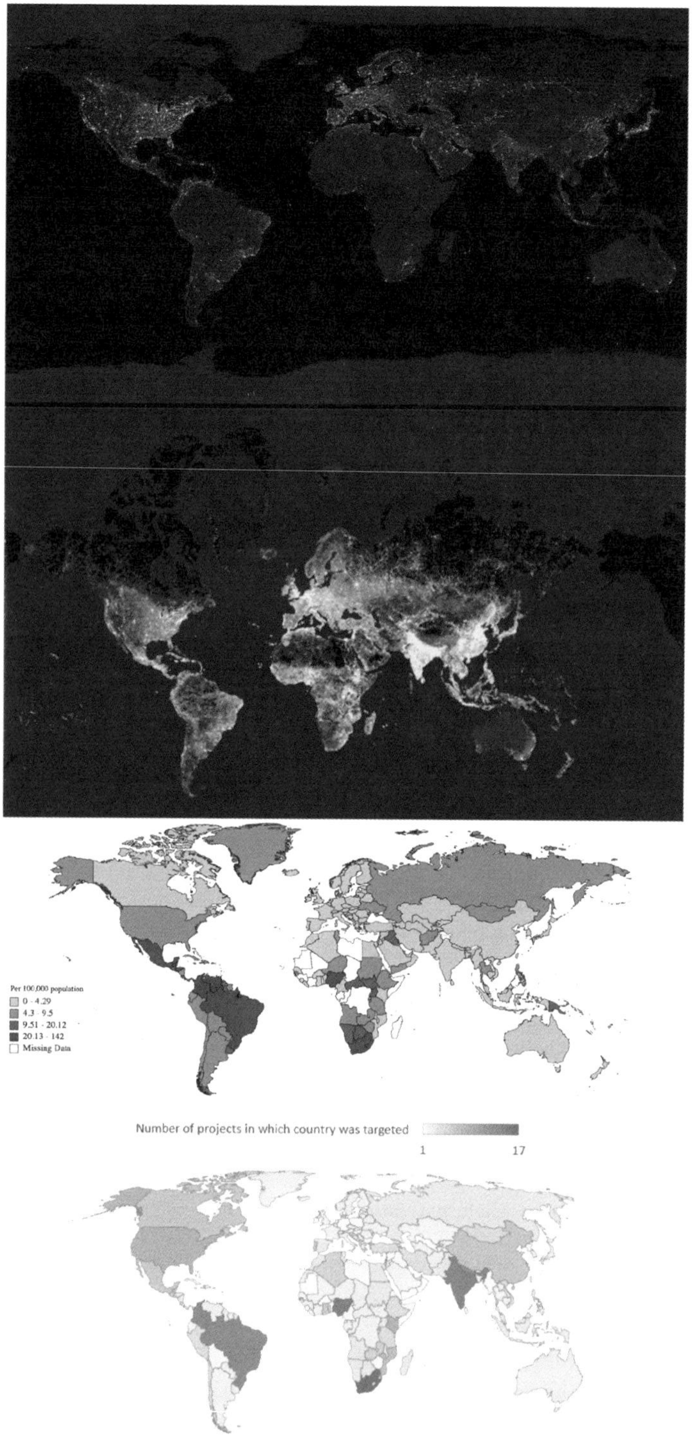

Figure 1. Top: A global view of Earth at night, compiled from over 400 satellite images (Image Credit: NASA/NOAA). Second row: Global population density, reference Period: March 11, 2020-November 01, 2023 (Image Credit `https://images.app.goo.gl/1T2a9nyfvMSnJAiT7`). Third row: Intentional homicides, per 100,000 population (Image Credit: World Bank SDGs database). Bottom: Number of OAD projects in different countries (Image Credit: `https://www.astro4dev.org/projects-impact/`).

as the restoration of dignity to 'other' conceptions of the world against the prejudices connected to a unimodal vision of history. For example, astronomy based projects have been supporting a multicultural approach to education, developing the synergy between scientific and cultural perspectives to produce an 'experimental togetherness' (Keller, Catherine & Daniell, Anne (eds.) 2002). Moreover, pioneers works have been promoting environment preservation, as by contributing to the world-wide knowledge of Brazilian indigenous lands, which are target of exploitation and deforestation.

In particular, the Office of Astronomy for Development† is a joint project of the International Astronomical Union and the South African National Research Foundation with the support of the Department of Science and Technology, which aims to pursue social development through funding and coordinating projects based on astronomy. Outcomes and deliverables of these projects, such as increasing in the literacy levels, or knowledge of astronomy, and production of novel curriculum resources, or teacher training material, encompass different perspectives. From a teaching/school perspective they support the training of teachers in the field of intercultural education, promoting the principle of inextricable connection between different areas of teaching, research and education of undergraduate students. From a community point of view, they promote a peaceful and welcoming environment in specific areas (such as marginalised and vulnerable communities), often suffering a historical profile of material and symbolic violence, leveling cultural and social differences, by increasing knowledge of cultural astronomy heritage, as a key aspect of the culture and daily life. From an academic perspective, debating, in an interdisciplinary way, scientific and cultural concepts on the visible sky, linking past and present, and the connections between the sky (cultural identity) and the Earth (territory, diaspora), these projects strengthen the relations between the University and School sectors, as well as with the Society at large. Moreover, given the world wide connections provided by the IAU/OAD, these innovative projects promote intercultural dialogues between knowledge among continents.

One of the countries hosting a high number of OADs projects is Brazil, see Figure 1, bottom panel, which due to its colonial past, suffered some of the most tragic episodes of human history, such as the transatlantic trade of enslaved people from Africa, leading to one of the largest African diaspora, the massacre of indigenous populations and a violent deforestation. Scars of this past still bleed in Brazilian present and are clearly visible in the inequality of the society, the racism and violence toward Black‡ and indigenous population, and the continuous devastation of the Amazon forest. Moreover, while astronomical outreach is becoming a fundamental step toward the integration of scientific concepts in everyday life and a point of connection between citizens and scientists (Simpson, Robert, Kevin R. Page, and David De Roure 2014), it is often restricted to the wealthy part of society (DAWSON, E. 2014). Recently, several projects started being created together with people that have long been kept out of the formal scientific process, fostering marginalised societies as examples where we can understand, learn and make new science (Benyei, P. 2023). In this work we present three projects developed in Brazil within the OAD/IAU framework and financial support, co-created in collaboration with marginalised communities, tackling several SDG goals such as quality education (SDG-4), reduced inequality within and among countries (SDG-10), promoting sustained, inclusive and sustainable economic growth, full and productive employment, and "decent work for all" (SDG-8), peace, justice, and strong institutions (SDG-17), "partnership for the Goals" (SDG-18), and gender equality (SDG-5)¶.

† `https://www.iau.org/development/oad/`
‡ `https://flacso.org.br/files/2016/08/Mapa2016_armas_web-1.pdf`
¶ See: `https://sdgs.un.org/goals` for more details on the SDG goals.

Figure 2. Left: A drawing representing the chant 'Brother Sun, brother moon'. Right: A drawing representing the chant 'The star women'.

2. Under other skies: dialogues of different cosmological paradigms

This project aims to bridge different visions of the Universe we live in by collecting, in a webpage, indigenous knowledge, as narrated in traditional chants (as sung by pajes - spiritual leaders of the villages), carried out by the Other Skies team in an indigenous village in Minas Gerais, Brazil. The webpage also contains drawings of the stories (chants) created by indigenous professors, during a workshop on illustrations (see Figure 2 as an example), developed in the context of the course Educação Indígena "Saberes Indígenas nas Escolas" at the Federal University of Minas Gerais (UFMG). The project is producing cultural and astronomical materials for indigenous and non-indigenous schools, and the participants are indigenous professors of Maxakali and other ethnic origins.

The Other Skies team is composed of two indigenous professors and chapes (leaders) of the Village Aldeia Verde (BR), four anthropologists from the department of education of UFMG (BR), four astronomers (BR and UK), one educator and one creative practitioner in community engagement and citizen science (UK).

The project was mostly developed during the COVID19 emergency, and the quarantine regime in the Brazilian territory. In the specific case of indigenous Villages in Brazil, FUNAI (Fundação nacional do Índio) with a 'Boletim de Serviço do 17 de março de 2020' resolved that: 'The granting of new authorisations to enter indigenous lands is suspended, with the exception of those necessary for the continuity of the provision of essential services to communities, as assessed by the competent authority of the Regional Coordination - CR'†. Due to complex conditions created in the first months of the isolation dictated by the pandemic, our collaborator professors of the village Aldeia Verde, together with dozens of families of the village, moved to a new village, with no infrastructure. As a consequence, to carry out the project as a virtual collaboration, it was necessary to install an internet connection in the new village and to provide instruments of communication. We applied for - and obtained - an extra-grant from IAU/OAD and we started looking for internet providers in this remote territory. Normally internet radio connection is used in this region of Brazil, but the existence of a gigantic stone between the transmitter and the village was rendering the use of the radio impossible. While we were looking for an alternative possibility, such as satellite internet (HUGHESNET) or

† Fica suspensa a concessão de novas autorizações de entrada nas terras indígenas, à exceção das necessárias à continuidade da prestação de serviços essenciais às comunidades, conforme avaliação pela autoridade competente da Coordenação Regional - CR.

Figure 3. Left: Two 10 meters high antennas for internet connection being built in the village Aldeia Nova, funded by the IAU/OAD extra grant. Right: Children at the artesian well in The Aldeia Escola Floresta.

bringing cable internet to the new village, the possibility arose that the indigenous community would move toward another land, due to the presence of a dam near the village that might compromise their safety and peaceful living. The internet installation was then paused, till the land problem was resolved. Even so, through the process of moving during the pandemic, several materials have been produced as a short movie shot by our collaborator Sueli Maxakali and edited by André Victor and Cristiano Araújo, which aimed to record an encounter of pajes in the village to discuss the COVID19 emergency† Our team also gave support to the preparation of English subtitles.

In April 2021, a new land was found, named Aldeia Nova, where the people could permanently reside, with running water and enough land to live, according to their way of life. We successfully installed two antennas and a stable connection for the entire community. Figure 3, left panel, shows pictures of the installation of the antennas. The connection was successfully working and used by the community. It made possible the discussion of the Undergraduate thesis of Sueli Maxakali transmitted live on YouTube (`https://www.youtube.com/watch?v=0fsc5M3af14`). It also allowed the realisation of several online courses and meetings with the authorities and other institutions (such as, for example, the organisation of the exposition of the Art Work by Sueli Maxakali, at the Biennale Art Exposition in São Paulo - September-December 2021).

On the 17th of September 2021 Dr. Roberto Romero visited the village Aldeia Nova in order to coordinate the collection of material (drawings and chants) in collaboration with four young professors of the village. During the visit of Dr. Romero, the community moved to a new Aldeia, where they are building the Village Forest School‡. With the OAD grant we were able to support the construction of an artesian well, lead by the Theofilo Otoni Caritas. Figure 3, right panel, pictures some children of the Aldeia using the well.

The result of the project, apart for being collected in the website, was published in a paper for an on-line blog, Big Data from the South Research Initiative (BigDataSur), 'a space for theoretical and empirical exchange on the challenges of datafication and massive data collection as they unfold in the plurality of South(s) inhabiting our increasingly complex world'. Specifically, we contributed to the section of the blog called 'COVID-19 from the margins' dedicated to forgotten and silenced voices of marginalized and disadvantaged communities and populations. Our contribution, entitled 'Under Other Skies:

† `https://drive.google.com/file/d/19jWg0bkVZNvFdCUN5-H_IQzsPGVclvsp/view?usp=sharing`.

‡ `https://aldeiaescolafloresta.org/`

Figure 4. A Screenshot of one of the webinars realised during the OruMbya project, picturing the different speakers present, representing different sectors of knowledge

Astronomy as a Tool to Face COVID-19-Induced Isolation in the Indigenous Village of Aldeia Verde, Brazil', reports the story of the project through the pandemic and importance of the support of IAU/OAD, as well as the ever-present sustained support of the department of education of UFMG, especially Roberto Romero, Ana Maria Gomes and Paola Gobetti. Our contribution was also published in the book 'COVID-19 from the margin, pandemic invisibilities, policies, and resistance in the datafied society', which resulted by collecting all the stories from the blog.

3. OruMbya - Astronomy as fuel of life: the resilience of stars in Yoruba, Afro-Brazilian and Indigenous Cosmogony

OruMbya (Orum, sky in Yorubá, and Mbya, a Brazilian Guarani ethnicity) is a project to celebrate Astronomy as the fuel of life, in which the stories of the stars are preserved in the resilience of people from three different continents (South America, Europe and Africa) and shared over months, through scientific and cultural activities focused on the dissemination of knowledge, promotion of social inclusion and sustainable development in the context of PLOAD (Portuguese Language Office of Astronomy for Development). In its first realisation, lead by Doctor Honoris Causa Gracy Mary Moreira, the hosts were the cultural centre "Remanescentes da Tia Ciata", whose aim is the defence and preservation of afro-brazilian memories in Rio, and the centenary Observatory of Valongo (OV), one of the oldest institutions of Astronomy in Brazil. The two institutions are located in Morro da Conceição, an iconic place of resistance and reaffirmation of black identity, one of the most socially vulnerable urban regions in Rio. UFRGS (The Federal University of Rio Grande do Sul) is the third partner of the project.

The project was developed by taking into account three possible degrees of impact of COVID-19 on social distancing: none, moderate and total. The rules of social distancing changed in Brazil during the nine months of development of the project. Specifically, we held all of the webinars online, see Figure 4, apart from the last seminar that was held in mixed mode (i.e., most of the participants of the projects joined together at the observatory, while the event was streamed in the usual platform). The 5 webinars (with teachers, students, Indigenous, Quilombolas and Favelas representatives and astronomers) connected people of very different cultural backgrounds, who share common goals of a just, peaceful and green future, telling stories and sharing knowledge about culture and the sky, creating new multicultural collaborations and alliances. We had more than 17 speakers from different segments (in even number) participating in the webinars and more than 1000 total views. Two hundreds and two persons filled the online questionnaire and sent us a brief summary of their thoughts on the project and the subjects discussed, actively contributing to the project.

At the observatory we held a workshop of plantation of species from the indigenous and Afro-Brazilian culture in collaboration with 15 children from the territory (the number is restricted to meet the measures of social distancing due to the pandemic) and their teacher, coming from a nearby favela (Favela da Providencia - ONG Impacto das Cores). Moreover, we offered 2 online extension courses of 2hrs each for teachers, creating new literature and enriching the possible way of study offered by the observatory, the university and the ORTC, creating new knowledge. Finally, we produced two videos to promote the project and the territory, changing the vision of the little Africa region of Rio de Janeiro, fighting for a renaissance of the area and preservation of its culture and monuments, as the world heritage Cais do Valongo, which risks losing this status. The pilot project sprouted in several subsequent projects as 'Orumbya -Mulheres do mundo sócio-cultural-tecnológico' (PI: Gracy Mary Moreira), a project aimed at girls aged between 14 and 20, interested in science. Designed in collaboration between Casa da Tia Ciata, the Valongo Observatory (OV/UFRJ), the Federal University of Rio Grande do Sul and the State University of Rio de Janeiro (UERJ), the project was awarded the 2nd edition of the "STEM Girls: training future scientists"† project, promoted by the British Council Brazil and the Carlos Chagas Foundation, see Figure 5 for an example of the flyer promoting the classes, presenting the two professors, from different fields of knowledge. In 2023, we are developing the project 'OruMbya - a library of silenced voices‡' (PI: Alan Alves Brito), whose main goal is to strengthen primary and secondary education in science, through equity and equal opportunities for children and young people living in extreme social vulnerability.

4. Closer to the Sky

This project aims at co-producing scientific knowledge in collaboration between astronomers and artists/educators living in the favela of Cantagalo Pavão e Pavãosinho (PPG), Rio de Janeiro (Brazil), for children, teenagers and young adults of the community. It is the result of the close collaboration between The PPG Astronomical Club, whose logo, see Figure 6, pictures an artistic view of the PPG community in the night sky, and the social project 'Ninho das aguias'¶, where classes and night sky observations are held.

Favelas in Rio de Janeiro state are often located on hills, which served as refuge for enslaved people - after the abolition of slavery (1888) - and immigrants, who worked for downtown citizens. The Law of lands (1850) prevented unoccupied lands to be owned through labour and provided government subsidies for the arrival of foreign settlers to be hired in the country, further devaluing the work of black men and women.As a result, favelas today are mostly composed of a black population, surviving decades of persecutions and low income while defending, preserving and creating a unique culture rooted in African origins that reverberates into music and the arts. Children in favelas, due to social and economical inequality and racial discrimination, have fewer opportunity for

† Science, Technology, Engineering and Mathematics
‡ `https://www.astro4dev.org/orumbya-library-of-silenced-voices/`
¶ `https://www.instagram.com/ninhodasaguiasppg/`

Figure 5. A flyer advertising the first class of the course 'Orumbya Mulheres' (`https://ov.ufrj.br/orumbya-mulheres-do-mundo-socio-cultural-tecnologico/`).

personal development and professional realization. They attend public schools where in 2021, according to SAEB†, students do not reach a satisfactory level in Portuguese language (69%) and mathematics (95%). They hardly have access to after-school courses and do not tend to see themselves represented in the academic community. This produces a disadvantage in access to higher education and consequently in opportunities for satisfactory employment. Offering extracurricular courses and cultural experiences to students in the PPG, we wish to enrich their school curriculum and strengthen the chance that they stay in education after secondary school. A key element of the courses is providing positive role models of scientists from afro-descendant backgrounds, reinforced by the presence of local artists and educators, thus endorsing their role within the academic community. Specifically, we aim at using the arts and the act of embodiment (Radford, Luis. 2011) as a tool to improve the learning experience (see Figure 7 for an example of a workshop on the stellar life cycle).

The project also creates work opportunities for local artists and educators, who will offer workshops rooted in favela culture, while at the same time creating novel, decolonial course ware based on contextualised science, i.e, materials that use the context

† `https://www.gov.br/inep/pt-br/areas-de-atuacao/avaliacao-e-exames-educacionais/saeb/resultados`

Figure 6. Artistic representation of the night sky in the favela do Cantagalo Pavão e Pavãozinho (Rio de Janeiro, Brazil), used as logo of the astronomical club.

of marginalised societies as examples where we can understand, learn and make science. The material developed within the project is shared as 'open educational resources'. In the next year, five students will be trained as astroguides, in collaboration with Astronera, a project committed to the scientifically accurate and innovative dissemination of astronomy, it was established by Shweta Kulkarni (Bangalore, India)†. Their training will benefit from visits and courses at the local Planetarium and Museum of Astronomy.

5. Discussion and conclusion

Stengers (2002) underlined how multicultural approaches to education are fundamental for pursuing sustainable development. The projects discussed here propose a dialogue between different visions of the sky, opposing the idea that one scientific paradigm is superior to another, following the steps of many fundamental works, see, for example, Hugh-Jones, S. (1979); Walmir Cardoso's (2007); Oscar T. Matsuura (2013); Afonso, G. B. (2014); Alan Alves-Brito et al. (2019). The team of researchers involved in all the projects is heterogeneous in gender, ethnicity and field of study (comprising astronomers, anthropologists, school teachers, indigenous school teachers and researchers, artists and museum managers), generating a fair and respectful approach to the subject, with participants carrying out the activities in full collaboration.

These projects are examples of the heterogeneity of astronomical knowledge. Through their intercultural approach, they promote an understanding of the different astronomical paradigms, and push back against a superficial approach to science and social biodiversity‡. Introducing those concepts in official centres of knowledge and publishing the material in university-based web pages, proceedings and various media of communication is a way of fighting stereotypes and reducing discrimination, contributing to a more

† `https://www.astronera.org/`

‡ We refer the readers to the projects listed in the OAD/IAU webpage (`https://www.astro4dev.org/projects-search/` for an extended and global perspective.

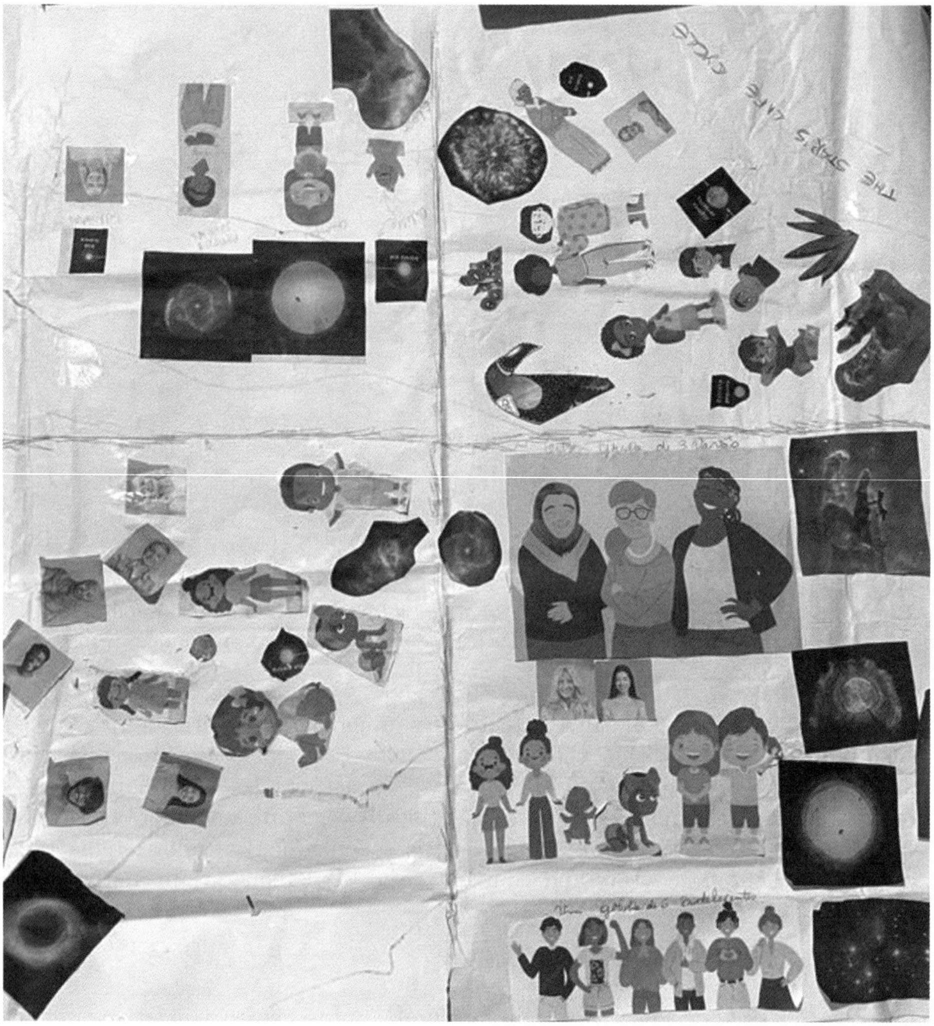

Figure 7. Example of a cooperative student work aimed at comparing the phases of life of stars and of humans.

informed understanding of indigenous people and marginalised communities and their way of life, increasing the inhabitants' political power. In addition, these projects raise awareness of exploitation and deforestation on national and global scales. The activities are included in the university programs, when possible, such as for example at FIEI (Intercultural Education for Indigenous Teachers) of the UFMG, opening new lines of academic study, and initiating a collaboration between the departments of astronomy and education.

The main challenges of these projects are (i) to promote, through Astronomy in Cultures, the intercultural dialogue between scientists and researchers from other fields and the general public; and (ii) to promote a new inclusive scientific literacy focused on the initial and continuing teaching training process in Brazil, where the contribution of underrepresented people (women, black and indigenous) are recognised and valued in the first place.

On the one hand, the objectives of social development, pursued by each institution independently, are supported and expanded through the collaboration between them, by promoting astronomy and science as part of the culture (race, gender, class, education) in Morro da Conceição, an iconic place of resistance and reaffirmation of black identity, one of the most socially vulnerable urban regions in Rio, in the favela of Cantagalo Pavão Pavãozinho (Rio de Janeiro, Bazil) and in the indigenous Florest School Village (Estado de Minas Gerais, Brazil). On the other hand, the virtual activities give the projects more visibility and allow us to invest not only in the training of teachers around Brazil, but also to expand our cultural/educational projects (black power, memory, cultural patrimony) to other lusophone countries (Portugal, and countries in Africa and Asia).

Focusing on the creation of a novel scientific literacy, teacher training, and the intercontinental cultural astronomy exchange, working with positive models of women and LGBT+ people in Astronomy, making their work visible, and helping people from different social backgrounds to develop their skills, opening access to the observatory to the afro-brasilian and indigenous communities, explicitly recognising the scientific and social relevance of their inherited knowledge, promoting the sustainable economic growth of ONGs, globally advertising the existence of these marginalised communities, creating a path towards the community revival of vulnerable areas of the city, are some of the main points tackled by these projects.

Astronomy is a unique science for its potential to inspire and fascinate people around the world. Recent studies, including an IAU OAD flagship project (Vertue, D. G. 2022), have been investigating the restorative power of stargazing and contemplating the universe to people's mental well-being. These initiatives promote local artists and educators and create a local network of cultural projects inspired by and making use of astronomical knowledge, putting them in contact with universities and research centres in the city of Rio and beyond, opening the possibility for future collaborations and employment. They support and foster local business, and create a safe knowledge space where youth feel welcome and have access to both material and immaterial resources, encouraging them to continue their studies in higher education, and achieve better paid jobs.

Measuring the impact of astronomy for development projects poses several challenges in terms of time, cost, accurate data and cooperation (Chapman, S. 2015). This is especially relevant when working with marginalised communities in fragile contexts, in order to protect these communities and their members. For the Orumbya projects, the participants, from very different segments, were encouraged to share narratives, videos and pictures, to capture their perception of the world. The webinars had more than a 1000 total views and the online courses were attended by 30 school professors and university stuff. Finally, we had the presencial participation of 15 children from a nearby favela, as well as their teacher, during the plantation of the allotment. Under Other Skies project is still ongoing. The stories of the Maxakali cosmogony as well as their culture and fight for land preservation have been presented in several conferences, as at the world's largest conference on astronomy communication: Communicating Astronomy with the Public 2022 (CAP 2022). Moreover, the project had a concrete impact in the day life of the indigenous village, with the construction of the two antennas for internet provision and the implementation of an artesian well. As for the more recent project, Closer to the Sky, a broader evaluation plan is envisioned, monitoring the wellbeing and self-esteem of children with support from medical and public anthropology, as well as course attendance of children and their long-term schooling activities, and the activities of the newly trained astroguides as they search for new work opportunities. The education interventions will be monitored with support from science education experts by evaluating the learning experience of children and teenagers pre- and post-course through questionnaires for self and peer assessment to empower learners and promote collaboration. We also envision conducting focus groups at the end with adults who have taken part in the project as collaborators, as well as families of children who have attended the course, to assess their perceptions of the project and of its impact on the children and the community.

By rediscovering cultural astronomy, for example traditional constellations, telling their stories - and the science underneath - in many different artistic formats, as well as empowering people often discriminated against on the basis of their colour and social origins, these projects centre them as the person of knowledge, promoting cultural dissemination, as well as opening the doors of Universities, Museums and Planetariums to people who are often excluded due to prejudice, cost and content perceived as "not for us" (DAWSON, E. 2014). These projects change who makes science, promoting self-representation among marginalised groups. Only co-creating knowledge by and for people that have long been kept out of the formal scientific process, will research truly be open.

We acknowledge funding from FAPERJ grant E-26/200.607 e 210.371/2022(270993) and of the OAD/IAU projects "Under Other Skies" and "OruMbya". We thank Ramasamy Venugopal for the kind support.

References

Alan Alves-Brito et al., Astronomy for development in Portuguese-speaking countries, Nature Astronomy, volume 3, pages 366–368 (2019)

Afonso, G. B., O céu dos índios do Brasil, Anais da 66ª reunião anual da SBPC - Rio Branco, AC - julho/2014

Benyei, P., Skarlatidou, A., Argyriou, D., Hall, R., Theilade, I., Turreira-García, N., Latreche, D., Albert, A., Berger, D., Cartró-Sabaté, M., Chang, J., Chiaravalloti, R., Cortesi, A., Danielsen, F., Haklay, M. (Mordechai)., Jacobi, E., Nigussie, A., Reyes-García, V., Rodrigues, E., Sauini, T., Shadrin, V., Siqueira, A., Supriadi, M., Tillah, M., Tofighi-Niaki, A., Vronski, N. and Woods, T., 2023. Challenges, Strategies, and Impacts of Doing Citizen Science with Marginalised and Indigenous Communities: Reflections from Project Coordinators. Citizen Science: Theory and Practice, 8(1), p. 21. DOI: https://doi.org/10.5334/cstp.514

Chapman S, Catala L, Mauduit J-C, Govender K, Louw-Potgieter J. (2015). Monitoring and evaluating astronomy outreach programmes: Challenges and solutions. S Afr J Sci. 111 (5/6), http://dx.doi.org/10.17159/sajs.2015/20140112

DAWSON, E. (2014), "Not Designed for Us": How Science Museums and Science Centers Socially Exclude Low-Income, Minority Ethnic Groups. Sci. Ed., 98: 981–1008. https://doi.org/10.1002/sce.21133

Hugh-Jones, S., The palm and the Pleiades: initiation and cosmology in northwest Amazonia. London: Cambridge University Press, 1979

Keller, Catherine & Daniell, Anne (eds.) (2002). Process and Difference: Between Cosmological and Poststructuralist Postmodernisms. State University of New York Press.

Oscar T. Matsuura, História da Astronomia no Brasil (2013), Capítulo 3. ASTRONOMIA INDÍGENA, MAST/MCTI

Radford, Luis. (2011). 4-17 EMBODIMENT, PERCEPTION AND SYMBOLS IN THE DEVELOPMENT OF EARLY ALGEBRAIC THINKING.

Simpson, Robert, Kevin R. Page, and David De Roure. 2014. Zooniverse: Observing the World's Largest Citizen Science Platform. In Proceedings of the 23rd International Conference on World Wide Web, 1049–54. New York, NY, USA: ACM. https://doi.org/10.1145/2567948.2579215.

I. Stengers, Beyond Conversation, Process and Difference, Chapter 10, C. Keller and A. Daniell, State University of New York (2002)

Dominic Gregory Vertue, The Intersection Between Astronomy and Mental Health, Mental Health Matters, 9, 4, 19-20, 2022, doi = 10.10520/ejc-menhm_v9_n4_a9

Walmir Cardoso's, O Céu dos Tukano na escola Yupuri, Construindo um calendário dinâmico, PhD thesis PUC/SP (2007)

Planetary Nebulae: A Universal Toolbox in the Era of Precision Astrophysics
Proceedings IAU Symposium No. 384, 2025
O. De Marco, A. Zijlstra & R. Szczerba, eds.
doi:10.1017/S1743921323005318

Exploring Planetary Nebulae in the dwarf galaxy VCC 1249 using MUSE data

Sophie Penger, Johanna Hartke, Magda Arnaboldi and Ana Inés Ennis

University of Cologne, Germany, European Southern Observatory, Germany, Finnish Centre for Astronomy with ESO (FINCA), Finland, Waterloo Centre for Astrophysics, Canada
email: sophie.antonia_penger@yahoo.de

Abstract. This study focuses on investigating planetary nebulae (PNe) within the dwarf galaxy VCC 1249, located in the halo of the early-type galaxy (ETG) M49, by utilizing data obtained from the Multi-Unit Spectroscopic Explorer (MUSE). The integral-field spectroscopy capabilities of MUSE enable the identification of individual planetary nebulae. The interaction of VCC 1249 with the cluster-dominant galaxy M49 in the Virgo Subcluster B is driving this project, as it offers a unique opportunity to explore how high-density environments influence the properties and fate of low-mass galaxies. To identify potential PNe candidates within VCC 1249, the method proposed by Roth et al. (2021) is employed. Through this approach, ten candidates exhibiting features consistent with PNe properties have been identified.

Keywords. galaxies: dwarf, halos; ISM: planetary nebula

1. Introduction

The dwarf irregular galaxy VCC 1249 (presented in figure 1) is located within the extended halo of the early-type galaxy (ETG) M49 in the Virgo Cluster. By exploring this interaction, we are particularly interested in understanding the shape of the dark matter potential-whether it is cuspy or cored (Errani et al. 2015). This factor significantly influences the survival of satellite galaxies, with studies indicating increased mass loss in dwarf galaxies within cored halos (Peñarrubia et al. 2010). This investigation serves as a robust foundation for comparing observational results with theoretical predictions from galaxy dynamics.

Here, we are using a cube from the Multi-Unit Spectroscopic Explorer (MUSE) (Bacon et al. 2010) centered on the dwarf galaxy VCC 1249. Planetary nebulae (PNe) are employed as tracers, using their 5007 Å [OIII] absorption line. This does not only provide insight into the interaction but also extends the existing PNe catalogue of M49 (Hartke et al. 2018), who initially detected three PNe within the field of view of the MUSE cube. Additionally we are utilizing the IFU data to measure absorption- and emission-line kinematics to map the interaction of the galaxies.

2. Methods

The MUSE data cube can be interpreted as a multitude of sliced wavelength images. Given the redshift and potential velocity variations in relation to the dwarf galaxy, we perform a detailed analysis at various wavelengths around 5007 Å. For this, we are employing the differential emission-line filtering (DELF) method (Roth et al. 2021). It is beneficial due to its high signal-to-noise ratio and accuracy compared to conventional PN detection using narrowband imaging. Other than in the original method, where archival data with

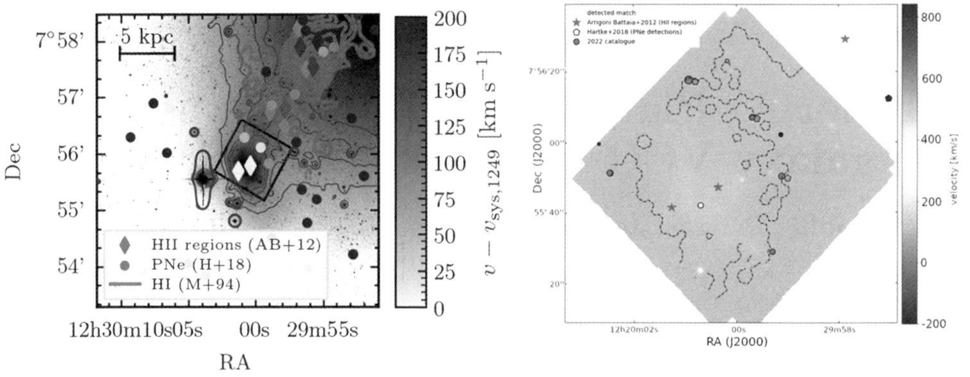

Figure 1. *Left panel:* VCC 1249 (g-band image, Ferrarese et al. (2012)). The grey contours show the stellar density, PNe marked as circles, HII and HI as diamonds and contours respectively. Adapted from (Hartke et al. (2018). *Right panel:* Velocities of PNe candidates plotted on the r-band image, color-coded from blue to red. Underlying contour corresponds to 510 km/s of the continuum velocity. PNe catalogue (Hartke et al. (2018), marked with pentagones) and the HII region catalogue (Arrigoni Battaia et al. (2012), marked as green stars).

lower resolution was used, we used two consecutive slices as a threshold to detect a PN candidate. The selection is based on the quality of Gaussian emission lines, resulting in a preliminary PNe catalogue (approximately 100 sources) shown in the right panel of figure 1.

3. Results

Upon comparing our catalogue with the existing work by Hartke et al. (2018), three matches are identified. Their velocities are suggesting the likely binding of these candidates to VCC1249 ($390 \pm 30\,\mathrm{km\ s^{-1}}$ (SDSS)). The right panel of figure 1 shows the $510\,\mathrm{km\ s^{-1}}$ continuum velocity contour of the dwarf that lies close to the candidates (their velocities with respect to the systemic velocity). We compare these detections to the HII region catalogue by Arrigoni Battaia et al. (2012) without detecting matches, suggesting that the candidates are genuine PNe.

4. Outlook

In the course of the Master thesis, the PNe detections will be further validated by measuring the abundance of strong [OIII] emitters and creating emission-line ratio diagrams (Ciardullo et al. 2002). Additionally, other emission-line objects in the cube will be looked for. Using the confirmed PNe detections, the Planetary Nebula Luminosity Function (PNLF) will be established. To describe the interaction, we will compare our observations with a dynamical model of the system that will be developed as in Errani et al. (2015).

Acknowledgements

Based on observations collected at the European Organisation for Astronomical Research in the Southern Hemisphere under ESO programme 108.21XS.001 (PI: Hartke).

Supplementary material

To view supplementary material for this article, please visit https://doi.org/10.1017/S1743921323005318

References

Arrigoni Battaia, F., Gavazzi, G., Fumagalli, M., et al. 2012, *A&A*, 543, A112
Bacon, R., Accardo, M., Adjali, L., et al. 2010, in Society of Photo-Optical Instrumentation Engineers (SPIE) Conference Series, Vol. 7735, Ground-based and Airborne Instrumentation for Astronomy III, ed. I. S. McLean, S. K. Ramsay, & H. Takami, 773508
Ciardullo, R., Feldmeier, J. J., Jacoby, G. H., et al. 2002, *ApJ*, 577, 31
Errani, R., Penarrubia, J., & Tormen, G. 2015, *MNRAS*, 449, L46
Ferrarese, L., Côté, P., Cuillandre, J.-C., et al. 2012, *ApJS*, 200, 4
Hartke, J., Arnaboldi, M., Gerhard, O., et al. 2018, *A&A*, 616, A123
Peñarrubia, J., Benson, A. J., Walker, M. G., et al. 2010, *MNRAS*, 406, 1290
Roth, M. M., Jacoby, G. H., Ciardullo, R., et al. 2021, *ApJ*, 916, 21

Planetary Nebulae: A Universal Toolbox in the Era of Precision Astrophysics
Proceedings IAU Symposium No. 384, 2025
O. De Marco, A. Zijlstra & R. Szczerba, eds.
doi:10.1017/S1743921323005331

Characterising Planetary Nebulae in the Large Magellanic Clouds

Silvia Tosi[1,2,3], Flavia Dell'Agli[2], Devika Kamath[2,4], Letizia Stanghellini[5], Paolo Ventura[2,6], Domingo Aníbal García-Hernández[7,8] and Stefano Bianchi[1]

[1]Dipartimento di Matematica e Fisica, Università degli Studi Roma Tre, via della Vasca Navale 84, 00100, Roma, Italy
email: silvia.tosi@uniroma3.it

[2]INAF, Osservatorio Astronomico di Roma, Via Frascati 33, 00077, Monte Porzio Catone, Italy

[3]Istituto Nazionale di Fisica Nucleare, section of Frascati, Via Enrico Fermi, 54, 00044 Frascati, Italy

[4]Department of Physics and Astronomy, Macquarie University, Sydney, NSW 2109, Australia

[5]NSF's NOIRLab, 950 Cherry Ave., Tucson, AZ 85719, USA

[6]Istituto Nazionale di Fisica Nucleare, section of Perugia, Via A. Pascoli snc, 06123 Perugia, Italy

[7]Instituto de Astrofísica de Canarias (IAC), E-38205 La Laguna, Tenerife, Spain

[8]Departamento de Astrofísica, Universidad de La Laguna (ULL), E-38206 La Laguna, Tenerife, Spain

Abstract. Planetary nebulae (PNe) represent the final link in the chain of the gas and dust enrichment of low- and intermediate-mass stars. We present a comprehensive study of the relevant observational data of 10 PNe of the Large Magellanic Cloud (LMC). Analysing them from the UV to the IR, we characterise the nature of the central star (CS) and the dust contribution. We link these results to the evolutionary history of these sources.

Keywords. planetary nebulae, stars: abundances - stars: evolution

1. Introduction

The asymptotic giant branch (AGB) phase, crossed by all the stars between 1 and 8$M_\odot$ (i.e. low- and intermediate-mass stars, LIMS), is characterized by the ejection of a large amount of reprocessed gas into the interstellar medium. These objects play a crucial role in the chemical evolution and enrichment of galaxies and are therefore considered one of the most important contributors to the interstellar medium. Their structure and evolutionary properties are still not fully understood due to the poor knowledge of some physical mechanisms, mainly convection and mass loss. A valuable help to overcome these limitations can be found in the later stages of evolution, as the planetary nebula (PN). This is because their spectra contain critical chemical fingerprints that serve as exquisite tracers of the evolution, nucleosynthesis, and dust production during the AGB phase. We present a comprehensive analysis, from the UV to the IR, of 10 PNe from the LMC with the aim to create a bridge to reconstruct the history of dust production and mass loss from the late AGB phase to the PN stage.

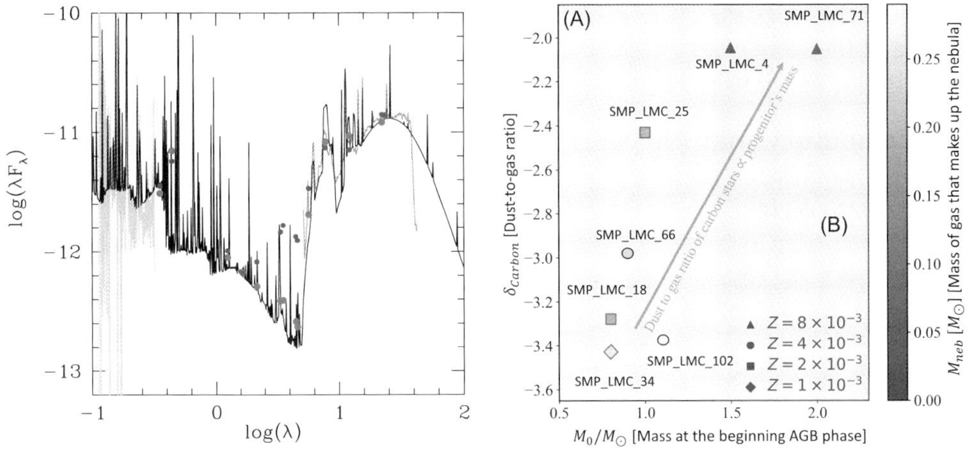

Figure 1. **Left**: SED of SMP-LMC-71, composed by the photometric data (blue dots) from Reid (2014), Cutri & et al. (2012) and Lasker et al. (2008), the *HST/STIS* UV spectrum taken from Stanghellini, Shaw, & Gilmore (2005) (in cyan) and the *Spitzer/IRS* spectrum (in magenta) from Stanghellini et al. (2007). The black line and red dots indicates the synthetic spectrum and photometry, respectively. **Right**: Mass of the CS, calculated at the beginning of the AGB phase, as a function of the dust-to-gas ratio and of the mass of gas that makes up the nebula. We report different symbols for different metallicities and we separated the diagram in two regions (A and B) according to the different evolutionary history.

2. Sample and Methodology

We select all the PNe from LMC characterized by a circular or elliptical shape, described in Stanghellini et al. (2007). We used the spectral synthesis code CLOUDY (v.22.0) (Ferland et al. 2017) to obtain a synthetic SED, which we compared with IR (Stanghellini, Shaw, & Gilmore 2005) and UV (Stanghellini et al. 2007) observational spectra and photometric data points (Reid 2014; Cutri & et al. 2012; Lasker et al. 2008) (see left panel, Fig. 1). The derived luminosity and effective temperature, with the chemical abundances, were used to infer the progenitor's mass (M_0) of the CS comparing the ATON (Ventura et al. 1998) evolutionary tracks computed from the main sequence to the PN phase.

3. Results

We find 7 PNe characterized by CSs that experienced several third dredge-up episodes (Iben 1974), reaching the carbon star stage and producing carbon dust. In 5 of them (SMP-LMC-25, -71, -18, -4 and -66) we highlight the presence of a near-IR bump visible from the photometry (see e.g. left panel Fig. 1). In the right panel of Fig. 1 we report for different metallicities (different symbols) the dust-to-gas ratio δ of carbon sources as a function of the progenitor's mass, that we calculated at the beginning of the AGB phase. We observe a linear dependence between those parameters and we note that the mass of gas that makes up the nebula in CS with $M \lesssim 1.3 M_{\odot}$ (region A in Fig. 1) is larger than the ones present in more massive CS (region B in Fig. 1). This behaviour can be linked to the history of mass loss: more massive stars have lost mass efficiently during several AGB pulses, while low-mass stars retain most of the mass until the last pulse, releasing it with lower wind velocity. In our sample we also find 3 objects that failed to become carbon stars and their IR spectra show traces of silicate dust.

We conclude that the dust surrounding the CS in the PNe records the previous evolution and therefore can be used to better understand some of the most unclear aspects of the LIMS, as the mass loss and the dust production history.

Supplementary material

To view supplementary material for this article, please visit https://doi.org/10.1017/S1743921323005331

References

Cutri, R. M. & et al. 2012, VizieR Online Data Catalog, II/311

Ferland G. J., Chatzikos M., Guzmán F., Lykins M. L., van Hoof P. A. M.,et al., 2017, RMxAA, 53, 385

Iben, I. Jr. 1974, ARA&A, 12, 215

Lasker B. M., Lattanzi M. G., McLean B. J., Bucciarelli B., et al., 2008, AJ, 136, 735

Reid W. A., 2014, MNRAS, 438, 2642.

Stanghellini L., Shaw R. A., Gilmore D., 2005, ApJ, 622, 294

Stanghellini L., García-Lario P., García-Hernández D. A. et al., 2007, ApJ, 671, 1669

Ventura P., Zeppieri A., Mazzitelli I., D'Antona F. 1998, A&A, 334, 953

Planetary Nebulae: A Universal Toolbox in the Era of Precision Astrophysics
Proceedings IAU Symposium No. 384, 2025
O. De Marco, A. Zijlstra & R. Szczerba, eds.
doi:10.1017/S174392132300515X

AI Techniques for Uncovering Resolved Planetary Nebula Candidates from the VPHAS+ Survey

Yushan Li[1], Quentin A. Parker[1], Peng Jia[2], Ruiqi Sun[2], Jaixin Li[2], Xu Li[2] and Liang Cao[2]

[1]Laboratory for space research, University of Hong Kong, HK SAR PRC

[2]Taiyuan University, PRC
email: quentinp@hku.hk

Abstract. AI and deep learning techniques are beginning to play an increasing role in astronomy as a necessary tool to deal with the data avalanche. We describe an application for finding resolved Planetary Nebulae (PNe) in crowded, wide-field, narrow-band Hα survey imagery in the Galactic plane.

Keywords. machine learning, artificial intelligence, planetary nebulae, wide-field surveys

1. Introduction

There are currently ~ 3800 Galactic planetary nebulae (PNe) known as recorded in the HASH database, e.g. Parker et al. (2016). These numbers fall far short of the numbers expected from population synthesis. Visual searching for PNe of narrow-band Hα surveys has provided most of the discoveries over the last 25 years, e.g. Parker et al. (2006), Miszalski et al. (2008), Sabin et al. (2014). This is time-consuming due to the large areal coverage and complex and varied nature of Hα emission in these Galactic plane surveys. To facilitate more objective, reproducible, efficient and reliable trawls for PNe candidates we have developed a new, deep learning algorithm for finding resolved Planetary Nebulae in crowded, wide-field, narrow-band Hα surveys in the Galactic plane. These techniques are beginning to play an increasing role in astronomy as a necessary tool to deal with the data avalanche.

Our approach uses a Swin-Transformer model based on Mask R-CNN (regions with convolutional neural networks), e.g. He et al. (2016). Specifically, we replaced the feature extraction network in Mask R-CNN with a transformer network, replaced the ResNet module with a Swin-Transformer, and then constructed a new 'bespoke' deep learning object detection method for PNe.

2. Our Results

We applied the algorithm to several Hα digital surveys, e.g. IPHAS (Drew et al. 2005) and VPHAS+ (Drew et al. 2014). The training and validation dataset was built with true PNe from the HASH database. After transfer learning, it was then applied to the VPHAS+ survey. We examined 979 out of 2284 survey fields with each survey field covering 1×1 degrees. With a sample of 454 PNe from the IPHAS as our validation set, our algorithm correctly identified 444 of these objects, with only 16 false positives. Our model returned $\sim$20,000 detections, including 2637 known PNe and many other

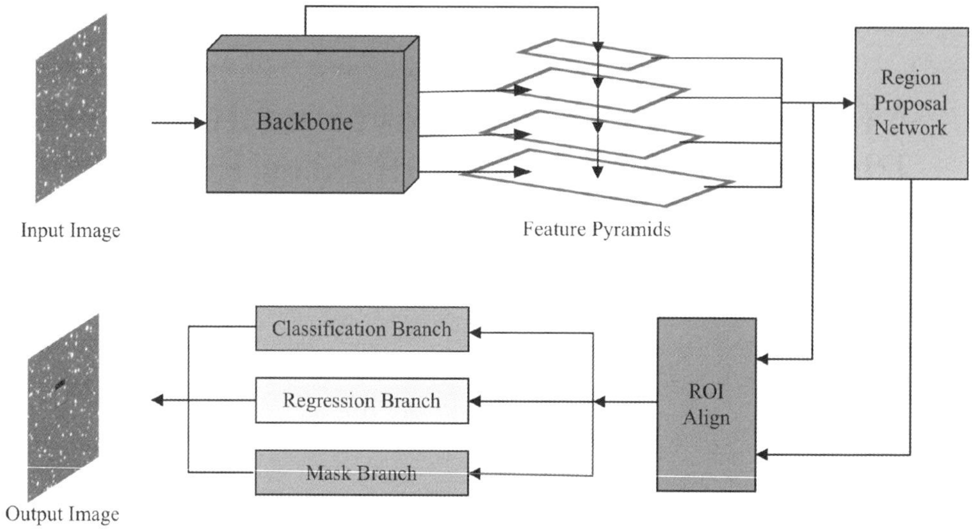

Figure 1. The schematic structure of the Swin-Transformer model used as the basis for this work.

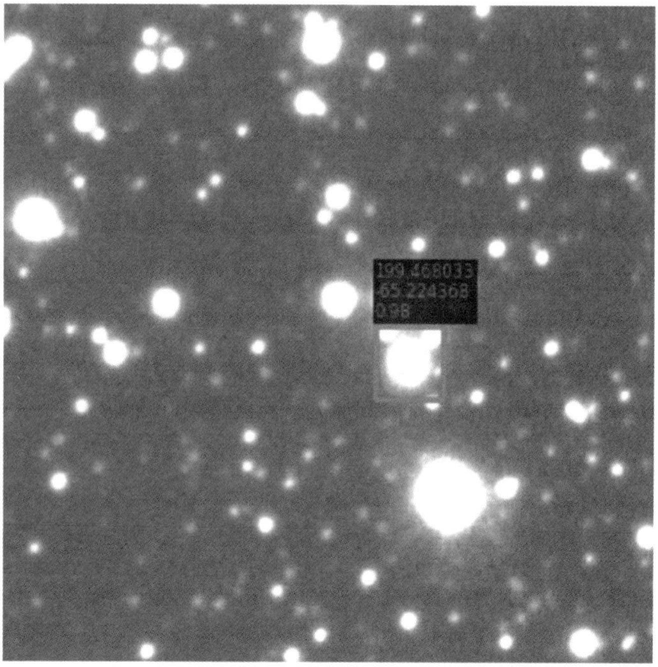

Figure 2. VPHAS+ image of a new PN found from our ML deep learning process.

kinds of catalogued non-PNe such as HII regions. A total of 815 new high-quality PNe candidates were found, 30 of which were selected as top-quality targets for subsequent optical spectroscopic follow-up on the SAAO 1.9m telescope in July 2023. Figure 1 shows the schematic structure of the Swin-Transformer model used as the basis for this work while Figure 2 shows a compact PN candidate uncovered in the VPHAS+ survey data by our process and finally Figure 3 shows a 2-D confirmatory SAAO 1.9m spectrum of one of the first PNe candidates found by our techniques.

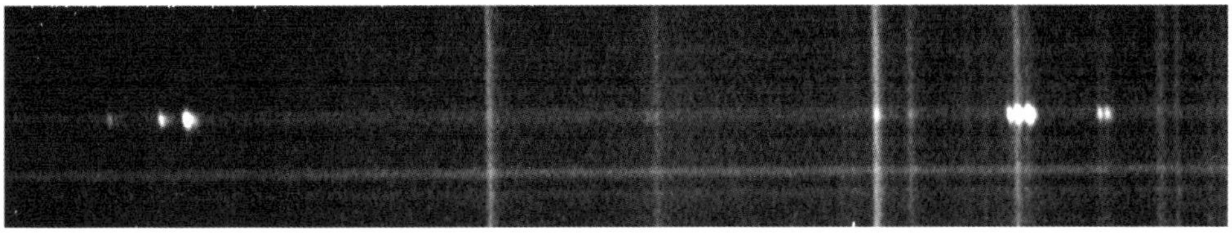

Figure 3. 2-D confirmatory SAAO 1.9m spectrum of a PNe candidate found by our techniques.

References

Drew, J. E., Greimel, R., Irwin, M. J. et al. 2005, *MNRAS*, 362, 753. doi: 10.1111/j.1365-2966.2005.09330.x

Drew, J. E., Gonzalez-Solares, E., Greimel, R. et al. 2014, *MNRAS*, 440, 2036. doi: 10.1093/mnras/stu394

He K., Zhang X., Ren S., Sun J., 2016, Proceedings of the IEEE conference on computer vision and pattern recognition. pp. 770–778

Miszalski, B., Parker, Q. A., Acker, A., Birkby, J. L., Frew, D. J. and Kovacevic, A., 2008, *MNRAS*, 384, 525. doi: 10.1111/j.1365-2966.2007.12727.x

Parker, Q.A., Bojičić, I. S. and Frew, D. J., 2016, *JPhCS*, 728, 32008. doi:10.1088/1742-6596/728/3/032008

Parker, Q. A., Acker, A., Frew, D. J. et al. 2005, *MNRAS*, 373, 79. doi:10.1111/j.1365-2966.2006.10950.x,

Sabin, L., Parker, Q.A., Corradi, R. L. M. et al. 2014, *MNRAS*, 443, 3388. doi: 10.1093/mnras/stu1404

Planetary Nebulae: A Universal Toolbox in the Era of Precision Astrophysics
Proceedings IAU Symposium No. 384, 2025
O. De Marco, A. Zijlstra & R. Szczerba, eds.
doi:10.1017/S174392132300580X

New Boundaries for Integral Field Spectroscopy

R. A. Pignata[1,2], V. Cristiani[2,3], D. Mast[1,2] and W. A. Weidmann[1,2]

[1]Observatorio Astronómico de Córdoba

[2]Consejo de Investigaciones Cientificas y Tecnicas de la Republica Argentina

[3]Instituto de Astronoma Teórica y Experimental

Abstract. The diagnostic diagrams are fundamental tools that require an upgrade, and this research marks the initial steps toward the development of advanced N-dimensional diagnostic charts by combining integral field spectroscopy and clustering techniques. Using this potent combination of methodologies, the preliminary findings have facilitated the precise differentiation of morphological components within NGC 3242, NGC 6369, NGC 6778, and NGC 7009 within a five-dimensional framework.

Keywords. (ISM:) planetary nebulae: general, techniques: spectroscopic, methods: statistical

1. Introduction

Integral Field Spectroscopy (IFS), a technology introduced just over 30 years ago, has transformed astronomy. However, its benefits are limited when combined with tools that fail to realise its full potential. Although diagnostic diagrams (DDs) have been valuable for assessing the physical conditions of planetary nebulae, they have failed to adapt to new observational and analytical capabilities. We use IFS data from MUSE and clustering techniques to explore new DDs to help fill this gap.

Finally, it is of utmost importance to note that we are not pursuing to perform a spaxel-by-spaxel analysis, this is not feasible, since the potential interference from sampling noise would not be considered. We aim to examine sets of spaxels that share common attributes. The MUSE data used to work with were extracted from the ESO processed data archive. The PNs are NGC 3242, NGC 6778, and NGC 7009 observed on 10/13/2016, and, NGC 6369 observed on 8/19/2018.

2. Methodology

The python package LIME (Fernández et al. 2023) was used to extract the Hβ, [OIII] $\lambda\lambda$ 4959, 5007, [NII] $\lambda\lambda$6548, 6584, Hα, and [SII] $\lambda\lambda$6717, 6731 lines. Extracted lines were extinction corrected using the PyNeb package (Luridiana et al. 2015).

A 5-dimensional parameter space were structured into a Pandas dataframe using the ratios Hα/[NII], Hα/[SII], 5007/Hβ, [NII]/5007, and [NII]/[SII]. Then Gaussian Mixture Model clustering was applied. For each nebula, the optimal number of clusters was obtained using Bayesian Information Criterion (BIC).

Finally, the NP image is reconstructed from the clustering data, thus determining the spatial distribution of each group.

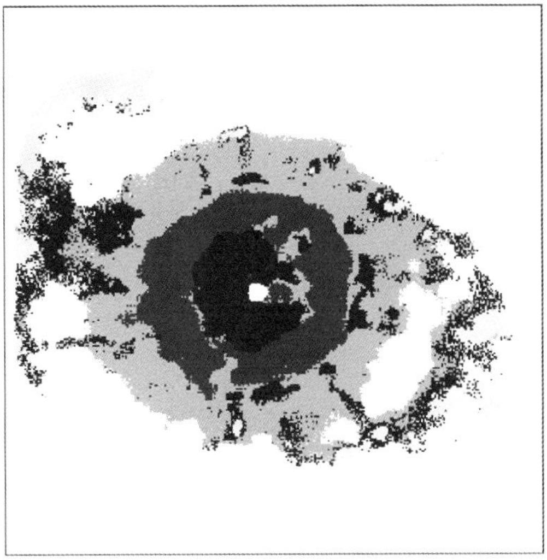

Figure 1. Results of clustering in 5-dimensional parameter space 4 clusters for 37380 spaxels of NGC 6369. More details in Sec. 3.

3. Results

NGC 6369 (Fig. 1): The number of groups determined through the BIC is 4. This process effectively separated the structures highlighted by Ramos-Larios et al. (2012) with remarkable consistency. These structures are the inner shell and envelope (blue and turquoise groups), the annular shell (red group), and the knots (yellow group). Notably, the blue structure even corresponds to certain filaments on the envelope.

NGC 3242 (Fig. 2 Top left): The number of groups determined through the BIC is 2. Compared with the work of Gómez-Muñoz et al. (2015) and considering the available biased data, we managed to discriminate the components K1 and K4 (yellow regions) and a small part of B1 and B2 (violet regions).

NGC 6778 (Fig. 2 Top right): The number of clusters determined by BIC is 3. Two regions are related to zones of higher emissivity in [NII] and [SII]. The purple one delimits a filamentary structure extending from the center to the left and right, which ends in three yellow regions, one to the left and two to the right of the nebula, in agreement with Guerrero & Miranda (2012). In addition, above and below, we have a light blue region corresponding to areas where [NII] and [SII] are considerably fainter.

NGC 7009 (Fig. 2 Bottom): The number of groups determined through the BIC is 3. We were able to separate structures located in the positions where the knots are found, colored in yellow and blue, and regions that are not part of the knots, colored in pink. These separations are in agreement with Gonçalves et al. (2006).

4. Conclusions and future work

Based on these initial results, the use of clustering in IFS data in parameter spaces with more than 2 dimensions is valuable for segmenting different morphological features. We will improve the selection of the parameter space by including variables such as temperature, density, and velocity. We also plan to carry out an analysis of the probability that the spaxels belong to each group, in order to eliminate those with unclear or ill-defined separations. All this will be done by incorporating more PN observed with multiple instruments.

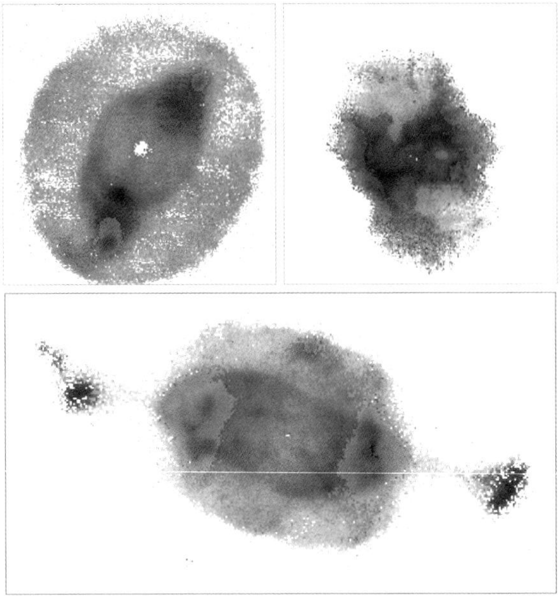

Figure 2. Clustering result in a 5-dimensional parameter space. An overlay of the emissivity in [NII] $\lambda\lambda6584$ and the regions corresponding to the clusters is shown in each of the images. Top left: NGC 3242, 2 groups. Top Right: NGC 6778, 3 groups. Bottom left: NGC 7009, 3 groups. More details in Sec. 3.

References

Fernández V., Amorín R., Sanchez-Janssen R., del Valle-Espinosa M. G., Papaderos P., 2023, MNRAS, 520, 3576

Gómez-Muñoz M. A., Blanco Cárdenas M. W., Vázquez R., Zavala S., Guillén P. F., Ayala S., 2015, MNRAS, 453, 4175

Gonçalves D. R., Ercolano B., Carnero A., Mampaso A., Corradi R. L. M., 2006, MNRAS, 365, 1039

Guerrero M. A., Miranda L. F., 2012, A&A, 539, A47

Luridiana V., Morisset C., Shaw R. A., 2015, A&A, 573, A42

Ramos-Larios G., Guerrero M. A., Vázquez R., Phillips J. P., 2012, MNRAS, 420, 1977

Planetary Nebulae: A Universal Toolbox in the Era of Precision Astrophysics
Proceedings IAU Symposium No. 384, 2025
O. De Marco, A. Zijlstra & R. Szczerba, eds.
doi:10.1017/S1743921323005550

Identification of post-AGBs from Gaia DR3 distances and morphology

Arturo Manchado[1,2,3], Minina Manteiga[4,5], Iker González-Santamaría[4,5] and Eva Villaver[1,6]

[1]Instituto de Astrofísica de Canarias, Vía Láctea S/N, E-38200 La Laguna, Tenerife, Spain
email: amt@iac.es

[2]Departmento de Astrofísica, Universidad de La Laguna (ULL), E-38206 La Laguna, Tenerife, Spain

[3]CSIC, Spain

[4]Universidade da Coruña (UDC), Department of Computer Science and Information Technologies, Campus Elviña s/n, 15071 A Coruña, Spain

[5]CIGUS CITIC, Centre for Information and Communications Technologies Research, Universidade da Coruña, Campus de Elviña s/n, 15071 A Coruña, Spain

[6]Agencia Espacial Española, 41015 Sevilla, Spain

Abstract. Gaia DR3 parallaxes of a sample of post-AGB candidates have allowed us to unequivocally establish their evolutionary stage. Making use of the available photometry, interstellar extinction, and parallax-derived distance, their spectral Energy Distributions (SED) were fitted. From this, luminosity and effective temperature were worked out, placing them in the Hertzsprung-Russell (HR) diagram. This allows direct comparison with updated post-AGB evolutionary tracks, and estimation of their masses and evolutionary ages. As a result of that they were classified as post-AGB, YSO, and supergiant. From a sample of 146 candidates, 63 are post-AGB, 27 YSO, 5 supergiants, and 51 unconfirmed candidates. In addition, there were HST images for some of them, finding that very few post-AGB show a bipolar or multipolar structure.

Keywords. ISM: planetary nebula: general, stars: AGB and post-AGB.

1. Introduction

Literature has a trend claiming that most of the post-AGBs are bipolar (e.g., Ueta, Meixner, & Bobrowsky (2000), Sahai *et al.* (2007), Siódmiak *et al.* (2008)). However, this is in contradiction with the observed morphologies of planetary nebula (PN) (e.g. Manchado (2003)), where bipolar only accounts for 17% of the sample. In this work, we see that only 3 in 12 (25%) post-AGBs are multi-polar.

2. Sample selection

One of the great problems in the study of the post-AGB phase is the correct classification. We started selecting objects from the Torun catalogue of galactic post-AGB stars (Szczerba *et al.* (2007)) the Simbad astronomical database and the spectroscopic atlas by Suárez *et al.* (2006) We cross-matched our list of objects with the Gaia DR3 archive, with the restriction that (UWE<1.96 or RUWE<1.4). After applying these constraints, we ended up with a set of 146 objects that we consider to have good astrometric measurements in DR3. Then the luminosity and Teff were worked out allowing us to place them in the HR diagram and then the unequivocal classification, as post-AGB (63),

Young Stellar Objects (27), 2 Super-Giant stars, and 51 were unconfirmed post-AGB candidates.

We have searched the HST database (`http://archive.stsci.edu/`) and downloaded images for 117 post-AGB stars obtained with the ACS, WFPC, and WFPC2 instruments onboard HST.

After the cross-match of both samples, 14 objects were identified with good distances from Gaia DR3 and HST images.

3. Results

When these 14 objects are located in the HR diagram 12 are classified as post-AGBs and 2 as supergiant. From the HST images of these 12 post-AGBs, their morphological class is as follows; 4 Stellar-like, 7 Round and 3 Multipolar. Though the sample is very small, the fraction of multipolar is very small just 25%, which is consistent, within the error, with the number of bipolar PN (17%).

References

Manchado A., 2003, *IAUS*, 209, 431

Sahai R., Morris M., Sánchez Contreras C., Claussen M., 2007, *AJ*, 134, 2200. doi:10.1086/522944

Siódmiak N., Meixner M., Ueta T., Sugerman B. E. K., Van de Steene G. C., Szczerba R., 2008, *ApJ*, 677, 382. doi:10.1086/529115

Suárez O., García-Lario P., Manchado A., Manteiga M., Ulla A., Pottasch S. R., 2006, *A&A*, 458, 173. doi:10.1051/0004-6361:20054108

Szczerba R., Siódmiak N., Stasińska G., Borkowski J., 2007, *A&A*, 469, 799. doi:10.1051/0004-6361:20067035

Ueta T., Meixner M., Bobrowsky M., 2000, *ApJ*, 528, 861. doi:10.1086/308208

Planetary Nebulae: A Universal Toolbox in the Era of Precision Astrophysics
Proceedings IAU Symposium No. 384, 2025
O. De Marco, A. Zijlstra & R. Szczerba, eds.
doi:10.1017/S1743921323005069

An evolved planetary nebula physically associated with the open cluster M37

Vasiliki Fragkou[1], Quentin A. Parker[2], Albert Zijlstra[3], Roberto Vázquez[4], Laurence Sabin[4], Jackeline S. Rechy-García[1] and Denise R. Gonçalves[1]

[1]Valongo Observatory, Federal University of Rio de Janeiro, Brazil
email: vfrag@physics.auth.gr

[2]Department of Physics, The University of Hong Kong, Hong Kong SAR

[3]Department of Physics and Astronomy, The University of Manchester, UK

[4]Instituto de Astronomía, Universidad Nacional Autónoma de México, Ensenada, Mexico

Abstract. We have found strong evidence that an extended bipolar planetary nebula (PN), lying in the line-of-sight of the Galactic open cluster M37, is actually its physical member. We estimated both the PN physical properties and the properties of its progenitor from cluster studies. The progenitor mass has been found to be around 2.8 $M_\odot$. There are only a handful of such confirmed associations and each of them provides valuable additional data to the initial-to-final-mass relation. The nebula has a major axis of 445 arcsec and a kinematical age of around 80 kyrs -the largest ever determined for a PN- suggesting that PNe in clusters do not dissipate as fast as field PNe.

Keywords. stars: planetary nebulae, open star clusters

1. Introduction

PNe that are physical members of star clusters, have many of their properties (e.g. distance, environment, progenitor star's initial mass and age) determined independently from cluster Color-Magnitude Diagrams (CMDs) and theoretical isochrones. These rare instances allow the study of the link between initial stellar mass and PN's chemical enrichment. Moreover, they provide additional, independent data for the, currently poorly constrained, Initial-to-Final-Mass Relation (IFMR, e.g. Cummings et al. 2018), which relates the central star's (CS) mass to its progenitor mass and is crucial for stellar evolution studies.

Only three PNe have been confirmed to be physically associated with Galactic open star clusters (Parker et al. 2011; Fragkou et al. 2019a,b, 2022). Such confirmations require good agreement in terms of the angular proximity, distance, reddening and most importantly radial velocities of the PN and the cluster.

2. A bipolar PN physically associated with the open cluster M37

The PN IPHASX J055226.2+32372 lies in a very close angular proximity to the well-studied open cluster M37. Multiple of their, reported in the literature, Gaia DR3 and estimated parameters (see Table 1, Fragkou et al. 2022) suggest that the two objects are physically associated. Crucially, the precise PN radial velocity, estimated using high resolution spectral data from MEGARA/GTC, is in an excellent agreement to that of the cluster, confirming that the PN is a physical member of M37.

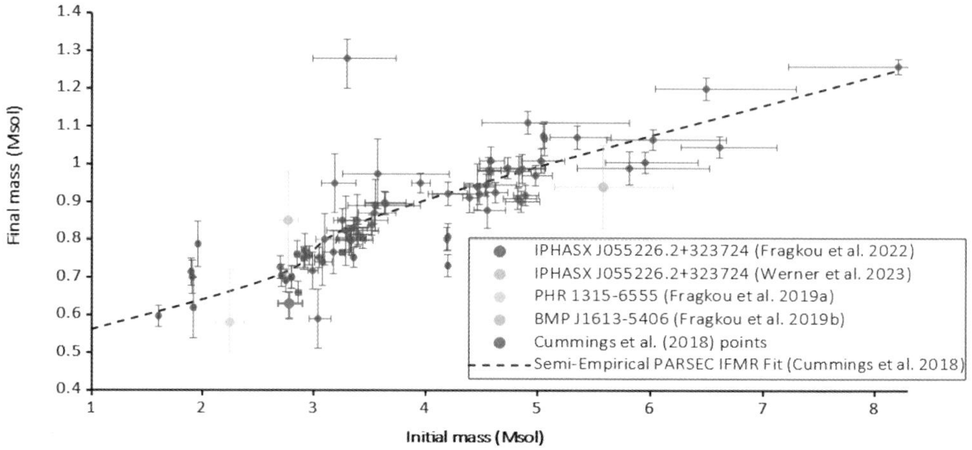

Figure 1. Our cluster PNe points plus the one estimated by Werner et al. (2023) over-plotted on the Cummings et al. (2018) white dwarf trend and points.

The nebular core is a hot hydrogen deficient PG1159 white dwarf (Griggio et al. 2022; Werner et al. 2023). The CS progenitor mass ($M = 2.78 \pm 0.12\,M_{\odot}$) has been estimated from theoretical predictions of the Padova theoretical isochrone that presents the best fit to the cluster Gaia DR3 CMD. Besides, the CS final mass ($M = 0.63 \pm 0.04\,M_{\odot}$) has been estimated from its V magnitude and nebular kinematical age using the latest evolutionary tracks (Miller Bertolami 2016). Recently, Werner et al. (2023) have estimated a higher final mass ($M = 0.85^{+0.13}_{-0.14}\,M_{\odot}$) from a detailed stellar spectral analysis.

A detailed study of this PN is currently underway. Deep long-slit GMOS/Gemini spectra, already partially acquired, will provide us with the necessary data to calculate the nebular abundances and precise nebular properties.

3. PNe in open clusters

All open cluster PNe confirmed so far are bipolar with enhanced nitrogen and relatively high-mass progenitors. Their estimated initial and final masses have been over-plotted along the latest IFMR estimates (see Figure 1). The cluster PNe represent generally well the previous trends Cummings et al. (2018) estimated from cluster white dwarfs and fill important gaps. The PN in NGC 6067 has the largest PN progenitor mass ($\simeq 5.6\,M_{\odot}$) ever determined. In the case of the PN in M37 its kinematical age was found to be 78 kyrs (or even larger according to Werner et al. 2023) - the largest ever determined for a PN. This suggests that PNe in clusters have a larger observable life time than field PNe, since they do not dissipate as fast due to the low velocity dispersion between cluster stars and the surrounding interstellar medium. In general the extreme characteristics of PNe in open clusters provide unique PN properties that deserve further studies.

VF acknowledges support from Brazilian research funding agencies CAPES (grant: 88887.838401/2023-00) and FAPERJ (grant: E26/210.847/2019). RV acknowledges support from UNAM-PAPIIT grant IN106720. LS is supported by the UNAM-PAPIIT grant IN110122. D.R.G acknowledges support from grants 200.527/2023 (FAPERJ) and 313016/2020-8 (CNPq).

Supplementary material

To view supplementary material for this article, please visit https://doi.org/10.1017/S1743921323005069

References

Cummings J. D., Kalirai J. S., Tremblay P.-E., Ramirez-Ruiz E., Choi J., 2018, *ApJ*, 866, 21
Fragkou V., Parker Q. A., Zijlstra A., Shaw R., Lykou F., 2019, *MNRAS*, 484, 3078
Fragkou V., Parker Q. A., Zijlstra A. A., Crause L., Barker H., 2019, *NatAs*, 3, 851
Fragkou V., Parker Q. A., Zijlstra A. A., Vázquez R., Sabin L., et al., 2022, *ApJL*, 935, L35
Griggio M., Bedin L. R., Raddi R., Reindl N., Tomasella L., et al., 2022, *MNRAS*, 515, 1841
Miller Bertolami M. M., 2016, *A&A*, 588, A25
Parker Q. A., Frew D. J., Miszalski B., Kovacevic A. V., Frinchaboy P. M., et al., 2011, *MNRAS*, 413, 1835
Werner K., Reindl N., Raddi R., Griggio M., Bedin L. R., et al., 2023, *A&A*, 678, A89

Planetary Nebulae: A Universal Toolbox in the Era of Precision Astrophysics
Proceedings IAU Symposium No. 384, 2025
O. De Marco, A. Zijlstra & R. Szczerba, eds.
doi:10.1017/S1743921323005021

Physics of the ionized gas in extremely young planetary nebulae

Lucero Uscanga[1], Jorge Cantó[2], James A. Green[3], José F. Gómez[4] Guillem Anglada[4], Luis F. Miranda[4], Roldán A. Cala[4], Olga Suárez[5] and Panayotis Boumis[6]

[1]Departamento de Astronomía, Universidad de Guanajuato, A.P. 144, 36000 Guanajuato, Gto., Mexico
email: luscag@gmail.com

[2]Instituto de Astronomía, UNAM, Ap. 70-264, 04510, Ciudad de México, Mexico

[3]ATNF, CSIRO Astronomy and Space Science, PO Box 76, Epping, NSW 1710, Australia

[4]Instituto de Astrofísica de Andalucía, CSIC, Glorieta de la Astronomía s/n, E-18008 Granada, Spain

[5]Université Côte d'Azur, Observatoire de la Côte d'Azur, CNRS, Laboratoire Lagrange, Bd de l'Observatoire, CS 34229, F-06304 Nice cedex 4, France

[6]IAASARS, National Observatory of Athens, 15236 Penteli, Greece

Abstract. We study the physics of the ionized gas in the last stages of evolution of low- and intermediate-mass stars that end their lives as planetary nebulae (PNe). Specifically, those that are in the earliest stages of the PN phase. For this purpose, we observed with the Australia Telescope Compact Array the spectra at radio frequencies of a sample of (H_2O and/or OH) maser-emitting PNe. We determined the spectral index of the radio continuum emission of these sources and the turnover frequency of the emission, which could be tied to the age of the sources.

Keywords. masers, radio continuum: stars, planetary nebulae: general, individual: IRAS 17393−2727.

1. Introduction

Maser-emitting PNe could be in their earliest phases since, e.g., H_2O masers are expected to extinguish shortly after ∼100 yr (Lewis 1989) from the end of the asymptotic giant branch phase. Their youth make them key objects for understanding the formation and evolution of PNe.

An important physical parameter of the ionized gas in PNe is the frequency at which its free-free emission changes from optically thick to thin. This turnover frequency is a direct estimator of the emission measure (EM), which is considered to be an age indicator (higher EM in younger PNe; Kwok *et al.* 1981; Aaquist & Kwok 1991). For example, an EM$\sim10^{10}$ cm^{-6}pc suggests an extremely young age ∼100 yr (Kwok & Bignell 1984). As a PN ages and expands, its electron density decreases, and the nebula becomes optically thin at increasingly lower frequencies. From the EM, it is also possible to estimate the electron density and mass of the ionized gas.

Previous studies toward H_2O maser-emitting PNe indicate that this turnover frequency is ≃10 GHz for K3−35 (Aaquist & Kwok 1991) and >20 GHz for IRAS 17347−3139 (Gómez *et al.* 2005; Tafoya *et al.* 2009). In the latter source, the flux density seems to

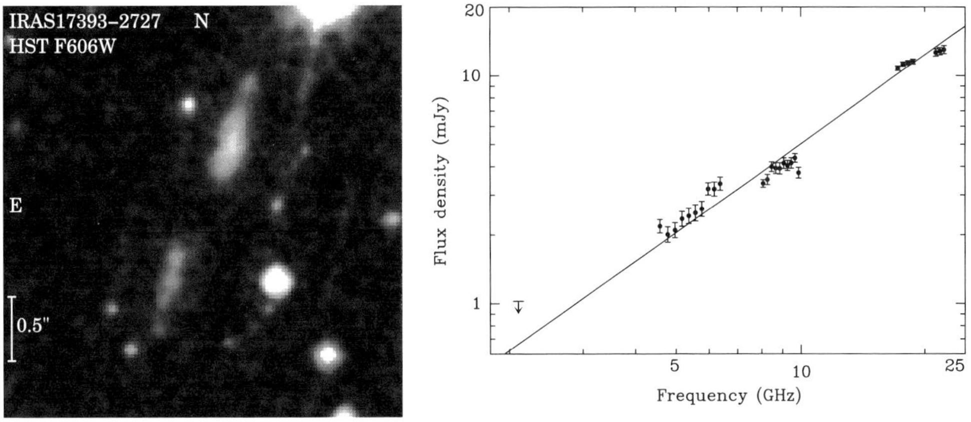

Figure 1. *Left*: *HST* image of I17393 taken from Hubble Legacy Archives. *Right*: Flux density of I17393 as a function of frequency in the range of ~ 2–22 GHz. The solid line is a linear fit to the data from our observations (spectral index = 1.29).

rapidly increase with time at all frequencies. This increase could be due to the expansion of the young ionized nebula within its circumstellar envelope (Gómez *et al.* 2005; Tafoya *et al.* 2009). The dynamical age of the ionized region of this source is estimated to be ≃120 yr (Gómez *et al.* 2005).

We carried out continuum observations at 2.1, 5.5, 9, 18, and 22 GHz with the Australia Telescope Compact Array in its 6A configuration on 2017 February, towards a sample of 3 maser-emitting PNe. Here we present the results of one of these sources: IRAS 17393−2727, hereafter I17393.

2. Spectrum at radio frequencies of I17393

The *Hubble Space Telescope* (*HST*) image of I17393 (Figure 1, left) shows a highly collimated bipolar outflow, as well as a dark lane that completely obscures the central region (Manteiga *et al.* 2011). The infrared spectrum of this source shows bright [Ne II] nebular emission, strongly suggesting that the ionization of its central region has already started (García-Hernández *et al.* 2007). This PN also harbors OH maser emission towards the center of the nebula (Zijlstra *et al.* 1989; Uscanga *et al.* 2012).

The radio-continuum emission of I17393 shows a spectral index $\alpha = 1.29 \pm 0.03$ ($S_\nu \propto \nu^\alpha$) between 2 and 22 GHz (Figure 1, right), consistent with a partially optically thick ionized region. The turnover frequency is > 22 GHz which is consistent with a very young PN. Moreover its EM $\gtrsim 2\times10^9$ cm^{-6}pc and its electron density is $\gtrsim 1.1\times10^6$ cm^{-3}.

Remarkably, the complete spectrum at radio frequencies would provide us with information on the emission processes (free-free, non-thermal and/or dust thermal emission) and thus, about the physical processes driving the transformation of these evolved objects into PNe. Given the physical parameters we have found, these maser-emitting PNe are among the youngest PNe.

L.U. acknowledges support from the University of Guanajuato (Mexico) grant No. CIIC 090/2023.

Supplementary material

To view supplementary material for this article, please visit https://doi.org/10.1017/S1743921323005021

References

Aaquist, O. B., Kwok, S. 1991, *ApJ*, 378, 599. doi:10.1086/170461

García-Hernández, D. A., Perea-Calderón, J. V., Bobrowsky, M., *et al.* 2007, *ApJL*, 666, L33. doi:10.1086/521673

Gómez, J. F., de Gregorio-Monsalvo, I., Lovell, J. E. J., *et al.* 2005, *MNRAS*, 364, 738. doi:10.1111/j.1365-2966.2005.09592.x

Kwok, S., Bignell, R. C. 1984, *ApJ*, 276, 544. doi:10.1086/161643

Kwok, S., Purton, C. R., Keenan, D. W. 1981, *ApJ*, 250, 232. doi:10.1086/159367

Lewis, B. M. 1989, *ApJ*, 338, 234. doi:10.1086/167194

Manteiga, M., García-Hernández, D. A., Ulla, A., *et al.* 2011, *AJ*, 141, 80. doi:10.1088/0004-6256/141/3/80

Tafoya, D., Gómez, Y., Patel, N. A., *et al.* 2009, *ApJ*, 691, 611. doi:10.1088/0004-637X/691/1/611

Uscanga, L., Gómez, J. F., Suárez, O., *et al.* 2012, *A&A*, 547, A40. doi:10.1051/0004-6361/201219760

Zijlstra, A. A., te Lintel Hekkert, P., Pottasch, S. R., *et al.* 1989, *A&A*, 217, 157

Planetary Nebulae: A Universal Toolbox in the Era of Precision Astrophysics
Proceedings IAU Symposium No. 384, 2025
O. De Marco, A. Zijlstra & R. Szczerba, eds.
doi:10.1017/S1743921323005070

On the significance of polarization of continuous spectrum in modelling of circumstellar dust shells

Juris Freimanis

Engineering Research Institute "Ventspils International Radio Astronomy Centre" of Ventspils University of Applied Sciences, Ventspils, Latvia
email: `jurisf@venta.lv`

Abstract. Radiative transfer in spherical circumstellar silicate dust envelope was modelled with and without accounting for polarization, using the code *RADMC-3D*. It was found that the influence of polarization on dust temperature and the mean intensity of shortwave radiation in spherically symmetric case is negligible, but neglecting for polarization does not give sensible economy of the computing time for the given signal to noise ratio. Construction of good virtual polarization images of the object can require much more computing time than good intensity images.

Keywords. radiative transfer, polarization, circumstellar matter

1. Introduction

AGB stars, post-AGB objects, protoplanetary nebulae and young planetary nebulae often have gas-dust shells of complex morphology and nontrivial geometry. Spherical, conical, toroidal and other structures are often observed, with highly polarized radiation.

Full modelling of such objects requires the solution of polarized radiative transfer equation. But often scalar radiative transfer equation is used, accounting only for tabulated phase function (in the best case) and neglecting polarization; this is not a theoretically sound approach (see, e.g., Mishchenko et al. (2006)).

Polarimetric observations and their analysis are very important tools for studying the structure of circumstellar shells, but the real importance of accounting polarization for modelling dust temperature distribution, as well as for the spatial distribution of the mean intensity of astrochemically active ultraviolet radiation, can be tested numerically. Such testing was done in this study using Monte Carlo radiative transfer code *RADMC-3D* (Dullemond 2020). Only continuum radiative transfer in dust was dealt with; spectral lines were not considered.

2. Modelling setup

Numerical radiative transfer models were constructed as follows:

• The dust cloud is spherically symmetric, but in two versions: either homogeneous, or with radially dependent Gaussian profile of dust density $\rho_d(r) = \rho_0 \exp(-r^2/2r_1^2)$.

• A star (a finite sphere) is in the centre of the cloud, in two versions: either with α Her parameters ($T_{\rm eff} = 3260\,{\rm K}$, $R = 284\,R_\odot$, $L = 8207\,L_\odot$), or alike O9V – B0V star ($T_{\rm eff} = 30000\,{\rm K}$, $R = 6.4\,R_\odot$, $L = 29,900\,L_\odot$). The star radiates as blackbody.

• The optical radius of the cloud in V band ($\lambda = 0.55\,\mu{\rm m}$) is either $\tau_V = 5$ or $\tau_V = 15$.

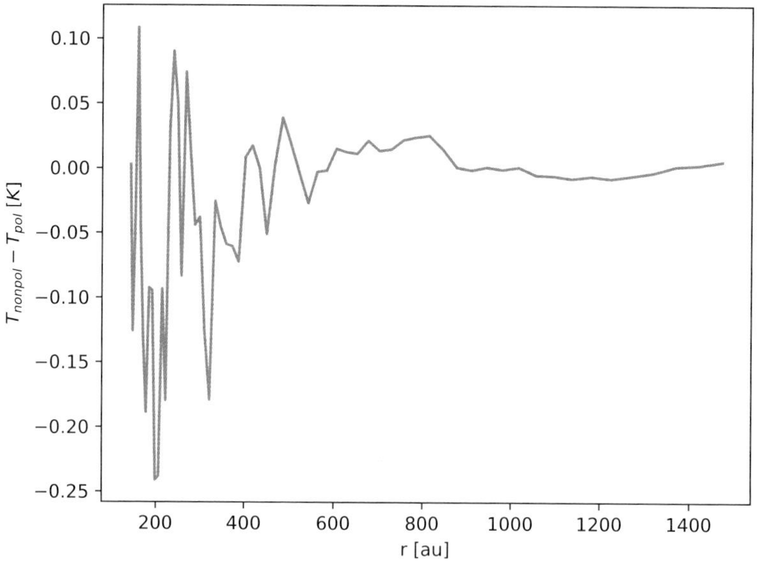

Figure 1. Difference of dust temperature profiles between unpolarized and polarized calculations. Gaussian dust density, $\tau_V = 5$, star with $T_{\rm eff} = 30000$ K in the centre.

Each combination of parameters mentioned above was modelled with *RADMC-3D* in two versions: fully accounting for polarization and neglecting for polarization but using tabulated phase function. The optical properties of dust were taken from the precalculated values given in downloadable examples to the *RADMC-3D* code. Namely, there are spherical grains of radius 0.1 μm, consisting of amorphous olivine with 50% Mg and 50% Fe. Radius of the inner boundary of the dust cloud was chosen so that the dust temperature does not exceed substantially 1000 K, and the outer radius of the cloud was 1500 au in all cases. Calculations were done in the 3D spherical spatial coordinate system, with typically 10^7 photon packages. Radial profiles of dust temperature and the mean intensities were averaged over the angular discretization, obtaining smooth functions of radius.

3. Results and conclusions

In all cases the difference between radial temperature profiles calculated with and without accounting for polarization did not exceed 1 K. An example of it is shown in Fig. 1. The relative differences of the mean spectral intensity profiles of chemically active shortwave radiation, calculated with and without accounting for polarization, did not exceed 1%.

The necessary computing time in order to achieve the prescribed signal to noise ratio in Monte Carlo modelling was approximately the same for calculations with and without accounting for polarization. It is preferable to account for polarization because this is more correct, and it can be essential for nonspherical models.

Often one needs to construct virtual image of the astronomical object, for comparison with observations. Good intensity images of spherically symmetric objects require about the same number of photon packages as good temperature profiles. Acceptable signal to noise ratio in polarization images can require much more photon packages and computing time.

This study was financed from the project "Desorption of icy molecules in the interstellar medium (DIMD)" (Latvian Council of Science grant No. lzp-2021/1-0076), the basic budget of Ventspils International Radio Astronomy Centre, as well as from co-sponsorship by Ventspils City Council. Competing interests: The author declare none.

Supplementary material

To view supplementary material for this article, please visit https://doi.org/10.1017/S1743921323005070

References

Mishchenko M. I., Travis L. D., Lacis A. A., 2006, *Multiple Scattering of Light by Particles*, Cambridge University Press

Dullemond C., 2020, RADMC-3D Version 2.0, `https://www.ita.uni-heidelberg.de/~dullemond/software/radmc-3d/`

Planetary Nebulae: A Universal Toolbox in the Era of Precision Astrophysics
Proceedings IAU Symposium No. 384, 2025
O. De Marco, A. Zijlstra & R. Szczerba, eds.
doi:10.1017/S174392132300532X

FAST Search for Atomic Hydrogen in Planetary Nebulae

Yong Zhang[1], Xu-Jia Ouyang[1], Albert Zijlstra[2], Chuan-Peng Zhang[3], Jun-ichi Nakashima[1] and Quentin A. Parker[4]

[1]School of Physics and Astronomy, Sun Yat-sen University, Guangdong Province, China
email: zhangyong5@mail.sysu.edu.cn

[2]Department of Physics and Astronomy, The University of Manchester, Manchester M13 9PL, UK

[3]National Astronomical Observatories, Chinese Academy of Sciences, Beijing 100101, China

[4]Faculty of Science, The University of Hong Kong, Hong Kong, China

Abstract. Due to the contamination from omnipresent interstellar 21 cm emission, atomic hydrogen (H I) associated with planetary nebulae (PNe) has been insufficiently investigated. In this proceeding we report a project of searching for H I surrounding PNe using the Five hundred-meter Aperture Spherical radio Telescope (FAST), which is the most sensitive single-dish telescope at L-band. The observations may offer new insights into the interaction processes between PNe and the interstellar medium.

Keywords. ISM: atoms, radio lines: stars, planetary nebulae

---

1. Introduction

Extensive observations of planetary nebulae (PNe) show that the total mass of the ionized material and the central star is much lower than the theoretical upper limit (the called 'PN missing mass problem') and the missing mass cannot be attributed to molecular gas and dust. There remains a vital nebular component that has not been sufficiently investigated and that could significantly contribute to the overall mass-loss budget: atomic hydrogen (H I). On a theoretical ground, Glassgold & Huggins (1983) suggest that for a photospheric temperature larger than 2500 K, the hydrogen flowing from an asymptotic giant branch (AGB) star is mainly atomic. Moreover, H I can be enriched by the photodissociation of H_2 and recombination of H^+. Therefore, H I observations of PNe can provide significant information on their early mass-loss history. The presence of H I can be indicated through the spin-flip transition at 21 cm wavelength in the radio regime. Unfortunately, the observation of circumstellar H I is extremely challenging because of heavy contamination from the interstellar medium (ISM) and the confusion due to ISM emission fluctuations (Gathier et al. 1986). To our best knowledge, there are only five PNe with detected H I emission and 11 with H I absorption. The limited number of measurements precludes us from performing a statistical analysis. To this end, we have been conducting a systematic search of H I associated with PNe using the Five-hundred-meter Aperture Spherical radio Telescope (FAST) in China.

2. Observations

The observations are performed using the tracking mode of the FAST 19-beam receiver, which enables us to sample the sky over a region of $15' \times 15'$ around the target. The

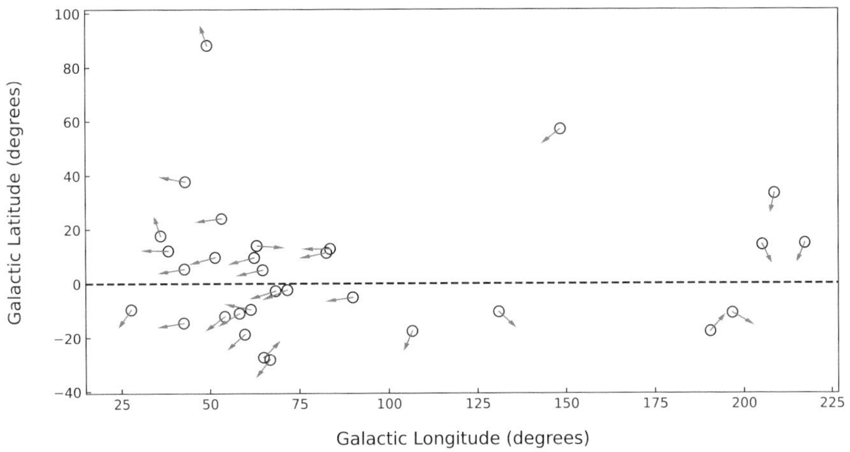

Figure 1. The locations of the observed PNe in the Galactic coordinate system. The arrows represent the directions of the proper motion, in which the interstellar H I may be swept up.

half-power beamwidth of each beam is about 3′ at 1420 MHz. The central beam is pointed toward the target. The other beams sample the adjacent off-source positions. We can simultaneously obtain the on- and off-source spectra covering a frequency range of 1.05–1.45 GHz at a velocity resolution of 0.01 $\mathrm{km\,s^{-1}}$, providing a fast way for searching for circumstellar H I. As part of an on-going long-term research project, we have observed 31 PNe, as shown in Figure 1. Half of the sample lie in the first or third quadrant of the Galactic plane within the solar circle and have a negative velocity of the local standard of rest (V_{LSR}) so that the circumstellar and interstellar H I features can be well separated in velocity space. Otherwise, we have a chance to discover the interstellar H I swept up by the PNe.

3. Results

The FAST observations confirm the presence of H I toward two young PNe IC 4997 and BD+30°3639 (Ouyang et al. 2022, 2023). Compared to the previous discoveries (Altschuler et al. 1986; Taylor et al. 1990), substantially more details are revealed by our new observations. The on-source spectrum of IC 4997 exhibits a dip at the blue side of its V_{LSR} with a depth smaller than the continuum emission, which does not appear in any off-source spectra. Therefore, we conclude that there is an expanding neutral shell generating the H I absorption against nebular free-free emission. Extended H I emission is detected surrounding BD+30°3639; its spatial distribution indicates to an interaction the moving PN and the ISM. The PN can carve a cavity in the interstellar atomic gas and sweep up ISM material in the leading edge. As a result of the PN-ISM interaction, the nebulosity can be been stripped and gradually incorporate into the downstream ISM. This provides a potential solution of the 'PN missing mass problem'. The single-dish telescope has a certain advantage to trace extended circumstellar structures that are likely to be filtered out by interferometers.

We acknowledge funding from the National Science Foundation of China through grant 11973099 and the China Manned Space Project through grants CMS-CSST-2021-A09 and CMS-CSST-2021-A10. This work has used the data from the Five-hundred-meter Aperture Spherical radio Telescope (FAST). FAST is a Chinese national mega-science facility, operated by the National Astronomical Observatories of Chinese Academy of Sciences (NAOC).

Supplementary material

To view supplementary material for this article, please visit https://doi.org/10.1017/S174392132300532X

References

Altschuler, D. R., Schneider, S. E., Giovanardi, C., et al. 1986, *ApJL*, 305, L85. doi:10.1086/184690

Gathier, R., Pottasch, S. R., & Goss, W. M. 1986, *A&A*, 157, 191

Glassgold, A. E. & Huggins, P. J. 1983, *MNRAS*, 203, 517. doi:10.1093/mnras/203.2.517

Ouyang, X.-J., Zhang, Y., Zijlstra, A., et al. 2022, *ApJ*, 933, 4. doi:10.3847/1538-4357/ac6fdb

Ouyang, X.-J., Zhang, Y., Zijlstra, A., et al. 2023, *ApJ*, 952, 166. doi:10.3847/1538-4357/acd761

Taylor, A. R., Gussie, G. T., & Pottasch, S. R. 1990, *ApJ*, 351, 515. doi:10.1086/168489

Planetary Nebulae: A Universal Toolbox in the Era of Precision Astrophysics
Proceedings IAU Symposium No. 384, 2025
O. De Marco, A. Zijlstra & R. Szczerba, eds.
doi:10.1017/S1743921324000978

Binary central stars of planetary nebulae in the Large Magellanic Cloud

Marcin Gładkowski[1], **Marcin Hajduk**[2], **Radosław Smolec**[3], **Ryszard Szczerba**[1] **and Igor Soszyński**[4]

[1]Nicolaus Copernicus Astronomical Center, Polish Academy of Sciences, ul. Rabiańska 8, 87-100 Toruń, Poland
email: seyfert@ncac.torun.pl

[2]Department of Geodesy, Institute of Geodesy and Civil Engineering, Faculty of Geoengineering, University of Warmia and Mazury, ul. Oczapowskiego 2, 10-719 Olsztyn, Poland

[3]Nicolaus Copernicus Astronomical Center, Polish Academy of Sciences, ul. Bartycka 18, 00-716 Warszawa, Poland

[4]Astronomical Observatory, University of Warsaw, Al. Ujazdowskie 4, 00-478, Warszawa, Poland

Abstract. We used the OGLE data to search for binary central stars of planetary nebulae (CSPNe) in the Large Magellanic Cloud (LMC). Nine binary CSPNe with periods between 0.24 and 23.6 days were discovered. The obtained fraction of binary CSPNe for the LMC PNe is $3.3^{+2.6}_{-1.6}\%$ without correcting for incompleteness.

Keywords. techniques: photometric, binaries: general, planetary nebulae: general, galaxies: individual (Large Magellanic Cloud)

1. Introduction

Large-scale photometric surveys like Optical Gravitational Lensing Experiment (OGLE) (Udalski et al. 1992) provide an excellent opportunity to improve our knowledge of the planetary nebulae (PNe) phenomenon. Some of PNe can be formed in binary systems through the common envelope interaction (Ivanova et al. 2013). The fraction of binary central stars of planetary nebulae (CSPNe) in the Milky Way was established as 12–21% towards the Galactic bulge (Miszalski et al. 2009) or 20.7% in the Galaxy using data from Kepler (Jacoby et al. 2021). A few attempts in searching for variability in the PNe beyond the Milky Way have been made so far, but only one binary CSPNe in the Small Magellanic Cloud was discovered (Hajduk et al. 2014).

2. PNe sample

Our sample of the PNe in the Large Magellanic Cloud (LMC) is based on the list of 605 PNe from Reid et al. (2014). We have positively identified 290 of them in the OGLE-III and OGLE-IV I-band reference images. This allowed us to get their light curves. However, in case of ten objects light curves were not accessible in the OGLE database. Therefore, our full sample for the further analysis consists of 280 objects.

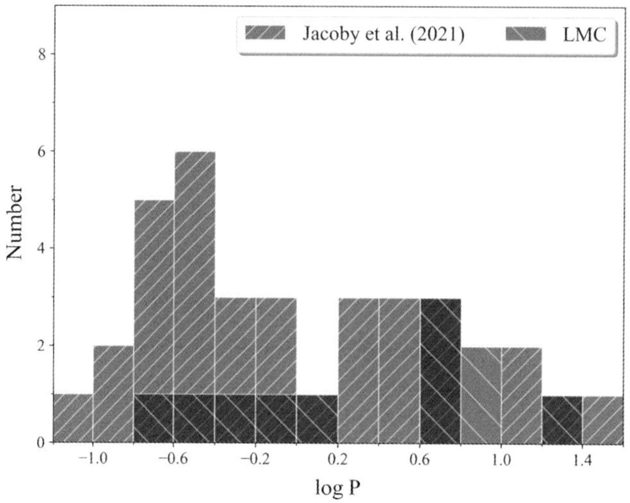

Figure 1. Comparison of the orbital period distribution of the new binaries in the LMC discovered by Gładkowski et al. (2024), and in the Milky Way found by Jacoby et al. (2021).

3. Data analysis and results

We have made an analysis of the I-band light curves using the Period04 (Lenz & Breger 2005) and our own software (Smolec 2017). We performed discrete Fourier transform up to a frequency of $10\,\mathrm{c\,d}^{-1}$ (cycles per day) to find the variability which can be assigned to the binary CSPNe. In total 32 variables were found: 27 belong to the LMC, and 5 are foreground objects. Among 27 LMC objects, 9 are binary CSPNe ([RP2006] 695, 979, 1429, 1488, 1773, SMP LMC 59, 64, MGPN LMC 55, and [M94b] 30), whereas 18 objects show the variability which cannot be attributed to the binarity of CSPNe. The binary CSPNe were selected on the grounds of derived periods which range from 0.24 up to 23.6 days with the obtained amplitudes 4-168 mmag. Figure 1 shows the period distribution of our new sample from Gładkowski et al. (2024), and 34 known Galactic binaries from Jacoby et al. (2021) with a chosen bin of $\Delta \log P = 0.2$. Two objects from the Galactic sample are not included in the histogram because their variability can be caused, for example, by stellar winds (Jacoby et al. 2021): PN H 2-48 with a period of 4.1 days and PN Th 3-14 with a period of 1.15 day. The shape of the period distributions seems to be different, with a lack of a well-defined maximum in the case of the LMC sample.

4. Conclusions

Our work led to discovery of nine binary CSPNe in the LMC with period ranging from 0.24 up to 23.6 days. The obtained period distribution in the LMC seems to be different to the one found by Miszalski et al. (2009) towards the Galactic bulge or Jacoby et al. (2021) in the Milky Way. In addition, the fraction of binary PNe which was determined by us as $3.3^{+2.6}_{-1.6}\%$ for the LMC is much lower than that established for the Milky Way, but it is uncorrected for incompleteness. Lower binary fraction suggests smaller efficiency of the common envelope phase producing close binaries in the LMC compared to the Galaxy (Gładkowski et al. 2024).

The work was financially supported by the National Science Centre (NCN) of Poland through grants: 2014/15/N/ST9/04629, 2016/23/B/ST9/01653, 2016/21/B/ST9/01626, 2022/45/B/ST9/00243, and 2018/30/E/ST9/00598.

Supplementary material

To view supplementary material for this article, please visit https://doi.org/10.1017/S1743921324000978

References

Udalski A., Szymański M., Kałużny J., Kubiak M., Mateo M., 1992, Acta Astron., 42, 253. adsurl: https://ui.adsabs.harvard.edu/abs/1992AcA....42..253U

Lenz P., Breger M., 2005, Communications in Asteroseismology, 146, 53. doi:10.1553/cia146s53

Miszalski B., Acker A., Moffat A. F. J., Parker Q. A., Udalski A., 2009, A&A, 496, 813. doi:10.1051/0004-6361/200811380

Ivanova N., Justham S., Chen X., 2013, A&A Rev., 21, 59. doi:10.1007/s00159-013-0059-2

Hajduk M., Gładkowski M., Soszyński I., 2014, A&A, 561, A8. doi:10.1051/0004-6361/201321682

Reid W. A., 2014, MNRAS, 438, 2642. doi:10.1093/mnras/stt2385

Smolec R., 2017, MNRAS, 468, 4299. doi:10.1093/mnras/stx679

Jacoby G. H., Hillwig T. C., Jones D., 2021, MNRAS, 506, 5223. doi:10.1093/mnras/stab2045

Gładkowski M., Hajduk M., Smolec R., Szczerba R., Soszyński I., 2024, A&A, 682, A70. doi:10.1051/0004-6361/202346540

Planetary Nebulae: A Universal Toolbox in the Era of Precision Astrophysics
Proceedings IAU Symposium No. 384, 2025
O. De Marco, A. Zijlstra & R. Szczerba, eds.
doi:10.1017/S1743921323005100

Stellar and circumstellar lines in the spectra of protoplanetary nebulae

Aija Grankina, Kārlis Puķītis and Laimons Začs

Laser Center, Faculty of Physics, Mathematics, and Optometry, University of Latvia, Raiņa bulvāris 19, LV-1586, Rīga, Latvia
email: aija.laure@gmail.com

Abstract. We present an analysis of high resolution spectra in the optical and near infrared wavelength region for cool protoplanetary nebulae with the goal to identify lines of carbon bearing molecules and some less studied neutron capture elements. The site of formation of CN and C_2 lines in the spectra of IRAS 22272+5435 and IRAS Z02229+6208 appears to be an extended stellar atmosphere and inner/outer CSE. The abundance of thulium was estimated for the first time in the photosphere of IRAS22272+5435, log $\epsilon(Tm) \simeq 1.5$.

Keywords. stars: AGB and post-AGB, stars: atmospheres, stars: circumstellar matter, stars: individual (IRAS 22272+5435, IRAS Z02229+6208), line: identification

1. Introduction

The atmospheres and circumstellar envelopes (CSEs) of AGB and post-AGB stars are the most remarkable chemical laboratories in the Galaxy. Many aspects of photospheric and circumstellar chemistry are still not understood, e.g. why some post-AGB stars are extremely s-process enriched while others are not enriched at all, where is the site of formation of broad unidentified features and what species take part in their formation.

2. Observations

Spectra of IRAS 22272+5435 and IRAS Z02229+6208 were monitored using the high-resolution spectrometer VUES of the Vilnius University installed on the 1.65 m telescope at the Moletai Observatory (Lithuania) and the CARMENES instrument on the 3.5 m telescope at the Centro Astronómico Hispano en Andalucía (CAHA) at Calar Alto.

3. Results and conclusions

Numerous lines of C_2 and CN molecules are seen in the spectra both in absorption and emission (Puķītis et al. 2023; Začs & Puķītis 2023). Figure 1 illustrates variability of IRAS Z02229+6208 spectra in the wavelength region redward of the CN Red system (2,0) bandhead at 7850 Å. The strongest blueshifted CN absorptions are seen in the two spectra observed near the light minima. The width of these CN lines is lower on average in comparison with that for the photospheric atomic lines, FWHM $\simeq$ 16 km s^{-1} and 23 km s^{-1}, respectively. In the spectra observed near the light maxima blueshifted emissions are seen. In addition, narrow blueshifted CN (2,0) system absorption lines are identified. The mean FWHM for these lines was found to be FWHM $\simeq$ 0.14 Å (5.4 km s^{-1}). The site of formation of the broad/variable molecular absorption and emission appears to be an extended atmosphere of a cool post-AGB star affected by stellar pulsation. The

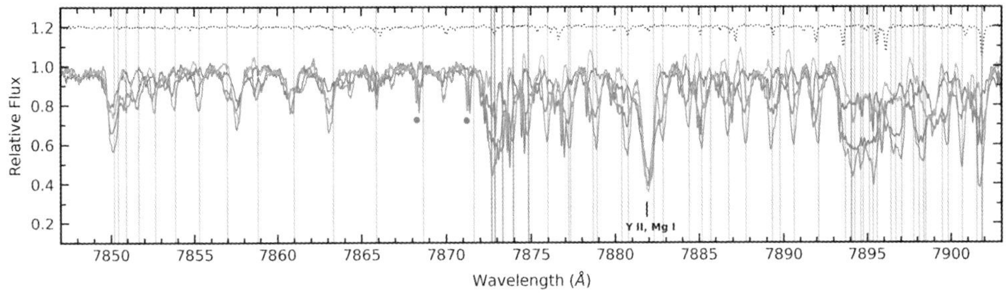

Figure 1. Time series of four IRAS Z02229+6208 spectra in the wavelength region from 7847 to 7903 Å observed from 2022 July 23 (red) to 2022 October 14 (blue). The telluric spectrum is shown by the dotted line on the top of the figure. Variable blueshifted CN Red system (2,0) lines, marked with vertical lines, are seen near the light minimum, along with narrow CN (2,0) CSE lines. Two less blended CSE lines are marked by red dots.

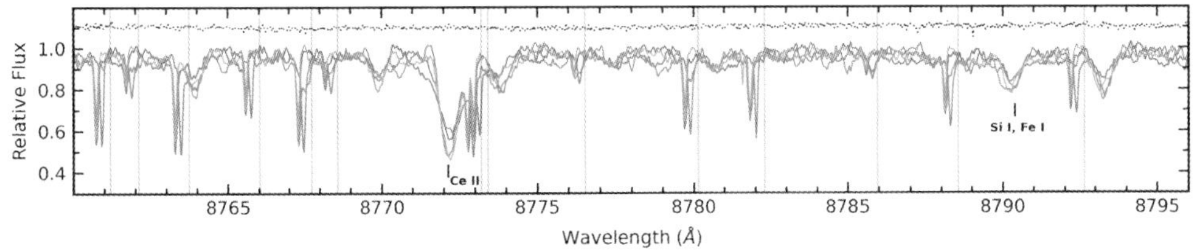

Figure 2. Same as Figure 1, but in the wavelength region from 8750 to 8800 Å. Narrow blueshifted C_2 Phillips system (2,0) lines are identified.

narrow CN (2,0) lines are formed most probably in the CSE produced during the AGB stage.

We examined two spectral regions in the near infrared wavelength region with the aim of finding the lines of C_2 Phillips system. Figure 2 illustrates the wavelengths region redward of the C_2 Phillips system (2,0) bandhead at 8750 Å, where the intensity of CN Red system lines is lower. A number of narrow blueshifted C_2 (2,0) lines are seen in the spectra. The mean radial velocity of the identified lines was found to be similar in all the spectra, δRV = -11.0 ± 0.2 km s^{-1}, relative to the mass center. The mean FWHM for selected lines was found to be $\simeq 0.14$ Å (5.4 km s^{-1}). Thus, the site of formation of the narrow Phillips system lines seems to be the CSE produced during the AGB stage.

Abundances of elements with the atomic numbers between Z = 64 and 69 are a good criteria to distinguish between nucleosynthesis in the s- and r-process. We inspected the spectra of IRAS22272+5435 in the optical wavelength region with the aim of finding the lines of less studied neutron capture elements thulium and holmium. Weak thulium lines are identified at 5009.77, 5346.49, and 5684.76 Å and the thulium abundance was estimated for the first time, log $\epsilon(Tm) \simeq 1.5$ on average. The method of model atmospheres and spectral synthesis was used for the abundance calculation.

We acknowledge support from the Latvian Science Council under the FLPP grant lzp-2020/1-0088 "Advanced spectroscopic methods and tools for the study of evolved stars".

References

Puķītis, K., Začs, L., & Sperauskas, J. 2023, *ApJ*, 948, 70. doi:10.3847/1538-4357/acc52b
Začs, L. & Puķītis, K. 2023, *ApJ*, 952, 49. doi:10.3847/1538-4357/acdcfe

Planetary Nebulae: A Universal Toolbox in the Era of Precision Astrophysics
Proceedings IAU Symposium No. 384, 2025
O. De Marco, A. Zijlstra & R. Szczerba, eds.
doi:10.1017/S1743921324000061

Disk-Driven Planetary Nebulae: Shapes and Spectra

Vincent Icke

Sterrewacht Leiden, Universiteit Leiden
email: icke@strw.leidenuniv.nl

Abstract. I have performed numerical hydrodynamical calculations of outflows driven by the evaporation of a pseudo-barotropic ring around a luminous central star. The outflow shapes and internal structures resemble known cylindrical nebulae. Some of the corresponding synthetic spectra show 'Hubble' type outflow.

Keywords. hydrodynamics, protoplanetary nebulae, evaporating disks

---

1. Introduction

Many bipolar (proto)planetary nebulae (pPN) have a pronounced cylindrical shape, but do not show an anisotropic stellar wind, or magnetic driving. In these cases there is clear evidence of a thick disk at the base of the nebula, and it would be quite remarkable if the outflow did not actually start there. Radiation from the central star is a plausible source of energy. Thus, I have computed a series of hydrodynamical models in which a dense gaseous ring around a luminous star is irradiated so fiercely that the disk surface blows off into space. The model generically produces well collimated cylindrical outflow patterns, with remarkable H-shocks along the axis. The first steps were published in Icke (2022). The present work is a continuation thereof, with emphasis on the velocity field.

2. Hydrodynamics

Single stars probably have planetary systems. When such a star becomes a pPN, its planets will be destroyed, especially if they are gaseous superjupiters. This gas forms an 'excretion disk', and the nascent white dwarf in its centre will fiercely irradiate the disk. The radiative influx energy is equal to the kinetic plus thermal energy of the evaporating gas. The launching conditions of the flow obey

$$\left(\frac{1}{2}\rho v^2 + \frac{1}{\gamma \mathscr{M}_0^2 \sqrt{r}}\right) v = \frac{\mathscr{L}}{\mathscr{L}_0} \frac{1}{r^2} \sin\left(\psi - \theta\right) \tag{1}$$

where ρ is the gas density, v the speed perpendicular to the disk surface, γ the adiabatic index of the gas, $\mathscr{M}_0$ the Mach number, $\mathscr{L}$ the luminosity, ψ the local inclination of the disk isodensity surface, θ the polar angle and r the radial distance from the star. In the derivation of Eq.(1), each variable V was replaced by $V_0 \times V$, in which V_0 is a fixed scaling quantity, and V is now dimensionless. The scaling quantities are related by

$$s_0^2 = \gamma P_0/\rho_0 \ ; \quad \mathscr{M}_0 = v_0/s_0 \ ; \quad \mathscr{L}_0 = 4\pi \rho_0 r_0^2 v_0^3 \tag{2}$$

In my computations, all variables are of order unity, so that the results may be scaled to the observations. For example, using the 'astronomical' units $\rho_A = 10^6$ H/cm^3,

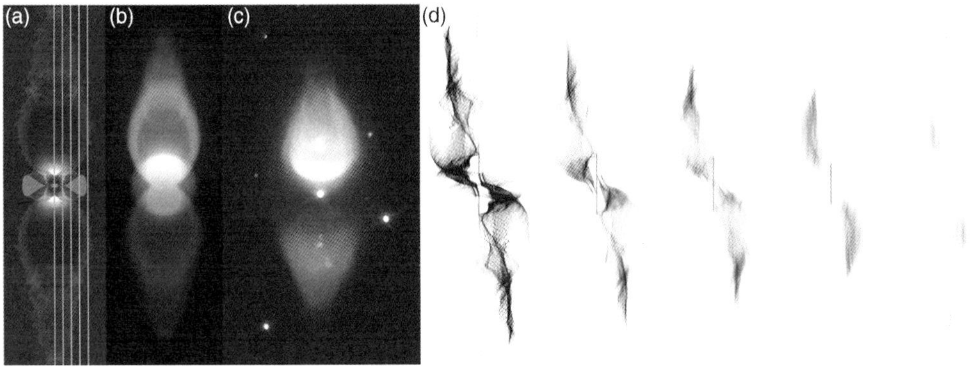

Figure 1. Results from one of my evaporating-disk models compared with M1-92. The mean values in this snapshot: $\rho = 0.66$, $P = 0.35$, $v = 0.71$. Maximum: $\rho = 18.7$, $P = 8.9$, $v = 4.0$. Luminosity $\mathscr{L}_0 = 1.2$. These must be scaled to the observed data (see text). Images, from left to right, **A:** Model Evap220818-d, with positions of the spectrograph slits. Red=density ρ, Green=pressure P, Blue=speed v; **B:** Projected gas density at 50° w.r.t. sky; **C:** M1-92 from Alcolea *et al.* (2022); **D:** synthetic long-slit spectra at the positions indicated in image A.

$r_A = 10^3$ AU, $v_A = 100$ km/s, it follows that $\mathscr{L}_A = 1226\,\rho r^2 v^3\ \mathrm{L}_\odot$. Also, $(4\pi/3)\rho_A r_A^3 = 12.4\ M_{\mathrm{Jup}}$, showing that a destroyed superjupiter provides enough matter for the evaporating disk.

3. Results

The overall appearance of my hydro models is encouraging. For quantitative comparison, I use the data assembled by Garcia-Lario *et al.* (1999), Bujarrabal *et al.* (2001), Muthumariappan *et al.* (2006), Hrivnak *et al.* (2008), Fang *et al.* (2018), and Balick *et al.* (2023). The dimensionless units in Eq.(1) make it easy to set up simulations, but the results must be converted into dimensional form for comparison with observations, e.g. the case of M1-92 (Alcolea *et al.* (2022); Figure 1). From their paper I take: speed $v_0 = 170$ km/s, size $r_0 = 3000$ AU and density $\rho_0 = 1.5 \times 10^5\ \mathrm{cm}^{-3}$. Eq.(2) then gives the scaling luminosity $\mathscr{L}_0 = 8100\,\mathrm{L}_\odot$. Because the dimensionless luminosity of the simulation is $\mathscr{L}_0 = 1.2$, my result corresponds to $\mathscr{L} = 9720\,\mathrm{L}_\odot$. This nicely matches their stellar luminosity: $\mathscr{L} = 10^4\,\mathrm{L}_\odot$.

The shapes of the nebulae Hen3-401, Hen3-1475, M1-92, Hen2-437, OH231.8 and V445Pup are reproduced quite well by my models. The axial features in M1-92 and Hen3-1475 agree with the H-shocks that always occur in the simulations, due to the focusing by the concave barotropic disk.

In many of the synthetic spectra, the outflow speed is proportional to the distance to the star, due to the conversion of thermal into kinetic energy downstream of the axial H-shocks. Such $v \propto z$ is in fact observed in some nebulae.

Acknowledgements. I thank my colleagues for the invitation to IAUS384, for their enlightening remarks, and for their patience. Once again, I am grateful to prof. Bruce Balick for his enthusiasm and encouragement. My research was supported by Universiteit Leiden, under the usual conditions for University employees.

Supplementary material

To view supplementary material for this article, please visit https://doi.org/10.1017/S1743921324000061

References

Alcolea, J., Agúndez, M., Bujarrabal, V., Castro-Carrizo, A., Desmurs, J.-F., Martínez-Fernández, J.-E., Sánchez Contreras, C., & Santander-García, M. 2022, *Galaxies*, 10, 47

Balick, B., Huehnerhoff, J. & Baerny, J. 2023, *The Catalog of Hubble Images of Nascent and Infantile Planetary Nebulae*

Bujarrabal, V., Castro-Carrizo, A., Alcolea, J. & Sánchez Contreras, C. 2001, *A&A*, 377, 868

Fang, X., Gomez de Castro, A. I., Toala, J. A., & Riera, A. 2018, *Ap.J.L.*, 865, L23

Garcia-Lario, P., Riera, A. & Manchado, A. 1999, *Ap.J.*, 526, 854

Hrivnak, B. J., Smith, N., Su, K. Y. L. & Sahai, R. 2008, *Ap.J.*, 688, 327

Icke, V. 2022, *Galaxies*, 10, 53

Muthumariappan, C., Kwok, S. & Volk, K. 2006, *Ap.J.*, 640, 353

Planetary Nebulae: A Universal Toolbox in the Era of Precision Astrophysics
Proceedings IAU Symposium No. 384, 2025
O. De Marco, A. Zijlstra & R. Szczerba, eds.
doi:10.1017/S1743921323004878

EXPLORE: The wide binary companions to the two Ring nebulae

Albert Zijlstra and Iain McDonald

Department of Physics and Astronomy, The University of Manchester, UK
email: albert.zijlstra@manchester.ac.uk

Abstract. Two planetary nebulae have sofar been observed with JWST. Both show stellar companions. The paper discusses how and what we can learn from the companions.

Keywords. Catalogs, Surveys, stars: binaries, planetary nebulae

1. Introduction

EXPLORE (https://explore-platform.eu) is an EU-funded project to develop tools to located and analyze on-line archival data, without the need to download these data. The philosophy is to bring the software to the data. EXPLORE is developing a set of scientific data applications (SDAs) on topics as diverse as Lunar crater classification, galactic archaeology, and 3-d extinction models.

We are developing an SDA called SPHOT which retrieves photometry for individual stars from a large number of surveys, with GAIA distances, and uses these to fit stellar atmosphere models. It is based on work in McDonald, Zijlstra, & Watson (2017).

The SDA can also be run off-line by installing the underlying `pyssed` package. It has two main modes, one for individual stars and one for fields. The package obtains an accurate position and proper motion for each star, and uses this to find the correct counterpart in various surveys, e.g. Sloan and IPHAS. The filter curves for each survey are retrieved and the stellar atmosphere models (BT-Settle by default) convolved with these. Extinction is obtained from 3-d extinction cubes in EXPLORE.

2. The two Ring Nebulae

We have used the SDA for stars associated with planetary nebulae. Two planetary nebulae have been observed with JWST: the Southern Ring (NGC 3132; De Marco et al. 2022) and the Ring Nebula (NGC 6720; Wesson et al. 2023). The central star of the Southern Ring has a bright A-type companion located at 1300 au from the central star. The pyssed fitting confirmed the temperature of 9200 K, from GAIA DR3 spectroscopy and was used to calibrate the photometry of the central star in these early JWST data. The companion star has evolved off the main sequence, allowing us to determine both the mass and age fron PARSEC isochrones: $2.4 \pm 0.15\,M_\odot$ and 530 Myr. Extrapolating the isochrone gives the progenitor mass of the PN central star: $2.86 \pm 0.05\,M_\odot$. Dartmouth isochrones yield masses lower by $0.15\,M_\odot$.

JWST shows that the central star has a resolved dust disk which is aligned with the companion star. The disk extends from 50 to 140 au from the star with an inner disk at 3 to 8 au seen in a hot dust excess (De Marco et al. 2022). Multiple arcs visible in the JWST images show evidence for an unseen close companion star, at ~ 50 au, around the inner edge of the disk. The close companion must be no more than $0.2\,M_\odot$ if Main Sequence or it would have been detected in pyssed.

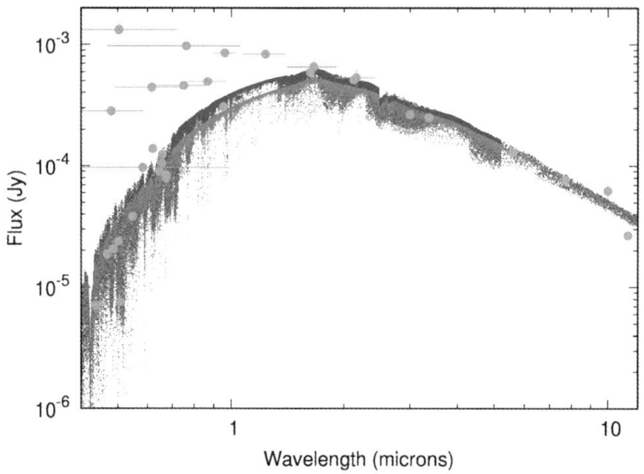

Figure 1. SED of the Ring Nebula companion star with BT-Settl models. The blue circles falling above the fit are affected by nebular emission and were excluded from the fitting.

A distant proper motion companion to the central star of the Ring Nebula (González-Santamaría et al. 2021) lies 18.5 arcsec from the central star, or a projected distance of 0.07 pc. It was proposed to be a white dwarf, based on the *Gaia* DR3 photometry. However, this photometry is badly affected by nebular emission lines. The pyssed fit (Fig. 1) gives $T_{\rm eff} = 3300$–3400 K. This indicates a main sequence star of approximate spectral type M2–M4 with a mass of 0.3–0.5 $M_{\odot}$.

The distant companion has remained bound to the central star over its life time. By estimating time scales for stellar encounters, we find that the mean survival time would 1 Gyr. This suggest a progenitor mass for the central star of $\sim 2\,M_{\odot}$.

JWST images show ~ 10 concentric arcs, interpreted as due to a companion star at 50 au. The star is not detected in photometry. Both ring nebulae therefore contain triple stellar systems with both closer and more distant companions. The more massive progenitors of 2–3 $M_{\odot}$ may have a higher chance of companions.

Companion stars can be important tools in deriving properties of the central stars. It is not clear how much tripe systems affect the structure of the nebulae. Angular momentum exchange between the outer and inner companions might amplify the angular momentum available to the wind of the mass losing star. However, this is speculative.

We acknowledge funding from the EU Horizon2020 program through grant 101004214.

Supplementary material

To view supplementary material for this article, please visit https://doi.org/10.1017/S1743921323004878

References

González-Santamaría I., Manteiga M., Manchado A., Ulla A., Dafonte C., López Varela P., 2021, *A&A*, 656, A51. doi:10.1051/0004-6361/202141916

De Marco O., Akashi M., Akras S., Alcolea J., Aleman I., Amram P., Balick B., et al., 2022, *NatAs*, 6, 1421. doi:10.1038/s41550-022-01845-2

McDonald I., Zijlstra A. A., Watson R. A., 2017, *MNRAS*, 471, 770. doi:10.1093/mnras/stx1433

Wesson R., Matsuura M., Zijlstra A. A., Volk K., Kavanagh P. J., García-Segura G., McDonald I., et al., 2023, *MNRAS*, subm. arXiv:2308.09027. doi:10.48550/arXiv.2308.09027

Planetary Nebulae: A Universal Toolbox in the Era of Precision Astrophysics
Proceedings IAU Symposium No. 384, 2025
O. De Marco, A. Zijlstra & R. Szczerba, eds.
doi:10.1017/S1743921323005525

A Multi-Wavelength Analysis of Planetary Nebula NGC 3132 using MUSE, JWST and SPITZER data

Konstantinos Bouvis and Stavros Akras

Institute for Astronomy, Astrophysics, Space Applications and Remote Sensing, National Observatory of Athens, GR 15236 Penteli, Greece
email: konos982@gmail.com

Abstract. MUSE data regarding NGC 3132 were used and analysed through SATELLITE in order to obtain 2D maps of the physico-chemical parameters of the nebula. Furthermore, our results were compared with a 3D photoionisation model built with MOCASSIN with the aim to constrain its parameters. Lastly, we utilized JWST and Spitzer IR data and examined their radial distribution.

Keywords. planetary nebulae: individual (NGC 3132), ISM: molecules, ISM: dust, extinction, ISM: abundances, infrared: ISM

1. Introduction

Integral field spectroscopy or imaging spectroscopy has been established in the last decade as an important technique for the spatial analysis of ionised gas such as HII regions, galaxies and planetary nebulae. MUSE, which is mounted on VLT, is one of the most capable integral field units available. In this study, a two-dimensional spectroscopic analysis has been performed on the PN NGC 3132 using the MUSE data from Monreal-Ibero & Walsh (2020) and SATELLITE code (Akras et al. 2020). This particular planetary nebula was selected for the early observing phase of JWST and significant emission from molecular hydrogen fragmented in clumps as well as a multiple stellar system at its centre have been found (De Marco et al. 2022).

2. Results

We utilised MUSE data with SATELLITE, and we examined several physico-chemical parameters of the nebula like $c(H_\beta)$, N_e, T_e, ionic and total elemental abundances (left panel Figure 1). The rims have $T_e \sim 10^4$ K and $N_e \sim 10^3$ cm^{-3}, while inside the elliptical ionized cavity $T_e \sim 9{,}700$ K and $N_e \sim 400$ cm^{-3} are found. Moreover, a 3D photoionization model build with MOCASSIN (Monteiro et al. in prep) was compared to MUSE's observational data in order to constrain its physical characteristics. The current model slightly underestimates N_e and overestimates T_e by a little. The ionic and total chemical abundances are in good agreement with the observational data.

From the radial analysis of the JWST data, it was found that H_2 gas shows two peaks at the inner and at the outer part of the rim as well. Extinction coefficient $c(H_\beta)$ and H_2 emission appear to be co-spatial, indicating the presence of dust that likely prevents the dissociation of H_2 (Akras et al. 2020, 2022; Aleman & Gruenwald 2011). Furthermore, according to Phillips et al. (2010), the Spitzer IRAC [8.0]/[4.5] ratio takes its lowest values at low ionisation regions. Interestingly enough, in our analysis, H_2 peaks at the

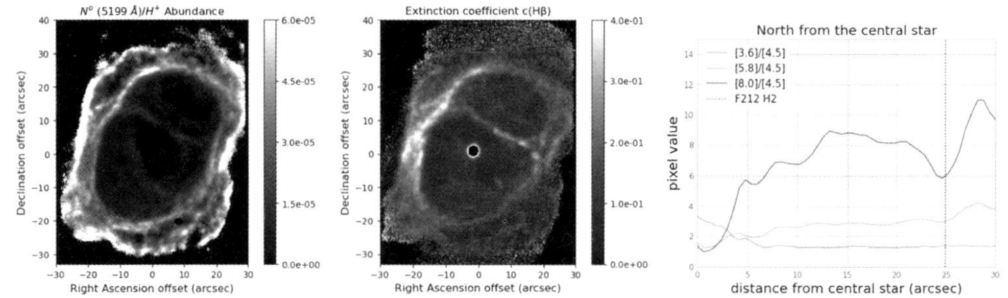

Figure 1. Left panel: 2D map of NGC 3132 for N^o/H^+ abundance. Middle panel: 2D map of NGC3132 for extinction coefficient $c(H_\beta)$. Right panel: Radial profiles for Spitzer IRAC channels ratios North from the central star of PN NGC 3132. The red dotted line represents the peak of 2.12 μm line of H_2 as obtained by JWST.

same distance from the central star where [8.0]/[4.5] ratio decreases (right panel Figure 1). Here, we provide for the first time confirmation between the link of H_2 2.12 μm emission line from JWST and infrared colours from Spitzer's IRAC [8.0]/[4.5] ratio.

3. Conclusions

The comparison of the MUSE data with the 3D photoionization modelled results of NGC 3132 with the SATELLITE code allow us to constrain and improve the model. In addition, this analysis will make possible the exploration of a potential spatial variation of ICFs throughout the nebula. Scrutinizing the JWST and Spitzer data, we verified the link between the H_2 emission line and the [8.0]/[4.5] ratio. On the other hand, the examination of the JWST and MUSE data revealed that c(Hb) and H_2 radial profiles peak at the exact same position, indicating that dust prevent the dissociation of H_2 and act as a catalyst for its formation.

The research project is implemented in the framework of H.F.R.I. call "Basic research Financing (Horizontal support of all Sciences)" under the National Recovery and Resilience Plan "Greece 2.0" funded by the European Union - NextGenerationEU (H.F.R.I. Project Number: 15665).

Supplementary material

To view supplementary material for this article, please visit https://doi.org/10.1017/S1743921323005525

References

Akras, S., Monteiro, H., Walsh, J. R., et al. 2022, *MNRAS*, 512, 2202. doi:10.1093/mnras/stac632

Akras, S., Gonçalves, D. R., Ramos-Larios, G., et al. 2020, *MNRAS*, 493, 3800. doi:10.1093/mnras/staa515

Aleman, I. & Gruenwald, R. 2011, *AAP*, 528, A74. doi:10.1051/0004-6361/201014978

Phillips, J. P., Cuesta, L. C., & Ramos-Larios, G. 2010, *MNRAS*, 409, 881. doi:10.1111/j.1365-2966.2010.17372.x

De Marco, O., Akashi, M., Akras, S., et al. 2022, *Nature Astronomy*, 6, 1421. doi:10.1038/s41550-022-01845-2

Monreal-Ibero, A. & Walsh, J. R. 2020, *AAP*, 634, A47. doi:10.1051/0004-6361/201936845

Planetary Nebulae: A Universal Toolbox in the Era of Precision Astrophysics
Proceedings IAU Symposium No. 384, 2025
O. De Marco, A. Zijlstra & R. Szczerba, eds.
doi:10.1017/S1743921323005082

3D photoionization and kinematical reconstruction of the Planetary Nebula H 2-18

K. Gesicki[1], A. Zijlstra[2], M. Hajduk[3], A. Iwanowska[1], K. Grzesiak[1], K. Lisiecki[1] and J. Lipinski[1]

[1]Institute of Astronomy, Faculty of Physics, Astronomy and Informatics, Nicolaus Copernicus University, ul. Grudziadzka 5, 87-100 Torun, Poland
email: kmgesicki@umk.pl

[2]Jodrell Bank Centre for Astrophysics, School of Physics & Astronomy, University of Manchester, Oxford Road, Manchester M13 9PL, UK

[3]Department of Geodesy, Faculty of Geoengineering, University of Warmia and Mazury, ul. Oczapowskiego 2, 10-719 Olsztyn, Poland

Abstract. The Planetary Nebula H 2-18 is analysed with the full-3D capabilities of the MOCASSIN code. The collected HST images help to constrain the density distribution while the ARGUS 2D spectroscopy provides a new and unique information on kinematics.

Keywords. planetary nebulae: individual: H 2-18

The Galactic Bulge Planetary Nebula H 2-18 was observed in 2002 with HST (program 9356). The Observing Run 099.D-0386 at ESO in 2017 provided high-resolution spatially resolved spectroscopy. The IFU images overplotted with the HST Hα contours are shown in Fig. 1. While both Hα images agree well, the [NII] 658.3 nm image is different and reveals intriguing separated blobs worth of a detailed analysis.

The photoionization modelling was performed with the publicly available MOCASSIN code (Ercolano et al. 2003). Codes for kinematical and spectral analysis were written in Python by the authors. We aimed at a model which fits the images and simultaneously reproduces the photoionization structure (verified by the line ratios) and the emission line profiles and their distribution on the sky.

With quite a number of trials and errors we deduced a fine tuned model structure. We cannot claim it to be unique however it is as simple as possible and when appropriately rotated and tilted it explains all observed features/components (1,2,3,4 indicated in Fig. 1). It has the following characteristics:

(1) A barrel-shaped outer nebula inclined by 40 deg to the sky plane, with a constant density inner region continued outwards with decreasing density, its almost cylindrical shape reproduces well the observed straight edges;
(2) An outer equatorial torus of very low density;
(3) inner bipolar narrow jets of high density, co-axial with the outer nebula. Both jets have the same extent and similar density and contain $\sim 5\%$ of nebular mass. The [NII] blobs form in a decreasing-ionization conditions at their tips;
(4) A single-sided plume of ejected gas inclined to the main axis, assumed as a flat fan-shaped structure with opening angle 90 deg, spatially extended but not too

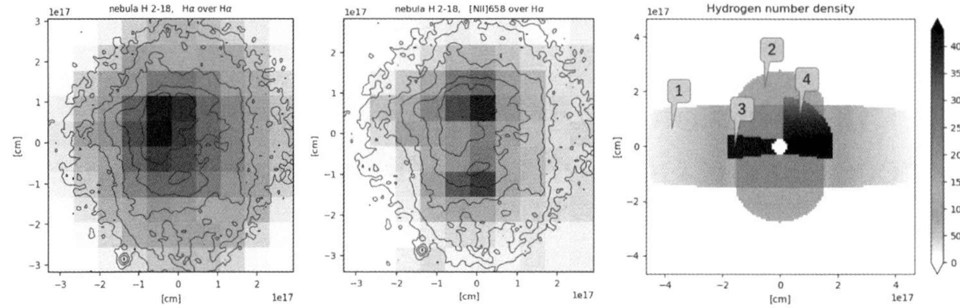

Figure 1. The nebula H 2-18 ARGUS/IFU image in Hα line (left panel) and in [NII] 658.3 nm (middle panel) with contours derived from HST Hα image. Right panel: the density structure of the model, the numbered components are described in the text. The axes are in [cm] assuming a distance of 8 kpc.

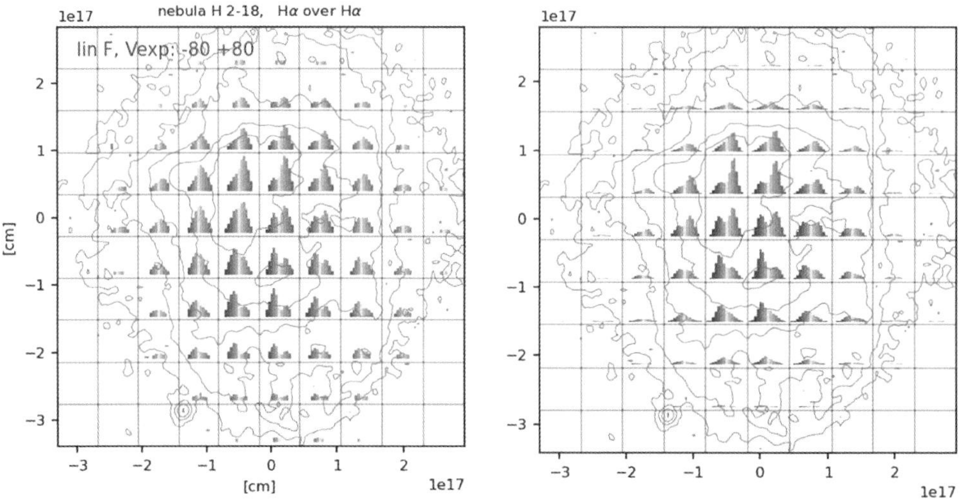

Figure 2. Left panel: The ARGUS IFU emission profiles in Hα line. Right panel: the Hα line shapes calculated from the proposed model. The contours are derived from the HST Hα image. The widths of the spectrum within each IFU pixel is from -80 to $+80$ km/s; colours indicate red- and blue-shift.

massive, $\sim 3\%$ of total mass, whose density is slowly decreasing away from the main axis. The plume seen at an angle produces the asymmetric broad central area in the Hα image.

The new model has higher stellar $T_{\rm bb}$ than our previous analyses (Gesicki et al. 2016) which better reproduces the [OIII] 500.7 nm emission. The advantage of 3D density (ionization) structure is obvious in this context. The expansion velocity of the main nebula and the velocity of the inner bipolar jets are typical for Planetary Nebulae, increasing from 15 to 60 km/s (Fig. 2). Even the [NII] jet-like or bullet-like structures are not exceptionally fast: the shaping of the nebula H 2-18 does not require particularly energetic processes.

For the outer nebula and its inner structures we assumed the same radial velocity field. A Hubble-type flow was not sufficient to reproduce the observed profiles, therefore we applied acceleration at the centre and an asymptotic value at larger distance. The contribution of 2D ARGUS/IFU spectroscopy is invaluable in this analysis (see Fig. 2).

The one-sided plume-like structure appears similar to the one observed in M 2-29 (Gesicki et al. 2010) however in H 2-18 it expands a little faster, is seen at different angle, and is located inside the main nebula although protruding a little out of it. The most likely explanation for the observed ejecta is a binary system, perhaps hidden in the central unresolved region. More details are presented in the online Supplementary Material.

We acknowledge financial support from the Nicolaus Copernicus University.

Supplementary material

To view supplementary material for this article, please visit https://doi.org/10.1017/S1743921323005082

References

Ercolano, B., Barlow, M. J., Storey, P. J. and Liu, X.-W., 2003, *MNRAS*, 340, 1136
Gesicki, K., Zijlstra, A. A., Szyszka, C., et al., 2010, *A&A*, 514, A54
Gesicki, K., Zijlstra, A. A., & Morisset, C., 2016, *A&A*, 585, A69

Planetary Nebulae: A Universal Toolbox in the Era of Precision Astrophysics
Proceedings IAU Symposium No. 384, 2025
O. De Marco, A. Zijlstra & R. Szczerba, eds.
doi:10.1017/S1743921324000024

NGC 3242 and the enigmatic nature of its Low Ionization Structures: A MUSE perspective

Lydia Konstantinou and Stavros Akras

Institute for Astronomy, Astrophysics, Space Applications and Remote Sensing, National Observatory of Athens, GR 15236 Penteli, Greece
email: lydiakonst@gmail.com

Abstract. The objective of our study was the spectroscopic analysis of the PN NGC 3242, which contains a pair of low-ionization structures (LISs). For our analysis, MUSE data were used in conjunction with the SATELLITE code for a spectroscopic analysis in two spatial dimensions. Additionally, infrared images from Spitzer Space Telescope (SST) were employed to search for potential H_2 emission at the LISs. The preliminary results revealed that the electron temperature calculated from [N II] diagnostics lines is approximately 12,000 K at the LISs, while the thorough examination of MUSE data has led to the identification of the [C I] 8727 Å emission line emitted only from the LISs. This result may imply that LISs are the optical counterpart of a dense molecular core. Spitzer's data didn't reveal the existence of H_2 at LISs, but three rings were identified around the main body of the PN.

Keywords. (ISM:) planetary nebulae: individual (NGC 3242), techniques: spectroscopic, ISM: atoms, ISM: abundances

1. Introduction

Planetary nebulae (PNe) are formed when low-to-intermediate mass stars expel their outer envelopes to the interstellar medium during the AGB phase. The intense ultraviolet (UV) radiation from the central star ionises the gas, leading to homogeneous nebular structures. However, in some PNe, distinct small-scale structures, characterized by lower ionization degree than the surrounding nebular gas, are observed. Although there are some theoretical scenarios for the origin of these low-ionisation structures (LISs), their nature remains poorly understood (Gonçalves et al. 2001; Mari et al. 2023; Akras & Gonçalves 2016). Our study is focused on the spectroscopic characterization in 2D of the multiple shell PN NGC 3242, which contains a pair of LISs. The SATELLITE code, developed from Akras et al. (2022), was used for the spatial analysis of the MUSE data and a physico-chemical analysis was carried out.

2. Results

2D maps for several nebular physico-chemical parameters were constructed. The electron temperature derived from [N II] diagnostic was representative only for the LISs with mean value 12,000 K (Fig. 1, left panel), which is in good agreement with the results from previous studies (e.g., Monteiro et al. 2013). Our analysis, also, revealed the existence of the far red atomic line [C I] 8727 Å , to originate only from the LISs (Fig. 1, right panel). This finding in conjunction with the enhanced low-ionisation lines such as [N II] and [O I] at LISs implies a partially ionised gas, which may surround a dense molecular core. The

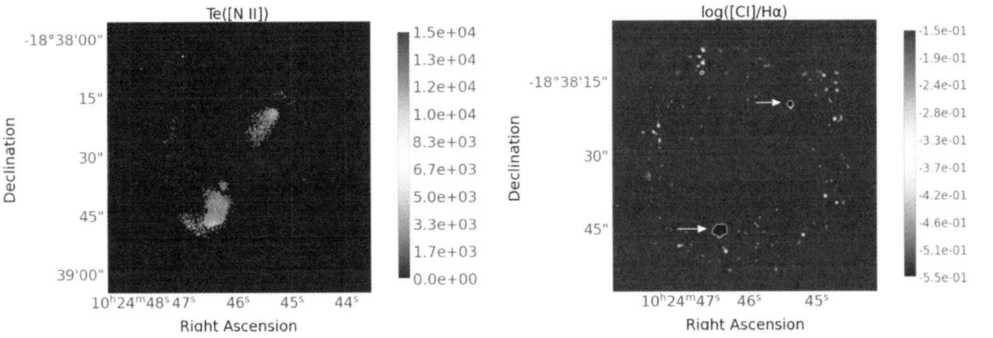

Figure 1. Left panel: electron temperature 2D map, calculated from [N II] emission lines. Right panel: smoothed 2D map of log([C I]/Hα). The white arrows point out the positions where atomic carbon was detected.

Figure 2. [4.5] Spitzer/IRAC band image of NGC 3242. Three rings are seen at the halo of the nebula. The colourbar indicates the surface brightness.

detection of the [C I] 8727 Å emission line at the pair of LISs provides further support of the scenario in which LISs are potentially mini photodissociation regions embedded in PNe.

In the investigation of Spitzer's image data, we couldn't find any evidence for H_2 emission to emanate from the LISs. We argue that the H_2 emission is either faint and not detectable by narrowband imaging or absent, but further investigation is required to confirm the presence of H_2 gas in the LISs of NGC 3242. In addition, three rings were identified around the main body of NGC 3242 (Fig. 2). These rings are probably related to different mass loss episodes during the AGB phase (Phillips et al. 2009).

This research project is implemented in the framework of H.F.R.I. call "Basic research Financing (Horizontal support of all Sciences)" under the National Recovery and Resilience Plan "Greece 2.0" funded by the European Union - NextGenerationEU (H.F.R.I. Project Number: 15665).

Supplementary material

To view supplementary material for this article, please visit https://doi.org/10.1017/S1743921324000024

References

Akras, S. & Gonçalves, D. R. 2016, *MNRAS*, 455, 930. doi:10.1093/mnras/stv2139
Akras, S., Monteiro, H., Walsh, J. R., et al. 2022, *MNRAS*, 512, 2202. doi:10.1093/mnras/stac632
Gonçalves, D. R., Corradi, R. L. M., & Mampaso, A. 2001, *APJ*, 547, 302. doi:10.1086/318364
Mari, M. B., Akras, S., & Gonçalves, D. R. 2023, *MNRAS*, 525, 1998. doi:10.1093/mnras/stad2256
Monteiro, H., Gonçalves, D. R., Leal-Ferreira, M. L., et al. 2013, *AAP*, 560, A102. doi:10.1051/0004-6361/201322220
Phillips, J. P., Ramos-Larios, G., Schröder, K.-P., et al. 2009, *MNRAS*, 399, 1126. doi:10.1111/j.1365-2966.2009.15379.x

Planetary Nebulae: A Universal Toolbox in the Era of Precision Astrophysics
Proceedings IAU Symposium No. 384, 2025
O. De Marco, A. Zijlstra & R. Szczerba, eds.
doi:10.1017/S1743921323005409

Discovery of hide-clumps of molecular hydrogen in the Owl nebula

G. Ramos-Larios[1], M. A. Guerrero[2], J. A. Toalá[3], S. Akras[4] and X. Fang[5]

[1]Instituto de Astronomía y Meteorología, CUCEI, Universidad de Guadalajara, Mexico
email: gerardo.astro@gmail.com

[2]Instituto de Astrofísica de Andalucía, IAA-CSIC, Granada, Spain

[3]Instituto de Radioastronomía y Astrofísica, UNAM, Morelia, Mich., Mexico

[4]Institute for Astronomy, Astrophysics, Space Applications and Remote Sensing, Penteli, Greece

[5]National Astronomical Observatories, Chinese Academy of Sciences, Beijing, China

Abstract. The recent acquisition of high-quality deep images of planetary nebulae (PNe) in world-class telescopes has allowed the detection for the first time of a wealth of small-scale morphological features and structures that highlight the complexity of their formation history and the physical processes modeling them. In this work we present the discovery of a series of clumps embedded within the ionized nebular shell of the evolved PN NGC 3587, the Owl Nebula, that had escaped previous detections. The multi-wavelength analysis provided by GEMINI, NOT and Aristarchos in the optical and CFHT and Spitzer infrared images indicates that these clumps are formed by denser and colder material, with a notable content of molecular H_2.

Keywords. (ISM:) planetary nebulae: general — planetary nebulae: individual: NGC 3587 — ISM: molecules — ISM: jets and outflows — ISM: lines and bands — infrared: ISM

1. Introduction

NGC 3587, a.k.a the Owl Nebula is a triple-shell PN consisting of an elliptical inner shell with the characteristic “owl eyes and beak”, a round envelope, and an outer halo (Guerrero et al. 2003). We report in this source the discovery of a number of clumps embedded within ionized material detected in optical low-excitation ionic and near-IR H_2 molecular line emission, which were undetected in early studies (Fig. 1).

Among the large number of molecules in the ISM, one of the most abundant is the molecular hydrogen (H_2), being the H_2 1−0 S(1) λ2.122 μm transition the most common to find in PNe (Guerrero et al. 2000; Ramos-Larios et al. 2017; Fang et al. 2018). Its formation occurs through reactions on the surface of dust grains, which act as catalyst to absorb the energy excess that is released when a new H_2 molecule is formed, surviving to photo-dissociation if the gas is dense enough. In order to study the spatial distributions of dust, ionized material and the newly discovered molecular hydrogen, we have collected a large amount of high-quality observational material in the optical and IR range that has allowed us to discern about the nature of the molecular material.

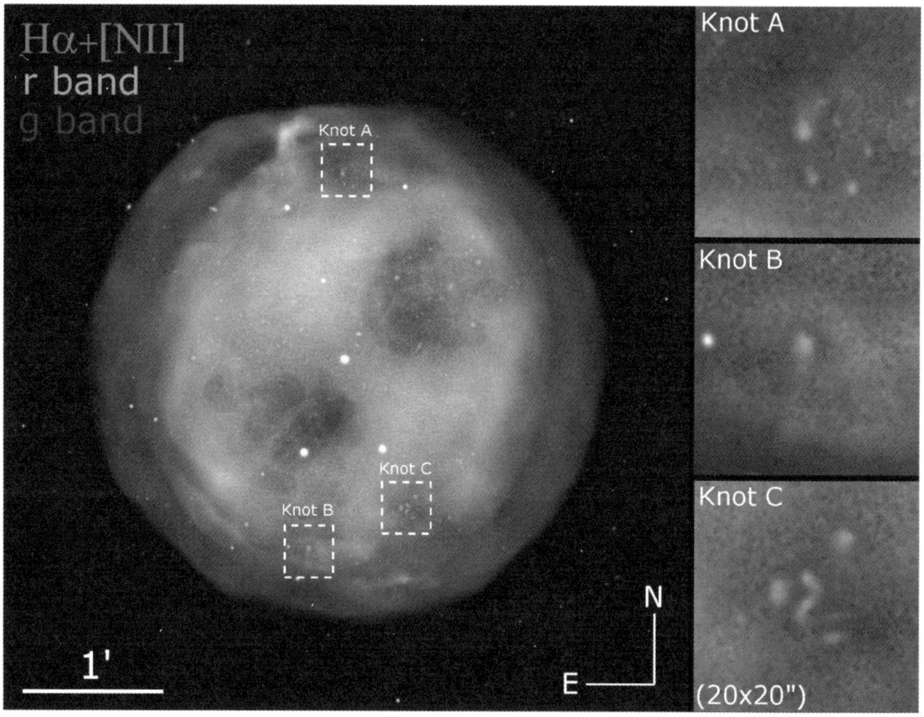

Figure 1. Gemini North GMOS high-resolution colour-composite picture of NGC 3587 in the light of the Hα+[NII] (red), r-SDSS (green), and g-SDSS (blue) filters. At the right side, insets of the 20×20 arcsec squared boxes overlaid on the picture around the position of the areas of lumpy material denoted as A, B and C. Their "unusual" shapes are emphasized in these zoomed views, with a bow-shock-like structure apparently associated with feature B.

2. The H_2 clumps

Pockets of molecular material embedded within ionized material are being detected in an increasing number of PNe as the quality of their H_2 observations improves (e.g. Akras et al. 2020; De Marco et al. 2022). May be the most prominent example of these structures is the myriad of H_2-emitting knots embedded within NGC 7293, the Helix Nebula (O'Dell, Henney, & Ferland 2007; Matsuura et al. 2009). These show morphologies that can easily match that of the knots detected in NGC 3587, as the cometary knots with tails (clump B) or multipeak knots (clump A) described by Matsuura et al. (2009).

The spatial distribution of the knots in the Helix Nebula, along an annular or ring-like structure, is otherwise notably different to that observed in the Owl Nebula. The detection of clumps of material where H_2 molecules are found in evolved PNe implies that compact, high-density structures are able to survive the whole PN evolution (and even after the PN dispersal).

We acknowledge funding from CONACyT grant 263373. MAG also acknowledges support of grant PGC2018-102184-B-100 co-funded with FEDER funds. JAT thanks support from the project UNAM PAPIIT IA101622.

Supplementary material

To view supplementary material for this article, please visit https://doi.org/10.1017/S1743921323005409

References

Akras S., Gonçalves D. R., Ramos-Larios G., Aleman I., 2020, *MNRAS*, 493, 3800

De Marco O., Akashi M., Akras S., Alcolea J., Aleman I., Amram P., Balick B., et al., 2022, *NatAs*, 6,1421

Guerrero M. A., Villaver E., Manchado A., Garcia-Lario P., Prada F., 2000, *ApJS*, 127, 125

Guerrero M. A., Chu Y.-H., Manchado A., Kwitter K. B., 2003, *AJ*, 125, 3213

Fang X., Zhang Y., Kwok S., Hsia C.-H., Chau W., Ramos-Larios G., Guerrero M. A., 2018, *ApJ*, 859, 92

Matsuura M., Speck A. K., McHunu B. M., Tanaka I., Wright N. J., Smith M. D., Zijlstra A. A., et al., 2009, *ApJ*, 700, 1067

O'Dell C. R., Henney W. J., Ferland G. J., 2007, *AJ*, 133, 2343

Ramos-Larios G., Guerrero M. A., Sabin L., Santamaría E., 2017, *MNRAS*, 470, 3707

Planetary Nebulae: A Universal Toolbox in the Era of Precision Astrophysics
Proceedings IAU Symposium No. 384, 2025
O. De Marco, A. Zijlstra & R. Szczerba, eds.
doi:10.1017/S1743921323005410

Variability and internal kinematics of the planetary nebula IC 4997

Luis F. Miranda

Instituto de Astrofísica de Andalucía-CSIC, Glorieta de la Astronomía s/n,
E-18008 Granada, Spain
email: lfm@iaa.es

Abstract. We present new high-spectral resolution échelle spectra of IC 4997 obtained in 2023 June to study the evolution of its recently reported variable Hα emission line profile. Compared with similar spectra from 2020 September, the new ones also show a single-peaked profile but the full velocity width of the Hα wings has increased by a factor of $\simeq$1.2. Besides, we use our high-resolution échelle spectra to investigate the internal kinematics of the nebula. Preliminary analysis suggests that the two shells of IC 4997 are kinematically resolved: the outer shell expands at $\simeq$10–14 km s^{-1} and the inner shell at $\simeq$25 km s^{-1}.

Keywords. Planetary nebulae:individual (IC 4997) – Circumstellar matter – ISM:jets and outflows

1. Introduction

IC4997 is a young double-shell planetary nebula with an outer bipolar and an inner very compact elliptical shell (Miranda et al. 1996; Miranda & Torrelles 1998). It presents variability in the emission line intensities, emission line intensity ratios, electron temperature, electron density, and radio continuum flux density, in some of these cases exhibiting episodic (perhaps periodic, $\simeq$50–60 yr) changes (Kostyakova & Arkhipova 2009; Arkhipova et al. 2020). Recently, Miranda et al. (2022) reported that the P Cygni Hα emission profile observed in 1990–1993 (Feibelman et al. 1992; Hyung et al. 1994) changed to a single-peaked profile in 2019–2020, and the very broad Hα wings ($\simeq$7000 km s^{-1}) narrowed by a factor $\simeq$2 between 1993 and 2019–2020. These changes have been attributed to an episodically variable stellar wind (Miranda et al. 2022). To follow up these changes, we have obtained new high-resolution échelle spectra in 2023. The high-resolution of our spectra also allows us to investigate the internal kinematics of IC 4997.

2. Observations and Results

The new spectra were obtained with the CARMENES échelle spectrograph at the 3.5 m telescope on Calar Alto Observatory in 2023 June 14. The aperture of the spectrograph (1.5 arcsec in diameter) was centered on the object. Both the visible (VIS, 5200–9600 Å) and near-infrared (NIR, 9600–17100 Å) bands of the spectrograph were used. The spectral resolution (FWHM) is $\simeq$2.4–3.2/4.3–5.4 km s^{-1} in the VIS/NIR band. Five spectra were obtained with an exposure time of 180 s each, and their median was used as the final spectrum.

The Hα emission line profile observed in 2023 is shown in Fig. 1 and presents a single-peaked profile as observed in 2019–2020 (Miranda et al. 2022). However, the wings of the Hα line seem to have broadened. By using the full velocity width of the Hα line at the 5σ level from the continuum as the width of the Hα wings, we obtain a value

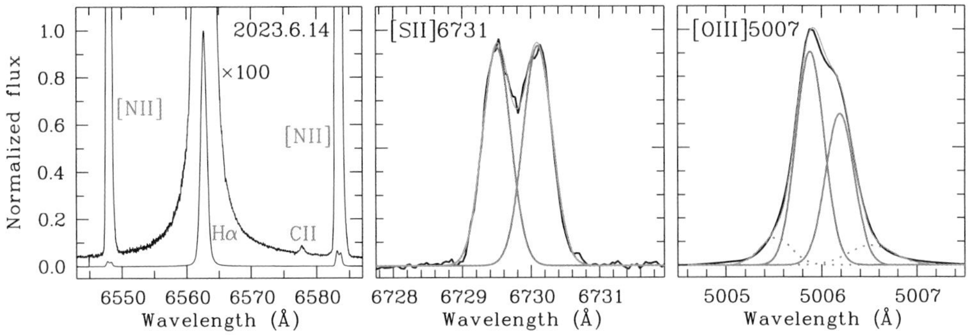

Figure 1. (*left:*) Normalized Hα emission line profile of IC 4997 observed in 2023 June 14. The observed emission lines are indicated. (*center and right:*) Normalized profiles of the [S II] and [O III] emission lines superimposed with gaussian fits using two and four components, respectively. Black is the observed spectrum, blue/red represents blueshifted/redshifted components with respect to the systemic velocity of IC 4997 (V(LSR)$\simeq-50\,\mathrm{km\,s^{-1}}$), solid/dotted line is used for the (presumably) inner/outer shell components, and magenta represents the sum of the gaussians.

of $2230\pm150\,\mathrm{km\,s^{-1}}$ in 2023, that is a factor $\simeq$1.2 larger than that of $1890\pm100\,\mathrm{km\,s^{-1}}$ in 2020 (Miranda et al. 2022). This increase could be due to small fluctuations of the stellar wind and/or of the physical conditions in the regions involved in the Rayleigh-Raman scattering process (Ouyang et al. 2022), or, alternatively, to the start of a new variability cycle, as it might be expected from the apparent relationship between the episodic variability of the [O III]4363/Hγ line intensity ratio and the Hα emission line profile (Arkhipova et al. 2020; Miranda et al. 2022).

We have started the kinematical analysis of the échelle spectra, including those obtained with the CAFE spectrograph in 2019 and 2020 (Miranda et al. 2022). Here we present some preliminary results. Fig. 1 also shows the [S II] and [O III] emission line profiles from the 2023 and 2020 spectra, respectively. The [S II] line presents two kinematical components separated by $\simeq27\,\mathrm{km\,s^{-1}}$. The [O III] line presents four kinematical components: the strong ones separated by $\simeq20\,\mathrm{km\,s^{-1}}$, the weak ones by $\simeq50\,\mathrm{km\,s^{-1}}$. Similar results to those in [S II]/[O III] are obtained from other low-/high-excitation emission lines. The velocity separation of the strong [O III] components is very similar to that of the [S II] components, strongly suggesting that they trace the same structure. The [S II] emission can hardly arise in the inner shell because of its high electron density of $\simeq2.6\times10^{6}\,\mathrm{cm^{-3}}$ (Gómez et al. 2002), but most probably in the outer shell. If so, the expansion velocity of the outer shell is $\simeq$10–14 $\mathrm{km\,s^{-1}}$. The weak components of the [O III] line may arise in the inner shell where this emission is not completely collisionally quenched at such a high electron density. This would imply that the inner shell expands at $\simeq25\,\mathrm{km\,s^{-1}}$, faster than the outer shell.

LFM acknowledges support from grants PID2020-114461GB-I00 and CEX2021-001131-S, funded by MCIN/AEI/10.13039/501100011033. He is grateful to Calar Alto Observatory for allocation of director's discretionary time to this program.

Supplementary material

To view supplementary material for this article, please visit https://doi.org/10.1017/S1743921323005410

References

Arkhipova V. P., et al., 2020, *Astron. Lett*, 46, 100. doi:10.1134/S1063773720020012
Feibelman W. A., et al. 1992, *PASP*, 104, 339. doi:10.1086/133003
Hyung S., et al., 1994, *ApJ*, 93, 465. doi:10.1086/192063
Kostyakova E. B., Arkhipova V. P., 2009, *Astron. Rep.*, 53, 1155. doi:10.1134/S1063772909120087
Gómez Y., et al., 2002, *MNRAS*, 336, 1139. doi:10.1046/j.1365-8711.2002.05843.x
Miranda L. F., Torrelles J. M., 1998, *ApJ*, 496, 274. doi:10.1086/305383
Miranda L. F., et al., 1996, *ApJ*, 461, L111. doi:10.1086/310017
Miranda L. F., et al., 2022, *A&A*, 657, L9. doi:10.1051/0004-6361/202142730
Ouyang X.-J., et al., 2022, *ApJ*, 933, id.4. doi:10.3847/1538-4357/ac6fdb

Planetary Nebulae: A Universal Toolbox in the Era of Precision Astrophysics
Proceedings IAU Symposium No. 384, 2025
O. De Marco, A. Zijlstra & R. Szczerba, eds.
doi:10.1017/S1743921324000012

Dual chemistry, high ADF and internal kinematics of the planetary nebula Vy 2-2

Roldán A. Cala, Luis F. Miranda and José F. Gómez

Instituto de Astrofísica de Andalucía (IAA-CSIC), Glorieta de la Astronomía s/n, 18008 Granada, Spain
email: rcala@iaa.es

Abstract. OH masers are signpost of planetary nebulae (PNe) at a very young stage. In particular, Vy 2-2 was the first OH maser-emitting PN ever identified. It consists of a bright compact shell and a faint bipolar structure. The reported values for its O^{+2}/H^{+} abundance discrepancy factor (ADF) are inconsistent: $\simeq$4.3, and $\simeq$11.8. To characterize the ionized gas and to redetermine the ADF(O^{+2}), we have obtained medium-resolution optical spectra. We found that the ionized gas is oxygen-rich (C/O$\simeq$0.15), and an ADF(O^{+2})$\simeq$13.6. Also, the N/O abundance ratio is $\simeq$0.39, implying a low-mass progenitor ($M_{\rm i} \leq 1.5\,{\rm M}_{\odot}$). Unexpectedly, the detection of stellar weak emission lines (*wels*) suggests that the central star is carbon-rich. Alternatively, the *wels* may be emitted by an irradiated companion in a post-common envelope system. We have also obtained high-resolution optical spectroscopy on Vy 2-2. Our spectra kinematically resolve the bright shell and bipolar structure. We found that these expand at $\sim$10 and $\sim$20 km s^{-1}, respectively.

Keywords. (ISM:) planetary nebulae: Vy 2-2, masers, techniques: spectroscopic, high angular resolution

1. Introduction

Circumstellar OH masers are expected to disappear in timescales of $\simeq 10^3$ yr after the end of the asymptotic giant branch (AGB; Gómez *et al.* 1990), while the planetary nebula (PN) starts $\simeq 10^3$-10^4 yr after the end of the AGB, depending on the initial mass ($M_{\rm i}$) of the star (Blöcker 1995). Thus, PNe showing OH masers (OHPNe) are thought to be young PNe. So far, There are only six confirmed OHPNe (Uscanga *et al.* 2012; Qiao *et al.* 2016), and several additional candidates (Cala *et al.* 2022). In particular, Vy 2-2 was the first one identified (Seaquist & Davis 1983). Its radio continuum emission (Fig. 1, left) originates from an angularly small ($\sim 0''.24$ in diameter) bright shell and a faint bipolar structure $\sim 2''$ in extent (Christianto & Seaquist 1998; Miranda & Solf 1991). All the available information indicates that its circumstellar environment is oxygen-rich (C/O < 1; e.g. Molster *et al.* 2002). Its abundance discrepancy factor (ADF), defined as ${\rm ADF} = {\rm O}^{+2}_{\rm RL}/{\rm O}^{+2}_{\rm CEL}$ to quantify the difference between the O^{+2}/H^{+} ionic abundance obtained from collisionally excited lines (CEL) and recombination lines (RL), has recently been found to be ADF(O^{+2}) $\simeq$ 4.3 (Ruiz-Escobedo & Peña 2022), which is inconsistent with the value of $\simeq$11.8 reported by Wesson *et al.* (2005).

2. Observations and Results

To characterize the physical properties of the ionized gas of Vy 2-2 and to redetermine the ADF(O^{+2}), we performed medium-resolution optical spectroscopy using CAFOS at

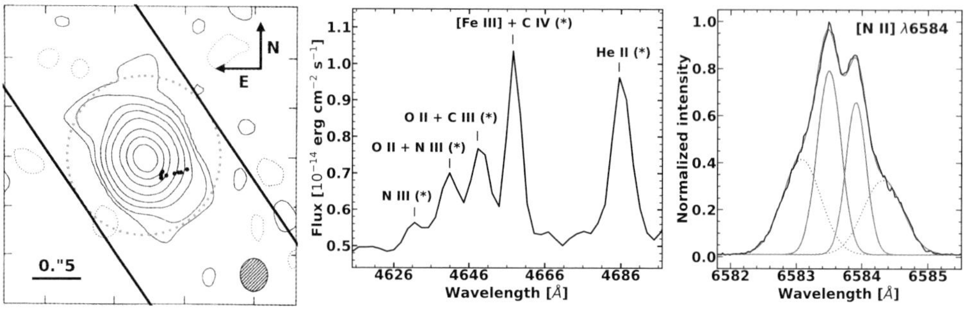

Figure 1. *Left.* Radio continuum emission of Vy 2-2 at 6 cm (Seaquist & Davis 1983), showing the long-slit (width=1.5 arcsec, PA=35°; solid lines) of CAFOS and the circular fiber of CARMENES (1.5 arcsec in diameter; red dotted lines). *Center.* Weak emission lines (*wels*, marked with *). *Right.* Emission profile of the [N II]λ6584 line. The solid and dotted lines correspond to the bright shell and bipolar structure, respectively. The red and blue colors correspond to the blueshifted and redshifted emission, with respect to the systemic velocity $V_{\rm sys} \simeq -50.7$ km s^{-1}. The magenta lines represent the sum of the four components.

the 2.2 m telescope at Calar Alto Observatory (CAHA). The spectra cover the 3200-9600 Å range at a 2 Å pix^{-1} dispersion. To study the internal kinematics of the ionized gas, we performed high resolution optical (5200-9600 Å) spectroscopy using CARMENES at the 3.5 m telescope also at CAHA, at a velocity resolution (FWHM) $\simeq$2.4-3.2 km s^{-1}. Fig. 1 (left) shows the CAFOS long-slit and the CARMENES circular fiber superimposed on the 6 cm radio continuum emission from Vy 2-2.

From the CEL we obtained a N/O abundance ratio $\simeq$0.39, implying a low-mass progenitor ($M_{\rm i}\leq1.5\,{\rm M}_\odot$), instead of the intermediate mass-star ones ($M_{\rm i}\geq4\,{\rm M}_\odot$) initially assumed for OHPNe (Uscanga *et al.* 2012). From the RL we obtained ionic abundances of $O^{+2}/H^{+}=15.23\pm1.27\,10^{-4}$ and $C^{+2}/H^{+}=2.34\pm0.25\,10^{-4}$, implying a C/O abundance ratio of $\simeq$0.15, which is similar to the value from Wesson *et al.* (2005). Using the CEL and RL, a high ADF(O^{+2})$\simeq$13.6 is obtained, which is similar to the $\simeq$11.8 from Wesson *et al.* (2005).

The most intriguing result is the detection of stellar weak emission lines (*wels*), which suggests an unexpected carbon rich nature of the central star (Fig. 1, center). Thus, Vy 2-2 would be an O-rich PN around a C-rich central star. It is possible that this is actually a common characteristic in OHPNe (Cala *et al.* 2023). Alternatively, the *wels* may be emitted by a companion, irradiated by the central star, as seen in post-common envelope binary systems (e.g., Miszalski *et al.* 2011). The binary evolutionary channel is further suggested by the extremely low C/O $\simeq$ 0.15 and the high ADF(O^{+2})$\simeq$13.6 (see De Marco 2009; Wesson *et al.* 2018).

Our CARMENES spectrum kinematically resolves the bright shell and bipolar structure observed in the radio continuum (Fig. 1, right). The strong components correspond to the bright shell and are separated by $\simeq$20 km s^{-1} in velocity; the faint components correspond to the bipolar lobes and are separated by $\simeq$40 km s^{-1}.

Authors acknowledge support from grants PID2020-114461GB-I00 and CEX2021-001131-S of MCIN/AEI/10.13039/501100011033, and PRE2018-085518 funded by MCIN/AEI and by ESF Investing in your future.

References

Blöcker, T., 1995, *A&A*, 299, 755
Cala, R. A., *et al.* 2022, *MNRAS*, 516, 2235. doi:10.1093/mnras/stac2341

Cala, R. A., *et al.* 2023, International Astronomical Union Symposium Proceedings, 380, in press
Christianto, H., Seaquist, E. R., 1998, *AJ*, 115, 246. doi:10.1086/300390
De Marco, O., 2009, *PASP*, 121, 316. doi:10.1086/597765
Gómez, Y., Moran, J. M., Rodríguez, L. F., 1990, *RevMexAA*, 20, 55
Miranda, L. F., Solf, J., 1991, *A&A*, 252, 331
Miszalski, B., *et al.* 2011, *A&A*, 531, 158. doi:10.1051/0004-6361/201117084
Molster, F. J., *et al.* 2002, *A&A*, 382, 222. doi:10.1051/0004-6361:20011551
Qiao, H.-H., *et al.* 2016, *ApJ*, 817, 37. doi:10.3847/0004-637X/817/1/37
Ruiz-Escobedo, F., Peña, M., 2022, *MNRAS*, 510, 5984. doi:10.1093/mnras/stac003
Seaquist, E. R., Davis, L. E., 1983, *AJ*, 274, 659. doi:10.1086/161478
Uscanga, L., *et al.* 2012, *A&A*, 547, 40. doi:10.1051/0004-6361/201219760
Wesson, R., *et al.* 2005, *MNRAS*, 362, 424. doi:10.1111/j.1365-2966.2005.09325.x
Wesson, R., *et al.* 2018, *MNRAS*, 480, 4589. doi:10.1093/mnras/sty1871

Planetary Nebulae: A Universal Toolbox in the Era of Precision Astrophysics
Proceedings IAU Symposium No. 384, 2025
O. De Marco, A. Zijlstra & R. Szczerba, eds.
doi:10.1017/S1743921323005161

Sakurai's object: a [WC] star in a new bipolar nebula after VLTP

G. C. Van de Steene[1], P. A. M. van Hoof[1], S. Kimeswenger[2,3], M. Hajduk[4], D. Tafoya[5], J. A. Toalá[6], A. Zijlstra[7] and D. Barría[8]

[1]Department of Astronomy & Astrophysics, Royal Observatory of Belgium, Ringlaan 3, 1180 Brussels, Belgium

[2]Universität Innsbruck, Institut für Astro- und Teilchenphysik, Technikerstr. 25, 6020 Innsbruck, Austria

[3]Instituto de Astronomía, Universidad Católica del Norte, Av. Angamos 0610, Antofagasta, Chile

[4]Department of Geodesy, Faculty of Geoengineering, University of Warmia and Mazury, ul. Oczapowskiego 2, 10-719 Olsztyn, Poland

[5]Department of Space, Earth and Environment, Chalmers University of Technology, Onsala Space Observatory, 439 92 Onsala, Sweden

[6]Instituto de Radioastronomía y Astrofísica, UNAM, Ant. Carretera a Pátzcuaro 8701, Ex-Hda. San José de la Huerta, Morelia 58089, Mich., Mexico

[7]Jodrell Bank Centre for Astrophysics, Alan Turing Building, University of Manchester, Manchester, M13 9PL, UK

[8]Facultad de Ingeniería y Arquitectura, Universidad Central de Chile, Av. Francisco de Aguirre 0405, La Serena, Coquimbo, Chile
email: `g.vandesteene@oma.be`

Abstract. Optical spectra of the Very Late Thermal Pulse (VLTP) object V4334 Sgr have shown a rapidly changing spectrum resulting from shocks in the outflow, which created a new bipolar nebula inside the old nebula. We see C II and C III emission lines emerging typical of a [WC 11-10]-type star. The strong increase of [O III] and [S III] emission lines indicate the possible onset of photoionisation in the new ejecta.

Keywords. stars: planetary nebulae, VLTP, bipolar

1. Introduction

V4334 Sgr (Sakurai's object) is the central star (CS) of an old Planetary Nebula (PN) that underwent a Very Late Thermal Pulse (VLTP) around 1996. The VLTP forced the star to briefly track back to the AGB and experience a second PN formation stage. High resolution ALMA continuum observations have shown the presence of a new bipolar PN inside the old one (Tafoya et al. 2023). We have been observing this object since 2006 to improve our understanding of PN formation and evolution.

2. Optical Monitoring

The first emission lines from the newly ejected gas were discovered in 1998 (Eyres et al. 1999) and 2001 (Kerber et al. 2002). We have been monitoring the changes in the optical emission line spectrum since 2006 using spectra obtained with FORS1&2 at ESO-VLT

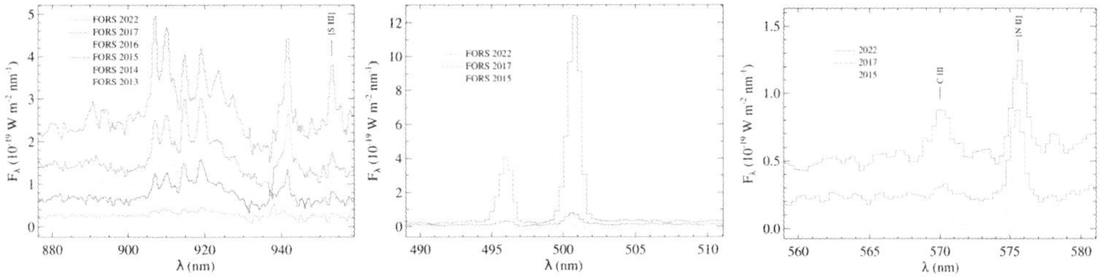

Figure 1. The emergence of WR lines since 2013 (left), the increase in [O III] emission lines (middle), and the emergence of the C IIIλ569.6 nm line (right).

(Reichel et al. 2022; van Hoof et al. 2007; Van de Steene et al. 2017). The goal of this monitoring program has been to derive the stellar temperature as a function of time in order to compare with stellar evolutionary models (Miller Bertolami et al. 2006; Herwig et al. 2014), which predict a fast reheating to 80 kK on a timescale of decades (Hajduk et al. 2005). Such fast evolution would cause the ejecta to be photoionised rapidly, resulting in observable, dramatic changes in the emission line spectrum.

3. Evolution of line fluxes

From 2001 to 2017 the data show a rapidly evolving spectrum that is completely produced by shocks. These shocks have been the result of the hydrodynamic shaping of the new bipolar nebula forming inside the old nebula. In van Hoof et al. (2007) we argued for the existence of a shock that occurred around 1998 and dissipated shortly afterwards based on the optical decline of the line flux values. In 2008 the spectrum changed dramatically. The [OII] λ732.5 nm lines increased almost tenfold in strength, and weak He I emission appeared. This sudden increase in excitation would have been caused by a second shock. However, unlike the first shock, there has been a gradual increase in line strengths since then (van Hoof et al. 2018). The evolution of the low-ionization forbidden lines is still dominated by these shocks in the most recent spectra. The emergence of a substantial stellar wind may have been the cause of the second shock, which is associated with the bipolar bow-shock features discovered in Hinkle & Joyce (2014). In 2014 there was another dramatic change in the spectrum with the emergence of a complex of emission lines mostly between λ905.0 and λ945 nm (Fig. 1, left). Many are identified as carbon lines (Williams et al. 2021). The flux evolution of these lines differs markedly from the shock excited helium and forbidden (nebular) lines. This points to a different origin and we assume that these lines are formed in the wind of the central star and are in fact WR features. The emergence of C III lines in the most recent spectra would confirm this assumption (Fig. 1, right). The presence of C II and C III lines, but the absence of C IV lines indicate a spectral type [WC 11-10] (Acker & Neiner 2003). This is the first sign of reappearance of the central star after the VLTP. In 2017 the spectra showed the first tentative signs of photoionisation (Fig. 1, middle) with a sudden increase in the flux of the [O III] λ495.9 and λ500.7 nm lines compared to 2015. This trend has continued in the spectra of 2022 where these lines showed another dramatic increase in strength. For the first time also the [S III] λ953.1 nm line appeared (Fig. 1, left). Its λ906.9 nm counterpart is blended. However, radio continuum observations have shown only a slight increase of flux density (M. Hadjuk, priv. Comm). It needs to be confirmed whether photoionisation of the new ejecta by the central star has started or this increase is due to strenghtening of the shock.

Supplementary material

To view supplementary material for this article, please visit https://doi.org/10.1017/S1743921323005161

References

Acker, A. & Neiner, C., 2003, *A&A*, 403, 659
Eyres, S. P. S., Smalley, B., Geballe, T. R., et al., 1999, *MNRAS*, 307, L11
Hajduk, M., Zijlstra, A. A., Herwig, F., et al., 2005, *Science*, 308, 231
Herwig, F., Woodward, P. R., Lin, P.-H., et al., 2014, *ApJL*, 792, L3
Hinkle, K. H. & Joyce, R. R. 2014, *ApJ*, 785, 146
Kerber, F., Pirzkal, N., De Marco, O., et al., 2002, *ApJL*, 581, L39
Miller Bertolami, M. M., Althaus, L. G., Serenelli, A. M., et al., 2006, *A&A*, 449, 313
Nakano, S., Sakurai, Y., Hazen, M., et al., 1996, *IAU Circ.*, 6322
Reichel, M., Kimeswenger, S., van Hoof, P. A. M., et al., 2022, *ApJ*, 939, 103
Tafoya, D., van Hoof, P. A. M., Toalá, J. A., et al., 2023, *A&A*, 677, L8
van de Steene, G. C., van Hoof, P. A. M., Kimeswenger, S., et al., 2017, *IAUS*, 323, 380
van Hoof, P. A. M., Hajduk, M., Zijlstra, A. A., et al., 2007, *A&A*, 471, L9
van Hoof, P. A. M., Kimeswenger, S., Van de Steene, G., et al., 2018, *Galaxies*, 6, 79
Williams, R., Manea, C., Margon, B., et al., 2021, *ApJ*, 906, 31

Planetary Nebulae: A Universal Toolbox in the Era of Precision Astrophysics
Proceedings IAU Symposium No. 384, 2025
O. De Marco, A. Zijlstra & R. Szczerba, eds.
doi:10.1017/S1743921323005574

Clues to PPN Chemical Evolution: The Unique Molecular Environment of V510 Pup

Mark A. Siebert[1] **and Anthony J. Remijan**[2]

[1]Department of Astronomy, University of Virginia, Charlottesville, VA 22904, USA
email: mas5fb@virginia.edu

[2]National Radio Astronomy Observatory, Charlottesville, VA 22903, USA

Abstract. V510 Pup (IRAS 08005-2356) is a binary post-AGB system with a fast molecular outflow that has been noted for its puzzling mixture of carbon- and oxygen-rich features in the optical and infrared. To explore this chemical dichotomy and relate it to the kinematics of the source, we present an ACA spectral line survey detailing fourteen newly detected molecules in this pre-planetary nebula. The simultaneous presence of CN/C_2H/HC_3N and SO/SO_2 support the previous conclusion of mixed chemistry, and their line profiles indicate that the C- and O-rich material trace distinct velocity structures in the outflow. This evidence suggests that V510 Pup could harbor a dense O-rich central waist from an earlier stage of evolution, which persisted after a fast C-rich molecular outflow formed. By studying the gas phase composition of this unique source, we aim to reveal new insights into the interplay between dynamics and chemistry in rapidly evolving post-AGB systems.

Keywords. stellar evolution, circumstellar matter, astrochemistry, post-AGB stars

1. Introduction

The nebulae surrounding evolved stars undergoing mass loss represent important sites of recycling for metal-rich gas and dust in our Galaxy. As low–intermediate mass stars leave the Asymptotic Giant Branch (AGB), their circumstellar envelopes undergo dramatic changes: transitioning from slow, spherical winds to complex bipolar/multipolar outflows seen in planetary nebulae (PNe) (Sahai *et al.* 2011). These dynamics are often met with a chemical transition as well, with molecules and dust being increasingly affected by conditions including high-velocity shocks, internal UV radiation, and AGB dredge up events (Pardo *et al.* 2007; Weiss *et al.* 2009). The mechanisms for the physical and chemical changes during the transitional pre-planetary nebula (PPN) phase are still not fully understood, but recent work has shown that binary and common envelope interactions are key to this evolution (e.g. Sahai *et al.* 2018).

One puzzling class of object that is critical to understanding the chemical output of evolved stars are PPNe showing signs of mixed chemistry. Stellar outflows are designated as either carbon- or oxygen-rich depending on the C/O ratio of the central star, which typically determines the molecular and dust grain composition throughout the wind (Höfner *et al.* 2018). However, it appears that this dichotomy is not universal, especially as stars evolve off the AGB. Evidence of this includes the widespread IR observations of fullerene and PAH features toward O-rich PNe (Gielen *et al.* 2011), as well as the existence of "silicate carbon stars" which have C-rich photospheres but are surrounded by O-rich circumstellar dust, and often show OH masers (Ohnaka *et al.* 2013).

V510 Pup (IRAS 08005-2356) is post-AGB star surrounded by a young high-velocity outflow that shows clear evidence of mixed chemistry. It exhibits OH maser emission typical of O-rich evolved stars (Zijlstra *et al.* 2001), but also shows optical absorption lines from C_2 and CN (Bakker *et al.* 1997). The extreme dynamics of V510 Pup were characterized recently by Sahai & Patel (2015), where broad (~200 km/s) line profiles were observed in CO and SiO using the Submillimeter Array (SMA). Analysis of the velocity gradient across the nebula showed that radiation pressure alone is insufficient to drive the outflow. Optical observations later discovered that V510 Pup is part of a radial-velocity binary, and that its Hα line profile modulates with the seven-year orbital period, confirming that the high-velocity bipolar outflow originates from accretion onto a close binary companion (Manick *et al.* 2021). This makes it the only extreme PPN whose jet origin is directly observed.

V510 Pup is at a critical point in its evolution to offer new insights into chemical transitions and binary interaction in exotic PPNe, but it lacks key constraints on its gas phase chemical inventory. To address this, a detailed spectroscopic study of this source is needed to determine the molecular abundances and their relationship to kinematic structures within the wind. We used interferometric observations from the Atacama Compact Array (ACA) to perform these measurements, and reveal the unique dynamics of C- and O-rich material in this source.

2. Observations

We utilize archival data from a Cycle 6 ACA filler program which observed 16 evolved stars transitioning between the AGB and PNe phases (Project code 2018.A.00047.S). These data include spectral line observations of V510 Pup covering the entirety of Bands 3 and 6 (85–115 GHz, and 211–274 GHz) at 1~3 km/s velocity resolution. Calibrated visibilities were produced using the standard pipeline of the Common Astronomy Software Application (CASA; McMullin *et al.* 2007), and each spectral window was then continuum-subtracted, then imaged and deconvolved using the `tclean` CASA task with briggs weighting. The resulting rms sensitivity ranges between 5 and 13 mJy/beam among the 56 spectral windows. Some spectral windows overlap in their frequency coverage, so these data were combined in the visibility plane to improve sensitivity. The ACA beam size is 10.1″–11.5″ and 4.3″–5.3″ at Bands 3 and 6, respectively. This is notably larger than the ~2″ nebular extent of V510 Pup observed by Sahai & Patel (2015), meaning a spatial analysis was not possible with these data, and our study is purely spectroscopic.

3. Results & Analysis

3.1. *Detected species and line profiles*

We detect emission from a total of 16 molecules and isotopologues toward V510 Pup, 13 of which have not yet been observed in this source. A list of all detected species is shown in Table 1, including the number of lines observed of each, and whether they are typically found in C- or O-rich sources, using Ziurys (2006) as reference. All these molecules are common in evolved stars environments, including "parent" molecules originating from the stellar atmosphere (e.g. SO, HCN, CS), as well as species produced through photochemistry like HCO^+, HNC, HC_3N, and C_2H (Woods *et al.* 2003). The remarkable result seen in Table 1 is the presence of characteristic O-rich molecules (SO, SO_2) paired with C-rich species (HNC, CN, C_2H, and HC_3N). This is the first AGB-related source with simultaneous detections of all these molecules, lending support to previous classifications of mixed chemistry.

Table 1. Summary of detected molecules and isotopologues.

Molecule	No. of transitions	Range in E_{up} (K)[a]	Velocity Component(s)[b]	Chemistry[c]
^{12}CO	2	10 – 30	CV, MV, HV	Both
^{13}CO	2	10 – 30	CV, MV, HV	Both
SiO	3	6 – 45	CV, MV, HV	Both
^{29}SiO	2	31 – 45	CV, MV, HV	Both
^{30}SiO	2	31 – 45	CV, MV, HV	Both
HCN	1	26	CV, MV	Both
$H^{13}CN$	1	25	CV, MV	Both
CS	1	35	CV(?), MV	C-rich
$C^{34}S$	1	28	MV	C-rich
HCO^+	1	26	CV, MV	Both
SO	5	44 – 56	CV	O-rich
SO_2	9	24 – 94	CV	O-rich
HNC	1	26	MV	C-rich
CN	1	16	MV	C-rich
C_2H	1	25	MV	C-rich
HC_3N	7	131 – 203	MV	C-rich

Notes: [a]Upper state energies obtained from Cologne Database of Molecular Spectroscopy (CDMS) Müller et al. 2005. [b]LSR velocity ranges of the CV, MV, and HV components are defined in Section 3.1 and shown in Fig. 1. [c]Denotes whether a particular molecule is typically associated with a carbon- or oxygen-rich surface chemistry in circumstellar envelopes, using the list from Ziurys (2006).

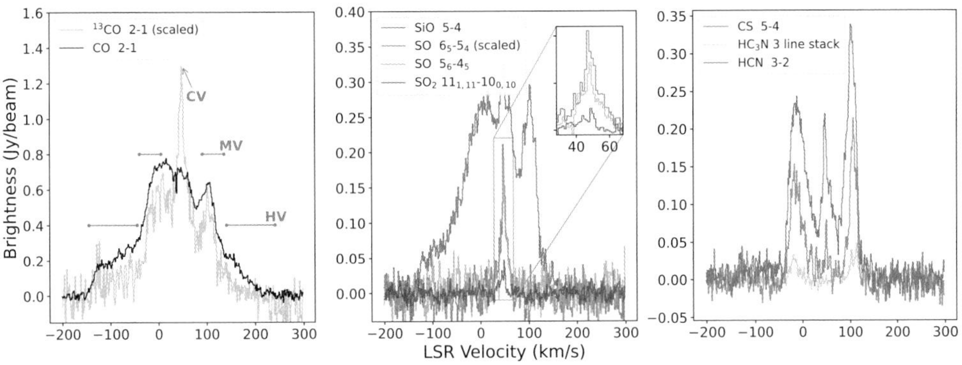

Figure 1. Emission line profiles of various molecules measured by the ACA toward V510 Pup. The central velocity (CV), medium-velocity (MV), and high-velocity (HV) components are defined in the left panel. Species that are typically associated with O- and C-rich evolved stellar outflows are shown in the middle and right panels, respectively. Spectra were extracted from an aperture with diameter 10″ centered on the position of the post-AGB star. Some transitions are scaled for comparison.

The peculiar chemistry of V510 Pup can be further explored using the kinematic information provided by molecular line profiles. Figure 1 shows a sample of these spectra. The full extent of the extreme outflow can be seen in the broad CO and SiO line profiles which span the range between -150 and 200 km/s. Following Sahai & Patel (2015), we decompose this into three main velocity components: a central component (CV) centered on the system velocity ($V_{sys} = 48$ km/s), a intermediate component (MV) at $V_{sys} \pm 50$ km/s, and high-velocity wings (HV) at $V_{sys} \pm 110$ km/s, all shown in Fig. 1. With the improved sensitivity on the ^{13}CO $J = 2-1$ line now available, we note that the CV component has a narrow feature (width < 10 km/s) appearing on top of the broad line profile, similar to how this transition was appears toward the similar extreme PPN HD 101584 (Olofsson *et al.* 2019). This narrow CV component is also observed isolated from the MV and HV components in the emission profiles of SO, SO_2, and HCN. Table 1

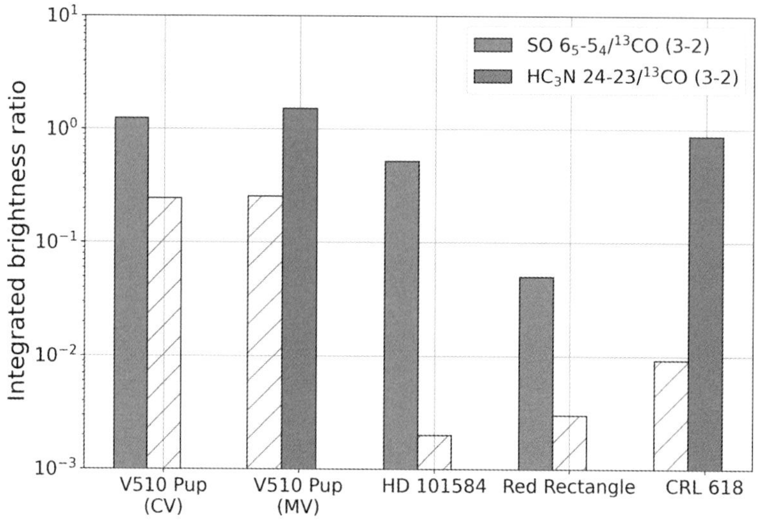

Figure 2. Comparison of integrated molecular line brightness (relative to ^{13}CO) for SO (red) and HC_3N (blue) among a sample of nearby PPNe. For V510 Pup, the O-rich central and C-rich medium velocity components are labeled CV and MV, respectively. Hatched regions denote upper limits, while solid regions indicate detected transitions. Data for sources other than V510 Pup adapted from Olofsson *et al.* (2019), Gallardo Cava *et al.* (2022), and Pardo *et al.* (2004).

also lists which velocity components are detected for each molecule. We find that all molecules which are primarily associated with carbon-rich outflows appear solely in the MV component, while oxygen-rich species are located in the narrow CV region. This can be seen in the middle and right panels of Fig. 1.

Figure 2 shows the measured brightnesses of SO (6_5–5_4) and HC_3N (24–23) relative to ^{13}CO compared with more well-studied PPNe for which these transitions have been observed previously (Olofsson *et al.* 2019; Pardo *et al.* 2004). From this, we see that the CV component of V510 Pup is chemically similar to O-rich sources like HD 101584, while the MV component is like the prototypical C-rich PPN CRL 618. Furthermore, this comparison provides evidence that the narrow CV is not depleted in its molecular chemistry as is the case for the Red Rectangle and other "disk-prominent" post-AGBs (Gallardo Cava *et al.* 2022).

3.2. *LTE modeling*

To obtain estimates on the abundances of detected molecules, we model the observed transitions assuming local thermodynamic equilibrium (LTE). This assumption is necessary since we lack spatial data and constraints on the physical conditions of the velocity components to perform a full radiative transfer analysis. To simulate line profiles and fit the transitions, we use the publicly available package `molsim` (Lee 2021). For each velocity component, we perform a least-squares minimization of the column density, rotational temperature, and line width of a given molecule. For species where only one transition was available, we fix the rotational temperature to that obtained for SO (CV) or HC_3N (MV). We employ the same procedure for ^{13}CO, simultaneously fitting the overlapping CV, MV, and HV components. Then, assuming a $^{13}CO/H_2$ ratio of 3.9×10^{-5} (Sahai & Patel 2015), we use the relative column densities to calculate final abundances. While this eliminates the need to adopt an explicit angular source size, it does assume that this size is equal to that of ^{13}CO emission (whether in the CV or MV component).

Table 2. Measurements on physical conditions of optically thin species in the outflow of V510 Pup.

Molecule	Component	T_{rot} (K)	f_{H2} (err.)
SO	CV	43 ± 13	4.5×10^{-6} (1.0)
SO_2	CV	57 ± 18	4.8×10^{-6} (0.9)
HC_3N	MV	63 ± 16	1.6×10^{-6} (0.6)
CS	MV	63^a	5.1×10^{-6} (0.5)
CN	MV	63^a	1.3×10^{-5} (0.1)
C_2H	MV	63^a	2.8×10^{-6} (0.3)

Notes: [a]Rotational temperature of HC_3N adopted for abundance calculation.

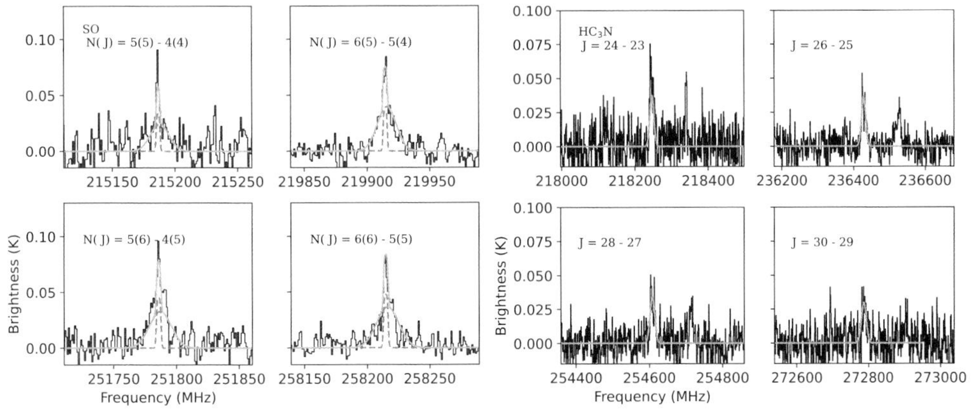

Figure 3. Examples of LTE emission line fits for SO (left panels) and HC_3N (right panels). ACA spectrum shown in black, while colored lines represent fitted `molsim` simulation. For SO, a narrow (magenta dashed) and wide (green dashed) gaussian were needed to reproduce the shape of the CV component. For HC_3N, one component was used, centered on the red-shifted side of the MV region.

The results of this analysis are shown in Figure 3 and Table 2. We find that the CV component exhibits excitation temperatures between 40–60 K, while the MV component (measured by HC_3N) is about 63 K. These values are in line with the temperatures found in the slowly expanding equatorial waist and the bipolar outflow of HD 101584 (Olofsson *et al.* 2019). The abundances of molecules observed in the MV component are close (within a factor of five) to their measured abundances in C-rich AGB stars (Agúndez *et al.* 2017; Massalkhi *et al.* 2019), indicating that this component does derive from acetylene-rich stellar material.

4. Conclusions

Using archival ACA observations, we analyzed the millimeter spectrum of V510 Pup to provide some of the first constraints on its molecular inventory. The new sensitivity and velocity information offered by our spectra indicate that not only does V510 Pup exhibit mixed chemistry in its outflow, but the carbon- and oxygen-rich material is separated into reservoirs of gas that are morphologically unique. The line profiles of the newly characterized CV component appear remarkably similar to the "disk-prominent" subclass of post-AGB stars (Gallardo Cava *et al.* 2022), as well as the central region of the similar PPN HD 101584 (Olofsson *et al.* 2019). These equatorial density enhancements (EDEs) are common in PPNe and PNe, and recent works suggest that they can form during the AGB phase through binary-shaping (Sahai *et al.* 2022; Decin *et al.* 2020). Thus, one possible explanation for the observed chemistry (summarized in Fig. 4) is that V510 Pup

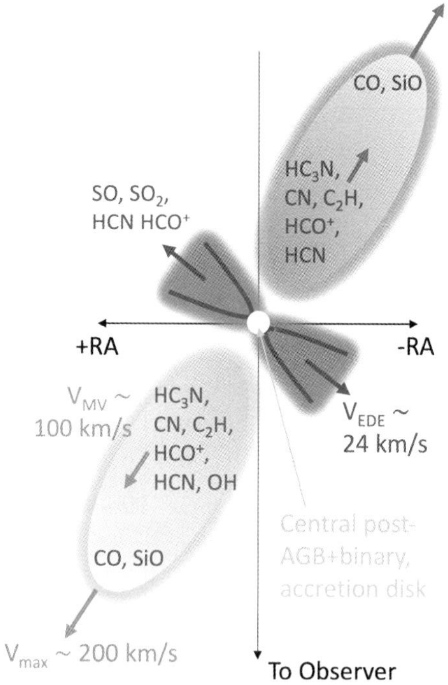

Figure 4. Diagram of the circumstellar environment of V510 Pup as suggested by our ACA analysis of its millimeter spectrum. Includes major morphological structures and their velocities, as well as the observed chemistry in each region. Proposed components include a carbon-rich bipolar outflow (red and blue), and a slowly expanding oxygen-rich equatorial waist surrounding the central binary (brown).

harbors a slowly expanding waist from an earlier stage of evolution when its surface chemistry was O-rich, then as its fast bipolar outflow formed it also underwent a transition to ejecting C-rich material. This scenario has been proposed to explain mixed dust features in silicate carbon stars (Ohnaka *et al.* 2013), but the observations presented here provide some of the first kinematic evidence for it. To confirm this, future observations of V510 Pup at higher resolution will be critical, as spatially resolving the chemically distinct CV, MV, and HV components will allow one to determine their physical conditions and dynamical histories.

This paper makes use of the following ALMA data: ADS/JAO.ALMA# 2018.A.00047.S. ALMA is a partnership of ESO (representing its member states), NSF (USA) and NINS (Japan), together with NRC (Canada), MOST and ASIAA (Taiwan), and KASI (Republic of Korea), in cooperation with the Republic of Chile. The Joint ALMA Observatory is operated by ESO, AUI/NRAO and NAOJ. The National Radio Astronomy Observatory is a facility of the National Science Foundation operated under cooperative agreement by Associated Universities, Inc. Support for this work and travel was provided to M. A. S. by the NSF through the Grote Reber Fellowship Program administered by Associated Universities, Inc./National Radio Astronomy Observatory.

References

Agúndez, M., Cernicharo, J., Quintana-Lacaci, G., *et al.* 2017, *A&A*, 601, A4
Bakker, E. J., van Dishoeck, E. F., Waters, L. B. F. M., *et al.* 1997, *A&A*, 323, 469
Decin, L., Montargès, M., Richards, A. M. S., *et al.* 2020, *Science*, 369, 1497
Gallardo Cava, I., Bujarrabal, V., Alcolea, J., *et al.* 2022, *A&A*, 659, A134
Fu, R. R., Moullet, A., Patel, N. A., *et al.* 2012, *ApJ*, 746, 42

Gielen, C., Cami, J., Bouwman, J., *et al.* 2011, *A&A*, 536, A54
Höfner, S., & Olofsson, H. 2018, *A&A Revs*, 26, 1
Lee, K. 2021, *Zenodo*, 10.5281/zenodo.4560750
Manick, R., Miszalski, B., Kamath, D., *et al.* 2021, *MNRAS*, 508, 2226
Massalkhi, S., Agúndez, M., Cernicharo, J. 2019, *A&A*, 628, A62
McMullin, J. P., Waters, B., Schiebel, D., *et al.* 2007, *Astronomical Society of the Pacific Conference Series*, 376, 127
Ohnaka, K., Boboltz, D. A., Mulitz-Schimel, G., *et al.* 2013, *A&A*, 559, A120
Olofsson, H., Khouri, T., Maercker, M., *et al.* 2019, *A&A*, 623, A153
Pardo, J. R., Cernicharo, J., Goicoechea, J. R., *et al.* 2004, *ApJ*, 615, 495
Pardo, J. R., Cernicharo, J., Goicoechea, J. R., *et al.* 2007, *ApJ*, 661, 250
Sahai, R., Claussen, M. J., Schnee, S., *et al.* 2011, *ApJL*, 739, L3
Sahai, R., & Patel, N. A., 2015, *ApJL*, 810, L8
Sahai, R., Sánchez Contreras, C., Mangan, A. S. *et al.* 2018, *ApJ*, 860, 2
Sahai, R., Huang, P. S., Scibelli, S., *et al.* 2022, *ApJ*, 929, 59
Weiss, A., & Ferguson, J. W. 2009, *A&A*, 508, 1343
Woods, P M., Millar, T. J., Herbst, E., *et al.* 2002, *A&A*, 402, 189
Zijlstra, A. A., Chapman, J. M., te Lintel Hekkert, P., *et al.* 2001, *MNRAS*, 322, 280
Ziurys, L. M. 2007, *PNAS*, 103, 12274

Planetary Nebulae: A Universal Toolbox in the Era of Precision Astrophysics
Proceedings IAU Symposium No. 384, 2025
O. De Marco, A. Zijlstra & R. Szczerba, eds.
doi:10.1017/S1743921324001479

Planetary Nebulae: A Universal Toolbox in the Era of Precision Astrophysics

Meeting (Quasi-)Summary

Joel H. Kastner

Rochester Institute of Technology, Rochester, USA
email: jhkpci@rit.edu

Abstract. Meeting number 384 in the IAU's Symposium series, *Planetary Nebulae: a Universal Toolbox in the Era of Precision Astrophysics*, featured an overwhelming array of exciting observational and theoretical developments in the study of planetary nebulae. I attempt to identify the themes and threads that ran through the meeting, some of them popping up in unexpected ways and connecting otherwise disparate science sessions. I also highlight key open questions that this meeting has raised for the benefit of future planetary nebula research.

Keywords. ISM: Planetary Nebula; hydrodynamics; astrochemistry; galaxies: stellar content

1. Introduction

Meeting number 384 in the IAU's Symposium series, *Planetary Nebulae: a Universal Toolbox in the Era of Precision Astrophysics*, featured an overwhelming array of exciting observational and theoretical developments in the study of planetary nebulae. Indeed, so many fascinating results were presented over the course of the meeting that, by the end of the symposium, there was the risk that the participants themselves might not have realized how IAUS 384 had largely succeeded in addressing its ambitious objectives. So, before vainly attempting to summarize this action-packed meeting, I offer a friendly reminder of those sweeping goals.

IAU Symposium 384 was aimed at understanding and exploiting planetary nebulae (PNe) in a wide variety of astrophysical contexts:

Planetary nebulae as tracers of stellar evolution. PNe facilitate studies of the giant branch-white dwarf connection, mass loss and stellar winds, binary interactions, and eruptive events and transients.

Planetary nebulae as hydrodynamics events. PNe provide unique insight into the shaping of stellar winds, dust in stellar winds, jet launching, jet-nebula interactions, the asterosphere, and outflow shaping by binary interactions.

Planetary nebulae as astrochemistry laboratories. PNe potentially offer rich targets for understanding molecular evolution, the origins of polycyclic aromatic hydrocarbons and fullerenes, dust formation and destruction, and photo-dissociation regions.

Planetary nebulae as unique tools to study the structure and evolution of galaxies. PNe can serve as vital, readily accessible probes to constrain galactic star formation histories, abundance gradients, structural components and dark matter, galaxy dynamics, and hierarchical mass assembly.

Or as put more succinctly during the meeting, by Jan Cami: "Planetary nebulae can solve any problem in astrophysics."

2. IAUS 384: Meeting "Takeaways"

Summarizing an entire 4-day meeting would be tedious at best, not to mention hazardous, if it were even possible. It is possible, however, to identify a number of themes and threads that ran through the meeting, some of them popping up in unexpected contexts and connecting otherwise disparate science sessions. The following briefly recaps these themes and threads — in no particular order — highlighting (in *italics*) speakers whose own work, or whose reviews of the work of others, addressed or touched on them. To learn more, please read their contributions to these Proceedings†.

Spectral multiplexing is driving the PN field forward. Integral field unit (IFU) and multi-object spectrometers (MOSs) are enabling studies of extragalactic PN kinematics and abundances aimed at connecting and enhancing cosmic abundance evolution and extragalactic stellar population studies. Our present-day workhorses in this domain are PN.S, MUSE, GTC/OSIRIS, and (soon) SITELLE (talks by *Cortesi, Ennis, Bureau, Fang, Hartke, Arnaboldi*). The future of PNe as extragalactic probes undoubtedly lies in the coming generation of 30-meter-class Extremely Large (optical/IR) Telescopes (ELTs), equipped with even more powerful IFUs and MOSs, that will enable higher-z studies (*Stanghellini*). A selfish aside here: the dependence of extinction on progenitor mass seen in M31 (*Bhattacharya*) ties in nicely with what we know about Galactic PNe; solar neighborhood studies have long shown that the dustiest, most molecule-rich PNe are descended from higher-mass progenitors (e.g., Kastner et al. 1996).

ESA's *Gaia* Mission is (still) changing everything. In addition to providing parallaxes for a growing number of planetary nebula central stars, the exquisite precision of *Gaia* data impacts studies of the PN luminosity function (PNLF; more on that later) and Local Group stellar populations (*Hernandez-Juarez, Chornay, Manteiga*). Even with the new Gaia-imposed constraints, the properties of PN central stars remain intriguing and (often) elusive (*Souropanis, Montoro Molina*), although there is potential to unlock the mystery of the ultra-high-excitation (UHE) lines that are detected both in certain white dwarfs and in certain PN central stars (*Reindl*).

Nature still likes to confound us with PN mysteries. There appears to be a statistically significant alignment of the symmetry axes of bipolar PNe in the Galactic Bulge. What physical mechanism could possibly accomplish such an effect, if real? Unclear. (*Parker*)

The PNLF: it's baaaack! Like a venerable old rock band, the PN [O III] luminosity function (PNLF) seems to be embarking on a (Universal) Reunion Tour. First described and proposed as a potential rung on the extragalactic distance ladder in the late 1980's by George Jacoby & Robin Cardiullo (e.g., Ciardullo et al. 1989), the aforementioned IFUs and MOSs are now reviving and refining the PNLF, presenting new opportunities for its application as a secondary external galaxy distance calibrator (*Chornay, Roth, Adhyaqsa Soemitro, Schlagenhauf, Jacoby*). But the apparent invariance of the PNLF from galaxy to galaxy remains somewhat mysterious — if not quite as mysterious as the possible alignment of bipolar PNe in the Bulge — and so clearly could stand some additional, firmer theoretical underpinnings.

We learned about some new steps in that direction at this meeting (*Valenzuela*) — including, during discussion time, what I have dubbed "Jacoby's Law" (with apologies to George): *there exists a delicate balance between a stellar population's peak PN [O III] luminosities and the extinction caused by the copious dust production of these most [O III]-luminous PNe.* The "poster child" for Jacoby's Law is NGC 7027, which is the

† To the dozens of poster presenters who also contributed mightily to the success of IAUS 384 and whose Proceedings contributions are also worthy of mention, but are omitted from this summary: my sincere apologies. You all deserve better than my neglect.

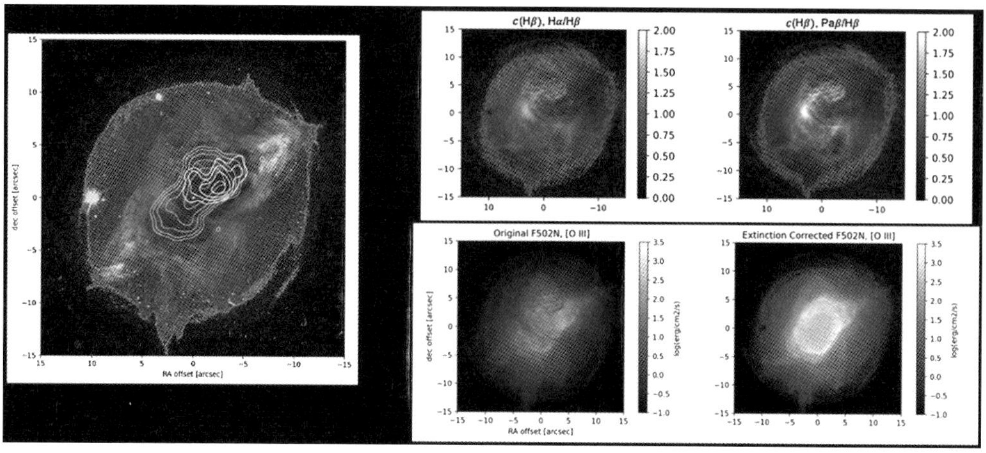

Figure 1. Recent *HST* imagery of the most [O III]-luminous known Galactic PN, the intensively studied NGC 7027, from Moraga Baez et al. (2023). This object features a superposition of almost every morphological feature known to occur in PNe: a system of concentric dust rings (or spiral pattern) surrounding an asymmetrically dust-obscured elliptical shell that has recently been punctured by fast, collimated outflows. The image on the left shows a color overlay of *HST* Wide Field Camera 3 (WFC3) emission line and line ratio images, highlighting both NGC 7027's complex pattern of dust extinction (red: Paβ/Hα) and shocks generated by the collimated outflows (green: [S II]/Hα; blue: [Fe II]); the strongest HST-imaged shocks are well aligned with shock-induced X-ray emission, as revealed by *Chandra* imaging (contours). The panels on the right display extinction maps as deduced from Hα/Hβ and Paβ/Hβ line ratios (top row); and the application of the resulting maps to effectively remove the strong imprint of dust extinction from the *HST*/WFC3 [O III] image, revealing NGC 7027's inner, elliptical, [O III]-luminous shell (bottom row).

most [O III]-luminous known PN in the Galaxy and is also certainly among its dustiest. But NGC 7027's dizzyingly complex structure and rapid structural evolution should give even PNLF "true believers" pause (Fig. 1). NGC 7027 makes clear how much more remains to work out theoretically, before we can understand why the PNLF appears to work as well as it does — and before it is even more widely applied, once ELT MOSs come on line.

PN abundance determinations are so essential, yet so tricky. As photoionization codes become increasingly sophisticated, even more care is required in interpretation of the results of such modeling (*Stasińska, Monteiro*). Extinction can be highly position-dependent, introducing additional complications (*Ueta*); NGC 7027 is again a case in point here (Fig. 1, right panels). And in this same vein...

The ADF: after all these years, it's still haunting us. The abundance discrepancy factor (ADF) parameterizes the systematic discrepancies between elemental abundances as determined from collisionally excited lines vs. recombination lines. Like the PNLF, the physical origin of ADFs continues to defy easy explanation, but — given PNe serve as exemplars of the determination of elemental abundances in the Universe — the ADF is more like a zombie coming to eat us than an aging rock band on a reunion tour. Models invoking strong plasma temperature inhomogeneities appear to mitigate ADFs, but the devil remains in the details (*Méndez Delgado, Morisset*).

High spectral resolution can reveal details that are in fact not details. Examples of the diagnostic power and discovery potential of high-resolution spectroscopy presented at the meeting included s-process nucleosynthesis, line broadening due to turbulence, 3D structural modeling of PNe, and dynamics in the atmospheres of post-AGB stars (*Sterling, Richer, Derlopa, Pukitis*).

We now know everything we need to know about AGB stars necessary to model the AGB/post-AGB/PN transition. Well, just kidding. But single-star AGB evolutionary models have become remarkably sophisticated and predictive, thanks to five decades of excellent, hard work in this particular area (*Ventura, Mendez*).

We are still struggling to disentangle shock excitation and photoionization within PNe. Case in point: low-ionization structures (LISs). Newly revealed connections between "classical" LIS tracers (such as [O I] and [S II]) and both more highly ionized and neutral (molecular) gas in PNe might help distinguish between the effects of shocks vs. central star UV in LISs; but, even in these regions, it remains difficult to assess whether and where one process dominates over the other (*Belén Mari, Akras, Gonçalves*). And speaking of shocks: nearly ten years after completion of the Chandra Planetary Nebula Survey (ChanPlaNS; Freeman et al. 2014), the ChanPlaNS X-ray data are still providing useful insight into PN shocks and, in particular, the shock-temperature-regulating effects of heat conduction (*Montez*).

Ring Nebulae Rule! Or should I say: two rings, NGC 6720 (the Ring) and NGC 3132 (the Southern Ring), now seem to rule the (PN) world, thanks in large part to dramatic new JWST infrared imaging of both nebulae (De Marco et al. 2022; Wesson et al. 2023). Despite (or perhaps because of) the fresh JWST-enabled insight into the morphologies and compositions of these two nebulae, the 3D structures of both PNe were the subject of much discussion and debate at the meeting (*Monteiro, Wesson*). It is worth pointing out that, in the case of the Ring Nebula, this debate has been raging since at least the end of the 19th century (Fig. 2). Fortunately, both NGC 6720 and NGC 3132 harbor large masses of cold molecular gas, such that mm-wave interferometric molecular line mapping — with its km s^{-1} radial velocity precision — likely offers our best hope of obtaining the detailed gas kinematics necessary to break the present morphological degeneracies between structural models for these two iconic Rings. Please read on...

Molecular line observations of PNe, especially by ALMA, are highly revealing. ALMA mm-wave molecular line and dust emission mapping is completely transforming the study of protoplanetary nebulae, PNe, and the AGB-PN connection. ALMA is dissecting "familiar" objects like M 1–92, M 2–9, AFGL 618, the Red Rectangle, and nearby bipolar nebulae (e.g., NGC 6445) to reveal their detailed kinematics and their molecular gas and dust structures and compositions (*Santander-García, Alcolea, Sánchez Contreras, Moraga Baez*). ALMA data is also further solidifying the connection between binary-induced spirals and detached envelopes in AGB ejecta, on the one hand, and spiral/arc/ring systems in PNe, on the other (*Kim, Toala*). More generally, molecular emission and absorption spectroscopy of PNe can shed light on UV- and X-ray-driven chemistry, making PNe excellent case studies through which to better understand photon-dominated regions and X-ray-dominated regions (*Ziurys, Black*).

Planetary nebulae remain essential laboratories for understanding the formation and survival of dust and complex organic molecules. PNe give us our last look at AGB-generated dust and simple molecules before these materials are incorporated into the interstellar medium (ISM) — and they offer our *only* look at the complex inventory of organics that is likely generated during the post-AGB/PN transition, and which then promptly seeds the ISM (*Dell'Agli, Huertas Roldán, Kwok, Cami, García Hernández, Matsuura, Bermúdez-Bustamante*).

Novae and supernovae can teach us a lot about PNe — and vice versa. We (still) stand to learn a great deal about PNe from efforts to observe and model these closely related objects, as well as stellar merger candidates (*Guerrero, Siebert, Quintana-Lacaci, Kamiński, Ritter, Hajduk*).

Oh yes, and jets. Noam Soker would never forgive me if I neglected to mention that all of these objects — novae, SN remnants, PNe — show evidence for jet activity (*Suzett,*

PLATE VII.

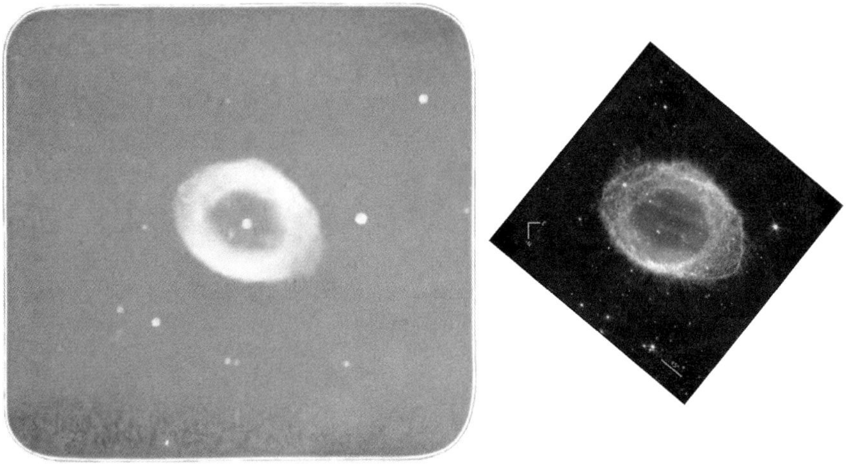

Ring Nebula in Lyra. Exposure 10m.
Photographed with the Crossley Reflector of the Lick Observatory.

Figure 2. The Ring Nebula (NGC 6720) as photographed in visible light using Lick Observatory's Crossley Reflector circa 1898 (left; Keeler 1899) and as imaged in the near-to-mid-IR by JWST in 2022 (right; Wesson et al. 2023). The JWST image has been rotated and scaled to approximately match the Crossley photograph (note the positions of field stars in both images). I highly recommend that all PN astronomers — students and veterans alike – read the highly informative (and downright entertaining) 12-page Keeler (1899) paper in its entirety. Like other papers of its early era, it provides important historical context for our beloved field of PN astrophysics.

Soker, Planquart) and so serve as potential touchstones to understand a wide variety of astrophysical jet sources, from young stellar objects to active galactic nuclei. New HST and ALMA results presented at IAUS 384 (*Balick, Sahai*) made clear that while such fast, collimated outflows are essentially a defining characteristic of bipolar/multipolar pre-PNe and PNe, the physics underlying the systems of "scattershot," episodic jets that shape these objects still remain to be worked out.

Last but by no means least, IAUS 384 made abundantly clear that **students and postdocs — and junior researchers more generally — are doing tremendously exciting and transformative work in the field of PNe.** We need to hear even more from these junior researchers, at these IAU meetings. We should continue to encourage their incisive questions concerning PN models, observations, and results and the myriad connections of PNe to other domains of astrophysics — and, indeed, we should invite junior researchers from adjacent fields to IAU PN meetings, so they can experience the excitement. As a relatively small (astrophysics) community, we very much need this sort of "renewal."

3. Open Questions and Potential Future Directions in Planetary Nebula Research

I close by posing what I believe are some key open questions in our field of PN research, and speculating about potential future studies and directions that might address these questions†.

† The only thing of which I'm certain, in writing down these questions and speculations, is that this list is woefully incomplete.

What can PNe tell us about the evolution of light-element and s-process element abundances over cosmic time? IAUS 384 demonstrated that the time is ripe for comprehensive molecular line studies aimed at elucidating PN molecular chemistry. Such work can inform a disparate range of studies, from the effects of irradiation on molecular chemistry to tracing the origin and evolution of C, N, and O isotopic ratios. Clearly, the field of cosmochemistry also stands to benefit greatly from ambitious programs of spectroscopy of PNe in external galaxies on the forthcoming generation of thirty-meter-class telescopes. In the meantime, we'd best continue to try to understand the origin(s) of the PN ADF "anomaly" and its implications for tracing the chemical evolution of the Universe, as well as the physical basis for the apparent wide applicability of the PNLF.

How long do jet-tracing, PN-shaping shocks persist? Improved constraints on the timescales and "duty cycles" of PN-shaping jets will require concerted campaigns of contemporaneous JWST+HST imaging and spectroscopy of multiple shock tracers (e.g., [S II], [N II], [Fe II]) in PNe, as well as JWST+HST nebular feature proper motion studies spanning long temporal baselines. In addition, forthcoming eROSITA all-sky survey X-ray data should be mined for PN X-ray detections/nondetections, to ascertain the lifetimes of shock-generated hot bubbles that reveal interactions between active fast PN central star winds and slower-moving pre-PN (AGB star) ejecta.

How do binary companions affect late AGB and post-AGB evolution? In the Gaia era, we can and should now revisit (ZA)MS star binary statistics — mass ratios, separations — to understand whether and when binary companions influence mass loss processes as intermediate-mass stars climb the RGB and then AGB. In parallel, we will need families of models invoking truncated AGB evolution and/or binary-assisted mass loss, and detailed simulations of AGB mass loss in interacting multiple star systems.

How can we distinguish between common envelope (CE) vs. detached companion PN shaping scenarios? We need CE evolution and jet interaction simulations spanning larger ranges of size scales and timescales. In parallel, we need multiwavelength studies at high spatial and spectral resolution (e.g., HST, MUSE, JWST, ALMA) that can establish, among other things, the masses of ionized gas, molecular gas, and dust in polar lobe vs. equatorial plane regions of bipolar and multipolar pre-PNe and PNe.

Is there a logarithmic relationship between the number of stars required to explain a given PN's complex shape and the number of coauthors on the paper invoking that multiple star system? This is one key question it seems we *can* answer at present — in the affirmative — given the extant data (i.e., De Marco et al. 2022). But perhaps this important issue is nonetheless worth revisiting, at the next IAU PN Symposium.

Acknowledgements

I wish to thank the organizers of IAUS 384, and especially Orsola De Marco, Ryszard Szczerba, and Albert Zijlstra, for their invitation to provide a summary of their well-organized and spectacularly successful Symposium. Support for my attendance of IAUS 384 was provided by NSF grant AST-2206033 to RIT.

References

Ciardullo R., Jacoby G. H., Ford H. C., Neill J. D., 1989, ApJ, 339, 53. doi:10.1086/167275

De Marco O., Akashi M., Akras S., Alcolea J., Aleman I., Amram P., Balick B., *et al.*, 2022, *Nature Astr*, 6, 1421. doi:10.1038/s41550-022-01845-2

Freeman M., Montez R., Kastner J. H., Balick B., Frew D. J., Jones D., Miszalski B., et al., 2014, ApJ, 794, 99. doi:10.1088/0004-637X/794/2/99

Kastner J. H., Weintraub D. A., Gatley I., Merrill K. M., Probst R. G., 1996, ApJ, 462, 777. doi:10.1086/177192

Keeler J. E., 1899, ApJ, 10, 193. doi:10.1086/140630

Moraga Baez P., Kastner J. H., Balick B., Montez R., Bublitz J., 2023, ApJ, 942, 15. doi:10.3847/1538-4357/aca401

Wesson R., Matsuura M., Zijlstra A. A., Volk K., Kavanagh P. J., García-Segura G., McDonald I., et al., 2023, MNRAS.tmp. doi:10.1093/mnras/stad3670

Author index